FINANCIAL ACCOUNTING

A CRITICAL APPROACH

SECOND EDITION

JOHN FRIEDLAN

University of Ontario Institute of Technology

 **McGraw-Hill
Ryerson**

Toronto   Montréal   Boston   Burr Ridge, IL   Dubuque, IA   Madison, WI   New York
San Francisco   St. Louis   Bangkok   Bogotá   Caracas   Kuala Lumpur   Lisbon   London
Madrid   Mexico City   Milan   New Delhi   Santiago   Seoul   Singapore   Sydney   Taipei

Financial Accounting:
A Critical Approach
Second Edition

ISBN-13: 978-0-07-095789-3
ISBN-10: 0-07-095789-4

1 2 3 4 5 6 7 8 9 10 TCP 0 9 8 7

Printed and bound in Canada

Care has been taken to trace ownership of copyright material contained in this text; however, the publisher will welcome any information that enables them to rectify any reference or credit for subsequent editions.

Editorial Director: Joanna Cotton
Sponsoring Editor: Colleen Henderson
Marketing Manager: Joy Armitage Taylor
Senior Developmental Editor: Denise Foote
Developmental Editor: Emma Gain
Senior Editorial Associate: Christine Lomas
Senior Production Coordinator: Madeleine Harrington
Senior Supervising Editor: Anne Nellis
Copy Editor: Gillian Scobie
Cover Design: Sharon Lucas
Interior Design: Sharon Lucas
Cover Image Credit: © Matthias Kulka/CORBIS
Composition: S R Nova Pvt Ltd., Bangalore, India
Printer: Transcontinental Printing Group

Library and Archives Canada Cataloguing in Publication

Friedlan, John Michael
    Financial accounting: a critical approach/John Friedlan.—2nd ed.

Includes bibliographical references and index.
ISBN-13: 978-0-07-095789-3
ISBN-10: 0-07-095789-4

    1. Accounting—Textbooks. I. Title.

HF5635.F76 2006   657'.044   C2006-902870-2

ABOUT THE AUTHOR

John Friedlan's favourite moments come in the quiet of night, such as on a deserted beach in Prince Edward Island, looking up at the stars over the ocean, and asking "Why?"

Questioning the obvious and always looking for the bigger picture are two critical skills Friedlan has tried to instill in generations of business students since he began teaching more than twenty-five years ago.

An award-winning professor at the Schulich School of Business at York University for thirteen years, Professor Friedlan has, since 2003, been Accounting Program Director in the Faculty of Business and Information Technology at Ontario's newest university, the University of Ontario Institute of Technology. In his classes, Friedlan challenges students to think critically about balance sheets, net income, and how accounting numbers can turn losses into profits, and vice versa.

A Montreal native, Friedlan originally wanted to be a scientist. After earning his Bachelor of Science at McGill University, he discovered that unlocking the mysteries of numbers was his true calling. He switched career paths and completed his MBA at York University in 1978. Friedlan entered the working world as an auditor with Deloitte and Touche (then Deloitte, Haskins and Sells, Chartered Accountants) in Toronto, and qualified as a CA two years later.

Friedlan gained real-world experience at Nabisco Brands, where he moved from bean counting to peanut counting as a manager with Planters Nuts. Next came a staff position with the Board of Examiners at the Canadian Institute of Chartered Accountants. In 1985, Friedlan moved to Seattle to pursue his Ph.D. at the University of Washington. After graduating in 1990, Friedlan returned to the classroom full time, this time as the teacher. He went on to win awards at York for his energetic lectures and his questioning of the whys behind corporate financial reporting choices. In 1992, Friedlan was awarded Educator of the Year for undergraduates. He also won the Seymour Schulich Award for Teaching Excellence in 2000.

For many years, Professor Friedlan has helped evaluate candidates taking their CA exams for the Canadian Institute of Chartered Accountants. He has also been involved with the Canadian Association of Insolvency Practitioners. Friedlan has been technical editor of the education section of *CA Magazine* and was chair of the education committee of the Canadian Academic Accounting Association.

Friedlan's expertise isn't limited to the academic world. His seminars on Financial Accounting for Lawyers teach the secrets of financial statements to top law firms on Bay Street. He's also lectured to municipal civil servants on accounting issues in the public sector.

Friedlan has been a commentator for ROBTV and CTV News' Canada AM, as well as on Canada's Business Report, on accounting issues such as Google's public offering and the collapse of Nortel.

Friedlan's articles have been published in top accounting journals including *Contemporary Accounting Research* and *Issues in Accounting Education*, and in practitioner journals *CGA Magazine* and *CA Magazine*. He has also presented papers at meetings of the American

Accounting Association, the Canadian Academic Accounting Association, and the Canadian Finance Association.

When he isn't teaching accounting in his public life, Professor Friedlan devotes his talent to helping his childrens' school, where he is treasurer of the Parent Council. He is an avid cyclist, runner, skier, and hiker and especially enjoys the solitude of the Washington State mountains.

His car radio is tuned to all-sports talk stations, and on his new toy, satellite radio, he sings along to folk music from the '60s (Peter, Paul and Mary, Simon and Garfunkel, and Bob Dylan). He also enjoys Green Day (thanks to his boys, Alex and Evan).

Friedlan lives with his wife, college professor and journalist Ellin Bessner, and their boys in Richmond Hill, Ontario, where asking "Why?" is a daily ritual.

BRIEF CONTENTS

Chapter 1

The Accounting Environment:
What is Accounting and Why is it Done?   1

Chapter 2

Financial Statements:
A Window on an Entity   32

Chapter 3

The Accounting Cycle   87

Chapter 4

Income Measurement and the
Objectives of Financial Reporting   167

Chapter 5

Generally Accepted
Accounting Principles   232

Chapter 6

Cash Flow, Profitability,
and the Cash Flow Statement   285

Chapter 7

Cash, Receivables, and the
Time Value of Money   335

Chapter 8

Inventory   392

Chapter 9

Capital Assets   453

Chapter 10

Liabilities   520

Chapter 11

Owners' Equity   597

Chapter 12

Investments in Other Companies   657

Chapter 13

Analyzing and Interpreting
Financial Statements   704

Appendix A Rogers Communications Inc.
              2005 Annual Report   A-1

Appendix B Comprehensive Cases   B-1

Photo Credits   PC-1

Glossary   G-1

Index   I-1

CONTENTS

Chapter 1

The Accounting Environment: What is Accounting and Why is it Done? 1

Introduction 2

A Challenge to the Reader 2

What is Accounting? 3

Why do People Need and Want Accounting Information? 3

The Two Fields of Accounting: Financial Accounting and Managerial Accounting 5

The Accounting Environment 5
  Environment 6
  Entities 6
  Stakeholders: Different Users, Different Decisions, Different Information 9
  Characteristics of Entities 10
  Constraints 10
  Stakeholders versus Preparers 11
  Accounting Scandals 13

Accounting is for Measurement 14

The Rules of the Game 18

Solved Problem 20

Summary of Key Points 23

Key Terms 23

Similar Terms 24

Assignment Materials 24
  Questions 24
  Exercises 25
  Problems 26

Endnotes 31

Chapter 2

Financial Statements: A Window on an Entity 32

Introduction 33

General Purpose Financial Statements 33

Rogers' Financial Statements: An Overview 34

The Balance Sheet 34
  Assets 38
  Liabilities 39
  Using Balance Sheet Information to Analyze Liquidity 40
  Owners' Equity 41

The Income Statement 44
  Rogers' Statement of Income (Income Statement) 47

Gross Margin and Gross Margin Percentage 48

The Statement of Retained Earnings 50

The Cash Flow Statement 51

The Relationship Among the Financial Statements 52

Notes to the Financial Statements 52

Users of Rogers' Financial Statements 54

Format of General Purpose Financial Statements 55

Other Accounting Information 56

Solved Problem 56

Summary of Key Points 59

Key Terms 60

Similar Terms 61

Assignment Materials 61
  Questions 61
  Exercises 63
  Problems 68
  Using Financial Statements 79
  Analyzing Rogers Communications Inc. 85

Endnotes 86

Chapter 3

The Accounting Cycle 87

Introduction 88

The Accounting Cycle 88

Accrual Accounting 90

A Question of Timing 93

Devices for Doing Accounting 93
  The Accounting Equation Spreadsheet 94
  Journal Entries 109

Adjusting Entries   112

Closing Journal Entries   120

Solved Problem   122

Summary of Key Points   127

Appendix: The Accounting Cycle   128

Key Terms   137

Similar Terms   138

Assignment Materials   138
   Questions   138
   Appendix Questions   139
   Exercises   140
   Problems   148
   Appendix Problems   159
   Using Financial Statements   161
   Analyzing Rogers Communications Inc.   165

Endnotes   166

Chapter 4

Income Measurement and the Objectives of Financial Reporting   167

Introduction   168

Revenue Recognition   168
   Criteria for Recognizing Revenue   170
   The Critical-Event Approach to Recognizing Revenue   171
   Why Does It Matter When a Company Recognizes Revenue?   176
   Google Inc.   179
   Why Do Managers Have So Much Choice?   181
   The Gradual Approach to Recognizing Revenue   182
   Accounting Innovation: Revenue Recognition at Microsoft Corporation   185

Gains and Losses   187

Expense Recognition   188

The Objectives of Financial Reporting   190
   Tax Minimization   192
   Stewardship   193
   Management Evaluation   193
   Performance Evaluation   193
   Cash Flow Prediction   193
   Monitoring Contract Compliance   193
   Earnings Management   194
   Minimum Compliance   195
   Reporting Impact   197

Can Managers Do Whatever They Want?   198

Solving Accounting Choice Problems   199
   Constraints, Facts, and Objectives   199
   Analyzing Accounting Problems   201

Solved Problem   202

Summary of Key Points   208

Key Terms   209

Assignment Materials   209
   Questions   209
   Exercises   211
   Problems   216
   Using Financial Statements   225
   Analyzing Rogers Wireless Communications   230

Endnotes   231

Chapter 5

Generally Accepted Accounting Principles   232

Introduction   233

What are Generally Accepted Accounting Principles (GAAP)?   234

The World According to GAAP   235
   Basic Assumptions of GAAP   236
   Qualitative Characteristics   239
   Measurement Conventions   244

The Audit Environment and the Auditors' Report   252
   A New Era for Financial Reporting   252
   The Auditors' Report   253
   Other Auditors' Reports   254
   Other Assurance Accountants Can Provide   255

Solved Problem   255

Summary of Key Points   263

Key Terms   263

Similar Terms   264

Assignment Materials   264
   Questions   264
   Exercises   265
   Problems   270
   Using Financial Statements   278
   Analyzing Rogers Communications Inc.   283

Endnotes   284

Chapter 6

Cash Flow, Profitability, and the Cash Flow Statement   285

Introduction   286

Cash Versus Accrual Accounting and the Cash Cycle   286
   The Cash Cycle   286
   Example: Cash Flow Scenarios at Peabody Corp.   289

Understanding the Cash Flow Statement: An Overview   293

Understanding the Cash Flow Statement: Specific Activities 296
    Cash from Investing and Financing Activities 296
    Cash from Operations 297
Interpreting and Using the Cash Flow Statement 306
Manipulating Cash Flow Information and the Effect of Accrual Accounting Choices on the Cash Flow Statement 308
Solved Problem 311
Summary of Key Points 314
Key Terms 315
Similar Terms 315
Assignment Materials 315
    Questions 315
    Exercises 317
    Problems 321
    Using Financial Statements 330
    Analyzing Rogers Communications Inc. 333
Endnotes 334

Chapter 7

Cash, Receivables, and the Time Value of Money 335

Introduction 336
Cash 336
    Cash Management and Controls Over Cash 338
    Is a Dollar a Dollar? 339
The Time Value of Money 341
    Future Value 341
    Present Value 343
    Present Value of an Annuity 346
Receivables 348
    Accounting for Uncollectible Receivables 353
    Long-Term Receivables 360
Financial Statement Analysis Issues 362
    Hidden Reserves 362
    Current and Quick Ratios 364
    Accounts Receivable Turnover Ratio 366
Solved Problem 368
Summary of Key Points 370
Key Terms 371
Similar Terms 371
Assignment Materials 371
    Questions 371
    Exercises 373
    Problems 379
    Using Financial Statements 387
    Analyzing Rogers Communications Inc. 391
Endnotes 391

Chapter 8

Inventory 392

Introduction 393
What is Inventory? 393
What Does GAAP Say? 394
Perpetual and Periodic Inventory Control Systems 395
    Internal control 397
Inventory Valuation Methods 397
    First In, First Out (FIFO) 399
    Last In, First Out (LIFO) 400
    Average Cost 400
    Specific Identification 401
    Comparison of the Different Cost Flow Assumptions 402
    Which Method is Best? 406
The Lower of Cost and Market Rule 409
Valuing Inventory at Other Than Cost 414
Examples of Inventory Disclosures in Financial Statements 415
Inventory and the Services Industry 416
Consignment Inventory 416
Inventory Accounting and Income Taxes 419
Financial Statement Analysis Issues 420
    A Banker's View of Inventory 423
Solved Problem 423
Summary of Key Points 426
Key Terms 427
Assignment Materials 428
    Questions 428
    Exercises 430
    Problems 436
    Using Financial Statements 448
    Analyzing Rogers Communications Inc. 451
Endnotes 451

Chapter 9

Capital Assets 453

Introduction 454
Measuring Capital Assets and Limitations to Historical Cost Accounting 454
What is Cost? 456
    Basket Purchases 459
Amortization 460
    Amortization and Market Values 461
    Amortization Methods 462
    Comparing Methods 466
    Financial Statement Disclosure 470
Intangible Assets 474
    Goodwill 477

A Contrast with Oil and Gas Accounting   479

Disposal of Capital Assets   481

Write-Downs   482

Capital Assets and the Cash Flow Statement   485

Does the Way Capital Assets are Accounted for Affect the
Cash Flow Statement?   485

Why Accounting Choice?   486

Financial Statement Analysis Issues   488

Solved Problem   489

Summary of Key Points   494

Appendix: Amortization and Taxes   495

Key Terms   496

Similar Terms   496

Assignment Materials   496

Questions   496

Exercises   499

Problems   505

Using Financial Statements   515

Analyzing Rogers Communications Inc.   518

Endnotes   519

Chapter 10

Liabilities   520

Introduction   521

What Are Liabilities?   521

Valuation of Liabilities   522

Current Liabilities   523

Bank and Other Current Loans   523

Accounts Payable   524

Collections on Behalf of Third Parties   524

Income Taxes Payable   525

Dividends Payable   525

Accrued Liabilities   525

Unearned Revenue   527

Disclosure   528

Bonds and Other Forms of Long-Term Debt   528

Characteristics of Bonds   530

Pricing of Bonds   531

Accounting for Bonds   533

Accruing Interest on Long-Term Debt   536

Early Retirement of Debt   537

Disclosure   537

Leases   538

Pensions and Other Post-Retirement Benefits   543

Contingencies   545

Commitments   547

Subsequent Events   549

Debt and Taxes   549

Financial Statement Analysis Issues   550

Debt-to-Equity Ratio   550

Interest Coverage Ratio   551

Other Issues   553

Solved Problem   553

Summary of Key Points   556

Appendix—Future Income Taxes   557

Key Terms   565

Similar Terms   566

Assignment Materials   566

Questions   566

Exercises   568

Problems   576

Using Financial Statements   586

Analyzing Rogers Communications Inc.   594

Endnotes   596

Chapter 11

Owners' Equity   597

Introduction   598

Corporations, Partnerships, and Proprietorships   598

Characteristics of Equity   603

Common and Preferred Shares   604

Share Repurchases   607

Retained Earnings, Dividends, and Stock Splits   608

Retained Earnings   608

Dividends   609

Stock Splits   612

Accounting Changes—Policies and Estimates   614

Comprehensive Income   616

Leverage   616

Employee Stock Options   619

Economic Consequences   622

Financial Statement Analysis Issues   623

Earnings Per Share   624

Return on Shareholders' Equity   625

Solved Problem   626

Summary of Key Points   629

Key Terms   630

Similar Terms   631

Assignment Materials   631

Questions   631

Exercises   633

Problems   640

Using Financial Statements   649

Analyzing Rogers Communications Inc.   655

Endnotes   656

Chapter 12

Investments in Other Companies 657

Introduction 658

Why Do Companies Invest in Other Companies? 658

Accounting for Investments in Other Corporations:
Introduction 659

Control: Accounting for Subsidiaries 660

    The Consolidated Balance Sheet on the Date the
Subsidiary is Purchased 663

    Non-Controlling Interest 665

    Are Consolidated Financial Statements Useful? 666

    Purchasing Assets Instead of Shares 668

Significant Influence 668

Passive Investments 669

Solved Problem 675

Appendix 677

Summary of Key Points 684

Key Terms 685

Similar Terms 685

Assignment Materials 685

    Questions 685

    Exercises 686

    Problems 690

    Using Financial Statements 697

    Analyzing Rogers Communications Inc. 702

Endnotes 703

Chapter 13

Analyzing and Interpreting Financial Statements 704

Introduction 705

Why Analyze and Interpret Financial Statements? 705

Know the Entity 707

Permanent Earnings and the Quality of Earnings 709

Permanent Earnings 709

Quality of Earnings 716

Using Ratios to Analyze Accounting Information 719

    Common Size Financial Statements and Trend
Analysis 721

    Evaluating Performance 727

    Liquidity 734

    Example: Analyzing Leon's Furniture Ltd.'s
Inventory 738

    Solvency and Leverage 739

    Other Common Ratios 741

Some Limitations and Caveats About Financial
Statements and Financial Statement Analysis 743

Earnings Management 745

Solved Problem 746

Summary of Key Points 753

Key Terms 754

Similar Terms 754

Assignment Materials 754

    Questions 754

    Exercises 756

    Problems 765

    Using Financial Statements 776

    Analyzing Rogers Communications Inc. 781

Endnotes 782

Appendix A Rogers Communications Inc.
2005 Annual Report A-1

Appendix B Comprehensive Cases B-1

Photo Credits PC-1

Glossary G-1

Index I-1

CONTENTS

PREFACE

OBJECTIVES

Welcome to the second edition of *Financial Accounting: A Critical Approach,* a text created to provide an accessible and insightful introduction to the real nature of accounting information. My hope is that any person who studies the book thoroughly will become a sophisticated user of financial statements and possess a solid understanding of the accounting issues, controversies, and scandals that are reported in the business press.

The title of the book requires some explanation. The *Critical Approach* to financial accounting guides students to look critically at accounting information. The book emphasizes the importance of accounting information as a decision-making tool, but also addresses the limitations, controversies, and problems with accounting and accounting information. Rather than accept the numbers in financial statements at face value, students learn that preparers of financial statements often choose from several acceptable ways of accounting for transactions and economic events, and that these choices can have economic consequences for an entity's stakeholders and for the entity itself. Students also learn that accounting information provided by an entity cannot be all things to all people. The information may be useful to some decision-makers, but not to others. Students learn to critically evaluate whether the information is appropriate for the decisions *they* are making.

The importance of using a *Critical Approach* to the study of accounting is more evident today than ever. For decades, accounting received little attention in the media beyond the regular earnings announcements made by public companies. Then, around the time I finished writing the first edition of *Financial Accounting: A Critical Approach,* Enron became a household name and accounting was headline news. Since the publication of the first edition, more accounting scandals have been brought to light (e.g., WorldCom, Nortel), the Sarbanes-Oxley Act has been enacted in the United States, and steps have also been taken in Canada to reassure users of the reliability and credibility of financial statements. Today people are much more aware of the importance of and the problems with accounting information. The approach I use in *Financial Accounting: A Critical Approach* fits well with the need for stakeholders to look critically and sceptically at the information in financial statements.

Many accounting textbooks classify themselves as having a "user" or a "preparer" orientation. In my view, these classifications are artificial, as a good introductory education in financial accounting requires elements of both. While the main purpose of this book is to make students literate readers of financial statements (a user orientation), it is difficult to understand financial statements without having some appreciation of how data are entered into an accounting system and converted into the information included in accounting reports. As a result, it is useful for introductory accounting students to have an understanding of basic bookkeeping (a preparer orientation). Without this familiarity, students will find it difficult to understand how and why accounting choices made by managers affect the financial statements.

Thus, while *Financial Accounting: A Critical Approach* is not primarily a book about how to do accounting, the "how to" part is fully covered. Chapter 3 explains how transactions and economic events are recorded and the data converted into financial statements. In the context of this book, understanding the procedural aspects of accounting is essential to understanding the relationship between transactions and economic events and the resulting financial statements.

One of the important features of *Financial Accounting: A Critical Approach* is the use of short, decision-oriented "mini-cases." The cases, and an approach for solving them, are first introduced in Chapter 4. Cases with solutions are provided as the Solved Problems in Chapters 4, 5, 6, 9, 10, 12, and 13. Cases for assignment and exam purposes appear in Appendix B of the book. Additional cases are provided in the Online Learning Centre. Many of the cases place the student in the role of a user or interpreter of financial statements. The cases serve three purposes: first, they help develop critical thinking and problem-solving skills; second, they help develop an appreciation of the context-specific nature of accounting; and third, they allow students to get "inside the heads" of preparers and users to understand how perspective affects the preparation and use of financial statements. Accounting comes to life as students are forced to think about alternative ways of accounting for transactions and economic events, and to consider the impact the different alternatives can have on decisions and economic outcomes.

CHANGES IN THE SECOND EDITION

I've made some significant changes in the second edition. My goal was to increase the focus on understanding the story financial statements convey to stakeholders and to remove some of the technical material that wasn't relevant to students' understanding of the statements. The book has also been shortened to make it more accessible. The table below summarizes the major reductions to the text.

Chapter 6	Removal of the section on preparation of the cash flow statement. This material can now be found in the text's Online Learning Centre.
Chapter 7	The material on bank reconciliations was removed. This coverage can now be found in the text's Online Learning Centre.
Chapter 8	Coverage of the inventory cost flow assumptions was shortened by excluding from the detailed example calculation of ending inventory and cost of sales using the perpetual inventory control method. The perpetual method is still described in general terms. In addition, coverage of direct and absorption costing has been removed.
Chapter 10	Coverage of bonds was significantly shortened and simplified, particularly the discussion of bond discounts and premiums. In addition, the material on mortgages was removed and coverage of future income taxes was moved to the chapter appendix.
Chapter 12	Coverage of consolidated financial statements was significantly simplified. The key topics are still presented (goodwill, intercompany transactions, non-controlling interest) but the examples have been simplified. In addition, the discussion of consolidated financial statements in periods after a subsidiary is purchased has been moved to the chapter appendix.

◇ ROGERS™

Further changes to the new edition include the use of Rogers Communications Inc. (Rogers) as the featured company. Rogers' businesses and financial information are integrated throughout the book to provide a continual focus from chapter to chapter. Some of the changes in coverage are dictated by using Rogers (instead of Mark's Work Wearhouse, the featured company in the first edition). For example, Chapter 11 discusses par value shares because Rogers' Class B non-voting shares have a par value. In contrast, coverage of the retail inventory method and sale-leaseback arrangements have been removed because these were used by Mark's Work Wearhouse, but not by Rogers.

A new feature to the book is the chapter-opening vignette. Each vignette discusses an aspect of Rogers and is designed to welcome the reader to the content of the chapter in a friendly and relevant way.

Of course, the text has been updated to reflect recent changes in accounting standards and in the accounting environment. Coverage of revenue recognition, passive investments, comprehensive income, and differential reporting has been updated or added. As well, references to Sarbanes-Oxley and the proposed harmonization of Canadian accounting standards with International Financial Reporting Standards have been added. New solved problems have been added to four chapters. These new solved problems are mini-cases that will provide more concrete examples of how to use and interpret accounting information. In addition, many other minor changes have been added to improve the text. Many of the exercises and problems in the end-of-chapter material have been revised, and many new problems and exercises added.

PEDAGOGICAL FEATURES OF *FINANCIAL ACCOUNTING: A CRITICAL APPROACH*

Besides the cases mentioned above, this text is full of other useful pedagogical tools.

- Learning Objectives and Summary—The Learning Objectives at the beginning of each chapter focus students' attention on what they will learn. The Chapter Summary at the end of each chapter outlines how each learning objective was addressed.

- Key Terms and Glossary—Key Terms are printed in bold in the text and are listed with page references at the end of each chapter. Key terms are defined in the text and appear with their definitions and a page reference in the Glossary at the end of the book.

- Rogers Communications Inc.—The financial statements of Rogers Communications Inc. are used as a focus for discussion throughout the book. Many of the topics discussed in the book are related to the accounting and presentation used by Rogers. Each chapter's Assignment Material contains a set of questions entitled *Analyzing Rogers Communications*, giving students the opportunity to apply the material from the chapter to Rogers' financial statements.

- Questions for Consideration—Each chapter contains a number of Questions for Consideration, providing opportunities for students to stop and think about what they have read so far in the chapter. The Questions for Consideration are designed as critical thinking questions requiring application of the material in the chapter. Solutions to these questions are provided.

- Knowledge Check—Each chapter contains a number of Knowledge Checks that give students a chance to stop and check their understanding of key points raised in the chapter. If a student can't answer the questions, they should go back and review the preceding sections. Solutions to the Knowledge Checks are provided in the text's Online Learning Centre.

- Insight boxes—Throughout the text, commentary on key points is provided in the Insight boxes. The Insight boxes provide additional details concerning the nature and interpretation of accounting information

- Use of extracts from actual entities' financial statements—Many of the issues, concepts, and points raised in the book are demonstrated through extracts from the financial statements of actual entities, presented as they appeared in the entity's annual report. Students are able to see first hand the presentation of the topic in a real-world setting.

- Solved problems—Each chapter provides a detailed problem with a solution. Many of the solved problems are cases that should help students develop their analytical skills.

- Similar Terms List—This unique feature provides a list of accounting terms used in the text compared to other terms with essentially the same meaning that students may encounter in the media, in financial documents, and in accounting practice.

- Using financial statements—Each chapter's Assignment Material provides extensive extracts from an entity's financial statements and a series of questions that provide students with the opportunity to work with actual financial statement material and to apply the chapter content in a realistic context.

- Assignment Material—Each chapter contains a large number of questions, exercises, and problems that provide students with the opportunity to apply the knowledge and skills they have gained from the chapter. Much of this material is keyed to the Learning Objectives in the text.

A NOTE ON COVERAGE

Financial Accounting: A Critical Approach provides considerable depth on a number of topics not normally covered in introductory accounting texts or courses. These topics include revenue recognition, leases, pensions, future income taxes (in an appendix), employee stock options, and consolidated financial statements. Coverage of revenue recognition is intended to introduce the concept of accounting choice and demonstrate the impact of different ways of reporting economic events on the financial statements. The other more complex topics are included because they are commonly reported in financial statements and often have large dollar amounts associated with them. If students are to make sense of the entire set of statements, they must have some familiarity and comfort with these topics, even if they tend to be complex. Some instructors may prefer not to cover some of the sections on leases, pensions, future income taxes, and investments in other companies. These topics can easily be skipped without having any impact on students' understanding of later chapters.

The material on liquidity and the cash flow statement appears early in the book, in Chapter 5. Consequently, coverage of the complete set of the financial statements is provided together and students are encouraged to think about cash flow as well as accrual accounting throughout the book.

NAMES OF ENTITIES

Some readers may wonder about the origins of the names given to the entities used in the examples and end-of-chapter material. *Financial Accounting: A Critical Approach* provides names for more than 500 entities throughout the book and virtually all are actual names of places in Canada!

SUPPLEMENTS

The supplements to support *Financial Accounting: A Critical Approach* have been completely revamped for the second edition. This exciting new package comprises the following elements:

Instructor's CD-ROM   The CD-ROM contains a complete support package that will cater to every instructor's needs.

Instructor's Manual   The thoroughly updated Instructor's Manual includes learning objectives, chapter overviews, classroom icebreakers, active learning techniques, comprehensive lecture notes, writing assignments, short cases based on the opening vignettes, and an assignment topic grid related to the coverage in the assignment material.

Computerized Test Bank   The brand new test bank was created from scratch by Julia Ann Scott of McGill University. It contains more than 1000 questions of the highest quality, varying in style and level of difficulty. The software allows instructors to choose questions, edit them, and even add new ones to create tests that are customized to fit each course.

Microsoft® PowerPoint® Presentations   With one presentation for every chapter of the text, instructors can guide their students through the text with ease. The slides have been adapted to fit the second edition, and the addition of figures and diagrams increases their visual appeal.

Solutions Manual   The fully revised Solutions Manual contains in-depth answers and step-by-step solutions for all assignment material included in the text.

ONLINE TECHNOLOGY
Online Learning Centre (OLC)

Both students and instructors will find the text's companion Online Learning Centre (OLC) to be an invaluable learning support tool. Also completely overhauled for the second edition, the OLC contains both a secure, password-protected section for both instructors and students.

Students can benefit from the following features for every chapter of the text:

Chapter overviews
Summaries of key points
Study tips
Interactive quizzes
Practice exams
Short cases
Knowledge Check solutions

The instructor's section contains all of this, plus the Instructor's Manual, Solutions Manual, and Microsoft® PowerPoint® presentations.

Go to www.mcgrawhill.ca/olc/friedlan today!

SUPERIOR SERVICE

iLearning Sales Specialist

Your Integrated Learning Sales Specialist is a McGraw-Hill Ryerson representative with the experience, product knowledge, training, and support to help you assess and integrate any of the following products, technology and services into your course for optimum teaching and learning performance. Whether it is using our test bank software, helping your students improve their grades, or putting your entire course online, your iLearning Sales Specialist is there to help you do it. Contact your local iLearning Sales Specialist today to learn how to maximize all of McGraw-Hill Ryerson's resources.

iLearning Services Program

McGraw-Hill Ryerson offers a unique iLearning Services package designed for Canadian faculty. Our mission is to equip providers of higher education with superior tools and resources required for excellence in teaching. For additional information, please visit http://www.mcgrawhill.ca/highereducation/iservices

COURSE MANAGEMENT

Visit www.mhhe.com/pageout to create a Web page for your course using our resources. **PageOut** is the McGraw Hill Ryerson Web site development centre. This Web page-generation software is free to adopters and is designed to help faculty create an online course, complete with assignments, quizzes, links to relevant Web sites, and more—all in a matter of minutes.

In addition, content cartridges are available for the course management systems **WebCT** and **Blackboard**. These platforms provide instructors with user-friendly, flexible teaching tools. Please contact your local McGraw-Hill Ryerson iLearning Sales Specialist for details.

ACKNOWLEDGEMENTS

Many people contributed to the development of this book and I take this opportunity to thank them.

Thanks to faculty reviewers who devoted significant time and effort to reading the manuscript as it developed and who provided valuable comments, suggestions, and criticisms, all of which served to make the book better:

M. Rick Bates, *University of Guelph*
Hilary Becker, *Carleton University*
Greg Berberich, *Wilfrid Laurier University*
Angela Downey, *University of Lethbridge*
Cameron Graham, *York University*
Gordon Holyer, *Malaspina University-College*
Cathie Hurley, *University of New Brunswick*
Stuart H. Jones, *University of Calgary*
Margaret Klatt, *University of Victoria*
Michael Konopaski, *Trent University*
Valorie Leonard, *Laurentian University*
Philippe Levy, *McGill University*
Patricia Mallia, *University of British Columbia*
Kevin Markle, *Schulich School of Business, York University*
Anthony Moung Yin Chan, *Ryerson University*
Shu-Lun Wong, *Memorial University of Newfoundland*
Lei Zhou, *McGill University*

Thanks to Rogers Communications Inc. and in particular John Gossling, Vice-President of Financial Operations, for their cooperation in providing information and pictures about Rogers. Thanks to Ellin Bessner who wrote the vignettes. Thanks to Christina Basanti, Chris Lazarte, and especially Tom Campbell, fourth year accounting students at the University of Ontario Institute of Technology for the work they did on the solutions. Also, thank you to Ingrid McLeod-Dick and Deborah Mortimer for their technical checks.

Various instructors assisted in preparing the set of supplements that accompany the book:

Michael Konopaski, *Trent University* (Instructor's Manual and Online Learning Centre)
Julia Ann Scott, *McGill University* (Computerized Test Bank)
Jane Bowen, *University of Ontario Institute of Technology* (Microsoft® PowerPoint® Presentations)

The staff at McGraw-Hill Ryerson provided outstanding support to help develop and market the book and were a pleasure to work with. Many thanks to:

Denise Foote
Emma Gain
Tom Gale
Madeleine Harrington
Colleen Henderson
Nicole Lukach
Anne Nellis
Gillian Scobie

Finally, a special acknowledgement to Professor Al Rosen who helped shape and develop the way I think about and teach accounting. His contribution to this book is significant.

Writing this book has been the greatest challenge of my professional life. It has also been one of the most exciting and fulfilling. I hope that all users of *Financial Accounting: A Critical Approach* find the book a valuable part of their study of accounting and business.

John Friedlan
Faculty of Business and Information Technology,
University of Ontario Institute of Technology

THE ACCOUNTING ENVIRONMENT: WHAT IS ACCOUNTING AND WHY IS IT DONE?

LEARNING OBJECTIVES

After studying the material in this chapter you will be able to:

▶ **LO 1** Explain accounting and its uses.

▶ **LO 2** Describe the accounting environment and understand that the accounting information an entity presents is affected by the accounting environment.

▶ **LO 3** Discuss how the interests of the people who prepare accounting information can conflict with the interests of the people who use the information.

▶ **LO 4** Understand the importance of accounting information for measuring the attributes of an entity.

▶ **LO 5** Describe generally accepted accounting principles in basic terms and identify the four qualitative characteristics that GAAP identify as necessary for accounting information to be useful.

There was a large crowd at the Rogers Centre in Toronto for the Sunday afternoon baseball game between the Toronto Blue Jays and the New York Yankees. Rogers Communications Inc. owns the Toronto major league baseball team and the stadium. The company had poured $8 million into the stadium that year to install a new set of jumbo video screens where fans could watch game statistics, as well as commercials from Rogers Sportsnet, one of over a dozen television stations the company owns. Red and white Rogers signs dotted the perimeter of the stadium. And some youngsters listened to the game's play-by-play on their portable radios, tuned to The Fan 590, a Rogers-owned AM radio station in Toronto. Here and there, women reached into their purses and men into their pockets to answer the ringing of their Rogers Wireless cell phones.

From cable television, to publishing, to mobile phones and the Internet, the Rogers Communications conglomerate is one of the country's most successful media empires. And it began with a single radio station in Toronto, named CHFI, bought in the 1960s by the founder, Ted Rogers, Jr. He found his calling in communications after the untimely death of his father, Edward Rogers, Sr., a media pioneer who invented the world's first battery-less radio.

Since the 1960s, Rogers Communications has grown into a $7-billion dollar company. It's Canada's largest cable television provider, with 2.3 million subscribers. Rogers Wireless boasts more than six million subscribers for voice, data, and one-way paging. Rogers Media, which includes the Rogers Centre and the Blue Jays, publishes 70 magazines, including *Macleans* and *L'actualité*, and operates more than 40 radio stations and several television channels, including Sportsnet. More recently, the family-owned business moved into the home telephone service, with the takeover of Call-Net Enterprises, the parent of Sprint Canada.

Rogers is based in Toronto and has about 18,000 employees. The Blue Jays won their game against New York, by a score of 6 to 5.

INTRODUCTION

Accounting is full of mystery and intrigue. The reader of an accounting report, like the reader of a good mystery, must sort through clues, interpret and analyze information, exercise judgment, decide which information is relevant and which should be ignored, and use the information to come to a conclusion. In an accounting mystery the question is not who the murderer or thief is. Instead, an accounting detective might have to decide whether to invest, lend, do business with a particular organization, or ask for an increase in wages.

Solving an accounting mystery requires detective work. The numbers tell a story, but it is usually necessary to read between the lines. You cannot just take the numbers at face value. Working with accounting information is not cold, calculating, and impersonal. The effective accounting detective must also understand human behaviour. *People* prepare accounting information—people who have their own interests regarding how the accounting information will be used.

Over the years accounting has endured a bad reputation. The stereotype conjures up dull people doing dreary work—people do not think of accounting as "sexy." Can you name any famous accountants? Have you ever heard of any television shows or movies about accounting? Probably the most famous accountants are the PricewaterhouseCooper representatives who deliver the results at the Academy Awards.

But accounting's dreary reputation is not fair. There may be some dull accountants; there may even be a lot of dull accountants. But accounting is definitely not dull. In fact, using, preparing, and understanding accounting information requires a set of high-level cognitive skills—skills that include judgment, analysis, synthesis, evaluation, problem solving, critical thinking, and creativity.

The goal of *Financial Accounting: A Critical Approach* is to help you become an effective accounting detective. You will examine accounting from the perspectives of the people who prepare the information and those who use it. You will learn to interpret and understand financial statements and financial reporting, and master the tools to unravel their mysteries.

Regardless of whether you plan to become a professional accountant, pursue a career in another business discipline, or just learn something about accounting, *Financial Accounting: A Critical Approach* will provide you with some tools to help you make sense of the information in accounting reports and understand the strengths and limitations of accounting information.

A CHALLENGE TO THE READER

Business and accounting are real-world subjects. The ideas and themes in an accounting textbook and course are easier to understand when you can connect them to real-world events. As we move through this book, links will be made with actual business problems and entities so that you can develop an understanding of accounting in context. You can help develop your own understanding of business by regularly reading the business press to learn about Canadian and international business issues, problems, and companies. Two excellent Canadian business newspapers are *The Globe and Mail's Report on Business* and *The National Post's Financial Post*. There are also many good business magazines and Web sites that will help you learn about Canadian and global business issues, personalities, and entities.

A sample of some well-known Canadian and international sources for business information follows on the next page.

In addition, the following Web sites are particularly helpful if you are looking for financial information about Canadian and U.S. publicly traded companies:

Canadian companies	www.sedar.com
U.S. companies	www.sec.gov/edgar.shtml

You should also observe the business world and economic activity as you go through your day. Business is everywhere. Think about the businesses you frequent (grocery stores, restaurants, clubs, gas stations, convenience stores, movie theatres, retail stores, pharmacies, and so on). Think about what makes them work. What are the keys to their success? How do they make money? What do they offer to customers? Talk to people about their businesses. You'll find that most business people enjoy discussing their companies.

Publication	Web Site
The Globe and Mail	www.theglobeandmail.com
The National Post	www.nationalpost.com
Canadian Business	www.canadianbusiness.com
The Wall Street Journal (U.S.)	www.wsj.com
The Financial Times (U.K.)	www.ft.com
The Economist (U.K.)	www.economist.com
CGA Magazine	www.cga-canada.org
CA Magazine	www.camagazine.com
CMA Management	www.managementmag.com
www.moneysense.ca	
Bloomberg.com (U.S.)	
money.cnn.com (U.S.)	

3

THE ACCOUNTING ENVIRONMENT: WHAT IS ACCOUNTING AND WHY IS IT DONE?

WHAT IS ACCOUNTING?

Accounting is a system for producing information about an **entity** (an entity is an economic unit of some kind, such as a corporation, university, government, or even a person) and communicating that information to people who want it so they can make decisions. As with any form of communication there are plenty of opportunities for misunderstanding, confusion, misinterpretation, and misdirection.

Like other forms of communication, accounting is not always straightforward. The people who prepare accounting information often have many choices and techniques available to them. This means that, depending on the choices they make, accounting reports could present the same situation in several different ways. If you don't know how to navigate through these differences, you could misunderstand, misinterpret, become confused, or be misdirected by accounting reports. As a result, you could make poor decisions that could result in economic losses.

WHY DO PEOPLE NEED AND WANT ACCOUNTING INFORMATION?

The more and better information or knowledge a person has about a situation, the better the decisions he or she can make. Without information, a "decision" is nothing more than a guess. For example, suppose you wanted to take a vacation over the winter break. You see an advertisement in the newspaper promoting Aruba as a fabulous winter vacation destination. Assuming you have never been to Aruba before and know little about it, would you simply accept the advertisement at face value? Most people wouldn't. You would probably want to find out whether Aruba offered what *you* wanted from a winter vacation. You might want to know about the weather, the beaches, the accommodations, the entertainment and activities available, and whether many people your age go there. You would also want to know whether the cost would fit your budget and if flight and hotel availability would suit your schedule. To obtain information you might ask friends and relatives if they know anything about Aruba. You could do research in the library or on the Internet. Or you could consult with expert sources that specialize in gathering travel information, such as a good travel agent or a travel guide published by an independent company. You would gather information until you were comfortable making a decision.

Not all information is equal. In making a decision, you will generally place more weight on the information that is the most reliable and most relevant to your needs. For example, travel brochures published by Aruba's government travel department will likely be very attractive, but would they be as credible as information provided by an independent travel company? Would you rely on the opinions of an acquaintance whose likes and dislikes are very different from yours, or trust the advice of a good friend with whom you share many similarities?

It is usually not possible or worthwhile to collect all the information available on a subject. First, gathering and analyzing information is costly and takes time. At some point the benefit of obtaining more information is not worth the cost. This is known as the **cost/benefit trade-off**. The cost/benefit trade-off is the concept of comparing the benefits of an action with the costs of the action, and taking the action only if the benefits are greater than the costs. Information should be collected only if the benefit is greater than the cost. (For example, it is probably not worth the cost in time and money to call a hotel to find out the colour of their carpeting.) Second, most people cannot effectively manage large quantities of information. Too much information, or information overload, can impair a person's ability to make decisions.

Question for Consideration

Explain why a potential vacationer to Aruba would likely find travel information published by Aruba's government travel department less credible than information provided by an independent travel company.

Answer: The objective of Aruba's government travel department is to encourage people to visit the island. It is likely that its publications will emphasize the favourable qualities of the island and downplay or ignore negative ones. In contrast, an independent travel company's objective is likely to provide a useful service to its customers that will encourage them to use the company's services again (the company will make more money if it can generate repeat business). As a result, the information from the independent travel agent is less likely to be biased. The vacationer is therefore likely to find the independent travel company's information more credible. This doesn't mean that the information provided by Aruba's government travel department wouldn't be useful. It means that a user of this information should recognize the probable bias and consider the implications of the bias when assessing the information.

What does a trip to Aruba have to do with studying accounting? Every day people make important decisions, both for themselves and on behalf of other entities. Individuals decide how to invest their retirement money. Bankers decide whether to lend money to struggling businesses. Labour union leaders assess how to approach negotiations with employers. Taxation authorities assess whether a taxpayer has paid the appropriate amount of tax. The point is, to make good decisions, whether they relate to a winter vacation or a business strategy, people must have good information available to them.

One important source of information for many business decisions is the accounting reports produced by entities. Accounting reports can be the standard financial statement package that most entities prepare each year, which includes balance sheets, income statements, statements of retained earnings, cash flow statements, and notes to the financial statements. Alternatively, accounting reports can be information that is designed for the use of a particular decision maker. (We will explore the standard financial statement package in depth in Chapter 2.)

Let's consider an example of how accounting information can help improve a business decision. Suppose you were approached by a person who was referred to you by a distant cousin and this person wanted you to lend a significant amount of your own money to her corporation. What would you want to know before you would agree to make the loan? Your first key question would be, "Will the company be able to pay back the money it borrowed, plus interest?" A second question would be, "If the company were unable to pay me back, what resources does it have that I could take and sell to recover my money?" What information would help you answer these questions? You could simply size up the person by examining how she is dressed, what she looks like, and how she speaks. However, this assessment would probably not tell you much that would allow you to answer the two questions we posed.

This is where accounting comes in. Accounting information could be very helpful for answering these two questions. Accounting could tell you how well the corporation has performed in the past and it could show you the amount of cash the company has been able to generate. Cash, of course, is important because that is what you hope to receive when the loan is paid back. You might also want a list of the resources the corporation owns so that you could see what would be available to you if the loan were not repaid. You might also like a list of to who else the corporation owes money. In addition, there is non-accounting information that would be helpful in your decision. For example, information about the people managing the corporation would be very useful. You can probably think of other information that would help you make your decision. Clearly, there is a wealth of information that could help you make an effective decision. A lot of this information is accounting information.

THE TWO FIELDS OF ACCOUNTING: FINANCIAL ACCOUNTING AND MANAGERIAL ACCOUNTING

The study of accounting is usually divided into two broad fields: financial accounting and managerial accounting. **Financial accounting** refers to the field of accounting that provides information to people who are external to an entity. These external users of accounting information include investors, lenders, taxation authorities (Canada Revenue Agency), competitors, and many others. Usually users of financial accounting information don't have direct access to information about the entity and must rely on the entity to provide information to them. This book focuses on financial accounting.

Managerial accounting refers to the field of accounting that provides information to the managers of the entity and other decision makers who work for the entity. This information assists them in making decisions related to operating the entity, including setting the price of products, deciding whether the company should expand, determining which products are successful and which are not, figuring out how much of a product should be produced, and so on.

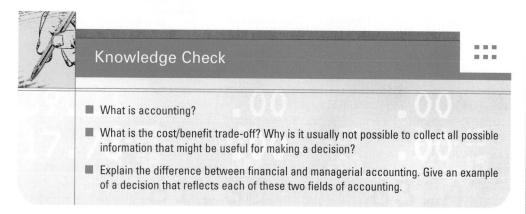

Knowledge Check

- What is accounting?

- What is the cost/benefit trade-off? Why is it usually not possible to collect all possible information that might be useful for making a decision?

- Explain the difference between financial and managerial accounting. Give an example of a decision that reflects each of these two fields of accounting.

www.mcgrawhill.ca/
olc/friedlan

THE ACCOUNTING ENVIRONMENT

Before we start our examination of accounting information, it is important to explore the environment in which accounting operates. It may come as a surprise that no single accounting report can suit all possible interested parties. An analogy may be useful in clarifying this point. Suppose your uncle approaches you to help him buy a car. He is very busy and has asked you to choose the car he should buy. What car would you suggest? Well, you might buy the car that appeals to you most, in the hope that he will let you borrow it. However, if you are going to buy a car that is suitable for your uncle, you will have to gather some information before you can decide. You will need to know how much he wants to spend, how many people will be travelling in the car, and how much importance your uncle places on characteristics such as safety, style, colour, make, fuel economy, speed, leg and head room, resale value, reliability, trunk/storage space, number of doors, and so on. If you don't consider these factors, your uncle might say, "Nice car, but a two-seater sports car doesn't leave any room for the baby," or "I love the Rolls-Royce, but I only make $35,000 a year. How will I pay for it?"

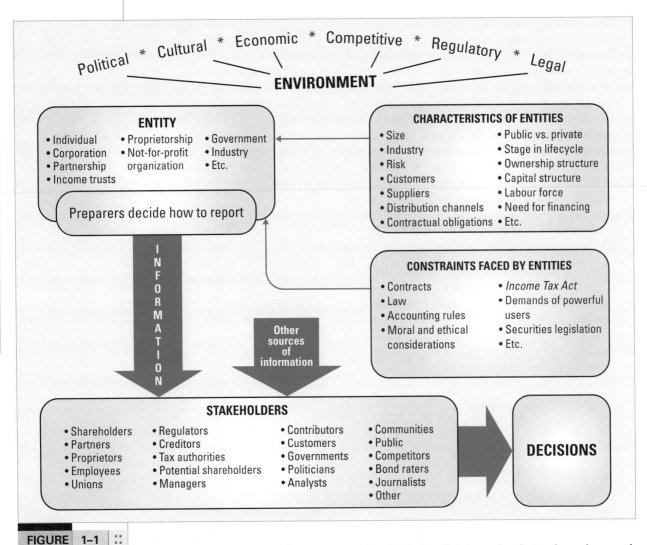

This example illustrates that no one car is suitable for all drivers: the choice depends on each driver's needs. Accounting is much the same. No one accounting report can provide the information that every decision maker needs. To best meet the needs of a decision maker, accounting information must be tailored. To do this, the people who prepare accounting information can often choose among alternative ways of doing their accounting so that they can tailor the information to the needs of the users (or, as we will see, to the needs of the preparers themselves!).

There are four key components of the accounting environment: entities, constraints, stakeholders, and overall environmental factors. These components are displayed in Figure 1–1 and discussed in detail below.

Environment

Every society has institutions that influence the way people live their lives. Canada, for example, is a constitutional democracy with a mixed economy and a legal system based on British common law. The environmental "umbrella" at the top of Figure 1–1 identifies some of the important societal parameters that establish the structure of a society: that is, the political, cultural, economic, competitive, regulatory, and legal parameters. Think of accounting as an activity that takes place within these environmental parameters.

Entities

An entity is an economic unit of some kind. An entity can be an individual, a business, part of a business, a charity, a school, a government, a club, or an industry—almost anything you care to define. Accounting can provide information about many different types of entities, including the four different types of business entities—corporations, proprietorships, partnerships, and income trusts—as well as not-for-profit organizations, governments, and individuals. Entities are central to the accounting environment because it is entities that provide accounting information to decision makers.

Corporations A **corporation** is a separate legal entity created under the corporation laws of Canada, a province, or some other jurisdiction in the world. A corporation has many of the same rights and responsibilities as an individual. For example, a corporation must file a tax return (unlike a proprietorship or a partnership), a corporation can be sued, and a corporation can enter into contracts (for example, to borrow money or to provide goods or services to a customer).

When a corporation is formed, shares in the corporation are issued to the owners. The **shares** represent ownership of the corporation. An entity that owns shares of a corporation is known as a **shareholder**. Shares can also be issued at any time through the life of a corporation.

One of the most important features of a corporation is that it provides **limited liability** to its shareholders. Limited liability means that the shareholders of a corporation are not liable for the obligations of the corporation or the losses it suffers. For example, if a corporation borrows money and is unable to repay the loan, the lender cannot demand repayment from the shareholders. The lender can take action only against the corporation. In effect, shareholders' liability is usually limited to the amount of money they invested in the corporation.

Another attractive feature of corporations is that it is relatively easy to transfer share ownership from one entity to another without any effect on the corporation. The corporation simply carries on business with a new owner. For other types of entities, a transfer of ownership can be more difficult.

Public corporations are corporations whose shares can be purchased by anyone who is interested in owning a piece of the entity and has the money to buy the shares. The shares of public corporations are usually traded on a **stock exchange** such as the Toronto Stock Exchange (TSX) or TSX Venture Exchange. A stock exchange is a place (physical or virtual) where entities can buy and sell shares and other securities of publicly traded entities.

Corporations can also be privately owned. A **private corporation** is one whose shares and other securities are not available for purchase unless the private corporation or its shareholders agree. For example, you might set up a corporation to run a small business. (The cost of setting up a corporation is relatively small, perhaps $1,500.) You could be the sole shareholder of the corporation and no one else could obtain shares of your corporation unless you wanted to sell them. Many small- and medium-sized businesses in Canada operate as private corporations. The most prominent corporations in Canada are public, but there are some well-known private corporations. Examples of some Canadian public and private corporations are shown in the table below.

www.tsx.ca

TABLE 1–1 ::: Examples of Public and Private Canadian Corporations			
Name of Corporation	**Ownership**	**Type of Business**	**Web site**
Canadian Tire Corporation	Public	Retail	www.canadiantire.ca
Research in Motion Limited	Public	Technology	www.rim.com
Westjet Airlines Ltd.	Public	Transportation	www.westjet.com
Loblaw Companies Limited	Public	Food Distribution	www.loblaw.ca
Petro-Canada	Public	Oil and Gas	www.petrocanada.ca
McCain Foods	Private	Food processing	www.mccain.com
Maple Lodge Farms Ltd.	Private	Food processing	www.maplelodgefarms.com
General Motors of Canada Limited*	Private	Auto Manufacturer	www.gmcanada.com
Irving Oil Limited	Private	Fuel Oil Dealer	www.irvingoil.com

*General Motors of Canada Limited is a private company owned by General Motors Corporation, which is a public company.

7

THE ACCOUNTING ENVIRONMENT: WHAT IS ACCOUNTING AND WHY IS IT DONE?

Proprietorships A **proprietorship** is an unincorporated business that has one owner. Unlike a corporation, a proprietorship is not a separate legal entity. A proprietorship doesn't pay taxes. Instead, the **proprietor**, the person who owns the proprietorship, includes the money made by the proprietorship in his or her personal tax return, along with money made from other sources, such as employment. If the proprietorship doesn't meet its obligations, the entities that are owed money can attempt to recover what is owed to them by seizing the proprietor's personal assets such as his or her house, car, or bank account. One of the attractive features of a proprietorship is that it is easy and inexpensive to set up.

Partnerships A **partnership** is an unincorporated business owned by two or more entities called **partners**. (Partners do not have to be people; they can be corporations.) A partnership is like a proprietorship except that there is more than one owner. Partnerships do not pay taxes. Instead, the money earned by the partnership is included in the income of the partners. A partnership does not have limited legal liability. A lawsuit against a partnership places the assets of at least some of the partners at risk. Like a proprietorship, a partnership is relatively easy and inexpensive to set up. However, since a partnership involves more than one person, it is wise to have a partnership agreement, which lays out the rights and responsibilities of the partners. A partnership agreement adds cost and complexity to this form of business. Many professional organizations such as accounting firms (for example, Deloitte and Touche) and law firms are organized as partnerships.

Income Trusts The income trust is a relatively new form of business organization that is becoming increasingly common. Business entities organize as income trusts instead of corporations, primarily for tax reasons. The money earned by an income trust is not taxed if paid out to the owners. However, on October 31, 2006, the Federal government announced major changes to the tax treatment of income trusts that will make it unattractive for corporations to convert to income trusts.

Not-for-profit Organizations A large part of the Canadian economy is not devoted to making money or a profit. These **not-for-profit organizations** provide social, educational, professional, religious, health, charitable, or other similar services in Canadian communities and around the world. Not-for-profit organizations include hospitals, charities, religious organizations, unions, clubs, daycare centres, universities, and many others.

Governments Government plays a large role in the lives of Canadians. The various levels of government in Canada raise and spend hundreds of billions of dollars each year, mainly through different types of taxes. Given the large amount of money governments manage, financial reporting by governments is important if citizens are to evaluate how their tax dollars are being spent.

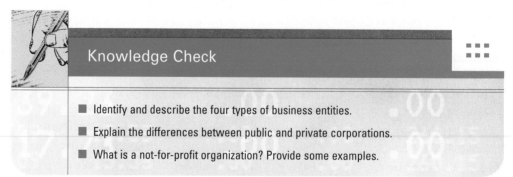

Knowledge Check

■ Identify and describe the four types of business entities.

■ Explain the differences between public and private corporations.

■ What is a not-for-profit organization? Provide some examples.

Individuals Individual people are also accounting entities. Individuals must often produce information in a quantitative form to meet the demands of everyday life. Consider the following examples:

■ Most individuals must file a tax return each year with the **Canada Revenue Agency (CRA)**, the Canadian government agency responsible for the administration and enforcement of Canadian federal tax laws. This requires the accumulation and organization of information to complete the return.

- Most people insure their homes and belongings. To determine the appropriate amount of home-owner insurance that is needed, an individual must list his or her personal belongings and estimate a value for them.
- Most people have a chequing account. The cheque register, where you record each cheque that you write, represents a simple accounting system that lets you know how much money is in your bank account.
- Many people prepare budgets. A student may want to estimate how much it will cost to attend university each year and thus plan monthly or weekly spending to ensure that enough money is available to meet all financial needs for the year.

Others Though most common entities have been identified, accounting information can be compiled on an endless list of entities, depending on the users' needs. For example, some people may want data on a particular industry. While industries do not prepare financial statements, useful information can sometimes be obtained from sources such as trade associations, industry publications, public interest groups, and Statistics Canada.

www.statcan.ca

Stakeholders: Different Users, Different Decisions, Different Information

There are many different groups and individuals that are interested in—or have a "stake" in—an entity. These groups and individuals are referred to as **stakeholders** and may include entities such as owners, lenders, taxation authorities, government, consumers, and regulators. (See Figure 1–1, page 6.) Of course, not every possible stakeholder will be interested in every possible entity. Each stakeholder has his or her own perspective on an entity and has specific decisions to make. An owner will be concerned about different things than a lender, who will be concerned about different things than the public, employees, or government. Therefore, the information that would be most useful to a particular stakeholder group would not be the same as the information some other stakeholder would find most useful.

Stakeholders are often people who do not have direct and unrestricted access to an entity's databases and must rely on the entity to provide information for decision making. Ideally, each stakeholder would receive information that is tailored to his or her own needs. More likely though, the information an entity provides will be designed with some other stakeholder or purpose in mind, or for general use by a variety of different stakeholders.

For example, imagine you are deciding which university's business program you should enrol in and you contact a number of schools for information. One university sends you information about the overall university instead of detailed information about the business program. While the general university calendar might have some information about the business program, it would not be as useful as the business program calendar. To make the most informed decision about the business program, you need its particular calendar.

Let's examine some of the stakeholders of an entity and look at how accounting information can be useful to them.

Owners Often, the owners of a business don't manage it and are not involved in its day-to-day affairs (for example, most shareholders of public corporations). When the owners do not manage a business, they need information from the company for a number of reasons, including: to evaluate how well their investment is doing; to determine whether management is doing a good job; to assess the effectiveness of business strategies; to consider whether they should sell their interest in the entity; or to decide if the managers should be replaced.

Lenders Most entities need to borrow money at one time or another. Before lending money, a prospective lender, such as a banker, would want to investigate whether the borrower would be able to pay back the loan and, if the loan is not paid back, whether the borrower has assets the lender could take and sell to recover the money it lent.

Suppliers Most entities use goods and services supplied by others. For example, a retail store obtains the goods it sells, the utilities it uses, the office supplies it needs, and the advertising it does from various third parties. Most of these goods and services are provided before they are paid for, so these suppliers might want to evaluate whether the entity will be able to pay for the goods and services before providing them.

Taxation Authorities The Canada Revenue Agency (CRA) uses accounting information to assess the taxes owed by a business or individual. In Canada each individual and corporation must file a tax return each year. The CRA requires taxpayers to calculate their taxes using methods that are consistent with the *Income Tax Act*, Canada's federal tax legislation. Provinces also have tax rules that must be followed.

Governments Other government departments also have an interest in accounting information. For example, governments may decide whether certain entities should receive government support or subsidies. Accounting information also has a political impact. Companies might attract the attention of politicians by making what the public perceives as "too much money."

Consumers When someone buys an expensive product such as a computer or car, he or she may be concerned about whether the company will be around in the future to support the product. While most people who make major purchases do not consult manufacturers' accounting reports, many sources can provide information about a manufacturer's financial status. These include television, newspaper, and radio reports. As a result, a potential customer might decide not to buy from a company in financial trouble even though the product is attractive for other reasons.

Regulators Some industries and businesses in Canada are regulated, including cable television providers and local telephone companies, which are regulated by the Canadian Radio-television and Telecommunications Commission (CRTC); pipeline companies that transport oil and natural gas, which are regulated by the National Energy Board (NEB); and even some transportation companies, for example BC Ferries (which provides transportation services on British Columbia's coastal waters). Accounting information prepared by the regulated companies is used to help regulators set rates so that customers pay a reasonable price for the service and investors receive a reasonable return on their investment. Regulators may sometimes even define the accounting rules that a regulated company can use.

Characteristics of Entities

Like people, no two entities are identical. Each has a set of characteristics that makes it unique. Some characteristics are obvious—for example, an entity's industry. Canada has businesses in a vast range of industries, including natural resources, agriculture, finance, manufacturing, high technology, hospitality, and services, to name a few. And even though several companies may be in the same industry, each may have different characteristics. Some may be public, others private, some may be large and others small, some may be unionized and others not, and each may do business in different markets. All of these characteristics are important for understanding an entity, what it does, and how it does its accounting.

Figure 1–1 (page 6) identifies a number of characteristics of entities. We will explore many of these as we proceed. At this point it is important to keep in mind that entities are not all the same and that the characteristics of an entity might influence the accounting choices it makes.

Constraints

How an entity does its accounting and what information it reports are not entirely up to the people who prepare the information. Often, the choices available are constrained by contracts, laws, accounting rules, and the information needs and demands of powerful users of accounting information. Consider the following examples:

- The *Income Tax Act* requires, for certain situations, that particular accounting methods be used to calculate the amount of income tax that an entity must pay.

- Corporations must meet the requirements of the law they are incorporated under (such as the *Canada Business Corporations Act*).

- Many companies must follow the accounting rules known as generally accepted accounting principles (GAAP).

- Companies that trade on Canadian stock exchanges must meet the requirements of the securities laws of their province and the rules of the stock exchange.

- Entities often enter voluntarily into contracts with other parties to do their accounting in a certain way.

Stakeholders versus Preparers

Accounting information must be considered from two perspectives: the stakeholders' perspective and the preparers' perspective. **Preparers** (or managers of an entity) are the people responsible for deciding what, how, and when information is going to be presented in an entity's financial statements and other accounting reports. Preparers are the people who make the decisions—senior managers such as controllers, chief financial officers, and even chief executive officers. They are not the people who physically prepare the statements.

It is important to recognize that preparers are not neutral providers of accounting information. Their own personal interests may influence their preparation of accounting reports. Consider the following situations:

- Managers' bonuses are sometimes based on the numbers contained in accounting reports. (A manager might want to enhance the accounting numbers to improve his or her bonus.)

- The amount of tax an entity pays is related to its accounting numbers. (The manager might account in a way so as to pay as little tax as is legally possible.)

- When a business is sold, the selling price can be based on the accounting numbers. (The manager might want to enhance the accounting numbers to increase the selling price of the business.)

There is clearly potential for conflict here. Stakeholders want information that will be useful for their decision making. Managers have an interest in supplying useful information to stakeholders, but they are also interested in acting on their own behalf. Making matters more complicated are the rules under which most Canadian entities report. Generally accepted accounting principles, or GAAP, provide managers a great deal of latitude in deciding what, how, and when information is presented in an entity's accounting statements. In other words, managers have the motivation and the ability to present accounting information in ways that do not necessarily meet the needs of stakeholders.

At this point, sirens might be going off in your head. "This doesn't sound very honest." "They cook the books!" "You can't trust accounting numbers." "Accountants are unethical." Sometimes these reactions are valid. However, the reality about accounting information is usually not so black and white. Preparers can often choose among different acceptable ways to account because trying to set rules that apply to all situations can be difficult and counterproductive. The diversity of entities, stakeholders, and entity characteristics, along with the complexity of economic activity, require flexibility—enough to allow information to be presented in an appropriate way for the circumstances as well as to allow accounting to adapt to new business arrangements and changes in the accounting environment. However, such flexibility also allows some managers to play fast and loose with the rules. Sometimes managers focus only on their personal interests and the interests of their entities rather than on ensuring that stakeholders get the information they need to make good decisions. To make matters worse, it is often difficult in this complex environment to figure out managers' motivations and the full impact of managers' accounting choices.

To place this discussion in context, consider this statement by Paul Beeston, former president of the Toronto Blue Jays Baseball Club, former president and chief operating officer of Major League Baseball, and an accountant:

> "Anyone who quotes profits of a baseball club is missing the point. Under generally accepted accounting principles, I can turn a $4 million profit into a $2 million loss, and I can get every national accounting firm to agree with me."[1]

www.mcgrawhill.ca/
olc/friedlan

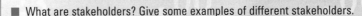

Knowledge Check

- What are stakeholders? Give some examples of different stakeholders.

- Provide some reasons why the personal interests of preparers may influence how they might prepare their financial statements.

- Entities have different characteristics. Identify some of the characteristics that distinguish one entity from another.

Question for Consideration

Consider the quote by Paul Beeston on page 11. In the context of our discussion of the accounting environment, what do you think Mr. Beeston meant by his statement?

Answer: Mr. Beeston was making the point that accounting rules, even under GAAP, are flexible and allow preparers considerable latitude in choosing how, what, and when accounting information is presented. This flexibility implies that the numbers reported in financial statements can vary depending on the choices that the preparers make and that a range of numbers can be considered as being "within the rules."

The apparent conflict between stakeholders and managers creates a need for independent people who can examine the information provided by the managers and offer assurance to the stakeholders that the information meets certain stated principles. The people who examine entities' financial information on behalf of external stakeholders are called **external auditors**. Their examination of an entity's information is known as an **external audit**. An external audit involves examining an entity's financial statements and the data supporting the information in the financial statements. Auditors audit to ensure that the financial statements are fair representations of the underlying economic activity of the entity and that the accounting is done in accordance with GAAP.

It is important that external auditors be independent of the entity they are auditing to add credibility to the information provided by an entity. That means an auditor cannot be involved in managing the entity, have an ownership interest, or participate in any type of relationship that will bring the independence of the auditor into question. For example, if you were buying a used car and wanted to be sure that the car you were interested in buying was in excellent condition, would you have more confidence in the opinion of the used car dealer or that of an independent mechanic? Clearly, the car dealer has an interest in making you believe that the car is of high quality since he or she will benefit from the sale.

There are other types of auditors in addition to the external auditors described above:

- Internal auditors are employed by an entity and conduct audits on behalf of the entity's management. Internal audits help ensure the credibility of the information produced by the entity for management decision making.

- The Canada Revenue Agency (CRA) has auditors whose job is to verify that taxpayers adhere to the *Income Tax Act* and pay the appropriate amount of tax.

Let's conclude this section with an accounting example. On December 15, 2008 a Toronto Blue Jays fan orders season tickets for the 2009 baseball season (the Blue Jays are owned by Rogers

Communications Inc. (Rogers)). The tickets cost $10,000 and the fan pays a $500 deposit when they're ordered. The rest must be paid in full on February 28, 2009. The baseball games will be played from April through October. When do you think the Blue Jays (and Rogers) should report that they've sold these season tickets? Should the Blue Jays report the sale when the tickets are ordered (December 15, 2008), when they're paid for (February 28, 2009), or when the games are actually played (April through October 2009)? Accountants can actually disagree as to when to report the sale. But the economic activity still proceeds while the accountants are scratching their heads figuring out when to report the sale. In other words, when the accountants decide to record this sale does not change when the order is received, when the cash is collected, or when the games are played.

While the actual economic activity is unaffected by how the Blue Jays do their accounting, how the accounting is done can affect the entity, the managers, and the stakeholders. The choice made can affect the amount of tax the Blue Jays pay, the size of bonus the sales manager earns, perhaps the terms of a bank loan, and even the price of Rogers' shares. Accounting information matters. Accounting information can affect the wealth and wellbeing of the preparers and the various stakeholders of an entity. (A term that is often used to describe an event that affects the wealth and wellbeing of an entity and its stakeholders is that the event has *economic consequences*. This term will be used frequently in *Financial Accounting: A Critical Approach*.) Because of these economic consequences it is essential for students of accounting to understand the nature of accounting information. It is also the economic consequences of accounting information along with the flexibility of accounting rules that make accounting such a fascinating discipline.

As we move through *Financial Accounting*, you'll see what choices are available to managers and how those different choices affect the information that is presented to stakeholders. The purpose for introducing this unexpected side of accounting is to make you aware of what accounting is really like. Accounting is not certainty, it is not truth, and there are few right answers.

Insight

This discussion of the accounting environment should make it clear that there is potential for significant and frequent ethical dilemmas. Managers, auditors, and accountants continually face choices about what, how, and when information should be presented in an entity's financial statements and other accounting reports. These choices are often difficult and usually are not simple choices between the right way and the wrong way. Economic activity can be complex and deciding how to account requires careful judgment. Managers have an ethical and moral responsibility to provide information that is a reasonable representation of the entity's economic activity. But it is important to understand that intelligent, ethical, and responsible managers, auditors, and accountants can have legitimate differences of opinion about how accounting should be done in a given situation. The "right" answer is not always obvious!

Accounting Scandals

In the last 10 years the business and accounting worlds have been rocked by scandals that have damaged the credibility of accounting information. Companies like Enron, Nortel, WorldCom, Parmalat, and Livent, have become notorious for their abuse of financial reporting. In each case stakeholders have suffered large economic losses. In addition, the prominent accounting firm of Arthur Andersen was effectively forced out of the public accounting business as a result of the Enron scandal.

Nortel Networks Corporation, long one of Canada's technology leaders and at one time the most valuable public company in the country, suffered through serious accounting problems in

13

THE ACCOUNTING ENVIRONMENT: WHAT IS ACCOUNTING AND WHY IS IT DONE?

the years after 2000. It took Nortel several years to get its accounting right—delaying, reissuing, and restating its financial statements a number of times because of accounting errors, violation of accounting rules and principles, and attempts by managers to mislead the people who used the company's financial statements so they could pursue their own interests. In 2004, for example, it was discovered that management used accounting "tricks" to report profits in 2003 that allowed bonuses to be paid to all Nortel employees, including significant bonuses to senior executives. Nortel's accounting woes occurred in the same period that its stock price fell from a high of over $120 per share in 2000 to a low of $0.67 in 2002 and then remained well under $10.00 from then on.

There has been a silver lining to these accounting scandals. People have become much more aware of how important good accounting information is and how detrimental poor-quality accounting information is to effective decision making. As a result of these scandals, laws affecting financial reporting and accountants have been tightened in the U.S. and subsequently in Canada. It is hoped that these laws will improve the integrity and reliability of financial statement information.

Professional Accountants in Canada

In Canada there are three groups of professional accountants: Certified General Accountants (CGAs), Certified Management Accountants (CMAs), and Chartered Accountants (CAs). A person with one of these designations has demonstrated that they have the knowledge, skills, and abilities required by the professional body. A member of the public who hires a professional accountant can be confident that he or she will be able to carry out his or her duties properly. Members of a professional accounting body have important responsibilities. They are expected to act in a professional, ethical, and competent manner at all times and to adhere to the code of conduct of their professional organization.

Becoming a professional accountant isn't easy. Each professional body has its own requirements but, in general, to earn an accounting designation it is necessary to:

■ receive a university degree;

■ complete specific course requirements to learn the body of knowledge needed to be an effective practitioner;

■ pass the examinations administered by the professional body;

■ obtain experience on the job.

ACCOUNTING IS FOR MEASUREMENT

Accounting systems are designed to accumulate data that are then organized, processed, and converted into information that is useful to stakeholders. The information produced by accounting systems allows stakeholders to measure different attributes of an entity, such as:

■ how it performed

■ how efficient it was

■ how its managers performed and how much bonus they should receive

■ how much it owes to lenders

■ how much it is worth

■ how much tax it should pay

Let's look at some examples of how accounting can be used for measuring. Suppose that over the summer you had a job in a mining town in northern Canada. You expected that you would earn enough money during the summer to pay for next year's tuition and be able to take a winter vacation with your friends. After the first couple of months you look at your bank account information on the Internet and become worried that you aren't saving enough money.

TABLE 1–2 ::: Your Summer Expenses: An Example of a Basic Accounting System

List of Money Spent During the Summer		
Date	**Purpose**	**Amount**
April 1	Rent	$300
•	•	•
•	•	•
•	•	•
April 13	Magazines	5.75
April 13	Entertainment	22.50
April 13	Groceries	44.85
•	•	•
•	•	•
•	•	•
May 17	Groceries	45.25
May 18	Entertainment	12.75
May 19	Miscellaneous	14.50
•	•	•
•	•	•
•	•	•
May 31	Clothes	47.99
May 31	Taxi	5.00

Fortunately, at the start of the summer you decided to keep track of the money you spent during the summer by recording the information in a notebook. An excerpt from the "book" for April and May is shown in Table 1–2. Your book represents a very basic accounting system.

The contents of the notebook are just raw data. To be useful, the data have to be organized, processed, and converted into information. You could go through your notebook and classify expenditures into categories such as food, entertainment, and rent. Table 1–3 shows an example of how you could organize the data in your book.

With the information organized as in Table 1–3 it is easy to see how much money you made, how much you spent and what you spent it on, and how much you have left over.

Next, we can consider how you could use the information in Table 1–3. Your concern is that you're not saving enough money, so you could use the information to identify ways you could reduce spending. For example, you might reduce the amount you're spending on entertainment by going out less often or finding less expensive forms of entertainment. Or you might consider ways to reduce the amount you're spending on groceries. Perhaps on reflection you find that you are buying expensive food items when less expensive (but equally nutritious) ones could be purchased. You might consider finding less expensive accommodation or even try to work more hours. Notice that Table 1–3 helps you identify ways that you can address your problem but it doesn't actually tell you what to do. The decision maker (you, in this case) must use the information to come up with a solution.

A crucial point to keep in mind is that how you organize the data depends on what you or some other stakeholder wants to know. If you didn't care how you spent your money, a statement like the one in Table 1–4 might suffice. On the other hand, Table 1–3 does not tell you the type of entertainment you enjoyed, what groceries you bought, or what the miscellaneous items represent, so you might find that Table 1–3 is not detailed enough.

You should also recognize that your ability to extract information from an accounting system is limited to the data entered into the system. For example, it would be possible to find out how much money you spent on different kinds of groceries only if you initially broke down your

TABLE 1–3 ::: Classifying Your Summer Earnings and Spending: An Example of a Basic Accounting Report

Summary of Earnings and Spending		
April and May		
Amount earned (gross pay)	$5,258.88	
Amount withheld*	946.60	
Deposited in the bank (net pay)		$4,312.28
Amounts spent		
Books, magazines, etc.	75.33	
Clothes	138.25	
Entertainment	221.55	
Groceries	327.58	
Local transportation	45.56	
Miscellaneous	99.98	
Rent	600.00	
Amount spent		1,508.25
Amount saved in April and May		$2,804.03

*Employers are required to withhold money from employees' pay for taxes, employment insurance, and Canada Pension Plan contributions. The amount earned before withholding is called gross pay. The amount after deductions is called net pay.

TABLE 1–4 ::: Summarizing Your Summer Earnings and Spending: An Example of a Basic Accounting Report

Summary of Summer Earnings and Spending		
Amount earned (gross pay)	$5,258.88	
Amount withheld*	946.60	
Deposited in the bank (net pay)		$4,312.28
Amount spent during April and May		1,508.25
Amount saved in April and May		$2,804.03

grocery spending in your notebook. That is, you couldn't find out how much money you spent on soft drinks if you didn't record soft drink spending separately in the notebook.

This example demonstrates how accounting can summarize information in a way that is useful for solving a problem. Let's consider an example that looks at another perspective on measurement.

Imagine that you are a first-year student who has just moved into a new apartment near your university or college. You need to get insurance for the apartment. You have furnished it with personal belongings, and it also has appliances supplied by the building's owner. How much insurance do you need? You want to have enough insurance to protect the things you own and the things you are responsible for, such as the building owner's appliances. The insurance company needs to know how much insurance you require so that it can write a policy and set a premium for you, based on the amount and type of insurance you want.

To estimate the amount of insurance you need, you will have to go through the apartment and take an "inventory" of the things you want to insure. (An inventory is a list of the items in your apartment, as shown in Table 1–5.)

Column 1 of Table 1–5 lists the contents of the apartment, but it doesn't say anything about how much insurance coverage you need. You have to assign a measure of value to each item so that you can "sum up" to a total. The total is important because if you don't know the worth of

| TABLE | 1–5 | ::: | Items in a Student's Apartment |

Inventory of Apartment Contents			
Column 1	Column 2	Column 3	Column 4
Item	What it cost	What it would cost to replace	What it could be sold for
Television	$ 500	$ 650	$ 225
Computer	1,900	1,500	700
Furniture	1,200	1,350	900
Books	750	875	300
Clothes	1,600	1,950	1,000
Stereo	900	1,100	700
Jewellery	500	625	300
Appliances	2,000	2,600	1,400
Art	300	300	200
Other	1,000	1,200	750
Total	$10,650	$12,150	$6,475

what you want to insure you may buy too little insurance, leaving you ill-prepared in the event of a fire or robbery. If you buy too much insurance you are wasting money on premiums, since the insurance company will not pay out more than the amount of the loss. (For example, if you have $50,000 of insurance coverage and everything you own is destroyed in a fire but is worth $10,000, the insurance company will pay you only $10,000.)

Now things get more complicated. What is the appropriate "value" to assign to each item? In Table 1–5 three different measurements of value have been used for each item, as follows:

■ Column 2 gives the amount paid for each item.

■ Column 3 shows the amount that would have to be paid to replace the item with an equivalent new item. (For example, the TV might be a ten-year-old model that is no longer made, so you would have to get something comparable that is available today.)

■ Column 4 is the amount each item could be sold for.

Notice that the total of each column is quite different from the others.

All of these amounts represent valid measures of the items in your apartment, but which would be appropriate for determining the amount of insurance that you need? That will depend on your needs. If you want the insurance to return you to the situation you were in before you suffered your loss then using the cost to replace amounts in Column 3 would be best. Using Column 3 would allow replacement of the items lost (this is called replacement cost insurance). For example, if your television was stolen, replacement cost insurance would allow you to obtain an equivalent television. If you wanted the insurance to simply compensate you for the loss you suffered, then Column 4 should be used. Using Column 4 would allow you to recover the cash value of the items you lost. So if your 10-year old television was stolen, your loss would be the market value of an identical 10-year-old TV. (The insurance company would not get estimates of the worth of the specific items, but would use a formula to estimate the extent to which they were used, based on the type of item and its age.)

There are two important points to note from our insurance example. The first is the importance of measurement. To decide on the amount of insurance needed it was necessary to come up with a measure of the total worth of the items in the apartment. The second point is that there is often more than one way to measure the same thing. We have easily come up with three ways to measure the "value" in terms of dollars of the items in your apartment. Which one is best? That question cannot be answered in absolute terms. The "best" one depends on the situation and the needs of the decision maker.

It is important to keep in mind that whereas most accounting reports use money as the basis for measurement, it is not the only possible basis. Accounting and accountants can provide information in many different ways. For example, accountants could be involved in providing information on the amount of pollution that a company produces. They could be involved in measuring the effectiveness of a medical care system (mortality rates, utilization of beds and equipment, etc.). Accountants could help develop measures of customer satisfaction or evaluate whether a government is getting value for the money it spends. These examples require measurements that are not stated in terms of money.

Question for Consideration

A few months ago you borrowed $1,000 from an acquaintance and now you don't have the cash to pay back the loan. In place of the cash you owe you have offered the acquaintance some of your personal belongings. If the list in Table 1–5 represents your belongings, which measurement basis (which column) would be most appropriate to use to determine which items the acquaintance could reasonably take?

Answer: Column 4, what the items could be sold for, would be most appropriate. Since you owe $1,000, the acquaintance should receive items that would allow her to receive the equivalent of $1,000 in cash. The acquaintance does not have to actually sell the items, but the items she receives could be sold for $1,000.

THE RULES OF THE GAME

Accounting is a tool that has been developed to provide information for decision making. Unlike gravity, accounting has no natural laws that define how it should be done. As a result, it is necessary to establish the rules of the game. If there were no rules it would be much more costly and difficult to make sense of the information contained in accounting reports because it would be necessary to learn and understand how each entity was doing its accounting.

The rules in accounting are known as **generally accepted accounting principles** or **GAAP**. GAAP are the principles, conventions, practices, procedures, and rules that define acceptable accounting practices and guide the preparation of financial statements in certain situations. In other words, GAAP represent a structure for preparing financial statements.

The importance of a set of rules can be demonstrated with an analogy. When we drive, there are certain conventions and rules that people follow that contribute to safe driving. In every community in Canada a red light means stop and a green light means go. A yellow light is a bit more ambiguous and different drivers respond differently to yellow lights. (This is actually just like GAAP, where some of the "rules" can be interpreted differently by different preparers of accounting information.) Everywhere in Canada we drive on the right side of the road. However, in some countries, such as the United Kingdom, Jamaica, and Zimbabwe, people drive on the left side of the road. In the same way that traffic rules can vary from one country to another, so can GAAP.

Now imagine the difficulty a driver would have if every community had different rules of the road—if there were different coloured lights in different positions. The result would be chaos. Traffic would move more slowly as visiting drivers tried to figure out the rules in each community. Getting around the community would be more costly in terms of time, fuel expense, insurance (since there would probably be more accidents), and fines (since people would likely violate the rules more often and there would be more tickets issued). In sum, the existence of standardized rules of the road reduces the cost of getting around.

Here are a few preliminary points to note about GAAP:

- GAAP are not universal. GAAP differ in each country. Canadian GAAP are quite similar but not identical to GAAP in the United States, but can be very different from GAAP in other countries in the world.

- Not every entity follows GAAP or has to follow GAAP. GAAP are followed by public corporations because it is required by securities and corporation law. However, GAAP do not have to be followed by private corporations, partnerships, or proprietorships unless there is some specific reason for doing so.

- GAAP are flexible. They offer preparers many choices that can affect the information contained in financial statements. The flexibility of GAAP requires that users be very careful when examining and interpreting financial statements.

- GAAP in Canada are the responsibility of the Accounting Standard Board of the Canadian Institute of Chartered Accountings (CICA) and the GAAP it lays down are published in the *CICA Handbook*. However, much of GAAP come from sources other than the *Handbook*, including the accounting methods actually used by entities. The *CICA Handbook* has the force of law behind it because the provincial securities commissions and the federal and provincial laws that regulate corporations recognize the *CICA Handbook* as the source of GAAP in Canada.

- In 2005 the CICA announced that it was getting out of the standard-setting business, at least for public companies, and would be adopting International Financial Reporting Standards (IFRS). IFRS are produced by the International Accounting Standards Board, which has worked for many years to develop a set of accounting standards that could be used by entities around the world. The CICA also indicated that it would try to create a new set of standards for private businesses that have significant external stakeholders and that it would work to remove GAAP requirements for private businesses with no external reporting requirements.

We will explore GAAP in depth in Chapter 5, but at this point we can take a look at some of the basic Canadian GAAP concepts. The *CICA Handbook* describes four qualitative characteristics that financial statement information must have if it is to be useful to users. The four characteristics are:

1. **Understandability.** Users must be able to understand information if it is to be useful to them. GAAP require that accounting information should be understandable to users who have a reasonable understanding of business and accounting, and a willingness to study the information provided.

2. **Relevance.** The information provided to users must be relevant or useful for the decisions they have to make. The *CICA Handbook* explains that relevant information is information that helps users make predictions about the future performance of the entity, provides feedback on decisions that were made in the past, and is provided to users in a timely manner so that it will be useful for decision making.

3. **Reliability.** For information to be useful to users, it must be a reasonable representation of the attribute being measured. The *CICA Handbook* identifies the components of reliability as verifiability, representational faithfulness, and freedom from bias. Information is verifiable if independent and knowledgeable people can come up with the same measurements for the attribute being measured. Financial statements are representationally faithful if they are a reasonable representation of the economic activity of an entity. Information is free from bias if it is not presented in a way that is designed to influence or manipulate users' decisions.

4. **Comparability.** Users should be able to compare the accounting information provided by different entities and the information of a particular entity from period to period.

19

THE ACCOUNTING ENVIRONMENT: WHAT IS ACCOUNTING AND WHY IS IT DONE?

www.cica.ca

For example, the ability to make predictions about the future performance of an entity can be helped by looking at historical performance trends of the entity. If the entity changes its accounting in each period the ability to interpret the trends would be impaired.

It is essential for any user or preparer of accounting information to know and understand GAAP. However, every user, preparer, and accountant must also understand that GAAP have significant problems and limitations. GAAP are not applicable to every user and every decision in every situation. Sophisticated users of financial statements will know when not to rely on GAAP-based statements, when to adjust the GAAP statements, and when to look elsewhere for information. Sophisticated users will also understand the flexibility that preparers of financial statements have, even under GAAP, and understand that this flexibility can have a significant effect on the information reported in the statements.

One of the main objectives of this book is to help readers understand and appreciate financial statements, with all their blemishes. We will look at accounting practice and accounting information with a critical eye so that you will become sophisticated users and preparers of accounting information.

▪▪ Solved Problem

Bayton Ltd.—Part 1

Bayton Ltd. (Bayton) is an operator of garbage dumps in western Canada. Bayton operates by purchasing land from private owners, having the land zoned for a garbage dump, and then developing and operating the dump. The planning and development of the dumps is done in close cooperation with the local communities that the dump will serve. Bayton does not provide garbage collection services; these are provided by local governments or by private companies that have contracts with local governments. The garbage collectors pay a fee to Bayton based on the weight of the garbage dumped.

Bayton is a privately owned corporation. The company has 15 investors who live all across Canada. A team of professional managers who have considerable experience in the waste management business runs Bayton. The managers are paid a salary plus a bonus based on the performance of the company, as measured by its accounting information. The company employs over 500 people, many of whom are unionized. In addition to money invested by the owners of the company, Bayton has borrowed heavily from several banks and other lenders.

Required:

Identify all of the stakeholders in Bayton and explain their "stake" in the company. Not all the stakeholders are explicitly referred to in the scenario. You will have to think about the business situation carefully to identify some of the stakeholders. (You may be able to identify other stakeholders in addition to those in the Solution.)

Solution:

Stakeholders	Stake
1. Shareholders (owners)	The shareholders are Bayton's owners. Part of their wealth is invested in the company.
2. Lenders	Bayton owes the lenders money. The lenders are concerned about Bayton's ability to repay amounts owed to them.
3. Managers	Managers are interested in maintaining their jobs and enhancing their reputations in the job market. In addition, part of the managers' compensation is based on the performance of Bayton.
4. Canada Revenue Agency (CRA)	Bayton Ltd. is a taxpaying entity and the CRA is interested in ensuring that it pays its taxes and complies with the *Income Tax Act*.

5. People located in communities where dumps are or will be located

Garbage dumps are often unpopular neighbours. People who live near existing garbage dumps want to ensure that the dumps are being managed responsibly and that Bayton will be able to carry out its obligations in the future. People living near prospective garbage dumps may want to take steps to prevent a dump from being set up near their homes.

6. Government

Garbage dumps can be politically very sensitive issues. Governments want to ensure that Bayton Ltd.'s garbage dumps do not cause them political problems.

7. Employees/unions

Bayton Ltd.'s employees rely on the company for their incomes. Unions negotiate contracts with Bayton Ltd. on behalf of their employees.

8. Environmental regulatory agencies

Because of the potential environmental problems associated with Bayton's garbage dumps, many jurisdictions have regulatory agencies whose responsibilities include monitoring the company's waste management practices, ensuring compliance with government standards, and reporting to the government and public.

9. Communities

Communities require a means of disposing of their garbage. Ensuring a reliable method of disposal is crucial for many communities. Bayton provides the means for these communities to dispose of their garbage.

10. Garbage collection companies

Garbage collection companies require a place to dump the garbage they collect and must pay fees to do so.

11. Environmental groups

Garbage dumps pose potentially serious environmental problems. Improper waste management practices can lead to contamination of land and ground water. Private environmental groups monitor the dumps and the companies operating them.

Bayton Ltd.—Part 2

In 1975 Bayton paid $250,000 ($500 per hectare) for a 500-hectare piece of land that it intended to develop into a garbage dump. For various reasons Bayton has not yet developed the land, but Bayton's president has stated that it will do so at the appropriate time. Over the last two years there have been two transactions involving the sale of land located near Bayton's property. In the first transaction, which occurred 20 months ago, the land was sold for $825 per hectare. In the second transaction, which occurred eight months ago, the land was sold for $730 per hectare.

Recently, a business person made an offer for Bayton's land of $690 per hectare or $345,000. The president of Bayton hired an independent appraiser to estimate the value of the land so that he could assess the offer. The appraiser estimated that the land was worth between $340,000 and $390,000. For the purpose of calculating municipal property taxes, two years ago the municipality where the land is located placed a value on it of $290,000. The president himself thinks that Bayton could sell the land for $410,000 if Bayton chose to sell it.

Required:

Identify and explain the different measurements of the value of Bayton's land. Discuss the relevance and reliability of the different measurements. Make sure you refer to the decisions that have to be made by some of the stakeholders.

Solution:

There are a number of different measurements available for valuing Bayton's land, none of which represent the actual current value of the land. The measurements are:

Measurement	Explanation	Relevance and Reliability
Cost: $250,000	The amount Bayton paid for the land.	Cost is a very reliable measure of the value of the land because documentation exists indicating the price that Bayton paid for the land in 1975. This measure will be verifiable, representationally faithful,

and unbiased. The cost is relevant for income tax purposes because the amount of tax paid when Bayton sells the land will be related to the price it paid for it. The cost may also be relevant to shareholders if they want to know how much profit Bayton made by holding the land since 1975 and then selling it. The cost of the land is not very relevant for most other decisions. Cost is not useful for determining whether or not the land should be sold, the amount of money that a lender would lend to Bayton based on the market value of land, or the amount that a buyer should pay for the land if Bayton decided to sell it. For these decisions the market value of the land is more relevant.

Property tax value: $290,000	The value assigned to the land by the municipality for determining the property taxes.	This amount is relevant for determining the amount of property tax that Bayton must pay. Otherwise this value does not likely have any other useful purpose. The value was determined two years ago, which makes it somewhat out of date, and since it is not clear how the amount was determined, its relevance for non-property-tax purposes is difficult to assess.
Bayton's president's estimate: $410,000	The amount that Bayton's president thinks the company can sell the land for.	This amount may be relevant as a benchmark for management for determining whether the land should be sold or kept. The value is not very reliable for prospective buyers of the land because it is biased, as it may be in the president's self-interest to make a high estimate.
Independent appraiser's estimate: $340,000–$390,000	The price range that an independent appraiser estimated the land is worth.	This estimate will be somewhat relevant and reliable to some stakeholders. The estimate is reliable because it comes from an unbiased source, but it is not very precise because the appraiser has given quite a broad estimate. It is also difficult to know what land will sell for before it is sold. The estimate would be relevant to lenders who are interested in lending money to Bayton because the lender would want to know how much money could be recovered if Bayton were unable to repay the loan. The estimate would also be relevant to Bayton itself and to prospective buyers of the land because it provides an unbiased estimate of the land's current market value.
Sale of nearby land: $412,500 based on the first sale and $365,000 based on the second sale.	These amounts are calculated by multiplying Bayton's 500 hectares by the price per hectare paid in the transactions for the nearby land.	The values for the land that was sold are reliable: they are supported by independent transactions and so there is no question about the amounts involved. However, these amounts are not necessarily reliable with respect to Bayton's land. There are three significant problems regarding the relevance of these amounts: (1) the transactions took place some time ago, so they may not reflect current market conditions, which would be an important concern to prospective lenders or buyers; (2) the land that was sold may not be similar to Bayton's land despite being nearby; and (3) the price does not inform us about the circumstances surrounding the sales (the seller in one of the transactions may have required cash urgently and therefore could not wait to get a higher price). These three factors limit the relevance of the selling price of the other pieces of land.

SUMMARY OF KEY POINTS

▶ **LO 1** Accounting is a system for producing information about an entity and communicating that information to people who want or need the information for making decisions. Effective decision making requires information, and accounting is a crucial source of information. The numbers in an accounting report tell a story but the numbers cannot be taken at face value. Using, preparing, and understanding accounting information requires a set of high-level cognitive skills, including judgment, analysis, synthesis, evaluation, problem solving, critical thinking, and creativity.

Preparers of accounting information often have considerable leeway and choice in how they will do their accounting. The existence of choices makes it necessary for users to exercise a great deal of care to ensure they are aware of the choices that the preparer made and of how those choices affect their decisions.

▶ **LO 2** Accounting does not operate in a vacuum. You cannot sensibly use or provide accounting information without considering the accounting environment, which includes the social, political, legal, cultural, and economic environment of a society; the types of entities that are of interest to stakeholders and the characteristics of those entities; the different stakeholders that may have an interest in an entity; and the constraints that limit the accounting choices an entity can make. The diversity of the accounting environment makes it impossible for a single accounting report to be appropriate for all situations. Accounting reports must be tailored to suit the circumstances of an entity's accounting environment.

▶ **LO 3** The stakeholders in an entity who require accounting information for their decision making rely on the entity to provide the information. The managers who prepare the information are not neutral. When preparing accounting reports, managers may be influenced by their own personal interests, and these interests may conflict with those of the stakeholders.

▶ **LO 4** Accounting systems are designed to accumulate data that are then organized, processed, and converted into information that is useful to stakeholders. The information produced by accounting systems allows stakeholders to measure different attributes of an entity.

▶ **LO 5** GAAP are the principles, conventions, practices, procedures, and rules that define acceptable accounting practices and guide the preparation of financial statements in certain situations. A set of rules for preparing accounting information can help reduce the cost and difficulty of communication between entities and users. Canadian GAAP describe four qualitative characteristics that financial statement information must have to be useful to users: understandability, relevance, reliability, and comparability. GAAP do not provide solutions to all accounting problems. GAAP are not universal, not every entity needs or is required to follow GAAP, and GAAP are flexible.

KEY TERMS

accounting, p. 3

Canada Revenue Agency (CRA), p. 8

comparability, p. 19

corporation, p. 7

cost/benefit trade-off, p. 4

entity, p. 3

external audit, p. 12

external auditors, p. 12

financial accounting, p. 5

generally accepted accounting principles (GAAP), p. 18

limited liability, p. 7

managerial accounting, p. 5

not-for-profit organization, p. 8

partner, p. 8

partnership, p. 8

preparers, p. 11

private corporation, p. 7

proprietor, p. 8

proprietorship, p. 8

public corporation, p. 7

relevance, p. 19

reliability, p. 19

share, p. 7

shareholder, p. 7

stakeholder, p. 9

stock exchange, p. 7

understandability, p. 19

SIMILAR TERMS

The left column gives alternative terms that are sometimes used for the accounting terms introduced in this chapter, which are listed in the right column.

non-profit organization	**not-for-profit organization, p. 8**
stockholder	**shareholder, p. 7**
stock market	**stock exchange, p. 7**

ASSIGNMENT MATERIALS

Questions

Q1-1. Provide a definition of accounting that someone without a business background would understand.

Q1-2. Explain the difference between managerial and financial accounting.

Q1-3. Explain why it is important when studying business and accounting to make links between the classroom and the real world.

Q1-4. There are many different stakeholders in an entity. Explain why the same information may not be suitable or appropriate for all stakeholders.

Q1-5. Distinguish between preparers and users of accounting information.

Q1-6. Explain why the self-interests of preparers of accounting information can affect what information is reported to stakeholders and how it is reported.

Q1-7. What is a corporation? What are the attractive features of organizing a business as a corporation?

Q1-8. What is a publicly owned corporation? How does it differ from a privately owned corporation?

Q1-9. What is a not-for-profit organization? Give an example of a not-for-profit organization. What is the purpose of the organization you identified?

Q1-10. Why is information important for good decisions?

Q1-11. Explain the cost/benefit trade-off. What are its implications for decision making?

Q1-12. When you make a decision, should you collect all possible related information? What limits would you set on the information you gather?

Q1-13. What are generally accepted accounting principles (GAAP)?

Q1-14. Why is it useful to have a set of rules such as GAAP to guide preparers of accounting information?

Q1-15. Why is it necessary for a user of accounting information to understand the rules (such as GAAP) that the preparer used when preparing the information?

Q1-16. According to the *CICA Handbook*, what are the four qualitative characteristics that financial statement information must have to be useful to users?

Q1-17. Describe and explain some of the limitations of GAAP that were described in this chapter.

Q1-18. What is an external audit of financial information and why can it be important for many stakeholders of an entity?

Q1-19. Why is it useful for non-accounting students to be familiar with and understand financial statements?

Exercises

E1-1. (**Consider the information relevant for making a decision, LO 2**) You meet a stranger on a street corner in Edmonton. She asks you for instructions on the best way to get from Edmonton to Ottawa. What would you tell her?

E1-2. (**Understanding the qualitative characteristics of accounting, LO 5**) According to the *CICA Handbook* there are four qualitative characteristics that financial statement information must have if it is to be useful to users. Describe these characteristics in detail:
a. Understandability.
b. Relevance.
c. Reliability.
d. Comparability.

E1-3. (**Considering the stakeholders in a university or college, LO 2**) Consider the university or college you attend. Who are the stakeholders in your university? Explain the interest or "stake" each stakeholder has in the university. What types of decisions would each of these stakeholders have to make regarding the university? What type of information would be useful to each of these stakeholders? Explain.

E1-4. (**Assessing the credibility of information, LO 3**) You are looking to buy a new computer. You read an advertisement in a computer newspaper that describes Aylsham Computer Products Inc.'s (Aylsham) computer as the best value for the money for students. Based on this advertisement, would you purchase the computer? Why? What additional information would you require to decide whether to buy an Aylsham computer?

E1-5. (**Assessing the credibility of information, LO 3**) A chain of donut shops claims to have the world's best coffee. Do you believe the claim? Explain. How would you go about determining whether the chain had the world's best coffee?

E1-6. (**Consider the information relevant for making a decision, LO 2**) Your brother has just asked you to lend him $5,000 to help him buy a car. Would you lend him the money? How would you decide? What would you want to know before you made a final decision?

E1-7. (**Consider the information relevant for making a decision, LO 2**) Your cousin is in her last year of high school and is in the process of deciding which university to attend. Since you went through the process just a few years ago, she has asked you for advice about the best university to attend. What would you tell your cousin? What questions would you ask her before you could provide an answer?

E1-8. (**Considering different ways of measuring, LO 4**) For each of the following situations, explain which method of valuing the item in question would be most useful:

Measurement method	Explanation of the method
Cost	What you paid for the item.
Replacement cost	What it would cost to replace the item with an identical item in the same condition.
Replacement cost new	What it would cost to replace the item with an identical item that is new.
Net realizable value	What the item could be sold for now.

a. You lost your favourite CD and want to get another copy of it.
b. You need to get some money fast and you have nothing in your bank account, so you are thinking of selling your car.

c. You purchased a DVD player from a store that had a special sale offering to let you "use it for a year and if you don't like it you can get your money back." You decide you don't like the DVD player.

d. Your 1995 Ford Mustang was stolen and you are looking to get another one just like it.

E1-9. (**Consider the different ways of measuring the attributes of a home, LO 4**) There are many attributes of an item that you can measure. For a car, you could measure how fast it can go, its gas mileage, the number of doors it has, what you could sell it for, and many more. Notice that only one of these measures is stated in terms of money. Now consider your home. How many different attributes of your home could you measure? What would be the use for each measurement? Which measure of your home is best? Explain.

E1-10. (**Consider different ways of organizing information, LO 4**) Your 99-year-old grandfather died recently and left you his beloved library of books. At the time of his death, your grandfather's library contained over 5,000 books. The books had been packed away in boxes and the boxes have been delivered to you. After opening the boxes you realize that the books were not organized in any particular way. You decide to build a library in your basement and organize and catalogue the books. What are some of the ways you could organize the books in the library? What are the benefits and limitations of the different ways of organizing the books? What are the benefits of organizing the books at all?

E1-11. (**Take a first look at an annual report, LO 1, 2, 3, 4, 5**) Read the Rogers Communications Inc. financial statements for 2005 provided in Appendix A. You can also look at the entire Rogers annual report on this text's Web site at www.mcgrawhill.ca/friedlan. List seven questions that came to mind while reading the financial statements (or the annual report). Your questions should cover topics such as why particular information is reported or what it means.

Problems

P1-1. (**Consider who should make accounting choices, LO 2, 3, 4, 5**) Figure 1–1 of the accounting environment and the chapter as a whole emphasized that it is the managers of an entity who choose the accounting methods that an entity uses. Do you think the managers should have this responsibility or should it belong to someone else? Who else could possibly fulfill this task? Explain your answer fully.

P1-2. (**Explain the reason stakeholders would want information about an entity, LO 2**) Consider the following stakeholders in an entity. Why would the stakeholder want information about the entity? Explain.
a. A customer considering a major purchase (such as a computer or an appliance).
b. A government minister evaluating whether to provide assistance to a business.
c. The head of the CRTC (the regulatory agency responsible for the cable industry) determining whether a rate increase should be awarded to a cable company.
d. A shareholder in a company.

P1-3. (**Explain the reason stakeholders would want information about an entity, LO 2**) Consider the following stakeholders in an entity. Why would the stakeholder want information about the entity? Explain.
a. A person considering making a donation to a charity.
b. Canada Revenue Agency (the federal government department responsible for tax collection).

c. A banker considering whether to lend money to a small business.

d. The head of a labour union preparing for negotiations with management of a company.

P1-4. **(Identify the stakeholders in an entity and the decisions they make, LO 2)** Consider the following entities. Identify the stakeholders in each of these entities. What types of decisions would each of these stakeholders want to make?

a. Air Canada.

b. Government of Canada.

c. The Canadian Cancer Society.

d. McCain Foods Limited.

P1-5. **(Identify the stakeholders in an entity and the decisions they make, LO 2)** Consider the following entities. Identify the stakeholders in each of these entities. What types of decisions would each of these stakeholders want to make?

a. A local convenience store owned and operated by a family.

b. A large, publicly owned company.

c. A private, not-for-profit golf club.

d. The government of a small Canadian city.

P1-6. **(Consider the decisions stakeholders make and the nature of the information they require, LO 1, 2)** Consider the following decisions that a stakeholder of an entity might have to make. For each decision, identify the stakeholder who would likely be making the decision and indicate whether the decision would be considered a financial or managerial accounting decision. Remember that the classification as financial or managerial accounting depends on who the decision maker is. Explain your answer.

a. The price a manufacturer's products should sell for.

b. Whether a loan should be made to a small business.

c. Whether a corporation has paid an appropriate amount of tax.

P1-7. **(Consider the decisions stakeholders make and the nature of the information they require, LO 1, 2)** Consider the following decisions that a stakeholder of an entity might have to make. For each decision, identify the stakeholder who would likely be making the decision and indicate whether the decision would be considered a financial or managerial accounting decision. Remember that the classification as financial or managerial accounting depends on who the decision maker is. Explain your answer.

a. Whether a local clothing store should move to a larger location so that it could sell a wider range of clothes.

b. Whether to purchase the shares of a large oil company.

c. Whether unionized employees should receive a significant wage increase.

P1-8. **(Considering the information needed to decide whether to invest in a business, LO 1, 2, 4)** A friend of yours has just called you up with "a great business opportunity." Your friend is starting up a new e-business and needs money to purchase computer equipment. Your friend says he is going to invest $10,000 in the business and wants to know whether you want to invest as well. Would you invest in the new e-business? Why or why not? What additional information would you want to have before making a decision?

P1-9. **(Considering the information needed to decide whether to invest in a business, LO 1, 2, 4)** Two of your friends own and operate a business that rents bicycles and inline skates at a local lake. They have told you that they want to expand the business but said they are short of the money needed for the expansion and have asked you to become a partner by investing $8,000. Would you invest the $8,000? How would you decide? What additional information would you want to have before making a final decision?

P1-10. **(Classify and organize information so that it is useful for decision making, LO 1, 4)**
Mike is a university student who is often short of cash. A month may pass and he has no idea where his money went. After suffering with this problem for several months, Mike decides to monitor his spending for the next month. He buys a small notebook to write down the amount spent and the purpose of the spending. The summary of Mike's spending for the month follows:

Date	Amount	Purpose
Feb 4	$8.75	Starting balance (cash in wallet)
Feb 4	50.00	Cash from ATM
Feb 4	−15.75	Movie and beer
Feb 6	−3.00	Photocopy of Steve's notes
Feb 6	−4.50	Lunch
Feb 10	−22.50	Book for course
Feb 11	−2.50	Snacks
Feb 12	50.00	Cash from ATM
Feb 12	−18.25	Date with Alexa
Feb 15	−10.00	Long-distance phone card
Feb 17	−3.00	Contribution to charity drive
Feb 19	50.00	Cash from ATM
Feb 19	−22.50	Card and gift for Dad
Feb 20	−8.75	Overdue fees at library
Feb 20	−17.40	Share of phone bill for dorm room
Feb 21	10.00	Borrow from Lisa
Feb 21	−23.00	Food/drink for dorm room
Feb 24	50.00	Cash from ATM
Feb 24	−10.00	Pay Lisa back
Feb 27	−18.75	Partying after exam
Feb 28	$38.85	Amount remaining in wallet

Required:

Prepare a statement that organizes the information from the month's spending in a useful way. Explain why you organized the information the way that you did. How could you use the information if you were Mike?

P1-11. **(Classify and organize information so that it is useful for decision making, LO 1, 4)**
Mei is a university student who has been unable, so far, to find a summer job. While she has enough money to pay for school next year, she is concerned that she is not managing her money as well as she could. She decides to monitor her spending for the next month so that she can get an idea of where her money is going. She buys a small notebook and writes down the amount spent and the purpose of the spending. Mei's summary of her spending for July is shown below:

Date	Amount	Purpose
July 4	$0.00	Starting balance (cash in purse)
July 4	100.00	Cash from ATM
July 4	−15.75	Partying with friends
July 6	−45.00	Clothes
July 6	−4.50	Lunch
July 10	−22.50	Novel

July 11	−8.50	Movie
July 12	70.00	Cash from ATM
July 12	−38.25	Software
July 15	−22.45	Gift for Dad's birthday
July 17	−3.00	Coffee and donuts with friends
July 19	50.00	Cash from ATM
July 19	−15.50	Beverages for party
July 20	−8.75	Snacks
July 20	−12.50	Monthly Internet access fee
July 21	−23.00	Cosmetics
July 21	100.00	Borrowed from Mom
July 24	50.00	Cash from ATM
July 24	−20.00	Tennis lesson
July 27	−125.00	Deposit for university courses in fall
July 31	$5.30	Amount remaining in purse

Required:

Prepare a statement that organizes the information from the month's spending in a useful way. Explain why you organized the information the way that you did. How could you use the information if you were Mei?

P1-12. (**Evaluate different ways of measuring the value of a house, LO 4**) Rajiv owns a home in suburban Ottawa. You obtain the following information about the home:

a. Purchase price in 1978		$175,000
b. Selling price of a similar house on another street last year		$625,000
c. Price offered (and turned down) for Rajiv's house two months ago		$575,000
d. What it would cost to rebuild the house if it were destroyed		$235,000

Required:

Explain how each of the measures of the "value" of Rajiv's house could be used by a decision maker. What decision would the person be making? How would the information be useful?

P1-13. (**Evaluate different ways of measuring the value of a vintage automobile, LO 4**) Otto Collector owns a vintage 1925 Ford automobile. You obtain the following information about the car:

a. What Otto paid for the car in 1983		$29,000
b. Selling price of a similar car one year ago		$80,000
c. Price offered (and turned down) by Otto for his car last month		$95,000
d. What the car sold for new in 1925		$800

Required:

Explain how each of the measures of the "value" of Otto's car could be used by a decision maker. What decision would the person be making? How would the information be useful?

P1-14. (**Consider the usefulness of audited information, LO 1, 2, 3**) For each of the following situations explain whether and why having an independent review of the information provided—that is, an audit—would be useful. Suggest the type of person who might be appropriate for conducting the audit.

a. A donut shop advertises that it has the world's best coffee.

b. A used car dealer says that a car you are interested in is in excellent condition.

c. A store's rent to the mall owner is $1,200 per month plus 5% of the amount of sales the store makes. For the year just ended the store reports to the mall owner that its sales were $250,000.

d. A graduate university program requests a list of grades a student earned in her undergraduate program.

P1-15. **(Consider the usefulness of audited information, LO 1, 2, 3)** For each of the following situations explain whether and why having an independent review of the information provided—that is, an audit—would be useful. Suggest the type of person who might be appropriate for conducting the audit.

a. An individual files an income tax return with the Canada Revenue Agency in which she reports the amount of money her business earned during the previous year.

b. An electronics store states that it has "the lowest prices, guaranteed!"

c. A public corporation predicts that it will double its profit next year.

d. A job applicant submits a résumé to a prospective employer outlining his employment history and educational background.

P1-16. **(Identify the characteristics of different entities, LO 2, 3)** Identify two distinct entities. These could be corporations, partnerships, proprietorships, not-for-profit organizations, or any other type of entity you are familiar with or can obtain information about. Identify the characteristics of each entity. (You can use the characteristics listed in Figure 1–1 on page 6.) Explain how the entities differ.

P1-17. **(Identify the characteristics of different entities, LO 2, 3)** Identify two different corporations that are in a similar business. Identify the characteristics of each corporation. (You can use the characteristics listed in Figure 1–1 on page 6 as a guide). Explain how the corporations are similar and how they differ.

P1-18. **(Identify the stakeholders in an accounting partnership, LO 2, 3)** Bricket, Brack, and Bosh (BBB) is a small accounting firm in Oshawa, Ontario. The firm has four partners and ten other employees. All of the partners belong to professional accounting organizations. The firm provides accounting, tax, and consulting services to small- and medium-sized businesses in the community. When the firm does work for clients it is often used by third parties such as banks or prospective investors. For example, BBB might audit a client's financial statements, which are then given to the bank as part of a loan application. BBB is also part of a group of independent accounting firms in Ontario that will do work for clients of other firms in the group. For example, if BBB has a client that has an office elsewhere in Ontario, it might use the services of a firm in the group to do necessary work at that office.

Required:

Identify all of the stakeholders in Bricket, Brack, and Bosh and explain their "stake" in the partnership. Not all the stakeholders are explicitly referred to in the scenario. You will have to think about the business situation carefully to identify some of the stakeholders.

P1-19. **(Identify the stakeholders in a not-for-profit organization, LO 2, 3)** Safety House provides shelter and services to homeless and runaway youth in Vancouver. Safety House began as a group home in the early 1980s that provided a safe haven to street children in the city but now provides additional services including a telephone support line, outreach programs, substance abuse programs, and other necessary community services. In recent years it has become an advocacy group for children, to make government and the public aware of the problems faced by youth, as well as working with government and community social service agency to improve the lives of children and families. Safety House is managed by people with experience in social services and employs about 100 people who fill a wide range of roles providing needed services to young people. Safety House raises money from the public through a variety of fundraising programs and receives a significant amount of money from the provincial government.

Required:

Identify all of the stakeholders in Safety House and explain their "stake" in the organization. Not all the stakeholders are explicitly referred to in the scenario. You will have to think about the situation carefully to identify some of the stakeholders.

ENDNOTES

1. Andrew Zimbalist, *Baseball and Billions*, updated ed. (New York: Basic Books, 1994), p. 62.

FINANCIAL STATEMENTS: A WINDOW ON AN ENTITY

ROGERS

Unsuspecting journalism student Justin Warner got a lot more than a trip to the bathroom when he walked into a washroom in the hallway of his Toronto community college. When Warner flicked on the light switch and closed the door, a riff of percussion with a steady beat began to play. He had unknowingly activated a large red poster, strategically placed above the single toilet. It was a Rogers' ad, part of the 2005 season's "LIVE OUT LOUD" marketing campaign for its wireless division, Rogers' growing mobile telephone division, which had more than six million subscribers by the end of that year. "LIVE OUT LOUD" offered cell phone users a host of services to spice up their handsets, including downloadable ring tones, celebrity voice mail, and the Rogers Ur Music store, where, for $1.25 a song, customers could have their favourite tunes sent directly to their handsets. Warner said he enjoyed the company's bold marketing foray into what usually is considered a private space.

It's not surprising Rogers was trolling for new business in the washrooms of Centennial College. It's exactly the kind of campus where the company sees growth for its myriad mobile services. Warner probably wasn't considering Rogers' financial health when deciding whether he should sign up for a new Motorola ROKR wireless MP3 phone. For him, it was probably more about cool and price. But investors and bankers certainly look carefully at Rogers' financial statements as a window into whether investing or lending money to the company is "cool." For them cool is about growth, the size of the company's debt, if there is a healthy cash flow, and if there are any significant one-time expenses that will shrink the company's profit.

Though Warner may not be interested in those things, he might notice the effect on the stock price of Rogers Communications Inc.'s shares, which scroll across the giant television screen down the hall in the Students' Lounge. A bad review from an analyst or a major research firm on the health of Rogers' financial statements one day could send the price of a Rogers' share significantly lower on the stock markets.

But the news for Rogers has been good. Company financial statements and reports on earnings, which come out four times per year, show that the wireless division has been the engine driving Rogers' overall growth since the division was founded in 1983, under the Rogers Cantel name. Back then, Rogers offered wireless cell phone service just in the Quebec City-Windsor corridor. Later, Rogers teamed up with several partners, including the American giant AT&T, to offer Rogers AT&T Wireless, expanded service nationwide, added paging, and adopted the latest technologies for its network. In November 2004, Rogers bought smaller rival FIDO, owned by Montreal's Microcell Telecommunications Inc., and bought out AT&T's stake in Rogers Wireless Communications.

Wireless accounted for 54 percent of Rogers Inc.'s revenue in 2005, worth over $4 billion, and contributed over $400 million to its bottom line.

INTRODUCTION

The most familiar products of accounting and accountants are financial statements. The financial statements most people see are published by public companies whose shares trade on stock exchanges. These companies are required to make this information publicly available so anyone who is interested can obtain it. But virtually all businesses, governments, and not-for-profit organizations in Canada produce a set of financial statements at least once a year. While financial statements are the most common products of accounting and accountants, they are by no means the only ones. Accounting systems can provide a wide range of information presented in an array of different forms.

In this chapter we will explore the five components of the financial statement package:

- the balance sheet

- the income statement

- the statement of retained earnings

- the cash flow statement

- the notes to the financial statements

The financial statements of Rogers Communications Inc. (Rogers) in Appendix A will be used to illustrate our discussion. The objective of this chapter is to familiarize you with the financial statement package and begin our investigation of how the information in financial statements can be used for decision making.

GENERAL PURPOSE FINANCIAL STATEMENTS

Rogers' financial statements are known as **general purpose financial statements** (GPFS). GPFS statements are intended for use by many different stakeholders and for many different purposes, and are not necessarily tailored to the needs of any or all stakeholders or purposes. In other words, GPFS are intended for no one in particular and for everyone in general. (The alternative to GPFS is special purpose reports, which provide information designed for a specific user and/or a specific use. We will discuss special purpose reports in more detail later in the chapter.)

A GPFS is like the jack of all trades but master of none—someone who can do many things, none of them expertly. You may be willing to trust a jack of all trades to change the oil in your car, but for a major problem you would probably prefer to use an expert mechanic, or bear the consequences later. The same is true for GPFS. A set of GPFS might provide a particular stakeholder with some of the information that stakeholder needs, but because the statements are not prepared with that particular stakeholder's needs in mind, they are not likely to be exactly what the stakeholder needs.

Every entity prepares a set of GPFS at least once a year, if for no other reason than it must be included with the entity's tax return. An entity can also produce any number of special purpose reports. The financial statements of public companies like Rogers are always general purpose and must be prepared in accordance with GAAP. Entities that are not publicly traded companies do not necessarily have to prepare their statements in accordance with GAAP.

An obvious question is, "If these statements are not especially useful for many of the decisions that users have to make, why devote an entire chapter, indeed a good chunk of a book, to examining them?" This is a good question. The answer is that an entity's stakeholders can usually count on receiving general purpose financial statements. As a result, if you are going to use these statements intelligently, you have to know their strengths and limitations. You have to know what questions to ask. And you have to know when to look elsewhere for information.

ROGERS' FINANCIAL STATEMENTS: AN OVERVIEW

Examining financial statements can be an intimidating task. What do the numbers mean? Where do they come from? The discussion below weaves a general discussion of each financial statement with an examination of Rogers' statements. Before we examine the financial statement package in detail, let's take a broad look at Rogers' financial statements. Four important points are worth noting:

1. Rogers' financial statements are **consolidated**. Consolidated means that the financial information of more than one corporation is combined into a single set of statements. Consolidated statements are prepared when a corporation controls another corporation (usually meaning it owns 50 percent or more of the other corporation). For example, Rogers Communications Inc. owns subsidiaries called Rogers Wireless Inc., Rogers Cable Inc., and the Toronto Blue Jays baseball team.

2. Financial statements are presented for two years. This provides the users of the financial statements with some context. It is very difficult to make sense of accounting information without some perspective on other companies, the industry, performance in other years, and the economy in general. As we will discuss in more detail as we proceed, making comparisons using accounting information can be very difficult and misleading. At the same time, not making comparisons makes it very difficult to interpret accounting information.

3. Rogers prepares its financial statements for a fiscal year. A **fiscal year** is the 12-month or 52-week period for which performance of an entity is measured and at the end of which a balance sheet is prepared. Rogers' fiscal year corresponds with the calendar year, running from January 1 to December 31. An entity can choose any 12-month or 52-week period as its fiscal year. For example, Bank of Montreal's fiscal year is from November 1 to October 31.

4. Everything in Rogers' financial statements is measured in terms of money, specifically in Canadian dollars. All amounts included in the statements must be reasonably measurable in dollars. (We will discuss what accountants consider reasonable as we proceed.) Numbers in Rogers' financial statements are rounded to the nearest thousand dollars. Rogers' balance sheet reports accounts receivable of $890,701,000, but because the thousands are dropped, the actual amount of accounts receivable could be anywhere between $890,700,500 and $890,701,500. The thousands are dropped to make the statements less cluttered in appearance. This rounding can be done only because dropping the thousands is not expected to affect the decisions of anyone using the information. For example, ignoring the thousands is not likely to affect whether an investor buys more Rogers shares or sell what he or she already owns.

THE BALANCE SHEET

Let's begin our tour of the financial statements by examining the balance sheet. The **balance sheet** provides information about the financial position of an entity at a specific point in time. The balance sheet is also known as the statement of financial position. (One of the confusing aspects of accounting is that different names are often given to the same thing. The confusion will pass with time, but be prepared to scratch your head sometimes when a new term is used to describe a familiar concept. The list of Similar Terms at the end of each chapter will help you sort out any confusion.)

In a balance sheet, financial position means information about assets, liabilities, and owners' equity. These terms are defined as follows:

■ **Assets** are economic resources that provide future benefits to an entity for carrying out its business activities.

- **Liabilities** are the obligations of an entity, such as to pay debts or provide goods or services to customers.

- **Owners' equity** is the investment the owners have made in the entity.

Look at Rogers' balance sheet and find these three headings—note that owners' equity is called shareholders' equity, because Rogers is a corporation and the owners of a corporation are called shareholders.

Rogers' balance sheet conforms to the **accounting equation**, which is the conceptual foundation of accounting. The accounting equation is:

$$\text{Assets} = \text{Liabilities} + \text{Owners' Equity}$$

The left side of the equation represents the assets, the entity's economic resources. The right side of the equation represents how those assets were financed; that is, how the entity was able to obtain the assets. Assets can be financed by **creditors** (entities to which money is owed) or owners. Financing by creditors results in liabilities. Financing by owners is represented by owners' equity. Any event that is entered into an accounting system must affect the accounting equation so that the equality between the left side and right side of the equation is maintained.

We can tie Rogers' balance sheet amounts into the accounting equation as follows:

Assets	=	Liabilities	+	Owners' (Shareholders') Equity
$13,834,289,000	=	$10,306,674,000	+	$3,527,615,000

Examine Rogers' balance sheet in Appendix A and find these amounts on the balance sheet.

All economic events that are entered into an accounting system are summarized in terms of the accounting equation; that is, each event is recorded based on its effect on assets, liabilities, and owners' equity. In this book we will use the accounting equation as the basis for a spreadsheet in which we will record transactions and economic events. The columns of the spreadsheet will represent assets, liabilities, and owners' equity, and each economic event that affects the entity will be recorded in a row of the spreadsheet based on its effect on each of the elements of the accounting equation. Ultimately, the spreadsheet will provide us with the information we need to prepare the financial statements. The spreadsheet will also provide us with a method for seeing how different accounting choices affect the financial statements. We will develop the spreadsheet method further in Chapter 3. For now, we will look at a simple example to learn about the balance sheet.

Suppose an entrepreneur named Tamara decides to start a house-painting business to earn money over the summer. In starting the business she has the following transactions. (See Table 2–1 for the spreadsheet summarizing the events.)

1. Tamara contributes $1,000 of her savings to the business. She sets up her business as a proprietorship (that is, a business that is not incorporated and is owned by one person) and opens a bank account under the name Tamara's Painting Business (TPB). As a result of this transaction the business now has $1,000 in cash. The cash is an asset because it is a resource that can be used to purchase the materials and equipment Tamara needs to paint houses. Owner's equity increases by $1,000 because Tamara, the proprietor, has invested $1,000 in the business.

2. Tamara then borrows $500 from her mother. Tamara promises to pay back the money at the end of the summer. Assets increase by $500, reflecting the money that has come into the company. This time, however, liabilities increase by $500 because a creditor, an entity that is owed money by the business, has supplied the money.

3. With $1,200 of TPB's cash Tamara purchases equipment for her business, including ladders, brushes, and trays. In this case there has been an asset exchange. One asset, cash, has been exchanged for other assets, equipment.

4. Tamara opens an account with a paint store. She plans to buy most of her paint from the store and the store allows her 60 days to pay her bills. She purchases $400 worth of supplies from the store. Assets increase because now TPB has supplies that are necessary for painting.

TABLE 2–1 ::: Spreadsheet for TPB

Tamara's Painting Business
Spreadsheet

	Assets	=	Liabilities	+	Owner's Equity
1.	+$1,000 cash				+$1,000 investment by owner
Balance	$1,000	=	$0	+	$1,000
2.	+$500 cash		+$500 loan from mother		
Balance	$1,500	=	$500	+	$1,000
3.	+$1,200 equipment −$1,200 cash				
Balance	$1,500	=	$500	+	$1,000
4.	+$400 supplies		+$400 account payable to paint store		
Balance	$1,900	=	$900	+	$1,000
5.	+$200 cash		+$200 service to be provided		
Balance	$2,100	=	$1,100	+	$1,000

Because the supplies were purchased on credit, TPB has a liability. It has to pay the paint store within the next 60 days for the supplies purchased.

5. After canvassing several houses in her neighbourhood, Tamara gets her first job. An elderly man wants the outside of his house painted and pays a $200 deposit. Tamara expects to begin work in about 10 days when the weather improves. Assets have increased by $200 because Tamara received cash. But Tamara also has a liability, which is to paint the elderly man's house. In this case the liability is to provide a service, not to pay back cash, as was the case in event 4.

For each entry made the accounting equation is maintained. We could expand the spreadsheet so that instead of a single column for each of assets, liabilities, and owner's equity, a separate column could be created for each type of asset, liability, and owner's equity. In this case we could have asset columns for Cash, Supplies, and Equipment, and liability columns for Accounts Payable, Loans, and Services to be Provided.

We can summarize the information in the spreadsheet into a balance sheet as shown in Table 2–2. The total assets, total liabilities, and total owner's equity correspond with the balances at the bottom of each column in Table 2–1. The total amounts have been separated on the balance sheet into the different types of assets and liabilities.

TABLE 2–2 ::: Balance Sheet for TPB

Tamara's Painting Business
Balance Sheet

Assets		Liabilities and Owner's Equity	
Cash	$ 500	Loans	$ 500
Supplies	400	Accounts payable	400
Equipment	1,200	Services to be provided	200
		Total liabilities	1,100
		Owner's equity	1,000
Total assets	$2,100	Total liabilities and owner's equity	$2,100

From Table 2–2 we see at a glance that when the balance sheet was prepared TPB had $500 in cash, supplies that cost TPB $400, and equipment that cost $1,200. Notice that the supplies and equipment are reported at their cost. This is important. According to Canadian GAAP, the basis for valuing an entity's assets is the transaction value—in the case of supplies and equipment the amount that was paid or the cost. The liabilities side of the balance sheet shows the $500 loan from the proprietor's mother, the $400 owed to the paint store, and the $200 advance from the customer. The liability to the customer is the amount of the deposit, not the value of the entire job. This again is the rule of GAAP (but not necessarily the only way to account for this event). The balance sheet also shows the $1,000 invested by Tamara.

Insight

It is important to recognize that the accounting equation is a tool for recording information in an accounting system. It is not unique to Canada or to GAAP. Recall the example in Chapter 1 where we valued the contents of an apartment in three different ways. All of these ways of valuing the items in the apartment are legitimate, although GAAP use cost as their basis of valuation. The accounting equation can accommodate all of these ways of measuring assets and others as well.

A balance sheet is like a photograph—it captures the scene at the moment the photo is taken. The scene could be dramatically different the moment before or after the picture is taken. For example, Rogers reports property, plant, and equipment of $6,151,526,000 on December 31, 2005. But it is possible that in early January 2006 Rogers could have purchased additional property, plant and equipment. The December 31, 2005 balance sheet would not show those new purchases.

Question for Consideration

Explain how the following events would affect the accounting equation for Tamara's Painting Business:

1. TPB pays $50 for some new paintbrushes.

2. TPB purchases $40 worth of new paintbrushes and promises to pay the store in 30 days.

3. Tamara contributes an additional $500 of her own money to ensure that TPB has enough cash to operate.

Answer:

1. No effect. This transaction simply transforms one asset, Cash (decreases by $50), into another asset, Equipment or Paintbrushes (increases by $50). There is no change in total assets or in liabilities or owner's equity.

2. Assets increase by $40 (the asset Equipment or Paintbrushes increases by $40) and liabilities increase by $40 (Accounts Payable, or amount owed to suppliers, increases by $40).

3. Assets increase by $500 (Cash) and owner's equity increases by $500 (Tamara, the owner, has contributed $500 to TPB).

Now let's take a closer look at assets, liabilities, and owners' equity.

◇ ROGERS™

Assets

Assets are economic resources available to an entity that provide potential future benefits to the entity. Let's look at some of the assets on Rogers' balance sheet and consider why they are assets (see the box below).

Type of Asset	What is it?	Why is it an asset?
Cash	Money.	Cash is used to buy needed goods and services, pay bills, pay debts, and pay dividends to shareholders.
Accounts receivable	Money owed by customers who received goods and services from Rogers before they paid for them.	Accounts receivables are assets because they represent the right to receive cash from customers.
Property, plant, and equipment	Includes the cable networks, wireless network and base station equipment, computer equipment, land and buildings, furniture, fixtures and office equipment and so on that allow Rogers to provide its goods and services to customers. These are the economic resources that are used on an ongoing basis to earn revenue, but that are not sold in the ordinary course of business.	These items are assets because they provide the resources that allow Rogers to provide the goods and services that customers want (such as the cable and cell phone services).

Believe it or not, accountants sometimes have a great deal of difficulty deciding what an asset is. Often our intuition about what an asset is may differ from what accountants define as an asset. For example, Rogers spends a great deal of money trying to attract new subscribers for its cell phone services. Many of the new subscribers may remain with Rogers for many years. The question then is, should money spent on advertising to attract subscribers be classified as an asset? The answer is usually no. Most of the time the money Rogers spends to attract subscribers does not appear on the balance sheet as an asset.

The reason that every economic resource with potential future benefits does not appear on the balance sheet has to do with how accountants define and measure assets. Because the financial statements of Rogers are prepared according to GAAP, GAAP's criteria must be followed. These criteria require that:

■ an asset must provide a future benefit to the entity and the benefit must be reasonably measurable (if you are not sure what the benefit is, the amount of the benefit, or that there will be a benefit, you cannot call an item an asset). The future benefit is that the asset helps the entity produce cash in the future

■ the entity has control over the benefits that will be obtained from the asset (this means that the entity is actually able to use the asset to make money)

■ an asset must be the result of a transaction or event that has already occurred

According to these criteria, Rogers does not classify the money it spends attracting new subscribers to its cable or cell phone services as an asset because the future benefit is very uncertain and difficult to measure. Other examples show how applying the criteria leads to accounting treatments that are not always consistent with our intuition. One of the most valuable resources any entity has, its employees, is not considered an asset. Even research, the lifeblood of many companies, is explicitly prohibited by GAAP from being called an asset.

An entity does not have to own an economic resource for it to be considered an asset. For example, according to GAAP, leased assets are sometimes classified as assets if the lease meets certain criteria.

Another way that GAAP's rules define an asset is the amount at which they are reported on the balance sheet. A piece of land purchased for $1,000,000 many years ago that has a market value today of $5,000,000 appears on the balance sheet at $1,000,000. This is because GAAP require that assets be recorded at their cost; the amount actually paid in a transaction with another entity. The land was purchased for $1,000,000 in a transaction, but there was no transaction supporting the $5,000,000 amount. As a result, the market value of the land does not appear in the financial statements.

It is important to understand that the assets and amounts reported on Rogers' balance sheet are the result of GAAP. If a different set of rules were used, you would get a different balance sheet. Accounting information is merely a representation of the economic activities of an entity. There are many different ways that assets and other financial statement components can be defined and measured. Canadian GAAP represent just one way.

Notice that Rogers' balance sheet classifies certain assets as **current assets**. Current assets are assets that will be used up, sold, or converted to cash within one year or one operating cycle. An **operating cycle** is the time it takes from the initial investment an entity makes in goods and services until cash is received from customers. Rogers would expect to sell its inventory of cell phones within one year, so its cell phone inventory is classified as current. Usually, amounts that customers owe Rogers must be paid in less than one year so its accounts receivable are considered current assets. The operating cycle of most businesses is a year or less. One exception is wine production, which has operating cycles of longer than one year because wine can be aged for many years before it is sold.

Assets that are not classified as current are **non-current assets**. These are assets that will not be used up, sold, or converted to cash within one year or one operating cycle. **Capital assets** (such as property, plant, and equipment and intangible assets on Rogers' balance sheet) are classified as non-current because they will provide benefits for more than one year. For example, Rogers would expect the cash registers in Rogers Video stores, the underground cables that provide cable services, and the broadcasting equipment of Rogers' radio stations to provide useful service for many years. Notice that on Rogers' balance sheet non-current assets are not specifically identified. This presentation is common in financial statements. If an asset is not identified as being current then it is understood to be non-current.

Liabilities

Liabilities are an entity's obligations to pay money or provide goods or services to suppliers, lenders, and customers. If an entity borrows money from a bank, the entity reports a liability because the amount borrowed is owed to the bank. The amount of the liability is the amount borrowed. If a customer pays an entity in advance for goods or services, such as paying in advance for tickets to a concert, the entity reports a liability. In that case the liability is to provide a concert to the ticket holder. The amount of the liability is the amount the customer paid for the ticket.

A liability does not have to be a legal obligation. For example, many companies provide warranties with their products. The warranty provides a customer with assurance that the company will repair certain problems with a product. When a product with a warranty is sold the company will record a liability for the estimated cost of repairing it. The company has no legal obligation to the customer when the product is sold. Only if and when a customer has a problem is there a legal obligation.

Like assets, liabilities are classified on Rogers' balance sheet as current and non-current. **Current liabilities** will be paid or satisfied within one year or one operating cycle. **Non-current liabilities** will be paid or satisfied in more than one year or one operating cycle. As was the case with assets, Rogers does not specifically identify non-current liabilities on its balance sheet. If a liability is not identified as a current liability, then it is understood to be non-current. Rogers reports $7,453,412,000 of long-term debt on its December 31, 2005 balance sheet. This means that this debt will not have to be paid until after December 31, 2006. Rogers reports a current liability called "current portion of long-term debt," which represents long-term debt that will have to be paid within the next year.

Explain why under GAAP an "asset" such as money spent on research does not appear as an asset on an entity's balance sheet, whereas insurance purchased in advance would be reported as an asset.

Answer: Under GAAP, three criteria must be met for an item to be considered an asset: an asset must provide a future benefit to the entity and the benefit must be reasonably measurable; the entity must have control over the benefits that will be obtained from the asset; and an asset must be the result of a transaction or event that has already occurred. For research, the second and third criteria are met (there will have been transactions with other entities—payment to researchers, purchase of supplies, etc. and the entity would have control over the research output), but the first criterion is not met. The future benefit of money spent on research is considered, under GAAP, to be too uncertain to classify as an asset, since it is hard to know whether the research will result in the entity making any money. In contrast, insurance paid for in advance meets all three criteria. The insurance provides the future benefit of insurance coverage and the amount of coverage is stated in the policy, the entity is entitled to any benefits under the policy, and the insurance is purchased from another entity (an insurance company).

Rogers' balance sheet reports several different liabilities including:

Type of Liability	What is it?	Why is it a liability?
Accounts payable and accrued liabilities	Amounts owed to suppliers for goods and services that Rogers purchased on credit.	Rogers buys goods and services from suppliers (for example, DVDs, digital terminals, cable). The suppliers of these goods and services give Rogers time to pay its bills. It may also owe money to employees for work they have done.
Unearned Revenue	Customers pay in advance for services to be provided later (prepaid cell phone services).	Rogers must provide the services to customers.
Long-term debt	Money borrowed that has to be repaid to lenders.	Rogers owes money to lenders.

Using Balance Sheet Information to Analyze Liquidity

The classification of assets and liabilities into current and non-current components is important because many users of financial statements want to assess an entity's liquidity. **Liquidity** is the entity's ability to pay its obligations as they come due; it refers to the availability of cash or near-cash resources to meet obligations. Liquidity is important to creditors who are expecting to be paid and to potential creditors who are considering extending credit. Liquidity is also important to shareholders because a company that is unable to meet its obligations is at significant risk of going out of business.

Current assets represent the resources that are or will soon be available to meet obligations that are coming due. Current liabilities represent the obligations that must be fulfilled soon. Taken together, current assets and current liabilities provide important information about the liquidity of an entity. Current assets minus current liabilities is called **working capital**. Rogers' working capital on December 31, 2005 was:

Working Capital	=	Current Assets	−	Current Liabilities
−$689,814,000	=	$1,301,697,000	−	$1,991,511,000

Positive working capital suggests that an entity has the resources to meet its upcoming obligations. Negative working capital means that the entity has more current liabilities than current assets and this could be an indication of liquidity problems, although this is not always true. In most cases, though, an entity's working capital is positive.

Another way of examining working capital is with a ratio. The ratio of current assets to current liabilities is called the **current ratio**, or **working capital ratio**, and is defined as:

$$\text{Current ratio} = \frac{\text{Current assets}}{\text{Current liabilities}}$$

Rogers' current ratio on December 31, 2005 was:

$$\text{Current ratio} = \frac{\text{Current assets}}{\text{Current liabilities}}$$

$$= \frac{\$1,301,697,000}{\$1,991,511,000}$$

$$= 0.65$$

The current ratio gives the relative amounts of current assets to current liabilities. The larger the ratio, the more current assets that are available to meet current liabilities. Therefore, on the surface at least, the entity is more likely to meet its obligations. On December 31, 2004, the current ratio was 0.52. The ratio shows that the relative amount of current assets to current liabilities is increasing, which could mean that Rogers' liquidity position is improving.

Ratios are attractive tools for analyzing a company's financial information because they eliminate the effect of size. Instead of having to evaluate the meaningfulness of negative working capital of $689,814,000 on December 31, 2005 versus negative working capital of $1,079,665,000 on December 31, 2004, we can evaluate the ratio of 0.65 versus 0.52. This makes comparisons with other years and other entities simpler.

Making sense of financial information is not usually straightforward; it can require a lot of detective work. The numbers in the financial statements can raise questions in the mind of a stakeholder, but they will rarely provide answers. Stakeholders must analyze, assess, evaluate, and compare the information in financial statements to make sense of it. Calculating ratios is a part of the analysis and assessment of financial data, but is often just a first step. After some preliminary investigation it may be necessary to gather more information. For example, is a current ratio of 0.65 bad news for Rogers? It is not possible to tell. Rogers has managed to operate successfully for several years with a current ratio of less than one (negative working capital) so that would suggest that it is not a big problem.

Insight

Often, people learn that a "good" current ratio is 2:1. This is false. Different industries have different norms. For example, industries that have very predictable cash flows, such as regulated utilities, can operate successfully with a lower current ratio than industries with more uncertain cash flows. Rogers' current ratio should make that clear since it has had negative working capital for a number of years but continues to operate successfully.

Owners' Equity

Owners' equity is the amount of investment that the owners have made in the entity. In terms of the accounting equation, owners' equity represents the amount of the assets financed by the owners. Equivalent terms you may see in a financial statement include:

- *shareholders' equity,* which refers to the owners' equity of a corporation

- *partners' equity,* which refers to the owners' equity of a partnership

- *owner's* or *proprietor's equity,* which refers to the owner's equity of a proprietorship

Owners' investments in entities can be direct or indirect. Owners can make direct investments by purchasing shares of a corporation or units in a partnership, or by contributing money to a proprietorship. Direct investments are usually cash, but sometimes other assets can be invested in exchange for an ownership interest. The investment is direct because the investors contribute their own assets directly to the entity.

Indirect investment occurs when an entity's net income or profit is not paid to the owners and is thus "reinvested" in the entity. If the net income is not paid to the owners, then it is kept in the entity. It can, therefore, be considered an investment in the entity by the owners.

In a corporation's financial statements the shareholders' equity section separates direct investments and the reinvestment of net income, as follows:

- Direct investments by shareholders are reported in the Capital Stock account. **Capital stock** represents the amount of money (or other assets) that shareholders have contributed to the corporation in exchange for shares in the corporation.

- Reinvested net incomes are accumulated in the Retained Earnings account. **Retained earnings** is the sum of all the net incomes a corporation has earned since it began, less the dividends paid to shareholders. (**Dividends** are payments of a corporation's assets, usually cash, to its shareholders.) Dividends represent distributions of the corporation's net income to the shareholders. The term retained earnings is descriptive because the account represents the net income or earnings that have been retained by the corporation. If retained earnings is a negative amount then it is referred to as the **deficit**.

The separation of investments by shareholders into capital stock and retained earnings is quite important, especially if the shareholders and managers are not the same people. Shareholders need to know whether the money being distributed to them is due to the profits earned by the corporation, or if it is just a return of the money that they invested.

Insight

A pyramid scheme is an example of how failure to know the source of payments can create problems. Consider the classic case of Ivar Kreuger, known as the Swedish Match King. In the early 1900s Kreuger raised money from new investors and used some of that money to pay dividends to existing investors. Investors found Kreuger's companies very attractive because of the high dividends they were paying. The high dividends attracted new investors, who in turn expected to be paid high dividends. This type of scheme requires a continual inflow of new capital, which, of course, becomes impossible once the number of investors gets too large. Kreuger's companies did not produce very much with the money they raised; they simply redistributed it among investors, with some finding its way into Kreuger's pocket. Investors were unable to detect what was going on because Kreuger's companies did not provide much financial information to them. Eventually the whole scheme collapsed and Kreuger committed suicide in disgrace.[1]

Rogers reports shareholders' equity on its December 31, 2005 balance sheet of $3,527,165,000. To find the components of shareholders' equity you have to look at Note 13 to the financial statements (see page A-30 of Appendix A). Rogers shareholders' equity section is quite complicated so we will focus on the key areas. From Note 13 we see that Rogers has two classes of common shares: Class A voting shares and Class B non-voting shares. The Class A shares are owned by a limited number of people (mainly members of the Rogers family) which allows these shareholders to control the decision making of the company without owning most of the common shares.

The Class B non-voting shares are the shares that are widely held by investors. These shareholders are not allowed to vote. For now, note that there is $72,311,000 associated with the Class A shares. This means that since the company's inception, Class A shareholders have paid Rogers $72,311,000 in exchange for the Class A Rogers shares. Things are a bit more complicated for the Class B shares where a portion of the amount contributed by shareholders goes to the share category and the remainder goes to the line called contributed surplus.

Notice in Note 13 that Rogers reports a deficit (negative retained earnings) on December 31, 2005 of $601,548,000. This means that since Rogers' inception the sum of net incomes and losses less dividends is negative (Rogers has had more losses than profits). You can see the relationship between retained earnings and net income by examining the following calculation for Rogers:

Deficit on December 31, 2004	$(519,441,000)
+ Net loss for the year ended December 31, 2005	(44,658,000)
− Amount paid in dividends and distributions during the year ended December 31, 2005	37,449,000
Deficit on December 31, 2005	$(601,548,000)

Dividends reduce the amount of retained earnings (or increase the deficit) because they represent distributions of the earnings of the entity back to the owners. (Be sure you can find these numbers Rogers' financial statements.)

Another common balance sheet analytical tool is the **debt-to-equity ratio**. The ratio provides a measure of how an entity is financed. The higher the ratio, the more debt an entity is using relative to equity. Rogers' debt-to-equity ratio on December 31, 2005 was

$$\text{Debt-to-equity ratio} = \frac{\text{Liabilities}}{\text{Shareholder's equity}} = \frac{\$10,306,674,000}{\$3,527,615,000} = 2.92$$

The debt-to-equity ratio is a measure of risk. The more debt an entity has the greater the risk, because regardless of whether it is doing well or poorly, it must make payments on its debt on time. Debt has a fixed cost associated with it called interest. **Interest** is the cost of borrowing money and is usually calculated as a percentage of the amount borrowed. For example, if an entity borrows $10,000 at a 10 percent interest rate, interest for the year would be $1,000 ($10,000 × 0.10). The amount borrowed is called the **principal**. An entity is legally required to make its interest and principal payments when they are due. If an entity does not pay on time the lenders can take action against it by compelling the borrower to sell assets, forcing it into bankruptcy, or requiring it to renegotiate the terms of the loan. In contrast, dividends are voluntary. An entity does not have to pay dividends at any time and shareholders cannot take any action if dividends are not paid.

A debt-to-equity ratio of 2.92 tells us that Rogers has about 2.9 times more liabilities than equity. The ratio has decreased from 4.56 on December 31, 2004, meaning that the amount of liabilities held by Rogers has decreased relative to the amount of equity. Is a ratio of 2.92 too high? Is the decrease from 2004 a good thing? Well, it depends. There is nothing wrong with financing with debt—in fact, in some ways it is attractive to do so. Careful analysis is necessary to decide when enough is too much, and even then it is a judgment call.

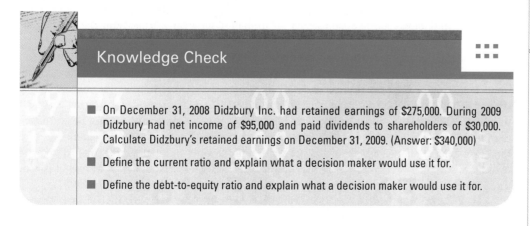

Knowledge Check

- On December 31, 2008 Didzbury Inc. had retained earnings of $275,000. During 2009 Didzbury had net income of $95,000 and paid dividends to shareholders of $30,000. Calculate Didzbury's retained earnings on December 31, 2009. (Answer: $340,000)

- Define the current ratio and explain what a decision maker would use it for.

- Define the debt-to-equity ratio and explain what a decision maker would use it for.

THE INCOME STATEMENT

If a balance sheet is like a photograph, then an income statement is like a movie: it shows events over a period of time. The **income statement** is a "how did we do?" statement, measuring the economic performance of the entity over a period of time such as a year. Performance measurement is considered an important use of accounting information. For example, stock prices often change when a company announces its net income. Managers' bonuses are often based on net income. Income taxes are related to net income and the selling price of a small business can be based on net income.

The income statement and net income are often referred to by many different names. The income statement is also known as the statement of income, statement of operations, statement of earnings, and the statement of profit and loss. Net income is also called income, earnings, net earnings, profit, net profit, and the bottom line. If a company "loses money" (that is, net income is negative), net income might be called a loss or net loss. Once again, don't be put off by the lack of consistent terminology.

Measuring the economic performance of an entity is more challenging than you might think. After all, what does economic performance mean? There are different ways performance can be measured. The two most commonly used methods in accounting are the cash basis of accounting and the accrual basis of accounting.

- The **cash basis of accounting** reports the cash flowing into and out of the entity. Under this method, economic performance represents the change in cash over the period.

- The **accrual basis of accounting** measures the economic impact of transactions and economic events, rather than cash flows. Accrual accounting, as we will refer to it throughout the book, measures economic changes rather than simply changes in cash.

Let's go back to our painting entrepreneur, Tamara, and see how the cash basis of accounting reports the performance for Tamara's Painting Business (TPB). TPB got off to a slow start in April and May, but by mid-June TPB was extremely busy. During July the following events occurred:

1. TPB started and completed seven painting jobs. TPB collected $2,500 for these jobs and was still owed $800 by one of its customers. The customer told Tamara that she would pay her on August 15. TPB also collected $500 during July for jobs completed during June.

2. TPB paid $1,450 to people Tamara hired to paint. At the end of July TPB owed its employees $450. TPB would pay the amount owed in early August.

3. TPB purchased and used $1,550 of paint for the seven jobs undertaken in July. Since TPB had credit terms from the paint store, it didn't pay for any of the paint used in July, but it did pay $900 for paint purchased before July.

An income statement for the month of July prepared on the cash basis is shown in Table 2–3.

Net income on the cash basis means that TPB had $650 more in cash at the end of July than at the beginning. By generating $650 in cash during July, Tamara knows that her business generated a cash surplus of $650 after paying all of its bills. Of course, TPB still has bills to pay (employees and paint) so the $650 doesn't mean that Tamara can spend it however she would like.

For general purpose reporting in Canada, accountants find the cash basis of accounting too limiting and an incomplete measure of performance. (This is not to understate how extremely important cash flow information is. Cash flow information is reported in depth in the cash flow statement, which is discussed on page 51.) Accountants generally prefer to use accrual accounting for general purpose reporting in Canada because it gives a broader measure of performance than is reflected by cash flows. Accrual accounting attempts to reflect economic changes rather than cash changes. For a complex entity, trying to reflect economic changes makes sense because cash flows do not always take place at the same time as economic changes, even though it is a lot more complicated than simply reporting cash flows.

TABLE 2-3 ::: Income Statement Prepared for TPB Using the Cash Basis

Tamara's Painting Business
Income Statement
For the Month Ended July 31

Revenue (cash collected)	$3,000
($2,500 for the seven July jobs plus $500 for jobs completed in June)	
Less: Expenses (cash spent)	
For employees	(1,450)
($1,450 paid to employees in July)	
For paint	(900)
($900 paid for paint purchased in previous months)	
Net income (cash flow)	$ 650

The format of the income statement can be stated as:

$$
\begin{array}{c}
\text{Revenue} \\
\underline{- \ \text{Expenses}} \\
\text{Net income}
\end{array}
$$

An entity can have many different types of revenues and expenses, but the structure of the income statement always comes down to this simple arrangement. This equation is an expansion of the owners' equity section of the balance sheet. Even though the income statement is always presented separately, it is really just a part of the owners' equity section of the balance sheet. We could rewrite the accounting equation to reflect the current year's income statement as:

Assets = Liabilities + Owners' Equity at the beginning of the period + Revenue − Expenses

or

Assets = Liabilities + Owners' Equity at the beginning of the period + Net income

Revenue (or sales or sales revenue) refers to economic benefits earned by providing goods or services to customers. Revenue results in an increase in owners' equity or the owners' investment in the entity. Revenue represents an increase in owners' equity because the revenue is associated with an increase in assets (usually cash or a promise of payment) or a decrease in liabilities. Under accrual accounting revenue does not have to be recorded at the same time cash is received. Consider the following arrangements Rogers could have for selling $500 of cell phones to a corporate customer:

	Assets	=	Liabilities	+	Owners' (Shareholders') Equity
The cell phones are sold for cash	+$500 (Cash)	=		+	+$500
The cell phones are sold for a promise of payment	+$500 (Accounts Receivable)	=		+	+$500
The cell phones are sold for some other asset such as furniture	+$500 (Furniture)	=		+	+$500
The cell phones are sold in exchange for the reduction in a liability		=	−$500 (Accounts Payable)	+	+$500

Expenses are economic sacrifices made or costs incurred to earn revenue. Expenses decrease owners' equity because some of the owners' investment is being sacrificed to earn the revenue. Rogers must provide goods or services in exchange for a customer's money. Thus owner's equity decreases because something of value—for example, Internet access—is being given up to make the sale. When an expense is incurred, assets must decrease or liabilities must increase to reflect the economic sacrifice. Like revenue, an expense does not have to correspond with a cash flow. Below are some examples of how the accounting equation can be affected by the different ways Rogers might pay employees for work that they did worth $500:

	Assets	=	Liabilities	+	Owners' (Shareholders') Equity
Employees are paid in cash for work they have done	−$500 (Cash)	=		+	−$500
Employees receive $500 worth of goods from a Rogers Video store	−$500 (Inventory)	=		+	−$500
Employees work but are promised payment later		=	+$500 (Wages Payable)	+	−$500

TABLE 2–4 ::: Income Statement Prepared for TPB Using the Accrual Basis

Tamara's Painting Business
Income Statement
For the Month Ended July 31

Revenue	$3,300
($2,500 for the six July jobs that were paid for plus $800 for the July job that was not paid for by the end of July)	
Less: Expenses	
Employees	(1,900)
($1,450 paid for work done by employees in July plus $450 owed for work done in July.)	
Paint	(1,550)
($1,550 for paint purchased and used in July. This paint will not be paid for until later.)	
Equipment	(50)
(Tamara estimates that she will be able to use the equipment for 24 painting months, after which time she will have to replace the equipment. The charge for the month is $1,200 ÷ 24 = $50.)	
Net loss	($200)

An income statement for Tamara's Painting Business for the month of July using the accrual method is shown in Table 2–4.

In the accrual statement, revenue reflects work done in July, not cash collected. Revenue includes all the money customers agreed to pay TPB for the seven jobs done in that month. The money collected for the June job is not included in July's revenue because it has nothing to do with the work done in July. The revenue for the June job would have been included in June's income statement. The expenses include the cost of paint used in July and the cost of the work done by employees in July even though these items were not fully paid for. Remember, these are costs that were incurred to earn the revenue in July—when cash changed hands doesn't matter.

One additional expense is included in TPB's income statement: the cost of the equipment. The equipment was bought and paid for when Tamara began her business, but it contributes to earning revenue in every month in which it is used. As a result, under accrual accounting a portion of the cost of the equipment is expensed or amortized each month. **Amortization** is the allocation of the cost of property, plant, and equipment to expense over the asset's useful life. Amortization reflects the "using up" of the asset in helping the entity to earn revenue. ("Depreciation" is a term often used to describe the using up of assets instead of amortization.)

What does net income mean in this statement? It is certainly more difficult to interpret than the cash flow statement, where the $650 bottom line represented the increase in cash. Here the negative net income or loss of $200 means that Tamara's business suffered an economic loss of $200 during July because the benefits (revenue) were exceeded by the costs of earning those benefits (expenses). The $200 loss does not, however, represent cash.

Question for Consideration

Examine the two income statements that were prepared for Tamara's Painting Business in Tables 2–3 (cash basis) and 2–4 (accrual basis). Explain why revenue in the two statements is different.

Answer: With the cash basis of accounting, revenue is the cash collected from an entity's customers during a period. In contrast, with accrual accounting revenue represents amounts earned from customers during the period, regardless of when the cash is collected. For TPB the difference in the amount of revenue between the two methods is the $500 that was collected in July for the job done in June and the $800 owed at the end of July. Revenue on the cash basis includes the $500 from June and excludes the $800 owing at the end of July. Revenue on the accrual basis excludes the $500 from June and includes the $800 owing at the end of July. Both methods include as revenue the amounts for jobs completed and paid for in July.

Rogers' Statement of Income (Income Statement)

Let's take a look at Rogers' statement of income (see page A-5). Rogers reported a loss of $44,658,000 for the year ended December 31, 2005. Remember that this does not mean that Rogers had $44,658,000 less in cash. In terms of the accounting equation, when a company reports net income, the shareholders' equity (shareholders' equity is used here because Rogers is a corporation) increases and **net assets** (assets − liabilities) must increase by the same amount. That is,

$$\underbrace{\text{Assets − Liabilities} \atop +\$3,527,615,000}_{\text{Net assets}} \quad = \quad \text{Shareholders' Equity} \atop = \quad +\$3,527,615,000$$

What does a loss of $44,658,000 mean? Standing alone, net income or loss is difficult to interpret. In an accrual accounting context it means that the investment of the shareholders of the entity has decreased by $44,658,000 or that the economic benefits enjoyed by Rogers were exceeded by the economic costs it incurred by $44,658,000. Suffering a loss isn't good news, but how bad is the news? That question must be evaluated in the context of how Rogers was expected to perform, how similar firms performed, and how Rogers performed compared with previous years. For example, if investors were expecting Rogers to lose $60,000,000, then the actual loss could be viewed favourably. Compared with 2004, when Rogers had a loss of $67,142,000, the 2005 result could be seen as a small improvement.

But there is more to Rogers' statement of income than net income; it also includes important information about how it earned the net income. Consider the following:

◆ ROGERS

- During fiscal 2005 Rogers sold $7,482,154,000 in services and goods (operating revenue).

- Rogers reported several different types of expenses for the year ended December 31, 2005 including:

  - **cost of sales** of $1,296,148,000—cost of items sold such as wireless equipment and video store merchandise;

  - sales and marketing expenses of $1,122,348,000—the costs to acquire new subscribers;

  - operating, general and administrative expenses of $2,853,613,000—all other expenses incurred to operate the business on a day-to-day basis;

  - depreciation and amortization of $1,478,011,000

When all of these expenses are deducted from operating revenue an amount Rogers calls operating income is obtained. **Operating income** is the income the entity earned from its main business activities. These expenses can be called operating expenses. **Operating expenses** are the usual expenses an entity incurs for its main business activities. Operating income can give stakeholders some insight into the performance of an entity's actual business activities. Rogers' operating income in 2005 was $665,558,000, meaning that it earned in excess of $665 million providing goods and service to customers.

Insight

Operating income is not a precisely defined term under Canadian GAAP or anywhere else. This means that managers can include whatever they want in the calculation of operating income or not even include a line called operating income in their income statements. As a result, operating income can represent different things for different entities. Stakeholders must be very careful how they interpret operating income because it can differ significantly from entity to entity.

Because Rogers is a corporation, it must pay taxes. For fiscal 2005 Rogers recorded an income tax expense of $2,155,000, which is deducted in the calculation of net earnings. Notice that the income tax expense is broken into two parts—a current portion and a future portion. The current portion represents the actual amount that Rogers has to pay to government for income taxes for 2005. The income statements of partnerships and proprietorships do not show an income tax expense because income taxes are the responsibility of the partners or the proprietor. Not-for-profit organizations do not have an income tax expense because they do not pay taxes.

GROSS MARGIN AND GROSS MARGIN PERCENTAGE

A very useful analytical tool for analyzing some companies' financial statements is the gross margin. **Gross margin** is sales less cost of sales (remember that cost of sales is the cost of the inventory an entity sells). The amount of gross margin is then available for covering the other costs of operating the business and for providing profit to the owners. A convenient way of analyzing gross margin is as a percentage of sales. The **gross margin percentage** is the ratio of gross margin to sales. It indicates the percentage of each dollar of sales that is available to cover other costs and return a profit to the entity's owners. Using the gross margin percentage makes it easier to compare the performance of different entities and the same entity year to year. Rogers is not a good type of business to demonstrate the gross margin and gross margin percentage because it is mainly a service business and therefore doesn't sell much inventory.

Consolidated statements of income & retained earnings

Years ended December 31

($ in thousands, except shares outstanding and earnings per share)	2005	2004
Sales	547,744	504,591
Cost of sales	323,629	295,241
Gross profit	224,115	209,350
Operating expenses (income)		
Salaries and commissions	81,364	75,394
Advertising	30,494	29,492
Rent and property taxes	9,518	9,579
Amortization	11,892	10,412
Employee profit-sharing plan	3,105	2,870
Other operating expenses	33,675	30,558
Interest income	(2,857)	(3,083)
Other income	(17,801)	(16,609)
	149,390	138,613
Income before income taxes	74,725	70,737
Provision for income taxes [note 3]	25,761	24,633
Net income for the year	48,964	46,104
Retained earnings, beginning of year	239,335	220,892
Dividends declared	(14,725)	(13,915)
Excess of cost of share repurchase over carrying value of related shares [note 8]	(24,104)	(13,746)
Retained earnings, end of year	249,470	239,335
Weighted average number of common shares outstanding		
Basic	17,962,580	18,485,248
Diluted	18,733,975	19,112,389
Earnings per share		
Basic	$ 2.73	$ 2.49
Diluted	$ 2.61	$ 2.41

To introduce gross margin we will look at the statement of income of Leon's Furniture Limited (Leon's), the Canadian furniture retailing chain (see Exhibit 2–1). Notice that Leon's separates its cost of sales from its other expenses and separately reports gross margin. For Leon's, cost of sales is the cost of the furniture it sold. Leon's gross margin for the year ended December 31, 2005 can be seen on its statement of income and is calculated as:

www.leons.ca

$$\text{Gross Margin} = \text{Sales} - \text{Cost of sales}$$
$$\$224,115,000 = \$547,744,000 - \$323,629,000$$

This calculation shows that Leon's sold its furniture for $224,115,000 more than what it cost. Leon's gross margin percentage is:

$$\text{Gross Margin Percentage} = \frac{\text{Gross margin}}{\text{Sales}} = \frac{\text{Sales} - \text{Cost of sales}}{\text{Sales}}$$
$$= \frac{\$224,115,000}{\$547,744,000} = \frac{\$547,744,000 - \$323,629,000}{\$547,744,000}$$
$$= 0.409, \text{ or } 40.9 \text{ percent}$$

Leon's gross margin percentage in 2005 was 40.9 percent, which means that for every dollar of sales, it has $0.409 to apply to costs other than the cost of sales and for profit. Leon's gross margin in 2004 was 41.5 percent (try to calculate this amount yourself), slightly higher than 2005. Higher gross margins are better than lower ones. In some businesses very small changes in the gross margin percentage can have a significant effect on net income.

EXHIBIT 2–2 :

Statement of Earnings of the Loblaw Companies Limited

Consolidated Statements of Earnings

For the years ended December 31, 2005 and January 1, 2005 ($ millions except where otherwise indicated)	2005 (52 weeks)	2004 (52 weeks)
Sales	$ 27,801	$ 26,209
Operating Expenses		
Cost of sales, selling and administrative expenses	25,716	24,084
Depreciation and amortization	558	473
Restructuring and other charges (note 3)	86	
Goods and Services Tax and provincial sales taxes (note 4)	40	
	26,400	24,557
Operating Income	1,401	1,652
Interest Expense (note 5)	252	239
Earnings before Income Taxes	1,149	1,413
Income Taxes (note 9)	400	445
Net Earnings before Minority Interest	749	968
Minority Interest	3	
Net Earnings	$ 746	$ 968
Net Earnings per Common Share ($) (note 6)		
Basic	$ 2.72	$ 3.53
Diluted	$ 2.71	$ 3.51

www.loblaw.com

Many companies are very secretive about their gross margins. They will combine cost of sales with other expenses to hide information from competitors. For example, the Statement of Earnings of the Loblaw Companies Limited (Loblaw) combines almost all of its expenses into a single line (see Exhibit 2–2). As a result it is not possible to calculate Loblaw's gross margin or gross margin percentage. Even in the section of Loblaw's annual report where management discusses its financial results, gross margin and gross margin percentage are discussed in general terms; specific amounts are not mentioned.[2]

www.mcgrawhill.ca/
olc/friedlan

Knowledge Check

- During the summer Hank operated a cart that sold hot dogs and cold drinks. At the end of the summer Hank had collected $6,500 from customers and paid $3,300 to suppliers. At the end of the summer Hank owed suppliers $500 and he was owed $200 from customers. The amortization on his cart for the summer was $800.

- What was Hank's net income on the cash basis for the summer?

- What was his accrual net income?

- Under accrual accounting why is amortization an expense?

THE STATEMENT OF RETAINED EARNINGS

The **statement of retained earnings** summarizes the changes to retained earnings during a period and serves as the bridge between the balance sheet and the income statement. Recall that earlier in the chapter it was pointed out that retained earnings represents the accumulation of an entity's net incomes over its life, less dividends paid. The statement of retained earnings shows all transactions and economic events that affected retained earnings during a period. In equation form the statement of retained earnings can be expressed as:

$$\text{Retained earnings at the end of the year} = \text{Retained earnings at the beginning of the year} + \text{Net income for the year} - \text{Dividends declared during the year}$$

To highlight the link between the income statement and the balance sheet this equation can be expanded to:

$$\text{Retained earnings at the end of the year} = \text{Retained earnings at the beginning of the year} + \text{Revenue} - \text{Expenses} - \text{Dividends declared during the year}$$

Have a look at Rogers' statement of deficit on page A-5 (remember that when retained earnings is negative it can be called a deficit).

Dividends are not treated as an expense when calculating net income. Dividends are not a cost of operating a business but are distributions of the owners' investment in the business back to the owners. A dividend does not affect the overall wealth of a shareholder. The dividend simply moves the wealth from the entity (which the shareholder owns) to the shareholder's bank account. In contrast, payments to stakeholders other than owners are treated as expenses because they reduce the overall wealth of the owners.

There are a number of other transactions and economic events that affect retained earnings but that are not reflected in these equations.

An expression commonly used to describe the payment of dividends is that "dividends are paid out of retained earnings." The expression means that when dividends are paid, retained earnings decreases. However, paying a dividend requires cash. If a company does not have enough cash it cannot pay a dividend, no matter how much it has in retained earnings. For example, Rogers is able to pay dividends because it has cash, even though its retained earnings is negative.

THE CASH FLOW STATEMENT

Readers of the business press might get the impression that the most important information about the performance of an entity comes from its income statement. This impression is far from accurate. While net income is an important indicator of performance, it is vital not to forget cash. As has been said and sung, money makes the world go round. Cash is necessary to pay bills and meet obligations as they come due. No matter how large a company's net income, if it does not have the cash to meet its obligations, it is in serious trouble.

Because of the importance of cash, the general purpose financial statement package usually includes a cash flow statement. The **cash flow statement** shows how cash was obtained and used during a period. The cash flow statement is another "how did we do?" statement. However, it measures "how we did" differently than the income statement. The cash flow statement shows users how the entity managed its cash during the reporting period. It is a source of information about an entity's liquidity.

The cash flow statement is broken down into three parts: (1) cash from operations, (2) investing activities, and (3) financing activities. Let's look at each part in more detail.

1. **Cash from operations (CFO)** is the cash an entity generates from or uses in its regular business activities. For Rogers, CFO is the cash it generates or uses to provide wireless communications, cable TV, and internet services, from its video retailing, broadcasting, and publishing businesses, and from the Toronto Blue Jays. CFO would include cash collected from customers for Rogers' services and goods, and money spent to provide those services and goods, such as paying employees, advertising, renting stores, buying equipment for sale to customers, fuel for service vehicles—anything spent on the day-to-day operation of the business.

   For fiscal 2005 Rogers had CFO of $1,227,407,000. (On Rogers' statement of cash flow on page A-6 the amount appears about half way down the statement on an unnamed line).

CFO means that during fiscal 2005 Rogers' regular business activities generated $1,227,407,000 in cash. This is internally generated cash that could be used for expansion, purchasing capital assets, retiring debt, paying dividends, and so on. Notice that CFO is much different from net earnings. Remember that under accrual accounting net income measures economic flows, not cash flows. That means that net income includes amounts that are not cash flows, whereas cash from operations simply reflects the movement of cash.

2. **Financing activities** is the cash an entity raises and pays to equity investors and lenders. Cash from financing activities includes cash raised from borrowing and from issuing shares, and cash paid for repaying loans, repurchasing shares, and paying dividends. (Interestingly, interest payments are usually included in CFO even though they are a cost of financing.)

   During fiscal 2005 Rogers had a net cash outflow of $139,804,000 from financing activities. The amount included repayment of $1,509,577,000 in long-term debt, the issuing of $1,369,208,000 in new long-term debt, and the issuance of $100,348,000 of capital stock.

3. **Investing activities** provides information about cash spent buying and cash received from selling capital and other long-term assets. For Rogers these investments include land and buildings, cable TV networks, cell phone network equipment, computer equipment and software, and so on. These types of assets contribute indirectly to the success of the entity over more than one period. These assets contribute indirectly because they are not bought and sold in the ordinary course of business, but are resources used in the operation of the business.

   During 2005 Rogers spent $1,435,477,000 in cash on investing activities, mainly on the purchase of new property, plant, and equipment.

   Overall, what does the Rogers' cash flow statement tell us? Internal generation of cash provided $1,227,407,000 (CFO) to pay for new property, plant, and equipment; reduce debt; and pay dividends. There was a net decrease in cash for 2005 (obtained by adding together cash from operations, financing activities, and investing activities) of $347,874,000.

THE RELATIONSHIP AMONG THE FINANCIAL STATEMENTS

It's probably not clear from the discussion of the individual financial statements but there is a close relationship among the four statements. The relationships are shown in Figure 2–1. At the top of Figure 2–1 is the balance sheet for Cupar Inc. (Cupar) on December 31, 2009. Below this balance sheet are the income statement, statement of retained earnings, and cash flow statement for 2010. Below these is Cupar's balance sheet on December 31, 2010. The arrows show how information flows from one statement to another. What you should notice is that the flow statements in the middle—the income statement, statement of retained earnings, and cash flow statement—capture the changes between the two balance sheets at the top and bottom. Thus the cash flow statement shows how the balance in the cash account on the balance sheet changed from December 31, 2009 to December 31, 2010. The income statement and statement of retained earnings show how retained earnings changed from December 31, 2009 to December 31, 2010.

The relationships among the statements are more extensive than cash and retained earnings. The recording of many transactions and economic events involves both the income statement and the balance sheet, so more relationships could be shown. These associations will become clearer as we proceed. For now, study Figure 2–1 to make sure that you understand the relationship among the financial statements.

NOTES TO THE FINANCIAL STATEMENTS

Some users of financial statements say that the notes to the financial statements provide more information than the statements themselves. It is certainly not possible to understand the financial statements without carefully reading the notes. The notes expand and explain the information in the statements and provide additional information that may help stakeholders assess an

FIGURE 2–1 ::

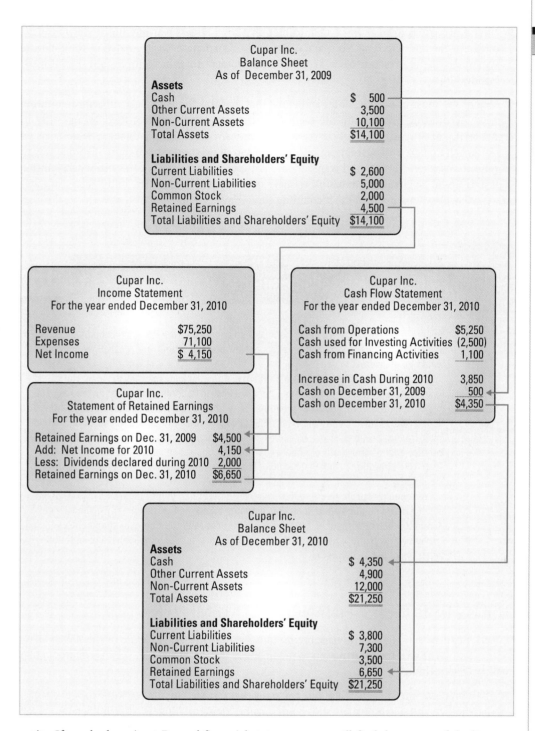

entity. If you look again at Rogers' financial statements you will find that many of the lines on each statement refer to specific notes.

Let's look at three examples of financial statement notes.

■ Note 5 (page A-18) lists the types of property, plant, and equipment that Rogers has. By examining Note 5, a stakeholder has an idea of the types of capital assets Rogers has, how much each type cost, and how much has been amortized.

■ Note 11 provides information about Rogers' long-term debt (page A-23). Whereas the balance sheet tells users that the company has $7,739,551,000 in long-term debt (long-term debt plus the current portion of long-term debt), the note lists the individual loans that Rogers has, when each is due, the interest rate, and other relevant terms. This information would be crucial if you were interested in predicting Rogers' future cash flows.

- Note 17 provides a breakdown of information about Rogers' various businesses (wireless, cable, media, and telecom) (see page A-39). This information is aggregated in the financial statements themselves but Note 17 allows stakeholders to gain some insight into Rogers' business lines.

One of the most important notes is the one that explains the entity's significant accounting policies. **Accounting policies** are the methods, principles, and practices used by an entity to report its financial results. Rogers describes its significant accounting policies in Note 2 (pages A-7 to A-14). Preparers of accounting information can often choose from more than one way to account for economic events and transactions. Without a description of the entity's accounting choices it would be virtually impossible to make any sense of the numbers in the financial statements. We will explore many of the accounting choices available to preparers as we move through this book.

Question for Consideration

You are a loan officer for a major bank and an executive from Rogers has come to ask for a $100,000,000 loan. What information on the balance sheet and cash flow statement would be of interest to you?

Answer: As a banker, your main concern is Rogers' ability to repay the loan. You would be interested in whether Rogers has the cash flow to support the interest on the loan and to pay back the principal when it is due. If the interest rate on the loan were 8 percent, Rogers would have to pay the bank $8,000,000 per year in interest. In 2005, Rogers had cash from operations of more than $1 billion, which is enough to cover the additional interest cost. If you were confident that Rogers could continue to generate that much cash from operations each year, you could assume that it would have little trouble paying the interest on the loan.

You would also be interested in knowing what other debts Rogers has. The liability section of the balance sheet identifies amounts owed to other creditors. The liability section of the balance sheet also refers you to the notes to the financial statements, which provide you with more details on the terms of Rogers' outstanding loans, and importantly, when they have to be repaid.

USERS OF ROGERS' FINANCIAL STATEMENTS

Rogers' financial statements give us some insights into the identity of some of the stakeholders of the company. From the information in the financial statements we can surmise that potential stakeholders include:

- **Shareholders.** Since Rogers is a public company that is traded on the Toronto Stock Exchange, shareholders are an important stakeholder group. Some of Rogers' shareholders are small investors who do not have access to information other than what is publicly available.

- **Creditors.** The balance sheet shows that Rogers has almost $8 billion in long-term debt (including the current portion). That means that there are lenders who will want to use the financial statements to evaluate the company to determine the status of their loans. The company also has a large amount owing to suppliers (accounts payable and accrued liabilities total more than $1.4 billion).

- **Regulators.** Some of Rogers' businesses are regulated by the Canadian Radio-television and Telecommunications Commission pursuant to and in accordance with requirements of the Telecommunications Act and the Broadcasting Act.

- **Canada Revenue Agency.** Rogers must file regular tax returns and the general purpose financial statements are required with the filing.

- **Potential Lenders.** Rogers seems to be continually borrowing new money which means that prospective lenders will want to examine the financial statements to assess the company.

FORMAT OF GENERAL PURPOSE FINANCIAL STATEMENTS

There is no one right way to organize a set of financial statements. Even under GAAP there are no requirements for how financial statements should be presented. The *CICA Handbook* requires that certain information be included in the financial statements, but it is the managers who decide how that information is presented. Managers' decisions about how to organize the financial statements can be influenced by what they are trying to emphasize in their statements and what is common practice in the entity's industry. Two examples of companies' balance sheets with formats quite different from Rogers' are shown in Exhibit 2–3.[3]

Panel A of Exhibit 2–3 shows the December 31, 2004 and 2005 balance sheets of Stelco Inc., Canada's largest steel producer.[3] Stelco did not use the Assets = Liabilities + Owners' Equity format of the accounting equation for its balance sheet. Instead, it rearranged the accounting equation so that one side showed "total investment" (working capital [current assets less current liabilities] plus non-current assets) and the other side showed other liabilities plus shareholders' equity. This arrangement emphasized the working capital position of the company, which is important because the company has ongoing liquidity problems and financial problems. The balance sheet, of course, still balances, but what is on each side is different.

Panel B of Exhibit 2–3 shows the balance sheet of Newfoundland Power Inc. (Newfoundland Power), a producer and supplier of electricity. Newfoundland Power arranges its balance sheet opposite to what we normally see. The fixed (capital) assets and other non-current assets are at the top of the asset side of the balance sheet, while current assets are at the bottom. One explanation for this arrangement is that non-current assets represent over 80 percent of the company's total assets, so management may want to give more prominence to the more significant asset classes.

EXHIBIT 2–3 :

Examples of General Purpose Financial Statements

Panel A: Stelco Inc.

Consolidated Statement of Financial Position
(under Creditor Protection as of January 29, 2004 – Note 1)

At December 31, (in millions)	2005 (Note 26)	2004 (Restated – Note 3)
Current assets		
Cash and cash equivalents	$ 25	$ 32
Restricted cash (Note 6)	17	11
Accounts receivable	294	470
Inventories (Note 12)	783	844
Prepaid expenses	29	38
Future income taxes (Note 11)	22	15
Assets held for sale (Note 10)	351	–
	1,521	1,410
Current liabilities		
Current liabilities not subject to compromise		
Bank and other short term indebtedness (Note 13)	191	216
Accounts payable and accrued	232	283
Employee future benefits (Note 22)	60	62
Income and other taxes	8	10
Long-term debt due within one year (Note 17)	23	44
Liabilities held for sale (Note 10)	206	–
	720	615
Working capital	801	795
Other assets		
Property, plant, and equipment (Note 14)	932	999
Intangible assets (Note 15)	72	66
Deferred pension cost (Note 22)	112	213
Future income taxes (note 11)	12	6
Other	21	24
	1,149	1,308
Total investment	1,950	2,103
Other liabilities		
Other liabilities not subject to compromise		
Employee future benefits (Note 22)	834	907
Long-term debt (note 17)	20	49
Future income taxes (Note 11)	92	120
Asset retirement obligations (Note 9)	15	12
	961	1,088
Liabilities subject to compromise (Note 7)	630	583
Shareholders' equity	$ 359	$ 432
Derived from:		
Convertible debentures conversion option (Note 17(b))	$ 23	$ 23
Capital stock (Note 19)	781	781
Contributed surplus	16	16
Retained deficit	(461)	(388)
	$ 359	$ 432

Panel B: Newfoundland Power Inc.

Balance Sheets As at December 31 ($thousands)	2005	2004[1]
Assets		
Capital Assets (Note 6)		
Property, plant and equipment	$ 1,085,106	$ 1,050,913
Less: accumulated amortization	433,648	420,836
	651,458	630,077
Current Assets		
Cash		467
Account receivable	58,730	59,571
Materials and supplies	5,206	5,419
Prepaid expenses	1,211	1,292
Regulatory assets (Note 3)	9,284	8,763
	74,431	75,512
Corporate Income Tax Deposit		6,949
Deferred and Other Charges (Note 7)	90,128	84,082
Regulatory Assets (Note 3)	34,042	28,690
	$ 850,059	$ 825,310
Shareholders' Equity and Liabilities		
Shareholders' Equity		
Common shares (Note 9)	$ 70,321	$ 70,321
Retained earnings	253,651	246,039
Common shareholder's equity	323,972	316,360
Preference shares (Note 8)	9,410	9,417
	333,382	325,777
Current Liabilities		
Bank indebtedness	772	
Short-term borrowings (Note 10)	11,040	58,109
Accounts payable and accrued charges	56,767	56,140
Income tax payable	1,726	728
Current portion of long-term debt (Note 11)	4,250	3,650
Regulatory liability (Note 3)	10,966	10,187
	85,521	128,814
Future Income Taxes (Note 2)	1,375	1,501
Long-term Debt (Note 11)	380,058	324,908
Other Liabilities (Note 12)	26,092	20,560
Regulatory Liability (Note 3)	23,631	23,750
	$ 850,059	$ 825,310

1 Certain comparative figures have been reclassified to conform with current year presentation.

On the liabilities and equity side, shareholder equity is on the top of the statement, not on the bottom as is usually seen. This format is quite common for electrical utilities and is common in the United Kingdom.

Financial statements are a method of communication between an entity and its stakeholders. As in any type of communication the preparer tailors the message to suit the situation. These examples highlight the variation that can exist in financial statements. How financial statements are formatted does not affect the information itself, only the appearance of the information.

OTHER ACCOUNTING INFORMATION

In addition to the general purpose financial statements accountants can prepare any type of report to satisfy the needs of stakeholders. The only limitations are the willingness of the entity to provide the information and the availability of the information in the accounting system (an accounting system can provide only information that is entered into it).

Accounting reports that are prepared to meet the needs of specific stakeholders and/or a specific purpose are called **special purpose reports**. Normally, special purpose reports would not be made publicly available even by public companies. For example, a creditor might want a statement of cash inflows and outflows, along with budgeted cash flows for the next year, to assess the borrower's ability to pay its debts. A property manager might want a statement of revenues from a retailer so that the appropriate amount of rent could be charged, if rent is based, in part, on the store's sales. The list of special purposes is endless. Special purpose reports, even by public companies, do not have to be prepared in accordance with GAAP.

:: Solved Problem

Snowflake's Snow Removal Company (SSRC)—Part 1

Stan Snowflake recently decided to start a new business clearing snow from residential driveways. Stan is a construction worker, and while he tends to have a lot of work during the spring, summer, and fall, he does not usually work during the winter months. Stan finds being idle quite frustrating, so after some thought he decided that a snow removal business would be a good way to make some money and keep busy during the winter. As a result he organized Snowflake's Snow Removal Company (SSRC), an unincorporated business. In October, before the first snowfall, SSRC entered into the following transactions:

1. Stan opened a bank account in the name of SSRC and deposited $10,000 of his savings into the account.

2. SSRC borrowed $5,000 from the bank.

3. SSRC purchased a used pickup truck and a snowplough attachment for $17,500. SSRC paid $11,000 in cash and promised to pay the remainder in four months.

4. SSRC purchased shovels and an axe for $200 cash.

5. Stan went door-to-door in his neighbourhood signing up people for SSRC. SSRC offered snow removal for $250 for the entire winter or $50 per month for the five months SSRC would be operating. Ten people paid for the entire winter. Other people will pay monthly beginning in November.

Required:

Record SSRC's transactions into a spreadsheet like the one in Table 2–1 on page 36. Use the spreadsheet to prepare a balance sheet as of October 31 (before the first snowfall).

Solution:

Snowflake's Snow Removal Company
Spreadsheet

	Assets	=	Liabilities	+	Owner's Equity
1.	+$10,000 cash				+$10,000 investment by owner
Balance	$10,000	=	$0	+	$10,000
2.	+$5,000 cash		+$5,000 bank loan		
Balance	$15,000	=	$5,000	+	$10,000
3.	+$17,500 equipment −$11,000 cash		+$6,500 payable to vendor of truck		
Balance	$21,500	=	$11,500	+	$10,000
4.	+$200 equipment −$200 cash				
Balance	$21,500	=	$11,500	+	$10,000
5.	+$2,500 cash		+$2,500 obligation to provide snow removal services		
Balance	$24,000	=	$14,000	+	$10,000

Snowflake's Snow Removal Company
Balance Sheet
As at October 31

Assets		Liabilities and Owner's Equity	
Cash	$ 6,300	Bank loan	$ 5,000
Equipment	17,700	Accounts payable	6,500
		Services to be provided	2,500
			14,000
		Owner's equity	10,000
Total assets	$24,000	Total liabilities and owner's equity	$24,000

Notice that the liabilities are broken down into three different types. This format allows Stan to see the different types of obligations that SSRC has.

Snowflake's Snow Removal Company (SSRC)—Part 2

November and December were very busy for Stan and SSRC. There were a number of snowfalls, two of them quite heavy.

1. SSRC had 75 regular customers (remember that 10 of the customers paid in full in October). By the end of December Stan had collected $5,600 from the customers who agreed to pay each month and was owed $900 by these customers. In addition, SSRC received $800 from people who stopped Stan on the street and asked him to clean their driveways during heavy snowfalls.

2. SSRC was so busy that Stan sometimes had to hire a person to help him do shovelling. He paid this person $450 for work done and owed her $100 at the end of December.

3. SSRC spent $700 on gas, oil, and service on the truck.

4. Stan estimates that the monthly amortization of the truck and other equipment should be $700.

Required:

Prepare income statements on the cash basis and on the accrual basis for the two months ended December 31.

Solution:

Snowflake's Snow Removal Company
Income Statement
For the Two Months Ended December 31
(Prepared using the cash basis)

Revenue (cash collected)	$6,400
($5,600 from customers who pay monthly plus $800 from people who stopped Stan on the street)	
Less: Expenses (cash spent)	
For employee	(450)
($450 paid to the person for work done)	
For oil, gas, and service	(700)
($700 for gas, oil, and service)	
Net income (cash flow)	$5,250

Snowflake's Snow Removal Company
Income Statement
For the Two Months Ended December 31
(Prepared using the accrual basis)

Revenue	$8,300
($5,600 from customers who pay monthly + $900 owed by customers who pay monthly + $1,000 for the people who paid in advance [10 customers × $50 per month × 2 months]* + $800 from people who stopped Stan on the street)	
Less: Expenses	
For employee	(550)
($450 paid to the person for work done + $100 owed)	
For oil, gas, and service	(700)
($700 for gas, oil, and service)	
Equipment	($1,400)
(Stan estimates that monthly amortization should be $700)	
Net income	$5,650

*Even though customers paid in advance, SSRC earns the money on a monthly basis. Therefore, one-fifth of advance payment should be recognized each month.

Snowflake's Snow Removal Company (SSRC)—Part 3

Required:

Use the information from SSRC's balance sheet on October 31 to calculate the following amounts. Discuss the information provided by these amounts.

a. Working capital.

b. Current ratio.

c. Debt to equity ratio.

Solution:

a. Working capital = Current assets − Current liabilities
   ($7,700) = $6,300 − $14,000

b. Current ratio $= \dfrac{\text{Current assets}}{\text{Current liabilities}} = \dfrac{\$6,300}{\$14,000} = 0.45$

c. Debt-to-equity ratio $= \dfrac{\text{Liabilities}}{\text{Owner's equity}} = \dfrac{\$14,000}{\$10,000} = 1.4$

The working capital calculation and current ratio show that SSRC has more current liabilities than current assets. This is potentially a cause of concern because if cash were not forthcoming in the near future, SSRC would not be able to pay the bank or the vendor of the truck. On October 31 this would not have been much of a concern because customers were expected to begin paying in November. The main concern on October 31 might have been signing up enough customers and ensuring that they paid the amounts they owed. The debt-to-equity ratio indicates that SSRC has more liabilities than equity. It is not possible to tell whether this is a problem because there is no benchmark for comparison. However, the more debt an entity has, the more risk it faces. In this case, if SSRC were not successful (if it didn't have enough paying customers), Stan would still be obliged to pay the bank and the vendor of the truck.

SUMMARY OF KEY POINTS

▶ **LO 1** There are five components of a set of general purpose financial statements: the balance sheet, the income statement, the statement of retained earnings, the cash flow statement, and the notes to the financial statements. The balance sheet summarizes the financial position of the entity—its assets, liabilities, and owners' equity—at a specific point in time. The income statement provides a measure of the economic performance of an entity over a period. The statement of retained earnings summarizes the changes to retained earnings during a period. The cash flow statement shows how cash during a period was obtained from and used for operating, investing, and financing activities. The notes to the financial statements expand and explain the information in the statements and provide additional information that may be helpful in assessing an entity.

General purpose financial statements are designed to suit a broad set of users and uses. General purpose financial statements are usually prepared according to GAAP.

▶ **LO 2** The accounting equation is the conceptual foundation of accounting and is defined as:

$$\text{Assets} = \text{Liabilities} + \text{Owners' Equity}$$

All economic events that are entered into an accounting system must be summarized in terms of the accounting equation. The equality between assets, and liabilities and equities must always be maintained.

▶ **LO 3** There are five basic elements in the financial statements: assets, liabilities, owners' equity, revenues, and expenses. Assets are economic resources that provide future benefits to an entity for carrying out its business activities. Liabilities are an entity's obligations to pay debts or provide goods or services. Owners' equity represents the owners' investment in an entity. Owners' investments can be made directly by contributing assets to the entity or indirectly by reinvesting profits back into the entity. Revenues represent economic benefits earned by providing goods and services to customers. Expenses are economic sacrifices made to earn revenue.

▶ **LO 4** While there are only five basic elements reported in financial statements (assets, liabilities, owners' equity, revenues, and expenses), entities maintain a large number of different types of these elements. The accounts reported on the financial statements are an aggregation of a much larger number of accounts in an entity's actual records.

▶ **LO 5** One of the main purposes of accounting is to record economic events and transactions in an accounting system so that the raw data can be converted into useful information for stakeholders in the form of financial statements and special purpose reports.

▶ **LO 6** Two of the most common methods of accounting are the cash basis of accounting and the accrual basis of accounting. The cash basis of accounting records only cash inflows and outflows. Under the cash basis of accounting, revenues are recorded when cash is received and expenses are recorded when cash is paid. The accrual basis of accounting attempts to measure the economic impact of transactions and economic events rather than cash flows. Under the accrual basis, revenue is recorded when it is earned and expenses are recorded when costs are incurred to earn the revenue, regardless of when the cash is received or spent.

▶ **LO 7** Obtaining and examining financial statements are often only the first steps in evaluating an entity. Financial statement numbers can be analyzed to obtain additional insights. One of the analytical tools available to financial statement users is ratios. The current ratio (current assets ÷ current liabilities) provides information about an entity's liquidity. The debt-to-equity ratio (debt ÷ equity) gives an indication of an entity's risk, and the gross margin percentage (gross margin ÷ sales) gives an indication of an entity's profitability.

KEY TERMS

accounting equation, p. 35
accounting policies, p. 54
accounts payable, p. 40
accounts receivable, p. 38
accrual basis of accounting, p. 44
amortization, p. 47
asset, p. 34
balance sheet, p. 34
capital assets, p. 39
capital stock, p. 42
cash basis of accounting, p. 44
cash flow statement, p. 51
cash from financing activities, p. 52
cash from investing activities, p. 52
cash from operations, p. 51
consolidated financial statements, p. 34
cost of sales, p. 48
creditor, p. 35
current asset, p. 39
current liability, p. 39
current ratio, p. 41
debt-to-equity ratio, p. 43
deficit, p. 42
dividend, p. 42
expense, p. 46

fiscal year, p. 34
general purpose financial statements, p. 33
gross margin, p. 48
gross margin percentage, p. 48
income statement, p. 44
interest, p. 43
liability, p. 35
liquidity, p. 40
long-term debt, p. 40
net assets, p. 47
non-current assets, p. 39
non-current liability, p. 39
operating cycle, p. 39
operating expenses, p. 48
operating income, p. 48
owners' equity, p. 35
principal, p. 43
property, plant, and equipment, p. 38
retained earnings, p. 42
revenue, p. 45
special purpose report, p. 56
statement of retained earnings, p. 50
working capital, p. 40
working capital ratio, p. 41

SIMILAR TERMS

The left column provides alternative terms that are sometimes used for the accounting terms introduced in this chapter. The accounting terms are listed in the right column.

accrual accounting	**accrual basis of accounting, p. 44**
cash accounting	**cash basis of accounting, p. 44**
cash from operating activities	**cash from operations, p. 51**
common stock	**capital stock, p. 42**
cost of goods sold	**cost of sales, p. 48**
depletion	**amortization, p. 47**
depreciation	**amortization, p. 47**
earnings, net earnings	
capital assets, fixed assets	**property, plant, and equipment, p. 38**
gross profit	**gross margin, p. 48**
long-term assets, long-lived assets	**non-current assets, p. 39**
partners' equity (for a partnership)	**owners' equity, p. 41**
profit, net profit	**net income, p. 44**
sales, sales revenue	**revenue, p. 45**
share capital	**capital stock, p. 42**
shareholders' equity (for a corporation)	**owners' equity, p. 41**
statement of cash flow	**cash flow statement, p. 51**
statement of earnings, statement of income, statement of profit and loss, statement of operations	**income statement, p. 44**
statement of financial position	**balance sheet, p. 34**
stockholders' equity (for a corporation)	**owners' equity, p. 41**

ASSIGNMENT MATERIALS

Questions

Q2-1. What are the components of a complete financial statement package?

Q2-2. Explain the difference between cash and accrual accounting.

Q2-3. Why is it important for direct and indirect investments by a corporation's shareholders to be reported separately on the balance sheet?

Q2-4. What are general purpose financial statements? What problems does any individual stakeholder have with using general purpose statements?

Q2-5. Why are the financial statements produced by public companies in Canada considered general purpose financial statements?

Q2-6. The balance sheet has been compared to a photograph. Explain.

Q2-7. Explain each of the following terms in your own words and give an example of each:
a. asset
b. liability
c. owners' equity
d. dividend
e. revenue
f. expense

Q2-8. Explain the following accounting measurements and explain how and why they would be used when evaluating an entity:
a. working capital
b. current ratio
c. debt-to-equity ratio
d. gross margin
e. gross margin percentage

Q2-9. Explain why each of the following would be classified as assets on an entity's balance sheet:
a. cash
b. rent paid for in advance
c. land
d. shares of other corporations owned by the entity

Q2-10. Explain why each of the following would be considered liabilities on an entity's balance sheet:
a. amounts owing to suppliers of inventory
b. advances received from customers for services to be provided in the future
c. long-term debt

Q2-11. Under GAAP, money spent on research by companies in the biotechnology, pharmaceutical, high technology, and other industries is not reported on the balance sheet as an asset. In your opinion, is the money companies spend on research an asset? Explain your thinking. Based on what you read in this chapter, why do you think money spent on research is not considered an asset under GAAP? What do you think the implications of this treatment of research costs are for users of the financial statements?

Q2-12. Explain the difference between capital stock and retained earnings in the shareholders' equity section of a corporation's balance sheet.

Q2-13. Explain the concept of liquidity. Why is evaluating liquidity important?

Q2-14. By law, distillers of Irish whiskey must age the whiskey for a minimum of three years, although the whiskey is often aged for a much longer time. If you were evaluating the liquidity of a distiller of Irish whiskey, how would you deal with the whiskey inventory?

Q2-15. Explain why net income results in an increase in owners' equity.

Q2-16. Explain why paying dividends results in a decrease in retained earnings of a corporation.

Q2-17. Readers of financial statements are always encouraged to read the notes to the statements. Why do you think the notes are considered so important? What impact would *not* reading the notes have on a user's ability to evaluate an entity? Use Roger's financial statements as a reference when answering this question.

Q2-18. Why is knowing the ability of an entity to generate cash flow so important to assessing the survival of the entity?

Q2-19. Virtually all entities prepare financial statements on an annual basis. For example, Rogers prepares its statements for a calendar year. Provide three reasons why entities report on an annual basis. In answering, consider the question from the point of view of the users of the information.

Q2-20. It is normal for entities to present financial statements for more than one year rather than for just the most recent year. Provide three reasons why it is useful to users of financial statements to receive more than one year's financial statements.

Q2-21. Explain why different entities will organize the presentation of their financial statements in different ways (use different formats). For example, why would some companies present a lot of detail in their statements, whereas others might present as little as possible? In answering, consider different users and uses of the statements.

Q2-22. Do you think all entities should be required to use the same format for financial statements? Explain.

Exercises

E2-1. (**Accounting equation, LO 2**) For each of the following independent situations, fill in the shaded area with the appropriate dollar amount.

	Assets	=	Liabilities	+	Owners' Equity
Situation 1	$255,000				$ 89,000
Situation 2			430,000		620,000
Situation 3	100,000		40,000		
Situation 4	680,000				295,000

E2-2. (**Accounting equation, LO 2**) For each of the following independent situations, fill in the shaded area with the appropriate dollar amount. You are provided with assets and liabilities on December 31, 2008, owners' equity on January 1, 2008, and revenue and expenses for 2008.

	Assets on Dec. 31, 2008	=	Liabilities on Dec. 31, 2008	+	Owners' Equity on Jan. 1, 2008	+	Revenue in 2008	−	Expenses in 2008
Situation 1	$		$29,000		$110,000		$295,000		$210,000
Situation 2	648,000				213,000		550,000		250,000
Situation 3	245,000		220,000		(50,000)				300,000
Situation 4	32,000		10,000		35,000		65,000		

E2-3. (**Determining the impact of transactions on the accounting equation, LO 2, 3**)
On July 1, 2009 Fairhaven Ltd. (Fairhaven) reported assets of $250,000, liabilities of $150,000, and shareholders' equity of $100,000. Indicate the amount of assets, liabilities, and shareholders' equity that Fairhaven has after accounting for each of the following events. Treat each event independently.
a. Fairhaven purchases $10,000 of new office furniture on credit.
b. Fairhaven pays $5,000 owing to a supplier.
c. Fairhaven sells shares of the company to investors for $6,000.
d. Fairhaven purchases inventory for $2,000 cash.
e. Fairhaven pays a $1,000 cash dividend to shareholders.
f. Fairhaven borrows $12,000 from the bank.

E2-4. (**Classification of balance sheet accounts, LO 1, 4**) Classify each of the following balance sheet accounts as a current asset, non-current asset, current liability, or non-current liability. Briefly explain your classification:
a. inventory
b. accounts payable that are usually paid within 60 days of receiving an invoice from a supplier
c. accounts receivable from customers that are expected to be paid within 30 days
d. land
e. furniture in the company's head office
f. bank loan that the bank can ask the company to repay at any time

g. account receivable that will be paid by the customer in two years

h. bank loan that must be repaid in full in three years

E2-5. **(Prepare a statement of retained earnings, LO 1, 5)** On December 31, 2008, Canmore Inc. (Canmore) reported retained earnings of $120,000. For the year ended December 31, 2009, Canmore had net income of $30,000 and paid dividends of $10,000.

Required:

Prepare a statement of retained earnings for Canmore for the year ended December 31, 2009.

E2-6. **(Prepare a statement of retained earnings, LO 1, 5)** Minden Corporation was incorporated on August 1, 2008 by five shareholders who each invested $100,000 in cash in exchange for common shares. Minden's year end is July 31. In its first year of business Minden had net income of $195,000. For its years ended July 31, 2010 and 2011, its second and third years of operation, Minden reported net income of $378,000 and $448,000 respectively. In its first year Minden did not pay any dividends, but in fiscal 2010 it paid $50,000 in dividends and in 2011 it paid $80,000 in dividends.

Required:

Prepare a statement of retained earnings for the year ended July 31, 2011.

E2-7. **(Classification of cash flows, LO 1)** Classify each of the following cash flows as operating, financing, or investing activities:

a. cash paid for inventory

b. cash collected from customers

c. cash paid to suppliers

d. repayment of a long-term loan

e. purchase of computer equipment

f. sale of a building for cash

g. sale of common stock to investors

h. cash spent to purchase advertising on radio

i. payment of a dividend to shareholders

E2-8. **(Prepare a balance sheet, LO 1, 4, 5)** You have received the following alphabetical list of balance sheet accounts for Picton Corporation (Picton). Organize the accounts into Picton's balance sheet.

Accounts receivable	$ 35,000	Insurance paid for in advance	$ 10,000
Advances paid by customers for goods to be provided in the future	20,000	Inventory	85,000
		Land	125,000
Amounts owed to suppliers	75,000	Loans made to the corporation by shareholders	50,000
Bank loan	100,000	Long-term debt	30,000
Capital stock	150,000	Retained earnings	80,000
Cash	12,000	Wages payable to employees	12,000
Furniture and fixtures	250,000		

E2-9. **(Complete statements of income and retained earnings, LO 1, 2, 3)** Selkirk Corporation began operations in 2008. Its summarized financial statements are presented on page 65. Fill in the shaded areas to complete the financial statements. Begin your work in 2008 and move forward from there.

	2010	2009	2008
Revenues	$	$412,500	$375,000
Expenses	352,500		297,000
Net income	97,500	90,000	
Retained earnings at the beginning of the year			0
Dividends declared during the year		27,000	
Retained earnings at the end of the year	187,500		60,000
Capital stock at the end of the year	135,000	112,500	
Liabilities at the end of the year	300,000		225,000
Assets at the end of the year	$	$520,500	$397,500

E2-10. **(Record the effect of transactions on the accounting equation, LO 2, 3, 4)** Show the effect that each transaction described below has on the elements of the accounting equation. Also, specify the type of asset, liability, or owners' equity account that would be affected. Set up your answer as shown in the example below.

	Transaction	Assets	=	Liabilities	+	Shareholders' Equity
	Example: Shareholders purchase shares for $10,000	$10,000 + Cash +				$10,000 + Capital stock +
a.	Equipment is purchased for $2,000 cash.					
b.	$3,000 cash is borrowed from a bank.					
c.	Goods are sold to customers for $4,000. The customer will pay in 45 days.					
d.	$4,500 cash is paid to employees for work done in the current year.					
e.	A cash dividend of $5,000 is paid to the shareholders.					

E2-11. **(Record the effect of transactions on the accounting equation, LO 2, 3, 4)** Show the effect that each transaction described below has on the elements of the accounting equation. Also, specify the type of asset, liability or owners' equity account that would be affected. Set up your answer as shown in the example below.

	Transaction	Assets	=	Liabilities	+	Partners' Equity
	Example: Partners purchase partnership units for $10,000.	$10,000 + Cash +				$10,000 + Partners equity +
a.	The partnership purchases new computer server and software for $25,000. The server and software will be paid for in 90 days.					
b.	Partners take out a $1,000,000 mortgage on a building that was purchased several years ago.					

Transaction	Assets	=	Liabilities	+	Partners' Equity
c. Services are provided to customers for $35,000. The customer paid in cash.					
d. $6,000 cash is paid to employees for work done last year.					
e. A customer pays $20,000 in advance for work that will be done next year.					
f. Last year, the partnership purchased liability insurance. The policy cost $12,000 and covered three years beginning at the start of the current year. The policy was paid for in cash.					

E2-12. **(Classification of cash flows, LO 1)** During 2009, Argentia Ltd. entered into the following cash transactions. Classify each transaction as operating, financing, or investing cash flows. Explain your thinking in each case.
a. Inventory is purchased for $100,000.
b. Dividends of $75,000 are paid to shareholders.
c. $500,000 is borrowed from the bank.
d. Office furniture is purchased for $20,000 to furnish the president's office.
e. Four delivery trucks are sold for $22,500.
f. Common shares are sold to investors for $500,000.
g. Payments of $30,000 are collected from clients.
h. Insurance for the next two years costing $8,000 is purchased.

E2-13. **(Classifying items on the financial statements, LO 3, 4)** State the financial statement on which each of the following items would appear (balance sheet, income statement, statement of retained earnings, statement of cash flows). Some items may appear on more than one statement:
a. Amounts owed by customers
b. Sales to customers
c. Amounts owed to employees
d. Cash from operations
e. Retained earnings
f. Land
g. Amount borrowed from the bank
h. Cash spent to purchase new equipment
i. Dividends paid
j. Cost of inventory sold to customers during the year

E2-14. **(Calculation of ratios, LO 4, 7)** Below is a simplified balance sheet for Summerside Inc. (Summerside):

Summerside Inc.

Balance Sheet

As at December 31, 2008

Assets		Liabilities and shareholders' equity	
Current assets	$2,250,000	Current liabilities	$1,750,000
Non-current assets	6,250,000	Non-current liabilities	2,500,000
		Shareholders' equity	4,250,000
Total assets	$8,500,000	Total liabilities and shareholders' equity	$8,500,000

Required:

Calculate the following on December 31, 2008, using Summerside's balance sheet. Provide an explanation for each:
a. working capital
b. current ratio
c. debt-to-equity ratio

E2-15. **(Calculation of ratios, LO 4, 7)** Consider the following alphabetic list of income statement accounts for Sussex Ltd. (Sussex) for the year ended September 30, 2009:

Advertising and promotion expense	$68,000
Amortization expense	45,000
Cost of sales	278,000
General and administrative expenses	82,000
Income tax expense	54,000
Interest expense	30,000
Research expense	100,000
Revenue	990,000
Salaries and wage expense	195,000
Selling expenses	70,000

Required:

a. Prepare an income statement for Sussex for the year ended September 30, 2009.
b. What is net income for the year?
c. What is Sussex' gross margin for 2009?
d. What is Sussex' gross margin percentage for 2009?

E2-16. **(Prepare income statements using cash and accrual accounting, LO 1, 6)** You have been provided the following information about Kedgwick Company, a small proprietorship, as of the end of its first year of operations. Assume that all supplies were used up at year end.

Cash collected from customers	$8,000
Amounts owing from customers	1,200
Amounts paid to suppliers	4,700
Amounts owing to suppliers	1,100

Required:

Calculate net income on the cash basis and on the accrual basis for Kedgwick Company. Explain why the cash basis and the accrual basis result in different amounts of income.

E2-17. **(Prepare income statements using cash and accrual accounting, LO 1, 6)** You have been provided the following information about Lunenberg Ltd. (Lunenberg) as of the end of its first year of operations. Lunenberg began business just over a year ago.

Cash collected from customers	$413,000
Amounts owing from customers	39,200
Amounts paid to suppliers for business supplies	121,450
Amounts owing to suppliers for business supplies	28,350
Business supplies on hand at the end of the year	9,800
Amounts paid to employees for work done	61,250
Amounts owing to employees for work done	7,700
Advances paid to employees for work that will be done in the future	3,500
Amortization of assets	14,000
Income taxes paid	26,250

Required:

Calculate net income on the cash basis and on the accrual basis of accounting for Lunenberg. Explain why the cash basis and the accrual basis result in different amounts of income.

E2-18. (**Prepare a personal balance sheet, LO 1, 3, 4, 5**) Make a list of your personal assets and liabilities and try to organize them into an accounting balance sheet format. Assign values to the assets and the liabilities. Answer the following questions about your balance sheet:

a. How did you determine your equity in your assets?
b. How did you decide what amount to assign to each asset and liability?
c. Did you include your education among your assets? Why or why not? If your personal balance sheet was being prepared according to GAAP, would your education be included as an asset? Explain.

Problems

P2-1. (**Complete a set of financial statements, LO 1, 2, 4**) Below are three years of balance sheets, income statements, and statements of retained earnings for Auburndale Ltd.

Required:

a. Replace the missing information in the shaded areas with the appropriate amount. Begin your analysis in 2008 and work forward.
b. If you were a banker, would you lend Auburndale Ltd. $5,000,000? Explain your answer. What additional information would you require to make your decision whether to lend? Explain.

Auberndale Ltd.
Balance Sheets
As at December 31
(in thousands of dollars)

	2010	2009	2008
Current Assets			
Cash	$	$	$
Accounts Receivable	22,134	19,992	17,850
Inventory	39,270	31,416	28,560
Prepaid Assets	2,142	714	1,428
Total Current Assets	70,686		50,694
Land	8,925	8,925	
Plant & Equipment	53,550	49,266	43,554
Accumulated Amortization		(22,134)	(19,278)
Other Assets	3,285	5,850	7,311
Total Non-Current Assets			40,512
Total Assets	$	$	$
Current Liabilities			
Accounts Payable	$	$ 20,703	$16,422
Bank Loan Payable	2,385	6,168	2,856
Total Current Liabilities	23,805	26,871	
Mortgage Payable	12,138		15,708
Total Liabilities	35,943		34,986
Shareholders' Equity			
Common Shares			12,138
Retained Earnings		52,452	
Total Shareholders' Equity	74,085	64,740	
Total Liabilities and Shareholders' Equity	$	$105,741	$

Auberndale Ltd.
Income Statement
For the Year Ended December 31
(in thousands of dollars)

	2010	2009	2008
Sales Revenue	$178,500	$	$146,370
Cost of Goods Sold		110,670	
Gross Margin		49,980	46,410
Expenses			
Selling	22,134	19,635	
Administrative	10,710		9,639
Amortization	4,641	3,570	2,856
Interest	1,785	2,712	2,856
Total Expenses		35,913	33,201
Income Before Income Taxes	14,280	14,067	
Income Taxes	5,427		4,113
Net Income	$	$	$ 9,096

Auberndale Ltd.
Statement of Retained Earnings
For the Year Ended December 31
(in thousands of dollars)

	2010	2009	2008
Retained Earnings, Beginning of year	$	$	$35,700
Net Income		9,156	
Dividends	786	786	714
Retained Earnings, End of year	$	$	$

P2-2. **(Preparing an income statement, LO 1, 4, 5)** The junior accountant for Josselin Ltd. was asked to prepare an income statement for the company for the year ended October 31, 2008. The accountant summarized the accounts he thought were necessary to prepare the statement but isn't sure how to proceed. Use the information provided by the junior accountant to prepare the income statement. Note that not all the information provided may be appropriate to use in the income statement.

Accounts receivable	$510,000	Property, plant, and equipment	$1,870,000
Amortization expense	224,000	Retained earnings	4,356,000
Cost of sales	2,800,000	Revenue	5,750,000
Dividends	300,000	Salaries and wage expense	545,000
Dividends payable	75,000	Selling, general, and	
Income tax expense	300,000	administrative expense	650,000
Interest expense	185,000	Wages payable	210,000

P2-3. **(Explaining assets, LO 3)** Explain why each of the following items would be considered an asset according to GAAP:
  i.   Inventory
  ii. Land
  iii. Money owed to an entity by its major shareholder
  iv. Prepaid rent
  v.   Computer equipment under lease

P2-4. (**Explaining liabilities, LO 3**) Explain why each of the following items would be considered a liability:
   i.   Wages payable
   ii. Warranty obligation
   iii. Advance received from a customer for services to be provided in the future
   iv. Current portion of long-term debt

P2-5. (**Prepare a balance sheet, LO 1, 2, 5**) Andrea Reed is in her fourth year at a business school in Nova Scotia. Recently Andrea was asked by her brother Nathan to help him prepare a personal balance sheet. Nathan needed the balance sheet because he was applying for a scholarship at a prestigious art school and the school required the information to help it assess Nathan' financial need. Andrea sat down with Nathan to go over his situation and she obtained the
following information:
   i.   Nathan's bankbooks show that he has $844 in his bank accounts.
   ii. Nathan purchased a used car from his uncle three years ago. He paid $4,500 for the car and he thinks he should be able to continue to use it for another two years.
   iii. Nathan is owed $750 for some decorating he did for a local social group's recent fundraising party.
   iv. Nathan owes $2,000 to a local bank for a job training program he took a couple of years ago. He must begin to pay back the money once he accepts a full-time job or in five years, whichever comes first.
   v.   About six months ago Nathan bought a computer from a local store. The computer cost $1,200 and he paid the seller $700 at the time he purchased it and he must pay $50 a month until the computer is paid for.
   vi. Nathan's personal property such as clothes, books, jewellery, etc., costs him about $6,000.

Required:

   a. Use the information provided to prepare a balance sheet for Nathan. Provide an explanation for why you classified each item as you did (asset, liability, equity). Remember that each item you include in your balance sheet must affect the accounting equation in two places to ensure that the equation balances.
   b. How do you think the balance sheet would help the art school assess whether Nathan should receive financial assistance?
   c. What additional information do you think the school would want to have before making a decision to offer financial assistance?

P2-6. (**Prepare a balance sheet, LO 1, 2, 5**) In addition to the information provided in Problem 2-5, you also learn the following about Nathan's assets:
   i.   Nathan thinks the car could be sold for about $2,200.
   ii. A friend of Nathan recently offered him $1,000 for the computer.
   iii. Nathan is unlikely to receive more than $1,000 for his personal property.

Required:

   a. Use the additional information along with the information provided in P2-5 to prepare a revised personal balance sheet for Nathan. Explain the choices you made in preparing the statement.
   b. Compare your balance sheet with the one you prepared in P2-5. Which do you think would be more useful to the art school in assessing Nathan's need for financial assistance? Explain.
   c. What problems arise when using market values of Nathan's assets instead of the cost? What are some of the benefits of using the cost of the assets? Is the balance sheet prepared using market value information more or less useful than the balance sheet prepared using the cost information?

P2-7. (**Prepare a balance sheet, LO 1, 2, 5**) Louis Davis is a dentist with a practice in a small town in Manitoba. Recently, he separated from his wife and they are currently negotiating how they will divide their assets when their divorce proceedings conclude. As part of the process, Louis' lawyer has asked for a balance sheet for his practice. The balance sheet will be used to help value Louis' practice. Louis has asked you to prepare the balance sheet. You gather the following information from Louis:

i. Louis purchased all his equipment eight years ago when he started his practice. The total cost of all the equipment was $100,000. He expects to replace all the equipment in four years.

ii. He purchased furniture and decorations for his office four years ago for $22,000. He expects the furniture and decorations to last for about ten years.

iii. Patients owe Louis $19,000.

iv. Louis owes various suppliers $12,000 for various goods and services that he used in his practice.

v. The practice has $4,750 in its bank account.

vi. Louis owes his staff $2,500. This amount will be paid on the next payday in two weeks.

vii. Louis has a bank loan outstanding for $10,000.

viii. Louis keeps various supplies that he needs in his practice. The cost of the supplies he currently has on hand is $750.

Required:

a. Use the information provided to prepare a balance sheet for Louis' dental practice. Provide an explanation for why you classified each item as you did (asset, liability, equity). Remember that each item you include in your balance sheet must affect the accounting equation in two places to ensure that the equation balances.

b. As a judge in this case, how would you use the balance sheet in deciding how to value Louis' practice?

c. What additional information do you think that you as judge might want to have before deciding how to value Louis' practice?

P2-8. (**Prepare a balance sheet, LO 1, 2, 5**) In addition to the information provided in Problem 2-7, you also learn the following about Louis' assets:

i. Louis thinks that if he closed his practice he could sell his list of patients to another dentist for $125,000.

ii. If Louis tried to sell his equipment he would receive about $25,000.

iii. Louis would be unlikely to receive any money if he tried to sell the furniture and decorations.

Required:

a. Use the additional information along with the information provided in P2-7 to prepare a revised personal balance sheet for Louis' dental practice. Explain the choices you made in preparing the statement.

b. Compare your balance sheet with the one you prepared in Problem 2-7. Which do you think would be more useful for valuing Louis' practice? Explain.

c. What problems arise when using market values of Louis' assets instead of the cost? What are some of the benefits of using the cost of the assets? Is the balance sheet prepared using market value information more or less useful than the balance sheet prepared using the cost information?

P2-9. (**Analyze financial information, LO 4, 7**) Below are the income statements and balance sheets for Penticton Inc. (Penticton) for 2008 and 2009:

Penticton Inc.
Balance Sheets
As of December 31

	2009	2008		2009	2008
Assets			**Liabilities and shareholders' equity**		
Cash	$ 5,000	$ 10,000	Bank loan	$ 100,000	$ 75,000
Accounts			Accounts payable	200,000	150,000
receivable	205,000	175,000	Goods to be provided		
Inventory	264,200	225,000	to customers	42,000	35,000
Equipment,			Long-term debt	250,000	150,000
furniture and					
fixtures (net of					
accumulated			Shareholders' equity		
amortization)	720,000	530,000	Capital stock	260,000	250,000
Other non-			Retained earnings	417,200	380,000
current assets	75,000	100,000			
			Total liabilities and		
Total assets	$1,269,200	$1,040,000	shareholders' equity	$1,269,200	$1,040,000

Penticton Inc.
Income Statements
For the Years Ended December 31

	2009	2008
Revenue	$2,475,000	$1,925,000
Cost of goods sold	1,350,000	1,098,000
Selling, general, and administrative expenses	550,000	495,000
Amortization expense	120,000	100,000
Interest expense	125,000	120,000
Tax expense	132,000	44,800
Net income	$ 198,000	$ 67,200

Required:

a. Calculate the following for Penticton for 2009 and 2008:
   i. working capital
   ii. current ratio
   iii. debt-to-equity ratio
   iv. gross margin
   v. gross margin percentage
b. Explain why the amounts you calculated in (a) changed from 2008 to 2009.
c. Comment on Penticton's liquidity position on December 31, 2009. As a prospective lender of money to Penticton, what concerns would you have about its current liquidity position?
d. What could Penticton's management do to improve liquidity?

P2-10. (**Record information in a simple spreadsheet and prepare a balance sheet, LO 2, 3, 4, 5**) Dennis Sonin had a great idea to make some extra money. He decided that he would sell holiday items in the local mall in the two months preceding Christmas. He set up a proprietorship that he called Dennis' Great Gifts, opened a bank account in the proprietorship's name, and deposited $10,000 of his savings into the account. He was also able to borrow $8,000 from his grandmother, which he also deposited into the bank accountant. He promised his grandmother that he would repay the money he borrowed by the end of January. On October 15 he came to terms with a mall manager to rent a small store in a good location for two months ending December 31, 2005. He paid the rent of $2,000 for the two month in full on October 15. Next Dennis purchased tables, shelving, and other materials that he needed to operate his store. The total cost of these purchases was $3,000. He spent as little money as possible on these items because he wanted to provide the merchandise to customers at low prices and this meant keeping the store simple. In the last week of October Dennis purchased merchandise to stock his store. He bought books, Christmas decorations, and other low cost items that he thought would be popular with his customers. In total, Dennis purchased merchandise costing $22,000. He paid the various suppliers $10,000 in cash and the rest on credit. He also purchased an advertisement in the community newspaper for $500 that would run in the first week of November. He paid for the advertisement on October 29.

Required:

    a. Set up a spreadsheet like the one in Table 2–1 on page 36 and record the transactions you find in the scenario. For each entry you make to your spreadsheet state the type of asset, liability, or equity that is affected (cash, accounts receivable, payable, etc.).

    b. Use the information in your spreadsheet to prepare a balance sheet for Dennis as of October 31.

P2-11. **(Record transactions and prepare income statements, LO 1, 6)** Refer to the information in P2-10. Dennis operated his business until December 31. In the two months he sold merchandise to customers for $52,000, all in cash, except for $1,200 that was owed by one customer. He sold all the inventory he originally purchased in October ($22,000) plus most of an additional $10,000 of inventory that he purchased in early December. As of the end of December he owed one of his suppliers $1,750. He paid the sales people he hired $3,000 in cash for their work and owed them $400 on December 31. He also incurred an additional $1,500 in advertising costs, all of which had been paid for as of the end of December. At the end of December he also owed about $500 for utilities and other miscellaneous costs that were incurred during November and December. At the end of December there was about $600 of inventory unsold, but Dennis thought he would be able to sell it in the future. Indeed, Dennis was so pleased about the performance of his business that he decided to continue operating in the new year selling other seasonal merchandise.

Required:

    a. Prepare income statements for Dennis' business for the period ending December 31 on the cash basis and on the accrual basis.

    b. Explain why the two income statements are different.

    c. Assess the performance of Dennis' business.

P2-12. **(Understanding the impact of transactions on financial ratios, LO 4, 7)** Victoria Ltd. (Victoria) is a small tool and die manufacturer in British Columbia. Victoria recently obtained financing from a local bank for an expansion of the company's facilities. The agreement with the bank requires that Victoria's current ratio and debt-to-equity ratio be within ranges stated in the agreement. If the ratios fall outside of these ranges Victoria would have to repay the new loan immediately. At this time Victoria has a current ratio of 1.80 (based on current assets of $900,000 and current liabilities of $500,000) and a debt-to-equity ratio of 2 to 1 (based on total liabilities of $2 million and total equity of $1 million). The chief financial officer of Victoria is concerned about the effect a number of transactions scheduled for the last few days of the year will have on the company's current ratio and debt-to-equity ratio.

Required:

Determine the effect that each of the following transactions will have on the initial current ratio and debt-to-equity ratio. Calculate what each ratio will be after each transaction takes place and state the effect each transaction has on the ratios (increase, decrease, or no effect). Treat each item independently.

	Transaction	Revised current ratio	Effect on the current ratio	Revised debt-to-equity ratio	Effect on the debt-to-equity ratio
		1.80	No effect	2 to 1	No effect
1.	Purchase of equipment for $150,000. The equipment supplier must be paid in two years.				
2.	Purchase of inventory for $40,000 cash. The inventory is not expected to be sold until after the year end.				
3.	Bonuses of $75,000 cash are paid to senior managers. (This one is tricky. Be sure to consider the effect of the transaction on net income and the resulting impact on equity.)				
4.	Declaration and payment of $100,000 of dividends.				
5.	Repayment of $150,000 on a long-term loan.				
6.	A $75,000 loan is arranged and the cash obtained. The loan must be repaid in 90 days.				
7.	Dividends of $50,000 are declared and will be paid after the year end. (Once the dividends have been declared they become a liability called Dividends Payable.)				

P2-13. (**Understanding the impact of transactions on financial ratios, LO 4, 7**) Longueuil Ltd. (Longueuil) is a small shirt manufacturer in Québec. Longueuil recently obtained financing from a local bank for an expansion of the company's facilities. The agreement with the bank requires that Longueuil's current ratio and debt-to-equity ratio be within ranges stated in the agreement. If the ratios fall outside of these ranges Longueuil would have to repay the new loans immediately. At this time Longueuil has a current ratio of 2.0 (based on current assets of $700,000 and current liabilities of $350,000) and a debt-to-equity ratio of 1.5 to 1 (based on total liabilities of $900,000 and total equity of $600,000). The chief financial officer of Longueuil is concerned about the effect a number of transactions that will be occurring in the last few days of the year will have on the company's current ratio and debt-to-equity ratio.

Required:

Determine the effect that each of the following transactions will have on the initial current ratio and debt-to-equity ratio. Calculate what each ratio will be after each transaction takes place and state the effect each transaction has on the ratios (increase, decrease, or no effect). Treat each item independently.

	Transaction	Revised current ratio	Effect on the current ratio	Revised debt-to-equity ratio	Effect on the debt-to-equity ratio
		2.0	No effect	1.5 to 1	No effect
1.	Purchase of equipment for $250,000. The supplier of the equipment must be paid within six months.				
2.	$10,000 owed by a customer is collected in cash.				
3.	Sale of capital stock to investors for $100,000 cash.				
4.	Declaration and payment of $100,000 of dividends.				
5.	A loan of $100,000 from a bank is arranged and the cash received. The loan must be repaid in 18 months.				
6.	A $50,000 short-term bank loan is repaid.				
7.	Merchandise is sold to a customer for $50,000. The customer must pay in two years. The inventory sold cost $20,000. (This one is tricky. Be sure to consider the effect of the transaction on net income and the resulting impact on equity.)				

P2-14. **(Prepare an income statement and balance sheet from a list of accounts, LO 4, 5)**
You have been provided with the following alphabetical list of accounts for Sudbury Ltd. for 2008. Use the information to prepare an income statement for the year ended December 31, 2008 and balance sheet as of December 31, 2008. You should be able to figure out how to treat accounts that have names that are unfamiliar to you by applying your understanding of the financial statements learned in this chapter.

Accounts payable	$ 183,750	Equipment, furniture and fixtures	$2,800,000
Accounts receivable	192,500	Income tax expense	525,000
Accrued liabilities	35,000	Income taxes payable	26,250
Accumulated amortization	2,625,000	Income taxes recoverable from government	15,750
Advances to employees	8,750	Interest expense	490,000
Advertising expenses	332,500	Interest revenue	3,500
Amortization expense	805,000	Inventory	297,500
Building	9,200,000	Investments in the shares of other corporations	420,000
Capital stock	3,500,000	Land	5,600,000
Cash	35,000	Long-term debt (non-current portion)	3,150,000
Cash revenue	787,500	Mortgage payable (non-current portion)	1,750,000
Charitable donations made	350,000	Other expense	70,000
Cost of assets lost in fire	315,000	Other non-current assets	175,000
Cost of sales	1,312,500	Patents	700,000
Credit revenue	5,075,000	Prepaid assets	7,000
Current portion of long-term debt	2,632,000	Retained earnings at the beginning of the year	2,632,000
Current portion of mortgage payable	75,000	Selling expenses	472,500
Deposits from customers	8,750	Wages expense	770,000
Dividends	87,500	Wages payable	12,250

P2-15. **(Prepare an income statement and balance sheet from a list of accounts, LO 4, 5)** You have been provided with the following alphabetical list of accounts for Thaxted Ltd. for 2009. Use the information to prepare an income statement for the year ended December 31, 2009 and balance sheet as of December 31, 2009. You should be able to figure out how to treat accounts that have names that are unfamiliar to you by applying your understanding of the financial statements learned in this chapter.

Accounts payable	$27,500	Interest revenue	$5,500
Accounts receivable	50,000	Inventory	75,000
Accrued liabilities	11,500	Investments in marketable securities	62,500
Accumulated depreciation and amortization	187,500	Loans to shareholders	6,250
Capital stock	375,000	Miscellaneous expenses	12,500
Cash	6,250	Notes payable (non-current portion)	312,500
Cost of closing west coast division	18,750	Other current assets	2,500
Cost of sales	237,500	Other non-current assets	18,750
Current portion of notes payable	12,500	Prepaid assets	13,000
Deposits from customers	6,250	Promotion and Advertising expenses	18,750
Depreciation and amortization expense	52,500	Property, plant, and equipment	500,000
Dividends	6,250	Research costs	237,500
General, and administrative expenses	68,750	Retained earnings at the beginning of the year	128,750
Income taxes payable	5,000	Revenue from sale of products	437,500
Income taxes recoverable from government	7,750	Revenue from sale of services	312,500
Intellectual property	300,000	Salaries and wages expense	105,000
Interest expense	26,250	Salaries and wages payable	3,750

P2-16. **(Evaluate the format of a balance sheet, LO 1, 5)** Look at the balance sheet of Stelco Inc. in Panel A of Exhibit 2–3 (page 55). Redo Stelco Inc.'s balance sheet in the more traditional format used by Rogers. How does your statement differ from the one prepared by the company? Which statement is more informative, the one you prepared or the one the company prepared? Should it make any difference to users how the balance sheet is formatted? Explain.

P2-17. **(Evaluate the format of a balance sheet, LO 1, 5)** Look at the balance sheet of Newfoundland Power Inc. in the Panel B of Exhibit 2–3 (page 55). Redo Newfoundland Power Inc.'s balance sheet in the more traditional format used by Rogers. How does your statement differ from the one prepared by the company? Which statement is more informative, the one you prepared or the one the company prepared? Should it make any difference to users how the balance sheet is formatted? Explain.

P2-18. **(Prepare a cash flow statement, LO 5)** The Pas Ltd. was organized on August 1, 2009 with a cash investment of $1,000,000 by its shareholders. The Pas arranged a mortgage with a local lender for $600,000 and purchased a warehouse for $900,000. During its fiscal year ended July 31, 2010 The Pas collected $425,000 in cash from customers, paid $270,000 in cash for operating expenses, and paid $60,000 in cash dividends to its shareholders.

Required:

a. Classify each of the cash flows described above as operating, investing, or financing.
b. Organize the cash flows into a cash flow statement.
c. Explain what your cash flow statement tells you that an income statement does not.

P2-19. **(Prepare a cash flow statement, LO 5)** Markham Ltd. was organized on September 1, 2008 with a cash investment of $350,000 by its shareholders. Markham arranged a long-term loan with a local bank for $250,000 and purchased a small office building for $400,000. During its fiscal year ended August 31, 2009 Markham collected $500,000 in cash from customers, paid $170,000 in cash for operating expenses, and paid $20,000 in cash dividends to its shareholders.

Required:

a. Classify each of the cash flows described above as operating, investing, or financing.

b. Organize the cash flows into a cash flow statement.

c. Explain what your cash flow statement tells you that an income statement does not.

P2-20. **(Explain whether and why an expenditure is an asset, LO 3)** For each of the following (a *and* b), explain whether and why each would be considered:

a. An asset by a non-accountant (use your intuition and judgment to decide whether the item in question should be considered an asset).

b. An asset according to GAAP (use the GAAP criteria that were discussed in the chapter).

  i. A large grocery store purchases land adjacent to the store for $300,000 so that it can expand its parking lot.

  ii. A company that operates call centres spends over $1 million per year providing training for staff so that they can provide informed and courteous service to the people they contact.

  iii. An auto parts manufacturer spends $200,000 to clear land to prepare it for construction of a new factory.

  iv. A metal fabricating shop is owed $25,000 by one of its customers. The customer recently filed for bankruptcy because it was unable to pay its debts.

  v. A student has paid university tuition totalling $15,000 to study business. The student plans to become a professional accountant in two years and hopes to open his own accounting practice within five years.

  vi. A major retailer is repeatedly found to have the most satisfied customers in its industry in surveys conducted by independent market research companies.

P2-21. **(Classify the effect of economic events on income on the cash and accrual bases, LO 3, 6)** Indicate whether each of the following events would be included in a calculation of net income on the cash basis, the accrual basis, or both. Provide a brief explanation for your treatment:

	Economic Event	Net income on the cash basis	Net income on the accrual basis
	Example: An entity sells merchandise for cash.	Yes, because cash is collected from a customer	Yes, because a sale with a customer has been completed.
a.	An entity sells merchandise on credit.		
b.	An entity collects cash for goods that were sold in a previous period.		
c.	Inventory that was paid for in a previous period is sold in the current period.		
d.	Dividends are declared and paid to shareholders.		
e.	Inventory is purchased and paid for in the current period but is unsold as of the year end.		
f.	A delivery vehicle is amortized.		

P2-22. **(Classify the effect of economic events on income on the cash and accrual bases, LO 3, 6)** Indicate whether each of the following events would be included in a calculation of net income on the cash basis, the accrual basis, or both. Provide a brief explanation for your treatment:

	Economic Event	Net income on the cash basis	Net income on the accrual basis
	Example: An entity sells merchandise for cash.	Yes, because cash is collected from a customer.	Yes, because a sale with a customer has been completed.
a.	An entity receives a deposit from a customer for services that will be provided in the future.		
b.	An entity provides services to a customer in the current period who paid in a previous period.		
c.	An advance is paid to an employee for work she will do in the future.		
d.	Supplies that were paid for in a previous period are used in the current period to provide services to a customer.		
e.	Supplies are bought, paid for, and used in the current period to provide services to a customer.		
f.	A delivery vehicle is purchased for cash.		

P2-23. **(Prepare balance sheets using different asset values, LO 5)** In Chapter 1 we asked you to imagine you were a student needing insurance on your apartment and examined different ways of valuing the contents of the apartment. We identified three different ways of valuing the contents of the apartment. Table 1–5 from Chapter 1 is reproduced next. All the items on the list are owned by you, except for the appliances, which are owned by the building.

Inventory of Apartment Contents			
Item	What it cost	What it would cost to replace	What it could be sold for
Television	$ 500	$ 650	$ 225
Computer	1,900	1,500	700
Furniture	1,200	1,350	900
Books	750	875	300
Clothes	1,600	1,950	1,000
Stereo	900	1,100	700
Jewellery	500	625	300
Appliances	2,000	2,600	1,400
Art	300	300	200
Other	1,000	1,200	750
Total	$10,650	$12,150	$6,475

In addition to the above, the following information is available:

Item	Amount
Student loans	$7,500
Loans from parents	3,000
Cash in bank	1,100
Owing from employer	800

Required:

a. Prepare three separate balance sheets using the information in each column above. Make sure to include the "other information" in each balance sheet.
b. Explain the benefits and limitations of each balance sheet to the people who might use them. Make sure to discuss specific entities that might use each balance sheet.
c. Which balance sheet do you think would be appropriate under GAAP?
d. Which balance sheet do you think is best? Explain.

Using Financial Statements

Dominion Citrus Limited (Dominion) is a leading diversified food company supplying fresh produce, premium juices, maple syrup, and Mediterranean food products to a wide variety of customers in retail, foodservice, and food distribution businesses. The Company provides procurement, processing, repacking, sorting, grading, warehousing, and distribution services to over 400 customers, with its major domestic markets being Ontario and Quebec. The Company also supplies products to customers in the United States and Europe.[4]

Dominion's consolidated balance sheets, statements of earnings, retained earnings, and cash flows, along with some extracts from the notes to the financial statements, are provided in Exhibit 2–4. Use this information to respond to questions FS2-1 to FS2-10.

FS2-1. Examine Dominion's balance sheet and confirm that the accounting equation equality holds (Assets = Liabilities + Owners' Equity). Show your work.

FS2-2. What is Dominion's year end?

FS2-3. Find the following information in Dominion's financial statements:
a. Revenue for the year ended December 31, 2005.
b. Warehouse and delivery expenses for the year ended December 31, 2005.
c. Total assets on December 31, 2005.
d. Long-term liabilities on December 31, 2005.
e. Total current liabilities on December 31, 2005.
f. Dividends paid to common shareholders during 2005.
g. The amount Dominion spent on additions to property, plant, and equipment during 2005.
h. The amount of long-term liabilities that was retired (paid off) during 2005.
i. The amount of cash raised by selling common shares during 2005.
j. What account on the balance sheet does the line on the statement of cash flows called "cash and cash equivalents (deficiency), end of year" correspond with?

FS2-4. Find the following information in Dominion's financial statements:
a. Net earnings (net income) for the year ended December 31, 2005.
b. Cost of goods sold for the year ended December 31, 2005.
c. Operating income for the year ended December 31, 2005.
d. Cash on December 31, 2005.
e. Capital stock on December 31, 2005.
f. Retained earnings on December 31, 2005.
g. Total liabilities on December 31, 2005.

h. Total current assets on December 31, 2005.
i. Cash from operations for 2005.
j. The amount Dominion received from the disposal of property, plant, and equipment during 2005.
k. The amount of long-term debt that was issued during 2005.

FS2-5. Use Dominion's financial statements to respond to the following:
a. Calculate the amount of working capital on December 31, 2004 and 2005.
b. Calculate the current ratio on December 31, 2004 and 2005.
c. How much did working capital change between the end of fiscal 2004 and the end of fiscal 2005?
d. What does the information you calculated in a. to c. above tell you about Dominon's liquidity?

FS2-6. Use Dominion's financial statements to respond to the following:
a. Calculate the debt-to-equity ratio on December 31, 2004 and 2005.
b. Explain why the debt-to-equity ratio changed from the end of fiscal 2004 to the end of fiscal 2005.
c. What comments can you make about Dominion based on your responses to a. and b. above?

FS2-7. Use Dominion's financial statements to respond to the following:
a. Calculate the gross margin for 2004 and 2005.
b. Calculate the gross margin percentage for 2004 and 2005.
c. Interpret your calculations in a. and b. above. What do they tell you about Dominion's performance? What additional information would you want to do a more thorough evaluation of Dominion's gross margin?

FS2-8. Examine the note to Dominion's financial statements that describes property, plant, and equipment. Describe the different types of property, plant, and equipment assets that the company has.

FS2-9. List five questions that you would ask Dominion's management if you were considering lending money to the company. Your questions should pertain to information that you cannot obtain from the financial statements.

FS2-10. Compare Dominion's balance sheet with Rogers'. Describe how the composition of assets differs between the two companies. Given the different industries that these two companies are in, does the difference make sense? Explain. In answering this question it may be helpful for you to calculate on a percentage basis what each asset represents as a proportion of total assets.

EXHIBIT 2–4 :

CONSOLIDATED BALANCE SHEETS

AS AT DECEMBER 31, 2005 AND 2004

	2005	2004 (Restated Note 1(q))
ASSETS		
CURRENT ASSETS		
Cash and cash equivalents	$ 3,034,000	$ —
Accounts receivable (Note 4)	15,571,000	12,288,000
Inventories	7,414,000	11,743,000
Portfolio investments, at market value	—	2,562,000
Prepaid expenses	426,000	203,000
	26,445,000	26,796,000
PROPERTY, PLANT AND EQUIPMENT (Note 5)	8,564,000	6,945,000
OTHER ASSETS (Note 6 (a))	1,393,000	232,000
GOODWILL (Note 6 (b))	4,827,000	4,652,000
FUTURE INCOME TAXES (Note 10)	—	2,000
	$ 41,229,000	$ 38,627,000
LIABILITIES		
CURRENT LIABILITIES		
Bank indebtedness (Note 7)	$ —	$ 705,000
Cheques in transit	3,641,000	1,291,000
Accounts payable and accrued liabilities	14,025,000	14,279,000
Current portion of long-term liabilities (Note 8)	48,000	979,000
Income taxes payable	180,000	59,000
Interest payable (Notes 1(q) and 11)	72,000	64,000
	17,966,000	17,377,000
LONG-TERM PAYABLE	427,000	401,000
LONG-TERM LIABILITIES (Note 8)	2,889,000	3,111,000
CONVERTIBLE DEBENTURE (Note 9)	4,813,000	4,752,000
PREFERENCE SHARES LIABILITY (Notes 1(q) and 11)	2,297,000	2,222,000
FUTURE INCOME TAXES (Note 10)	269,000	—
	28,661,000	27,863,000
Contingencies and commitments (Note 13)		
Subsequent events (Note 18)		
SHAREHOLDERS' EQUITY		
CAPITAL STOCK (Note 11)	6,942,000	6,481,000
CONTRIBUTED SURPLUS	27,000	15,000
EQUITY COMPONENT OF DEBENTURE (Note 9)	425,000	425,000
RETAINED EARNINGS	5,174,000	3,843,000
	12,568,000	10,764,000
	$ 41,229,000	$ 38,627,000

EXHIBIT 2–4 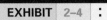 :

(continued)
Dominion Citrus Limited
Extracts from Financial Statements

CONSOLIDATED STATEMENTS OF EARNINGS

YEARS ENDED DECEMBER 31, 2005 AND 2004

	2005	2004 (Restated Note 1(q))
REVENUE	$ 125,849,000	$ 131,619,000
COST OF GOODS SOLD	102,721,000	107,763,000
GROSS MARGIN	23,128,000	23,856,000
EXPENSES		
Warehouse and delivery	12,707,000	12,192,000
Selling	2,540,000	2,702,000
General and administrative	4,430,000	4,496,000
	19,677,000	19,390,000
OPERATING INCOME	3,451,000	4,466,000
OTHER INCOME (EXPENSE)		
Foreign exchange gain	604,000	531,000
Interest expense – current	(82,000)	(139,000)
Interest expense – long-term	(839,000)	(852,000)
Interest expense - preference shares (Notes 1(q) and 11)	(141,000)	(136,000)
Interest income	65,000	17,000
Other income (Note 14)	385,000	244,000
	(8,000)	(335,000)
INCOME BEFORE PORTFOLIO & CATANTI RELATED INCOME (EXPENSE)	3,443,000	4,131,000
PORTFOLIO & CATANTI RELATED INCOME (EXPENSE)		
Dividend income	—	10,000
Income (loss) on disposal/write-down of portfolio investments (Note 2)	21,000	(1,184,000)
Catanti write-down and provision (Note 3(b))	—	(475,000)
	21,000	(1,649,000)
EARNINGS BEFORE INCOME TAXES	3,464,000	2,482,000
INCOME TAXES (Note 10)	1,143,000	1,294,000
NET EARNINGS FOR THE YEAR	$ 2,321,000	$ 1,188,000
EARNINGS PER SHARE (Note 12)		
Basic	$ 0.12	$ 0.06
Fully diluted	$ 0.11	$ 0.06

CONSOLIDATED STATEMENTS OF RETAINED EARNINGS

YEARS ENDED DECEMBER 31, 2005 AND 2004		2005		2004 (Restated Note 1(q))
RETAINED EARNINGS–BEGINNING OF YEAR	$	3,843,000	$	3,644,000
Net earnings for the year		2,321,000		1,188,000
Dividends paid – common shares		(990,000)		(989,000)
RETAINED EARNINGS–END OF YEAR	$	5,174,000	$	3,843,000

CONSOLIDATED STATEMENTS OF CASH FLOWS

YEARS ENDED DECEMBER 31, 2005 AND 2004		2005		2004 (Restated Note 1(q))
CASH PROVIDED BY (USED IN)				
OPERATIONS				
Net earnings for the year	$	2,321,000	$	1,188,000
Items not involving current cash flows:				
Amortization of property, plant and equipment		923,000		918,000
Amortization of deferred financing costs		150,000		144,000
Amortization of debenture discount		61,000		61,000
Write-off of Catanti trademarks		—		359,000
Loss (income) on portfolio investments		(21,000)		1,184,000
Gain on disposal of property, plant and equipment		(21,000)		(43,000)
Stock-based and other compensation expense		38,000		41,000
Future income taxes		271,000		(187,000)
		3,722,000		3,665,000
Net change in non-cash working capital:				
Accounts receivable		(3,283,000)		202,000
Inventories		4,329,000		89,000
Prepaid expenses		(223,000)		(38,000)
Cheques in transit		2,350,000		273,000
Accounts payable and accrued liabilities		(2,035,000)		281,000
Interest payable (Notes 1(q) and 11)		8,000		(14,000)
Income taxes		121,000		76,000
		4,989,000		4,534,000
FINANCING ACTIVITIES				
Repayment of long-term liabilities		(1,693,000)		(883,000)
Proceeds from long-term liabilities		540,000		—
Net proceeds from issue of common shares		461,000		21,000
Net proceeds from issue of preference shares		75,000		4,000
Other		—		(51,000)
Dividends paid		(990,000)		(989,000)
		(1,607,000)		(1,898,000)
INVESTING ACTIVITIES				
Proceeds on disposal of portfolio investments		2,583,000		167,000
Acquisition of property, plant and equipment		(2,091,000)		(1,191,000)
Acquisition of Bo-Fruits, net of cash acquired (Note 3(a))		(175,000)		(1,203,000)
Investment in Catanti		—		(9,000)
Proceeds on disposal of property, plant and equipment		40,000		103,000
		357,000		(2,133,000)
CHANGE IN CASH		3,739,000		503,000
INDEBTEDNESS – BEGINNING OF YEAR		(705,000)		(1,208,000)
CASH (INDEBTEDNESS) – END OF YEAR	$	3,034,000	$	(705,000)
SUPPLEMENTAL CASH FLOW INFORMATION				
Interest paid	$	726,000	$	769,000
Income taxes paid	$	751,000	$	1,362,000

EXHIBIT 2-4 :

(continued)
Dominion Citrus Limited
Extracts from Financial Statements

5. PROPERTY, PLANT AND EQUIPMENT

	2005		
	Cost	Accumulated Amortization	Net Book Value
Land, building and leasehold improvements	$ 4,489,000	$ 1,445,000	$ 3,044,000
Trucks and automobiles	806,000	763,000	43,000
Manufacturing equipment	11,369,000	6,428,000	4,941,000
Other equipment and furniture	1,480,000	944,000	536,000
	$ 18,144,000	$ 9,580,000	$ 8,564,000

	2004		
	Cost	Accumulated Amortization	Net Book Value
Land, building and leasehold improvements	$ 4,294,000	$ 1,245,000	$ 3,049,000
Trucks and automobiles	938,000	856,000	82,000
Manufacturing equipment	8,548,000	5,272,000	3,276,000
Other equipment and furniture	1,973,000	1,435,000	538,000
	$ 15,753,000	$ 8,808,000	$ 6,945,000

8. LONG-TERM LIABILITIES

	2005	2004
Non-revolving term credit facility, at prime plus 0.50%, repayable in quarterly principal installments of $200,000 commencing September 2003 and originally maturing May 15, 2006. The effective interest rate at December 31, 2005 was 5.50% (2004 - 4.75%). Subsequent to year-end, the loan was refinanced. Also see subsequent event note 18(b).	$ 2,400,000	$ 3,800,000
Mortgages, at prime plus 2.00%, repayable in monthly principal installments of $3,000 maturing in 2020 and principal installments of $1,000 maturing in 2011, secured by a hypothec on certain land and building.	537,000	126,000
8.16% chattel mortgage, repayable in monthly installments of $8,000 principal plus interest, maturing December 2005, secured by certain manufacturing equipment.	—	164,000
	2,937,000	4,090,000
	(48,000)	(979,000)
Deduct: Current portion	$ 2,889,000	$ 3,111,000

Principal repayments of the long-term liabilities are as follows:

2006	$	48,000
2007		48,000
2008 (see subsequent event note 18(b))		2,448,000
2009		48,000
2010		48,000
Thereafter		297,000
	$	2,937,000

Analyzing Rogers Communications Inc.

Read the Rogers Communications Inc. annual report provided in Appendix A including the financial statements, notes, and management discussion and analysis and discuss the following questions. (Instructors may supplement the Rogers annual report with one they obtain themselves directly from an alternative company or download from the Internet at www.sedar.com.)

R2-1. What is the purpose of the annual report?

R2-2. How much credibility do you attach to the financial statements and related notes? Explain. What about the management discussion and analysis?

R2-3. What do the financial statements tell you? Explain. How would you use the information contained in the statements for decision making? What additional information would you want?

R2-4. Among the "Deferred charges" of $129,119,000 that Rogers reports on its December 31, 2005 balance sheet is $12,126,000 for "Pre-operating costs" (see Note 8 of the financial statements in Appendix A). Note 2h explains that when Rogers is developing new products or businesses it calls certain costs that it incurs assets. For example, if Rogers is about to launch a new product it might incur costs such as staff training, advertising and promotion of the product, and similar costs.

Required:

Do you think that these pre-operating costs are assets? Explain. Consider the definition of an asset and GAAP's criteria for assets in your answer, and also express your opinion.

R2-5. Find the following amounts in Rogers' financial statements:
   a. Accounts receivable on December 31, 2005.
   b. Total liabilities on December 31, 2005.
   c. Long-term debt on December 31, 2005.
   d. Operating revenue during the year ended December 31, 2005.
   e. Loss on repayment of long-term debt during the year December 31, 2005.
   f. Interest on long-term debt for the year ended December 31, 2005.
   g. Amount of cash Rogers spent on new property, plant and equipment during the year ended December 31, 2005.

R2-6. Find the following amounts in Rogers' financial statements:
   a. Property, plant, and equipment on December 31, 2005.
   b. Total assets on December 31, 2005.
   c. Accounts payable and accrued liabilities on December 31, 2005.
   d. Retained earnings on December 31, 2005.
   e. Operating, general and administrative expenses for the year ended December 31, 2005.
   f. Net income for the year ended December 31, 2005.
   g. Amount of cash Rogers raised issuing capital stock during the year ended December 31, 2005,

ENDNOTES

1. Summarized from Dale L. Flesher and Tonya K. Flesher, "Ivar Kreuger's Contribution to U.S. Financial Reporting," *The Accounting Review*, Vol. 61 (July 1986), p. 421.

2. Extracted from Loblaw Companies Ltd.'s 2005 annual report.

3. Panel A extracted from Stelco Inc.'s 2005 annual report. Panel B extracted from Newfoundland Power Inc.'s 2005 annual report.

4. Extracted from Dominion Citrus Limited's 2005 annual report.

THE ACCOUNTING CYCLE

It's 7 a.m. on a Saturday morning in Halifax, in May 2006. The theme music plays for all-news radio station 95.7 FM. Then news anchor Tim Rozsell turns on his microphone and launches into his hourly newscast.

"The Premier is coy about what he'll say when he speaks outside the Legislature today," says Rozsell, as he runs through the top story, which was the imminent calling of an election in Nova Scotia.

The newscast ends about five minutes later, after a look ahead to later in the evening, when the Rogers Communications-owned station plans to broadcast the Rogers-owned Blue Jays' baseball game against the Tampa Bay Devil Rays. Then Rozsell gives a time check and a weather update.

"Right now in downtown Halifax, it's foggy and 7 degrees," he says.

Mike Eppel—680 News in Toronto

News 95.7 is part of the Rogers Media subsidiary of the Canadian communications giant, which operates some 40-plus radio stations across the country, including similar all-news formats in Montreal (940 AM), Moncton (News 91.9) and Saint John (News 88.9). Rogers launched its three all-news radio stations in the Maritimes in the fall of 2005. They follow the successful formula of Rogers' flagship all-news radio station, Toronto's 680 News.

Newscasts air all day and night, traffic and weather every 10 minutes, sports at :15 and :45 past each hour, entertainment, and business reports at :26 and :56 past each hour.

Like most reporters at the all-news radio stations, 680's business anchor Mike Eppel follows a predictable process or cycle for his work: an event happens in the business world, such as one company buying another, or the stock market losing 200 points. Eppel takes notes, and then edits those notes to make sure his story is accurate and objective. Next, he types his finished article into the computer beside his microphone. When he's ready, he broadcasts the finished story over the airwaves.

The Rogers' accountants at the radio stations follow a similar process. An event happens, such as the sale of a 60-second block of airtime on the radio station to a company, such as itravel2000.com, a Canadian Internet travel agency. itravel2000.com wants the radio station to run a commercial. Sales executives at

Rogers record the transaction with itravel2000.com in the company computer system. They make adjustments, such as whether itravel2000.com gets a discount if it buys commercials on radio stations in more then one city. Eventually, when Rogers Communications publishes its financial statements the dollar value of those commercials will be included as part of the line called Revenue—it's all part of the accounting cycle.

INTRODUCTION

In Chapter 2 we became familiar with financial statements. In this chapter we will examine in detail how transactions and other economic events are recorded in an accounting system, and how these raw data are organized, processed, and converted into information that is useful to stakeholders.

The recording and processing of transactions and economic events is an essential part of accounting. They provide the data that is used to prepare the information needed by managers and stakeholders for decision making. Procedures for recording and processing accounting data are the heart and soul of many accounting courses. Some students find a focus on accounting procedures attractive because there is little judgment, analysis, and evaluation required. Once you know the rules, you follow the recipe and presto … you have the "one right answer." Unfortunately, just focusing on procedures ignores the judgment that is required to decide how *to apply* the rules. Learning accounting procedures is useful and if you decide to pursue a career in accounting, essential. But to understand financial statements and other accounting information you must do more than simply learn the procedures. You have to understand why they are being used. And that's important for accountants and non-accountants alike. As historian Diane Ravitch put it, "The person who knows HOW will always have a job. The person who knows WHY will always be his boss." A bookkeeper knows "how," but an accountant or sophisticated user of financial statements knows "why."

In the main body of this chapter, a "short-cut" approach is used to explain the accounting cycle. This approach will show you the "how" of accounting and provide you with the tools you need to understand accounting and work through the material in the rest of the book. For the reader who requires a more traditional approach to the accounting cycle, the appendix to this chapter on pages 128–137 provides full coverage of the accounting cycle.

THE ACCOUNTING CYCLE

The **accounting cycle** is the process by which data about economic events are entered into an accounting system, processed, organized, and used to produce information, such as financial statements. It would be very difficult for anyone to understand and use the data if it wasn't organized in some useful way. Suppose you wanted to track the amount of money you spent in a month and how you spent it. Each time you spend money you get a receipt and put it in an envelope. You can't determine the amount of money you spent or how you spent it until you classify the receipts by type of spending—entertainment, meals, clothing, transportation, etc.—and determine the amount that was spent in each category. The data do not become useful until they have been processed and organized into a useful format. The process of organizing the data from your receipts represents a simple accounting system. Even a chequebook represents an accounting system because it allows you to keep track of whom you paid, what you paid, and how much money you have.

Figure 3–1 provides a schematic overview of the role of an accounting system in capturing raw data, processing it, and producing financial statements and other financial information. Let's look at each step of the process. Economic events occur around an entity continuously. Some economic events are transactions the entity enters into with others, such as buying and selling assets, incurring and settling liabilities, raising capital, and supplying its goods and services to clients and customers and incurring the costs of doing so. Many economic events affect an entity but are not the result of transactions involving the entity. For example, decisions by competitors and government, technological changes, and economic conditions all have economic effects on an entity.

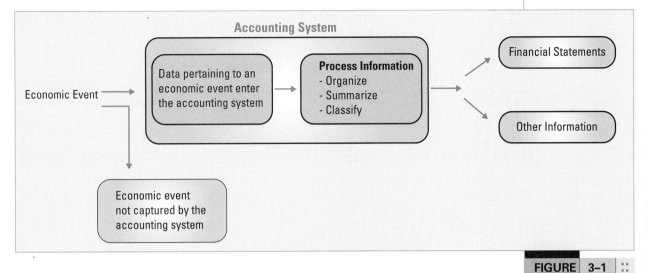

An accounting system is designed to capture economic events that affect the entity. However, as shown in Figure 3–1, not all economic events are captured by the accounting system. An entity's managers decide which economic events and transactions will be captured by the accounting system, based on the information the managers want the system to produce.

In Canada, financial reporting by most entities is based on transactions that have actually occurred. Amounts recorded in these accounting systems are the transaction values. This means that if a piece of land is purchased for $2,000,000, the land is recorded in the accounting system at $2,000,000 and remains at that amount for as long as it is owned by the entity. Economic events that the accounting system is not designed to capture are ignored. For example, the accounting systems of most Canadian entities would not capture an increase in the value of land. However, an accounting system does not have to be limited in this way. The designers of the accounting system can include and exclude any economic events that affect the entity. The key is for the accounting system to meet the decision-making needs of the users and the reporting requirements of the entity.

An economic event that is relevant to an entity must be entered into the accounting system in some way. An accounting system does not capture data automatically. Each sale or purchase, payment or collection, and change in the value of an asset must be recorded. Once entered into the accounting system, the data are processed so that useful information can be produced. Processing involves organizing, classifying, and summarizing the data into a useful form.

An accounting system operates in a way that is similar to the editorial process of a newspaper. (Figure 3–2 shows a schematic overview of the newspaper editorial process.) Each day the editors of the newspaper assign reporters to cover stories. Many newsworthy events take place in the world each day and it is not possible to cover or report all the stories. A newspaper will cover the stories that the editors think are most relevant to its readers. If a story is not covered, it cannot appear in the newspaper.

Think of a newspaper as a general purpose report. All people who buy the newspaper get the same paper regardless of their interests or information needs. The newspaper is designed for a wide range of different readers. However, newspapers can also provide special purpose reports by using the Internet to allow readers to "build their own papers." Readers decide which topics are of particular interest to them and the newspaper sends them e-mail reports that are tailored to their needs.

The fact that accounting systems do not capture all economic events that affect the entity (in the same way that newspapers do not report all newsworthy stories) highlights a very important point. Financial statements cannot give a complete picture of the entity, just as newspapers cannot give a complete picture of what's going on in the world. Financial statements can report only information that is entered into the accounting system: If the accounting system does not gather information on the current market value of land, that information cannot be presented in the financial statements.

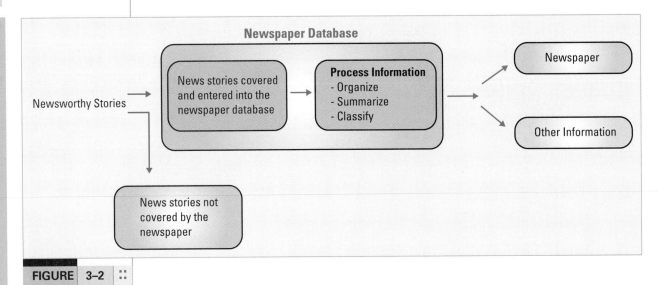

FIGURE 3-2 ::

**Newspaper
Editorial Process**

90

CHAPTER 3

ACCRUAL ACCOUNTING

In Chapter 2 accrual accounting was introduced as one of the commonly used methods of accounting. Now we are going to explore accrual accounting in more detail.

Accrual accounting measures economic activity and economic changes rather than cash and cash flows, which is the basis of cash accounting. Accountants believe that by measuring economic activity and economic changes, they will provide more relevant information to users of the financial statements. A good way to explain accrual accounting is to contrast it with cash accounting. Under cash accounting the economic event that triggers recording in the accounting system is the exchange of cash. A sale is recorded when the customer pays cash; an expense is recorded when cash is paid to a supplier. With accrual accounting the exchange of cash is not necessarily the economic event that triggers recording (although it may). If inventory were purchased on credit, the inventory would be recorded as an asset and the obligation to pay the supplier would be recorded as a liability. The purchase of the inventory is reflected in the financial statements even though no cash is involved in the transaction. With accrual accounting, revenues and expenses can be recorded before, after, or at the same time cash changes hands. Because revenues and expenses can be recognized at times other than when cash is exchanged, accounts receivable and accounts payable arise. These don't occur with cash accounting.

If you think about it, a cash system provides incomplete information about an entity's activities. Consider the following situations where economic events do not occur at the same time as the cash flow:

■ Exchanges between entities are often done on credit.

■ Entities usually have assets that are paid for when they are purchased but contribute to the entity's success over many years.

■ Customers sometimes pay for goods or services in advance.

An accrual accounting system captures these economic events.

○ ROGERS™

Let's use Rogers Communications (Rogers) to demonstrate how the recording of revenue differs under cash and accrual accounting. Typically (but not always) under accrual accounting, revenue is recorded when goods are delivered to customers. In December 2009, Rogers receives a large order for cell phones from a corporate customer. The phones are delivered to the customer in November 2010. Figure 3–3 shows three different payment arrangements for this sale:

■ Situation 1: cash is received when the order is placed (in December 2009).

■ Situation 2: cash is received on delivery of the goods to the customer (in November 2010).

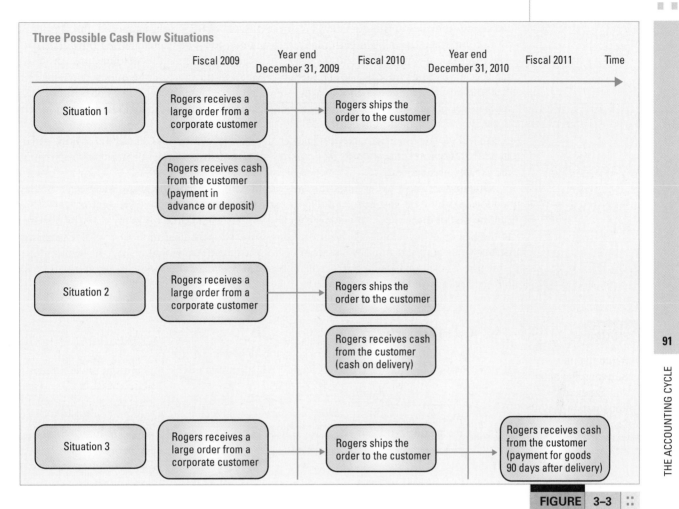

Three Possible Cash Flow Situations

	Fiscal 2009	Year end December 31, 2009	Fiscal 2010	Year end December 31, 2010	Fiscal 2011	Time

Situation 1: Rogers receives a large order from a corporate customer → Rogers ships the order to the customer

Rogers receives cash from the customer (payment in advance or deposit)

Situation 2: Rogers receives a large order from a corporate customer → Rogers ships the order to the customer

Rogers receives cash from the customer (cash on delivery)

Situation 3: Rogers receives a large order from a corporate customer → Rogers ships the order to the customer → Rogers receives cash from the customer (payment for goods 90 days after delivery)

FIGURE 3–3

Cash versus Accrual Accounting

- Situation 3: the customer agrees to pay for the goods 90 days after delivery (in February 2011) (remember that Rogers' year end is December 31).

With accrual accounting the revenue would be reported in fiscal 2010 (when the cell phones are delivered) regardless of when the cash is received. The reason is that the key economic event in accrual accounting is delivery of goods.

A similar story exists for expenses. Under accrual accounting accountants try to expense the costs incurred to earn revenue in the same period that the revenue is recorded. The term **matching** is used to describe the process of recording and reporting expenses in the same period as the revenue that those expenses help earn is recorded and reported. Matching is a fundamental concept of accrual accounting. The association between economic benefits (revenues) and economic costs (expenses) is necessary if profit is to be used as a measure of performance. For the sale of phones to its corporate customer, Rogers would expense the cost of the phones at the same time it recorded the revenue from the sale, regardless of when it paid for the phones.

While accrual accounting may provide more relevant information to users in many situations, it introduces the need for judgment. With cash accounting, an economic event or transaction is simply recorded when cash changes hands. With accrual accounting, revenue is recognized when an entity enjoys an economic benefit; however, someone has to decide when the benefit occurs.

Revenue recognition refers to the point in time when revenue is recorded in the accounting system and is reported in the income statement. Determining when revenue should be recognized is not always straightforward. Sometimes there are choices. It is easy for a hotdog vendor with a cart on a street corner to recognize revenue. When a customer turns over her money and

91

THE ACCOUNTING CYCLE

the vendor provides the hotdog, the vendor is better off—revenue has happened. But consider a more complicated example. A customer places an order for some merchandise from a manufacturer, but doesn't want the goods delivered for several months. The manufacturer produces the goods when the order is placed and stores them until the customer requests shipment. The customer inspects the goods once they have been produced and pays within 30 days if the goods meet its specifications. When should the manufacturer recognize revenue? On production? On inspection? On payment? On delivery?

We will explore how managers decide when to recognize revenue in Chapter 4. For now, understand that *when* an entity should recognize revenue is not always straightforward and can require the exercise of judgment.

Matching expenses to revenues can also be difficult, even for the above mentioned hotdog vendor. Matching the cost of the hotdog to a sale is easy, but what about the vendor's cart? How can the cost of the cart, which will probably be used to sell hotdogs for many years, be matched to the sale of a single hotdog, or to the hotdogs sold in a particular month or year? The answer isn't obvious but has significant implications for the income statement.

Figure 3–4 summarizes the relationship between revenue and expense recognition and cash flow under cash and accrual accounting.

FIGURE 3–4 ::

Relationship Between Revenue and Expense Recognition and Cash Flow

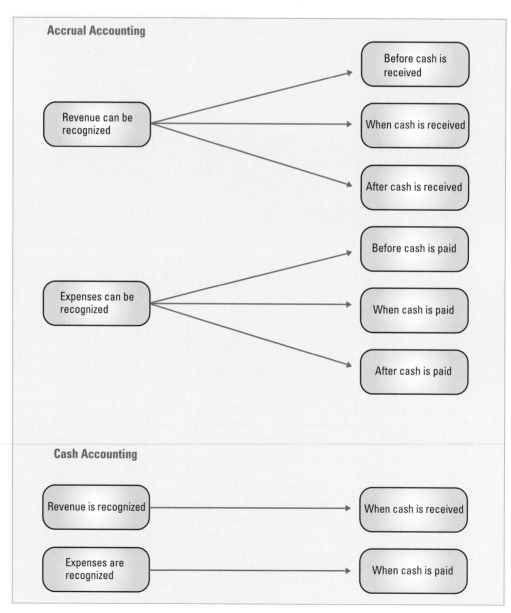

A QUESTION OF TIMING

We saw in the last section that, under accrual accounting, it can be a matter of judgment when revenues and expenses are reported in the income statement. Sooner or later all transactions and economic events get reflected in the financial statements. It's mainly a matter of when. And the "when" matters a lot because the accounting choices an entity makes can have economic consequences for stakeholders and influence the decisions they make.

If an entity had to prepare financial statements only at the end of its life, the job of an accountant would be much simpler because, over the life of an entity, accrual accounting and cash accounting provide the same results—there would be no need to decide when to recognize revenue and expenses. Indeed, the cause of many accounting scandals and controversies is that financial statements are prepared periodically—monthly, quarterly, or annually.

In the 15th and 16th centuries the need to measure income periodically during the life of a business was not particularly important. At that time many business opportunities were operated as short-term ventures. Investors would put money in a venture such as a trade voyage to the New World. The organizers would purchase all they needed for the venture, including a ship. At the end of the venture, everything would be sold off and the proceeds would be distributed among the investors. Income measurement during the trade voyage was not necessary.

As business became more complex and business itself became continuous, it was no longer possible or appropriate to sell all of a company's resources from time to time. But stakeholders wanted to know how the entity was doing, so the need for a periodic statement of performance arose.

DEVICES FOR DOING ACCOUNTING

We will use two devices to show the effect of transactions and economic events on financial statements. Both devices will be used throughout the book to show the effect economic events can have on an entity's accounting information.

The first device is the *accounting equation spreadsheet* that was introduced in Chapter 2 (see page 36). The spreadsheet captures the full accounting cycle in an easy-to-use way, and preparation of financial statements is straightforward. A spreadsheet is not very practical for an entity with large numbers of transactions in a year, and hundreds or thousands of different types of asset, liability, and equity accounts. Nonetheless, it is a convenient device for learning accounting.

The second device is the **journal entry**. Journal entries are used *in practice* to enter information about economic events into the accounting system. Whenever an economic event or transaction occurs that is to be entered into the accounting system, a journal entry is made. We will use journal entries because they summarize the effect of an economic event in a compact and concise way that makes it easy to see and understand the effect of the event on the financial statements.

No matter what device is used, for any economic event that is to be entered into an accounting system, the following needs to be determined:

1. Which elements of the accounting equation are affected—assets, liabilities, and/or owners' equity, including revenues and expenses?

2. Which specific asset, liability, owners' equity, revenue, and expense accounts have been affected?

3. How are the accounts affected—that is, does the amount in each account increase or decrease?

4. By how much has each specific asset, liability, owners' equity, revenue, and expense account increased or decreased?

By answering these questions we will ensure that economic events are properly recorded in the accounting system. We answered these questions implicitly in Chapter 2 when we examined Tamara's Painting Business. Now we will consider them explicitly.

All but the simplest accounting systems employ what is known as **double-entry bookkeeping**. In the double-entry system, each transaction or economic event is recorded in two places in the accounts. This is necessary to keep the accounting equation in balance. We will use this double-entry system to discuss the accounting equation spreadsheet and journal entries.

The Accounting Equation Spreadsheet

The accounting equation spreadsheet was introduced in Chapter 2 when we recorded events for Tamara's Painting Business. In that situation the spreadsheet was very simple: we classified economic events by their effect on the broad categories of assets, liabilities, and owners' equity. The format introduced in Chapter 2 was:

$$\text{Assets} = \text{Liabilities} + \text{Owners' Equity}$$

In practice, asset, liability, and owners' equity are divided into separate categories called *accounts* to reflect an entity's different types of assets, liabilities, and owners' equity. Instead of having a single column for assets, the assets column is divided into categories such as Cash, Accounts Receivable, Inventory, Furniture, Land, and any other assets that the managers would like identified specifically. The number and type of separate accounts that an entity has is determined by the information managers want to have in their accounting system. The division of assets, liabilities, and owners' equity into a larger number of accounts makes more detailed information available. The cost of having more accounts is that the accounting system may be more complicated and more costly to set up and run.

Let's use the accounting equation spreadsheet in a realistic business setting. In June 2008, two friends from business school, Filomena and Teresa, decide to open a small restaurant near the campus. The friends think that the variety of food available to students and faculty on campus is limited and they believe that by offering large portions of good quality, fresh food at reasonable prices, their restaurant will be successful.

Filomena and Teresa develop a business plan and set to work opening their restaurant, which they are going to call Strawberries. They will use July and August to ready the restaurant and will open for business on September 1. Filomena and Teresa decide that their restaurant's accounting system will be designed to provide the information they need to prepare tax returns and to evaluate the performance of the restaurant. Thus, the accounting system will process mainly transactional information and historical costs.

The accounting equation spreadsheet that will be used for this example is:

Transaction		Assets					=	Liabilities		+	Shareholders' Equity	
	Cash	Accounts Receivable	Food, Drinks, and Supplies Inventory	Prepaid Rent	Renovations, Equipment, and Furniture			Bank Loan	Accounts Payable		Capital Stock	Retained Earnings
Balance before transaction												
Transaction												
Balance after transaction												

The very top line of the spreadsheet states the accounting equation in the familiar format, with the difference that owners' equity has been replaced by shareholders' equity. This is because Filomena and Teresa are going to operate their restaurant as a corporation, and as you'll recall from Chapter 2, the owners of a corporation are called shareholders.

Under each of the accounting equation categories, the different asset, liability, and shareholders' equity accounts relevant to Strawberries are shown. When a transaction or economic event affects an account, the dollar amount will be placed in that account's column. (An **account** is a category of asset, liability, or owners' equity. Each column in an accounting equation spreadsheet represents an account.) This format will be used to record each transaction and economic event in the example.

At this stage of the discussion the income statement accounts are not shown. Revenue and expense transactions will be included in the retained earnings account at first. The income statement details will be shown later.

To record transactions in the spreadsheet we will follow these procedures:

■ The row just under the account headings shows the balance in each account before the transaction being discussed is recorded in the spreadsheet.

■ The transaction under discussion will be recorded in the next row and given a number for easy reference.

■ The "balance after transaction" row will give the balance in each account after the transaction is recorded. This row is the sum of the beginning balance and the current transaction. The amounts in this row are carried forward to the next transaction as the amounts in the "balance before transaction" row.

Now let's look at the specific transactions.

1. The first step Filomena and Teresa take is to set up a corporation because they have decided that the corporate form of organization is the most appropriate for both tax and for legal liability purposes. Filomena and Teresa each contribute $20,000 to the corporation and each receives 1,000 of the corporation's shares in exchange. They name their corporation Strawberries Inc. and their restaurant Strawberries. The entry to the spreadsheet is:

Transaction	Assets					=	Liabilities		+	Shareholders' Equity	
	Cash	Accounts Receivable	Food, Drinks, and Supplies Inventory	Prepaid Rent	Renovations, Equipment, and Furniture		Bank Loan	Accounts Payable		Capital Stock	Retained Earnings
Balance before transaction											
1	$40,000									$40,000	
Balance after transaction	$40,000									$40,000	

Strawberries Inc.'s Cash (an asset) has increased by $40,000 because Filomena and Teresa contributed $40,000 in cash. In exchange for their $40,000, Filomena and Teresa received shares of Strawberries Inc. The shares represent an ownership interest in Strawberries, so the Capital Stock account increases by $40,000 because the investment was a purchase of company shares.

2. Filomena and Teresa realize that they probably do not have enough cash to start their business. They approach a banker for a loan to provide additional cash. The banker examines their business plan and is satisfied that it is reasonable. The banker offers a $20,000 loan. Interest of $150 must be paid to the bank at the end of each month, beginning in September. Strawberries Inc. must begin paying back the loan in one year.

Transaction	Assets					=	Liabilities		+	Shareholders' Equity	
	Cash	Accounts Receivable	Food, Drinks, and Supplies Inventory	Prepaid Rent	Renovations, Equipment, and Furniture		Bank Loan	Accounts Payable		Capital Stock	Retained Earnings
Balance before transaction	$40,000									$40,000	
2	$20,000						$20,000				
Balance after transaction	$60,000						$20,000			$40,000	

The money from the bank loan increases Strawberries Inc.'s cash by $20,000. Strawberries Inc. now has a liability—it owes the bank $20,000. As a result of the loan, Cash and Bank Loan each increase by $20,000. The cost of borrowing the money, the interest, is not recorded at this time because under accrual accounting the cost of using money occurs with the passage of time. Therefore, an interest expense will be recorded only after Strawberries Inc. has had the use of the money for some period of time. We will record the interest cost later.

3. Now Filomena and Teresa get to work setting up their business. They find a suitable space in a shopping centre near the campus and Filomena negotiates a two-year lease with the owner. The lease requires Strawberries Inc. to pay $1,250 per month in rent. Rent is due on the first day of each month, with the first three months' rent due on signing of the lease. Filomena

writes a cheque for $3,750 when she signs the lease. The owner of the shopping centre has agreed that Strawberries Inc. will be charged rent beginning in September. The entry is made in the cash column because a cheque is equivalent to cash. When a cheque is cashed, the amount is removed from the bank account of the entity that wrote the cheque.

	Assets					=	Liabilities		+	Shareholders' Equity	
Transaction	Cash	Accounts Receivable	Food, Drinks, and Supplies Inventory	Prepaid Rent	Renovations, Equipment, and Furniture		Bank Loan	Accounts Payable		Capital Stock	Retained Earnings
Balance before transaction	$60,000						$20,000			$40,000	
3	($3,750)*			$3,750							
Balance after transaction	$56,250			$3,750			$20,000			$40,000	

*Brackets indicate a decrease in an account.

The payment to the owner of the shopping centre represents an asset to Strawberries. The $3,750 gives Strawberries Inc. the right to use the location for three months beginning in September, so when the payment is made in early July it represents a future benefit and, therefore, an asset. Strawberries Inc. has exchanged one asset, Cash, for another asset, the right to use the location for three months, which we call Prepaid Rent. As a result Cash decreases by $3,750 and Prepaid Rent increases by $3,750. (A decrease in an account is recorded in brackets on the spreadsheet.)

Only the amount paid to the property owner is recorded as an asset. Even though the lease is for two years, only the portion actually paid in cash is typically recorded under accrual accounting in Canada. The right to use the location for two years at an agreed-upon price is not recorded, even though having the lease is a benefit to Strawberries. This is an example of a type of future benefit that does not usually appear on the financial statements of Canadian entities.

4. To get the restaurant ready for business, Filomena and Teresa undertake some renovations, including painting, refinishing the floors, and adding appropriate décor. In addition, some plumbing and electrical work is done. The total cost of renovations is $15,000, all of which is paid in cash.

	Assets					=	Liabilities		+	Shareholders' Equity	
Transaction	Cash	Accounts Receivable	Food, Drinks, and Supplies Inventory	Prepaid Rent	Renovations, Equipment, and Furniture		Bank Loan	Accounts Payable		Capital Stock	Retained Earnings
Balance before transaction	$56,250			$3,750			$20,000			$40,000	
4	($15,000)				$15,000						
Balance after transaction	$41,250			$3,750	$15,000		$20,000			$40,000	

The renovations are an asset because they will contribute to the environment of the restaurant while it is in business—after all, a restaurant's ambiance is part of the attraction of dining out. The renovations were paid for in cash so Cash decreases by $15,000. The renovations cost was $15,000, so the asset Renovations, Equipment, and Furniture increases by $15,000.

5. Teresa buys equipment, furniture, dishes, and other necessary materials from a restaurant supply company. The total cost of the purchase is $25,000. Half of the purchase is paid in cash. The remainder is owed to the supplier and must be paid in 90 days.

Transaction	Assets					=	Liabilities		+	Shareholders' Equity	
	Cash	Accounts Receivable	Food, Drinks, and Supplies Inventory	Prepaid Rent	Renovations, Equipment, and Furniture		Bank Loan	Accounts Payable		Capital Stock	Retained Earnings
Balance before transaction	$41,250			$3,750	$15,000		$20,000			$40,000	
5	($12,500)				$25,000			$12,500			
Balance after transaction	$28,750			$3,750	$40,000		$20,000	$12,500		$40,000	

This is a slightly more complicated transaction because more than two accounts are affected, reflecting the fact that the items were paid partly in cash and partly on credit. As a result, Cash decreases by $12,500, the amount that was paid to the supplier, and there is a liability, Accounts Payable, to pay the supplier $12,500 in 90 days. Accounts Payable are amounts owed to suppliers for goods or services purchased on credit. Accounts Payable are usually classified as current liabilities.

The items Teresa purchased are capital assets because they will help Strawberries Inc. earn revenue by providing the equipment to prepare meals, the dishes on which to serve meals, and so on, over several years. They will not be used up, sold, or converted to cash within one year. The assets purchased are recorded at their cost of $25,000. Cost is the usual basis for initially recording an asset in the accounting system. The cost recorded is the full economic sacrifice that the entity will make; it doesn't matter that the full amount wasn't paid in cash at the time of purchase.

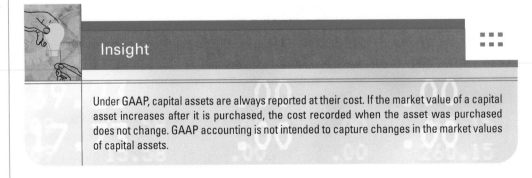

Insight

Under GAAP, capital assets are always reported at their cost. If the market value of a capital asset increases after it is purchased, the cost recorded when the asset was purchased does not change. GAAP accounting is not intended to capture changes in the market values of capital assets.

Notice that the Renovations, Equipment, and Furniture account includes several different kinds of capital assets. In practice, the different types of capital assets would probably be placed in separate accounts if for no other reason than different types of capital assets receive different treatments for tax purposes and, therefore, separate classification would be useful.

Insight

An entity doesn't have to pay in cash for everything it buys. Strawberries Inc. could even have paid the restaurant supply company in meals at the restaurant. Trading goods or services instead of paying cash is called a **non-monetary transaction**. The word barter is often used to describe trades of goods or services.

6. As opening day approaches, Strawberries Inc. hires staff, including a server and kitchen help. The new employees will begin work when Strawberries Inc. opens. The restaurant also purchases non-perishable food items and supplies for $900. Strawberries pays using its debit card. (A **debit card** allows a customer to pay for goods and services by transferring money directly from the customer's bank account to the vendor's bank account. Payment by debit card is equivalent to payment by cash.)

Transaction	Assets					=	Liabilities		+	Shareholders' Equity	
	Cash	Accounts Receivable	Food, Drinks, and Supplies Inventory	Prepaid Rent	Renovations, Equipment, and Furniture		Bank Loan	Accounts Payable		Capital Stock	Retained Earnings
Balance before transaction	$28,750			$3,750	$40,000		$20,000	$12,500		$40,000	
6	($900)		$900								
Balance after transaction	$27,850		$900	$3,750	$40,000		$20,000	$12,500		$40,000	

The purchase of food items and supplies for cash reduces Strawberries Inc.'s Cash by $900 and increases another asset, Food, Drinks, and Supplies Inventory, by $900. The food items and supplies will contribute to making meals for customers, so they are assets. The food items and supplies will become expenses when they are used. The inventory is recorded at its cost.

The hiring of employees is not recorded because the employees haven't done any work yet and Strawberries Inc. hasn't paid them. If one or both of the parties had fulfilled its part of the contract—by the employees working, or by Strawberries Inc. paying them—an entry would have been made in the accounting system. Under GAAP, these executory contracts are not usually recorded in the accounting system. (An **executory contract** is an exchange of promises in which one party promises to supply goods or services and the other party promises to pay for them, but neither side has fulfilled its side of the bargain. We will see situations later in the book where this GAAP treatment may not provide the most useful information to the users.)

7. Strawberries Inc. is open for business! The restaurant becomes popular with students, staff, and faculty almost immediately, attracting large crowds, especially at lunch and on weekends. During September, Strawberries Inc. purchases $12,000 of food and drinks to serve to customers. The food and drinks are paid for by debit card.

The food and drinks are recorded as inventory when they are purchased because they are available for sale to customers. Cash decreases by $12,000 and Food, Drinks, and Supplies Inventory increases by $12,000. Under accrual accounting, inventory is an asset until it is sold. The food and drinks that Strawberries Inc. has will be expensed when they are sold to people who eat at the restaurant. In contrast, if Strawberries Inc. were using a cash accounting system, the purchase of food and drinks would be treated as an expense when they are paid for.

	Assets					=	Liabilities		+	Shareholders' Equity	
Transaction	Cash	Accounts Receivable	Food, Drinks, and Supplies Inventory	Prepaid Rent	Renovations, Equipment, and Furniture		Bank Loan	Accounts Payable		Capital Stock	Retained Earnings
Balance before transaction	$27,850		$900	$3,750	$40,000		$20,000	$12,500		$40,000	
7	($12,000)		$12,000								
Balance after transaction	$15,850		$12,900	$3,750	$40,000		$20,000	$12,500		$40,000	

8. During September, Strawberries had sales of $17,900. $17,200 of these sales were meals served in the restaurant and were paid for by cash, credit card, or debit card. Strawberries also catered a faculty party, for which it charged $700. Payment from the faculty is due in the middle of October.

Sales represent an economic benefit to the entity, so Retained Earnings increases by $17,900. The amount owed for catering is an asset because it represents cash that will be received in the future, so $700 has been entered in Accounts Receivable, the usual account name for amounts owed by customers. Sales of $17,200 were for cash, so Cash increases by $17,200.

The time when an entity should record its revenue is not always obvious. For example, did Strawberries Inc. enjoy an economic benefit from catering the faculty party when the order was received, when the food was delivered, or when the cash was collected? Arguments can be made in support of each.

Under GAAP and accrual accounting, it is not necessary to wait until cash is received to record a sale. On the other hand, GAAP encourage caution in deciding when to record a sale. According to GAAP, if revenue is recorded too soon, the information could be unreliable. For example, if the faculty party was cancelled at the last minute and Strawberries Inc. recorded the revenue when the order was received, revenue would be reported that never actually happened.

In contrast, the only logical time to recognize revenue for the people who eat at Strawberries is when they pay at the end of their meals. It is not possible to anticipate that a person will have a meal at Strawberries until he or she actually comes to the restaurant and

	Assets					=	Liabilities		+	Shareholders' Equity	
Transaction	Cash	Accounts Receivable	Food, Drinks, and Supplies Inventory	Prepaid Rent	Renovations, Equipment, and Furniture		Bank Loan	Accounts Payable		Capital Stock	Retained Earnings
Balance before transaction	$15,850		$12,900	$3,750	$40,000		$20,000	$12,500		$40,000	
8	$17,200	$700									$17,900
Balance after transaction	$33,050	$700	$12,900	$3,750	$40,000		$20,000	$12,500		$40,000	$17,900

orders. But once the customer has paid the bill and left the restaurant, both Strawberries and the customer have fulfilled their part of the bargain.

Although the $17,900 of sales was recorded on a single line on the accounting equation spreadsheet, in fact a separate line would be added for each individual sale or each day's sales. Since the sales represent hundreds of separate transactions with customers, it is not practical to include each one in the example.

9, 10. At the end of September, Strawberries Inc. pays $525 for utilities and $925 in wages to its employees. Strawberries transfers the money electronically to the utilities using Internet banking. Payments to employees were deposited directly into their bank accounts by the bank.

Transaction	Assets					=	Liabilities		+	Shareholders' Equity	
	Cash	Accounts Receivable	Food, Drinks, and Supplies Inventory	Prepaid Rent	Renovations, Equipment, and Furniture		Bank Loan	Accounts Payable		Capital Stock	Retained Earnings
Balance before transaction	$33,050	$700	$12,900	$3,750	$40,000		$20,000	$12,500		$40,000	$17,900
9	($525)										($525)
10	($925)										($925)
Balance after transaction	$31,600	$700	$12,900	$3,750	$40,000		$20,000	$12,500		$40,000	$16,450

The utilities and wages payments are costs of operating the restaurant in September and represent expenses for the month. Expenses reduce retained earnings because they represent economic sacrifices or costs to the entity. Therefore, Retained Earnings decreases by $1,450 ($525 + $925). Since these expenses were paid in cash, Cash decreases by $1,450.

11. At the end of September, Strawberries Inc. pays the bank $150 interest for the loan.

Transaction	Assets					=	Liabilities		+	Shareholders' Equity	
	Cash	Accounts Receivable	Food, Drinks, and Supplies Inventory	Prepaid Rent	Renovations, Equipment, and Furniture		Bank Loan	Accounts Payable		Capital Stock	Retained Earnings
Balance before transaction	$31,600	$700	$12,900	$3,750	$40,000		$20,000	$12,500		$40,000	$16,450
11	($150)										($150)
Balance after transaction	$31,450	$700	$12,900	$3,750	$40,000		$20,000	$12,500		$40,000	$16,300

Interest is the cost of using the bank's money. The $150 is a cost of doing business during September and so is treated as an expense in September. Therefore, Retained Earnings decreases by $150, as does Cash, since the interest was paid to the bank in cash.

If Strawberries Inc. had not made the interest payment to the bank at the end of September, the interest would still be recorded as an expense in the spreadsheet. Under accrual accounting, it doesn't matter whether the interest was paid in cash. Accrual accounting records as expenses any costs incurred to earn revenue during the period, regardless of whether cash is paid at the time. Since Strawberries Inc. had the use of the bank's money during September, the cost of using the money is reported as an expense in September's income statement. If Strawberries Inc. had not paid the interest, an increase in a liability, Interest Payable, would have been recorded on the spreadsheet, instead of a decrease in Cash.

12. One of Strawberries' major operating costs is the food, drinks, and supplies used in preparing meals for customers. One way of determining the amount of food, drinks, and supplies used is to subtract the amount of Food, Drinks, and Supplies Inventory on hand at the end of the month from the amount available for sale during the month. At the end of September, Teresa counted the Food, Drinks, and Supplies Inventory and found that there were items costing $1,000 on hand. Because Strawberries Inc. had $12,900 of food, drinks, and supplies available during September and there was $1,000 left in inventory at the end of the month, this means that $11,900 ($12,900 − $1,000) was used.

Transaction	Assets					=	Liabilities		+	Shareholders' Equity	
	Cash	Accounts Receivable	Food, Drinks, and Supplies Inventory	Prepaid Rent	Renovations, Equipment, and Furniture		Bank Loan	Accounts Payable		Capital Stock	Retained Earnings
Balance before transaction	$31,450	$700	$12,900	$3,750	$40,000		$20,000	$12,500		$40,000	$16,300
12			($11,900)								($11,900)
Balance after transaction	$31,450	$700	$1,000	$3,750	$40,000		$20,000	$12,500		$40,000	$4,400

It is important for readers to understand that GAAP and accrual accounting do not necessarily serve all stakeholders in all situations. There are many situations where GAAP doesn't apply or doesn't make sense. For example, financial statements prepared primarily for tax purposes must comply with the requirements of the *Income Tax Act,* which is not the same as GAAP. For many decisions, GAAP accounting can be inappropriate or misleading. Users of financial statements must be able to understand the shortcomings of GAAP-based financial statements as well as how they can be effectively used for decision making. This is a theme that will be repeated throughout this book.

To reflect the use of food, drinks, and supplies, Food, Drinks, and Supplies Inventory must be decreased by $11,900. The food, drinks, and supplies were used to prepare meals that were sold to customers, so they are an expense incurred to earn the revenue that was recorded in Transaction 8. As a result, Retained Earnings decreases by $11,900. By expensing the $11,900, we are *matching* the cost of the meals served to the revenue earned from providing those meals.

13. Strawberries Inc. must account for the use of the space leased in the shopping centre. When Filomena paid $3,750 to the shopping centre owner, the amount was recorded as an asset because it represented a future benefit—the right to use the space from September through November. Now, at the end of September, Strawberries Inc. has used up part of its right to occupy that space. When an asset is used up or consumed, it becomes an expense. (This is another example of matching.) Since one of the three months that were paid for has passed, it makes sense to match the $1,250 cost of leasing the space in September to revenues recorded in September. The remaining $2,500 balance in Prepaid Rent represents the right to use the space in the shopping centre in October and November, so it is still an asset. To reflect the fact that one month of Prepaid Rent has been used up, Prepaid Rent is reduced by $1,250 and Retained Earnings is decreased by $1,250 because the rent is an expense for September.

	Assets					=	Liabilities		+	Shareholders' Equity	
Transaction	Cash	Accounts Receivable	Food, Drinks, and Supplies Inventory	Prepaid Rent	Renovations, Equipment, and Furniture		Bank Loan	Accounts Payable		Capital Stock	Retained Earnings
Balance before transaction	$31,450	$700	$1,000	$3,750	$40,000		$20,000	$12,500		$40,000	$4,400
13				($1,250)							($1,250)
Balance after transaction	$31,450	$700	$1,000	$2,500	$40,000		$20,000	$12,500		$40,000	$3,150

14. During September, Strawberries Inc. will have consumed some of its capital assets—renovations, equipment, and furniture—in the process of operating its business. The renovations to the restaurant space have future benefit to Strawberries Inc. as long as the restaurant occupies that particular location. As the lease period expires, so do the bene-

	Assets					=	Liabilities		+	Shareholders' Equity	
Transaction	Cash	Accounts Receivable	Food, Drinks, and Supplies Inventory	Prepaid Rent	Renovations, Equipment, and Furniture		Bank Loan	Accounts Payable		Capital Stock	Retained Earnings
Balance before transaction	$31,450	$700	$1,000	$2,500	$40,000		$20,000	$12,500		$40,000	$3,150
14					($1,042)						($1,042)
Balance after transaction	$31,450	$700	$1,000	$2,500	$38,958		$20,000	$12,500		$40,000	$2,108

fits associated with the renovations. The equipment and furniture will eventually wear out, break down, or become obsolete. As a result, an amortization expense should be recorded to reflect consumption of these assets.

Amortization (or depreciation) is the allocation of the cost of a capital asset to expense over the capital asset's useful life. Amortization is another example of matching. Since capital assets help an entity earn revenue, their cost should be matched to the revenue they help earn. This type of matching can be hard to do. After all, how does a chair or an oven or paint on a wall contribute to revenue? Still, the job has to be done, so accountants or managers have to estimate for how long a capital asset will be used (its useful life) and choose a method for amortizing the cost of the capital assets.

First, we'll consider the renovations. They will be amortized over two years, which is the period of the lease Strawberries Inc. signed. Other amortization periods are possible. For example, if the lease had an option that allowed Strawberries Inc. to renew its lease, it might amortize the renovations over two lease periods. Since we don't know whether Strawberries Inc. can or will remain in its present location beyond the two-year lease period, we will amortize the renovation costs over two years. Since it is not possible to determine the contribution that the renovations will make to earning revenue each month, we will simply amortize an equal amount of the cost each month, $625 ($15,000 ÷ 24 months) (the method that amortizes an equal amount of the cost of an asset each period is called straight-line amortization).

This decision represents a conservative approach to reporting. **Conservatism** is a fundamental GAAP accounting concept that serves to ensure that assets, revenue, and net income are not overstated and that liabilities and expenses are not understated. The implication is that when preparers are faced with reasonable alternative accounting treatments, they should choose the one that is more conservative. In the case of renovations, a two-year amortization is more conservative because it is not clear that Strawberries will be in its present location for more than two years. Amortizing the renovations over two years rather than, say, three or four years is more conservative because the renovations are expensed more quickly.

The approach is similar for the equipment and furniture. However, the useful lives of equipment and furniture are not limited to the term of the lease because they could be moved if the restaurant changed locations. Therefore, to calculate an amortization expense we must make an assumption about how long the furniture and equipment will provide future benefits to Strawberries Inc. We will assume that the useful life of the equipment and furniture is five years (this assumption is a simplification because it is likely that the individual assets have a variety of useful lives) and amortize it using the straight-line method over 60 months. The amount of amortization that should be expensed in September for the equipment and furniture is $417 ($25,000 ÷ 60 months). Therefore, the total amortization expense for September is $1,042 ($625 + $417). The amortization expense reduces retained earnings (since it is an expense) and reduces the amount in Renovations, Equipment, and Furniture. In practice, the amortization is usually accumulated in a separate account called Accumulated Amortization (more will be said about this later in the chapter).

15. At the end of September Filomena and Teresa decide to declare and pay a dividend of $0.50 per share, or $1,000 ($0.50 × 2,000 shares). The two friends need some money to meet personal expenses and are satisfied that the restaurant can afford to pay out the cash. A dividend is a distribution of the assets of the corporation to its shareholders.

	Assets					=	Liabilities	+	Shareholders' Equity	
Transaction	Cash	Accounts Receivable	Food, Drinks, and Supplies Inventory	Prepaid Rent	Renovations, Equipment, and Furniture		Bank Loan	Accounts Payable	Capital Stock	Retained Earnings
Balance before transaction	$31,450	$700	$1,000	$2,500	$38,958		$20,000	$12,500	$40,000	$2,108
15	($1,000)									($1,000)
Balance after transaction	$30,450	$700	$1,000	$2,500	$38,958		$20,000	$12,500	$40,000	$1,108

When a dividend is paid, Retained Earnings decreases because some of the shareholders' investment is being returned to them. (Remember from Chapter 2 that earnings represents an indirect investment in the company by the owners and that retained earnings is the accumulated earnings of a business over its life, less dividends paid.) Cash decreases by $1,000 because the dividend is paid in cash. A dividend is not an expense.

We have now considered all the transactions and other economic events that affected Strawberries Inc. in September and have recorded them in its accounting system. The accounting equation spreadsheet makes it very simple to prepare the balance sheet for the end of September. The bottom line of the spreadsheet provides the total in each balance sheet account on September 30, 2008. To create the balance sheet, we reorganize the information into a more traditional format. For example:

Strawberries Inc.
Balance Sheet
As of September 30, 2008

Assets		Liabilities and Shareholders' Equity	
Cash	$30,450	Bank Loan	$20,000
Accounts Receivable	700	Accounts Payable	12,500
Food, Drinks, and Supplies Inventory	1,000	Total Liabilities	32,500
Prepaid Rent	2,500	**Shareholders' Equity**	
Renovations, Equipment, and Furniture	38,958	Capital Stock	40,000
		Retained Earnings	1,108
		Total Shareholders' Equity	41,108
		Total Liabilities and	
Total assets	$73,608	Shareholders' Equity	$73,608

The account names and amounts on the balance sheet correspond with the columns on the accounting equation spreadsheet. In practice, a balance sheet will aggregate many of the accounts in the accounting system. For example, the accounting system might have separate accounts for renovations, equipment, and furniture but the balance sheet might aggregate them in a single line.

For space reasons we recorded all revenue and expense transactions directly to the Retained Earnings account on the spreadsheet. We really should have had separate accounts for these items. Table 3–1 (below) expands the Retained Earnings account to include the revenue and expense accounts. Now the balances in each of the revenue and expense accounts can be easily found on the bottom line of the spreadsheet and placed in the income statement.

Strawberries Inc.

Income Statement

For the Month Ended September 30, 2008

Sales		$17,900
Expenses		
Cost of sales	$11,900	
Rent	1,250	
Amortization	1,042	
Wages	925	
Utilities	525	
Interest	150	
Total expenses		15,792
Net income		$ 2,108

Notice that dividends are not included in the calculation of net income. Net income represents the amount that is left for the owners after all other stakeholders (such as employees, lenders, and suppliers) have been considered, so payments of dividends are not included.

Also notice that the ending balance in the retained earnings account in Table 3–1 is not the same as the amount on the balance sheet. If you added the balances in the revenue and expense

---

TABLE 3–1 ::: **Complete Accounting Equation Spreadsheet for Strawberries Inc.**

	Assets					=	Liabilities	
Transaction	**Cash**	**Accounts Receivable**	**Inventory**	**Prepaid Rent**	**Renovations, Equipment, and Furniture**		**Bank Loan**	**Accounts Payable**
1	$40,000							
2	$20,000						$20,000	
3	($3,750)			$3,750				
4	($15,000)				$15,000			
5	($12,500)				$25,000			$12,500
6	($900)		$900					
7	($12,000)		$12,000					
8	$17,200	$700						
9	($525)							
10	($925)							
11	($150)							
12			($11,900)					
13				($1,250)				
14					($1,042)			
15	($1,000)							
Balance	**$30,450**	**$700**	**$1,000**	**$2,500**	**$38,958**		**$20,000**	**$12,500**

accounts to retained earnings you will get the correct amount. (This process will be discussed later in this chapter in the section on closing entries.)

Now that we have prepared Strawberries Inc.'s balance sheet and income statement, what do we do with them? What do they tell us? In general, financial statements raise questions rather than provide definite answers. Strawberries Inc.'s financial statements must be used with special care because they provide information for only the first month of operations. Nonetheless, a number of questions can be asked and observations made.

1. How well has Strawberries Inc. done? It is difficult to say. We have only one month's performance, the first month, and nothing to compare it with. Perhaps if we had information about how restaurants do when they first begin operations we would have a better idea. After Strawberries Inc. has been operating for a few years, we will be better able to compare its performance with other years or other restaurants. It is important to recognize that a user must be very cautious when making comparisons using the accounting information of different entities. As we will discover, managers have many ways to account for similar situations. Nonetheless, it is not possible to make sense of accounting information without some benchmarks or bases of comparison.

2. Some analysis we can do suggests that Strawberries Inc. has done reasonably well in its first month:

   ■ It has "turned a profit" of $2,108 for the month, which is good news. It is very difficult to succeed in the restaurant business.

   ■ The net income of $2,108 represents a return on equity of about 5 percent on Filomena and Teresa's $41,108 equity in Strawberries Inc. (return on equity = net income ÷ shareholders' equity = $2,108 ÷ $41,108). **Return on equity (ROE)** is a measure of the profitability of an entity and its effectiveness in using the assets provided by the owners of the entity to generate net income.

   ■ Strawberries Inc.'s profit margin ratio (net income ÷ sales) is almost 12 percent, meaning that for every dollar of sales, it earns $0.12. The **profit margin ratio** is a measure of how effective the entity is at controlling expenses and reflects the amount of income earned for each dollar of sales.

+				Shareholders' Equity				
Capital Stock	Retained Earnings	Sales	Cost of Sales	Rent Expense	Wages Expense	Utilities Expense	Amortization Expense	Interest Expense
$40,000								
		$17,900						
						($525)		
					($925)			
								($150)
			($11,900)					
				($1,250)				
							($1,042)	
	($1,000)							
$40,000	($1,000)	$17,900	($11,900)	($1,250)	($925)	($525)	($1,042)	($150)

However, as we have already pointed out, it is very difficult to draw conclusions from this analysis without benchmarks or bases for comparison.

3. Why does Strawberries Inc. have so much cash? The new restaurant borrowed $20,000 from the bank, yet it has more than that amount in cash on September 30. Strawberries Inc. owes $12,500 to the restaurant supply company that it must repay in two months, so at this point it has the cash to meet that obligation. Should Strawberries Inc. reduce its bank loan? Or do Teresa and Filomena have plans for the money? Perhaps major purchases are still required. Certainly some of the cash will be needed to buy more food inventory. We need more information to answer some of these questions.

4. While Strawberries Inc. seems to have a large cash balance, starting up the business and operating it for a month consumed a significant amount of cash. Table 3–2 shows Strawberries Inc.'s cash flow since it was incorporated. This statement was prepared by organizing the transactions in the Cash column of the accounting equation spreadsheet.

   The cash flow situation is not nearly as favourable if you remember that $60,000 of this cash came from the bank and the owners. If we ignore these inflows, net cash flow is negative (cash inflows from sales − cash outflows = $17,200 − $46,750 = $ − 29,550).

   Also, cash from operations (cash from or used by an entity's regular business activities) is negative, which shows that business operations are using more cash than they are generating. Cash from operations for Strawberries Inc. is shown in Table 3–3.

5. Strawberries Inc.'s large cash balance means it can easily pay the accounts payable as well as purchase needed inventory. Therefore, Strawberries Inc.'s liquidity position appears to be solid because it will be able to pay its debts as they come due. Strawberries Inc.'s current ratio (current assets ÷ current liabilities = $34,650 ÷ $32,500) is 1.07 to 1, which is usually not considered to be very high. But the bank loan does not have to be paid for almost a year, which suggests that the low current ratio is not a significant problem yet.

6. The income statement doesn't tell us much about how Strawberries Inc. will perform in the next month or the next year. September was the first month of operations and Strawberries' encouraging performance may have been due to curiosity by local people who may not come back. Alternatively, next month may be even better as more people learn about the new restaurant. It is not possible to predict what will happen based on the first month's performance of a restaurant.

| TABLE 3–2 ::: Strawberries Inc.'s Cash Flow |

Strawberries Inc.
Cash Flow Statement
For the Period Ended September 30, 2008

Cash inflows:		
Shareholders	$40,000	
Bank	20,000	
Sales	17,200	
Total cash inflows		$77,200
Cash outflows		
Capital assets	27,500	
Inventory	12,900	
Rent	3,750	
Utilities	525	
Wages	925	
Interest	150	
Dividends	1,000	
Total cash outflows		46,750
Net cash flow		$30,450

TABLE 3–3 ::: Strawberries Inc.'s Cash from Operations

Strawberries Inc.		
Cash from Operations		
For the Period Ended September 30, 2008		
Cash inflows from sales		$17,200
Cash outflows		
Inventory	12,900	
Rent	3,750	
Utilities	525	
Wages	925	
Interest	150	18,250
Net cash flow		($ 1,050)

In general, one of the limitations of general purpose financial statements is that they are prepared mainly on the basis of transactional information and historical costs. They do not tell us very much about the future. Historical cost, transactional-based statements can sometimes be used as a starting point to predict the future. However, in the case of new entities such as Strawberries Inc., or even for established entities facing significant change, the statements may not be very helpful for predicting the future.

Journal Entries

The accounting equation spreadsheet is one device for recording the effects of economic events and for showing the effects of accounting choices on financial statements. The second device that will be used extensively in this book is the journal entry. Journal entries are used in practice as the method of initially recording a transaction or economic event into the accounting system. For learning purposes, journal entries will be used to summarize transactions or other economic events so that the effects on the financial statements can be easily seen. The appendix to this chapter on pages 128–137 shows how journal entries fit into the complete accounting cycle.

A journal entry accomplishes exactly the same thing as an entry to an accounting equation spreadsheet, but in a different format. The format of a journal entry is:

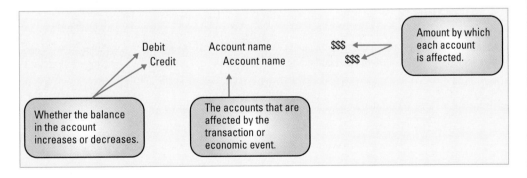

A journal entry provides the following information:

■ the accounts that are affected by the transaction or economic event

■ whether the balance in each account increases or decreases

■ the amount by which each account is affected

The account name identifies the account that is affected by the transaction or economic event and $$$ is the amount by which each account is affected. The account names correspond to the column headings on the spreadsheet. The terms **debit** and **credit** tell whether the balance in the account has increased or decreased. These terms have very precise meanings in accounting. The precise meanings of debit and credit are described in the following list:

Debit (Dr.)	Credit (Cr.)
Increase assets	Decrease assets
Decrease liabilities	Increase liabilities
Decrease owners' equity	Increase owners' equity
Decrease revenues	Increase revenues
Increase expenses	Decrease expenses

At first these terms may be confusing and cumbersome to work with. You might want to memorize their meaning so that you will understand them right from the start. As you work with journal entries, the terms will become second nature to you. In a journal entry the debits must equal the credits. Journal entries are manipulations of the accounting equation, so if the debits do not equal the credits, the accounting equation will not balance.

Let's return to Strawberries Inc. to show how journal entries work. Journal entries will be recorded for each of the transactions that were recorded in the spreadsheet. The number of each journal entry corresponds to the number assigned to each transaction in the spreadsheet. In the first transaction, Filomena and Teresa each contributed $20,000 cash in exchange for shares of Strawberries Inc. The journal entry to record this transaction is:

1. Dr. Cash (asset +) 40,000
   Cr. Capital stock (shareholders' equity +) 40,000
   To record the sale of shares for cash.

Cash is debited because the amount of cash has increased and an increase in an asset is a debit.

Teresa and Filomena purchased shares of Strawberries Inc., which means that Capital Stock, a shareholders' equity account, increases, requiring a credit entry. Note that the debits equal the credits. At this point you might find it helpful to keep track of the type of account (asset, liability, shareholders' equity) that is being affected in the journal entry and the direction of the change on that account.

The journal entry corresponds to the entry made to the accounting equation spreadsheet: The $40,000 debit to Cash corresponds to the $40,000 added to the Cash column. The $40,000 credit to Capital Stock corresponds to the $40,000 added to the Capital Stock column.

Transaction	Assets					=	Liabilities		+	Shareholders' Equity	
	Cash	Accounts Receivable	Inventory	Prepaid Rent	Renovations, Equipment, and Furniture		Bank Loan	Accounts Payable		Capital Stock	Retained Earnings
Balance											
1	$40,000									$40,000	
Balance	$40,000									$40,000	

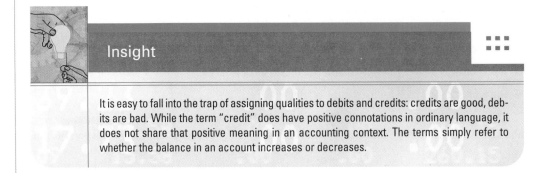

Insight

It is easy to fall into the trap of assigning qualities to debits and credits: credits are good, debits are bad. While the term "credit" does have positive connotations in ordinary language, it does not share that positive meaning in an accounting context. The terms simply refer to whether the balance in an account increases or decreases.

www.mcgrawhill.ca/
olc/friedlan

Knowledge Check

■ What is amortization and why are capital assets amortized?

■ What is the profit margin ratio and what does it mean?

■ Describe the effect (increase or decrease) that debits and credits have on asset, liability, owners' equity, revenue, and expense accounts.

The second transaction was the loan Strawberries Inc. obtained from the bank. Cash is debited because Strawberries Inc.'s cash has increased by $20,000. Strawberries Inc. also has a liability to repay the bank $20,000. As a result, the Bank Loan account is credited for $20,000 because liabilities have increased and an increase in a liability is a credit.

2. Dr. Cash (asset +)   20,000
    Cr. Bank loan (liability +)   20,000
    To record the acquisition of a $20,000 bank loan.

The journal entries for the remainder of Strawberries Inc.'s transactions are shown below. Make sure you can explain the debits and credits in each entry.

3. Dr. Prepaid rent (asset +)   3,750
    Cr. Cash (asset −)   3,750
    To record the prepayment of three months' rent.

4. Dr. Renovations, equipment, and furniture (asset +)   15,000
    Cr. Cash (asset −)   15,000
    To record the cost of renovating the restaurant.

5. Dr. Renovations, equipment, and furniture (asset +)   25,000
    Cr. Cash (asset −)   12,500
    Cr. Accounts payable (liability +)   12,500
    To record the purchase of equipment and furniture.

6. Dr. Food, drinks, and supplies inventory (asset +)   900
    Cr. Cash (asset −)   900
    To record the purchase of inventory.

7. Dr. Food, drinks, and supplies inventory (asset +)   12,000
    Cr. Cash (asset −)   12,000
    To record the purchase of food during September. (In practice,
    each purchase of food inventory would require a
    separate journal entry, but for the purpose of the example,
    all purchases are recorded in a single entry.)

Journal entries 8 through 15 affect income statement accounts. Recall that income statement accounts are actually sub-accounts of the shareholders' equity section of the balance sheet. For clarity, the type of account (asset, liability, shareholders' equity, revenue, or expense) and the direction of the change are shown. For income statement accounts, the effect on the income statement account (revenue or expense) and the effect on shareholders' equity (retained earnings) are shown. However, you should recognize that these are two ways of describing the same thing.

8. Dr. Cash (asset +)   17,200
    Dr. Accounts receivable (asset +)   700
    Cr. Sales (shareholders' equity +, revenue +)   17,900
    To record sales for the month of September.

9, 10. Dr. Utilities expense (shareholders' equity −, expense +)   525
      Dr. Wage expense (shareholders' equity −, expense +)   925
        Cr. Cash (asset −)   1,450
      To record the utilities and wages expenses for the
      month of September.

11. Dr. Interest expense (shareholders' equity −, expense +)   150
      Cr. Cash (asset −)   150
    To record the interest expense for the month of September.

12. Dr. Cost of sales (shareholders' equity −, expense +)   11,900
      Cr. Food, drinks, and supplies inventory (asset −)   11,900
    To record the cost of food, drinks, and supplies used to
    provide meals to customers.

13. Dr. Rent expense (shareholders' equity −, expense +)   1,250
      Cr. Prepaid rent (asset −)   1,250
    To record the rent expense for September.

14. Dr. Amortization expense (shareholders' equity −, expense +)   1,042
      Cr. Renovations, equipment, and furniture (asset −)   1,042
    To record the amortization of renovations, equipment, and furniture.

15. Dr. Retained earnings (shareholders' equity −)   1,000
      Cr. Cash (asset −)   1,000
    To record the payment of a dividend of $0.50 per share.

One final point: for both journal entries and the accounting equation spreadsheet, making sure that the debits equal the credits or that the accounting equation equality is maintained does not guarantee that your accounting decisions make sense. You could incorrectly classify an asset as an expense or a liability as revenue, and your entries would balance but not necessarily make sense.

ADJUSTING ENTRIES

An entry into an accrual accounting system is usually triggered by a transaction—an exchange between the entity and a party external to the entity. In the Strawberries Inc. example most of the entries to the spreadsheet represented exchanges with outside parties (bankers, shareholders, suppliers, and customers) (entries 12, 13, and 14 are exceptions). But sometimes economic changes occur that are not triggered by transactions. These changes must sometimes be recorded in the accounting system.

Entries to an accrual accounting system that are not triggered by exchanges with outside entities are called **adjusting entries**. At the end of each reporting period, managers must identify economic changes that have occurred during the period but that have not been reflected in the accounting system, and make any adjustments that are necessary. Adjusting entries are not required in a cash accounting system because recording is triggered only by the exchange of cash, which must involve an outside entity.

Insight

Adjusting entries are not intended to capture all economic changes that are not the result of transactions. The adjusting entries only reflect the changes that the method of accounting is designed to capture. For example, according to GAAP, adjusting entries are not recorded to recognize increases in the market value of property that has not been sold as of the end of the period.

TABLE 3–4 ::: **Four Types of Adjusting Entries**

Type	Situation	Example	Entry made in the current or previous period (Transactional Entry)	Entry made at the end of the current period (Adjusting Entry)	Entry made in the next period (Transactional Entry)
Deferred expense/ prepaid expense	Cash is paid before the expense is recognized	Prepaid insurance Prepaid rent Capital assets	Dr. Asset Cr. Cash	Dr. Expense Cr. Asset	No entry
Deferred revenue	Cash is received before revenue is recognized	Deposits Subscriptions Advances Gift certificates	Dr. Cash Cr. Liability	Dr. Liability Cr. Revenue	No entry
Accrued expense/ accrued liability	Expense is recognized before cash is paid	Wages Utilities Interest expense	No entry	Dr. Expense Cr. Liability	Dr. Liability Cr. Cash
Accured revenue/ accrued asset	Revenue is recognized before cash is received	Interest earned	No entry	Dr. Asset Cr. Revenue	Dr. Cash Cr. Asset

Adjusting entries are necessary in accrual accounting because recognition of revenues and expenses does not always correspond with cash flows. Once again, recall Strawberries Inc. In July, Filomena signed a two-year lease and paid rent for September, October, and November. As a result of that exchange between Strawberries Inc. and the property owner, we recorded an asset called Prepaid Rent. At the end of September we had to reduce the amount of Prepaid Rent and record a rent expense because one month of the prepaid rent asset had been used up. This event did not involve an exchange with another entity. The owner of the shopping centre didn't phone us and tell us to record the event. However, there was clearly a change that had to be reflected in the accounting records.

There are four types of adjusting entries. (See the summary in Table 3–4.) Before discussing adjusting entries in detail, you should note the following general points:

1. Adjusting entries are required because revenue and expense recognition can happen at a different time than cash flows.

2. Each adjusting entry involves a balance sheet account and an income statement account.

3. Each adjusting entry is associated with a transaction that is recorded before or after the adjusting entry. A **transactional entry** is a journal entry that is triggered by an exchange with another entity.

Here are three tips to keep in mind as you study adjusting entries:

1. Adjusting entries are required only when financial statements are prepared.

2. Adjusting entries never involve cash. If cash is part of the entry, it is not an adjusting entry.

3. Adjusting entries always include at least one balance sheet account and one income statement account.

Question for Consideration

Why are adjusting entries required when using accrual accounting? Why are they not necessary when using cash accounting?

Answer: Accrual accounting attempts to measure economic changes. Not all economic changes are triggered by an interaction with an outside entity. As a result it is necessary to "adjust" the accounts for economic changes that occur during a period but are not triggered by interactions with outside entities. Adjusting entries are not required in a cash accounting system because recording in the accounting system is triggered only by an exchange of cash, which always involves an outside entity.

Let's examine the four types of adjusting entries in detail.

1. Deferred Expense/Prepaid Expense   Entities often purchase assets that provide benefits for more than one period, including insurance policies, equipment, buildings, and patents. Usually, as time passes or as an asset is used by the entity, these future benefits are consumed. As a result, the portion consumed in a period must be expensed so that the cost can be matched to the revenue the asset helped earn.

The terms **deferred expense** and **prepaid expense** apply to assets that are acquired in one period but not expensed, at least in part, until a later period or periods. These entries reduce the amount of the asset that is reported on the balance sheet and recognize an expense for the portion of the asset that has been consumed in the period.

On January 5, 2009 Dahlia Ltd. (Dahlia) purchases three years of insurance coverage for $9,000 cash. The insurance covers the period January 1, 2009 to December 31, 2011. Dahlia's year end is December 31.

When Dahlia purchases the insurance it makes the following journal entry:

Dr. Prepaid insurance (asset +)	9,000	
Cr. Cash (asset −)		9,000
To record the purchase of insurance for the period		
January 1, 2009 to December 31, 2011.		

This is a transactional entry because an exchange has taken place between Dahlia and the insurance company. The insurance is set up as an asset because the policy will provide Dahlia with three years of coverage, a future benefit.

On December 31, 2009 an adjusting entry is required because one year of the insurance coverage has been used up. If no adjusting entry is made, Dahlia's balance sheet would report $9,000 of insurance coverage, implying that there are three years of coverage available when there are really only two. What the balance sheet should report on December 31, 2009 is $6,000 of prepaid insurance, representing two years of coverage. Therefore, Prepaid Insurance must be decreased by $3,000. Dahlia must also report an expense of $3,000 to reflect the cost of insurance consumed in 2009. The adjusting entry that Dahlia would make on December 31, 2009 is:

Dr. Insurance expense (expense +, shareholders' equity −)	3,000	
Cr. Prepaid insurance (asset −)		3,000
To record the cost of insurance used in the year ended		
December 31, 2009. ($9,000 ÷ 3 years of coverage = $3,000).		

This is an adjusting entry because Dahlia makes it without the involvement of another entity. The adjusting entry assumes that the cost of the insurance in each year of the policy is the same.

One year later, on December 31, 2010, an identical adjusting entry is required to reflect the insurance coverage used in 2010. The December 31, 2010 balance sheet would now show prepaid insurance of $3,000 ($9,000 − $3,000 − $3,000). The same adjusting entry would be required on December 31, 2011. The financial statement effects are shown using the summarized spreadsheet in Table 3–5.

Note that the insurance expense column in the spreadsheet doesn't accumulate over the three years. As will be explained later in the chapter, expense (and revenue) accounts are always zero at the beginning of a new year, so the balance at the end of a year is just the amount expensed during that year.

If Dahlia's insurance policy came into effect on July 1, 2009 and ran until June 30, 2012, the adjusting entry would be a bit different. In that case, on December 31, 2009, only half of a year's insurance would have been used up. The amount expensed would be $1,500 because one year's coverage costs $3,000, so half a year's coverage is $3,000 ÷ 2 or $1,500. Therefore, the adjusting entry would be:

Dr. Insurance expense (expense +, shareholders' equity −)	1,500	
Cr. Prepaid insurance (asset −)		1,500
To record the cost of insurance used from		
July 1, 2009 to December 31, 2009.		
([$9,000 ÷ 3 years of coverage] ÷ 1/2 year = $1,500).		

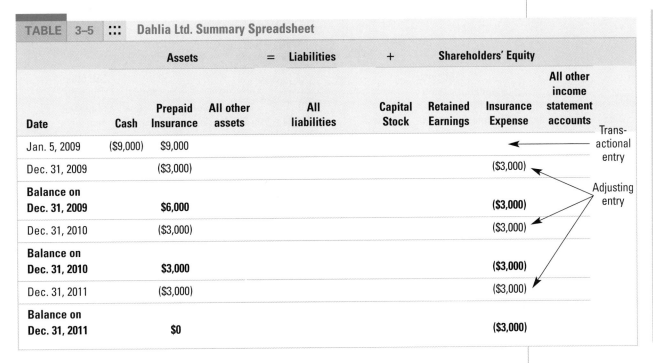

TABLE 3–5 ::: Dahlia Ltd. Summary Spreadsheet

		Assets		= Liabilities	+	Shareholders' Equity		
Date	Cash	Prepaid Insurance	All other assets	All liabilities	Capital Stock	Retained Earnings	Insurance Expense	All other income statement accounts
Jan. 5, 2009	($9,000)	$9,000						
Dec. 31, 2009		($3,000)					($3,000)	
Balance on Dec. 31, 2009		$6,000					($3,000)	
Dec. 31, 2010		($3,000)					($3,000)	
Balance on Dec. 31, 2010		$3,000					($3,000)	
Dec. 31, 2011		($3,000)					($3,000)	
Balance on Dec. 31, 2011		$0					($3,000)	

Transactional entry

Adjusting entry

The transactional entry would be the same in this scenario.

Another example of this type of adjusting entry is the amortization of capital assets. Capital assets are the assets an entity uses to produce or supply the goods or services it offers to its customers. These assets contribute indirectly to the earning of revenue—indirectly, because they are not sold in the ordinary course of business. Examples include buildings, vehicles, machinery, patents, copyrights, and so on. Capital assets contribute to earning revenue over more than one period and the cost of these assets must be expensed over the asset's life. Conceptually, amortizing the cost of a capital asset is the same as expensing prepaid insurance over the life of a policy.

There are many different ways that an asset can be amortized. We will discuss some of these methods in Chapter 9. In the following example, straight-line amortization is used. **Straight-line amortization** allocates an equal amount of the cost of a capital asset to expense in each year of the asset's life.

On January 2, 2007, Kaslo Ltd. (Kaslo) purchased a new delivery truck for $50,000 cash. Kaslo's management estimates that the truck will have a useful life of five years. The adjusting entry that would be recorded at the end of each year is:

Dr. Amortization expense (expense +, shareholders' equity −)   10,000
   Cr. Accumulated amortization (asset −)   10,000
Adjusting entry to record amortization of the truck
(Cost of the asset ÷ estimated useful life = $50,000 ÷ 5 years = $10,000 per year).

The accumulated amortization account is referred to as a contra-asset account. A **contra-asset account** is an account that is used to accumulate amounts deducted from a related asset account. Thus, the **accumulated amortization** account accumulates deductions from capital asset and other amortizable asset accounts. Instead of crediting the asset account directly for the period's amortization, the credit is made to the accumulated amortization account. This treatment makes information about the cost of an asset readily available from the accounting system. Knowing the original cost of an asset can be important for various reasons, including for tax purposes. The balance in the accumulated amortization account is not meaningful by itself. Taken together, the cost of a capital asset less the accumulated amortization gives the asset's **net book value (NBV)**.

The spreadsheet for Kaslo is shown in Table 3–6. Notice that the balance in the capital asset account itself remains at $50,000 all the time. The accumulated amortization increases by $10,000 each year, the amount of the annual amortization expense. On December 31, 2007 the

TABLE 3–6 ::: Spreadsheet for Kaslo Ltd.: Amortization of its Truck										
	Assets				**= Liabilities +**		**Shareholders' Equity**			
Date	**Cash**	**Capital Assets (Vehicles)**	**Accumulated Amortization**	**All other assets**	**All liabilities**	**Capital Stock**	**Retained Earnings**	**Amortization Expense**	**All other income statement accounts**	
Jan. 2, 2007	($50,000)	$50,000								Transactional entry
Dec. 31, 2007			($10,000)					($10,000)		
Balance on Dec. 31, 2007		$50,000	($10,000)					($10,000)		
Dec. 31, 2008			($10,000)					($10,000)		
Balance on Dec. 31, 2008		$50,000	($20,000)					($10,000)		
Dec. 31, 2009			($10,000)					($10,000)		Adjusting entry
Balance on Dec. 31, 2009		$50,000	($30,000)					($10,000)		
Dec. 31, 2010			($10,000)					($10,000)		
Balance on Dec. 31, 2010		$50,000	($40,000)					($10,000)		
Dec. 31, 2011			($10,000)					($10,000)		
Balance on Dec. 31, 2011		$50,000	($50,000)					($10,000)		

NBV of the truck is $40,000 ($50,000 − $10,000) and on December 31, 2010 the NBV is $10,000 ($50,000 − $40,000).

If you look at Rogers' consolidated balance sheet on page A-4 you will see that $6,151,526,000 in property, plant, and equipment is reported. (Check Note 5 to the financial statements, page A-18) and you will see that the cost of that property, plant, and equipment was $13,677,008,000. The difference between the cost and the amount reported on the balance sheet, $7,525,482,000, is the accumulated amortization.

2. Deferred Revenue   Sometimes an entity will receive payment for goods or services before it recognizes the revenue. For example, a fan might purchase tickets to a concert months before the performance, or a customer might pay a deposit to ensure delivery of goods some time later. In these examples, the entity might recognize revenue when the concert is performed or the goods are delivered. When the payment is received the entity records a liability. The liability represents the obligation to provide the good or service that the customer has paid for. An adjusting entry is necessary when the revenue is recognized and the obligation is fulfilled.

On May 20, 2009 Fatfish Magazine Ltd. (Fatfish) received $52 for a new two-year subscription to its popular monthly magazine. The subscription begins in the first week of July. When Fatfish received the credit card information from the new subscriber, it made the following journal entry. Fatfish's year end is December 31:

Dr. Cash (asset +)	52
Cr. Unearned revenue (liability +)	52

To record cash received for a two-year subscription.

This is a transactional entry because it involves an interaction with an outside entity, namely the new subscriber. When Fatfish received the new subscriber's credit card information, revenue was not recognized because the company had not yet provided magazines to the subscriber. The unearned revenue liability means that Fatfish has an obligation to deliver the magazine to

◆ ROGERS™

the subscriber over the next two years. **Unearned revenue** is a liability that is recorded when cash is received before revenue is recognized.

In this scenario, revenue is recognized when the magazine is delivered. At the end of the year, Fatfish would make an adjusting entry to recognize revenue. Since 25 percent of the subscription will have been delivered as of December 31, 2009, 25 percent of the revenue can be recognized. The journal entry would be:

Dr. Unearned revenue (liability −) 13
   Cr. Revenue (revenue +, shareholders' equity +) 13
To record revenue earned from subscriptions.
(Percentage of subscription delivered × price of subscription
= 6 months ÷ 24 months × $52 = $13.)

This is an adjusting entry because it doesn't involve an outside entity. Adjusting entries would be required on December 31, 2010 and December 31, 2011 to recognize the revenue earned in 2010 and 2011 respectively. The effects on the balance sheet and income statement for each year of the subscription are summarized in the condensed spreadsheet in Table 3–7. Note that these entries assume that financial statements are prepared only at the end of the year. If financial statements were prepared monthly, an adjusting entry would be required at the end of each month to recognize the revenue earned in that month.

3. Accrued Expense/Accrued Liability   An **accrued expense** is an expense that is recognized and recorded in the financial statements before the cash payment is made. The accrued expense/accrued liability type of adjusting entry is needed when an entity has incurred an expense, but the recording of the expense and related liability have not been triggered by an external event such as receipt of an invoice. Recognition of the expense gives rise to a liability to pay for the resource that was consumed. This type of adjusting entry is necessary to ensure that all resources consumed in a period are expensed in that period—in other words, to ensure that expenses are matched to revenues. It is important to understand that an adjusting entry is not required if the entity has received an invoice (an external trigger). If there is an external trigger, the expense and liability are accrued, but as a result of receiving the invoice, not by an adjusting entry.

Babbit Inc. (Babbit) pays its employees every two weeks. Every other Thursday, employees are paid for the two weeks ended the previous Friday. On June 26, 2008 employees were paid for the two weeks ended June 20. The next pay period runs from June 21 through July 4. Babbit's year end is June 30. From June 21 through June 30 employees earned $22,500. Because the year end falls in the middle of a pay period it is necessary to make an adjusting entry to record the wage

TABLE 3–7 ::: Fatfish Magazine Ltd. Spreadsheet Summary

	Assets	=	Liabilities	+		Shareholders' Equity		
Date	**Cash**	**All other assets**	**Unearned revenue**	**All liabilities**	**Capital Stock**	**Retained Earnings**	**Revenue**	**All other income statement accounts**
May 20, 2009	$52		$52					
Dec. 31, 2009			($13)				$13	
Balance on Dec. 31, 2009			$39				$13	
Dec. 31, 2010			($26)				$26	
Balance on Dec. 31, 2010			$13				$26	
Dec. 31, 2011			($13)				$13	
Balance on Dec. 31, 2011			$0				$13	

Trans-actional entry

Adjusting entry

expense for the last 10 days of June and to record the liability for the money owed the employees on June 30. Even though the employees will not be paid until July 10, they earned $22,500 in the fiscal year ending June 30, 2008 and the cost of this work should be expensed in fiscal 2008. Babbit would make the following adjusting entry on June 30, 2008:

Dr. Wage expense (expense +, shareholders' equity −)	22,500	
Cr. Accrued wages payable (liabilities +)		22,500
To accrue wage expense for the last 10 days of June.		

The transactional entry is recorded when the pay period ends and employees are paid.

Dr. Accrued wages payable (liabilities −)	22,500	
Dr. Wage expense (expense +, shareholders' equity −)	10,000	
Cr. Cash (assets −)		32,500
To record payment of wages for the last 10 days of June and the first four days of July.		

There are two things happening in this entry:

1. Payment of the amount that was accrued for June. This part of the entry removes the wages payable liability that was accrued for the last 10 days of June.

2. The recording of the expense and payment of wages earned in the first four days of July. The July wages are earned, expensed, and paid in July (fiscal 2009), so this entry is not related to the adjusting entry.

The July 2008 entry is a transactional entry because it is triggered by the completion of the pay period and payment of the employees. The effects of the accrued expense/accrued liability adjusting entry on the balance sheet and income statement are summarized in the condensed spreadsheet in Table 3–8.

An important point to note about adjusting entries and accrual accounting in general is that estimates are often required. In the Babbit example, the amount that employees earned would have been known from the work records, but there are many situations where the amounts are not known. For example, if Babbit was billed for its utilities two or three months after the end of fiscal 2008, it would have to estimate the cost of utilities used in 2008 to prepare its financial statements—the amount of the liability and the expense would be an "educated guess." Financial statements are filled with estimates like these. Other examples of estimates used in accounting are the useful lives of capital assets (what is the life of a delivery truck?) and the amount of accounts receivable that will be collected (not everyone pays their debts).

Because estimates represent uncertain future amounts, you cannot assume that numbers in financial statements are exact. Keep in mind too the fact that estimates are made by managers,

	TABLE	3–8	:::	**Babbit Inc. Summary Spreadsheet**							

	Assets	=	Liabilities	+		Shareholders' Equity			
Date	**Cash**	**All other assets**	**Accrued liabilities**	**All other liabilities**	**Capital stock**	**Retained earnings**	**Wage expense**	**All other income statement accounts**	
June 30, 2008			$22,500				($22,500)		Adjusting entry
Balance on June 30, 2008			**$22,500**				**($22,500)**		Trans-actional entry
July 10, 2008	($32,500)		($22,500)				($10,000)		

Notice that the balance in the accrued liability account is zero after the employees has been paid

The expense recorded on July 10, 2008 is for work done by employees in July 2008 (fiscal 2009).

A sports fan buys tickets for a game. The game will be played in six months, which is in the team's next fiscal accounting year. When the fan purchases the ticket the team records the following journal entry:

Dr. Cash   xxx
   Cr. Unearned revenue   xxx

The team recognizes revenue from its games when the games are actually played. Explain why an adjusting entry is necessary to recognize revenue when the game is played.

Answer: The exchange between the fan and the team occurs when the fan pays money for the tickets. There is no exchange or interaction between the fan and the team when the game is actually played. However, the team recognizes the revenue from tickets sold for the game when the game is played. Therefore, an adjusting entry is required so that the revenue can be reported in the income statement for the period in which the game is played.

and managers may have reporting objectives such as maximizing their own bonuses, satisfying lenders so they keep lending money, and maximizing profits to keep investors happy. Thus the need for careful detective work when you examine a company's financial statements.

4. Accrued Revenue/Accrued Asset **Accrued revenue** is revenue that is recorded before cash is received. The accrued revenue/accrued asset type of adjusting entry is required when an entity has earned revenue but no transaction with another entity has triggered the recording of the revenue. Recognizing the revenue gives rise to a receivable that reflects that payment is forthcoming. As was the case for accrued liabilities, the adjusting entry is recorded before the transactional entry.

On October 1, 2009 Jalobert Ltd. (Jalobert) invested $1,000,000 of surplus cash in Government of Canada bonds that have an interest rate of 5 percent. Interest on the bonds is paid semi-annually on September 30 and March 31 of each year. Interest revenue is earned simply by the passage of time. Jalobert earns interest for each minute it holds the bonds. On December 31, 2009 (Jalobert's year end), Jalobert Ltd. should recognize the interest it earned by holding the bonds from October 1 to December 31. The adjusting entry is:

Dr. Interest receivable (asset +)   12,500
   Cr. Interest revenue (revenue +, shareholders' equity +)   12,500
To record accrual of revenue earned from October 1 to December 31
from investment in Government of Canada bonds
(3 months ÷ 12 months × $1,000,000 × 5 percent).

The entry recognizes interest revenue earned over the three months from October through December and the interest receivable. While the government does not have an obligation to pay the interest until March 31, 2010, Jalobert has earned interest revenue by owning the bonds. When a cheque is received from the government on or about March 31, 2010, Jalobert would record the following transactional entry:

Dr. Cash (asset +)   25,000
   Cr. Interest revenue (revenue +, shareholders' equity +)   12,500
   Cr. Interest receivable (asset −)   12,500
To record cash received for interest earned from investment in
Government of Canada bonds between October 1, 2009
and March 31, 2010 [(6 months ÷ 12 months) × $1,000,000 × 5 percent].
The October 1, 2009 to December 31, 2009 portion of the
payment had been accrued on December 31, 2009.

		Assets		=	Liabilities	+			Shareholders' Equity	

TABLE 3–9 ::: **Jalobert Ltd. Summary Spreadsheet**

Date	Cash	Interest Receivable	All other assets	All liabilities	Capital Stock	Retained Earnings	Interest Revenue	All other income statement accounts	
Dec. 31, 2009		$12,500					$12,500		Adjusting entry
Balance on Dec. 31, 2009		**$12,500**					**$12,500**		Trans- actional
Mar. 31, 2010	$25,000	($12,500)					$12,500		entry

Notice that the balance in the interest receivable account is zero after the payment has been received from the government.

The revenue recorded on March 31, 2010 is for interest earned between January 1 and March 31, 2010.

The transactional entry reflects two events:

1. Collection of the interest revenue that was earned in the last three months of 2009 and recorded as a receivable for the December 31, 2009 year end.

2. Recognition and collection of the interest revenue earned during the first three months of 2010.

The effects on the balance sheet and income statement of the accrued asset are summarized in the condensed spreadsheet in Table 3–9.

CLOSING JOURNAL ENTRIES

All accounts that are reported on the income statement are referred to as **temporary accounts**. They are temporary because at the end of each period they are reset to zero so that accumulation of revenues and expenses can begin anew in the next period. The balances in temporary accounts are not carried forward from one period to the next. This is important because an income statement reports results for a period of time. For example, a year-end income statement reports revenues and expenses "For the Year Ended December 31, 2009." If the income statement accounts are not reset to zero, then the revenues and expenses for the year ended December 31, 2010 would be combined with those of 2009, making it almost impossible to understand what amounts belonged to which year.

Consider the analogy of the trip odometer in a car. You want to find out how many kilometres you are able to travel per litre of gas. When you fill up your car you set the trip odometer to zero. The next time you fill up you note the distance travelled and the amount of gas that you used so that you can do the calculation. If you wanted to repeat the test, you would have to reset the trip odometer to zero when you fill up the car. Otherwise you would not know how far you travelled on the second tank of gas because the trip odometer would reflect the distance travelled on two fill-ups.

Setting each of the income statement accounts to zero simply involves making an entry to the accounting equation spreadsheet that is opposite in amount to the ending balance in each account. So if the ending balance in sales is $1,000,000, an entry of −$1,000,000 is made. But how do we make the accounting equation's equality hold? Remember that the income statement accounts are part of the shareholders' or owners' equity section of the balance sheet. When the income statement accounts are set to zero, or *closed*, the amounts in those accounts are moved to owners' or shareholders' equity. For a corporation, the income statement accounts are closed to Retained Earnings. For a partnership or proprietorship, the amounts are closed to the owners' capital accounts. The process of resetting temporary account balances to zero and transferring the balances in the temporary accounts to Retained Earnings or Owners' Equity is accomplished using **closing journal entries**.

Let's return to the Strawberries Inc. example. Table 3–10 shows the bottom line of the Shareholders' Equity section of the spreadsheet from Table 3–1. For each of the temporary accounts (that is, the income statement accounts), an entry is made that is equal and opposite in amount to the ending balance for the month (that is, the amounts on the last line of the spreadsheet). The "other side" of each entry is made to Retained Earnings. The final balance in Retained Earnings now corresponds to the amount we included in the balance sheet. The income statement accounts are now at zero so the accounting records are ready to accumulate amounts for the next period. The end result is that we have "transferred" the balances in each income statement account to Retained Earnings.

The corresponding journal entry would be:

Dr. Sales	17,900	
Cr. Cost of sales		11,900
Cr. Rent expense		1,250
Cr. Wages expense		925
Cr. Utilities expense		525
Cr. Amortization expense		1,042
Cr. Interest expense		150
Cr. Retained earnings		2,108

To record the closing entry at September 30, 2008.

TABLE 3–10 ::: Strawberries Inc. Spreadsheet: Shareholders' Equity Section

	Shareholders' Equity								
	Capital Stock	Retained Earnings	Sales	Cost of Sales	Rent Expense	Wages Expense	Utilities Expense	Amortization Expense	Interest Expense
Balance before closing entry on Sept. 30, 2008	$40,000	($1,000)	$17,900	($11,900)	($1,250)	($925)	($525)	($1,042)	($150)
Closing entry		$17,900	($17,900)						
Closing entry		($11,900)		$11,900					
Closing entry		($1,250)			$1,250				
Closing entry		($925)				$925			
Closing entry		($525)					$525		
Closing entry		($1,042)						$1,042	
Closing entry		($150)							$150
Ending balance on Sept. 30, 2008	$40,000	$1,108	$0	$0	$0	$0	$0	$0	$0

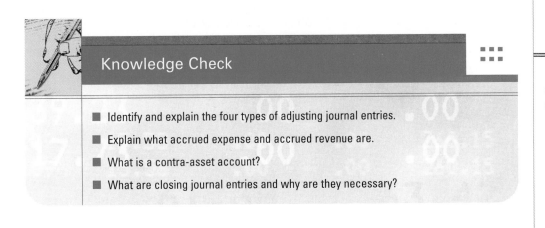

Knowledge Check

- Identify and explain the four types of adjusting journal entries.
- Explain what accrued expense and accrued revenue are.
- What is a contra-asset account?
- What are closing journal entries and why are they necessary?

www.mcgrawhill.ca/
olc/friedlan

Solved Problem

Child First Safety Ltd. (CFS) is a small business that provides safety advice and equipment to parents and daycare centres that want to have a safe, childproofed environment for infants and toddlers. The company has been in business for approximately two years. CFS is owned and operated by Yehuda Bigalli, who owns 100 percent of the shares of the company. Yehuda has never been much of a bookkeeper and his accounting system has tended to be a bag where he puts all information pertaining to CFS, including receipts, invoices, cancelled cheques (a cheque that has been cashed and returned by the bank to the cheque writer), and so on. At the end of the year he brings the bag to an accountant friend, who organizes the information and prepares financial statements that Yehuda uses for calculating his taxes and to show his bank, because he has a bank loan.

In answering the question, we will play the role of Yehuda's accountant friend.

We begin by examining the October 31, 2009 (last year's) balance sheet, which is shown in Table 3–11.

We organize and summarize the data in the bag and determine the following:

1. On November 1, 2009 CFS purchased a two-year insurance policy for $3,000 cash.

2. During the year CFS sold safety equipment and advising services to customers for $199,000; $140,000 of the sales were for cash, with the remainder on credit.

3. CFS purchased $65,000 of inventory during the year. All purchases were on credit.

4. CFS paid $62,000 during the year to suppliers for inventory purchases.

5. On November 15, 2009 CFS purchased a used car for $12,000 in cash. Yehuda uses the car for service calls and deliveries instead of using his personal vehicle. He estimates that the car will last for four years.

6. During the year CFS paid Yehuda and a part-time sales person $70,000 in salary and commission.

7. During the year, CFS collected $45,000 from customers for purchases they had made on credit.

8. On October 31, 2010 CFS paid interest of $900 for the year on its bank loan.

TABLE 3–11 ::: Child First Safety Ltd. Balance Sheet

Child First Safety Ltd.
Balance Sheet
As of October 31, 2009

Assets		Liabilities and Shareholders' Equity	
Current assets		**Current liabilities**	
Cash	$ 12,800	Bank loan	$15,000
Accounts receivable	22,000	Accounts payable	49,000
Inventory	52,000	Taxes payable	5,000
	86,800	Unearned revenue	3,000
			72,000
Non-current assets		**Shareholder's equity**	
Capital assets	24,000	Capital stock	15,000
Accumulated amortization	(8,000)	Retained earnings	15,800
	16,000		30,800
		Total liabilities and	
Total assets	$102,800	shareholder's equity	$102,800

9. On October 31, 2010 CFS repaid $2,000 of its bank loan.

10. During the year, CFS incurred other expenses of $20,000, all paid in cash.

11. CFS paid a dividend of $15,000 on September 15, 2010.

12. During the year CFS paid the $5,000 in taxes payable that was owing to the federal and provincial governments on October 31, 2009.

13. In November 2009 CFS supplied $3,000 of equipment to a large daycare centre. The daycare centre had paid in advance for the equipment in October 2009. The payment was reported as unearned revenue on the October 31, 2009 balance sheet.

14. At the end of the year, CFS owed the part-time sales person $1,500 in salary and commissions. The amount owing will be paid in mid-November 2010.

15. Amortization of capital assets is $6,000, including the used car that was purchased on November 15, 2009.

16. The cost of the safety equipment sold during the year was $72,000.

17. CFS will have to pay $6,700 in income taxes for the 2010 fiscal year. No payments had been made with respect to the 2010 fiscal year as of October 31, 2010.

Required:

Use an accounting equation spreadsheet to record all of the above events and transactions for CFS during 2010. Make sure to include the adjusting and closing entries. Prepare the balance sheet as of October 31, 2010 and the income statement and the statement of retained earnings for the year ended October 31, 2010. Also discuss CFS's performance for the year ended October 31, 2010.

Solution:

To prepare the balance sheet as of October 31, 2010 and the income statement and statement of retained earnings for the year ended October 31, 2010, we will use an accounting equation spreadsheet to record all of the above transactions and events. Table 3–12 (pages 124–125) provides the completed spreadsheet for the year ended October 31, 2010. Most of the entries should be clear, but note the following points:

■ The first line of the spreadsheet, which is called "beginning balance," contains the values on the balance sheet on October 31, 2009. Remember that balance sheet accounts are permanent, so the ending balances in last year's balance sheet are always the beginning balances in this year's balance sheet. The income statement accounts all have beginning balances of zero. This is because the income statement accounts are closed each year to retained earnings.

■ The amortization expense in item 15 is the portion of the cost of capital assets that is matched to sales in fiscal 2010. The amortization of the capital assets is accumulated in a separate contra-asset account and not directly to the capital asset account itself.

■ Item 18 is tricky because the question does not specifically state that part of the prepaid insurance has to be expensed at year end. This is typical of adjusting entries. Because adjusting entries are generated within the entity, the accountant or bookkeeper has to examine the accounts and decide when an adjusting entry is necessary.

The balance sheet, income statement, and statement of retained earnings are shown in Table 3–13 (page 126).

How Did Child First Safety Ltd. (CFS) Do?

Since we have put these financial statements together on behalf of Yehuda, who does not seem too concerned about the accounting information, we should probably give him some insights

TABLE 3–12 ::: Child First Safety Completed Spreadsheet

Transaction	Type of entry	Cash	Accounts Receivable	Inventory	Prepaid Insurance	Capital Assets	Accumulated Amortization	=	Bank Loan	Accounts Payable	Salaries Payable
Beginning Balance		12,800	22,000	52,000	0	24,000	(8,000)		15,000	49,000	0
1	Transactional	(3,000)			3,000						
2	Transactional	140,000	59,000								
3	Transactional			65,000						65,000	
4	Transactional	(62,000)								(62,000)	
5	Transactional	(12,000)				12,000					
6	Transactional	(70,000)									
7	Transactional	45,000	(45,000)								
8	Transactional	(900)									
9	Transactional	(2,000)							(2,000)		
10	Transactional	(20,000)									
11	Transactional	(15,000)									
12	Transactional	(5,000)									
13	Adjusting										
14	Adjusting										1,500
15	Adjusting						(6,000)				
16	Adjusting			(72,000)							
17	Adjusting										
18	Adjusting				(1,500)						
		7,900	36,000	45,000	1,500	36,000	(14,000)		13,000	52,000	1,500
19	Closing										
Ending Balance		7,900	36,000	45,000	1,500	36,000	(14,000)		13,000	52,000	1,500

into what these statements say. We should warn Yehuda that the financial statements do not provide clear-cut answers to questions about an entity's situation. The statements raise flags for further investigation.

1. As was the case with Strawberries Inc., our ability to analyze the performance of CFS is hampered by the absence of comparable income statement data. We do have the October 31, 2009 balance sheet for making comparisons between balance sheet accounts.

2. It can be difficult to evaluate the financial statements of an entity when the owner also manages the entity. One reason is that the salary the owner receives may not bear any relationship to the market value of the work he or she provides to the entity. That is because owner-managers are free to pay themselves any amount they choose and the payments can take different forms, including salary, dividends, and loans. Remember that only salary reduces net income so different combinations of payments made to owner-managers will affect net income differently. Often, an important objective of owner-managers of private corporations is to minimize the overall tax burden on themselves and their corporation.

3. Without knowing his share of the salaries expense, we cannot make a conclusive statement about how well-paid Yehuda was this year, but it appears that he had a reasonably good year. If we assume that Yehuda's share of the Salaries Expense was $45,000 (which is probably a reasonable assumption given that the sales person was a part-time employee), Yehuda took home $60,000 in salary and dividends ($45,000 in salary + $15,000 in dividends). In addition, his business made money so that also added to his wealth.

Liabilities (cont'd)		+			Shareholders' Equity						
Taxes Payable	Unearned Revenue	Capital Stock	Retained Earnings	Sales	Cost of sales	Insurance Expense	Salaries Expense	Amort. Expense	Other Expenses	Tax Expense	Interest Expense
5,000	3,000	15,000	15,800								
				199,000							
							(70,000)				
											(900)
									(20,000)		
			(15,000)								
(5,000)											
	(3,000)			3,000							
							(1,500)				
								(6,000)			
					(72,000)						
6,700										(6,700)	
						(1,500)					
6,700	0	15,000	800	202,000	(72,000)	(1,500)	(71,500)	(6,000)	(20,000)	(6,700)	(900)
			23,400	(202,000)	72,000	1,500	71,500	6,000	20,000	6,700	900
6,700	0	15,000	24,200	0	0	0	0	0	0	0	0

4. At first glance, CFS's liquidity position seems adequate. Its current ratio has been stable for the two years available (1.23 in 2010, 1.21 in 2009). We would need to compare these current ratios with other businesses of this type to get some perspective of the adequacy of this current ratio. Of some concern is the low amount of cash and receivables (current assets that are cash or will be cash very soon) relative to the liabilities that will require cash very soon (accounts payable, salaries payable, and taxes payable). If sales slow down, there may be a cash problem since the sale of inventory generates cash. However, CFS's liquidity position was similar a year ago and the company seems to have managed.

5. CFS generated a return on equity of about 67 percent (Net income ÷ Average shareholders' equity), a very good return on investment. The profit margin for the year is 11.6 percent. This ratio is difficult to assess without some comparative data from similar businesses.

6. Compared with October 31, 2009, the amount of inventory on hand on October 31, 2010 has decreased, while the amount of accounts receivable has increased. Without comparable income statements to tell us how sales changed from fiscal 2009, it is difficult to interpret these changes. For example, the increase in accounts receivable could be due to higher sales, more generous credit terms being offered to customers to attract more business, customers paying more slowly than last year, or other reasons.

TABLE 3–13 ::: Child First Safety Ltd. Balance Sheet, and Income Statement and Statement of Retained Earnings

Child First Safety Ltd.
Balance Sheet
As of October 31, 2010

Assets		Liabilities and Shareholders' Equity	
Current assets		**Current liabilities**	
Cash	$ 7,900	Bank loan	$ 13,000
Accounts receivable	36,000	Accounts payable	52,000
Inventory	45,000	Salaries payable	1,500
Prepaid insurance	1,500	Taxes payable	6,700
	90,400		73,200
Non-current assets		**Shareholder's equity**	
Capital assets	36,000	Capital stock	15,000
Accumulated amortization	(14,000)	Retained earnings	24,200
	22,000		39,200
		Total liabilities and	
Total assets	$112,400	shareholder's equity	$112,400

Child First Safety Ltd.
Income Statement and Statement of Retained Earnings
For the Year Ended October 31, 2010

Sales		$202,000
Cost of sales		72,000
Gross margin		130,000
Expenses		
Insurance expense	$1,500	
Salaries expense	71,500	
Amortization expense	6,000	
Other expenses	20,000	
Interest expense	900	
Total expenses		99,900
Income before taxes		30,100
Income tax expense		6,700
Net income		23,400
Retained earnings at the beginning of the year		15,800
Dividends		(15,000)
Retained earnings at the end of the year		$ 24,200

Insight

Analyzing accounting information can be difficult. There are rarely answers and usually many questions. You should already see that the numbers reported in financial statements cannot simply be taken at face value. When managers have choices about how to account for transactions and other economic events, the choices they make will affect the accounting numbers that are reported, which in turn may affect how the numbers are interpreted and what decisions stakeholders make. That is why it is always necessary to look behind the numbers.

SUMMARY OF KEY POINTS

▶ **LO 1** The key to producing accounting information is having an accounting system that captures raw data and organizes, summarizes, and classifies the data into a form that is useful for decision making. The information provided by an accounting system is limited by the data that are entered into it.

The accounting cycle is the process by which data about economic events are entered into an accounting system, processed, organized, and used to produce information, such as financial statements. An accounting system is very important because if data were not processed and organized it would be very difficult for anyone to understand and use it.

▶ **LO 2** The accounting equation spreadsheet is a device that is used to record transactions and economic events in a way that allows the information to be conveniently collected and organized, and then presented in financial statements. The accounting equation spreadsheet has columns for each account in the entity's records. Each transaction or economic event is recorded on a separate line in the spreadsheet. Each entry to the spreadsheet must maintain the accounting equation of Assets = Liabilities + Owners' (Shareholders') Equity. The ending balance in each column of the spreadsheet represents the ending balance in that account at a point in time and can be used to prepare the balance sheet, income statement, and statement of retained earnings.

▶ **LO 3** The journal entry is the method used in practice to enter information about economic events into the accounting system. Whenever an economic event or transaction occurs that is to be entered into the accounting system, a journal entry is made. Journal entries provide compact and concise summaries of economic events in a way that makes it easy to see and understand the effect the event has on the financial statements. Debits and credits are the notations used to record the effects of an economic event on the accounts. Debits represent increases in assets and expenses, and decreases in liabilities, owners' (shareholders') equity, and revenue. Credits represent decreases in assets and expenses, and increases in liabilities, owners' (shareholders') equity, and revenue.

▶ **LO 4** Devices such as accounting equation spreadsheets and journal entries are only means to an end. These devices give us the ability to record and organize, summarize, and classify data into information that is useful for decision making. Accounting methods such as accrual accounting and GAAP often provide preparers of accounting information with choices for how to record and report transactions and economic events. When managers have choices for how to account for transactions and other economic events, their decisions will affect the accounting numbers that are reported, which in turn may affect how the numbers are interpreted and the decisions stakeholders make.

▶ **LO 5** Accrual accounting attempts to measure the economic activity and economic changes of an entity. An entry into an accrual accounting system is usually triggered by a transaction—an exchange between the entity and a party external to the entity. Sometimes, however, economic changes occur that affect the entity but that are not triggered by transactions. These changes must be recorded in the accounting system. Entries to the accrual accounting system that are not triggered by exchanges with outside entities are called adjusting entries.

There are four types of adjusting entries:

1. Deferred expense/prepaid expense where cash is paid before the expense is recognized;

2. Deferred revenue where cash is received before revenue is recognized;

3. Accrued expense/accrued liability where the expense is recognized before cash is paid; and

4. Accrued revenue/accrued asset where revenue is recognized before cash is received.

▶ **LO 6** Income statement accounts are sub-accounts of an entity's owners' equity account (retained earnings in the case of a corporation). At the end of each period the balances in the income statement, or temporary accounts, must be set to zero and the balances in those accounts transferred to their permanent place in the owners' equity section of the balance sheet. The balances in the income statement accounts are set to zero so that they can accumulate information about transactions and economic events that pertain only to the next period. The setting of temporary accounts to zero and the transferring of the balances in those accounts to owners' equity is achieved by a closing journal entry.

APPENDIX: THE ACCOUNTING CYCLE

Introduction

The accounting equation spreadsheet approach discussed in the main part of Chapter 3 is a straightforward method to show how transactions and economic events affect the financial statements. The spreadsheet approach provides a technique for preparing financial statements without getting into many of the details of bookkeeping. This appendix will go through the steps that are followed in keeping formal accounting records so those students who wish to learn the complete accounting cycle may do so. The steps in the accounting cycle are shown in Figure 3–A1.

Prepare Journal Entries

As described in the main part of Chapter 3, the initial recognition of a transaction or other economic event is made by a journal entry. The journal entry is recorded in the **general journal**, a chronological record of the journal entries that have been entered into the accounting system. The general journal is referred to as the book of original entry because an event is first recorded in the accounting system in the general journal. The general journal can be an actual book where entries are written down or a computerized accounting package.

FIGURE 3–A1 ::

The Accounting Cycle

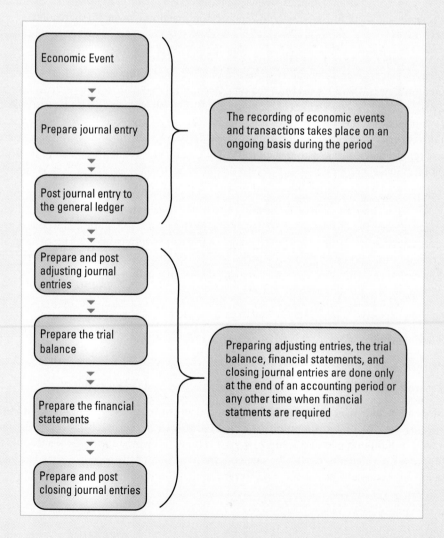

Economic Event

↓

Prepare journal entry

↓

Post journal entry to the general ledger

The recording of economic events and transactions takes place on an ongoing basis during the period

↓

Prepare and post adjusting journal entries

↓

Prepare the trial balance

↓

Prepare the financial statements

Preparing adjusting entries, the trial balance, financial statements, and closing journal entries are done only at the end of an accounting period or any other time when financial statments are required

↓

Prepare and post closing journal entries

FIGURE 3–A2 ::

The General Journal

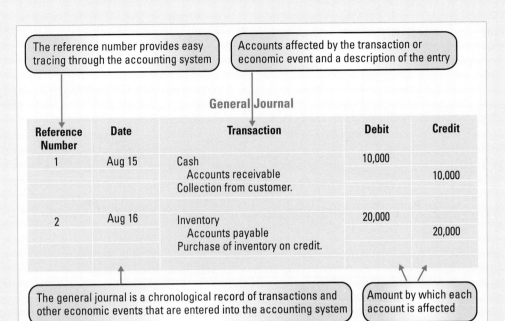

The reference number provides easy tracing through the accounting system

Accounts affected by the transaction or economic event and a description of the entry

General Journal

Reference Number	Date	Transaction	Debit	Credit
1	Aug 15	Cash	10,000	
		Accounts receivable		10,000
		Collection from customer.		
2	Aug 16	Inventory	20,000	
		Accounts payable		20,000
		Purchase of inventory on credit.		

The general journal is a chronological record of transactions and other economic events that are entered into the accounting system

Amount by which each account is affected

An example of a general journal is shown in Figure 3–A2. Figure 3–A2 shows that the general journal is a dated list of the journal entries that are made by the entity. The reference number is useful because it allows for easy tracing of entries as they proceed through the accounting system. Regardless of whether data are recorded in the accounting system manually or with software, the process of the accounting cycle is the same. Review the section on journal entries on pages 109–112 to ensure you understand them.

Post Journal Entries to the General Ledger

The next step in the accounting cycle is posting the journal entry to the general ledger. The **general ledger** is a record of all the accounts of an entity. **Posting** a journal entry to the general ledger is the process of transferring each line of a journal entry to the corresponding account in the general ledger. You can picture the general ledger as a book where each page represents a different account, although again computerized general ledgers are common. There will be a page for Cash, a page for Inventory, a page for Sales, and so on. The general ledger organizes information on an account-by-account basis, rather than on a transaction-by-transaction basis as is the case with the general journal. In the spreadsheet method, each column represents a general ledger account.

In accounting textbooks a device called the **T-account** is used to represent general ledger accounts. (The name "T-account" is used because the device has the shape of the letter T.) Each T-account corresponds with a general ledger account.

The structure of the T-account is shown in Figure 3–A3. The name of the account is written on the horizontal line at the top. The vertical line separates the debits and credits made to the account. The beginning balance—the balance in the account at the beginning of the period—is shown between the horizontal lines at the top of the T-account. The ending balance is shown below the horizontal lines at the bottom. If an account has a debit balance at the beginning or end of the period, the balance is recorded on the left side of the vertical line. If an account has a credit balance at the beginning or end of the period, the balance is recorded on the right side of the vertical line.

When a journal entry is posted to the T-accounts, debits are recorded on the left side of the vertical line and credits on the right side. The sum of the debits and credits plus the beginning balance gives the ending balance in the account. Usually, asset accounts have debit balances and liability and owners' equity accounts have credit balances, although there are exceptions. The posting process is shown in Figure 3–A4.

Whereas a journal entry allows you to see which accounts a transaction or economic event affects, a general ledger account allows you to see the activity in the account over time. If you

FIGURE 3–A3 ::

The T-Account

Account Name	
Beginnning Balance	
Debits	Credits
Ending Balance	

FIGURE 3–A4 ::

The Posting Process

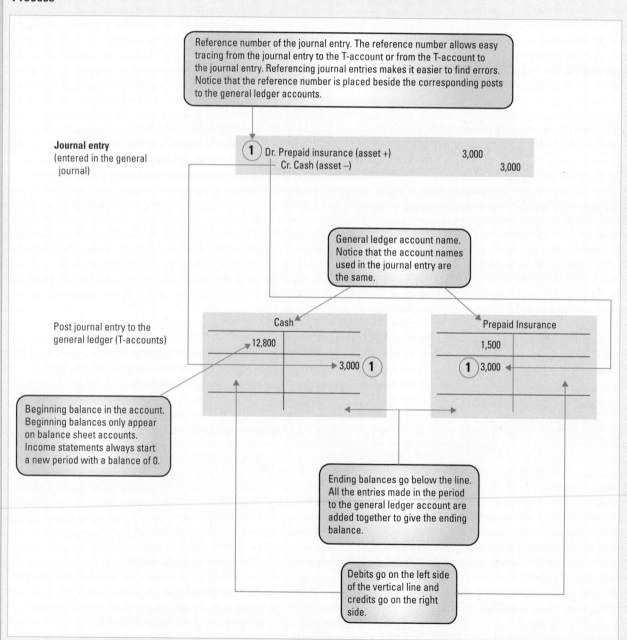

Reference number of the journal entry. The reference number allows easy tracing from the journal entry to the T-account or from the T-account to the journal entry. Referencing journal entries makes it easier to find errors. Notice that the reference number is placed beside the corresponding posts to the general ledger accounts.

Journal entry (entered in the general journal)

1 Dr. Prepaid insurance (asset +)   3,000
    Cr. Cash (asset –)   3,000

General ledger account name. Notice that the account names used in the journal entry are the same.

Post journal entry to the general ledger (T-accounts)

Cash	
12,800	
	3,000 **1**

Prepaid Insurance	
1,500	
1 3,000	

Beginning balance in the account. Beginning balances only appear on balance sheet accounts. Income statements always start a new period with a balance of 0.

Ending balances go below the line. All the entries made in the period to the general ledger account are added together to give the ending balance.

Debits go on the left side of the vertical line and credits go on the right side.

wanted to examine the activity in inventory over the last year, you would look at the inventory general ledger account. If you then wanted to examine the individual events that were recorded in the general ledger account, you would go back to the journal entry, which describes the specific event.

Prepare and Post Adjusting Journal Entries

Preparing journal entries and posting them to the general ledger occurs on an ongoing basis during a reporting period. The remaining steps in the accounting cycle occur at the end of a period when the entity wants to prepare financial statements.

Adjusting journal entries were discussed in detail on pages 112–120. At the end of the period the managers examine the general ledger accounts and determine the adjusting entries that must be made. Many adjusting entries are automatic, as managers know that certain adjustments have to be made each period. Other adjustments do not occur regularly and managers must be careful to make sure that these are also recorded.

Prepare the Trial Balance

The **trial balance** is a listing of all the accounts in the general ledger with their balances. The main purpose of the trial balance is to ensure that the debits equal the credits and to provide a summary of the balances in each account. If debits and credits are unequal there is an error somewhere in the accounts that must be corrected.

However, having equal debits and credits does not mean that the accounting has been done properly. It simply means that all journal entries and postings to the general ledger accounts were balanced. For example, if an entity purchases land and promises to pay for the land in one year, the correct entry would be to debit Land (asset) and credit Payables (liability). But if the accountant incorrectly debited the Cash account instead of the Land account, the debits and credits would still balance but the account balances would not be correct.

Sometimes several trial balances are prepared at the end of a period. Trial balances are sometimes prepared before and after preparation of the adjusting entries, as well as after the closing entry has been prepared. Each trial balance helps ensure that the posting of the journal entries balances at each step.

Prepare the Financial Statements

The trial balance provides all the information required to prepare the balance sheet and income statement. To prepare these statements the accounts in the trial balance have to be aggregated and organized into the format desired by the managers. At this point the ending balance in Retained Earnings that will be reported on the year-end balance sheet is not known because the income statement accounts have not been closed. Once the income statement accounts have been closed, the ending balance in Retained Earnings is available for inclusion on the balance sheet.

Prepare and Post Closing Journal Entries

Preparation and posting of the closing journal entry is the last step in the accounting cycle. The closing entry sets the income statement accounts to zero and updates the balance in retained earnings to its year-end balance. (Closing entries are discussed on pages 120–121).

COMPREHENSIVE EXAMPLE

The description of the accounting cycle has so far been rather abstract. We will now work through the full accounting cycle using the Child First Safety Ltd. (CFS) example developed in the main body of Chapter 3. The mechanics of the accounting cycle are relatively straightforward. Learning them is just a matter of practice.

Prepare Journal Entries

1. Dr. Prepaid insurance (asset +)   3,000
        Cr. Cash (asset −)   3,000
    To record the purchase of insurance for two years.

2. Dr. Cash (asset +)   140,000
    Dr. Accounts receivable (asset +)   59,000
        Cr. Sales (revenue +, shareholders' equity +)   199,000
    To record sales for the year.

3. Dr. Inventory (asset +)   65,000
        Cr. Accounts payable (liability +)   65,000
    To record the purchase of inventory on credit.

4. Dr. Accounts payable (liability −)   62,000
        Cr. Cash (asset −)   62,000
    To record the payment to suppliers for inventory purchased.

5. Dr. Capital assets (asset +)   12,000
        Cr. Cash (asset −)   12,000
    To record the purchase of a car.

6. Dr. Salaries expense (expenses +, shareholders' equity −)   70,000
        Cr. Cash (asset −)   70,000
    To record salaries paid.

7. Dr. Cash (asset +)   45,000
        Cr. Accounts receivable (asset −)   45,000
    To record collection of accounts receivable.

8. Dr. Interest expense (expense +, shareholders' equity −)   900
        Cr. Cash (asset −)   900
    To record the payment of interest on the bank loan.

9. Dr. Bank loan (liability −)   2,000
        Cr. Cash (asset −)   2,000
    To record payment of principal on the bank loan.

10. Dr. Other expenses (expense +, shareholders' equity −)   20,000
        Cr. Cash (asset −)   20,000
    To record the payment of other expenses.

11. Dr. Retained earnings (shareholders' equity −)   15,000
        Cr. Cash (asset −)   15,000
    To record the payment of a dividend.

12. Dr. Taxes payable (liability −)   5,000
        Cr. Cash (asset −)   5,000
    To record the payment of taxes payable.

Post Journal Entries to the General Ledger

Next, the elements of each journal entry are posted to the appropriate general ledger accounts. T-accounts will be used to represent the general ledger accounts. The T-accounts are shown in Figure 3–A5. On the left side of each line in each T-account there is a number that corresponds to the number of the journal entry. This cross-referencing is important because it makes it easy to trace back from the general ledger account to the journal entry. This is important because it is

Cash

	Debit	Credit	
Bal	12,800	3,000	1
2	140,000	62,000	4
7	45,000	12,000	5
		70,000	6
		900	8
		2,000	9
		20,000	10
		15,000	11
		5,000	12

Accounts Receivable

	Debit	Credit	
Bal	22,000		
2	59,000		
7		45,000	

Inventory

	Debit	Credit	
Bal	52,000		
3	65,000		
16		72,000	

Prepaid Insurance

	Debit	Credit
Bal	0	
1	3,000	

Capital Assets

	Debit	Credit
Bal	24,000	
5	12,000	

Accumulated Amortization

	Debit	Credit
		8,000 Bal

Bank Loan

	Debit	Credit
Bal		15,000
9	2,000	

Accounts Payable

	Debit	Credit	
Bal		49,000	
3		65,000	
4	62,000		

Salaries Payable

	Debit	Credit
Bal		0

Taxes Payable

	Debit	Credit
Bal		5,000
12	5,000	

Unearned Revenue

	Debit	Credit
Bal		3,000

Capital Stock

	Debit	Credit
Bal		15,000

Retained Earnings

	Debit	Credit
Bal		15,800
11	15,000	

Sales

	Debit	Credit
2		199,000

Cost of Sales

Insurance Expense

Salaries Expense

	Debit	Credit
6	70,000	

Amortization Expense

Other Expenses

	Debit	Credit
10	20,000	

Tax Expense

Interest Expense

	Debit	Credit
8	900	

FIGURE 3–A5

T-Accounts for Child First Safety Ltd. before Adjusting Entries are Posted

easy to make posting errors. Cross-referencing makes it easy to find the journal entry associated with each ledger entry when you are trying to find errors.

In addition, for each balance sheet T-account a beginning balance is shown. This is the amount that was in the account on October 31, 2009. Remember that income statement accounts do not have beginning balances because they were set to zero on October 31, 2009 when the temporary accounts were closed. Ending balances are shown at the bottom of each T-account.

Prepare and Post Adjusting Journal Entries

At the end of the period the accounts are examined and any necessary adjusting entries are made. The adjusting entries are then posted to the corresponding general ledger accounts. The adjusting journal entries are shown below and posting of the adjusting entries to the T-accounts is shown in Figure 3–A6. The adjusting entries in Figure 3A–6 are posted to the T-accounts in bold.

13. Dr. Unearned revenue (liability −)   3,000
    Cr. Sales (revenue +, shareholders' equity +)   3,000
    Adjusting entry to record recognition of revenue
    on merchandise paid for in advance.

14. Dr. Salaries expense (expense +, shareholders' equity −)   1,500
    Cr. Salaries payable (liability +)   1,500
    Adjusting entry to accrue salaries owed but not paid.

15. Dr. Amortization expense (expense +, shareholders' equity −)   6,000
    Cr. Accumulated amortization (contra-asset +)   6,000
    Adjusting entry to record the amortization of capital assets.

16. Dr. Cost of sales (expense +, shareholders' equity −)   72,000
    Cr. Inventory (asset −)   72,000
    Adjusting entry to record cost of sales.

17. Dr. Tax expense (expense +, shareholders' equity −)   6,700
    Cr. Taxes payable (liability +)   6,700
    Adjusting entry to record income tax expense and
    accrue the liability for income taxes.

18. Dr. Insurance expense (expense +, shareholders' equity −)   1,500
    Cr. Prepaid insurance (asset −)   1,500
    Adjusting entry to record insurance used during the year.

Prepare the Trial Balance

The ending balance in each general ledger account (T-account) is organized into a trial balance. The ending balance in each T-account with a debit balance is placed in the left column of the trial balance and the ending balance in each T-account with a credit balance is placed in the right column. The trial balance is shown in Table 3–A1. The trial balance in Table 3–A1 was prepared after the adjusting journal entries had been made and posted to the appropriate ledger accounts. It would also be appropriate to prepare a trial balance before the adjusting entries were made.

FIGURE 3–A6 ::

T-Accounts for Child First Safety Ltd. After Adjusting Entries Are Posted

Cash				Prepaid Insurance				Salaries Payable				Cost of Sales		
Bal	12,800			Bal	0			Bal		0		16	72,000	
1		3,000		1	3,000			14		1,500		Bal	72,000	
2	140,000			**18**		**1,500**		Bal		1,500				
4		62,000		Bal	1,500								Insurance Expense	
5		12,000							Taxes Payable			**18**	**1,500**	
6		70,000			Capital Assets			Bal		5,000		Bal	1,500	
7	45,000			Bal	24,000			12		5,000				
8		900		5	12,000			**17**		**6,700**			Salaries Expense	
9		2,000		Bal	36,000			Bal		6,700		6	70,000	
10		20,000										**14**	**1,500**	
11		15,000			Accumulated Amortization				Unearned Revenue			Bal	71,500	
12		5,000		Bal		8,000		Bal		3,000				
Bal	7,900			**15**		**6,000**		13	3,000				Amortization Expense	
				Bal		14,000		Bal		0		**15**	**6,000**	
	Accounts Receivable											Bal	6,000	
Bal	22,000				Bank Loan				Capital Stock					
2	59,000			Bal		15,000		Bal		15,000			Other Expenses	
7		45,000		9	2,000			Bal		15,000		10	20,000	
Bal	36,000			Bal		13,000						Bal	20,000	
	Inventory								Retained Earnings					
Bal	52,000				Accounts Payable			Bal		15,800			Tax Expense	
3	65,000			Bal		49,000		11	15,000			**17**	**6,700**	
16		**72,000**		3		65,000		Bal		800		Bal	6,700	
Bal	45,000			4	62,000									
				Bal		52,000			Sales				Interest Expense	
								2		199,000		8	900	
								13		**3,000**		Bal	900	
								Bal		202,000				

TABLE 3-A1 ::: **Child First Safety Ltd. Trial Balance**

Child First Safety Ltd.
Trial Balance
October 31, 2010

	Debits	Credits	
Cash	$ 7,900		
Accounts receivable	36,000		
Inventory	45,000		
Prepaid insurance	1,500		
Capital assets	36,000		
Accumulated amortization		$ 14,000	Balance sheet
Bank loan		13,000	accounts
Accounts payable		52,000	
Salaries payable		1,500	
Taxes payable		6,700	
Unearned revenue		0	
Capital stock		15,000	
Retained earnings		800	
Sales		202,000	
Cost of sales	72,000		
Insurance expense	1,500		
Salaries expense	71,500		Income statement
Amortization expense	6,000		accounts
Other expenses	20,000		
Tax expense	6,700		
Interest expense	900		
	$305,000	$305,000	→ Debits = Credits

Prepare the Financial Statements

The balances listed in the trial balance can be used to prepare the financial statements. (The financial statements are the same as the ones in Table 3–13 on page 126.) The financial statements are prepared before the closing entry because at this stage the balances in the income statement accounts are still shown. Once the closing entry is made, the balances in the income statement accounts will be zero. However, preparing the statements before the closing entry is made means that the ending balance in retained earnings is not known from the trial balance. (Ending retained earnings can be calculated by using the following formula: Ending retained earnings = beginning retained earnings + total revenues − total expenses − dividends.)

Prepare and Post Closing Journal Entries

The last step in the accounting cycle is the closing entry that sets all the income statement accounts to zero and transfers those amounts to retained earnings. The closing journal entry is shown on page 137 and the T-accounts after the closing entry has been posted are shown in Figure 3–A7 (the closing posts are shown in bold). The after-closing trial balance (the trial balance prepared after the closing entry has been posted) is shown in Table 3–A2. Notice that the income statement accounts all have zero balances and the balance in the Retained Earnings corresponds with the amount on the October 31, 2010 balance sheet.

FIGURE 3–A7 ::

**Post-closing
T-Accounts
for Child First
Safety Ltd.**

Cash

Bal	12,800	
1		3,000
2	140,000	
4		62,000
5		12,000
6		70,000
7	45,000	
8		900
9		2,000
10		20,000
11		15,000
12		5,000
Bal	7,900	

Accounts Receivable

Bal	22,000	
2	59,000	
7		45,000
Bal	36,000	

Inventory

Bal	52,000	
3	65,000	
16		72,000
Bal	45,000	

Prepaid Insurance

Bal	0	
1	3,000	
18		1,500
Bal	1,500	

Capital Assets

Bal	24,000	
5	12,000	
Bal	36,000	

Accumulated Amortization

Bal		8,000
15		6,000
Bal		14,000

Bank Loan

Bal		15,000
9	2,000	
Bal		13,000

Accounts Payable

Bal		49,000
3		65,000
4	62,000	
Bal		52,000

Salaries Payable

Bal		0
14		1,500
Bal		1,500

Taxes Payable

Bal		5,000
12	5,000	
17		6,700
Bal		6,700

Unearned Revenue

Bal		3,000
13	3,000	
Bal		0

Capital Stock

Bal		15,000
Bal		15,000

Retained Earnings

Bal		15,800
11	15,000	
19		23,400
Bal		24,200

Sales

2		199,000
13		3,000
Bal		202,000
19	202,000	
Bal		0

Cost of Sales

16	72,000	
Bal	72,000	
19		72,000
Bal	0	

Insurance Expense

18	1,500	
Bal	1,500	
19		1,500
Bal	0	

Salaries Expense

6	70,000	
14	1,500	
Bal	71,500	
19		71,500
Bal	0	

Amortization Expense

15	6,000	
Bal	6,000	
19		6,000
Bal	0	

Other Expenses

10	20,000	
Bal	20,000	
19		20,000
Bal	0	

Tax Expense

17	6,700	
Bal	6,700	
19		6,700
Bal	0	

Interest Expense

8	900	
Bal	900	
19		900
Bal	0	

TABLE 3–A2 ::: Post-Closing Trial Balance

Child First Safety Ltd.
Post-Closing Trial Balance
October 31, 2010

	Debits	Credits	
Cash	$ 7,900		
Accounts receivable	36,000		
Inventory	45,000		
Prepaid insurance	1,500		
Capital assets	36,000		
Accumulated amortization		$ 14,000	Balance sheet accounts
Bank loan		13,000	
Accounts payable		52,000	
Salaries payable		1,500	
Taxes payable		6,700	
Unearned revenue		0	
Capital stock		15,000	
Retained earnings		24,200	
Sales		0	
Cost of sales	0		
Insurance expense	0		
Salaries expense	0		Income statement accounts
Amortization expense	0		
Other expenses	0		
Tax expense	0		
Interest expense	0		
	$126,400	$126,400	→ Debits = Credits

19. Dr. Sales	202,000	
Cr. Cost of sales		72,000
Cr. Insurance expense		1,500
Cr. Salaries expense		71,500
Cr. Amortization expense		6,000
Cr. Other expense		20,000
Cr. Tax expense		6,700
Cr. Interest expense		900
Cr. Retained earnings		23,400

To close income statement accounts to retained earnings.

KEY TERMS

account, p. 95

accounting cycle, p. 88

accrued expense, p. 117

accrued revenue, p. 119

accumulated amortization, p. 115

adjusting entry, p. 112

closing journal entry, p. 121

conservatism, p. 104

contra-asset account, p. 115

credit, p. 109

debit, p. 109

debit card, p. 99

deferred expense, p. 114

double-entry bookkeeping, p. 94

executory contract, p. 99

general journal, p. 128

general ledger, p. 129

journal entry, p. 93

matching (matching concept), p. 91

net book value (NBV), p. 115

non-monetary transaction, p. 98

posting, p. 129

prepaid expense, p. 114

profit margin ratio, p. 107

return on equity (ROE), p. 107

revenue recognition, p. 91

straight-line amortization, p. 115

T-account, p. 129

temporary accounts, p. 120

transactional entry, p. 113

trial balance, p. 131

unearned revenue, p. 117

SIMILAR TERMS

The left column gives alternative terms that are sometimes used for the accounting terms introduced in this chapter, which are listed in the right column.

carrying value	**net book value (NBV), p. 115**
barter transaction	**non-monetary transaction, p. 93**
deferred expense, deferred charge, deferred cost, deferred debit	**prepaid expense, p. 114**
nominal account	**temporary accounts, p. 120**
deferred revenue	**unearned revenue, p. 117**
depreciation	**amortization, p. 104**

ASSIGNMENT MATERIALS

Questions

Q3-1. Explain why much more judgment is required with accrual accounting than with cash accounting.

Q3-2. What are closing journal entries and why are they necessary? When do closing entries have to be prepared?

Q3-3. In 2009 Taymouth Inc. reported net income of $100,000. What would be the effect on retained earnings on Taymouth's 2009 balance sheet and on its 2010 income statement if it did not record a closing journal entry?

Q3-4. Explain why adjusting entries are necessary in accrual accounting, but not required when the cash basis of accounting is used.

Q3-5. Explain the difference between transactional journal entries and adjusting journal entries.

Q3-6. Identify the four types of adjusting entries and explain why each type is necessary.

Q3-7. For each type of adjusting entry, explain the impact on assets, liabilities, owners' equity, revenue, expenses and net income if the required adjusting entry were not made.

Q3-8. When do adjusting entries have to be made? Explain.

Q3-9. What do the terms *debit* and *credit* mean?

Q3-10. What is a contra-asset account? Why are contra-asset accounts used?

Q3-11. When a dividend is declared and paid by a corporation, a debit is made to retained earnings. Explain.

Q3-12. Describe the two devices used in Chapter 3 for recording accounting information.

Q3-13. If cash increases when a debit is made to the cash account, why does the bank credit your account when you make a deposit?

Q3-14. What is an executory contract? How do GAAP usually account for executory contracts?

Q3-15. Identify and explain the four things that must be known if data are to be entered into an accounting system.

Q3-16. Why do entities divide assets, liabilities, and owners' equity into sub-accounts rather than accumulating data simply as assets, liabilities, and owners' equity?

Q3-17. How should an entity determine the number of accounts it should keep in its general ledger?

Q3-18. Why can preparers sometimes choose among alternative ways of accounting for transactions and economic events when accrual accounting is used? What are the implications of these choices on the financial statements and to the users of financial statements?

Q3-19. Figure 3–1 (page 89) shows that not every economic event that has an effect on an entity is entered into the entity's accounting system. What do you think are the implications for financial statements and financial statement users of not having every economic event recorded in the accounting system?

Q3-20. Figure 3–1 shows that not every economic event that has an effect on an entity is entered into the entity's accounting system. Give three examples of economic events that might have an effect on an entity but are not recorded in the entity's accounting system.

Q3-21. Explain the matching concept. Give some examples of matching. Why is matching important for financial accounting? Why is matching sometimes difficult to do in practice?

Appendix Questions

Q3-22. Identify and explain the steps of the accounting cycle.

Q3-23. What is a T-account? Why are T-accounts used?

Q3-24. What does "posting" journal entries to the general ledger mean? Why are journal entries posted to the general ledger?

Q3-25. What is a trial balance and what is its purpose? Why doesn't a trial balance guarantee that your accounting is "correct?"

Q3-26. Why is it useful to cross-reference journal entries to the posting to the general ledger account (T-account)?

Q3-27. Explain how information that is recorded in the general journal (using journal entries) is organized differently from the information in the general ledger (posted from the general journal).

Exercises

E3-1. **(Types of events, LO 5)** For each of the events listed below, indicate whether the event will give rise to a transactional entry, an adjusting entry, or not result in any entry in the accounting system. Assume that the accounting system is designed to collect information on an accrual and a GAAP basis.

  a. Amortization of equipment.
  b. Collection of accounts receivable from a customer.
  c. Increase in the market value of a building while it continues to be owned.
  d. Recognition of revenue for work done in the current period but paid for in the previous period.
  e. Hiring of a new vice-president of finance.
  f. Purchase of inventory on credit from a supplier.
  g. Earning of interest on an investment. The interest will not be paid until next year.
  h. Customer pays in advance for work to be done next year.
  i. Sale of land to a buyer in exchange for a promise to pay $1,000,000 in cash in two years.
  j. Payment of a dividend to shareholders.
  k. Company agrees to supply cleaning services to a customer. The customer agrees to pay each time the work is done.

E3-2 **(Creating transactions and economic events from accounting equation effects, LO 2, 3)** Below are pairs of changes that affect elements of the accounting equation. Give an example of a transaction or economic event that reflects each:

  a. Asset increases, asset decreases
  b. Asset increases, liability increases
  c. Asset increases, shareholders' equity increases
  d. Asset increases, revenue increases
  e. Liability decreases, asset decreases
  f. Asset decreases, expense increases
  g. Liability decrease, revenue increase
  h. Asset decreases, shareholders' equity decreases
  i. Liability increase, expense increase

E3-3. **(Preparing closing entries using spreadsheets and journal entries, LO 2, 3, 6)** Below is a summarized income statement for St. Bruno Inc. (St. Bruno).

St. Bruno Inc.
Income Statement for the Year Ended December 31, 2008

Revenue	$5,125,000
Expenses	3,225,000
Net income	$1,900,000

  a. Prepare a spreadsheet and make the entry that is necessary to close the temporary accounts. Assume that the balance in retained earnings on December 31, 2007 was $17,500,000.
  b. Prepare the journal entry necessary to close the temporary accounts.
  c. Explain why closing entries are necessary and when they should be recorded.
  d. What would be the effect on net income in 2009 if St. Bruno Inc. forgot to prepare a closing entry?

E3-4. **(Preparing closing entries using spreadsheets and journal entries, LO 2, 3, 6)** Below is Niagara Falls Ltd.'s (Niagara Falls) summarized income statement for the year ended August 31, 2010, its first year in business.

Niagara Falls Ltd.
Income Statement for the Year Ended August 31, 2010
(in thousands of dollars)

Sales		$225,720
Cost of sales		76,200
Gross margin		149,520
Expenses		
Selling and marketing	$22,740	
General and administrative	15,450	
Research and development	9,675	
Amortization	9,420	
Interest	4,500	
Other	3,315	65,100
Income before taxes		84,420
Income taxes		30,390
Net income		$54,030

a. Prepare a spreadsheet and make the entries that are necessary to close the temporary accounts.

b. Prepare the journal entry necessary to close the temporary accounts.

c. Explain why closing entries are necessary and when they should be recorded.

d. What would be the effect on net income in 2011 if Niagara Falls Ltd. forgot to prepare a closing entry?

E3-5. (**Recognizing the effects of debits and credits, LO 3**) Indicate whether each of the following would be treated as a debit or a credit in a journal entry.

a. Increase in accounts receivable.

b. Decrease in unearned revenue.

c. Decrease in prepaid rent.

d. Increase in revenues earned from services.

e. Increase in cost of goods sold.

f. Increase in capital stock.

g. Decrease in amortization expense.

h. Decrease in accounts payable.

E3-6. (**Identifying different types of adjusting entries, LO 5**) Refer to Table 3–4 in this chapter (page 113). For each of the situations described below, identify the type of adjusting entry that would ultimately be required as a result of the event. Explain the reason for your choice.

	Type	Situation
Example	Deferred expense/ prepaid expense	Two years' rent is paid in advance
a.	_____	Water used by the company has not yet been billed or paid for.
b.	_____	Rent is owed by a tenant but not yet paid.
c.	_____	A customer pays in advance for services to be rendered.
d.	_____	Salaries earned by employees are not yet paid.
e.	_____	Computers are purchased.
f.	_____	Interest earned on an investment is not due to be received until next year.
g.	_____	Membership to a golf club is paid in advance.
h.	_____	A golf club receives membership fees in advance.

E3-7. **(Recording transactions using an accounting equation spreadsheet, LO 2)** Set up an accounting equation spreadsheet and enter each of the following independent economic events into the spreadsheet.

a. A car is purchased for $25,000 cash.

b. A car is purchased for $15,000 cash and $10,000 financed through the dealer.

c. A corporation sells shares to investors for $100,000.

d. A corporation pays dividends to shareholders of $1,000,000.

e. A corporation declares dividends of $1,000,000. The dividends will be paid in 30 days.

f. A corporation pays $1,000,000 of dividends that were previously declared.

g. A company sells goods to a customer for $300 cash. The goods cost $200. (Hint: the company records the reduction in inventory and cost of sales at the time the sale is recorded.)

h. A company sells goods to a customer for $300. The goods cost $200. The customer promises to pay in 30 days. (Hint: the company records the reduction in inventory and cost of sales at the time the sale is recorded.)

i. A company collects $1,000 that is due from a customer.

E3-8. **(Recording transactions using journal entries, LO 3)** For each of the events described in Exercise E3-7, make the journal entry necessary to record the event.

E3-9. **(Recording transactions using an accounting equation spreadsheet, LO 2)** Set up an accounting equation spreadsheet and enter each of the following independent economic events into the spreadsheet:

a. A company pays $5,000 in cash to consultants for services provided in the current period.

b. A company buys equipment and the vendor takes a note payable for the full amount of $300,000. The note must be repaid in two years.

c. A company purchases inventory for $100,000. The company will pay in 30 days.

d. A partnership exchanges land worth $1,000,000 for machinery worth the same amount.

e. A proprietorship repays a $10,000 bank loan plus $1,000 interest on the loan.

f. An employee earns $5,000 in commissions for selling products during the month. The commission will be paid in one month.

g. A company pays a $5,000 deposit to a law firm that will provide legal services next year.

h. A company receives a $3,000 deposit from a customer for services that will be provided next year.

E3-10. **(Recording transactions using journal entries, LO 3)** For each of the events described in Exercise E3-9, make the journal entry necessary to record the event.

E3-11. **(Calculate inventory related amounts, LO 4)** In each of the following situations, calculate the missing information.

a. Beginning inventory = $ 312,500
   Purchases = 1,312,500
   Ending inventory = 337,500
   Cost of goods sold =

b. Beginning inventory = 312,500
   Purchases = 1,312,500
   Ending inventory =
   Cost of goods sold = 1,487,500

c. Beginning inventory = 1,062,500
   Purchases =
   Ending inventory = 212,500
   Cost of goods sold = 2,437,500

E3-12. (**Explaining journal entries, LO 3, 4, 5**) Provide a description of the event represented by each of the following journal entries.

a.	Dr. Cash	1,000,000	
	Cr. Land		1,000,000
b.	Dr. Accounts receivable	20,000	
	Cr. Revenue		20,000
c.	Dr. Cash	7,500,000	
	Cr. Capital stock		7,500,000
d.	Dr. Capital assets—equipment	350,000	
	Cr. Notes payable		350,000
e.	Dr. Rent expense	5,000	
	Cr. Prepaid rent		5,000
f.	Dr. Unearned revenue	10,000	
	Cr. Revenue		10,000
g.	Dr. Accounts payable	15,000	
	Cr. Cash		15,000
h.	Dr. Supplies expense	2,000	
	Cr. Supplies inventory		2,000

E3-13. (**Explaining journal entries, LO 3, 4, 5**) Provide a description of the event represented by each of the following journal entries.

a.	Dr. Equipment	1,100,000	
	Cr. Cash		350,000
	Cr. Notes payable		750,000
b.	Dr. Interest receivable	25,000	
	Cr. Interest revenue		25,000
c.	Dr. Cash	1,500,000	
	Dr. Long-term receivable	3,500,000	
	Cr. Land		5,000,000
d.	Dr. Wages expense	8,500	
	Cr. Wages payable		8,500
e.	Dr. Sales commissions	21,000	
	Cr. Commissions payable		21,000
f.	Dr. Bond payable	250,000	
	Cr. Capital stock		250,000
g.	Dr. Cash	35,000	
	Cr. Revenue		25,000
	Cr. Unearned revenue		10,000
h.	Dr. Rent expense	2,500	
	Cr. Prepaid rent		2,500

E3-14. (**Recording economic events in an accounting equation spreadsheet and preparing financial statements, LO 2, 4, 5, 6**) Fitness For All Ltd. is a new health club operating in a suburb of Winnipeg. The following transactions take place in September and October 2009:

i. September 1: Fitness For All Ltd. is incorporated. The owner pays $125,000 for 5,000 shares of company stock.

ii. September 3: Fitness For All Ltd. signs a three-year lease for space for the club in a strip mall. The owner pays $3,000 cash in rent for October and November.

iii. September 3-20: Renovations on the location are carried out at a cost of $20,000 cash.

iv. September 21: Equipment worth $125,000 is purchased from a supplier. Fitness For All Ltd. pays $75,000 in cash and promises to pay the remainder in six months. The estimated life of the equipment is five years.

v. September 25: Supplies are purchased on credit for $5,000.

vi. During September and October: Memberships to the club are sold to 300 people at $350 per person. Members pay 50 percent immediately and promise to pay the remainder in 30 days. Fitness for All Ltd. records sales when a new member joins.

vii. During September and October: Employees are paid wages of $10,000. At the end of October Fitness For All Ltd. owes employees $1,200.

viii. During September and October: Utilities costing $2,000 are paid.

ix. During September and October: Fitness For All Ltd. pays $2,700 toward the supplies purchased on credit on September 25.

x. During September and October: Fitness For All Ltd. collects $30,000 owed by members.

xi. During September and October: $3,900 of supplies was used.

Required:

a. Use an accounting equation spreadsheet to record the transactions that occurred during September and October.

b. Make adjusting entries for amortization of equipment and renovations, expensing of rent, use of supplies, and wages owing to employees for September and October.

c. Make the closing entry.

d. Prepare the balance sheet as of October 31, 2009 and an income statement and statement of retained earnings for the period ending October 31, 2009.

E3-15. **(Recording adjusting entries, LO 2, 3, 5)** For each of the following situations prepare the required adjusting entries. Also show the related transactional entries and the date the entries would be made. Assume a December 31 year end. This question can be done using an accounting equation spreadsheet or journal entries.

a. On June 30 a company purchases a building for $10,000,000. The estimated life of the building is 25 years.

b. A company pays its salaried employees monthly, on the 15th of the month. On December 31 the company owes its employees $4,500.

c. On July 10 a company received a $10,000 deposit for services that were to be provided over the next 10 months, beginning on August 1. The services provided are worth the same amount each month.

d. On October 1 a company invested $100,000 in an investment account that pays interest of 6 percent per year, payable on March 31 and September 30.

e. On January 1 the office supplies account had a balance of $4,300. During the year office supplies costing $7,000 were purchased. A count of office supplies on December 31 found supplies worth $2,100 on hand.

E3-16. **(Recording adjusting entries, LO 2, 3, 5)** For each of the following situations prepare the required adjusting entries. Also show the related transactional entries and the date the entries would be made. Assume a July 31 year end. This question can be done using an accounting equation spreadsheet or journal entries.

a. On February 15 a company pays $100,000 in advance for goods that it will receive over the next six months. As of July 31, 60 percent of the goods had been received.

b. As of July 31 a company estimates that it owes $5,000 to its natural gas supplier for gas used in July. The company won't be billed until early September.

c. A company earns $5,000 per month in royalty revenue from another company that has rights to use one of the company's patents. The full amount for the year must be paid on December 31.

d. Amortization expense for the year is $125,000.

e. On September 1 a company purchased a one-year insurance policy for $6,000.

E3-17. **(Recording adjusting entries, LO 3, 5)** The account balances before and after the adjusting entries have been made are presented below for a number of accounts. For each account, prepare the adjusting entry that gave rise to the change in the account balance and provide an explanation for each entry.

Account	Balance before adjusting entry	Balance after adjusting entry
Accumulated amortization	$250,000	$320,000
Deposits from customers	20,000	15,000
Interest receivable	0	4,000
Interest payable	0	5,000
Prepaid insurance	16,000	10,000
Supplies inventory	30,000	16,000
Utilities payable	0	9,000

E3-18. (**Understanding the relationship between closing entries and the income statement, LO 6**) Below is the closing journal entry prepared by Bellburn Ltd. on December 31, 2009. Use the closing journal entry to prepare Bellburn Ltd.'s income statement for the year ended December 31, 2009.

Dr. Sales	650,000	
Dr. Interest revenue	3,000	
Cr. Retained earnings		112,000
Cr. Wage expense		125,000
Cr. Advertising expense		35,000
Cr. Amortization expense		25,000
Cr. Cost of goods sold		225,000
Cr. Selling and administrative expense		32,000
Cr. Interest expense		12,500
Cr. Rent expense		18,000
Cr. Income tax expense		59,000
Cr. Miscellaneous expense		9,500

E3-19. (**Evaluating the effect that not recording adjusting entries has on net income, LO 4, 5**) For each of the following situations, indicate whether not recording the necessary adjusting entry will result in (i) an overstatement of net income (net income is higher than it would otherwise be), (ii) an understatement of net income (net income is lower than it would otherwise be), or (iii) no effect on net income. Provide an explanation for your conclusion.

a. Amortization expense is not recorded.

b. Interest is earned on a bond but the cash will not be received until next year. The interest earned is not recorded.

c. A company takes a deposit from a customer for services that will be provided in the following year. When the services are provided in the following year the company does not make an adjusting entry.

d. A company purchases a two-year insurance policy on the first day of the year and records the purchase as prepaid insurance. At the end of the year no adjustment is made to reflect the portion of the policy that was consumed.

e. Interest on a loan that is incurred but is not payable until next month is not recorded.

f. Wages are earned by employees in the last week of the year but will not be paid until next year. The wages earned are not recorded.

E3-20. (**Using an accounting equation spreadsheet to determine the opening balance in an account, LO 2**) The chief financial officer of Afton Ltd. (Afton) is trying to determine the amount of cash the company had on hand one month ago on March 1, 2010. A problem with the company's computer system resulted in the loss of the information. Use an accounting equation spreadsheet and the following information to determine the information the chief financial officer requires. Afton Ltd. had a cash balance of $125,000 on March 31, 2010.

a. On March 15 Afton purchased equipment costing $100,000 by paying $20,000 in cash and promising to pay the remainder in 90 days.

b. On March 20 Afton made payments of $10,000 on its bank loan.

c. During March Afton had sales of $175,000. $25,000 of the sales were for cash, the rest on credit.

d. During March Afton collected $110,000 from customers who had made credit purchases and paid suppliers $90,000.

e. During March Afton paid employees $32,000.

f. During March Afton had other cash revenue of $4,500 and other cash expenses of $8,000.

E3-21. (**Using an accounting equation spreadsheet to determine missing information, LO 2**) Use an accounting equation spreadsheet and the following information to determine the amount of credit sales to customers that occurred during November 2009:

a. On November 1, 2009 the balance in the accounts receivable account was $350,000.

b. During November, 2009, $410,000 was collected from customers.

c. The balance in the accounts receivable account on November 30, 2009 was $380,000.

E3-22. (**Using an accounting equation spreadsheet to determine missing information, LO 2**) Use an accounting equation spreadsheet and the following information to determine the amount paid to suppliers during June 2010:

a. On June 1, 2010 the balance in the accounts payable account was $150,000.

b. During June 2010, there were credit purchases from suppliers of $760,000.

c. The balance in the accounts payable account on June 30, 2010 was $180,000.

E3-23. (**Effect of adjustments on financial ratios, LO 4, 5**) For each of the following adjusting entries, state whether the entry increases, decreases, or has no effect on the following financial ratios: current ratio, debt-to-equity ratio, profit margin ratio, and return on equity. Assume that the current ratio and debt-to-equity ratio are greater than one and the profit margin ratio and return on equity are less than one before each of the adjusting entries is considered.

a. Dr. Amortization expense	10,000	
Cr. Accumulated amortization		10,000
b. Dr. Unearned revenue	5,000	
Cr. Revenue		5,000
c. Dr. Interest receivable	2,000	
Cr. Interest revenue		2,000
d. Dr. Utilities expense	500	
Cr. Accrued utility expense payable		500
e. Dr. Rent expense	1,000	
Cr. Prepaid rent		1,000

E3-24. (**Effect of adjustments on financial ratios, LO 4, 5**) Examine the adjusting entries provided in exercise E3-23. Indicate the impact that **not** making each of the entries would have on the following financial ratios: current ratio, debt-to-equity ratio, profit margin ratio, and return on equity. Assume that the current ratio and debt-to-equity ratio are greater than one and the profit margin ratio and return on equity are less than one before each of the adjusting entries is considered.

E3-25. (**Correcting errors, LO 2, 3, 4**) Zhoda Ltd. (Zhoda) has been having problems with its bookkeeper. Recently errors have been observed in the bookkeeper's work. Examine each of the items below and make any journal entry that is necessary to correct the entries originally made. This question can also be answered using an accounting equation spreadsheet.

a. Zhoda received an advance from a customer for work that was going to be done in the next fiscal year. The bookkeeper debited Cash and credited Revenue for $10,000.

b. Zhoda sold shares to investors for $200,000. The bookkeeper debited Cash and credited Revenue for $200,000.

c. Zhoda purchased four computers for $10,000. The bookkeeper debited Computer Expense and credited Cash for $10,000.

d. Zhoda paid a supplier $5,000 for services previously received. The bookkeeper debited Services Expense and credited Cash.

E3-26. **(Correcting errors, LO 2, 3, 4)** Examine the accounting errors described in Exercise E3-25. For each error explain the impact the error (and failure to correct the error) would have on the financial statements.

E3-27. **(Correcting errors, LO 2, 3, 4)** Grosswerder Ltd. (Grosswerder) has been having problems with its bookkeeper. Recently errors have been found in the bookkeeper's work. Examine each of the items below and make any journal entry that is necessary to correct the entries originally made. This question can also be answered using an accounting equation spreadsheet.
a. Grosswerder received a $3,000 payment from a customer for goods previously delivered. The bookkeeper debited Cash and credited Revenue.
b. Grosswerder repaid $100,000 of its long-term debt. The bookkeeper debited Interest Expense and credited Cash.
c. Grosswerder paid a dividend to shareholders of $50,000. The bookkeeper debited Dividend Expense and credited Cash for $50,000.
d. Grosswerder purchased a $1,500 insurance policy that would provide coverage in the next fiscal year. The bookkeeper debited Insurance Expense and credited Cash.

E3-28. **(Correcting errors, LO 2, 3, 4)** Examine the accounting errors described in Exercise E3-27. For each error explain the impact the error (and failure to correct the error) would have on the financial statements.

E3-29. **(Preparing a balance sheet and income statement using a trial balance, LO 3, 4, 6)**
Below is Kuskonook Inc.'s (Kuskonook) December 31, 2009 trial balance that was prepared before the closing journal entry was recorded. Use the trial balance to prepare Kuskonook's balance sheet as of December 31, 2009 and the income statement for the year ended December 31, 2009. The accounts in the trial balance are listed alphabetically.

Kuskonook Inc.
Trial Balance
December 31, 2009

Account	Debit	Credit
Accounts payable	$	$ 200,000
Accounts receivable	125,000	
Accrued liabilities		18,000
Accumulated amortization		825,000
Amortization expense	250,000	
Bank loan payable		150,000
Buildings	3,000,000	
Capital stock		1,250,000
Cash	25,000	
Cost of sales	2,445,000	
Current portion of long-term debt		300,000
Furniture and equipment	2,075,000	
Income tax expense	350,000	
Income taxes payable		15,000
Interest expense	180,000	
Interest payable		12,000
Inventory	224,000	
Land	750,000	
Loan receivable	48,000	
Long-term debt		2,100,000
Long-term loan receivable	110,000	
Other expenses	182,000	
Prepaid assets	18,000	
Retained earnings		808,000
Revenue		5,750,000
Selling, general, and administrative expense	725,000	
Wages and salaries expense	950,000	
Wages and salaries payable		29,000
	$11,457,000	$11,457,000

Problems

P3-1. (**Prepare adjusting entries, LO 3, 5**) For each of the following situations provide the necessary adjusting entries for Truax Ltd. (Truax) for the year ended June 30, 2010. (These situations are tricky. When preparing each adjusting entry, compare what is recorded in the accounting system before you make your entry with what you think should be in the accounting system. Your adjusting entry should take the accounting system from "what is" recorded to "what should be" recorded.)

a. On January 2, 2010 Truax purchased a two-year insurance policy for $15,000 cash. The transactional journal entry debited Insurance Expense for $15,000 and credited Cash for $15,000.

b. On April 1, 2010 Truax received $25,000 for goods that it would produce and deliver to a customer. Truax would deliver $5,000 of the goods each month beginning in May 2010. Truax recorded the transaction by debiting Cash for $25,000 and crediting Revenue for $25,000.

c. On March 1, 2010, Truax invested $100,000 of surplus cash in a one-year investment certificate that paid 0.5 percent per month. The $100,000 initial investment plus the interest of $6,000 were to be paid on February 28, 2011. On March 1, 2010 Truax recorded the investment by debiting Investments for $100,000 and crediting Cash for $100,000. It also debited Interest Receivable for $6,000 and credited Interest Revenue for $6,000.

P3-2. (**Prepare adjusting entries, LO 3, 5**) For each of the following situations provide the necessary adjusting entries for Carberry Inc. for the year ended December 31, 2009. (These situations are tricky. When preparing each adjusting entry, compare what is recorded in the accounting system before you make your entry with what you think should be in the accounting system. Your adjusting entry should take the accounting system from "what is" recorded to "what should be" recorded.)

a. On April 1, 2009, Carberry Inc. paid $25,000 cash for the right to use a vacant lot to store some of its equipment for the next two years. The transactional journal entry debited Prepaid Rent for $25,000 and credited Cash for $25,000.

b. On November 1, 2009, Carberry Inc. received $10,000 as an advance for services to be rendered in 2010. Carberry Inc. recorded the transaction by debiting Cash for $10,000 and crediting Revenue for $10,000.

c. On July 2, 2009, Carberry Inc. purchased equipment with a five-year life for $50,000. Carberry Inc. debited Equipment Expense and credited Cash to record the transaction.

P3-3. (**The effect of different lease arrangements on the financial statements, LO 3, 4, 5**) Liscomb Consulting is a partnership of business consultants located in Halifax. The company has been successful since it began business five years ago and the partners have decided to move into new offices. On August 20, 2010, the partners came to terms with a property owner and signed a three-year lease for space at a prestigious address. Liscomb Consulting occupied its new offices on September 1, 2010. Monthly rent is $1,000. For each situation below show what would appear on Liscomb Consulting's balance sheet and income statement if these statements were prepared on September 1, 2010 and on September 30, 2010. For each situation show all journal entries prepared in August and September 2010. Indicate whether each journal entry is a transactional or adjusting journal entry. Consider each situation separately.

a. On August 20, 2010 Liscomb Consulting pays the property owner rent for September and agrees to pay each month's rent on the first day of the month (so October's rent is due on October 1).

b. The property owner agrees to allow Liscomb Consulting to pay its rent in arrears so that the rent is due on the first day of the next month (so September's payment is due October 1, and so on).

c. The property owner agrees to allow Liscomb Consulting to pay its rent on the 15th of each month. The first month's rent is paid August 20 (so the payment on September 15 is for October).

d. The property owner agrees to allow Liscomb Consulting to pay its rent on the 15th of each month. The first month's rent is paid on September 15 (so the payment on September 15 is for September).

P3-4. **(The effect of different lease arrangements on the financial statements, LO 3, 4, 5)** Kashabowie Properties Ltd. (Kashabowie) owns and operates several commercial real estate properties in Halifax. On August 20, 2009 Kashabowie signed a three-year lease with a consulting firm for space in one of its buildings. Monthly rent is $1,000. For each situation below show what would appear on Kashabowie's balance sheet and income statement if these statements were prepared on September 1, 2009 and on September 30, 2009. For each situation show all journal entries prepared in August and September 2009. Indicate whether each journal entry is a transactional or adjusting journal entry.

a. On August 20, 2009 Kashabowie receives the $1,000 rent payment for September. The lease agreement requires the consulting firm to pay each month's rent on the first day of the month (so October's rent is due on October 1).

b. Kashabowie agrees to allow the consulting firm to pay its rent in arrears so that its rent is due on the first day of the next month (so September's payment is due October 1 and so on).

c. Kashabowie agrees to allow the consulting firm to pay its rent on the 15th of each month. The first month's rent is paid on August 20 (so the payment on September 15 is for October).

d. Kashabowie agrees to allow the consulting firm to pay its rent on the 15th of each month. The first month's rent is paid on September 15 (so the payment on September 15 is for September).

P3-5. **(Understanding the effect of errors on the elements of the accounting equation, LO 4, 5)** For each of the following situations, state how the recording errors affect the amount of assets, liabilities, owners' equity, revenues, and expenses reported in the 2010 financial statements. Indicate whether assets, liabilities, equity, revenues, and expenses are overstated (too high), understated (too low), or unaffected by the error. Assume that the year end is June 30. Briefly explain why the effects occur and state any assumptions that you make.

a. On January 3, 2010 a company purchased a new delivery truck for $35,000. The company estimates the truck will be used for five years. No adjusting entry was made at year end.

b. On June 15, 2010 a sports fan purchased seasons tickets for her city's hockey team's games for $6,000 cash. The hockey season begins in October and the team recognizes its revenue when the hockey games are played. The bookkeeper credited revenue for $6,000 when the cash was received.

c. On June 30, 2010 no entry was made to reflect the use of water during June. The water bill will not be received until late August. In June 2009, the company used $5,000 of water and the managers estimate that about the same amount of water was used this year.

d. On September 1, 2009 a company borrowed $1,000,000 from a private lender. The interest rate on the loan is 6 percent per year. Interest must be paid on August 31 and February 28 of each year. The loan principal must be paid in full on August 31, 2014. No adjusting entry was made by the borrower with respect to the loan and interest on June 30, 2010.

e. On April 17, 2010 a $7,970 cash expenditure for capital assets was recorded as $9,770.

P3-6. **(Understanding the effect of errors on the elements of the accounting equation, LO 4, 5)** For each of the following situations, state how the recording errors affect the amount of assets, liabilities, owners' equity, revenues, and expenses reported in the 2010 financial statements. Indicate whether assets, liabilities, equity, revenues, and expenses are overstated (too high), understated (too low), or unaffected by the error. Assume that the year end is December 31. Briefly explain why the effects occur and state any assumptions that you make.

a. On January 3, 2010 a three-year insurance policy was purchased for $9,000 cash. The bookkeeper debited Prepaid Insurance for $9,000 when the policy was purchased. No adjusting entry was made at year end.

b. On December 15, 2010 $400 was received from a customer paying in advance for lawn care services that were going to be provided in 2011. The bookkeeper credited Revenue for $400 when the cash was received.

c. On December 31, 2010 no entry was made to reflect the use of electricity during the month of December. The bill for electricity will not be received until late February. In December 2009 the company used $2,000 of electricity and management estimates that about the same amount was used this year.

d. On September 1, 2010 the company invested $1,000,000 in government bonds that pay interest on September 1 and March 1 of each year. The interest rate is 5 percent per year. No adjusting entry was made.

e. On July 17, 2010 a $5,750 cash expense for casual labour was recorded as $7,570.

P3-7. **(Using the accounting equation spreadsheet to record transactions and prepare financial statements, LO 1, 2, 5, 6)** Paul Byrne is a first-year student in a business program in Toronto. Toward the end of the academic year he was approached by a friend who offered to sell him his hot dog vending cart. The friend was finishing his university studies and was going to be starting a permanent job in the summer, so he no longer needed the cart. Paul thought about the offer for a few days and decided to buy the cart. He thought that it would be a way to make money to finance his education and learn how to manage a business at the same time.

Paul operated his business from late April, when the weather started to warm up, to early September, when it was time to get back to school. Paul was so busy running the business, he had no time to keep any accounting records. So on September 10, after he had put away the cart until the next year, he sat down with all the data he had carefully collected throughout the summer about his business and placed in a shoebox. From the information in the shoebox he obtained the following:

a. On April 1, Paul opened a bank account in the name of his company Paul's Dogs. He deposited $2,000 from his bank account into the account. Paul decided he would operate the business as a proprietorship. (Remember, in a proprietorship the owners' equity section of the balance sheet includes only a single account called Owner's Equity or Owner's Capital. This is different from a corporation where there will be a Capital Stock account and a Retained Earnings account.)

b. Paul purchased the cart from his friend on April 8 for $1,500. He gave his friend $1,000 in cash and promised to pay him the rest at the end of the summer. The cart was already four years old and Paul's friend said it should be good for another three or four years, after which time it would probably be junk.

c. Paul took the cart to a repair shop. He had the cart painted, serviced, and repaired. Paul paid the shop $300 in cash.

d. Paul went to city hall and obtained a licence to operate his cart in the city. The license cost $250 and Paul paid with his debit card. The licence is valid for two years and expires at the end of the next calendar year.

e. During the summer Paul sold hot dogs and drinks for $15,750.

f. In late August Paul was asked to bring his cart to a softball tournament where he would be the official supplier of hot dogs to participants. The agreement was that Paul would keep track of the hot dogs and drinks he handed out to the players and send a bill to the tournament organizers. At the end of the tournament Paul sent a bill to the organizers for $1,115. The organizers said they would pay on September 20.

g. During the summer Paul bought hot dogs, buns, drinks, condiments, napkins, plastic cutlery, paper plates, and other supplies for $8,525. All of these items were paid for in cash.

h. At the end of the summer Paul had about $750 in non-perishable items stored in his basement at home (he had used $7,775 of the supplies he had bought).

i. On several days during the summer Paul was unable to operate the cart himself. On those days he hired his brother to do it. During the entire summer Paul paid his brother $375 cash. As of today Paul still owes him $75.

j. During the summer Paul incurred $1,000 in other expenses. All of these were paid in cash.

k. On August 15 Paul withdrew $1,500 from the business to pay for tuition and other school-related items.

l. On September 5 Paul paid his friend the $500 he owed him.

Required:

a. Enter each of the transactions onto an accounting equation spreadsheet. You can use a computer spreadsheet program or create a spreadsheet manually, although the computer spreadsheet will probably be easier because you will be able to correct mistakes more easily. Create a separate column on the spreadsheet for each account.

b. Provide explanations for each of your entries. You should explain why you have treated the economic events as you have (that is, why you have recorded an asset, liability, etc.).

c. Prepare a balance sheet as of September 10 and an income statement for the period ended September 10 from your spreadsheet. Make sure to make a closing entry.

d. Explain why the financial statements you have prepared would be useful to Paul.

e. If Paul asked you for some feedback on his business from examining the financial statements, what would you be able to tell him from your examination?

P3-8. **(Using the accounting equation spreadsheet to record transactions and prepare financial statements, LO 1, 2, 5, 6)** We've Got Wheels, Inc. (Wheels) was formed on May 1, 2008 by two university friends who thought they could make money renting bikes and inline skates to visitors at a busy lake-front area near their homes. The friends thought the business would be a good way to spend their summer near the beach while making enough money to finance next year's university costs. If the business is successful the friends hope to operate it for as long as they attend university.

The two owners closed down Wheels for the year after the Labour Day weekend. It was a very hectic summer and they didn't have nearly as much time to have fun as they thought they would. They were also so busy that they didn't pay much attention to keeping any accounting records. They did, however, keep all the receipts, invoices, and deposit slips that accumulated over the summer.

It is now September 10. The owners have asked you to compile useful information about Wheels for them. After summarizing the data they provided, you have the following information for the summer of 2008:

i. May 1: Each friend contributed $7,500 in cash to Wheels in exchange for stock in the company.

ii. May 5: Purchased 15 new and used bicycles for a total of $5,250. Wheels agreed to pay $3,000 immediately and the remainder on September 30, 2008. The owners think the bikes will last for at least three summers, after which time they will no longer be useful for the business.

iii. May 9: Obtained a permit to operate a business at the lake. The cost of the permit was $75 for the summer.

iv. May 10: Purchased 25 sets of inline skates and 25 sets of protective equipment for $3,375 in cash. The owners think that the most they will get out of this equipment is about two summers of use.

v. During the summer: Wheels rented bicycles and skates to customers for $20,813 cash.

vi. During the summer: Purchased packaged snacks for $900 cash. At the end of the summer there were $206 of snacks left over. The snacks were sold to customers through the summer for $1,350 cash.

vii. During the summer: Purchased advertising on a local radio station. Advertising was paid for by cheque once an ad was played. Total amount spent during the summer was $675. Nothing was owing at the end of the Labour Day weekend.

viii. During the summer: Wheels provided inline skating lessons to children on behalf of the local Parks and Recreation Department. Wheels billed the department $3,375 for the lessons. As of September 10, $1,125 was still owed to Wheels. The amount owed is due on October 15.

ix. During the summer: Wheels incurred other expenses amounting to $9,525. All were paid in cash.

x. During the summer: The owners took $3,750 each to meet their personal needs.

Required:

a. Enter each of the transactions onto an accounting equation spreadsheet. You can use a computer spreadsheet program or create a spreadsheet manually, although the computer spreadsheet will probably be easier because you will be able to correct mistakes more easily. Create a separate column on the spreadsheet for each account.

b. Provide explanations for each of your entries. You should explain why you have treated the economic events as you have (that is, why you have recorded an asset, liability, etc.).

c. Prepare a balance sheet as of September 10, 2008 and an income statement for the period ended September 10, 2008 from your spreadsheet. Make sure to make a closing entry.

d. Explain why the financial statements you have prepared would be useful to the owners of Wheels.

e. Compare Wheels' net income with the amount of cash that was generated by the business. Which is a better indicator of how Wheels did? Why are they different? (When looking at the cash flow, consider the cash flows after the owners made their initial $15,000 investment.)

f. If Wheels' owners asked you to evaluate the financial statements for them, what would you be able to tell them based on your evaluation?

P3-9.   **(Using the accounting equation spreadsheet to record transactions and prepare financial statements, LO 1, 2, 5, 6)** Austin Chhor is the owner and operator of Austin's Appliance Emporium Ltd. (AAEL), Yarksis' largest independent household appliance store. AAEL supplies appliances to retail customers as well as to builders of the many new homes and apartments that are going up in the community. Sales to builders have grown substantially in the last year. AAEL has been in business for five years and Austin has been happy with its performance.

AAEL's balance sheet for August 31, 2009, the company's year end, is shown below. Austin uses the financial statements mainly for tax purposes and to show the holders of the long-term notes.

Austin's Appliances Emporium Ltd.
Balance Sheet
As of August 31, 2009

Assets		Liabilities and shareholders' equity	
Cash	$ 60,000	Accounts payable	$ 530,000
Accounts receivable	246,000	Taxes payable	40,000
Inventory	893,000	Interest payable	17,000
Prepaids	28,000	Long-term notes payable	200,000
Furniture and fixtures	380,000	Capital stock	220,000
Accumulated amortization	(80,000)	Retained earnings	520,000
	$1,527,000		$1,527,000

It is now mid-September 2010. AAEL needs to prepare its financial statements for the year ended August 31, 2010. The following information has been obtained about the fiscal year just ended:

i.   AAEL purchased appliances from suppliers for $1,700,000. All purchases were made on credit.

ii. Sales during the year were $2,700,000. Cash sales were $1,550,000. The remainder was on credit, mainly to builders.

iii. The cost of the appliances sold during fiscal 2010 was $1,490,000.

iv. AAEL paid salaries and commissions to employees of $400,000. On August 31, 2010, employees were owed $15,000 by AAEL.

v.   AAEL collected $750,000 during the year from customers who purchased on credit.

vi. AAEL paid suppliers $1,200,000 for appliances it purchased on credit.

vii. During the year AAEL paid the taxes it owed at the end of fiscal 2009. During fiscal 2010 AAEL paid $30,000 in instalments on its 2010 taxes. At year end it is estimated that AAEL owes an additional $24,000 in taxes.

viii. AAEL accepted $20,000 in deposits from customers who wanted a guarantee that their appliances would be delivered when they needed them. The deposits pertained to a particularly hard-to-get appliance. AAEL expects that the appliances will be delivered in early November 2010.

ix. Beginning July 1, 2010 AAEL pays $8,000 a month for the rent of its store. The terms of the lease require that rent be paid six months in advance on January 1 and July 1 of each year. Before July 1, 2010 AAEL paid $7,000 a month in rent. In addition, the new lease requires that AAEL must pay 2 percent of annual sales to the property owner 60 days after the year end (this was not required under the old lease).

x.   Austin recently redecorated his kitchen at home. He took a refrigerator, stove, and microwave that cost $9,000 from the store and installed them in his new kitchen.

xi. During 2010 AAEL purchased new capital assets (furniture and fixtures) for $50,000 cash.

xii. Amortization expense for 2010 is $44,000.

xiii. During the year AAEL paid $17,000 in interest to the holders of the long-term notes. Interest is paid annually on September 1. In addition to the interest payment, AAEL paid $40,000 on September 1, 2009 to reduce the balance owed on the long-term notes. The interest rate on the notes is 8.5 percent.

xiv. AAEL paid $450,000 in cash for other expenses related to operating the business in fiscal 2010.

Required:

a. Enter each transaction onto an accounting equation spreadsheet. Create a separate column on the spreadsheet for each account. Make sure to prepare all adjusting entries and the closing entry to the spreadsheet. Indicate whether each entry to the spreadsheet is a transactional entry, an adjusting entry or a closing entry.

b. Provide explanations for each of your entries. You should explain why you have treated the economic events as you have (that is, why you have recorded an asset, liability, etc.).

c. Prepare a balance sheet, an income statement, and a statement of retained earnings from your spreadsheet.

d. Austin is considering expanding AAEL to include a wider range of products. Austin has approached you about purchasing common shares of AAEL to help finance the expansion. Based on your examination of the statements, what can you tell about AAEL that would be useful to your decision to invest? Also, list five questions you might ask Austin that would help you use the financial statements more effectively.

P3-10. (Using the accounting equation spreadsheet to record transactions and prepare financial statements, LO 1, 2, 5, 6) Majestic Trucking Inc. (Majestic) is a small trucking company that carries freight between centres in central Canada and the northeastern United States. The Mozart family of Cobourg owns Majestic, but professional managers manage it. One member of the Mozart family serves as the chair of the board of directors. No other family members are actively involved with Majestic.

Majestic's balance sheet for December 31, 2009, the company's year end, is shown below. Majestic uses its financial statements for tax purposes, to show to the holders of the long-term notes that the company issued to finance the purchase of some of its trucks, and to provide information to the shareholders.

Majestic Trucking Inc.
Balance Sheet
As of December 31, 2009

Assets		Liabilities and Shareholders' Equity	
Cash	$ 77,340	Accounts payable	$ 42,220
Accounts receivable	81,500	Taxes payable	15,000
Prepaid insurance	18,000	Wages payable	10,000
Capital assets	465,000	Customer deposits	27,000
Accumulated amortization	(201,700)	Interest payable	11,900
		Long-term notes payable	140,000
		Capital stock	80,000
		Retained earnings	114,020
	$440,140		$440,140

It is now January 2011. Majestic needs to prepare its financial statements for the year ended December 31, 2010. The following information has been obtained about the fiscal year just ended:

i. Shipping revenue for the year was $1,065,225. Majestic gives credit to all its customers and there were no cash sales during the year.

ii. Majestic purchased $275,000 worth of fuel during the year. All purchases were on credit. At the end of 2010 Majestic had not been billed for an additional $10,000 of fuel that it purchased.

iii. Majestic incurred maintenance costs of $125,000 during 2010. At the end of 2010 Majestic owed mechanics $8,000.

iv. Majestic paid salaries and bonuses of $475,000 to employees. At December 31, 2010 Majestic owed employees $27,500.

v. During the year Majestic collected $1,075,000 from customers.

vi. Majestic paid its fuel suppliers $250,000 during 2010.

vii. During the year Majestic paid the taxes it owed at the end of 2009. It also paid $11,000 in instalments on its 2010 income taxes. It is estimated that Majestic owes an additional $12,000 in income taxes for 2010.

viii. The deposits reported on the 2009 balance sheet pertained to customers who were perceived to be high risk and to whom Majestic was not prepared to offer credit. These customers were required to give deposits against shipping to be done during 2010. These customers used shipping services during 2010 in excess of the amount of the deposits. Majestic decided in 2010 to offer credit to these customers.

ix. Members of the Mozart family sometimes used Majestic employees for personal work at their homes and cottages. Usually the work was done on weekends and the employees were paid at overtime rates. Majestic pays the employees' wages for the work done for the family members and accounts for the cost as a wage expense. The wages paid for work done on behalf of Mozart family members was $11,000.

x. During 2010 Majestic purchased a new truck for $98,000 in cash.

xi. Amortization expense for 2010 was $48,000.

xii. Prepaid insurance pertains to insurance on its truck fleet and premises. During 2010 it used $15,000 of insurance that was recorded as prepaid on December 31, 2009. In late 2010 Majestic purchased and paid for insurance for 2011. The insurance cost $21,000.

xiii. During the year Majestic paid $11,900 in interest to the holders of the long-term notes. Interest is paid annually on January 2. In addition to the interest payment, Majestic paid $20,000 on January 2, 2010 to reduce the balance owed on the long-term notes. The interest rate on the notes is 8.5 percent.

xiv. Majestic paid $75,000 in cash for other expenses related to operating the business in fiscal 2010.

xv. Majestic paid dividends of $55,000 to shareholders.

Required:

a. Enter each of the transactions onto an accounting equation spreadsheet. You can use a computer spreadsheet program or create a spreadsheet manually, although the computer spreadsheet will probably be easier because you will be able to correct mistakes more easily. Create a separate column on the spreadsheet for each account. Make sure to prepare all adjusting entries and the closing entry to the spreadsheet. Indicate whether each entry to the spreadsheet is a transactional entry, an adjusting entry or a closing entry.

b. Provide explanations for each of your entries. You should explain why you have treated the economic events as you have (that is, why you have recorded an asset, liability, etc.).

c. Prepare a balance sheet as of December 31, 2010 and an income statement for the year ended December 31, 2010 from your spreadsheet.

d. The North American economy is booming and there is a lot of work for shipping companies like Majestic. However, the competition is fierce and success and failure are defined by how efficient a company is and how well it services its customers. Majestic's managers would like to upgrade its fleet by adding two new trucks and making significant improvements to its existing vehicles. Based on your examination of the statements, what can you tell about Majestic that would be useful to your decision to lend it $125,000? Also, list five questions you might ask Majestic's management that would help you use the financial statements more effectively.

P3-11. **(Using the accounting equation spreadsheet to record transactions and prepare financial statements, LO 1, 2, 5, 6)** Gary's Computer Maintenance Ltd. (GCML) is a small computer repair shop owned and operated by Gary Armstrong. Gary's wife Susan is a 50 percent shareholder in GCML but she is not involved in the operations of the company. GCML has been in business for three years since being incorporated in 2006. Because he has been so busy recently and lacks expertise in financial matters, Gary has asked you to prepare the financial statements for GCML for 2009. Gary provides you with the company's balance sheet for the year ended December 31, 2008 and the following information about GCML's activities in the year.

Information about GCML's activities during 2009:

1. In August 2009 GCML signed a lease for a new shop on the main street in town. Monthly rent is $1,200. GCML paid six months' rent in advance when it signed the lease. The lease came into effect when GCML occupied the new shop on November 1, 2009. GCML paid rent of $10,000 in cash from January though October 2009 for its previous location.

2. During 2009 GCML earned revenues of $188,000. Credit sales accounted for $56,000 of the revenues earned.

3. GCML purchased capital assets for $12,000 cash during 2009.

4. During 2009 GCML purchased inventory of parts and supplies for $52,000. All inventory purchases were on credit.

5. During 2009 GCML collected $65,000 in amounts due from customers.

6. GCML paid suppliers $24,000 for inventory it purchased during 2009. It also paid $26,000 to suppliers for amounts owing on December 31, 2008.

Gary's Computer Maintenance Ltd.
Balance Sheet
As of December 31, 2008

Assets			Liabilities and Shareholders' Equity		
Current assets			**Current liabilities**		
Cash		$ 12,000	Bank loan		$ 15,000
Accounts receivable		47,000	Accounts payable		26,000
Inventory		38,000	Taxes payable		3,000
		97,000	Interest payable		400
					44,400
Non-current assets			**Shareholders' equity**		
Capital assets		22,000	Capital stock		30,000
Accumulated amortization		(10,000)	Retained earnings		34,600
		12,000			64,600
Total assets		$109,000	Total liabilities and shareholders' equity		$109,000

7. On March 2, 2009 GCML borrowed an additional $8,000 from the bank.
8. During 2009 GCML paid cash dividends of $30,000 to its shareholders.
9. GMCL paid employees salaries of $45,000. In addition, Gary was paid a salary of $25,000. All salaries paid pertained to work done in 2009. At the end of 2009 GMCL owed employees $1,000.
10. During 2009 GMCL incurred other expenses of $27,000, all paid in cash.
11. During the year GCML paid the $3,000 in taxes payable that was owing to the federal and provincial governments on December 31, 2008.
12. In December 2009 GCML signed a number of one-year contracts to provide ongoing 24-hour service to customers' computers at their places of business. All of the contracts take effect in January 2010. The customers paid $10,000 in cash to GCML in December 2009 as deposits against future services to be provided.
13. During 2009 GCML paid the bank $2,000 in interest. Of that amount, $1,600 pertained to 2009 and the remainder was owed to the bank from fiscal 2008. On December 31, 2009 GCML owed the bank $600 in interest, which will be paid in March 2010.
14. On December 31, 2009 Gary counted the inventory of parts and supplies on hand. His count showed that there was $41,000 of inventory on hand. (Use this information to figure out how much inventory was used during 2009.)
15. Amortization of capital assets was $5,000.
16. GCML will have to pay $3,200 in income taxes for the year. No payments had been made with respect to the fiscal 2009 year as of December 31, 2009.

P3-12

	Assets					=	Liabilities		
Transaction	Cash	Supplies Inventory	Prepaid Rent	Capital Assets	Accumulated Amortization		Accounts Payable	Unearned Revenue	Wages Payable
Balance before adjusting entries	$30,000	$22,000	$3,000	$40,000	($14,000)		$8,000	$14,000	
Balance after adjusting entries	$30,000	$10,000	$1,000	$40,000	($22,000)		$8,000	$6,000	$4,000

P3-13

	Assets					=	Liabilities		
Transaction	Cash	Inventory	Prepaid Insurance	Capital Assets	Accumulated Amortization		Bank Loan	Accounts Payable	Salaries Payable
Balance before adjusting entries	$50,000	$325,000	$25,000	$120,000	($44,000)		$58,000	$78,000	
Balance after adjusting entries	$50,000	$145,000	$15,000	$120,000	($69,000)		$58,000	$78,000	$12,000

Required:

a. Enter each of the transactions onto an accounting equation spreadsheet. You can use a computer spreadsheet program or create a spreadsheet manually, although the computer spreadsheet will probably be easier because you will be able to correct mistakes more easily. Create a separate column on the spreadsheet for each account. Make sure to prepare all adjusting entries and the closing entry to the spreadsheet. Indicate whether each entry to the spreadsheet is a transactional entry, an adjusting entry or a closing entry.

b. Provide explanations for each of your entries. You should explain why you have treated the economic events as you have (that is, why you have recorded an asset, liability, etc.).

c. Prepare a balance sheet as of December 31, 2009 and an income statement for the year ended December 31, 2009 from your spreadsheet.

d. Gary is pleased with the performance of his business and he is considering opening a second location. He would like to get another investor to purchase an equity interest in GCML and operate the new location. Based on your examination of the statements, what can you tell about GCML that would be useful to your decision to purchase an equity stake in GCML? Also, list five questions you might ask Gary that would help you use the financial statements more effectively.

P3-12. **(Reconstructing adjusting entries, LO 2, 4, 5)** The spreadsheet below provides the balances in Takhini Inc.'s accounts on December 31, 2009, before and after the adjusting entries have been made.

Required:

Reconstruct the adjusting entries that were made to Takhini Inc.'s spreadsheet on December 31, 2009.

P3-13. **(Reconstructing adjusting entries, LO 2, 4, 5)** The spreadsheet below provides the balances in Smithers Inc.'s accounts on May 31, 2010, before and after the adjusting entries have been made.

Required:

Reconstruct the adjusting entries that were made to Smithers Inc.'s spreadsheet on May 31, 2010.

+	Shareholders' Equity						
	Capital Stock	Retained Earnings	Services Revenue	Supplies Expense	Rent Expense	Wage Expense	Amortization Expense
	$10,000	$12,000	$58,000		$5,000	$16,000	
	$10,000	$12,000	$66,000	$12,000	$7,000	$20,000	$8,000

Liabilities (cont'd)		+			Shareholders' Equity					
Unearned Revenue	Interest Payable		Capital Stock	Retained Earnings	Revenue	Cost of Goods Sold	Insurance Expense	Salaries Expense	Interest Expense	Amortization Expense
$55,000			$50,000	$55,000	$258,000			$78,000		
$55,000	$6,000		$50,000	$55,000	$258,000	$180,000	$10,000	$90,000	$6,000	$25,000

P3-14. **(Evaluating the effect that not recording adjusting entries has on financial statements, LO 4, 5)** For each of the following economic events, indicate the effect that *not* recording the necessary adjusting entry at year end would have on the financial statements. Indicate whether not recording the required adjusting entry would result in:

    (i) an overstatement of assets, liabilities, owners' equity, or net income (they are higher than they would be otherwise),

    (ii) an understatement of assets, liabilities, owners' equity, or net income (they are lower than they would be otherwise), or

    (iii) no effect on assets, liabilities, owners' equity, or net income.

Provide an explanation for your conclusion and state any assumptions you make. Assume a December 31 year end. To respond it is necessary to determine the required journal entry.

a. Equipment costing $100,000 is purchased.

b. Work is performed for a customer who paid for the work in a previous period.

c. An investment in a long-term government bond pays interest on March 31 and September 30 of each year. (Consider this from the perspective of the entity investing in the bond.)

d. A company purchases a two-year insurance policy for $5,000. Coverage begins on July 1.

e. Wages earned by employees in the last week of the year are not paid until next year.

P3-15. **(Evaluating the effect that not recording adjusting entries has on financial statements, LO 4, 5)** For each of the following economic events, indicate the effect that *not* recording the necessary adjusting entry at year end would have on the financial statements. Indicate whether not recording the required adjusting entry would result in:

    (i) an overstatement of assets, liabilities, owners' equity, or net income (they are higher than they would be otherwise),

    (ii) an understatement of assets, liabilities, owners' equity, or net income (they are lower than they would be otherwise), or

    (iii) no effect on assets, liabilities, owners' equity, or net income.

Provide an explanation for your conclusion and state any assumptions you make. Assume a December 31 year end. To respond it is necessary to determine the required journal entry.

a. A travel company sells packaged vacations to customers in advance and recognizes revenue when the customer departs on the vacation.

b. An investment in a long-term corporate bond pays interest on March 31 and September 30 of each year. (Consider this from the perspective of the entity issuing the bond.)

c. On October 1 a tenant pays $12,000 to cover six months' rent. The tenant records the payment as prepaid rent.

d. A retail store pays a percentage of its sales as rent to the property owner. The payment is made three months after its year end, when the financial statements are released. (Respond from the property owner's perspective.)

e. A retail store pays a percentage of its sales as rent to the property owner. The payment is made three months after its year end, when the financial statements are released. (Respond from the retail store's perspective.)

P3-16. **(Understanding the effect of different estimates on net income, LO 4)** In 2009 Otis Knight opened a small business that he called The Corner Coffee Cart. The Corner Coffee Cart sells a variety of coffee-based beverages from a portable cart that Otis can move from place to place. Otis purchased the cart for $12,000 cash when he began the business.

All of The Corner Coffee Cart's transactions are for cash. Otis pays cash for all supplies and all sales to customers are for cash. At the end of 2009 Otis decided he wanted to get an idea about how well The Corner Coffee Cart performed in its first year. He assembled the following information:

i. Sales to customers $22,000 (all in cash)
ii. Cost of providing coffee to customers $13,000 (all in cash, includes coffee, milk, cups, stir sticks, etc.)

From this information Otis concluded that he had made $9,000, which he was satisfied with. A friend who had recently taken an accounting course told Otis that his profit of $9,000 was not correct because he did not amortize the cost of the coffee cart. Otis asked his friend to help him calculate the "correct" amount of profit based on the friend's knowledge of accounting.

Required:

a. Why did Otis's friend tell Otis that his measure of profit was not correct without an amortization expense for the cart? Do you agree with the friend's position?
b. If Otis assumes that the useful life of the cart is six years and he amortizes the cost of the cart using the straight-line method (an equal amount is expensed each year), what would The Corner Coffee Cart's net income for 2009 be? Assume that the cart would not have any value at the end of its life.
c. Calculate The Corner Coffee Cart's net income assuming that the cost of the cart is amortized over three years. Calculate net income assuming the cost of the cart is amortized over ten years. Assume straight-line amortization in both cases.
d. What is the difference in The Corner Coffee Cart's net income using the three different periods for amortizing the cart in (b) and (c)?
e. How is your evaluation of how The Corner Coffee Cart performed during 2009 affected by using different periods for amortizing the cart?
f. Assume that the different periods used for amortizing the cart simply represent different reasonable estimates of the cart's useful life. Is the actual performance of The Corner Coffee Cart really different even though the net income under each estimate is different? Explain.
g. What is the "correct" number of years over which to amortize the cart?

Appendix Problems

P3-17.   **(Following the steps of the accounting cycle, LO 1, 3, 5, 6)** Use the information provided in Problem P3-7 about Paul's Dogs to do the following:
a. Prepare all necessary journal entries until September 10.
b. Prepare T-accounts and post each journal entry to the appropriate T-account.
c. Prepare and post adjusting journal entries to their appropriate T-accounts. Adjusting entries are needed for the cart and the license.
d. Prepare a trial balance as of September 10.
e. Prepare a balance sheet for Paul's Dogs as of September 10 and an income statement covering the period until September 10.
f. Prepare the closing journal entry and post the closing entry to the appropriate T-accounts.
g. Prepare a trial balance as of September 10, after the closing entry has been prepared.
h. If Paul asked you for some feedback on his business from examining the financial statements, what would you be able to tell him from your examination?

P3-18. (**Following the steps of the accounting cycle, LO 1, 3, 5, 6**) Use the information provided in Problem P3-8 about We've Got Wheels, Inc. (Wheels) to do the following:

a. Prepare all necessary journal entries until September 10, 2008.

b. Prepare T-accounts and post each journal entry to the appropriate T-account.

c. Prepare and post adjusting journal entries to their appropriate T-accounts. Adjusting entries are needed for the bikes, inline skates and equipment, and the permit.

d. Prepare a trial balance as of September 10, 2008.

e. Prepare a balance sheet as of September 10, 2008 and an income statement for the period ended September 10, 2008 from your spreadsheet. Prepare the closing journal entry and post the closing entry to the appropriate T-accounts.

f. Prepare a trial balance as of September 10, 2008, after the closing entry has been prepared.

g. Compare Wheels' net income with the amount of cash that was generated by the business. Which is a better indicator of how Wheels did? Why are they different? (When looking at the cash flow, consider the cash flows after the owners made their initial $20,000 investment.)

h. If Wheels' owners asked you evaluate the financial statements for them, what would you be able to tell them based on your evaluation?

P3-19. (**Following the steps of the accounting cycle, LO 1, 3, 5, 6**) Use the information about Austin's Appliance Emporium Ltd. (AAEL) provided in Problem P3-9 to do the following:

a. Prepare all necessary transactional journal entries for the year ended August 31, 2010.

b. Prepare T-accounts and post each journal entry to the appropriate T-account.

c. Prepare and post adjusting journal entries to their appropriate T-accounts.

d. Prepare a trial balance as of August 31, 2010.

e. Prepare a balance sheet for AAEL as of August 31, 2010 and an income statement and statement of retained earnings for the year ended August 31, 2010.

f. Prepare the closing journal entry and post the closing entry to the appropriate T-accounts.

g. Prepare a trial balance as of August 31, 2010, after the closing entry has been prepared.

h. Austin is considering expanding AAEL to include a wider range of products. Austin has approached you about purchasing common shares of AAEL to help finance the expansion. Based on your examination of the statements, what can you tell about AAEL that would be useful to your decision to invest? Also, list five questions you might ask Austin that would help you use the financial statements more effectively.

P3-20. (**Following the steps of the accounting cycle, LO 1, 3, 5, 6**) Use the information about Majestic Trucking Inc. (Majestic) provided in Problem P3-10 to do the following:

a. Prepare all necessary transactional journal entries for the year ended December 31, 2010.

b. Prepare T-accounts and post each journal entry to the appropriate T-account.

c. Prepare and post adjusting journal entries to their appropriate T-accounts.

d. Prepare a trial balance as of December 31, 2010.

e. Prepare a balance sheet for Majestic as of December 31, 2010 and an income statement and statement of retained earnings for the year ended December 31, 2010.

f. Prepare the closing journal entry and post the closing entry to the appropriate T-accounts.

g. Prepare a trial balance as of December 31, 2010, after the closing entry has been prepared.

h. The North American economy is booming and there is a lot of work for shipping companies like Majestic. However, the competition is fierce and success and failure are defined by how efficient a company is and how well it services its customers. Majestic's managers would like to upgrade its fleet by adding two new trucks and making significant improvements to its existing vehicles. Based on your examination of the statements, what can you tell about Majestic that would be useful to your decision to lend it $125,000? Also, list five questions you might ask Majestic's management that would help you use the financial statements more effectively.

P3-21. **(Following the steps of the accounting cycle, LO 1, 3, 5, 6)** Use the information about Gary's Computer Maintenance Ltd. (GCML) provided in Problem P3-11 to do the following:

a. Prepare all necessary transactional journal entries for the year ended December 31, 2009.

b. Prepare T-accounts and post each journal entry to the appropriate T-account.

c. Prepare and post adjusting journal entries to their appropriate T-accounts.

d. Prepare a trial balance as of December 31, 2009.

e. Prepare a balance sheet for GCML as of December 31, 2009 and an income statement and statement of retained earnings for the year ended December 31, 2009.

f. Prepare the closing journal entry and post the closing entry to the appropriate T-accounts.

g. Prepare a trial balance as of December 31, 2009, after the closing entry has been prepared.

h. Gary is pleased with the performance of his business and he is considering opening a second location. He would like to get another investor to purchase an equity interest in GCML and operate the new location. Based on your examination of the statements, what can you tell about GCML that would be useful to your decision to purchase an equity stake in GCML? Also, list five questions you might ask Gary that would help you use the financial statements more effectively.

Using Financial Statements

WestJet is Canada's leading low-fare airline, serving 33 destinations with its fleet of Boeing-Next-Generation 737 jet aircraft. With a strong focus on safety, and through its high-efficiency structure, motivated people, and the provision of unmatched customer service, WestJet has grown from a Western Canadian regional carrier to a coast-to-coast low-fare airline with scheduled service to the United States. WestJet's ticker symbol on the Toronto Stock Exchange is WJA.[1]

www.westjet.com

WestJet's consolidated balance sheets, statements of earnings, and retained earnings along with some extracts from the notes to the financial statements, are provided in Exhibit 3–1.[2]

Use this information to respond to questions FS3-1 to FS3-9.

FS3-1. Examine WestJet's balance sheets. Which accounts do you think would require adjustments at the year end? Explain.

FS3-2. WestJet includes among its current liabilities $127,450,000 for "Advance Ticket Sales." Note 1(c) provides some additional information about this account.

a. When does WestJet recognize its revenue?

b. What does Advance Ticket Sales represent?

c. Why is Advance Ticket Sales reported as a liability? Describe the circumstances that would give rise to an increase in this account.

d. What journal entry would be made to record an increase in Advance Ticket Sales? (Alternative approach: Use an accounting equation spreadsheet to record an increase in Advance Ticket Sales.)

e. What circumstances would give rise to a decrease in Advance Ticket Sales?

f. What journal entry would be made to record a decrease in Advance Ticket Sales? (Alternative approach: Use an accounting equation spreadsheet to record a decrease in Advance Ticket Sales.)

EXHIBIT 3–1 :

**WestJet Airlines
Ltd. Extracts
from Financial
Statements**

CONSOLIDATED BALANCE SHEETS

WestJet Airlines Ltd.

December 31, 2005 and 2004
(Stated in Thousands of Dollars)

	2005	2004
Assets		
Current assets:		
Cash and cash equivalents	$ 259,640	$ 148,532
Accounts receivable	8,022	12,814
Income taxes recoverable	13,909	2,854
Prepaid expenses and deposits	31,746	25,493
Inventory	6,259	5,382
	319,576	195,075
Property and equipment (note 2)	1,803,497	1,601,546
Other assets (note 3)	90,019	80,733
	$ 2,213,092	$ 1,877,354
Liabilities and Shareholders' Equity		
Current liabilities:		
Accounts payable and accrued liabilities	$ 100,052	$ 91,885
Advance ticket sales	127,450	81,991
Non-refundable guest credits	32,814	26,704
Current portion of long-term debt (note 4)	114,115	97,305
Current portion of obligations under capital lease (note 6)	2,466	6,564
	376,897	304,449
Long-term debt (note 4)	1,044,719	905,631
Obligations under capital lease (note 6)	1,690	–
Other liabilities (note 5)	16,982	10,000
Future income tax (note 8)	102,651	67,382
	1,542,939	1,287,462
Shareholders' equity:		
Share capital (note 7(b))	429,613	390,469
Contributed surplus (note 7(g))	39,093	21,977
Retained earnings	201,447	177,446
	670,153	589,892
Subsequent events (note 6)		
Commitments and contingencies (notes 6 and 9)		
	$ 2,213,092	$ 1,877,354

See accompanying notes to consolidated financial statements.

EXHIBIT 3–1 :

(continued)
WestJet Airlines
Ltd. Extracts
from Financial
Statements

CONSOLIDATED STATEMENTS OF EARNINGS (LOSS) AND RETAINED EARNINGS

WestJet Airlines Ltd.

Years ended December 31, 2005 and 2004
(Stated in Thousands of Dollars, Except Per Share Amounts)

	2005	2004
Revenues:		
Guest revenues	$ 1,207,075	$ 933,407
Charter and other	181,641	119,332
Interest income	6,308	5,251
	1,395,024	1,057,990
Expenses:		
Aircraft fuel	354,065	241,473
Airport operations	219,144	173,604
Flight operations and navigational charges	183,463	148,706
Sales and marketing	124,154	85,186
Depreciation and amortization	106,624	126,338
Maintenance	75,717	78,903
General and administration	69,552	60,953
Aircraft leasing	65,647	41,239
Interest expense	55,496	44,109
Inflight	53,005	43,808
Customer service	27,322	23,570
	1,334,189	1,067,889
Earnings (loss) from operations	60,835	(9,899)
Non-operating income (expense):		
Loss on foreign exchange	(2,729)	(3,224)
Gain (loss) on disposal of property and equipment	(98)	63
	(2,827)	(3,161)
Employee profit share (note 9(b))	6,033	2,916
Earnings (loss) before income taxes	51,975	(15,976)
Income tax expense (recovery) (note 8):		
Current	(7,367)	(4,771)
Future	35,341	5,963
	27,974	1,192
Net earnings (loss)	24,001	(17,168)
Retained earnings, beginning of year	177,446	204,731
Change in accounting policy (note 1(l))	–	(10,117)
Retained earnings, end of year	$ 201,447	$ 177,446
Earnings (loss) per share (note 7(d)):		
Basic	$ 0.19	$ (0.14)
Diluted	$ 0.19	$ (0.14)

See accompanying notes to consolidated financial statements.

EXHIBIT 3–1 :

1. **Significant accounting policies:**

(c) Revenue recognition:

Guest and charter revenue is recognized when air transportation is provided. Tickets sold but not yet used are included in the consolidated balance sheet as advance ticket sales.

The Corporation earns revenue under the tri-branded credit card agreement and is included in other revenue. Net retail sales revenue is recognized at the time the transaction occurs. Revenue related to account activations is deferred and not recognized until the credit file issued for the new activation is used or expires.

(d) Non-refundable guest credits:

The Corporation, under certain circumstances, may issue future travel credits which are non-refundable and which expire one year from the date of issue. The utilization of guest credits is recorded as revenue when the guest has flown or upon expiry.

(g) Deferred costs:

Sales and marketing and customer service expenses attributed to advance ticket sales are deferred and expensed in the period the related revenue is recognized. Included in prepaid expenses and deposits are $13,236,000 (2004 - $7,400,000) of deferred costs.

(h) Property and equipment:

Property and equipment are recorded at cost and depreciated to their estimated residual values. Aircraft under capital lease are initially recorded at the present value of minimum lease payments at the inception of the lease.

Asset	Basis	Rate
Aircraft net of estimated residual value – Next-Generation	Cycles	Cycles flown
Live satellite television included in Aircraft – Next-Generation	Straight-line	10 years/lease term
Aircraft net of estimated residual value – 200-series	Flight hours	Hours flown
Ground property and equipment	Straight-line	5 to 25 years
Spare engines and parts net of estimated residual value – Next-Generation	Straight-line	20 years
Spare engines and parts net of estimated residual value – 200-series	Flight hours	Fleet hours flown
Aircraft under capital lease	Straight-line	Term of lease
Other assets under capital lease	Straight-line	Term of lease
Buildings	Straight-line	40 years
Leasehold improvements	Straight-line	Term of lease

For the year ended December 31, 2003

(i) Maintenance costs:

Costs related to the acquisition of an aircraft and preparation for service are capitalized and included in aircraft costs. Heavy maintenance ("D" check) costs incurred on aircraft are capitalized and amortized over the remaining useful service life of the "D" check.

All other maintenance costs are expensed as incurred.

FS3-3. WestJet includes among its current liabilities $32,814,000 for "Non-refundable guest credits." Note 1(d) provides some additional information about this account.

    a. What journal entry would WestJet record when a traveller makes the initial reservation? Remember that when a traveller pays for a ticket in advance of a flight the amount is credited to "Advance Ticket Sales" (see Note 1(c)). (Alternative approach: In each of parts a–d, use an accounting equation spreadsheet to record the entry that would be made to record the transaction or economic event that is described.)

    b. What adjusting entry is required if a traveller cancels his or her flight but WestJet grants the traveler a "guest credit"?

    c. What journal entry would WestJet make if a traveller who has a travel credit calls to book another flight?

    d. What journal entry would WestJet make if a traveller who has a guest credit allows it to expire without using it?

FS3-4. Read note 1(g) to WestJet's financial statements. The note explains how WestJet accounts for "Deferred Costs."

    a. Where on WestJet's balance sheet are the deferred costs reported?

    b. What amount of deferred costs is reported on WestJet's December 31, 2005 balance sheet?

    c. What are the deferred costs?

    d. WestJet's treatment of the deferred costs can be considered an application of the matching principal. Explain.

e. What journal entry would WestJet make to record the deferred costs? (Alternative approach: Use an accounting equation spreadsheet to record the entry WestJet would make to record the deferred costs.)

f. What journal entry would WestJet make when it was time to expense the deferred costs? (Alternative approach: Use an accounting equation spreadsheet to record the entry WestJet would make when it was time to expense the deferred costs.

FS3-5. Note 1(i) explains that WestJet expenses all maintenance and repairs costs it incurs. Compare that note with a similar note from WestJet's 2003 annual report where it is explained that the company capitalizes some of the maintenance costs that it incurs and expenses others. How do you think these different ways of accounting for maintenance and repairs would affect WestJet's financial statements? When answering consider how financial statements would differ under one accounting treatment versus the other. Would a different accounting treatment change the actual economic activity and performance of WestJet? How might the perceptions of users of the financial statements be affected by different accounting treatments?

FS3-6. Calculate the following ratios for WestJet for 2004 and 2005:
a. Profit margin.
b. Return on equity.
c. Current ratio.

FS3-7. Prepare the closing journal entry that WestJet would make on December 31, 2005. (Alternative approach: Set up an accounting equation spreadsheet using WestJet's financial statements and record the closing entry that WestJet would make on December 31, 2005.)

FS3-8. How much inventory does WestJet report on its December 31, 2005 balance sheet? Why do you think WestJet has so little inventory?

FS3-9. Compare WestJet's balance sheet and income statement with Rogers'. Describe how the statements differ. Explain. In responding, consider the different types and relative amounts of assets, liabilities, revenues, and expenses that are reported on the statements. In answering this question consider current assets as a percentage of total assets, current liabilities as a percentage of total liabilities and shareholders' equity, and expenses as a percentage of revenues.

Analyzing Rogers Communications Inc.

ROGERS

R3-1. See Appendix A for the Rogers Communications Inc. Annual Report. Examine Rogers' balance sheet and income statement for the year ended December 31, 2005 (pages A-4 to A-5). What adjusting journal entries do you think Rogers had to make when preparing the statements? Explain. (Reading the notes associated with some of the balance sheet and income statement items might help in answering this question.)

R3-2. How much would Rogers "close" to retained earnings at the end of its 2005 fiscal year? Explain.

R3-3. Prepare the closing journal entry that Rogers would make on December 31, 2005, using the information provided in the financial statements. (Alternative approach: Use an accounting equation spreadsheet to record Rogers' closing entry on December 31, 2004.)

R3-4. What accounts on Rogers' income statement and balance sheet indicate that it is using accrual accounting? Explain.

R3-5. How much depreciation and amortization did Rogers expense in the year ended December 31, 2005? What journal entry would Rogers make to record the depreciation and amortization expense? (Alternative approach: Use an accounting equation spreadsheet to record Rogers' depreciation and amortization expense for 2005.) What amount is in the accumulated depreciation account for Rogers' property, plant, and equipment on December 31?

R3-6. Note 4 to Rogers' financial statement provides information about the company's prepaid expenses. Assume that during 2005 Rogers spent $75,540,000 on prepaid items. Prepare the journal entry that Rogers would record when it spent this money. Record the adjusting entry that would be required on December 31, 2005 to record the consumption of prepaid expenses during the year. (Alternative approach: Use an accounting equation spreadsheet to record the entry Rogers would make to record the $75,540,000 it spent on prepaid items and the adjusting entry that would be required on December 31, 2005 to record the consumption of prepaid expenses during the year.)

ENDNOTES

1. Extracted from WestJet Airlines Ltd.'s Web site at www.westjet.com

2. Extracted from WestJet Airlines Ltd.'s 2005 audited consolidated financial statements.

INCOME MEASUREMENT AND THE OBJECTIVES OF FINANCIAL REPORTING

LEARNING OBJECTIVES

After studying the material in this chapter you will be able to:

▶ **LO 1** Explain and apply the GAAP criteria for revenue recognition.

▶ **LO 2** Describe the critical-event and gradual approaches of recognizing revenue.

▶ **LO 3** Explain the effects that different approaches to recognizing revenue have on the income statement and on financial ratios.

▶ **LO 4** Describe expense recognition and the matching principle.

▶ **LO 5** (a) Understand how the constraints, economic facts surrounding a transaction or economic event, and the managers' objectives of financial reporting affect the accounting choices made by an entity.

(b) Understand the reasons for, the economic consequences to stakeholders of, and limitations to, flexible accounting rules that give managers the opportunity to choose how they account for transactions and economic events.

▶ **LO 6** Apply an approach to solving accounting choice problems.

It's a Monday afternoon on March 13, 2006, at the Grosvenor Park Rogers Video store on 8th St East, in Saskatoon. The store is the second largest one in the city, and one of close to 300 in the Rogers Video chain across Canada.

At the cash register, some customers prepare to pay for their selections with a red coupon they received in their newspapers a few weeks ago. These coupons offer $45 in savings on various deals, including two new-release movie rentals for a special price and "2 for 1" seven-day game rentals.

But it's not just videos, DVDs, and games that are for rent or sale at the Rogers Video outlet.

Customers can also sign up for Rogers Wireless cell phone service and order handsets. Many other stores also sell complementary products, including Rogers Cable and Rogers Yahoo Hi Speed Internet.

When a customer pays for the latest releases that week, the Harry Potter movie, "The Goblet of Fire" and EA Sports' "Fight Night Round 3," Rogers Video's computerized system records the payments as they are made. The company says it "recognizes the revenue" for video rentals when the rentals are provided.

In some Rogers Video stores in Ontario, Blue Jays fans can even buy their tickets for home games at the Rogers Video stores months in advance. Yet Rogers only recognizes the revenue from the tickets on the day the games are played at the Rogers Centre in Toronto.

Why this delayed revenue recognition for the ball game? According to company officials, Rogers provides the service when the videos are rented. For the Jays, Rogers recognizes the revenue when the service is provided, i.e., when the game is played. In theory, if the game wasn't played, Rogers would have to give back the cash.

Rogers Video is part of the parent company's cable subsidiary. Rogers Video bills itself as the largest Canadian-owned specialty video store chain in the country, and the fifth-largest in North America. Founded in 1988, Rogers Video is based in Richmond, B.C., and has 4,500 employees. In June 2005, the company moved from the traditional bricks-and-mortar business to meet the demand of viewers who prefer to do their video ordering from the comfort of their home computers, and launched Rogers Video Direct, with a catalogue of 40,000 titles. DVDs are delivered by mail to customers' doors for a monthly subscription fee, no return deadlines, and no late fees—and revenues are recognized at time of payment.

INTRODUCTION

We have now covered the fundamentals of accounting. In Chapters 1 to 3 we explored the accounting environment, became familiar with financial statements, and learned the basics of the accounting cycle. We can now begin our exploration of accounting information in depth. In the remainder of the book we will examine how economic events are reported (and not reported) in financial statements. It is now time to don our detective gear and learn how to sleuth through accounting information.

In the first part of this chapter we will explore revenue and expense recognition. The term *recognition* refers to when revenues and expenses appear on the income statement. (Actually, the term *recognition* has a broader application in accounting. *Recognition* more generally refers to when a transaction or economic event is recorded in an entity's accounting system.) There are different ways of recognizing revenues and expenses, and the methods chosen can affect the amount of revenues, expenses, and net income that an entity reports in a period. Different revenue and expense recognition methods also affect many accounting and financial ratios—tools that stakeholders often use to analyze an entity. When there are alternative ways of recognizing revenues and expenses, managers must decide which one to choose (remember from Chapter 1 that managers decide how to report accounting information).

Throughout the remainder of *Financial Accounting*, we will see that managers often have the opportunity to choose among alternative ways of accounting. Chapter 4 provides some explanations as to why managers are allowed to choose as well as some of the implications of allowing them to choose. Chapter 4 and the rest of the book also address some important questions about allowing managers to make accounting choices. You may have thought of some of these questions already. For example, how do managers choose among legitimate alternatives? What motivates managers' choices? Which user group's interests should be considered most important if managers have to choose among competing interests?

At this point we can say that managers must often make difficult decisions about what information to present in the general purpose financial statements and how to present that information. These choices may make the financial statements more useful and informative to some stakeholders, and less useful and less informative to others. The choices may have different economic consequences for different stakeholders.

The second part of this chapter examines the objectives of financial reporting. This material is designed to help readers understand the factors that influence the accounting choices managers make, including the incentives for managers to pursue their self-interests. Most often managers make accounting choices that are within the rules (rules such as GAAP). But because managers are often able to choose among acceptable alternatives, they can design their choices to satisfy their own interests while still meeting the rules. Some readers may be uncomfortable with the ethical implications of this situation. This discomfort is understandable. But it is the reality of accounting. This material is **not** intended to be a guide or encouragement to misuse accounting information. It is intended to help you understand, be a savvy user of, and avoid being deceived by accounting information. For better or for worse, empirical evidence and casual observation suggest that when people have choices, the choices they make are the ones that are best for them. This applies to accounting too.[1]

However, an entity's managers are still responsible for supplying relevant and reliable information to stakeholders. This responsibility must be carried out to the highest ethical standards. Failure to do so has significant consequences for society, the economy, stakeholders, and individuals. Accounting scandals at Enron, WorldCom, Nortel, and Tyco have highlighted how managers can use accounting information unethically as well as the consequences of unethical behaviour. There are also many other accounting controversies that are not clear violations of accounting rules but that can raise questions about the intent of management when making accounting choices.

REVENUE RECOGNITION

When revenue recognition was introduced in Chapter 3 we learned that under accrual accounting, revenue is an economic gain earned by an entity from providing goods or services to customers. However, it is not always obvious when an economic gain "happens." Someone has to decide what the economic event is that triggers revenue recognition. *When* revenue is recognized and *how* expenses are matched to revenue have a significant impact on the amounts reported on the financial statements, the value of financial ratios, and can affect a person's perception of how an entity is performing. Once you determine *when* revenue should be recognized, the journal entry to record revenue is straightforward. The journal entry is:

Dr. Cash (asset +) or Accounts Receivables (asset +)   xxx
    or Unearned Revenue (liabilities −)
      Cr. Revenue (revenue +, owners' equity +)   xxx
    To record revenue.

When revenue is recognized, an income statement account for revenue (or sales or sales revenue) is credited and a balance sheet account is debited. The entry to the balance sheet account either increases assets (accounts receivable or cash usually) or decreases liabilities.

Earning revenue is a continuous process. Each activity an entity undertakes that increases the economic value of a good or service represents revenue, because by adding value an entity makes its goods or services more valuable to consumers and thereby increases the amount that customers will pay (remember that revenue is the amount consumers pay for a good or service).

For Rogers Communications Inc. (Rogers), a subscriber making a cell phone call is the culmination of a series of actions. Before a subscriber can make a call using the Rogers' network, Rogers must:

- acquire spectrum and licences to operate cell phone service in Canada

- construct a cell phone network

- advertise its services

- provide the facilities necessary for customers to sign up with Rogers

- provide or sell a phone to a customer (this would require Rogers to purchase inventory from suppliers and distribute the inventory to outlets)

- set up the subscriber's account and provide him/her with a phone number, etc.

Each of these steps adds value to Rogers' services by making them more attractive and available to customers and by making customers aware of the services. Each step along the way represents revenue to Rogers, at least in a conceptual sense, i.e., the real economic process of earning revenue as opposed to how revenue is accounted for. As a practical matter, it is very difficult for accountants to determine *when* and *how much* revenue should be recognized over the series of actions that culminates in an actual sale to a customer. For example, how much revenue does a particular television advertisement broadcast at 8:13 PM on Thursday create? It is impossible to know. Despite these difficulties, revenue must somehow be reflected in the income statement in a logical and rational way. Accountants have devised two broad approaches for recognizing revenue.

The first approach for recognizing revenue we can call the **critical-event approach**. Under the critical-event approach, an entity chooses an instant in the earnings process that it considers an appropriate time to recognize revenue. That instant is called the critical event. When the critical event occurs, 100 percent of the revenue is recognized. The critical-event approach is "all or nothing." Before the critical event occurs there is no revenue. Once the critical event has occurred, all the revenue is recognized. With the critical-event approach, the continuous nature of the revenue-earning process is ignored.

The second approach recognizes revenue gradually over a period of time. We can call this approach the **gradual approach**. The gradual approach is often used when an entity provides services or signs long-term contracts, such as construction projects, that last for more than one accounting period. With the gradual approach, revenue is recognized little by little as a project progresses. The entity must identify a basis for determining how much revenue to recognize each period. The gradual method is also used when revenue is earned continuously over time. For example, interest earned on a bank account is recognized based on the number of days the money is deposited.

Both revenue recognition approaches will be discussed in more detail later in this chapter. First, we will discuss some criteria that can be used to decide when to recognize revenue.

Criteria for Recognizing Revenue

To recognize revenue in a logical and rational manner we need some criteria to guide our choice. Without some guidance, financial reporting could become a free-for-all that could impair the usefulness of financial statements. (Some critics argue that financial reporting is already a free-for-all!) The criteria are:

1. Performance has occurred.

2. The amount of revenue can be reasonably measured.

3. The costs required to earn the revenue can be reasonably measured.

4. Collection of payment is reasonably assured.

These are the criteria according to GAAP. We use GAAP as our benchmark because GAAP-based financial statements are the types of statements that we most commonly encounter. Remember, however, that we are examining financial reporting with a critical eye, so it is important not to think of these criteria as the best or only criteria for recognizing revenue.

The first criterion requires that performance has occurred. According to the *CICA Handbook*, performance has been achieved when the significant rights and risks of ownership have been transferred from the seller to the buyer. This means that the seller has done most or all of what it is supposed to do to be entitled to payment. The first criterion is usually the most difficult to apply. In many situations, performance is fairly easy to identify but sometimes transactions can be structured in new and unusual ways, which makes it challenging to determine when performance has occurred.

Criteria two and three deal with measurability. For revenue to be recognized it must be measurable—the entity must be able to make a reasonable estimate of the amount of revenue. In addition, the costs associated with earning the revenue must be measurable so that they can be matched to the revenue—the entity must be able to make a reasonable estimate of the costs. Remember that matching is a key accrual accounting concept.

The fourth criterion is collectability. The entity must have a reasonable expectation that it will be paid.

These criteria provide guidance to managers, but they require interpretation and judgment. Interpretation and judgment are necessary because business transactions don't always fit into convenient categories. Transactions sometimes have terms that make them challenging to assess. After all, at what point has performance "occurred"? When have the "significant rights and risks of ownership" been transferred? For criteria two through four, what does "reasonably" mean? What determines whether there is a reasonable expectation of collection? These fairly vague terms provide flexibility for choosing when to recognize revenue. We will see later that this vagueness serves a purpose.

The criteria are fairly *conservative* in that they tend to delay the recognition of revenue until fairly late in the revenue-generating process. The intent of this more conservative approach is to reduce the uncertainty surrounding the numbers in the financial statements so that the information reported can be meaningful. Financial statement numbers that are too uncertain do not provide financial statement users with much useful information for decision making. On the other hand, waiting until there is no uncertainty may not be useful either because the users will not receive the information in time to influence their decisions. While the criteria listed above tend to reduce uncertainty, they do not eliminate it. For uncertainty to be eliminated, revenue would have to be recognized very late—in most cases long after cash is collected.

Here is one more criterion that we can add: the revenue-recognition point selected should provide a reasonable and fair representation of the entity's activities, given the needs of the people who will be using the accounting information. This means that after deciding that a revenue recognition point satisfies the criteria described above, the manager should step back and assess whether the choice is reasonable and fair. If the manager believes that the choice of revenue recognition point may be misleading or confusing, an alternative should be considered. We can think of this criterion as pervasive and overriding. Remember that accounting information must, above all, provide useful information about an entity to stakeholders so that they can make informed decisions. As our discussion proceeds, we will refer mainly to the first four criteria. However, this fifth criterion should always be kept in mind.

Knowledge Check

- What are the two approaches that accountants have devised for recognizing revenue?

- What are the four criteria for recognizing revenue under GAAP? Explain each criterion.

- What is the "fifth" criterion for revenue recognition and why is it so important?

Question for Consideration

Evarts Ltd. (Evarts) is a retail store that sells clothing to men and women. Evarts has been in business for 15 years. Customers pay by cash or major credit card at the time they purchase and take their merchandise. Customers are allowed to return merchandise within 15 days of purchase if it has not been used. On occasion, Evarts replaces or repairs goods that are damaged or that customers are otherwise dissatisfied with. Evarts recognizes its revenue at the time the customer pays and takes the merchandise. Use the revenue recognition criteria to support when Evarts recognizes its revenue.

Answer: At the time of payment the four revenue recognition criteria are clearly met. The amount of revenue is known since the customer has paid the agreed price. The price will not change. Most costs have been incurred at the time. The cost of the merchandise sold will be known as well as any other costs directly associated with the sale, such as the sales person's commission. There are some uncertainties about costs, such as the cost of replacements and repairs, as well as returns. However, these costs are likely small and given the length of time Evarts has been in business, can be reasonably estimated. Collection is not an issue since the customer has paid cash or with a credit card, which is equivalent to cash. Any doubt about the appropriateness of recognizing the revenue is related to whether Evarts has "performed" when the merchandise is exchanged for payment. The risks and rewards of ownership seem to have been transferred at this time. The customer has taken possession of the goods and can use them in any way he or she chooses. While Evarts will accept responsibility for manufacturer's defects and certain repairs, it would not take the goods back if a garment became stained or torn as a result of use by the customer. Notice that at the time merchandise is exchanged for cash it is reasonable to recognize revenue even though some uncertainties (returns, exchanges, repairs) remain.

One final remark on these revenue-recognition criteria: they are not universal. One could devise a different set of criteria that would be equally appropriate for particular stakeholders in particular situations. For example, stakeholders in a real estate company might benefit from having the increases in the value of the property owned by the company reported as revenue. Recognizing increases in value before property is sold would not meet our GAAP revenue-recognition criteria. However, alternative criteria could be set up that would allow these increases in value to be recognized. The reason other sets of criteria are possible is that there is no natural set of accounting rules. People create accounting rules to suit their needs and the environments in which they function.

The Critical-Event Approach to Recognizing Revenue

Under the critical-event approach to recognizing revenue, when a critical event occurs, it triggers the recording of revenue and the matching of the related expenses. The critical event is the instant in the earnings process that an entity considers an appropriate time to recognize revenue. Revenue is recognized in full when the critical event occurs. Until the critical event occurs, revenue is not recorded and there is no effect on the income statement.

In some situations, there is not just one and only one possible critical event. Alternatives may exist because the circumstances surrounding a transaction may be ambiguous and different people may reasonably be able to identify and support different critical events. In these situations, managers must choose among the most reasonable and supportable alternatives. When there is more than one possible critical event, the one an entity chooses will be influenced by the entity's accounting environment—factors such as the characteristics of the entity (industry, type of transactions, risk, and so on), constraints, stakeholder needs, and the interests of the mangers. (See Figure 1–1 on page 6.)

If the entity is following GAAP, the critical event must meet the revenue-recognition criteria and must occur at a reasonable and fair point in the earnings process. One of the most common critical events used by companies is when the goods or services are delivered to the customer. However, different critical events are seen in practice and these critical events can be before or after the goods or services are delivered. Let's take a look at some of the critical events that trigger the recognition of revenue.

Delivery Delivery occurs when the buyer takes possession of the goods being sold or receives the service being purchased. When a Rogers Cable customer uses the "video-on-demand" (VOD) service, the revenue-recognition criteria are met when the customer views the video. (VOD allows customers to view at home the videos they want to see when they want to see them.) Customers can't ask for their money back if they didn't like the movie. By ordering the video customers have also agreed to the price, so the amount of revenue is known at the time the video is ordered. Once the show is viewed there are almost no uncertainties. A customer could claim there was a billing error or that the show ordered was not actually delivered, but that's about it.

A university course is another example of recognizing revenue on delivery. Revenue for student tuition is recognized when the course is delivered. Suppose you register in March 2008 for a summer course at your university. You pay your tuition using your credit card when you register. The summer course begins in May. If the university has March 31 as its year end (as many Canadian universities do), revenue would be recognized in fiscal 2009 (because that's when the course is given) even though cash is collected in fiscal 2008. For tuition, performance means offering the course to students, rather than collecting the revenue from it.

Most retail, manufacturing, and service businesses use delivery as their critical event because the revenue-recognition criteria are not met until delivery occurs. There is too much uncertainty before delivery, and recognizing revenue after delivery would delay recognition beyond a reasonable time. However, there are exceptions, as we will see.

Completion of Production In some situations, the four revenue-recognition criteria are met as soon as the product is produced, even if it has not been delivered to the customer. If the sale of the product is assured and the costs of selling and distributing it are minor, revenue can be reasonably recognized when production is complete. An example is a bill and hold arrangement. In a bill and hold arrangement, a customer orders merchandise but requests that it not be delivered until a later date (perhaps because the customer doesn't have enough space to store it). If the customer asks the seller to hold the goods, the seller can still recognize the revenue if certain conditions are met, including that the risks of ownership have been transferred to the customer, the order from the customer is firm, the seller has fulfilled all its obligations (other than delivery), and the goods are segregated from the seller's inventory and can't be used to fill other orders.

Recognizing revenue on production provides an example of how accounting rules evolve. Until 2003, Canadian GAAP allowed mining companies to recognize revenue when the ore had been extracted from the ground and refined into the finished product. This was common practice in the gold mining industry. The principle was that because there is a ready market for gold (you don't have to look for a customer for commodities such as gold) most of the effort required to sell the gold was done when production had been completed. Recent rule changes

EXHIBIT 4–1 ⋮

Aurizon Mines Ltd.

Extract from the December 31, 2003 Annual Report

2. **SIGNIFICANT ACCOUNTING POLICIES (Continued)**

i) Revenue Recognition

The Company recognizes revenue from metals when they have been extracted and processed at the mill facilities. Revenue amounts recognized but not settled are classified as bullion settlements.

Extract from the December 31, 2003 Annual Report

2. **SIGNIFICANT ACCOUNTING POLICIES (Continued)**

i) Revenue Recognition

The Company recognizes revenue from metals when they have been delivered and title has passed to a purchaser.

Royalty income is recognized on an accrual basis when the Company has reasonable assurance with respect to measurement and collectability.

3. **CHANGE IN ACCOUNTING POLICIES**

a) Revenue Recognition

Effective January 1, 2004, the Company has elected to apply a new CICA Accounting Standard, EIC 141, for revenue recognition, on a prospective basis.

Previously the Company recognized revenue from metals when they had been extracted and processed at the mill facilities. Under the new standard, revenue is recognized when the metals have been delivered, and title is passed to a purchaser.

The adoption of the new standard has resulted in an increase in inventories of $284,725 as at December 31, 2004, and an increase in the net loss of $14,900 in 2004.

now require mining companies to recognize their revenue when the refined metal is delivered to a customer. The rule changes reduce the amount of latitude that managers have as to when they can recognize revenue.

Exhibit 4–1 shows the revenue recognition note from the financial statements of Aurizon Mines Ltd. (Aurizon), which operates mines in Quebec and Newfoundland.[2] The Exhibit shows Aurizon's note describing its revenue recognition policy in its 2003 financial statements and its 2004 statements. The exhibit also provides the note that explains the change in accounting policy in 2004. Notice the change and consider the impact on the financial statements.

Cash Collection Sometimes it is very difficult for an entity to reasonably estimate the amount that will be collected from customers. In these situations collection becomes the critical event because the fourth criterion for revenue recognition requires that collection of payment be reasonably assured. For example, a retail business that sells to high-risk customers on credit (customers who have a high likelihood of not paying) could reasonably delay recognizing revenue until cash is collected. The key is that it is difficult to estimate the amount that will be collected.

With most credit sales, there is some risk of non-collection. However, just because there is some chance that money owed will not be collected does not mean that revenue recognition should be delayed. *If* the amount that *will be* collected can be reasonably estimated, then revenue can be recognized before collection. Most companies that sell goods on credit recognize their revenue on delivery, but they record an expense that is an estimate of the amount that is not expected to be collected.

On the other hand, receiving cash does not automatically mean that revenue can be recognized. Collection is only one of the revenue-recognition criteria, and all of the criteria must be met before revenue can be recognized. If the other criteria are not satisfied when the cash (or other compensation) is received, then revenue recognition should be deferred.

EXHIBIT 4–2 :

Revenue Recognition Method Used by WestJet

NOTES TO CONSOLIDATED FINANCIAL STATEMENTS

WestJet Airlines Ltd.

Years ended December 31, 2005 and 2004
(Tabular Amounts are Stated in Thousands of Dollars, Except Share and Per Share Data)

1. Significant accounting policies:

(c) Revenue recognition:

Guest and charter revenue is recognized when air transportation is provided. Tickets sold but not yet used are included in the consolidated balance sheet as advance ticket sales.

Consider air travel. Many travellers pay for their plane tickets in advance of their flights, but airlines such as WestJet Airlines Ltd. (WestJet) recognize revenue only when the flight occurs, not when they receive payment. As shown in Exhibit 4–2, WestJet does not recognize revenue when it receives cash from its guests[3] (i.e., customers). WestJet faces many uncertainties before a flight occurs which might prevent the earning of revenue, including the possible cancellation of a flight or cancellations by travellers. The flight itself represents WestJet's performance. Without the flight, WestJet has not met the revenue recognition criteria.

Sometimes a customer does not make full payment all at once. For example, it is common to see advertisements for a range of products that allow customers to make their purchases in "five easy payments." If the entity cannot reasonably determine the collectability of the amounts owed by customers, then a method known as the **instalment method** can be used. The instalment method recognizes revenue when each payment is received. The expenses incurred to earn the revenue are matched on a proportional basis. For example, if an instalment payment is received that represents 20 percent of the expected revenue, then 20 percent of the expenses are matched to the revenue. The instalment method is not, strictly speaking, a critical-event approach because 100 percent of the revenue is not recognized when the critical event occurs. However, because revenue is recognized on the occurrence of a critical event (the collection of cash), the instalment method is a critical-event method.

Completion of Warranty Period or Right-of-Return Period When there are significant uncertainties that may not be resolved until after delivery, it may be appropriate to recognize revenue only when those uncertainties have been resolved. For example, a company develops a sophisticated product that relies on a new technology and sells the product with an unconditional warranty. (A **warranty** is a promise by a seller or producer of a product to correct specified problems with the product.) If it is impossible to estimate the cost of repairing any problems that may arise, it would be appropriate to defer revenue recognition until the warranty period ends because criterion three (that costs required to earn the revenue can be reasonably measured) is not fulfilled.

However, the existence of a warranty does not usually justify delaying revenue recognition. Revenue can be recognized earlier if the warranty costs associated with a product can be reasonably estimated. To satisfy the matching principle it is necessary to accrue the estimated warranty costs when the revenue is recognized, even though the warranty costs will not actually be incurred until a later period.

Similarly, if a customer has the right to return merchandise and it is not possible for the seller to come up with a reasonable estimate of the amount that will be returned, it would be appropriate for the selling entity to defer recognizing revenue until the end of the return period.

A similar situation is a **consignment sale**. In a consignment sale the producer or distributor transfers merchandise to another entity for sale. The other entity is responsible for selling the merchandise, and only when merchandise is sold is it responsible for making payment to the producer or distributor. In a consignment sale the other entity can return the merchandise at any time without penalty. As a result, it would be appropriate for the producer or distributor to recognize revenue when the other entity actually sells the merchandise to somebody else, because the producer or distributor still retains the rights and risks of ownership.

Production (before delivery), delivery, cash collection (after delivery), and completion of the warranty period/right-of-return period (after delivery) represent most of the critical events one would observe in practice under GAAP, though other critical events could arise in special circumstances. Absent a GAAP constraint, more critical events would be possible. It is important to keep in mind when assessing possible critical events under GAAP that the four revenue-recognition criteria must be met if revenue is to be recognized. However, when the criteria are met in a given situation is not always clear and judgment may be necessary to decide the appropriate critical event.

Unrealized Gains—A Non-GAAP Critical Event The revenue-recognition criteria used under GAAP do not capture all of an entity's economic gains and losses. Sometimes the market value of an entity's assets can change while the entity continues to own them. That is, the market value of inventory, capital assets, investments, and other assets can increase and decrease over time. Increases or decreases in the market value of assets that are not supported by a transaction with an outside party are called **unrealized gains and losses**. A gain or loss is *realized* when there is a transaction—that is, when the asset is sold. Under GAAP, gains on most assets are recognized only when they are realized. (Because of conservatism, unrealized losses are sometimes recognized before they are realized.) An unrealized gain is not recognized because most or all of the four revenue-recognition criteria are not met. This accounting treatment for unrealized gains represents a limitation of GAAP. The change in market value of an entity's assets could be useful information for some stakeholders, but it is not provided in GAAP financial statements.

www.genesisland.com

Now let's consider a real example. Companies in the real estate industry can hold land and buildings for a long time before they are sold. Exhibit 4–3 shows the notes to the financial statements of Genesis Land Development Corp. (Genesis) that explain its revenue recognition policies and valuation policy for real estate held for development and sale.[4] When Genesis purchases land it is recorded at cost. All costs incurred over the years prior to the land being developed are added to the cost of the land. Even if the land is held for many years, there is no income statement impact reported until the land is sold.

INCOME MEASUREMENT AND THE OBJECTIVES OF FINANCIAL REPORTING

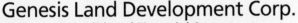

Genesis Land Development Corp.
Notes to Consolidated Financial Statements
December 31, 2004 and 2003

EXHIBIT 4–3 :

Revenue Recognition Policies at Genesis Land Development Corp.

1.   Significant accounting policies

   (c)   Revenue recognition

      (i)   Residential and commercial lot sales

         Revenue is recognized when a contract for sale is signed, a minimum of 15% of the sale proceeds have been received and the sale is unconditional and the purchaser can commence construction.

         Non-refundable deposits received upon signing of contracts and receipt of a minimum of 15% of the contract amount is recorded as deferred revenue until the builder is able to commence construction.

      (ii)   Housing and construction sales

         The sale is recognized when the completed unit is conveyed to the purchaser.

   (d)   Real estate held for development and sale

      Land under development, land held for future development and housing projects under development are recorded at lower of cost and estimated net realizable value.

      Capitalized costs include all direct costs related to development and construction, carrying costs including interest on debt used to finance projects, property taxes and land acquisition costs. Land acquisition costs are prorated to a phase of a project on an acreage basis when the first sale occurs in the phase.

      No general and administration costs are capitalized.

As you can imagine, the market value of land can change dramatically over the years. A non-GAAP approach could recognize the gains on land held as income in the year the gains occur. However, GAAP-based financial statements provide very little information about the changing value of land, even though these changes can be economically significant to the entity and the information could be valuable to some stakeholders.

Insight

In most situations the critical event for a transaction is not controversial. The nature of most revenue transactions is similar or the same as transactions that have been encountered by other entities, so there is no need to determine the appropriate critical event. However, when a transaction occurs that has not been seen before (either because it is completely new or because it is a variation of an existing transaction), management will have to assess the facts of the new transaction to determine an appropriate critical event. The facts may require management to choose from among reasonable, supportable alternative critical events.

www.mcgrawhill.ca/
olc/friedlan

Knowledge Check

■ What does the term "revenue recognition" mean?

■ What happens when the critical event for revenue recognition occurs?

■ What are some examples of critical events?

Why Does It Matter When a Company Recognizes Revenue?

Let's look at an example to show the effects on the income statement of using different critical events for recognizing revenue. Escuminac Manufacturing Ltd. (Escuminac) makes sophisticated heavy equipment for manufacturing facilities. Equipment is made on a special-order basis to meet the specifications of each customer. Customers usually order equipment from Escuminac well in advance of when it will be needed. It is typical in this industry for a manufacturer to store equipment that it makes for up to several months before it is actually delivered to the customer. Customers usually make a payment to Escuminac when the contract to produce equipment is signed and then pay at milestones that are specified in the contract. In 2008 through 2010, the following dollar amounts of equipment were produced and delivered. (For this example, a number of assumptions are made to keep things simple. The key one is that while Escuminac would likely be a continuing business, it is assumed here that there is no business activity before 2008 and effects after 2010 are not considered.)

	2008	2009	2010
Produced by Escuminac	$10,000,000	$12,000,000	$8,000,000
Delivered to customers	$7,500,000	$11,500,000	$9,000,000

Now let's look at Escuminac's financial results in the years 2008 to 2010. Two sets of income statements have been prepared and are shown in Table 4–1. The first set assumes that the critical

TABLE 4–1 ::: Income Statements for Escuminac Manufacturing Ltd

	1. Revenue recognized when the equipment is produced			2. Revenue recognized when the equipment is delivered		
	2008**	**2009**	**2010**	**2008**	**2009**	**2010**
Revenue*	$10,000,000	$12,000,000	$8,000,000	$7,500,000	$11,500,000	$9,000,000
Production Expenses	6,000,000	7,200,000	4,800,000	4,500,000	6,900,000	5,400,000
Gross Margin	4,000,000	4,800,000	3,200,000	3,000,000	4,600,000	3,600,000
Other Expenses (assumed)	3,000,000	3,000,000	3,000,000	3,000,000	3,000,000	3,000,000
Net Income	$1,000,000	$1,800,000	$200,000	$0	$1,600,000	$600,000
Financial Ratios						
Gross Margin Percentage	40.0%	40.0%	40.0%	40.0%	40.0%	40.0%
Profit Margin Percentage	10.0%	15.0%	2.5%	0.0%	13.9%	6.7%

* The total amount of revenue, expenses, and net income over the three years is different for the two critical events because some of the equipment will not be delivered until 2011, so recognition of some of the revenue at the delivery points will not be recognized until 2011. If results for 2011 were also shown for these contracts, the total of revenue, expenses, and net income over 2008 through 2011 would be the same. Over the term of the contracts, the amount of revenue, expenses, and net income reported are not affected by the critical event chosen. Only the timing of when the revenue, expenses and net income is affected.

**Below are sample calculations for the amounts shown in the exhibit. Calculations are shown for 2008 when revenue is recognized when the equipment is produced.

Production Expenses = 60% × Revenue = 60% × $10,000,000 = $6,000,000
Gross Margin = Revenue − Production Expenses = $10,000,000 − $6,000,000 = $4,000,000
Other Expenses = $3,000,000 (fixed amount)
Net Income = Gross Margin − Other Expenses = $4,000,000 − $3,000,000 = $1,000,000
Gross Margin Percentage = Gross Margin/Revenue = $4,000,000 ÷ $10,000,000 = 0.40 = 40%
Profit Margin = Net Income ÷ Revenue = $1,000,000 ÷ $10,000,000 = 0.10 = 10.0%

event for recognizing revenue is when the equipment is produced and the second set when the equipment is delivered.

Both statements assume that the cost of producing the equipment, called *production expenses* in Table 4–1, is 60 percent of the revenue. These costs are expensed when the revenue is recognized, as required by the matching concept. In addition, there are $3,000,000 of other costs, such as executive salaries, cost of support staff, and so on, that are expensed in the period the work is done. The example ignores income taxes.

The numbers in each set of income statements are different. In 2008, revenue is $10,000,000 using production as the critical event versus $7,500,000 when delivery is the critical event. Net income in 2008 is $1,000,000 using production as the critical event and zero using delivery as the critical event. Revenue and net income in 2009 and 2010 are also different with each of the critical events. The gross margin percentage is the same across years and critical events because it is assumed that Production Expenses were a constant percentage (60 percent) of revenue. The profit margin percentage differs across years and critical events because Other Expenses is a constant $3,000,000 per year. A key point to recognize is that using different critical events for recognizing revenue yields very different financial statements *but* the underlying economic activity of Escuminac is the same regardless of which statement is prepared. In other words, regardless of how the financial statements are prepared, it is exactly the same company.

Many of Escuminac's other financial ratios will also be affected, depending on the critical events used to recognize revenue. For example, the current ratio (current assets ÷ current liabilities) will be different because the amount of accounts receivable, inventory, and liabilities will be different with each critical event. The debt-to-equity ratio (debt ÷ equity) will also be affected by the different critical events. Escuminac's shareholders' equity will be different because net income is different in each year. Retained earnings is, therefore, different under each method.

Now we can consider some important questions. Which critical event for recognizing revenue is best? Which one reports the "right" amount of revenue? How do these different critical events affect users of Escuminac's financial statements?

First, recognizing revenue on production or on delivery are both potentially reasonable alternatives for Escuminac, depending on the details of the contract between the company and its customers. The business arrangement used by Escuminac is an example of the bill and hold arrangement described earlier. Accounting standards address the appropriateness of recognizing revenue on production in situations such as this one, but ultimately professional judgment by managers and accountants is needed to interpret the facts. Reasonable arguments in favour of more than one alternative can be made.

Which critical event is *best* is a question that cannot be answered. The best or most appropriate choice of critical event depends on the situation—the stakeholders, the managers, and the facts underlying the entity's economic transactions. The accounting environment plays an important role in determining the best critical event.

Which critical event reports the "right" amount of revenue and income? This is another question that has no correct answer. The two critical events discussed above are different ways of measuring the same underlying economic activity and both can be supported. Because revenue is earned continuously, using a critical event is a convenient way to overcome the difficulty of measuring revenue as it is earned in an economic sense. However, using a critical event to recognize revenue is convenient but arbitrary. And, most important, regardless of which critical event is selected, Escuminac Manufacturing Ltd. is the same. The accounting choices an entity makes do not change the underlying economic activities that an entity is reporting. Different accounting choices simply change how the underlying economic activities are reported. This is not to say, however, that different accounting choices do not have economic consequences for the entity and its stakeholders. They certainly do.

This leads us to the final question: How are stakeholders affected by these alternative critical events? If there are contracts or agreements that are based on accounting numbers such as revenue or net income, the accounting choices an entity makes can have an effect on the stakeholders. If the president of Escuminac receives a bonus of 1 percent of net income, her bonus is directly affected by the critical event that has been chosen for recognizing revenue. The amount of tax that Escuminac pays may be related to the critical event chosen. Unionized employees might feel more confident about seeking wage increases if Escuminac reported net income that had been determined using production as the critical event, because the higher net income suggests a more successful company and a greater ability to pay higher wages. In fact, there are many different contracts and agreements that rely on accounting numbers, which makes accountants' measurement of things like revenue very important.

Even more subtle is the effect that different choices have on the perceptions of users. Does a more "rosy" income statement make a company more attractive to investors and lenders? Do higher revenues and higher net incomes make stakeholders think that managers have done a better job, even if the difference in the numbers was due to an entity's accounting choices, rather than real economic differences? While it is hard to give definite answers, there is some evidence that managers concerned about the numbers that are reported will use accounting flexibility to report numbers more to their liking.

In summary, here are some of the important issues to keep in mind while you think about the Escuminac Manufacturing Ltd. example:

1. When you receive an income statement, you are not shown what revenue or net income would have been under alternative choices of critical events. That means the income statement you receive shapes your perceptions of the entity.

2. The managers choose the critical event for recognizing revenue. That means that the self-interest of Escuminac's management can affect its choice. (Self-interest in an accounting choice situation means that the managers would choose accounting methods that, for example, give them higher bonuses rather than providing more useful information to stakeholders.)

3. The economic activity of Escuminac is not affected by how or when it recognizes revenue. Regardless of which critical event is chosen, the same amount of equipment was produced each year, the same amount of equipment was delivered each year, and the same amount of cash was collected each year. What is affected is how the activities are accounted for and reported.

Question for Consideration

Suppose you are an investor who is interested in making an investment in a manufacturing company. Examine the two sets of income statements provided for Escuminac Manufacturing Ltd. in Table 4–1 and choose which of the sets of statements represent a better investment. Explain your choice.

Answer: This is a trick question. The two financial statements represent exactly the same company at exactly the same time in exactly the same circumstances. The underlying economic activity of Escuminac is not affected even though the choice of critical event affects how that economic activity is represented in the financial statements. Thus, regardless of how revenue is recognized, the same amount of equipment was produced each year, the same amount of equipment was delivered to customers each year, and the same amount of cash was collected each year. Thus, your perceptions, as an individual investor of Escuminac, may be influenced by how the economic activity is represented in the financial statements.

Google Inc.

Now let's look at a real example of how different revenue recognition methods can affect a company's financial statements. Google Inc. (Google) is the well-known company that offers free online search services. In 2004, Google became a public company by offering its shares to investors (the shares were sold by the company itself and by its shareholders). When a company "goes public" it must file a document with the securities regulator called a prospectus. A **prospectus** is a legal document that provides detailed information about a company that is offering its securities for public sale.

On July 12, 2004 Google filed a prospectus with the Securities and Exchange Commission (SEC) (the securities regulator in the United States). The income statements in that prospectus can be found in Panel A of Exhibit 4–4. Notice that for the year ended December 31, 2003 revenue was $961,874,000, cost of revenues was $121,794,000, and net income was $105,648,000. Just two weeks later on July 26, 2004 Google filed an amended prospectus with the SEC. The income statements from that prospectus can be seen in Panel B of Exhibit 4–4. Now, for the year ended December 31, 2003 Google's revenue has increased to $1,465,934,000 and cost of revenues has increased to $625,854,000. Net income is unchanged. In the space of two weeks Google's revenue increased by over $500,000,000, an increase of over 50 percent![5] What happened? A colossal error? An obvious fraud? No, it's nothing but accounting at work.

What caused this dramatic change was a change in how Google recognized its revenue. One of the ways Google makes money is by placing ads for advertisers on other companies' Web sites. Each time a Web user clicks on an ad, Google is entitled to payment from the advertiser. Google must then make a payment to the owner of the Web site where the ad appeared. Suppose Google gets $3 each time an Internet user clicks on an ad and from that amount it must pay $2 to the Web publisher on whose site the ad appears. For each click on the ad, how much revenue should Google recognize? Should it recognize $3 of revenue and a $2 expense for the payment to the Web publisher (this is called the gross method because the amount reported as revenue is the full amount owed by the advertiser)? Or should it simply recognize $1 in revenue (called the net method because the amount reported as revenue is the net amount owed by the advertiser after deducting the amount owed to the Web publisher)?

In its July 12, 2004 prospectus, Google used the net method for recognizing its revenue, whereas in the July 26 prospectus it switched to the gross method. By making this change, revenues and cost of revenues increased by the same amount (this is why net income didn't change). No explanation was given. A possible reason is that Google wanted to use the same accounting method as its competitor, Yahoo. In any case, Google's income statement looks quite different as a result of the change. Whereas there is no effect on the company's net income, there are significant effects on revenues, expenses, and on financial ratios such as

Panel A From the prospectus issued July 12, 2004

| GOOGLE INC.
CONSOLIDATED STATEMENTS OF INCOME
(IN THOUSANDS, EXCEPT PER SHARE AMOUNTS)			
	Year Ended December 31		
	2001	**2002**	**2003**
Net revenues	$86,426	$347,848	$961,874
Costs and expenses:			
Cost of revenues	14,228	39,850	121,794
Research and development	16,500	31,748	91,228
Sales and marketing	20,076	43,849	120,328
General and administrative	12,275	24,300	56,699
Stock-based compensation (1)	12,383	21,635	229,361
Total costs and expenses	75,462	161,382	619,410
Income from operations	10,964	186,466	342,464
Interest income (expense) and other, net	(896)	(1,551)	4,190
Income before income taxes	10,068	184,915	346,654
Provision for income taxes	3,083	85,259	241,006
Net income	$6,985	$99,656	$105,648

Extract from the notes to the financial statements:
Google AdSense is the program through which the Company distributes its advertisers' text-based ads for display on the Web sites of the Google Network members. The Company recognizes as revenues the fees charged advertisers net of the portion shared with its Google Network members under its AdSense program.

Panel B From the prospectus issued July 26, 2004

| GOOGLE INC.
CONSOLIDATED STATEMENTS OF INCOME
(IN THOUSANDS, EXCEPT PER SHARE AMOUNTS)			
	Year Ended December 31		
	2001	**2002**	**2003**
Revenues	$86,426	$439,508	$1,465,934
Costs and expenses:			
Cost of revenues	14,228	131,510	625,854
Research and development	16,500	31,748	91,228
Sales and marketing	20,076	43,849	120,328
General and administrative	12,275	24,300	56,699
Stock-based compensation (1)	12,383	21,635	229,361
Total costs and expenses	75,462	253,042	1,123,470
Income from operations	10,964	186,466	342,464
Interest income (expense) and other, net	(896)	(1,551)	4,190
Income before income taxes	10,068	184,915	346,654
Provision for income taxes	3,083	85,259	241,006
Net income	$6,985	$99,656	$105,648

Extract from the notes to the financial statements:
Google AdSense is the program through which the Company distributes its advertisers' text-based ads for display on the web sites of the Google Network members. In accordance with Emerging Issues Task Force ("EITF") Issue No. 99-19, *Reporting Revenue Gross as a Principal Versus Net as an Agent*, the Company recognizes as revenues the fees it receives from its advertisers. This revenue is reported gross primarily because the Company is the primary obligor to its advertisers.

profit margin. In the July 12, 2004 prospectus Google's profit margin percentage for 2003 is 11.0 percent ($105,648,000/$961,784,000) while in the July 26, 2004 prospectus the profit margin percentage is 7.2 percent ($105,648,000/$1,465,934,000).

It is crucial to recognize that Google is the same company in the two prospectuses. Suddenly having an extra $500,000,000 of revenue changed nothing. Google's underlying economic activity is exactly the same. What has changed is the accounting representation of that economic activity.

Why Do Managers Have So Much Choice?

The discussion of Escuminac Manufacturing Ltd. and Google Inc. might make you wonder why managers are given so much power over the way they choose to report the information in financial statements. Can't rules be established to limit choices and effectively capture economic reality? Wouldn't it be easier if there were just one way to recognize revenue? Accounting standard setters and regulators often try to restrict or eliminate the accounting choices available to managers by issuing accounting standards that entities adhering to GAAP must observe. That's one of the roles of the *CICA Handbook*. However, while eliminating choice may make all financial statements consistent in how and when they recognize revenue, the same critical event may not make statements comparable. The fact is that all sale transactions are not identical. The terms of sale can vary widely, such that the same critical event would not make sense for every sale. For example, consider the following two transactions. In the first, a producer ships goods on consignment to the customer. The customer only pays if it sells the goods and the goods can be returned at any time without penalty to the producer. In the second case, the producer ships the goods to the customer on a final sale basis. The goods cannot be returned for any reason and they must be paid for in full within 30 days. Does it make sense to use the same critical event in both cases to recognize revenue? After all, the transactions are different and the financial statements would probably be more informative if different critical events were used.

In theory, allowing choice for recognizing revenue and for other accounting issues is sensible because the economic activities of the Canadian and world economies are too complex to precisely define accounting rules to suit every situation. The challenge with accounting choice is ensuring that the people who prepare accounting information provide the most useful information to stakeholders instead of focusing on their own interests. This is an ethical challenge faced by accountants and other financial professionals.

Consider this analogy: When most people look for a job they create a résumé to show to prospective employers. A résumé is usually a short, concise document describing a person's experience, education, skills and abilities, interests, activities, and any other information considered appropriate by the job hunter. When preparing a résumé, you would presumably try to highlight your strengths and downplay your weaknesses. You wouldn't add false university degrees or work experience, but you would certainly organize the information and describe your accomplishments in ways that would put you in the best light. Further, if you were applying for several quite different jobs (perhaps in accounting, marketing, and finance), it is possible that you might even prepare a different résumé for each job, with each résumé highlighting the attributes best suited for each job.

Is it dishonest to give different résumés to different prospective employers, provided that the information in each résumé is truthful? Given that there are many ways that a résumé can be written and organized, how would you describe the "right" way to prepare one? Should there be international rules that dictate how every résumé should be prepared? In many ways, preparing financial statements is like writing a résumé. Most people have an honest desire to provide useful and relevant information to the users of the financial statements or résumés. At the same time, the people who prepare financial statements, like a person preparing a résumé, will want to put themselves in a good light. Without strict rules about the right way to prepare financial statements or résumés, a lot of power and judgment is given to the people preparing the information. Even under GAAP, the rules are not strict. GAAP provide considerable room for judgment and flexibility. In the absence of GAAP, flexibility is even greater. However, with GAAP or in the absence of GAAP, while there can be many acceptable or "right" ways to prepare financial statements, there are also many unacceptable or "wrong" ways.

The Gradual Approach to Recognizing Revenue

The gradual approach recognizes revenue bit by bit over the entire earnings process rather than when a particular critical event occurs. The gradual approach is consistent with the conceptual nature of the revenue-earning process because it reflects earnings as a continuous rather than a discrete process. As we discussed earlier, in most situations recording revenue gradually is not practical. However, in a number of situations the gradual method is practical and necessary for providing useful information to users of the financial statements. In these situations, the gradual approach is not an *alternative* to the critical-event approach; rather, it is used in situations where the critical-event approach is not appropriate.

We have already considered one example of the gradual approach to revenue recognition. In Chapter 3 we examined how adjusting journal entries are made to accrue interest earned on investments such as bonds and bank accounts. These adjusting entries, referred to as the accrued revenue/ accrued asset type, are made so that the income statement will reflect interest earned to date even though cash has not been received and is not owed as of the date on which the financial statements are being prepared. With this type of revenue, there is no critical event triggering revenue recognition and recognition is not all-or-nothing. Instead, the revenue is earned gradually over time.

The gradual approach to revenue recognition is appropriate for providing useful and timely information to stakeholders regarding delivery of services and long-term construction projects such as dams and large buildings. With a long-term contract, an entity is earning revenue in more than one reporting period. If a critical-event approach were used, revenues and earnings would tend to be more erratic. Since the revenue-recognition criteria usually lead to later rather than earlier revenue recognition, the early years of long-term contracts would have no revenue or income and a later or the final year would have it all. As a result, stakeholders would be prevented from receiving timely and relevant information for their decision making.

The Percentage-of-Completion Method A gradual-approach method that is used for recognizing revenue on long-term contracts is known as the percentage-of-completion method. With the **percentage-of-completion method**, revenues and expenses associated with a long-term contract are spread over the life of the contract, based on a measure of the effort completed in each period. This approach reduces the erratic reporting of revenues and earnings, and provides useful economic information to stakeholders on a timelier basis. The percentage-of-completion method can be considered a compromise because the four revenue-recognition criteria are usually not met when revenue is recognized early on in the contract. For a long-term project such as the construction of a dam, the entity will not have performed in the early periods of the contract (because the dam has not been built). Also, in most cases, there will be uncertainties about future costs to be incurred and possibly uncertainty about the amount of revenue that will be earned. Notice that the description of the percentage-of-completion method requires allocation of both revenues and expenses. Remember that under accrual accounting and the matching concept, expenses must be recognized in the period when the revenues they helped earn are recognized.

To use the percentage-of-completion method, it is necessary to have a way of determining how much revenue to recognize in each period. One of the most common ways is to base the estimate on the proportion of total costs incurred to date on the contract. This can be done by using the ratio of the actual costs incurred on the project during the period to the project's total estimated costs. Thus, the revenue recognized in a period is:

$$\text{Revenue for the period} = \frac{\text{Cost incurred during the period}}{\text{Total estimated costs for the project}} \times \text{Estimated revenue for the project}$$

Note that it is necessary to estimate total revenues as well as total costs for the project to calculate the revenue that should be recognized in a period.

As long as a project is profitable, the percentage-of-completion method is used as described above. However, if a project is found to be unprofitable—that is, if the expenses are expected to be greater than the revenue—then 100 percent of the loss is recognized immediately. The loss is not spread over the entire contract. The reason this treatment is used is conservatism. Conservatism requires a cautious approach to reporting, so whenever a loss becomes known it is accounted for in full immediately, even though reporting 100 percent of the loss is not consistent with the percentage-of-completion method

The Completed-Contract Method Sometimes it is not possible to use the percentage-of-completion method for a long-term contract. If the revenues or expenses cannot be reasonably estimated, or if it is difficult to estimate the portion of the project that has been completed, then the **completed-contract method** is used instead. The completed-contract method is a critical-event approach that recognizes revenue in full when a contract is completed. The income statement is not affected until the contract is complete. All the costs incurred are accumulated in balance sheet asset accounts until the revenue is recognized. When the revenue is recognized, the balances in these asset accounts are expensed and matched to the revenue. Conservatism also affects reporting when the completed-contract method is used. Under the completed-contract method a loss is also reported as soon as it is known. That means that the loss would be reported before the contract is completed.

Comparing the Completed-Contract and Percentage-of-Completion Methods Let's compare the effects on the income statement of the completed-contract and percentage-of-completion methods. On December 15, 2008 Judique Construction Corporation (Judique) entered into a three-year contract to build a factory for Hallam Corp. (Hallam). Hallam agreed to pay $75,000,000 for the factory, from which Judique would cover all costs of construction. Hallam paid $5,000,000 when it signed the contract and agreed to pay $20,000,000 on July 2 of each of the next three years. The final $10,000,000 is to be paid six months after the factory is completed. The expected completion date is August 1, 2011. Table 4–2 shows Judique's estimated annual costs and the amount of revenue that would be recognized each year using the percentage-of-completion method. Judique's year end is December 31. It is important to recognize that cash flows and revenue and expense flows do not have to correspond. Revenue is recognized based on the portion of the job that has been completed, not when payment is made.

For the completed-contract method, all the revenue would be recognized in 2011 when the factory is completed. Net income under the percentage-of-completion method and the completed-contract method for each year of the contract is shown in Table 4–3 (page 184). The total amount of revenue and expense under the two methods is the same. What differs is the amount that is reported in each period.

The problem with the completed-contract method is clear. In years when no contracts are completed, no revenue and no expenses are reported on the income statement, making

---

TABLE 4–2 ::: Judique Contruction Corporation: Amount of Revenue Recognized Using Percentage-of-Completion Method

	Column A	Column B	Column C	Column D	
Year	Cash payments by Hallam to Judique	Judique's estimated annual cost of building the factory	Percentage of project completed each year based on estimated costs	Amount of revenue recognized each year Calculated as: $\dfrac{\text{Year's cost}}{\text{Total estimated cost}} \times \text{Total revenue}$	
2004	$ 5,000,000				
2005	$20,000,000	$ 9,000,000	18.8%*	$14,063,000	$\dfrac{\$9,000,000}{\$48,000,000} \times \$75,000,000$
2006	$20,000,000	$18,000,000	37.5%*	$28,125,000	$\dfrac{\$18,000,000}{\$48,000,000} \times \$75,000,000$
2007	$20,000,000	$21,000,000	43.7%*	$32,812,000	$\dfrac{\$21,000,000}{\$48,000,000} \times \$75,000,000$
2008	$10,000,000				
Total	$75,000,000	$48,000,000	100%	$75,000,000	

*The percentage of the project completed each year $= \dfrac{\text{Year's cost (Column B)}}{\text{Total estimated cost (total of Column B)}}$

TABLE 4–3 ::: Judique Construction Corporation: Percentage-of-Completion versus Completed-Contract Methods for Accounting for Long-Term Contracts										
Judique Construction Corporation **Income Statements** **(thousands of dollars)**										
	Percentage-of-Completion Method					**Completed-Contract Method**				
	2008	**2009**	**2010**	**2011**	**Total**	**2008**	**2009**	**2010**	**2011**	**Total**
Income Statements										
Revenue	$0	$14,063	$28,125	$32,812	$75,000	$0	$0	$0	$75,000	$75,000
Expenses	0	9,000	18,000	21,000	48,000	0	0	0	48,000	48,000
Net income	$0	$ 5,063	$10,125	$11,812	$27,000	$0	$0	$0	$27,000	$27,000

Judique appear to be an inactive company. This could be very misleading to users who are unaware of how Judique conducts its business. At a minimum, the financial statements are not very informative. If a company is involved in a small number of long-term contracts at any one time, the completed-contract method can produce wild fluctuations in earnings, depending upon when the contracts are completed.

The percentage-of-completion method gives a more realistic indication of Judique's economic activity. Over the term of the contract, Judique is earning revenue by building the factory. The percentage-of-completion method reflects this economic activity in the financial statements. The disadvantage of the percentage-of-completion method is that it allows managers some latitude in deciding how much revenue and income to report in each period. This latitude exists because estimates are required to determine the amount of revenue to be reported in a period. The completed-contract method reduces managers' latitude because revenues and expenses are known when the contract is completed, so with the completed-contract method we are giving up relevance to get more reliability.

In practice, the accounting for long-term contracts can get much more complicated than the example indicates. For instance, the example assumes that actual costs equal estimated costs. In most cases, actual costs will differ from estimated costs, sometimes dramatically. Many other problems can arise over the course of a long-term contract that can affect the accounting for the project.

www.mcgrawhill.ca/
olc/friedlan

Knowledge Check

- What is the gradual approach to recognizing revenue?

- How do you determine the percentage of a project that has been completed?

- How does conservatism affect the application of the percentage-of-completion method?

One of the reasons an entity would choose to use the completed-contract method rather than the percentage-of-completion method is that Canada Revenue Agency allows the use of completed-contract accounting for contracts less than two years long. The benefit of the completed-contract method for tax purposes is that it delays payment of taxes. The *Income Tax Act* requires that the percentage-of-completion method be used for contracts that are longer than two years. The following example shows the tax benefit of using the completed-contract method.

Joynt Corp. (Joynt) signs a contract to do major renovations to an office building. The work will be completed over two fiscal years. Joynt estimates that half the work will be done in 2009 and half in 2010. Joynt's year end is December 31. Joynt will be paid $300,000 for the job and will incur tax-deductible costs of $120,000. If Joynt uses the percentage-of-completion method, it will report $90,000 of income in each year that can be taxed. At a tax rate of 25 percent, Joynt will pay tax of $22,500 each year. If Joynt uses the completed-contract method, it will pay no tax in 2009, since it will not report any income in that year, but will pay $45,000 in tax in 2010. The income statements for Joynt showing these results are given in Table 4–4. While Joynt pays the same amount of tax over the two years, the company defers the payment of $22,500 in tax for a year without any penalty by using the completed-contract method. This deferral means that Joynt has an extra $22,500 to use or invest for a year. If cash were tight, the $22,500 would be useful. It could reduce the amount of borrowing that is required or be invested to earn additional money.

Accounting Innovation: Revenue Recognition at Microsoft Corporation

Revenue recognition for most companies is not very controversial. But from time to time, a completely new business arrangement or a significantly different variation of an existing arrangement occurs. When this happens, accountants and managers must figure out an appropriate way of accounting and create and innovate new solutions.

Let's take a look at an example of accounting innovation. When Microsoft Corporation (Microsoft) sells its Windows® operating system or software such as Excel® or PowerPoint®, it doesn't recognize 100 percent of the selling price as revenue in the year that the software is sold. Instead, it defers a portion of the revenue because customers are entitled to additional services and products, such as technical support and product upgrades, that will be provided to customers in future periods. The traditional accounting treatment in this type of situation would be to recognize

www.microsoft.com/msft

| TABLE | 4–4 | ::: | **Tax Benefits of Using the Completed-Contract Method** |

Joynt Corp.
Income Statements

	Percentage-of-Completion Method		Completed-Contract Method	
	Years Ended		Years Ended	
	2009	**2010**	**2009**	**2010**
Revenue	$150,000	$150,000	$0	$300,000
Expenses	60,000	60,000	0	120,000
Taxes	22,500	22,500	0	45,000
Net income	67,500	67,500	$0	$135,000

Knowledge Check

:::

www.mcgrawhill.ca/olc/friedlan

Ryley Inc. (Ryley) recently entered into a three-year contract to build a small office building for a growing law firm. The law firm will pay Ryley $7,000,000 for the building. Ryley is required to pay all costs. Ryley estimates that its total cost to build the building will be $5,200,000. It estimates the cost to be $1,700,000 in the first year, $2,500,000 in the second year, and $1,000,000 in the third year. Assuming that Ryley's cost estimates prove to be correct, how much revenue will it recognize in each year of the contract using (1) the percentage-of-completion method and (2) the completed-contract method?

EXHIBIT 4–5 :	
Microsoft Corporation's Revenue Recognition Policies	

REVENUE RECOGNITION

Revenue is recognized when persuasive evidence of an arrangement exists, delivery has occurred, the fee is fixed or determinable, and collectability is probable. We enter into certain arrangements where we are obligated to deliver multiple products and/or services (multiple elements). In these arrangements, we generally allocate the total revenue among the elements based on the sales price of each element when sold separately (vendor-specific objective evidence).

Revenue for retail packaged products, products licensed to original equipment manufacturers (OEMs), and perpetual licenses for current products under our Open and Select volume licensing programs generally is recognized as products are shipped, with a portion of the revenue recorded as unearned due to undelivered elements including, in some cases, free post-delivery telephone support and the right to receive unspecified upgrades/enhancements of Microsoft Internet Explorer on a when-and-if-available basis. The amount of revenue allocated to undelivered elements is based on the vendor-specific objective evidence of fair value for those elements using the residual method. Under the residual method, the total fair value of the undelivered elements, as indicated by vendor-specific objective evidence, is recorded as unearned, and the difference between the total arrangement fee and the amount recorded as unearned for the undelivered elements is recognized as revenue related to delivered elements. Unearned revenue due to undelivered elements is recognized ratably on a straight-line basis over the related product's life cycle.

UNEARNED REVENUE

Undelivered elements — Represents free post-delivery telephone support and the right to receive unspecified upgrades/enhancements of Microsoft Internet Explorer on a when-and-if-available basis. The amount recorded as unearned is based on the sales price of those elements when sold separately and is recognized ratably on a straight-line basis over the related product's life cycle. The percentage of revenue recorded as unearned due to undelivered elements ranges from approximately 15 percent to 25 percent of the sales price for Windows XP Home, approximately 5 percent to 15 percent of the sales price for Windows XP Professional, and approximately 1 percent to 15 percent of the sales price for desktop applications, depending on the terms and conditions of the license and prices of the elements. Product life cycles are currently estimated at three and one-half years for Windows operating systems and two years for desktop applications.

the full selling price as revenue when the product was shipped, despite the additional products and services. When Microsoft ships certain products, it makes a journal entry similar to this:

Dr. Accounts receivable	100	
Cr. Revenue		80
Cr. Unearned revenue		20

The effect of this entry is that some of Microsoft's revenue is deferred to later periods. As a result of this treatment, Microsoft reported unearned revenue of $2.1 billion on June 30, 2005. Extracts from notes to Microsoft's financial statements explaining its revenue recognition policies are shown in Exhibit 4–5.[6]

Is Microsoft's treatment justifiable? The answer is yes. That is the problem. In effect, Microsoft is arguing that when it sells some of its products, it is really selling a series of products and services that are provided over more than one period. Microsoft contends that when it ships the initial product, it has not earned the revenue on the product and services that will be delivered later. Microsoft's position has merit. The approach is more conservative than recognizing 100 percent of the selling price as revenue when a product is shipped to a customer, which is usually very appealing to accountants. The approach also recognizes the more complex nature of the product being sold.

However, some critics have argued that Microsoft's accounting treatment is really designed to allow it to "smooth" its earnings, report steadily increasing profits, and meet the earnings targets set by financial analysts. ("Smoothing income" refers to managing revenues and expenses to smooth out the "peaks" and "valleys" that can appear in reported earnings from period to period.) When Microsoft releases a new version of some of its products, there is a sales spike as people rush to purchase the latest software. The spike adds significantly to revenue and earnings when the product is released, but revenue and earnings may be lower in the next period once that initial burst of demand has been satisfied. By deferring revenue, Microsoft takes some of that sales spike and moves it and the related profits into later periods, thereby "smoothing" its earnings. As it turned out, there was merit to the critics' concerns. In 2002, the SEC and Microsoft settled accounting charges that the SEC had brought against Microsoft, suggesting that Microsoft may have used accounting choices to smooth its income.

Is Microsoft's accounting bad or wrong? No, it was just new and different. Their approach, in changing the way it recognizes its revenue, does make it more difficult to use financial statements because similar companies may be using different accounting policies. On the other hand, the software business is relatively new and it is not surprising that new accounting approaches are arising to meet different circumstances. This is one of the ways new accounting approaches become generally accepted. GAAP in particular, and accounting principles in general, are evolving. As changes take place in the world that affect how entities operate and transact, and as the needs of stakeholders change, accounting must respond to keep up with the changes.

GAINS AND LOSSES

A gain or loss arises when an entity sells an asset that it does not usually sell in the ordinary course of its business for an amount that is different from the net book value of the asset. For example, if Rogers sells furniture and fixtures or old computers, a gain or a loss arises rather than revenue and expenses because Rogers is not in the business of selling these things.

Let's consider some examples. An entity owns land that has a net book value of $500,000. If the land is sold for more than $500,000 a gain results; if it is sold for less than $500,000 a loss results. For example:

1. If the land were sold for $600,000, a gain of $100,000 would be reported on the income statement (selling price − net book value = $600,000 − $500,000 = $100,000).

2. If the land were sold for $425,000, a loss of $75,000 would be reported (selling price − net book value = $425,000 − $500,000 = − $75,000). The journal entries to record the gain and loss would be:

        1. Dr. Cash   600,000
              Cr. Gain on sale of land (income statement)   100,000
              Cr. Land   500,000
           To record the gain on the sale of land.
        2. Dr. Cash   425,000
           Dr. Loss on sale of land (income statement)   75,000
              Cr. Land   500,000
           To record the loss on the sale of land.

In both cases, the land account must be credited for $500,000, the book value of the land. The difference between the amount received and the amount recorded in the accounting system is the gain or loss.

The difference between the income statement presentation of the sale of an asset that results in a gain or loss and the sale of inventory is one of detail. When inventory is sold, the revenue and the cost of the inventory are shown separately (revenue − cost of sales). When the sale of an incidental asset occurs, the proceeds from the sale and the cost of the asset sold are shown net— only the net amount, the gain or loss, is shown. The examples here are limited to the sale of land—an asset that is not amortized. Gains and losses also arise when assets that are amortized are sold. We will look at the accounting for the sale of amortizable assets in Chapter 9. For now, recognize that the net book value of an asset that is amortized equals the cost of the asset less the amount of the asset that has been amortized up to the date the asset is sold.

A couple of points are worth mentioning:

1. The amount of a gain or loss is related to the accounting choices that were made regarding the asset. The costs that were capitalized, the amortization method selected, and the estimates of residual value and useful life will all affect the net book value of the asset and, therefore, the gain or loss.

2. Proceeds from the sale of a capital asset should not be affected by the book value. The price a buyer will pay for an asset will be based on the economic value of the asset to the buyer. The net book value of the asset will make no difference to the buyer. Sellers may be affected by the accounting effect of a potential sale because they may be concerned about the impact of

the gain or loss on the financial statements. This behaviour by sellers (managers) is not especially prudent because they should focus on the economic effects of a transaction, not its accounting effects.

Generally, gains and losses should be reported separately from revenues and expenses on the income statement. Disclosing gains and losses separately is important because if they are included in normal operating revenues and expenses, it can be much more difficult for financial statement users to assess the performance of the entity. Gains and losses are different from ordinary revenue and expenses, and users such as investors should interpret them differently. For example, if a gain is included in revenue, the amount of operating revenue reported by the entity is overstated, which would make it difficult for an investor to predict future earnings.

Exhibit 4–6 (next page) provides an example of how a gain is reported on the income statement.[7] In 2005 Peace Arch Entertainment Group Inc., a media company that finances, packages, and distributes movies and television programs reported a number of gains and a loss in the three years reported, including a $98,000 gain on the sale of assets and a $2,560,000 gain on the settlement of obligations.

www.peacearch.com

EXPENSE RECOGNITION

A key concept in accrual accounting for determining income is the matching concept, which was introduced in Chapter 3. According to the matching concept, expenses are reported on the income statement in the same period as the revenue that those expenses helped earn. The order of the accounting is important: *expenses* are matched to *revenues*. First, revenue is recognized and then the costs incurred to earn that revenue are expensed. This process is generally the reverse of actual economic activity. Usually an entity first incurs the costs that will help generate revenues and then later earns the revenue. For example, Rogers must acquire spectrum and licenses to operate cell phone service in Canada, construct a cell phone network, and advertise its services before it can provide cell phone services to its customers.

The matching principle makes sense, at least for some uses and users of accounting information. If the purpose of an income statement is to provide information about the economic (as opposed to cash flow) activity and performance of an entity, it makes sense to associate costs and benefits. If you sell a cell phone and want to know how much better off you are as a result of the sale, it makes sense to subtract the cost of the phone, along with any other costs incurred to sell it, from the revenue that you earned. Accrual accounting requires that all costs be matched to the revenue—regardless of whether cash was paid before, at the same time as, or after the revenue is recognized.

In a perfect accrual accounting world, all costs could be matched to the related revenues. Practically speaking, that can't be done. The problem is that often there are many costs that are difficult to match. Consider the costs that a retail clothing store incurs to sell a pair of pants. First, there is the cost of the pants. This cost is easy to match to the revenue earned from selling the pants. Then there are wages to salespeople and rent for the stores. But how do you match a salesperson's wage or the store rent to the sale of a particular pair of pants? It is even more difficult to match the cost of the capital assets used in the store. For example, how can the cost of display cases be matched to the sale of a particular item? As you can see, many costs do not lend themselves well to matching.

The result is that the income statement does not perfectly match costs and benefits. That is, when it is difficult or impossible to reasonably match costs and benefits, accountants do not try to force a match. Instead, costs that cannot be reasonably matched to revenue are expensed in the period in which they are incurred. The wages the retail clothing store pays to its store employees and the rent it pays for its stores are expensed when the employees do their work or when the space being rented is used. Costs that are expensed in the period that they are incurred are called **period costs**. Costs that can be matched to specific revenues, such as the cost of pants that are sold, are called **product costs**. Product costs are expensed when the revenue they help generate is recognized. Product costs are usually accumulated in inventory on the balance sheet (or in some other balance sheet account) until the revenue is recognized. Note that the distinction between

Peace Arch Entertainment Group Inc.
Consolidated Statements of Earnings (Loss)
For the years ended August 31, 2005, 2004 and 2003

EXHIBIT 4-6 :

**Peace Arch
Entertainment
Group Inc.**

(expressed in thousands of Canadian dollars, except per share amounts)

	2005 $	2004 $	2003 $
Revenue	10,747	21,236	21,465
Expenses			
Amortization of investment in film and television programming and other production costs (note 4)	8,636	18,774	18,827
Selling, general and administrative	3,888	3,370	3,088
	12,524	22,144	21,915
Earnings (loss) from operations before the undernoted	(1,777)	(908)	(450)
Interest income (note 12)	818	39	125
Interest expense (note 17)	(953)	(220)	(495)
Other amortization	(74)	(17)	(230)
Provision for obligation to issue shares (note 9(d))	–	(207)	–
Gain on sale of asset (note 8)	98	–	127
Foreign exchange gain (loss)	679	(575)	778
Gain on settlement of obligations (note 11)	2,560	–	–
Loss on disposal of subsidiary	–	–	(164)
Gain on modification of debt	–	–	3,094
Recovery of selling, general and administration expenses (note 10)	145	427	–
Non-controlling interest (note 2(b))	(47)	–	–
Earnings (loss) before income taxes	1,449	(1,461)	2,785
Income tax recovery	–	(977)	(74)
Net earnings (loss) for the year	1,449	(484)	2,859
Net earnings (loss) per common share (note 18)			
Basic	0.07	(0.03)	0.24
Diluted	0.07	(0.03)	0.19

product costs and period costs is not always clear. One cannot say that a certain type of cost will always be a product cost or a period cost.

It is also necessary to estimate costs that have not yet been incurred so that they can be matched to revenues. For example, bad debts, returns, and warranty costs are usually incurred after revenue is recognized. Let's look at these situations in more detail.

- The bad debt expense is an estimate of the amount that will not be collected from customers who purchased on credit. Of course, it is not possible to identify the customers who are not going to pay at the time of the transaction because if you could, you wouldn't sell to those customers. However, bad debts are a cost of selling on credit and should, under accrual accounting, be matched to the related revenue.

- When merchandise is returned it represents revenue that never happened. As a result, an estimate of returns should be accrued in the period the related revenue is recognized.

- Many businesses offer to repair, adjust, or service their goods or services after a customer buys them—sometimes for a long time after the sale. For example, many new cars come with a 36-month-or-60,000-kilometre warranty covering the complete vehicle against defects in factory-supplied materials or workmanship. Warranty costs should be accrued when the revenue from the product or service under warranty is sold. The difficult part of accounting for these costs is estimating how much they will be. Managers rely on historical information and their knowledge of the business and products to come up with estimates.

It is important to remember that not all stakeholders or uses of accounting information benefit from matching. For example, recognizing expenses as early as possible, regardless of matching, reduces the amount of income tax that has to be paid. Lenders might be interested in cash flow information so that they can assess the liquidity of the entity, again regardless of matching. One must always keep in mind that the usefulness of information has to be assessed in the context of the needs of the user. As a result, it cannot be said that GAAP financial statements are the best way to present accounting information to all users or in all situations. However, for accrual accounting and GAAP, matching is a central concept.

THE OBJECTIVES OF FINANCIAL REPORTING

Managers can often choose from a number of reasonable accounting treatments for transactions and other economic events, even under GAAP. The discussion of revenue recognition in this chapter highlights this idea. But how do managers decide which accounting methods to choose?

Managers' choices are influenced by two factors: the information needs of stakeholders and their own self-interest. Providing relevant information to stakeholders is the reason for financial accounting, but as we have seen managers may take their own needs into consideration when making accounting choices. Managers' needs include maximizing compensation, job security, increasing share price or the apparent value of the business, and so on. The information needs of stakeholders and manager self-interest often conflict. The accounting choice that provides the "best" information to stakeholders (or at least to particular stakeholders) will not always be the one that best satisfies the interests of managers. Ideally, self-interest should not play a role in the accounting choices a manager makes, but given human nature, self-interest can be a factor. In fact, there is considerable evidence that managers' accounting choices are influenced by self-interest. Given the reality of self-interested behaviour by managers, it is crucial for users of accounting information to understand the nature of this behaviour and the impact it can have on their ability to analyze and interpret financial statements. The factors that affect accounting choice are shown in Figure 4-1.

Figure 4–1 shows the two factors that influence managers' accounting choices and lists some of the managers' self-interests. Stakeholders who require information for decision making are also shown (these were first shown in Figure 1–1 on page 6). While managers often have choice in how to account, they usually can't account any way they want. There are mechanisms in place to limit managers' accounting choices and their self-interest. These mechanisms include the following:

- GAAP

- the involvement of independent accountants and auditors who assess, on behalf of stakeholders, the accounting choices made by the managers

- contract terms

- the information demands of powerful stakeholders who may dictate accounting treatments and disclosures

- the facts surrounding an economic event or transaction that is being accounted for

Determining the extent to which self-interest influences accounting choices is a challenge. But even if managers considered only the information needs of stakeholders when making accounting choices, they would still have choices to make and stakeholders would not be assured of receiving information that was most useful for their decisions. The reason for this is that, as we saw in Chapter 1, there are many stakeholders who can use accounting information, and the information appropriate for each stakeholder group is not necessarily the same. However, an entity can prepare only one set of general purpose financial statements. That means that some stakeholders' information needs are not going to be satisfied by an entity's general purpose report. (An entity can produce any number of special purpose reports that are designed for a specific purpose, but special purpose reports will be prepared only for powerful stakeholders who have the ability to demand information that is tailored to their needs.)

Factors Influencing Managers' Accounting Choices

Stakeholder information needs   Managers' self interests

Stakeholders
- Shareholders
- Partners
- Proprietors
- Employees
- Unions
- Regulators
- Creditors
- Taxation authorities
- Potential shareholders
- Managers
- Contributors
- Customers
- Governments
- Politicians
- Communities
- Public
- Competitors
- Analysts
- Bond raters
- Journalists
- Other stakeholders

Managers' self interests
- Compensation
- Job security
- Power and influence
- Maintaining share price
- Increasing wealth
- Providing information to stakeholders
- Other interests

Factors limiting Managers' accounting choices
- Constraints (GAAP, auditors and independent accountants, contractual terms, etc.)
- Powerful stakeholders
- Facts defining the events and transactions being accounted for

ENTITY

Managers decide how to report

Objectives of financial reporting
- Tax minimization
- Stewardship
- Management evaluation
- Performance evaluation
- Cash flow prediction
- Income smoothing (smoothing income)
- Bonus plan management
- Income maximization (increasing income)
- Minimum compliance
- Monitoring contract compliance
- Income minimization (reducing income)
- Etc.

Reporting

Special Purpose Reports   General Purpose Reports

Knowledge Check

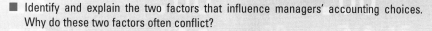

- Identify and explain the two factors that influence managers' accounting choices. Why do these two factors often conflict?

- What are some of the factors that limit the choices that managers can make?

www.mcgrawhill.ca/olc/friedlan

For example, consider a small business owned and managed by Ellin Bamboo. Ms. Bamboo's company's financial statements are used primarily for tax purposes. When a Canadian business files a tax return, it must include its general purpose income statement and balance sheet. In many instances the same accounting methods are used for tax purposes as are used in the general purpose statements. If choosing one accounting treatment over another reduces the amount of tax that has to be paid, it makes sense to use the tax-lowering treatment. This is not illegal, dishonest, or unethical. If Canada Revenue Agency allows you to choose among alternatives, you should do so. If Ms. Bamboo uses the completed-contract method of revenue recognition for her business's long-term contracts that are less than two years in duration, she legitimately delays paying tax and keeps cash in her business.

Insight

Tax law sometimes specifies the accounting treatment that an entity must use to calculate the amount of tax it should pay. In those situations a manager is free to choose any accounting method for the entity's general purpose financial statements. But when it comes time to calculate the amount of tax it should pay, an adjustment must be made so that the calculation of tax is consistent with tax law. Tax law does not impose accounting rules for preparing general purpose financial statements. Federal and provincial tax laws apply only to the calculation of the amount of tax that must be paid.

Now suppose that Ms. Bamboo decides to sell her business. Prospective buyers would want to examine the financial statements as part of their assessment of the business. Would the financial statements that were prepared for tax purposes be appropriate for a person evaluating a business? No, because the financial statements prepared using the completed-contract method could misstate the economic activity of Ms. Bamboo's business. This is because recognition of activity in the statements is delayed until a contract is completed. The financial statements prepared for tax purposes may not give a fair and reasonable reflection of Ms. Bamboo's business even though they are perfectly acceptable for tax purposes. If these financial statements were used to set the price for Ms. Bamboo's business without taking into consideration the fact that the statements were prepared to minimize taxes, it is possible that Ms. Bamboo would not receive, and the buyer would not pay, a fair price for the business.

This example demonstrates that one set of financial statements may not satisfy all users and uses. But because only one set of general purpose financial statements can be prepared, some stakeholders may have to be satisfied with statements that have not been tailored to their specific needs. A manager's accounting choices will affect the usefulness of the financial statements to stakeholders and may have economic consequences for them.

Figure 4–1 lists some of the objectives of reporting that an entity can have. Let's look at these in detail.

Tax Minimization

When a taxpayer pursues the objective of *tax minimization*, the taxpayer will follow the tax laws to pay as little tax as possible. The accounting choices an entity makes can have a bearing on the amount of tax it pays because the policies used in general purpose financial statements are often also used for tax purposes. A business's general purpose financial statements must be filed with its tax return. (In the case of partnerships or proprietorships, the general purpose financial statements must be filed along with the tax return of the partners or proprietor.) To minimize its taxes, an entity will make accounting choices that lower taxable income. In principle, this objective makes good economic sense because it keeps cash in the hands of the entity for as long as possible. However, many entities do not pursue this objective because they believe that the lower income that results from minimizing taxes may jeopardize other objectives.

Stewardship

When the people who provide money or other resources to an entity are different from the people who manage the resources, a stewardship relationship exists. People want to know how the resources they have invested in an organization have been handled. Has the money been used efficiently and effectively and in a way that is satisfactory to the investors? A stewardship relationship can exist for businesses, governments, and not-for-profit organizations. Information provided for this purpose should allow the stakeholders to understand easily what has taken place during the reporting period. Stewardship is one of the explicit objectives of Canadian GAAP as stated in the *CICA Handbook*.

Management Evaluation

Stakeholders often want to evaluate the performance of the people managing an entity. The financial statements should provide information that reflects the decisions of an entity's managers and the effects of those decisions on the performance of the entity. Information should be provided to allow stakeholders to separate the effects of management's decisions from the effects of luck and other factors beyond management's control.

Performance Evaluation

Performance evaluation is similar to management evaluation but broader in scope, in that the stakeholders want to evaluate the overall performance of the entity. People are interested in evaluating the performance of the corporations in which they have invested so they can decide whether they should continue to invest, invest more, or invest less in these corporations. For a charity, performance evaluation may involve evaluating whether the organization is spending an appropriate proportion of the money it raises for the cause, rather than for fundraising and administration.

Cash Flow Prediction

Many decisions that stakeholders make are future-oriented. The cash flows an entity will generate in the future are especially important. Knowledge of future cash flows can help a lender evaluate whether a borrower will be able to pay back the interest and principal on a loan, assist an investor estimate future dividends, or help a prospective buyer of a business evaluate whether the purchase price is reasonable. Prediction of future cash flows is explicitly stated in the *CICA Handbook* as one of the objectives of accounting information. However, information that is presented in accordance with GAAP in general purpose financial statements is historical in nature—it reflects what *has already happened*, not what *will happen*. Stakeholders who want to predict future cash flows can use the information in GAAP financial statements as a basis for predicting the future, but they would need additional information to do so.

Monitoring Contract Compliance

Entities often enter into contracts that require them to meet certain terms and conditions. These terms and conditions are intended to limit the actions that management can take and they are often stated in terms of financial statement numbers. For example, a lending agreement may require that a borrower maintain its current ratio above a specified amount or its debt-to-equity ratio below a specified amount. Failure to meet these requirements could mean repaying or renegotiating the loan. Another condition often seen in contracts restricts the payment of dividends if retained earnings are not above a specified amount. Covenants are included in contracts to restrict the behaviour of an entity so that, for example, a lender is not exposed to unforeseen risks when making a loan, such as the entity taking on additional debt. When contract terms and conditions are based on financial statement numbers, the financial statements serve as tools for monitoring compliance with the terms of the contract by the entity.

Earnings Management

The objectives listed to this point represent reasons stakeholders might have to see a set of financial statements. In a perfect accounting world, stakeholders would receive the information they require to make their decisions, for example to evaluate performance or predict future cash flows. However, managers might not want to fully cooperate with the needs of stakeholders. Because managers have their own interests to pursue, they may, for example, use their ability to make accounting choices to influence or manipulate stakeholders' evaluation of entity performance or their predictions about future cash flows. Or managers may make accounting choices that are simply in their own interests.

What is earnings management? Our definition is that if managers can choose from *acceptable* alternative ways of accounting, they will likely choose the ways that satisfy the objectives or self-interests of the entity or its managers. This explanation means that managers will be making their accounting choices from those that are acceptable under GAAP or whatever set of accounting principles is being applied. This definition of earnings management does not include fraud, or accounting choices that are not acceptable under GAAP, or whatever set of accounting principles being used.

While the term *earnings management* suggests a focus that is exclusively on earnings, it really applies to any accounting choices made by managers to affect *any* financial statement numbers with the intent of satisfying their self-interests. For example, accounting choices made to prevent an entity from violating a current ratio or debt-to-equity requirement that is specified in a contract would be considered earnings management. However, remember that earnings management has no impact on the underlying economic activity of the entity, though it will likely have economic consequences.

Now we will look at some of the reasons why managers manage their accounting information.

Managing Earnings to Reduce Income It may come as a surprise, but there are situations in which managers want to manage earnings downward. Companies in politically sensitive businesses may find themselves under pressure from politicians and citizens if they make "too much money." One way that managers can ease this pressure is by making accounting choices that reduce what might otherwise be seen as excessive profits. Another situation when reducing income might be a good strategy for an entity is if the entity is looking for government support or subsidies. By making the entity's performance appear poor, the entity might be more likely to convince governments to provide support. Lower reported earnings could also be used to influence the outcome of labour negotiations by convincing workers and unions to accept lower wage settlements. Tax minimization would also be a motivation for reducing income.

On an ongoing basis, reducing income can be achieved by recognizing revenue late in the earnings cycle and recognizing expenses early. Managers can significantly lower earnings in a particular period by taking a "big bath." A **big bath** is the expensing of a significant amount of assets that normally would have been amortized or otherwise expensed in future periods. The benefit of a big bath is that while net income is lowered in the current period, income will be higher in future periods compared with what it would have been had there not been a big bath. Income will be higher in the years after a big bath because assets that were expensed as part of the big bath do not have to be expensed in those later periods (because they were already expensed). In other words, there are fewer expenses in later periods. Big baths are sometimes seen when a company replaces its management. The new management blames poor performance on the previous management, takes a big bath, and then takes the credit when earnings improve subsequently.

Even not-for-profit organizations can benefit from this strategy, even though they do not report earnings. (Remember that not-for-profit organizations do not operate to make a profit and, therefore, do not report earnings. However, they do report surpluses or deficits, which reflect the extent to which their "revenues" are greater than or less than their "expenses.") If the revenues of a not-for-profit organization exceed its expenses by a large amount, contributors might doubt the organization is in need and make their donations elsewhere. Managers of not-for-profit organizations might use accounting choices to make their organizations look less successful and more in need of contributions.

Managing Earnings to Increase Income At the other end of the spectrum are managers who want to make accounting choices that increase reported income. Situations in which managers might manage earnings to increase earnings include the following:

- Managers may try to influence the stock price of publicly traded companies. There is a well-established relationship between accounting earnings and stock prices, and managers might believe that by increasing reported earnings they can increase the stock price.

- Before a private company is sold, managers might make accounting choices that increase income to increase the selling price. Accounting information is crucial for determining the market value of a private company, and managing earnings may increase the amount of money sellers receive.

- Managers might manage accounting information to increase the likelihood of receiving a loan.

- By managing earnings upwards, managers may influence some stakeholders' perceptions about how well the entity and its managers are performing.

- Managers who have bonus plans that are based on net income or other accounting numbers might use accounting choice to increase their bonuses.

- Managers might manage earnings to avoid violating the terms of debt agreements or other kinds of contractual agreements.

Managing Earnings to Smooth Income As we saw earlier in the discussion of Microsoft's accounting, "smoothing" income refers to managing revenues and expenses to smooth out the "peaks" and "valleys" that can appear in reported earnings from period to period. Fluctuating net income can be an indicator of risk, and many managers would prefer to avoid having stakeholders believe that their companies are risky. Research has found that the stock prices of public companies benefit from having smooth earnings. As discussed in the section about Microsoft's accounting, some critics have suggested that Microsoft's revenue recognition policy for some of its products was chosen to smooth income.

The list of circumstances where the managers of financial statements would have incentives to manage earnings and other financial statement numbers is endless and well documented. It is important at this point to recognize that managing earnings and other accounting information can be beneficial to managers. Managing earnings is also at the heart of the accounting scandals that have occurred.

It is important to understand that by managing earnings, managers may be undermining the objectives of stakeholders. For example, by making certain accounting choices, managers might use earnings management to make an entity look less risky and more financially secure. As a result, a prospective lender might over-estimate future cash flows and thereby make a loan that it might not have made otherwise. Thus, by managing earnings, managers undermine the cash flow prediction objective of the prospective lender but help the managers achieve their objective of obtaining new financing.

Managing earnings is complex. It is usually not obvious what the motivation is for accounting choices. Stakeholders have to be aware that managers have the ability to manage earnings and keep in mind the impact that different choices can have on financial statements.

Minimum Compliance

Managers sometimes provide the minimum amount of information necessary to comply with reporting requirements. Minimum reporting requirements are defined in various pieces of federal and provincial legislation. All corporations are subject to the requirements of the *Canada Business Corporations Act* or the equivalent provincial corporations act. Public companies must also meet the requirements of the relevant provincial securities act and of the stock exchange, if any, on which the company's securities trade.

Some public companies will pursue minimum compliance if they are concerned about providing information to competitors or if they are not concerned about negative reactions by

EXHIBIT 4–7 :

Shoppers Drug Mart Corporation's Statement of Earnings

SHOPPERS DRUG MART

Consolidated Statements of Earnings

52 weeks ended December 31, 2005 and January 1, 2005
(in thousands of dollars, except per share amounts)

	2005	2004
		(Note 2)
Sales	$ 7,151,115	$ 6,566,399
Operating expenses		
Cost of goods sold and other operating expenses	6,430,933	5,927,548
Amortization	120,937	102,157
Operating income	599,245	536,694
Interest expense (Note 4)	48,649	60,872
Earnings before income taxes	550,596	475,822
Income taxes (Note 5)		
Current	177,197	160,093
Future	8,905	8,407
	186,102	168,500
Net earnings	$ 364,494	$ 307,322
Net earnings per common share (Note 11):		
Basic	$ 1.72	$ 1.48
Diluted	$ 1.69	$ 1.43

www.shoppersdrugmart.ca

the stock markets to supplying limited information. Private companies may prepare minimum compliance statements if the shareholders are active in the entity and, therefore, have other sources of information, or if other stakeholders are able to receive the information they require in special purpose reports. Also, by providing as little information as they can, managers make it even more difficult for users to figure out how managers' accounting choices affect the financial statements, thereby making it difficult for users to make good decisions. Exhibit 4–7 shows the December 31, 2005 statement of earnings of Shoppers Drug Mart Corporation (Shoppers).[8] Shoppers' income statement provides the minimum amount of information that is required under GAAP. Notice that the statement reports only four lines of expenses: cost of goods sold and other operating expenses, amortization expense, interest expense, and income tax expense. This lack of detail is not very informative for decision making.

When you begin the study of accounting, it is easy to get the impression that all the accounting choices managers can make are transparent to users of the information. You might believe that a stakeholder who carefully examines financial statements and notes can find any skulduggery that the managers have chosen to pursue. This is far from true. Accounting policies *do* have to be disclosed in the notes to the financial statements, so a stakeholder will know, for example, how an entity recognizes revenue. However, it is not always easy to figure out what effect these choices have on the reported numbers.

Accounting estimates pose even bigger challenges for stakeholders than accounting policies. **Accounting estimates** (in contrast with accounting policies) are estimated amounts that must be used when financial statements are prepared because the actual amounts pertaining to many economic events and transactions are not known with certainty at the time. Examples of accounting estimates include the amount of accounts receivable that will not be collected, the useful lives of capital assets, and the cost of warranty services that have not yet been provided. Many (if not most) financial statement numbers are based on estimates, but entities are not usually

Insight

After reading this discussion of the different objectives of financial reporting, especially earnings management, one might come to the conclusion that accounting information cannot be relied on or used for decision making. This is not true. Accounting information is an absolutely essential source of information for most decisions regarding an entity. It would be a mistake to ignore accounting information. The message that readers should take from this discussion is that accounting information must be analyzed and interpreted carefully before decisions are made. Understanding the nature of accounting information and the motivations of the managers will help make you a more sophisticated user whose decisions are less likely to be affected by managers' accounting choices.

It is also important to recognize that accounting is not any different from any other business discipline or, for that matter, any other form of communication. Take advertising, for example. When a company advertises a product, it tries to project an image of the product that makes it attractive to consumers. Advertisers do not go out of their way to highlight the shortcomings of their products. They highlight the positive aspects, and minimize or even ignore the negative. Sometimes advertising is considered misleading, but most of the time it isn't. It is the responsibility of consumers to do their research to assure themselves they are getting what they bargained for. Accounting is no different.

required to disclose their estimates. Accounting estimates provide managers with a powerful tool for managing financial statement numbers in ways that can't be easily observed by the stakeholders.

Reporting Impact

The objective of financial reporting that is chosen by an entity's managers can have a significant impact on the financial statements. The table below gives an indication of how managers would approach the preparation of financial statements with particular objectives in mind. The table is not comprehensive but gives an idea of how different objectives might affect financial reporting.

Objective	Reporting Approach
Tax minimization	Recognize revenue as late as possible and recognize expenses as as possible while being consistent with Income Tax Act.
Cash flow predication	Choose accounting policies that correlate current earnings with future cash flows and provide extensive disclosure of information about future cash flows. Provide forecasts (not part of GAAP).
Minimum compliance	Provide the minimum amount of information in the financial statements and notes that is required by any constraints.
Performance evaluation	Associate economic costs and economic benefits. Separate items that are unusual, are less likely to occur in future, and are not the result of managerial decisions.
Stewardship	Provide historical, reliable information that will allow stakeholders to see how managers have managed entity resources over the reporting period.

CAN MANAGERS DO WHATEVER THEY WANT?

One could get the impression from our discussion that managers of accounting information are completely unconstrained when they prepare their financial statements and that they can do whatever they want to accomplish their accounting objectives. This is not true. As was mentioned earlier in the chapter, constraints, powerful stakeholders, and the economic circumstances surrounding transactions and economic events limit managers' choices.

The constraints managers could face include GAAP, securities laws, tax laws, corporation laws, and the terms of contracts. (Note that different entities face different constraints. For example, not all entities are constrained by GAAP or have contractual constraints.) Constraints may reduce or eliminate choice in some circumstances. For example, Canadian GAAP require that money spent on research be expensed—entities have no choice. However, it is rarely possible to limit completely by law or by contract all or even most of the accounting choices managers have. The economy is far too complex and dynamic to have rules that can apply to every possible situation.

Even companies that are not constrained by GAAP are really not free to do whatever they want. It is unlikely that an entity would invent a radically new set of accounting rules on which to base its financial statements because it would be very difficult for users to understand them. Remember that accounting is a means of communication. If the people receiving the accounting information can't understand it, then it serves no purpose. Imagine receiving a set of financial statements prepared in a language that you didn't understand. Those statements would be of no use to you.

Sometimes, powerful stakeholders can make reporting demands on an entity. If an entity needs a loan, a banker can demand information and special reports that meet the specific information needs of the bank. The entity isn't required to meet the information demands of the bank, but the bank isn't required to make a loan. Another example of a powerful stakeholder is a shareholder of a corporation who owns a large proportion of the shares of the company. A large shareholder may be able to demand special purpose reports that provide information not available in the general purpose report. A shareholder that controls the majority of the shares of a corporation may be able to determine the objectives of the corporation and the accounting policies it uses. In contrast, a small shareholder in a public company—for example, a person who owned 100 shares of Rogers—would not be able to obtain information beyond what was in the general purpose financial statements.

The economic circumstances surrounding transactions can also impose some limits on the choices managers have. Consider a vendor selling hotdogs for cash from a mobile cart on the street. No matter what objectives of reporting the hotdog vendor might have, it is hard to imagine recognizing revenue at a time other than when a hotdog is exchanged for cash. On the other hand, in the case of Escuminac Manufacturing Ltd. (pages 176 to 178) two viable alternatives for recognizing revenue were presented. Though there are other alternatives that could be identified for Escuminac, for example when the order was made, when the contract was signed, or when cash was received, these would be less viable, especially if GAAP were a constraint. An entity that is not constrained by GAAP may have a wider range of accounting alternatives to choose from, but there still has to be a link between the economic circumstances and the choice made.

SOLVING ACCOUNTING CHOICE PROBLEMS

This chapter has examined two important accounting topics: revenue and expense recognition, and the objectives of financial reporting. These two topics will be linked in this section, where we develop a problem-solving technique that will help you understand how managers make accounting choices and how users of accounting information can both use and are limited by the information provided to them by entities.

Constraints, Facts, and Objectives

Before looking at the problem-solving approach, let's examine the factors that guide the accounting choices made by entities and that will form the central analytical tool for making accounting choices. The accounting choices made by managers are affected by three factors:

1. The *constraints* that formally limit the choices that are available to managers.

2. The *facts* surrounding the transaction or economic event that is being accounted for.

3. The *objectives* of financial reporting.

   The application of the constraints, facts, and objectives is shown schematically in Figure 4–2.

Constraints are specific external limitations on the accounting choices that managers can make, including legal requirements, GAAP, or the terms of contracts. Constraints can eliminate choice by requiring that a particular economic event or transaction be treated in one and only one way, or limit choice by reducing the set of available alternatives. For example, GAAP limit the choices available for recognizing revenue. As we discussed earlier, under GAAP, changes in the market value of assets cannot be recognized as revenue. If the constraints limit or eliminate choice, there is little purpose in considering alternatives that violate the constraints because those alternatives cannot be used. If the constraints require a manager to use one and only one method, then that method must be used—no further evaluation is necessary. If there are no constraints, or if the constraints allow more than one alternative, then the facts can be examined.

The *facts* are the economic circumstances that surround a transaction or economic event. The facts must be interpreted to determine an appropriate accounting method. A key question to address is: What do accounting principles, fair reporting and ethics, and common sense tell us about how the accounting should be done? The facts can be ambiguous. Ambiguity allows for different interpretations of the facts, which leads to more than one possible, reasonable accounting method. For example, in the Escuminac Manufacturing Ltd. example (pages 176 to 178), more than one reasonable point for recognizing revenue could be justified. On the other hand, it would be difficult for Rogers to justify recognizing revenue at a time other than when a customer rents a movie at a Rogers Video store and pays her MasterCard®. When the facts are binding (that is, when the facts point to one and only one accounting treatment), then that treatment must be used. If the facts allow for more than one possible accounting treatment for a transaction or economic event, then the final choice depends on the managers' *objectives* of financial reporting. From the remaining alternatives, the managers choose the one that best suits the objectives. It is crucial to remember that the remaining alternatives have survived scrutiny in light of the constraints and the facts. That means that each is justifiable in terms of the constraints and the facts. To be acceptable, a recommendation that satisfies the objectives *must* satisfy the constraints and the facts. For example, if we have a GAAP constraint, we must be able to justify the choice of revenue-recognition method in terms of the revenue-recognition criteria.

◇ ROGERS™

It should be clear from this discussion that managers do not always get to choose the alternative that best meets their objectives. Before the objectives of financial reporting play a role, the constraints and the facts surrounding the transaction or economic event must be satisfied. The constraints and facts may prevent managers from selecting the best alternative for satisfying the objectives. Being able to justify an accounting choice in terms of the constraints and facts is important for another reason: an accounting choice will rarely be justified in terms of the objectives of financial reporting. Managers would not say that they had made an accounting choice to maximize income. Instead, the choice would be couched in terms of accounting concepts—in other words, in terms of the facts.

Analyzing Accounting Problems

The constraints, facts, and objectives model can be used in a decision-making approach to understand how accounting choices are made. The steps described below attempt to formalize the problem-solving process so that all important constraints, facts, and objectives are identified and integrated into the analysis. Note that this approach to problem solving is not unique to accounting—it can be used for any type of problem.

Also note that the steps in the approach take the perspective of the managers: they follow a process that managers might follow in making their accounting choices. This is an important perspective because even as a user it is important to understand the process that managers use to make their accounting choices. Later in the book, we will take a close look at solving problems from the perspective of the users of the financial statements.

The steps are:

1. Assess the entity and its environment. What are the entity's key characteristics (industry, size, ownership, management, and so on)? What problems is it facing? What are the entity's crucial success factors (what are the keys to the entity's success)? How does the business make money (if it is a for-profit organization)? The purpose is to understand the entity from an operational perspective (rather than an accounting perspective) so that you can make accounting choices that suit the needs of the organization. Remember that accounting serves the needs of an entity and its stakeholders. It is not an end in itself.

2. Create a framework for analyzing the accounting issues. The framework provides the parameters by which the accounting problems will be analyzed. The framework should include the following:

   a. Identify the users and uses of accounting information.

   b. Identify the objectives of financial reporting, based on the users and uses of the accounting information.

   c. Rank the objectives in order of importance and explain the ranking. (The ranking is necessary so that the analysis can be directed toward accomplishing the most important objective.)

   d. Consider the accounting implications of the objectives. That is, you must understand how the objectives will affect *accounting* choices.

   e. Identify constraints that can limit or eliminate accounting choices.

   When managers rank the objectives, the ranking is done from their perspective. Managers determine what they believe is most important for the entity (and perhaps themselves) and proceed accordingly. As a result, the needs of some stakeholders may not be served since the decisions (accounting and otherwise) that managers make may not be the ones that are in the best interests of a particular stakeholder. This point highlights the difference between a manager's perspective and a user's perspective.

3. Identify the accounting problems. Sometimes the accounting problems an entity faces are clearly laid out. Other times problems may be hidden and need to be detected through analysis and inference.

4. Rank the problems in order of importance and emphasize the more important problems in the analysis. More time and effort should be spent on the accounting problems that have the greatest impact on the entity. There is not much point in devoting resources to solving problems that do not matter.

5. Analyze the accounting problems. For each accounting problem:

   a. Identify possible alternative accounting treatments.

   b. Determine which alternatives, if any, violate the constraints and eliminate them. If the constraints allow only a single alternative, then the analysis of the problem is complete because the accounting treatment is determined by the constraints.

c. Analyze each alternative to determine whether it can be supported by the facts. This means that you must use information about the transaction or economic event and relevant accounting rules/principles/concepts to provide support for the alternative. For example, analyzing a revenue recognition problem for an entity that is constrained by GAAP requires applying the revenue-recognition criteria discussed in this chapter.

The existence of an alternative does not automatically make it acceptable. For an alternative to be acceptable, it must be supportable and justifiable by the facts. If the facts do not support an alternative, it must be discarded. If the facts support only one alternative, then that alternative must be used regardless of whether it is useful for meeting the objectives. If the facts support an alternative that is not allowed by the constraints, then that alternative cannot be used because constraints take precedence over the facts.

d. From the remaining alternatives, determine the one that best suits the objective or objectives of financial reporting that were identified and ranked in step 2.

6. Link the solution to each accounting problem back to the framework by explaining why the solution addresses the main objectives. Often you will not be able to come up with a solution that best serves the objective. That's ok. Explain to the reader why you weren't able to satisfy the objective.

When you work on textbook problems there are some additional points to remember:

- First, play your role. Normally, when you face a real-life problem you will implicitly understand the perspective from which you are supposed to tackle the problem. However, in a textbook problem you have to play an assigned role. Make sure you understand what the role means so you can play it effectively. Roles that you can be asked to play include advisors to management, or the board of directors, various user groups, arbitrators (a person who helps resolves disputes between parties), external auditors, and auditors for the Canada Revenue Agency.

- Second, in any problem situation, real or textbook, it is never possible to have all the possible information. Time, cost, and limitations to a person's ability to process information prevent this. As a result, it is necessary to make assumptions—to fill in the blanks—when information is missing. It is very important to recognize when you make assumptions and to state them explicitly. Knowing when assumptions are being made and what those assumptions are is not always easy—it takes skill and practice to do it well.

- Third, many accounting problems do not have a single, correct answer. The appropriateness of a response depends on the weightings given to various factors, the assumptions made, and the interpretation of events. There can also be many wrong answers. It is also possible to come up with a reasonable recommendation that is poorly supported. The quality and usefulness of a recommendation lies in the support provided for it, not in the recommendation itself.

The following solved problem shows an application of this decision-making approach. This solved problem and the one in Chapter 5 take a manager's (preparer's) perspective. User-perspective cases are the solved problems in Chapters 6, 9, 10, and 12.

:: Solved Problem

Pizzazz Pizza Parlours Ltd. (PPPL) is a small chain of take-out/delivery pizza shops located in Atlantic Canada. The Pizzazz family owns the chain. Until recently, the company was managed by several members of the Pizzazz family. Many other family members are passive shareholders who are not involved in managing PPPL, including some who rely on the company for their incomes.

In early fiscal 2009, PPPL underwent a number of organizational and strategic changes. First, the family decided that instead of only opening pizza parlours they owned themselves, PPPL would also sell franchises to people interested in owning their own businesses. (In a franchise arrangement, an individual or company (the franchisee) would approach PPPL about purchasing the right to operate a Pizzazz Pizza Parlour in a particular area. The franchisee would pay PPPL a fee and would receive the rights to sell Pizzazz Pizzas in the agreed area. PPPL would help the franchisee find a good location, help it set up the shop, advertise, and provide business advice. The franchisee would also pay PPPL a percentage of the revenue it earned selling pizzas and buy certain supplies from PPPL.)

Next, the members of the family who were running the business realized that they were not fully qualified to manage the business they envisioned. As a result, PPPL's board of directors, which is made up mostly of members of the Pizzazz family, hired as president a person with many years of experience in the pizza industry. The new president signed an employment contract that entitled him to a salary plus a bonus based on net income. Some of the Pizzazzes remained as part of the management team. One of the first actions taken by the new president was to arrange a large bank loan to finance the expansion of the company.

As of PPPL's year end on August 31, 2009, PPPL's new strategy was developing nicely. Fourteen Pizzazz Pizza Parlour franchises had been sold, of which eight were already operating. The remaining six are expected to open by the end of December 2009. Franchises are sold for $70,000. A franchise owner pays PPPL $5,000 when the franchise agreement is signed, $15,000 when the restaurant opens, and $10,000 per year for five years on the anniversary of the opening of the pizza parlour. In addition, franchises pay PPPL a royalty of 5 percent of sales and are required to purchase pizza dough, sauce, cheese, and some other items either from PPPL or from designated suppliers.

Franchises receive help from PPPL in selecting a location, advice on operating the business, training, policy manuals, and the benefits of centralized purchasing, advertising, and centralized order taking from customers.

PPPL's 2009 fiscal year has just ended and it has not yet determined how to recognize revenue on the franchises it sells. You have been asked by PPPL's board of directors to prepare a report that responds to the following questions:

Required:

1. What business is PPPL in? How does it make its money? What do you think are some crucial success factors for PPPL's franchise business?

2. Who are the likely users of PPPL's financial statements? For what purposes will these users want the financial statements?

3. From the perspective of the board of directors of PPPL (which we will assume is responsible for approving major accounting policies used by PPPL), what are the possible objectives of financial reporting? The discussion in part (2) should help answer this question. Which objective of financial reporting do you think is most important? Explain. How would you rank the remaining objectives? Are there any conflicts among the objectives?

4. Are there any constraints that limit the accounting choices that PPPL can make?

5. What are some possible alternatives for when PPPL could recognize the revenue from the sale of franchises? (You should be able to identify at least three different revenue-recognition points.)

6. Do any of the revenue-recognition points you identified in (5) violate the constraints? Which of the alternatives can be justified and supported by the facts?

7. For each revenue-recognition alternative you identify, calculate the amount of franchise fee revenue that would be recognized in the years ended August 31, 2009 and 2010, for franchise agreements signed during fiscal 2009 and assuming that all payments are received on time.

8. Which revenue-recognition method would you recommend PPPL use to recognize franchise fee revenue? Explain.

9. What information about the franchise revenue would it be important to disclose in the financial statements for the users? Explain.

Solution:

1. PPPL is in three businesses:

   a. It owns and operates pizzerias, making money by selling pizzas to customers.

   b. It sells franchise rights to people who are interested in operating their own Pizzazz Pizza Parlour, making money from the franchise fees and royalties paid by the Pizzazz Pizza Parlour franchises.

   c. PPPL is also a supplier of ingredients to the franchised pizzerias, possibly making money by selling the ingredients at a profit.

   For the franchise business, the crucial success factors include:

   ■ Having strong management to run the company, especially during this period of strategic change. Strong management is crucial because the Pizzazz family did not feel it had the ability to manage the expansion of the business on its own through franchises.

   ■ Availability of financing for the franchising program. The franchise business requires cash because the pizzerias open before most of the cash is received from the franchises. For the expansion to continue successfully, credit must be available as required.

   ■ Capable people with adequate resources to buy and operate the franchises. The franchises must be successful so that money will be available to pay debts and royalties to PPPL and to help attract new franchises in the future.

   ■ PPPL must successfully promote its name so that people will have a preference for eating at a Pizzazz Pizza Parlour.

2. There are a number of possible users and uses of PPPL's financial statements:

Possible users	Decisions that will be assisted by the financial statements and how the information will help users make the decisions
Pizzazz family members	Pizzazz family members will have a number of uses that could be helped by financial statements:
	■ They will want to evaluate the performance of the new president to decide whether he is managing the company well. Since the president's bonus is based on net income, they will want the income statement to reflect the president's accomplishments.
	■ Pizzazz family members, especially those who depend on PPPL for their incomes, will want information that will allow them to assess the performance of PPPL and evaluate the amount of cash that will be available to pay dividends.
	■ Family members who are not involved in management will want information for stewardship purposes.
	■ From PPPL's perspective, the board of directors may want to show the Pizzazz family members that PPPL is performing well.
Lenders and potential lenders	■ Existing lenders will want to assess whether their loans are safe and check whether any restrictions (such as current-ratio or debt-to-equity ratio restrictions), if any, have been violated.
	■ Additional loans might be required if the franchising program continues. Potential lenders will want to assess PPPL's ability to generate the cash flows necessary to make interest and principal payments. They will also be interested in the market value of available collateral, which would have to be sold in the event that PPPL were unable to pay back the loan. Potential lenders would want to know the terms of existing loans

such as amounts already borrowed, the interest rate, repayment schedule, and collateral pledged to other lenders.

- From PPPL's perspective, the company will want the financial statements to indicate to lenders that existing loans are and future loans would be secure, and that any restrictions have not been violated.

Canada Revenue Agency (CRA)
- The CRA will want to ensure PPPL complies with the *Income Tax Act*.

- From PPPL's perspective, the company will want to pay as little tax as possible and still comply with the *Income Tax Act*.

New president of PPPL
- The president receives a bonus based on net income so he will want to see high net income.

- From PPPL's perspective, the company would want the president to receive a fair bonus that reflects his contribution to the performance of the company.

Prospective franchise owners
- Prospective franchise owners may want to assess the financial position of PPPL to obtain some confidence that the company is financially solid. If a franchise is purchased, but PPPL is unable to support it, the franchise owner does not benefit from owning a PPPL pizzeria. Depending on the level of sophistication, prospective franchise owners may want information about cash flows, the number of franchises sold and being negotiated, expansion plans, and information on the performance of operating franchises. PPPL is under no obligation to provide its financial statements to prospective franchisees unless it chooses to do so as part of its effort to sell franchises.

- From PPPL's perspective, the company will want to give prospective franchise owners confidence that PPPL will be able to support its franchises and that a PPPL franchise is a good investment.

Suppliers
- If they are major suppliers, they may want assurances that PPPL will be able to pay for goods and services purchased. They will be interested in cash flows and liquidity.

- From PPPL's perspective, the company will want to give confidence to the suppliers that it is able to meet its obligations to pay for supplies. PPPL is under no obligation to provide its financial statements to suppliers, unless it chooses to do so.

3. From the analysis of the users and uses of accounting information, a number of possible objectives emerge. Based on our analysis of the crucial success factors in part (1), the important users from PPPL's perspective are:

- prospective lenders, because additional loans will be required if PPPL continues to sell franchises
- new franchise owners, who are key to PPPL's expansion strategy
- the president of PPPL, who has been hired to implement the new business strategy

Of these three groups, the president is most important because PPPL's board chose him to lead the company in this phase of its development. To lose him at this stage would probably be a serious blow to PPPL's new strategy. A good president will probably be able to effectively manage the relationship with the bank and help attract good franchise owners. Without good management, borrowing from the bank would likely be much more difficult.

Therefore, the objective of financial reporting should be to ensure that the financial statements reflect the performance of management and adequately compensate the president for his accomplishments—that is, the objective of management evaluation. The board would probably want to make sure that the net income of PPPL was a reasonable reflection of the president's actions so that he would receive a bonus that he felt was fair. The needs of lenders would probably be satisfied by the statements used for management evaluation along with supplementary information on cash flows. While people who buy franchises are important users, PPPL would probably not be making financial statement information available to them.

Members of the Pizzazz family are also important and powerful users, but their needs must be considered secondary to the users who are important to expanding PPPL. In addition, the board could provide special purpose reports to members of the family to satisfy their information needs.

Everything else being equal, all businesses want to pay as little tax as possible, and PPPL's need for cash makes the objective of tax minimization even more important. However, the need for strong management also makes tax minimization a secondary objective.

Suppliers are a minor user and will not likely be granted access to the financial statements.

Note that there are conflicts among the objectives. In particular, the tax minimization objective, which suggests lower net income, conflicts with the management evaluation objective, which suggests "fair" or net income that is representative of the entity's underlying economic activity.

It is interesting to note that had we examined the objectives from the perspective of the president of PPPL rather than from that of the board of directors, the primary objective might have been bonus maximization rather than management evaluation. The president's self-interest might have had a stronger influence since he would have been making accounting choices that directly affected his personal wealth.

Finally, remember that this ranking is not the only one or the best one. Many other rankings are possible, reasonable, and supportable. However, any proposed ranking must be supported.

4. There do not appear to be any statutory constraints stated in the question. PPPL is a private company and therefore it does not have to provide audited financial statements. Some users may prefer audited, GAAP-based financial statements, such as the bank, the shareholders who are not involved in management, and prospective franchise owners. For purposes of preparing tax returns, PPPL will have to comply with the *Income Tax Act*. The lending agreement with the bank may have minimum requirements for accounting ratios, such as the current ratio or the debt-to-equity ratio, but without any information about these ratios it is not possible to make a reasonable assumption regarding specific amounts. Given the number of external users of the financial statements, it will be assumed that GAAP financial statements will be prepared.

5. Possible points for recognizing revenue from the sale of franchises include:

- when a franchise agreement is signed with a new owner of a franchise
- when a franchised Pizzazz Pizza Parlour opens
- when cash is collected from a franchise (instalment method)
- when full payment is received from a franchise

6. Since it was assumed that GAAP will be followed, each revenue-recognition point must be evaluated in relation to the four revenue-recognition criteria:

- *When a franchise agreement is signed with a new owner of a franchise.* It may be difficult to argue that revenue should be recognized at this point. PPPL offers support getting a franchise location started and it has not performed those obligations, so the first criterion is not likely to be met. The amount of revenue is known when the contract is signed because the amount is specified in the contract. Costs are uncertain because PPPL still has work to do providing assistance to the franchisee. These costs may be fairly predictable, although at this stage PPPL has no history on which to base its estimates. Collection is a potential problem because payment depends on the success of the franchises and PPPL has no track record for evaluating how successful the franchised pizzerias will be, so it is not clear how much will actually be collected from the franchisees. This alternative does not meet the revenue-recognition criteria.

- *When a franchised Pizzazz Pizza Parlour opens.* PPPL has probably performed as of this point since once a pizza parlour is open, most of what PPPL has agreed to do has been done (though there are ongoing responsibilities). In addition, the franchise owner has an operating business at this point so one could argue that the risks and rewards of ownership are with the owners of the franchise restaurant. The amount of revenue is specified in the franchise agreement. Most costs are probably known at this time, although some cost uncertainty likely exists regarding the cost of the support that must be provided to the franchisee (especially given that PPPL is new to the franchising business), which may make estimating future costs difficult. Of course, at some point the support provided by PPPL can be considered paid for by the royalties paid by the franchises rather than from the initial franchise fee. Collection from the franchises is still an open question. At the time the pizza parlour opens, the franchise will have paid $20,000 of the $70,000 of the franchise fee. The fact that PPPL is new to the business makes it difficult to estimate the amount that will not be collected. This alternative meets the four criteria, provided that a reasonable estimate of the amounts that will not be collected from the franchises can be made.

■ *When cash is collected from a franchise.* Restaurants are a notoriously risky business and franchises can fail. As a result, collection is not a foregone conclusion. Waiting until cash is in hand is conservative but not unreasonable because collection may prove to be unpredictable. Except for the payment received when the franchise agreement is signed, the instalment method meets the four revenue-recognition criteria. The $5,000 received when the contract is signed would probably have to be deferred until the pizza parlour opened because if the opening does not go as planned PPPL might have to return the initial payment.

■ *When full payment is received from a franchise.* This method is very conservative. It would require that there be significant and unpredictable costs occurring in the later years of the contract, or that PPPL had not earned the revenue once a restaurant opened or once it had been opened for a few months. The most likely reason for delaying revenue recognition for this long would be for tax purposes. However, this method would not be allowed under the *Income Tax Act.*

7. Amount of revenue that would be recognized in the years ended August 31, 2009 and 2010, using each revenue recognition point:

   ■ When a franchise agreement is signed with a new owner of a franchise

   Revenue in 2009: $980,000 (14 stores × $70,000 per store)
   Revenue in 2010: $0

   ■ When a franchised Pizzazz Pizza Parlour opens

   Revenue in 2009: $560,000 (8 × $70,000)
   Revenue in 2010: $420,000 (6 × $70,000)

   ■ When cash is collected from a franchise (except for the payment on signing of the franchise agreement, which must be recognized when the franchise restaurant opens—see the discussion above)

   Revenue in 2009: $160,000 (8 × $20,000)
   Revenue in 2010: $200,000 (6 × $20,000 + 8 × $10,000)

   ■ When full payment is received from a franchise

   Revenue in 2009: $0
   Revenue in 2010: $0

8. The analysis above supports using either the opening of a Pizzazz Pizza Parlour or collection of cash as acceptable points to recognize revenue. Because more than one alternative is available after the constraints and the facts are addressed, the objectives of financial reporting can be considered. To satisfy the the primary objective, the objective of management evaluation, revenue should be recognized when a franchised Pizzazz Pizza Parlour opens. While cash collection is a significant uncertainty in PPPL's earnings process, using cash collection as the basis for evaluating and rewarding the president would likely undermine the incentive value of the bonus plan because the bonus would be significantly delayed. While recognizing revenue when the store opens might make the president less selective in choosing franchise owners (he may focus more on making sure the franchises open rather than making sure that the franchises are able to pay their debts), the disincentive overrides this problem. When a restaurant opens, the president has done his job of expanding the chain. At this point, the franchise

owners have made a significant financial investment and would likely work hard to make sure that their restaurants succeed.

9. Information that would be important to users includes, but is not limited to, the following:

- The revenue-recognition method used.
- When cash will be received from franchisees.
- Collectability of receivables.
- Costs to PPPL of selling franchises.
- Whether PPPL can generate the cash flow to support the expansion.
- Whether PPPL has enough credit/cash available to meet the needs of the franchise business.
- How many franchises have been sold and how many have been opened.

(Note: The usefulness of any piece of information would depend on who the user is.)

Reminder: This is one possible solution to this case. Other rankings of objectives, evaluation of alternatives, and recommendations are possible and acceptable provided they are well supported.

SUMMARY OF KEY POINTS

▶ **LO 1** To recognize revenue in a logical and rational matter we need some criteria to guide the choice. Under GAAP the following four criteria are used:

1. Performance has occurred.
2. The amount of revenue can be reasonably measured.
3. The costs required to earn the revenue can be reasonably measured.
4. Collection of payment is reasonably assured.

These criteria provide guidance to managers, but they are open to interpretation and require judgment. An additional, overriding criterion requires that the revenue recognition point selected provide a reasonable and fair representation of the entity's activities, given the needs of the people who are using the accounting information.

▶ **LO 2** Conceptually, earning revenue is a continuous process. Each activity an entity undertakes that increases the value of a good or service represents an economic benefit to the entity. It can be very difficult for accountants to determine when and how much revenue should be recognized along the series of actions leading to a sale to a customer. Accountants have devised two approaches for recognizing revenue: the critical-event approach and the gradual approach.

Under the critical-event approach, an entity chooses a "critical event" in the earnings process that it considers an appropriate time to recognize revenue. When the critical event occurs, 100 percent of the revenue is recognized.

Under the gradual approach, revenue is recognized gradually over a period of time. The gradual approach, which is often used when an entity provides services or enters into long-term contracts, provides useful and timely information to stakeholders about long-term contracts.

▶ **LO 3** There are different ways and times that revenues and expenses can be recognized, and the methods chosen can affect the amount of revenue, expense, and net income that an entity reports. Different revenue and expense recognition methods also affect many accounting and financial ratios. Even though the financial statements will be affected by using different revenue and expense recognition methods, the underlying economic activity of the entity is the same regardless of the methods chosen.

▶ **LO 4** Accrual accounting requires that all costs be matched to revenue in the same period as that in which the revenue that those expenses helped earn is recognized—whether the expenditures occur before, at the same time as, or after the revenue is recognized. Not all costs are easy to match to revenue. Costs that are expensed in the period that they are incurred are called period costs. Costs that can be matched to specific revenues are called product costs. Product costs are expensed when the revenue they help generate is recognized.

▶ **LO 5** Managers of accounting information can often choose from a number of reasonable accounting treatments for transactions and other economic events, even under GAAP. Flexible accounting rules are needed because of the complexity of economic activity. The choice of accounting methods by managers is influenced by the constraints, facts, and objectives that are relevant to the situation. Managers themselves are influenced by their need to provide information to stakeholders and by their own self-interests.

▶ **LO 6** The existence of alternative accounting treatments makes it necessary to decide which accounting alternative to choose. Choosing among accounting alternatives requires consideration of the relevant constraints, facts, and objectives, and application of a problem-solving approach that incorporates the following steps:

1. Assess the entity and its environment.

2. Create a framework for analyzing the accounting issues.

3. Identify the accounting problems.

4. Rank the problems in order of importance and emphasize the more important problems in the analysis.

5. Analyze the accounting problems.

6. Make a recommendation and explain why the recommendation is consistent with the main objectives.

KEY TERMS

accounting estimate, p. 196
big bath, p. 194
completed-contract method, p. 183
consignment sale, p. 174
critical-event approach, p. 169
gradual approach, p. 169
instalment method, p. 174

percentage-of-completion method, p. 182
period costs, p. 188
product costs, p. 188
prospectus, p. 179
unrealized gain (loss), p. 175
warranty, p. 174

ASSIGNMENT MATERIALS

Questions

Q4-1. Explain why it is not possible to have a single set of financial statements that will satisfy all the stakeholders of an entity.

Q4-2. Explain the difference between period and product costs. How is each type of cost accounted for?

Q4-3. Explain what is meant by the accounting term "revenue recognition."

Q4-4. How is the balance sheet affected when revenue is recognized? Explain your answer and give examples.

Q4-5. The revenue-recognition criteria introduced in this chapter require that revenue should be recognized when "performance has occurred." Explain what "performance" means.

Q4-6. Do you think it is good or bad that entities have flexibility in choosing when to recognize revenue? Explain.

Q4-7. Costs can be classified as period costs or product costs. How are the income statement and balance sheet affected by the classification? How might the objectives of accounting be affected by the classification?

Q4-8. Does the percentage-of-completion method of recognizing revenue meet the revenue-recognition criteria discussed in the chapter? Explain. How do accountants justify using the percentage-of-completion method for recognizing revenue on long-term contracts?

Q4-9. What effects do the objectives of financial reporting have on when an entity recognizes revenue? Explain.

Q4-10. What are constraints, facts, and objectives? How does each affect the accounting methods an entity uses? Why does each have to be considered when making an accounting choice?

Q4-11. What is the matching concept? Why is it relevant to revenue recognition?

Q4-12. Can a single set of financial statements satisfy all objectives of financial reporting? Explain.

Q4-13. Explain why recognizing revenue and expenses in different ways has no effect on the underlying economic activity of an entity.

Q4-14. Why can it be difficult for accountants to determine when revenue should be recognized under accrual accounting?

Q4-15. What is the instalment method of recognizing revenue? Under what circumstances should it be used?

Q4-16. Why is determining when to recognize revenue more difficult under accrual accounting than under cash accounting?

Q4-17. Distinguish between the percentage-of-completion method and the completed-contract method of revenue recognition. Which method requires the exercise of more judgment by managers? Explain.

Q4-18. Do you think that the managers of entities should be responsible for selecting the accounting methods and estimates that they use, or should that responsibility be given to an independent third party? Explain your view. Make sure you consider both sides of the argument.

Q4-19. Do you think accounting would be more useful and reliable if only a single method of revenue recognition were allowed, such as when cash is collected or when the goods or services are provided to the customer? Explain.

Q4-20. Identify and explain the four revenue-recognition criteria.

Q4-21. Does it matter how and when a company recognizes its revenue? How and why does it matter? Explain.

Q4-22. Under what circumstances should the completed-contract method of revenue recognition be used instead of the percentage-of-completion method?

Q4-23. What are gains and losses? How do they arise? How are gains and losses reported in the financial statements?

Q4-24. Why are gains and losses usually shown separately from revenues and expenses from ordinary business activities? What are the implications to the users of the financial statements if gains and losses are included in revenues and/or expenses?

Q4-25. Identify and explain the two factors that influence the accounting choices that are made by the managers who prepare the financial statements.

Q4-26. Why does self-interest play a role in accounting choice? Should it, in an ideal world?

Q4-27. Why do managers have the opportunity to choose some of the accounting methods they use? Should managers have a choice? Explain.

Q4-28. Conceptually, why can the earning of revenue be considered to be a continuous process? In spite of the continuous conceptual nature of revenue, why is revenue usually recognized at a single instant in time?

Q4-29. Why is it not possible to use the gradual approach to revenue recognition for sales of appliances by a retailer?

Q4-30. Explain what each of the following objectives of financial reporting means:
a. Tax minimization.
b. Management evaluation.
c. Minimum compliance.
d. Cash flow prediction.
e. Stewardship.
f. Earnings management.

Q4-31. What is an unrealized gain? Why are unrealized gains not usually recorded under GAAP?

Q4-32. What does it mean when accountants refer to recognizing revenue when a "critical event" occurs?

Exercises

E4-1. **(Classifying period and product costs, LO 4)** Oxbow Toy Ltd. (Oxbow) develops, manufactures, markets, and distributes a broad range of toys and games for children, from newborns to teenagers. The principal markets for Oxbow's products are Canada, the United States, and Australia, where Oxbow markets and distributes both company-developed and licensed products. In addition to sales in these countries, Oxbow's products are marketed in more than 50 countries worldwide. For each of the costs described below, state whether you would treat the cost as a product cost or a period cost. Explain your choices.
a. Plastic, wood, metal, and other materials that are used to produce toys.
b. Commissions paid to salespeople who sell toys to distributors and retailers.
c. Salaries paid to head office staff and senior executives.
d. Electricity and other utilities used in the manufacturing plant.
e. Amortization of equipment used to manufacture toys.
f. Amounts paid to trucking companies for delivering toys to customers.
g. Amounts paid to research and develop new toys.
h. Television and print advertising to promote one of Oxbow Toy Ltd.'s toys.
i. Television and print advertising to promote the entire line of Oxbow Toy Ltd.'s toys.

E4-1a. **(Identify reasonable methods for determining the proportion of a long-term contract that has been completed, LO 2)** For each of the following long-term projects, provide a basis for estimating the percentage of the job that has been completed. In the text, the main emphasis is on the proportion of total estimated cost incurred during a particular year for the percentage completed. For this exercise, identify bases other than cost for estimating the percentage completed.
a. Construction of a 50 kilometre stretch of highway;
b. Contract to remove contaminated earth from a factory that had been dumping toxic waste over a factory site for many decades;
c. Contract to do an overhaul of a large shipping vessel.

E4-2. **(Recording journal entries for recording revenue at different critical events, LO 1, 2, 4)**
Risteen Telephone Services Ltd. (Risteen) designs and installs telephone systems for commercial customers. For example, in December 2009, Risteen signed a contract with Yarm Telemarketing Systems Ltd. (Yarm) to design and install a phone system for Yarm's new call centre in New Brunswick. The following events pertain to the contract with Yarm:

i. December 13, 2009: The contract between Risteen and Yarm is signed. Yarm will pay $750,000 for the system and the system will cost Risteen $450,000 to design, produce, and install. The contract provides an 18-month warranty to make any repairs or adjustments required. Yarm will pay within 90 days of completion of the installation of the system.

ii. October 15, 2010: Installation of the system is completed.

iii. December 12, 2010: Warranty work costing $22,500 is performed.

iv. January 8, 2011: Risteen receives payment in full from Yarm.

v. April 15, 2011: Warranty expires.

Required:

Prepare the journal entries required for the above events assuming that:

a. Revenue is recognized when the contract is signed.
b. Revenue is recognized when installation of the system is complete.
c. Revenue is recognized when cash is collected.
d. Revenue is recognized when the warranty period expires.

E4-3. **(Identifying the objectives of financial reporting, LO 5, 6)** For each of the following entities, identify the objectives of financial reporting that the entity's managers might have. In answering, consider who the users of the financial statements might be and which user(s) would be most important to the managers. Explain how the objectives of financial reporting would influence the accounting choices made by the managers.

a. A private company with a large labour union that is preparing for negotiations with the union.
b. An accounting firm partnership that uses accounting income to determine the amount of tax the partners pay and the compensation the partners receive.
c. A private corporation that repairs commercial vehicles. The company has one shareholder who is also president of the company. The company urgently needs cash.
d. A public company planning to borrow a large amount of money to finance an expansion.
e. A not-for-profit golf club. Membership fees, green fees, dining room charges, and pro shop sales are used to operate the club. Club members are elected to sit on the board of directors of the club.

E4-4. **(Identifying the objectives of financial reporting, LO 5, 6)** For each of the following entities, identify the objectives of financial reporting that the entity's managers might have. In answering, consider who the users of the financial statements might be and which user(s) would be most important to the managers. Explain how the objectives of financial reporting would influence the accounting choices made by the managers.

a. A family-owned corporation that is planning to sell shares to the public and become a public company that is traded on a stock exchange.
b. A municipal government.
c. A public company that has been adversely affected by international competition and that is trying to receive subsidies from government.
d. A charity that raises money to buy and distribute food to hungry children around the world.
e. A private corporation that provides consulting services to restaurants. The company has one shareholder who is also president of the company. The company has a small bank loan and no other major creditors.

E4-5. **(Determining when to recognize revenue, LO 1, 2)** For each of the following situations, use the four GAAP revenue-recognition criteria to determine when revenue should be recognized. Explain your reasoning.

a. A customer purchases $100 of groceries for cash at a local grocery store.

b. A theatre goer purchases tickets for the entire season of plays at the local theatre. Theatre goers pay the full price of the tickets before the season begins and receive tickets for all of the plays.

c. A software manufacturer sells a computer game. The company promises to provide the next two upgrades to the program free of charge.

d. A jewellery store offers a lay-away plan whereby a customer pays 10 percent of the purchase price of an item and the store holds the item until the customer has paid 60 percent of the selling price.

E4-6. **(Determining when to recognize revenue, LO 1, 2)** For each of the following situations, use the four GAAP revenue-recognition criteria to determine when revenue should be recognized. Explain your reasoning.

a. A lender makes a loan to a borrower with an excellent credit rating. Interest is paid annually and the principal must be paid in full in three years.

b. A lender makes a loan to a borrower. The borrower is now suffering significant financial problems and has not made interest payments for several months. Collection of interest and principal from this borrower is considered unlikely.

c. A land developer sells small parcels of undeveloped land to prospective home owners. People who buy land from the developer make a 5 percent down payment with the remainder due when development of the land begins. Buyers have three years to begin development. If development does not begin by the end of three years, the land reverts back to the developer. The down payment is not returned.

d. A company sells a licence to a clothing manufacturer to make certain clothing items with its well-known logo. The licence is for three years. The clothing manufacturer has paid the full amount at the beginning of the three-year period.

e. An airline sells a ticket to a traveller for travel that will take place next year. The traveller pays in full at the time of purchase, using his MasterCard. The ticket is non-refundable.

E4-7. **(Determining when to recognize revenue, LO 1, 2)** For each of the following situations, use the four GAAP revenue-recognition criteria to determine when revenue should be recognized. Explain your reasoning.

a. A furniture store has a "don't pay for a year" event. Customers take delivery of their furniture immediately but do not have to pay until twelve months later.

b. A parents' magazine sells a three-year subscription to a new subscriber for $33. The subscriber makes the payment when she subscribes.

c. An auto parts manufacturer sells wheel assembly parts to a major car manufacturer. The car manufacturer pays for the parts within 60 days of delivery. The manufacturer must approve the parts to ensure that they meet specifications before the sale is finalized.

d. An electronics store sells customers extended warranties on the products that it sells. The extended warranty provides "free" parts and labour for three years beyond the one-year warranty that is provided by the manufacturer. The warranty is purchased and paid for at the time the product is purchased.

E4-8. **(Determining when to recognize revenue, LO 1, 2)** For each of the following situations, determine an appropriate time to recognize revenue. Provide support for your recommendations. Also, prepare any journal entries that would be required on the date of the transaction. Assume that in each case the year end is December 31.

a. On February 19, 2008 a publisher received a cheque for $75 for a three-subscription to *Good Health*, a monthly newsletter about healthful living. The first issue will be sent to the subscriber in April 2008.

b. On June 8, 2009 an auto parts manufacturer delivered an order of $100,000 of parts to the distribution centre of a large national company. The order for the parts was made on June 3, 2009. Terms of payment are that the national company will pay in full within 30 days.

c. On December 15, 2007 an equipment manufacturer agreed to sell a piece of specialized equipment to a customer for $68,000. At the time of the agreement the buyer paid $15,000 with the remainder to be paid on delivery. The equipment is to be delivered on January 10, 2008.

E4-9. **(Calculating revenue using the percentage-of-completion and completed-contract methods, LO 2)** Whipporwill Ltd. (Whipporwill) is a small construction company in northern Ontario. Whipporwill recently signed a contract to build a new town hall in one of the region's larger cities. Whipporwill will receive $25,000,000 from the city for building the town hall and will have to pay the costs of construction from that amount. Construction will begin in September 2009 and is expected to be completed in March 2011. Whipporwill's year end is December 31. Whipporwill estimates that construction costs in each year will be:

	2009	2010	2011	Total
Estimated costs	$3,500,000	$9,000,000	$4,400,000	$16,900,000

The town paid $7,000,000 when the contract was signed and will pay $6,000,000 on January 1, 2010, 2011, and 2012.

Required:

Calculate the amount of revenue and expense that Whipporwill would recognize in each year of the contract using the percentage-of-completion method and the completed-contract method. Assume the actual costs incurred equal the estimated costs.

E4-10. **(The effect of using different ways of estimating the proportion of a long-term contract that has been completed on the amount of revenue recognized, LO 2, 3)** Hectanooga Ltd. (Hectanooga) is a large construction engineering company. In 2010, Hectanooga was awarded a contract to build a small hydroelectric generating plant adjacent to an aluminium smelting plant. The aluminium company decided that it would be cheaper to generate its own power than to buy power from a supplier, so it is having a generating plant built. Hectanooga will receive $31,000,000 to build the dam, from which it must pay the costs of construction. Information regarding the yearly progress of the contract measured in different ways is provided below:

	2010	2011	2012	2013	Total
Costs	$4,000,000	$6,500,000	$8,000,000	$2,500,000	$21,000,000
Percentage completed in each year as estimated by an independent engineering expert	12%	38%	40%	10%	100%
Labour hours worked	10,000	25,000	50,000	18,000	103,000

Required:

Hectanooga's new vice-president of finance understands that there are different ways to calculate the percentage-of-completion of a project. The vice-president has asked you to calculate the amount of revenue that would be recognized in each year of the contract using three different methods of estimating the percentage completed:

a. Costs incurred.

b. Percentage completed in each year as estimated by an independent engineering expert.

c. Labour hours worked.

The vice-president would also like you to explain how he should choose among the three methods.

E4-11. **(Understanding the impact of self-interest on decision making, LO 5)** Different stakeholders of an entity will view the entity's goals and objectives in different ways, in part (at least), influenced by their personal goals and objectives (their self-interests). For each of the following situations, explain what the stakeholder would want to accomplish in its dealings with the entity. Explain how the interests of the identified stakeholder could conflict with the interests of other stakeholders.

a. Leaders of a union about to negotiate a new contract for its members.

b. A lender considering making a large loan to an entity.

c. President and CEO of a public company who holds a significant number of the company's shares.

d. A financial analyst preparing a report for investors on a company that her employer does corporate work for.

E4-12. **(Using the instalment method, LO 2)** Red Pheasant Inc. (Red Pheasant) sells a range of consumer products. The company buys half-hour blocks of time on local television stations to promote the products to potential buyers. For example, recently Red Pheasant has been promoting a sophisticated home gym. Customers can purchase the home gym for 36 monthly payments of $100. The cost of a home gym to Red Pheasant is $1,000. Red Pheasant uses the instalment method for recognizing revenue.

Required:

a. Why do you think that Red Pheasant uses the instalment method to recognize revenue on the sale of its home gym?

b. What journal entries would Red Pheasant record when it receives a payment from a customer?

E4-13. **(Accounting for gains and losses, LO 4)** For each of the following land sales, prepare the journal entry that would be recorded and indicate the amount of the gain or loss that would be reported. Assume that in each case the sale of land is not a main business activity of the entity.

a. Land costing $500,000 is sold for $410,000.

b. Land costing $1,300,000 is sold for $4,000,000.

c. Land costing $1,800,000 is sold for $1,800,000.

E4-14. **(Explaining and understanding different roles that accounting problems can be viewed from, LO 5, 6)** Listed below are some of the roles that a person addressing accounting problems can have. The role can affect how the role-player approaches and analyzes an accounting problem. For each role listed below, explain the perspective that the role brings to the analysis. (Example: an auditor for the Canada Revenue Agency examines accounting information to ensure that an entity complies with the *Income Tax Act* and, as a result, pays an appropriate amount of tax.) In answering, consider the entity the person in the role is working for and the objectives of that entity, and apply these factors to explain how the role-player would approach providing advice on accounting problems.

a. Arbitrator. (An arbitrator is a person who helps resolve disputes between parties. In an accounting setting, an arbitrator might be asked to resolve disagreements over the accounting choices an entity made when, for example, the selling price of the entity is based on net income.)

b. Advisor to management of the entity.

c. Advisor to the board of directors of the company.

d. External auditor.

e. Advisor to a prospective lender.

f. Advisor to a major shareholder who is not involved in the day-to-day management of the entity.

E4-15. **(Choosing when to recognize revenue according to the objectives of financial reporting, LO 1, 2, 6)** Pisquid Ltd. (Pisquid) is a manufacturer of kitchen furniture. In November 2009, Pisquid received an order for 15,000 sets of specially designed furniture from a large retail chain. The contract with the retail chain guaranteed the price that the retailer would pay and the quantity it would buy from Pisquid. The furniture is to be delivered monthly, in equal quantities each month, beginning in March 2010 and continuing through August 2011. The retail chain is to pay Pisquid within 45 days of receiving each shipment. Because Pisquid had excess capacity in its plant when the contract was signed, it decided to manufacture the full order as soon as it could. Pisquid began producing the furniture in January 2010 and completed making the 15,000 sets in November 2010.

Required:

a. Identify the different possible critical events that could be used to recognize revenue.

b. For the purposes of satisfying each of the following objectives, which critical event would you recommend for recognizing revenue? Explain. For purposes of answering, do not consider the constraints and the facts.
   i.   Tax minimization.
   ii. Evaluation of management by outside shareholders.
   iii. Income smoothing.
   iv. Managing earnings to increase income.
   v.   Cash flow prediction.

c. Which of the revenue-recognition methods that you identified in (a) satisfy the four revenue recognition criteria? Explain.

E4-16. **(Assessing different ways of recognizing revenue, LO 1, 2, 5)** Valhalla Furniture Emporium Ltd. (Valhalla) sells poor-quality furniture at low prices. Customers take delivery of their furniture after making a down payment of 10 percent of the selling price. The customers agree to pay the balance owing in 36 equal monthly payments. Valhalla repossesses between 40 percent and 60 percent of the furniture sold because customers default on their payments. Repossessed furniture can be resold if it requires only minor repairs and cleaning. Some repossessed furniture is unsaleable and must be disposed of.

Required:

a. What are the possible points at which Valhalla could recognize revenue?

b. Explain what objectives of reporting each revenue-recognition point would satisfy?

c. Which revenue-recognition points can you support with the four GAAP criteria?

Problems

P4-1. **(Choosing a revenue-recognition point to achieve an objective of financial reporting, LO 1, 2, 3, 5, 6)** For each of the following independent situations, recommend how you would want to recognize revenue if your objective of financial reporting were to minimize taxes. Support your answer. (To respond, you should identify alternative points for recognizing revenue and choose the one that best satisfies the objective of minimizing taxes *and* can be reasonably supported.)

a. A construction company signs a contract to build a warehouse for a food distribution company. The project is to take 18 months from the signing of the contract and the construction company will receive $10,000,000. At the construction company's fiscal year end, 60 percent of the project has been completed.

b. An investment company purchases shares of publicly traded companies for its portfolio. During the year, the market value of the portfolio increases from $2,300,000 to $3,745,000. None of the shares were sold during the year.

c. A national bus company sells passes that allow the passenger unlimited travel on the company's buses for 60 days from the day the pass is first used. Passes must be purchased at least 90 days before they are first used. Once purchased, the passes are not refundable.

d. A computer software company sells a software package that entitles the owners to receive the next two upgrades of the package at no additional charge, plus technical support for 18 months from the date of purchase.

e. A law firm charges clients who wish to have legal advice available to them 24 hours a day, seven days a week, a fee of $10,000 per year for the service. (The $10,000 fee is simply for the privilege of having a lawyer available all the time. These clients then have to pay the lawyer's hourly rate for the advice given.)

P4-2. **(Evaluating when to recognize revenue to try to achieve an objective of financial reporting, LO 1, 2, 3, 5, 6)** For each of the following independent situations, recommend how you would want to recognize revenue if you were the president of the company, you received a significant bonus based on net income, and your objective of financial reporting was to receive as high a bonus as is reasonably possible. Support your answer. (To respond, you should identify alternative points for recognizing revenue and choose the one that best satisfies the objective of achieving a high bonus *and* can be reasonably supported.)

a. A construction company signs a contract to build a warehouse for a food distribution company. The project is to take 18 months from the signing of the contract and the construction company will receive $10,000,000. At the construction company's fiscal year end, 60 percent of the project has been completed. The construction company receives payments of $500,000 on the first day of each month. The remaining amount is due one month after completion of the warehouse.

b. A national bus company sells passes that allow the passenger unlimited travel on the company's buses for 60 days from the day the pass is first used. Passes must be purchased at least 90 days before they are first used. Once purchased, the passes are not refundable.

c. A computer software company sells a software package that entitles the owners to receive the next two upgrades of the package at no additional charges plus technical support for 18 months from the date of purchase.

d. A law firm charges clients who wish to have legal advice available to them 24 hours a day, seven days a week, a fee of $10,000 per year for the service. (The $10,000 fee is simply for the privilege of having a lawyer available all the time. These clients then have to pay the lawyer's hourly rate for the advice given.)

P4-3. **(Observing the effects of different revenue-recognition methods on financial ratios, LO 1, 2, 3, 4, 5)** On November 15, 2008 Desert Renovations Ltd. (Desert) signed a contract to renovate a 75-year-old building so that it would be suitable to house the head office of a real estate company. Desert has provided you with the following information about the contract:

i. Desert expects the renovations to take three years.

ii. Desert will receive $20,000,000 for the renovations. Desert will receive payments on the following schedule:

  ■ $5,000,000 when the contract is signed.
  ■ $6,000,000 on September 1, 2009.
  ■ $6,000,000 on June 1, 2010, the expected completion date of the project.
  ■ $3,000,000 on January 15, 2011.

iii. The total cost of the renovations is expected to be $13,000,000:
- 2008: $0
- 2009: $4,800,000
- 2010: $8,200,000
- 2011: $0

iv. Other costs associated with the contract are $1,400,000 in each of 2009 and 2010. These costs are treated as period costs in the calculation of income.

v. Desert's year end is December 31.

Required:

a. Calculate revenue, expenses, gross margin, and net income for each year using the following revenue-recognition methods:
   i. Percentage-of-completion.
   ii. Completed-contract.
   iii. Cash collection. (Hint: match expenses based on the proportion of cash collected in each year).
b. Calculate the gross margin percentage and the profit margin percentage for each year.
c. Does it matter how Desert accounts for its revenue from the renovation contract? To whom does it matter and why?
d. Is the actual economic performance of Desert affected by how it accounts for the revenue from the renovation contract? Explain.

P4-4. **(Observing the effects of different revenue-recognition methods on financial ratios, LO 1, 2, 3, 4, 5)** On, July 15, 2009 Tidnish Vessel Refitters Ltd. (Tidnish) signed a contract to refit a 25-year-old supertanker to meet new environmental standards and operate more efficiently. Tidnish has provided you with the following information about the contract:

i. Tidnish expects the refitting to take three years.

ii. Tidnish will receive $20,000,000 for the refitting. Tidnish will receive payments on the following schedule:
- $4,000,000 when the contract is signed.
- $4,800,000 on June 1, 2010.
- $8,000,000 on February 1, 2011, the expected completion date of the project.
- $3,200,000 on July 15, 2012.

iii. The total cost of the renovations is expected to be $12,800,000:
- 2009: $0
- 2010: $8,000,000
- 2011: $4,800,000
- 2012: $0

iv. Other costs associated with the contract are $1,600,000 in each of 2010 and 2011. These costs are treated as period costs in the calculation of income.

v. Tidnish's year end is July 31.

Required:

a. Calculate revenue, expenses, gross margin, and net income for each year using the following revenue-recognition methods:
   i. Percentage-of-completion.
   ii Completed-contract
   iii. Cash collection. (Hint: match expenses based on the proportion of cash collected in each year).
   iv. Calculate the gross margin percentage and the profit margin percentage for each year.

b. Does it matter how Tidnish accounts for its revenue from the refitting contract? To whom does it matter and why?

c. Is the actual economic performance of Tidnish affected by how it accounts for the revenue from the refitting contract? Explain.

P4-5. **(Observing the effects of different revenue-recognition methods on financial ratios, LO 2, 3, 4, 5)** Antler Manufacturing Ltd. (Antler) is a newly formed company specializing in the production of high-quality machine parts. Paul Wayne incorporated Antler on the understanding that it would receive a large contract from his previous employer, Pocologan Inc. (Pocologan), to manufacture parts. Antler has rented the space and equipment it needs to operate its business. During Antler's first year of operations, the following transactions and economic events take place:

i. January 3, 2008: Paul Wayne contributes $1,000,000 cash in exchange for 100,000 common shares in Antler.

ii. January 5, 2008: Antler borrows $500,000 from Pocologan. The loan carries an interest rate of 10 percent per year. No interest or principal needs to be paid until 2011.

iii. January 8, 2008: Antler rents space and equipment to operate the business. Rent of $400,000 for two years is paid.

iv. January 10, 2008: Antler signs the contract with Pocologan. The contract requires that Antler manufacture and deliver $8,000,000 in parts over the period July 1, 2008 to December 31, 2010. The contract requires payment by Pocologan within 90 days of each delivery by Antler. The selling price of all parts is specified in the contract. Antler begins production of the parts immediately. Pocologan operates a just-in-time inventory system, which requires that Antler be ready to deliver parts within three hours of being notified by Pocologan that parts are required. As a result, Antler is required to keep an adequate supply of parts on hand to meet demand.

v. During 2008 Antler produced and delivered parts, and collected cash in the following amounts:

Selling price of parts *produced* during 2008 $2,800,000
Cost of parts *produced* during 2008 1,680,000
Selling price of parts *delivered* to Pocologan during 2008   1,800,000
Cost of parts *delivered* to Pocologan during 2008   1,080,000
Cash collected from Pocologan during 2008 1,050,000
Cost of parts that were paid for by Pocologan during 2008   630,000

vi. All costs incurred to produce the parts were purchased on credit. Of the $1,680,000 incurred to produce parts in 2008, $1,520,000 had been paid by December 31, 2008.

vii. During 2008 Antler incurred additional costs of $420,000, all on credit. As of December 31, 2008, $350,000 of these costs had been paid. Because these costs were not directly related to the production of parts, Antler plans to expense them in full in 2008. This amount does not include the amount paid for rent and the interest expense.

viii. Antler has a December 31 year end.

Required:

a. Use an accounting equation spreadsheet to record the transactions and economic events that occurred in 2008 for Antler. Prepare a separate spreadsheet using the following critical events for recognizing revenue:
   i. Production.
   ii. Delivery.
   iii. Collection of cash.

b. Prepare Antler's income statement for 2008 and its balance sheet as of December 31, 2008, using each of the three critical events (production, delivery, and collection of cash). Your income statements should show revenue, cost of goods sold, gross margin, other expenses, and net income.

c. Calculate the gross margin percentage, profit margin percentage, current ratio, and the debt-to-equity ratio for 2008 for each critical event.

d. Which method of revenue recognition in (c) gives the best indication of Antler's performance and liquidity? Explain.

e. Does it matter how Antler recognizes revenue? To whom does it matter and why?

f. Is the actual economic performance of Antler affected by how it recognizes revenue? Explain.

P4-6.   (**Recognizing revenue in a bill and hold arrangement, LO 1, 4**) Josselin Inc. (Josselin) is a manufacturer of computer game consoles. The company's products are designed to the specifications of each customer. In 2009, Josselin entered into a number of bill and hold arrangements with customers. Each arrangement is a bit different and management isn't sure when revenue should be recognized in each case. Provide a report to management explaining when you think revenue should be recognized for each arrangement (or perhaps whether revenue should be recognized on production, delivery, or some other point). Josselin's year end is December 31.

a. The customer signed a contract to purchase 100,000 consoles to meet expected increased demand for its products. The customer asked that the consoles be produced as soon as possible but that they not be delivered until early the next year because of a shortage of space in its warehouse. The customer paid a deposit of 25 percent of the selling price and the contract states that the customer must pay the agreed to price in full for the consoles whether it needs them or not. The contract also specifies that 25,000 consoles are to be delivered on the 15th day of each the first four months of 2010. Josselin completed production of the consoles in mid-December and they are awaiting shipment. The price has been agreed to and normal payment terms apply.

b. The customer ordered 50,000 consoles and paid a deposit of 30 percent of the selling price. The deposit must be refunded if the customer decides to cancel the order. The order can be cancelled at the option of the customer for any reason. The units ordered can be easily modified by Josselin and sold to distributors if need be. The contract also specifies that 12,500 consoles are to be delivered on the 15th day of each the first four months of 2010. Josselin completed production of the consoles in mid-December and they are awaiting shipment. The price has been agreed to and normal payment terms apply.

c. To take advantage of some excess production capacity that is temporarily available at its factory, Josselin produced 200,000 consoles for one of its regular customers. The customer indicated in a conversation with Josselin's president that it was highly likely that the units would be needed but the customer would not make a commitment to purchase the consoles. Josselin's management expects that the units will be shipped to the customer by October of 2010 at the latest.

P4-7.   (**Evaluating when to recognize revenue, LO 1**) Happy Snacks Ltd. (HSL) is a distributor of snack products to various retail stores in Toronto. HSL establishes agreements with stores whereby it places racks in the stores that display HSL's products. HSL is responsible for stocking and maintaining the racks. The retail merchant does not pay for the snacks and earns a commission for any snacks sold. The merchant pays HSL monthly for any snacks sold during the month, less commission.

Required:

When should HSL recognize its revenue? Explain your answer.

P4-8.   (**Evaluating when to recognize revenue, LO 1**) Fair Jewelers is a retail jewelry store. Fair offers a program to its customers that allows them to make a down payment on an item in the store, with the store holding the item for the customer until it is paid for in full. Customers are required to complete the purchase (meaning payment in full) within 180 days of inception. Customers do not have to sign a formal agreement to pay or purchase for the selected item. The merchandise is generally not released to the customer until the full purchase price is paid. If the customer fails to pay the remaining purchase price, the customer loses the cash deposit. If the merchandise is lost, damaged, or destroyed, Fair must either refund the cash deposit to the customer or provide replacement merchandise.

Required:

When should Fair Jewelers recognize its revenue? Explain your answer.

P4-9. (**Evaluating when to recognize revenue, LO 1**) In late December 2009, Alpha Inc. made a large shipment of goods to a new customer. Alpha had been in negotiations with the customer for some time and the final agreement was an important step in its planned expansion into western Canada. The agreement was unusual in that it allowed the customer to return any and all of the goods shipped at any time up until March 1, 2010. The customer is not required to pay for the goods until March 2010. Alpha recognizes its revenue when goods are delivered to the customer and normally provides 30 days to pay. Alpha's year end is December 31.

Required:

When should Alpha Inc. recognize its revenue? Explain your answer.

P4-10. (**Considering how to recognize expenses, LO 4, 5, 6**) Duthil Ltd. is a small public company that publishes a variety newsletters and magazines. The CEO and founder of Duthil owns 35 percent of the shares of the company with the remainder owned by public investors. Duthil makes money through the sale of subscriptions and individual issues of its magazines and newsletters (revenue is recognized when a publication is mailed to a subscriber or an individual issue is sold) and through the sale of advertising in the publications. In late 2008, Duthil conducted a campaign to increase subscriptions to its publications. The company engaged a telemarketing firm, which called potential subscribers in the desired demographic group. The cost of the campaign was $66,000. As a result of the campaign several hundred new subscriptions were obtained. The subscriptions will come into effect in fiscal 2009 and will generate about $75,000 for the year. All the new subscriptions are for one year but management expects that approximately 50 percent of those subscriptions will be renewed for the next year and then for each year after that approximately 75 percent of the subscribers will renew. Duthil's yearend is December 31.

Required:

a. Who are the possible users of Duthil's financial statements and what use do they have for the statements?
b. What objectives of financial reporting might Duthil's management consider when preparing the financial statements? Explain.
c. How would you recommend the objectives be ranked? Explain.
d. Prepare a report to Duthil's management explaining how to account for the costs incurred to increase the number of subscribers. In your answer, be sure to consider your responses to (a), (b), and (c) above. Also consider whether the costs incurred should be considered an asset or an expense when incurred, and if considered an asset when incurred, over what period the asset should be expensed. Explain your response.

P4-11. (**Evaluating objectives of financial reporting and recommending how to recognize revenue, LO 1, 2, 5**) Opeongo Construction Ltd. (Opeongo) is a recently formed company that builds commercial and industrial buildings in the Ottawa area. All of Opeongo's common stock is owned by five people: Adam and Nikki, a brother and sister who operate the company; two cousins of Adam and Nikki who live and work in Vancouver; and a wealthy aunt who is retired and lives in Europe. Opeongo borrowed money from the bank to cover the costs of starting the business. All the money that was initially borrowed from the bank has been spent.

In October 2008, Opeongo won a contract to build a warehouse in suburban Ottawa. This will be its first large job. The warehouse will take about 18 months to build and construction is scheduled to begin in late March 2009. Opeongo will receive $5.88 million to build the warehouse. The contract specifies the following payment schedule:

■ On commencement of construction	$300,000
■ On the first day of each month beginning with the month after construction begins ($210,000 per month for 18 months)	3,780,000
■ On completion of construction	1,200,000
■ 90 days after the purchaser takes possession of the warehouse	600,000
■ Total	$5,880,000

From this amount Opeongo will have to pay the costs of construction, which it estimates to be about $4,500,000. Construction costs are expected to be incurred evenly over the construction period. Opeongo's year end is December 31.

Required:

a. What do you think Opeongo's objectives of accounting could be? Explain.
b. How would you rank the objectives? Explain.
c. What different revenue recognition methods could Opeongo consider for the warehouse project? How much revenue would be recognized in 2008, 2009, and 2010 under the different methods you identified? Show your work.
d. When would you recommend that revenue be recognized on the warehouse construction project? Explain your recommendation. Make sure that you consider the constraints, facts, and objectives in your answer.

P4-12. (**Considering when to recognize revenue, LO 1, 2, 5, 6**) Teslin Inc. (Teslin) is a medium-sized manufacturer of plastic storage containers. Teslin is a private corporation that is owned entirely by a single shareholder, Rima Ishtiaque. Ms. Ishtiaque is not involved in the day-to-day management of Teslin, but she does speak regularly with Teslin's president, Mr. Krajden. Mr. Krajden is compensated with a salary plus a bonus based on Teslin's net income.

On October 1, 2009 Teslin signed a $1,000,000 contract with the Government of Canada to design and manufacture storage containers for all the tax dollars they collect from Canadians. The storage containers must be delivered by April 1, 2011. The government will pay $250,000 on April 1, 2010, $250,000 on January 15, 2011, and the balance 30 days after all the containers have been delivered. Teslin plans to begin production of the containers in early 2010. Teslin plans to ship 10 percent of the contracted number of containers per month beginning in September 2010. The contract stipulates that Teslin pay a penalty of $20,000 per week if the containers are not completely delivered by April 1, 2011. Teslin had to borrow $300,000 from the bank to provide cash to finance the project. Teslin expects to earn $225,000 from this contract.

You have been hired by Mr. Krajden to provide advice to him on how to recognize revenue on the contract with the government. Teslin's year end is December 31.

Required:

    a. Who are the possible users of Teslin's financial statements and what use do they have for the statements?

    b. What objectives of financial reporting would you suggest that Mr. Krajden consider when preparing Teslin's financial statements? Explain.

    c. How would you advise Mr. Krajden to rank the objectives? Explain.

    d. What possible critical events for recognizing the revenue on the container contract can you identify for Mr. Krajden? Explain.

    e. When would you recommend that Teslin recognize the revenue on the contract? Make sure that you consider the constraints, facts, and objectives when responding.

P4-13. **(Evaluating when a partnership of lawyers should recognize revenue, LO 1, 2, 3, 5, 6)**
Elnora and Partners is a recently formed partnership of lawyers. The partnership has ten partners (all of whom are practising lawyers) and 15 associate lawyers (lawyers who work for the partnership but who are not partners), along with 12 other employees. The partnership's financial statements will be used to determine:

- the amount of income tax that each partner pays (remember, partners, not the partnership, pay income tax).
- the amount of money that is paid to each partner, based on the net income of the partnership.
- the amount that a new partner pays to join the partnership and the amount a departing partner is paid for his or her partnership interest. In addition, the financial statements are provided to the bank because the partnership has a large line of credit available to it.

    The partnership's September 30 year end has just passed and the managing partner of the firm has asked for your advice on how to recognize revenue. The managing partner provides you with the following information on how the partnership generates revenue:

    i. Some clients are billed at the completion of a case, based on the number of hours lawyers worked on the case. (Each lawyer has an hourly billing rate.) Lawyers keep track of the time they spend on each case and report the number of hours each month to the accounting department, which keeps track of the hours spent on each case by each lawyer. The amount actually billed to a client may differ from the actual charges generated by the lawyers who worked on the case. (That is, the amount billed may differ from the number of hours worked multiplied by the hourly billing rate.) The final amount billed is based on the judgment of the partner in charge of the case. Clients have 60 days from receipt of their bill to pay.

    ii. Some clients pay only if their cases are successful. The partnership receives a percentage of the settlement if the client wins the case. It can be difficult to determine whether a client will win a case and the amount that will be received if the client does win.

    iii. Some clients pay amounts called retainers, which is an amount paid to the partnership before services are provided. The retainer is used to pay for legal services as they are provided. If the amount of retainer is not used by the end of the year, the remaining amount is applied against future years' legal services.

    iv. Clients who wish to have legal advice available to them 24 hours a day, seven days a week, pay a fee of $10,000 per year for the service. (The $10,000 fee is simply for the privilege of having a lawyer available all the time. These clients then have to pay the lawyer's hourly rate for the advice given.)

a. What are the possible objectives of financial reporting? Explain each objective that you identify. Are there any conflicts among the objectives? Explain.
b. Rank the objectives in order of importance. Explain your ranking.
c. When should the partnership recognize its revenue? Explain your recommendations fully. Make sure to discuss constraints, facts, and objectives in your answer.

P4-14. **(Selecting and justifying revenue-recognition alternatives to suit the objectives of financial reporting, LO 2, 3, 5, 6)** Eyebrow Technologies Ltd. (Eyebrow) is a Canadian-owned developer of computer hardware and software. Eyebrow is owned by 20 private investors, most of whom are not involved in the day-to-day management of the company. Eyebrow has borrowed extensively from banks, and management believes that additional loans will be required in the near future. Senior executives own a small number of Eyebrow's shares and are compensated with a salary plus a bonus based on the performance of the company.

Eyebrow is completing development of a new product. The product combines a modification of Eyebrow's existing computer hardware with a newly developed proprietary software program. The new product is targeted at firms in the financial services industry (firms such as Canadian banks, mid- to large-sized trust companies, and insurance companies). The design of the product requires that customers purchase both Eyebrow's hardware and software (a customer cannot purchase only the software, and the hardware is not useful without the software).

The new product (hardware and software) sells for $325,000. Eyebrow has 12 firm orders for the new product. In January 2009, Eyebrow shipped the computer hardware component to the 12 customers. The software will be provided to customers when it is completed in May 2009. The software was originally expected to be ready in February 2009, but unexpected programming problems delayed its completion. Eyebrow now expects to complete testing and debugging of the software in time to meet the May shipping date. Costs of the product include the hardware, software development, and marketing, sales and administrative costs.

Customers have already paid 25 percent of the cost of their orders. They will pay an additional 60 percent 30 days after the product is delivered and operating, and the balance six months after that.

Eyebrow's year end is February 28.

Required:

a. Identify the stakeholders who would have an interest in the financial information of Eyebrow. Explain each stakeholder's interest in the information (i.e., why would they want it?).
b. Identify possible objectives of financial reporting that Eyebrow's management might have. Explain why each objective might be relevant.
c. Identify possible critical events that Eyebrow could use to recognize the revenue on the new product. (In answering this question, consider whether the new product is really two products instead of one.)
d. Select two of the stakeholders and recommend a revenue and expense recognition policy to Eyebrow's management that could be used to satisfy the information needs of each of the two stakeholders. (Note: You should come up with two *different* policies, one for each stakeholder.) Fully explain your choices by justifying them in terms of the constraints, facts, and objectives.

Using Financial Statements

PET VALU, INC

Pet Valu, Inc. is a specialty retailer of pet food and pet supplies. As of December 31, 2005, it had 351 franchised and company-owned stores located in Canada and the U.S. Pet Valu is a public company traded on the Toronto Stock Exchange. The Canadian affiliated stores operate under the names Pet Valu, Paulmac's Pet Food, and Pet Food Plus, and together comprise the largest retail operation in Canada dedicated to the sale of food and supplies for dogs, cats, caged birds, wild birds, fish and small animals. Pet Valu's philosophy is to provide pet owners with a wide selection of pet food and supply products at competitive prices, together with friendly customer service and convenience of store location.

Pet Valu's consolidated balance sheets and statements of operations, along with some extracts from the notes to the financial statements and an excerpt from Pet Valu's Management Discussion & Analysis of Operating Results, are provided in Exhibit 4–8. Use this information to answer questions FS4-1 to FS4-13.

FS4-1. According to what accounting principles are Pet Valu's financial statements prepared? In what currency are the amounts in the financial statements stated? Do you think it is important to know the accounting principles and currency used to prepare the financial statements? Explain.

FS4-2. Examine Pet Valu's income statements and the accompanying notes to the financial statements and respond to the following:
   a. For its year ended December 31, 2005, how much did Pet Valu reported as "Sales and revenue?"
   b. By what percentage did "Sales and revenue" increase from the year ended January 1, 2005 to the year ended December 31, 2005?
   c. How much of Pet Valu's "Sales and revenue" was earned from its Canadian franchise operation? (Be careful here!)
   d. By what percentage did "Sales and revenue" from the Canadian franchise operation change from the year ended January 1, 2004 to the year ended December 31, 2005?

FS4-3. Examine Notes 1 and 3 to Pet Valu's financial statement and the excerpt from Pet Valu's "Management Discussion & Analysis of Operating Results" and respond to the following:
   a. What are the different sources of revenue from Canadian franchise stores? Give a brief explanation of what each type of revenue represents?
   b. What is the major source of revenue from the Canadian franchise stores? The financial statements do not explain how Pet Valu recognizes this revenue. When do you think Pet Valu would recognize this revenue? Explain.
   c. How does the way Pet Valu earns money from the sale of merchandise differ between Canadian and U.S. franchise stores?
   d. How does Pet Valu recognize revenue from royalties from Canadian franchise stores?
   e. How do you think Pet Valu recognizes revenue from sales in corporate-owned stores?

FS4-4. How does Pet Valu account for store pre-opening costs? How would you justify the treatment of these costs? Some businesses capitalize and amortize pre-opening costs. How would you justify that treatment? What are the implications of these different treatments of store pre-opening costs to you as a user of the financial statements?

EXHIBIT 4–8 :

**Pet Valu, Inc. Extracts
from Financial Statements**

Consolidated Balance Sheets

In accordance with accounting principles generally accepted in the United States of America
(In U.S. dollars)

	December 31, 2005		January 1, 2005
Assets			
Current assets			
Cash	$ 1,673,708	$	51,839
Accounts receivable	1,945,004		1,622,856
Other receivables (Note 3)	1,201,325		1,331,778
Inventories	23,803,567		22,365,496
Prepaid expenses	929,033		2,718,325
Deferred income tax assets (Note 13)	828,570		678,395
Total current assets	30,381,207		28,768,689
Notes receivable (Note 4) (Less allowances of $37,833, 2004 - $36,605)	66,379		167,446
Deferred charges (Note 1)	1,686,220		1,464,698
Property and equipment, net of accumulated depreciation and amortization (Note 5)	4,905,029		5,261,243
Goodwill (Note 1)	13,592,915		13,021,307
Deferred income taxes (Note 13)	3,977,741		2,742,104
Total assets	$ 54,609,491	$	51,425,487
Liabilities and Shareholders' Equity			
Current liabilities			
Bank overdraft	$ 1,559,421	$	3,710,327
Bank operating loans (Note 6)	1,862,419		2,691,935
Current portion of long-term debt including capital lease obligations (Note 7)	559,672		581,867
Current portion of deferred gain on warehouse sale (Note 5)	225,576		215,354
Trade accounts payable	5,201,056		4,311,514
Accrued liabilities (Note 8)	3,708,713		3,066,492
Accrued wages and benefits	2,459,436		2,405,662
Income taxes payable (Note 13)	2,602,198		1,747,247
Subordinated debentures (Note 9)	12,896,691		3,017,554
Total current liabilities	31,075,182		21,747,952
Deferred franchise revenue (Note 3)	20,039		104,897
Deferred gain on warehouse sale (Note 5)	605,419		804,034
Deferred rent payable	2,054,679		1,943,967
Long-term debt including capital lease obligations, less current maturities (Note 7)	1,203,785		1,406,017
Subordinated debentures (Note 9)	15,567,178		27,328,353
Total liabilities	50,526,282		53,335,220
Commitments and contingencies (Notes 6, 14 & 15)			
Minority interest in subsidiaries (Note 10)	-		1,118,388
Shareholders' Equity (Deficit)			
Capital stock (Notes 10 & 11)	963		963
Additional paid in capital	12,453,589		12,384,686
Accumulated deficit	(2,296,046)		(9,550,223)
Accumulated other comprehensive loss	(5,383,312)		(5,171,562)
Treasury stock – exchangeable shares, at cost	(691,985)		(691,985)
Total shareholders' equity (deficit)	4,083,209		(3,028,121)
Total liabilities and shareholders' equity (deficit)	$ 54,609,491	$	51,425,487

Consolidated Statements of Operations

In accordance with accounting principles generally accepted in the United States of America
(In U.S. dollars, except number of shares)

	Fiscal Years Ended	
	December 31, 2005	January 1, 2005
Sales and revenue (Note 3)	$ 134,405,802	$ 128,212,055
Cost of sales including occupancy costs	97,069,899	95,903,926
Gross profit	37,335,903	32,308,129
Store operating expenses excluding occupancy costs	14,057,272	12,757,603
General and administrative expenses	10,947,027	11,244,380
	12,331,604	8,306,146
Net interest expense (Note 12)	3,901,664	3,572,408
Loss on extinguishment of debt (Note 9e)	-	210,543
Gain on foreign exchange (Note 1)	-	(141,666)
Income before income taxes	8,429,940	4,664,861
Income taxes provision (Note 13)	1,175,763	932,100
Net income	$ 7,254,177	$ 3,732,761
Basic EPS (Note 2)	$ 0.97	$ 0.50
Diluted EPS (Note 2)	0.84	0.45
Weighted average number of common stock and exchangeable shares outstanding:		
Basic (Note 2)	7,497,586	7,496,418
Diluted (Note 2)	8,902,695	9,007,219

1. Significant Accounting Policies

Revenue Recognition The Company recognizes revenue from retail sales through company-owned stores, wholesale sales to other retailers, and revenues from its franchise operations.

The Company has individual franchise agreements, which grant the individual franchisees the exclusive right to operate a franchise store. Initial site development fees, established business fees and franchise fees are collected in advance and recorded as income when the store commences operations as a franchise location. All initial fees are earned on the date of the store opening. On the sale of an existing company-owned store to a franchisee, costs relating to the sale of the store are charged to expense as incurred and proceeds (excluding fees) in excess of the net book value of store assets are recorded as a gain on the date of sale.

Ongoing revenue from Canadian franchise operations are comprised of royalties, percentage rents, franchise fees, fees for services, and wholesale merchandise sales. Royalties and percentage rents are based on the gross sales or imputed gross sales of the franchise and are recorded in income as earned. Franchise fees are non-refundable. Accordingly, revenue is recognized when the fees are collected. Fees for service are recognized when the service has been performed by the Company. Canadian franchisees purchase the majority of their inventory requirements from the Company. Accordingly, the Company recognizes revenue from the wholesale sale of merchandise to these franchisees.

Under the U.S. franchising system, the Company retains ownership of all inventories and recognizes revenue and records related expenses upon the sale of merchandise at the retail level. U.S. franchisees purchase the store equipment and are responsible for store operating costs, including labour for which they receive an allowance from the Company. In addition, U.S. franchisees are paid a royalty based on merchandise sales and compliance with operational standards. Royalties and store operating cost allowances paid by the Company to U.S. franchisees are recorded as store operating expenses.

Store Pre-opening Costs All costs associated with the opening of new stores are charged to expense as incurred.

Advertising Costs Advertising costs are charged to expense as incurred. Advertising expense was $1,635,581 $1 012,195 in fiscal 2005 and 2004, respectively.

EXHIBIT 4–8 :

(continued)
Pet Valu, Inc. Extracts
from Financial Statements

3. Franchise Operations

Included in other receivables were net amounts due from franchisees of $1,077,217 and $1,143,897 as of December 31, 2005 and January 1, 2005, respectively. An amount due in respect of a deficit balance in the franchise promotion fund of $170,892 was included in the net amount due from franchisees as of January 1, 2005.

Included in sales and revenue were the following amounts with respect to Canadian franchise operations:

	Fiscal Years Ended	
	December 31, 2005	January 1, 2005
Merchandise sales to franchises	$ 61,520,000	$ 58,016,000
Distribution charges	5,149,000	4,836,000
Initial franchise fees	368,000	415,000
Gain on sale of company-owned stores	147,000	5,000
Franchise royalties and other revenues	10,547,000	10,432,000
	$ 77,731,000	$ 73,704,000

In fiscal 2005 and 2004, the Company earned initial franchise fees and gains on the sale of company-owned stores of $51,791 and $18,533 respectively, through its U.S. franchise operations. Retail sales of merchandise through U.S. franchise stores were $2,202,629 and $2,910,488 in fiscal 2005 and 2004, respectively, and were included in sales and revenue. Royalties and other fees paid to U.S. franchisees in the amount of $482,419 for fiscal 2005 and $628,086 for fiscal 2004 were included in store operating expenses excluding occupancy costs.

Promotion Fund

The Company's Canadian franchisees contribute a percentage of their weekly merchandise purchases to a promotion fund. This fund is used to offset marketing and advertising activities performed by the Company. Collections for this fund are made in accordance with the terms of applicable agreements made with each franchisee. The percentage of franchise merchandise purchases designated for the promotion fund is determined at the discretion of the Company, subject to certain restrictions contained in the franchise agreements.

17. Segmented Financial Information

The Company operates exclusively in the pet product retail industry. The Company's reportable segments are based on geographic area. All intercompany revenues and expenses are eliminated in computing revenues and operating income. The accounting policies of the segments are the same as those described in Note 1 - Significant Accounting Policies.

Operating results and other financial data by segment for fiscal 2005 and 2004 were as follows:
(in thousands of U.S. dollars)

	Fiscal years ended	
	December 31, 2005	January 1, 2005
Sales and revenue to external customers		
Canada	$ 100,555	$ 95,334
U.S.	33,851	32,878
Total sales and revenue	$ 134,406	$ 128,212
Net interest expense		
Canada	$ 3,891	$ 3,501
U.S.	11	71
Total net interest expense	$ 3,902	$ 3,572
Net Income		
Canada	$ 4,622	$ 2,352
U.S.	3,100	1,883
Intersegment elimination	(468)	(502)
Total net income	$ 7,254	$ 3,733
Depreciation and amortization		
Canada	$ 1,412	$ 1,163
U.S.	357	366
Total depreciation and amortization	$ 1,769	$ 1,529
Purchases of property and equipment		
Canada	$ 653	$ 525
U.S.	353	184
Total purchases of property and equipment	$ 1,006	$ 709

Excerpts from Pet Valu's Management Discussion & Analysis of Operating Results

Franchising

In Canada, Company revenues in relation to franchise operations are generated from fees and gains on the sale of franchises, from ongoing merchandise sales to franchisees, and from royalty and other income from franchise operations.

Under the U.S. franchising system, as distinct from the Canadian franchise program, the Company retains ownership of all inventories and records as revenue the full amount of store sales at the retail level. As well, the franchisee does not sublet the premises; instead, Pet Valu International Inc. pays the rent and normal operating expenses. U.S. franchisees purchase the store equipment and are responsible for certain store operating costs, including labour, for which they receive an allowance from the Company. In addition, U.S. franchisees are paid a royalty based on merchandise sales and compliance with operational standards. Royalties and store operating cost allowances paid by the Company to U.S. franchisees are recorded by the Company as store operating expenses. The Company is not currently offering new PET VALU franchises in the U.S. nor PAULMAC'S franchises in Canada.

Reniching project

During the last two fiscal years, the Company continued to pursue a long-term objective of shifting its product offering to higher-margin, high-quality pet products, which include pet specialty brands and private label products featuring a wellness focused approach to pet nutrition. Initiatives implemented to achieve this objective included the refinement and testing of marketing strategies, a shift in the in-store presentations, and the introduction of new pet foods in the wellness focused categories. While this component of our reniching may result in temporary same store sales declines, it is also expected to improve operating profits and enhance the image of the Company as a specialty retailer. The other key component of the Company's reniching project involves the development of revised or new store location and store image strategies reflecting changes in consumer traffic patterns, shopping centre developments, and competitive dynamics between mass merchandiser's and specialty stores. This resulted in certain store closures in Canada and certain store openings in the U.S. during fiscal 2005.

During fiscal 2005, the Company commenced rebranding efforts with the introduction of its new PET VALU BETTER PET NUTRITION trademark, now used in addition to the PET VALU trademark and name. This new mark, together with the expected gradual elimination of the "discount" image in association with the PET VALU business, highlight efforts to transform the Company's image from discount retailer to purveyor of higher quality products.

Comparison of Fiscal 2005 to Fiscal 2004

Sales and revenue

Sales and revenue represent retail sales through company-owned stores in Canada and the U.S., retail sales through franchise stores in the U.S., merchandise sales to franchisees in Canada, initial and continuing franchise fees in both countries, and wholesale sales to third parties. The Company's sales and revenue increased by $6.2 million or 4.8% in fiscal 2005 as compared to fiscal 2004. In fiscal 2005, the change in foreign exchange rates resulted in an increase in sales and revenue of $6.9 million. Before the effects of the change in foreign exchange rates, the sales and revenue in the Canadian operations decreased by $1.7 million or 1.8%. The sales and revenue in the U.S. operations increased by $1.0 million or 3.0%. A reduction in the average number of stores in operation contributed to the decrease in sales and revenue in Canada. In the U.S., an increase in the average number of stores in operation and an increase in the comparable store sales contributed to the increase in sales and revenue.

In fiscal 2005, total merchandise sales through company-owned stores increased by $2.5 million to $53.0 million, accounting for an increase of 1.8% in consolidated sales and revenue. In fiscal 2005, the change in foreign exchange rates resulted in an increase of $1.5 million in merchandise sales through company-owned stores. Before the effects of the change in foreign exchange rates, the merchandise sales through company-owned stores in the Canadian operations decreased by $0.6 million or 3.1%. In the U.S. operations, merchandise sales through company-owned stores increased by $1.7 million or 5.5%. The decrease in merchandise sales through company-owned stores in fiscal 2005 in Canada was due to a decrease in the average number of company-owned stores. The increase in fiscal 2005 in the U.S. was primarily due to an increase in the average number of company-owned stores and the increase in comparable store sales.

Merchandise revenue from franchisees includes (1) merchandise sales at U.S. franchise stores; and (2) merchandise sold to Canadian franchisees together with related franchise distribution charges, royalty revenue and percentage rent revenue. Total merchandise revenue from franchise stores increased by $3.5 million to $79.2 million, accounting for a 2.7% increase in consolidated sales and revenue. In fiscal 2005, the change in foreign exchange rates resulted in an increase of $5.3 million in merchandise revenue from franchise stores. Before the effects of the change in foreign exchange rates, the merchandise revenue from franchise stores in the Canadian operations decreased by $1.1 million or 1.5%. In the U.S. operations, merchandise revenue from franchise stores decreased by $0.7 million or 24.3%. A reduction of two franchises during the year in the U.S. operation and a decrease of 1.3% in the average number of franchise stores open in the Canadian operation contributed to the decrease in merchandise revenue from franchisees.

Initial fees and gains on the sale of franchises in fiscal 2005 of $1.1 million was $0.2 million greater than the prior year.

Wholesale revenue in fiscal 2005 of $0.9 million increased by $0.1 million as compared to the prior year.

FS4-5. What are the different sources of Pet Valu's revenue? How does it recognize the revenue from each source? Do you think that Pet Valu's revenue-recognition policies meet the four revenue recognition criteria? Explain.

FS4-6. Examine note 17 to Pet Valu's financial statements and respond to the following questions:
a) What is segmented financial information and why do you think it is provided (consider how it will help you as a user of the financial statements)?
b) How does Pet Valu define its segments? Why?
c) How much sales and revenue did Pet Valu earn in Canada and the U.S. in the fiscal years ended January 1, 2005 and December 31, 2005? How much net income was earned in each segment each year? What is the profit margin percentage in each segment in each year?

FS4-7. How does Pet Valu account for the money it spends on advertising? Why do you think these costs are accounted for this way? How much did Pet Valu spend for advertising in fiscal 2004 and 2005?

FS4-8. Examine the part of the extracts from Pet Valu's Management Discussion and Analysis that addresses the "Reniching Project." What is the Reniching Project? How do you think Pet Valu should account for the costs incurred for the Reniching Project? Explain.

FS4-9. What is the promotion fund? How do you think Pet Value accounts for amounts contributed to the promotion fund?

FS4-10. Read Note 3 to Pet Valu's financial statements. What makes up most of the amount that is included in "Other receivables" in the December 31, 2005 balance sheet?

FS4-11. Calculate the gross margin percentage for the fiscal years ended January 1, 2005 and December 31, 2005. What explanations can you give for the differences between the two years? (In answering, give consideration to the different ways that Pet Valu makes money as well as to the actual operations of the business.)

FS4-12. What was Pet Valu's net income for the years ended December 31, 2005 and January 1, 2005? In the year ended December 31, 2005, net income almost doubled from the previous year. Examine Pet Valu's statements of operations and provide some possible explanations for the higher net income in fiscal 2005.

FS4-13. Examine the extract from Pet Valu's Management Discussion and Analysis that provides a comparison of fiscal 2005 sales and revenue with fiscal 2004. Explain the difference in sales and revenue in the two years.[9]

◇ ROGERS — Analyzing Rogers Wireless Communications

R4-1. What do you think Rogers' objectives of financial reporting are? Explain.

R4-2. How much unearned revenue does Rogers report on its December 31, 2005 balance sheet? What does the unearned revenue represent? In responding you should specifically discuss how Rogers recognizes its revenue.

R4-3. How much revenue did the Toronto Blue Jays generate for Rogers in 2005? How do the Blue Jays earn revenue for Rogers (how does the team make money)? How do you think the Blue Jays recognize its revenue from its different business activities? Explain your reasoning.

R4-4. What different businesses does Rogers operate in? How does Rogers make money in each of those businesses? How is revenue recognized for each of those businesses (some businesses may have more than one revenue recognition policy)? Do those revenue-recognition policies meet the four revenue recognition policies? Explain.

R4-5. Examine Rogers' income statement. Which costs that are shown on the income statement could be reasonably matched to the revenue Rogers earns? Which costs would be difficult to match? Explain. In answering you should consider how Rogers makes money and the relation between the revenue it earns and the costs it incurs to earn that revenue.

R4-6. How much revenue did Rogers report for the year ended December 31, 2005? What different sources of revenue did Rogers report? What was Rogers' largest source of revenue? How much did it earn from that source during 2005? By what percentage did Rogers' total revenue increase from 2004 to 2005? Which type of revenue grew at the fastest rate?

R4-7. When a Rogers Cable customer signs up for service the customer usually pays an installation fee. How are these fees accounted for in Canada? How are these fees accounted for in the United States? How much more revenue was recorded in the U.S. than in Canada for installation fees? Which method makes more sense, the U.S. approach or the Canadian approach? Explain you reasoning.

ENDNOTES

1. For a fascinating look at how people respond to incentives, see the book *Freakonomics* by Steven D. Levitt and Stephen J. Dubner, published by HarperCollins.

2. Extracted from Aurizon Mines Ltd's 2003 and 2004 annual reports.

3. Extracted from WestJet Airlines Ltd.'s 2005 annual report.

4. Extracted from Genesis Land Development Corp.'s 2004 annual report.

5. Extracted from Google Inc.'s July 12, 2004 and July 26, 2004 prospectuses.

6. Extracted from Microsoft Corporation's 2005 annual report.

7. Extracted from Peace Arch Entertainment Group Inc.'s 2005 annual report.

8. Extracted from Shoppers Drug Mart Corporation's 2005 annual report.

9. Extracted from Pet Valu Inc.'s 2005 annual report.

GENERALLY ACCEPTED ACCOUNTING PRINCIPLES

LEARNING OBJECTIVES

After studying the material in this chapter you will be able to:

▶ **LO 1** Explain the need for and the applicability of GAAP.

▶ **LO 2** Describe the four basic assumptions that underlie GAAP.

▶ **LO 3** Recognize the strengths and limitations of the four qualitative characteristics of GAAP.

▶ **LO 4** Explain the measurement conventions that determine the amounts that are reported in the financial statements.

▶ **LO 5** Interpret the meaning of an unqualified audit report and understand why audited information is important.

At 9:30 a.m., early in March 2006, the red Rogers corporate symbol beamed over the television monitors on the floor of the New York Stock Exchange. Seconds later, CEO Ted Rogers rang the opening bell to start the trading day on Wall Street at the world's most important stock exchange. It was an anniversary party for Rogers and his business, Rogers Communications Inc., celebrating the company's 10 years as a publicly traded company in the U.S. (Rogers has been listed on the Toronto Stock Exchange in Canada since 1971.)

Being publicly traded has its own complications for the company, not the least of which is complying with ever-changing rules and regulations about how to prepare financial statements.

To do this, says Rogers Vice President of Financial Operations, John Gossling, the company has a staff of about 1,500 finance people. Of these, about 100 are executives at Rogers' head office in Toronto who make sure the company's financial statements are properly prepared. Of those 100, six or seven Chartered Accountants work on making sure the company complies with Generally Accepted Accounting Principles (GAAP) set by the Accounting Standards Board of the Canadian Institute of Chartered Accountants (CICA). The CAs cover everything from when revenue can be recognized to how to handle stock options and company pension liabilities.

There are six thick binders of CICA documents lined up on the bookshelf of Gossling's 10th floor office, just beside a book called "The Financial Numbers Game," which he said he's never read. Probably a good thing.

Playing games with financial statements led to the collapse of several high-profile U.S. corporate empires in recent years, such as Enron, WorldCom, and Adelphia. It also led American lawmakers to pass the Sarbanes-Oxley (SOX) legislation of 2002. That law forces CEOs and other top corporate executives who trade in the U.S. to personally sign off on all financial statements and to be held criminally liable if those declarations are found later to be false or if someone was cooking the books.

To ensure Rogers complies with SOX, the company's internal audit department had to triple in size, to 30 people.

Because Rogers' shares are traded on Bay Street and Wall Street, the company must report accounting numbers in accordance with both Canadian and U.S. GAAP, which can differ substantially from one another. For instance, under

Canadian GAAP, Rogers Communications lost $44 million in 2005. Under U.S. GAAP, the loss was $312.5 million.

Yet, despite the enormous resources Rogers devotes to compliance and following GAAP rules, Rogers' management also publishes key internal performance measures, which do not comply with GAAP, but are frequently used by analysts, investors, and Rogers' competitors to measure how well the company is doing.

INTRODUCTION

Financial reporting in Canada and in most places around the world is played by a set of rules. These rules are known as generally accepted accounting principles or GAAP. We have mentioned GAAP several times so far. In this chapter we will take a more comprehensive look at GAAP.

GAAP represent the rules of the accounting game. In most games, the rules are subject to interpretation. For example, hockey has a detailed set of rules about how the game is to be played. Some rules are straightforward and not subject to judgment: if an offensive player precedes the puck over the offensive zone blue line, the linesman must blow the whistle and stop play because the play is offside. Other hockey rules are subject to the referee's interpretation: a player who holds an opponent with hands, stick, or in any other way will receive a minor penalty for holding. Hockey fans know that a holding penalty is not given every time holding occurs. The referees exercise judgment in applying the holding rule. They take into consideration the extent of the holding, the impact a particular holding infraction has on the play, and when the infraction occurs.

Without rules, a hockey game would be chaotic. Some players might choose to pick the puck up in their hands and skate with it until an opposing player tackled them. Other players might think that the best way to stop opponents is to club them over the head with a stick. The rules of hockey add order to the play and make the game understandable to the people who watch it.

The rules of hockey are not universal. Hockey organizations modify the rules to meet their own needs. For example, younger children's leagues and some recreational leagues do not allow physical contact. Many leagues below the professional level require players to wear full facial protection. In Europe, the game is played on a larger ice surface and players who fight are thrown out of the game.

So it is with accounting. Accounting needs rules to ensure that, in broad terms at least, all participants and observers can know and understand how the game is played. At the same time, it is very difficult to establish a set of rules that can be uniformly applied without any judgment or interpretation. The circumstances surrounding economic events and transactions are so varied that if rigid rules were created there would be uniformity in financial reporting, but the accounting itself would not necessarily provide a reasonable representation of the economic activity.

In this chapter, we will look at the assumptions, characteristics, and conventions that form the foundation of GAAP in Canada and that define Canadian financial reporting. Having a common basis of communication that all stakeholders can know and understand makes it easier and more straightforward for an entity to communicate with its stakeholders. Like hockey, without a set of "rules," financial reporting would be chaotic. It would be very costly in time and money for stakeholders to learn and understand the accounting of each entity they are interested in. Many stakeholders would decide that the benefit was not worth the cost.

Despite the importance and the value of a somewhat standardized set of rules, it is important to look at GAAP critically. GAAP are not perfect. GAAP do not satisfy the information needs of all stakeholders in all situations. GAAP are sometimes abused by managers who are looking out for their own interests. This book offers a critical examination of accounting, with the objective to make readers sophisticated users of accounting information. This means recognizing that GAAP have significant limitations as well as benefits. It is also important to remember that not every entity follows GAAP.

WHAT ARE GENERALLY ACCEPTED ACCOUNTING PRINCIPLES (GAAP)?

Chapter 1 explained that accounting is a tool that has been developed by people as a means of providing information for decision making. There are no natural laws that define how accounting should be done. As a result, it is necessary to create rules for accounting. If there were no rules, it would be much more costly and difficult to make sense of the information contained in accounting reports because it would be necessary to learn and understand the rules that each entity was using. These rules are known as generally accepted accounting principles (GAAP). **GAAP** can be defined as the broad principles and conventions that provide guidance to accountants and managers for making accounting choices, as well as rules and procedures that are established as accepted accounting practices at a particular time.

Despite the prominence and wide use of GAAP, it is not possible to point to a single source that documents all GAAP. In fact, much of GAAP are not recorded at all. The most prominent source of GAAP is the *CICA Handbook*. The *CICA Handbook* is a thick document that contains the broad principles and conventions and some of the rules and procedures that make up GAAP. The *CICA Handbook* is the first place someone should look when trying to determine how to account according to GAAP, but it is certainly not the only source. Section 1100 of the *CICA Handbook* describes what constitutes Canadian generally accepted accounting principles and its sources, and provides guidance on sources to consult when making accounting choices that are not dealt with explicitly in the primary sources of GAAP.

Much of GAAP are simply what entities actually do in practice. If an accounting practice is used successfully by an entity, that practice becomes generally accepted. An accounting practice does not have to be widely used to be considered a GAAP, and there can be more than one way acceptable under GAAP of accounting for a particular type of economic event or transaction (think back to our discussion of revenue recognition in Chapter 4 and recall that a number of acceptable ways to recognize revenue were available so that financial statements could reflect the economic substance of transactions and economic events). Some accounting methods are GAAP only in specific industries—a certain accounting treatment might be acceptable in one industry, but not used or generally acceptable in others. And because the world is always changing, accountants and managers are often faced with new and different transactions and economic events for which to account. As a result, GAAP are always evolving and changing to meet the changing environment.

Federal and provincial corporations acts (for example, the *Canada Business Corporations Act*) and the provincial securities acts require that financial statements comply with GAAP. This suggests that all corporations in Canada must comply with GAAP. However, this is not the case. Public companies must follow GAAP. If a public company does not follow GAAP, the securities regulators have the authority to intervene. For private entities, the situation is less clear. If a private company is audited, its financial statements will likely comply with GAAP. However, while the corporations acts apply to private corporations and require them to provide audited financial statements to their shareholders, the shareholders are entitled to waive this requirement if they unanimously agree. Private corporations might not obtain unanimous consent of the shareholders if, for example, some shareholders are not involved in day-to-day management of the corporation. Private corporations might prepare GAAP statements if they are required as part of a borrowing agreement with a bank.

Partnerships and proprietorships are not required to follow GAAP. Following GAAP is voluntary for these types of entities. The decision to do so will be motivated by the needs of the stakeholders.

However, even when entities do not follow GAAP, they will generally not abandon them entirely. (That would mean inventing an entirely new and different method of accounting.) Rather, these entities are likely to follow some, but not all, GAAP. For example, most entities will use historical cost and accrual accounting (these are used for tax purposes and all businesses must file tax returns). Most will do some matching of expenses to revenues. Some may not provide as extensive note disclosure as is provided with GAAP statements. But private companies may choose not to follow GAAP because some of the standards may be too complex and may not help the entity achieve its reporting objectives, or because alternative accounting methods are more appropriate for the information needs of the stakeholders. (For example, if an entity has tax minimization as its primary objective, the entity might use accounting policies that are allowed by the *Income Tax Act*, even if the policies are not consistent with GAAP.) It is worth remembering that most entities in Canada are private. Therefore, most entities in Canada do not *have* to follow GAAP.

Canadian GAAP are not the same as GAAP in other countries. Accounting principles in countries evolve as they do for many reasons, including the economic, political, and social conditions that exist. Because of the close relationship between Canada and the United States, Canadian GAAP have many similarities to U.S. GAAP but are not identical. One of the major differences between accounting in Canada and the U.S. is that Canadian accounting standards emphasize professional judgment, whereas U.S. standards tend to be much more rule-oriented.

Recognizing that there are differences in the GAAP used in different countries helps one understand that there is no one right or best way to account. Exhibit 5–1 (page 236) shows income statements for the Canadian National Railway Company (CN) prepared under Canadian GAAP and U.S. GAAP.[1] CN provides both statements in its annual report. Notice that net income is different in each of the three years under U.S. and Canadian GAAP, sometimes by a fairly large amount. Which measure is right? Probably the best way to answer that question is to say that the amounts shown for Canadian GAAP are acceptable under Canadian GAAP and the amounts shown under U.S. GAAP are acceptable under U.S. GAAP. You can't say that one is better than the other. They're just different ways of measuring the same thing.

www.cn.ca

The Accounting Standards Board (ASB) of the Canadian Institute of Chartered Accountants (CICA) is responsible for setting the accounting standards that are included in the *CICA Handbook*. The ASB is made up mainly of Chartered Accountants, but it also gives representation to the groups that have an interest in accounting standards, such as financial executives, financial analysts, accounting academics, and the other two major accounting groups in Canada, the Certified General Accountants (CGA) and Certified Management Accountants (CMA). The process of setting standards is fairly elaborate and provides opportunities for interested parties to respond to proposed accounting standards before they are approved and included in the *CICA Handbook*.

www.cica.ca
www.cga-canada.org
www.cma-canada.org

The Future of Canadian GAAP: GAAP in Canada are changing. In 2005, the CICA released a strategic plan that proposes that International Financial Reporting Standards (IFRS) will become Canadian GAAP for Canadian public companies. IFRS are produced by the International Accounting Standards Board and are used in many countries around the world as the basis for preparing financial statements. For example, all public companies in Europe are required to prepare their financial statements according to IFRS. Australia and New Zealand use IFRS as their national reporting standards.

www.iasb.org

This means that for most Canadian public companies, Canadian GAAP would be replaced with IFRS. Canadian public companies that trade in the U.S. would be allowed to use U.S. GAAP. The strategic plan also proposes that for private companies with significant external stakeholders (such as bankers), a new set of accounting standards would be established, designed to meet the needs of these private business entities. For private entities whose financial statements are not used for external reporting purposes, the strategic plan proposes removing GAAP as a constraint altogether. In addition, GAAP for not-for-profit organizations are expected to converge with the international standards. The *CICA* intends to have its plan implemented by 2011.

The purpose of this chapter is to introduce the underpinnings of GAAP. However, it is crucial that you not look at GAAP as the one, the only, or the best way to account. Despite the usefulness of having a set of guidelines and rules for preparing financial statements, GAAP are not without flaws. To be a sophisticated user of financial information, you need to know and understand what GAAP-based information tells you, how it can help you, and what its limitations are.

THE WORLD ACCORDING TO GAAP

In this section we will examine three groups of accounting principles that form the essence of GAAP. The three groups of principles are:

1. The basic assumptions.

2. The qualitative characteristics.

3. The measurement conventions.

Consolidated Statement of Income – Canadian GAAP

In millions, except per share data	Year ended December 31,	2005	2004	2003
Revenues		$7,240	$6,548	$5,884
Operating expenses				
Labor and fringe benefits		1,873	1,838	1,929
Purchased services and material		814	746	879
Depreciation and amortization		510	517	472
Fuel		725	528	471
Equipment rents		192	244	299
Casualty and other		417	445	466
Total operating expenses		4,531	4,318	4,516
Operating income		2,709	2,230	1,368
Interest expense		(299)	(282)	(317)
Other income (loss)		12	(20)	21
Income before income taxes		2,422	1,928	1,072
Income tax expense		(819)	(631)	(338)
Net income		$1,603	$1,297	$ 734

Consolidated Statement of Income – U.S. GAAP

In millions, except per share data	Year ended December 31,	2005	2004	2003
Revenues				
Petroleum and chemicals		$1,096	$1,059	$1,013
Metals and minerals		837	714	527
Forest products		1,738	1,505	1,320
Coal		331	284	261
Grain and fertilizers		1,119	1,063	947
Intermodal		1,270	1,117	1,101
Automotive		514	510	525
Other items		335	296	190
Total revenues		7,240	6,548	5,884
Operating expenses				
Labor and fringe benefits		1,841	1,819	1,698
Purchased services and material		814	746	703
Depreciation and amortization		627	598	554
Fuel		725	528	469
Equipment rents		192	244	293
Casualty and other		417	445	390
Total operating expenses		4,616	4,380	4,107
Operating income		2,624	2,168	1,777
Interest expense		(299)	(294)	(315)
Other income (loss) (Note 14)		12	(20)	21
Income before income taxes and cumulative effect of change in accounting policy		2,337	1,854	1,483
Income tax expense (Note 15)		(781)	(596)	(517)
Income before cumulative effect of change in accounting policy		1,556	1,258	966
Cumulative effect of change in accounting policy (net of applicable taxes) (Note 2)		–	–	48
Net income		$1,556	$1,258	$1,014

As you read about these principles, keep in mind that they do not always work in harmony. The principles often conflict, which makes it difficult to develop consistent, coherent solutions to accounting problems. These conflicts help explain how it is possible to have more than one solution to an accounting problem while still being consistent with the accounting principles. One could argue that these principles are flawed because they do not provide a consistent basis for resolving accounting issues and problems. The groups of principles are shown in Figure 5–1.

Basic Assumptions of GAAP

Four basic assumptions underlie financial reporting under GAAP. We have discussed three of the four assumptions—the unit-of-measure, entity, and periodic-reporting assumptions—in the first four chapters. The fourth basic assumption is the **going-concern assumption**.

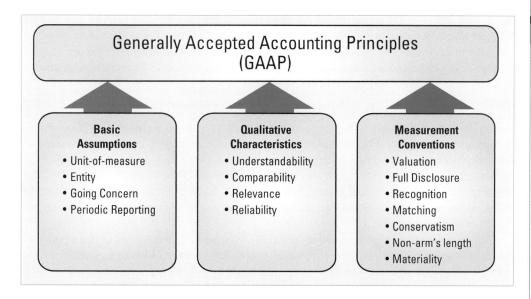

FIGURE 5–1 ::

Generally Accepted Accounting Principles (GAAP)

Basic Assumptions	Qualitative Characteristics	Measurement Conventions
• Unit-of-measure	• Understandability	• Valuation
• Entity	• Comparability	• Full Disclosure
• Going Concern	• Relevance	• Recognition
• Periodic Reporting	• Reliability	• Matching
		• Conservatism
		• Non-arm's length
		• Materiality

Unit of Measure The **unit-of-measure assumption** states that the economic activity of an entity can be effectively stated in terms of a single unit of measure. The unit of measure that is almost always used is money, and in Canada the monetary unit used is usually the Canadian dollar (although some Canadian companies, for example Nortel Networks Corporation and Research In Motion Limited, use the U.S. dollar as their unit of measure).

There are benefits and drawbacks to using a single unit of measure. The major benefit of using a single unit of measure is that it allows diverse information to be aggregated and summarized. If a single unit of measure were not used, Rogers could not calculate total assets, because different types of assets such as cash, intangible assets, and property, plant, and equipment could not be added together into a single amount. It would also not be possible to calculate net income.

There are also drawbacks to using a single unit of measure:

■ By stating everything in terms of money, considerable information is lost about the individual items being measured. For example, when cost of goods sold is reported as a single dollar amount on the income statement, it is not possible to tell the quantity or type of inventory that was sold.

■ Characteristics that are not easily measured in terms of dollars are not accounted for. For example, intellectual and human capital and social costs are typically not reported in GAAP financial statements.

■ Canadian GAAP ignore the changing purchasing power of the dollar over time. The unit of measure required under Canadian GAAP is not simply the Canadian dollar, it is the *nominal* Canadian dollar. The term *nominal dollar* means that no consideration is given to the fact that the purchasing power of money changes over time. Because of inflation, the quantity of goods an amount of money will buy decreases with time. In other words, $100 today will buy fewer groceries than $100 purchased 25 years ago.

Entity An accounting entity is any economic unit that is of interest to a stakeholder. An accounting entity does not have to be a separate legal entity. Partnerships and proprietorships are legitimate entities of interest, but they aren't separate legal entities; they are simply extensions of the partners or proprietor. Corporations are separate legal entities but sometimes the information about a group of corporations with common ownership is combined into a single accounting entity for reporting purposes. For example, Rogers' consolidated financial statements shown in Appendix A are the aggregation of the financial statements about 15 different corporations, including Rogers Wireless Communications Inc., Rogers Cable Inc., Rogers Sportsnet Inc., and Blue Jays Holdco Inc.

The financial statements of an entity should only provide information about that entity. Transactions and economic events that do not pertain to that entity should be excluded. This exclusion does not always occur. For example, in some proprietorships and private corporations, the personal transactions of the owners are intermingled with the entity's business activities.

www.nortelnetworks.com
www.researchinmotion.com

Sometimes it may be difficult to determine whether an expense is a personal or a business expense. In those circumstances, the shareholder or proprietor might make choices that serve his or her self-interests, perhaps to reduce taxes. For example, it may be difficult to separate the personal and business costs associated with operating a business from home. Users of financial statements need to be aware of the possibility that transactions that do not belong to the entity are included in the statements.

Going Concern In accounting, a going concern is an entity that will be continuing its operations for the foreseeable future. GAAP accounting assumes that, if there is no evidence to the contrary, an entity operates as a going concern. This means that an entity is expected to complete its current plans, use its existing assets, and meet its obligations in the normal course of business. For Rogers, operating as a going concern means that it will provide its services, collect its receivables, use its property, plant, and equipment for the purposes they were acquired, and settle its liabilities as they come due.

If the going-concern assumption does not apply—for example, because an entity is going out of business or because an entity was formed as a short-term venture, such as a summer business set up by a student—then the primary valuation method used in GAAP accounting—historical cost—should not be used. If an entity is not a going concern, then assets and liabilities are valued on a liquidation basis: assets at the amount that will be received from their immediate sale and liabilities at the amount that they will be settled for. The reason for this treatment is that if an entity is closing down, assets will be disposed of to raise cash and not used as intended and liabilities will be paid as soon as possible. When an entity is not a going concern, all assets and liabilities are classified as current because they are expected to be liquidated or settled in the short term. Capital assets are not amortized when an entity is not a going concern because there is not expected to be any revenue to match the costs with.

An interesting problem that accountants sometimes face is deciding when the going-concern assumption no longer applies. There is always some probability that an entity will go out of business but when is that probability significant enough to decide that the going-concern assumption no longer applies? Waiting until the entity is actually out of business is too late to provide useful information to stakeholders. Making the decision too early can force a struggling entity out of business if stakeholders such as creditors act on the information and take steps to protect their own interests.

Periodic Reporting The **periodic-reporting assumption** states that meaningful financial information about an entity can be provided for periods of time that are shorter than the life of an entity. Accounting would be much easier if entities only had to prepare financial information at the end of their life. At the end of an entity's life, everything about its activities is known with certainty and there are no decisions or estimates to make about when and how much to record of assets, liabilities, revenues, and expenses. The problem with waiting until the end of an entity's life is that stakeholders need information for making decisions more frequently and more regularly.

Waiting until the end of some entities' lives can take a long time. Molson's Breweries, now part of the Molson Coors Brewing Company, was founded in 1786; The Hudson's Bay Company was founded in 1670. While these are extreme examples, they highlight the fact that an entity's life can be very long. It's unlikely that governments would be willing to wait for centuries to collect income taxes from these entities!

Providing information to stakeholders frequently and regularly is crucial for the efficient operation of the economy. Stakeholders need and want up-to-date information to allow them to make the best possible decisions. At a minimum, financial statements are prepared annually, although it is common for entities to produce financial statements more often than that. Some stakeholders, such as banks, may require monthly or quarterly statements as part of a loan agreement, and some stock exchanges and securities commissions require quarterly reports from public companies. Rogers provides financial statements for each calendar year and issues quarterly financial statements as well.

However, reporting periodically instead of at the end of an entity's life has many problems. Once the life of an entity is broken down into small pieces, there can be difficulty determining in which periods revenues, expenses, assets, and liabilities should be reported. The underlying economic activity is not affected by the different choices, but the representation of that economic

Knowledge Check

- Do all corporations have to follow GAAP? Explain.

- What organization is responsible for setting accounting standards (GAAP) in Canada? What are its strategic plans for GAAP over the next few years?

- Identify and briefly explain the four basic assumptions that underlie GAAP.

www.mcgrawhill.ca/
olc/friedlan

activity in financial statements can differ significantly, which could impact the decision making of stakeholders. As we pointed out in Chapter 3, the requirement to report periodically over the life of an entity is at the heart of many accounting problems and controversies.

Qualitative Characteristics

Chapter 1 introduced the four qualitative characteristics that the *CICA Handbook* states financial information should have if it is to be useful to stakeholders. The four characteristics are understandability, comparability, relevance, and reliability. Let's review these characteristics in more detail.

Understandability Imagine having to study from a textbook written in a language you do not understand. It would be virtually impossible for you to learn anything from that book. The same difficulties apply to working with accounting, the language of business. Users must be able to understand the information presented to them in financial statements if it is to be useful to them. The *CICA Handbook* states that accounting information should be understandable to people who have a reasonable understanding of business and accounting, and a willingness to study the information provided. If they do not, it is assumed that they will obtain advice.

Targeting accounting information at moderately sophisticated users is a choice made by standard setters. There is no compelling reason why moderately sophisticated users should represent the appropriate audience for accounting information. The choice has implications for the nature and sophistication of the information that is presented. If information were targeted at the least sophisticated users, financial statements would have to be much simpler than they are now, but they would have a wider audience. If accounting information were targeted at the most sophisticated users (financial analysts, mutual fund and pension fund managers, accountants, and other experts) the financial statements could be much more detailed and sophisticated, but many people who might have an interest in examining financial statements would be excluded and forced to rely more on experts for their information.

Comparability Accounting numbers are very difficult to evaluate in absolute terms. It is necessary to have benchmarks or bases of comparison to make sense of the numbers. Broadly, users can make two types of comparisons:

1. An entity's accounting numbers can be compared with the accounting numbers of other similar entities.

2. The entity's accounting numbers can be compared with its own accounting numbers from previous years.

Comparisons are easier to make if the entities being compared use the same accounting methods and if the entity itself uses the same accounting methods every year. If different accounting methods are used, it is difficult to know whether differences in the numbers are due to real economic differences or to the different accounting methods. If managers change the accounting practices each year, it is impossible to draw sensible inferences from any patterns that are observed. Accountants often use the term **consistency** to describe the use by an entity of the same accounting policies from period to period.

Ensuring that financial statements are consistent and comparable is a worthwhile goal in principle. In practice, however, there are many challenges in achieving comparability. As we have discussed, GAAP frequently provides managers with legitimate alternative accounting treatments for certain types of transactions. If managers make different choices for similar transactions and economic events, comparability is impaired. As a result, one must use a great deal of caution when comparing the financial information of different entities. You can't assume that different entities prepare their statements on the same basis. Indeed, if entities do not have the same set of constraints, facts, and objectives, it's not reasonable to expect them to use the same accounting methods.

GAAP provide some protection for users by requiring entities to disclose the accounting policies they choose. This disclosure allows users to assess whether comparable accounting policies are being used (for example, Note 2 to Rogers' financial statements describes the company's significant accounting policies). However, the disclosure of the accounting policies being used does not tell users what the accounting numbers would be using different accounting policies. And while GAAP require that entities disclose the accounting policies that they use, GAAP do not require entities to disclose much information about any estimates they make. (For example, an entity does not have to disclose the amount of its accounts receivable that it does not expect to collect.) Differences among entities in the estimates they make can have a significant effect on the accounting numbers the entities report, which can then make comparisons difficult, especially since it can be very difficult for users to determine the existence and extent of the differences.

GAAP also provide some protection to users from arbitrary changes in accounting policies. GAAP do not allow entities to change accounting policies without good reason. According to the *CICA Handbook,* a change in accounting policy must result in a more appropriate presentation of events or transactions in the financial statements. However, it is usually not very difficult for managers to come up with a good reason for a desired accounting change.

When a change in policy is made, the existence of the change and its effect on the current period must be disclosed. As well, the effects of the change must be made *retroactively.* This means that the entity has to present its financial statements for previous years as if it had been using the new accounting policy all along. For example, if Rogers changed the way it recognized its revenue in its 2005 financial statements, the financial statements for 2004 that are included in the 2005 annual report for comparative purposes would have been restated to reflect the new accounting policy for revenue recognition.

Unlike a change in an accounting policy, a change in an accounting estimate is done *prospectively.* A prospective change means that the change is applied to the current year's financial statement, then in future years' statements. Previous years' statements are not restated. If an entity changes an estimate, the financial statements may not be consistent and users may not be aware of the fact.

Relevance It should be self-evident that accounting information must be relevant to the people who use it. If accounting information is not relevant—if it doesn't influence stakeholders' decisions—then what is the point of producing it?

However, relevance according to GAAP is set in a limited context. Unlike the broad set of users and objectives of financial reporting presented thus far in this book, according to GAAP, the users and objectives are narrowly defined. For profit-oriented entities, the users that the *CICA Handbook* focuses on are primarily existing and potential debt and equity investors. The *CICA Handbook* goes on to state that the objective of debt and equity investors is the prediction of future earnings and cash flows. Indeed, the *CICA Handbook* is explicit that it is not practical for financial statements to satisfy all the information needs of all users. These limitations on the focus of GAAP may be realistic, reasonable, and practical. However, they highlight the importance of recognizing that the relevance of financial reporting is not universal: GAAP financial statements are not designed to be relevant for all uses and to all users.

In this context, the *CICA Handbook* describes three characteristics that contribute to the relevance of information. These characteristics are:

- *Predictive value:* Many decisions that stakeholders make involve predicting the future. For example, lenders want to estimate future cash flows to determine whether an entity will be able to meet the repayment schedule required by a loan. Equity investors often want to predict future earnings as a basis for predicting the future stock price of public companies.

Curiously, despite the stated importance of prediction, GAAP are backward-looking. GAAP financial statements focus on reporting transactions and economic events that have happened, not those that will happen. GAAP financial statements are useful for prediction because they can be used as a benchmark for predicting the future; the financial statements are not themselves predictions. Users are expected to begin with previous periods' financial statement information. By incorporating future-oriented information from other sources and by making assumptions, they can then make the predictions they require.

This approach can probably be used effectively for entities that are relatively stable and established, However, for new entities and for entities that are subject to significant change, such as high-technology, Internet, and high-growth companies, the task can be difficult because historical financial statements may not provide a relevant basis upon which to predict the future. Also, it is important to remember that managers make accounting choices that can affect the relationship between present accounting information and future information.

■ *Feedback value:* When users make predictions, they require information that allows them to evaluate their predictions and to revise, update, correct, and adjust them. GAAP-based accounting is reasonably well suited for providing feedback because it presents the results of what happened. Stakeholders are then able to compare the actual results with their predictions. It's important to remember though, that managers have the ability, through their accounting choices, to influence the financial statement numbers, so that they can make choices that help the entity achieve stakeholders' predictions.

■ *Timeliness:* For information to be useful for decision making it must be available to stakeholders in time to influence their decisions. Information that does not arrive on a timely basis will have little impact on decision making. Timeliness is the reason that financial statements are prepared periodically. But some people argue that financial statements provided by entities are not timely at all. For example, Rogers' 2005 fiscal year end was December 31, but its financial statements were not made available to the public until March 2006. (This long time lag is not unique to Rogers. Most public companies have a similar lag.) One can question the timeliness and usefulness of information that arrives in the hands of stakeholders more than three months after the year end. This is especially true for businesses of the new economy—that is, knowledge-based industries—where change takes place very quickly.

Reliability For information to be useful to users, it must provide a reasonable representation of what it is intended to measure. The *CICA Handbook* identifies the components of reliability as verifiability, representational faithfulness, and neutrality (freedom from bias). Let's examine these components more closely.

■ *Verifiability:* Information is verifiable if independent and knowledgeable observers can come up with the same results for the measurement of an attribute. If a group of people were asked to measure the height and weight of the members of a sports team, it is likely that each person would come up with very similar results. Measurement of height and weight would be considered verifiable and therefore reliable. Now suppose the same group of people were asked to rate the ability of the players on the team. It is likely that this measurement would be more diverse. The measurements of ability are not as easily verified and are therefore less reliable than the measurements of height and weight.

In an accounting context, historical-cost, transaction-based information is quite verifiable. Because financial statement amounts can be traced back to documents that underlie a transaction, the amounts are relatively easy to verify. For example, the amount paid for inventory can be traced to the invoice sent by the supplier. While there can be some variation in the amount that different people would come up with, the variation would normally fall within a narrow range. In contrast, measures of financial statement elements that are not supported by transactions would have much more variation, since the amounts would be based on individual judgments rather than on observations of what actually took place—for example, the market value of land. Verifiability is one of the main reasons why historical cost is the primary method of valuation used under GAAP.

■ *Representational faithfulness:* If you examine a map of Canada, you expect the provincial boundaries and the locations of cities and towns on the map to be an accurate reflection of where the boundaries and the cities and towns are. Representational faithfulness refers to the association between underlying information being represented (the actual locations of boundaries and communities) and the representation of that information (the map). Financial statements are a representation of the underlying economic activity of an entity. If the statements are to be representationally faithful, then they must capture the economic activity of an entity. This means that all the assets, liabilities, revenues, and expenses must be reflected in the statements.

As we discussed in Chapter 2, not all of an entity's assets are reflected on a GAAP balance sheet. For example, brand names are usually not reflected on an entity's balance sheet. For some entities, the brand name is their most valuable asset, yet traditional GAAP accounting does not reflect this asset (a brand name will only show up on a balance sheet if it has been purchased). This would be equivalent to not showing the capital city of each province on a map. The difficulty of verifying the amount that should be reported for a brand makes accounting for the brand inappropriate under GAAP. Curiously, problems with one dimension of reliability (verifiability) make it difficult to achieve another dimension of reliability (representational faithfulness).

■ *Neutrality or freedom from bias:* Information is neutral or free from bias if it is not presented in a way that is designed to bias or manipulate users' decisions. This characteristic seems to be inconsistent with the objectives of financial reporting that we discussed in Chapter 4. The discussion in Chapter 4 stated that managers can often select accounting methods that allow them to achieve their objectives of accounting—objectives that can be in the self-interests of the entity and its managers rather than in the interests of stakeholders. In contrast, neutrality suggests that accounting information should be presented in a way that does not serve any of the managers' objectives. It is definitely desirable that accounting information be neutral. Unfortunately, evidence from research and casual observation of events reported in the popular press strongly suggest that managers do use the accounting choices available to them to pursue their own objectives.

Neutrality is sometimes misinterpreted to mean that accounting information should have no effect on the decisions that users make. If this were the case, there would be no point in preparing accounting information because it would not serve a useful purpose: it would not have any impact on users' decisions. For information to be useful to a decision maker, it must have the possibility of influencing decisions.

Relevance versus Reliability: A Conflict Relevance and reliability are both necessary if information is truly going to be useful to stakeholders. Information that is relevant but not reliable—that is, stakeholders can't be confident that the measurements provided are a reasonable representation of the underlying economic activity—is not going to be useful to stakeholders. Information that is reliable but not relevant—that is, stakeholders can have confidence in the measurement, but the measurement is not appropriate for the decision being made—is also not going to be useful to stakeholders. Ideally, all information that is provided to stakeholders should be both relevant and reliable. Unfortunately, in many situations this is not possible and as a result there is a trade-off between these crucial characteristics.

If stakeholders were free to choose the information they receive from entities, they could deal with this trade-off in a way that satisfied their needs. However, most stakeholders have to rely on general purpose financial statements for their information. This is why GAAP are so important. GAAP define the information in general purpose financial statements and therefore define the information that all stakeholders who rely on the general purpose financial statements receive. Thus, GAAP must also define how to resolve the trade-off between relevance and reliability. GAAP accounting tends to favour reliability over relevance. For example, GAAP use historical costs as the primary measurement method, even though it is widely acknowledged that for many decisions, historical cost information is not very relevant.

Consider a lender who has been asked to make a large loan to a new borrower. Lenders often ask for **collateral** from a borrower in the event a loan can't be repaid. Collateral is assets that are

Knowledge Check

■ What is comparability and why is it important according to GAAP?

■ Identify and briefly explain the characteristics that, according to the *CICA Handbook* and GAAP, make accounting information relevant.

■ Identify and briefly explain the characteristics that, according to the *CICA Handbook* and GAAP, make accounting information reliable.

pledged by a borrower and that are turned over to the lender if the borrower is unable to repay the loan. Lenders want to know the market value of the collateral so they will have an idea of how much they will receive if and when the collateral has to be sold. What information might satisfy the needs of the lender on the date the loan is made?

Figure 5–2 shows how different pieces of information reflect the relevance-reliability trade-off in the context of a lender's evaluation of collateral. Figure 5–2 shows that information can be considered to have low or high relevance and low or high reliability. Information that is in the top-right quadrant is best because it is both highly relevant and highly reliable. The market value of publicly traded shares fits into this quadrant for a lender because the current value of the shares provides current information on what the shares could be sold for. This information is reliable because the current market value of a share of a public company as set by a stock market is representationally faithful, verifiable, and neutral.

The most interesting quadrants are the lower-right and the upper-left quadrants because this is where we see the trade-offs. The information in the lower-right quadrant is relevant because the market value of real estate gives the lender an idea of what the real estate could raise in cash if sold today. The problem with determining the market value of real estate without actually selling it is that the information can be very unreliable. After all, how sure can you be about the selling price of land and buildings, until they are sold? In contrast, the information in the upper-left quadrant is highly reliable because the cost of the real estate is fairly easy to check by examining documents that support the original purchase of the real estate. But it is unlikely that the historical cost of real estate is relevant to the lender, especially if the real estate was purchased a long time ago. Historical cost tells the lender very little about the amount the real estate could be sold for today or in the future.

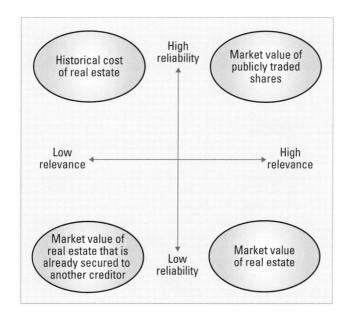

FIGURE 5–2

The Relevance-Reliability Trade-Off

The information in the lower-left quadrant is of little interest because it is not relevant or reliable. A stakeholder would not be interested in that information at all. For example, the current market value of real estate that is secured to another creditor could be placed in this quadrant. Real estate that is secured to another creditor has little relevance to our lender because the proceeds of sale would go to the other creditor. The market value of real estate has low reliability because it is difficult to estimate what it could be sold for.

Measurement Conventions

We can now examine the conventions that define the measurements recorded in an accounting system and reported in the financial statements. Ultimately, accounting is about measurement. GAAP have a number of conventions that help determine the amounts reported in financial statements.

Valuation There are many different ways that assets and liabilities can be valued. These methods include historical cost, replacement cost, net realizable value, and the value-in-use. While historical cost is the primary valuation method used in GAAP financial statements, the other methods are legitimate measurement alternatives, some of which are generally accepted in some situations.

The **replacement cost** of an asset is the current price that would have to be paid to purchase an identical or equivalent asset. Replacement cost is a market-value measure, not a historical measure. Under certain circumstances, replacement cost can be used under GAAP for reporting inventory on the balance sheet. According to GAAP, inventory should be valued at the lower of its historical cost and market value on the balance sheet date. If the market value is lower than the cost, the inventory would be reported on the balance sheet at the market value. One of the definitions of market value commonly used for inventory is replacement cost. This approach to valuing inventory is known as the lower of cost and market rule (LCM) and it will be discussed in detail in Chapter 8.

Net realizable value is the amount of cash that is expected to be received from the sale or realization of an asset, after taking into consideration any additional costs. Accounts receivable are normally valued at their net realizable value on the balance sheet. Under GAAP, an entity reduces the actual amount that customers have promised to pay by an estimate of the amount of those receivables that are not expected to be collected. Thus, the amount that appears on the balance sheet will be an estimate of the amount of cash that will actually be collected or realized. Net realizable value is also one of the methods used to estimate the market value of inventory when using the lower of cost and market rule. Net realizable value is also used to value assets and liabilities when the going-concern assumption is deemed not to apply.

Question for Consideration

Which characteristic is more valuable in financial statements: relevance or reliability? Explain.

Answer: This question does not have an answer. Both characteristics are important and ideally all financial statement information should be both relevant and reliable. Unfortunately, there is often a trade-off between these two characteristics. If a stakeholder must use GAAP-based general purpose financial statements, then the trade-off is resolved by the GAAP constraint (that is, the trade off between relevance and reliability is settled by what GAAP says) and by the managers' accounting choices. If stakeholders can obtain the information they need, they could resolve the tradeoff themselves. Some stakeholders would choose more relevance at the expense of less reliability (perhaps an estimate of the market value of real estate rather than the real estate's historical cost). Other stakeholders might find reliability more valuable (for example, reliable information might be considered more appropriate by some users for purposes of evaluating how well the managers have done managing the entity).

The value-in-use of an asset is its value when an entity uses it for its intended purpose. For example, the value-in-use of an airplane, for an airline, is the amount of cash flow the plane would generate less the cash expended to operate it. Value-in-use is probably the most relevant measure of value for purposes such as estimating what an entity is worth. It is also a very subjective measure because often many individual assets do not generate cash flows on their own (for example, delivery vehicles are part of a chain of activities that generates cash, but they do not generate cash on their own) and future cash flows can be difficult to estimate.

Historical cost or transaction cost is the primary method used to measure financial statement elements under GAAP. **Historical cost** requires that transactions and economic events be valued in the financial statements at the actual dollar amounts involved when the transaction or economic event took place. For example, if Rogers purchases new display cases for its Rogers Video stores for $1,000,000, the display cases will be reported on Rogers' balance sheet at $1,000,000. The cost of the display cases will be amortized over their useful lives to match the cost to revenues. But remember that amortization under GAAP is simply the allocation of the cost of an asset to expense over time for matching purposes. Amortization is not a change in the valuation method of an asset or a reflection of any change in its market value.

The dominance of historical cost emerges from the assumptions and qualitative characteristics described earlier in this chapter. Historical cost is consistent with *reliability*. In almost all situations, the historical cost of an asset, liability, revenue, or expense is at least as reliable as any of the other possible alternatives. The terms of most transactions and economic events are usually easily determined at the time they occur and can usually be readily verified. Other possible measures can be difficult to determine and verify. For example, determining the replacement cost or net realizable value of an old building can be difficult and is certainly less reliable than determining what the building cost. The use of historical cost in GAAP accounting indicates that the frequently occurring trade-off between reliability and relevance is often resolved in favour of reliability. Historical cost is the primary measurement method used under GAAP despite its limited usefulness for many users and uses of accounting information.

Historical cost is also supported by the going-concern assumption. Recall that under the going-concern assumption it is assumed that an entity will continue its operations for the foreseeable future. Therefore, according to GAAP, market value estimates of financial statement elements are not necessary because assets will be used up in the ordinary course of business and liabilities will be settled. This means that the cost of assets can be expensed as they are used up so that income can be determined.

Tax requirements provide a practical reason for using historical cost for financial reporting in Canada. In most cases, income for tax purposes requires a transaction (something has to be sold) and the amount of income is the amount received, less the costs incurred. For example, if a taxpayer purchases shares in a company for $10 per share, no income is reported for tax purposes until the shares are sold, regardless of any changes in the market value of the shares year to year. If the taxpayer sells the shares several years later for $25 per share, the amount of income reported is $15 per share ($25 − $10). If the shares pay dividends, the taxpayer would have to declare the dividends as income in the year received. Since the tax system is based on transactions and historical costs, an accounting system based on that approach makes sense.

While cost is generally the most reliable of the valuation methods, it is not always straightforward to determine what the cost is. There is general agreement about what should be included in cost, but practical problems often intervene, and, as a result, different entities may include different costs in, for example, the cost of inventory or capital assets. For example, remember from our discussion in Chapter 4 that it can sometimes be difficult to attach some costs to the inventory and it is common to simply treat difficult-to-attach costs as period costs. Also note that such differences across entities make comparability difficult to achieve.

Full Disclosure   For financial statements to fulfil their objective of providing relevant information to users, the statements must include all relevant information about the economic activities of the entity. The principle that financial statements should provide this information is known as **full disclosure**. In reality, financial statements do not provide all the information users require. Some of the information that users might want would represent deviations from GAAP. For example, some users might want the market values of capital assets, but this information would not be allowable

◆ ROGERS™

according to GAAP. Some information might be inappropriate to disclose outside the entity for competitive reasons. Other information might be too voluminous to include in a traditional set of financial statements and would thereby violate the understandability criterion.

Thus, once again GAAP come with a practical constraint. In principle it is certainly desirable for users to receive all relevant information, but in practice there are limits. Under GAAP, certain disclosures are explicitly required, while in other cases the managers must use their judgment to determine what and how information should be disclosed in the financial statements.

Information can be disclosed in financial statements in a number of ways:

1. Quantified information can be incorporated into the financial statements without further explanation. For example, Rogers shows its accounts payable and accrued liabilities on the balance sheet with no additional explanation. What you see on the balance sheet is all you get.

2. Quantified information can be incorporated into the financial statements and supplementary information provided in the notes. Many of the items in Rogers' financial statements reference specific notes. For example, long-term debt on the balance sheet refers the reader to Note 11, which describes the type, maturity, interest rate, and provides other information about Rogers' long-term debt. (See pages A-23 and A-29).

3. Information may be provided only in the notes to the financial statements without being included in the financial statements themselves. Note 21 (page A-44) provides information about guarantees that Rogers has made that may have financial consequences for the company but are not reflected in the financial statements.

Whether an economic event is disclosed only in the notes or measured and incorporated in the financial statements will affect the financial statement numbers and may thereby have an economic impact on the entity and its stakeholders. Measurement is important if financial statement numbers are used to determine an outcome—for example, managers' bonuses, the selling price of a business, whether a borrower has met the terms of a loan agreement (such as a minimum current ratio), or the amount of tax that should be paid.

For highly sophisticated users of accounting information (for certain types of decisions) and for the capital markets, how the information is incorporated into the financial statement package is less important than whether it is incorporated. Sophisticated users can readily take information from various sources, including the financial statements and the notes, and organize it in ways that are appropriate for their decisions. How securities are priced on the capital markets, such as the Toronto Stock Exchange, is captured by a theory known as the Efficient Market Hypothesis.

The **Efficient Market Hypothesis** (EMH) states that all publicly available information is reflected quickly in the price of publicly traded securities such as stocks and bonds. According to the EMH, it does not make any difference how information is made available to the public. The information can be included in the financial statements, in the notes to the financial statements, or made available in some other way, such as an announcement to the media by the company. It is important to emphasize that the EMH only applies to the prices set for publicly traded securities in the capital markets. The EMH is not relevant for purposes of setting the prices of the securities of private companies, or for outcomes that depend on actual financial statement numbers.

Recognition We explored revenue recognition in depth in Chapter 4. Revenue recognition represents the point when a sale transaction is recorded. The term **recognition** alone has a more general meaning in accounting. It refers to when any financial statement element—asset, liability, equity, expense or revenue—is entered into the accounting system and reported in the financial statements. Disclosing information in the notes to the financial statements is not recognition. Recognition only occurs when an item is included in the financial statements.

Matching Recall that net income is a measure of the economic performance of an entity over a period of time. Under GAAP, matching is the process of associating costs (based on the historical costs) with the revenue the costs help generate so that net income can be determined. However, there are many practical problems with matching that are important to understand if GAAP financial statements are to be understood.

◇ ROGERS™

The process of matching means that expenditures are not reported as expenses until the expenditures have contributed to the generation of revenue. Determining when an expense should be recorded is straightforward for some costs. For example, when Rogers sells a cell phone and the revenue is recognized, the cost of the phone sold is expensed and matched to the revenue in the period in which the revenue is recognized. As long as the inventory is unsold, it is accounted for as an asset and is not expensed. As long as there is a clear link between the revenue and the costs, there is no problem with matching.

Matching the cost of capital assets to revenues is more problematic. Clearly, capital assets contribute to the generation of revenue, and they do so over a number of periods, so it makes sense that the cost of capital assets should be expensed over the life of the assets. This gives rise to amortization. In most cases, it is very difficult to establish a relationship between the cost of a capital asset and the revenue the asset helps earn. As a result, the amount that is amortized in a given period can be thought of as being somewhat arbitrary.

Another difficulty with matching is that some costs are difficult to associate with revenue. These are the period costs we discussed in Chapter 4. Period costs can include head office administration costs, compensation to senior executives, advertising, salaries to salespeople, research, and so on.

Matching also gives rise to the need to estimate expenses. Some expenditures are not made until after the revenue is recognized. For example, warranty costs on consumer goods and technical support costs for computer hardware and software are usually incurred after the revenue is recognized. Since these types of future costs are part of the cost of earning the revenue, good matching requires that they be matched against the revenue when it is recognized. This means that the expense must be estimated at the time that the revenue is recognized.

Conservatism We first discussed the accounting concept of conservatism in Chapters 3 and 4. Conservatism requires that measurements in financial statements should be made to ensure that assets, revenues, and net income are not overstated and that liabilities and expenses are not understated. Conservatism does not mean that there should be a deliberate understatement of assets, revenues, and net income, or a deliberate overstatement of liabilities and expenses. In principle, there is no problem with using a conservative approach to accounting (although one should recognize that a conservative approach is only one of a number of approaches to accounting that can be legitimately used). One reason a conservative approach to accounting might make sense is because the managers who are usually responsible for an entity's financial statements tend to be optimistic about the prospects for the entities they manage. The managers also have incentives to act in their self-interest when making accounting choices. Conservatism can serve to dampen the effects of managerial optimism and self-interest.

Conservatism manifests itself in different ways in financial statements. Under normal circumstances inventory is valued at its historical cost. However, if the market value of inventory is below its cost as of the year end, the inventory is recorded on the balance sheet at its market value. Similarly, if capital assets are impaired as of year end, it is appropriate (and conservative) under GAAP to reduce the book value of the capital assets to a measure of their market value. If the book value of assets were not reduced, the value of the assets on the balance sheet would be overstated. In contrast, if the market value of these assets increased, under GAAP there would be no recognition of the increases until the assets were sold and the increases in value realized. It would not be conservative to recognize a gain until it was realized.

One of the problems with conservatism is that today's conservative choices can lead to the opposite effects in later periods. For example, in 2009 Carcajou Ltd. (Carcajou) purchased computer equipment for $210,000. Carcajou's management decides to amortize the equipment over two years, a period of time that it believes was a reasonable but conservative estimate of the equipment's useful life. Carcajou's summarized income statements for the years ended December 31, 2009, 2010, and 2011 are shown in Panel A of Table 5–1. As it turns out, the computer equipment is actually used by Carcajou for three years.

Now, let's assume that Carcajou's management had decided instead to amortize the computer equipment over three years rather than two, a less conservative estimate of the equipment's useful life. Carcajou's income statements under this assumption are shown in Panel B of Table 5–1. When we use the more conservative two-year estimate of the useful life of the computer equipment,

TABLE 5-1 ::: **CARCAJOU LTD. INCOME STATEMENTS**

Panel A

Carcajou Ltd.

Income Statements

For the Years Ended December 31

	2009	2010	2011	Total
Revenue	$750,000	$800,000	$825,000	$2,375,000
Expenses	620,000	660,000	680,000	1,960,000
Amortization of computer equipment*	105,000	105,000	0	210,000
Net income	$ 25,000	$ 35,000	$145,000	$ 205,000

*Computer equipment cost $210,000 and is amortized over two years.

Panel B

Carcajou Ltd.

Income Statements

For the Years Ended December 31

	2009	2010	2011	Total
Revenue	$750,000	$800,000	$825,000	$2,375,000
Expenses	620,000	660,000	680,000	1,960,000
Amortization of computer equipment*	70,000	70,000	70,000	210,000
Net income	$ 60,000	$ 70,000	$ 75,000	$ 205,000

*Computer equipment cost $210,000 and is amortized over three years.

net income in the first two years is lower than when the three-year estimate is used, a more conservative result. However, in the third year, net income is much higher than when the three-year estimate is used. The reason for this is that the computer equipment is fully amortized after two years in the first case, so there is no amortization expense needed in the third year. As a result, net income gets a boost in the third year when the more conservative estimate of the useful life of the equipment is used. This is why conservatism today can lead to the opposite effect in later periods. It is important to note that over the three years, total revenue, expenses, amortization, and net income are the same. It is also important to recognize that at the time Carcajou purchased the equipment it was making an estimate—an educated guess—about what the useful life of the equipment would be.

Another example of conservative accounting is write-downs and write-offs. Sometimes situations arise that impair the value of an asset. For accounting purposes, an asset is impaired when the future benefits that the asset will provide over its remaining life are less than its net book value (NBV) (NBV of a capital asset = cost − accumulated amortization). For example, a building could be destroyed by fire, market demand could reduce the production of a plant, declines in commodity prices could reduce the revenues to be earned from a mine, oil well, or forest, or the market value of inventory could fall. When assets become impaired, a write-down of the assets is required. A **write-down** is a reduction in the net book value of an asset to some measure of the market value of the asset. A write-down is achieved by debiting an expense and crediting the asset. When an asset is written down to zero, the event is referred to as a **write-off**. Writing down an asset does not mean the asset is no longer used by the entity. It just means that the amount the asset is recorded at in the financial records has decreased. A write-down does not affect cash. It is merely a bookkeeping entry that reduces assets and net income. Write-downs can be very subjective. Management can have a lot of influence over the timing and amount of a write-down.

Let's look at an actual example. In its year ended December 31, 2004 Camco Inc. (Camco) reported costs of $24,067,000 related to the closure of its Hamilton, Ontario plant. This followed costs of $77,627,000 in 2003. Camco's income statements and the related note to the financial statements are shown in Exhibit 5–2.[2] The write-down is considered conservative accounting

EXHIBIT 5–2 :

CAMCO INC.
Plant Closure
Costs

Consolidated Statements of Operations and Retained Earnings (Deficit)

Years ended December 31 (in thousands of dollars)	2004	2003
Sales of Products and Services	$ 642,635	$ 594,570
Operating Costs		
Employee compensation including benefits	150,096	141,445
Material, supplies, services and other costs	482,615	447,802
	632,711	589,247
Income from Operations Before Undernoted Items	9,924	5,323
Writedown of Retail Advances (Note 10)	297	3,395
Hamilton Plant Closure Costs (Note 3)	24,067	77,627
Loss from Operations	(14,440)	(75,699)
Interest and Other Expenses, net	(1,220)	(1,972)
Loss Before Income Taxes	(15,660)	(77,671)
Income Taxes (Note 11)	4,917	25,143
Net Loss	$ (10,743)	$ (52,528)
Loss Per Share, Basic and Diluted (Note 12)	$ (0.54)	$ (2.63)
Retained Earnings (Deficit), Beginning of Year	$ (49,578)	
Net Loss	(10,743)	
Deficit, End of Year	$ (60,321)	

3. Hamilton Plant Closure Costs

As a result of the October 2003 decision to close the Hamilton manufacturing and distribution facility, the Company recorded $24,067 in closure costs for the year ended December 31, 2004 (2003 – $77,627). The components of the recorded closure costs as at December 31, 2004 and 2003 are as follows:

	2004	2003
Writedown of plant and equipment	$ –	$ 34,969
Pension plan curtailment	2,933	33,080
Employee severance	18,692	9,051
Other	2,442	527
	$ 24,067	$ 77,627

because it is recorded as soon as the costs associated with the closure of the Hamilton plant were known. The Hamilton plant didn't actually close until well into 2004 but the costs associated with the closure were first recorded in 2003, when the closure was announced.

Conservatism tends to be one of the dominant accounting conventions. It can be used to justify deviating from the historical cost convention (assets such as inventory and capital assets are recorded at their market values in certain circumstances) and reliability (market values are used for assets such as inventory and capital assets even though there is no supporting transaction). One of the problems with conservatism is that it requires judgment by the managers and these judgments can be highly subjective and open to abuse.

Non-Arm's Length Transactions Financial reporting under GAAP assumes that the transactions that give rise to assets, liabilities, revenues, and expenses occur at arm's length. An **arm's length transaction** is a transaction that takes place between unrelated parties, each of whom is acting in their own self interest and therefore trying to get the best deal for themselves. When a transaction takes place at arm's length, the exchange amount is considered to be the fair market value. The exchange or transaction amount is the basis of most valuations in GAAP accounting.

A non-arm's length transaction occurs between **related parties**. Related parties exist when one entity has the ability to influence the decision making of another. Examples of related parties include close family members, corporations owned or controlled by a single shareholder, and senior management. When transactions take place between related parties it can't be assumed that the transaction amount is the fair market value. As we will see, non-arm's-length transactions can cause serious problems for interpreting financial statements.

Suppose you decide that you are going to buy a used car and you find one that appears to meet your needs. When you negotiate with the person selling the car, you try to get the best deal for yourself, while the person selling the car tries to get the best deal for himself. Since each of you is trying to get the best deal, if you come to an agreement it is assumed that the agreed price is a reasonable representation of the fair market value of the car. For accounting purposes, the car would be reported at its cost—which is assumed to be a reasonable estimate of its fair market value.

Now, suppose instead that you were not buying the used car from a stranger but from your parents. In this case, it is not possible to assume that the price you pay for the car is its fair market value. There are factors other than getting the best deal for yourself that could have come into play in determining the selling price. For example, your parents may have been interested in helping you out by giving you a deal on the car (something a stranger would not do). Or you may have been helping out your parents by paying more than the fair market value. The point is that in this situation, it's not possible to be sure whether the transaction took place at fair market value.

It's crucial for financial statement users to be aware of the existence and the terms of non-arm's length transactions because they can have serious implications for interpreting the financial statements. Consider the owner-manager of a small manufacturing business. As the owner, she can choose to pay herself as much or as little as she thinks appropriate. She can choose to pay herself a salary, which is an expense on the income statement, or pay herself a dividend, which has no effect on net income. The payment she receives can be considered a non-arm's length transaction. Table 5–2 shows the income statement for such a small business under three scenarios:

- In Scenario A the owner-manager does not pay herself a salary. The wage and salary expense pertains to employees.

- In Scenario B the owner-manager pays herself a large, above-market-value salary of $200,000 (the wage and salary expense is $200,000 higher in Scenario B than in Scenario A). This means that the owner-manager is receiving a larger salary than she would receive if she were an employee in a similar capacity for a similar business.

- In Scenario C the owner-manager is receiving a fair market salary for the work she does.

For purposes of evaluating the performance of this entity, the net income under each of the scenarios tells a different story. Net income ranges from −$30,000 to $170,000 and the profit margin ranges from −1.7 percent to 9.7 percent. If you were interested in buying this business and hiring a manager to operate it, the most useful measure of performance would be Scenario C because it indicates what the entity would earn if a manager were paid the fair market value for his or her services. When investigating a business, it is crucial to ask questions about the existence of non-arm's-length transactions because they can distort the financial statements.

The *CICA Handbook* requires that information about non-arm's length or **related party transactions** be disclosed in the financial statements. These disclosures include information

TABLE 5–2 ::: Non-Arm's Length Transactions: The Effect on Net Income of Different Methods of Compensating an Owner-Manager			
	Scenario A Owner-manager receives no salary	Scenario B Owner-manager receives a salary that is greater than the market value for the work done	Scenario C Owner-manager receives a reasonable salary
Revenue	$1,750,000	$1,750,000	$1,750,000
Cost of goods sold	675,000	675,000	675,000
Gross margin	1,075,000	1,075,000	1,075,000
Expenses:			
Wage and salary	370,000	570,000	470,000
Selling and marketing	275,000	275,000	275,000
Amortization	110,000	110,000	110,000
Interest	45,000	45,000	45,000
Taxes	105,000	105,000	105,000
Net income	$ 170,000	$ (30,000)	$ 70,000

about the existence of these transactions, descriptions of the relationship between the parties, and the amount of the transactions. It is important to note that it is not necessary to disclose whether exchanges between related parties took place at fair market value or whether special arrangements were made between the parties. In other words, entities record transactions in the ordinary course of business at the actual exchange amount, regardless of whether the transaction took place at fair market value. As a result, it is difficult for a user to determine the effect that the non-arm's length transactions have on the financial statements.

Note 18 to Rogers' financial statements provides an example of the information that companies disclose about their related party transactions (see page A-41). The note explains Rogers' related party activities and discloses amounts. Notice that at the end of section (a) of the note it says "these transactions are recorded at the exchange amount, being the amount agreed to by the related parties." It is not clear whether these related party transactions took place at fair market value or something else. There is not enough information to assess these transactions.

Non-arm's length transactions are not illegal or unethical. However, their existence can have significant implications for the financial statements and users should be very aware of that fact.

Knowledge Check

- What is matching? Why does matching make it necessary to estimate future costs in some situations?

- What is conservatism? Why does conservative accounting in the present sometimes lead to non-conservative results in the future?

- Why does the existence of non-arm's length or related party transactions make it possible that the reporting entity's financial statements will be difficult to interpret?

www.mcgrawhill.ca/olc/friedlan

GENERALLY ACCEPTED ACCOUNTING PRINCIPLES

Materiality If you look at Rogers' financial statements you will notice that all the numbers in the statements are rounded to the nearest thousand. Amounts in the financial statements of some very large entities, such as BCE Inc. or Bank of Montreal, are rounded to the nearest million. Why are amounts in financial statements rounded at all? Why not show amounts right to the dollar, or even the cent? The reason is materiality. **Materiality** describes the significance of financial information to users. Information is material if its omission or misstatement affects the judgment of a user of the information. All material information should be disclosed in financial statements because its absence may affect the decisions made by users. For entities like Rogers, BCE Inc., and the Bank of Montreal, rounding the thousands or the millions is not expected to affect any of the decisions that users want to make. In fiscal 2005, Rogers reported a loss of $44,658,000. The fact that this amount is rounded to the nearest thousand means that the managers do not think that the decisions of any users will change if the actual amount of the loss was $44,657,501 or $44,658,499.

Think of materiality from a personal standpoint. If you lost a dollar, would it have any impact on your life? Probably not. Your behaviour, your plans, and your activities would probably stay the same. Suppose, instead, that you lost $1,000. Would there be any impact on your life? For many people there would be. You might have to forgo a vacation, computer equipment, some entertainment, or even education. The loss of one dollar would not be considered material, whereas the loss of $1,000 would be.

We can link materiality back to *full disclosure*. The need to disclose all relevant information to users is constrained by materiality. If certain information is not considered material, then it does not have to be disclosed because it will not have an effect on users' decisions.

Matters that are not material do not have to be treated in accordance with GAAP. For example, Rogers may expense the cost of inexpensive capital assets that, strictly speaking, should be capitalized. Staplers should be capitalized and amortized over their useful lives. However, because of their relatively small cost, the staplers might be expensed when they are purchased. The question

www.bce.ca
www.bmo.com

then is, does this "incorrect" GAAP accounting mislead or confuse users in any way, or have an impact on their decisions? If the answer is no, then the accounting used is acceptable. In contrast, suppose Rogers decided to expense the $1,000,000 cost of new furniture and fixtures when they were acquired. Would this accounting treatment potentially mislead or confuse users in any way, or have an impact on their decisions? In this case the answer is probably yes, so expensing would not be appropriate.

What, then, should be considered material? Materiality is a matter of judgment and it is difficult to establish firm rules. Materiality depends on who will be using the financial statements and what they will be using them for. Depending on the decision, materiality could be as low as a dollar. Some information considered immaterial for purposes of preparing an entity's financial statements might be regarded as material by some users.

THE AUDIT ENVIRONMENT AND THE AUDITORS' REPORT

A New Era for Financial Reporting

One part of Rogers' annual report that we didn't examine in Chapter 2 was the auditors' report. The auditors' report gives the *external auditors' opinion* on the entity's financial statements. Remember from Chapter 1 that the external auditor is an independent person who adds credibility to an entity's financial information by assessing the information in relation to some standard, such as GAAP, and expressing an opinion on the information.

Audits are essential in an economy like Canada's, where the management of an entity is often separate from the owners and the other stakeholders. The owners and other stakeholders need information about the entity for decision making, and this information will almost always be produced by the entity itself. An audit adds credibility to information that could be biased by the managers, who may be inclined to pursue their own interests rather than the interests of the stakeholders. Without an external audit, information would be less reliable and stakeholders would have less confidence in it. However, despite the importance of audited information, the work of the auditor is heavily constrained by the rules that auditors report under. As we will see, a satisfactory opinion does not provide a guarantee.

In the last few years, the world of the auditor and financial reporting have undergone dramatic structural changes. These changes have had significant implications for the managers of companies and their auditors, and for the governance of these entities. The changes followed in the wake of the bankruptcy of Enron Corporation (Enron) in the United States, which at the time was one of the largest companies in that country. Enron's collapse exposed a huge accounting fraud and resulted in the demise of one of the largest accounting firms in the world, Arthur Andersen. As a result of the Enron collapse, there was a loss of confidence in financial reporting by stakeholders, who wondered whether they could trust and rely on the information that was provided in general purpose financial statements and audited by so-called independent auditors. As a result, lawmakers and regulators in the U.S., and later in Canada, imposed tighter restrictions and increased responsibilities on companies, their senior managers, and their accountants.

In the U.S., the law that changed the reporting environment is known as the Sarbanes-Oxley Act, which was enacted in 2002. In Canada, steps were taken by organizations in the Canadian environment to restore investor confidence and protect the public interest by making sure that the quality of financial information in Canada meets the highest possible standards. The government of Ontario passed legislation that increased the power and authority of the Ontario Securities Commission, the body that oversees the sale of securities to the public.

The Canadian Public Accountability Board (CPAB) was created by the Canadian Securities Administrators, Office of the Superintendent of Financial Institutions, and the Chartered Accountants. The CPAB is intended to provide more control and oversight of auditing firms.

In addition, new rules were established to ensure that Canadian Chartered Accountants who provide assurance services to clients maintained their independence from those clients. Independence means that the auditors should be free of any conflicts of interest that may impair their ability to do their work unbiasedly and impartially. These rules make it easier for auditors to maintain their independence by prohibiting auditing firms from offering certain services to clients (before these changes it was common for audit firms to offer lucrative services such as IT, bookkeeping, and corporate finance services), by requiring the audit partner in charge of an engagement to switch every five years, and by restricting the ability of an auditor to be employed by a client for a year after leaving the auditing firm.

The Auditors' Report

Auditors examine an entity's financial statements and the accounting records to evaluate whether the financial statements are properly prepared in accordance with the relevant accounting rules. Based on the audit, an auditor issues an opinion on the financial statements. There are four opinions that auditors can give on financial statements: an unqualified opinion, which says the financial statements satisfy the standards the auditor is using, and three opinions that indicate problems with the financial statements or the audit. The audit opinions that indicate problems are a qualified opinion, an adverse opinion, and a denial of opinion.

Our discussion will focus on the unqualified opinion because that is the one most commonly seen. (Rogers' financial statements received an unqualified opinion.) For entities that follow GAAP, an **unqualified opinion** means that the auditors are satisfied that the financial statements present the financial situation of the entity fairly and that the statements follow GAAP.

Rogers' auditors' report, prepared by the accounting firm KPMG, is on page A-3 in the appendix. Refer to it as we proceed through the discussion.

Rogers' auditors' report is addressed to Rogers' shareholders. The auditors' report is always addressed to the entity that appointed the auditor. In the case of a public company, it is the shareholders that appoint the auditor. Management nominates the auditor but it is up to the shareholders to vote for the auditor, which they do at the entity's annual general meeting. A possible conflict of interest for auditors exists because, whereas the auditors' report is usually addressed to some entity other than the management, the auditors' fee is authorized by management and paid by the entity being audited.

The auditors' report usually follows a standard format, making it easy for users to see at a glance whether the entity has received an unqualified opinion. An unqualified auditors' report always consists of three paragraphs. The other opinions always have more than three paragraphs, which is why it is easy to tell whether an entity received an unqualified opinion or not.

The first paragraph of an unqualified auditors' report is known as the introductory paragraph. The introductory paragraph tells the reader what the auditor did. This paragraph explains that an audit was conducted, identifies the financial statements that were audited, and describes the periods that were audited. The introductory paragraph of Rogers' auditors' report says that the auditors' audited Rogers' consolidated balance sheets as of December 31, 2005 and 2004 and its consolidated statements of income, deficit, and cash flows for each of those years. The auditor also audited the notes to the financial statements, although this is not explicitly stated.

The introductory paragraph also tells readers that preparation of the financial statements is the responsibility of the management of the entity. The auditor does not prepare the financial statements—the auditor only audits and expresses an opinion on them. The entity's management makes all the accounting choices required when preparing the financial statements. The auditors do not have the authority to change the financial statements that have been prepared by management. The auditors will discuss any concerns they have with management, but it is up to management to make any changes. Ultimately, if the auditors are not satisfied that the financial statements meet the appropriate standards, they can express their dissatisfaction only in the auditors' report.

The second paragraph of an unqualified auditors' report is called the scope paragraph. The scope paragraph describes the nature of an audit. The paragraph states that the auditors "conducted our audits in accordance with Canadian generally accepted auditing standards." **Generally accepted auditing standards (GAAS)** is a set of general guidelines that are stated in the *CICA Handbook* and that provide guidance to auditors when they conduct their audits. GAAS do not provide specific details as to how to do an audit, but offer a broad overview of how auditors should approach audits to ensure that they are done properly and that enough evidence is obtained to give on opinion on the financial statements. The *CICA Handbook* also provides more specific guidance to auditors, but, ultimately, how an audit is done is left to the professional judgment of the auditor.

The scope paragraph includes a number of terms that give valuable insights into the nature of an audit and the meaning of an audit opinion. The scope paragraph says that GAAS require that an audit be planned and performed to obtain "reasonable assurance" that the financial statements are free of "material misstatement." The use of the term "material" means that the auditor is only looking for errors and misstatements that will have an effect on the decisions of users, not minor mistakes that have no effect on users' decisions. This has two implications:

1. The financial statements cannot be considered precise or exact because the auditors' report acknowledges that there may be errors in the statements that are not material.

2. The notion of materiality assumes that the same level of materiality applies to all users. This is not necessarily the case. An error that is not material for one user of the financial statements may be material to another.

The term "reasonable assurance" means that an audit does not eliminate the possibility that there is a material error or misstatement in the financial statements. An audit means that there is a very good chance that the financial statements are free of material errors, but an audit is not a guarantee.

The scope paragraph also states that "an audit includes examining, on a test basis, evidence supporting the amounts and disclosures in the financial statements." This statement means that auditors do not examine every transaction and economic event in which an entity was involved. Instead, it means that a sampling of transactions and economic events is examined to reach an opinion on the financial statements. Auditors use their professional judgment to decide how many and which transactions and economic events should be audited. The last sentence of the scope paragraph explains that auditors assess the accounting principles used, estimates made by management, and the overall financial statement presentation.

In the third paragraph of an unqualified auditors' report, the auditors' opinion on the financial statements is expressed. The opinion paragraph states that the financial statements present fairly, in all material respects, the financial situation of the entity, in accordance with GAAP. Once again it is important to emphasize that the auditor is offering an opinion, not a guarantee. There *appear* to be two elements to the opinion—that the financial statements present the financial situation of the entity fairly and that the financial statements comply with GAAP. In fact, there is only one element. The fairness of the financial statements is evaluated in relation to GAAP. In other words, financial statements must comply with GAAP to be fair. If they do not comply with GAAP, they aren't fair.

Within GAAP, auditors must evaluate whether the choices made among alternative available accounting methods result in a fair representation of the entity's economic activities. In other words, simply because an entity chooses an alternative that is in accordance with GAAP does not automatically mean that the choice results in fair financial statements. The opinion paragraph also states that the financial statements present fairly "in all material respects the financial position of the company." The phrase "in all material respects" reiterates the point that the financial statements are not precise or exact.

Other Auditors' Reports

The three other opinions that auditors can give on financial statements, in addition to an unqualified opinion, are described briefly as follows:

Qualified Opinion A **qualified opinion** is used when, the financial statements present the entity's situation fairly overall, but the statements do deviate from GAAP (or from whatever set of accounting standards the auditor is auditing to). A qualified audit opinion always contains the term "except for," which prefaces the explanation as to why the qualified audit report was given.

Adverse Opinion An **adverse opinion** is given when the financial statements are so materially misstated or misleading that they do not fairly present the financial position, results of operations, and/or cash flows of the entity. Adverse opinions are rare and would never be given to a public company because an adverse opinion would be unacceptable to the securities regulators. If an adverse opinion were expressed on the financial statements of a private entity, the statements would likely be seen as having limited usefulness to the stakeholders receiving them.

Denial of Opinion When auditors cannot obtain enough evidence to support an opinion on the financial statements, then the auditors do not give one. This is a **denial of opinion**. Instead, the auditors state in their report that they are unable to express an opinion as to whether the financial statements are fair and in accordance with GAAP.

When the opinion given on financial statements is something other than an unqualified opinion, the format of the auditors' report is different than the three-paragraph format used with an unqualified auditors' report. In these cases, there will always be more than three paragraphs. Extra paragraphs are necessary to explain why an unqualified opinion was not given. The different format highlights the fact that the opinion is not the standard, unqualified opinion.

Other Assurance Accountants Can Provide

Audits are only one of the forms of assurance that accountants can provide. A **review engagement** provides less assurance to users about whether an entity's financial statements are in accordance with GAAP than an audit does. The benefit of a review engagement is that it is much less expensive than an audit and therefore saves the entity money. When an accountant performs a review, the report that the accountant prepares is called a review engagement report. Review engagements are never performed on public companies because securities laws require audits. A review will be done for private companies when external stakeholders require some assurance, but these stakeholders are satisfied with less assurance than is provided by an audit.

Accountants can also provide reports on financial information other than financial statements (for example, a shopping mall may want a report on the amount of sales a store made because the rent the mall receives is based on sales) or in compliance with an agreement or regulations (for example, to see whether an entity has met the current-ratio requirement of a lending agreement).

Question for Consideration

You are the property manager for a large mall. Most of the tenants in the mall pay a fixed amount of rent each month based on the number of square metres rented plus a percentage of sales made in the store each year. Would you require the stores in the mall to have their sales audited by an independent auditor? Explain.

Answer: An audit would be essential. Since the people managing and owning the stores in the mall prepare the accounting information that you rely on to determine the amount of rent, there is a possibility that some of these people might understate the amount of sales. The benefit to stores' understating their sales is a smaller rent payment. An audit would add reliability to the accounting information that the store presented. Audited sales figures would provide you with greater assurance that the amount of sales a store was reporting in its statement to you represented the actual sales the store earned during the year.

Solved Problem

The solved problem in this chapter will build on the problem-solving skills that were developed in Chapter 4. Some of the issues raised in this and similar types of questions may have actual rules that GAAP prescribe. However, at this stage of the book it is not necessary for you to be aware of the rules. Instead, you want to apply the principles you have learned to come up with sensible responses to accounting issues. For example, if you are faced with a situation in which an entity chooses to conform with GAAP, proposed accounting treatments should be assessed in relation to the GAAP discussed in this chapter. When reviewing the problem, keep in mind that the objective is to provide a well-reasoned and well-supported set of recommendations that address and attempt to resolve the accounting issues faced by the entity in the context of the role you are assigned.

Savoy Health Club Ltd.

Fred Irving, the founder, owner and operator of the Savoy Health Club Ltd. (Savoy or the club) recently agreed in principle to sell Savoy to Jim Floor. The parties have agreed in principle to make the purchase price equal to five times net income for the year ended June 30, 2008. However, the deal cannot be finalized until Jim Floor receives the June 30, 2008 financial statements and agrees to them. In the event that Jim Floor does not agree to the financial statements, outstanding accounting issues can be submitted to an independent arbitrator for resolution. Until the agreement in principle was signed, Savoy's financial statements were prepared exclusively for tax purposes. Fred Irving is in the process of finalizing the June 30, 2008 financial statements, but he is unsure about how to account for a number of issues.

Fred Irving has hired you to prepare a report explaining appropriate accounting treatments for the issues he is concerned about. Fred wants full explanations and justifications for the recommendations you make so that he can explain them to Jim Floor and to the arbitrator, if necessary. Your discussions with Fred Irving provide the following information:

1. People join the club by paying an initiation fee of $600. The initiation fee is paid only once when the member joins. Provincial legislation requires that health clubs allow members to pay their initiation fees in equal instalments over 12 months. Most new members pay their initiation fees monthly. Historically, between 10 percent and 20 percent of people who join the club stop paying their initiation fees sometime during the year.

   In addition, each member must pay a monthly fee of $80. Members can pay their continuing monthly fees on the first day of each month or they can pay the full annual amount on the renewal date of their contract, in which case they receive a $160 reduction in their annual fee. (Members sign a one-year contract each year.) Approximately 40 percent of members pay in a lump sum at the start of the year. Some members who pay their monthly fees each month stop paying sometime during the year.

2. During fiscal 2008, the club began selling passes that allow non-members to participate in aerobics classes put on by the club. Passes for individual classes can be purchased for $8 each, or monthly passes can be purchased for one month ($70), three months ($200), or six months ($375). A monthly pass allows the holder to attend 15 classes per month, but the pass can only be used in the month for which it was issued. Aerobics instructors receive $1.50 for each participant in their classes.

3. Normal maintenance work on some of the athletic equipment has been delayed for the last two months. The work will cost about $4,000. The delay is apparently due to scheduling problems with the contractor. The work is now scheduled for July 2008.

4. During the year, three pieces of equipment were damaged by vandals and cannot be repaired for a reasonable price. The equipment cost $5,000 and has a net book value of $2,200. The cost to replace the equipment is $6,500.

5. The club pays monthly rent of $3,000. Rent is paid six months in advance on October 1 and April 1.

6. Fred Irving has never taken a salary.

Required:

Prepare the report requested by Fred Irving.

Insight

When you examine this solution, it is important to remember that there is not a single right answer to this question. There are many wrong answers, but more than one good answer. The thinking that goes into supporting the recommendations that are made is the most important quality needed to respond to this type of question, not the recommendations themselves. A recommendation that is not well supported is not part of a good answer. In supporting your recommendations, you should try to use the accounting assumptions, qualitative characteristics, and measurement conventions discussed in this chapter, as well as the principles raised in earlier chapters.

The answer below is prepared as a report to Fred Irving. It is useful to respond to these types of questions in the role you are asked to play. Comments on the answer, which are not part of the report itself, but provide some additional explanation, are found throughout the report.

Solution:

Mr. Fred Irving
2334 Piché St.
Bordeaux, Québec

Dear Mr. Irving:

Attached is the report you requested recommending accounting treatments for unresolved items in the financial statements of Savoy Health Club Ltd. In preparing this report I have attempted to provide reasonable, justified alternatives for the outstanding accounting issues that were identified. There is often more than one reasonable choice for treating accounting problems. In situations where there is more than one acceptable alternative, I have attempted to choose the one that serves the objective of increasing net income and thereby increasing the selling price of Savoy.

In previous years, Savoy's financial statements have been prepared primarily for income tax purposes. Presumably, the accounting choices made for those statements served to legitimately reduce Savoy's tax burden. Financial statements prepared for tax purposes meet the requirements of the *Income Tax Act* but are often not appropriate for determining the selling price of a business. Financial statements prepared for tax purposes will tend to understate income because they are designed to reduce taxes. Using such statements for determining the selling price of a business will unfairly reduce the proceeds you receive from the sale of Savoy.

Financial statements prepared for determining the selling price of a business should provide a reasonable representation of the ongoing and continuing earning ability of the business. Because these financial statements will be used by Mr. Jim Floor, the prospective buyer of Savoy, and potentially by an arbitrator, it is important to use a recognized standard as the basis for preparing the statements. Accordingly, I recommend using GAAP (generally accepted accounting principles). While GAAP are not necessarily the best criteria for setting the selling price of a business, GAAP are widely known and recognized. It is possible that the buyer will reject some of the accounting choices that you incorporate into the financial statements. You may have to concede some issues to come to an agreement. However, all recommendations made in this report are supportable in terms of GAAP, fairness, and accrual accounting.

If you have any questions, please contact me.

Yours truly,

John Friedlan, CA

Insight

The letter to Fred Irving, the person who engaged the accountant, lays out the perspective that the accountant will take in pursuing the engagement. The letter is an important part of effective role-playing and serves the purpose of providing a vehicle for discussing the constraints, facts, and objectives that are relevant to the case. In this case, the objective of preparing financial statements for determining the selling price of Savoy is clearly the most important objective. The perspective that the accountant brings to the report is to work within the constraints and the facts, but, when possible, to attempt to serve the objectives of the client to get a good price for Savoy. Clearly, the financial statements that Savoy has been preparing to date are not appropriate for the intended purpose. Using them would be unfair to Mr. Irving. Some might contend that it is not appropriate to change accounting methods because consistency would be violated. However, because the objectives of financial reporting have changed, the change in accounting approach is justifiable. As a result, the accountant should advise Mr. Irving to make accounting choices that produce a fair price for the sale of his business. This is not to imply that the managers will intentionally misstate the financial statements. Rather, when there are legitimate alternatives, the ones that are more favourable will be selected. It is reasonable to assume that the other parties will take a similar position—that Jim Floor will argue for accounting treatments that will tend to lower the selling price of Savoy.

REPORT TO FRED IRVING

Terms of Reference

You have asked me to prepare a report recommending appropriate accounting treatments for a number of issues that must be resolved before presenting the financial statements of Savoy Health Club Ltd. (Savoy) to Mr. Jim Floor, who has agreed in principle to purchase Savoy from you. The financial statements, specifically net income, will be used to determine the final selling price of Savoy. I understand that if Mr. Floor does not accept the financial statements as presented to him, you and Mr. Floor will attempt to resolve any differences through negotiations. If outstanding issues cannot be resolved through negotiations, the remaining issues will be presented to an arbitrator for resolution.

My objective in preparing this report is to come up with reasonable and justified treatments for the accounting problems that will result in an income measure that reflects normalized earnings (earnings that can reasonably be expected to repeat in future years). Generally accepted accounting principles will be used as the basis for my evaluation of the accounting issues.

Insight

Materiality will be low in this situation. Each dollar change in net income has a five-dollar effect on the price of Savoy. That is, if an accounting choice results in a $1,000 increase in net income, the selling price of Savoy increases by $5,000. Also, disclosure cannot be used to resolve any accounting issues. Because the selling price of Savoy depends on net income, measurement of all accounting events is necessary for them to be relevant.

Issues

Revenue Recognition There are three revenue recognition issues that must be addressed: initiation fees, monthly membership fees, and aerobics fees, as follows:

1. *Initiation fees:* Under GAAP, there are four criteria that must be met if revenue is to be recognized. The first criterion is that the entity must have performed. Initiation fees allow an individual to be a member of the club for however long the person wishes, provided that he or she pays the monthly fee. However, access to the club is restricted by the requirement to pay the monthly fee. If a member stops paying the monthly fee, he or she will not be able to use the club, even though the initiation fee has been paid. In effect, Savoy earns this revenue over the life of the membership, even though the fee is not refundable. Since memberships are variable in length, I would recommend that you recognize the initiation fee revenue at the start of each month over a reasonable period. Since for many people attendance at health clubs tends to be fleeting, one year is probably reasonable.

   The second criterion requires that the amount of revenue be known. Since new members must sign contracts in which they agree to pay the $600 initiation fee, the amount of revenue is known when the member joins.

   The third criterion is that the costs of earning the revenue must be known when revenue is recognized. The costs of recruiting new members include advertising, salespeople, promotions, office space for meeting with prospective members, and so on. These costs are treated as period costs and are expensed when incurred. No portion of the costs incurred in recruitment are carried forward to future periods.

   The fourth criterion for recognizing revenue is collectability of amounts owing. Collectability is an issue because a significant number of people do not pay their initiation fees in full. As long as the amount that is uncollectible can be estimated, it will be acceptable for Savoy to recognize the revenue as proposed. There is no uncertainty about amounts that will be received if a new member pays in full when the contract is signed.

Insight

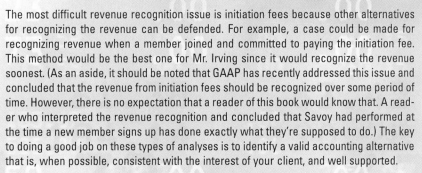

The most difficult revenue recognition issue is initiation fees because other alternatives for recognizing the revenue can be defended. For example, a case could be made for recognizing revenue when a member joined and committed to paying the initiation fee. This method would be the best one for Mr. Irving since it would recognize the revenue soonest. (As an aside, it should be noted that GAAP has recently addressed this issue and concluded that the revenue from initiation fees should be recognized over some period of time. However, there is no expectation that a reader of this book would know that. A reader who interpreted the revenue recognition and concluded that Savoy had performed at the time a new member signs up has done exactly what they're supposed to do.) The key to doing a good job on these types of analyses is to identify a valid accounting alternative that is, when possible, consistent with the interest of your client, and well supported.

2. *Monthly membership fees:* Monthly fees should be recognized as time passes and members have access to the club. The monthly fee entitles members to use the club for a period of time. This means that revenue is earned as time passes. Therefore, revenue should be accrued to reflect portions of monthly membership fees earned as of the date the financial statements are prepared. This accounting approach should be used regardless of whether a member pays monthly or at the start of the year. If the member pays in full on the renewal date of the contract, the amount paid should be treated as unearned revenue and an adjusting entry should be prepared to recognize the appropriate amount of revenue when the financial statements are prepared.

There are no legitimate alternatives for recognizing revenue for the monthly fees. Revenue is earned as members have access to the club. The revenue is known because the monthly fee is set in the contract signed by the member. Costs of earning the revenue are known because these are the costs of operating the club. Collection may be an issue for some members, although it should be possible to make an estimate of the amounts that will not be collected, based on past experience.

Insight

Accounting for the monthly membership fees is an example of a situation where the facts dictate the accounting method. It would be desirable from Mr. Irving's point of view to recognize revenue earlier, say when a member signs a contract, because this would place more revenue in the current period. However, these choices would not be appropriate under GAAP (our constraint) because the revenue has not been earned before the members can use the club (the facts).

3. *Aerobics fees:* Non-members can attend aerobics classes at the club by purchasing passes for individual classes, or monthly passes that entitle a person to attend 15 aerobics classes per month. Payment is made when the pass is purchased. Clearly, revenue is earned when a person attends a class. The service being provided is an aerobics class, and it is difficult to argue that revenue is earned at any other time. The fee earned by the instructor should be matched to the revenue when it is recognized.

The difficult problem is how to handle classes not attended. Some people will not attend all 15 classes they are entitled to attend by the end of a month. The revenue from the unattended classes should be recognized in the month for which the pass was purchased, because classes cannot be carried forward to another month. Unattended classes do not incur an instructor fee because instructors only get paid for classes attended by the client. The four revenue-recognition criteria are clearly met at the time the class is given (or at the end of the month for unattended classes) because: (a) performance is achieved when the class is given (or the month ends for unattended classes); (b) the amount of revenue is known because the price of the passes is specified; (c) costs are known (most costs are club operating costs that must be treated as period costs plus the fee paid to the instructor, which is known once a class is given); and (d) collection is not an issue because people pay in advance.

Insight

The timing of aerobics fee revenue is also dictated by the facts. An alternative might be to recognize revenue when passes are purchased, but under the GAAP criteria, point of purchase is too early because the service being purchased has not been provided when a pass is purchased. Considerable effort is still required to put on the aerobics class. An aggressive accountant might try to use point of purchase as the revenue recognition point, which would increase club revenue and net income, but Mr. Floor would likely challenge it.

Maintenance Costs Maintenance costs are incurred to ensure that the equipment lives up to its operating potential. Without proper maintenance, the useful lives of the equipment will be shorter than expected. While regularly scheduled maintenance is necessary for proper operation of the equipment and for customer satisfaction, the judgment of management is the ultimate determinant for whether maintenance is required at a point in time. It is senseless from a business perspective to do maintenance unless it is required.

In this case, we must rely on management's judgment that maintenance was not required at the time and therefore should not be included as an expense in the income statement in the current period. This is not a situation where an expense should be accrued, such as a good or service consumed but not billed (such as electricity costs), or an expense that should be matched to revenue recognized in the current period but that will not be incurred until a future period (such as a warranty expense). This is an independent transaction that has not taken place. GAAP are a transactions-based accounting system. Since there has been no transaction, it is inappropriate under GAAP to accrue the maintenance costs.

Insight

Strictly speaking, the maintenance expense should be recorded when it is incurred. There are many uncertainties surrounding this cost, including the amount and whether it will be incurred (perhaps Mr. Floor will decide, should he buy Savoy, that this particular service call is not necessary). Since GAAP record transactions and economic events that have happened, it is easy to make a case that these maintenance costs should not be accounted for in 2008.

However, as the accountant explained in the letter to Mr. Irving, the financial statements should be a reasonable representation of the ongoing and continuing earning ability of the business. After all, Mr. Floor is buying future earnings and future cash flow. Maintenance is an ongoing and regular cost of operating a health club. By excluding this particular maintenance cost in fiscal 2008, net income is overstated in relation to ongoing and continuing earnings (although the accounting is consistent with GAAP). So, while the treatment proposed by the accountant is consistent with GAAP, we can question whether it is fair. The accountant's choice is consistent with Mr. Irving's objectives and with the constraints, and perhaps the facts, and therefore is a reasonable recommendation. Mr. Floor and the arbitrator may see things differently. This demonstrates some of the practical limitations of using GAAP accounting for setting the price of a business. Similar problems are seen with the vandalized equipment and Mr. Irving's compensation.

Vandalized Equipment The vandalized equipment appears to be of no value to Savoy because it cannot be repaired at a reasonable cost. Therefore, the equipment does not meet the definition of an asset because it does not provide any future benefit. According to conservatism, the equipment should be written down to its net realizable value—the amount that it could be sold for. The problem is that while recognizing a loss in the June 30, 2008 financial statements is consistent with GAAP, it does not result in a net income that is representative of ongoing and continuing earnings. Any loss suffered by writing down the vandalized equipment is a cost that is not likely to recur on an ongoing basis. By recognizing the loss in the June 30, 2008 financial statements, the price that will be received for Savoy will be lower than is appropriate. This is an undesirable and unfair outcome for Mr. Irving.

One alternative would be to contend that the equipment is serviceable and should not be written off. However, given my understanding of the situation, this treatment would be a misrepresentation of the facts and is therefore unethical. Also, Mr. Floor would certainly discover that the equipment could not be used once he took over the club. A reasonable approach to take would be to argue that because the loss on the vandalized equipment is unusual, it should not be included in the amount that is used to calculate the selling price. Since the loss is a one-time event, the loss should be subtracted from the selling price but not subject to the five-times multiplier.

The costs associated with the vandalized equipment are a non-recurring item that reduces net income. This item shows the problems with using net income in a single year to set the selling price of a business. There will sometimes be non-recurring items that can distort the representativeness of net income of ongoing and continuing earnings. The proposed solution addresses this problem, but, strictly speaking, it is not consistent with the agreement in principle since the agreement bases the price on net income, which should include this loss. Mr. Irving and Mr. Floor will have to do some negotiating to resolve this issue.

Rent Costs Clearly, rent should be accrued on a monthly basis. Rent expense should reflect the cost of the space used during the period in question because it is only that cost that contributed to earning revenue. Savoy paid $18,000 to the property owner on April 1, 2008 to cover rent for April 1 to September 30, 2008. A rent expense of $9,000 should be accrued in the June 30, 2008 income statement.

Insight

This is a clear application of accrual accounting. The rent should be expensed in the period when the space was used, regardless of when the cash is expended.

Owner's Salary The owner's salary is a non-existent expense. Over the life of the business, Mr. Irving never took a salary so it is inappropriate to include it in the calculation of net income. Historical cost financial statements are intended to be representations of what happened. Including a salary for Mr. Irving means that the statements would include something that did not happen.

Insight

The issue here is whether the selling price should include a cost of management. An owner manager has the option of removing money from the company as salary or dividend (a question that has significant tax implications), or not at all. From an entity standpoint, the financial statements do not reflect all the costs of operating Savoy because the cost of management is a part of the cost. The method and amount of compensation received by an owner-manager is a non-arm's length transaction and can distort net income for purposes of setting the price of Savoy. There is no simple solution to this issue. The treatment recommended by the accountant is consistent with GAAP and is the best choice to achieve Mr. Irving's objectives. Ultimately, this issue, along with the accounting for the maintenance cost and the vandalized equipment, may be better resolved through negotiations.

SUMMARY OF KEY POINTS

▶ **LO 1** The rules of accounting are known as generally accepted accounting principles or GAAP. GAAP are the broad principles and conventions that provide guidance to accountants and managers for making accounting choices as well as rules and procedures that are established as accepted accounting practices at a particular time. It is not possible to point to a single source that documents all GAAP. In fact, much of GAAP are not recorded at all, but are simply what is done in practice. GAAP often allow more than one way of accounting for a particular type of economic event or transaction.

All public companies must adhere to GAAP. However, private companies can waive compliance with unanimous consent of all shareholders. Partnerships and proprietorships are not required to use GAAP unless they choose to.

▶ **LO 2** There are four basic assumptions that underlie GAAP. The assumptions are: unit of measure, entity, going concern, and periodic reporting.

▶ **LO 3** The *CICA Handbook* defines four qualitative characteristics that financial information should have if it is to be useful to users. The four qualitative characteristics are: understandability, comparability, relevance, and reliability. According to the *CICA Handbook* and GAAP, relevant information must have predictive value, feedback value, and timeliness. According to the *CICA Handbook* and GAAP, reliable information must be representationally faithful, verifiable, and neutral/free from bias.

▶ **LO 4** Accounting is about measurement. GAAP have a number of conventions that help determine the amount at which financial statement elements will be recorded. The conventions are: valuation, full disclosure, recognition, matching, conservatism, non-arm's length transactions, and materiality.

▶ **LO 5** An audit adds credibility to information that could be biased by the managers, who may be inclined to pursue their own interests rather than the interests of the users. Without an external audit, information would be less reliable and users would have less confidence in the information. However, audits are not guarantees that the financial statements are true, exact, precise, or correct.

There are four opinions that auditors can give on financial statements. The most common opinion is an unqualified opinion, which says the financial statements satisfy the standards the auditor is using (GAAP, for example). The three other opinions indicate that there are problems with the financial statements or the audit. These opinions are a qualified opinion, an adverse opinion, and a denial of opinion.

KEY TERMS

adverse opinion, p. 254

arm's length transaction, p. 249

collateral, p. 242

comparability, p. 239

consistency, p. 240

contingent liability, p. 283

denial of opinion, p. 255

Efficient Market Hypothesis (EMH), p. 246

full disclosure, p. 245

generally accepted auditing standards (GAAS), p. 253

going-concern assumption, p. 236

historical cost, p. 245

materiality, p. 251

net realizable value, p. 244

periodic-reporting assumption, p. 238

qualified opinion, p. 254

recognition, p. 246

related parties, p. 249

related party transactions, p. 250

relevance, p. 240

reliability, p. 241

replacement cost, p. 244

review engagement, p. 255

understandability, p. 239

unit-of-measure assumption, p. 237

unqualified opinion, p. 253

write-down, p. 248

write-off, p. 248

The left column gives alternative terms that are sometimes used for the accounting terms introduced in this chapter, which are listed in the right column.

clean audit opinion	**unqualified audit opinion, p. 253**
non-arm's length transactions	**related party transactions, p. 250**

ASSIGNMENT MATERIALS

Questions

Q5-1. Which entities are required to follow GAAP? Which entities do not have to follow GAAP? Why would entities that do not have to follow GAAP choose to follow GAAP? Explain your answers.

Q5-2. What are the benefits of having a set of rules like GAAP to guide financial reporting in Canada? What are some of the drawbacks? Explain.

Q5-3. Where do GAAP come from? Who decides what GAAP are?

Q5-4. You are a fairly sophisticated Canadian investor who has experience investing in Canadian companies. You have been asked in a phone solicitation to invest in a small distributing company. You receive the financial statements and discover they are not prepared according to Canadian GAAP. What problems does the fact, that the statements are not prepared in accordance with GAAP, create for you? Explain.

Q5-5. How is it possible that GAAP are different in different countries? Shouldn't GAAP be the same in all countries? Do you think it is a problem that GAAP are different in different countries? Explain your response.

Q5-6. Explain the historical cost convention. Why is historical cost the primary valuation method used under GAAP?

Q5-7. Explain conservatism. Which accounting principles are sometimes violated when conservative accounting is used?

Q5-8. Why do making conservative accounting choices today sometimes result in non-conservative effects in later periods?

Q5-9. Explain the conflict that sometimes exists between relevance and reliability. Provide examples of the conflict.

Q5-10. Identify and explain the four assumptions that underlie GAAP accounting.

Q5-11. Explain why the periodic reporting assumption is the cause of many of the problems and controversies that face the accounting professions today.

Q5-12. Explain what accountants mean when they speak of a going concern. What are the implications for financial reporting of an entity not being a going concern? Do you think these implications make sense? Explain.

Q5-13. Explain how the going-concern assumption is used as a justification for using historical cost for valuing capital assets.

Q5-14. What is the unit of measure that is typically used in the financial statements of Canadian companies? What are the some of the benefits and drawbacks of using the Canadian dollar as the unit of measure?

Q5-15. Identify and explain the characteristics that make information (i) relevant and (ii) reliable.

Q5-16. What do accountants mean when they say that an accounting change is made retroactively? What kinds of accounting changes are made retroactively?

Q5-17. What do accountants mean when they say that an accounting change is made prospectively? What kinds of accounting changes are made prospectively?

Q5-18. What is the Efficient Market Hypothesis (EMH)? Explain why the EMH does not apply to situations where the numbers in the financial statements are used to determine an outcome such as a manager's bonus or the selling price of a business.

Q5-19. According to the Efficient Market Hypothesis (EMH), does it matter whether an entity provides information to the capital markets in the financial statements or the notes to the financial statements? Explain.

Q5-20. Identify and explain each of the audit opinions that an auditor can express on an entity's financial statements.

Q5-21. As a prospective investor in a company, would you be concerned if the company did not receive an unqualified audit opinion? Explain.

Q5-22. What is comparability? Why is it important to users that financial statements be comparable?

Q5-23. One of the qualitative characteristics of GAAP accounting is that financial information must be understandable. Should financial information be tailored such that it is understandable to the most unsophisticated possible users? Explain.

Q5-24. Despite what some people think, an audit does not provide a guarantee that the financial statements are perfect, correct, or exact. Explain.

Q5-25. Neutral information is sometimes interpreted to mean that the information does not influence the decisions made by the users of the information. Why would it be appropriate to conclude that accounting information should not be neutral according to this definition? Explain.

Q5-26. Based on what we have discussed thus far in the book, do you think that accounting information is likely to be neutral? Explain.

Q5-27. What is a non-arm's length transaction? Why do non-arm's length transactions present serious problems for users of financial statements?

Exercises

E5-1. **(Examining relevance and reliability, LO 3)** You are trying to decide which business school to attend. You receive a package of information from one of the schools that contains the following:
a. A list of some graduates and their current jobs.
b. An article from a major Canadian newsmagazine with a ranking of all business schools in Canada.
c. Letters from existing students and recent graduates praising various aspects of the school's academic and non-academic programs.
d. A catalogue of courses offered by the Physical Education department.
e. A letter from the dean of the school stating that the school is the best in Canada.
f. A list of faculty and some background information on them.
g. A brief history of the school.
h. An article from the university newspaper that claims the university is the "best party university in the province."

Required:

Evaluate the relevance (including predictive value, feedback value, and timeliness) and reliability (including representational faithfulness, verifiability, and neutrality/ freedom from bias) of each piece of information for purposes of choosing a business school.

E5-2. **(Examining relevance, LO 3)** For each of the following situations, indicate the information that the specific user would require. Explain. Do you think the information required would be available in general purpose GAAP financial statements? Explain.

a. A banker is asked to lend money and accept a building as collateral for the loan. The banker can lend only 90 percent of the fair market value of the collateral.

b. A tenant in a mall must pay 5 percent of its gross sales in a year as rent to the mall owner. The rent must be paid within 60 days of the end of the year.

c. An investor wants to predict the amount of cash a company will have to spend on replacing old equipment.

d. An investor wants to know the current market value of the Loblaw Companies Limited shares that she owns.

E5-3. **(Examining the entity assumption, LO 2)** Mazeppa Ltd. (Mazeppa) is a producer of electronic parts that it sells to manufacturers of electronic equipment. Mazeppa has organized itself by setting up a number of separate corporations to operate different parts of its business. The corporate organization chart is shown below. Each box represents a separate corporation and the percentage shown represents the percentage of that corporation that is owned by the corporation above it in the chart. For example, Mazeppa Ltd. owns 100 percent of Mazeppa US Ltd. and Mazeppa Distributing Ltd. owns 60 percent of Mazeppa Retail Ltd. (The other 40 percent of Mazeppa Retail Ltd. is owned by other investors).

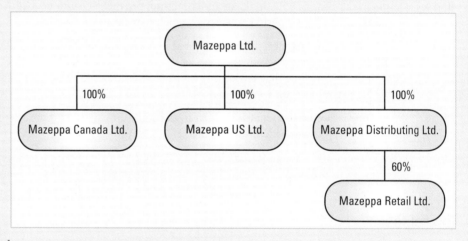

Required:

For each of the following situations, indicate which entity the party described would want information about. Explain your answer:

a. An investor purchases shares in Mazeppa Ltd. and wishes to evaluate the performance of the company.

b. A bank is evaluating a loan application from Mazeppa US Ltd. The loan will not be guaranteed by any other entity.

c. The 40 percent shareholders in Mazeppa Retail Ltd. wish to evaluate their investment in that company.

d. The Canada Customs and Revenue Agency is assessing the tax return filed by Mazeppa Distributing Ltd.

E5-4. **(Examining neutrality, LO 3)** In each of the following situations, indicate whether the information being provided is neutral. Explain your reasoning.

a. A newspaper publishes an editorial recommending that readers vote for a particular political party.

b. Environment Canada reports that 15 centimetres of snow fell overnight.

c. An advertisement for a donut shop states that it has the "world's best coffee."

d. An arbitrator issues a report based on her meetings with disputing parties that makes recommendations designed to help the parties come to an agreement.

e. A candidate for employment prepares a résumé for a prospective employer.

f. A manager prepares the financial statements that will be presented to the board of directors and the shareholders of the company.

E5-5. **(Identifying accounting assumptions, qualitative characteristics, and measurement conventions, LO 2, 3, 4)** For each of the following situations, identify the accounting assumptions, qualitative characteristics, and/or measurement conventions that Exmoor Corp. (Exmoor) would be violating by the accounting choices that it made. Explain your answer.

a. The president of Exmoor decided to increase the value of land the company was holding for resale because the amount originally recorded significantly understated its current value.

b. Exmoor's sole shareholder used Exmoor personnel, material, and equipment to build his mansion. All costs incurred were reported on Exmoor's income statement as other expenses.

c. A foreign government has threatened to expropriate some of Exmoor's production facilities in that country without compensation. The country has a history of expropriating the assets of foreign corporations. Exmoor has not provided any information about this possibility in its financial statements because the company is still having discussions with the government and is hopeful that "things will work out."

d. Exmoor recently signed a contract to sell specially designed equipment to a poor developing country for use in agriculture. Exmoor's engineering staff just began working on the design and it is hoped that the equipment will be delivered in four years. Exmoor recognized the revenue when the contract was signed with the country.

e. Exmoor expenses the cost of inventory when the inventory is received from the supplier.

f. Exmoor decided to change the method for recognizing revenue on some of its long-term contracts from the completed-contract method to the percentage-of-completion method to be consistent with its competitors. Due to certain complexities, Exmoor is not changing the revenue reported in previous years.

g. Exmoor purchased new computer equipment for its head office. The equipment itself cost $250,000. Delivery, installation, and renovations to the office to allow the computer equipment to be installed and operated cost an additional $175,000, which were expensed when incurred.

h. Some of Exmoor's inventory was seriously damaged in a fire. The company is currently looking for a buyer and is hoping to receive about 25 percent of the original cost of the inventory. Exmoor's controller is not writing down the inventory because "it has not been sold yet."

E5-6. **(Identifying accounting assumptions, qualitative characteristics, and measurement conventions, LO 2, 3, 4)** Identify the accounting assumption, characteristic, or convention that provides the best reason for each of the statements below. Explain your choice.

a. Financial statements should include all relevant information about the economic activity of an entity.

b. The financial statements of a proprietorship should exclude the personal assets, liabilities, revenues, and expenses of the proprietor.

c. Capital assets are reported at their historical cost.

d. Shareholders receive an annual report from the corporation each year.

e. A company uses the percentage-of-completion method for recognizing revenue on long-term projects. The company determines that one of the projects is generating a loss and so recognizes the full amount of the loss immediately, rather than spreading the loss over the life of the contract.

f. Financial statement analysis is easier if similar entities use similar accounting methods.

g. The financial statements of most Canadian companies are presented in Canadian dollars.

h. The financial statements of many entities round amounts to the nearest thousand or even the nearest million.

i. A business that is ceasing operations values its assets and liabilities on a liquidation basis.

j. The cost of inventory sold is reported in the income statement in the same period in which the revenue that the inventory helped earn is recognized.

k. The cost of some low-cost assets is expensed when they are purchased, even though they have useful lives of more than one year.

E5-7. (**Examining verifiability, LO 3**) For each of the following transactions and economic events involving Hybla Ltd. (Hybla), indicate whether you think the amounts involved are easy to verify, moderately easy/moderately difficult to verify, or difficult to verify. Explain your reasoning.

a. Hybla purchases land from a developer for $5,000,000.

b. Land that Hybla has owned for 25 years has an estimated market value of $1,200,000.

c. Hybla trades a piece of land that it has owned for many years for shares in a privately held company. Hybla records the shares on its books at $5,000,000.

d. Hybla purchases a delivery vehicle and estimates that it will have a useful life of six years for purposes of calculating amortization.

e. Hybla sells merchandise to a customer for $100,000 and recognizes the revenue when the goods are delivered. The customer promises to pay in 90 days.

f. Hybla reports that it has $124,000 cash.

g. Hybla recognizes revenue on a percentage-of-completion basis on some of its long-term projects. For one project, Hybla estimates that 32 percent of the project was completed during the current year.

E5-8. (**Examining the periodic reporting assumption, LO 3**) For each of the following situations, explain the accounting problems and difficulties created because of the requirement for periodic reporting. Include other accounting assumptions, qualitative characteristics, and measurement conventions in your discussion if they are relevant.

a. An airline amortizes its Boeing 787 Dreamliner on a straight-line basis over 20 years.

b. An engineering company decides to recognize revenue on a large dam project in a developing country using the percentage-of-completion method.

c. A button manufacturer sells to clothing manufacturers around the world. Customers are required to pay within 60 days of delivery. The button manufacturer recognizes revenue when buttons are shipped to customers.

d. An oil refiner produces gasoline from crude oil and sells it to independent gas stations across Ontario. The crude oil is purchased at market prices and stored in large containers until it is refined. A single container mixes together different batches of crude oil that cost significantly different amounts because the price of crude can vary greatly.

e. Rogers Communications Inc. expenses the cost of its senior executives' salaries in the year the employees earn them (when answering think about matching and what the function of senior executives is).

E5-9. (**Examining materiality, LO 4**) For each of the following situations, explain whether you think the amount involved is material.

a. Students in an accounting course receive a grade of A if they get 80 percent or more on the final exam. A student receives 79 percent on the final exam, but the instructor made an adding error and the actual grade is 80 percent. Is the one-mark adding error material?

b. Students in an accounting course receive a grade of A if they get 80 percent or more on the final exam and a grade of B if they get between 65 percent and 79 percent. A student receives a 69 percent on the final exam, but the instructor made an adding error and the actual grade is 70 percent. Is the one-mark adding error material?

c. A company with annual sales of $1,000,000, net income of $150,000, and total assets of $500,000 accidentally did not include a $100,000 sale made near the end of the year in its current year's income statement. All costs associated with the sale were expensed in the current year's income statement. Is the $100,000 omission material?

d. A company with annual sales of $1,000,000, net income of $150,000, and total assets of $500,000 accidentally did not include a $1,000 sale made near the end of the year in its current year's income statement. All costs associated with the sale were expensed in the current year's income statement. Is the $1,000 omission material?

e. An agreement to sell a business sets the selling price at five times average net income. A $10,000 expenditure that is normally expensed when incurred was capitalized. Net income, without considering the capitalized $10,000 item, was $200,000.

f. In 2009 a company spent $200,000 on advertising and promotion. In 2010, because the company was short of cash, it spent $30,000 on advertising and promotion. Since the amount spent in 2010 was relatively small, management decided to include advertising and promotion in the general and administrative account on the income statement instead of reporting it separately as it did in its 2009 financial statements. In the 2010 financial statements, the 2009 amount was restated for consistency purposes so that it was also included in general and administrative expenses.

g. A company paid $500 for inventory it purchased from another company owned by the same shareholder.

E5-10. **(Examining non-arm's length transactions, LO 4)** For each of the following transactions entered into by Nootka Ltd. (Nootka), indicate whether it should be considered a non-arm's length transaction. In each case, indicate whether information about the transaction should be disclosed separately according to GAAP. Explain your thinking. Assume you are a small shareholder in Nootka.

a. The CEO of Nootka purchases land owned by Nootka so that she can build a home.

b. Forty percent of Nootka's sales are to a single customer.

c. Nootka obtains consulting services from a firm operated by the majority shareholder's brother. All transactions occur at standard terms for the industry.

d. A number of Nootka's employees are close relatives of the majority shareholder. These people receive compensation that is the same as other employees carrying out similar duties.

e. The husband of Nootka's CEO is the "special consultant to the CEO." The special consultant receives a fee of $100,000 annually. The special consultant does not have special training or experience in the field and is rarely seen in Nootka's offices.

f. A friend of the CEO is Nootka's main supplier of office equipment.

g. Nootka sells goods to the Government of Canada and several of the provinces.

E5-11. **(Applying accounting assumptions, characteristics, and measurement conventions, LO 2, 3, 4)** What accounting assumption, characteristic, or measurement convention would Pilger Ltd. (Pilger) use to justify the following accounting treatments for the year ended June 30, 2008?

a. Pilger writes down inventory to its net realizable value if the net realizable value is less than the cost of the asset.

b. Pilger discloses in the notes to the financial statements the fact that a fire destroyed a major production facility in July 2008. The effect of the fire is not recorded in Pilger's financial statements for the year ended June 30, 2008.

c. Pilger records the purchase of inventory at the amount of money it paid.

d. Pilger expenses the cost of inventory when the inventory is sold to a customer and the revenue is recognized.

e. Pilger allocates the cost of its amortizable assets over the estimated life that Pilger expects each asset to contribute to earning revenue.

E5-12. **(Examining conservatism, LO 4)** Anvil Ltd. (Anvil) adheres to GAAP in its financial statements. For each of the following independent situations, explain how Anvil should account for the transaction or economic event. Explain your reasoning. In each case, provide the journal entry that Anvil should prepare.

a. A piece of equipment that was purchased for $25,000 was destroyed in an accident during initial installation. The equipment had not yet been amortized.

b. Inventory with a cost of $100,000 has gone out of style and it will have to be sold at a discount. Management estimates that Anvil will be able to sell the inventory for $60,000.

c. Equipment used by one of the divisions of Anvil has become technologically obsolete because a new generation of equipment has been introduced that is more efficient and produces output of higher quality. Anvil's existing equipment can still be used (it still functions) but is used infrequently because of the lower quality output it produces.

d. Last year Anvil loaned $300,000 to a biotechnology company. Last week, the biotechnology company announced that it was bankrupt and would be liquidating all of its assets and going out of business. Anvil expects to receive nothing from the biotechnology company for the loan.

E5-13. **(Audit opinions, LO 5)** For each of the following situations, indicate the type of audit opinion that you think would be appropriate. The possible audit opinions are unqualified, qualified, adverse, and denial of an opinion.

a. Instead of using historical cost to value its inventory and capital assets on its balance sheet, Chocolate Cove Corp. used net realizable value, which was significantly higher than the cost of these assets.

b. Kitchimanitou Ltd. complied with GAAP in all material respects except that it expensed $330 worth of office supplies (staplers, hole punches, etc.) rather than capitalizing and amortizing them over their useful lives.

c. The auditor of Salt Harbour Inc. was prevented from determining the amount of inventory the company had at year end and as a result was unable to verify the amount of cost of goods sold, net income, and total assets.

d. Heart's Desire Inc. refused to write off inventory that, in the auditor's opinion, could not be sold. The amount is material and, as a result, the amount of inventory on the balance sheet is overstated and net income is overstated. In the auditor's opinion, except for this item, the financial statements are fair and are in accordance with GAAP.

E5-14. **(Evaluating independence, LO 5)** The chapter discussed the importance of an auditor being independent of the entity being audited. Without independence the credibility of the financial statements and the auditors' report would be impaired. For each of the following situations explain whether the auditor would be considered independent of the client being audited.

a. The auditor owns 35 percent of the company being audited.

b. The auditor has invested in a mutual fund that owns 0.1 percent of the shares of the company being audited.

c. The auditor is married to the brother of the vice-president of marketing of the company being audited.

d. The auditor lives next door to the president of the company being audited.

e. The auditor's firm has a large consulting contract with the company being audited.

Problems

P5-1. **(Examining relevance and reliability, LO 3)** You are a corporate loan officer at a major bank. Itivia Inc. (Itivia) has applied to your bank for a $1,000,000 line of credit to finance operations. You have been given Itivia's file and find the following information:

a. Audited financial statements for the last three years.

b. Forecasted financial statements for the next two years prepared by management.

c. A letter from management providing assurances that Itivia is a solid company in good financial position.

d. A letter from the major shareholder offering a portfolio of securities as collateral against the loan.

e. Job descriptions and biographies of Itivia's senior executives.

f. A credit history (including a listing of loans obtained during the last 10 years) prepared by Itivia's management.

Required:

Evaluate the relevance (including predictive value, feedback value, and timeliness) and reliability (including representational faithfulness, verifiability, and neutrality/freedom from bias) of each piece of information in Itivia's file for the purpose of making the lending decision.

P5-2. **(Examining relevance and reliability, LO 3)** You are a prospective investor contemplating purchasing shares in Whyac Ltd. (Whyac), a publicly traded Canadian corporation. In the course of your research, you obtain the following information:

a. Whyac's audited financial statements for the last three years.

b. The remainder of Whyac's annual report, including the president's letter and management's discussion and analysis.

c. A tip from a broker friend of yours indicating that "some big things are about to happen at Whyac."

d. A research report prepared by an independent financial research company that does in-depth analyses of companies and their prospects.

e. A research report prepared by a brokerage firm. The brokerage firm is in the process of finalizing a deal with Whyac that will have the brokerage firm selling Whyac's new issue of shares to the public.

f. An anonymous tip from an Internet investment chat room.

g. A newspaper item assessing the future prospects of Whyac's industry.

h. An economic outlook written by the chief economist of one of Canada's major banks.

Required:

Evaluate the relevance (including predictive value, feedback value, and timeliness) and reliability (including representational faithfulness, verifiability, and neutrality/freedom from bias) of each piece of information for the purpose of deciding whether to invest in Whyac.

P5-3. **(Considering comparability, LO 3)** Thoburn Ltd. (Thoburn) and Nitro Inc. (Nitro) are two companies in the same industry. The net incomes for the year ended October 31, 2009 for the companies are shown below:

	Net income for the year ended October 31, 2009
Thoburn Ltd.	$375,000
Nitro Inc.	$225,000

Upon reviewing the financial statements, you discover that the two companies use identical accounting policies except for inventory and amortization of capital assets. Thoburn uses a method for accounting for inventory called FIFO, while Nitro uses a method called average cost (these methods will be discussed in Chapter 8). Also, Thoburn uses a method called straight-line amortization for amortizing its capital assets whereas Nitro uses a method called accelerated amortization (these methods of accounting for amortization will be discussed in Chapter 9).

Had Thoburn used average cost for accounting for inventory, its net income would have been $90,000 lower than it reported in its financial statements. Had Nitro used FIFO instead of average cost for accounting for inventory, its net income would have been $90,000 higher than it reported in its financial statements. Had Thoburn used accelerated amortization instead of straight-line amortization, its net income would have been $60,000 lower than it reported in its financial statements. Had Nitro used straight-line amortization instead of accelerated amortization, its net income would have been $60,000 higher than it reported in its financial statements.

Required:

a. Compute net income for Thoburn and Nitro under the following circumstances:

Inventory Method	Amortization Method	Net Income for Thoburn Ltd.	Net Income for Nitro Inc.
FIFO	Straight line		
FIFO	Accelerated		
Average cost	Straight line		
Average cost	Accelerated		

b. Which company performed better during the year ended October 31, 2009? Explain.

c. Why do you think the managers of Thoburn and Nitro selected the accounting policies they did? Explain.

d. What are the implications of having more than one acceptable accounting method under GAAP on a user's ability to use the financial statements?

P5-4. (**Applying accounting assumptions, qualitative characteristics, and measurement conventions, LO 2, 3, 4**) For each of the following items pertaining to Dollarton Ltd. (Dollarton), indicate which accounting assumptions, qualitative characteristics, and measurement conventions are influencing the accounting treatment used. Explain your reasoning.

a. A corporation that is owned by Dollarton is going out of business and values its assets and liabilities at their net realizable value. Dollarton and the other companies owned by it do not value their assets and liabilities at their net realizable value.

b. Dollarton records the purchase of new heavy equipment at $22,000,000, the price paid. The $20,000 cost of inspecting the equipment is expensed when the equipment was purchased as a maintenance expense.

c. Dollarton prepares financial statements for its December 31 year end and amounts in the statements are stated in U.S. dollars.

d. Because of zoning problems with a piece of land, Dollarton writes down the cost of the land to $500,000 from its cost of $1,200,000.

e. A person who claims to have been injured using one of Dollarton's products launches a lawsuit against the company. Dollarton includes a note describing the lawsuit in its financial statements but does not accrue any amount in the financial statements themselves.

P5-5. (**Applying accounting assumptions, qualitative characteristics, and measurement conventions, LO 2, 3, 4**) For each of the following items pertaining to Magpie Ltd. (Magpie), indicate which accounting assumptions, qualitative characteristics, and measurement conventions are influencing the accounting treatment used. Explain your reasoning.

a. During the year just ended, Magpie changed the method it uses to account for inventory. Magpie restated previous years' financial statements so that all years in the financial statements would reflect the same accounting method. As a result of the change, Magpie now uses the same accounting policy as its major competitors.

b. Magpie, which has assets of $3,000,000 and revenues of $4,000,000, includes the $20,000 cost of renting storage space in general and administrative expenses rather than providing a separate line on the income statement for the amount.

c. Magpie receives an advance payment from a customer for goods that will be delivered in four months. The payment is credited to the unearned revenue account.

d. The cost of capital assets is amortized over their useful lives.

e. For the year just ended, Magpie recorded a bad debt expense of $20,000, which is its estimate of the amount of accounts receivable that will not be collected. The $20,000 was credited to the allowance for doubtful accounts account, which is a contra-asset account to accounts receivable.

f. Some land owned by Magpie has more than doubled in value since it was purchased two years ago. Magpie plans to sell the land in the next year, but to date the increase in the value of the land has not been reflected in the financial statements.

P5-6. (**Examining conservatism, LO 4**) Kitscoty Inc. (Kitscoty) is a chain of retail sporting goods stores located across western Canada. Kitscoty has a policy of capitalizing the cost of opening new stores and amortizing the cost over four years. In the last year and a half, Kitscoty has not been performing well and in late 2008 the shareholders of the company, none of whom are involved in the management, decided to replace the existing management with a new team of managers. Kitscoty is in the process of preparing its December 31, 2008 financial statements. In light of the company's recent poor performance, the new management has decided to write off the entire $2,600,000 of store opening costs that were recorded as an asset on the balance sheet.

a. If a new store incurred $200,000 in opening costs, what journal entity would Kitscoty make to capitalize the cost of the store opening cost as an asset? Assume that $125,000 of the opening costs was in cash and the remainder are liabilities.

b. What journal entry would Kitscoty record when it writes off the $2,600,000 in store opening costs? What is the effect on income in 2008 of writing off the store opening costs?

c. What accounting principles justify the write-off of the store opening costs?

d. What possible motivations could Kitscoty's new management have for writing off the store opening costs in 2008?

e. If Kitscoty had not written off the store opening costs, it would have incurred $650,000 in amortization expense for the store opening costs in each of fiscal 2008, 2009, 2010, and 2011. Assuming that income including all revenues and expenses except for the store opening costs in 2008 was $2,300,000, and was estimated to be the same for 2009, 2010, and 2011 calculate net income in 2008, 2009, 2010, and 2011:

i. Assuming that Kitscoty wrote off the store opening costs in 2008.

ii. Assuming that Kitscoty did not write off the store opening costs in 2008 and amortized $650,000 in each year.

f. Using your results in (e), explain the effect of the write off in 2008 on future years' earnings, and the problems that users might have interpreting financial statements as a result of the write-off.

P5-7. (**Applying accounting assumptions, qualitative characteristics, and measurement conventions, LO 2, 3, 4**) Internet Access Ltd. (IAL) is a large Canadian Internet service provider (ISP). A key to success for IAL is enlisting new customers and the company aggressively markets its service by sending out free IAL Internet Access Software in newspapers, magazines, and direct mailings. The software allows potential customers to gain access to the Internet at no charge and IAL hopes that after the trial period expires the potential customers will become paying customers by signing up with

IAL as their ISP. The costs of attracting new customers in this way include printing, production, and distributing the Internet Access Software. IAL capitalizes theses costs of attracting new customers and amortizes them over 24 months. The 24-month amortization period is used because IAL estimates that the customers will generate revenue for IAL for an average of 24 months.

IAL is the only company in the industry that accounts for attracting customers in this way; in general, most companies expense these types of costs when they are incurred. IAL's costs of attracting new customers have increased significantly in each of the last five years.

Required:

a. Explain the effect on IAL's earnings of capitalizing the costs of attracting new customers and amortizing them over 24 months.
b. Use the accounting assumptions, qualitative characteristics, and measurement conventions identified in this chapter to make a case for:
i. Capitalizing the costs of attracting new customers and amortizing them over a reasonable period.
ii. Expensing the costs of attracting new customers as they are incurred.

P5-8. **(Applying accounting assumptions, qualitative characteristics, and measurement conventions, LO 2, 3, 4)** Live Theatre Productions Ltd. (LTPL) produces major theatrical productions in major centres across Canada. Usually LTPL selects shows that have had or are having successful runs in the United States or in Europe, and then mounts Canadian productions of the show. Most productions that are successful outside of Canada do well in Canada, but this is not always the case.

It can take well over a year from the time LTPL decides to put on a show to the first performance. Many costs must be incurred before the show is ever performed, including purchasing the rights to the show, paying performers and other personnel, creating costumes and sets, holding rehearsals, and so on. LTPL capitalizes all costs incurred before a show begins its run and classifies them as an asset on the company's balance sheet. LTPL then amortizes these costs over the estimated life of the show.

Required:

Use the accounting assumptions, qualitative characteristics, and measurement conventions identified in this chapter to make a case for:
a. Capitalizing the costs incurred before a show begins and amortizing them over the estimated life of the show.
b. Expensing the costs as they are incurred, before a show begins.

P5-9. **(Applying accounting assumptions, qualitative characteristics, and measurement conventions, LO 2, 3, 4)** Companies in the oil and gas exploration industry can choose the method they use to account for the cost of finding oil or gas. The cost of finding these resources is very expensive and significant amounts of money must be spent before a single drop of oil or gas finds its way to market.

The first method available to oil and gas exploration companies is the successful-efforts method. When oil and gas companies explore, they often look in a number of places and find the resource in only some of the places. Thus, a company may drill a dozen wells and find oil or gas in five of them. Under the successful efforts method of accounting, only the costs incurred to find wells that actually contain oil or gas are capitalized. The costs incurred to find wells that are empty are expensed once it is known that a well is empty. The capitalized costs are then amortized over the estimated amount of oil or gas that will be extracted from the well. (If a well is estimated to have 1,000,000 barrels of oil and the well cost $5,000,000 to find and develop, then $5 is expensed for each barrel of oil that is removed from the well. If at the same time another $5,000,000 were spent on a well that proved to be empty, the $5,000,000 would be expensed immediately.)

The second method of accounting for the costs of exploring for oil and gas is called the full-cost method. Under the full-cost method, all costs incurred to find oil or gas are capitalized regardless of whether the wells explored for are full or empty. All of the costs incurred would be amortized over the estimated amount of oil or gas that will be extracted from the successful wells. (Thus, if a well is estimated to have 1,000,000 barrels of oil in it and that well and an unsuccessful well cost $10,000,000 to find and develop, then $10 is expensed for each barrel of oil that is removed from the successful well.)

Required:

a. Explain the effect on earnings that using the successful efforts method would have versus the full costing method. Which method do you think entities would prefer to use? Explain.

b. You have been asked to prepare a brief for the accounting standard-setters that argues in favour of using successful efforts accounting for oil and gas exploration costs and against the full cost method. Use the accounting assumptions, qualitative characteristics, and measurement conventions identified in this chapter as appropriate to develop your arguments.

c. You have been asked to prepare a brief for the accounting standard-setters that argues in favour of using full cost accounting for oil and gas exploration costs and against the successful efforts method. Use the accounting assumptions, qualitative characteristics, and measurement conventions identified in this chapter as appropriate to develop your arguments.

P5-10. **(Case analysis, LO 2, 3, 4)** Re-read the Savoy Health Club Ltd. case that was given as the Solved Problem in this chapter (see pages 256–262).

Required:

Jim Floor has approached you to advise him regarding his pending acquisition of Savoy Health Club Ltd. Mr. Floor has become familiar with the accounting concerns being addressed by Fred Irving and he would like you to prepare a report explaining appropriate accounting treatments for the accounting issues. Mr. Floor wants full explanations and justifications for the recommendations you make so that he can explain them to Fred Irving and to the arbitrator, if necessary.

P5-11. **(Case analysis, LO 2, 3, 4)** Re-read the Savoy Health Club Ltd. case that was given as the solved problem in this chapter (see pages 256–262).

Required:

You are an arbitrator who has been engaged by Fred Irving and Jim Floor to help resolve the outstanding accounting issues that are delaying the completion of the deal that will sell Savoy Health Club Ltd. to Mr. Floor. Prepare a report recommending appropriate accounting treatments for the accounting issues. Mr. Irving and Mr. Floor would like full explanations and justifications for the recommendations you make.

P5-12. **(The impact of non-arm's length transactions and entity assumption, LO 2, 4)** Norboro Software Development Inc. (Norboro) is a small software development company that specializes in customizing computer software for small- to medium-sized professional practices. Norboro has developed a number of proprietary software packages that it modifies for clients. Norboro also modifies existing commercial packages to suit the needs of clients. Norboro is owned by James and Anita Norboro; each owns 50 percent of the shares of the company. Recently, the Norboros were approached about selling their business to a competitor that is looking to expand. The Norboros are thinking seriously about selling and they have provided the following income statement for the year ended September 30, 2008:

Norboro Software Development Inc.		
Income Statement		
For the Year Ended September 30, 2008		
Revenue		$1,237,500
Expenses:		
Salaries and wages	$487,500	
Amortization	112,500	
Advertising and promotion	90,000	
Other	52,500	
Interest	6,750	
Utilities	18,000	
Administration	15,000	
Consulting fees	120,000	902,250
Income before income taxes		$335,250

In discussions with the Norboros, the prospective buyer has obtained some important information about the business. Norboro was originally financed five years ago by a $300,000 interest free loan from Anita Norboro's parents. An equivalent loan from the bank would have an interest rate of about 10 percent. The loan has not yet been repaid. The salaries and wages expense includes $90,000 per year that is paid to James and $90,000 per year that is paid to Anita. Anita does not work in the business, except to help out from time to time with some of the administration. If Norboro had to hire an employee to do the work done by Anita, the cost would be about $25,000. Hiring a person to do the work James does would cost about $120,000. Norboro's offices are located in a building owned by Anita. The company pays no rent for the space. Equivalent space in the building rents for about $120,000 per year. The consulting fees pertain to service provided by another company owned by James Norboro. These services are provided to Norboro Software Development Inc. at about 10 percent below the usual market rate.

Required:

a. Are the financial statements as shown above an appropriate basis for the prospective buyer to assess Norboro? Explain.

b. You have been asked by the prospective buyer of Norboro to recast the financial statements for the year ended September 30, 2008 as if the buyer had operated the company.

P5-13. (Case analysis, LO 2, 3, 4) Wanda's Fashions is a small tailor's shop located in the centre of a medium-sized community. The shop is owned and operated by Wanda. Wanda makes alterations to clothing, tailors clothing to the specification of customers, and carries a line of ready-made clothing that she designs and makes herself. Wanda also makes all the uniforms worn by the employees of her brother Wendel's businesses. Wanda has been in business for over 20 years and has many loyal customers. Wanda has a list of over 200 people who use her services regularly, both for tailoring new clothes and for repairing and altering clothes.

The store owns several sewing machines, pressing equipment, mannequins, and furniture and fixtures in the showroom portion of the store. There is also a large sign in front of the store. All capital assets are amortized using the rates required by the *Income Tax Act*.

Wanda has a large quantity of fabrics in stock so she can provide selection to customers who wish to have clothes made for them.

Wanda operates the store on her own. She has two tailors who work for her part-time, based on how busy she is. Her children, Wendy and Webster, sometimes work in the store when it is busy. Webster also helps his mother do alterations and some of the tailoring. The children are not paid for their work but Wanda pays for their university tuition fees and last year bought them a car.

The shop is located in a three-storey building owned by Wanda and her husband Willie. In addition to Wanda's shop, the building houses three other storefront businesses (a fruit store, a butcher shop, and a video store) and has two businesses and three apartments on the second floor. Each of the tenants (except Wanda's Fashions) pays a monthly rent.

Wanda, Willie, and their family live on the third floor of the building.

Wanda and Willie prepare a single set of financial statements that are used for tax purposes. The statements encompass all income and expenses generated by Wanda and Willie's business activities (all of which are unincorporated), including Wanda's Fashions, building operations, and some of Willie's unincorporated business ventures.

Wolfgang Wondergarment has expressed interest in purchasing Wanda's shop. Wolfgang is an experienced tailor who arrived in Canada three years ago from an eastern European company. He has been working as a tailor for a major chain but he feels he is ready to have his own business. He will be meeting with Wanda next week to discuss the sale. Wanda has indicated that she will provide any information that is required.

Required:

Wolfgang Wondergarment has asked you for help in preparing for the meeting. Wolfgang would like a report outlining the information that should be requested from Wanda, including questions and concerns he should have about the financial statements that Wanda will show him. Wolfgang believes that Wanda's accountant (actually her cousin Wesley) will be present, so Wolfgang wants full explanations of what is needed and why it is required.

P5-14. **(Auditor independence, LO 5)** Etna and Partners (Etna) is a firm of accountants located in a medium-sized town in Quebec. Recently, the senior partner of the firm was approached by the CEO of Dyment Inc. (Dyment) to discuss the possibility of becoming Dyment's auditor. Dyment is a private corporation with about 150 shareholders, none of whom are involved in the management of the company. In addition, the company has several large loans from banks and other private lenders. Management has recently come under considerable criticism from the shareholders about the poor performance of the company and the CEO has assured the shareholders that a turn-around plan is in place. In the meeting **with Etna**, the CEO offered the information that, in addition to the audit engagement, Dyment could benefit from Etna's expertise in a number of other areas. In particular, as part of the turn-around plan, the CEO said there was a need for a complete review and overhaul of Dyment's accounting systems. The CEO also felt that Etna could provide expert advice on the turn-around plan itself and ongoing financial and management advice in the future. The audit fee for this client is estimated to be $40,000 per year, which would make Dyment one of Etna's largest clients. The additional work in the first three years could be as much as $100,000 per year.

Required:

The senior partner will be meeting with his partners to discuss the Dyment engagement. Prepare a report that discusses the appropriateness of accepting the audit engagement and the consulting engagement.

Using Financial Statements

CLEARLY CANADIAN BEVERAGE CORPORATION

Clearly Canadian Beverage Corporation (CCBC) was incorporated in 1981. CCBC produces, distributes, and markets bottled water and other flavoured sparkling beverages under the names Clearly Canadian, Clearly Canadian O+2, Cascade bottled water, Battery, Orbitz and Clearly Canadian Refresher. The Company's products are distributed in various countries worldwide including Canada, the United States, the United Kingdom, the Caribbean, France, the Philippines, Portugal, Turkey and others. The company's shares trade in the United States on the OTC Bulletin Board. Its head office is in Vancouver.

CCBC's consolidated balance sheets and statements of operations, along with some extracts from the notes to the financial statements, are provided in Exhibit 5–3. Use this information to respond to questions FS5-1 to FS5-13. Incorporate the relevant GAAP assumptions, qualitative characteristics, and measurement conventions discussed in this chapter, when appropriate, in your answers.[3]

FS5-1. What is the unit of measure used by CCBC in its financial statements? How do you know? Why is it important that this information be provided? Why do you think it uses the unit of measure it does?

FS5-2. Why does CCBC round the dollar numbers in its financial statements to the nearest thousand? Does this rounding result in users of CCBC's financial statement losing important information? Could it? Explain.

FS5-3. What is the entity that CCBC's financial statements report on? Is this entity a single legal entity? Explain.

FS5-4. How is the periodic reporting assumption reflected in CCBC's financial statements? Explain. How is accounting for capital assets such as property, plant, and equipment affected by the periodic reporting assumption? (When answering the latter question, consider how the cost of property, plant, and equipment is expensed over its life and the difficulty that might exist in estimating the amount to expense.)

FS5-5. Examine CCBC's statement of operations. Do you think this statement satisfies the four qualitative characteristics discussed in this chapter? Explain.

FS5-6. Read Note 1 to CCBC's financial statements entitled "Going Concern" and respond to the following questions:
  a. What principles are used in the preparation of the financial statements?
  b. Why has CCBC included this note in the financial statements (what principles from the chapter make this note necessary)? Wouldn't it be better for the company if the note was not included? Explain.
  c. What are the company circumstances that make this note necessary (i.e. what is it about CCBC's financial situation that makes it necessary to include this note in the financial statements)? What steps is management taking to overcome the problem? What must happen if the problem is to be overcome?

FS5-7. Read the description of CCBC's accounting for Distribution Rights in Notes 2 and 8 to the financial statements. What are distribution rights? Why do you think they are reported as assets on the financial statements? Why did CCBC write down the distribution rights during 2004? What was the amount of the write down? What accounting principles discussed in this chapter justify this treatment?

FS5-8. Examine Notes 2d and 6 to CCBC's financial statements. How are CCBC's property, plant, and equipment valued on the financial statements? Do you think the information provided about property and equipment is relevant, reliable, or both? Explain.

FS5-9. Read Note 2(e) to CCBC's financial statements. Why do you think this note is necessary? What are the implications of this note to readers of the financial statements? In answering, refer to relevant accounting principles that were raised in the chapter.

Clearly Canadian Beverage Corporation
Consolidated Balance Sheets
For the years ended December 31, 2005 and 2004
(in thousands of United States dollars, except where indicated)

	2005 $	2004 $
Assets		
Current assets		
Cash and cash equivalents	520	78
Accounts receivable (notes 5 and 6)	475	600
Inventories (notes 5 and 6)	781	524
Prepaid expenses, deposits and other assets	803	167
	2,579	1,369
Long-term investments (note 7)	29	29
Assets held for sale (note 6)	343	415
Property, plant and equipment (note 6)	1,831	2,252
Prepaid contracts (note 16(b))	1,477	116
	6,259	4,181
Liabilities		
Current liabilities		
Bank indebtedness (note 5)	361	272
Accounts payable and accrued liabilities (note 6)	2,094	4,150
Customer deposits (note 6)	-	69
Capital lease obligation, current portion (note 9)	3	-
Short-term debt (note 6)	567	1,248
	3,025	5,739
Capital lease obligation, net of current portion (note 9)	9	-
Long-term debt (note 10)	1,501	1,957
	4,535	7,696
Shareholders' (Deficiency) Equity		
Capital stock (notes 12 and 13)		
Authorized		
Unlimited common shares without par value		
2,000,000 Class A preferred shares		
2,000,000 Class B preferred shares		
Outstanding - 2,000,000 (2004 - NIL) Class B preferred shares	2,000	-
Issued - 6,901,652 (2004 - 1,033,868) common shares without par value		
Outstanding - 6,864,352 (2004 – 9,965,682) common shares without par value	64,311	58,590
Share subscription receivable	(198)	-
Contributed surplus (note 3)	4,809	1,037
Cumulative translation account	(929)	(1,253)
Deficit	(68,269)	(61,889)
	1,724	(3,515)
	6,259	4,181

Clearly Canadian Beverage Corporation
Consolidated Statements of Operations
For the years ended December 31, 2005, 2004 and 2003
(in thousands of United States dollars, except where indicated)

	2005 $	2004 $	2003 $
Sales	9,141	11,586	13,270
Cost of sales	6,349	8,048	9,960
Gross profit	2,792	3,538	3,310
Selling, general and administration expenses	5,592	5,587	5,554
Amortization of property, plant and equipment	122	130	294
Royalty revenue (note 4)	(76)	(133)	(163)
Other expense	203	270	161
Financing costs	-	208	-
Interest on short-term debt (note 6)	172	174	141
Interest on long-term debt (note 10)	49	52	4
Loss on sale of assets held for sale (note 6)	-	56	328
Stock-based compensation	1,709	23	13
Write-down of property, plant and equipment (note 6)	382	721	272
Write-down of distribution rights (note 8)	-	1,536	500
Write-down of investments	28	-	-
Gain on settlement of convertible debenture (note 11)	-	-	(81)
Restructuring	680	-	-
	8,861	8,624	7,023
Loss for the year	(6,069)	(5,086)	(3,713)
Basic and diluted loss per share (note 2) (expressed in dollars)	(1.06)	(6.56)	(5.48)

EXHIBIT 5-3 :

(continued)
Clearly Canadian
Beverage
Corporation
Extracts from
Financial
Statements

Going concern (note 1)

Clearly Canadian Beverage Corporation

Consolidated Statements of Cash Flows

For the years ended December 31, 2005, 2004 and 2003

(in thousands of United States dollars, except where indicated)

	2005 $	2004 $	2003 $
Cash flows from operating activities			
Loss for the year	(6,069)	(5,086)	(3,713)
Items not involving cash (note 18(a))	2,790	2,534	1,921
Changes in non-cash working capital balances related to operations (note 18(b))	(2,376)	1,094	2,005
	(5,655)	(1,458)	213
Cash flows from investing activities			
Proceeds from sale of property, plant and equipment	-	543	202
Proceeds from sale of long-term investment	-	85	-
Purchase of property, plant and equipment	-	(44)	-
	-	584	202
Cash flows from financing activities			
Proceeds on issuance of short-term debt	1,277	1,943	-
Proceeds from issuance of capital stock and warrants	6,516	216	66
Increase (decrease) in bank indebtedness	89	(206)	(224)
Repayment of short-term debt	(446)	(1,081)	(6)
Repayment of long-term debt	(1660)	-	-
	5,776	872	(164)
Effect of exchange rates on cash and cash equivalents	321	(47)	(124)
Increase (decrease) in cash and cash equivalents	442	(49)	127
Cash and cash equivalents - Beginning of year	78	127	-
Cash and cash equivalents - End of year	520	78	127
Interest paid	191	226	145
Income taxes paid	-	-	-

Supplementary cash flow information (note 18(c))

CLEARLY
CANADIAN.
Annual report 2005

1   Going concern

The accompanying financial statements have been prepared using Canadian generally accepted accounting principles applicable to a going concern.

While these accompanying financial statements have been prepared on the assumption that the Company is a going concern and will be able to realize its assets and discharge its liabilities in the normal course of business, certain events and conditions cast substantial doubt on this assumption. The Company had a loss of $6,069,000 for the year ended December 31, 2005 and a working capital deficit of $446,000, an accumulated deficit of $68,269,000 and a shareholders' equity of $1,724,000 at year end. Operations for the year ended December 31, 2005 have been funded primarily from the issuance of capital stock, the net proceeds of short-term debt financing of $831,000 and the continued support of creditors.

Management has continued to take steps to try to improve the Company's financial results and cash flows. These steps include listing for sale its land and water rights in Ontario, analyzing liquidation of non-core investments and pursuing debt and/or equity financing to fund working capital requirements (see Subsequent Events). The Company's ability to continue operations is contingent on its ability to obtain financing. Management believes that it will be able to secure the necessary financing; however, there is no assurance that management will be successful in achieving these objectives.

These financial statements do not reflect adjustments to the carrying value of assets and liabilities, the reported revenues and expenses and balance sheet classifications used that would be necessary if the going concern assumption were not appropriate. Such adjustments could be material.

Summary of significant accounting policies

Principles of accounting

These consolidated financial statements have been prepared in accordance with accounting principles generally accepted in Canada (Canadian GAAP). These principles differ in certain respects from those accounting principles and practices that the Company would have followed had its consolidated financial statements been prepared in accordance with accounting principles and practices generally accepted in the United States (U.S. GAAP). The differences as they affect the Company are described in note 20.

Consolidation

These consolidated financial statements include the accounts of Clearly Canadian Beverage Corporation and its wholly owned subsidiaries, Clearly Canadian Beverage (International) Corporation, CC Beverage (US) Corporation and Blue Mountain Springs Ltd.

In view of the consolidated nature of these financial statements, the term "Company", as used herein, is sometimes used to refer to all of the consolidated companies collectively and, where the context or specific transactions require, is sometimes used to refer to certain of the consolidated companies individually.

Distribution rights

Distribution rights, relating to the acquisition of certain territorial rights to distribute beverage products, have an indefinite life and are recorded at cost. Management reviews the carrying value of the distribution rights at least annually for impairment. Distribution rights are written down when declines in value are considered to be other than temporary based upon forecast future cash flows.

Property, plant and equipment

Property, plant and equipment are recorded at cost less accumulated amortization. Amortization is provided on a straight-line basis over the following periods which represent estimated useful life:

Buildings	30 years
Equipment	5 - 15 years
Leasehold improvements	term of the lease

These assets will be written down to the recoverable amount if carrying value exceeds that amount.

Use of estimates

The preparation of financial statements in accordance with Canadian generally accepted accounting principles requires management to make estimates that affect the reported amounts of assets and liabilities and disclosure of contingent liabilities at the dates of the financial statements, and the reported amounts of revenues and expenses during the reporting periods. Significant areas requiring the use of management estimates relate to the assessment of the fair market value of stock options, land and water sources ($1,900,000) and the accrual for local marketing fees ($474,000). Actual results could differ materially from those estimates.

Prior year comparatives

Certain comparative figures have been reclassified to conform to the current year's presentation.

3 Changes in accounting policies

The Company has a stock option plan which is described in note 13. Effective January 1, 2004, the Company adopted the new provisions of the Canadian Institute of Chartered Accountants (CICA) Handbook Section 3870 on "Stock-Based Compensation and Other Stock-Based Payments", which now requires companies to adopt the fair value based method for all stock-based awards granted on or after January 1, 2002. As a result, the Company is required to expense stock options issued to employees and directors. Previously, the Company was only required to disclose the pro forma effect of stock options issued to employees and directors in the notes to the financial statements.

The Company has applied the new provisions retroactively by a charge to retained earnings and a corresponding increase to contributed surplus in the amount of $523,000 on January 1, 2004 with respect to employee stock options granted in 2003 and 2002 (refer to note 13).

EXHIBIT 5-3 :

(continued)
Clearly Canadian
Beverage
Corporation
Extracts from
Financial
Statements

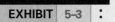

EXHIBIT 5-3 :

(continued)
Clearly Canadian
Beverage
Corporation
Extracts from
Financial
Statements

6 Balance sheet components

Accounts receivable

	2005 $	2004 $
Trade accounts receivable - net of allowance of $36,000 (2004 - $25,000)	435	525
Other receivables	40	75
	475	600

Inventories

	2005 $	2004 $
Finished goods	586	247
Raw materials	195	277
	781	524

Property, plant and equipment and assets held for sale

				2005
	Cost $	Accumulated amortization $	Write-down $	Net $
Land and water sources	1,603	-	-	1,603
Buildings	1,326	996	280	50
Equipment	1,116	938	-	178
Leasehold improvements	67	67	-	-
	4,112	2,001	280	1,831

8 Distribution rights

During 2004, the Company undertook its annual review of the carrying value of distribution rights and determined that the value of the distribution rights was impaired. As a result, $1,536,000 (2003 - $500,000) was recorded as an impairment. See note 2.

15 Related party transactions

In the ordinary course of business, the Company enters into transactions with related parties. All related party transactions are recorded at their exchange amounts.

During the year ended December 31, 2005, the Company paid $185,000 (2004 - $168,000; 2003 - $137,000) for the lease of its office premises to a limited partnership in which certain directors and a company with common directors own limited partnership interests. In addition, the Company in 2003 received a deposit of $200,000 from related parties on the building held for sale. In 2004, the building held for sale was sold to a non-related party and the $200,000 was reclassified to short-term debt.

16 Commitments and contingencies

d) Dispute with D. Bruce Horton and Continental Consulting Ltd.

In August 1999, a claim was filed against the Company in the Supreme Court of British Columbia by D. Bruce Horton and his company, Continental Consulting Ltd. (Continental). Mr. Horton is claiming compensation from the Company for allegedly constructively dismissing him as an officer of the Company. Continental is claiming compensation from the Company alleging that the Company terminated its management agreement without cause. Mr. Horton and Continental are claiming an aggregate of CA $2,400,000 plus interest and costs. The Company does not accept Mr. Horton's and Continental's allegations, and has filed statements of defence and has further filed counterclaims against Mr. Horton and Continental for monies owed and damages. The Company has made an accrual based on its expected costs.

22 Subsequent events

a) On February 22, 2006, the Company issued 200,000 common shares on the exercise of two stock options at a price of $1.00 per share, netting the Company $200,000.

b) On February 27, 2006, the Company issued 100,000 common shares to convert CA $222,570 of the Global (GMPC) Holdings Inc. short-term debt (note 6).

c) On March 1, 2006, the Company signed a Letter of Intent relating to the sale of Innisfill water equipment, storage tanks and water source at the Thornton well site for CA $400,000.

FS5-10. Read Note 3 to CCBC's financial statements. What is a change in accounting policy? Which of the qualitative characteristics is violated by such a change? If a change in accounting policy violates this characteristic, why is the company allowed to do it? Describe the accounting policy change that CCBC made. How did it account for the change?

FS5-11. Examine Note 15 to CCBC's financial statements. What are related party transactions? Why are they reported in the financial statements? Describe the related party transaction that CCBC reports. Explain why this particular information is useful to users of the financial statements. What are the limitations to this information?

FS5-12. Examine Note 16(d) to CCBC's financial statements, which describes a contingent liability. A contingent liability is a liability that may arise in the future if certain future events occur.
a. What is the nature of the economic event described in Note 16?
b. Why do you think this information is included in the notes to the financial statements even though it is not incorporated in the financial statements themselves?

FS5-13. Examine Note 22 to CCBC's financial statements. As the title of the note, "Subsequent Events" suggests, it provides information about events that took place after CCBC's December 31, 2005 year end. Describe the subsequent event that CCBC reports in the notes to its financial statements. Since the events described in Note 22 occurred after CCBC's year end, why is this note included in the financial statements? Tie your answer to the accounting assumptions, qualitative characteristics, and measurement conventions described in the chapter.

Analyzing Rogers Communications Inc.

◇ROGERS

R5-1. Examine Rogers' financial statements and give examples of how each of GAAP's basic assumptions is reflected in the statements.

R5-2. Examine Rogers' financial statements, including the notes, and give examples of how each of GAAP's qualitative characteristics of accounting is reflected in the statements and notes.

R5-3. Examine Rogers' financial statements, including the notes, and give examples of how each of GAAP's measurement conventions is reflected in the statements and notes.

R5-4. Examine Note 18 of Rogers' financial statements (page A-41) on related-party transactions. Describe the related-party transactions that Rogers was involved in during 2005. Explain why this note is included in the statements. In your answer, refer to the relevant GAAP assumptions, qualitative characteristics, and measurement conventions that were discussed in the chapter. Is information about these related party transactions important to Rogers' stakeholders? Explain why and tie your discussion specifically to Rogers.

R5-5. Examine Note 17 of Rogers' financial statements (pages A-39 to 40) on segmented information. Describe the information that is provided in this note. Explain why this note is included in the statements. In your answer, refer to the relevant GAAP assumptions, qualitative characteristics, and measurement conventions that were discussed in the chapter. Is information about Rogers' business segments important to its stakeholders? Explain why and tie your discussion specifically to Rogers.

R5-6. Read Notes 1 and Note 2(a) to Rogers' financial statements (page A-7). What is the entity that Rogers' financial statements are reporting on?

R5-7. Note 20 to Rogers' financial statements (page A-43) provides information on Rogers' commitments. A commitment is an executory contract.
a. Describe the commitments that Rogers has.

b. Why is the information supplied in this note useful to users? Include in your answer a discussion of the relevant accounting assumptions, qualitative characteristics, and measurement conventions that were raised in this chapter.

R5-8. Note 22 to Rogers' financial statements (pages A-44 to 45) provides information on Rogers' contingent liabilities. A contingent liability is a liability that may arise in the future if certain future events occur.
a. Describe Rogers' contingent liabilities.
b. Why is the information supplied in this note useful to users? Include in your answer a discussion of the relevant accounting assumptions, qualitative characteristics, and measurement conventions that were raised in this chapter.

R5-9. Examine Rogers' balance sheet and explain how the statement would change if it was determined that Rogers was no longer a going concern.

ENDNOTES

1. Extracted from the Canadian National Railway Company's 2005 annual report.

2. Extracted from Camco Inc.'s 2004 annual report.

3. Extracted from Clearly Canadian Beverage Company, Limited 2005 annual report.

CASH FLOW, PROFITABILITY, AND THE CASH FLOW STATEMENT

LEARNING OBJECTIVES

After studying the material in this chapter you will be able to:

▶ **LO 1** Understand the importance of cash flow and distinguish cash from operations and net income.

▶ **LO 2** Describe the cash cycle.

▶ **LO 3** Read and interpret the cash flow statement.

▶ **LO 4** Explain how cash flow information can be manipulated and how accrual accounting policy choices affect the cash flow statement.

When Blue Jays general manager J.P. Ricciardi signed free-agent B.J. Ryan to a 5-year, $47 million dollar (USD) contract in the fall of 2005, it made Ryan the highest-paid relief pitcher in Major League Baseball history. But the Toronto baseball club defended the steep price for its newest employee. According to Ricciardi, it put the team within striking distance of being a contender against the richer clubs in the American League division, such as the New York Yankees and the Boston Red Sox.

Pitcher Roy Halladay of the Toronto Blue Jays

"From our end," Ricciardi told the *Philadelphia Daily News* Web site, "we just say 'We want to have a chance.' And that's what we have now, a chance."

And the spending spree didn't end with leftie Ryan.

Ricciardi also collected starting pitcher A.J. Burnett at $55 million over five years, and a trio of infielders: Benjie Molina, Troy Glaus, and Lyle Overbay. He also extended star pitcher Roy Halladay's contract for another three years, through 2010. In all, Ricciardi raised the Blue Jays' 2006 payroll to over $71 million dollars and committed to team salaries of over $250 million over the next five years.

Rogers is committed to paying its roster of 24 Blue Jays players every year, no matter how well the team does, or how much money Rogers Communications makes as a whole. But J.P. Ricciardi could be confident in seeking out fresh talent, because Rogers had $1.2 billion left over in cash from operating activities at the end of 2005. The company generates this money from selling cable TV services, wireless services, magazine subscriptions, and, of course, Blue Jays home game tickets at the Rogers Centre, and other baseball-related sales, like beer and popcorn, and team merchandise.

But Rogers is hoping to recover the cash it's committed to paying its ballplayers by fielding a winning team that will fill more seats in the Rogers Centre. The team would like to get back its early 1990s glory when it regularly drew over four million fans a year. It's also trying to attract fans by spending money on sales and marketing initiatives. For instance, it was hard to miss the teams' new batch of commercials for the Jays' 2006 season: the ads featured All Stars Vernon Wells, Roy Halladay, and Troy Glaus playing with an unfair advantage against a bunch of ordinary kids. Another television commercial, shot during spring training in Dunedin, Florida, had pitcher Roy Halladay, the 2003 American League Cy Young Award winner, showing off his pitching arm to some kids trying to hit a beehive with rocks.

ROGERS

INTRODUCTION

Money—cash money, that is—makes the world go round. A company like Rogers Communications (Rogers) must have cash to pay for operating costs such as maintenance on their wireless and cable networks, employees, rent, and advertising. Rogers also needs cash to repay its debts, upgrade its technology, and expand the geographical reach of its services. Without cash, business will quickly grind to a halt.

When it comes to assessing an entity, however, it seems that net income and accrual information are the main criteria. Unfortunately, focusing on accrual information can be a very narrow and naïve way to view an entity for many of the decisions and assessments that stakeholders have to make. It is important to remember that earnings is a very abstract concept. Earnings reflects economic performance; *earnings does not pay the bills*. Paying bills and operating a business require cash. A business can survive quite nicely without showing a profit, provided it has adequate cash inflows or reserves. Conversely, as we will discover in this chapter, it is very possible for an entity to have good earnings and poor cash flow. An entity that cannot generate enough cash will eventually find itself in trouble because it will be unable to meet its financial obligations. Clearly, focusing only on earnings can give a misleading picture of how an entity is doing.

In this chapter, we will explore the importance of cash flow and liquidity to an entity. Managing the liquidity of an entity is crucial to its success and survival. If an entity is too liquid (in other words, if it has too much cash), it stands to be unprofitable or less profitable than it could be. If it is not liquid enough, it can suffer financial distress. A useful source of information about the cash flow and liquidity of an entity is the cash flow statement. In this chapter you will learn how to read and interpret a cash flow statement. (This chapter will not cover the preparation of the cash flow statement. However, readers who are interested in reading about how to prepare the cash flow statement can visit the text Web site at www.mcgrawhill.ca/olc/friedlan.)

CASH VERSUS ACCRUAL ACCOUNTING AND THE CASH CYCLE

Accrual accounting is the primary accounting method used in Canada. While there are some exceptions—primarily small, simple businesses—accrual accounting is used by the vast majority of entities. Once the economic environment an entity faces becomes the least bit complex, there is a need for at least some elements of accrual accounting. For example, if an entity buys or sells on credit, there is a need for payables or receivables, both of which are accrual concepts. With accrual accounting, revenue is recognized when it is earned and expenses are matched to the revenue. Cash flows can occur before, after, or at the same time that revenues and expenses are recognized.

Cash accounting is much simpler than accrual accounting and requires far less judgment. In cash accounting, the concepts of revenue and expense are replaced by receipt and disbursement, which simply reflect cash received and cash expended. Receivables and payables do not exist at all under cash accounting. Accrual accounting requires judgment as to when revenue should be recognized and how costs should be matched to revenues. Cash receipts are recorded when cash is received and disbursements are recorded when cash is paid—there is little room for judgment in either case. The standard measure of performance under accrual accounting, earnings, is a slippery, abstract economic concept that is intended to measure the economic performance of a profit-oriented entity. Earnings is not designed to reflect flows of cash. Cash flow is a much more concrete concept than earnings. This is not to say that cash flow is a better or worse measure than earnings. Cash flow is just different from earnings, and each has its role to play.

In sum, cash accounting and accrual accounting tell us different things. Cash accounting provides information about the movement of cash in and out of an entity. This information is crucial for assessing liquidity. Accrual accounting provides information that can give a bigger economic picture. Both cash information and accrual information can be useful to stakeholders and it can be unwise to ignore either.

The Cash Cycle

Being in business costs money. And entities usually have to spend money before generating cash from customers. There is almost always a lag between the expenditure of cash and the receipt of cash. For example, before a single DVD or game is rented at a new Rogers Video store, Rogers has to locate, rent, design, decorate, and equip the store, stock it with inventory, hire and train employees, and so on. Once the store is operating, DVDs must be continually replaced with the newest releases. Many of the DVDs will be bought and paid for before they are rented very many times. Even a relatively simple business, such as a street-side hot dog vendor, requires up-front investment for the cart and a supply of hot dogs, drinks, and condiments before business can begin.

We can get a better understanding of the lag between the expenditure and receipt of cash by looking at some numbers. The cash lag is shown in Figure 6-1. Yellowknife Corp. (Yellowknife) is a distributor of outdoor clothing and equipment. On average, Yellowknife has inventory in stock for 180 days before it is sold (inventory conversion period). In other words, the average length of time between Yellowknife receiving inventory from its suppliers and selling it to customers is 180 days. Yellowknife pays for its inventory, on average, 90 days after it receives goods from a supplier (payables deferral period). The average length of time between delivery of goods to customers and receipt of cash by Yellowknife is 40 days (receivables conversion period).

Figure 6–1 shows that 220 days pass from the time Yellowknife receives inventory from a supplier to when it receives cash from a customer. For 90 days Yellowknife does not have to pay for its inventory—suppliers finance the purchases. For the remaining 130 days, Yellowknife has cash invested in inventory (inventory self-financing period). Even though Yellowknife will not have sold most of its inventory once it is paid for, the company must have cash available to pay for the inventory as well as other costs of operating the business, such as wages, rent, utilities, and so on. If Yellowknife does not have the cash to meet these obligations, suppliers may stop shipping inventory, employees may refuse to work, utilities may cut off their services, and property owners may evict the occupant. These outcomes would be disastrous for Yellowknife's business.

The length of the lag will vary depending on the industry, customers, terms and conditions of transactions, and so on. For example, in the mining industry huge amounts of money must be spent to find the resource and develop the mine before any cash is generated from selling the mine's production. Similarly, a manufacturer will have to invest a significant amount of capital to establish the manufacturing capacity to produce goods before sales can be made to customers. In contrast, some service businesses require little initial investment before they can provide service to customers.

The cycle by which an entity begins with cash, invests in resources, provides goods or services to customers using those resources, and then collects cash from customers is called the **cash cycle**.

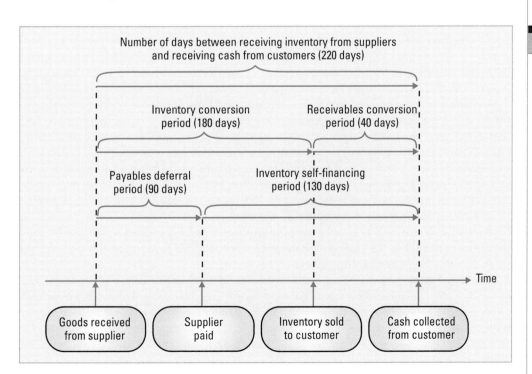

FIGURE 6–1 ::

The Cash Lag for Yellowknife Corp.

FIGURE 6–2 ::

The Cash Cycle

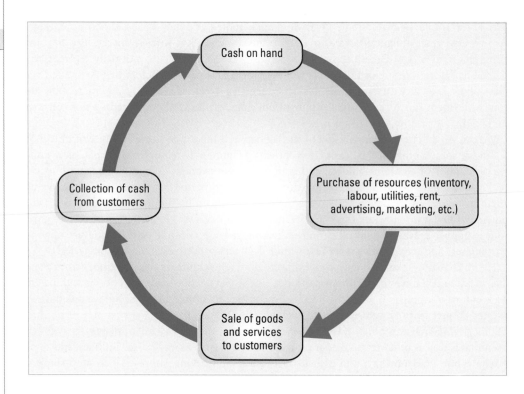

The cash cycle is shown in Figure 6–2. When you examine Figure 6–2, it is crucial to recognize that the cash that is expended purchasing resources usually occurs before the entity receives any cash from customers.

If the future were perfectly predictable, there would be few entities facing liquidity problems. Liquidity problems occur because what actually happens is not always the same as what managers expect to happen. For example, a clothing store manager must buy merchandise for his or her store many months before the clothing will be made available for sale. When making buying decisions, the manager must predict customers' tastes, economic conditions, and so on, to stock appropriate merchandise in the right quantities for sale at the right price. But many things can go wrong. If there is a downturn in the economy, there will be less demand for fashions because people will have less money to spend. If the store purchases lines of merchandise that are not popular with customers, that merchandise will not sell very well. The upshot is that if any of these circumstances arise, the clothing store will have less cash coming in than expected. However, the suppliers of the merchandise still have to be paid.

Growing businesses can also face serious liquidity problems. Expansion and growth are positive times for businesses, but poor planning and excessive optimism can lead to serious cash shortages. Consider a successful restaurant that expands to accommodate all the people the owners think are clamouring to eat at the restaurant. Expansion requires upfront capital costs to renovate the new space, purchase furniture and fixtures, perhaps buy additional kitchen equipment, and so on. Ongoing operating costs will increase with expansion as well. The owners may have to pay additional rent and increased utilities costs, hire more staff, and carry an increased amount of inventory. What happens if customers do not come to the expanded location? Many of the higher operating costs still have to be paid. If loans were obtained to finance the upfront costs, interest must be paid on the loans. If cash inflows are not adequate to meet the cash requirements of the business, financial distress may occur.

Ensuring that an entity has enough cash resources on hand or available to it is a crucial task for management. If cash inflows from customers do not occur as expected, the ability of an entity to meet its obligations can be impaired. In an economic slowdown, cash inflows may be reduced because customers are slow in paying their debts (perhaps they themselves have cash flow problems). If cash inflows are reduced, there might not be enough cash to pay suppliers, employees, and other creditors.

■ Ushta Ltd. is a manufacturer of auto parts. The company purchases materials from suppliers and stores them in a warehouse. Materials are held for an average of 30 days, until they are used in the manufacturing process, and then the manufactured auto parts are held for an average of 15 days until they are sold and shipped to customers. Ushta pays its suppliers 40 days after receiving the goods, and receives payments from customers 30 days after delivering auto parts. Calculate the following for Ushta and explain the cash implications of the inventory self-financing period:

a. Payables deferral period.
b. Inventory self-financing period.
c. Inventory conversion period.
d. Receivables conversion period.
e. Number of days between receiving inventory from suppliers and receiving cash from customers.

Example: Cash Flow Scenarios at Peabody Corp.

Let's look at an example that demonstrates the cash flow problems an entity can face and the differences that can exist between earnings and cash flow. Peabody Ltd. (Peabody) began operations on January 1, 2009. Peabody purchases various types of candy in bulk from producers, packages the candy, and sells it to corporate customers. The corporate customers use the packaged candy as gifts for customers, suppliers, and employees. Peabody must maintain an inventory of candy and packaging so that it can meet the orders of customers quickly. The following information is available about Peabody's operation:

■ All of Peabody's inventory purchases are for cash because suppliers are not ready to extend credit to the new company.

■ Peabody allows customers up to 90 days to pay for their purchases. For the purpose of the example, assume that customers always pay in the quarter after they make their purchases.

■ The amount of inventory Peabody has on hand at the start of a quarter is based on management's forecast of the amount of sales that will be made in the next quarter. All purchases of inventory are made on the first day of each quarter.

■ Peabody has a mark-up on its product of 100 percent. (If a customer purchases candy, that costs Peabody $100. The customer pays $200.)

■ Operating costs, other than the cost of product sold, are $12,000 per quarter. These costs are paid in cash during the quarter.

■ Peabody began operations with $40,000 in cash contributed by its shareholders.

■ Peabody purchased $16,000 worth of inventory when it started operations.

■ Sales by quarter for 2009 were:

1st Quarter	2nd Quarter	3rd Quarter	4th Quarter	Total sales in 2009
$20,000	$24,000	$27,500	$31,500	$103,000

Peabody's quarterly income statements for 2009 are shown in Table 6–1. Information about Peabody's inventory purchases are shown in Table 6–2 (page 290).

The income statements show that Peabody suffered a loss of $2,000 in the first quarter, broke even in the second quarter, and made profits in the third and fourth quarters. For the entire year Peabody made a profit of $3,500. The inventory information shows that the amount of inventory that

TABLE 6–1 ::: Peabody Ltd. Quarterly Income Statements for 2009

Peabody Ltd. Quarterly Income Statements for 2009					
	1st Quarter	2nd Quarter	3rd Quarter	4th Quarter	Total 2009
Sales	$20,000	$24,000	$27,500	$31,500	$103,000
Cost of sales	10,000	12,000	13,750	15,750	51,500
Other costs	12,000	12,000	12,000	12,000	48,000
Net income	$(2,000)	$ 0	$ 1,750	$ 3,750	$ 3,500

TABLE 6–2 ::: Peabody Ltd. Inventory Information for 2009

Peabody Ltd. Inventory Information for 2009					
	1st Quarter	2nd Quarter	3rd Quarter	4th Quarter	Total 2009
Beginning inventory	$ 0	$ 6,000	$ 7,200	$ 8,250	$ 0
+ Purchases	16,000	13,200	14,800	16,950	60,950
− Cost of sales	10,000	12,000	13,750	15,750	51,500
= Ending inventory	$ 6,000	$ 7,200	$ 8,250	$ 9,450	$ 9,450

TABLE 6–3 ::: Peabody Ltd. Quarterly Cash Flow Statements and Cash Flow Balances for 2009

Peabody Ltd. Quarterly Cash Flow Statements for 2009 and Quarterly Cash Balances					
	1st Quarter	2nd Quarter	3rd Quarter	4th Quarter	Total 2009
Collections*	$ 0	$20,000	$24,000	$27,500	$ 71,500
Disbursements**	28,000	25,200	26,800	28,950	108,950
Cash flow	(28,000)	(5,200)	(2,800)	(1,450)	(37,450)
Beginning cash balance	40,000	12,000	6,800	4,000	40,000
Ending cash balance	$ 12,000	$ 6,800	$ 4,000	$ 2,550	$ 2,550

*Collections equal the amount of sales in the previous quarter.
**Disbursements equal the amount spent purchasing inventory plus $12,000 per month in other costs.

Peabody has on-hand increased over the year. This makes sense because Peabody's sales are growing. As sales increase it is necessary to maintain more inventory to meet the needs of customers. The increasing amount of inventory means that more and more cash must be invested in inventory.

Let's now compare these income statements with the cash flow statements for the same periods. Peabody's quarterly cash flow statements and beginning and ending cash balances for each quarter are shown in Table 6–3.

Peabody's cash flow statements tell a different story than the income statements. During 2009, Peabody expended considerably more cash than it collected, and at the end of 2009 most of the $40,000 it began operations with was gone. In every quarter during 2009 cash flow was negative. Over the entire year Peabody had a negative cash flow of $37,450 but a net income of $3,500. Why? Because Peabody is a new business, it was necessary to make a large initial purchase of inventory and then allow the inventory to increase as sales increased so that customer orders could be met.

TABLE 6–4 ::: Peabody Ltd. Financial Information for 2010: Scenario 1 (Sales Table)

Peabody Ltd. Quarterly Income Statements for 2010					
	1st Quarter	2nd Quarter	3rd Quarter	4th Quarter	Total 2010
Sales	$31,500	$31,500	$31,500	$31,500	$126,000
Cost of sales	15,750	15,750	15,750	15,750	63,000
Other costs	12,000	12,000	12,000	12,000	48,000
Net income	$ 3,750	$ 3,750	$ 3,750	$ 3,750	$ 15,000

TABLE 6–5 ::: Peabody Ltd. Inventory Information for 2010

Peabody Ltd. Inventory Information for 2010					
	1st Quarter	2nd Quarter	3rd Quarter	4th Quarter	Total 2010
Beginning inventory	$ 9,450	$ 9,450	$ 9,450	$ 9,450	$ 9,450
+ Purchases	15,750	15,750	15,750	15,750	63,000
– Cost of sales	15,750	15,750	15,750	15,750	63,000
= Ending inventory	$ 9,450	$ 9,450	$ 9,450	$ 9,450	$ 9,450

TABLE 6–6 ::: Peabody Ltd. Quarterly Cash Flow Statements for 2010 and Quarterly Cash Balances

Peabody Ltd. Quarterly Cash Flow Statements for 2010 and Quarterly Cash Balances					
	1st Quarter	2nd Quarter	3rd Quarter	4th Quarter	Total 2010
Collections*	$31,500	$31,500	$31,500	$31,500	$126,000
Disbursements**	27,750	27,750	27,750	27,750	111,000
Cash flow	3,750	3,750	3,750	3,750	15,000
Beginning cash balance	2,550	6,300	10,050	13,800	2,550
Ending cash balance	$ 6,300	$10,050	$13,800	$17,550	$ 17,550

*Collections equal the amount of sales in the previous quarter.
**Disbursements equal the amount spent purchasing inventory plus $12,000 per month in other costs.

The build-up in inventory is not reflected in the income statement because only goods sold are expensed in an accrual income statement. However, the build-up of inventory did use cash.

If a user focused only on the income statement and ignored Peabody's cash flow statement, Peabody's performance would look positive, despite the fact that Peabody had just about run out of cash. If in late 2009 Peabody had to make a $5,000 cash payment, it would be unable to do so. This example highlights how earnings and cash flow can differ dramatically, and how important it is to examine both cash and accrual information.

Now let's look at 2010, Peabody's second year of operation. We will look at Peabody under two scenarios. The first scenario assumes that Peabody reached its maximum level of sales in the fourth quarter of 2009 and that level of sales ($31,500 per quarter) will continue in each quarter for the foreseeable future. Peabody's income statements, inventory information, cash flow statements, and cash balances by quarter for 2010 under this scenario are shown in Tables 6–4, 6–5, and 6–6 respectively.

TABLE 6–7 ::: Peabody Ltd. Financial Information: Scenario 2 (Sales Decrease)

Peabody Ltd.
Quarterly Income Statements for 2010

	1st Quarter	2nd Quarter	3rd Quarter	4th Quarter	Total 2010
Sales	$28,500	$27,500	$26,500	$26,000	$108,500
Cost of sales	14,250	13,750	13,250	13,000	54,250
Other costs	12,000	12,000	12,000	12,000	48,000
Net income	$ 2,250	$ 1,750	$ 1,250	$ 1,000	$ 6,250

Peabody Ltd.
Inventory Information for 2010

	1st Quarter	2nd Quarter	3rd Quarter	4th Quarter	Total 2010
Beginning inventory	$ 9,450	$10,950	$12,950	$15,450	$ 9,450
+ Purchases	15,750	15,750	15,750	15,750	63,000
– Cost of sales	14,250	13,750	13,250	13,000	54,250
= Ending inventory	$10,950	$12,950	$15,450	$18,200	$18,200

Peabody Ltd.
Quarterly Cash Flow Statements for 2010 and Quarterly Cash Balances

	1st Quarter	2nd Quarter	3rd Quarter	4th Quarter	Total 2010
Collections*	$31,500	$28,500	$27,500	$26,500	$114,000
Disbursements**	27,750	27,750	27,750	27,750	111,000
Cash flow	3,750	750	(250)	(1,250)	3,000
Beginning cash balance	2,550	6,300	7,050	6,800	2,550
Ending cash balance	$ 6,300	$ 7,050	$ 6,800	$ 5,550	$ 5,550

*Collections equal the amount of sales in the previous quarter.
**Disbursements equal the amount spent purchasing inventory plus $12,000 per month in other costs.

When Peabody's sales stabilized at $31,500 per quarter, net income (Table 6–4) and cash flow (Table 6–6) were the same in each quarter. The reason is that Peabody simply has to replace the inventory it sells so that the amount of inventory sold is the same as the amount of inventory purchased. With a stable level of sales, Peabody no longer has to spend money building up inventory (Table 6–5). An important point to note: the balance in the cash account in this situation builds up during the year such that at the end of 2010 there is an ending cash balance of $17,550. Cash builds up at this point because Peabody is selling the inventory for more than it costs, so cash levels increase.

The second 2010 scenario assumes that sales decline. After reaching a peak in the fourth quarter of 2009, interest in Peabody's products declines. Perhaps the attraction of offering candy as a gift has lost its appeal and is being replaced by something else, or competitors have moved into the market. Whatever the case, sales decline in 2010. However, management does not see that demand for its product is declining—perhaps management believes that the decline will be short-lived or there is not enough information to identify the problem. Consequently, management targets its inventory levels to the level of sales in the fourth quarter of 2009. As a result, inventory builds up during 2010.

Peabody's income statements, inventory information, cash flow statements, and cash balances by quarter for 2010 under the sales decline scenario are shown in Table 6–7.

In this scenario, we can see the effect of the sales decline and management's planning error. Peabody's management expected sales to level off at $31,500 per quarter, but instead they declined throughout the year. As a result, inventory increased significantly over the year to an amount greater than what was needed to run the business. Despite the decrease in sales during 2010, Peabody was profitable in every quarter. However, cash flow declined through the year and in the last two quarters cash flow was negative.

If this trend continues, Peabody could run out of cash. What would happen then? Perhaps as a result of the build-up in inventory, it would not have enough cash to pay its rent or employees. The company would have to take steps to come up with cash. There are a number of possible sources of cash. The owners could contribute additional cash in exchange for shares or as a loan. Peabody could approach a bank for a loan. (Of course, bankers may be reluctant to lend money to a company that is in financial difficulty, so a bank loan may not be a viable option.) Another alternative would be for Peabody to have a sale by lowering the prices of its products. A sale would lower or eliminate profits, but it would generate cash.

UNDERSTANDING THE CASH FLOW STATEMENT: AN OVERVIEW

Our discussion of the differences between cash and accrual accounting and the cash cycle leads to an important conclusion: financial statement users need to pay attention to cash and liquidity. The source of cash flow information in a set of general purpose financial statements is the **cash flow statement**. (The cash flow statement is also known by other names, including the statement of cash flows and the statement of changes in financial position.) The cash flow statement is intended to provide users with information about the historical changes in an entity's cash position.

While a document like the cash flow statement has long been part of the financial statement package, the emphasis on cash flow is actually relatively recent. Previous forms of the cash flow statement focused on broader definitions of liquidity than cash, such as working capital. However, a number of high-profile business failures, where the entity in question was profitable and working capital indicated that the entity was liquid, led standard setters to conclude that cash flow information should be the basis for preparing the cash flow statement.

It is interesting to note that the *CICA Handbook* does not require private companies to include a cash flow statement in their financial statement packages, provided that the required cash flow information is available from the other financial statements and the notes to the statements. This means that while cash flow statements will always be available in the annual reports of public companies, they may not be included in the financial statements of private companies. This does not mean that the cash flow statement is unimportant, but it may mean that additional work is needed by a stakeholder to find the cash flow information in the statement.

The cash flow statement was introduced in Chapter 2. Before reading on, take another look at Rogers' cash flow statement (which Rogers calls the statement of cash flows) on page A-6 in Appendix A.

The cash flow statement provides information on an entity's historical cash flows. Cash flows are grouped into three categories: cash from operations, cash from investing activities, and cash from financing activities. Let's look at these categories in more detail:

1. **Cash from operations (CFO)** is the cash an entity generates from, or uses in, its regular business activities. Cash inflows from operations include cash collected from customers, along with other receipts of cash that are related to operations. Cash outflows from operations include cash payments made to generate operating cash inflows; for example, payments to suppliers and employees.

2. **Cash from investing activities** is the cash an entity spends on buying capital and other long-term assets and the cash it receives from selling those assets.

3. **Cash from financing activities** is the cash an entity raises from and pays to equity investors and lenders.

A question that might not seem interesting is, what does the *cash* in the cash flow statement include? Naturally, the answer is not as straightforward as one might think. A term that is often seen in cash flow statements is "cash and cash equivalents." Look at Rogers' cash flow statement,

○ ROGERS™

| FIGURE | 6–3 | :: |

Examples of Cash Flows

Examples of Cash Flows by Category	
Cash From Operations	
Cash inflows	**Cash outflows**
Amounts received from customers	Payments for inventory
Tax refunds	Payments to other suppliers
Interest collected	Payments to employees
	Taxes paid
	Interest paid
Cash From Investing Activities	
Cash inflows	**Cash outflows**
Sale of capital assets	Purchase of capital assets
Collection of principal on loans made by the entity	Loans made to other entities
Proceeds from the sale of securities held for investment by the entity (i.e., stocks and bonds)	Purchase of securities of other entities made for investment purposes
	Cash expended and capitalized as intangible assets (e.g., pre-opening costs, oil and gas exploration costs)
Cash From Investing Activities	
Cash inflows	**Cash outflows**
Proceeds from the sale of shares to investors	Dividends paid to shareholders
Proceeds from the issuance of debt to investors	Repurchase of the entity's shares from investors
Amounts received from bank loans	Repayment of debt principal
	Repayment of bank loans

Insight

The classification of the payment and collection of interest as cash flows from operations is debatable for most entities. According to the *CICA Handbook*, these cash flows should be classified as cash from operations. However, interest collected often relates to activities that would be classified as investing activities, such as investments in bonds. Interest payments clearly pertain to borrowed amounts and borrowings are classified as cash from financing activities. An exception would be banks, where interest received and paid is a part of their regular business activities.

including the first footnote at the bottom of the page in the small print to see the use of this term and the definition that Rogers uses (page A-6). The term suggests that there is more to cash than the loose change in the owner's pocket. Some possible items that could be included in a definition of cash in the cash flow statement include:

■ Cash on hand and cash in bank accounts.

■ Short-term liquid investments—these are investments that can be easily converted to a known amount of cash, where there is little risk that the amount of cash to be received will change. For example, a short-term guaranteed investment certificate that will mature within about three months would qualify. Bonds wouldn't be included because the market value of a bond changes with interest rates. Equity investments cannot be included.

■ Certain types of bank loans such as bank overdrafts and lines of credit where the loans are used as part of the day-to-day cash management of the entity. (A **bank overdraft** occurs when an entity writes cheques for amounts that exceed the balance in its bank account, creating a liability to the bank. For example, if an entity has $20,000 in its bank account and it writes cheques on the account for $30,000, the account will be overdrawn by $10,000. The $10,000 is treated as a liability. A **line of credit** is a prearranged loan that can be drawn on as required by an entity.)

GAAP, as stated in the *CICA Handbook*, are not specific as to the definition of cash, so managers who are constrained by GAAP have some discretion as to the exact definition they use. The notion behind this section in the *CICA Handbook* is that the cash flow statement should show the movement of readily available cash resources, even if some of the cash is not on hand. Bank overdrafts and lines of credit can be included in the definition of cash because these bank loans are sometimes used as pools of cash that can be used as needed. For example, seasonal businesses will use their lines of credit to finance inventory build up to meet the demand of the busy

Question for Consideration

Classify the following cash flows of Quick Motors Ltd. (Quick), a new car dealership, as operating, investing, or financing. Quick sells new cars and services cars. Explain your reasoning.

a. Quick purchases a number of cars and vans for resale to customers for $375,000 cash.

b. Quick purchases a van for $40,000 cash that it will use to carry customers who leave their cars at the dealership for servicing to and from their homes.

c. Quick sells a car to a customer for $32,000 cash.

d. Quick repays a $500,000 loan from a bank that was used to renovate the showroom.

e. Quick sells old furniture and computers that were used by its salespeople for $25,000 cash.

f. Quick sells infrequently-sold inventory from its auto parts department to a parts dealer that specializes in parts for older cars.

g. Quick sells a number of cars that were used by its salespeople to a charitable organization. The organization is given 12 months to pay for the cars.

Answer:

a. Operating: Cars and vans are Quick's inventory. Sales of these are its business. Clearly, this is an operating cash flow.

b. Investing: This van will not be resold, but rather is a capital asset that will be used to help generate revenue by providing convenience to customers.

c. Operating: Quick's line of business is selling cars. Cash received from a sale is an operating item.

d. Financing: Repayment of a loan is a financing activity.

e. Investing: Quick is in the car business, not the furniture and computer business. Selling furniture and computers is not part of Quick's regular business activities. When these assets were purchased they would have been considered capital assets and the cash spent on them classified as an investing activity.

f. Operating: Sale of auto parts is part of the regular business activities of a car dealership.

g. None: No cash is involved in this transaction so it does not appear on the cash flow statement.

period. Cash collected from sales in the busy period is then used to pay back the bank. When bank overdrafts and the amount borrowed on a line of credit are included in the definition of cash and cash equivalents, the amount of the overdraft or amount borrowed on the line of credit is subtracted from the amount of cash and cash equivalents when determining the amount of cash an entity has.

For example, Rogers defines cash and cash equivalents as cash and short-term deposits. But also notice that Rogers' definition of cash includes bank overdrafts (or bank advances, as it calls them). Rogers' December 31, 2005 balance sheet reported no cash and cash equivalents. Anyone who's been to a Rogers Video store knows that the company always has some cash. What Rogers does is combine its actual cash and cash equivalents with its bank advances. If the cash and cash equivalents is greater than the bank advances, the net amount is shown as a current asset. If the reverse is true, as was the case in 2005, the net amount appears on the balance sheet as a current liability.

UNDERSTANDING THE CASH FLOW STATEMENT: SPECIFIC ACTIVITIES

This section will focus on understanding the cash flow statement. The main emphasis of the section will be on the CFO section because it is more difficult to understand than cash from investing and financing activities.

Cash from Investing and Financing Activities

Cash flows from investing and financing activities are quite straightforward. The items in the financing activities section simply show changes in the financing accounts on the balance sheet—accounts such as long-term debt, bank loans, mortgages, capital stock—and dividends. The items in the investing activities section show changes in the investment accounts on the balance sheet—accounts such as capital assets, intangibles, other long-term assets, and investments. In essence, these two sections reorganize the information that is presented in the balance sheet to reflect the cash flows related to investing and financing activities. However, if all the cash flow statement provided was a reorganization of the balance sheet accounts, there would be little benefit to having it at all. Users could simply reorganize the information themselves in a way that suited their needs.

One of the ways that the financing and investing activities sections provide additional information over and above what is in the balance sheet is by not combining positive and negative changes in balance sheet accounts. For example, Rogers reports separate lines in the financing activities section for "issue of long-term debt" and "repayment of long-term debt." It can sometimes be very difficult, if not impossible, to determine these more detailed changes from the information in the balance sheet and notes to the financial statements.

Another way that the cash flow statement provides information that cannot be determined from changes in balance sheet accounts is by including only transactions affecting cash. For example, if an entity purchases an asset and pays for it by issuing shares of the entity, that transaction is not reflected in the cash flow statement because cash is not involved. Or, if a capital asset is sold and the entity takes a mortgage back from the buyer instead of cash, that too is a transaction that would not be reflected in the cash flow statement. However, while these transactions are not included in the cash flow statement, their existence is disclosed. For example, Rogers provides in Note 10(c) "Supplemental disclosure of non-cash transactions," (page A-22) a summary of non-cash investing and financing activities. For Rogers in 2005, these non cash transactions were reported at almost $1.3 billion.

A look at Rogers' cash flow statement during the year ended December 31, 2005 shows that it expended $1,435,477,000 in cash on investing activities, mainly on additions to property, plant and equipment. Rogers had a net outflow from financing activities of $139,804,000. It issued $1,369,208,000 of new long-term debt and repaid $1,509,577,000 existing long-term debt. The company also issued $100,348,000 of new capital stock.

Cash from Operations

Cash from operations (CFO) is the cash that an entity generates from and consumes in its ordinary, day-to-day operations. For example, CFO for Rogers includes the cash from selling wireless and cable services, baseball tickets, and advertising on its radio and television stations, less the cash spent generating those cash flows.

There are two ways that CFO can be reported in a cash flow statement:

1. The **indirect method** reconciles from net income to CFO by adjusting net income for non-cash amounts that are included in the calculation of net income, and for operating cash flows that are not included in the calculation of net income.

2. The **direct method** reports CFO by showing cash collections and cash disbursements related to operations during the period.

Rogers uses the indirect method. If you look at Rogers' cash flow statement you will see that the starting point for calculating CFO is the net income or loss for the year followed by a series of adjustments. These adjustments reconcile net income to a cash number. In fiscal 2005, Rogers had CFO of $1,227,407,000. (CFO is an untitled line about mid-way down the cash flow statement, just before the "financing activities" section.) If Rogers used the direct method, it would show cash collected from customers, and show cash expended on inventory, employees, and so on.

While the direct method has more intuitive appeal, it is rarely used in practice. *Financial Reporting in Canada* reports that of 200 Canadian public companies surveyed in 2004, only one used the direct method.[1] A possible reason for the popularity of the indirect method is that it links the cash flow statement to the income statement. By starting with net income, a user can see a relationship between income and cash flow. The *CICA Handbook* permits the use of both the direct and indirect methods, although the *Handbook* encourages the use of the direct method. The direct and indirect methods are compared schematically in Figure 6–4.

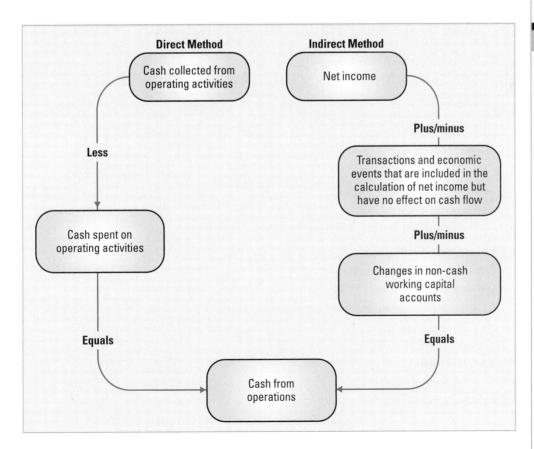

FIGURE 6–4

Comparison of the Direct and Indirect Methods of Calculating Cash from Operations

Table 6–8 provides an example of cash from operations calculated using the direct method. Azcar Technologies Incorporated (Azcar) provides the broadcast and communications industries with consulting, engineering, systems design, integration, project management, and the supply of related materials and equipment. In contrast with the indirect method, CFO calculated using the direct method is simply a listing of operating cash inflows from customers and outflows paid to various sources (mainly employees and suppliers). Azcar doesn't provide very much detail about its cash outflows, but it is one of the few Canadian examples of the direct method.

Now we'll examine the indirect method of calculating CFO. Broadly, there are two types of adjustments that must be made when reconciling from net income to CFO using the indirect method. The first type of adjustment removes transactions and economic events that are included in the calculation of net income but have no effect on cash flow. A simple way to conceptualize this adjustment is to imagine two sets of balls—a red set and a blue set. The red balls represent transactions that involve cash and the blue balls represent transactions that do not affect cash. If you mix the balls together, you have a set of balls that reflects all transactions—cash and non-cash. If you were then asked to provide information only on cash transactions, it would be necessary to remove the blue balls. In effect, you are removing the blue balls that you previously added in.

The most common example of this type of adjustment is the amortization expense. Amortization does not involve cash—it is the allocation of the cost of a capital asset to expense over the life of the asset. Since net income includes the non-cash amortization expense, it is necessary to remove the expense when reconciling from net income to CFO. The same is true for any transaction or economic event that doesn't involve cash. The amortization expense is eliminated from net income by adding it back because the amortization expense was subtracted in the

TABLE 6–8 ::: Azcar Technologies Incorporated		
Consolidated Statements of Cash Flow **Year Ended December 31**		
	2005	**2004**
Cash flows from operating activities		
Cash receipts from customers	$48,776	$54,234
Cash paid to suppliers and employees	(51,604)	(52,309)
Net change in short-term investments	136	0
Income taxes recovered (paid)	(148)	58
Interest (paid) net of interest received	(176)	(4)
	(3,016)	1,979
Cash flows from financing activities		
Bank indebtedness	1,249	(100)
	1,249	(100)
Cash flows from investing activities		
Purchases of property and equipment, net	(409)	(378)
Purchase of Procom assets	(61)	0
Receipt of partial payment on loan to shareholder	50	0
	(420)	(378)
Foreign exchange loss on foreign currencies held	(139)	(113)
Net increase (decrease) in cash	(2,326)	1,388
Cash at beginning of period	3,593	2,205
Cash at end of period	$ 1,267	$ 3,593

calculation of net income. (Think of net income as the combined set of red and blue balls, and amortization as the blue balls.)

Let's consider an example. The income statement of Moose Jaw Company (Moose Jaw) is presented as follows:

Moose Jaw Company
Income Statement
For the Year Ended December 31, 2008

Revenue	$35,000
Expenses	18,000
Amortization expense	8,000
Net income	$ 9,000

All of Moose Jaw's revenues and expenses are in cash except for amortization. All of its cash flows are operating cash flows. It should be clear that Moose Jaw's CFO for 2008 is $17,000 ($35,000 − $18,000). However, we can see this directly by using a spreadsheet:

	Cash	Capital Assets	Accum. Amort.	Owners' Equity	Revenue	Expenses	Amort. Expense
Balance on December 31, 2007	5,000	80,000	(16,000)	69,000			
Revenue during 2008	35,000				35,000		
Expenses during 2008	(18,000)					(18,000)	
Amortization expense for 2008			(8,000)				(8,000)
Pre-closing balance on December 31, 2008	22,000	80,000	(24,000)	69,000	35,000	(18,000)	(8,000)
Closing entry for 2008				9,000	(35,000)	18,000	8,000
Balance on December 31, 2008	22,000	80,000	(24,000)	78,000	0	0	0

The Cash column of the worksheet gives us the information we need about cash flow. Since cash increased from $5,000 to $22,000, the CFO for the year is $17,000. (Remember, there were no cash flows from financing or investing activities.)

The difference between net income and CFO is simply the amount of the amortization expense. If we are trying to calculate CFO starting with net income, we adjust net income by adding back the amortization that was expensed in calculating net income in the first place. For Moose Jaw,

Net income	$ 9,000
Add: Amortization expense	8,000
Cash from operations	$17,000

The thinking is straightforward. If a non-cash item is subtracted in the calculation of net income (such as amortization), then it must be added back when reconciling from net income to CFO. Similarly, if a non-cash item is added in the calculation of net income, then it must be subtracted when reconciling from net income to CFO. If we were calculating CFO using the direct approach, we would not consider these non-cash items at all. We would simply prepare a statement that reflected operating cash inflows and outflows:

Revenue (all cash)	$35,000
Expenses (all cash)	18,000
Cash from operations	$17,000

Note that we get the same CFO by ignoring the non-cash items in the first place.

A list of non-cash items that are included in net income and that must be adjusted for when calculating CFO using the indirect method is given in Figure 6–5. (Some of the items on the list will not be discussed in detail until later in the book.)

The second type of adjustment for the calculation of CFO using the indirect method adjusts accrual revenues and expenses that are associated with current asset and liability balance sheet accounts so that only the cash flows associated with these revenues and expenses are reflected. These adjustments are necessary because revenues and expenses are recognized on an accrual basis. This means that the cash flows associated with the revenues and expenses may occur before, after, or at the same time as recognition on the income statement. As we will see below, changes in the non-cash current operating accounts (non-cash working capital accounts such as accounts receivable, inventory, prepaids, accounts payable, wages payable, and accrued liabilities) over a period provide the information needed to make these adjustments. You can see this type of adjustment on Rogers' cash flow statement in Note 10(a) (see page A-22). The total shown in Note 10(a) can be found in the calculation of CFO in the Statement of Cash Flows on the line named "Change in non-cash working capital."

One might think that the simplest way to obtain this information is to identify operating cash inflows and outflows directly from the accounting system. However, accounting systems designed

FIGURE 6–5

Non-Cash Items and Their Treatment in CFO Calculation Using the Indirect Method

Expense	Description	Treatment (Add to or subtract from net income when reconciling net income to CFO)
Amortization	Allocation of the cost of a capital asset to expense over the asset's life.	Add
Gains	The amount by which the selling price of an asset is greater than its net book value.	Subtract
Losses	The amount by which the selling price of an asset is less than its net book value.	Add
Future (deferred) taxes	Difference between how taxes are calculated for accounting purposes versus how they are calculated for the taxation authorities. Future taxes will be discussed later in the book.	Add or subtract
Write-offs and write-downs of assets	Occurs when an asset's book value is decreased to reflect a decline in market value that is not supported by a transaction.	Add

Insight

The treatment of gains and losses can be a bit confusing. When an asset is sold and gives rise to a gain or loss, there is often cash involved in the transaction. The cash component of the sale is classified as an investing activity. The gain or loss is just the difference between the book value of the asset and the proceeds from the sale; it does not represent cash. Net income, however, includes the gain or loss. If the cash proceeds from the sale are classified as an investing activity and if the reconciliation from net income to CFO does not remove the gain or the loss, there will be double counting (i.e., the same amount will be included twice in the statement). Double counting occurs because CFO will reflect the gain or loss, and the full amount of the proceeds will be reported as an investing activity—the total will be different from the actual amount of cash actually received.

For example, Rife Inc. (Rife) sells land that cost $10,000 for $25,000 cash. This is the only transaction Rife has for the year. The gain on the sale of the land is $15,000 ($25,000 − $10,000) and that would be its net income, since there are no other transactions. CFO would be

Net income	$15,000
Less: Gain on sale of land	15,000
Cash from operations	$ 0
Cash from investing activities:	
Sale of land	$25,000

If the gain were not subtracted from net income when reconciling to CFO, CFO would be $15,000 and cash from investing activities would be $25,000, for total inflow of $40,000. This is clearly wrong, since Rife only received $25,000. This is why it is necessary to adjust for gains and losses.

Knowledge Check

www.mcgrawhill.ca/
olc/friedlan

In 2009 Baltic Ltd. (Baltic) reported net income of $16,000, based on revenues of $100,000, expenses other than amortization of $70,000, amortization of $6,000, and a loss on the sale of a piece of land of $8,000. All of these revenues and expenses (other than amortization) were for cash. Assuming that there are no other transactions or economic events, calculate Baltic's CFO for 2009 using the indirect method.

for accrual accounting purposes are usually unable to easily provide this information. As a result, it is necessary to make these adjustments by using changes in an entity's non-cash current operating accounts. Even when the direct approach is used, it is necessary to determine cash inflows and outflows in this roundabout way.

Converting accrual income statement amounts to cash flow amounts is actually quite straightforward. Understanding why the adjustments are made is less obvious. First, let's look at the process. Figure 6–6 (page 302) shows the adjustments that must be made when reconciling from net income to CFO. The box in Figure 6–6 entitled "Adjustments for non-cash transactions" represents the first type of adjustment that we discussed above. The remaining adjustments are the changes in the non-cash current operating accounts on the balance sheet. When calculating CFO using the indirect method, increases in current operating asset accounts such as accounts receivable, inventory, and prepaids are subtracted from net income and decreases in these accounts are added. Increases in current operating liability accounts such as accounts payable, wages payable, and accrued liabilities are added to net income and decreases are subtracted.

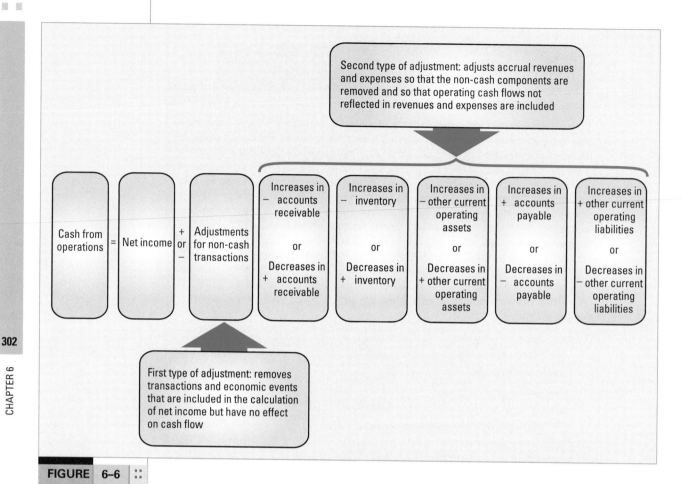

Second type of adjustment: adjusts accrual revenues and expenses so that the non-cash components are removed and so that operating cash flows not reflected in revenues and expenses are included

| Cash from operations | = | Net income | + or − | Adjustments for non-cash transactions | Increases in − accounts receivable or Decreases in + accounts receivable | Increases in − inventory or Decreases in + inventory | Increases in − other current operating assets or Decreases in + other current operating assets | Increases in + accounts payable or Decreases in − accounts payable | Increases in + other current operating liabilities or Decreases in − other current operating liabilities |

First type of adjustment: removes transactions and economic events that are included in the calculation of net income but have no effect on cash flow

FIGURE 6–6

Calculating Cash from Operations Using the Indirect Approach

At this point, take another look at Rogers' cash flow statement and Note 10(a) to see this type of adjustment. [Note that if you try to compare the changes in the current operating accounts as reported in Note 10(a) with the changes in those accounts as reported on the balance sheet, you will find that the two are not the same. For Rogers, part of the reason for this difference is due to how the acquisition of subsidiaries is accounted for in the cash flow statement.]

Our next question is, why do these adjustments convert accrual revenues and expenses into cash flows? The reason is that differences between the accrual income statement numbers and the cash flow numbers are represented in the changes in these accounts. That is, the non-cash components of accrual revenues and expenses are reflected on the balance sheet. These effects can best be shown with examples. We will examine three examples. The first looks at cash collections and revenue; the second looks at cash disbursements and wage expense; and the third looks at cash flow for inventory and cost of goods sold.

Example 1: Kamloops Inc. Consider the following information for Kamloops Inc. in Table 6–9 and the partial accounting equation spreadsheet in Table 6–10 on p. 303. The spreadsheet summarizes the entries that would have been made in 2009 regarding revenue, cash, and accounts receivable. Examine the spreadsheet to see how these entries affected the Revenue account in comparison with the Cash account.

The difference between revenue recognized during 2009 and cash collected from customers during 2009 ($525,000 − $496,000 = $29,000) is the same amount as the increase in Accounts Receivable in 2009 ($89,000 − $60,000 = $29,000). This is not a coincidence. An increase in accounts receivable means that credit sales in the current year that are uncollected as of the year end are greater than the amount of cash collected in the current year from credit sales that were recognized in a previous year. When accounts receivable decrease, the opposite is true. The difference between these two amounts is the difference between the beginning and ending balances

TABLE 6–9 ::: Kamloops Inc. Financial Information

Kamloops Inc. Information About the Year 2009			
Cash on December 31, 2008	$ 70,000	Cash on December 31, 2009	$566,000
Accounts receivable on December 31, 2008	60,000	Accounts receivable on December 31, 2009	89,000
Sales during 2009	525,000	Collections from customers in 2009	496,000

TABLE 6–10 ::: Kamloops Inc. Partial Accounting Equation Spreadsheet

Kamloops Inc. Partial Spreadsheet for 2009	Cash	Accounts receivable	Revenue
Balance on December 31, 2008	70,000	60,000	
During 2009—revenue		525,000	525,000
During 2009—collection of receivables	496,000	(496,000)	
Balance on December 31, 2009	566,000	89,000	525,000

of accounts receivable and the difference between cash collections and revenue during the period. This effect can be expressed as follows:

$$\begin{array}{l} \text{Cash collected from} \\ \text{customers during} \\ \text{the period} \end{array} = \begin{array}{l} \text{Revenue in} \\ \text{the period} \end{array} + \begin{array}{l} \text{Cash collections during the period} \\ \text{that were recognized as revenue} \\ \text{in a previous period (beginning} \\ \text{accounts receivable)} \end{array} - \begin{array}{l} \text{Credit sales during the year} \\ \text{that were not collected at} \\ \text{year end (ending accounts} \\ \text{receivable)} \end{array}$$

The difference between these two amounts is the difference between beginning and ending Accounts Receivable

Applying this equation to Kamloops Inc., cash collected from customers during 2009 is:

$$\begin{aligned} \text{Cash collected from customers} &= \$525,000 + 60,000 - 89,000 \\ &= \$496,000 \end{aligned}$$

This is the same amount that was calculated in the spreadsheet. Therefore, by subtracting an increase in accounts receivable from net income or by adding a decrease in accounts receivable, we have adjusted revenues (which are included in net income) so that cash collections rather than accrual revenue is reflected.

Example 2: Yoho Ltd. For this example we will examine cash expanded to pay employee wages. Consider the information about Yoho Ltd. in Table 6–11 and the partial accounting equation spreadsheet in Table 6–12. The spreadsheet summarizes the entries that would have been made in 2010 regarding wage expense, cash, and wages payable. Examine the spreadsheet to see how these entries affected the wage expense account compared with the cash account.

Notice that the difference between the wage expense in 2010 and cash expended on wages during 2010 ($88,000 − $93,000 = $−5,000) is the same as the amount of the decrease in wages payable in 2010 ($8,000 − $13,000 = $−5,000). Once again, this is not a coincidence. A decrease in wages payable means that the entity paid employees more during the year than it expensed in

TABLE 6–11 ::: Yoho Ltd. Financial Information

Yoho Ltd. Information About the Year 2010			
Cash on December 31, 2009	$98,000	Cash on December 31, 2010	$ 5,000
Wages payable on December 31, 2009	13,000	Wages payable on December 31, 2010	8,000
Wage expense for 2010	88,000	Wages paid to employees during 2010	93,000

TABLE 6–12 ::: Yoho Ltd. Partial Accounting Equation Spreadsheet

Yoho Ltd. Partial Spreadsheet for 2010	Cash	Wages payable	Wage expense
Balance on December 31, 2009	98,000	13,000	
During 2010—wage expense		**88,000**	(88,000)
During 2010—wages paid to employees	**(93,000)**	(93,000)	
Balance on December 31, 2010	5,000	8,000	**(88,000)**

wages. The relationship is reversed if wages payable increased. So when a decrease in wages payable is subtracted from net income when reconciling from net income to CFO, we are adjusting wage expense (which is reflected in net income) so that wages paid are reflected instead of the accrual expense.

Example 3: Rollingdam Ltd. For the third example we will examine cash disbursed for inventory and cost of goods sold. Consider the following information about Rollingdam Ltd. in Table 6–13 and the partial accounting equation spreadsheet in Table 6–14. The spreadsheet summarizes the entries that would have been made in 2008 regarding cost of goods sold, cash, inventory, and accounts payable. Examine the spreadsheet to see how these entries affected the cost of goods sold account in comparison with the cash account. This example is a bit more complicated than the Kamloops and Yoho examples because cash disbursed for inventory requires that we look at two balance sheet accounts—inventory and accounts payable—instead of one. The example assumes that accounts payable pertains only to inventory purchases.

Notice that the difference between cost of goods sold in 2008 and cash expended on inventory during 2008 ($325,000 − $270,000 = $55,000) is the same as the amount of the decrease in inventory in 2008 ($125,000 − $100,000 = $25,000) plus the amount of the increase in accounts payable in 2008 ($90,000 − $60,000 = $30,000) ($25,000 + $30,000 = $55,000). A decrease in the amount of inventory means that the entity sold inventory acquired in previous periods. If inventory were paid for in cash when purchased, a decrease in inventory would mean that less cash was spent on inventory in the current year than the amount that was expensed as cost of goods sold. An increase in the amount of inventory means that the entity was building up its inventory. Again, if inventory were paid for in cash when purchased, an increase in inventory would mean that more cash was spent on inventory in the current year than was expensed as cost of goods sold. (Remember that inventory is not expected until it is sold.)

Of course, most inventory is not paid for in cash when it is purchased, but is purchased on credit. As a result, accounts payable has an effect on the amount of cash that is expended in a period for inventory. Credit terms delay the payment of cash to suppliers. When accounts payable increases during a period, the amount of financing provided by suppliers has increased. The additional financing means that less cash is needed to buy inventory (or other goods and services). When accounts payable decreases, the amount of financing provided by suppliers has declined so, in effect, the entity must use cash to reduce the amount of money owing.

TABLE 6–13 ::: Rollingdam Ltd. Financial Information

Rollingdam Ltd.
Information About the Year 2008

Cash on December 31, 2007	$340,000	Cash on December 31, 2008	$ 70,000
Inventory on December 31, 2007	125,000	Inventory on December 31, 2008	100,000
Accounts payable on December 31, 2007	60,000	Accounts payable on December 31, 2008	90,000
Payments made to inventory suppliers during 2008	270,000	Inventory purchased during 2008 (All inventory is purchased	
Cost of goods sold during 2008	325,000	on credit)	300,000

TABLE 6–14 ::: Rollingdam Ltd. Partial Accounting Equation Spreadsheet

Rollingdam Ltd.
Partial Spreadsheet for 2008

	Cash	Inventory	Accounts payable	Cost of goods sold
Balance on December 31, 2007	$340,000	$125,000	$ 60,000	
During 2008—inventory purchases		300,000	300,000	
During 2008—payments made for inventory	(270,000)		(270,000)	
During 2008—cost of goods sold		(325,000)		$(325,000)
Balance on December 31, 2008	70,000	100,000	90,000	(325,000)

Therefore, to determine the amount of cash spent on inventory during a period, we adjust cost of goods sold for the change in the inventory and accounts payable accounts on the balance sheet. The adjustment is achieved by subtracting from net income increases in inventory and decreases in accounts payable, and by adding to net income decreases in inventory and increases in accounts payable.

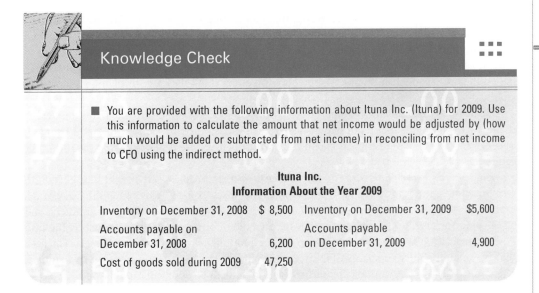

Knowledge Check

■ You are provided with the following information about Ituna Inc. (Ituna) for 2009. Use this information to calculate the amount that net income would be adjusted by (how much would be added or subtracted from net income) in reconciling from net income to CFO using the indirect method.

Ituna Inc.
Information About the Year 2009

Inventory on December 31, 2008	$ 8,500	Inventory on December 31, 2009	$5,600
Accounts payable on December 31, 2008	6,200	Accounts payable on December 31, 2009	4,900
Cost of goods sold during 2009	47,250		

www.mcgrawhill.ca/olc/friedlan

◇ **ROGERS**™

INTERPRETING AND USING THE CASH FLOW STATEMENT

The cash flow statement provides important information to many users of an entity's financial statements. Cash flow is an important indicator of liquidity. In Chapter 2, the current ratio was introduced as a commonly used measure of liquidity. There are limits to the current ratio because it is static—it is based on balance sheet elements. CFO, if it is regular and predictable, is a crucial indicator of liquidity because it shows the amount of cash an entity can generate to meet its requirements.

Prediction of future cash flows is key for estimating the value of an entity and its shares. Bankers and other lenders and creditors are interested in cash flow so they can evaluate whether the entity will be able to meet its obligations. Of course, the cash flow statement in a set of GAAP-based general purpose financial statements is a *historical* statement—it provides information about cash flows that have already occurred, not cash flows that will occur. However, as was the case with earnings and the income statement, it is expected that users can use historical cash flow information as a starting point for predicting future cash flows. The usefulness of historical cash flows to predict future cash flows depends on the entity and its circumstances. A new or rapidly growing entity's historical cash flows may not be a good indication of its future cash flows. The cash flow statement would probably be a good starting point for an established, stable entity.

Rogers' cash flow statement (see page A-6) shows that during fiscal 2005 it had CFO of $1,227,407,000. This means that Rogers' ordinary business activities produced enough cash to pay the operating cash flows and have over $1.23 billion left to apply to other purposes. The CFO allowed Rogers to purchase additions to property, plant, and equipment and reduce its debt load slightly. Without its CFO, Rogers would have had to borrow more money and/or sell additional shares.

CFO provides cash that can be used for paying dividends, acquiring capital assets, paying off liabilities, financing expansion, and so on. CFO is valuable because it provides cash internally, without having to go to lenders or prospective shareholders. Companies with good opportunities will be able to raise money from lenders and equity investors. On the other hand, struggling companies will have difficulty raising debt and equity capital. Lenders will demand higher interest rates to compensate them for the risk of lending to a struggling company. Equity investors will not be prepared to pay very much for the shares of companies that don't have much promise of providing a reasonable return on their investment.

Because CFO is an important source of cash, negative CFO is cause for concern. Negative CFO means that operating the business uses cash. If an entity has negative CFO, it must have sources of cash to make up the shortfall. In the short run, negative cash from operations can be covered by drawing on cash reserves, using available lines of credit, borrowing or raising equity capital, or selling capital assets. As with so many situations we have seen already, negative CFO is not necessarily bad news. Entities that are just starting up or are in a growth phase could be expected to have negative CFO because growth or expansion requires investment in current assets such as inventory and accounts receivable. Also, a new or expanding business does not reach its maximum sales capacity immediately. However, many operating costs will still have to be incurred regardless of the amount of sales. As a result, the business may be operating at a loss (in accrual accounting terms) and have negative CFO. Debt and equity investors are often very willing to provide cash to new or growing businesses that have good prospects. Struggling companies may have difficulty raising cash if lenders and equity investors think they are "throwing good money after bad."

Like most accounting information, the cash flow statement does not provide many answers—it only raises questions that require further investigation. An inventory build-up that is using up cash can indicate that a business is expanding (which is likely good news) or that the inventory cannot be sold (which is bad news).

While operating cash flows are crucial to an entity's main business activities, it is important to recognize that entities must regularly spend on capital assets to maintain their ability to operate. Even if an entity is not growing, equipment, buildings, furniture and fixtures, computers, and other capital assets must be replaced as they become old or out of date. When evaluating the cash flow of an entity, it is necessary to consider cash requirements to replace capital assets. The cash that is remaining after reducing CFO by cash spent on capital expenditures and dividends is called free cash flow. (A **capital expenditure** is money spent to purchase capital assets.)

> Free cash flow = CFO – capital expenditures – dividends

Free cash flow represents the cash that is available for use by the entity after required expenditures for capital assets and dividends have been made. Free cash flow can be used as management chooses, for example to increase dividends, acquire companies, reduce debt, buy back shares, and so on. Rogers' free cash flow for 2005 is:

> Free cash flow = CFO – capital expenditures – dividends
> = $1,227,407,000 – $1,353,796 – $26,209,000
> = $(152,598,000)

There are many combinations of cash flows from operations, investing activities, and financing activities that an entity can have, and each combination tells a different story. For example, one would expect that a new, fast-growing company would have negative CFO, cash inflows from financing activities, and cash outflows for investing activities. A new, fast-growing company would be spending cash on establishing itself and would need to raise financing to cover the CFO shortfall and to purchase needed capital assets. A stable, mature entity might have positive CFO, negative cash from investing activities (meaning that the entity is investing in capital assets, presumably replacing assets as required), and negative cash from financing activities (meaning that the entity is paying down debt and/or paying dividends). Figure 6–7 shows the patterns of the components of cash flow for several Canadian firms. GGL Diamond Corp., a diamond mining company, shows the pattern of a growing company, with negative CFO and cash from investing activities, and positive cash from financing activities.

Let's take a look at the cash flow statements of a Canadian start-up company. (**Start-up** or **development-stage** companies are companies that are in the process of developing their products and markets, and have not yet begun their planned business activity.) Hemosol Corp. (Hemosol) is a biopharmaceutical company focused on the development and manufacturing of biologics, particularly blood-related proteins. The company is located in Mississauga, Ontario.

Company and year end	Net Income (000)	Cash from Operations (000)	Investing Activities (000)	Financing Activities (000)	Net Change in Cash (000)
Rogers Communications December 31, 2005	$(44,658)	$1,227,407 +	$(1,435,477) −	$139,804 −	$(347,874)
Nortel Networks Corporation December 31, 2004	(100,000)	(184,000) −	(127,000) −	(110,000) −	(311,000)
CanWest Global Communications Corp. August 31, 2004	(13,478)	327,745 +	175,594 +	(546,558) −	(40,830)
GGL Diamond Corp. November 30, 2004	(1,244)	(564) −	(2,599) −	2,470 +	(693)
Clearly Canadian Corporation December 31,2004	(5,086)	(1,458) −	584 +	872 +	(49)
Sleeman Breweries Ltd. January 1, 2005	$14,426	13,199 +	(53,554) −	40,355 +	0

+ Indicates a net cash inflow.
− Indicates a net cash outflow.

Cash from operations + cash from investing activities do not necessarily add to the Net change in cash because of adjustments not included in the table.

FIGURE 6–7

Cash Flow Patterns of Selected Canadian Corporations

◇ **ROGERS**

Since 1995, Hemosol has been attempting to develop marketable products, but without commercial success. It has never made a profit, and as of December 31, 2004 had accumulated negative retained earnings of $266,255,000. Hemosol has been able to raise over $300 million from shareholders to finance the development of its products. Exhibit 6–1 (page 309) provides Hemosol's statements of cash flow for the years ended December 31, 2001 through 2004.[2] Notice how operations used huge amounts of cash and the company had to go to shareholders when cash reserves got low. The only way Hemosol could survive for as long as it did was because of shareholders were willing to purchase the equity of the company when it was offered. In late 2005, Hemosol filed for bankruptcy.

So far we have focused on the cash flow statements of businesses. Cash flow is also a relevant topic for governments and not-for-profit organizations. Exhibit 6–2 (page 310) shows the statement of cash flow for the Government of Canada for the year ended March 31, 2005.[3] The statement has the same structure as the statements for profit-oriented entities. In fiscal 2005 the Canadian Government generated CFO of $6.138 billion. In fiscal 2004 CFO was $13.114 billion. The CFO numbers show that the government is generating huge cash surpluses, which can be used to reduce taxes, reduce debt, and invest in programs that the Canadian people would value. The financing section of the statement shows that in fiscal 2005 Canada reduced its national debt by $4.771 billion.

MANIPULATING CASH FLOW INFORMATION AND THE EFFECT OF ACCRUAL ACCOUNTING CHOICES ON THE CASH FLOW STATEMENT

We have already spent a good deal of space in this book discussing how the preparers of accounting information can use the availability of alternative accounting methods and the judgment that is required by accrual accounting to manage earnings and other financial statement numbers. One of the attractions, it is said, of cash accounting and the information in a cash flow statement is that it cannot be managed or manipulated the way accrual information can be.

This conclusion is not true. Cash information can be manipulated. It's certainly true that cash information cannot be manipulated in the same way as accrual information, where managers must decide the timing of revenue and expense recognition. Cash information is "cleaner" in the sense that a transaction has an impact on cash flow only if cash is involved. As a result, managers cannot exercise any judgment on the accounting for cash *once a transaction involving cash has occurred*. However, managers can manipulate cash by influencing the timing of cash flows.

One way an entity can affect the timing of cash flows is by reducing "discretionary" spending on research and development, advertising and promotion, marketing, or maintenance. These spending reductions increase CFO, but such decisions by management to reduce the spending might not be in the interests of the entity. For example:

■ The reduction of maintenance spending by a company that relies on its production facilities would increase CFO in the short term, but could contribute to higher costs in the future. Equipment would eventually require more costly maintenance or need replacing sooner than would have been necessary had the equipment been properly maintained. Poorly maintained equipment could also reduce the efficiency of operations or the quality of the goods produced, which would increase costs and reduce revenues.

■ An entity could also increase CFO by delaying payments to suppliers. The payments to suppliers would have to be made eventually, which would have consequences on cash flows in future periods, but by deferring the payment, CFO increases in the period when the payment is not made.

■ Management decisions could also influence cash flow if it decides to sell some of its capital or other long-term assets. Such sales would increase cash from investing activities, but may result in the disposal of assets that could generate revenue and profit.

■ Management could decide to sell the entity's accounts receivable to a third party that takes responsibility for collection. This is a legitimate way to raise cash but it would have the effect of significantly increasing CFO in the period the plan to sell receivables was implemented.

EXHIBIT **6–1** :

Cash Flow Statements of a Development Stage Company: Hemosol Corp.

Hemosol Corp. [A Development Stage Company]

CONSOLIDATED STATEMENTS OF CASH FLOWS

Years ended December 31

[in thousands of dollars]

	2004 $	2003 $	2002 $	2001 $
OPERATING ACTIVITIES				
Net loss for the year	(10,148)	(34,942)	(54,834)	(38,577)
Add (deduct) items not involving cash				
Amortization of property, plant and equipment	2,156	2,276	2,450	2,303
Write-off of property, plant and equipment *[note 5[v]]*	—	4,654	—	—
Amortization of license technology	260	—	—	—
Amortization of patents and trademarks	204	134	115	74
Write-off of patents and trademarks *[note 6]*	—	846	—	—
Amortization of deferred charges	2,150	5,009	1,587	360
Write-off of deferred charges *[note 8]*	—	—	6,453	—
Write-off of inventory *[note 4]*	—	1,676	—	(1,189)
Gain on sale of equipment *[note 5[iii]]*	—	(1,100)	—	(1,096)
Stock-based compensation	2,972	—	—	134
Future income taxes	(3,723)	—	—	—
Minority interest	(1,074)	—	—	—
Net gain on Arrangement *[note 9[d]]*	(6,838)	—	—	—
Foreign currency translation loss (gain)	31	(79)	52	(42)
	(14,010)	(21,526)	(44,177)	(35,748)
Net change in non-cash working capital balances related to operations *[note 19]*	(542)	(5,129)	3,818	99
Cash used in operating activities	(14,552)	(26,655)	(40,359)	(37,934)
INVESTING ACTIVITIES				
Patent and trademark costs	—	(172)	(327)	(568)
Purchase of license technology *[note 7]*	(1,502)	—	—	—
Proceeds on sale of tax losses *[note 9[d]]*	12,898	—	—	—
Proceeds on sale of equipment	—	1,100	—	(87,647)
Sale of short-term investments	—	—	67,052	20,595
Purchase of property, plant and equipment	(1,379)	(8,361)	(31,699)	(38,415)
Cash provided by (used in) investing activities	10,017	(7,433)	35,026	(106,035)
FINANCING ACTIVITIES				
Proceeds on issuance of common shares	223	—	22,170	113,078
Proceeds on issuance of Series A special warrants	—	5,021	—	—
Proceeds on issuance of Series B special warrants	—	448	—	—
Proceeds from short-term debt	—	20,000	—	—
Payment of share issue costs	—	(466)	(1,351)	(8,393)
Payment of debentures	—	(5,000)	—	—
Payment of debt issue costs	—	—	(640)	113,078
Proceeds on issuance of debentures	—	—	5,000	—
Cash put in escrow *[note 10]*	—	(448)	(5,000)	—
Cash released from escrow *[notes 10 and 14]*	448	5,000	—	—
Cash provided by financing activities	671	24,555	20,179	104,685
Effect of exchange rates on cash and cash equivalents	(31)	79	(52)	42
Net increase (decrease) in cash and cash equivalents during the year	(3,895)	(9,454)	14,794	(39,284)
Cash and cash equivalents, beginning of year	8,125	17,579	2,785	42,027
Cash and cash equivalents, end of year	4,230	8,125	17,579	2,785

See accompanying notes

GOVERNMENT OF CANADA

Statement of Cash Flow
for the Year Ended March 31, 2005

(in millions of dollars)

	2005	2004
OPERATING ACTIVITIES —		
ANNUAL SURPLUS	**1,630**	**9,083**
Items not affecting cash —		
Share of annual profit in enterprise Crown corporations and other government business enterprises	-4,855	-3,711
Amortization of tangible capital assets	3,696	3,502
Loss on disposal of tangible capital assets	317	231
Gain on disposal of investments	-2,562	
Changes in inventories and prepaid expenses	414	133
Changes in pension and other liabilities	-1,090	2,611
Changes in foreign exchange accounts	3,442	4,637
Net change in other accounts	5,146	-3,372
CASH PROVIDED BY OPERATING ACTIVITIES	*6,138*	*13,114*
CAPITAL INVESTMENT ACTIVITIES —		
Acquisitions of tangible capital assets	-4,619	-4,535
Proceeds from disposal of tangible capital assets	144	91
CASH USED BY CAPITAL INVESTMENT ACTIVITIES	*-4,475*	*-4,444*
INVESTING ACTIVITIES —		
Enterprise Crown corporation and other government business enterprise net repayments	1,861	2,034
Other loans, investments and advances issued	-8,139	-9,366
Other loans, investments and advances repayments	9,435	4,907
CASH PROVIDED OR USED (-) BY INVESTING ACTIVITIES	*3,157*	*-2,425*
TOTAL CASH GENERATED BEFORE FINANCING ACTIVITIES	*4,820*	*6,245*
FINANCING ACTIVITIES —		
Canadian currency borrowings issued	335,454	336,148
Canadian currency borrowings repayments	-335,969	-337,734
Foreign currencies borrowings issued	13,608	14,227
Foreign currencies borrowings repayments	-17,864	-14,826
CASH USED BY FINANCING ACTIVITIES	*-4,771*	*-2,185*
NET INCREASE IN CASH	**49**	**4,060**
CASH AT BEGINNING OF YEAR	*20,546*	*16,486*
CASH AT END OF YEAR	*20,595*	*20,546*
SUPPLEMENTARY INFORMATION		
Cash used for interest[1]	21,006	22,977

EXHIBIT 6–2 :

Cash Flow Statement of the Government of Canada

Of course, in all these examples it is difficult to be sure what is motivating management to make its decisions, which makes understanding the cash flow statement numbers more difficult.

One way for a cash flow statement user to overcome the difficulties caused by preparers who manage the timing of their cash flows is to examine cash flow statements for a number of periods. Many of these manipulations are simply moving cash flows among periods, which an alert user can observe by carefully examining a number of cash flow statements.

Another question about the cash flow statement is whether accrual accounting policy choices have an effect on cash flow. The answer to this question is no. Accrual accounting policy choices do not affect total cash flows for a period, but the choices may affect how the cash flows are classified in the cash flow statement. Note that this conclusion refers to the actual cash flows of a transaction, not the cash flow *implications* of an accounting choice. In other words, an accounting policy choice could affect the amount of tax an entity pays or the amount of bonus its managers receive.

For example, if an entity can choose between capitalizing a cash expenditure and amortizing it over a period of time, and expensing the expenditure when it is incurred, there will be an effect on CFO and cash from investing activities in the period that the expenditure is made. The reason is that if an expenditure is capitalized it is treated as an investing activity, whereas if it is expensed it is treated as CFO. Total cash flow is not affected, but the classification of cash flows is. By capitalizing an expenditure (rather than expensing it) managers can increase CFO. (We will examine a detailed example of this effect in Chapter 9.)

Solved Problem

This solved problem is another case analysis that will allow you to learn and develop the problem-solving skills that were introduced in Chapter 4. In the following situation, a student operating a small business comes to you for an explanation for the poor cash position of the business despite a good net income. You should attempt to solve the case on your own before reading the solution.

TRENDY TEE-SHIRTS INC.

In spring 2009, Denis Sonin decided that instead of finding a summer job working for someone else, he would start a business of his own to make money to finance his education. He decided that he would design and sell tee-shirts to the residents and the many vacationers visiting the area near where Denis lived.

Denis incorporated a company called Trendy Tee-Shirts Inc. (Trendy). He decided that he would operate the business out of a modified van that Trendy purchased. The van would allow him to move around from location to location so he could be where the customers were. Denis used his own computer to create designs and purchased equipment to print the designs on the shirts. To start up the business, Denis invested $6,000 of his own money and borrowed $10,000 from his parents. His parents told him that they had to have the money repaid in the next two to three years.

Denis thought that Trendy's first year in business was successful. He earned enough money to pay for his schooling and to take a nice vacation during the winter. In fact, Denis thought Trendy was so successful that he expanded the business in 2010. For 2010, Denis bought a second van that was operated by an employee and some additional equipment. He also increased the number of designs and the quantity of tee-shirts he produced, because in the summer of 2009 he found himself running short of shirts. Trendy financed the purchase of the second van and the equipment and was able to repay the loan quickly out of operating cash flows.

It is now October 2010 and Trendy has ceased operations for the year. Denis feels very satisfied with the performance of his business for the year. Trendy had net income of $14,250 for the year ended September 30, 2010. (Denis' father is a bookkeeper and he prepared an income statement for him.) However, Denis was shocked to find that when he finally got around to looking at Trendy's bank statements for the last few months (he didn't bother to look at them over the summer because he was so busy) that there was only $2,820 in the bank. There was not enough money to pay for school, to take another vacation, or to repay the bank. Trendy's cash flow statements for the last two years (shown in Exhibit 6–3) confirmed his fears—there isn't enough cash to meet his needs—and Denis can't figure out why.

Required:

a. Use the cash flow statement to explain to Denis how his business can be successful yet he doesn't have enough cash to meet his needs. Be sure to consider Trendy's activities and Denis' decisions for both 2009 and 2010.

b. Denis is thinking about going to the bank to borrow additional money. If you were the banker, would you lend money to Trendy? Explain.

<table>
<tr><td colspan="3">

EXHIBIT 6–3 :

Cash Flow Statements for Trendy Tee-Shirts Inc.

</td></tr>
</table>

TRENDY TEE-SHIRTS INC.
CASH FLOW STATEMENT FOR THE YEARS ENDED OCTOBER 31

	2010	2009
Operations		
Net income	$14,250	$9,430
Add: amortization expense	8,100	3,250
Less: increase in inventory	3,510	1,250
Cash from operations	18,840	11,430
Financing		
Loan from parents	(6,000)	10,000
Bank loan	7,500	
Van and equipment loan	(18,000)	
Van and equipment loan repayment	18,000	
Common stock issued		6,000
Dividends paid		(12,500)
Investing		
Purchase of van	17,000	11,000
Purchase of equipment	2,200	2,250
Increase in cash	1,140	1,680
Cash balance at the beginning of the year	1,680	0
Cash balance at the end of the year	$2,820	$1,680

Solution:

Part a)

Report to Denis Sonin regarding the performance of Trendy Tee Shirts Inc.

Dear Denis:

I am writing to try to clarify your confusion regarding the cash position of Trendy Tee Shirts Inc. compared with its accrual accounting performance. Your business performed well in 2010—earning an income of $14,250—but your cash position is poor—only $2,820 is on hand at the end of the year before paying yourself a dividend. To explain, it is first important to understand the difference between accrual accounting and cash flow. Accrual accounting reflects economic flows and economic activity, not just cash and the change in cash. As a result, the amount of income you report does not necessarily correspond with your business' cash flow.

During 2009, Trendy generated cash from operations—the cash an entity generates from its ordinary business activities—of $11,430. This means that Trendy generated from operations $11,430 in cash that could be used for purposes such as paying off debts, paying dividends, expanding operations, making investments in capital assets, and so on. This amount was different from your net income of $9,430 for two reasons. First, in the calculation of net income, an amortization expense of $3,320 was deducted. This amount does not involve an outlay of cash; it is simply part of the cost of the van and equipment that is deducted in calculating net income. The idea is to expense each year part of the cost of assets that help earn revenue over more than one year. (It is important to note that Trendy did spend $13,250 in cash on the van and equipment in 2009. I will have more to say about this shortly.) The second difference between cash from operations and net income was the $1,250 investment in inventory you had at the end of the year. This inventory had been paid for by the end of 2009 but it had not been expensed in 2009 because it had not been sold.

A similar analysis can be provided for 2010. Your cash from operations in 2010 was $18,840, a fair bit higher than in 2009. The same adjustments that I described above were needed to explain the difference between cash from operations and net income. Trendy's income statement reported $8,100 in non-cash amortization expense and an additional $3,510 was invested in inventory that was unsold as of the end of the year. The bottom line is that your business is generating decent cash flow. So why don't you have enough cash on hand to meet your needs?

There are several reasons. First, you have spent a significant amount of money purchasing assets that will help you make money over an extended period of time—i.e., the vans and the equipment. So, while your business is generating cash, you have had to invest a significant amount of money to get your business going. If you do not expand in future years, these assets will contribute to sales without costing you any cash. However, when a business first starts up or expands, cash outlays are required. In your first two years in business Trendy spent $32,450 on these assets.

Second, Trendy has $4,760 in cash invested in inventory. This seems like a lot of money to be tied up in inventory. Does this amount represent plain tee-shirts or ones that are designed? If it is the latter, will these shirts be saleable? Don't designs go out of style? If this is the case and the inventory cannot be sold, the income of your business may, in fact, be overstated because the cost of unsaleable inventory should be expensed. If the inventory is shirts without designs then it can be used in future, but it seems like a lot of money to be tied up in materials that can be easily purchased at any time. You might consider returning some of these goods if you can to free up some cash.

Third, in 2009 Trendy paid at $12,500 dividend, probably one that the company couldn't afford. In 2009 Trendy was able to pay for the van and equipment ($13,250) and for the dividend ($12,500) by generating cash from operations ($11,430), borrowing ($10,000), and from your own investment ($6,000). In 2010 you generated the cash to pay for the second van and some additional equipment ($19,200) and to repay the van and equipment loan and the loan from your parents ($24,000) by generating cash from operations ($18,840) and borrowing ($25,500). The problem in 2010 was that Trendy spent about the same amount of money as it generated from all sources. There was nothing left over to pay a dividend. In contrast, in 2009 the amount of money spent before paying the dividend was significantly less than the amount generated from operations and financing activities. In essence, your dividend in 2009 was paid for by borrowing from your parents and from the money you invested in Trendy to start with, not with cash from operations.

This should be a short-term problem for you. Assuming that your business continues to be as successful as it has been, and if you control your inventory, Trendy should be generating about $20,000 a year in cash from operations. That amount will allow you to pay off your $7,500 bank loan in 2011 and have plenty of cash available for your own needs. This also assumes that you will not be spending significant amounts of cash on additional assets such as vans and equipment. In the meantime, you will have to find an alternative source of cash to meet your personal needs this year. Perhaps you can borrow from your parents or obtain a bank loan.

Part b)

As a banker, I would give serious consideration to providing a loan to Trendy on the basis of its operations. Trendy generates a lot of cash and it would be able to support a loan—both the interest and principal—assuming that it continues to perform as it did in 2010. That said, tee-shirts can be a risky business. What is popular one year might not be popular another, so there are some risks should the business become less successful. On the other hand, over the years, tee-shirts have enjoyed sustained popularity so this fact mitigates some of the risk. Even if the business were to contract by 25 percent, there would still be significant cash flow to support the loan. Trendy has its two vans and the equipment along with the inventory to use as collateral for a loan. It is not clear, however, how much cash those items would raise if they had to be sold. An estimate would have to be made to determine the amount. Of significant concern is that Trendy does not really needed cash for the business. Assuming that no additional purchases of capital assets are required (no additional expansion is planned) and that little cash is needed for working capital (for example to purchase inventory and supplies) the main purpose of the loan would be to allow Trendy to pay a dividend. If that is the case, the amount of equity that Denis would have in the business would be $7,180 (initial equity investment + net incomes − dividends = $6,000 + $9,430 + $14,250 − $12,500 − $10,000 (assuming an additional bank loan of $10,000)). This would be in comparison with liabilities of $21,500 ($4,000 + $7,500 + $10,000 (assuming an additional bank loan of $10,000)). This represents a relatively small amount of equity relative to debt (debt-to-equity ratio = $21,500/$7,180 = 2.99). If Denis neglects his business for some reason in the future or chooses not to continue in business, our bank and the other lenders stand to lose much more than Denis does (although Denis' parents will lose $4,000 of their money).

All told, I would be inclined to recommend a loan to Trendy. I think that the business has shown an ability to generate cash in the past and stands to do so in the future. I recommend that, if any assets have not been secured against the other bank loan, we should take those assets as security against our loan. In addition, we should obtain personal guarantees from Denis and from his parents, if possible. This will provide the bank with additional protection. Finally, the terms of the loan should prevent Trendy from purchasing additional capital assets until the bank loans have been reduced or paid off. This is appropriate because additional purchases will use up cash from operations and reduce or eliminate cash needed to pay off the bank loan. Additional purchases will also result in a repetition of the current situation where Denis is not able to draw enough cash from Trendy to meet his personal needs. In addition, further expansion may add to the bank's risk since it is not known whether there is enough demand for more of Trendy's products and it is not clear whether Denis will be able to effectively manage an expanded business.

Insight

Notice that the focus of the discussion banker's response in part b) is on what will happen, not what has happened. This is very important to keep in mind. Historical information can sometimes be a useful basis for predicting future cash flows (and earnings) but the future will usually not be the same as the past. As a result, the bank must consider "what if" scenarios. What if sales decrease? What if profit margins decrease? Without this type of assessment, it is difficult for the bank to evaluate the risks that it is facing. Also recognize that the banker's response is only one of many possible ones. For example, some bankers might decline to make the loan because it is for personal rather than business reasons. That conclusion would be fine but it would still have to be supported by a similar type of analysis as in part b.

SUMMARY OF KEY POINTS

▶ **LO 1** Cash flow is essential for an entity. Without adequate cash flow, an entity will not be able to operate because it will not be able to meet its obligations as they come due. If an entity cannot generate enough cash from its business activities to meet its needs, it will have to raise cash by borrowing, selling shares, or selling assets. Cash flow is often not given enough attention by stakeholders evaluating an entity. The standard measure of performance under accrual accounting, earnings, is not designed to reflect flows of cash, but rather economic activity. It is crucial not to ignore cash flow when analyzing an entity. Cash flow is not a better or worse measure than earnings; it's just a different measure of performance than earnings and each has its role to play.

▶ **LO 2** The cycle of how an entity begins with cash, invests in resources, provides goods or services to customers using those resources, and then collects cash from customers is called the cash cycle. Entities usually have to invest cash in resources before cash is received from customers— there is almost always a lag between the expenditure of cash and the receipt of cash.

▶ **LO 3** The cash flow statement provides information on an entity's historical cash flows. Cash flows in the cash flow statement are grouped into three categories: cash from operations (CFO), cash from investing activities, and cash from financing activities. CFO can be calculated and reported in two ways on the cash flow statement. The indirect method reconciles net income to CFO by adjusting net income for non-cash amounts that are included in the calculation of net income and for operating cash flows that are not included in the calculation of net income. The direct method reports CFO by showing cash collections and cash disbursements related to operations during the period.

▶ **LO 4** Some argue that one of the attractions of cash accounting information over accrual accounting information is that cash accounting information cannot be managed or manipulated. Cash accounting information cannot be manipulated the same way as accrual information, where preparers must decide the timing of revenue and expense recognition. Cash information is "cleaner" in the sense that a transaction has an impact on cash flow only if cash is involved in the transaction. However, preparers can manipulate cash information by influencing the timing of cash flows. Also, some accrual accounting choices made by preparers affect the classification of cash flows in the cash flow statement, but not the actual amount of the cash flow.

KEY TERMS

bank overdraft, p. 295

capital expenditure, p. 306

cash cycle, p. 287

cash flow statement, p. 293

cash from financing activities, p. 293

cash from investing activities, p. 293

cash from operations (CFO), p. 293

development-stage company, p. 307

direct method (of calculating cash from operations), p. 297

free cash flow, p. 307

indirect method (of calculating cash from operations), p. 297

line of credit, p. 295

start-up company, p. 307

SIMILAR TERMS

The left column gives alternative terms that are sometimes used for the accounting terms introduced in this chapter, which are listed in the right column.

statement of cash flows, statement of changes in financial position   **cash flow statement, p. 293**

cash flow from operating activities   **cash from operations, p. 293**

ASSIGNMENT MATERIALS

Questions

Q6-1.   Explain the difference between cash accounting and accrual accounting.

Q6-2.   Why is the cash flow statement included in the general purpose financial statement package? Explain your answer fully.

Q6-3.   What are some of the possible components that can be included in the definition of "cash" in the cash flow statement? Explain the usefulness and limitations of including each of the components in the definition.

Q6-4.   Explain each of the following:
a. Payables deferral period.
b. Inventory self-financing period.
c. Inventory conversion period.
d. Receivables conversion period.

Q6-5.   What is cash from operations?

Q6-6.   Which should be more important to a shareholder of a company: cash flow or net income? Explain your answer.

Q6-7. Why is amortization added back to net income when cash from operations is calculated using the indirect method?

Q6-8. Why are losses added back to and gains subtracted from net income when cash from operations is calculated using the indirect method?

Q6-9. What does it mean when an entity has negative cash from operations? What are the reasons for negative cash from operations? Why is negative cash from operations cause for concern? Is negative cash from operations necessarily bad news for an entity? Explain.

Q6-10. Which should be more important to the management of an entity: cash flow or income? Explain your answer.

Q6-11. Explain the three types of activities that are reported in a cash flow statement. Give examples of each and explain the classification for each example.

Q6-12. New businesses frequently fail because of poor cash flow. Explain why you think new businesses have this problem.

Q6-13. What are the two methods for calculating and reporting cash from operations? Explain how each arrives at cash from operations. As a user of financial statements, which method of calculating cash from operations would you prefer to see in a cash flow statement? Explain.

Q6-14. How is interest paid classified in a cash flow statement prepared according to GAAP? Does this treatment make sense? Explain.

Q6-15. How are dividends paid classified in a cash flow statement prepared according to GAAP? Does this treatment make sense? Explain.

Q6-16. What information does the cash flow statement provide to users that is not in the income statement?

Q6-17. What is the cash cycle? Describe the cash cycle for a wine maker.

Q6-18. An entity has a very profitable year, yet its cash flow and cash from operations are negative. Explain how this can happen.

Q6-19. An entity reports a loss for the year. Explain how the entity could have positive cash flow and positive cash from operations in that year.

Q6-20. What does the term "cash" in the cash flow statement refer to? Explain.

Q6-21. Why does an increase in accounts receivable imply a decrease in cash from operations? Explain.

Q6-22. Why does a decrease in inventory imply an increase in cash from operations? Explain.

Q6-23. How is it possible for managers to manipulate the information in the cash flow statement?

Q6-24. What type of manipulation of accounting information do you think is more likely to cause operational problems for an entity: the manipulations that are done with accrual accounting, or the manipulations that are done with cash accounting? Explain your answer.

Q6-25. Managers often receive bonuses based on the net income of the entities they manage. Do you think that it would be better to use cash from operations as a basis to award bonuses rather than net income? Explain your answer.

Q6-26. What objectives of financial reporting does the cash flow statement serve? Explain.

Q6-27. One way for a biotechnology, software, or other high-technology company to increase cash from operations would be to reduce spending on research. Explain why reducing spending on research (which is expensed when incurred according to GAAP) would increase cash from operations. Explain why reducing spending on research is potentially a serious problem for these types of entities. Respond by discussing the business implications of reducing spending on research.

Q6-28. In a recent negotiation between labour and management of a major corporation, management argued that the company's low earnings made it imprudent to grant the requested wage increase. The labour union disagreed and argued that the company had ample resources to meet the wage demands of the union. What do you think might have been the basis of the union's argument? Do you think that it is adequate to base the ability of a company to grant a wage increase only on net income? Explain.

Q6-29. Give examples of the circumstances that could cause cash flow problems for an airline.

Q6-30. Explain why growing companies sometimes face cash flow problems.

Exercises

E6-1.   (Calculating the cash lag, LO 2) Dickens Tailor Shop (Dickens) makes tailored-to-measure suits, jackets, and pants for men and women. Customers who are interested in purchasing tailored-to-measure clothing make an appointment with one of Dickens' tailors, at which time the customer decides on the style of clothing he or she wishes to buy, selects an appropriate fabric, and is measured by the tailor. Dickens keeps a large selection of fabrics so customers can see the actual fabric their clothing will be made from. A bolt of fabric is, on average, held in inventory for seven months before it is used to make a garment. Dickens pays for its fabric 30 days from the time it is received from the supplier. The time from a customer's first appointment to the completion and delivery of the garment is, on average, 45 days. Customers receive an invoice when the garment is delivered and payment is received from the customer, on average, 20 days from the time of delivery.

Required:

Calculate the following for Dickens Tailor Shop:
a. Payables deferral period.
b. Inventory self-financing period.
c. Inventory conversion period.
d. Receivables conversion period.
e. Number of days between receiving inventory from suppliers and receiving cash from customers.

E6-2.   (The effect of amortization on cash from operations, LO 1, 3) In 2011, Anyox Ltd. (Anyox) reported net income of $200,000. All revenues and expenses were in cash, except for a $30,000 amortization expense.

Required:

a. Calculate cash from operations for Anyox in 2011.
b. Suppose that instead of a $30,000 amortization expense in 2011, Anyox expensed $44,000 for amortization. Assume that all other revenues and expenses remained the same. What would Anyox's net income be in 2011? What would its cash from operations be in 2011? Explain the reasons for any differences or similarities in your answer for when the amortization expense was $30,000 and when it was $44,000.

E6-3.   (The effect of asset write-offs on cash from operations, LO 1, 3) In the year ended December 31, 2008 Hexham Inc. (Hexham) reported net income of $7,400,000, which included a write off of $2,000,000 of company assets. During 2008 accounts receivable increased by $200,000, inventory increased by $350,000, and accounts payable decreased by $30,000. Amortization expense in 2008 was $556,000.

Required:

a. What journal entry did Hexham make to record the write-off of the assets?

b. Calculate cash from operations using the indirect method.

c. Suppose that at the last minute, Hexham's management decided to delay writing off the assets from its books:
  i. What would Hexham's net income be in 2008?
  ii. What would Hexham's cash from operations be in 2008?

d. Explain the differences you found between what net income Hexham originally reported and the net income you calculated under c(i).

e. Explain the differences you found between the cash from operations numbers you calculated under b and c(ii).

E6-4. **(Classifying transactions for a cash flow statement, LO 3)** For each of the following transactions and economic events, classify each as an operating, investing, or financing cash flow, or whether the item has no effect on cash flow. Also, indicate whether each item increases or decreases cash.

a. Equipment is purchased for cash.

b. Capital assets are amortized.

c. Cash dividends are paid to shareholders.

d. Interest is paid on a bond.

e. Accounts receivable are collected from customers.

f. Land is purchased in exchange for shares in the company.

g. Cash is obtained from a lender in exchange for a long-term note payable.

h. A bank loan is repaid.

i. Suppliers of inventory are paid in cash.

j. Inventory is purchased on credit.

E6-5. **(Classifying transactions for a cash flow statement, LO 3)** Mamalilaculla Ltd. (Mamalilaculla) is a small retail jewellery store. For each of the following, specify whether the item should be classified as an operating, financing, or investing cash flow, whether the item represents a cash inflow or outflow, and the amount of the transaction. Explain your reasoning.

a. Mamalilaculla paid $20,000 cash for a shipment of cut diamonds for engagement rings.

b. Mamalilaculla's amortization expense for the year was $8,000.

c. Mamalilaculla purchased new display cases for the store for $13,500 cash.

d. Mamalilaculla sold a number of old display cases for $3,500. The loss on the sale of the display cases was $2,000.

e. Mamalilaculla sold a pendant to a customer for $2,000. The customer paid with a Visa credit card.

f. Mamalilaculla's shareholder purchased additional shares of the corporation for $100,000. The cash will be used to purchase additional inventory.

g. Mamalilaculla repaid a $50,000 loan from the bank.

E6-6. **(Determining missing information, LO 3)** Calculate the missing information (indicated by shaded areas) from the following cash flow statements:

Cash from (used by)	Company 1	Company 2	Company 3	Company 4	Company 5
Operations	$ 30,000	($ 36,000)	$	$ 48,000	$
Investing activities	(13,500)		1,500	(30,000)	(15,000)
Financing activities		45,000	(30,000)	(18,000)	6,000
Net increase (decrease) in cash	3,000	(15,000)	18,000		(24,000)

E6-7. (**Calculating cash from operations, LO 3**) You are provided the following information about Joggins Inc. (Joggins) for 2010:

Net income	$ 437,500
Accounts receivable on January 1, 2010	1,375,000
Accounts receivable on December 31, 2010	1,562,500
Inventory on January 1, 2010	1,750,000
Inventory on December 31, 2010	1,525,000
Accounts payable on January 1, 2010	1,187,500
Accounts payable on December 31, 2010	1,437,500
Amortization expense	262,500

Required:

Calculate cash from operations for Joggins for 2010.

E6-8. (**Organize information into a cash flow statement, LO 3**) Use the following information to prepare a well-organized cash flow statement for Quesnel Ltd. for the year ended December 31, 2009. Use the information to calculate net income for the year.

Amortization	$ 258,000
Cash and cash equivalents at the beginning of the year	100,000
Cash and cash equivalents at the end of the year	519,000
Decrease in prepaids	15,000
Decrease in taxes payable	35,000
Dividends	75,000
Increase in accounts payable	65,000
Increase in accounts receivable	75,000
Increase in inventory	110,000
Issuance of common shares	500,000
Issuance of long-term debt	250,000
Loss on the sale of land	100,000
Net Income	?
New bank loans	125,000
Proceeds from the sale of property, plant, and equipment	356,000
Purchase of property, plant, and equipment	1,750,000
Retirement of long-term debt	410,000
Sale of long-term investments	205,000

E6-9. (**Adjustments to net income when using the indirect method of calculating cash from operations, LO 3**) Tracadie Inc. (Tracadie) uses the indirect method to calculate and report cash from operations in its cash flow statement. For each of the following items, indicate whether the item would be added to net income, deducted from net income, or not be relevant when calculating cash from operations.
a. Loss on the sale of office furniture used in Tracadie's executive offices.
b. Dividends paid.
c. Purchase of a building.
d. Increase in accounts payable.
e. Decrease in inventory.
f. Sale of land.

g. Decrease in accrued liabilities.

h. Increase in long-term debt.

i. Gain on the sale of equipment that was used by Tracadie to provide its services.

j. Increase in accounts receivables.

k. Amortization expense.

E6-10. **(Calculate cash from operations using the indirect method, LO 1, 3)** Consider the following non-cash current operating account information of Yahk Ltd. (Yahk):

	2010	2009		2010	2009
Accounts receivable	$ 60,000	$ 47,500	Accounts payable	$130,000	$117,500
Inventory	187,500	217,500	Wages payable	22,500	30,000
Prepaids	25,000	20,000	Taxes payable	40,000	25,000
			Interest payable	23,750	32,500
Total current operating assets	$272,500	$285,000	Total current operating liabilities	$216,250	$205,000

Yahk's net income for 2010 was $180,000. In addition, Yahk reported an amortization expense of $50,000 and a loss on the sale of capital assets of $25,000.

Required:

a. Calculate cash from operations for Yahk using the indirect method and prepare the cash from operations section of Yahk's cash flow statement.

b. Explain why cash from operations is different from net income in 2010.

E6-11. **(Calculate cash collections using the direct method, LO 3)** In its April 30, 2010 annual report, Ebbsfleet Inc. (Ebbsfleet) reported a beginning Accounts Receivable balance of $363,000 and an ending Accounts Receivable balance of $456,000. Ebbsfleet reported Credit Sales for the year ended April 30, 2010 of $4,626,000.

Required:

Calculate the amount of cash Ebbsfleet collected from customers during fiscal 2010.

E6-12. **(Calculate cash payments using the direct method, LO 3)** In its May 31, 2009 annual report, Maloneck Ltd. (Maloneck) reported that it had Inventory of $175,000 and Accounts Payable of $104,000 on May 31, 2008, and Inventory of $196,000 and Accounts Payable of $122,000 on May 31, 2009. Maloneck's income statement for the year ended May 31, 2009 reported Cost of Goods Sold of $1,220,000.

Required:

Calculate the amount of cash that Maloneck paid to suppliers for purchases of inventory during fiscal 2009. Assume that accounts payable pertain only to the purchase of inventory on credit.

E6-13. **(Calculate cash payments made to employees using direct method, LO 3)** In its August 31, 2011 annual report, Pitquah Corp. (Pitquah) reported Wages Payable on August 31, 2010 of $87,500, and Wages Payable on August 31, 2011 of $112,500. Pitquah's income statement reports Wages Expense of $1,173,000.

Required:

Calculate the amount of cash that Pitquah paid in wages to employees in fiscal 2011.

Problems

P6-1. **(Calculating missing information about balance sheet accounts, LO 3)** The following general equation can be used to determine missing information about balance sheet accounts:

Ending balance in the account	=	Beginning balance in the account	+	Transactions and economic events that increase the balance in the account	−	Transactions and economic events that decrease the balance in the account

Use the above equation to determine the missing information in each of the following independent situations. For each case, assume that the year end is December 31. You can also use an accounting equation spreadsheet to obtain the missing information.

a. On January 1, 2008 Ewart Ltd. (Ewart) had $350,000 of Inventory on hand. During 2008 Ewart sold $1,040,000 of inventory and purchased $1,230,000 of inventory. How much inventory did Ewart have on December 31, 2008?

b. On January 1, 2009 Peno Inc. (Peno) had $1,000,000 of Accounts Receivable and on December 31, 2009 it had $900,000 of Accounts Receivable. During 2009 Peno collected $4,900,000 from customers. What amount of credit sales did Peno make during 2009?

c. Noir Inc. (Noir) capitalizes its store opening costs and amortizes them over five years. On January 1, 2008 the balance in Noir's unamortized Store Opening Costs account on the balance sheet was $150,000. On December 31, 2008 the balance in the account was $170,000. During 2008 the amortization expense for store opening costs was $40,000. What amount of store opening costs did Noir capitalize to the Store Opening Cost account on the balance sheet during 2008? Assume that Noir does not have a separate contra-asset account for accumulating amortization for this account.

d. On December 31, 2009 Hythe Ltd. (Hythe) owed its employees $44,000. During 2009 Hythe's employees earned $400,000 and were paid $420,000. How much did Hythe owe its employees on December 31, 2008?

e. Cadzow Inc. (Cadzow) purchases all of its inventory on credit. On January 1, 2008 Cadzow had $2,500,000 of Inventory on hand and on December 31, 2008 it had $3,000,000 of Inventory. Cost of Goods Sold during 2008 was $10,700,000. The balances in Cadzow's Accounts Payable account on January 1, 2008 and December 31, 2008 were $1,900,000 and $2,200,000 respectively. How much did Cadzow pay its suppliers during 2008?

P6-2. **(Calculating missing information about balance sheet accounts, LO 3)** The following general equation can be used to determine missing information about balance sheet accounts:

Ending balance in the account	=	Beginning balance in the account	+	Transactions and economic events that increase the balance in the account	−	Transactions and economic events that decrease the balance in the account

Use this equation to determine the missing information in each of the following independent situations. For each case, assume that the year end is June 30. You can also use an accounting equation spreadsheet to obtain the missing information.

a. On July 1, 2008 Zincton Ltd. (Zincton) had $975,000 of Inventory on hand. During fiscal 2009 Zincton sold $2,940,000 of Inventory and purchased $2,445,000 of inventory. How much inventory did Zincton have on June 30, 2009?

b. On July 1, 2007 Winsloe Inc. (Winsloe) had $1,110,000 of Accounts Receivable and on June 30, 2008 it had $1,260,000 of accounts receivable. During fiscal 2008 Winsloe collected $6,450,000 from customers. What amount of credit sales did Winsloe make during fiscal 2008?

c. Union Inc. (Union) capitalizes its store opening costs and amortizes them over five years. On July 1, 2008 the balance in Union's unamortized Store Opening Costs account on the balance sheet was $345,000. On June 30, 2009 the balance in the account was $285,000. During fiscal 2009 the amortization expense for store opening costs was $90,000. What amount of store opening costs did Union capitalize to the Store Opening Costs account on the balance sheet during fiscal 2009? Assume that Union does not have a separate contra-asset account for accumulating amortization for this account.

d. On June 30, 2008 Sawbill Ltd. (Sawbill) owed its employees $456,000. During fiscal 2008, Sawbill's employees earned $3,750,000 and were paid $3,360,000. How much did Sawbill owe its employees on July 1, 2007?

e. Otter Inc. (Otter) purchases all of its inventory on credit. On July 1, 2008 Otter had $750,000 of Inventory on hand and on June 30, 2009 it had $600,000 of Inventory. Cost of Goods Sold during fiscal 2009 was $2,850,000. The balances in Otter's Accounts Payable account on July 1, 2008 and June 30, 2009 were $405,000 and $309,000 respectively. How much did Otter pay its suppliers during fiscal 2009?

P6-3. (Interpreting cash flow patterns, LO 1, 3) Viewmont Inc. is a small manufacturing company. You have been presented with the following summarized information from Viewmont Inc.'s cash flow statement:

Cash from operations	$(1,247,500)
Cash from investing activities	(3,675,000)
Cash from financing activities	5,098,000

Required:

Examine the cash flow pattern for Viewmont Inc. What does the pattern say about the situation that the company finds itself in? (That is, consider what type of circumstances would give rise to a situation in which CFO and investing activities would have net cash outflows and financing activities would have a net cash inflow.)

P6-4. (Interpreting cash flow patterns, LO 1, 3) You have been presented with the following summarized information from Inverness Ltd.'s cash flow statement:

Cash from operations	$5,354,000
Cash from investing activities	(7,580,000)
Cash from financing activities	2,500,000

Required:

Examine the cash flow pattern for Dunvegan Ltd. What does the pattern say about the situation that the company finds itself in? (That is, consider what type of circumstances would give rise to a situation in which CFO and financing activities would have net cash inflows and investing activities would have a net cash outflow.)

P6-5. (Interpreting cash flow patterns, LO 1, 3) You have been presented with the following summarized information from Dunvegan Ltd.'s cash flow statement:

Cash from operations	$4,250,000
Cash from investing activities	(2,450,000)
Cash from financing activities	(1,610,000)

Examine the cash flow pattern for Dunvegan Ltd. What does the pattern say about the situation that the company finds itself in? (That is, consider what type of circumstances would give rise to a situation in which CFO would have a net cash inflow and investing and financing activities would have net cash outflows.)

P6-6. (**Organize information into a cash flow statement, LO 3**) Use the following alphabetical list of information to prepare a well-organized cash flow statement for Winkler Ltd. for the year ended July 31, 2010. The bookkeeper who prepared the information wasn't sure about exactly what information to provide to you so there may be information that should not be included in the cash flow statement.

Accounts receivable	$ 560,000
Amortization	852,000
Cash and cash equivalents at the beginning of the year	450,500
Cash and cash equivalents at the end of the year	9,500
Decrease in accounts payable	44,000
Decrease in accounts receivable	51,000
Dividends paid	750,000
Dividends declared but not paid	350,000
Gain on the sale of equipment	225,000
Increase (decrease) in cash	(441,000)
Increase in inventory	96,000
Increase in prepaids	12,000
Increase in taxes payable	77,000
Issuance of common shares	1,000,000
Issuance of long-term debt	3,000,000
Land	1,000,000
Loss on the sale of land	100,000
Net Income	750,000
Proceeds from the sale of property, plant, and equipment	356,000
Purchase of long-term investments	1,355,000
Purchase of property, plant, and equipment	1,750,000
Repayment of bank loans	955,000
Retirement of long-term debt	1,750,000
Shares exchanged for equipment	500,000
Write-down of assets	310,000

P6-7. (**Calculating cash from operations using both the direct and indirect methods, LO 1, 3, 4**) You are provided with the following balance sheet information and summarized income statement for Rivulet Inc.:

Rivulet Inc.
Current Operating Assets and Liabilities as of December 31, 2009 and 2010

	2010	2009		2010	2009
Accounts receivable	$248,000	$202,000	Accounts payable	$384,000	$434,000
Inventory	550,000	630,000	Accrued liabilities	98,000	64,000

Rivulet Inc.
Income Statement For the Year Ended December 31, 2010

Revenue	$2,150,000
Cost of goods sold	1,064,000
Gross margin	1,086,000
Other expenses	784,000
Amortization expense	430,000
Loss on sale of capital assets	50,000
Net loss	$ 178,000

All sales are credit sales. Accounts Payable pertains exclusively to the purchase of inventory and Accrued Liabilities pertains exclusively to Other Expenses.

Required:

a. Prepare Rivulet's cash from operations section of the cash flow statement using the direct method.

b. Prepare Rivulet's cash from operations section of the cash flow statement using the indirect method.

c. Which method do you think is more informative to users of the cash flow statement? Explain. What information is available when the direct method is used that is not available when the indirect method is used?

d. Explain the difference between net income and cash from operations. Why did Rivulet have a loss on its income statement but positive cash from operations?

e. What are the implications of having a loss on the income statement but positive cash from operations?

P6-8. **(Calculating cash from operations using both the direct and indirect methods, LO 1, 3)** You are provided the following balance sheet information and summarized income statement for Katrime Ltd.:

Katrime Ltd.
Current Operating Assets and Liabilities as of May 31, 2010 and 2011

	2011	2010		2011	2010
Accounts receivable	$427,000	$278,000	Accounts payable	$392,000	$315,000
Inventory	818,000	566,000	Wages payable	72,000	85,000
Prepaid insurance	72,000	35,000			

Katrime Ltd.
Income Statement For the Year Ended May 31, 2011

Revenue	$1,381,000
Cost of goods sold	735,500
Gross margin	645,500
Wages expense	(333,000)
Amortization expense	(42,500)
Insurance expense	(30,000)
Other expenses	(137,500)
Gain on sale of capital assets	27,500
Net income	$130,000

All sales are credit sales. Accounts payable pertains exclusively to the purchase of inventory. Other Expenses were fully paid in cash during the year.

Required:

a. Prepare Katrime's cash from operations section of the cash flow statement using the direct method.

b. Prepare Katrime's cash from operations section of the cash flow statement using the indirect method.
c. Which method do you think is more informative to users of the cash flow statement? Explain. What information is available when the direct method is used that is not available when the indirect method is used?
d. Explain the difference between net income and cash from operations. Why did Katrime have a profit on its income statement but negative cash from operations?
e. What are the implications of showing a profit on the income statement but negative cash from operations?

P6-9. (Interpreting the cash flow statement, LO 1, 3) Chilliwack Ltd. (Chilliwack) is a small specialty lumber mill located in the interior of British Columbia. The company is private and has one shareholder. Chilliwack has been very successful in the last few years with high demand from both the Canadian and international markets. The company has been unable to keep up with customer demand and is concerned that it will be losing business to competitors, even those that have inferior products. Chilliwack's sales have increased over the last few years by almost 300 percent and profits have increased from $75,000 in 2005 to $1.2 million in the year ended December 31, 2009. Despite its success, Chilliwack is using up cash very quickly and management is worried that it will not have enough cash to operate successfully. You have been provided with Chilliwack's cash flow statements for the years ended December 31, 2008 and 2009. Prepare a report to management explaining the reasons for the company's cash problems despite its profitability. Management has also asked for any suggestions you might have to improve the situation.

Required:

Prepare the report.

Chilliwack Ltd.
Statement of Cash Flows
For the Years Ended December 31,

	2009	2008
Net Income	$1,200,000	$825,000
Items not affecting cash: Amortization	250,000	200,000
	1,450,000	1,025,000
Changes in non-cash working capital accounts		
Accounts receivable	(350,000)	(200,000)
Inventory	(410,000)	(290,000)
Prepaids	7,000	(15,000)
Accounts payable and accrued liabilities	175,000	125,000
	872,000	645,000
Financing activities		
Issue of long-term debt	1,000,000	
Bank loans	425,000	500,000
Repayment of long-term debt	(225,000)	(225,000)
Issue of shares		1,500,000
Dividends paid	(100,000)	(100,000)
	1,100,000	1,675,000
Investing activities		
Purchase of plant, property, and equipment	(2,750,000)	(1,250,000)
	(2,750,000)	(1,250,000)
Increase in cash and cash equivalents	(778,000)	1,070,000
Cash and cash equivalents, beginning of year	1,220,000	150,000
Cash and cash equivalents, end of year	$442,000	$1,220,000

P6-10. **(Interpreting the cash flow statement, LO 1, 3)** Iqaluit Water Company Ltd. (Iqaluit) is a bottler and marketer of bottled water. Iqaluit was established many years ago in response to the demand for healthful, refreshing drinks. Iqaluit sells its products to distributors in Canada, the United States, and Europe. In the last few years, Iqaluit's performance has deteriorated significantly in the face of increased competition and high marketing and promotion costs. Management is concerned that the company is in financial distress and may be headed for serious problems that will threaten its survival. Some of Iqaluit's shareholders have approached you for advice about the company's status. They have provided you with Iqaluit's most recent cash flow statements and have asked you to prepare a report that addresses the prospects for the company.

Required:

Prepare the report.

Iqaluit Water Company Ltd.
Statement of Cash Flows For the Years Ended July 31,

Operations	2010	2009
Net Loss	($512,000)	($952,000)
Items not affecting cash		
Amortization	278,500	310,000
Losses on disposal of assets	110,000	225,000
Write-down of assets	150,000	95,000
	26,500	(322,000)
Changes in non-cash working capital accounts		
Accounts receivable	208,000	242,000
Inventory	150,000	90,000
Prepaids	85,000	101,000
Accounts payable and accrued liabilities	(88,000)	(110,000)
	381,500	1,000
Financing activities		
Issue of short-term debt	300,000	225,000
Bank loans	425,000	500,000
Repayment of long-term debt	(450,000)	(450,000)
Dividends paid	(1,000,000)	(1,000,000)
	(725,000)	(725,000)
Investing activities		
Purchase of plant, property, and equipment	(72,000)	(12,000)
Proceeds from sale of plant, property, and equipment	950,000	485,000
Purchase of long-term investments	(625,000)	(85,000)
	253,000	388,000
Decrease in cash and cash equivalents	(90,500)	(336,000)
Cash and cash equivalents, beginning of year	139,000	475,000
Cash and cash equivalents, end of year	$48,500	$139,000

P6-11. **(Preparing and interpreting financial statements, LO 1, 3)** Souvenirs-On-The-Go Ltd. (Souvenirs-On-The-Go) is a mobile souvenir stand that moves around the city to be "where the action is." Souvenirs-On-The-Go was started this summer by Evan Shayne as a way to earn money in the summer months to help pay for his education. Evan registered his corporation and contributed $20,000 of his savings to Souvenirs-On-The-Go in exchange for shares in the company. Souvenirs-On-The-Go borrowed $5,000 from Evan's parents to provide additional cash. Souvenirs-On-The-Go purchased a used cart for $15,000 cash. If it is successful, Evan hopes to operate Souvenirs-On-The-Go for four years, until he graduates from university. Souvenirs-On-The-Go obtained a municipal vending license for $500 that allows the cart to operate in designated areas around the city. The license is valid for two years.

Over the summer, Souvenirs-On-The-Go sold $25,400 in souvenirs, all for cash. Souvenirs-On-The-Go purchased $10,200 worth of souvenirs, including $1,800 in souvenirs that were not paid for by the end of the summer. Souvenirs-On-The-Go incurred $1,050 of maintenance and repairs on the cart and $2,100 of miscellaneous expenses during the summer. As of the end of the summer, the maintenance and repairs had been fully paid for and $500 of the miscellaneous expenses was still owed to the suppliers. At the end of the summer, unsold souvenirs costing $1,200 remained. However, Evan thinks he will be able to sell them next summer. Also, Souvenirs-On-The-Go owes Evan's parents $600 in interest.

Required:

The summer is now over and Evan is back at school. Evan has not yet had a chance to evaluate the performance of Souvenirs-On-The-Go. Evan has asked you to prepare an income statement, balance sheet, and cash flow statement for the summer just ended. Use the financial statements you prepared to assess the financial situation of Souvenirs-On-The-Go. Your assessment should consider information from all of the financial statements. (To prepare the cash flow statement, identify Souvenirs-On-The-Go cash transactions and organize them into the different categories (operating, investing, financing).)

P6-12. **(The effect of accrual accounting policies on the cash flow statement, LO 5)** The chief accountant of Phidias Publications Ltd. (Phidias) is thinking about how accrual accounting policy choices affect the cash flow statement. Phidias publishes a number of newspapers in mid-sized Canadian communities. One of the key success factors of the newspaper business is the circulation of the papers. Phidias spends a significant amount of money recruiting and maintaining subscribers. The accountant thinks that sound arguments could be made for both expensing the cost of recruiting and maintaining subscribers when they are incurred, and capitalizing the costs and amortizing them over a number of years.

The accountant has prepared the following cash flow statement, which is complete except for how to account for the cost of recruiting and maintaining subscribers. During 2010 Phidias spent $67,500 recruiting and maintaining subscribers.

Phidias Publications Ltd.
Cash Flow Statement For the Year Ended December 31, 2010

Cash from operations:		
Cash collected from customers	$1,173,000	
Cash paid to employees	(562,500)	
Cash paid to suppliers	(452,500)	
Cash paid in interest	(26,000)	
Cash from operations		$132,000
Cash from investing activities:		
Proceeds from sale of capital assets	55,000	
Purchase of capital assets	(150,000)	
Cash from investing activities		(95,000)
Cash from financing activities:		
Dividends paid	(37,500)	
Repayment of bank loan	(87,500)	
Proceeds of long-term debt	162,500	
Cash from financing activities		37,500
Cash generated during the year		74,500
Cash on hand on December 31, 2009		18,500
Cash on hand on December 31, 2010		$93,000

Required:

a. Present arguments for and against the two proposed accounting treatments for the cost of recruiting and maintaining subscribers.

b. Explain the effect of the two accounting alternatives on Phidias' income statement.

c. Complete Phidias' cash flow statement assuming that cash spent on recruiting and maintaining subscribers is expensed when incurred.

d. Complete Phidias' cash flow statement assuming that cash spent on recruiting and maintaining subscribers is capitalized and amortized over three years.

e. Discuss the difference between the statements you prepared in (c) and (d) above. What are the implications of the different treatments to the underlying cash flow and liquidity of Phidias?

f. Which cash flow statement do you think the managers of Phidias would prefer? Explain.

P6-13. **(Accrual and cash flow information analysis, LO 1, 3)** In December 2009 Alexander Bedlam organized Soldit Properties Ltd. (Soldit), a company that sells real estate on behalf of clients. Alexander exchanged $40,000 in cash for 1,000 common shares of Soldit. When business actually began in January 2010 Alexander was very busy—so busy that he did not bother keeping any records. At the end of the month, Alexander noticed that he had less than the $40,000 in cash that he started business with. He did not understand how he could have been so busy and still have lost money. Alexander has come to you for help to understand his situation. From your conversation with Alexander, you obtain the following information:

i. During the month, five properties were sold with a sales value of $1,200,000. Soldit earns a commission of 5 percent of the sales value of the property.

ii. Sales assistants sold three of the five properties sold in January. These three properties had a total sales value of $800,000. Sales assistants receive a commission of 4 percent of the sales value of the properties they sell.

iii. The commission on one of the properties has not yet been received. The client owes Soldit $16,000.

iv. During January Soldit made the following payments in cash:

Salaries	$4,400
Commissions to sales assistants	32,000
Down payment on car	6,000
Rent	2,400
Purchase of computer, fax, and copier	4,000
Utilities	1,000

v. Soldit has taken delivery of the car and the computer, fax, and copier. The price of the car was $40,000 and the price of the computer, fax, and copier was $10,000.

Required:

a. Prepare an income statement for the month of January for Soldit.

b. Prepare a cash flow statement for January for Soldit. (To prepare the statement, organize the amounts into the different cash flow categories.)

c. How did Soldit perform in January? How should Alexander interpret these two statements? Did Soldit perform as badly as Alexander seems to think? Explain your answer.

P6-14. **(Interpreting the cash flow statement, LO 1, 3)*** Anna Malover is a full-time veterinarian who started her own business five years ago. Anna felt that the market for doggie fashions had a lot of promise, based on her clients' complaints about fashionable

*This question was written by Angela Kellett of the University of Ontario Institute of Technology and is used with permission.

doggie clothes being so hard to find. She decided to start a business to design, make and sell a line of high fashion doggie clothes including hats, booties, sweaters, and co-coordinating accessories under the name Doggie Duds.

Anna wanted to continue her career as a full-time veterinarian and hired a full-time manager to manage Doggie Duds on a day-to-day basis. Anna has never been involved in the daily operations of the company, relying on periodic meetings with the manager and the company's annual financial statements. Since the business started, it has grown to be the number one provider of dog clothes and accessories in the country, with seven stores in locations across Ontario and Quebec. Anna has come to rely on the cash flow generated by Doggie Duds to support her lifestyle and usually pays herself a significant cash dividend each year.

After seeing the cash flow statement for 2008, Anna was very disappointed that the cash balance had decreased for the first time since the business began. As a result, she fired the manager for his poor performance and hired a new manager, Hue Gego, to "turn around" the company in 2009. In fact, Anna offered Hue a bonus based on the increase in total cash from 2008 to 2009.

It is now January 2010. Upon seeing the 2009 financial statements, Anna is very pleased with her decision, noting that cash increased significantly during the year. As a result, Anna was able to increase her dividend for the year to $90,000.

Doggie Duds Inc.
Cash Flow Statement For the Years Ended December 31,

	2009	2008
Operations		
Net income	$116,020	$133,500
Add: amortization expense	27,600	25,300
Less: gain on sale of land*	150,000	0
Cash from operations	(6,380)	158,800
Financing		
Repayment of Bank Loan**	0	(85,000)
Dividends	(90,000)	(50,000)
Investing		
Sale of Land	200,000	0
Purchase of new computer system***	0	(40,000)
Increase (decrease) in cash	103,620	(16,200)
Cash balance at the beginning of the year	22,200	38,400
Cash balance at the end of the year	$125,820	$22,200

*In 2001, Doggie Duds purchased a vacant lot beside one of its stores for future expansion. As of 2009, the land was still vacant. It was purchased for $50,000 and sold in 2009 for $200,000.
**In 2007, Doggie Duds borrowed $85,000 from the bank to open its seventh store. The loan was fully repaid in 2008. Doggie Duds has an additional loan of $250,000 still outstanding. The full balance is due on December 31, 2010.
***In 2008, Doggie Duds replaced its aging computer system with a new system which includes integrated sales, accounting and inventory tracking systems, and state of the art registers in all stores. The system is expected to last five years.

Required:

a. Who are the users of the Doggie Duds financial statements? What will they be using the statements for? Discuss the possible objectives of financial reporting for Doggie Duds.

b. Do you think that Anna was justified in firing the manager based on poor performance in 2008? Why or why not?

c. Do you think that the company performed as well as Anna thinks in 2009? Why or why not?

d. Do you think it is wise of Anna to offer a bonus based on the overall increase in cash? Why or Why not?

Using Financial Statements

BALLARD POWER SYSTEMS INC.

Ballard Power Systems Inc. (Ballard) is recognized as the world leader in the design, development, and manufacturing of proton exchange membrane ("PEM") fuel cells. The company operates in three market segments:

Transportation: PEM fuel cell products and electric drive systems;

Power Generation: PEM fuel cell products and power electronics; and

Material Products: Carbon fiber products primarily for automotive transmissions, and gas diffusion layers ("GDL") for PEM fuel cells.

www.ballard.com

Ballard is based in Canada, with its head office, research and development, and manufacturing facilities in Burnaby, British Columbia. In addition, the company has research and development and manufacturing facilities in the United States and Germany. Ballard's shares trade on the Toronto Stock Exchange and on the NASDAQ in the U.S.[4]

Ballard's consolidated statements of cash flows and earnings, along with extracts from the notes to the financial statements, are provided in Exhibit 6-3.[5] Use this information to respond to questions FS6-1 to FS6-11.

EXHIBIT 6-4

Ballard Power Systems Inc. Extracts from Financial Statements

BALLARD POWER SYSTEMS INC.

CONSOLIDATED STATEMENTS OF OPERATIONS

(Expressed in thousands of U.S. dollars, except per share amounts and number of shares)
Years ended December 31

	2005	2004	2003
Revenues:			
Product revenues.	$ 37,366	$ 67,575	$ 79,828
Engineering service and other revenue	16,367	13,798	39,738
Total revenues.	53,733	81,373	119,566
Cost of revenues and expenses:			
Cost of product revenues	31,292	59,594	76,063
Research and product development	75,492	91,737	103,863
General and administrative	17,543	15,671	17,711
Marketing	8,012	10,028	9,454
Depreciation and amortization.	26,094	40,094	46,408
Total cost of revenues and expenses.	158,433	217,124	253,499
Loss before undernoted	(104,700)	(135,751)	(133,933)
Investment and other income	11,153	3,670	29,191
Loss on disposal and write-down of long-lived assets (notes 7, 8 and 9)	(7,787)	(17,678)	(13,274)
Gain (loss) on assets held for sale (note 2)	18,294	(23,051)	—
Equity in loss of associated companies	(3,738)	(2,175)	(2,067)
Minority interest.	—	—	4,578
Business integration and restructuring costs.	—	—	(8,838)
Loss before income taxes	(86,778)	(174,985)	(124,343)
Income taxes (note 15)	205	422	749
Net loss for the year	(86,983)	(175,407)	(125,092)
Accumulated deficit, beginning of year.	(663,264)	(487,857)	(362,765)
Accumulated deficit, end of year.	$ (750,247)	$ (663,264)	$ (487,857)
Basic loss per share.	$ (0.73)	$ (1.48)	$ (1.07)
Weighted average number of common shares outstanding	119,701,260	118,461,114	117,438,962

EXHIBIT 6-4 :

(continued)
Ballard Power
Systems Inc.
Extracts from
Financial
Statements

BALLARD POWER SYSTEMS INC.

CONSOLIDATED STATEMENTS OF CASH FLOWS

(Expressed in thousands of U.S. dollars)
Years ended December 31

	2005	2004	2003
Cash provided by (used for):			
Operating activities:			
Net loss for the year	$ (86,983)	$(175,407)	$(125,092)
Items not affecting cash:			
Compensatory shares	5,483	5,091	7,837
Depreciation and amortization	29,234	45,313	54,421
Loss on disposal and write-down of long-lived assets	7,787	17,678	13,274
(Gain) loss on assets held for sale (note 2)	(18,294)	23,051	—
Equity in loss of associated companies	3,738	2,175	2,067
Minority interest	—	—	(4,578)
Other	(361)	(278)	(375)
	(59,396)	(82,377)	(52,446)
Changes in non-cash working capital:			
Accounts receivable	(4,400)	4,175	4,252
Inventories	(790)	7,560	2,498
Prepaid expenses and other current assets	987	(75)	(174)
Accounts payable and accrued liabilities	1,351	(2,789)	(758)
Deferred revenue	(3,048)	213	54
Accrued warranty liabilities	(9,480)	1,217	1,554
Net current assets and liabilities held for sale (note 2)	(1,953)	(6,181)	2,254
	(17,333)	4,120	9,680
Cash used by operations	(76,729)	(78,257)	(42,766)
Investing activities:			
Net (increase) decrease in short-term investments	(32,603)	(2,498)	90,624
Additions to property, plant and equipment	(6,613)	(7,087)	(5,714)
Additions to intangible assets	—	(411)	(557)
Proceeds on sale of long-lived assets	485	529	897
Proceeds on sale of subsidiary (note 2)	21,458	—	—
Investments	(677)	(2,751)	(2,016)
Acquisition of other businesses (note 3)	—	—	(1,879)
Other long-term assets	2,689	(1,932)	(53)
Long-term liabilities	441	1,826	846
	(14,820)	(12,324)	82,148
Financing activities:			
Net proceeds on issuance of share capital	50,668	1,234	1,519
Other	1,052	(4)	(35)
	51,720	1,230	1,484
(Decrease) increase in cash and cash equivalents	(39,829)	(89,351)	40,866
Cash and cash equivalents, beginning of year	188,748	278,099	237,233
Cash and cash equivalents, end of year	$ 148,919	$ 188,748	$ 278,099

FS6-1. What amounts does Ballard report in its December 31, 2004 and December 31, 2005 statement of cash flow for each of the following?
   a. Cash provided by (used for) operating activities.
   b. Cash provided by (used for) investing activities.
   c. Cash provided by (used for) financing activities.

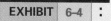

EXHIBIT 6-4 :

(continued)
**Ballard Power
Systems Inc.
Extracts from
Financial
Statements**

1. **SIGNIFICANT ACCOUNTING POLICIES (cont'd):**

   (d) Cash and cash equivalents:

   Cash and cash equivalents consist of cash on deposit and highly liquid short-term interest-bearing securities with maturities at the date of purchase of three months or less. Interest earned and any market value losses are recognized immediately in the statement of operations.

17. **SUPPLEMENTAL DISCLOSURE OF CASH FLOW INFORMATION:**

	2005	2004	2003
Income taxes paid..........................	$ 145	$ 289	$ 147
Non-cash financing and investing activities:			
Compensatory shares	$ 2,510	$ 3,526	$ 5,549
Accrued disposition costs (note 2)	$ 2,341	$ —	$ —
Shares cancelled from disposition of assets			
held for sale (note 2)	$ 73,800	$ —	$ —
Shares cancelled upon release of Ford from			
certain future obligations (note 2).........	$ 12,500	$ —	$ —
Issuance of common shares on acquisition of			
other businesses (note 3)	$ —	$ —	$ 30,386
Issuance of common shares for intellectual			
property (note 16)	$ —	$ —	$ 2,403
Acquired intellectual property accrued in other			
liabilities (note 16)	$ —	$ 1,116	$ —

FS6-2. How much did Ballard spend/raise from investing activities in each of the years reported in its statement of cash flows? Describe Ballard's main investing activities during these years. Why do you think these activities were necessary?

FS6-3. What method does Ballard use to calculate cash flows from operating activities? How can you tell?

FS6-4. Ballard's statement of cash flows uses the term cash and cash equivalents.
   a. What does Ballard include in its definition of cash equivalents?
   b. Does it make sense to include cash and cash equivalents in a statement of cash flow, or would using cash only make better sense? Explain your answer.

FS6-5. Ballard reported losses on its statement of operations in excess of $US85,000,000 in each of the three years reported on, but cash used by operations is significantly smaller (cash used by operations is less negative than the net losses). Explain why these differences exist between the accrual measure of performance and cash used by operations.

FS6-6. In each of the three years reported on in Ballard's statement of cash flows, cash from operations is negative. Over the three years, operations consumed almost $US200,000,000. How has Ballard been able to survive over this period in the face of such large negative cash from operations? Explain fully.

FS6-7. During 2005 Ballard reported a loss on the disposal and write-down of long-lived assets of $US7,787,000. Explain why the loss and the write-down are added back in the calculation of cash used by operations.

FS6-8. Note 17 describes "non-cash financing and investing activities." These activities are not included in the statement of cash flows, but are reported in a separate schedule. In 2003, how much does Ballard report as "issuance of common shares on acquisition of other businesses." What do you think these amounts represent? If they were to be reflected in the statement of cash flows how would they be reported? Why do you think the amounts are not included in statement of cash flows? (When answering, give thought to what the statement of cash flows is designed to report and different ways that capital assets can be purchased.)

FS6-9. Suppose that on December 31, 2004 Ballard had $US10,266,000 of accounts receivable and $US13,057,000 of inventories. Use the information in Exhibit 6–3 to determine the amount of accounts receivable and inventories on December 31, 2005.

FS6-10. Explain how Ballard's non-cash working capital accounts affected cash flows from operating activities during 2005. Explain why changes in non-cash working capital accounts affect cash flows from operating activities.

FS6-11. Calculate Ballard's free cash flow for 2004 and 2005. What does the free cash flow tell you about Ballard?

Analyzing Rogers Communications Inc.

◇**ROGERS**

R6-1. In its 2005 statements of cash flow, Rogers reported cash from operations of $1,227,407,000. How did Rogers use this cash?

R6-2. What does Rogers include in its definition of cash and cash equivalents?

R6-3. What amounts does Rogers report in its 2004 and 2005 statements of cash flows for each of the following?
a. Cash from operating activities.
b. Cash from investing activities.
c. Cash from financing activities.

R6-4. In its December 31, 2005 financial statements, Rogers reported a net loss of $44,658,000 but cash from operating activities of $1,227,407,000. Explain why there was such a big difference between the accrual loss and cash from operating activities in 2005.

R6-5. Examine Note 10(c) to the financial statements:
a. Why do you think the information in the note is included in the financial statement package? What information does the schedule provide that is not included in the cash flow statement?
b. Describe the activities that are reported in the schedule of non-cash investing and financing activities.

R6-6. Note 2(h) explains that Rogers defers (capitalizes) incremental costs related to the development and pre-operating phases of new products and businesses and amortizes them over periods of up to five years.
a. Explain how capitalizing incremental costs associated with new products and businesses and amortizing them affects the cash flow statement in comparison with simply expensing these costs as they occur.
b. Would changing the method of accounting for these costs affect Rogers' cash flow? Explain.
c. How might a stakeholder's interpretation of Rogers' cash flows be affected by the accounting treatment for incremental costs associated with new products and businesses?
d. Assume that during 2005 Rogers incurred $2,000,000 in incremental costs associated with new products and businesses and during the year amortized $1,500,000 of these costs that it previously capitalized. Recalculate Rogers' cash from operations, assuming that it simply expensed these incremental costs as incurred.

R6-7. How much did Rogers pay in cash for income taxes and interest in 2005 and 2004? How do you know? Explain. How much did Rogers expense for interest in 2005 and 2004? Why are these amounts different from the amounts actually paid?

R6-8. Read Note 23(p)(ii) to the financial statements. Explain the difference between Canadian and US GAAP that is described. If Rogers statement of cash flows was prepared using US GAAP how would it differ from the Canadian version?

ENDNOTES

1. Clarence Byrd, Ida Chen, and Joshua Smith, *Financial Reporting in Canada*, 30th Edition. The Virtual Professional Library. 2005.

2. Extracted from Hemosol Corp.'s 2004 and 2001 annual reports.

3. Extracted from the Public Accounts of Canada, 2005, Volume I.

4. Extracted from Ballard Inc.'s Web site at www.ballard.com (accessed April 2, 2006).

5. Extracted from Ballard Power Inc.'s 2005 annual report.

7

CASH, RECEIVABLES, AND THE TIME VALUE OF MONEY

LEARNING OBJECTIVES

After studying the material in this chapter you will be able to:

▶**LO 1** Discuss how cash is accounted for in financial statements and recognize the importance of cash management and internal controls over cash.

▶**LO 2** Explain the concept of the time value of money and its relevance to accounting, and be able to do some basic time value of money calculations.

▶**LO 3** Describe accounting for receivables and uncollectible amounts.

▶**LO 4** Analyze and interpret information for evaluating the liquidity of an entity and understand how managers can use accounting estimates to create hidden reserves to manage earnings.

The January 2005 issue of *Flare* magazine boasts a photo of Canadian supermodel Maria D. on the runway at a Just Cavalli fashion show. Flipping through the eye-catching beauty and fashion publication, one of 70 owned by the Rogers Media subsidiary, and attracting 1.8 million readers, readers can peruse articles about the latest hair styles from the haute couture world or essential beauty must-haves.

A single copy of *Flare* magazine sells for about $4.00 on the newsstand (165,000 copies sell that way each month), but *Flare* sells pieces of each monthly issue for thousands of dollars more. To who? Advertisers. That's where *Flare* makes most of its money. Interspersed with articles are glossy advertisements promoting everything from Herbal Essences shampoo to Maybelline mascara to the latest perfume.

Fashion and beauty businesses such as L'Oréal who want to advertise in Flare are charged a rate based on where the ad runs in the magazine that month, how many colours the ad will use, and how big a space on the page the ad takes up. In 2006, a full-page full-colour ad on the outside back cover of an issue cost more than $24,000.

An issue of *Flare* might include more than 100 advertisements. So how do *Flare's* accounting people keep track of who owes them how much, and when L'Oréal or Neutrogena, or their ad agencies, are supposed to pay for those ads?

That's where Lisa Scott comes in. Scott is a supervisor with *Flare's* credit department in Toronto. She uses a tracking system called MSG that documents who bought what ad, when it was created, and when it was approved and sent to *Flare's* printing plant. The system issues a separate invoice for each ad running that particular month, even if a cosmetics giant buys different ads for different products (one ad for a lip liner and another for mascara) in the same issue of the magazine. The invoices have 30-day terms and if clients don't send in the money on time, the account is sent to Rogers' collection department.

INTRODUCTION

So far, we have examined accounting and accounting information from a broad perspective. For the remaining chapters we will delve more deeply into the accounting used for the major components of the financial statements. Do not be misled by the apparent focus of these chapters on the balance sheet. Never forget that the financial statements are all closely linked and accounting choices that affect one of the statements will invariably have an impact on others. Therefore, our discussion will look at the effect of accounting information on the income statement and the cash flow statement as well as on the balance sheet.

In this chapter, we will examine some of an entity's most liquid assets: cash and receivables. Cash, of course, is the most liquid of assets and is vital for the effective operation and survival of an entity. Yet, understanding accounting for cash is not always as straightforward as counting the amount of money in your pocket. Receivables represent amounts owed to the entity, usually, but not always, by customers. Our examination of receivables will show the effect that estimates have in determining the values that are assigned to the assets on the balance sheet and to the amount of income an entity reports.

The chapter also introduces a powerful tool used in accounting and for financial analysis that takes into consideration the "time value of money"—the fact that money received today is more valuable than the same amount of money received sometime in the future.

CASH

Cash is a crucial asset. If an entity does not have enough cash, or at least access to enough cash, the consequences could be dire. Without cash, an entity cannot pay its bills or meet other obligations, and as a result operations may grind to a halt if suppliers refuse to do business with the cash-strapped entity. We discussed the importance of cash and cash flow at length in Chapter 6. This chapter will cover some of the accounting issues pertaining to cash. Accounting for cash is relatively straightforward and does not generate much controversy, although there are some twists and turns that you should be aware of.

Rogers' December 31, 2005 balance sheet reported no cash and cash equivalents. This doesn't mean that Rogers has no cash at all. As was explained in Chapter 6, cash and cash equivalents on the balance sheet can be shown net of certain types of bank loans, such as bank overdrafts (or advances as Rogers calls them) and lines of credit, when the loans are used as part of the day-to-day cash management of the entity. Rogers includes bank advances in its definition of cash and cash equivalents (see the first note at the bottom of Rogers Statements of Cash Flows (page A-6). If the cash and cash equivalents is greater than the bank advances, the net amount is shown as a current asset. If the reverse is true, as was the case in 2005, the net amount appears on the balance sheet as a current liability. Including bank advances in the definition of cash and cash equivalents makes it impossible to know how much cash Rogers actually has and affects the current ratio.

In its December 31, 2004 balance sheet Rogers Communications Inc. (Rogers) reports cash and cash equivalents of $243,993,000 as a current asset. The cash part of this amount represents all of the cash that Rogers has in its bank accounts, cash registers, and safes throughout the organization. As long as the cash is readily available for use, it can be classified as a current asset. Cash equivalents represent short-term investments that can be converted into a known amount of cash easily and quickly. Cash equivalents can include securities such as treasury bills, guaranteed investment certificates (GICs), and money market funds. Cash equivalents exclude equity investments such as common and preferred shares because the price of equity investments fluctuates day to day, which means that the amount of cash that would be received from selling these securities is uncertain until they are sold.

Sometimes an entity's cash is restricted in some way, perhaps because there is a legal or contractual obligation to use it in a particular way. For example, Geac Computer Corporation Limited (Geac) reports $4,808,000 of restricted cash as a current asset and $3,039,000 of restricted cash as a non-current asset on April 30, 2005. This means that this cash cannot be used for day-to-day purposes and cannot be considered a liquid asset. The non-current portion of the restricted cash will not be used for more than one year. Exhibit 7–1 shows the asset side of Geac's balance sheet and the notes to the financial statements that explain the restricted cash balance.[1]

EXHIBIT 7–1 :

CONSOLIDATED BALANCE SHEETS | AS AT APRIL 30, 2005 AND 2004

(amounts in thousands of U.S. dollars)

	April 30, 2005	April 30, 2004
		(Revised – see note 2)
Assets		
Current assets:		
Cash and cash equivalents	$ 188,242	$ 86,050
Restricted cash	4,808	95
Short-term investments	–	26,500
Accounts receivable and other receivables (note 3)	56,853	55,837
Future income taxes (note 20)	8,292	15,247
Prepaid expenses and other assets (note 4)	8,230	8,437
Total current assets	266,425	192,166
Restricted cash	3,039	1,781
Future income taxes (note 20)	34,558	21,741
Property, plant and equipment (note 5)	22,005	23,843
Intangible assets (note 6)	23,841	32,628
Goodwill (note 7)	110,142	128,366
Other assets	6,156	6,378
Total assets	$ 466,166	$ 406,903
Liabilities and Shareholders' Equity		
Current liabilities:		
Accounts payable and accrued liabilities (note 9)	$ 73,373	$ 79,691
Income taxes payable	22,997	34,538
Current portion of long-term debt (note 12)	424	391
Deferred revenue (note 10)	112,605	117,927
Total current liabilities	209,399	232,547
Deferred revenue (note 10)	2,058	2,256
Employee future benefits (note 15)	26,334	23,967
Asset retirement obligations (note 14)	1,678	1,648
Accrued restructuring (note 19)	1,769	5,864
Long-term debt (note 12)	4,630	4,550
Total liabilities	245,868	270,832
Shareholders' Equity		
Preference shares; no par value;		
unlimited shares authorized; none issued or outstanding	–	–
Common shares; no par value; unlimited shares authorized;		
issued and outstanding as at April 30, 2005 - 86,377,012 (2004 - 85,174,785)	131,445	124,019
Treasury shares; issued and outstanding as at April 30, 2005 - 816,598 (2004 - nil)	(6,979)	–
Common stock options	12	44
Contributed surplus	6,353	2,368
Retained earnings	111,541	34,517
Cumulative foreign exchange translation adjustment	(22,074)	(24,877)
Total shareholders' equity	220,298	136,071
Total liabilities and shareholders' equity	$ 466,166	$ 406,903

Commitments and contingencies (notes 12, 16 and 22)

CASH AND CASH EQUIVALENTS

Cash and cash equivalents are composed of non-restricted cash and short-term, highly liquid investments with an original maturity of 90 days or less. Cash equivalents are stated at amounts that approximate fair value, based on quoted market prices.

RESTRICTED CASH

Cash is considered to be restricted when it is subject to contingent rights of a third party, including customers, vendors, or government agencies. As at April 30, 2005, $250 of the Company's restricted cash balance was related to customer holdbacks, lease and other deposits, and funds held in escrow related to a legal settlement. An additional $2,823 was related to cash collateralization of bank guarantees issued for leased office space, vendor, customer and government agency obligations, and $4,774 was related to cash segregated by the Company to purchase common shares for its restricted share unit plan. As at April 30, 2004, $367 of the Company's restricted cash balance was related to bid proposal deposits, customer holdbacks, lease and other deposits. Additionally, $1,509 was related to cash collateralization of bank guarantees issued for leased office space, vendor, customer and government agency obligations.

Cash Management and Controls Over Cash

It would be easy to conclude that the more cash an entity has on hand, the better. That is far from true. Having too little cash, of course, is a potential threat to the survival of the entity. But having too much cash can be a problem as well. While cash provides insurance for the unexpected, cash is an unproductive asset. Businesses do not make money by holding cash. Business chequing accounts typically pay no interest. At best, cash will earn a very small return in an interest bearing account, but those earnings would be far less than what could be earned if the cash were invested in the business. If a business is unable to find productive ways to use its cash, it would probably be best if the surplus cash were returned to shareholders, who could find more effective investments for their money. Or the surplus cash could be used to retire outstanding liabilities. Effective cash management is a key function for an entity's management. A balance must exist between having too little cash and too much.

One of the important stewardship responsibilities of management is to ensure that the entity maintains an adequate system of internal controls. **Internal controls** are the processes that management implements to provide reasonable assurance that an entity will be able to achieve its objectives regarding the reliability of financial reporting, the effectiveness and efficiency of its operations, and compliance with relevant laws and regulations. Strong internal controls provide assurance to stakeholders that the entity's assets cannot be stolen, used inappropriately, or used without proper authorization, and that the information produced by the accounting system can be relied on. (For example, many retail stores place devices on more expensive inventory items that set off an alarm if the item is removed from the store without being paid for. The use of these devices is an internal control that helps prevent theft.) In general, poor internal controls can lead to significant losses.

From an external stakeholders' perspective, good internal controls should be very important. External stakeholders rely on management to protect their "stake" in the entity. If good internal controls don't exist, how can stakeholders rely on the financial statements for decision making? If good internal controls don't exist, how can stakeholders be confident that the assets in the care of management are protected from theft or misuse?

A relatively new part of public companies' annual reports is the statement of management's responsibility for financial reporting. You can find Rogers' statement on page A-3. This statement explains that the financial statements are the responsibility of management and describes the steps that have been taken to ensure the integrity of the financial statements, including a system of internal controls. In the wake of the Enron and other financial reporting scandals, legislators in the U.S. passed the Sarbanes-Oxley Act, which requires CEOs and CFOs to certify the information contained in their entities' annual reports. Canada is a few steps behind the U.S. in this area, but proposals similar to the Sarbanes-Oxley Act should ultimately be in place.

An important area for an entity to control is cash. Cash is attractive to thieves because it is easy to hide and it cannot be identified once it is stolen. Most entities do not leave cash lying around so it is easy for a thief to take, although entities that handle a lot of cash, such as retail stores, casinos, arcades, and laundromats, need internal controls to protect their cash. There are many ways that cash can be stolen, in addition to being physically taken. Money can be stolen if weak internal controls allow an employee to make payments by cheque to non-existent suppliers and then cash the cheques him- or herself. Weak internal controls might also allow an employee to alter a payment so that a supplier receives more than is actually owed, or to alter records to cover up a theft of cash.

There are many controls that can be put in place to limit the likelihood that cash will somehow be stolen. One of the most important and effective controls that can be implemented for cash (and other assets as well) is **segregation of duties**. Segregation of duties means that people who handle an asset should not also be responsible for record keeping for that asset. If duties are not segregated, an employee may be able to steal cash and cover up the theft by making fictitious entries to the accounting records. For example, consider a person who receives mailed-in cheques from customers and deposits the cheques in the bank, and who is also responsible for recording the deposit in the accounting system. That person might be able to deposit some of the cheques in his or her own bank account and cover up the theft by making a journal entry that writes off accounts receivable in the amount stolen.

(A bank reconciliation is an important internal control tool for cash used by management to explain differences between an entity's accounting records and its bank account. Readers who are interested in learning about the bank reconciliation and how to prepare it can visit the text Web site at www.mcgrawhill.ca/olc/friedlan.)

An in-depth discussion of internal controls is not an appropriate part of an introductory financial accounting course. However, it is important for stakeholders to understand the importance of internal controls.

Is a Dollar a Dollar?

One of the fundamental GAAP accounting concepts explained in Chapter 5 was the unit-of-measure assumption. The unit-of-measure assumption requires that financial statement information must be measurable and stated in monetary units, such as Canadian dollars. A dollar of cash reported on a balance sheet means a dollar in hand. But is a dollar always really worth a dollar? In fact, the value of a dollar is not constant over time. While the face value of a dollar is always the same, the value of a dollar will vary relative to what it can buy and relative to other currencies.

The Effect of Changes in Purchasing Power If you take $10,000 and hide it under your mattress, your GAAP financial statements will always show that you have $10,000 in cash. While you will always have the $10,000, as time passes you will be less and less well off. Why? Because, with the passage of time, the purchasing power of cash declines because of **inflation**. Inflation refers to a period when, on average, prices in the economy are rising. If the amount of goods and services you can buy with your money declines, the value of the money has declined even though the face value of the money stays the same. The reverse logic is true if there is **deflation**, but deflation is far less common than inflation. Deflation refers to a period when, on average, prices in the economy are falling.

Using Canada's inflation rate as the base, let's say you hid your $10,000 under your mattress at the beginning of 1990. At the end of 2005, your $10,000 would purchase what $7,424 would have purchased in 1990. In other words, while the absolute or nominal number of dollars you had in 1990 and 2005 is the same, the amount of goods and services those dollars can buy is different. You would be able to buy fewer groceries in 2005 than you could in 1990.

Canadian GAAP doesn't take into consideration the changing purchasing power of money over time. The unit of measure is the "nominal" dollar, which means that no adjustment is made for changes in purchasing power. Yet losses in the purchasing power of money represent a real

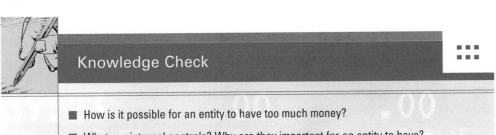

Knowledge Check

- How is it possible for an entity to have too much money?
- What are internal controls? Why are they important for an entity to have?
- How does GAAP deal with the effect that inflation has on the purchasing power of money? What is the economic impact of inflation on the purchasing power of money?

CASH, RECEIVABLES, AND THE TIME VALUE OF MONEY

www.mcgrawhill.ca/
olc/friedlan

Question for Consideration

As an investment, you purchased a vending machine that sells a variety of drinks. The machine is located in a busy suburban mall. As owner, you are responsible for purchasing and stocking the machine with drinks, collecting the cash, and maintaining the machine. Because you are busy, you have hired a person who works near the mall to stock the machine, collect the cash, and report maintenance problems to you.

Explain why internal controls are important in this situation and why hiring a person to handle all the tasks mentioned represents weak internal controls. What kinds of internal controls would help protect you?

Answer: Internal controls are important to protect your assets—in this case, the drinks and the cash. Because you have hired someone to stock the machine and collect the cash, it is possible that the person could steal the drinks, the cash, or both. Without proper controls, it would be difficult to know whether your employee was stealing. That person could pocket the cash and take the drinks without your knowledge.

The easiest way to ensure that cash or drinks are not stolen is to stock the machine and collect the cash yourself (you cannot steal from yourself). But because you are busy, this does not appear to be a viable solution. Control would be stronger if you used different people to stock the machine and collect the cash (segregation of duties). By using different people, you would be able to compare the number of drinks sold (this would be the number of drinks placed in the machine) with the amount of cash collected. You would receive a report of the number of drinks sold from the person stocking the machine, and the cash from the person collecting the cash. If sales and cash collections did not match, it would be an indication of a problem.

If you must use the same person for both stocking and collection, it is important to keep control of the inventory. Controlling the inventory means that your employee would only use inventory supplied by you, meaning that you would know the number of drinks that went into the machine and, therefore, the amount of cash you should receive. This is a weak control because there is nothing to prevent the person from buying drinks, placing them in the machine, and keeping the cash from those sales. This kind of theft is very difficult to detect. Another possible control would be an electronic counter that would keep track of the number of drinks sold but that is not accessible to your employee. With this control, you would be able to compare the number of drinks sold with the cash collected. This control would require that you inspect the machine from time to time to check the counter.

economic cost to an entity. While this approach to accounting is not used in Canada, it is used in countries that have had high inflation, for example, Israel and Brazil.

How could a change in purchasing be reflected in the financial statements? One way would be to record the decrease in purchasing power as a loss. If an entity held $10,000 over a period where the purchasing power decreased by 10 percent, a loss of $1,000 would be reported on the income statement. By doing this, the financial statements would reflect the cost of holding cash.

The Effect of Changing Prices of Foreign Currencies Canada is a trading nation. Much of its economic activity involves transactions with entities in foreign countries and in foreign currencies. Many Canadian companies have business operations in other countries. Transactions involving foreign currencies and foreign operations can have an impact on an entity's financial statements, including the amount of cash it reports.

For example, Quarry Ltd. (Quarry) has a bank account in which it has U.S. dollars. Because of the unit-of-measure assumption, all amounts reported in the financial statements must be stated in a single currency. If Quarry's financial statements are presented in Canadian dollars, its U.S. cash must be stated in Canadian dollars. Since **exchange rates** of currencies fluctuate, the number of Canadian dollars that a U.S. amount represents will vary. (The exchange rate is the price to buy one currency, stated in terms of another currency.)

Suppose that on December 31, 2009 Quarry had U.S.$1,000,000 and the exchange rate was $1.10—that is, US$1 could be exchanged for Cdn$1.10. When Quarry prepares its financial statements, it must convert its U.S.$1,000,000 into the equivalent amount in Canadian dollars. This means that on its December 31, 2009 balance sheet Quarry would report $1,100,000 of Canadian cash (exchange rate × amount of foreign currency = $1.10 × U.S.$1,000,000). This amount is reported even though the money is still actually in U.S. dollars. If one year later, on December 31, 2010, Quarry's U.S. bank account still has U.S.$1,000,000, but the exchange rate is $1.15, on its December 31, 2010 balance sheet Quarry would report $1,150,000 of Canadian cash.

The effect is that when exchange rates change, the amount of Canadian dollars reported changes even though the quantity of the foreign currency stays the same. The change in the exchange rate from December 31, 2009 to December 31, 2010 has resulted in Quarry having $50,000 more in Canadian dollars, even though the amount of U.S. dollars has not changed.

THE TIME VALUE OF MONEY

Would you rather receive $1,000 today or $1,000 a year from now? The answer to that question should be easy. It is better to have cash now rather than the same amount of cash later. There are a number of reasons why:

1. Having the money sooner allows you to earn a return on the money. By investing in a one-year investment certificate that offers 4 percent interest per year, your $1,000 would turn into $1,040 in a year. You would have an extra $40. By waiting a year to receive the $1,000 you would lose the opportunity to earn that $40.

2. By getting the money today, you can spend and enjoy it now. A person is likely to prefer having a plasma TV or taking a holiday sooner rather than later, or at least have the option of doing so.

3. As explained in the previous section, because of inflation the purchasing power of money declines over time. With inflation of 2 percent, $1,000 in one year will only buy what $980 would have bought today.

4. Getting the money sooner reduces the likelihood that you are not going to be paid.

However you look at it, it should be clear that you are ahead of the game if you get your money sooner. This does not mean that a person will never decide to receive his or her money later rather than sooner. However, the delay should come with a price. The concept that people would prefer to receive a given amount of money sooner rather than later is known as the **time value of money**.

While conceptually it should make sense that it is preferable to receive a given amount of money sooner rather than later, how do you choose among different amounts that can be received at different times? For example, suppose you won a contest that allowed you to choose among receiving $10,000 today, $4,000 at the end of each of the next three years, or $14,000 in three years. Which would you choose?

It is hard to make a decision by just looking at these three alternatives. However, there is a powerful tool that allows you to evaluate this choice and other business and accounting problems that involve cash flows that occur at different times. Valuing cash flows that occur at different times can be viewed from two perspectives: the future value and the present value. The **future value** of cash flows is the amount of money you will receive in the future by investing today at a given interest rate. The **present value** of cash flows is the value today of money that will be received in the future.

The coverage in this book will be limited to a brief introduction of these time-value-of-money tools. The objective is to give you enough background to be able to understand the financial reporting topics that are affected by the time value of money and to understand the usefulness of these tools.

Future Value

We will begin our discussion with future value because it is a concept that most people are familiar with. The way that money in a bank account grows with the passage of time is an application of the future value concept. If you put $1,000 in a bank account that pays interest of 5 percent per year, in one year your bank account will have $1,050. You will have earned $50 in interest during the year. The amount of interest earned is calculated by multiplying the amount in your bank account by the interest rate. In this case, the calculation is $1,000 \times 0.05 = 50. The amount of money in the bank account at the end of the year is calculated by multiplying the amount in the account by one plus the interest rate $(1 + 0.05)$. For our example, the balance in the account would be $1,000 \times 1.05 = $1,050$. In time-value-of-money terms, the future value of $1,000 invested at 5 percent for one year is $1,050.

If you leave your $1,050 in the bank for another year and continue to receive interest at 5 percent per year, at the end of the second year you will have $1,102.50 ($1,050 \times 1.05$). During the second year, you will have earned $52.50 of interest ($1,050 \times 0.05$). The reason that you earned more than $50 in interest in the second year is that you earned compound interest. **Compound interest** is interest that is calculated on the principal amount and on interest accumulated in previous periods. In the second year, interest was not only earned on the original $1,000, but also on the $50 in interest that you earned in the first year. In time value of money terms, the future value of $1,000 invested at 5 percent for two years is $1,102.50. (If the interest were only calculated using the initial investment of $1,000, the interest every year would be $50. This type of interest is called simple interest. **Simple interest** is interest paid or earned on the principal amount only.)

The formula for calculating the amount that you will receive at some future time with an investment today is:

$$FV_{n,r} = (1 + r)^n \times \text{Amount invested}$$

FV (future value) is the amount you will receive in the future by investing an amount (amount invested) for n periods at an interest rate of r per period. This formula incorporates the compounding of interest.

Using the formula to calculate the future value of an investment of $1,000 at 5 percent for two years, we find

$$
\begin{aligned}
FV_{2,0.05} &= (1 + 0.05)^2 \times $1,000 \\
&= 1.1025 \times $1,000 \\
&= $1,102.50
\end{aligned}
$$

This is the same amount that we calculated earlier.

If you wanted to find out how much you would have if you invested $1,000 at 8 percent for 25 years, the formula would give you:

$$
\begin{aligned}
FV_{n,r} &= (1 + r)^n \times \text{Amount invested} \\
FV_{25,0.08} &= (1 + 0.08)^{25} \times $1,000 \\
&= 6.84848 \times $1,000 \\
&= $6,848.48
\end{aligned}
$$

The future value technique is very useful and powerful. There are many questions that can be answered by using it. Let's look at a couple of examples.

Example 1: The Mayos In 2009 Mr. and Mrs. Mayo received $2,500 from Mr. Mayo's parents as a gift in honour of the birth of their first daughter, Ellin. Mr. and Mrs. Mayo plan to invest the money to help pay for Ellin's university education. They would like to know how much Ellin will receive if they invest the $2,500 in a 20-year investment certificate that earns 6 percent interest per year.

$$
\begin{aligned}
FV_{n,r} &= (1 + r)^n \times \text{Amount invested} \\
FV_{20,0.06} &= (1 + 0.06)^{20} \times $2,500 \\
&= $8,017.84
\end{aligned}
$$

Therefore, Ellin will receive $8,017.84 when the investment certificate matures in 2029.

Example 2: Ms. Secretan Ms. Secretan recently purchased a new car to replace her rusting 13-year-old vehicle. Ms. Secretan arranged a $35,000 three-year loan at 10 percent per year from the bank to pay for the car. Under the terms of the loan, Ms. Secretan does not have to make any payments until the end of the three-year term, at which time she must pay the bank the principal and interest in full. Ms. Secretan would like to know how much she will have to pay the bank when the loan must be repaid.

$$FV_{n,r} = (1 + r)^n \times \text{Amount invested}$$
$$FV_{3,0.10} = (1 + 0.10)^3 \times \$35,000$$
$$= \$46,585.00$$

Therefore, Ms. Secretan will have to pay the bank $46,585.00 in three years when the loan must be repaid.

In these examples the periods are years, but periods could be days, weeks, months, or anything else. However, the interest rate selected must be appropriate for the period (that is, you wouldn't use the annual interest rate if you were measuring the number of periods in months).

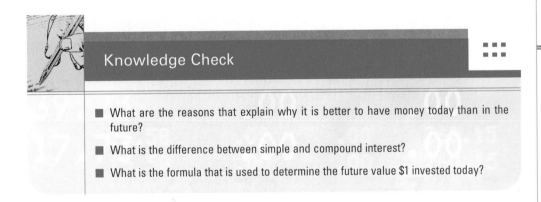

Knowledge Check

■ What are the reasons that explain why it is better to have money today than in the future?

■ What is the difference between simple and compound interest?

■ What is the formula that is used to determine the future value $1 invested today?

www.mcgrawhill.ca/
olc/friedlan

Present Value

The present value technique looks at what cash received in the future is worth today. The present value technique is a very powerful tool that allows comparisons of alternative cash flow arrangements and the valuation of securities. Consider the $1,102.50 that you had in your bank account after two years invested at 5 percent per year (this is the example that introduced the discussion of future values). The question asked in a present value analysis is, "At an interest rate of 5 percent, how much is the $1,102.50 that you will receive in two years equivalent to today?" Another way of posing the question is, "How much would you pay or invest today to receive $1,102.50 in two years, if the interest rate was 5 percent?" Based on the earlier example, you should guess that the present value of $1,102.50 to be received in two years at 5 percent is $1,000. This result can be shown by using the following formula:

$$PV_{n,r} = \frac{1}{(1+r)^n} \times \text{Amount to be received or paid}$$

where n is the number of periods and r is the interest rate. Note that the term discount rate is often used instead of interest rate in a present value analysis. The **discount rate** is the rate used to calculate the present value of future cash flows.

Present value is nothing more than the amount that would be received in the future less the interest that would be earned on the money over the investment period. Applying this formula to the example gives:

$$PV_{2,\,0.05} = \frac{1}{(1+0.05)^2} \times \$1{,}102.50$$
$$= \$1{,}000$$

What this calculation tells us is that at a discount rate of 5 percent, having $1,000 now is equivalent to receiving $1,102.50 in two years. In other words, if you were offered a choice between $1,000 now and $1,102.50 in two years and your discount rate was 5 percent, you would be indifferent—the two amounts are equally valuable to you. However, if instead you were offered $1,100 in two years, you would prefer the $1,000 now. And if you were offered $1,110 in two years, you would prefer the $1,110 to $1,000. Remember that when the time-value-of-money concept was first introduced, it was explained that people would accept money later rather than sooner, but at a price. That price is a larger amount of money.

Question for Consideration

Your aunt recently won $100,000 in a lottery. She has approached you for advice on which of two investments she should place her money. Your aunt wants to invest for ten years, at which time she plans to retire. Your aunt is only interested in investments that she considers safe, so she has narrowed her choice to two investments with large banks. The first investment is a ten-year investment certificate that bears an interest rate of 8 percent, with interest calculated annually. The second investment is also a ten-year certificate, but interest on that investment is calculated and compounded at the rate of 4 percent every six months (this means that there are 20 six-month investment periods at 4 percent rather than 10-one year investment periods at 8 percent).

Which investment would you recommend to your aunt? Explain your answer. Make sure to explain why the quantitative result you obtain occurs.

Answer: Your aunt would be better off with the investment that has 4 percent interest calculated and compounded every six months. Quantitatively,

Investment 1: $FV_{n,\,r}$ $= (1+r)^n \times$ Amount invested
 $FV_{10,\,0.08}$ $= (1+0.08)^{10} \times \$100{,}000$
$\phantom{Investment 1:FV_{10,\,0.08}}$ $= \$215{,}892$

Investment 2: $FV_{n,\,r}$ $= (1+r)^n \times$ Amount invested
 $FV_{20,\,0.04}$ $= (1+0.04)^{20} \times \$100{,}000$
$\phantom{Investment 2:FV_{20,\,0.04}}$ $= \$219{,}112$

Investment 2 is more attractive because compounding occurs more often. Even though the interest rate appears to be the same for both investments, more interest is earned with Investment 2. For example, in the first year, your aunt earns 8 percent on $100,000 with Investment 1. But with Investment 2, she earns 4 percent on $100,000 in the first half of the first year ($4,000) and then 4 percent on $104,000 in the second half ($4,160) of year one, which gives a total of $8,160 of interest in the first year. The effect of the more frequent compounding builds over the life of the investment.

Suppose that instead of using a discount rate of 5 percent to determine the present value of $1,102.50 to be received in two years, you decide that 7 percent is the appropriate discount rate. Then the present value of $1,102.50 to be received in two years is:

$$PV_{2,\,0.07} = \frac{1}{(1+0.07)^2} \times \$1,102.50$$
$$= \$962.97$$

In other words, if your discount rate were 7 percent, the present value of the $1,102.50 would be $962.97. You would only be willing to pay up to $962.97 to receive $1,102.50 in two years. Having to pay anything more than $962.97 would not be satisfactory. To put it another way, you would prefer receiving any amount more than $962.97 today rather than $1,102.50 in two years. Anything less than $962.97 today would make $1,102.50 in two years preferable. At a discount rate of 7 percent you would be indifferent between $1,102.50 in two years and $962.97 today.

It is important to recognize the crucial role the discount rate plays in determining the present value. The higher the discount rate, the lower the present value of a future amount. This corresponds to the future-value effect whereby the higher the interest rate paid on an investment, the more money received in the future. The selection of the discount rate is somewhat subjective and there are many considerations that go into the choice, including risk and expected inflation. Further discussion about determining the discount rate is beyond the scope of this book.

Let's look at two examples of the present value technique.

Example 1: Phil Maybutt Phil Maybutt has decided to give his new nephew a gift of a university education. Phil estimates that it will cost $150,000 for a four-year education at a good school, including tuition and living expenses, when his nephew is ready for university in 18 years. Phil has an investment opportunity that will earn 8 percent per year. How much must Phil invest today to have the $150,000 required in 18 years? In other words, what is the present value of $150,000 to be received in 18 years using a discount rate of 8 percent?

$$PV_{n,\,r} = \frac{1}{(1+r)^n} \times \text{Amount to be received or paid}$$
$$PV_{18,\,0.08} = \frac{1}{(1+0.08)^{18}} \times \$150,000$$
$$= \$37,537.35$$

Therefore, Phil would have to invest $37,537.35 today at 8 percent so that his nephew would have $150,000 in 18 years to pay for his university education.

Example 2: Quyon Ltd. Quyon Ltd. (Quyon) recently purchased a machine for $500,000. The purchase agreement allows Quyon to pay for the machine in three years with no interest. What would be the equivalent price if Quyon had to pay for the machine in cash today, if the appropriate discount rate was 6 percent? In other words, what is the present value of $500,000 to be paid in three years using a discount rate of 6 percent? Using the formula:

$$PV_{n,\,r} = \frac{1}{(1+r)^n} \times \text{Amount to be received or paid}$$
$$PV_{3,\,0.06} = \frac{1}{(1+0.06)^3} \times \$500,000$$
$$= \$419,809.64$$

Therefore, the current cash amount that is equivalent to paying $500,000 in three years at a discount rate of 6 percent is $419,809.64.

Question for Consideration

You have the option of receiving $1,000 today, $1,500 in four years, or $1,700 in six years. Which would you choose? Assume a discount rate of 6 percent. Explain your choice.

Answer: To answer the question it is necessary to compare the present values of each of the cash flows and select the one with the highest present value. The cash flow with the highest present value is the most valuable. The present value of cash today is that amount of cash:

$$\text{Option 1:} \quad PV_{n,r} = \frac{1}{(1 + r)^n} \times \text{Amount to be received or paid}$$

$$PV_{0,\,0.05} = \frac{1}{(1 + 0.06)^0} \times \$1,000$$

$$= \$1,000$$

$$\text{Option 2:} \quad PV_{4,\,0.06} = \frac{1}{(1 + 0.06)^4} \times \$1,500$$

$$= \$1,188.14$$

$$\text{Option 3:} \quad PV_{6,\,0.06} = \frac{1}{(1 + 0.06)^6} \times \$1,700$$

$$= \$1,198.43$$

Option 3 is the best one because it has the largest present value. Note that the present value of a cash flow to be received or paid now is always the actual amount of the cash flow, regardless of the discount rate.

Discounting, which is another term used for determining the present value of a future cash flow, is a very powerful tool because it allows comparisons of cash flows received at different times and in different amounts. So far, we have looked at simple situations involving a single cash flow sometime in the future. The present-value technique can be used in more complex situations. Let's add a fourth option to the three prizes offered in the previous Question for Consideration. Option 4 is that you could receive $250 per year for six years, beginning in one year. How would option 4 stack up against receiving $1,700 in year six, the best option of the first three?

This calculation is a bit more complicated, but the concepts are the same. Option 4 requires that we determine the present value of a series of six cash flows occurring at different times. The approach is the same as with the simpler examples, but more calculations are involved. The calculation of the present value of this series of cash flows is shown in Table 7–1.

Since the present value of the cash flows in Option 4 is the largest of the four offered, it should be selected.

Present Value of an Annuity

For Option 4 in the example we've just discussed, you would receive a $250 payment at the end of each of the next six years. A series of equal cash flows (inflows or outflows), made at equally spaced time intervals, is known as an **annuity**. To calculate the present value of the series of six $250 payments requires the following steps:

1. Find the discount rate for each of the six years.

2. Multiply the cash flow in each year by the appropriate discount rate to determine the present value of the cash flow in each year.

TABLE 7–1 ::: Option 4: Calculation of Present Value			
Calculation of Present Value of Option 4 **(Receive $250 per year for six years, beginning one year from now,** **at a discount rate of 6 percent)**			
Cash received	**Amount of cash received**	**Discount factor** $\frac{1}{(1+r)^n}$	**Present Value of cash flow**
Now	$0		
In one year	250	0.9434	$ 235.85
In two years	250	0.8900	222.50
In three years	250	0.8396	209.90
In four years	250	0.7921	198.02
In five years	250	0.7473	186.81
In six years	250	0.7050	176.24
Totals		4.91734	$1,229.33

3. Add up the present values from each year to get the present value of the entire series of cash flows. These three steps were what we did in Table 7–1.

This process can be summarized in the following equation:

$$PV_{n,r} = \sum \left[\frac{1}{(1+r)^n} \right] \times \text{Amount to be received or paid in each period}$$

$$= \frac{1}{r} \times \left[1 - \frac{1}{(1+r)^n} \right] \times \text{Amount to be received or paid in each period}$$

The first line of the formula sums the discount factors for each year of the annuity (see the third column of Table 7–1). The second line is the formula for the sum of a geometric series. Applying this formula for Option 4:

$$PV \text{ of an annuity}_{6,\,0.06} = \frac{1}{0.06} \times \left[1 - \frac{1}{(1+0.06)^6} \right] \times \$250$$

$$= \$1,229.33$$

This is the same amount that we calculated in Table 7–1. Note that the n in this formula refers to the number of periods for which the cash flow will be received. Also, this formula can only be used if the following conditions are met:

■ the cash flow is the same in each year;

■ the same discount rate is applied to each year's cash flow; and

■ the cash flow occurs in every year beginning one year from the present.

If *any* of these conditions is not met, the formula does not apply and the individual cash flows must be evaluated on a year-by-year basis. Let's look at an example of an annuity.

Example 1: Tuttle Inc. Tuttle Inc. (Tuttle) can invest in a business opportunity that will pay it $5,000,000 at the end of each of the next five years. Assuming that the appropriate discount rate is 12 percent, what is the present value of the payments Tuttle would receive by investing in the opportunity? What is the maximum amount that Tuttle should pay to invest in the business opportunity?

The answer can be obtained by applying the formula for the present value of an annuity.

$$\text{PV of an annuity}_{n,\,r} = \frac{1}{r} \times \left[1 - \frac{1}{(1+r)^n}\right] \times \begin{array}{c}\text{Amount to be received or paid}\\ \text{in each period}\end{array}$$

$$\text{PV of an annuity}_{5,\,0.12} = \frac{1}{0.12} \times \left[1 - \frac{1}{(1+0.12)^5}\right] \times \$5{,}000{,}000$$

$$= \$18{,}023{,}881$$

The present value of a series of $5,000,000 payments to be received at the end of each of the next five years, at a discount rate of 12 percent, is $18,023,881. This means that Tuttle would pay no more than $18,023,881 to invest in this business opportunity. By paying $18,023,881 Tuttle is earning exactly 12 percent on its investment, which is what it requires (that's why the 12 percent discount rate is used). If Tuttle had to pay more than $18,023,881, it would earn less than 12 percent, which would not be acceptable.

Discounting is relevant for a number of accounting issues. For example, if a company makes sales on credit, where payment is not due for a long time and no interest is payable on the debt, discounting helps determine how much revenue should be recognized. Discounting is also relevant for many liabilities, such as leases, pensions, and other long-term obligations. Later in this chapter, we will examine an accounting application of the time value of money.

Comment: This discussion of the time value of money is intended to briefly introduce the topic. For the purpose of this text it, is necessary that you understand the fundamentals so that you can understand how the time value of money affects financial reporting. Any further discussion is beyond the scope of this text.

www.mcgrawhill.ca/
olc/friedlan

Knowledge Check

■ What is the formula used to determine the present value of $1 to be received sometime in the future?

■ What is the present value of $100 to be received in ten years if the discount rate is 9 percent? ($42.24)

■ What is an annuity?

RECEIVABLES

Receivables represent amounts owing to an entity. Usually the amounts owing will be received in cash, but goods and services can also be receivable or owing. Most receivables result from selling goods and services to customers on credit. These are usually referred to as *accounts receivable.* Receivables can also represent amounts owing by shareholders and employees (shareholder/employee loans receivable), tax refunds (taxes receivable), amounts owing from investments (interest and dividends receivable), proceeds due from the sale of capital assets, and so on. Receivables are usually current assets, but if an amount owing is to be received in more than a year, it would be classified as non-current.

Exhibit 7–2 provides information about the receivables of Canadian Tire Corporation, Limited (Canadian Tire).[2] The exhibit shows that Canadian Tire has different types of receivables, including amounts owing on the company's own credit card and amounts owing from associate dealers (the Canadian Tire stores), as well as personal loans (loans to credit cardholders) and mortgages receivable. Also notice that some of the receivables are not current because

A famous professional athlete recently signed a one-year contract with his team for $15,000,000. Because the team was having financial problems, the athlete agreed to accept the $15,000,000 in equal payments of $750,000 over the next 20 years. The team stated at a press conference that the $15,000,000 justly rewarded the best player in the game with the highest one-year salary in the history of the sport, exceeding the previous high salary of $9,500,000.

Do you agree with the team's statement that the salary is the highest in the history of the sport? Explain your answer. Assume a discount rate of 10 percent and that payments are received at the end of each year.

Answer: If the previous high salary of $9,500,000 was paid in one year, the $15,000,000 salary is nowhere near the previous high. The present value of a series of $750,000 payments received over 20 years is:

$$PV_{n,\,r} = \frac{1}{r} \times \left[1 - \frac{1}{(1+r)^n}\right] \times \text{Amount to be paid in each period}$$

$$PV \text{ of an annuity}_{20,\,0.10} = \frac{1}{0.10} \times \left[1 - \frac{1}{(1+0.10)^{20}}\right] \times \$750,000$$

$$= \$6,385,173$$

Because the payments on the contract are spread over 20 years, the present value of the athlete's salary is $6,385,173. That means that receiving $750,000 over 20 years is equivalent to receiving $6,385,173 today. In nominal dollar terms, the athlete is receiving more money than any athlete before him. However, comparing the present value of the payments made under different contracts is a more legitimate way of comparing the contracts.

Consolidated Balance Sheets

As at (Dollars in millions)	January 1, 2005		January 3, 2004
			(Restated – Note 1)
ASSETS			
Current assets			
Cash and cash equivalents (Note 12)	$	802.2	$ 726.6
Accounts receivable (Note 12)		370.7	508.3
Credit card receivables and personal loans (Note 2)		592.4	562.8
Merchandise inventories		620.6	465.9
Prepaid expenses and deposits		24.1	27.9
Total current assets		2,410.0	2,291.5
Long-term receivables and other assets (Note 3)		129.7	64.1
Goodwill (Note 4)		41.7	40.6
Intangible assets (Note 4)		52.0	52.0
Property and equipment (Note 5)		2,585.2	2,444.9
Total assets	$	5,218.6	$ 4,893.1

EXHIBIT 7–2 :

Canadian Tire

www.canadiantire.ca

EXHIBIT 7–2 :

(continued)
Canadian Tire

Credit card receivables and personal loans   Credit card receivables are recorded at cost net of allowances established for credit losses, bankruptcy and fraud. Personal loans are recorded at cost net of allowances established for credit losses. The allowance for credit losses is calculated using the historical loss experience of account balances based on the aging and arrears status, with certain adjustments for other relevant circumstances influencing the recoverability of the loans. The allowance for bankruptcy is recorded as the average number of months in arrears of bankrupt accounts multiplied by the average monthly bankruptcy charge-off. Historical bankruptcy data for the past 12 months is used to calculate the averages. The allowance for fraud is recorded as three months of the average monthly fraud charge-offs, which is calculated using historical fraud charge-off data for the past 12 months. Credit card receivables in arrears for over 180 days are written off. Personal loans are classified as impaired when the principal or interest payments are over 90 days in arrears, and are written off when they are 365 days in arrears.

Effective July 1, 2001, the Company adopted the Canadian Institute of Chartered Accountants' Accounting Guideline 12 ("AcG-12"), "Transfers of Receivables." Under the new policy, the Company is required to recognize gains or losses on its credit card securitizations subsequent to June 30, 2001 that qualify as sales. Sales of credit card receivables prior to July 1, 2001 were accounted for under the accounting guidelines in effect at that time. The gain or loss on the sale of the credit card receivables depends in part on the previous carrying amount of the receivables involved in the sale. The carrying amount is allocated between the assets sold and the retained interests based on their relative fair value at the date of sale. The Company estimates fair value based on the present value of future expected cash flows using management's estimates of the key assumptions (see Note 2).

2. CREDIT CARD RECEIVABLES AND PERSONAL LOANS

During the year ended January 1, 2005, the Company sold undivided co-ownership interests in certain pools of credit card receivables (the "Receivables") to an independent trust, Glacier Credit Card Trust ("GCCT"), formerly known as Canadian Tire Receivables Trust, in transactions known as securitizations. Securitizations transfer to GCCT ownership interests in certain pools of the Receivables previously wholly owned by the Company that provide GCCT with (i) ownership of a share of the service charges generated by the pool up to a stipulated amount, and (ii) ownership of a share of the principal payments generated by the pool, both computed on a monthly basis. The Company retains any income in excess of GCCT's share of service charges on the Receivables. In these transactions, the Company also assumes responsibility for servicing the Receivables for which it will not receive any direct compensation. GCCT's recourse to the Company is generally limited to its income earned on the Receivables, although unexpected sizeable losses could also result in a reduction in the value of the co-ownership interest retained by the Company.

As the Company does not control GCCT, it has not been consolidated in these financial statements. The Company has reflected the transfer of the co-ownership interest to GCCT as a sale in accordance with AcG-12, "Transfers of Receivables," which became effective on July 1, 2001. In accordance with this Guideline, the proceeds of the sale to GCCT were deemed to be the cash received from GCCT plus the estimated fair value of the Company's retained interest in the service charges of the pool, net of the servicing obligation assumed. The excess of the estimated fair value of the proceeds over the carrying value of the interests in Receivables sold is reflected in these financial statements as a gain on the date of disposition. For the year ended January 1, 2005, the Company has recognized pre-tax gains of $22.6 million (2003 - $16.8 million) on such securitization transactions. The Company recognizes gains from securitization transactions prior to July 1, 2001, as the service charges are realized.

For transfers of Receivables occurring after July 1, 2001, the Company has computed the estimated fair values of its retained interest by discounting the expected future cash flows from the retained interest.

Quantitative information about net credit card receivables and net personal loans managed by the Company is as follows:

(Dollars in millions)	Total principal amount of receivables		Average balances	
	2004	2003	**2004**	2003
Total net managed credit card portfolio	$ **2,789.2**	$ 2,433.3	$ **2,512.6**	$ 2,035.2
Credit card receivables sold[1]	**(2,209.3)**	(1,870.5)	**(1,889.5)**	(1,475.5)
Credit card receivables held	**579.9**	562.8	$ **623.1**	$ 559.7
Personal loans[2]	**64.0**	–		
Total	**643.9**	562.8		
Less: long-term portion of personal loans[3]	**51.5**	–		
Credit card receivables and current portion of personal loans	$ **592.4**	$ 562.8		

Includes receivables sold pre and post adoption of AcG-12 "Transfers of Receivables" on July 1, 2001.
Personal loans are provided to qualified existing credit cardholders for terms of three to five years. Personal loans have fixed monthly payments, however, the personal loans can be repaid at any time without penalty.
The long-term portion of personal loans is included in "Long-term receivables and other assets" (see Note 3).

Net credit losses for the year ended January 1, 2005 were $149.6 million (2003 - $121.9 million). Net credit losses are charge-offs net of recoveries and are based on the total managed portfolio of credit card receivables and personal loans.

The fair value of future cash flows of the Company's retained interest at January 1, 2005 was $67.0 million (2003 - $44.4 million).

The following table shows the key economic assumptions used in measuring the retained interests at the date of securitization resulting from securitizations completed during the year. The table also displays the sensitivity of the current fair value of residual cash flows to immediate 10 percent and 20 percent adverse changes in the 2004 key economic assumptions.

(Dollars in millions)	Assumptions	Effects of adverse change on $100 million of GCCT debt[1]		Assumptions
	2004	10%	20%	2003
Yield	**16.50%**	$ (0.7) $	(1.4)	17.01%
Liquidation rate (% of sold receivables per month)[2]	**23.01%**	(0.5)	(1.0)	24.53%
Expected credit losses	**5.60%**	–	–	5.85%
Discount rate	**12.00%**	–	–	12.00%
Service costs[3]	**2.00%**	(0.1)	(0.2)	2.00%

[1] These sensitivities are hypothetical and should be used with caution. As the figures indicate, changes in fair value based on a 10 percent or 20 percent variation in assumptions generally cannot be extrapolated because the relationship of the change in assumption to the change in fair value may not be linear. Also, in this table, the effect of a variation in a particular assumption on the fair value of the retained interest is calculated without changing any other assumption; in reality, changes in one factor may result in changes in another (for example, increases in market interest rates may result in lower payments and increased credit losses), which might magnify or counteract the sensitivities.
[2] Based on historical patterns the full receivable is estimated to be collected in 12 months.
[3] The servicing liability as at January 1, 2005 was $13.5 million (2003 - $8.8 million).

Details of cash flows from securitizations[1]:

(Dollars in millions)	2004	2003
Proceeds from new securitizations	$ **625.0**	$ 570.0
Proceeds from collections reinvested in previous credit card securitizations	**5,601.0**	4,099.3
Other cash flows received on retained interests[2]	**1,335.3**	953.6

[1] Cash flows from securitizations include securitizations before and after the adoption of AcG-12 on July 1, 2001.
[2] Retained interests represent receivables held by the Company in addition to those sold to GCCT.

EXHIBIT 7-2 :

(continued)
Canadian Tire

12. *Notes to the Consolidated Statements of Cash Flow*

Sale of Associate Dealer receivables   In December 2004, the Company sold certain Associate Dealer receivables to independent investors. According to the terms of the sale, the Company retained full servicing responsibilities for which it received no compensation. For the year ended January 1, 2005, the Company has recognized a loss of $2.1 million (2003 – $0.7 million) on the sale of the Associate Dealer receivables, which assumes no expected credit losses and a servicing liability of 1.0 percent. Quantitative information about accounts receivable managed by the Company is as follows:

		Total principal amount of receivables	
(Dollars in millions)		**2004**	2003
			(Restated – Note 1)
Associate Dealer receivables	$	**543.3**	$ 462.3
Associate Dealer receivables sold		**(323.2)**	(98.7)
Other accounts receivable		**150.6**	144.7
Receivables held	$	**370.7**	$ 508.3

they don't have to be repaid within a year. Exhibit 7–2 also shows that Canadian Tire has *securitized* (sold to investors) some of the amounts owing on the customer credit cards and by the associate dealers as a way to raise cash to meet its needs. Indeed, Canadian Tire has sold over $2.2 billion of its credit card receivables and over $323 million of the amounts owed by associate dealers. The receivables that have been sold are not reported on Canadian Tire's balance sheet.

Our discussion will focus on accounts receivable because these are the most common and most significant receivables reported on financial statements. The concepts discussed will generally apply to all types of receivables. Accounts receivable arise when revenue is recognized but payment is not received. As we discussed in Chapter 4, the journal entry to record revenue that is recognized before payment is received is:

Dr. Accounts receivable (asset +)	xxx
Cr. Revenue (revenue +, owners' equity +)	xxx

When the customer pays the amount owed, the journal entry recorded is:

Dr. Cash (asset +)	xxx
Cr. Accounts receivable (asset −)	xxx

Accounts receivable are essentially loans made by an entity to its customers. Most businesses would probably prefer to do business on a cash basis because selling on credit lengthens an entity's cash cycle and introduces the risk that amounts owed will not be collected. Selling on credit also incurs costs to administer the credit program—costs such as setting policies for determining whether customers are eligible for credit, doing credit checks on prospective credit customers, processing billings and collections, and pursuing customers that do not pay. However, if a company does not offer credit, some customers may take their business elsewhere. In many business situations, credit terms are an important part of the "package" that an entity offers its customers, especially for non-retail transactions.

For most retail businesses, credit is offered through major credit cards such as MasterCard and Visa. However, credit can be an important and lucrative business in the retail industry. That is why companies such as Sears Canada Inc., Home Depot, Canadian Tire, and Hudson's Bay Company offer their own credit cards to their customers. These companies earn interest from customers who do not pay for their purchases within the allowed period of time.

GAAP financial statements report receivables at their net realizable value (NRV); that is, at the estimated amount that will be collected. When a company sells on credit, a number of events can reduce the amount that will actually be collected, including the following:

■ Customers might not pay what they owe. Failure to pay may be due to financial problems, disputes over whether the goods or services were delivered or acceptable, or simply because some customers are dishonest.

■ Some customers may demand refunds if they are not satisfied with the goods or services provided. Most people have purchased items or received gifts that they have returned for a refund or credit.

- Customers may receive a discount if they pay their bills early. For example, an entity may offer a customer a 2 percent discount if the amount owed is paid within 10 days. Thus, if the customer owes $1,000, only $980 has to be paid if payment is made within 10 days. If the customer waits until the payment is actually due, perhaps 30 or 60 days from the date of purchase, then the full amount must be paid.

Under accrual accounting, bad debts, returns, and discounts are costs of doing business in the period when the revenue is recognized. The effect of accounting for bad debts, returns, and discounts is to reduce net income (by reducing sales or increasing expenses) and reduce accounts receivable. Each of these items is not usually known at the balance sheet date, so the amounts have to be estimated.

Reporting receivables at their NRV makes sense for many users and uses of financial statements. For cash flow prediction and liquidity analysis, the NRV provides the most useful information because the amount represents the cash that will likely be received. For the stewardship and management evaluation objectives, knowing the actual amount owed by customers and the estimated amount that will be collected are useful for assessing how well receivables, credit and collection, returns, and discounts are being managed. GAAP do not cooperate fully in providing this stewardship information. Under GAAP, it is necessary to account for uncollectible receivables, sales returns, and discounts, but there is no requirement that information on these estimates be disclosed. As a result, there is wide variation among entities for dealing with adjustments to accounts receivable.

For private companies, where adherence to GAAP may not be required, the amount reported for accounts receivable could represent gross receivables, net receivables, or receivables net of some estimates (such as bad debts), but not of others (such as returns). A user must be very careful to understand exactly what is represented by the numbers being reported. This is especially true for financial statements that are prepared primarily for tax purposes. Estimates such as returns and discounts cannot be deducted when calculating taxable income, so a preparer may not include these estimates when preparing the financial statements. For tax purposes, an allowance for uncollectible accounts can be deducted.

◇ ROGERS

When a Rogers' customer makes a purchase using a credit card such as Visa or MasterCard, the amount does not appear as a receivable. The credit card receipt is equivalent to cash; Rogers just has to take the receipt to the bank to receive cash. The account receivable belongs to the credit card company. Rogers pays the credit card company a percentage of each sale as a fee for being able to accept the credit card. For example, a $100 purchase made using a MasterCard might cost Rogers 1 percent of the charged amount, or $1. When Rogers presents the credit card receipt at the bank, it would receive $99 instead of $100.

A credit card transaction could be recorded in two ways. The first way would be to simply record the sale in the amount of the cash received. For a $100 sale with a service charge of $1, the journal entry would be:

Dr. Cash (asset +)	99	
Cr. Revenue (revenue +, owners' equity +)		99
To record the sale of goods using a credit card at the net amount.		

The second way to record a credit card transaction would be to record the sale at the amount the customer agreed to pay and to create a separate account for the service charge. In this case, the journal entry would be:

Dr. Cash (asset +)	99	
Dr. Credit card service fee (expense +, owners' equity –)	1	
Cr. Revenue (revenue +, owners' equity +)		100
To record the sale of goods using a credit card at the gross amount.		

The second entry provides information about the cost of allowing customers to use credit cards. With the first entry, this information is lost. The amount of revenue reported is not affected by how the customer paid. In other words, with the second entry, $100 of revenue would be recorded, regardless of whether the customer paid by cash, cheque, or credit card.

Accounting for Uncollectible Receivables

A cost of doing business on credit is that some customers don't pay what they owe and this cost must be accounted for. Accounting for uncollectible receivables must address two effects. First, an expense must be recorded to reflect the amounts that will not be collected. Second, accounts receivable must be decreased by the estimated amount that will not be collected so that the amount on the balance sheet reflects the amount the entity will collect from its customers.

The easiest way to account for uncollectible receivables, or bad debts, is to simply write off a receivable when it becomes clear that a customer will not be paying. This method is known as the direct write-off method. With the **direct write-off method**, a receivable is removed from the list of receivables and an expense recorded when management decides that the receivable will not be collected. The journal entry that would be recorded is:

Dr. Bad debt expense (expense +, owners' equity −)	xxx	
Cr. Receivables (assets −)		xxx

For example, in September 2009 the management of Killowen Inc. (Killowen) decided that $10,000 owed to it by Fredericton Ltd. would not be paid. The amount had been in dispute for 18 months and management decided that it was not worthwhile pursuing the matter any further. Killowen has a December 31 year end. If Killowen used the direct write-off method to account for bad debts, it would make the following journal entry in September 2009, when management decided that the amount owing would not be collected:

Dr. Bad debt expense (expense +, owners' equity −)	10,000	
Cr. Accounts receivable (assets −)		10,000
To write off an uncollectible account receivable.		

While the direct write-off method is simple and straightforward, it's not good matching. In the example, the expense for the bad debt would be recognized over 18 months after the transaction had taken place. Matching requires that the cost of bad debts be expensed in the period when the related revenue is recognized. In other words, if Killowen is using accrual accounting, it shouldn't wait until it is clear that a customer is not going to pay. Another problem with the direct write-off method is that it is easily manipulated, because management can pick and choose exactly when it wants to write off accounts receivable.

If we are going to match and expense bad debts in the period in which the related revenue is recognized, an obvious question is, "How do we know which accounts to write off?" We don't. If we knew at the time of the transaction that a customer was not going to pay, we would not have offered the customer credit. Under accrual accounting, an estimate of the amount that will not be collected is made without knowing which specific receivables will not be collected. We have to wait to find out which receivables will not be collected.

There are two methods used to estimate the cost of bad debts:

1. The percentage-of-receivables method.

2. The percentage-of-credit-sales method.

With either of these two methods, the following journal entry is made each period to account for bad debts:

Dr. Bad debt expense (expense +, owners' equity −)	xxx	
Cr. Allowance for uncollectible accounts (contra-asset +)		xxx

The bad debt expense is a cost of selling on credit during the period. The **allowance for uncollectible accounts** is a contra-asset account to accounts receivable or another receivables account that represents the amount of the receivables that management estimates will not be collected. A contra-asset account is used because it is not possible to identify the specific receivables that will not be collected when the estimate is made. The Accounts Receivable account represents a listing of the amount owed by each customer. For example, an extract from the detailed list for Killowen Inc. is presented in Table 7–2. Considered together, Accounts Receivable and Allowance for Uncollectible Accounts give an estimate of the NRV of accounts receivable.

TABLE 7-2 ::: Killowen Inc.: Selected Accounts Receivable

Killowen Inc.
Accounts Receivable Ledger
December 31, 2009

Customer	Accounts Balance
Charlottetown Inc.	$ 31,200.05
Dartmouth Ltd.	157,000.10
Fredericton Ltd.	25,000.92
Gander Inc.	38,500.68
Moncton Ltd.	22,250.25
Saint John Inc.	117,410.41
St. John's Ltd.	57,200.09
Total	$1,194,000.00

The Percentage-of-Receivables Method With the **percentage-of-receivables method**, managers estimate the amount of receivables at the end of the period that won't be collected. This approach provides an estimate of the NRV of the ending balance of receivables. To achieve this result, the allowance for uncollectible accounts is debited or credited for whatever amount is needed to bring the balance in the account to the amount estimated by management. This entry is an adjusting entry.

For example, Killowen Inc.'s management estimates that $71,500 of its ending accounts receivable of $1,194,000 on December 31, 2009 will not be collected. The balance in the allowance account before the end-of-period adjusting entry is recorded is a credit of $5,000. (The reason why there might be a balance in the allowance account before the adjusting entry is made will be made clear shortly.) To bring the balance in the allowance account to the desired credit balance of $71,500, a credit to the allowance account of $66,500 is required. The following journal entry is recorded:

> Dr. Bad debt expense (expense +, owners' equity –)   66,500
>   Cr. Allowance for uncollectible accounts (contra-asset +)   66,500
> To record the bad debt expense for 2009.

With the percentage-of-receivables method, the bad debt expense is not calculated directly. The bad debt expense is simply "the other side of the journal entry" that is required to bring the Allowance account to the desired amount. If, as in the example, a credit of $66,500 is required to bring the Allowance account to the desired amount, the bad debt expense is debited for $66,500. This focus on the Allowance account is why the percentage-of-receivables method is called a *balance sheet approach*. The effect on the accounts can be seen in the partial spreadsheet in Table 7–3.

The NRV of Killowen's accounts receivable is $1,122,500 ($1,194,000 − $71,500). There is a balance in the Allowance for Uncollectible Accounts before the adjusting entry is made on December 31, 2009 because management's estimate of the amount of receivables that would not be collected during 2009 was not correct. That is, the estimate Killowen's management made on December 31, 2008 was $5,000 too high. An incorrect estimate is a reflection of the difficulty in predicting the future. When the adjusting entry is made, management is making an educated guess of the amount of receivables that won't be collected. What the actual amount of receivables is that won't be collected is only known long after the end of the period. As we will see later in this chapter, managers can use estimates as a way of achieving their reporting objectives.

TABLE 7–3 ::: Partial Spreadsheet for Killowen Inc.

Killowen Inc. Partial Spreadsheet December 31, 2009			
	Accounts Receivable	**Allowance for Uncollectible Accounts**	**Bad Debt Expense**
Balances on December 31, 2009, before adjusting entry	$1,194,000	$ (5,000)	
Adjusting entry		(66,500)	66,500
Ending balances on December 31, 2009	1,194,000	(71,500)	66,500

TABLE 7–4 ::: Aging Schedule for Killowen Inc.

Killowen Inc. Aging Schedule December 31, 2009					
	Current	**1 to 30 days overdue**	**31 to 90 days overdue**	**Over 90 days overdue**	**Total**
Amount	$950,000	$125,000	$72,000	$47,000	$1,194,000
Percentage estimated to be uncollectible	1%	4%	40%	60%	
Amount estimated to be uncollectible	$9,500	$5,000	$28,800	$28,200	$71,500

How does management estimate the amount of receivables that will not be collected? One way is to use an aging schedule. An **aging schedule** classifies accounts receivable by the length of time they have been outstanding. Current receivables are ones that are due within the period that the entity allows customers to pay. If the entity allows customers to pay within 30 days, receivables that have been outstanding for 30 days or less are current. The remaining receivables are then classified by how long overdue they are.

Management uses its historical information about the proportion of each category of receivables that has been collected in the past, along with its knowledge of factors that might cause those historical percentages to change, to estimate the amount of end-of-period accounts receivable that will not be collected. Typically, the older a receivable, the less likely it is to be collected. An aging schedule for Killowen is shown in Table 7–4.

Based on the aging schedule, Killowen would report gross accounts receivable of $1,194,000, less an allowance for uncollectible accounts of $71,500. How this information is disclosed in the financial statements varies. Killowen could disclose the allowance on the balance sheet, in the notes to the statements, or not at all. According to GAAP, entities are not required to disclose their bad debt expense in the income statement or in the notes to the financial statements. In 2004, 152 of 200 firms surveyed in *Financial Reporting in Canada* did not disclose or refer to the allowance for uncollectible accounts in their financial statements.[3] As a result, it can be difficult for a user to assess the efficiency and effectiveness of an entity's credit and collection policies. Exhibit 7–3 shows how two companies provide information about their accounts receivable in their financial statements and notes.[4]

It is important to remember that an estimate is a prediction of what will happen—in this case, the amount of receivables that will not be collected. Historical information might be helpful for making a prediction, but that does not mean it will happen in the future. For

December 31, 2005 and 2004
(In thousands of US dollars (note 1(a))

	2005	2004
Assets		
Current assets:		
Cash and cash equivalents	$ 242,178	$ 226,377
Receivables (note 2)	69,690	81,541
Inventory	7,326	1,439
Prepaid expenses	2,950	2,981
	322,144	312,338
Long-term receivables (note 3)	175,374	179,060
Investments in hotel partnerships and corporations (note 4)	99,928	131,338
Fixed assets (note 5)	64,850	59,939
Investment in management contracts (note 6)	164,932	181,273
Investment in trademarks and trade names (note 7)	4,210	4,424
Future income tax assets (note 8)	14,439	3,711
Other assets	34,324	30,064
	$ 880,201	$ 902,147

2. **Receivables:**

	2005	2004
Trade accounts of consolidated hotels	$ 1,526	$ 4,331
Receivables from hotel partnerships, affiliates and managed hotels	52,684	56,674
Receivables relating to stock options exercised (note 11(a))	–	5,708
Taxes receivable	6,647	2,735
Other	8,833	12,093
	$ 69,690	$ 81,541

Receivables at December 31, 2005 are recorded net of an allowance for doubtful accounts of $2,792 (2004 - $2,535). The net bad debt expense for the year ended December 31, 2005 was $18 (2004 - $10).

Comment: Four Seasons Hotels Inc. reports the net amount of accounts receivable in its balance sheet and breaks down the different types of receivables in the note. The amount of each type of receivable is shown in the note net of the allowance for doubtful accounts but the balance in the allowance for doubtful accounts is given. The amount of the bad debt expense is also provided.

example, circumstances such as a slowdown in the economy or a change in the credit terms an entity offers suggest that simply using the historical rate of bad debts is not always appropriate.

Users of financial statements are not likely to see the accounts receivable aging schedule unless they are powerful enough to successfully demand information from an entity. Banks will usually require a schedule of aged receivables if the receivables are used as collateral for a loan and the maximum amount that can be borrowed is a percentage of receivables. Banks will want an aging schedule because they will not usually accept as security receivables that are more than 90 days old, since these receivables have a high risk of being uncollectible.

EXHIBIT 7–3 :

(continued)
Panel B: Eldorado
Gold Corporation

Consolidated Balance Sheets

As at December 31 (Expressed in thousands of US dollars)

		2005	2004
ASSETS			
Current Assets			
Cash and cash equivalents		$ 33,826	$ 135,390
Accounts receivable		8,264	8,705
Prepaids		2,024	–
Inventories	Note 5	7,597	5,927
		51,711	150,022
Property, plant and equipment	Note 6	186,610	52,337
Other assets		6,288	–
Mineral properties and deferred development	Note 6	23,326	22,676
Investments and advances	Note 9	562	1,224
Deposits	Note 4	50,000	
Goodwill	Note 3	2,238	–
		$ 320,735	$ 226,259

Comment: Eldorado Gold Corporation provides an amount for accounts receivable on its balance sheet with no additional explanation. We can assume that the amount is net of the allowance for doubtful accounts since Husky follows accrual accounting. No information is provided about the bad debt expense for the year.

Comment: Also look at Rogers' balance sheet on page A-4. Roger discloses its allowance for doubtful accounts parenthetically on the balance sheet. No information about the bad debt expense is provided.

Percentage-of-Credit-Sales Method With the **percentage-of-credit-sales method** of estimating uncollectible receivables, managers estimate the amount of credit sales recognized during the period that won't be collected. With this method, the bad debt expense is estimated by taking a percentage of credit sales recognized in the period. The logic is that in each period, some portion of credit sales will not be collected. That percentage is the bad debt expense for the period. Only credit sales are considered because cash sales are, of course, 100 percent collected. Again, management bases its estimate on the historical collection rate of credit sales and knowledge of any changes that might cause the collection rate to change.

For example, if Killowen had credit sales of $9,375,000 during 2009 and management estimated that 0.8 percent of credit sales would not be collected, then the adjusting journal entry that Killowen would make on December 31, 2009 would be:

Dr. Bad debt expense (expense +, owners' equity −)	75,000	
Cr. Allowance for uncollectible accounts (contra-asset +)		75,000
To record the bad debt expense for 2009.		

Unlike the percentage-of-receivables method, which takes a balance sheet approach, the percentage-of-credit-sales method takes an *income statement approach*. The focus of this method is the bad debt expense. By calculating the amount of credit sales that will not be collected, the "right" amount of bad debt expense is obtained. This method results in a better matching of costs and benefits because the amount expensed is directly related to the amount of credit sales in the period. With the percentage-of-credit-sales method, the bad debt expense is calculated and the amount of the expense for the period is credited to the allowance account to complete the journal entry. Because the percentage-of-credit-sales method focuses on the income statement, the estimate of the NRV of accounts receivable may not be as accurate as with the percentage-of-receivables approach.

Sometimes, the annual estimate that management makes to determine the bad debt expense is consistently too high or too low. The percentage of credit sales that management uses may be above or below the actual amount of bad debts the entity incurs each year. This may occur if management doesn't change the assumptions for estimating bad debts in response to a change in the economy (for example, an improvement or deterioration in the economy). The result is that

Knowledge Check

■ You have been given the following list of aged accounts receivable for Onward Inc. (Onward) on December 31, 2010:

Current	$175,000
1–30 days overdue	32,000
31–60 days overdue	12,500
61–90 days overdue	5,700
Over 90 days overdue	2,300

Onward's management estimates that it will collect 98 percent of the current accounts receivable, 94 percent of the receivables that are 1–30 days overdue, 80 percent of the receivables that are 31–60 days overdue, 65 percent of the receivables that are 61–90 days overdue, and 30 percent of the receivables that are more than 90 days overdue.

Onward uses the percentage-of-receivables method for estimating bad debts. There is a credit balance of $1,025 in Allowance for Uncollectible Accounts on December 31, 2010, before the adjusting entry is made.

■ How much of each category of accounts receivable does Onward not expect to collect?

■ Prepare the journal entry that Onward should make on December 31, 2010 to record the bad debt expense.

there will be a build-up in the Allowance account. If the bad debt expense is consistently higher than the amount of receivables that are actually written off, then a credit balance builds up in the allowance account. If the bad debt expense is consistently less than the actual amount written off, then a debit balance builds up. In either case, an adjusting entry must eventually be made that puts the balance in the allowance account in line with the actual economic situation. It would probably take management a few years before it realizes that there is a problem with its estimate since for any given year one wouldn't expect the estimate to be exactly correct. If there is a credit balance build-up in the Allowance account, the adjusting entry is:

Dr. Allowance for uncollectible accounts (contra-asset −)   xxx
     Cr. Bad debt expense (expense −, owners' equity +)   xxx

The entry reduces the credit balance in the allowance account to a level that reflects the NRV of accounts receivable. The entry also reduces the bad debt expense, which increases net income for the period. In effect, in the previous years when the misestimate was being made, net income was lower than it would have been had a better estimate of bad debts been made. The effect of these estimation errors is being corrected in the current period's income statement. If the Allowance account is not adjusted, the balance does not give a reasonable estimate of the NRV of accounts receivable. The opposite is true of the effect for a debit build-up in the Allowance account.

The adjusting journal entry in the event of a debit balance build-up is:

Dr. Bad debt expense (expense +, owners' equity −)   xxx
     Cr. Allowance for uncollectible accounts (contra-asset +)   xxx

In principle, errors in estimates are not a major concern. Predicting the future is difficult, so there should be no expectation that management will get the estimate "right" each time. However, if managers make errors in the same direction each year (that is, every year the estimate is higher (or lower) than what the actual amount turns out to be, amounts in the financial statements can be significantly misstated. By making estimates that are biased (have intentional "errors"), managers can manage earnings.

From a user's perspective, financial statements usually do not provide enough information to allow effective analysis of credit and collection policies. It is rare for an entity to break down its sales into cash and credit components. Entities usually don't disclose their bad debt expenses, and almost never disclose how uncollectibles are estimated or how the percentages are used to make the estimates.

Writing Off a Receivable The percentage-of-receivables and the percentage-of-credit-sales methods are used to estimate uncollectible accounts. But what happens when we finally know who is not going to pay? For both methods of estimating uncollectible accounts, when a specific account receivable is identified as not being collectable, that receivable is removed from the receivables listing, thereby reducing the balance in the Receivables account. The balance in the Allowance account is also reduced or debited. The Allowance account is reduced because when a specific uncollectible account is identified, that part of the estimate has become reality. Therefore, the amount of the estimate that has happened is transferred from the "estimate account" (Uncollectibles) to the "actual account" (Receivables).

Once Killowen Inc.'s management decides that the $10,000 owing from Fredericton Ltd. is not going to be collected, it will make the following entry:

Dr. Allowance for uncollectible accounts (contra-asset −)   10,000
   Cr. Accounts receivable—Fredericton (asset −)   10,000
To write off a $10,000 account receivable from Fredericton Ltd.

Writing off an account receivable has no effect on the net balance of Accounts Receivable (Accounts Receivable − Allowance for Uncollectibles). This can be seen by comparing Killowen's receivables before and after the write-off of the $10,000 owed by Fredericton. The comparison is shown in Table 7–5. Allowance for Uncollectible Accounts and Accounts Receivable both decrease by $10,000, but net Accounts Receivable remains the same.

If we examined the accounts receivable ledger shown in Table 7–2 (page 354) after the write-off, we would find that the amount owing by Fredericton is $15,000.92 instead of $25,000.92.

Notice that the write-off of an account receivable has no effect on the income statement. The income statement effect occurs when the adjusting entry that records the bad debt expense and the adjustment to Allowance for Uncollectible Accounts is made.

Comparison of the Methods The three methods that have been discussed—direct write-off, percentage-of-receivables, and percentage-of-credit sales—all address the problem of accounting for uncollectible amounts. Under accrual accounting, the direct write-off method is not acceptable because it does not match expenses to revenues. The two estimation methods are different ways of achieving the same purpose of providing a bad debt expense and the NRV of accounts receivable. Both methods are used in practice. Both methods require judgement by the managers to determine the amount of the bad-debt expense, the adjustment to the Allowance for Uncollectibles, and the decision to write off a specific account receivable. As a result of the need for judgment, estimating bad debts is a tool that managers can use to "manage the numbers" in the financial statements.

It's also worth noting that the amount that will be expensed each year with the three methods will usually be different, although over the life of the entity the amount expensed will be the same, regardless of the method. It is important to recognize that an entity's net income in a

TABLE 7–5 ::: Killowen Inc.: Accounts Receivable Before and After Write-Off	Before Write-Off	After Write-Off
Accounts receivable	$1,194,000	$1,184,000
Less: Allowance for uncollectible accounts	71,500	61,500
Accounts receivable, net	$1,122,500	$1,122,500

period may be affected by the method used, even though the underlying economic circumstances of the entity are not affected by the method. However, outcomes that are based on net income and other accounting numbers that are affected by the accounting choice may be affected in turn—for example, management bonuses may differ with different net incomes.

Returns: At the end of a period, it is necessary to adjust the financial statements for estimated returns. Like uncollectable amounts, estimated returns are recorded in a contra-asset account (contra-accounts receivable). Unlike uncollectables, returns are not shown as an expense but are netted against revenue. When you look at the amount of revenue reported on an entity's income statement, the amount is normally after returns have been deducted, so a user doesn't see the amount of returns (which could be useful information). If estimated sales returns are not recorded, accounts receivable and revenue will be overstated.

Long-Term Receivables

Receivables do not always have to be current assets. Even amounts owing from customers can be due in more than a year or an operating cycle. An entity can enter into any type of payment arrangement with customers that it chooses. If a receivable is due in more than a year or an operating cycle, it is classified as a long-term asset. Look again at Panel A of Exhibit 7–3. Notice that Four Seasons Hotel's balance sheet reports long-term receivables in the amount of $175,374,000.

An interesting question surrounding the accounting for long-term receivables is the amount that should be reported on the balance sheet. When payment is not due for a long time, or if payment is spread out over a long period of time, then the time value of money becomes an issue. If a long-term receivable does not require the payment of interest or if the interest rate is less than the market rate, then the amount of revenue that is recognized and the receivable are too high if the time value of money is ignored.

Let's look at an example. On December 31, 2007 Winnipeg Inc. (Winnipeg) sold goods to Regina Ltd. (Regina) for $200,000. Because of Regina's financial difficulties, Winnipeg agreed to accept payment in full in three years, on January 2, 2011. The agreement does not require Regina to pay interest. Winnipeg was confident that it would receive its money because Regina's owners have personally guaranteed the debt, so Winnipeg recognized the revenue when the goods were shipped.

How much revenue should Winnipeg recognize when the goods are shipped and how should the receivable be accounted for in its accounting records? Clearly, Winnipeg has not earned $200,000 because the time value of money concept means the present value of the money Regina will pay in three years is less than $200,000.

For this example, assume that a discount rate of 8 percent is appropriate. The present value of $200,000 to be received in three years can be determined using the formula:

$$PV_{n,r} = \frac{1}{(1+1r)^n} \times \text{Amount to be received or paid}$$

$$PV_{3,\,0.08} = \frac{1}{(1+0.08)^3} \times \$200,000$$

$$= \$158,766$$

This means that if we consider the time value of money, Winnipeg should recognize $158,766 of revenue in 2007 for the sale to Regina. The journal entry that Winnipeg would make in 2007 to record the revenue is:

Dr. Long-term receivable (asset +)	158,766	
Cr. Revenue (revenue +, shareholders' equity +)		158,766
To record the sale of goods to Regina Ltd.		

The spreadsheet entries for the sale to Regina are shown in Table 7–6. The difference between the $158,766 that Winnipeg recognizes as revenue in 2007 and the $200,000 in cash that it will receive in January 2011 is the interest implicit in the agreement between Winnipeg and Regina.

TABLE 7–6 ::: Partial Spreadsheet for Winnipeg Inc.

Winnipeg Inc.
Partial Spreadsheet

	Cash	Current accounts receivable	Long-term receivable	Revenue	Interest revenue	
Ending balance sheet December 31, 2007			158,766	158,766		Recognition of revenue on sale of goods to Regina Ltd.
December 31, 2008 (adjusting entry)			12,701		12,701	Recognition of interest revenue earned in 2004. Interest is calculated based on the receivable on December 31, 2007. The interest is added to the long-term receivable account. Interest earned = $158,766 × 0.08. Note that amounts are rounded to the nearest dollar.
Ending balance sheet December 31, 2008			171,467			
December 31, 2009 (adjusting entry)			13,718		13,718	Recognition of interest revenue earned in 2008. Interest earned = $171,467 × 0.08.
Ending balance sheet December 31, 2009			185,185			
December 31, 2010 (adjusting entry)			14,815		14,815	Recognition of interest revenue earned in 2009. Interest earned = $185,184 × 0.08.
December 31, 2010 (adjusting entry)		200,000	(200,000)			To reclassify the receivable as current.
Ending balance sheet December 31, 2010		200,000				
January 2, 2011	200,000	(200,000)				Collection of the $200,000 from Regina Ltd.

Over the three-year period, Winnipeg will recognize $41,234 in interest on this receivable. Each year, Winnipeg will recognize interest revenue and increase the long-term receivable. The journal entry made each year would be:

Dr. Long-term receivable (asset +)   xxx
    Cr. Interest revenue (revenue +, shareholders' equity +)   xxx
    To accrue interest revenue on the long-term receivable from Regina Ltd.

Note that revenue from the sale of goods is reduced and is replaced with interest revenue. In other words, the sale to Regina is equivalent to selling the goods for $158,766 on the date of the transaction and then earning $41,234 in interest by financing the sale. Over the three years $200,000 of revenue is recognized, but taking the time value of money into consideration changes the timing and type of the revenue. Table 7–6 shows the amount of interest revenue that Winnipeg would recognize each year as a result of the contract with Regina. Notice that the amount of interest accrued each year is added to the long-term receivable column. On December 31, 2010 the amount of the receivable reported on the balance sheet is $200,000, the amount that Regina is expected to pay. On Winnipeg's December 31, 2010 balance sheet, the long-term receivable would be classified as a current asset because it is then due within one year.

If Winnipeg's agreement with Regina required the payment of interest at the market rate, it would be unnecessary to discount the cash flow. The revenue and receivable could be set up at $200,000 in 2007 and the interest revenue would be recorded each year.

FINANCIAL STATEMENT ANALYSIS ISSUES

Hidden Reserves

Hidden reserves are undisclosed accounting choices used to manage earnings and other financial information with the intention of satisfying the self-interests of the preparers. Using hidden reserves is an abuse of accounting information; hidden reserves undermine the usefulness and credibility of financial statements. It is strongly suspected that hidden reserves are in wide use by many entities. Securities commissions in Canada and the U.S. have taken direct aim on this manipulation of financial statements. While hidden reserves are inappropriate, their apparent wide use makes them an interesting area of accounting and one that users of accounting information need to understand.

A simple example will show how management can use accounting estimates to manage earnings. The example uses the allowance for uncollectible accounts and bad debt expense to show how profits can be moved from one period to another. Remember, under GAAP there are minimal disclosure requirements about the estimates that management makes when preparing the financial statements.

In 2010, Discovery Ltd. (Discovery), a public company, enjoyed its most successful year ever. Its performance exceeded the expectations of management as well as investors and stock market watchers. Sales in 2010 were $50,000,000 and net income should have been $3,000,000. However, in late 2010, management recognized that 2011 would be less successful and they feared that the poorer performance would have a negative effect on Discovery's stock price and management's bonuses. Historically, Discovery had set up an allowance for uncollectible accounts equal to 3 percent of its year-end accounts receivable. Over the years the 3 percent estimate had proven to be a reasonable estimate of amounts that would not be collected from customers.

For its December 31, 2010 financial statements, Discovery's management decided to increase the allowance for uncollectible accounts to 4.5 percent of the ending balance of accounts receivable. Management justified the change in estimate by arguing that it was concerned about the collectability of a number of receivables and as a result, a more conservative allowance for uncollectibles was appropriate. Remember from Chapter 5 that conservatism is an easily abused accounting principle. Add to that the bias that exists in GAAP accounting towards conservative measurements and the fact that accounting estimates can be very difficult for auditors to verify, and you have a situation that managers can use to their advantage.

By increasing the percentage-of-receivables that was expected to be uncollectible, Discovery's bad debt expense is higher and its net income lower than what would have been reported had Discovery continued to use the 3 percent estimate. The change in the estimate of uncollectibles increased the bad debt expense from $405,000 to $607,500 and decreased net income by $202,500. Table 7–7 provides a partial worksheet for Discovery Ltd. that shows the entries it would have made if it were creating a hidden reserve.

In 2011, as expected, Discovery's performance was not as strong as in 2010. Sales declined to $47,000,000. During 2011, $405,000 of accounts receivable were written off (which turned out to be 3 percent of the December 31, 2010 accounts receivable). At the end of 2011, management decided that the receivables it was "concerned" about a year earlier were no longer a problem and, accordingly, Discovery would return to the 3 percent estimate that it had used in previous years. Because only $405,000 of accounts receivable had to be written off during 2011, the balance in the Allowance account, before making the adjusting entry at the end of 2011, was a credit of $202,500. For the Allowance account to have the desired balance of $397,500 at the end of 2011 (representing 3 percent of the 2011 year-end accounts receivable—$13,250,000 × 3 percent), the Allowance account would have to be increased by $195,000 and the Bad Debt Expense for 2011 would be $195,000. These entries can be seen in Table 7–7.

Table 7–8 (page 364) compares summarized income statements and accounts receivable information when Discovery creates a hidden reserve and when it doesn't create a hidden reserve (it uses the 3 percent estimate in both years). By using a hidden reserve, Discovery Ltd. is able to report a profit increase of $207,500 from 2010 to 2011, an increase of over 7 percent, instead of a decline in profit of $197,500, a decline of almost 7 percent. By using a hidden reserve, Discovery is able to show a positive earnings trend rather than a negative trend. Note that total income over

TABLE 7–7 ::: **Discovery Inc.: Partial Spreadsheet Showing How Hidden Reserves Can Be Used to Manipulate Earnings**

The zero balance in the Allowance account means that during 2010 the exact amount of the estimate of bad debts made at December 31, 2011 was written off during 2010.

The pre-adjusting balance in the Bad Debt Expense account is zero because the account would have been closed at the end of 2009 and no entries would be made to the account until the adjusting entries were made.

The balance in Allowance for Doubtful Accounts is equal to 4.5% of closing Accounts Receivable.

	Cash (B/S)	Accounts Receivable (B/S)	Allowance for Doubtful Accounts (B/S)	Revenue (I/S)	Bad Debt Expense (I/S)
31/12/10 (pre-adjusting entries)		13,500,000	0		0
31/12/10 adjusting entries			(607,500)		(607,500)
31/12/10 (final)		13,500,000	(607,500)		(607,500)[1]
During 2011					
Sales		47,000,000		47,000,000	
Collections	46,845,000	(46,845,000)			
Bad debts written off		(405,000)	405,000		
31/12/11 (pre-adjusting balances)		13,250,000	(202,500)		
31/12/11 adjusting entries			(195,000)		(195,000)
31/12/11 (final)		13,250,000	(397,500)		(195,000)[1]

[1] The balance in the Bad Debt Expense account would become zero when the closing entry is made. The closing entry is not shown in this example.

During 2011 management writes off $405,000 in receivables that it decides are uncollectable.

The amount that must be added to the allowance account for it to have the desired balance of 3% of year-end accounts receivable at the end of 2011. By making too large an estimate of uncollectables in 2010, the expense required in 2011 is lower than it would have been.

the two years is the same under both scenarios. But by altering the allowance for uncollectible accounts, Discovery is able to shift income from 2010 to 2011.

This example is set up to allow you to see how management can use the flexibility of accounting to satisfy its self-interests. The example makes the problem, the motivation, and effect transparent. In reality, users of financial statements cannot see these hidden choices that management makes so it is very difficult to know that anything unusual is occurring. This is why these types of manipulations are called hidden reserves.

You might be wondering how managers can get away with behaviour that is clearly unethical, violates the spirit of fair presentation of the financial statements, and, as a result, is inconsistent with GAAP. One of the reasons is that it can be difficult to evaluate the reasonableness of estimates. As long as an estimate falls within a reasonable range and managers can provide a reasonable explanation for it, a change can be difficult to quarrel with. After all, management knows the entity best, is best able to make estimates, and is responsible for the financial statements.

CASH, RECEIVABLES, AND THE TIME VALUE OF MONEY

TABLE 7–8 ::: Discovery Ltd. Extracts from Financial Statements				
Discovery Limited **Extracts from the December 31, 2010 and 2011** **Financial Statements (in thousands)**				
	No hidden reserves		Using hidden reserves	
	2010	2011	2010	2011
Revenue	$50,000	$47,000	$50,000	$47,000
Expenses (except bad debts)	46,595	43,800	46,595	43,800
Bad debt expense	405	397.5	607.5	195
Net income	$ 3,000	$ 2,802.5	$ 2,797.5	$ 3,005
Accounts receivable	$13,500	$13,250	$13,500	$13,250
Allowance for uncollectible accounts	405	397.5	607.5	397.5

Insight

Are hidden reserves a real problem? Arthur Levitt, then-chairman of the Securities and Exchange Commission in the United States, commenting on the problems with financial reporting, said:

"Companies stash accruals in "cookie jar" reserves during the good economic times and reach into them when necessary in the bad times."[5]

Mr. Levitt's comments highlight the problem of entities using the flexibility available in GAAP to manage the information reported in their financial statements. While many years have passed since Mr. Levitt made his comment, examples continue to arise of managers using hidden reserves to manage the earnings of their companies. The hidden reserve is a problem that all financial statement users should be aware of.

It is important to emphasize that the problem in the example is not that the estimate of uncollectibles changed. The problem is the motivation for the change. For financial statement information to be useful, it must reflect current economic circumstances. If management were legitimately concerned about the collectability of receivables, then increasing the allowance for uncollectibles would be appropriate and would provide useful information to the stakeholders. The problem is that it can be difficult to tell whether management's intention is to provide information or to satisfy its self-interests.

The allowance for the uncollectible accounts estimate is only one of many estimates available to management to create hidden reserves. Managers can use estimates like sales returns and warranty liabilities, among many others, to create hidden reserves. The procedure and effect for these other examples is similar to the treatment shown for the allowance for uncollectible accounts. The use of hidden reserves is not limited to public companies only. Many different scenarios could explain why preparers would want to have a "rainy day" fund.

Current and Quick Ratios

In this chapter we have examined two of an entity's most liquid assets—cash and receivables. One other liquid asset, passive investments, will be discussed in Chapter 12. As we have discussed in a number of places in this book, liquidity is a crucial consideration when evaluating an entity. In Chapter 2, we examined the current ratio, an indicator of an entity's ability to meet its current obligations. The current ratio was defined as current assets divided by current liabilities.

Explain why managers would create hidden reserves and why securities commissions, in the case of public companies, would be so concerned about them.

Answer: Managers create hidden reserves because it gives them the ability to manage earnings and other financial statement numbers in a way that is very difficult for financial statement users to detect. If users are not able to detect management of earnings, then managers are better able to use accounting information to achieve their self-interests. For public companies, hidden reserves can be used to influence investors' perceptions of the company and possibly its stock price. Hidden reserves would be useful to management in any situation where earnings management would be beneficial—situations such as maximizing management bonuses, avoiding violation of covenants, and so on.

Securities commissions are concerned about the use of hidden reserves by entities because they undermine the integrity of the financial statements. If preparers are able to use hidden reserves to achieve their self-interests, then financial statements will be less useful for communicating with stakeholders and stakeholders will have less confidence in the information.

A potential problem with the current ratio is that the numerator includes all current assets and all current assets may not be liquid.

Let's look at Rogers Communications as an example. Note 4 to Rogers' financial statements (page A-18) describes the "Other current assets" that are reported on Rogers' balance sheet. These other assets include prepaid expenses, representing items like insurance and rent paid in advance, inventory, and acquired program rights (the right to broadcast particular programming on company television stations). Property owners are unlikely to return rent paid in advance, and while it might be possible to get a refund on an insurance policy, it would probably be unwise to operate Rogers without insurance. One could also question the liquidity of Rogers' inventory. In general, inventory can sometimes be difficult to sell quickly. For example, Rogers' inventory of cell phones could probably be sold quickly by offering a low price, but even that might take some time. Rogers' inventory would also include supplies for its cable business. These would likely also be difficult to sell quickly.

To compensate for these problems with the current ratio, the **quick** or **acid test** ratio can be used as a stricter test of an entity's liquidity. The quick ratio is a stricter test because it excludes less liquid assets such as inventory, prepaids and acquired program rights. The quick or acid test ratio is defined as

$$\text{Quick ratio} = \frac{\text{Quick assests}}{\text{Current liabilities}} = \frac{\text{Cash} + \text{Cash equivalents} + \text{Temporary investments} + \text{Receivables}}{\text{Current liabilities}}$$

Quick assets are assets that are cash or can or will be realized in cash fairly quickly. For Rogers, the quick ratio for 2005 is:

$$\text{Quick ratio} = \frac{\$890,701,000}{\$1,991,511,000} = 0.45$$

Rogers' quick ratio seems quite low. In Chapter 2 we also observed that its current ratio was also low. It was pointed out in Chapter 2 that Rogers has managed to succeed despite its low current ratio and the same is true for its quick ratio. Since 1996, Rogers' quick ratio has ranged from a high of 0.68 to a low 0.24. Clearly, Rogers has been able to function well with a low quick ratio. An explanation might be that because of its cable business, Rogers has a reliable cash flow, which reduces the likelihood that the company will be unable to meet its obligations. Remember from

FIGURE 7–1 ::

Seven-Year
Averages for
Current and Quick
Ratios for
Selected Canadian
Industries

Seven-Year Averages (1999–2005) for Selected Industries*		
Industry	**Current Ratio**	**Quick Ratio**
Biotechnology	10.13	9.80
Computers and Electronic Equipment	2.91	1.99
Food and Staples Retailing	0.98	0.48
Gold	5.55	4.81
Media	1.31	0.92
Oil, Gas, and Consumable Fuels	2.16	1.78
Paper and Forest Products	1.73	0.85
Retailing	2.27	0.57
Software	3.86	3.30
Telecommunications Services	0.86	0.62
Utilities	1.41	1.20

*Data obtained from the 2006 Industry Reports published by the Financial Post

Chapter 6 that cash flow is a crucial indicator of liquidity. The evaluation of liquidity should include an assessment of the ability of an entity to generate cash from operations, along with an assessment of its current and quick ratios.

The implication is that evaluation of a quick ratio (or any other ratio) must be done in the broader context of the overall financial health of the entity and the economic environment it faces. Figure 7–1 shows the current and quick ratios for a number of Canadian industries. These ratios are the averages for the firms in the industry over seven years, 1999 through 2005. Notice the wide variation in both ratios across the industries. If the table presented the ratios for each year, you would also see variation within each industry across time and across the companies in each industry.

Accounts Receivable Turnover Ratio

An important responsibility of management is to effectively manage the entity's credit program. The **accounts receivable turnover ratio** is one tool users have to assess how well credit is being managed. The ratio is defined as:

$$\frac{\text{Accounts receivable}}{\text{turnover ratio}} = \frac{\text{Credit sales}}{\text{Average accounts receivable}}$$

This ratio provides information on how quickly the entity is collecting its receivables. The higher the ratio, the more quickly the entity is collecting its receivables. The term *turnover* means how quickly receivables are collected and replaced by new receivables. An accounts receivable turnover ratio of eight means that the entity incurs, collects, and replaces its receivables eight times a year. The higher the turnover ratio, the more quickly the entity is able to get cash from its customers.

Average accounts receivable is calculated by adding the balances in the accounts receivable account at the beginning and end of the year and divide by two. For Rogers, the average for fiscal 2005 would be calculated by using accounts receivable on December 31, 2004 and December 31, 2005. Using this approach, the average accounts receivable would be $782,318,500 ([$673,936,000 + $890,701,000] ÷ 2).

A more intuitive measure can be obtained by dividing the accounts receivable turnover ratio into 365 to give the **average collection period of accounts receivable.**

$$\frac{\text{Average collection period}}{\text{of accounts receivable}} = \frac{365}{\text{Accounts receivable turnover ratio}}$$

The average collection period of accounts receivable gives the number of days, on average, it takes to collect receivables. Table 7–9 shows the accounts receivable turnover ratio and the average collection period of accounts receivable for Rogers for 2001 to 2005.

TABLE 7–9 :::	Rogers Communications Inc.: Accounts Receivable Turnover Ratio and Average Collection Period of Accounts Receivable			
	Average Accounts Receivable (000)	Sales (000)	Accounts Receivable Turnover Ratio	Average Collection Period of Accounts Receivable
For the year ended December 31, 2005	$782,318,500	$7,482,154,000	9.56	38.16
For the year ended December 31, 2004	612,383,000	5,608,249,000	9.16	39.86
For the year ended December 31, 2003	531,478,500	4,791,856,000	9.02	40.48
For the year ended December 31, 2002	503,740,000	4,266,785,000	8.47	43.09
For the year ended December 31, 2001	498,453,000	3,912,656,000	7.85	46.50

Table 7–9 shows that there was a gradual increase in the accounts receivable turnover ratio and a gradual decrease in the average collection period from 2001 to 2005. On the surface, this is good news because a shorter collection period means that cash is realized more quickly, which shortens the cash cycle. However, a great deal of caution must be exercised when one uses and interprets this ratio. Let's look at some potential problems:

■ First, correct application of the ratio requires credit sales. Table 7–9 uses total sales as reported in Rogers' income statement because the financial statements of most companies do not provide separate credit and cash sales numbers. We can assume that most of Rogers' business is on credit but Rogers Video and some of the wireless business is on a cash basis.

A quick example will demonstrate the problem. Castor Inc. (Castor) reported total sales in 2009 of $875,000 and in 2010 of $941,000. Average receivables were $132,500 and $150,000 in 2009 and 2010 respectively. Using this information, we find that the accounts receivable turnover ratio was 6.60 in 2009 and 6.27 in 2010. This result indicates that receivables management has deteriorated somewhat over the last two years. Now suppose we learn that in 2009 credit sales made up $700,000 of the $875,000 total and in 2010 credit sales were $800,000 of the $941,000 total. (Average receivables, of course, would not be affected by this additional information.) Now, if we calculate the accounts receivable turnover ratio, we find that it was 5.28 in 2009 and 5.33 in 2010—a much more stable situation than was previously found. We would expect the level of the accounts receivable turnover ratio to be different using the two sets of data. However, the trends using the two sets suggest different situations. The reason for the difference is that in 2010 the proportion of credit sales increased to 85 percent of total sales from 80 percent in 2009. Without the credit sales information, we could easily misinterpret Castor's credit management situation.

■ Second Rogers' financial statements combine the financial information of a number of different businesses. In any consolidated set of financial statements, ratios will be affected by the relative contribution of the different businesses in the group. Much of the cable and wireless businesses likely offer payment terms of about 30 days. Terms for the media business may differ.

■ Third, using the year-end accounts receivables balances to calculate average receivables may not provide a good estimate of the average for the year. For seasonal businesses, accounts receivable will fluctuate, sometimes significantly, during the year. In fact, for fiscal 2005, Rogers demonstrates only minor seasonality, with about 28.3 percent of sales being made in the 4th quarter and about 21.1 percent of sales being made in the first quarter. (Quarterly information is available from Rogers' *quarterly financial statements*, which are public documents and available at www.sedar.com.) Some businesses are highly seasonal, which means that ratios will be sensitive to how they are calculated. For example, using annual data will ignore the seasonality of a business and will affect the ratios. Retail businesses are often highly seasonal with a significant proportion of business occurring just before Christmas.

If a stakeholder is powerful, it will be able to get additional detail to carry out any analysis it deems necessary. For example, an entity's lenders could probably overcome many of the problems described above by requiring that certain information be provided as part of the loan agreement. Despite these limitations, the accounts receivable turnover ratio is a useful tool for assessing an entity's credit management. The limitations may make it difficult to compare different entities, but examining trends for an entity may be a reasonable way to apply this tool. Changes in the ratio will raise questions for further investigation but will likely not provide any definitive answers.

:: Solved Problem

You are provided with the following information about Nuwata Inc.'s (Nuwata) sales and accounts receivable:

1. On October 31, 2009 (Nuwata's year end), the balance sheet reported gross accounts receivable of $27,250 and an allowance for uncollectible accounts of $1,300.

2. During fiscal 2010 Nuwata wrote off $1,100 in bad debts.

3. During fiscal 2010 Nuwata had total sales of $347,000, including cash sales of $52,000.

4. Nuwata uses the percentage-of-credit-sales method for accounting for uncollectible receivables. For 2010 Nuwata's management will base the bad debt expense on 1.2 percent of credit sales for the year.

5. During fiscal 2010 Nuwata collected $285,000 from customers who purchased merchandise on credit.

6. Nuwata's credit terms require customers to pay outstanding amounts within 25 days of receiving merchandise. For 2009 Nuwata's average collection period of accounts receivable was 32.5 days.

Required:

a. Use an accounting equation spreadsheet to determine the balances in Accounts Receivable and Allowance for Uncollectible Accounts on October 31, 2010, and the bad debt expense for the year ended October 31, 2010.

b. Calculate Nuwata's accounts receivable turnover ratio and the average collection period of accounts receivable for fiscal 2010. Interpret the ratios you calculated.

Solution

a. Spreadsheet results:

	Cash	Accounts Receivable	Allowance for Uncollectible Accounts	Revenue	Bad Debt Expense
Balances on October 31, 2009		$27,250	($1,300)		
Sales during 2010	$52,000	295,000		$347,000	
Cash collections during 2010	285,000	(285,000)			
Accounts written off during 2010		(1,100)	1,100		
Adjusting entry accruing bad debt expense for 2010			(3,540) [$295,000 × 1.2%]		($3,540)
Balances on October 31, 2010	$337,000	$36,150	($3,740)	$347,000	($3,540)

b. Accounts receivable turnover ratio and average collection of accounts receivable:

$$\frac{\text{Accounts receivable}}{\text{turnover ratio}} = \frac{\text{Credit sales}}{\text{Average accounts receivable}}$$

$$= \frac{\$295,000}{(($27,250 - \$1,300) + (\$36,150 - \$3,740)) \div 2}$$

$$= \frac{\$295,000}{\$29,180}$$

$$= 10.11$$

$$\frac{\text{Average collection period}}{\text{of accounts receivable}} = \frac{365}{\text{Accounts receivable turnover ratio}}$$

$$= \frac{365}{10.11}$$

$$= 36.10 \text{ days}$$

Nuwata's collection period has deteriorated from 2009. In 2009, Nuwata, on average, collected its receivables in 32.5 days. This year the collection period has increased by almost four days to 36.1 days. This increase is of concern because it delays the receipt of cash from customers and lengthens the cash cycle. This in turn may impair Nuwata's liquidity.

An increase in the average collection period may occur for a number of reasons:

1. Nuwata may have eased its credit terms, meaning that it grants credit to less credit-worthy customers. Easing credit terms can increase sales, but it comes at the potential cost of increasing the amount that is not collected from customers. This can be a reasonable business strategy for an entity to pursue, but the costs and benefits of the strategy must be assessed.

2. Nuwata's internal controls over some aspect of the credit process may not be working effectively. For example, credit may have been given to inappropriate customers or the accounts receivable department may not be following up on unpaid accounts promptly or thoroughly.

3. Existing customers are having difficulty paying their bills, perhaps because of an economic slowdown in general or because of problems faced by the particular customers.

From the information given, it is not possible to tell what the cause of the increase is in the average collection period. It is necessary to understand the cause before conclusions can be drawn about the implications for stakeholders.

In the case of explanation 1, the increase in the average collection period is reasonable and would be expected under the circumstances. In the case of explanation 2, steps could be taken to tighten the internal controls over credit and collections to ensure that company policies are being followed. Explanation 3 is most problematic. If customers are facing financial problems or if there is an economic downturn, the flow of cash through the whole economy is affected. Nuwata should aggressively pursue the amounts owed to it so that if customers are choosing which suppliers to pay, Nuwata will be one they choose first. Nuwata should also take steps to ensure that it will be able to meet its obligations even if the cash cycle is lengthened.

SUMMARY OF KEY POINTS

LO 1 Cash reported on the balance sheet often includes cash equivalents, which includes short-term investments that can be converted into a known amount of cash easily and quickly. Good management requires that there be enough cash available to meet obligations, but not too much as to result in the inefficient use of the entity's resources.

An important responsibility of management is to protect the entity's assets. Internal controls are the processes that management implements to provide reasonable assurance that an entity will be able to achieve its objectives regarding the reliability of financial reporting, the effectiveness and efficiency of its operations, and compliance with relevant laws and regulations. Strong internal controls provide assurance to stakeholders that the entity's assets cannot be stolen, used inappropriately, or used without proper authorization, and that the information produced by the accounting system can be relied on.

The amount of cash reported on the balance sheet represents the face value of an entity's cash. GAAP in Canada do not consider changes in the purchasing power of cash. Also, because financial statements are stated in a single currency, cash held in foreign currencies must be translated into Canadian dollars so that they can be reported on the balance sheet.

LO 2 The time value of money is the concept that cash received in the future is not worth as much as the same amount of cash today. The future value of cash flows is the amount of money you will receive in the future by investing it today at a given interest rate. The present value of cash flows is the equivalent value today of money that will be received in the future, discounted to the present at a particular discount rate. Present and future value analyses are valuable tools for comparing the values of cash flows that occur at different times and in different amounts.

LO 3 Receivables represent amounts owing to an entity. Under accrual accounting, receivables should be valued at their net realizable value (NRV). This means that uncollectibles, discounts, and returns can reduce the amount of cash the entity will actually realize. There are three ways to account for uncollectible amounts:

- the direct write-off method
- the percentage-of-receivables method
- the percentage-of-credit-sales method

The percentage-of-receivables and percentage-of-credit-sales methods are accrual methods that attempt to match the cost of offering credit to customers to the revenue in the period. The direct write-off method does not result in the matching of costs and revenues. The three methods can lead to very different bad debt expenses in a given year, although over the life of an entity the amount expensed will be the same.

LO 4 Hidden reserves are undisclosed accounting choices used to manage earnings and other financial information with the intention of satisfying the self-interests of the preparers. Two factors contribute to the existence of hidden reserves: the need for estimates and the fact that many of the estimates that managers make do not have to be disclosed in the financial statements.

The current ratio has limitations because current assets often include assets that are not very liquid. The quick or acid test ratio is sometimes used to overcome this problem by including only liquid assets in the numerator of the ratio. The accounts receivable turnover ratio and the average collection period of accounts receivable provide information on how well management is managing the entity's credit program.

KEY TERMS

accounts receivable turnover ratio, p. 366

acid test ratio, p. 365

aging schedule, p. 355

allowance for uncollectible accounts, p. 353

annuity, p. 346

average collection period of accounts receivable, p. 366

compound interest, p. 342

deflation, p. 339

direct write-off method, p. 353

discount rate, p. 343

exchange rate, p. 340

future value, p. 341

hidden reserves, p. 362

inflation, p. 339

internal control, p. 338

percentage-of-credit-sales method, p. 357

percentage-of-receivables method, p. 354

present value, p. 341

quick or acid test ratio, p. 365

receivables, p. 348

segregation of duties, p. 339

simple interest, p. 342

time value of money, p. 341

SIMILAR TERMS

The left column gives alternative terms that are sometimes used for the accounting terms introduced in this chapter, which are listed in the right column.

discounting	**discount rate, p. 343**
interest rate	**allowance for uncollectible accounts, p. 353**
allowance for doubtful accounts, allowance for bad debts	

ASSIGNMENT MATERIALS

Questions

Q7-1. What is meant by the term "internal control"? Why are strong internal controls important to an entity?

Q7-2. What is meant by the term "segregation of duties"? Why is it important for internal control purposes that people who physically handle an asset not also be responsible for accounting for the asset?

Q7-3. Why is cash considered an unproductive asset?

Q7-4. How is it possible that an entity can have too much cash?

Q7-5. You are examining the financial statements of a company in which you are interested in investing. The company reports a negative balance in the cash account (the cash account on the balance sheet is reported as a negative amount on the asset side of the balance sheet). How would you interpret the negative balance in the cash account?

Q7-6. In August 2008, you received a birthday gift of $500 in cash from a generous uncle. Your uncle wanted you to have the money so that you could enjoy yourself as you were beginning your studies at university. Unfortunately, you lose the $500 in your very messy room in your residence hall. In June 2012, when you graduate, you find the $500 when you clean out your room as you prepare to move out. With respect to the $500, are you as well off on the day you found the $500 as you were on the day you received it? Explain your answer.

Q7-7. According to GAAP in Canada, the unit of measure that is used is the *nominal* dollar. What is a nominal dollar? What real economic costs are ignored by using a nominal dollar as the unit of measure, rather than using a unit of measure that takes into consideration the changing purchasing power of a dollar?

Q7-8. What does it mean when cash on an entity's balance sheet is classified as restricted? What are the implications of restricted cash for users of the financial statements?

Q7-9. Why is a certain amount of cash today more valuable than the same amount of cash in the future?

Q7-10. What is the difference between compound interest and simple interest? Would you receive more interest from an investment that pays compound interest or from one that pays simple interest? Explain.

Q7-11. Which investment would be more attractive: 8 percent per year compounded annually or 8 percent per year compounded quarterly? Explain.

Q7-12. Explain the terms *present value* and *future value*. Give an example of when each measurement would be appropriate.

Q7-13. What is a "receivable"? How are receivables classified on a balance sheet? What are some of the different types of receivables that can be reported on a balance sheet?

Q7-14. How is the reported liquidity of an entity affected by how it recognizes revenue? Explain. Is the liquidity in an economic rather than an accounting sense affected by how revenue is recognized?

Q7-15. What is the relationship between an account receivable and the income statement? What is the relationship between an account receivable and the revenue recognition criteria discussed in Chapter 4?

Q7-16. What are some of the benefits and drawbacks to a business of offering credit terms to customers? Would a business prefer to do business in cash or on credit? Explain.

Q7-17. Why is the amount reported on a balance sheet for receivables usually not the same as the sum of the amounts that customers and other people who owe the entity money have promised to pay?

Q7-18. When a customer makes a purchase from Rogers using a credit card such as Visa or MasterCard, why does Rogers not include the sale as an account receivable?

Q7-19. What are the three methods available for accounting for uncollectible amounts from customers? Explain each of the three methods.

Q7-20. Why is the direct write-off method of accounting for bad debts not appropriate in accrual accounting or GAAP?

Q7-21. Why is the percentage-of-credit-sales method of accounting for bad debts referred to as an income statement approach, whereas the percentage-of-receivables method is referred to as a balance sheet approach?

Q7-22. Explain why the percentage-of-credit-sales and the percentage-of-receivables methods do not usually give the same bad debt expense or the same balance in the allowance for uncollectible accounts.

Q7-23. If an entity uses the percentage-of-credit-sales method of accounting for uncollectible accounts, what are the effects on the financial statements if the entity consistently uses too low a percentage of credit sales for estimating bad debts? What are the effects on the financial statements if it consistently uses too high a percentage? Consider the effects on both the income statement and the balance sheet.

Q7-24. What is an aging schedule? How is the aging schedule used for calculating the bad debt expense?

Q7-25. How does management decide what percentage of receivables or what percentage of credit sales should be used to calculate the bad debt expense and the balance in the allowance for uncollectibles account? Is this a subjective or objective decision? Explain.

Q7-26. How does management decide when to write off an account receivable or some other receivable? Is this an objective or subjective decision? Explain. How can management use the judgment required to decide when to write off a receivable to affect the numbers in the financial statements? Explain.

Q7-27. Canadian GAAP do not require companies to disclose the amount of the bad debt expense or the balance in the allowance for uncollectible accounts. Would this information be useful to users of financial statements? Why do you think some entities would not want to disclose this information?

Q7-28. Verlo Ltd. recently made a $100,000 sale to a customer. Terms of the sale agreement permit the customer to pay the $100,000 in two years. The customer will not have to pay any interest. If Verlo Ltd. recognizes the revenue in the current period, why should the amount of revenue recorded be less than $100,000? Explain.

Q7-29. What is a hidden reserve? Why would management create hidden reserves? Why is it possible for managers to create hidden reserves? Why is the existence of hidden reserves a problem for users of financial statements?

Q7-30. What is the quick or acid test ratio? How does the quick or acid test ratio differ from the current ratio? What would be a better measure of liquidity for a jewellery store, the quick ratio or the current ratio? Explain. What would be a better measure of liquidity for a mine holding a large inventory of gold bullion, the quick ratio or the current ratio? Explain.

Exercises

E7-1. (**Classifying cash on the balance sheet, LO 1**) For each of the following items, explain whether the amount described should be included in "Cash and Cash Equivalents" on Jelly Inc.'s (Jelly) December 31, 2009 balance sheet:
  a. $22,300 in Jelly's chequing account at the bank.
  b. An investment certificate that will pay $10,000 plus accrued interest on the date it is cashed. The certificate can be cashed at any time by Jelly.
  c. A guaranteed investment certificate that matures on July 15, 2011. Jelly will receive $11,000 when the certificate matures.
  d. $250 kept in the office to pay for incidentals such as office supplies.
  e. $12,500 kept in a savings account at the bank.
  f. $7,000 of cheques received from customers in mid-December, 2009, but not yet cashed.
  g. $10,000 held by Jelly's lawyer for purposes of paying a particular supplier when equipment ordered is delivered. The supplier required that the lawyer hold the money so that it would be assured of payment. The equipment is due to be delivered in February 2010.
  h. $4,200 that is owed by a senior executive. The amount is to be paid on January 5, 2010.
  i. £3,000 (British pounds) held in an account at a major British bank.

E7-2. (**Calculating future values, LO 2**) Calculate the future value in each of the following situations:
  a. A senior citizen purchases a Canada Savings Bond for $5,000 that pays 3 percent interest per year for eight years, compounded annually. How much will the senior citizen receive when the Savings Bond matures in eight years?
  b. An investor purchases a long-term investment for $70,000 that pays 7 percent interest per year for 12 years, compounded semi-annually. How much will the investor receive when the investment matures in 12 years?

c. An entity borrows $100,000 at 10 percent for four years. Interest and principal must be paid in full in four years, at the end of the term of the loan. How much will the entity have to pay the lender in four years?

d. A parent lends her child $15,000 to help finance his education. The loan bears no interest, but must be repaid in six years. How much will the parent receive from the child in six years?

E7-3. (**Calculating present values, LO 2**) Answer the following questions:

a. A customer purchases $20,000 of goods. The goods will be paid for in cash in three years. How much revenue should be recorded on the date the goods are delivered, assuming a discount rate of 8 percent?

b. You are presented with an investment opportunity that will pay you $4,000 in one year, $3,000 in two years, and $2,000 in three years. At a discount rate of 12 percent, would you pay $7,000 for this investment? Explain.

c. A "zero coupon bond" is a type of long-term debt that pays no interest, but simply pays a single amount on the date the bond matures. Your broker offers you a zero coupon bond that will pay $5,000 in 20 years. How much would you pay for the bond today, if your discount rate were 10 percent?

d. You are presented with an investment opportunity that will pay you $6,000 in one year, $4,000 in two years, and $8,000 in three years. At a discount rate of 8 percent, what is the maximum amount you would pay for this investment?

E7-4. (**Calculating the present value of annuities, LO 2**) Answer the following questions:

a. A contest advertises that the winner wins $1,000,000. The $1,000,000 prize is paid in equal instalments over 25 years, with the first payment being made one year from the date the contest winner is announced. What is the "real" (present) value of the prize? Assume a discount rate of 8 percent.

b. You have the option of receiving $2,000,000 today or $250,000 a year for 15 years, beginning one year from now. If your discount rate is 12 percent, which would you choose?

c. A store allows you to purchase a new computer for $200 down and $50 a month for 36 months. If the appropriate discount rate is 1 percent per month, what would be the equivalent cash price today for the computer?

d. An investor can purchase an investment that pays interest of $200 per year for ten years as well as paying the investor $2,500 in the tenth year. If the appropriate discount rate for an investment of this type is 10 percent, what is the maximum amount that the investor should pay for the investment? (When answering, remember that calculating an annuity only applies to equal payments. In this question, the present value of the additional $2,500 received in the tenth year must be determined separately.)

E7-5. (**Calculating the future value, present value, and present value of annuities, LO 2**) Use the tools introduced in the chapter to answer the following questions. You have to decide which tool to use in each case:

a. An investor purchases a $5,000 investment certificate that pays 8 percent interest per year, compounded semi-annually. How much will the investor receive when the certificate matures in five years?

b. An investor is offered a choice of three possible investments. In each case the investor must invest $1,000. The first investment will pay the investor $2,500 at the end of year 5. The second investment will pay the investor $500 in one year, $650 in two years, $800 in three years, $200 in four years, and $100 in five years. The third alternative will pay the investor $400 at the end of each of the next five years. Assume that the investor's discount rate is 10 percent. Which is the most attractive investment? Explain.

c. A retiring teacher has the opportunity to receive $10,000 per year for the next 20 years. If the teacher's discount rate is 7 percent what is the most she should pay for this investment?

d. An entity borrows $50,000 at 9 percent for three years. Interest and principal must be paid in full in three years, at the end of the term of the loan. How much will the entity have to pay the lender in three years?

e. You are offered a choice of receiving $1,000 today or $1,500 in three years. If your discount rate is 10 percent, which alternative would you prefer? Would your choice change if your discount rate is 15 percent?

E7-6.   (**Basic journal entries, LO 3**) Prepare the journal entries necessary to record the following transactions and economic events for Sahali Ltd. (Sahali):

a. During 2009 Sahali had cash sales of $175,000 and credit sales of $625,000.

b. During 2009 $405,000 of accounts receivable were collected.

c. Management estimated that 5 percent of credit sales would not be collected.

d. During 2010 Sahali wrote off $34,000 of accounts receivables.

E7-7.   (**Writing off an account receivable, LO 3**) Malagash Ltd. (Malagash) recently learned that a major customer would be permanently shutting down its operations within 30 days. The reason for the shut-down was not clear, but Malagash's management assumed that there were probably financial problems underlying the decision. As of Malagash's year end it was not clear whether it would receive any of the $50,000 owed to it by the customer. Despite the uncertainty regarding collection, Malagash's management decided that it would write off the $50,000 receivable in the current fiscal year.

Required:

a. Prepare the journal entry that Malagash would prepare if it were using the direct write-off method of accounting for uncollectible amounts. What would be the effect on net income of the entry?

b. Prepare the journal entry that Malagash would prepare if it were using the percentage-of-credit-sales method of accounting for uncollectible amounts. What would be the effect on net income of the entry?

c. Prepare the journal entry that Malagash would prepare if it were using the percentage-of-receivables method of accounting for uncollectible amounts. What would be the effect on net income of the entry?

d. Why do you think that Malagash decided to write off the receivable in the current fiscal year, even though it did not know whether it would be paid or not? In answering, consider accounting principles and the objectives of accounting.

E7-8.   (**Accounting for long-term receivables, LO 2, 3**) On May 31, 2010 Namaka Ltd. (Namaka) sold an office building to Audy Inc. (Audy) for $16,000,000. The sale agreement required that Audy pay $4,000,000 to Namaka on May 31, 2010, and then $4,000,000 on each of May 31, 2011, 2012, and 2013. Namaka decided to recognize the sale of the building in the year ended May 31, 2010.

Required:

a. How much revenue should Namaka recognize as a result of its sale of the office building to Audy? Prepare the journal entry that Namaka should prepare to record the sale. Assume a discount rate of 14 percent.

b. How much interest revenue will be reported on Namaka's income statement for the years ended May 31, 2011, 2012, and 2013 as a result of the sale to Audy? Prepare the journal entry that should be prepared each year to record the interest revenue.

c. How much would be reported as receivable from Audy on Namaka's balance sheets for the years ended May 31, 2010, 2011, 2012, and 2013? How would the receivable be classified on each year's balance sheet? Explain your answer.

d. Suppose Namaka insisted on recognizing $16,000,000 as revenue in 2010. What would be the implications for users of its financial statements? Why might Namaka's management want to report the full $16,000,000 immediately?

E7-9. **(Calculating accounts receivable, LO 3)** Use an accounting equation spreadsheet and the following information to calculate accounts receivable on July 31, 2010 and the amount of accounts receivable written off in 2010:

	July 31,	
	2010	2009
Accounts receivable	$?	$ 75,800
Allowance for uncollectible accounts	(3,300)	(3,000)
Revenue recognized during 2010	350,000	
Collections of accounts receivable during 2010	375,000	
Bad debt expense for 2010	3,500	
Amount of accounts receivable written off during 2010	?	

E7-10. **(Calculating accounts receivable, LO 3)** Use an accounting equation spreadsheet and the following information to calculate accounts receivable on December 31, 2009 and the amount of accounts receivable written off in 2009:

	December 31,	
	2009	2008
Accounts receivable	$?	$134,750
Allowance for uncollectible accounts	(8,712)	(7,062)
Unearned revenue	40,040	56,100
Revenue recognized during 2009*	949,300	
Collections of accounts receivable during 2009	847,000	
Bad debt expense for 2009	9,130	
Amount of accounts receivable written off during 2010	?	
Cash received from customers in 2009 for services to be provided in the future during 2010	31,240	
Amount of accounts receivable written off during 2009	?	

*Includes recognition of revenue classified as unearned in previous periods. All other revenue is on credit.

E7-11. **(Calculating the bad debt expense and the allowance for uncollectible accounts, LO 3)** You are provided with the following information about Nyanza Corp.:
i.   Accounts Receivable on December 31, 2010 = $287,500.
ii. Sales during the year ended December 31, 2010 = $2,262,500 (all sales are on credit).
iii. Accounts Receivable written off during 2010 = $39,600.
iv. Balance in Allowance for Uncollectible Accounts on December 31, 2009 = $38,150.
v.   Historically, an average of 2 percent of credit sales has been uncollectible.

Required:

Calculate Nyanza's bad debt expense for the year ended December 31, 2010 and the allowance for uncollectible accounts on December 31, 2010, and prepare the journal entry that should be prepared to record the bad debt expense.

E7-12. **(The effect of errors on net income, LO 3)** Capstick Ltd. (Capstick) uses the percentage-of-credit-sales method of estimating the bad debt expense. Since 2004 Capstick has used too low a percentage in calculating the bad debt expense each year. In 2008 management realized the error and decided to make an adjusting entry to correct it. Credit sales every year from 2004 through 2008 were $500,000. Capstick determined the bad debt expense using 2 percent of revenue as the basis of its estimate each year. Management decides it will use 2.3 percent beginning in 2009 (and should have done since 2004). Capstick has written off $11,500 of accounts receivable each year from 2004 through 2008. The balance in the allowance account on January 1, 2004 (the first day of Capstick's fiscal year) was $11,500.

a. What bad debt expense did Capstick record in each year from 2004 to 2008?
b. What was the effect on net income each year of using too low a bad debt expense estimate?
c. What was the balance in the allowance account at the end of each year?
d. What effect does correcting the error have on net income in 2008?
e. Prepare the journal entry that Capstick would make in 2008 to correct the error and leave an appropriate balance in the allowance account. Assume the adjusting entry to correct the error is made after the entry to record the 2008 bad debt expense.

E7-13. **(Comparing the percentage-of-receivables and percentage-of-credit-sales methods, LO 3)** The following information has been obtained about Elzevir Inc. (Elzevir) for 2010. The information was obtained before any year-end adjusting entries were made. Elzevir's year end is March 31:

Accounts receivable on March 31, 2010	$1,575,000
Credit sales for the year ended March 31, 2010	9,361,500
Allowance for uncollectible accounts on March 31, 2010 (credit balance)	11,250

Required:

a. Calculate the bad debt expense that Elzevir would record for the 2010 fiscal year, assuming that management expects that 6 percent of year-end accounts receivable will not be collected. What would be the balance in allowance for uncollectible accounts on March 31, 2010? Prepare the journal entry to record the bad debt expense.
b. Calculate the bad debt expense that Elzevir would record for the 2010 fiscal year, assuming that management expects that 1.5 percent of credit sales during fiscal 2010 will not be collected. What would be the balance in allowance for uncollectible accounts on March 31, 2010? Prepare the journal entry to record the bad debt expense.
c. What would your answers in (a) and (b) be if the balance in allowance for uncollectible accounts on March 31, 2010 (before any year-end adjusting entries) was a debit of $11,250? Explain any differences you find.

E7-14. **(Using an aging schedule to calculate the bad debt expense, LO 3)** Pipestone Ltd. (Pipestone) uses an aging schedule to estimate the amount of receivables that will not be collected. Pipestone allows its customers up to 60 days to pay amounts owed. Any receivable outstanding for more than 60 days is considered overdue. Based on historical information, management estimates that it will collect 97.5 percent of current accounts receivable, 90 percent of receivables overdue by between 1 and 30 days, 75 percent of receivables overdue by between 31 and 90 days, and 40 percent of receivables overdue by more than 90 days. Management has provided you with the following aged receivable schedule:

Account age	Balance on January 31, 2010
Current	$700,000
1–30 days overdue	288,000
31–90 days overdue	128,400
More than 90 days overdue	58,800

The balance in allowance for uncollectible accounts before the period-end adjusting entry is made is a debit of $10,800.

Required:

a. What amount of closing accounts receivable is estimated to be uncollectible on January 31, 2010?
b. Prepare the journal entry required to record the bad debt expense for Pipestone for the year ended January 31, 2010.

E7-15. **(Compute the accounts receivable turnover ratio and the average collection period for accounts receivable, LO 4)** The following information was obtained from Acamac Corp.'s (Acamac) 2011 financial statements:

Sales (all sales are on credit)	$4,150,000
Accounts receivable on March 31, 2011	520,000
Accounts receivable on March 31, 2010	475,000

Required:

a. Calculate Acamac's accounts receivable turnover ratio for 2011.
b. Calculate the average collection period for accounts receivable during 2011.
c. Is Acamac's average collection period for 2011 reasonable? What information would you require to answer this question? Explain.

E7-16. **(Correcting the balance in Allowance for Uncollectible Accounts, LO 3)** Trilby Inc. (Trilby) uses the percentage-of-credit-sales method for estimating its bad debt expense. The percentage that Trilby uses is based on historical information. Trilby's management has not revised the percentage for several years, a period during which a number of environmental and business factors have changed. Trilby's management recently realized that over the last three years, the percentage of credit sales that the company used was too high. As a result, the balance in Allowance for Uncollectible Accounts is $53,000 higher than it would have been had a better estimate of bad debts been used each year.

Required:

a. Prepare the adjusting journal entry that Trilby must make to have an appropriate balance in Allowance for Uncollectible Accounts.
b. What is the effect of the error in estimating bad debts in each of the years the error is made? What is the effect of the adjusting entry on net income? Answer the question by comparing the reported net income with what net income would have been had the error not been made and the adjusting entry not required.
c. What is the impact of this error and the adjusting entry on the users of the financial statements? Explain fully.

E7-17. **(Identifying quick assets, LO 4)** Which of the following assets would you classify as quick assets for purposes of calculating the quick ratio? Explain your reasoning.
a. Accounts receivable
b. Prepaid insurance
c. Current portion of a long-term note receivable
d. Interest receivable
e. Inventory of gold bars
f. An investment certificate that matures in 12 months
g. Inventory of gravel
h. Shares in Rogers Communications Inc.
i. A term deposit that matures in one month
j. Shares in a privately owned corporation

E7-18. **(Compute current and quick ratios, LO 4)** Following are the balance sheets for the years ended June 30, 2010 and 2009 for Seahorse Inc.:

				2010	2009
Seahorse Inc.					
Balance Sheets					
As of June 30, 2009 and 2010					
	2010	**2009**		**2010**	**2009**
Assets			**Liabilities and Shareholders' Equity**		
Current assets			*Current liabilities*		
Cash and cash equivalents	$ 95,000	$ 105,000	Accounts payable	$175,000	$173,750
			Accrued liabilities	30,000	47,500
Accounts receivable	237,500	145,000	Unearned revenue	25,000	30,000
Inventory	275,000	245,000	Current portion of		
Prepaids	20,250	18,750	long-term debt	112,500	150,000
Current assets	627,750	513,750	Current liabilities	342,500	401,250
Capital assets (net)	932,250	1,025,000	Long-term debt	275,000	387,500
			Capital stock	412,500	312,500
			Retained earnings	530,000	437,500
			Total liabilities and		
Total assets	$1,560,000	$1,538,750	shareholders' equity	$1,560,000	$1,538,750

Required:

a. Calculate the current ratio and the quick ratio on June 30, 2009 and 2010.
b. Assess the change in the liquidity position of Seahorse Inc.
c. Can you think of any circumstances where a significant increase in the quick ratio could be an indicator of a deteriorating liquidity position?

E7-19. **(Working with the accounts receivable turnover ratio, LO 4)** During 2008 Oderin Inc. (Oderin) reported revenue of $1,178,000. Oderin's accounts receivable turnover ratio for 2008 was 4.92. What was Oderin's average amount of accounts receivable during 2008?

Problems

P7-1. **(Thinking about internal controls, LO 1)** For the following two scenarios, describe what you think are the weaknesses in the internal controls and explain the implications of the weaknesses:

a. The administrative assistant to the corporate controller keeps a cash box with up to $500 of company money in her desk so that she can pay for incidental expenses as they occur. These expenses include paying couriers, reimbursing other employees for expenditures that they make on behalf of the company, paying for food ordered for meetings and people who work late, and so on. The cash is kept in a locked box in a locked drawer in the administrative assistant's desk. The cash in the box is replaced when the administrative assistant tells the corporate controller that more is required. The administrative assistant has been with the company for over 20 years and is highly respected and trusted by all members of senior management.

b. A religious centre collects cash contributions from people who attend services. The cash is stored in the religious centre's office in an unlocked drawer until later in the week, when the volunteer treasurer takes the money and deposits it in the centre's bank account. The office is located near the entrance to the religious centre and visitors to the centre usually go to the office. Many of the members of the religious centre know where the money is stored because they have filled volunteer positions and so are familiar with the procedures the centre follows.

P7-2. **(Thinking about internal controls, LO 1)** For the following two scenarios, describe what you think are the weaknesses in the internal controls and explain the implications of the weaknesses:

a. A travelling amusement park hires people in the towns the park visits to operate the rides on the midway. A person hired is given full responsibility for the ride. Responsibility includes collecting cash from the people who want to take the ride, making sure people get on and off the rides safely, and operating the ride. At the end of the day, the person gives the cash collected from customers to the park manager.

b. Because of its small size, Hochelaga Ltd. has only one person, Mathew Jordan, in its accounting department. For accounts payable, Mr. Jordan is responsible for ensuring that goods and services that have been ordered are received, authorizing payments to suppliers, preparing cheques, and entering transactions into the accounting system. He also prepares the bank reconciliation. The owner of the company signs all cheques and frequently reviews Mr. Jordan's work. The owner is often out of the country on business, sometimes for up to two weeks. Office staff are always aware of when the owner will be returning.

P7-3. **(Interpreting current and quick ratio data, LO 4)** Refer to Figure 7–2. Why do you think retailing businesses have such a large difference between their quick ratios and their current ratios? To answer, think about what the balance sheet of a retail business would look like, particularly the types of current assets that it has.

P7-4. **(Time value of money calculations, LO 2)** For each of the following situations, do the calculations necessary to make a decision:

a. An entity purchases equipment for $75,000. The entity is to pay $15,000 on the delivery date, $22,500 one year from the delivery date, and $37,500 two years from the delivery date. How much should the entity record as the cost of the equipment? The purchase agreement does not require that the entity pay interest. Assume a discount rate of 10 percent.

b. A woman saving for her retirement invests $50,000 in a long-term investment certificate. The certificate pays 5 percent interest per year compounded annually for 18 years. How much money will the woman receive when she retires in 18 years?

c. An investment promises to pay investors $25,000 per year for 12 years. The first payment will be received one year from the date the investment is made. If an investor has a discount rate of 8 percent, what is the maximum amount that the investor should pay for the investment?

d. A company borrows $500,000 for four years from a group of lenders. The company does not have to pay interest each year but must pay the principal and interest back at the end of the loan term. Assuming an interest rate of 9 percent, how much will the company have to give the lenders when the loan comes due in four years?

e. Would you prefer to receive $30,000 today, $50,000 in five years, or $8,000 at the end of each of the next five years? Assume a discount rate of 10 percent.

P7-5. **(Analyzing changes to credit policy, LO 3, 4)** Magundy Inc. (Magundy) imports high-end merchandise from Europe and distributes it to retailers across eastern Canada. Magundy has tended to be very conservative in managing its operations. In late 2008, the shareholders of Magundy decided that they were not satisfied with the performance and growth of the company, and they decided to replace the president with a younger, more aggressive person whom they believed would be better able meet their performance and growth objectives.

In early 2009, the new president decided that Magundy had been too cautious in granting credit to customers and he implemented a new credit policy that significantly increased the number of retailers who would be able carry Magundy's merchandise. The new president thought the new credit policy would increase sales significantly, which would meet the objectives of the owners. The new credit policy allowed businesses that were considered higher credit risks (customers that were more likely to not pay their debts) to obtain credit from Magundy. The new credit policy also allowed all customers more time to pay Magundy for purchases.

By the end of 2009, it appeared that the new president's strategy was working. Sales during the year had increased 20 percent over the previous year, to $2,395,000.

Required:

You have been asked by the shareholders to prepare a report evaluating certain aspects of Magundy's performance during 2009. Your report should consider the following:
a. What should be Magundy's bad debt expense for 2009? In previous years Magundy calculated its bad debt expense based on 2 percent of credit sales during the year. Explain your answer.
b. How would you expect Magundy's accounts receivable turnover ratio to change from 2008 to 2009? Explain.
c. How would the new credit strategy affect Magundy's liquidity?
d. Do you think the new president's credit strategy is a good one? What are the risks and benefits of the new strategy?

P7-6. **(Comparing the effects of different methods of accounting for bad debts, LO 3)** You have obtained the following information about Eskasoni Inc. (Eskasoni) from the company's 2009 annual report:
   i. Eskasoni's year end is November 30.
   ii. Sales for the year ended November 30, 2009 were $8,470,000; 85 percent of sales are credit sales.
   iii. The balance in Accounts Receivable on November 30, 2009 was $1,220,000.
   iv. The balance in Allowance for Uncollectible Accounts on November 30, 2008 was $96,000.
   v. During fiscal 2009, Eskasoni wrote off $84,000 of accounts receivable.
   vi. The bad debt expense can be estimated as 1.5 percent of credit sales or 9.5 percent of year-end accounts receivable.
   vii. Net income for the year ended November 30, 2009, including all revenues and expenses except for the bad debt expense, was $500,000.

Required:

a. Determine the bad debt expense for the year ended 2009, assuming that Eskasoni used:
   i. the direct-write-off method for accounting for uncollectible accounts.
   ii. the percentage-of-credit-sales method for accounting for uncollectible accounts.
   iii. the percentage-of-receivables method for accounting for uncollectible accounts.
b. What would be the balance in Allowance for Uncollectible Accounts on November 30, 2009 using the three methods identified in part (a)?
c. Prepare the journal entry required to record the bad debt expense under each of the three methods identified in part (a).
d. What would net income be for 2009 under each of the three methods identified in part (a)?
e. Explain why the three methods identified in part (a) provide different bad debt expenses.
f. Which method of determining the bad debt expense and the allowance for uncollectible accounts is best? Explain.

P7-7. **(Comparing the effects of different methods of accounting for bad debts, LO 3)** You have obtained the following information about Dogwood Inc. (Dogwood) from the company's 2010 annual report:
   i. Dogwood's year end is April 30.
   ii. Sales for the year ended April 30, 2010 were $750,000; 85 percent of sales are credit sales.

iii. The balance in accounts receivable on April 30, 2010 was $145,000.
iv. The balance in allowance for uncollectible accounts on April 30, 2009 was $13,500.
v. During fiscal 2010 Dogwood wrote off $18,000 of accounts receivable.
vi. The bad debt expense can be estimated as 2.5 percent of credit sales or 10 percent of year-end accounts receivable.
vii. Net income for the year ended April 30, 2010, including all revenues and expenses except for the bad debt expense, was $45,000.

Required:

a. Determine the bad debt expense for the year ended 2010, assuming that Dogwood used:
   i. the direct-write-off method for accounting for uncollectible accounts.
   ii. the percentage-of-credit-sales method for accounting for uncollectible accounts.
   iii. the percentage-of-receivables method for accounting for uncollectible accounts.
b. What would be the balance in Allowance for Uncollectible Accounts on April 30, 2010 using the three methods identified in part (a)?
c. Prepare the journal entry required to record the bad debt expense under each of the three methods identified in part (a).
d. What would net income be for 2010 under each of the three methods identified in part (a)?
e. Explain why the three methods identified in part (a) provide different bad debt expenses.
f. Which method of determining the bad debt expense and the allowance for uncollectible accounts is best? Explain.

P7-8. **(Observing the effect of errors in estimating the bad debt expense and the allowance of uncollectible accounts on the financial statements, LO 3, 4)** Since 2006, Kyuquot Inc. (Kyuquot) has estimated that its bad debt expense would be approximately 3 percent of credit sales each year. In late 2007, Kyuquot made a number of changes to its internal control procedures that increased the effectiveness of its credit granting and receivables collection. As a result, in 2008 uncollectibles decreased to about 2 percent of credit sales. However, the accounting department never bothered to lower the 3 percent rate that had been implemented in 2006.

The following information is also available about Kyuquot's receivables and bad debts:
   i. Kyuquot's year end is December 31.
   ii. The balance in Kyuquot's allowance account on January 1, 2006 was $39,200.
   iii. Credit sales and write-offs by year and accounts receivable on December 31 of each year were:

Year	Credit sales made during the year	Write-offs during the year	Accounts receivable on December 31*
2006	$1,500,000	$39,200	$526,000
2007	1,650,000	45,100	562,000
2008	1,860,000	35,750	614,000
2009	2,100,000	32,896	672,000
2010	2,390,000	45,998	752,000
2011	2,600,000	47,800	806,000

*Accounts receivable is the gross amount, before deducting the allowance for doubtful accounts.

Required:

    a. Calculate the bad debt expense Kyuquot's accounting department would have made in each year from 2006 through 2011.

    b. Calculate the balance in allowance for uncollectible accounts on December 31 of each year, after the adjusting entry recording the bad debt expense for the year was made by the accounting department.

    c. Examine the balance in the allowance account over the period from 2006 through 2011. Explain what is happening to the allowance account as a result of using a percentage of credit sales that is consistently too high. (To answer, it may help to look at the balance in the allowance account as a percentage of Accounts Receivable.)

    d. What is the effect on income each year of using a percentage of credit sales that is consistently too large? Explain.

    e. What is the net amount of accounts receivable (accounts receivable − allowance for uncollectibles) on Kyuquot's balance sheet on December 31, 2011? Does the balance on the balance sheet represent the net realizable value of the accounts receivable on December 31, 2011? Explain.

    f. What would the balance in the allowance account be on December 31, 2011, after the adjusting entry for bad debts is made, if Kyuquot expensed 2 percent of credit sales as bad debts beginning in 2008?

    g. Suppose that in 2011 management become aware of the error it was making estimating bad debts each year by using 3 percent of credit sales instead of 2 percent. What journal entry would Kyuquot have to make to reduce the balance in the allowance account to the amount calculated in part f ? What would be the effect of this journal entry on net income in 2011? What are some of the implications of these errors on users of the financial statements?

P7-9. **(The effect of transactions on ratios, LO 1, 3, 4)** Indicate whether each of the following transactions will increase, decrease, or have no effect have on the current ratio, quick ratio, accounts receivable turnover ratio, and the average collection period of accounts receivable. Assume that the current and quick ratios are greater than 1.0 before each of the items is considered.

    1. Collection of accounts receivable
    2. Recording the bad debt expense
    3. Writing off an uncollectible account
    4. Credit sale
    5. Cash sale
    6. Purchase of inventory on credit
    7. A new short-term bank loan
    8. Reclassification of a long-term receivable as current (because it will come due within 12 months)

P7-10. **(Determine missing information, LO 4)** Use the information provided to determine the values for the missing information (indicated by shaded boxes):

Current assets on December 31, 2010 = $

Current ratio on December 31, 2010 = 1.15

Current liabilities on December 31, 2010 = $1,325,000

Quick assets on December 31, 2010 = $850,000

Quick ratio on December 31, 2010 =

Accounts receivable on December 31, 2010 = $

Accounts receivable on December 31, 2009 = $207,000

Revenues (all on credit) during 2010 = $2,750,000

Average collection period of accounts receivable for 2010 = 32 days

Accounts receivable turnover ratio for 2010 =

P7-11. **(Determine missing information, LO 4)** Use the information provided to determine the values for the missing information (indicated by shaded boxes):

Current assets on December 31, 2010 = $275,000

Current ratio on December 31, 2010 = 1.25

Current liabilities on December 31, 2010 = $

Quick assets on December 31, 2010 = $

Quick ratio on December 31, 2010 = 0.85

Accounts receivable on December 31, 2010 = $55,000

Accounts receivable on December 31, 2009 = $45,000

Revenues (all on credit) during 2010 = $

Average collection period of accounts receivable for 2010 =

Accounts receivable turnover ratio for 2010 = 5.75

P7-12. **(The effect of transactions on ratios, LO 3, 4)** For the year ended December 31, 2008 Alpena Inc. (Alpena) had revenues (all on credit) of $2,456,000. Its average collection period of accounts receivable for 2008 was 62 days. Accounts receivable on December 31, 2008 was $420,000.

Calculate the effect on the average collection period of accounts receivable and the accounts receivable turnover ratio if the following additional transactions occurred during 2008. Consider the effect of each transaction or economic event separately.
a. Alpena, which uses the percentage-of-credit-sales method of estimating the bad debt expense, wrote off an additional $7,000 of accounts receivable.
b. Alpena collected an additional $80,000 of accounts receivable from customers.
c. Alpena recognized additional cash revenue of $125,000.
d. Alpena recognized additional credit revenue of $125,000.

P7-13. **(Accounting for long-term receivables, LO 2, 3)** On July 31, 2010 Romanace Ltd. (Romanace) agreed to sell Youbou Inc. (Youbou) $4,500,000 of specialized equipment for use at its newly developed mine site in northern Manitoba. Because the mine had not yet begun to produce any metal, Youbou negotiated that it would pay for the equipment on August 6, 2012, at which time the mine would be generating the cash flow required to pay Romanace. Despite the fact that Romanace would not be receiving its cash for two years, it decided to recognize the revenue from the sale during the year ended July 31, 2010. The agreement between Romanace and Youbou states that Youbou does not have to pay any interest on the amount owed.

Required:

Use a spreadsheet similar to the one in Table 7–6 (page 361) to answer the following:
a. How much revenue should Romanace recognize in the year ended July 31, 2010 for the sale to Youbou? Prepare the journal entry that Romanace should prepare to record the sale. Assume a discount rate of 8 percent.
b. What amount would be reported on Romanace's July 31, 2010 balance sheet for accounts receivable as a result of the sale to Youbou? How would the receivable from Youbou be shown in the balance sheet? Explain your answer.
c. How much interest revenue would Romanace report on its July 31, 2011 income statement as a result of the sale to Youbou? Prepare the journal entry that Romanace would make to record the interest revenue. What amount would be shown as receivable from Youbou on Romanace's July 31, 2011 balance sheet? How would the receivable from Youbou be classified on the balance sheet?
d. How much interest revenue would Romanace report on its July 31, 2012 income statement as a result of the sale to Youbou? Prepare the journal entry that Romanace would make to record the interest revenue. What amount would be

shown as receivable from Youbou on Romanace's July 31, 2012 balance sheet? How would the receivable from Youbou be classified on the balance sheet?

e. What journal entry would Romanace make when it received payment in full on August 6, 2012?

P7-14. (**Using an** aging **schedule to calculate the bad debt expense, LO 3**) Examine the following information about Weyakwin Inc. (Weyakwin):

i. Ending balance in Allowance for Uncollectible Accounts on April 30, 2009 = $67,800 (credit balance).

ii. Accounts receivable written off during the year ended April 30, 2010 = $58,000.

iii. Aging schedule for accounts receivable outstanding on April 30, 2010:

Account age	Balance on April 30, 2006	Percent estimated to be uncollectable
Current	$288,000	1%
1–30 days overdue	112,000	5%
31–60 days overdue	60,000	15%
61–120 days overdue	40,000	40%
More than 120 days overdue	60,000	75%

Required:

a. What amount of closing accounts receivable is estimated to be uncollectible on April 30, 2010?

b. Prepare the journal entry required to record the bad debt expense for Weyakwin for the year ended April 30, 2010.

c. What are some possible explanations for the change in the allowance account between April 30, 2009 and April 30, 2010?

P7-15. (**Correcting the balance in Allowance for Uncollectible Accounts, LO 3**) Trilby Inc. (Trilby) uses the percentage-of-credit-sales method for estimating its bad debt expense. The percentage that Trilby uses is based on historical information. Trilby's management has not revised the percentage for several years, a period during which a number of environmental and business factors have changed. Trilby's management recently realized that over the last three years the percentage of credit sales that the company used was too high. As a result, the balance in Allowance for Uncollectible Accounts is $53,000 higher than it would have been had a better estimate of bad debts been used each year.

Required:

a. Prepare the adjusting journal entry that Trilby must make to have an appropriate balance in allowance for uncollectible accounts.

b. What is the effect of the error in estimating bad debts in each of the years the error was made? What is the effect of the adjusting entry on net income? Answer the question by comparing the reported net income with what net income would have been had the error not been made and the adjusting entry not required.

c. What is the impact of this error and the adjusting entry on the users of the financial statements? Explain fully.

P7-16. (**Managing accounts receivable, LO 4**) A financial analyst is comparing the credit management of two companies, Zealand Inc. (Zealand) and Manotick Ltd. (Manotick). The two companies are in the same industry, but operate in different parts of the country. Through conversations with representatives of each of the companies, the analysts learned that Zealand gives its customers 45 days to pay for purchases, while Manotick gives its customers 60 days to pay. By examining the companies' financial statements, the analyst found that during 2008 Zealand had revenues of $4,950,000, of which 85 percent were on credit, while Manotick had revenues of $5,900,000, of which 70 percent were on credit. Average accounts receivable during 2008 were $572,000 for Zealand and $980,000 for Manotick.

Required:

a. Calculate the accounts receivable turnover ratio for Zealand and Manotick.
b. Calculate the average collection period of accounts receivable for Zealand and Manotick.
c. Which company does a better job managing its receivables? Explain.

P7-17. **(Creating hidden reserves, LO 4)** The president of Remo Ltd. (Remo) wants to use hidden reserves to "save" income for a year when the company is not performing very well. To accomplish this objective, the president instructed the accounting department to over-estimate the bad debt expense each year. Instead of using the historical norm of 1.5 percent of credit sales, the president suggested using 1.75 percent of credit sales. Remo commenced this "policy" in 2007 and it has continued through 2011, a period in which Remo has been very successful. The following information about Remo is available:

	2007	2008	2009	2010	2011
Credit sales	$5,054,000	$6,317,500	$7,265,126	$8,572,848	$9,858,774
Net income, excluding the bad debt expense	464,968	631,750	690,186	797,274	887,290
Accounts receivable write-offs	63,000	75,810	94,762	108,976	128,592

The balance in Remo's Allowance for Uncollectible Accounts on January 1, 2007 was $63,000.

Required:

a. Prepare a table that shows:
   i. Remo's bad debt expense from 2007 through 2011 using the 1.5 percent rate.
   ii. Remo's bad debt expense from 2007 through 2011 using the 1.75 percent rate.
   iii. The Allowance for Uncollectible Accounts at the end of each year using each of the estimates.
   iv. Net income for each year using each of the two estimates.
b. How could the president of Remo justify using the 1.75 percent rate for estimating bad debts?
c. In 2012, Remo's net income fell slightly and the president was concerned about a negative response from shareholders and creditors. He was especially concerned that Remo was planning to approach new equity investors to invest in Remo. Credit sales during 2012 were $10,382,000 and net income, excluding the bad debt expense, for the year was $882,820. At this point the president "recognized" the error that had been made over the previous five years and decided it was time to correct it. The president instructed the accounting department to reduce the balance in the Allowance account to the level that would have existed had Remo used 1.5 percent of credit sales as the basis of calculating the bad debt expense each year.
   i. What journal entry would be prepared to reduce the balance in the Allowance account to the desired level?
   ii. What would be the effect on net income of making this journal entry?
d. Why are hidden reserves a serious problem that undermines the integrity and usefulness of accounting information?

P7-18. Zbaraz Bank Ltd. (Zbaraz) lends money to borrowers around the world. One of the major areas of concern to management and stakeholders is what's called the loan loss provision, (which is equivalent to the bad debt expense for non-banking companies) and the allowance for loan losses (which is equivalent to the allowance for uncollectible accounts for non-banking companies). You are provided with the following information about Zbaraz loan situation:

Zbaraz Bank Ltd. Allowance for Loan Losses			
	2010	2009	2008
Beginning balance	$17,615,000	$17,770,000	$18,450,000
Loan losses (write-offs of loans)			
Consumer loans	5,425,000	5,115,000	3,805,000
Canadian commercial loans	770,000	1,315,000	1,175,000
International commercial loans	330,000	195,000	75,000
Total	6,525,000	6,625,000	5,055,000
Loan loss recoveries			
Consumer loans	1,110,000	1,155,000	710,000
Canadian commercial loans	775,000	580,000	905,000
International commercial loans	135,000	300,000	495,000
Total	2,020,000	2,035,000	2,110,000
Loan loss provision	?	?	?
Ending balance	$17,500,000	$17,615,000	$17,770,000

a. Calculate the loan loss provision for Zbaraz for 2008, 2009, and 2010.
b. Examine the information about Zbaraz's loan losses and the loan loss provision you calculated in Part (a). Interpret and discuss any trends that you see in the data.
c. At the end of 2010, Zbaraz had a total of $835,555,000 of loans in its portfolio and reported on its balance sheet. The loan portfolio was broken down as follows:

Consumer loans	$370,545,000
Canadian commercial loans	322,350,000
International commercial loans	142,660,000
Total	$835,555,000

Which of the categories of loans is the most risky? Explain. Given the risk of that category, why does Zbaraz lend to this group?
d. The portfolio of loans could be further broken down in countries loaned to, industries, purpose of the consumer loan (car loan, home renovation loan, etc.), and so on. What additional information would you want about Zbaraz's loan portfolio as a stakeholder in the bank? Explain your answer.

Using Financial Statements

COTT CORPORATION

Cott Corporation is one of the world's largest retailers of brand beverage producers. Cott manufactures carbonated soft drinks and other non-alcoholic beverages for leading supermarkets, mass merchandisers, drug stores and convenience stores in its core geographies of Canada, the United States, the United Kingdom and Mexico. The Company also develops formulas and sells

www.cott.com

concentrates to bottlers in more than 60 countries outside North America who produce the RC® family of soft drinks.

Cott's commitment to customer service is supported by exceptional research and development, concentrate manufacturing, 22 beverage manufacturing plants and over 3,400 employees. The Company is headquartered in Toronto, Canada, with offices and operations in the United States, Canada, the United Kingdom and Mexico. Its over 3,400 employees include professionals in research, procurement, manufacturing, distribution, marketing and customer service.[6]

Cott's consolidated balance sheets, statements of earnings, and statements of cash flow, along with some extracts from the notes to the financial statements are provided in Exhibit 7–6. Use this information to respond to questions FS7-1 to FS7-7.

EXHIBIT 7–6 :

Cott Corporation Financial Statements

Consolidated Statements of Income

	For the years ended		
(IN MILLIONS OF U.S. DOLLARS, EXCEPT PER SHARE AMOUNTS)	December 31, 2005	January 1, 2005	January 3, 2004
Sales	$ 1,755.3	$ 1,646.3	$ 1,417.8
Cost of sales	1,505.8	1,362.6	1,141.0
Gross profit	249.5	283.7	276.8
Selling, general and administrative expenses	138.6	138.1	126.1
Unusual items – note 2			
Restructuring	3.2	—	—
Asset impairments	33.5	0.9	1.8
Other	0.8	—	—
Operating income	73.4	144.7	148.9
Other expense (income), net – note 3	0.8	(0.1)	0.5
Interest expense, net – note 4	28.8	26.0	27.5
Minority interest	4.5	4.0	3.2
Income before income taxes and equity loss	39.3	114.8	117.7
Income taxes – note 5	(14.7)	(35.8)	(40.1)
Equity loss	—	(0.7)	(0.2)
Net income – note 6	$ 24.6	$ 78.3	$ 77.4

Consolidated Balance Sheets

(IN MILLIONS OF U.S. DOLLARS)	December 31, 2005	January 1, 2005
ASSETS		
Current assets		
Cash	$ 21.7	$ 26.6
Accounts receivable – note 8	191.1	184.3
Inventories – note 9	144.2	122.8
Prepaid expenses and other assets	9.5	9.7
	366.5	343.4
Property, plant and equipment – note 11	394.2	313.7
Goodwill – note 12	150.3	88.8
Intangibles and other assets – note 13	260.4	276.1
	$ 1,171.4	$ 1,022.0
LIABILITIES		
Current liabilities		
Short-term borrowings – note 14	$ 157.9	$ 71.4
Current maturities of long-term debt – note 15	0.8	0.8
Accounts payable and accrued liabilities – note 16	182.5	145.2
	341.2	217.4
Long-term debt – note 15	272.3	272.5
Deferred income taxes – note 5	53.5	51.0
	667.0	540.9
Minority interest	22.5	23.8
SHAREOWNERS' EQUITY		
Capital stock – note 17		
Common shares – 71,711,630 (2004 – 71,440,020) shares issued	291.4	287.0
Retained earnings	186.2	161.6
Accumulated other comprehensive income	4.3	8.7
	481.9	457.3
	$ 1,171.4	$ 1,022.0

Consolidated Statements of Cash Flows

EXHIBIT 7-6 :

(continued)
Cott Corporation
Financial
Statements

		For the years ended	
(IN MILLIONS OF U.S. DOLLARS)	December 31, 2005	January 1, 2005	January 3, 2004
OPERATING ACTIVITIES			
Net income	$ 24.6	$ 78.3	$ 77.4
Depreciation and amortization	70.2	60.0	51.0
Amortization of financing fees	0.8	0.7	1.7
Deferred income taxes – note 5	(6.5)	9.1	9.6
Minority interest	4.5	4.0	3.2
Equity loss	—	0.7	0.2
Asset impairments	33.5	1.5	1.8
Other non-cash items	3.0	0.8	1.6
Net change in non-cash working capital – note 19	(1.0)	(52.4)	(3.8)
Cash provided by operating activities	129.1	102.7	142.7
INVESTING ACTIVITIES			
Additions to property, plant and equipment	(75.8)	(50.3)	(39.6)
Acquisitions – note 20	(135.1)	(34.6)	(49.8)
Acquisition of production capacity	—	(3.8)	—
Notes receivable	—	—	(2.5)
Other investing activities	(6.8)	(4.7)	(9.9)
Cash used in investing activities	(217.7)	(93.4)	(101.8)
FINANCING ACTIVITIES			
Payments of long-term debt	(0.9)	(3.5)	(90.2)
Short-term borrowings	91.8	(7.0)	55.8
Distributions to subsidiary minority shareowner	(5.8)	(5.9)	(4.1)
Issue of common shares	3.6	14.3	12.3
Financing costs	(3.8)	—	—
Other financing activities	(0.4)	(0.4)	(0.4)
Cash used in financing activities	84.5	(2.5)	(26.6)
Effect of exchange rate changes on cash	(0.8)	1.4	0.8
Net increase (decrease) in cash	(4.9)	8.2	15.1
Cash, beginning of year	26.6	18.4	3.3
Cash, end of year	$ 21.7	$ 26.6	$ 18.4

Note 8
Accounts Receivable

(IN MILLIONS OF U.S. DOLLARS)	December 31, 2005	January 1, 2005
Trade receivables	$ 178.7	$ 154.2
Allowance for doubtful accounts	(7.8)	(12.1)
Other	20.2	42.2
	$ 191.1	$ 184.3

Note 14
Short-Term Borrowings

Short-term borrowings include bank overdrafts, and borrowings under our credit facilities and receivables securitization facility.

On March 31, 2005, we entered into committed senior secured credit facilities that provide for financing in North America, the U.K. and Mexico expiring on March 31, 2010. The facilities replaced our former committed senior secured credit facility in the U.S. and Canada and our demand bank credit facility in the U.K. These multicurrency facilities were amended on August 10, 2005 to increase the facilities to $225.0 from $100.0 million, to add Macaw (Soft Drinks) Limited as a co-borrower, to consent to the Macaw Acquisition, and to increase the maximum facility amount to $350.0 million.

The amended facilities allow for revolving credit borrowings in a principal amount of up to $225.0 million provided we are in compliance with the covenants and conditions of the agreement. The amended facilities include two separate facilities:

(1) a $220.0 million multicurrency facility made by certain lenders to us and our indirect wholly-owned subsidiaries, Cott Beverages Inc., Macaw (Soft Drinks) Limited and Cott Beverages Limited as co-borrowers, and

(2) a $5.0 million Mexican facility made by certain lenders to our indirect 90% owned subsidiary Cott Embotelladores de Mexico, S.A. de C.V. ("CEMSA").

Each facility includes subfacilities for swingline loans and letters of credit. The $225.0 million facilities can be increased up to an additional $125.0 million at our option if the lenders agree to increase their commitments or new lenders join the facility and we satisfy certain conditions. Within such $125.0 million of extra availability, and subject to certain other limitations, we can establish additional revolving loan facilities in an aggregate amount not to exceed $30.0 million to be provided in various currencies as agreed upon for additional subsidiaries designated by us. Wachovia Bank, National Association acts as administrative agent and security trustee for lenders under these facilities.

The facilities are collateralized by substantially all our personal property with certain exceptions including the receivables sold as part of our receivables securitization facility discussed below.

FS7-1. How much does Cott report on its balance sheet for accounts receivable on December 31, 2005? What does that amount represent (how would you explain its meaning to a novice user of financial statements)? How much cash does Cott report on December 31, 2005?

FS7-2. What currency does Cott prepare its financial statements? Why do you think it uses that currency as opposed to some other currency? If the exchange rate in December 2005 was $1.10 (every US$ is worth $1.10 in Canadian funds), how many Canadian dollars did Cott have on December 31, 2005? Because Cott does business around the world, it will have many transactions in currencies other than Canadian dollars. What are the risks to Cott with doing business with customers that pay in a currency other than Canadian dollars?

FS7-3. What is the balance in Allowance for Doubtful Accounts on December 31, 2005 and January 1, 2005? What is the gross amount of accounts receivable (before deducting Allowance for Doubtful Accounts) each year? Is it useful to know the gross and net amount of accounts receivables, or is knowing just the net amount enough? Explain. Propose some possible reasons for the change in the ending balance in the Allowance for Doubtful Accounts from fiscal 2004 to 2005.

FS7-4. Read Note 14 to Cott's financial statements. Explain the content of the note. What has Cott pledged as collateral for its $225 million borrowing facility? What does this mean? Which of these pledged current assets do you think is more attractive as collateral to the bank? Explain. Why does the bank want collateral for the loans it makes? What benefits do you think exist to the borrower of providing collateral to a lender?

FS7-5. Calculate Cott's current and quick ratios, and the amount of working capital on hand on December 31, 2005 and January 1, 2005. Using the current and quick ratios, the amount of working capital, and the information in the statements of cash flow, provide an assessment of Cott's liquidity position.

FS7-6. Calculate Cott's accounts receivable turnover ratio for the years ended December 31, 2005 and January 1, 2005.
   a. Which receivables did you include in the calculation of the accounts receivable turnover ratio? Explain.
   b. What is the average collection period of accounts receivable for the two years?
   c. Do the accounts receivable turnover ratio and the average collection period indicate that Cott is managing its receivables well? Explain. Assume that Cott allows its customers to pay within 30 days of delivery.

FS7-7. Suppose that instead of showing cash separately on the balance sheet, Cott combined its cash with its short-term borrowings.
   a. How would the balance sheet be affected by this treatment of cash?
   b. How would the current and quick ratios be affected by this treatment?
   c. How would the debt-to-equity ratio be affected by this treatment?
   d. Do you think this approach to reporting cash is confusing or misleading? Explain.
   e. Why do you think some entities combine cash and bank borrowing and others report them separately? Explain.

Analyzing Rogers Communications Inc.

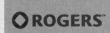

R7-1. What amount of Cash and Cash Equivalents did Rogers report on its December 31, 2005 and 2004 balance sheets? Explain your answer.

R7-2. By how much did accounts receivable increase from the end of fiscal 2004 to the end of fiscal 2005? Is this increase in accounts receivable surprising? Explain. What are some possible explanations for the increase? Support your explanations with evidence from the financial statements.

R7-3. What would be considered *quick assets* on Rogers' balance sheet? Explain your answer. What amount of quick assets did Rogers report on its December 31, 2005 and 2004 balance sheets? Calculate Rogers' quick and current ratios for fiscal 2005 and 2004.

R7-4. Provide the following information for December 31, 2005 and 2004:
a. Amount of accounts receivable reported on the balance sheet.
b. Allowance for doubtful accounts.
c. Gross amount of accounts receivable

R7-5. How much in long-term receivables does Rogers report in its December 31, 2005 balance sheet? Suppose the long-term receivables are due to be paid on December 31, 2010. Assuming that the receivables are interest free, how much would Rogers expect to collect when the receivables become due? If the receivables paid a market rate of interest each year how much would Rogers expect to collect when the receivables come due? Assume an appropriate interest/discount rate for Rogers is 12 percent.

ENDNOTES

1. Extracted from GEAC Computer Corporation Limited's 2005 annual report.

2. Extracted from Canadian Tire Corporation, Limited's 2004 annual report.

3. Clarence Byrd, Ida Chen, and Joshua Smith, *Financial Reporting in Canada*, 30th Edition. The Virtual Professional Libarary. 2005.

4. Panel A extracted from Four Seasons Hotels Inc.'s 2005 annual report. Panel B extracted from Eldorado Gold Corporation's 2005 annual report.

5. Arthur Levitt, speech to the Financial Executives Institute, New York, New York, November 16, 1998, quoted at the United States Securities and Exchange Commission Web site, http://www.sec.gov/news/speech/speecharchive/1998/spch227.htm (accessed April 18, 2002).

6. Extracted from Cott Corporation's 2005 annual report.

INVENTORY

It's the morning of his monthly appearance on The Shopping Channel for Canadian makeup artist and hairstylist Pierre Lalande. Lalande, who has created his own line of cosmetics and beauty products, will drive from his downtown Toronto hair salon to the Rogers' owned The Shopping Channel (TSC) television studios in Mississauga, in the city's west end.

He'll be a guest on a series of live shows that run in prime time on Canada's only nationally televised shopping channel, a 24-hour, seven-day-per-week broadcast retailer available on a variety of cable channels as well as Star Choice, ExpressVu, and Look TV satellite throughout Canada. TSC peddles everything from jewellery to cosmetics to home electronics.

Pierre Lalande

For Lalande, each show is a chance to promote his shampoo, lipstick, and foundation to a nationwide audience of home shoppers who can either call in to purchase or order from the Web site. Lalande will tell the audience why they need to buy his white cardboard peek-a-boo packages of liquid foundation make-up.

"No need for hosiery," he says. "You can put the foundation on your legs, too."

And when customers call in to order, TSC is ready to ship out the merchandise right away.

That's because two weeks before every show, Lalande has to fill the $25,000 purchase order from TSC, and deliver a shipment of 2,000 or 3,000 of his products, all pre-packaged with shrink wrap, to the massive Shopping Channel warehouse in Mississauga.

His products will then sit in the warehouse until they are sold. Once TSC customers pay for shipping and handling, the cosmetics are sent out within a few days.

Lalande is one of hundreds of Canadian retailers who sell their products through TSC, but he says everyone has to abide by the same inventory rules: delivery to the warehouse two weeks before show time.

The Shopping Channel's warehouse keeps some of Rogers' inventory, while Rogers Video has a distribution centre in Calgary where it keeps stock of videos and DVDs in inventory as well. In total, in 2005, Rogers reported $152 million worth of inventory from all subsidiaries. Is that a lot? Not really, according to company officials, because they say Rogers is mostly in the business of selling services (downloadable music, cellphone and cable services, Internet access, airtime, etc.) unlike retailers such as Canadian Tire or Loblaw's, which actually have to stock tens of thousands of products.

LEARNING OBJECTIVES

After studying the material in this chapter you will be able to:

▶ **LO 1** Understand the nature, purpose, and importance of inventory to an entity.

▶ **LO 2** Distinguish between the perpetual and periodic methods of inventory control.

▶ **LO 3** Distinguish among the different cost flow assumptions that are used to determine the amount of inventory that is reported on the balance sheet and cost of sales on the income statement, and understand the impact that the different cost flow assumptions have on the amounts reported in the financial statements.

▶ **LO 4** Explain the lower of cost and market rule.

▶ **LO 5** Recognize the issues, choices, and effects on the financial statements of using market values instead of cost for valuing inventory.

▶ **LO 6** Discuss the relationship between accounting and income tax.

▶ **LO 7** Analyze and interpret inventory information in financial statements.

INTRODUCTION

For many entities, inventory *is* the business. Without inventory, many businesses cannot operate. What's a clothing store without clothes? What's a car dealership without cars? What is an appliance manufacturer without the parts to build the appliances? What's a fast food outlet without burgers, fries, or the ingredients to make pizza? In each case, it is the inventory that is directly responsible for the generation of revenue. Even some service businesses rely on inventory to provide their services to customers. Painters require paint. Lawn care companies require fertilizer.

Accounting for inventory can be surprisingly tricky. Our exposure to accounting for inventory so far in the book has simply involved recording inventory in the accounting records at its cost, and then expensing the cost of that particular inventory when it was sold. Pretty straightforward. But imagine an entity with thousands of identical units of inventory that didn't all cost the same amount. How do we know the cost of the particular unit that was taken from the warehouse? The fact is, in many cases we don't. However, we still have to determine a cost of the inventory sold so that an income statement and balance sheet can be prepared. This is one of the challenges that accountants face—determining the value of inventory on hand and the cost of inventory sold when we do not know the cost of the specific inventory sold to customers, used up in the production process, or consumed in providing services to customers.

This chapter examines the issues that affect accounting for inventory and the effect the resolution of those issues has on the numbers reported in the financial statements. The chapter also discusses a number of other issues designed to broaden our perspective of accounting information. Throughout the book, the point has been made that historical cost, transactions-based accounting is not the only way to account, although it is the method that dominates financial reporting in Canada. In this chapter we will take a quick look at non-cost-based methods for accounting for inventory to see how financial statements would be affected by using alternatives to cost. We will also discuss the close link that exists between accounting and tax. We have already identified tax minimization as an important objective of financial reporting. In this chapter we will see how the Canadian income tax system has an effect on accounting choices and financial reporting by entities.

WHAT IS INVENTORY?

Inventory is goods that are available for sale by an entity, or goods that will be used to produce goods that will be sold. Inventory can also include materials used in supplying a service to customers. The type of inventory an entity has depends on what it does: different types of entities have different inventories.

Rogers has a relatively small inventory, made up of DVDs and video games in Rogers Video stores, supplies for its cell phone and cable businesses (phones, digital cable boxes, parts, and supplies), merchandise for The Shopping Channel, and so on. Service businesses like Rogers tend to have relatively lower amounts of inventory since their businesses don't involve providing goods to customers. Another example of a service company is WestJet Airlines Inc. (WestJet), which has inventory that consists primarily of spare parts, fuel, and supplies. WestJet also has relatively low levels of inventory. Table 8–1 shows the dollar value of the inventory of companies in five different industries along with the proportion inventory is of current assets and total assets. At the other end of the spectrum are retail businesses that have very large inventories. For example, Indigo Books & Music Inc.'s (Indigo) inventory is 85.4 percent of current assets and 52.8 percent of total assets. Indigo must have adequate inventory to meet the needs of its customers but doesn't need the large investment in capital assets that manufacturers do, and the retail nature of the business keeps accounts receivable low (retail customers mainly pay cash or use major credit cards).

Other types of entities have different kinds of inventory. Property development companies' inventory is the land and buildings that are under development. A forestry company like Canfor Corporation, a Canadian producer of lumber and other wood products, has inventory that

TABLE 8–1 ::: Inventory in Different Companies				
Company	**Type of Business**	**Dollar value of inventory**	**Inventory as a percentage of current assets**	**Inventory as a percentage of total assets**
Canfor Corporation	Forest products	$ 600,900,000	46.5%	15.7%
Indigo Books & Music Inc.	Retail	207,643,000	85.4%	52.8%
Magna International Inc.	Auto parts manufacturer	1,388,000,000	21.0%	11.3%
Rogers Communications Inc.	Diversified communications and media	117,182,000	9.0%	0.8%
WestJet Airlines Ltd.	Airline	6,259,000	2.0%	0.3%

includes logs, lumber, and pulp and paper. For entities that manufacture or process inputs into finished goods that are sold to customers, inventory is usually broken down into three sub-categories on the balance sheet or in the notes to the financial statements. These sub-categories of inventory are:

1. **Raw materials inventory:** the inputs into the production process of a manufacturer or processor. For example, raw materials inventory for a furniture manufacturer includes the wood that is used to build the furniture.

2. **Work-in-process** inventory or **WIP:** inventory that is partially completed on the financial statement date. For a car manufacturer, a partially completed car would be classified as WIP inventory.

3. **Finished goods inventory:** inventory that has been completed and is ready for sale.

One entity's inventory can be another entity's capital asset. For example, Rogers accounts for televisions in its Rogers Sportsnet studios as capital assets. But for companies that manufacture televisions, the televisions are inventory because they are the goods that are sold to customers. For some types of entities, it is not obvious whether an item is inventory or something else. Rogers Video stores purchase large quantities of the latest DVDs for rental to customers. As time passes, the demand for a once-popular DVD declines and the stores sell them as "previously viewed" DVDs. Are these DVDs capital assets (because they are rented to customers) or inventory (because they are sold)? We will discuss this question further in Chapter 9.

WHAT DOES GAAP SAY?

Canadian GAAP provides us with surprisingly little guidance about how to account for inventory. As a result, there are many acceptable ways of accounting for inventory, which allows for many different measurements of the same underlying economic resource. The *CICA Handbook* requires that inventory be accounted for at cost. It uses the term "laid-down cost" to describe the costs that should be included in inventory.

Laid-down cost can be interpreted to include all costs that are incurred to purchase or make the products and get them ready for sale to customers. For retailers and wholesalers, laid-down cost should include the actual cost of the product purchased, plus shipping and handling, and any taxes. Of course, things are not always straightforward. Consider a company that takes delivery of a variety of goods in a single shipment. It may not be practical to allocate the cost of shipping individual products. Similarly, it may be difficult to allocate the cost of employees who stock the shelves of a store with the individual products. In these cases, the costs might not be allocated to inventory but instead expensed as incurred.

For manufacturers, laid-down cost would include the cost of the materials that go into the production of the product, direct labour costs that can be traced to the product, and a share of overhead. The *CICA Handbook* is ambiguous about how much of overhead costs should be included in inventory. As a result, in practice there can be considerable variability in the allocation of overhead to inventory. (**Overhead** is the costs in a manufacturing process other than direct labour and direct materials. Overhead costs are more difficult or even impossible to associate directly with the product being made.)

While it is usually easy to identify the costs that should be included in inventory, it is not always practical to include all these costs. Recall our discussion of period and product costs in Chapter 4. It can be difficult to attach some costs to the inventory and it is common to simply treat difficult-to-attach costs as period costs. What makes the situation most difficult from a user's standpoint is that different entities may treat similar types of costs differently. This makes comparability difficult to achieve.

PERPETUAL AND PERIODIC INVENTORY CONTROL SYSTEMS

There are two ways in which accounting systems are designed to keep track of or "control" transactions affecting inventory during a period: perpetual systems and periodic systems.

A **perpetual inventory control system** keeps an ongoing tally of purchases and sales of inventory, with the Inventory account adjusted to reflect changes as they occur. When inventory is purchased or sold, the Inventory account is immediately debited or credited to record the change. When inventory is sold, Cost of Sales is debited immediately. A perpetual system can determine cost of sales at any time.

The journal entry to record the purchase of inventory using a perpetual inventory control system is:

Dr. Inventory (asset +)	xxx	
Cr. Accounts payable (liability +) or Cash (asset −)		xxx
To record the purchase of inventory using a perpetual inventory control system.		

When inventory is sold, the entity would record the following journal entry:

Dr. Cash (asset +) or Accounts receivable (asset +)	yyy	
Cr. Revenue (revenue +, owners' equity +)		yyy
To record the sale of inventory.		

Dr. Cost of sales (expense +, owners' equity −)	xxx	
Cr. Inventory (asset −)		xxx
To record the sale of inventory using a perpetual inventory control system and the corresponding cost of goods sold.		

Because the recording of cost of sales with a perpetual system occurs when the actual exchange with the customer takes place, the entry that records cost of sales is a transactional entry.

With a **periodic inventory control system,** the Inventory account is not adjusted whenever a transaction affects inventory. The balance in the Inventory account at the end of an accounting period is determined by actually counting the inventory. Purchases of inventory are not recorded directly to the Inventory account but instead are accumulated in a separate "Purchases" account. With a periodic inventory control system, cost of sales is determined indirectly using the following equation:

Cost of sales = Beginning inventory + Purchases − Ending inventory

Cost of sales is determined by finding out the beginning and ending Inventory balances (which are known from the inventory counts) and the amount of inventory purchased during the period (from the "Purchases" account). Because it is necessary to count the inventory to calculate cost of sales, it isn't possible to determine cost of sales from the accounting system before the end of a period. If an entity's accountant received an urgent call in the middle of an accounting period from the president asking for the entity's gross margin to date, the accountant could only shrug. (The accountant might be able to estimate the gross margin indirectly, but the cost of sales information would not be directly available from the accounting system.)

The journal entry to record the purchase of inventory using a periodic inventory control system is:

Dr. Purchases (asset +)	xxx	
Cr. Accounts payable (liability +), Cash (asset –)		xxx

To record the purchase of inventory using a periodic inventory control system. (Note that the Purchases account is not the same as the Inventory account.)

When inventory is sold, the following journal entry is made:

Dr. Cash (asset +)	yyy	
Cr. Revenue (revenue +, owners' equity +)		yyy

To record the sale of inventory. (This entry is the same as with the perpetual system. The sale transaction is not affected by the inventory control system being used.)

No entry is made to record cost of sales. Cost of sales is recorded at the end of the period after the inventory has been counted. Because the recording of cost of sales occurs separately from the sale of inventory, it is an adjusting entry—it is not triggered by an external transaction.

The journal entries that would be made at the end of the period under a periodic system would be:

Dr. Inventory	zzz	
Cr. Purchases		zzz

To transfer the inventory purchased during the period that is recorded in the Purchases account to the Inventory account.

Dr. Cost of sales	www	
Cr. Inventory		www

To record cost of sales for the period.

Remember, with a periodic system the debit to Cost of Sales and the credit to Inventory is simply the amount that is necessary to make the ending balance in the Inventory account equal to the amount determined from the inventory count.

www.mcgrawhill.ca/
olc/friedlan

Knowledge Check

- Describe the three subcategories of inventory that manufacturing firms would usually report in their financial statements.

- Describe the two inventory control systems that are used to keep track of inventory transactions. How do the two differ?

- Trenche Ltd. provides you with the following information about its inventory:

Inventory on December 31, 2008	$ 175,000
Purchases during 2009	1,245,000
Inventory on December 31, 2009	210,000

Trenche uses a periodic inventory control system. Use this information to calculate Trenche's cost of sales for 2009.

Internal Control

A perpetual inventory control system does not eliminate the need for counting the inventory from time to time. The selling of inventory is not the only way inventory is consumed. Inventory can also be stolen, lost, damaged, or destroyed. A perpetual system will only account for the cost of inventory actually sold. Only a physical count of inventory will identify that inventory has been consumed for reasons other than a sale.

For example, if $5,000 of inventory had been stolen during the year, the perpetual inventory records would show that there was $5,000 more inventory than there was in fact. This is because the theft would not be recorded in the accounting system (thieves don't usually report their activities). If the inventory were not physically counted, the amount of inventory on the balance sheet at the end of the period would be overstated by $5,000 and expenses would be understated by $5,000. (Stolen inventory is an expense in the period the theft occurs or is discovered.) Differences between the accounting records and the count can also occur because of errors in recording transactions. Once the inventory is counted, the accounting records should be adjusted so that they correspond with the actual amount of inventory on hand.

Counting the inventory and discovering differences between the accounting records and the count is valuable for internal control purposes. Differences between the count and the accounting records allow management to identify the "disappearance" of inventory. With this information, management is able to investigate the cause of the difference and take steps to reduce or eliminate the problem. For example, if management discovered that inventory was being stolen, it could consider steps to better protect the inventory from theft. Information about the amount of inventory being stolen could help stakeholders assess how management is fulfilling its stewardship responsibilities. However, information on the amount of stolen inventory is rarely, if ever, reported in a set of financial statements. The amount of stolen inventory is usually included in cost of sales.

It is important to note that with a periodic inventory control system, it is not possible to determine whether any theft has taken place, because there are no records with which to compare the physical count. Therefore, the cost of stolen items is included, by default, in cost of sales. More important, it is not possible to tell from the accounting records that there is a problem with stolen inventory. This is one of the weaknesses of a periodic inventory control system. The periodic system does not allow for as effective control over inventory as a perpetual system.

Let's consider another situation. It is very common to see scanners in retail and grocery stores. The scanners provide detailed information about what is being sold and quantities on hand. This information is invaluable for management decision-making—including decisions such as when merchandise should be reordered and whether particular products should be stocked. However, the information about physical quantities of inventory may not be integrated with the entity's financial accounting records. The inventory control system might keep track of quantities, but it might not record the financial effect of a sale by crediting Inventory and debiting Cost of Sales when an item is sold. In other words, even though an entity might be collecting information about physical quantities on a continuous or perpetual basis, it might still be using a periodic system for determining the cost of inventory and cost of sales.

The choice between a periodic and perpetual inventory control system is thus an internal control issue, not an accounting issue. Managers choose between periodic and perpetual inventory control systems based on the costs and benefits of the two systems. However, their choice can have an effect on the amount of inventory reported on the balance sheet and cost of goods sold for the period.

INVENTORY VALUATION METHODS

So far, the description of how inventory costs are accounted for has been straightforward. We have assumed that when inventory is sold, we know the actual cost of that specific inventory. In fact, the actual cost of the specific inventory sold is often not known. When inventory is purchased or manufactured, the cost is recorded in the Inventory account (or in the Purchases account). From then on, the flow of costs from the balance sheet to the income statement (from the Inventory account to Cost of Sales) does not necessarily correspond with the physical flow of the actual goods sold. The Cost of Inventory reported on the balance sheet may not be the actual cost of the physical items in inventory. Also, the Cost of Sales that is reported on the income statement may not be the actual cost of the physical units that were received by customers. The reason why the flow of costs through the financial statements does not usually match the physical flow of goods is because in most cases it is not practical, cost effective, or even possible to track the cost of individual units of inventory.

For example, consider inventories of nails, lumber, flower seeds, tennis balls, or plastic furniture—inventory that is relatively low in cost and homogeneous (that is, the items are virtually identical). To track the cost of individual items would require that the entity be able to identify the cost of each individual nail, seed, or tennis ball. It is difficult to imagine a situation where it would be worthwhile to incur the costs of doing so. Or consider a company that refines crude oil to produce a range of petroleum-based products. The price of crude oil is continually fluctuating. The refiner buys crude oil on the open market and stores it in large storage tanks at the refinery. Batches of oil that cost different amounts will be mixed together in the storage tanks. Once the batches are mixed together, it's impossible to know the cost of the oil that is being removed from the storage tanks for use in the production process.

Clearly, it's not practical or even possible in many cases for accountants to keep track of the costs associated with individual units of inventory. But it's necessary to somehow assign costs; otherwise it won't be possible to prepare financial statements. As a result, accountants have developed methods, called *cost flow assumptions*, for moving costs through the Inventory account to Cost of Sales without regard for the actual physical movement of the inventory. There are a number of cost flow assumptions that are currently used. The *CICA Handbook* identifies four:

1. specific identification   2. average cost

3. first in, first out (FIFO)   4. last in, first out (LIFO)

The *CICA Handbook* and GAAP in general do not state a preference for one of these cost flow assumptions over any other. The *CICA Handbook* only requires that inventory be valued at cost and that the method an entity uses to value its inventory be the one that results in the "fairest" matching of costs to revenues. In most cases, it is difficult to argue conclusively that one of the cost flow assumptions results in a fairer matching than the others, so the choice is up to the preparer of the financial statements.

The choice of cost flow assumption does not have any effect on the underlying economic activity of the entity (though it may have tax implications, as we will see below), but the numbers reported on the balance sheet and the income statement can be significantly different depending on the cost flow assumption used. The cost flow assumption that an entity uses must be disclosed in the notes to the financial statements.

Figure 8–1 shows the flow of inventory costs through the accounting system. The cost of inventory available for sale during a period is made up of inventory on hand at the beginning of

FIGURE 8–1

FIFO Inventory Valuation System

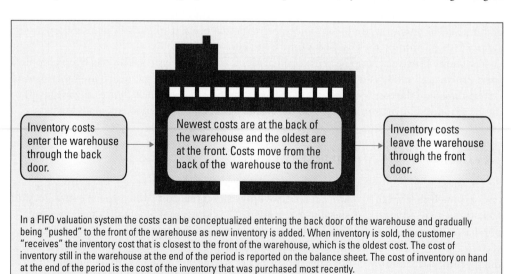

Inventory costs enter the warehouse through the back door.

Newest costs are at the back of the warehouse and the oldest are at the front. Costs move from the back of the warehouse to the front.

Inventory costs leave the warehouse through the front door.

In a FIFO valuation system the costs can be conceptualized entering the back door of the warehouse and gradually being "pushed" to the front of the warehouse as new inventory is added. When inventory is sold, the customer "receives" the inventory cost that is closest to the front of the warehouse, which is the oldest cost. The cost of inventory still in the warehouse at the end of the period is reported on the balance sheet. The cost of inventory on hand at the end of the period is the cost of the inventory that was purchased most recently.

the period plus the cost of inventory purchased during the period. The cost of inventory available for sale during the period is associated either with inventory that was sold during the period (cost of goods sold on the income statement) or with inventory that is on hand (unsold) at the end of the period (ending inventory on the balance sheet). In Figure 8–1, the cost of the goods available for sale is the same under each of the cost flow assumptions, but how that cost is split between the income statement and balance sheet will depend on the cost flow assumption used.

Cost is not the only basis for valuing inventory. There are methods that use measures of current market value to value inventory, such as replacement cost and net realizable value. These methods are not acceptable according to GAAP in most cases because they violate the historical cost measurement convention. (These methods will be examined later in the chapter.)

The remainder of this section will be devoted to discussing the four common cost flow assumptions. When you study the assumptions, remember that their purpose is to provide a way of moving costs from the balance sheet to the income statement. The flow of costs provided by the assumptions does not necessarily reflect or affect the physical flow of inventory.

Let's begin our look at the four common cost flow assumptions.

First In, First Out (FIFO)

Under **first in, first out** or **FIFO**, the cost associated with the inventory that was purchased or produced first is expensed first. For raw materials that are used in a manufacturing process, the cost associated with the raw materials that were purchased first is the cost that is charged to the production process first.

With FIFO, the cost of inventory reported on the balance sheet represents the cost of inventory that was most recently purchased or produced. The inventory cost that has been on hand for the least amount of time is the inventory cost that will still be on hand at the end of the period. Oldest costs are the first ones matched to revenue.

We can conceptualize FIFO by imagining a warehouse where new purchases of inventory are placed in the warehouse from a loading dock at the back and where customers receive the inventory they buy at the front of the warehouse. This conceptualization is shown in Figure 8–1. When new inventory is purchased and placed in the warehouse, it "pushes" the inventory that was purchased earlier toward the front of the warehouse. The inventory gradually moves from the back of the warehouse to the front. When the inventory reaches the front of the warehouse, it can be sold to customers. The result is that the "oldest" costs (the costs that entered the accounting system the longest time ago) are expensed first, while the "newest" costs (the costs associated with the most recently acquired inventory) remain in inventory at the end of the period. This conceptualization uses the physical flow of goods through a warehouse as an analogy for how costs move through a FIFO inventory system. However, remember that FIFO and the other cost flow assumptions address the flow of costs, not the physical flow of goods.

Question for Consideration

Thessalon Inc. (Thessalon) manufactures gumballs. Its most popular product is a one-quarter-inch gumball that comes in six colours. This size gumball is commonly found in dispensers in stores, malls, and so on, as well as in candy stores. Thessalon can have as many as 1,000,000 of these gumballs in inventory at a point in time, depending on the time of year. Once they are made, the gumballs are stored in large containers that hold up to 50,000 gumballs. The gumballs are then packaged into smaller containers for shipment to customers. The cost of gumballs can vary because some of the inputs used in the production of gumballs are commodities whose price can vary from day to day.

Why is it unlikely that Thessalon would know the exact cost of a particular order of one-quarter-inch gumballs? Why is it likely that Thessalon would use a cost flow assumption to determine the value of its inventory and its cost of sales?

(continued)

Answer: With the cost of gumballs varying because of changing input prices and the vast number of gumballs on hand at anytime, it would be impossible to determine the cost of any particular gumball under the current storage arrangement. Once they are produced, gumballs with different costs are presumably mixed together in the large containers, at which time it becomes impossible to distinguish gumballs of different costs (but identical appearance), unless each gumball were given an identifying mark that would allow Thessalon's management to determine its cost. However, giving each gumball an identifying mark would be impractical and costly.

It is likely that gumballs of different costs will be drawn from the large storage containers for packaging. Without being able to identify the cost of individual gumballs, it is impossible for Thessalon to determine the cost of a particular gumball order. However, for accounting purposes Thessalon needs to have a cost associated with the gumballs that are sold so that net income and the value of ending inventory can be determined. As a result, it is necessary to use a method of estimating the cost of the gumballs sold.

This is where a cost flow assumption becomes useful. With a large amount of low-cost, identical inventory it would be cost effective and practical for Thessalon to use a cost flow assumption rather than trying to determine the exact cost of the gumballs sold.

Last In, First Out (LIFO)

Under the **last in, first out** or **LIFO** cost flow assumption, the cost associated with the inventory that was purchased or produced most recently is matched to revenue (expensed) first. For raw materials that are used in a manufacturing process, the cost associated with the raw materials that were purchased last or most recently is the cost that is charged to the production process first. With LIFO, the cost of inventory reported on the balance sheet represents the cost of old, sometimes very old, inventory. Because under LIFO the cost of the newest inventory is expensed first, as long as new inventory keeps being purchased the cost of the older inventory may not be expensed for a long time.

We can also conceptualize LIFO using the warehouse analogy. In a LIFO warehouse, new purchases of inventory enter and inventory that is sold leaves the warehouse through the same door. This conceptualization of a LIFO inventory system is shown in Figure 8–2. When new inventory is purchased, it is placed closest to the door so that when a customer comes to purchase inventory it is conveniently available to be sold to the customer. The older inventory that was previously closest to the door is "pushed" toward the back of the warehouse. As older inventory is pushed to the back, the only way it can be sold is if the inventory in front of it is sold first. In Figure 8–2, the only way the inventory costs from two years ago could be expensed is if the costs associated with the inventory from last year, last month, last week, and today were sold first. As an entity expands, the amount of inventory it will have increases, so it is unlikely that costs associated with the older inventory that has been pushed back in the warehouse will be expensed. The inventory cost that is expensed first is the cost associated with the newest inventory—the inventory that was placed in the warehouse most recently.

Average Cost

With the **average cost method**, the average cost of all inventory on hand during the period is calculated and that average is used to calculate cost of sales and the balance in ending inventory. The average cost method does not attempt to distinguish among units of inventory that have different costs and make assumptions about when costs move from Inventory to Cost of Sales (as FIFO and LIFO do). Instead, the average cost method simply assumes that all the inventory units have the same cost. In an average cost system, all units of inventory at a point in time are

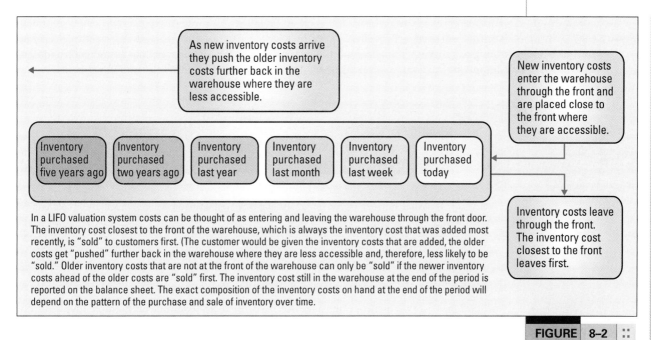

As new inventory costs arrive they push the older inventory costs further back in the warehouse where they are less accessible.

New inventory costs enter the warehouse through the front and are placed close to the front where they are accessible.

| Inventory purchased five years ago | Inventory purchased two years ago | Inventory purchased last year | Inventory purchased last month | Inventory purchased last week | Inventory purchased today |

Inventory costs leave through the front. The inventory cost closest to the front leaves first.

In a LIFO valuation system costs can be thought of as entering and leaving the warehouse through the front door. The inventory cost closest to the front of the warehouse, which is always the inventory cost that was added most recently, is "sold" to customers first. (The customer would be given the inventory costs that are added, the older costs get "pushed" further back in the warehouse where they are less accessible and, therefore, less likely to be "sold." Older inventory costs that are not at the front of the warehouse can only be "sold" if the newer inventory costs ahead of the older costs are "sold" first. The inventory cost still in the warehouse at the end of the period is reported on the balance sheet. The exact composition of the inventory costs on hand at the end of the period will depend on the pattern of the purchase and sale of inventory over time.

FIGURE 8–2 ⠿ 401

LIFO Inventory Valuation System

INVENTORY

assigned the same cost: the average cost of the inventory on hand. With an average cost system, the cost of individual units of inventory is lost.

We have to conceptualize the average cost inventory cost flow assumption differently than we did LIFO and FIFO. Consider a large storage tank at an oil refinery. The refinery purchases crude oil at market prices and stores the oil in the storage tank. Crude oil prices fluctuate daily, so it is necessary to mix crude oil purchased at different prices in the tank. When oil is taken from the tank it is impossible to tell what priced oil is coming out of the tank. In fact, all the differently priced oil mixes together and each litre drawn will be a combination of the oil costs that were put in the storage tank.

Specific Identification

The **specific identification method** assigns the actual cost of a particular unit of inventory to that unit of inventory. Unlike the average cost, FIFO, and LIFO cost flow assumptions, when specific identification is used, the physical flow of inventory matches the flow of costs that are recorded in the accounting system. As a result, the inventory cost reported on the balance sheet is the actual cost of the specific items that are in inventory, and cost of sales is the actual cost of the specific items of inventory that were sold during the period. (Strictly speaking, specific identification should not be referred to as a cost flow assumption because it reflects the actual flow of costs and the physical flow of inventory.)

Specific identification has appeal because the physical flow of inventory and the flow of costs correspond. However, aside from the practical problems with using specific identification for homogeneous inventories, specific identification allows for easy manipulation of financial information by managers. If there are a number of identical items in inventory that have different costs, managers could choose to sell the inventory items that would have a desired effect on the financial statement.

For example, a car dealer might have two of the same model car, each the same colour and with the same features. The two cars may have been purchased from the manufacturer for different amounts. A car buyer is unlikely to be able to differentiate between the vehicles and may not care which vehicle he or she receives. However, if the dealer sells the more expensive car, net income is lower. If the less expensive model is sold, income increases. Simply by choosing the "appropriate" unit of inventory, the dealer can help achieve an objective of financial reporting.

The other cost flow assumptions are less subject to manipulation than specific identification because these other methods have defined flows of costs that are not subject to arbitrary choices. (Nonetheless, LIFO can be manipulated if managers allow the level of inventory to decrease so that the entity is expensing the costs associated with inventory from much earlier periods.) FIFO and average cost are much more difficult to manipulate.

The specific identification method is suitable for more expensive inventory that is unique (such as works of art or some types of jewellery) or for inventory that is relatively easy to distinguish among individual units (such as cars, major appliances, and home entertainment equipment, which have serial numbers that make it easy to identify the individual items).

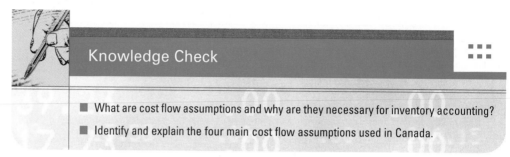

Knowledge Check

- What are cost flow assumptions and why are they necessary for inventory accounting?
- Identify and explain the four main cost flow assumptions used in Canada.

Comparison of the Different Cost Flow Assumptions

Now that the cost flow assumptions have been explained, let's examine an example that will allow us to see the effects that they have on the financial statements. Information about the purchases and sales of inventory made by Woolchester Inc. (Woolchester) during October 2010 is shown in Figure 8–3. We will use this information to calculate ending inventory on October 31, 2010, and the cost of sales and the gross margin for October 2010. We will calculate these amounts for each cost flow assumption, but only using a periodic inventory control system. While different inventory control systems can result in different amounts for inventory and cost of sales, the main focus is understanding the effect that the different cost flow assumptions have on the financial statements. The mechanics of periodic and perpetual systems are essentially the same. The difference is that with a perpetual system the cost of sales and changes to inventory are calculated with each transaction, whereas with a periodic system these calculations are only done at the end of the period.

We will also see that cash flow is not affected by the choice of inventory cost flow assumption and control method.

FIGURE 8–3

Purchases and Sales of Inventory at Woolchester Inc.

Woolchester Inc. Information about the Purchases and Sales of Inventory During October 2010			
	Number of units	Price per unit	Total
Inventory balance on September 30, 2010	0	$	$ 0
Purchases:*			
October 3	100	50	5,000
October 15	125	55	6,875
October 25	75	59	4,425
Sales:**			
October 8	80	125	10,000
October 20	130	125	16,250
*All purchases of inventory are made for cash. **All sales are for cash.			

FIFO The spreadsheet entries for Woolchester for October 2010 using FIFO are shown in Table 8–2. On October 31 Woolchester has to make the entry to record cost of sales and inventory used during the period. We determine the costs that should be expensed for October by looking at the units and costs available for sale during the month in the order the inventory was purchased.

TABLE 8–2 ::: Woolchester Inc.: Spreadsheet 1—FIFO

Woolchester Inc.
Spreadsheet for Inventory Transactions for October 2010 Using FIFO Periodic

		Cash	Inventory*	Revenue	Cost of sales
October 3	Purchase 100 units @ $50	$(5,000)	$5,000		
October 8	Sell 80 units @ $125	10,000		$10,000	
October 15	Purchase 125 units @ $55	(6,875)	6,875		
October 20	Sell 130 units @ $125	16,250		16,250	
October 25	Purchase 75 units @ $59	(4,425)	4,425		
October 31	Inventory on hand on October 31 (before recording cost of sales): 100 units @ $50 125 units @ $55 75 units @ $59	Inventory expensed for October 2010: 100 units @ $50 + 110 units @ $55		(11,050)		$(11,050)
October 31	**Ending balances** Remaining in inventory: 15 units @ $55 = $ 825 } 75 units @ $59 = $4,425 }	$ 9,950	$5,250	$26,250	$(11,050)

*In this table purchases are made directly to the Inventory account. These should have been made to the Purchases account. However, for clarity the step of recording purchases to the Purchases account and then moving them to the Inventory account is ignored.

During October, Woolchester had on hand (in order of acquisition) 100 units at $50, 125 units at $55, and 75 units at $59. Under FIFO, to record the cost of selling 210 units during October, Woolchester would expense the cost associated with the 100 units purchased for $50 each on October 3 and the cost associated with 110 of the units purchased for $55 each on October 15. Under FIFO, the total cost of sales for October was $11,050. If Woolchester had a beginning inventory balance at the start of October, the costs associated with that inventory would be expensed first under FIFO.

LIFO With LIFO the first inventory costs to be expensed are the costs that were most recently added to inventory. During October, Woolchester had available for sale inventory costs of 100 units at $50, 125 units at $55, and 75 units at $59. The most recent costs are the $59 units, so these are expensed first, followed by the $55 units, and then by the $50 units. Since 210 units were sold during October, Cost of Sales must be debited and Inventory credited for the cost of the 75 $59 units, the 125 $55 units, and 10 of the $50 units. At the end of October the costs remaining in inventory are associated with 90 units with a cost of $50 each. The spreadsheet entries for Woolchester for October using LIFO are shown in Table 8–3.

Average Cost When the average cost method is used, the average cost of the inventory available for sale is determined when the entry that records cost of sales and the reduction to inventory is made. The average cost is then applied to the inventory sold and the inventory on hand at the end of the period.

The spreadsheet entries for Woolchester for October using average cost periodic are shown in Table 8–4. For Woolchester, the average cost per unit of the inventory available for sale during October is $54.33 ([(100 units at $50) + (125 units at $55) + (75 units at $59)] ÷ 300 units). Cost of sales for October is simply $11,409.30, the product of the average cost and the number of units sold ($54.33 × 210). The $54.33 becomes the cost associated with each of the 90 units of inventory on hand at the start of the next period.

TABLE 8–3 ::: Woolchester Inc.: Spreadsheet 2—LIFO

Woolchester Inc.
Spreadsheet for Inventory Transactions for October 2010 Using LIFO Periodic

		Cash	Inventory*	Revenue	Cost of sales
October 3	Purchase 100 units @ $50	$(5,000)	$5,000		
October 8	Sell 80 units @ $125	10,000		$10,000	
October 15	Purchase 125 units @ $55	(6,875)	6,875		
October 20	Sell 130 units @ $125	16,250		16,250	
October 25	Purchase 75 units @ $59	(4,425)	4,425		
October 31 Inventory on hand on October 31 (before recording cost of sales): 100 units @ $50 125 units @ $55 75 units @ $59	Inventory expensed for October 2010: 75 units @ $59 + 125 units @ $55 + 10 units @ $50		(11,800)		$(11,800)
October 31 **Ending balances** Remaining in inventory:} 90 units @ $50 = $4,500		$9,950	$4,500 ↑	$26,250	$(11,800)

*In this table purchases are made directly to the Inventory account. These should have been made to the Purchases account. However, for clarity the step of recording purchases to the Purchases account and then moving them to the Inventory account is ignored.

TABLE 8–4 ::: Woolchester Inc.: Spreadsheet 3—Average Cost

Woolchester Inc.
Spreadsheet for Inventory Transactions for October 2010 Using Average Cost Periodic

		Cash	Inventory*	Revenue	Cost of sales
October 3	Purchase 100 units @ $50	$(5,000)	$5,000		
October 8	Sell 80 units @ $125	10,000		$10,000	
October 15	Purchase 125 units @ $55	(6,875)	6,875		
October 20	Sell 130 units @ $125	16,250		16,250	
October 25	Purchase 75 units @ $59	(4,425)	4,425		
October 31	Cost of sales for October 2010: 210 units @ $54.33		(11,409.30)		$(11,409.30)
Average cost = [(100 units @ $50) + (125 units @ $55) + (75 units @ $59)] / 300 units = $54.33					
October 31 **Ending balances** Remaining in inventory: 90 units @ $54.33 = $4,890.70		$9,950	$4,890.70 ↑	$26,250	$(11,409.30)

*In this table purchases are made directly to the Inventory account. These should have been made to the Purchases account. However, for clarity the step of recording purchases to the Purchases account and then moving them to the Inventory account is ignored.

Specific Identification When the specific identification method is used, cost of sales is the actual cost of the particular units of inventory that were sold and the balance in Inventory at the end of the period is the actual cost of the units of inventory that have not yet been sold. As a result, the cost remaining in ending inventory at the end of the period and cost of sales for the period will depend on which physical units are sold.

The spreadsheet entries for Woolchester for October using specific identification are shown in Table 8–5. When Woolchester sold 80 units on October 8, the cost of each of the units sold had to be $50. For the sale that occurred on October 20, if we assume that Woolchester sold 12 of the $50 units and 118 of the $55 units, then cost of sales for that transaction would be $7,090. The cost that would be reported in Inventory on October 31 would be $5,210, which would be the cost associated with the eight $50 units, the seven $55 units, and the 75 $59 units that were on hand on October 31.

If on October 20, either by design or by chance, Woolchester sold 124 of the $55 units and only six of the $50 units, cost of sales would be $11,120 instead of $11,090. In this case, ending inventory would be $5,180 instead of $5,210. Simply by changing the actual physical units that were given to customers, amounts reported on the income statement and the balance sheet change. One can see that the specific identification method can be easily manipulated by the managers to achieve their reporting objectives.

TABLE 8–5 ::: Woolchester Inc.: Spreadsheet 4—Specific Identification

Woolchester Inc.
Spreadsheet for Inventory Transactions for October 2010 Using specific identification

		Cash	Inventory	Revenue	Cost of sales
October 3	Purchase 100 units @ $50	$(5,000)	$5,000		
October 8	Sell 80 units @ $125	10,000		$10,000	
October 15	Purchase 125 units @ $55	(6,875)	6,875		
October 20	Sell 130 units @ $125	16,250		16,250	
October 25	Purchase 75 units @ $59	(4,425)	4,425		
October 31 Inventory on hand during October 2010 (before recording cost of sales): = [(100 units @ $50) + (125 units @ $55) + (75 units @ $59)]	Sell 210 @ $54.33 Inventory expensed for October 2010: 80 units @ $50 + 12 units @ $50 + 118 units @ $55		(11,090)		$(11,090)
October 31 Ending balances Remaining in inventory: 8 units @ $50 = $ 400 7 units @ $55 = $ 385 75 units @ $59 = $4,425		$9,950	$5,210	$26,250	$(11,090)

Summary of the Comparison of Different Cost Flow Assumptions Figure 8–4 summarizes the results from each of the cost flow assumptions discussed above. Figure 8–4 highlights a number of important points:

■ Cash flow is not directly affected by the cost flow assumption used. In all of the situations described, there is a net increase in cash of $9,950 from the purchase and sale of inventory during October. The choice of cost flow assumption can have secondary effects on cash flow because outcomes based on financial statement numbers may be affected. For example, the cost flow assumption used for financial reporting purposes is usually also used for tax purposes. Methods that yield higher cost of sales and, therefore, lower income before tax will have a smaller cash outflow because less tax will have to be paid. Outcomes such as management bonuses, compliance with debt covenants, and selling prices of businesses, among others, may also be affected by the cost flow assumption used.

- Cost of Sales and Inventory are affected by the choice of cost flow assumption. While there is an effect on the numbers reported in the financial statements, the underlying economic activity of the entity is the same regardless of the method used. That means that the number of units sold during the period, the number of units in inventory on hand at the end of the period, the number of units purchased during the period, and the number of transactions during the period are the same regardless of the cost flow assumption used.

- Because the amounts reported for Inventory and Cost of Sales differ under the different cost flow assumptions and inventory valuation methods, many other financial accounting measures and ratios are also affected. For example, gross margin and the gross margin percentage will change with the methods, as will net income, return on assets and return on equity, profit margin, current ratio, and debt-to-equity ratio. Again, it is important to emphasize that the underlying economic activity of the entity is not affected by these different methods. However, the representations of the underlying economic activity are affected, which may affect the perceptions, interpretations, and inferences of users of the information.

Woolchester Inc. Summary Information on Inventory Transactions for the Month Ended October 31, 2010						
	Revenue	Cost of sales	Gross margin	Gross margin percentage	Cash flow	Ending inventory
FIFO	26,250	11,050	15,200	57.90%	9,950	5,250
Average cost	26,250	11,409.30	14,840.70	56.54%	9,950	4,890.70
LIFO	26,250	11,800	14,450	55.05%	9,950	4,500
Specific identification	26,250	11,090	15,160	57.75%	9,950	5,210

FIGURE 8-4

Woolchester Inc.: Summary

- The sum of cost of sales and ending inventory in each case is $16,300. This is not a coincidence. The different cost flow assumptions affect the allocation of the cost of inventory available for sale during a period between the balance sheet and the income statement but they do not affect the total amount.

- When inventory prices are rising, FIFO will always give the lowest cost of sales (and the highest gross margin and net income), while LIFO will always give the highest cost of sales (and the lowest gross margin and net income). Average cost will always be between these two. This point will be discussed further later in this chapter.

Which Method Is Best?

That takes care of the mechanics. We now have to figure out what all this means for the numbers that appear in financial statements and for users of financial statements. How and why does an entity choose one cost flow assumption over another? Do GAAP provide any direction for the choice? Is one cost flow assumption better than the others?

According to the *CICA Handbook* and GAAP, none of the cost-based cost flow assumptions described above are recommended or preferred. The *CICA Handbook* merely requires that the method an entity chooses for determining inventory costs should be "one which results in the fairest matching of costs against revenues." The requirement of fair matching is very ambiguous and pretty much allows the managers to choose the cost flow assumption they prefer, as long as it is a cost-based method. The problem with the matching argument is that it is not clear what it is we are trying to match. All of the cost flow assumptions match a cost to the revenue—what is being matched depends on the method.

Question for Consideration

Figure 8–4 shows that cost of sales and gross margin are different with cost flow assumption, while cash flow is the same for each. Explain why this is the case.

Answer: The cost flow assumptions are accounting methods for allocating the cost of inventory between the balance sheet and the income statement. They are accrual accounting concepts that involve economic flows, not necessarily cash flows. The cost flow assumption an entity selects has no effect on the amount of cash that is paid to suppliers of inventory or for the inputs used for producing inventory. The actual amount of cash paid is not affected by accrual accounting choices made by the preparers of the financial statements. Therefore, cost of sales and gross margin will change with the cost flow assumption, but cash flows will remain the same. Alternative cost flow assumptions may affect secondary cash flows, however.

Over the years, accountants have developed many arguments for and against the various cost flow assumptions. None of these arguments has conclusively proved that one cost flow assumption is always better than the others. The implication is that we can't say that one of the cost flow assumptions is best in all situations. Each cost flow assumption has strengths and weaknesses, and the choice depends on the information the preparers want to convey to stakeholders. In many cases an entity will choose the method that is used by other similar entities for comparison purposes.

The *CICA Handbook* also states that the cost flow assumption that is used does not have to correspond with the physical flow of the inventory. This means that the physical flow of goods is not a criterion that managers have to consider when choosing the cost flow assumption.

We will now discuss the implications of each cost flow assumption for the financial statements.

FIFO When FIFO is used, the costs in inventory at the end of a period are the costs associated with the inventory that was purchased or produced most recently. This means that the amount reported on the balance sheet for Inventory is as close an approximation of the replacement cost of the inventory that is possible while still using a cost-based inventory valuation method. This is a useful feature of FIFO because it provides users more relevant information about the current value of an entity's inventory.

Users of financial statements who are interested, for example, in predicting future cash flows might find a FIFO-based inventory value more useful than the alternatives because it gives a more current indication of what it would cost to replace the entity's inventory. When FIFO is used in periods when prices are rising, the reported amount for ending inventory will be higher than with average cost and FIFO because the newest costs are in inventory at the end of a period. Because the more recent, higher costs are reported on the balance sheet, the current ratio will be higher when FIFO is used in a period of rising prices.

On the other hand, the costs associated with the oldest inventory are expensed to cost of sales first under LIFO. The implication of this treatment is that cost of sales is more out of date with FIFO, compared with average cost and LIFO. Being out of date means that the most current cost of inventory is not being matched to the current revenue. As a result, gross margin and net income are poorer indications of economic performance than when FIFO or average cost are used. This effect could be misleading to a user who is attempting to predict future profitability. Future profitability is based on what inventory will cost in the future, not what it cost in the past. If inventory costs are rising and the entity cannot raise prices to offset the increase in costs, the gross margin calculated under FIFO is not as representative of the future as the alternative cost flow assumptions. Consequently, users who base their predictions about future profitability on an income statement that is based on FIFO might overestimate future profitability.

Despite the fact that the flow of inventory costs and the physical flow of inventory do not have to correspond, one of the appeals of FIFO seems to be that in most cases it does follow the physical flow of goods. The use of FIFO provides an approximation of the specific identification method, where there is a matching of the actual cost of the item sold to the revenue recognized. In many situations, good inventory management requires that the oldest inventory be sold to customers first. This is, of course, crucial for perishable goods.

From the managers' standpoint, FIFO can be attractive because when prices are rising it will result in a higher asset valuation for inventory on the balance sheet and higher net income. The higher asset valuation can be beneficial if, for example, the size of an entity's bank loan is related to the amount of inventory (say the bank will lend $0.30 for each $1.00 of inventory). The higher asset value would also provide a higher current ratio, which could be valuable in some circumstances.

LIFO LIFO matches the most recent inventory costs to revenue first. This means that when the prices of an entity's inputs are rising, cost of sales will be higher and net income, gross margin, and profit margin will be lower than with the other cost flow assumptions. This result will not be attractive for objectives of financial reporting that are served by higher net income, such as management bonuses.

On the other hand, by matching the newer, more current costs to revenue, the LIFO income statement gives a better approximation of the current cost of operations—a more relevant and current gross margin, profit margin, and net income. This can be useful. One can argue that the wealth of an entity only increases once it is able to replace the resources it has consumed earning the current revenue. In other words, if an entity is going to continue in business, it must replace the inventory that it uses. That inventory must be replaced at the current market price, not at some historical cost.

LIFO can create some big problems on the balance sheet. The almost-current cost of sales number on the income statement comes at the expense of the balance sheet. As we discussed earlier in the chapter, the costs in inventory under LIFO can be very, very old. They will certainly not approximate the replacement cost of inventory. If a bank lends money to an entity based on the amount of inventory reported on the balance sheet, LIFO would allow for a smaller amount of borrowing than FIFO would, again assuming that prices are rising. This conclusion assumes that no consideration was given to the cost flow assumption used by the entity when the terms of the loan were established. The lower inventory value would also result in a lower current ratio. Overall, when prices are rising, LIFO paints a poorer picture of an entity.

There is an additional problem associated with LIFO that can play havoc with the financial statements. The problem arises when an entity reduces the amount of inventory being held. An entity might reduce its inventory levels for efficiency purposes or because it has decided to eliminate some of its products. Whatever the reason, when the amount of inventory is reduced significantly, the entity expenses older costs, which are likely much lower than current costs. The effect will be to match low, old costs with current revenues, which will result in unusually high gross margin and net income. With LIFO, managers can intentionally deplete their inventory to boost net income. Therefore, the benefits of using LIFO for income measurement can be lost if inventory levels fluctuate significantly.

Some readers might logically conclude that one of the attractions of LIFO when prices are rising is that it would reduce the amount of tax the entity would have to pay, because income is lower. While this conclusion makes sense, it is not correct because LIFO is not allowed for tax purposes in Canada. This issue will be discussed further later in the chapter.

Average Cost Average cost provides results that fall in between FIFO and LIFO. That means the cost of sales is not as current as would be achieved when LIFO is used, but not as old or out of date as is achieved when FIFO is used. Conversely, average cost does not provide balance sheet information that is as current as FIFO, but it is not as out of date as LIFO. As a result of this "in the middle" effect, gross margin, net income, current ratio, and many other financial measurements fall between LIFO and FIFO.

Because average cost yields an income figure that is lower than FIFO, it is attractive in Canada for tax purposes. (Remember that LIFO is not acceptable for tax purposes in Canada.) Entities that have a tax minimization objective would choose average cost over FIFO in periods when prices are rising. One would expect that private companies would tend to prefer average cost because the tax minimization objective is more likely to be dominant. This will not always be the case, since some private firms may be interested in maximizing their net income to satisfy lenders or because of an upcoming sale of shares.

Insight

This section has highlighted the fact that different cost flow assumptions can have a significant effect on the cost of inventory that is reported on the balance sheet and the amount of cost of sales. It is crucial to understand that the different cost flow assumptions provide different results only if the cost of inventory is changing. If the cost of inventory remains constant over a period of time, all the methods will yield the same results. However, it is unusual for the price of anything to remain constant for any length of time. Even in periods of very low inflation, the prices of individual goods and services are rising and falling.

It is important for users of financial statements to be aware of the accounting choices made by the preparers of the statements. As our discussion of cost flow assumptions has shown, the choice of accounting policies can have significant effects on many of the accounting numbers that stakeholders use to analyze an entity. Without knowing the accounting policy choices that an entity has made, it is virtually impossible to make any sense of the information in the financial statements.

Comparisons among entities are very difficult at the best of times. Comparisons are invalid when the entities being compared use different accounting policies. The *CICA Handbook* provides some assistance here because entities are required to disclose the cost flow assumption they use. For comparisons of an entity's accounting information over time, consistency requires that an entity use the same set of accounting policies year after year. While changes in accounting policies are allowable, it is not possible to change accounting policies every period and still adhere to GAAP. In addition, when accounting policies change, it is necessary to restate the financial statements so they present prior years' statements using the new accounting policies.

THE LOWER OF COST AND MARKET RULE

In the fashion business, what is popular today might be virtually unsellable in a couple of months. A clothing chain might buy a large supply of fashionable styles for the 2008 fall season, but when the spring 2009 merchandise arrives, it may still have some inventory left over from fall that might not be easy to sell at the full retail price. From a business standpoint, it makes sense for the clothing chain to sell those fall fashions for whatever it can get—even if it means selling them for less than their cost.

But how should the chain account for clothes that cannot be sold for more than what they cost? According to GAAP, inventory on hand at the end of a period must be evaluated according to the lower-of-cost-and-market rule. The **lower of cost and market (LCM) rule** requires that when the market value of inventory at the end of a reporting period is lower than its cost, the inventory must be reported on the balance sheet at its market value. If the market value of inventory is less than its cost, the inventory must be written down to its market value. The amount of the write-down is the difference between the inventory's cost and its market value, and it is reported as a loss on the income statement in the period that the market value of the inventory falls, not when the inventory is sold. This treatment is a departure from what is ordinarily done under GAAP, where inventory remains at its cost until it is sold. Remember that if inventory is written down, it is still on hand and can be sold. What has changed is the amount that the inventory is recorded at in the accounting records.

If the inventory must be written down, the following journal entry is recorded:

Dr. Cost of sales (expenses +, owner's equity –)   xxx
    Cr. Inventory (asset –)   xxx
To record a write-down of inventory.

The effect of this journal entry is to reduce the balance in the Inventory account and increase expenses, and thereby decrease net income. This journal entry buries the loss suffered on the decline in the value of inventory in Cost of Sales. The amount of the write-down could also be disclosed separately in the income statement, either on a separate line in the income statement or in the notes.

If the write-down is included in Cost of Sales, a financial statement user will not be able to determine if an inventory write-down has occurred or the amount of the write-down. And when the amount of the write-down is included in Cost of Sales, financial ratios such as gross margin percentage might be distorted. Without adequate disclosure of the existence of the write-down, it is not possible for a user to understand why the gross margin percentage has changed from previous years. Once inventory is written down to its market value, it cannot be written back up in the event that the market price of the inventory increases.

For some entities, writing down inventory is a regular occurrence. For example, most entities that sell fashion goods will have out-of-style merchandise every year that has to be written down to market value. If such write-downs are normal and in the ordinary course of business, then not separately disclosing information about them is probably not a serious problem, although knowing about any material write-downs would provide some insight into management's ability. However, it would be valuable for users of the financial statements to be aware of unusual write-downs of inventory. Separate disclosure of an unusual inventory write-down would be helpful to users for evaluating the performance of management and for predicting future earnings of the entity.

Let's consider an example. In its fiscal year ended December 31, 2004 Digital Theater Systems, Inc. (DTS), a U.S. company that specializes in entertainment technology, took a $3,871,000 write-down of its inventory. Exhibit 8–1 provides extracts from DTS's 2004 annual report.[1] The write-down represents 6 percent of total revenues, almost 39 percent of net income, and is greater than the amount of inventory reported on the December 31, 2004 balance sheet. Notice that there is no mention of the write-down on the balance sheet or statement of operations. The existence of the write-down is clearly disclosed on the statement of cash flow, the notes to the financial statements, and in the management discussion and analysis. Also notice the discussion of the impact of the write-down on gross profit.

As we discussed in Chapter 5, the reason for this departure from the usual transactions-based accounting approach is conservatism. When conservatism is applied to inventory, the historical cost, transactions-based valuation of inventory is replaced with a market value that is not supported by a transaction if the market value of the inventory is less than the cost. If there were no LCM rule and the market value of inventory were below cost, the value of inventory on the balance sheet would be overstated. That is, the actual future benefit associated with the inventory would be less than the amount reported on the balance sheet. From this perspective, the LCM rule makes sense.

Probably the major criticism with the use of the LCM rule and conservatism is that decreases in the value of inventory are recognized, whereas increases are not recognized until the inventory is sold. Also, applying the LCM rule sacrifices consistency, because cost is not being applied consistently from period to period.

There are many circumstances in which the market value of inventory can fall, in addition to clothing going out of style. Technological change is another reason. For example, the selling price of last year's leading-edge computer equipment will usually fall dramatically when faster and more powerful computers come on the market. Another example is goods that are damaged. If the market value of damaged goods is less than cost, the inventory should be written down to market. For commodities, such as lumber or minerals, market prices rise and fall with market conditions, and in some circumstances the market price may fall below the cost of producing or extracting the commodity.

CONSOLIDATED BALANCE SHEETS

ASSETS	As of December 31, 2003	2004
	(Amounts in thousands, except share and per share amounts)	
Current assets:		
Cash and cash equivalents	$ 39,243	$ 21,271
Short-term investments	60,146	93,040
Accounts receivable, net of allowance for doubtful accounts of $429 and $402 at December 31, 2003 and 2004, respectively	3,962	4,649
Inventories	7,552	3,669
Deferred tax assets, net	6,025	9,144
Prepaid expenses and other	1,846	3,651
Income tax receivable	660	72
Total current assets	119,434	135,496
Long-term investments	2,998	2,657
Property and equipment, net	3,092	3,539
Intangible assets, net	424	1,779
Deferred tax assets	1,527	500
Other assets	20	718
Total assets	$127,495	$144,689

CONSOLIDATED STATEMENTS OF OPERATIONS

	For the Years Ended December 31, 2002	2003	2004
	(Amounts in thousands, except share and per share amounts)		
Revenues:			
Technology and film licensing	$ 31,906	$ 42,229	$ 49,920
Product sales and other revenues	9,150	9,473	11,511
Total revenues	41,056	51,702	61,431
Cost of goods sold:			
Technology and film licensing	3,687	4,281	4,451
Product sales and other revenues	6,949	6,751	11,711
Total cost of goods sold	10,636	11,032	16,162
Gross profit	30,420	40,670	45,269
Operating expenses:			
Selling, general and administrative	16,379	20,473	27,644
Research and development	3,754	4,987	6,131
Total operating expenses	20,133	25,460	33,775
Income from operations	10,287	15,210	11,494
Interest income (expense), net	(94)	271	1,447
Other expense, net	(255)	(214)	(31)
Income from legal settlement (Note 20)	—	—	2,601
Income before provision for income taxes	9,938	15,267	15,511
Provision for income taxes	3,688	5,368	5,535
Net income	6,250	9,899	9,976
Accretion and accrued dividends on preferred stock	(1,848)	(1,234)	—
Net income attributable to common stockholders	$ 4,402	$ 8,665	$ 9,976

EXHIBIT 8-1 :

Digital Theater Systems, Inc.

411

INVENTORY

EXHIBIT 8–1 :

(continued)
Digital Theater
Systems, Inc.

CONSOLIDATED STATEMENTS OF CASH FLOWS

	For the Years Ended December 31,		
	2002	2003	2004
	(Amounts in thousands)		
Cash flows from operating activities:			
Net income	$ 6,250	$ 9,899	$ 9,976
Adjustments to reconcile net income to net cash provided by operating activities:			
Depreciation and amortization	902	910	1,298
Stock-based compensation charges	138	497	273
Allowance for doubtful accounts	10	114	61
Loss on disposal of property and equipment	—	93	—
Deferred income taxes	(3,141)	(374)	(2,092)
Tax benefit from employee stock plans	—	3,384	4,348
Write-down of projector inventory	—	—	3,871
Changes in operating assets and liabilities:			
Accounts receivable	(1,855)	1,542	(748)
Inventories	(1,736)	(2,906)	12
Prepaid expenses and other assets	3	(1,121)	(1,245)
Accounts payable and accrued expenses	1,460	359	713
Deferred revenue	—	—	519
Income taxes	2,527	(3,187)	588
Net cash provided by operating activities	$ 4,558	$ 9,210	$17,574

FROM THE NOTES TO THE FINANCIAL STATEMENTS

Inventories

Inventories are stated at the lower of cost or market. Cost is determined using the first-in, first-out method. The Company evaluates its ending inventories for estimated excess quantities and obsolescence. The Company's evaluation includes the analysis of future sales demand by product, within specific time horizons. Inventories in excess of projected future demand are written down to net realizable value. In addition, the Company assesses the impact of changing technology on inventory balances and writes-down inventories that are considered obsolete. The Company recorded an inventory write-down of $3,871 related to its monochrome projector inventory during the year ended December 31, 2004 due to declines in future demand and technological obsolescence.

FROM THE MANAGEMENT DISCUSSION AND ANALYSIS

Inventories

Inventory levels are based on projections of future demand and market conditions. Any sudden decline in demand and/or rapid product improvements and technological changes can result in excess and/or obsolete inventories. On an ongoing basis, inventories are reviewed and written down for estimated obsolescence or unmarketable inventories equal to the difference between the costs of inventories and the estimated net realizable value based upon forecasts for future demand and market conditions. If actual market conditions are less favorable than our forecasts, additional inventory reserves may be required. Estimates could be influenced by sudden declines in demand due to economic downturns, rapid product improvements, and technological changes. During the fourth quarter of 2004, we recorded a write-down of approximately $3.9 million related to our monochrome projector inventory as a result of our revised outlook based on declines in future demand and technological obsolescence.

Gross Profit

Consolidated gross profit decreased to 74% of revenues for the year ended December 31, 2004, from 79% for the year ended December 31, 2003. The decrease is primarily due to the write-down of our monochrome projector inventory of approximately $3.9 million that was a result of our revised outlook based on declines in future demand and technological obsolescence. We expect consolidated gross margins in the 70% to 75% range in 2005, as we incorporate the activities of LDI into our consolidated results.

The definitions most commonly used for market are replacement cost and net realizable value.

■ **Replacement cost** is the amount that an entity would have to pay to replace its existing inventory (or other asset).

■ **Net realizable value (NRV)** is the amount that the entity would receive from selling the inventory (or other asset) less any additional selling costs that would have to be incurred.

The *CICA Handbook* does not provide much guidance on what definition of market should be used. It merely requires that entities explicitly state their definition of market. *Financial Reporting in Canada*, 30th Edition, reports that of 92 companies surveyed in 2004 that reported inventory and used only one definition of market, 76 used NRV and 12 used replacement cost. Sixty-two other companies used more than one definition, most commonly replacement cost and NRV.[2]

Let's consider an example to show how the LCM rule is applied. Sangree Ltd. (Sangree) values its inventory at the lower of cost and net realizable value (NRV). Sangree carries three types of inventory items: type 1, type 2, and type 3. The cost and NRV of Sangree's inventory on December 31, 2009, are shown in Figure 8–5. Column 1 in Figure 8–5 shows the cost of each type in inventory, column 2 provides the NRV of each type, and column 3 shows the lower of cost and NRV for each type.

There is actually more than one approach for applying the LCM rule, and the approach used can affect the amount of the write-down and the value of ending inventory. One approach compares the cost and market for the entire inventory. Another approach compares cost and market type by type. Both methods are used in practice.

If cost and market are compared for the entire inventory, the total cost of inventory—the cost of types 1, 2, and 3 in total—is compared with the market value of the entire inventory. For Sangree, we compare the total cost in column 1 with the total NRV in column 2 in Figure 8–5. Since the total NRV is lower than total cost, the LCM rule requires that the inventory be written down to its NRV. The amount of the write-down required is $3,950 ($145,500 − $141,550).

Sangree Ltd. Inventory Information on December 31, 2009			
	Column 1	**Column 2**	**Column 3**
	Cost	**Net realizable value**	**Lower of cost and net realizable value**
Type 1	$ 72,300	$ 69,250	$ 69,250
Type 2	21,200	22,400	21,200
Type 3	52,000	49,900	49,900
Total	$145,500	$141,550	$140,350

FIGURE 8–5 ::

Inventory Information for Sangree Ltd.

Applying LCM on a type-by-type basis is a bit trickier. Instead of looking at the cost and NRV for the entire inventory, we compare cost and NRV for each type of inventory. Whichever of cost and market is lower for each item is used as the basis for determining the value of the inventory. For inventory Types 1 and 3, NRV is lower than cost, so NRV is used and included in column 3, while for inventory Type 2, cost is lower than NRV, so cost is used. The total of column 3 is the amount that will appear on the balance sheet for inventory. Since the inventory is recorded at cost, a write-down of $5,150 ($145,500 − $140,350) is required. The type-by-type method provides the lowest possible value for inventory and, therefore, is considered more conservative than looking at the inventory in total.

If Sangree used the total inventory approach to determine the market value of its inventory, the journal entry it would make to record the loss on its inventory would be:

Dr. Cost of sales (expense +, shareholders' equity −)   3,950
    Cr. Inventory (asset −)   3,950
To record the write-down of inventory to market.

It is important to remember that the LCM rule is not intended to find the lowest possible value for inventory. The comparison of cost and market is based on whatever definition of cost the entity chooses (cost based on FIFO or LIFO or average cost) and whatever definition of market it chooses. If an entity uses average cost as its cost flow assumption and NRV as its definition of market, then those two measures are compared. If, for example, replacement cost gave a lower market value than NRV, the entity would not switch its market definition to replacement cost so that it could obtain the lowest possible valuation. In each period, the comparison would be based on the definitions that the entity selected. These measures should be applied consistently.

For tax purposes, entities are allowed to deduct write-downs of inventory to market.

www.mcgrawhill.ca/
olc/friedlan

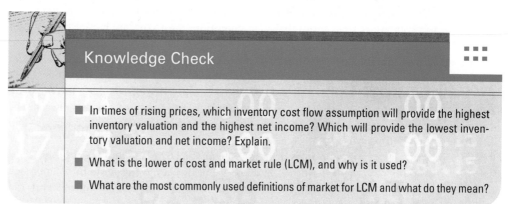

Knowledge Check

■ In times of rising prices, which inventory cost flow assumption will provide the highest inventory valuation and the highest net income? Which will provide the lowest inventory valuation and net income? Explain.

■ What is the lower of cost and market rule (LCM), and why is it used?

■ What are the most commonly used definitions of market for LCM and what do they mean?

VALUING INVENTORY AT OTHER THAN COST

It is easy to forget that it is possible to value inventory and other assets in ways other than cost. Many people who become comfortable with accounting information prepared in accordance with GAAP, or at least in accordance with the cost concept, may forget that there are legitimate, often useful alternatives to cost for valuing assets and liabilities. For many stakeholders, these alternative valuation methods can provide information that is relevant for their decision making. GAAP's general reluctance to embrace market value accounting for inventory is because of the trade-off that exists between relevance and reliability. While many users and uses of accounting information might benefit from the market value of inventory, a market value measure is often less reliable than cost, sometimes much less reliable. Accounting standard setters have concluded that the loss of reliability from having to estimate current values is not worth any benefits that could be derived from having the more relevant information.

The market value measures that are usually given consideration when accountants talk about alternatives to cost are the same ones that were discussed when we examined the lower of cost and market rule—replacement cost (what you can buy the inventory for) and net realizable value (what you can sell it for). What is different between the LCM rule and using market value for valuing inventory is that the LCM rule only applies when market value is less than cost. When market value accounting is used for inventory, the market value is always used, regardless of the cost of the inventory.

When inventory is valued using replacement cost, the amount reported on the balance sheet is the amount that it would cost to replace the inventory on hand on the balance sheet date. This means that when financial statements are prepared, it is necessary to adjust the balance in the inventory account for changes in the replacement cost of the inventory since it was purchased. At the time inventory is purchased or manufactured, the cost and the replacement cost are the same. After that, the cost to buy or make the same item can change. For example, if an entity purchased inventory for $1,000 and then at year end the inventory had a replacement cost of $1,100, the entity would make the following journal entry to record the change in the replacement cost. This example assumes that none of the inventory had been sold by the end of the year.

Dr. Inventory (assets +)   100
    Cr. Holding gain (income statement +, owner's equity +)   100
To record the increase in the replacement cost of inventory.

The amount by which the replacement cost of the inventory changes from the date it was purchased to either the date it was sold or the end of the period is called a **holding gain or loss**. This terminology makes sense. If the replacement cost of inventory, or any asset, increases while you own it, you are better off. If the price falls, you are worse off. This change in well-offness occurred by simply owning or "holding" the inventory—thus the term holding gain or loss. When replacement cost accounting is used, a holding gain or holding loss is recognized in the financial statements regardless of whether the inventory is sold. This is a major departure from transactions-based, historical cost accounting where gains are recognized only if there is a transaction. If a holding gain or loss occurs on inventory that has not been sold by the end of the period, it is an **unrealized holding gain or loss**. Realization of a gain or loss occurs when there is a transaction or exchange supporting the change in value. If the replacement cost of inventory changes from the date it is purchased (or from the beginning of the period) to the date it sold, there is a holding gain or loss, but it is a **realized holding gain or loss** because the inventory has been sold. Traditional historical cost accounting recognizes realized holding gains when the inventory is sold, but the holding gains are not identified separately in the income statement. Information about holding gains and losses can help stakeholders assess how well inventory is being managed and predict future cash flows.

Valuing inventory at its NRV (selling price less additional selling costs) is equivalent to recognizing the revenue from the sale of the inventory as soon as it is received from the supplier. The profit that will be earned from the sale of the inventory is recognized when the inventory is acquired. However, because there is no actual buyer for the inventory, the debit increases the value of inventory rather than accounts receivable. By recording the inventory at NRV, users get an idea of the amount of cash that will be realized from the sale of the inventory. This would be useful information for predicting cash flows. Of course, estimating the selling price of inventory can be difficult in many situations.

By using market value methods for valuing inventory, there is no need for a cost flow assumption. All inventory is valued at the same amount at a point in time, so it is not necessary to make assumptions as to which inventory cost is "sold" first.

Finally, while cost does rule for most of an entity's assets reported according to GAAP, GAAP does require that certain investments in securities like stocks and bonds be valued at their fair value. As a result, GAAP financial statements now recognize unrealized holding gains and losses that occur on these investments. We will explore this topic further in Chapter 12.

EXAMPLES OF INVENTORY DISCLOSURES IN FINANCIAL STATEMENTS

When you read the annual report of a company that follows Canadian GAAP, what can you expect to find about inventory? The *CICA Handbook* requires that an entity disclose the method it uses to value its inventory—that is, its cost flow assumption. The *CICA Handbook* goes on to state that if "cost" is not significantly different from the "recent" cost of inventory, then the cost flow assumption used does not have to be stated. Entities are encouraged (not required) to disclose the amounts of major categories of inventory, such as finished goods, supplies, raw materials, etc.

Exhibit 8–2 provides three examples from companies in three different industries of the type of information about inventory that appears in entities' financial statements.[3]

■ Panel A provides information about Magna International Inc.'s (Magna) inventory. Magna is a large international auto parts manufacturer. Magna's balance sheet for the year ended December 31, 2005 reports inventory of $1,388,000,000 representing about 21.0 percent of current assets and about 11.3 percent of total assets. The balance sheet only reports a single number for the entire inventory held by Magna.

To get more detail about Magna's inventory, it is necessary to examine Note 7 to the financial statements. Note 7 shows that Magna's inventory is made up of several components—raw materials and supplies, WIP, finished goods, and tooling and engineering inventory. To understand the numbers on the balance sheet and in Note 7, it is necessary to know the accounting

policies Magna uses to account for its inventory. The policy is explained under inventories in the significant accounting policies note. The note discloses that inventory is valued at the lower of FIFO cost and NRV. The note also provides a broad indication of what production costs are included in inventory. The explanation is not very specific but it does comply with GAAP

www.genesisland.com

- Panel B provides information about Genesis Land Development Corp. (Genesis). Genesis is a Calgary-based real estate company that develops planned communities.

What is interesting about real estate development companies is that they have inventory, but it is not usually described as inventory in the financial statements. On Genesis' balance sheet is an account called "Real estate held for development and sale." This is Genesis' inventory. The accounting for this asset is described in Note 1d. The note explains that properties held under development, construction and held for sale are valued at the lower of cost and net realizable value. The note also describes the costs that are included in the account. Note 4 shows the components of the real estate held for development and sale account and explains that there was a write-down of a property in 2003.

Genesis does not state a cost flow assumption because specific identification is likely used. Each house or building is unique and identifiable so it is possible and appropriate to keep track of each separately.

- Panel C provides information about the inventory of Canfor Corporation, a company in the forestry business. The company harvests trees and processes them into a variety of wood and paper products. Note 4 describes the different categories of inventory that Canfor holds. The accounting policy note says that Canfor uses average cost for all types of inventory but uses different definitions of market for different types of inventory. This demonstrates that different categories of inventory can be accounted for in different ways. Canfor (or any entity) can also use different cost flow assumptions for different categories of inventory.

INVENTORY AND THE SERVICES INDUSTRY

For the most part in this chapter, the discussion of inventory has focused on entities that sell physical goods to customers. A large part of the Canadian economy is made up of entities that provide services to customers. Examples of service businesses include banks, insurance companies, hotels, professional services (for example, accountants and lawyers), and airlines. The not-for-profit sector also provides many services in the Canadian economy—hospitals, for example. One characteristic of service businesses is that they don't have inventory to provide to customers. The services that these entities provide can't be stored. An empty seat on a plane or an empty hotel room can't be saved for when there is more demand. An hour of an accountant's or lawyer's time can't be stored for the busy season.

However, if you examine the balance sheet of a service provider like an accounting firm you would find a kind of an inventory. The inventory of an accounting firm represents the costs the firm has accumulated by providing services to clients. For example, the accounting firm would record in its accounting records the cost of employee and partner time worked on an engagement. Other costs such as travel costs, administration costs, supplies, printing, and any other costs incurred to provide services to the client would be accumulated as assets until the revenue earned from the client is recognized, at which time the accumulated costs would be expensed and matched to the revenues. Accumulation of costs by client engagement is important for internal control purposes so that management can have information to base billings to clients as well as to assess the profitability of different engagements.

CONSIGNMENT INVENTORY

Sometimes an entity (the owning entity) provides its inventory to another entity (the selling entity) to sell, but the selling entity doesn't buy, own, or assume the rights and risks of ownership of the inventory. Inventory that is held for sale by the selling entity, but not owned by the selling

Panel A: Magna International Inc.

Consolidated Balance Sheets

Magna International Inc.
[U.S. dollars in millions]

As at December 31,

	Note	2005	2004 [restated – note 2]
ASSETS			
Current assets			
Cash and cash equivalents		$ 1,682	$ 1,519
Accounts receivable		3,436	3,276
Inventories	7	1,388	1,376
Prepaid expenses and other		97	110
		6,603	6,281
Investments	13, 20	142	139
Fixed assets, net	3, 8	4,124	3,967
Goodwill	9	918	747
Future tax assets	10	208	199
Other assets	11	326	282
		$ 12,321	$ 11,615

1. SIGNIFICANT ACCOUNTING POLICIES

Inventories

Production inventories and tooling inventories manufactured in-house are valued at the lower of cost and net realizable value, with cost being determined substantially on a first-in, first-out basis. Cost includes the cost of materials plus direct labour applied to the product and the applicable share of manufacturing overhead.

Outsourced tooling inventories are valued at the lower of subcontracted costs and net realizable value.

7. INVENTORIES

Inventories consist of:

	2005	2004
Raw materials and supplies	$ 449	$ 474
Work-in-process	208	229
Finished goods	201	186
Tooling and engineering	530	487
	$ 1,388	$ 1,376

Tooling and engineering inventory represents costs incurred on separately priced tooling and engineering services contracts in excess of billed and unbilled amounts included in accounts receivable.

Panel B: Genesis Land Development Corp.

Genesis Land Development Corp.
Consolidated Balance Sheets
Dec 31, 2004 and 2003

	2004	2003
Assets		
Real estate held for development and sale (note 4)	$ 88,868,045	$ 80,630,368
Amounts receivable (note 5)	42,654,876	47,796,149
Other assets (note 6)	5,121,726	5,693,970
Cash and cash equivalents	3,356,931	5,519,627
Investments (note 7)	264,418	2,244,116
Income taxes recoverable	-	12,905
Future income taxes (note 8[a])	682,552	1,273,844
	$ 140,948,548	$ 143,170,979

EXHIBIT 8–2 :

Magna International Inc. Genesis Land Development Corp. Examples of Inventory Disclosures

417

INVENTORY

EXHIBIT 8–2 :

(continued)
Genesis Land
Development Corp.
Canfor Corporation
Examples of
Inventory
Disclosures

1. Significant accounting policies

(d) Real estate held for development and sale

Land under development, land held for future development and housing projects under development are recorded at lower of cost and estimated net realizable value.

Capitalized costs include all direct costs related to development and construction, carrying costs including interest on debt used to finance projects, property taxes and land acquisition costs. Land acquisition costs are prorated to a phase of a project on an acreage basis when the first sale occurs in the phase.

No general and administration costs are capitalized.

4. Real estate held for development and sale

	2004	2003
Land held for future development	$ 76,954,901	$ 75,325,890
Land under development	11,729,767	5,117,532
Housing projects under development	183,377	186,946
	$ 88,868,045	$ 80,630,368

During the year ended December 31, 2004, interest of $ 2,104,194 (2003- $2,880,623) and other carrying costs of $ 154,068 (2003 - $178,433) were capitalized to real estate held for development and sale.

During 2003, the carrying value of certain property located in British Columbia was determined to be impaired due to a continuing deterioration in regional markets. Appraisals were obtained and one specific property was written down by $3,536,004 to estimated fair value based on the discounted expected future cash flows from the property.

Panel C: Canfor Corporation

CONSOLIDATED BALANCE SHEETS

As at December 31 (millions of dollars)	2005	2004
ASSETS		
Current assets		
Cash and temporary investments (Note 2)	$ 306.3	$ 438.5
Accounts receivable		
Trade	205.4	224.9
Other	79.8	58.1
Income taxes recoverable	-	14.7
Future income taxes (Note 21)	23.9	32.5
Inventories (Note 4)	600.9	573.8
Prepaid expenses	36.2	39.1
Current assets of discontinued operations (Note 3)	39.8	85.3
Total current assets	1,292.3	1,466.9
Long-term investments and other (Note 5)	186.5	196.8
Property, plant, equipment and timber (Note 6)	2,211.1	2,141.7
Deferred charges (Note 7)	96.9	96.1
Non-current assets of discontinued operations (Note 3)	43.7	78.1
	$ 3,830.5	$ 3,979.6

December 31, 2005

1. SIGNIFICANT ACCOUNTING POLICIES

VALUATION OF INVENTORIES

Inventories of lumber, panels, pulp and kraft paper are valued at the lower of average cost and net realizable value. Logs and chips are valued at average cost or the greater of net realizable value and replacement cost if lower than average cost. Processing materials and supplies are valued at the lower of average cost and replacement cost.

4. INVENTORIES

(millions of dollars)	2005	2004
Lumber	$ 212.1	$ 237.2
Logs	199.0	144.3
Pulp	51.8	56.2
Panel products	20.9	20.7
Chips	9.4	15.3
Paper	11.5	10.7
Processing materials and supplies	96.2	89.4
	$ 600.9	$ 573.8

entity, is known as **consignment inventory**. For example, it is very common for art dealers to accept works of art from artists on consignment. The art dealer displays the art and tries to sell it to customers. If a particular piece of art doesn't sell, it is returned to the artist. If a customer purchases a piece of art, the art dealer receives a commission and the artist receives the selling price of the art, less the commission. (A **commission** is a payment made to a seller as compensation for making a sale. A commission can be based on the selling price of the item, on the gross margin, or be a fixed fee.)

Consignment selling is attractive to the selling entity because it does not have to invest in inventory, so cash is conserved. The risk to the seller is lower because he or she can't get "stuck" with the inventory since it can always be returned to the owner. On the other hand, the inventory's owner has a continuing investment in the inventory and greater risk than with a traditional sale because the owner retains ownership of the inventory.

From an accounting standpoint, consignment inventory is included in the inventory account of the owning entity (not in the inventory account of the selling entity). Revenue on the sale of consignment inventory is only recognized when the inventory is sold by the selling entity to a customer. It is important for the owning entity to remember to include the consignment inventory in its year-end financial statements, even though it does not have physical custody of the inventory.

INVENTORY ACCOUNTING AND INCOME TAXES

The accounting choices that the preparers of financial statements make frequently have tax implications. Often, as we have discussed, preparers must choose among accounting alternatives that can lower the entity's tax burden or achieve some other objective of financial reporting. In situations where the *Income Tax Act (ITA)* doesn't specify a treatment, the method used for financial reporting purposes will often be selected for tax purposes. Inventory accounting is one such situation. The *ITA* is not very specific about how to account for inventory for tax purposes. Therefore, entities will usually, for tax purposes, use the inventory accounting methods selected for the general purpose financial statements, which means that these accounting choices can have a bearing on the amount of tax an entity pays.

The Canada Revenue Agency (CRA), the Canadian government agency responsible for the administration and enforcement of the Canadian federal tax laws, suggests that the same cost flow assumption that is used for financial reporting purposes should also be used for tax purposes. While, in principle, using different methods for financial reporting and tax is allowable, using different methods might raise a red flag that encourages the CRA to investigate. However, the CRA does not automatically accept the method being used for financial reporting purposes. The CRA has stated that "the method used for income tax purposes should be the one that gives the truer picture of the taxpayer's income."[4] Even if the method used for financial reporting purposes is acceptable according to GAAP, the CRA can challenge the choice if it believes that the method is not the one that "gives the truer picture of taxpayer income."

The LIFO cost flow assumption can't be used in Canada for tax purposes. LIFO is not allowed because it tends to lower taxable income unreasonably, at least in the eyes of the CRA and the courts. If an entity chooses LIFO for financial reporting purposes, it must switch to an alternative method such as FIFO, average cost, or specific identification, to determine cost of sales for tax purposes. As a result, LIFO is rarely used in Canada. *Financial Reporting in Canada*, 30th Edition, reports that in 2004 only two of 161 firms used LIFO.[5]

In contrast, in the United States LIFO is allowable for tax purposes, provided that the entity also uses it for financial reporting purposes. As a result, the use of LIFO is much more widespread in the U.S. because LIFO can defer taxes for a long time. However, preparers in the U.S. are faced with the conflict of lower tax payments by using LIFO versus lower accounting income, which may be inconsistent with other objectives. The fact that so many entities in the U.S. use LIFO suggests how important the tax minimization objective is to many managers.

The definition of cost for tax purposes is similar to that used for accounting purposes. The CRA explains that for inventories of merchandise purchased for resale or raw materials acquired

www.cra-arc.gc.ca

for a manufacturing process, cost means laid-down cost. Laid-down cost includes invoice cost, customs and excise duties, transportation and other acquisition costs and, where they are significant, storage costs.[6]

Entities are also allowed to use the lower of cost and market rule for inventory valuation purposes. If the fair market value of inventory at the end of a year is less than its cost, then the taxpayer can use fair market value. This treatment allows the taxpayer to reduce income by writing down the value of inventory to fair market value. Taxpayers are expected to use the same definition of market for tax purposes as they do for financial reporting purposes.

The CRA requires that methods used to account for inventory for tax purposes be applied consistently from period to period. Once a method is used for tax purposes, it can only be changed with the permission of the Minister of National Revenue. The Minister will usually approve a change if the new method proposed by the taxpayer:

a. is a more appropriate way of determining income,

b. will be used for financial reporting purposes, and

c. will be used consistently in future years.[7]

This constraint on the ability of taxpayers to change methods of accounting for inventory is intended to limit an entity's ability to make changes simply to avoid tax.

Insight

The difference in use of LIFO between Canada and the U.S. highlights the role that the objectives of financial reporting play in the selection of accounting policies. The extensive use of LIFO in the U.S. provides some evidence that managers are willing to sacrifice higher net income for lower taxes when given the choice. In Canada, the low use of LIFO could be due to the fact that LIFO generally allows for lower net income or that companies don't want to have to use two parallel inventory accounting systems (one for tax and one for financial reporting).

FINANCIAL STATEMENT ANALYSIS ISSUES

For many businesses, management of inventory is a crucial management responsibility. Management's effectiveness and efficiency in managing inventory can have a significant impact on the performance of the entity. Managing inventory requires careful balance. Carrying too much or too little inventory can be costly. Remember from Chapter 6 that, usually, at least some of an entity's inventory has been fully paid for. That means that an entity's cash must be invested in inventory and is not available for other purposes. The more inventory an entity has, the more cash that is tied up. Also, higher levels of inventory may mean that the entity may be unable to sell some of the inventory, or may have to sell it at a discount.

On the other hand, too little inventory may mean that an entity runs out of the inventory that it requires to meet customers' needs on a timely basis. When an entity is out of stock, customers may take their business elsewhere, which means a loss of revenue for that particular transaction. The impact may be more serious than the loss of a single sale. The customer may be lost permanently, which means that the stream of revenue that the customer would have generated is lost. Thus, the impact of not carrying enough inventory is that revenues will decline. If a manufacturing company runs out of inventory required in its production process, the entire production process may be forced to stop, which would be very costly.

A ratio that is often used to evaluate how well inventory is being managed is the inventory turnover ratio. The **inventory turnover ratio** provides information on how efficiently inventory is being managed by measuring how quickly the entity is able to sell its inventory. The inventory turnover ratio is defined as:

$$\text{Inventory turnover ratio} = \frac{\text{Cost of sales}}{\text{Average inventory}}$$

Average inventory can be calculated by summing the amount in the Inventory account at the beginning and the end of the period and dividing by two. A better measure of average inventory can be obtained by using quarterly or monthly data if they are available. This is especially important for entities that are seasonal. Many retail businesses have their lowest amount of inventory in January, after the Christmas season, and the highest amount just before the winter and Christmas seasons.

The inventory turnover ratio indicates the number of times during a period the entity is able to purchase and sell its stock of inventory. Usually, the higher the inventory turnover ratio, the better, because a higher ratio indicates that the entity can sell or "turn over" the inventory more quickly. A high turnover ratio indicates that the inventory is more liquid because the inventory is sold more quickly and therefore cash will be realized sooner than with slower-moving inventory. A lower inventory turnover ratio may indicate that inventory is not selling or is slow moving, that there is obsolete inventory, or that there is low demand for the inventory. However, a decreasing inventory turnover ratio could indicate that inventory is being built up in anticipation of increasing sales or because of an expansion of the business.

As with other financial ratios, it is not possible to make sense of the inventory turnover ratio in absolute terms. The ratio must be considered in comparison with other, similar entities, or for a particular entity over time. Inventory turnover ratios can vary significantly from industry to industry.

Another measure used to evaluate the efficiency of inventory management is the average number of days inventory on hand. The **average number of days inventory on hand** indicates the number of days it takes an entity to sell its inventory. The average number of days inventory on hand is defined as:

$$\text{Average number of days inventory on hand} = \frac{365}{\text{Inventory turnover ratio}}$$

An average number of days inventory on hand of 105 means that the entity holds its inventory for an average of 105 days before it is sold. This measure is another way of presenting the inventory turnover ratio and is interpreted in the same way as the inventory turnover ratio, except that a lower average number of days inventory on hand measure indicates better and more efficient inventory management.

The inventory turnover ratio can be difficult to interpret if an entity has many different types of inventory. Different types of inventory may turn over at different rates. The figure obtained using the aggregate total reported on the balance sheet will just be an average of the turnover ratios of all the different types of inventory. A manufacturer will likely have finished goods, work-in-process, and raw materials. If the total amount of inventory on the balance sheet is used to calculate the inventory turnover ratio, the ratio will reflect the turnover rate of the entire inventory. If a manufacturer breaks down the components of inventory in the notes to the financial statements, for example as Magna International Inc. does (see Exhibit 8–2, Panel A, page 417), it is possible to calculate an inventory turnover ratio for finished goods.

Since Rogers has so little inventory, we will look at Leon's Furniture Limited (Leon's) to demonstrate the calculation of inventory turnover and the average number of days of inventory on hand. We will look at these measures over a number of years to see if there are any trends in the data. Year end inventory balances for Leon's for 2000 through 2005 and cost of sales for each of those years are presented on the next page:

	2000	2001	2002	2003	2004	2005
Inventory	$49,171,000	$51,079,000	$55,047,000	$58,841,000	$71,279,000	$72,644,000
Cost of sales	234,798,000	248,445,000	261,265,000	267,323,000	295,241,000	323,629,000
Inventory turnover ratio	4.75	4.96	4.92	4.69	4.54	4.50
Average number of days inventory on hand	76.8	73.6	74.1	77.8	80.4	81.2

The calculation of the 2005 inventory turnover ratio and average number of days inventory on hand is shown below:

$$\text{Inventory turnover ratio} = \frac{\text{Cost of sales}}{\text{Average inventory}}$$

$$= \frac{\$323,629,000}{(\$71,279,000 + 72,644,000)/2}$$

$$= 4.50$$

$$\text{Average number of days inventory on hand} = \frac{365}{\text{Inventory turnover ratio}}$$

$$= \frac{365}{4.50}$$

$$= 81.2 \text{ days}$$

Over the six years shown, the inventory turnover ratio has steadily declined after increasing from 2000 to 2001. The average number of days inventory on hand has steadily increased after a decrease from 2000 to 2001. Because it has to carry its inventory for increasing amounts of time, the cost of carrying inventory will be increasing. There are many possible reasons why Leon's inventory turnover ratio has been falling. For example, it may have to carry more inventory to meet the demands of customers and the competition. Also, the mix of inventory may be changing (each category of Leon's inventory may not have the same turnover ratio). It's also possible that Leon's isn't managing its inventory as well. At this point we can't determine the reason.

Interpreting these measures can be challenging. There are entities that sell inventory of very different types. For example, a department store will carry a vast range of different products from furniture to art to clothing to jewellery to appliances. Each of these product categories is very different and can be expected to have different inventory turnover ratios. Yet, despite the different types of inventory, a department store like Sears Canada Inc. provides a single amount in its financial statements for inventory. If the composition of the inventory changes (for example, if the proportion of one product type increased and another was reduced), the inventory turnover ratio can change without any change in how inventory is being managed. Also, many entities don't co-operate by providing adequate disclosure of cost of sales. For example, if you look back at Exhibit 2–1 in Chapter 2 you see how Loblaw combines most of its expenses, including cost of sales, in a single line on the income statement. As a result, it is impossible to calculate a meaningful inventory turnover ratio.

Like other information in the financial statements, information about inventory and cost of sales raises questions and does not necessarily provide answers. For example, the existence of inventory doesn't mean that the inventory can be sold. Suppose that at the end of a year you notice that the amount of inventory reported on the balance sheet had increased significantly from previous years. How can that change be interpreted? If sales had increased along with inventory, we might conclude that inventory has increased to support the increased level of sales. If there was no increase in the amount of sales, then we could conclude that management was building up inventory in anticipation of an expansion or to reflect anticipated sales growth. On the other hand, the increase might reflect over-purchasing of inventory or obsolete inventory that had not yet been written off.

Insight

It should be clear from the discussion of the different inventory cost flow assumptions that financial analysis and financial ratios will be affected by the cost flow assumption used by an entity. This means that it may be difficult to make comparisons among firms in an industry if the amount of inventory reported differs because the entities are using different cost flow assumptions or treating similar costs in different ways. The effect of different treatments can have an impact on the inventory turnover ratio, current ratio, gross margin, and profit margin, to name a few. However, analyzing an entity over time is not affected by differences in accounting treatments for inventory, provided the entity has applied its inventory accounting policies consistently over the period being examined.

It is important to recognize that while the different accounting methods affect our accounting measures, they do not affect the concept that is being measured. Whether a company uses LIFO, FIFO, or average cost does not affect the actual liquidity or profitability of the entity.

A Banker's View of Inventory

When entities borrow money, it is common for the lender to request that collateral be provided in the event that the borrower can't repay the loan. Inventory would seem like a sensible asset to use as collateral, but in general banks do not welcome inventory for this purpose. The reason is that inventory can be difficult to dispose of if the borrower is unable to meet its obligations. After all, if the borrower can't sell the inventory, how will a bank sell it? What will a bank do with large quantities of toasters, shirts, or machine-tooled dies? Generally, banks recover as little as five or ten cents for each dollar of inventory that is reported on the balance sheet.

All the same, many businesses require financing for their inventory. This is especially true for seasonal businesses. For example, consider a business that produces Christmas decorations. The decoration maker would build up its inventory during the year until it begins shipping its products as the holiday season approached. Most seasonal businesses will not have a stockpile of cash available to self-finance the inventory build-up. Instead, many businesses in this situation will use bank credit to finance the inventory build-up and, despite their concerns, banks will lend against inventory. However, when a bank lends against inventory, it generally expects the loan to be repaid in full at the end of the entity's operating cycle. In other words, inventory loans are not permanent. They must be fully repaid each year. In contrast, when accounts receivable is the collateral, the amount borrowed can remain outstanding permanently, based on the amount of receivables the entity has.

Solved Problem

In November 2010 Chedder Inc. (Chedder) set up operations as the exclusive western Canada distributor of Pligs, the newest children's toy sensation. Pligs first became popular in Europe and then the fad came to North America. Chedder's lone shareholder contributed $37,000 of her own money to purchase shares in Chedder and borrowed $50,000 from the bank. The terms of the loan required that Chedder have a current ratio of greater than 1.4 on December 31, 2011 or the loan is fully repayable immediately. Chedder began selling Pligs in early 2011. For its December 31, 2010 year end Chedder did not select an inventory cost flow assumption because it had not yet sold anything.

Chedder's December 31, 2010 balance sheet is shown in Table 8–6 and information on sales and purchases of Pligs in fiscal 2011 is shown in Table 8–7. During 2011, Chedder's other expenses (all expenses other than the cost of sales) were $150,000. The balances in Chedder's current asset and liability accounts (except for inventory) on December 31, 2011 are shown in Table 8–8.

TABLE 8–6 ::: Balance Sheet for Chedder Inc.

Chedder Inc. Balance Sheet For the Year Ended December 31, 2010			
Assets		**Liabilities and shareholders' equity**	
Current assets		*Current liabilities*	
Cash	$44,000	Bank loan	$50,000
Accounts receivable	0	Accounts payable	10,000
Inventory	24,000	Total current liabilities	60,000
Other current assets	9,000		
Total current assets	77,000		
Capital assets (net)	20,000	Capital stock	37,000
		Retained earnings	0
Total assets	$97,000	Total liabilities and shareholders' equity	$97,000

TABLE 8–7 ::: Purchasing Information for Chedder Inc.

Chedder Inc. Purchasing Information For the Year Ended December 31, 2011 (including inventory purchased in December 2010)		
Date	**Quantity purchased**	**Purchase price per unit**
December 28, 2010	15,000	$1.60
April 1, 2011	25,000	$1.75
July 1, 2011	20,000	$1.90
October 1, 2011	40,000	$2.00

Chedder Inc. Sales Information For the Year Ended December 31, 2011		
Period	**Quantity sold**	**Selling price per unit**
January 1–March 31, 2011	8,000	$3.75
April 1–June 30, 2011	20,000	$3.75
July 1–September 30, 2011	17,000	$4.00
October 1–December 31, 2011	45,000	$4.00

TABLE 8–8 ::: Current Asset and Liability Account Balances for Chedder Inc.

Chedder Inc. Current Asset and Liability Account Balances (Excluding Inventory) As of December 31, 2011	
Cash	$13,000
Accounts receivable	88,250
Other current assets	2,000
Bank loan	50,000
Accounts payable	38,000

Required:

a. What might be Chedder's objectives of financial reporting? Briefly explain your reasoning.

b. Calculate ending inventory, cost of sales, gross margin, and net income for Chedder under FIFO, average cost, and LIFO assuming a periodic inventory control system. Calculate the gross margin percentage, inventory turnover, and current ratio under each cost flow assumption.

c. Comment on the financial statement amounts and the ratios calculated in (b) above. What are the implications of the amounts calculated under each of the methods?

d. Which inventory cost flow assumption do you recommend for Chedder?

e. Suppose that on December 31, 2011 the replacement cost of the Pligs was $1.86. Assuming that Chedder decided to use replacement cost as its definition of market for purposes of the lower of cost and market rule, what would the financial statement implications under each inventory cost flow assumption be?

Solution:

a. Because Chedder is a small, privately owned corporation with a single shareholder who operates the business, the owner would likely want to minimize tax payments. This would mean choosing accounting treatments that lower income for tax purposes. However, Chedder's bank loan has a restrictive covenant that requires that it have a current ratio that is greater than 1.4. Therefore, Chedder would want to ensure that it does not violate the covenant because doing so would likely create financial problems for the company and its owner.

b. Calculation results:

	FIFO	LIFO	Average Cost
Revenue	$353,000	$353,000	$353,000
Cost of sales	165,750[1]	169,750[3]	167,175[5]
Gross margin	187,250	183,250	185,825
All other expenses	150,000	150,000	150,000
Net income	$37,250	$33,250	$35,825
Gross margin percentage	0.53	0.519	0.526
Ending inventory	$20,000[2]	$16,000[4]	$18,575[6]
Current assets except for inventory (from Table 8–10)	$103,250	$103,250	$103,250
Total current assets	$123,250	$119,250	$121,825
Total current liabilities (from Table 8–10)	$88,000	$88,000	$88,000
Current ratio (Current assets/Current liabilities)	1.401	1.355	1.384
Inventory turnover (Cost of sales/Average inventory)	7.534	8.488	7.853

[1] Expense:
15,000 @ $1.60 +
25,000 @ $1.75 +
20,000 @ $1.90 +
30,000 @ $2.00

[2] Ending inventory: 10,000 @ $2.00

[3] Expense:
40,000 @ $2.00 +
20,000 @ $1.90 +
25,000 @ $1.75 +
5,000 @ $1.60

[4] Ending inventory: 10,000 @ $1.60

[5] Expense: $185,750 ÷ 100,000 × 90,000 [total cost of inventory purchased ÷ no. of units purchased × no. of units sold]

[6] Ending inventory: $185,750 ÷ 100,000 × 10,000 [total cost of inventory purchased ÷ no. of units purchased × no. of units in ending inventory]

c. While each of the methods produces different numbers, each is actually measuring the same underlying economic phenomenon. For many users and uses of financial information, this can be an inconvenience because it impairs the ability to compare the financial information of different entities. In some situations, these differences can have serious consequences.

For example, if Chedder uses an inventory cost flow assumption other than FIFO, it is in violation of its current ratio covenant, which would mean that it would have to repay its bank loan immediately. The economic consequence of this violation could be significant. If Chedder uses FIFO, there is no problem with the loan. Either way, it is the same company, yet with FIFO it has no (immediate) problems with the bank, whereas with any of the others it has a potentially large problem. The gross margin is slightly different under each of the methods. This can lead to different conclusions about the profitability of Chedder. A 1 percent difference in margins may not seem significant, but in some industries a 1 percent difference can have a dramatic effect on the profitability of the entity.

d. Chedder should use FIFO. The other cost flow assumptions result in the current ratio falling below 1.4, which would require that it repay its bank loan. This could be an especially serious problem because Chedder only had $13,000 cash on hand on December 31, 2011. To meet the repayment requirement, Chedder would have to obtain cash from the shareholder or from another investor, or obtain a new loan from a bank or another lender. Clearly, in this situation, ensuring that the current ratio covenant is met is more important than minimizing taxes.

e. If the replacement cost of a single unit of inventory is $1.86, then the replacement cost of the 10,000 units on hand on December 31, 2011 is $18,600. The replacement cost of the inventory is less than the cost when FIFO is used. If Chedder were using FIFO, it would be appropriate to write down the inventory on the balance sheet to the market value. In the case of FIFO, the write-down would be $1,400. If the write-down were required, Chedder would be in violation of its current ratio covenant and it would be required to pay back the bank loan immediately.

SUMMARY OF KEY POINTS

▶ **LO 1** Inventory is goods that are available for sale by an entity, or goods that will be used to produce goods that will be sold. Inventory can also include materials used in supplying a service to customers. According to GAAP, inventory is valued at cost, where cost includes all costs that are incurred to purchase or make the products and get them ready for sale to customers.

▶ **LO 2** There are two types of inventory control systems for keeping track of inventory transactions: perpetual systems and periodic systems. A perpetual inventory control system keeps an ongoing tally of purchases and sales of inventory, and the inventory account is adjusted to reflect changes as they occur. With a periodic inventory control system, the balance in the Inventory account at the end of period is determined by actually counting the inventory on hand at the end of a period, and Cost of Sales is determined indirectly using the equation Cost of Sales = Beginning Inventory + Purchases − Ending Inventory. The choice between a periodic and perpetual inventory control system is an internal control issue, not an accounting issue. However, the choice can have an effect on the amount of inventory reported on the balance sheet and cost of goods sold for the period.

▶ **LO 3** Usually accountants do not keep track of the costs associated with individual items of inventory. Instead, they have developed methods called cost flow assumptions for moving costs through the Inventory account to Cost of Sales without regard for the actual physical flow of the inventory. There are a number of cost flow assumptions that are currently in use, including FIFO, LIFO, average cost, and specific identification, all of which are acceptable under GAAP. The choice of cost flow assumption does not directly affect the cash flow of the entity, but the information reported on the balance sheet and the income statement can be significantly different depending on the cost flow assumption used. When inventory prices are rising, FIFO will always give the lowest cost of sales and the highest inventory value, whereas LIFO will always give the highest cost of sales and the lowest inventory value. Average cost will always be between these two.

▶ **LO 4** According to GAAP, inventory on hand at the end of a period must be reported at the lower of cost and market. If the market value of inventory at the end of a reporting period is lower than its cost, the inventory must be written down to its market value. The amount of the write-down is expensed in the period of the write-down. The LCM rule is an application of conservatism. Once inventory is written down to its market value, it is not written back up in the event that the market price of the inventory increases. Net realizable value and replacement cost are the most commonly used definitions of market.

▶ **LO 5** Historical cost, transactions-based accounting is not the only accounting model available. For many users of financial statements, alternative valuation methods, such as replacement cost accounting, can provide useful information for decision making. These alternative methods are not in use in Canada for inventory because accounting standard setters have concluded that the loss of reliability from having to estimate current values is not worth any benefits. When inventory is valued using replacement cost, the amount reported on the balance sheet is the amount that it would cost to replace the inventory on hand on the balance sheet date.

▶ **LO 6** The accounting choices that the preparers of financial statements make often have tax implications. In situations where the *Income Tax Act* does not specify a treatment, the method used for financial reporting purposes will often be used for tax purposes. The Canada Revenue Agency suggests that the same cost flow assumption that is used for financial reporting purposes should also be used for tax purposes. However, LIFO is not allowed for tax purposes in Canada. For tax purposes, entities can apply the lower of cost and market rule. The CRA requires that methods used to account for inventory for tax purposes be applied consistently.

▶ **LO 7** Management's effectiveness and efficiency in managing inventory can have a significant impact on the performance of the entity. Managing inventory requires careful balance. Carrying too much or too little inventory can be costly. The inventory turnover ratio and the number of days inventory on hand provide information on how efficiently and effectively inventory is being managed. A low or decreasing inventory turnover ratio can indicate that inventory is not selling or is slow moving or obsolete, or that there is low demand for the inventory. Generally, a higher inventory turnover ratio indicates better management of inventory.

KEY TERMS

average cost method of inventory valuation, p. 400

average number of days inventory on hand, p. 421

commission, p. 419

consignment inventory, p. 419

finished goods inventory, p. 394

first-in, first-out (FIFO), p. 399

holding gain or loss, p. 415

inventory, p. 393

inventory turnover ratio, p. 421

laid-down cost, p. 394

last-in, first-out (LIFO), p. 400

lower of cost and market (LCM) rule, p. 409

net realizable value (NRV), p. 413

overhead, p. 395

periodic inventory control system, p. 395

perpetual inventory control system, p. 395

raw materials inventory, p. 394

realized holding gain or loss, p. 415

replacement cost, p. 413

specific identification method, p. 401

unrealized holding gain or loss, p. 415

work-in-process inventory (WIP), p. 394

ASSIGNMENT MATERIALS

Questions

Q8-1. For each of the following entities, describe the type of inventory you would expect the entity to have:
  a. Future Shop (an electronics retailer)
  b. Loblaw Companies Limited (a grocery chain)
  c. Barrick Gold Corporation (a gold mining company)
  d. Torstar Corporation (a newspaper publisher)
  e. Magna International Inc. (an auto parts manufacturer)
  f. Andrés Wines Ltd. (a vintner)
  g. Burger King Corporation (a fast-food chain)

Q8-2. For each of the following entities, describe what would be included in raw materials inventory, work-in-process inventory, and finished goods inventory:
  a. an auto manufacturer
  b. a producer of concentrated orange juice
  c. a tailor shop
  d. a grower of trees (trees often take many years to mature before they are available for sale)
  e. a miner and refiner of gold

Q8-3. Explain why it is not possible to calculate cost of goods sold when a periodic inventory control system is used if the inventory is not counted.

Q8-4. Explain and give examples of the following types of inventory:
  a. raw materials
  b. work-in-process
  c. finished goods
  d. supplies

Q8-5. Why is it not possible to determine the amount of inventory that was stolen during a period when a periodic inventory control system is used?

Q8-6. Explain the difference between periodic and perpetual inventory control systems. Which do you think is the better system to use? Why?

Q8-7. Why is it necessary to use a cost flow assumption in many situations for valuing inventory and determining cost of sales? Why can't the actual cost of the goods sold be used to calculate cost of sales in these situations?

Q8-8. Regardless of the cost flow assumption being used (FIFO, average cost, LIFO, specific identification), the sum of cost of sales plus ending inventory will be the same. Explain why.

Q8-9. Explain why a FIFO inventory system gives higher inventory valuation and lower cost of sales than LIFO when prices are rising.

Q8-10. Explain how costs flow through the following cost flow systems: a LIFO versus a FIFO versus an average cost versus a specific identification cost flow system.

Q8-11. What is the lower of cost and market rule? Why is it used? What is meant by the term "market" in lower of cost and market?

Q8-12. Why might it be difficult to actually determine the market value of inventory when applying the lower of cost and market rule? Provide some examples of when determining market might be difficult.

Q8-13. What is a holding gain? How are holding gains accounted for when traditional historical cost, transactions-based accounting is used?

Q8-14. Under the traditional historical cost, transactions-based accounting model, are holding gains and losses always treated the same way? Describe the difference in the accounting treatment used for each and explain the reason for the difference.

Q8-15. The *CICA Handbook* is quite unclear with respect to exactly how preparers of financial statements should account for their inventory. Explain the areas where the *CICA Handbook* is unclear and explain what the implications of this lack of clarity are for users of financial statements.

Q8-16. Why is it necessary to count inventory when a perpetual inventory control system is used? Explain. Why is it necessary to count inventory when a periodic inventory control system is used? Explain.

Q8-17. Explain how the specific identification method of valuing inventory works. Why do many entities not use this method? Under what circumstances is the method useful? Why is it sometimes easy to manipulate the financial statements when the specific identification method is used?

Q8-18. Why is the choice of the inventory cost flow assumption important for tax purposes? Explain.

Q8-19. Why is it not possible to satisfy a tax minimization objective and an income maximization objective when selecting the inventory cost flow assumption that the entity should use?

Q8-20. Onslow Ltd. (Onslow) is a small public company trading on a Canadian stock exchange. Onslow's managers have a bonus plan that is based on net income and the managers believe that the amount of reported earnings is important for maintaining the company's stock price. Assume that whether Onslow uses FIFO or average cost will have a significant effect on reported earnings (FIFO earnings being higher) and the amount of assets it reports on its balance sheet. Discuss the issues that Onslow's management must consider when choosing between FIFO and average cost.

Q8-21. Why is LIFO so commonly used in the United States but rarely used in Canada?

Q8-22. Does it matter which cost flow assumption an entity uses if the price an entity pays for its inventory is stable? Explain.

Q8-23. How does the choice of cost flow assumption affect financial ratios such as the inventory turnover ratio and the current ratio? Does the choice have any effect on the actual rate at which an entity's inventory turns over or the entity's actual liquidity? Explain.

Q8-24. What is inventory turnover? What does it tell a user of financial statements about how the entity is managing its inventory? What could be some reasons for a decreasing inventory turnover ratio? What could be some reasons for an increasing inventory turnover ratio?

Q8-25. Which cost flow assumption for valuing inventory is best? Explain.

Q8-26. What is inventory that is on consignment? Which entity should report consignment inventory on its balance sheet: the entity that has the inventory and is selling it or the entity that owns the inventory? Explain.

Q8-27. Ayr Inc. (Ayr) uses a periodic inventory control system. During Ayr's inventory count on December 31, 2009, $100,000 of the inventory was counted twice in error. What effect would the double counting of this inventory have on net income for the year ended December 31, 2009 and on the amount of inventory reported on the balance sheet on December 31, 2009? Explain your answer.

Q8-28. Explain why the cash spent on inventory is not affected by the cost flow assumption used for valuing ending inventory and determining cost of sales.

Exercises

E8-1. **(Determine cost of units sold and cost of units remaining in inventory using average cost, FIFO, and LIFO cost flow assumptions, LO 2, 3)** The following information is provided for Badger Inc. (Badger):

Badger Inc. Inventory Information For October 2009	Number of units purchased	Price paid per unit
Purchased on October 8, 2009	2,200	$ 8
Purchased on October 17, 2009	1,650	$ 9
Purchased on October 25, 2009	1,800	$10

On October 30, 2009, Badger sold 4,800 units of inventory to customers.

Required:

Identify which inventory costs would be expensed in October 2009 and which costs would be in inventory on October 31, 2009 using the average cost, FIFO, LIFO, and specific identification cost flow assumptions. Assume Badger had no inventory on hand at the beginning of October.

E8-2. **(Calculating cost of sales and ending inventory using different flow assumptions, LO 3)** You are provided the following information about Chetwynd Ltd. (Chetwynd) for June 2009. Assume that Chetwynd uses a periodic inventory system and that during June the company sold 100 units of inventory:

Date	Description	Number of units	Cost per unit	Total cost
June 1	Opening inventory	50 units	$10	$ 500
June 12	Purchase	35 units	$11	385
June 22	Purchase	45 units	$12	540
	Total	130 units		$1,425

Required:

Calculate cost of goods sold and ending inventory on June 30, 2009 for Chetwynd using the FIFO, average cost, and LIFO cost flow assumptions. How many units of inventory are on hand at the end of June under each cost flow assumption?

E8-3. **(Calculating cost of sales and ending inventory using different flow assumptions, LO 3)** You are provided the following information about Klemtu Inc. (Klemtu) for April 2010. Assume that Klemtu uses a periodic inventory system and that during April the company sold 10,000 units of inventory:

Date	Description	Number of units	Cost per unit	Total cost
April 1	Opening inventory	7,000 units	$1.00	$ 7,000
April 13	Purchase	4,200 units	1.10	4,620
April 21	Purchase	2,700 units	1.25	3,375
	Total	13,900 units		$14,995

Required:

Calculate cost of goods sold and ending inventory on April 30, 2010 for Klemtu using the FIFO, average cost, and LIFO cost flow assumptions. How many units of inventory are on hand at the end of June under each cost flow assumption?

E8-4. **(Calculating cost of sales and ending inventory using average cost, FIFO, and LIFO cost flow assumptions, LO 2, 3)** Information is provided for Olds Ltd. below.

Date	Purchases	Sales	Balance
December 31, 2009			55 units @ $2.50
January 5, 2010	40 units @ $3		
January 8, 2010		30 units @ $4	
January 15, 2010	60 units @ $3.50		
January 20, 2010		60 units @ $5	
January 22, 2010	50 units @ $4		
January 29, 2010		40 units @ $5.50	
January 31, 2010			75 units @ $

Required:

Calculate cost of goods sold and ending inventory for Olds Ltd. using the average cost, FIFO, and LIFO cost flow assumptions.

E8-5. **(Classifying different types of inventory, LO 1)** Whonock Ltd. (Whonock) is a manufacturer of fine wood furniture. Indicate whether Whonock would classify the costs associated with each of the following types as inventory and, if it should be classified as inventory, whether it would be considered raw materials, work-in-process, finished goods, or supplies. Provide a brief explanation for each classification.
a. lumber
b. unpainted furniture
c. furniture makers' tools
d. fabric
e. sandpaper
f. furniture awaiting shipment on the loading dock
g. crates used for packing furniture for shipment
h. storage containers for parts (nails, screws, etc.) used to build the furniture

E8-6. **(Classifying different types of inventory, LO 1)** Quesnel Inc. (Quesnel) is a burger joint that claims to have the best burgers in the world. For each of the following items, indicate whether Quesnel would classify the costs as inventory and, if it should be classified as inventory, how you would classify the inventory. Provide a brief explanation for each classification.
a. wrappers for burgers
b. plastic cutlery
c. brooms and mops
d. oil for cooking the French fries
e. raw meat
f. cooking implements
g. ketchup, mustard, and relish
h. cleaning supplies (soap, disinfectant, etc.)

E8-7. **(Classifying different types of inventory, LO 1)** For each of the following, explain whether the asset can be classified as inventory on the entity's balance sheet. This is a tricky question that requires some careful thought:

Entity	Asset
a. Bank	cash
b. Equipment rental store	chain saw
c. Farm	cows
d. Commercial real estate developer	shopping centre

E8-8. **(Calculating cost of sales and ending inventory using average cost, FIFO, and LIFO cost flow assumptions when prices are stable, LO 2, 3)** The following information is provided for Exlou Ltd. (Exlou):

	Number of units	Purchase price per unit	Selling price per unit
Inventory on hand on January 1, 2008	20,000	$5	
Inventory purchases during 2008	80,000	$5	
Inventory purchases during 2009	100,000	$5	
Sales during 2008	76,000		$11
Sales during 2009	108,000		$11

Required:

a. Calculate ending inventory on December 31, 2008 and 2009 and cost of sales and gross margin for the years ended December 31, 2008 and 2009 for Exlou using FIFO, LIFO, and average cost. Assume that Exlou uses a periodic inventory control system.

b. Explain the results you obtained in (a). Do you find anything unusual about the amounts you calculated for ending inventory, cost of sales, and gross margin under each of the cost flow assumptions?

E8-9. **(Manipulating income with specific identification, LO 3)** Baddeck Antiques Ltd. (Baddeck) sells rare antiques to discriminating clients. Over the years Baddeck has acquired four essentially identical vases from one of the ancient dynasties in China. The cost of the vases are as follows:

Vase A	$11,200
Vase B	10,950
Vase C	13,150
Vase D	9,250

Recently, a customer purchased one of the vases for $25,000.

Required:

a. If Baddeck wanted to minimize its profit on this sale, which of the vases would it have sold to the customer? Calculate gross margin and ending inventory at the end of the period.

b. If Baddeck wanted to maximize its profit on this sale, which of the vases would it have sold to the customer? Calculate gross margin and ending inventory at the end of the period.

c. What is the impact on ending inventory of your choices in a. and b.? Under what circumstances might Baddeck's management want to maximize profit? Under what circumstances might it want to minimize profit? In reality, would it be possible for Baddeck's management to have the opportunity to manage the financial statements in this way? Explain.

E8-10. **(Calculating inventory turnover ratio and the average number of days inventory on hand, LO 7)** You are provided with the following information about Kepenkeck Inc. (Kepenkeck):

Cost of sales for the year ended November 30, 2010	$27,050,000
Inventory balance on November 30, 2009	$ 6,900,000
Inventory balance on November 30, 2010	$ 7,800,000

Required:

a. Calculate Kepenkeck's inventory turnover ratio for the year ended November 30, 2010.

b. What is the average length of time that it took Kepenkeck to sell its inventory in 2010?

c. Is Kepenkeck's inventory turnover ratio satisfactory? What would you need to know to fully answer this question?

E8-11. **(Lower of cost and market, LO 4)** Massawippi Inc. (Massawippi) uses the lower of cost and market rule to value its inventory. Massawippi defines market as net realizable value. Massawippi's inventory on February 28, 2011 had a cost of $1,125,000 and a NRV of $1,035,000.

Required:

a. By how much should Massawippi's inventory be written down?
b. Prepare the journal entry that Massawippi should prepare to record the write-down.
c. What amount should be reported for inventory on Massawippi's February 28, 2011 balance sheet?

E8-12. **(Lower of cost and market, LO 4, 7)** Wolf Ltd. (Wolf) reports its inventory at the lower of cost and market. You obtain the following information about Wolf for its year ended August 31, 2010:

Inventory, at cost on August 31, 2009	$1,503,000
Inventory, at cost, on August 31, 2010	1,575,000
Inventory, at NRV, on August 31, 2010	2,985,000
Inventory, at replacement cost, on August 31, 2010	1,491,000
Sales during the year ended August 31, 2010	7,020,000
Cost of sales for the year ended August 31, 2010	3,270,000
[Before any write down]	

Required:

a. If Wolf defines market as replacement cost, by how much should Wolf's inventory be written down?
b. If Wolf defines market as NRV, by how much should Wolf's inventory be written down?
c. If Wolf knew the replacement cost and NRV of its inventory on August 31, 2010, which should it use to determine the lower of cost and market?
d. What would be the effect of applying the lower of cost and market rule on Wolf's gross margin and inventory turnover ratio?

E8-13. **(Working with the inventory turnover ratio and the average number of days inventory on hand, LO 7)** Use the information provided in each row to calculate the missing values (shaded boxes). Each row is an independent situation.

	Cost of sales	Average inventory	Inventory turnover ratio	Average number of days inventory on hand
a.	$625,000	$		46.1
b.		4,312,000	4.77	
c.		152,100		11.0
d.	4,875,000	2,900,000		

E8-14. **(Identifying and calculating holding gains and losses, LO 5)** For each of the following situations, indicate whether the event gives rise to a gain or a loss and whether the gain or loss is realized or unrealized.

a. In 1995, a land development company purchased raw land for later development for $5,000,000. In 2008, development of the land had not yet begun. The company had recently received an offer for the land of $14,000,000.
b. In November 2008, a jeweller purchased $10,000 of gold for making jewellery. In May 2009, when the jeweller sold the jewellery made from the gold, the same amount of gold would have cost $9,000.
c. In March 2010, a company purchased a large supply of lumber for $200,000. By the end of the year, the market price of the lumber had doubled because of high demand in the United States.

E8-15. (**Compute missing information, LO 2**) Complete the following table by calculating the missing values (shaded boxes).

	Dec. 31, 2008	Dec. 31, 2009	Dec. 31, 2010	Dec. 31, 2011
Beginning inventory	$100,000	$	$	$
Purchases		775,000	1,200,000	1,300,000
Ending inventory	150,000		200,000	
Cost of sales	900,000	800,000		1,310,000

E8-16. (**The effect of different cash flow assumptions on liquidity, LO 3, 7**) The balances in the current asset and liability accounts for Feeder Ltd. (Feeder) are provided below. The balances in the inventory account are provided under the FIFO, average cost, and LIFO cost flow assumptions.

Cost flow assumption	Inventory balance on December 31, 2010
FIFO	$222,500
Average cost	170,000
LIFO	117,500

Account	Account balance on December 31, 2010
Cash	$ 30,000
Accounts receivable	62,500
Prepaid assets	17,500
Bank loan	87,500
Accounts payable and accrued liabilities	150,000

Required:

a. Calculate Feeder's current ratio on December 31, 2010 using the three cost flow assumptions.
b. How do you explain the results you obtained in (a)?
c. What are the implications for analyzing Feeder Ltd.'s financial statements of the different results you obtained in (a)?
d. Which current ratio provides the best measure of Feeder's liquidity? Explain.

E8-17. (**Effect of transactions and economic events on ratios, LO 4, 7**) Complete the following table by indicating whether the following transactions or economic events would increase, decrease, or have no effect on the financial ratios listed. Assume that the current ratio is greater than 1.0 and the quick ratio less than 1.0 before considering the effect of each transaction or economic event.

	Current ratio	Quick ratio	Gross margin percentage	Inventory turnover ratio	Profit margin percentage	Debt-to-equity ratio
a. Inventory is written down						
b. Inventory is sold at its cost						
c. Inventory is stolen						
d. The amount of inventory carried by the entity is increased						
e. Inventory is purchased on credit						

E8-18. **(Recording inventory transactions, LO 2, 3, 4)** For each of the following transactions and economic events, prepare the necessary journal entries. Provide a brief explanation for each journal entry and state any assumptions that you make.
  a. Inventory costing $20,000 is purchased on credit.
  b. Inventory costing $15,000 is written off because it has become unsaleable.
  c. Inventory costing $10,000 is sold to a customer for $22,000 cash. The entity uses a periodic inventory control system.
  d. Inventory costing $8,000 is sold to a customer on credit for $20,000, with the amount due in 30 days. The entity uses a perpetual inventory control system.
  e. Management discovers that the NRV of its inventory is $200,000 and its cost is $215,000.
  f. A supplier is paid $5,000 for inventory purchased on credit.

E8-19. **(Inventory cost flow assumptions when prices are falling, LO 3, 4)** Azilda Inc. (Azilda) operates in a part of the computer industry where the cost of inventory has been falling recently. The **cost** of inventory purchased by Azilda over the last year is summarized below. Azilda values its inventory at the lower of cost and market and defines market as net realizable value. Assume that purchases are made at the start of a month before any sales occur during that month.

Date	Quantity	Cost per unit	Selling price per unit
Purchases			
Opening inventory	70	$ 950	
October 1, 2008	144	900	
January 2, 2009	108	860	
April 1, 2009	84	810	
July 2, 2009	170	775	
Sales			
October-December, 2008	162		$1,710
January-March, 2009	116		1,620
April-June, 2009	86		1,550
July-September, 2009	158		1,390

Required:

  a. Calculate cost of sales for the year ended September 30, 2009 and ending inventory on September 30, 2009 for Azilda using the FIFO, average cost, and LIFO cost flow assumptions.
  b. Which cost flow assumption is most attractive for an accounting objective of income maximization?
  c. Which cost flow assumption is most attractive for an accounting objective of tax minimization?
  d. Compare the relative values under the three cost flow assumptions of ending inventory and cost of sales in this situation versus a situation where prices are rising. What is different between the two situations?
  e. Apply the lower of cost and market rule to the year-end inventory. Assume that Azilda's selling costs for inventory are $300 per unit.

E8-20. **(Inventory cost flow assumptions and taxes, LO 3, 6)** Sayabec Ltd.'s (Sayabec) purchases for 2010 were:

Date	Quantity purchased	Cost per unit
March 1	16,000	$5.50
June 4	20,000	6.00
September 9	30,000	6.30
December 4	14,000	6.60

The beginning balance in inventory on January 1, 2010 was 24,000 units with a cost of $5.00 per unit. The inventory count on December 31, 2010 found that there were 22,000 units on hand at the end of the year. Sayabec uses a periodic inventory control system. During 2010, Sayabec had revenues of $984,000 and expenses other than the cost of sales and taxes of $400,000. Saybec pays taxes equal to 20 percent of its income before taxes.

Required:

a. Prepare income statements for 2010 for Sayabec using FIFO and average cost. Your income statements should show the amount of taxes that the company has to pay for the income it earned in 2010. Taxes are calculated by multiplying income before taxes (revenue − all expenses except taxes) by the tax rate.

b. Which method would you recommend that Sayabec use if its primary objective of financial accounting is to minimize taxes? Explan your answer.

c. What are possible explanations as to why Sayabec would choose not to use the method you recommended in (b)?

E8-21. **(Considering the impact of valuing inventory at replacement cost, LO 5)**
Kapuskasing Inc. (Kapuskasing) imports widgets from China for sale in the Canadian market. You are provided with the following information about Kapuskasing's inventory for 2008:

Beginning inventory	5,000 units @ $5.25 per unit
Purchases during 2008	48,000 units @ $5.80 per unit
Sold during 2008	46,000 units for $11.75 when the replacement cost per unit was $6.10.
Ending inventory	7,000 units with replacement cost of $6.25 per unit

In addition, Kapuskasing incurred $125,000 in other costs to operate its business. The company's year end is December 31.

Required:

a. Prepare an income statement for Kapuskasing for 2008. Show the gross margin and net income for the year on your income statement. Assume that Kapuskasing uses FIFO to account for its inventory.

b. Prepare an income statement for Kapuskasing for 2008, assuming that it values its inventory at replacement cost. Prepare the journal entries you require to record the ending inventory at replacement cost at the end of 2008.

c. What amount would be reported on the December 31, 2008 balance sheet for inventory:
   i) If Kapuskasing uses FIFO to value its inventory;
   ii) If Kapuskasing uses replacement cost to value its inventory.

d. Explain the differences between the two income statements you prepared. How would a stakeholder interpret these income statements?

Problems

P8-1. **(Calculating cost of sales and ending inventory using average cost, FIFO, and LIFO cost flow assumptions, LO 1, 2, 3)** Adamo Limited (AL) is a wholesaler of machine parts. Jacob Avery recently purchased AL. Previously, Mr. Avery was an employee of AL. Mr. Avery purchased AL from the original owner, Mr. Adam, who is retiring. Mr. Avery has come to you for advice on how to calculate ending inventory and cost of goods sold. He has asked you to explain your reasoning for any choices you make.

Mr. Avery provided you with the following example of his inventory costs using Part 17592a.

Inventory Information for Part 17592a

	Number of units	Date of purchase/sale	Cost per unit	Selling price per unit
Opening inventory	250 units	various	$13.00	
Purchase	200 units	Nov. 10	$13.50	
Sale	160 units	Nov. 12		$30.00
Purchase	150 units	Nov. 20	$13.75	
Sale	320 units	Nov. 22		$60.00
Purchase	180 units	Nov. 25	$14.00	

Required

Calculate ending inventory as at November 30 and cost of goods sold for Part 17592a for November. Provide the explanations requested by Mr. Avery.

P8-2. **(The impact of cost flow assumptions on ratios, LO 3, 7)** Cardigan Corp. (Cardigan), Huskisson Ltd. (Huskisson), and Mallet Inc. (Mallet) are small distribution companies. They are identical in every respect—same amount of sales, same quantity of inventory sold, same number of employees. Everything is the same except that Cardigan uses FIFO as its cost flow assumption, Huskisson uses average cost, and Mallet uses LIFO.

Balance Sheets As of December 31, 2009			
	Cardigan (FIFO)	Huskisson (Average cost)	Mallet (LIFO)
Assets			
Cash	$ 142,200	$ 142,200	$ 142,200
Accounts receivable	378,000	378,000	378,000
Inventory	1,582,500	1,176,750	824,250
Other current assets	63,000	63,000	63,000
Total current assets	2,165,700	1,759,950	1,407,450
Capital assets (net)	2,260,500	2,260,500	2,260,500
Total assets	$4,426,200	$4,020,450	$3,667,950
Liabilities and Owners' Equity			
Bank loan	$ 225,000	$ 225,000	$ 225,000
Accounts payable	1,132,500	1,132,500	1,132,500
Other current liabilities	97,500	97,500	97,500
Total current liabilities	1,455,000	1,455,000	1,455,000
Long-term debt	393,000	393,000	393,000
Other non-current liabilities	75,000	75,000	75,000
Total liabilities	1,923,000	1,923,000	1,923,000
Capital stock	300,000	300,000	300,000
Retained earnings	2,203,200	1,797,450	1,444,950
Total liabilities and owners' equity	$4,426,200	$4,020,450	$3,667,950

| Income Statements | | | |
| For the Year Ended December 31, 2009 | | | |
	Cardigan (FIFO)	Huskisson (Average cost)	Mallet (LIFO)
Revenue	$5,310,000	$5,310,000	$5,310,000
Cost of sales	2,548,800	2,867,400	3,079,800
Gross margin	2,761,200	2,442,600	2,230,200
Other expenses	2,175,000	2,175,000	2,175,000
Net income	$ 586,200	$ 267,600	$ 55,200

You also learn that on December 31, 2008 the balances in Inventory for the three companies were:

| Ending Inventory Balances on December 31, 2008 | | | |
	Cardigan (FIFO)	Huskisson (Average cost)	Mallet (LIFO)
Inventory	$1,432,650	$1,071,300	$757,800

Required:

a. Calculate the following ratios for each of the three companies:
   i. current ratio
   ii. quick ratio
   iii. inventory turnover ratio
   iv. average number of days inventory on hand
   v. gross margin percentage
   vi. profit margin percentage
b. Which of the three companies has the strongest liquidity position?
c. Which of the three companies is the most profitable?
d. Which of the three companies manages its inventory most effectively?
e. The three companies' bankers lend money based on the amount of accounts receivable and inventory on hand. Which company will be able to obtain the largest loan? From the banks' point of view, is the company that receives the largest loan the best credit risk? Explain.

P8-3. **(The impact of cost flow assumptions on ratios, LO 3, 7)** Weybridge Corp. (Weybridge), Kennetcook Ltd. (Kennetcook), and Aaskana Inc. (Aaskana) are small retail stores. They are identical in every respect—same amount of sales, same quantity of inventory sold, same number of employees. Everything is the same except that Weybridge uses FIFO as its cost flow assumption, Kennetcook uses average cost, and Aaskana uses LIFO.

| Income Statements | | | |
| For the Year Ended December 31, 2011 | | | |
	Weybridge (FIFO)	Kennetcook (Average cost)	Aaskana (LIFO)
Revenue	$885,000	$885,000	$885,000
Cost of sales	552,240	621,270	667,290
Gross margin	332,760	263,730	217,710
Other expenses	242,000	242,000	242,000
Net income (loss)	$90,760	$21,730	($24,290)

Balance Sheets
For the Year Ended December 31, 2011

	Weybridge (FIFO)	Kennetcook (Average cost)	Aaskana (LIFO)
Assets			
Cash	$23,700	$23,700	$23,700
Accounts receivable	63,000	63,000	63,000
Inventory	263,750	196,126	137,376
Other current assets	10,500	10,500	10,500
Total current assets	360,950	293,326	234,576
Capital assets (net)	376,750	376,750	376,750
Total assets	$737,700	$670,076	$611,326
Liabilities and Owners' Equity			
Bank loan	$37,500	$37,500	$37,500
Accounts payable	188,750	188,750	188,750
Other current liabilities	16,250	16,250	16,250
Total current liabilities	242,500	242,500	242,500
Long-term debt	65,500	65,500	65,500
Other non-current liabilities	12,500	12,500	12,500
Total liabilities	320,500	320,500	320,500
Capital stock	50,000	50,000	50,000
Retained earnings	367,200	299,576	240,826
Total liabilities and owners' equity	$737,700	$670,076	$611,326

You also learn that on December 31, 2010 the balances in Inventory for the three companies were:

Ending Inventory Balances on December 31, 2010

	Weybridge (FIFO)	Kennetcook (Average cost)	Aaskana (LIFO)
Inventory	$240,000	$178,474	$125,012

Required:

a. Calculate the following ratios for each of the three companies:
   i. current ratio
   ii. quick ratio
   iii. inventory turnover ratio
   iv. average number of days inventory on hand
   v. gross margin percentage
   vi. profit margin percentage
b. Which of the three companies has the strongest liquidity position?
c. Which of the three companies is most profitable?
d. Which of the three companies manages its inventory most effectively?
e. The three companies' bankers lend money based on the amount of accounts receivable and inventory on hand. Which company will be able to obtain the largest loan? From the banks' point of view, is the company that receives the largest loan the best credit risk? Explain.

P8-4. **(Recommending inventory accounting policies, LO 1, 2, 3, 4, 6)** Tesseralik Inc. (Tesseralik) is a small private manufacturing company that makes inexpensive laptop computers. Tesseralik is owned by three brothers who converted their interest in computers into a business. All three brothers are involved in the management of the company. The company is relatively free of debt, with only a small bank loan outstanding, which is personally guaranteed by the brothers. Tesseralik purchases all component parts from independent manufacturers and assembles them into the laptops.

The company has been successful because it has been able to provide a good-quality product at a low price. Management searches extensively to find the lowest-cost components that meet its quality standards. Tesseralik employs 14 people, mainly assemblers who put together the computers. The major costs that Tesseralik incurs are the cost of labour and parts for the computers. There is as well a significant amount of both fixed and variable overhead that is incurred by the business. While the company has been successful, it is often short of cash.

Required:

Prepare a report to Tesseralik's management recommending accounting policies for inventory. Your report should fully explain your recommendations.

P8-5. **(Recommending inventory accounting policies, LO 1, 2, 3, 4)** Howser Ltd. (Howser) is a Canadian manufacturer of wooden shingles. Howser purchases lumber from saw mills and manufactures the shingles in one of its two factories. The shingles are used in house construction, mainly in the southern and western United States. Howser is owned by 20 investors, not all of whom are involved in the day-to-day management of the company. The professional management team that manages the company receives salary, plus bonuses based on company performance as compensation. Howser has a large loan outstanding from the bank. The amount of the loan is based on accounts receivable and inventory outstanding on the last day of each calendar month. Howser has usually borrowed the maximum amount allowable under the borrowing agreement with the bank. Howser pays surplus cash (cash that is not required for operations and that is available after paying of debts) out to its shareholders.

Required:

Prepare a report to Howser's management recommending accounting policies for inventory. Your report should fully explain your recommendations.

P8-6. **(Considering the effect of inventory errors, LO 1, 2, 7)** Abney Ltd. (Abney) is a small manufacturing company. In the fiscal year just ended, a number of errors were made in accounting for inventory. For each of the following errors, indicate their effect on the financial statement elements and ratios shown in the table below. Indicate whether the financial statement element or ratio would be overstated (higher than it would have been had the error not occurred), understated (lower than it would have been had the error not occurred), or not affected by the error. Abney uses a periodic inventory control system. Abney applies the lower of cost and market rule on a type-by-type basis. The initial ratios before considering the adjustments are shown in bold in the table on the next page.
a. Some of the inventory in Abney's warehouse was not counted during the year-end inventory count.
b. Certain costs that are normally expensed as incurred were included in inventory.
c. The purchase of some inventory on credit was not recorded (both the inventory and the payable) but the inventory was included in the year-end inventory count.
d. Damaged inventory that cannot be sold was included in the year end inventory amount.

	Net income	Cost of sales	Total assets	Owners' equity	Current ratio [1.65]	Inventory turnover ratio [4.3]	Debt-to-equity ratio [1.25]
a.							
b.							
c.							
d.							

P8-7. (**Considering the effect of inventory errors, LO 1, 2, 4, 7**) Cariboo Ltd. (Cariboo) is a small manufacturing company. In the fiscal year just ended a number of errors were made in accounting for inventory. For each of the following errors, indicate their effect on the financial statement elements and ratios shown in the table below. Indicate whether the financial statement element or ratio would be overstated (higher than it would have been had the error not occurred), understated (lower than it would have been had the error not occurred), or not affected by the error. Cariboo uses a periodic inventory control system. Cariboo applies the lower of cost and market rule on a type-by-type basis. The initial ratios before considering the adjustments are shown in bold in the table.

a. Inventory that was on consignment with one of Cariboo's customers was not included in inventory.

b. Certain costs that are normally included in inventory were expensed by mistake.

c. Several inventory items whose market value was less than cost were not written down to market.

d. Some of the inventory in Cariboo's warehouse was counted twice during the year-end inventory count.

	Net income	Cost of sales	Total assets	Owners' equity	Current ratio [1.31]	Inventory turnover ratio [2.4]	Debt-to-equity ratio [0.52]
a.							
b.							
c.							
d.							

P8-8. (**Determining the amount of inventory on hand when a periodic inventory control system is used, LO 2, 7**) On March 24, 2009 Enterprise Inc. (Enterprise) suffered a serious fire that destroyed its entire inventory of fine paper products. Enterprise uses a periodic inventory control system and as a result does not keep track of the amount of inventory that has been removed from inventory. Enterprise last counted its inventory on December 31, 2008, its year end. At that time there was $900,000 of inventory on hand. Enterprise's records indicate that sales from January 1 to March 24, 2009 were $740,000 and that during that time additional inventory was purchased for $650,000. Enterprise's usual gross margin on its sales of fine paper is 48 percent.

Required:

Enterprise has insurance that covers it fully for losses suffered by fire, except for a $50,000 deductible. Prepare a report to Enterprise's management that computes the amount of the loss that should be claimed from the insurance company as a result of the fire. Explain any factors that management should be aware of that would change the amount of the claim.

P8-9. (**Determining the amount of inventory on hand when a periodic inventory control system is used, LO 2, 7**) On February 19, 2010 Exploits Inc.'s (Exploits) entire inventory was stolen in a daring daylight robbery. The thieves held warehouse personnel at gunpoint while they methodically loaded trucks with the contents of the warehouse. There were no injuries.

Exploits is fully insured against theft and so must file a claim with its insurance company for the loss suffered. Because Exploits uses a periodic inventory control system, it does not know for certain the amount of inventory that was stolen. However, from your discussions with company personnel, you have learned that Exploits has two categories of inventory. Category one inventory usually generates a gross margin of 60 percent, while the category two usually generates a gross margin of 40 percent. Sales of category one since the company's year end on October 31, 2009 were about $425,000. Sales of category two over the same time period were about $877,500. During the period since the year end, Exploits purchased $162,500 of category one inventory and $400,000 of category two inventory. The financial records show that on October 31, 2009 there was $225,000 of category one inventory and $500,000 of category two inventory on hand.

Required:

Prepare a report to Exploits' management that computes the amount of the loss that should be claimed from the insurance company as a result of the robbery. Explain any factors that management should be aware of that would change the amount of the claim.

P8-10. **(Lower of cost and market, LO 4, 7)** Tumbell Corp. (Tumbell) reports its inventory at the lower of cost and market, where market is defined as net realizable value. Tumbell has five inventory categories. You are provided with the following cost and NRV information about each category:

Inventory category	Cost	Net realizable value
Category 1	$201,600	$180,000
Category 2	415,800	588,000
Category 3	134,100	189,000
Category 4	176,580	265,500
Category 5	264,600	252,000

Required:

a. What amount should Tumbell report on its balance sheet for inventory if it determines the lower of cost and market for the inventory as a whole? What is the amount of write-down that is required?

b. What amount should Tumbell report on its balance sheet for inventory if it determines the lower of cost and market category by category? What is the amount of write-down that is required?

c. What is the effect on Tumbell's cash flow of determining the lower of cost and market for the inventory as a whole versus on a category-by-category basis?

d. What are the implications of the two methods on the inventory turnover ratio and the gross margin percentage? Explain. Assume that the inventory turnover ratio before considering the write down is 3.1.

e. Should Tumbell use the inventory-as-a-whole approach or the category-by-category approach to determine the lower of cost and market of its inventory? Explain your answer.

P8-11. **(Lower of cost and market, LO 4, 7)** Wolverine Corp. (Wolverine) reports its inventory at the lower of cost and market, where market is defined as replacement cost. Wolverine has five inventory categories. You are provided with the following cost and replacement cost information about each category:

Inventory category	Cost	Replacement cost
Category 1	$168,000	$187,500
Category 2	346,500	322,500
Category 3	111,750	112,800
Category 4	147,150	117,750
Category 5	220,500	228,000

Required:

a. What amount should Wolverine report on its balance sheet for inventory if it determines the lower of cost and market for the inventory as a whole? What is the amount of write-down that is required?

b. What amount should Wolverine report on its balance sheet for inventory if it determines the lower of cost and market category by category? What is the amount of write-down that is required?

c. What is the effect on Wolverine's cash flow of determining the lower of cost and market for the inventory as a whole versus on a category-by-category basis?

d. What are the implications of the two methods on the inventory turnover ratio and the gross margin percentage? Explain. Assume that the inventory turnover ratio before considering the write down is 3.9.

e. Should Wolverine use the inventory-as-a-whole approach or the category-by-category approach to determine the lower of cost and market of its inventory? Explain your answer.

P8-12. (**Determine the amount of inventory lost due to theft, LO 1, 2**) Wekusko Ltd. (Wekusko) is a wholesaler of electronic equipment that it imports from Asia. Recently, the manager of Wekusko's warehouse in Winnipeg became concerned that a significant amount of goods was being stolen from the warehouse. He wanted to know the extent of the problem so he could take steps to remedy the problem, if necessary. He spoke with the company accountant, who told the warehouse manager that if he would count the inventory on hand, the accountant could give him an idea of how much inventory was being stolen.

The manager closed the warehouse and had the inventory counted. The warehouse manager advised the accountant that there was $3,066,896 of inventory on hand on the date of the count. The manager also told the accountant that since the last year end, goods costing $15,688 had been damaged and had to be thrown away. The accountant examined the financial records pertaining to the Winnipeg warehouse and found that since the last year end, goods costing $1,244,550 had been purchased and stored in the warehouse, and that goods costing $1,319,320 had been shipped to customers over the same period. The inventory count at the end of the previous reporting period reported inventory of $3,279,706.

Required:

a. Estimate the amount of electronic equipment that might have been stolen from the Winnipeg warehouse.

b. Is it possible to conclude with certainty the amount you calculated in (a) was due to theft? Explain.

c. Why was it necessary to count the inventory to estimate the amount of inventory that was stolen?

P8-13. (**Determine the amount of inventory shrinkage, LO 1, 2**) Magyar Ltd. (Magyar) is a large retail clothing store located in a suburban mall. Recently, the store manager became concerned that a significant amount of goods was being stolen from the store and she wanted an idea of how much was being stolen so that she could decide whether it was worthwhile to install theft-prevention equipment. The accountant told the store manager that if she would count the inventory on hand, the accountant could give her an idea of the amount of inventory being stolen.

The manager had the inventory counted after store closing one Sunday. According to the count there was $240,000 of inventory on hand. The manager also told the accountant that since the year end, $21,000 of merchandise had been returned to suppliers. At the last year end, Magyar had $210,000 of inventory. Since the year end, the store had purchased $202,500 of inventory and had sales of $305,000. The gross margin that Magyar usually earns is 55 percent.

Required:

a. Determine the amount of clothing that might have been stolen from the store.
b. Is it possible to conclude with certainty that the amount you calculated in (a) was due to theft?
c. Why was it necessary to count the inventory to estimate the amount of inventory that was stolen?
d. If Magyar had used a perpetual inventory control system, would a count of the inventory have been required to provide the manager with the information she required?

P8-14. **(Consider the effect of different inventories on the inventory turnover ratio, LO 7)**
Xena Inc. (Xena) is an importer of gift items from Europe and Asia. Xena classifies its inventory into three categories: porcelain figurines, toys, and linens. Over the years, Xena's management has found that the success of the three categories has tended to vary, sometimes quite significantly, although, fortunately for the company, poor performance of one category seems to be offset by success in another. On its balance sheet and income statement, Xena does not break down its Inventory, Sales, and Cost of Sales into the three categories.

For its years ended October 31, 2008 and 2009, Xena reported inventory of $417,500 and $433,250 respectively. For the fiscal year ended October 31, 2009, Xena reported sales of $1,961,000 and cost of sales of $963,625. However, the following breakdown of Inventory, Sales, and Cost of Sales has been made available to you:

Category	Inventory balance on October 31, 2008	Inventory balance on October 31, 2009	Sales for the year ended October 31, 2009	Cost of Sales for the year ended October 31, 2009
Porcelain figurines	$146,250	$159,500	$862,500	$345,000
Toys	168,750	126,250	692,750	415,750
Linens	102,500	147,500	405,750	202,875

Required:

a. Calculate the gross margin percentage, inventory turnover ratio, and the average number of days inventory on hand for the year ended October 31, 2009, using the aggregated amounts reported for inventory, sales, and cost of sales on Xena's balance sheet and income statement.
b. Calculate the gross margin, inventory turnover ratio, and the average number of days inventory on hand for the year ended October 31, 2009 for each category of inventory that Xena carries.
c. What are the implications of the results you obtained in parts (a) and (b) of the question?
d. How is your ability to analyze Xena affected by the aggregated information presented in the company's balance sheet and income statement versus the information that was made available to you? Explain fully.

P8-15. **(Consider the effect of different inventories on the inventory turnover ratio, LO 7)**
Herschel Inc. (Herschel) is a small chain of convenience stores. Herschel classifies its

inventory into three categories: perishable items, packaged goods, and household items. On its balance sheet and income statement, Herschel does not break down its Inventory, Sales, and Cost of Sales into three categories.

For its years ended December 31, 2010 and 2011, Herschel reported inventory of $671,000 and $873,500 respectively. For the fiscal year ended December 31, 2011, Herschel reported sales of $7,013,000 and cost of sales of $5,575,000. However, the following breakdown of Inventory, Sales, and Cost of Sales has been made available to you:

Category	Inventory balance on October 31, 2010	Inventory balance on October 31, 2011	Sales for the year ended October 31, 2011	Cost of Sales for the year ended October 31, 2011
Perishable items	$50,000	$42,500	$2,375,000	$2,000,000
Packaged goods	183,500	306,000	2,013,000	1,650,000
Household items	437,500	525,000	2,625,000	1,925,000

Required:

a. Calculate the gross margin percentage, inventory turnover ratio, and the average number of days inventory on hand for the year ended December 31, 2011 using the aggregated amounts reported for Inventory, Sales, and Cost of Sales on Herschel's balance sheet and income statement.

b. Calculate the gross margin percentage, inventory turnover ratio, and the average number of days inventory on hand for the year ended December 31, 2011 for each category of inventory that Herschel carries.

c. What are the implications of the results you obtained in parts (a) and (b)? How is your ability to analyze Herschel affected by the aggregated information presented in the company's balance sheet and income statement versus the information that was made available to you? Explain fully.

P8-16. (Cost flow assumptions, LO 2, 3, 4, 6) The purchase and sale of inventory by Yearly Inc. (Yearly) during the year ended November 30, 2009 is summarized below. Assume that purchases are made on the first day of each quarter and sales on the last day of each quarter. Yearly pays for all its inventory in cash when it is delivered.

Economic event	Quantity	Purchase price per unit	Selling price per unit
Opening inventory	5,000	$6.00	
Purchases—first quarter	4,000	$6.15	
Purchases—second quarter	5,500	$6.45	
Purchases—third quarter	9,500	$6.60	
Purchases—fourth quarter	3,500	$6.80	
Sales—first quarter	6,500		$11.00
Sales—second quarter	5,000		$11.00
Sales—third quarter	11,000		$11.50
Sales—fourth quarter	2,500		$11.50

Required:

a. Determine cost of sales for the year ended November 30, 2009 and ending inventory on November 30, 2009 using FIFO, LIFO, and average cost, assuming that Yearly uses a periodic inventory control system.

b. How much cash was spent on inventory during 2009 under each cost flow assumption? Is the amount of cash spent on inventory under each cost flow assumption the same or different? Explain.

c. Which cost flow assumption would you recommend if the objective of the entity were to minimize taxes? Explain.

d. Which cost flow assumption would you use if you were Yearly's CEO and your bonus were based on net income? Explain.

e. Which cost flow assumption would you recommend if the amount of Yearly's bank loan were a percentage of inventory? Explain.

f. Yearly uses the lower of cost and market to value its inventory and defines market as net realizable value. Suppose that on November 30, 2009 the NRV of Yearly's inventory plummeted to $6.25 per unit. What would you do under each cost flow assumption?

g. Does it matter which cost flow assumption Yearly uses? Explain fully.

P8-17. **(Cost flow assumptions, LO 2, 3, 4, 6)** The purchase and sale of inventory by Ripple Inc. (Ripple) during the year ended April 30, 2010 is summarized below. Assume that sales are made on the first day of each quarter and purchases are made on the last day of each quarter. Ripple pays for all its inventory in cash when it is delivered.

Economic event	Quantity	Purchase price per unit	Selling price per unit
Opening inventory	150,000	$5.50	
Purchases—first quarter	180,000	$7.00	
Purchases—second quarter	102,000	$8.00	
Purchases—third quarter	140,000	$8.50	
Purchases—fourth quarter	160,000	$7.40	
Sales—first quarter	136,000		$16.00
Sales—second quarter	176,000		$16.00
Sales—third quarter	110,000		$16.00
Sales—fourth quarter	134,000		$16.00

Required:

a. Determine cost of sales for the year ended April 30, 2010 and ending inventory on April 30, 2010 using FIFO, LIFO, and average cost, assuming that Ripple uses a periodic inventory control system.

b. How much cash was spent on inventory during 2010 under each cost flow assumption? Is the amount of cash spent on inventory under each cost flow assumption the same or different? Explain.

c. Which cost flow assumption would you recommend if the objective of the entity were to minimize taxes? Explain.

d. Which cost flow assumption would you use if you were Ripple's CEO and your bonus was based on net income? Explain.

e. Which cost flow assumption would you recommend if the amount of Ripple's bank loan were a percentage of inventory? Explain.

f. Ripple uses the lower of cost and market to value its inventory and defines market as replacement cost. Is it necessary to make any adjustments to inventory on April 30, 2010 to ensure compliance with the lower of cost and market rule? Explain.

g. Does it matter which cost flow assumption Ripple uses? Explain fully.

P8-18. **(Problems with LIFO, LO 3)** Iffly Ltd. (Iffly) uses LIFO to account for its inventory. Beginning in April 2009, the start of its fiscal year, Iffly's management began to reduce the amount of inventory it carried. Management felt that with the new inventory control techniques it recently implemented that it would be able to safely operate with 40 percent less inventory. Iffly uses a periodic inventory control system. The listing of the costs associated with the inventory on hand on March 31, 2009 is provided on the next page:

Iffly Ltd.
LIFO Inventory Listing—Costs Remaining in Inventory
March 31, 2009

Year acquired	Number of units	Cost per unit
2009	10,000	$4.80
2004	10,000	3.90
2001	46,000	3.10
1998	170,000	2.50
1994	182,000	2.20
1993	160,000	2.10
1992	84,000	2.00
Total	662,000	

During fiscal 2010, Iffly purchased an additional 860,000 units of inventory for $4.80 per unit and sold 1,120,000 units for $10.00 per unit. During fiscal 2009, Iffly sold 1,100,000 units for $10.00 per unit and purchased 1,100,000 units for $4.80 per unit. In each of 2009 and 2010, Iffly incurred $2,000,000 in other expenses.

Required:

a. What amount did Iffly report for inventory on its March 31, 2010 balance sheet?
b. Prepare income statements for fiscal 2009 and 2010.
c. What was Iffly's gross margin percentage in 2009 and 2010?
d. Assess Iffly's performance in 2010 versus 2009. How do you explain the improvement in the company's performance? Do you think the company is more attractive to investors in 2010 than it was in 2009? Explain.
e. What would Iffly's net income and gross margin percentage have been if Iffly's cost per unit for all units sold in 2010 had been $4.80? Explain why net income in this part is different from what you calculated in (b) for net income in 2010.

P8-19. **(Problems with LIFO, LO 3)** Joyvista Ltd. (Joyvista) uses LIFO to account for its inventory. In early 2010, Joyvista's management realized that it would be difficult to meet earnings targets set by its parent company in the United States that were key for evaluating the performance of the managers and determining their annual bonuses. As a result, Joyvista's management decided to reduce the amount of inventory it was carrying so that it would be able to expense "less expensive" inventory. Joyvista uses a periodic inventory control system. The listing of the costs associated with the inventory on hand on December 31, 2009 is provided below:

Joyvista Ltd.
LIFO Inventory Listing—Costs Remaining in Inventory
December 31, 2009

Year acquired	Number of units	Cost per unit
2009	200	$11.50
2008	300	11.25
2007	1,000	10.00
2006	2,000	6.90
2005	10,000	6.50
2004	10,000	6.75
2003	7,500	6.75

During fiscal 2010, Joyvista purchased an additional 10,000 units of inventory for $11.50 per unit and sold 17,500 units for $25.00 per unit. During fiscal 2009 Joyvista sold 15,000 units for $24.00 per unit and purchased 15,000 units for $11.50 per unit. In each of 2009 and 2010, Joyvista incurred $125,000 in other expenses.

Required:

    a. What amount did Joyvista report for inventory on its December 31, 2010 balance sheet?

    b. Prepare income statements for 2009 and 2010.

    c. What was Joyvista's gross margin percentage in 2009 and 2010?

    d. Assess Joyvista's performance in 2010 versus 2009. How do you explain the improvement in the company's performance? Do you think the company is more attractive to investors in 2010 than it was in 2009? Explain.

    e. What would Joyvista's net income and gross margin percentage have been if Joyvista's cost per unit for all units sold in 2010 had been $11.50? Explain why net income in this part is different from what you calculated in (b) for net income in 2010.

Using Financial Statements

ATI TECHNOLOGIES INC.

www.ati.com

ATI Technologies Inc. (ATI) is a world leader in the design and manufacture of innovative 3D graphics and digital media silicon solutions. An industry pioneer since 1985, ATI is the world's foremost graphics processor unit provider. ATI is dedicated to delivering leading-edge performance solutions for the full range of PC and Mac desktop and notebook platforms, workstation, digital television, game console, and handheld markets. With 2005 revenues of approximately $2.2 billion, ATI has more than 3,300 employees in the Americas, Europe and Asia. ATI common shares trade on NASDAQ and the Toronto Stock Exchange.[8]

    ATI's consolidated balance sheets and statements of earnings, along with extracts from the notes to the financial statements and extracts from Management's Discussion and Analysis from the annual report, are provided in Exhibit 8–3. Use this information to respond to questions FS8-1 to FS8–8.

FS8-1. What amount of inventory did ATI report on its August 31, 2005 balance sheet? What proportion of current assets and what proportion of total assets did inventory comprise? What is the breakdown of ATI's inventory? As a user of the financial statements, do you find knowing the breakdown useful? Explain.

FS8-2. Describe the accounting policies that ATI uses to account for its inventory. Why do you think that raw materials and finished goods are not accounted for in exactly the same way? Do you think all the inventory should be accounted for using the same accounting policies? Do you think it would be appropriate if an entity used different cost flow assumptions for different categories of inventory? Explain.

FS8-3. Note 1(d) identifies specific factors that are taken into consideration when determining the NRV of the finished goods and work-in-process inventories. What are these factors? Do you think these factors are especially relevant to ATI and similar companies or are they equally relevant to all companies? Explain.

FS8-4. Note 1(p) provides an explanation of how ATI's management uses estimates in the preparation of the financial statements. What important information for readers of the financial statements does this note provide? Why is it important for users to understand this note? What are some of the estimates that ATI's management must make when preparing the financial statements? What are the specific issues raised with respect to inventory?

FS8-5. Calculate ATI's inventory turnover ratio and the number of days inventory on hand for 2005, 2004, and 2003. Assume that inventory on August 31, 2003 was $176,494,000 and on August 31, 2002 was $192,121,000. How would you interpret the change in the inventory turnover ratio over the three-year period? Explain. You might have noticed that in the extracts from Management's Discussion and Analysis the number of days inventory on hand at the end of fiscal 2005 is stated as 85 days. Speculate on the difference between your calculation and the calculation by the company.

Consolidated Balance Sheets

(In thousands of U.S. dollars)

EXHIBIT 8–3 :

**ATI Technologies
Extracts from
Financial
Statements**

August 31	2005	2004
ASSETS		
Current assets:		
Cash and cash equivalents	$ 223,277	$ 359,608
Short-term investments (note 3)	363,370	189,308
Accounts receivable	386,264	365,644
Inventories (note 4)	348,209	254,867
Prepayments and sundry receivables	24,463	22,395
Future income tax assets (note 13)	5,348	8,022
Total current assets	1,350,931	1,199,844
Capital assets (note 5)	112,875	86,943
Intangible assets (note 7)	17,631	5,558
Goodwill (note 7)	190,095	190,095
Long-term investments (note 8)	291	2,751
Tax credits recoverable	59,080	29,149
Future income tax assets (note 13)	12,588	1,114
Total assets	$ 1,743,491	$ 1,514,454
LIABILITIES AND SHAREHOLDERS' EQUITY		
Current liabilities:		
Accounts payable	$ 362,926	$ 274,772
Accrued liabilities	302,028	219,607
Deferred revenue (note 10)	24,576	29,131
Current portion of long-term debt (note 11)	1,852	1,571
Total current liabilities	691,382	525,081
Long-term debt (note 11)	29,110	28,053
Future income tax liabilities (note 13)	8,861	16,632
Total liabilities	729,353	569,766
Shareholders' equity (note 12):		
Share capital:		
Authorized:		
Unlimited preferred shares		
Unlimited common shares		
Issued and outstanding:		
251,473,305 common shares (2004 – 249,287,125)	665,566	638,985
Treasury stock	(14,867)	(22,100)
Contributed surplus	61,795	10,704
Retained earnings	293,370	308,825
Currency translation adjustment	8,274	8,274
Total shareholders' equity	1,014,138	944,688
Total liabilities and shareholders' equity	$ 1,743,491	$ 1,514,454

Consolidated Statements of Operations and Retained Earnings

(In thousands of U.S. dollars, except per share amounts)

Years ended August 31	2005	2004	2003
REVENUES	$ 2,222,509	$ 1,996,717	$ 1,385,293
Cost of revenues	1,608,582	1,303,802	956,116
Gross margin	613,927	692,915	429,177
OPERATING EXPENSES:			
Selling and marketing	146,352	117,597	92,810
Research and development	327,017	265,491	212,976
Administrative	61,808	46,702	39,413
Amortization of intangible assets (note 7)	8,919	6,115	10,767
Stock-based compensation	42,504	7,583	–
Other charges (recoveries) (note 16)	2,508	(304)	28,724
	589,108	443,184	384,690
Income from operations	24,819	249,731	44,487
Interest and other income, net (note 8)	14,935	2,950	4,382
Interest expense (note 11)	(2,096)	(2,058)	(1,899)
Income before income taxes	37,658	250,623	46,970
Income taxes (note 13)	20,729	45,824	11,741
NET INCOME	16,929	204,799	35,229
RETAINED EARNINGS, beginning of year	308,825	104,026	68,797
Adjustment to opening retained earnings:			
Change in accounting policy on stock-based compensation (note 1(o))	(13,843)	–	–
Repurchase of common shares (note 12(a))	(18,541)	–	–
Retained earnings, end of year	$ 293,370	$ 308,825	$ 104,026
NET INCOME PER SHARE (note 14):			
Basic	$ 0.07	$ 0.84	$ 0.15
Diluted	0.07	0.80	0.14
WEIGHTED AVERAGE NUMBER OF SHARES (000s):			
Basic	250,680	245,257	238,251
Diluted	258,314	256,208	244,353

EXHIBIT 8–3 :

(continued)
ATI Technologies
Extracts from
Financial
Statements

NOTE 1.

Significant accounting policies

(d) Inventories

Raw materials are stated at the lower of cost and replacement cost. Finished goods and work in process are stated at the lower of cost and net realizable value. In determining net realizable value, the Company considers factors such as market conditions, the aging of inventory and forecasted future demand. Cost is determined on a first-in, first-out basis.

(p) Use of estimates

The preparation of consolidated financial statements requires management to make estimates and assumptions that affect the reported amounts of assets and liabilities and disclosure of contingent assets and liabilities at the dates of the consolidated financial statements and the reported amounts of revenue and expenses during the reporting years presented. Significant estimates are used in determining the allowance for doubtful accounts, provision for inventory obsolescence, useful lives of long-lived assets, goodwill and long-lived asset impairment testing, valuation of long-term investments, realization of future tax assets, and estimates for sales returns and allowances, price protection and sales rebates. Management makes its estimates based on historical experience and on various other assumptions it believes are reasonable. Actual results could differ from those estimates.

NOTE 4.

Inventories

	2005	2004
Raw materials	$ 32,599	$ 44,882
Work in process	193,448	122,020
Finished goods	122,162	87,965
	$ 348,209	$ 254,867

At August 31, 2005, the Company had non-cancellable inventory purchase commitments totalling $223.6 million (2004 – $181.1 million).

Management's Discussion and Analysis

FINANCIAL RESULTS ANALYSIS

Quarterly Financial Data

(Unaudited) (In thousands of U.S. dollars, except per share amounts)

	Fiscal 2005				Fiscal 2004			
	Aug. 31 2005	May 31 2005	Feb. 28 2005	Nov. 30 2004	Aug. 31 2004	May 31 2004	Feb. 29 2004	Nov. 30 2003
Revenues	$ 470,227	$ 530,235	$ 608,188	$ 613,859	$ 572,218	$ 491,457	$ 463,337	$ 469,705
Gross Margin[1]	42,345	154,429	208,303	208,850	192,382	172,539	160,423	167,571
Operating Expenses	159,085	157,057	141,867	131,099	119,958	112,355	103,561	107,310
Net Income (Loss)	(103,522)	(445)	57,193	63,703	61,156	48,619	47,585	47,439
Net Income (Loss) per Share (Basic)	$ (0.41)	$ 0.00	$ 0.23	$ 0.26	$ 0.25	$ 0.20	$ 0.19	$ 0.20
Net Income (Loss) per Share (Diluted)	$ (0.41)	$ 0.00	$ 0.22	$ 0.25	$ 0.24	$ 0.19	$ 0.19	$ 0.19

[1] Gross margin for the fourth quarter of fiscal 2005 includes an inventory write-down of $67 million.

Inventories

Inventory at August 31, 2005 increased 36.6% to $348.2 million from $254.9 million in fiscal 2004. Our inventory position at fiscal year-end includes the impact of an inventory write-down of $67.4 million in the fourth quarter of fiscal 2005 consisting predominantly of mid- to high-end PCI Express and AGP desktop discrete products. Following the inventory write-down, days of inventory on hand at the end of fiscal 2005 were 85 as compared with our long-term target of 70 days.

Accounts Payable and Accrued Liabilities

Accounts payable increased 32.1% to $362.9 million in 2005 from $274.8 million in 2004 as a result of increased inventory purchases required to support our sales increase.

Accounts payable are within our target range for current sales levels.

Inventory Valuation

We record raw materials at the lower of cost and replacement cost. Finished goods and work in process are stated at the lower of cost and net realizable value. Cost is determined on a first-in, first-out basis. We write down our inventory for estimated obsolescence, and excess inventories based upon assumptions about future demand and market conditions. The business environment in which we operate is subject to rapid change in technology and customer demand. If actual market conditions are less favorable than those estimated or if our future product purchase commitments to our suppliers exceed our forecasted future demand for such products, additional material inventory write-downs may be required.

FS8-6. At the bottom of Note 4 to ATI's financial statements, the note states "At August 31, 2005, the Company had non-cancellable inventory purchase commitments totalling $223.6 million (2004 – $181.1 million)." The statement means that ATI is obligated by contract to buy almost $224 million of inventory in the future, whether the inventory is needed or not. How is this information useful to stakeholders? Explain. How do you think ATI would account for an agreement that requires the company to buy inventory in the future? Explain.

FS8-7. During fiscal 2005 ATI reported an inventory write-down. What is a write-down and why was it necessary for ATI to write down some of its inventory? What was the amount of the write-down? Where is the write-down reflected in the income statement? What impact does the write-down have on ATI's cash flow? Explain. What impact did the write-down have on gross margin for fiscal 2005 and for each of the quarters? How is comparability affected by how ATI accounts for the write-down?

FS8-8. Why is careful management of inventory so important for a company like ATI?

Analyzing Rogers Communications Inc.

◇ ROGERS

R8-1. Suppose Rogers decided to write off some of its inventory because it could not be sold (perhaps it was damaged or destroyed).
   a. What journal entry (or worksheet entry) would Rogers make to record the write-off?
   b. Suppose the amount of the write-off was sizable (material to Rogers). How or where would you report the write-off in the income statement? Explain why.
   c. Are there any alternatives as to how the amount of the write-off could be reported?
   d. How would different ways of reporting the write-off affect stakeholders' interpretations of the statements?

R8-2. Given the type of business it is in, do you think that Rogers is likely to have to address lower of cost and market (LCM) problems on a regular basis? Explain.

R8-3. Most companies report inventory on their balance sheets. Rogers doesn't. Explain why. What types of firms do you think would not report inventory on the balance sheet itself?

R8-4. How much does Rogers report for video rental inventory? Where is this amount reported in the financial statements? Do you think the video rental inventory is properly classified as inventory? Explain. How is the video rental inventory accounted for? Is this accounting treatment consistent with how inventory is typically accounted for? Should the video rental inventory be classified as current or non-current? Explain.

ENDNOTES

1. Extracted from Digital Theater Systems, Inc. 2004 10-k filing with SEC.

2. Clarence Byrd, Ida Chen, and Joshua Smith, *Financial Reporting in Canada*, 30th Edition. The Virtual Professional Library. 2005.

3. Panel A extracted from Magna International Inc.'s 2005 annual report. Panel B extracted from Genesis Land Development Corp.'s 2004 annual report. Panel C is extracted from Canfor Corporation's 2005 annual report.

4. Interpretation Bulletin IT473R "Inventory Valuation." Published by the Canadian Customs and Revenue Agency, December 21, 1998; http://www.cra-arc.gc.ca/E/pub/tp/it473r/it473r-e.html.

5. Clarence Byrd, Ida Chen, and Joshua Smith, *Financial Reporting in Canada*, 30th Edition. The Virtual Professional Library. 2005.

6. Interpretation Bulletin IT473R "Inventory Valuation." Published by the Canadian Customs and Revenue Agency, December 21, 1998; http://www.cra-arc.gc.ca/E/pub/tp/it473r/it473r-e.html.

7. Interpretation Bulletin IT473R "Inventory Valuation." Published by the Canadian Customs and Revenue Agency, December 21, 1998; http://www.cra-arc.gc.ca/E/pub/tp/it473r/it473r-e.html.

8. Extracted from ATI Technologies Inc.'s 2005 annual report.

CHAPTER

9

CAPITAL ASSETS

LEARNING OBJECTIVES

After studying the material in this chapter you will be able to:

▶ **LO 1** Explain the strengths and limitations of the different bases for valuing capital assets on the balance sheet.

▶ **LO 2** Recognize how to account for the purchase of capital assets.

▶ **LO 3** Describe the different methods of amortizing capital assets and understand the implications of the different methods for financial statements and for the users of the statements.

▶ **LO 4** Discuss the problems with accounting for intangible assets and understand that many of an entity's intangible assets are not reported on its balance sheet.

▶ **LO 5** Explain how to account for disposals of amortizable capital assets and for writedowns of capital assets.

▶ **LO 6** Explain how the cash flow statement is affected by whether expenditures are expensed or capitalized.

▶ **LO 7** Analyze and interpret information about capital assets in financial statements.

▶ **LO 8** (appendix). Differentiate between capital cost allowance for tax purposes and amortization for financial reporting purposes.

I n late October 2005, Rogers did a return of sorts to its roots, buying a ninety-three-thousand—square-metre (one million square feet) facility in Brampton, Ontario (west of Toronto), for $100 million. The seller? Troubled telecom equipment maker Nortel, whose shrunken workforce could no longer afford the former manufacturing plant's 24-foot-high ceilings, huge skylights, and basketball and volleyball courts. The deal with Nortel gave Rogers not only the building, but the land, including 63 acres of walking paths, ponds, and waterfalls.

For CEO Ted Rogers, it was clearly more then just a business decision to move 3,500 people to Brampton.

"We're excited to return to Brampton," he said in a news release. "the city where our cable operations began in 1967."

Fresh out of law school in the 1960s, and busy starting to assemble a media empire, a young Ted Rogers acquired his first cable company, based in Brampton, in March 1967. It was called Bramalea Telecable Limited. He had 300 subscribers. In 2005, Rogers Cable was the largest cable company in Canada, with over 2.26 million subscribers to basic cable television, home movies, high-definition programs on digital cable, Internet access, and home phone service. Rogers Cable subscribers are based mainly in urban Canada, in southern Ontario, Ottawa, and two Atlantic provinces, Newfoundland and Labrador and New Brunswick.

The reels of cable, the computer equipment, even the cable company's network of buildings across the country, are all known as "capital assets." Rogers Communications financial statements call them property, plant, and equipment or PP&E. In 2005, the company reported $6.2 billion of PP&E.

In the fall of 2005, Rogers Communications and its main rival Bell Canada agreed to create and build a Canada-wide wireless broadband network which will cover 45 cities and approximately 100 unserved rural and underserved communities across Canada by 2008. The joint venture is called Inukshuk Wireless and is expected to cost the pair $200 million over three years to build and operate. Both companies will use their existing cellular phone towers and their wireless networks to give rural customers who have cell phones or laptops access to voice, video streaming, and data on the Internet and provide secure wireless data transmission over spectrum licences. The wireless network radio base stations in Inukshuk Wireless are also considered capital assets.

www.indigo.ca
www.viarail.ca
www.timberwest.com
www.opentext.com

INTRODUCTION

Capital assets are resources that contribute to the earning of revenue over more than one period by helping an entity to produce, supply, support, or make available the goods or services it offers to its customers. Capital assets contribute indirectly to the earning of revenue—indirectly, because selling capital assets is not part of the ordinary activities of the entity (although capital assets are sometimes sold).

For example, Rogers is a capital-intensive business. That means that it must make large investments in capital assets to provide its services to customers. Consider what is needed to provide cable and wireless services. For its cable services, Rogers must install cable that is accessible to all its customers. It must have a sophisticated system for managing and distributing cable signals to customers. Rogers has invested over $13.5 billion in property, plant, and equipment (see Note 5 to Rogers financial statement (Page A-18)), most of which is for its cable and wireless businesses. In addition, Rogers has about $6 billion invested in intangible assets and goodwill. Indeed, over 85 percent of Rogers' total assets are property, plant, and equipment, intangible assets, and goodwill.

Virtually all entities need some investment in capital assets. In the last chapter, we saw that retail businesses have a much smaller proportional investment in capital assets than Rogers does and a much larger investment in inventory. Entities in different industries require different capital assets to operate. Indigo Books & Music Inc.'s capital assets are furniture and fixtures for its stores, the cost of renovating and decorating stores, and computer equipment. Via Rail's capital assets include its trains. TimberWest Forest Corp.'s capital assets include the rights to harvest timber from government land, privately-owned timberland, saw and pulp mills, and logging roads. The capital assets of Open Text Corporation (a software company) include computer equipment and software. In each case, the capital assets are essential if these companies are going to be able to carry on their business. What would Via Rail do if it had no trains or TimberWest Forest if it had no land from which to harvest trees?

Capital assets take many forms. They can be tangible—have physical existence—like land, buildings, equipment, and furniture. They can be intangible, like patents, copyrights, brands, and trademarks. Capital assets can be oil in the ground or trees in a forest. Capital assets can have very long lives—like land, which lasts forever, or buildings, which can last for decades. Or they can have relatively short lives—like computer hardware and software.

Not all of an entity's capital assets appear on its balance sheet. The traditional accounting model sometimes has difficulty with certain types of capital assets. As a result, assets that most people, including accountants, agree would have future benefit to an entity do not appear on the balance sheet. For example, many software and biotechnology companies do not report the software and pharmaceuticals that they develop as capital assets. Some of the aircraft flown by airlines do not appear as assets because they are leased. Many companies' brand names are not recorded. The investments that entities make in their employees rarely appear as assets.

In this chapter, we will take a close look at the accounting for capital assets. We will investigate what amounts are recorded on the balance sheet as capital assets and how these amounts are expensed. We will look at the challenges that contemporary accounting faces with accounting for intangible or "knowledge" assets. And we will evaluate the usefulness of information about capital assets when it is presented on a historical cost basis.

MEASURING CAPITAL ASSETS AND LIMITATIONS TO HISTORICAL COST ACCOUNTING

GAAP require that entities report their capital assets at historical cost. This means that the purchase price of a capital asset, plus any costs incurred to get the asset ready for use, should be **capitalized**—recorded on the balance sheet as an asset. From the date a capital asset is recorded on the balance sheet, the cost of the asset is the basis of its valuation. For example, a piece of land purchased in 1953 for $25,000 would be reported on the 2009 balance sheet at $25,000. It makes no difference that the market value of the land may have increased to $1,000,000 in the years after the purchase—the land would be reported at its cost. As we will see in this chapter, only when a capital asset is impaired is its basis of valuation something other than cost.

One has to wonder about the usefulness of historical cost information about capital assets. How useful is it today to know that land cost $25,000 when it was purchased in 1953? The purpose of historical cost accounting is to match the cost of capital assets to revenue earned over the life of the asset. But for the purpose of making projections or other future-oriented decisions, it is difficult to understand how the historical cost of capital assets—costs that are sometimes very old—can be useful for most uses and to most users of financial statements. While inventory is also reported at cost, in most cases inventory is bought and sold in a relatively short period of time, so historical information and trends can be used as a basis for making projections and future-oriented decisions. In contrast, capital assets can remain in an organization for a long time, which limits the usefulness of the cost of those assets for making projections and future-oriented decisions. (However, the historical cost of capital assets is relevant for tax purposes because the tax treatment of capital assets is based on their cost.)

There are three alternatives to historical cost accounting for capital assets: net realizable value (NRV), replacement cost, and value-in-use. It is important to recognize that each of these alternatives has shortcomings of its own, and none is ideal for all uses. Of course, the usefulness of any method of accounting for capital assets depends on the decisions a particular user has to make. It should also be remembered that historical cost is the "law of the land," so despite its limitations it is necessary to understand and be able to work with the information presented in traditional financial statements.

NRV and replacement cost were discussed in Chapter 8. Here we will look at them from the perspective of capital assets.

NRV is the amount that would be received from the sale of an asset after the selling costs are deducted. For example, it is common for a bank to have a property appraised when a person is buying a home so the bank can have an idea of what the property is worth when it makes its lending decision. NRV is more useful than historical cost in this situation because it gives the lender a current estimate of what would be received if the property had to be sold. Historical cost will likely provide no information about a capital asset's NRV. NRV is less objective and less reliable than historical cost because the amount is an estimate—it is not supported by a transaction. It may be difficult to come up with a reasonable estimate of the NRV of capital assets because many used and even new capital assets are not bought and sold very often. Also, NRV does not tell the lender what the asset could be sold for in the future. It is only an estimate of the current NRV.

Replacement cost is the amount that would have to be spent to replace a capital asset. Replacement cost can take a number of forms. It can be the cost of replacing an existing asset with a new identical one. It can be the cost of replacing an existing asset with an equivalent one—for example, if the existing asset were no longer available, it would be necessary to consider an asset with similar capabilities and features. The replacement cost of an asset can be useful for predicting future cash flows associated with replacing an existing asset. Most capital assets have to be replaced from time to time and the timing and amounts involved in replacing assets can have significant consequences for the cash flow of the entity, as well as implications for a user's evaluation of the performance of the entity and its management. Replacement cost has some of the same problems that were noted with NRV. Replacement cost is less objective than historical cost because there is no transaction supporting the amount. Replacement cost today also doesn't say anything about what the asset will cost to replace in the future, when actual replacement is required.

Another method of valuing capital assets is the value-in-use—the value the asset has for doing what it was purchased to do. **Value-in-use** is the net present value of the cash flow that the asset will generate over its life, or the net present value of the cash flow that the asset would allow the entity to avoid paying. Value-in-use would be useful to investors who are trying to figure out the value of an entity. Conceptually, value-in-use is an attractive method, but practically it has severe limitations. First, individual assets are rarely responsible for generating cash on their own. They interact with other assets to generate cash flows. For example, what is the value-in-use of a computer that contributes to the development of some software? Second, estimating the future cash flows that an asset will generate can be difficult, requiring many assumptions and estimates that can make the value-in-use estimate very unreliable.

Historical cost also has its uses, although not for future-oriented decisions. Historical cost measures can be used for users interested in evaluating historical performance, such as calculating return on investment,. Historical cost information is also of use for the stewardship objective of accounting. As mentioned earlier, historical cost is also appropriate for tax purposes.

Question for Consideration

For each of the following, specify which measurement basis—historical cost, NRV, replacement cost, or value-in-use—is most appropriate for the purpose described. Provide a brief explanation why you chose the measurement basis in each case.

a. Determine the amount of fire insurance needed for a building.

b. Prepare a balance sheet according to GAAP.

c. Determine the value of the assets of an entity going out of business.

d. Evaluate whether the entity should purchase a particular capital asset.

Answer:

Situation	Measurement basis	Explanation
a. Determine the amount of fire insurance needed for a building.	Replacement cost	Fire insurance is intended to allow the insured to replace a building destroyed by fire. Therefore, the replacement cost of a building is the appropriate measurement basis.
b. Prepare a balance sheet according to GAAP.	Historical cost	GAAP require the use of historical cost, transactions-based accounting.
c. Determine the value of the assets of an entity going out of business.	NRV	An entity that is going out of business will likely be looking to sell its assets so that it can satisfy its creditors and/or allow the owners to receive cash from the liquidation of the business. NRV gives the current selling price of assets.
d. Evaluate whether the entity should purchase a particular capital asset.	Value-in-use	The managers should evaluate the present value of the cash flows the asset will generate to assess whether the purchase is desirable. By evaluating the present value of the cash flows, management is measuring the value in use of the asset.

WHAT IS COST?

For better or worse, historical cost is the measurement basis that is used for capital assets in almost all financial statements in Canada. It is therefore necessary to have a good understanding of the workings of historical cost accounting for capital assets as well as the issues and problems surrounding its use.

The cost of an asset that is reported on an entity's balance sheet should include all the costs associated with purchasing the asset and getting it ready for use. This definition casts a fairly broad net around the costs that should be capitalized and includes more than just the purchase price of the asset. Amounts that can be included in this definition of cost are the purchase price of the asset; architectural design and engineering fees; taxes; delivery costs; insurance costs; duties, testing and preparation charges; installation costs; and legal costs—any and all costs incurred to get the asset up and running. Costs incurred by employees of the purchasing entity to get the asset ready for use, including their wages, should also be capitalized. Only necessary costs should be capitalized. Costs that are not related to the acquisition—such as repairs or unnecessary work caused by poor planning, etc.—should not be capitalized.

Interest can be capitalized up until an asset is ready for use. Once an asset is ready for use, interest incurred is expensed. Capitalizing interest is most common when an entity is constructing an asset itself. For example, if an entity is using its own personnel to build an extension to its warehouse, the interest incurred to finance the extension can be capitalized up until the time the extension is complete and ready for use.

Sometimes it is difficult to determine whether certain costs should be capitalized and judgment must be exercised in deciding how to treat those costs. This need for judgment introduces the possibility that different managers will account for similar costs differently. For example, it may be difficult to determine the amount of employees' wages that should be capitalized as part of the cost of preparing an asset for use. Of course, any time ambiguity exists, the choices made by managers may be influenced by their self-interests. For example, if an entity has tax minimization as its main objective, it may expense as much and as many of the costs incurred to acquire the asset as it reasonably can. On the other hand, if the entity prefers to maximize current income, then it will capitalize as much as it can to defer expensing the costs. The WorldCom scandal is an extreme example of a company that tried to maximize its income by capitalizing most of the costs it incurred.

Let's look at an example. Aillik Corp. (Aillik) purchases a new machine for $700,000 plus $45,000 in taxes. Aillik pays $5,000 to have the machine delivered and $50,000 to have it installed and tested. Legal fees associated with the contract with the seller of the machine are $10,000. According to GAAP, all of these costs should be capitalized as part of the cost of the machine. The journal entry to record the purchase of the machine would be:

Dr. Machine (asset +)	810,000	
Cr. Accounts payable—machine manufacturer (liability +)		700,000
Cr. Taxes payable (liability +)		45,000
Cr. Accounts payable—delivery (liability +)		5,000
Cr. Accounts payable—installation (liability +)		50,000
Cr. Accounts payable—legal fees (liability +)		10,000
To record the purchase of a machine.		

The $810,000 cost of the machine would be recorded as a capital asset on the balance sheet and the cost would be amortized over its expected useful life.

However, suppose that instead of using outsiders to deliver and install the new machine, Aillik used its own personnel and equipment. If the wages Aillik paid to deliver and install the machine were $25,000, it could make the following journal entry:

Dr. Machine (asset +)	780,000	
Cr. Accounts payable—machine manufacturer (liability +)		700,000
Cr. Taxes payable (liability +)		45,000
Cr. Wages payable (liability +)		25,000
Cr. Accounts payable—legal fees (liability +)		10,000
To record the purchase of a machine.		

Or if it was too difficult or troublesome to identify the costs of these internally provided services, and if Aillik had tax minimization as it main objective, it might make this journal entry:

Dr. Machine (asset +)	755,000	
Dr. Wage expense (expense +, shareholders' equity −)	25,000	
Cr. Accounts payable—machine manufacturer (liability +)		700,000
Cr. Taxes payable (liability +)		45,000
Cr. Wages payable (liability +)		25,000
Cr. Accounts payable—legal fees (liability +)		10,000
To record the purchase of a machine.		

In this case, only $755,000 is capitalized, and the $25,000 that is paid to Aillik's employees is expensed. There is nothing inherently inappropriate about this accounting treatment. Aillik may not have been able to determine the cost of the employees' work to deliver and install the machine.

Or the company may have felt that because the employees would have been paid regardless of whether the machine was acquired, it was not appropriate to capitalize the cost.

This example again highlights the fact that different possible accounting treatments exist for similar transactions. The motivation for different treatments may be the result of several factors:

a. The cost of gathering the information may not be worth the benefit,

b. There may be different, legitimate interpretations of GAAP,

c. There may be different objectives of accounting at play, or

d. A combination of all three factors.

So what theoretically should be capitalized under GAAP, and what is capitalized in fact, may depend on a number of factors, including the reporting objectives of the entity. That's why it is important not to take for granted how an entity has accounted for a transaction. It is important to find out the accounting choices an entity has made if the information is relevant to a decision.

Sometimes expenditures are made that improve an existing capital asset. These types of investments are called betterments. A **betterment** makes a capital asset more valuable to the entity, perhaps by increasing the asset's useful life, or by improving its efficiency or effectiveness. In other words, the betterment stands to make the entity more profitable. Because betterments provide future benefits, the cost is capitalized and amortized over the remaining life of the asset.

In contrast, expenditures that allow an asset to operate as intended—to do what it is designed to do—are considered **repairs** or **maintenance** and should be expensed when incurred. Changing a car's oil regularly does not make the car better—it allows it to operate as intended by the manufacturer. The same goes for brakes. Car brakes wear out from time to time and have to be replaced. Replacing worn brakes does not improve the car; it simply makes the car drivable. On the other hand, the cost of rebuilding an engine so that it is more powerful and efficient should be capitalized. A more powerful, efficient engine might allow the vehicle to do more work (carry heavier loads) and use less fuel, both of which are beneficial to the entity.

While some expenditures can easily be classified as betterments or maintenance, the treatment is not always obvious. As a result, managers' choices may be motivated by their reporting objectives. When tax minimization is the primary objective, managers would expense as much of the expenditures as they could reasonably justify because the accounting treatment might make expensing those outlays for tax purposes more justifiable. If management is more concerned with the bottom line, it would be inclined to capitalize as much of the outlays as possible. The financial statement effect of treating an expenditure as a betterment is that the cost of the betterment is capitalized and amortized over the remaining life of the asset. Treating an expenditure as a repair or maintenance increases expenses and reduces income by the full amount of the expenditure in the period in which it is incurred. In general, it can be assumed that expenditures made on existing capital assets are much more likely to be repairs or maintenance than betterments.

Question for Consideration

Meadow Inc. (Meadow) recently acquired a new computer server for its head-office network. The server had a list price of $50,000, but the head of the computing department was able to negotiate a price of $46,900. Taxes added $7,035 to the price and delivery cost $2,000. Replacement of the cables in the offices to meet the needs of the new server cost $8,000. A planning error by Meadow's management made it necessary for most of the cabling work to be redone, which cost an additional $2,100. Installation of the server cost $3,000, but once it was installed, management realized that the site for the server was inappropriate because the ventilation was not adequate. Moving and reinstalling the server cost an additional $2,600. Meadow purchased a three-year insurance policy for the server for $3,600.

Calculate the amount that should be capitalized for the purchase of the new server. Also, indicate which cost items should not be included in the capitalized amount. Explain your reasoning.

(continued)

Solution:

Cost	Amount Capitalized	Explanation
Purchase price	$46,900	The only price that is relevant is the amount actually paid. The list price does not matter.
Taxes	7,035	Taxes are a part of the cost of the server.
Delivery	2,000	Delivery costs are necessary to get the server ready for use. The server must be delivered to be useful.
Cabling	8,000	Cabling costs are necessary to get the server ready for use. The server cannot do its job without adequate cabling.
Cabling required due to error	Not capitalized	The additional costs were incurred due to a mistake. These costs were not required to get the server ready for use and do not add anything to the value of the server. These costs should be expensed when incurred.
Installation	3,000	Installation costs are necessary to get the server ready for use. It cannot serve its purpose if it is not installed.
Reinstallation	Not capitalized	Reinstallation was required because of poor planning. The cost incurred was not necessary and does not make the server more valuable to the entity.
Insurance	Not capitalized	Insurance is not a cost required to get the server ready for use. It is a cost incurred to provide insurance protection for the server when it is operating. The insurance should be recorded as a prepaid asset and expensed as it is used.
Total amount to be capitalized for acquisition of the server	$66,935	

Basket Purchases

Sometimes an entity will purchase a "basket," or bundle of assets, at a single price. The price of individual assets will not be stated anywhere. Basket purchases raise the problem of how to allocate the cost of the whole basket to each of the assets in the bundle. Good accounting requires that the purchase price be allocated in proportion to the market values of the assets in the bundle. The allocation is important because the different assets in the bundle may be accounted for differently, and different allocations will result in different financial statement effects (as we will see below).

For example, suppose that Pockwock Ltd. (Pockwock) purchases land and a building for $25,000,000. If the land were worth 40 percent of the total cost and the building 60 percent, the journal entry would be

Dr. Land (asset +)	10,000,000	
Dr. Building (asset +)	15,000,000	
Cr. Cash (asset −)		25,000,000

To record the basket purchase of land and building.

In practice, the problem is knowing exactly what the market values of the land and building are as separate assets. Consequently, as long as the amount assigned to each asset is reasonable, managers have the flexibility to make the allocation in a way that suits their reporting objectives. If the manager's main concern were minimizing taxes, it would be preferable to allocate more of the cost to the building because buildings can be deducted for tax purposes whereas land cannot. By allocating more of the cost to the building, the company will have more to deduct to reduce taxes. If management were more concerned about increasing net income, it could allocate more of the cost of the basket to land, which is not amortized.

If Pockwock obtained independent appraisals that estimated the value of the land at between $9,000,000 and $12,000,000, it could justifiably assign any amount between those two values to the land. If Pockwock's reporting objective were tax minimization, it would allocate $9,000,000 of the purchase price to land and $16,000,000 to the building. This treatment would maximize the amount of expenses available for tax purposes, thereby permanently reducing the amount of tax Pockwock would have to pay. The downside of this choice would be that it would result in lower net income as well as lower taxes. If, instead, management wanted to minimize the effect of the purchase on income, it would allocate $12,000,000 to the cost of the land and $13,000,000 to building. This treatment would minimize the amount that would have to be amortized.

Remember, the choice being made here is not strictly arbitrary—it is not pure self-interest by the managers. The amounts in both cases can be justified because they fall within the ranges of the independent appraisals. A reader might be suspicious of any choice management makes in circumstances such as these, but it is important to remember that it is usually not possible to know exactly what the "truth" is. The actual market value of the land and building individually are just not known and cannot be known unless they are sold separately. The portion of cost that is assigned to each asset is an informed estimate.

AMORTIZATION

Most capital assets get used up. A truck, a machine, a building, a mine, even an idea don't last forever. The truck eventually breaks down and can deliver no more merchandise. The machine is no longer able to produce goods effectively and has to be replaced by technologically up-to-date equipment. The building no longer meets the needs of the entity. The resource in the mine is exhausted and the patent for the idea expires. Because capital assets get used up while helping to earn revenue, it makes sense that under historical cost accrual accounting the cost of the capital assets should somehow be matched to the revenues they help earn. Expensing the cost of a capital asset is no different conceptually from expensing the cost of inventory when it is sold or salaries when the work is done. It is an application of the matching concept. The hard part about expensing the cost of a capital asset is figuring out a way of doing it. Because capital assets contribute to the earning of revenue indirectly and over more than one period, it is necessary to have a way of allocating the cost to each of the periods that the asset contributes to earning revenue.

The process of allocating the cost of a capital asset to expense over time to reflect the consumption of the asset while it helps to earn revenue is known as **amortization**. There are also specific terms used for the amortization of different types of capital assets. **Depreciation** is usually used to describe the amortization of the cost of tangible assets. **Tangible assets** are capital assets that have physical substance, such as buildings, equipment, vehicles, and furniture. The term *amortization* is also used specifically to refer to the amortization of intangible assets. **Intangible assets** are capital assets that do not have physical substance, such as patents, copyrights, trademarks, and brand names. A third term—**depletion**—is used to describe the amortization of the cost of natural resources. Note that amortization is the more general term, encompassing depreciation and depletion. The types of capital assets and the associated terms used to describe the amortization of those capital assets are summarized in Figure 9–1.

As mentioned earlier, the hard part about expensing the cost of a capital asset is figuring out a way of doing it. Authoritative sources provide very little specific guidance about how to amortize capital assets. According to the *CICA Handbook,* the cost of an asset less its **residual value** (the amount the asset can be sold for at the end of its useful life) should be amortized over its useful life in a "systematic and rational" manner. There are several difficulties: What is a systematic and rational way of amortizing the cost? What is the useful life? What is the residual value?

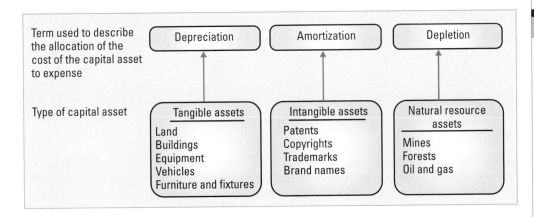

These difficulties do not have definitive solutions. Managers must use their knowledge and judgment in resolving these difficulties, and users must recognize that there is considerable scope for different reasonable decisions. For example, could anyone strongly argue with the assumption that the useful life of a car is three years or five years or seven years? An asset does not come with a tag advising owners how long the asset will last and how much it will be worth when it is sold. The useful life, residual value, and the contribution an asset makes to revenue depend on how the asset is used, what it is used for, and how it is cared for. As long as the estimates are reasonable, any choice is likely acceptable.

We will now look at different methods for amortizing capital assets. First, let's consider the conceptual reasoning behind amortization.

There are two main reasons that explain why capital assets are amortized: physical use and obsolescence. Physical use refers to the effects that the passage of time, wear and tear, and exposure to the elements have on the ability of a capital asset to make a contribution to earning revenue. The effectiveness and efficiency of a machine decreases with use. As the machine gets older and is used a lot, it may break down more often, use more energy to operate, and produce less and lower-quality output. Eventually, the machine is not worth operating and must be replaced.

Assets become obsolete because of changes in technology as well as shifts in the business environment. Computers are an excellent example. Most computers purchased three or more years ago can probably still do now what they did when they were purchased. However, often advances in technology have rendered those computers obsolete. These computers may be inadequate because they are too slow, don't have enough memory or multi-media capabilities, or are unable to handle some software applications. They have less to contribute to the moneymaking activities of the business than state-of-the-art equipment.

Consider your wardrobe as an analogy. Clothes wear out because they are used: they fade, they tear, and they pill. However, you may own an article of clothing that is in excellent condition but that you never wear because the style, colour, or pattern is no longer considered fashionable. That article of clothing has become obsolete.

Not all assets are amortized. Land is usually not amortized because it does not wear out and does not become obsolete. The buildings that are constructed on a piece of land may come and go, but the land on which the buildings were constructed will always be there to receive the next construction project. An exception to this treatment is land that is used for extracting natural resources. In that case, the cost of the land is expensed as the resource is taken from the land. In the case of a mine, the land is "used up" as the resource is removed. Intangible assets are not amortized when there are no factors that limit their useful lives. For example, the cost of Rogers' spectrum licences (which provide the right to use airwaves for wireless communications) is not amortized. Goodwill is also not amortized.

Amortization and Market Values

According to GAAP, the purpose of amortization is to allocate the cost of an asset to expense in a "rational and systematic manner." Amortization is not intended to reflect the change in a capital asset's market value. The net book value (NBV) of the asset (cost less amortization to date) is not intended to be an estimate of its market value. New accounting students are tempted to think that the NBV of a capital asset is an estimate of market value. Resist the temptation.

Amortization Methods

Now let's look at how capital assets are amortized. There are several methods that are generally accepted in Canada as systematic and rational. These methods can be grouped into three major categories:

1. straight-line
2. accelerated
3. usage-based

Each method allocates the cost of a capital asset to expense in a different pattern and, as a result, each will provide a different net income in each year over the asset's life and different NBVs.

We will discuss each method. For this discussion, we will use an example of a capital asset with a cost of $1,200,000, residual value of $200,000, and useful life of ten years. Figure 9–2 shows plots of the annual amortization expense over the useful life of the asset under each of the four methods (Panel A) and shows how the NBV of the asset declines under each method (Panel B). Refer to Figure 9–2 when you study the discussion of each amortization method.

When you study the different amortization methods, remember that they all result in the same amount of amortization over the life of the asset. Only the timing of the expense is affected. Also, while these choices do not affect cash flow, they can affect outcomes that are based on financial statement numbers, such as management bonuses and debt covenants.

Now let's look at the example. When the asset is purchased, the following journal entry is made:

Dr. Capital Assets—equipment (assets +)	1,200,000	
Cr. Cash (assets –) or Liability (liability +)		1,200,000
To record the purchase of a capital asset.		

Under any amortization method, the form of the journal entry that will be made each period to record the amortization expense is:

Dr. Amortization expense (expense +, owners' equity –)	xxx	
Cr. Accumulated amortization (contra-asset +)		xxx
To record the amortization expense and the increase in the accumulated amortization account for the year.		

FIGURE 9–2

Annual Amortization Expense Example

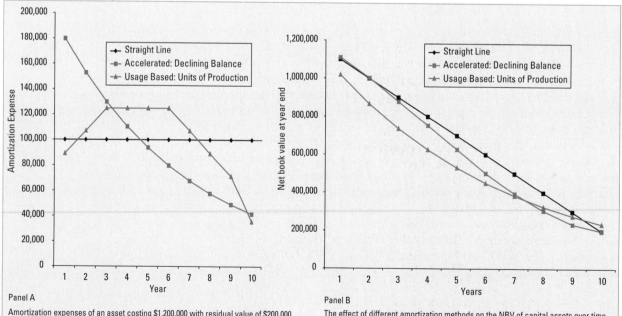

Panel A

Amortization expenses of an asset costing $1,200,000 with residual value of $200,000 and estimated useful life of ten years. The amount that is amortized in any year differs widely depending on the method. The straight-line method has equal amortization in each year, declining balance has decreasing amounts over time, decelerated methods have an increasing amortization pattern, and the units of production method depends on the amount of production in each year.

Panel B

The effect of different amortization methods on the NBV of capital assets over time. All methods approach the residual value of the asset at the end of the asset's life, but the NBV of the asset at any time during its life will differ.

The amortization expense is the portion of the cost of the capital asset that is being matched to revenues earned during the period. The credit entry represents the portion of the capital asset that was consumed during the period, so the credit acts to reduce assets on the balance sheet. Notice that the credit is made to a contra-asset account, not to the capital asset account itself. Recall from Chapter 3 that a contra-asset account is used to accumulate reductions in the related asset account. That means that the capital asset itself remains in the capital asset account at full cost while amortization accumulates in the contra-asset account. To obtain the NBV of a capital asset, the cost recorded in the capital asset account must be considered together with the credit balance in the contra-asset account.

Finally, before we examine the different methods, Figure 9–3 shows the relative use of each of the amortization methods in Canada, as reported in *Financial Reporting in Canada 2004*, 30th Edition.[1] Figure 9–3 shows that straight-line amortization is by far the most commonly used method by public companies in Canada.

Straight-Line Amortization With **straight-line amortization**, the amortization expense is the same in each period. This method is straightforward and simple to use, which makes it appealing. The method implies that the contribution that the capital asset makes to revenue generation is the same each period. This assumption is probably not entirely valid because the capability of most assets declines with time, repairs and maintenance increase with time, and sales tend to vary over time. However, since it can be so difficult to reasonably estimate the contribution an asset makes in each period, this approach is reasonable (or as reasonable as any other). The equation for calculating amortization using the straight-line method is:

$$\text{Amortization Expense} = \frac{\text{Cost} - \text{Estimated residual value}}{\text{Estimated useful life}}$$

For our asset costing $1,200,000, with an estimated residual value of $200,000 and estimated useful life of 10 years, the annual amortization expense is $100,000.

$$\text{Amortization Expense} = \frac{\$1,200,000 - \$200,000}{10 \text{ years}}$$
$$= \$100,000 \text{ per year}$$

Figure 9–4 shows the amortization schedule for the life of the asset.

The annual amortization expense will change if different estimates of the asset's useful life and residual value are made. If we estimated the useful life to be 12 years and the residual value to be $300,000, the annual amortization expense becomes $75,000. If everything else stays the same, these changes will result in net income being $25,000 higher in each of the first ten years than with our original estimates. These changes have no direct economic impact on the entity, but they may affect the outcome of contracts that are based on net income and other financial statement measures. From a user's standpoint, this example shows that the estimates made by management can affect numbers that may influence perceptions of the entity and possibly decisions that a user makes. As we will discuss in the appendix to this chapter, the choice of amortization method has no tax implications.

Accelerated Amortization **Accelerated amortization** methods allocate more of the cost of a capital asset to expense in the early years of its life and less in the later years. When an asset's

	Number of Firms	**Percentage***
Straight-line	185	93%
Accelerated: Declining Balance	47	24%
Usage-Based: Unit-of-production	52	26%
Other	8	4%

*Results are from 2004 annual reports. Percentages are greater than 100% because some firms use more than one amortization method.

FIGURE 9–3

Relative Use in Canada of Each of the Four Amortization Methods for Property, plant, and Equipment

FIGURE 9–4 ::

Amortization
Schedule Using
Straight-Line
Amortization

		Balance Sheet		Income statement
Year	Cost	Accumulated amortization on December 31	NBV on December 31 (cost – accumulated amortization)	Amortization expense for the year ended December 31
1	$1,200,000	$100,000	$1,100,000	$100,000
2	1,200,000	200,000	1,000,000	100,000
3	1,200,000	300,000	900,000	100,000
4	1,200,000	400,000	800,000	100,000
5	1,200,000	500,000	700,000	100,000
6	1,200,000	600,000	600,000	100,000
7	1,200,000	700,000	500,000	100,000
8	1,200,000	800,000	400,000	100,000
9	1,200,000	900,000	300,000	100,000
10	1,200,000	1,000,000	200,000	100,000
Total				$1,000,000

contribution to the revenue-generating ability of the entity is greater in the early part of its life, an accelerated method of amortization makes sense. Accelerated amortization would be appropriate for assets that are sensitive to obsolescence, such as computers, and assets that clearly lose efficiency and/or effectiveness with the passage of time, producing less or lower quality output. Look at Figure 9–2 to see the pattern of accelerated amortization in graphic form.

The most common accelerated amortization method used in Canada is the **declining balance** method. This method applies an amortization rate to the NBV of the asset at the beginning of the year to calculate the amortization expense. That is,

> Amortization Expense = (Cost − Accumulated amortization) × Rate
> = NBV at the beginning of the period × Rate

Because a fixed rate is being applied to a declining balance, an asset is never amortized to zero. This is one of the reasons why the residual value is usually ignored with this method.

The amortization schedule for our $1,200,000 asset is shown in Figure 9–5. The rate that is being applied to this asset is 15 percent. The amortization expense in the first year is $180,000 ($1,200,000 × 0.15). In the second year the amortization expense is $153,000 ([$1,200,000 − $180,000] × 0.15). You can see how the amortization expense is lower than the year before. You can also see that at the end of Year 10 only $963,751 of the cost has been amortized. If the residual value is estimated to be $200,000 in Year 10, the remaining $36,249 would then be expensed, assuming that the estimate of a ten-year useful life still applies.

For managers who are concerned about the level of income of their company, accelerated amortization is less attractive than straight-line because the amortization expense is larger in the first years of an asset's life, which makes net income lower. Of course, straight-line eventually catches up, so in later years, when the accelerated amortization expense is lower than straight-line amortization, net income will be higher with accelerated amortization. The effect, where the accelerated amortization expense eventually becomes less than the straight-line expense, can be seen in the plots in Figure 9–2, Panel A. While this pattern applies to single assets, if an entity is growing and continually purchasing and replacing capital assets, the amortization expense using straight-line will almost always be lower than with declining balance. If an entity is not growing, declining balance eventually produces lower amortization expenses.

There are other accelerated amortization methods, but these methods are rarely used in Canada and will not be discussed further.

FIGURE 9–5 ::

Amortization
Schedule Using
Accelerated
Amortization

	Balance Sheet				Income statement
Year	Cost	Accumulated amortization December 31	NBV on December 31	Amortization rate	Amortization expense for the year ended December 31
1	$1,200,000	$180,000	$1,020,000	15%	$180,000
2	1,200,000	333,000	867,000	15%	153,000
3	1,200,000	463,050	736,950	15%	130,050
4	1,200,000	573,593	626,408	15%	110,543
5	1,200,000	667,554	532,446	15%	93,961
6	1,200,000	747,421	452,579	15%	79,867
7	1,200,000	815,307	384,693	15%	67,887
8	1,200,000	873,011	326,989	15%	57,704
9	1,200,000	922,060	277,940	15%	49,048
10	1,200,000	963,751	236,249	15%	41,691
Total					$963,751

Usage-Based Amortization: Unit-of-Production If the consumption of an asset can be readily associated with its use and not to the passage of time or obsolescence, then an amortization method based on the actual use of the asset can be employed. One of the more common usage-based methods is unit-of-production. To use unit-of-production, the manager must be able to estimate the number of units that the asset will produce over its life. The amortization expense in a year is the proportion of units produced in the year to total estimated number of units to be produced over the asset's life. In our example, if the estimated production of the asset over its useful life is 280,000 units and 25,000 are produced in the first year, the amortization expense in the first year would be:

$$\text{Amortization Expense} = \frac{\text{Number of units produced in the period}}{\text{Estimated number of units produced over the asset's life}} \times (\text{Cost} - \text{Estimated residual value})$$

$$= \frac{25,000 \text{ units}}{280,000 \text{ units}} \times (\$1,200,000 - \$200,000)$$

$$= \$89,286$$

The amortization schedule using this method is shown in Figure 9–6. Note that it is assumed that the actual production over the asset's life equals the estimated production. In practice, this assumption will often not be true.

Other measures of assets' use are also available. For example, the number of kilometres a delivery truck travels and the number of hours equipment is used are possible measures of use.

There are a number of difficulties with applying an amortization method that is based on actual use:

■ First, it can be difficult to make a reasonable estimate of the production or usage of an asset. Is it possible to make a reasonable, justifiable estimate of the number of kilometres a vehicle will travel, the number of units a machine will produce, or the number of hours equipment will function over their useful lives? For most assets, the answer is probably no. But the estimate is crucial for determining the amount of amortization that will be expensed in a period. For example, estimating that a truck will travel 200,000 kilometres rather than 150,000 will have a significant effect on the amortization expense.

	Balance Sheet			Percentage of total		Income Statement
Year	Cost	Accumulated amortization	NBV	production in year	Production	Amortization expense
1	$1,200,000	$ 89,286	$1,110,714	0.089	25,000	$ 89,286
2	1,200,000	196,429	1,003,571	0.107	30,000	107,143
3	1,200,000	321,429	878,571	0.125	35,000	125,000
4	1,200,000	446,429	753,571	0.125	35,000	125,000
5	1,200,000	571,429	628,571	0.125	35,000	125,000
6	1,200,000	696,429	503,571	0.125	35,000	125,000
7	1,200,000	803,572	396,428	0.107	30,000	107,143
8	1,200,000	892,858	307,142	0.089	25,000	89,286
9	1,200,000	964,287	235,713	0.071	20,000	71,429
10	1,200,000	1,000,000	200,000	0.036	10,000	35,713
Total				1.000	280,000	$1,000,000

FIGURE 9–6

Amortization Schedule Using Unit-of-Production Amortization

■ Second, the usage-based amortization method is not appropriate for many types of assets. For example, buildings or office equipment do not lend themselves well to this method as there is no obvious unit of measurement that could be applied. Could we measure the use of a chair by the number times it is sat on?

■ Third, unit-of-production allocates an equal amount of amortization per unit, but the revenue per unit may vary over time. In that case the amortization expense is not a constant proportion of revenue, which will affect ratios such as operating margin and return on investment.

An attractive aspect of usage-based amortization methods, if reasonable measures of usage can be made, is that they result in good matching. With usage-based methods, there is a direct association between the amount of amortization and the consumption of the asset. Unfortunately, the difficulties described above limit the usefulness of the methods.

However, Figure 9–3 shows that the unit-of-production method is used quite widely in Canada, by 26 percent of the firms in the survey. One of the main reasons for its fairly high use is that it is popular in natural resources industries such as mining, oil and gas, and forestry. In these industries, it is possible to estimate the amount of the resource that is available. The estimated amount of the resource is used as the basis for amortizing the costs of discovering and developing the mine, oil and gas reserve, or forest (costs such as the purchase of the land or rights to the land, the cost of finding the resource, and the cost of developing it.)

Exhibit 9–1 provides a note to the financial statements of Aur Resources Inc. (Aur), which uses the unit-of-production amortization method.[2] Aur is a Canadian copper mining company. The note explains how the company accounts for its mineral exploration costs and how it amortizes its capital assets. Aur uses unit-of-production amortization for some of its plant and equipment, certain development costs, and some of its financing costs. Other capital assets are amortized using the straight-line method.

www.aurresources.com

Comparing Methods

Let's now look at an example of how different amortization methods affect a company's financial statements.

In 2009, Vermilion Corp. (Vermilion) began operations and purchased capital assets for $1,000,000. Vermilion estimated that the assets would have no residual value and that their useful lives would be four years, after which Vermilion would terminate operations. Table 9–1 (page 468) shows summarized income statements, year-end capital assets, and total assets for years 2009 through 2012 using three different amortization methods: straight-line, declining balance (40 percent per year), and unit-of-production.

Vermilion's revenues and expenses, other than the amortization expense, are identical regardless of the method of amortization. The tax expense is based on the actual rules stated in the *Income Tax Act (ITA)* and is the same under all three methods. In the fourth year, the unamortized portion of

EXHIBIT 9–1

Aur Resources
Inc.: Example of
the Unit-of-
Production
Amortization
Method

Notes to Consolidated Financial Statements

For the years ended December 31, 2005 and 2004 (in thousands of United States dollars except where otherwise noted)

1. **Accounting policies**

   (g) Property, plant and equipment

   i) Mineral property and exploration costs
   Mineral property and exploration expenditures are charged to earnings when incurred except for certain expenditures on specified properties identified through pre-feasibility or other assessments as having mineral reserves and/or resources with the potential of being developed into a mine, and/or have the characteristics of property, plant and equipment, in which case the expenditures are capitalized and are not amortized until commercial production is achieved. These costs are transferred to development costs once the development of the mine commences.

   ii) Plant and equipment
   Plant and equipment are recorded at cost and are amortized once commercial production is achieved, using the units-of-production method based on the estimated life of the mine. Other equipment with useful lives less than the estimated life of the mine are depreciated using the straight-line method over 3 to 8 years, but not to exceed the estimated life of the mine.

   iii) Development costs
   Development costs incurred to bring a mining property into production, expand the capacity of an operating mine, develop new orebodies or develop mine areas substantially in advance of current production are capitalized and charged to operations using the units-of-production method based on the estimated life of the mine. Amounts shown as development costs are net of metal recoveries prior to commercial production.

   iv) Mining equipment under capital lease
   Leases that transfer substantially all of the benefits and risks of ownership of property to Aur are accounted for as capital leases. At the time a capital lease is entered into, an asset is recorded together with the related long-term obligation. Mining equipment acquired under capital lease is amortized using the straight-line method over the estimated life of the leased asset, but not to exceed the life of the mine. Lease payments under operating leases are charged to earnings as incurred.

   v) Corporate
   Corporate fixed assets are recorded at cost and are depreciated using the straight-line method based on the estimated useful life of the asset. The estimated useful life for buildings is 20 years and for corporate equipment is 3 to 5 years.

the capital assets under the declining balance method is fully expensed so that the NBV of the capital assets is zero at the end of the fourth year, the assumed residual value. That's why the amortization expense in the fourth year with the declining balance method is larger than in the third year with the declining balance method. For the unit-of-production method, it is assumed that the number of units produced equals the number of units sold in each year. In the example, there were 30,000 units produced and sold in 2009, 45,000 in 2010, 60,000 in 2011, and 35,000 in 2012.

Notice the significant effect that the amortization method has on Vermilion's net income, net capital assets, and total assets. In 2009, for example, net income ranges from a loss of $63,500 to a profit of $160,029. What does this tell a user? Is Vermilion profitable or is it losing money? Is Vermilion doing well, as might be suggested by the $160,029 profit, or poorly, as indicated by the loss? These questions are not easy to answer because while the numbers are quite different in each of the income statements, the underlying economic position of Vermilion is the same. Accounting choices affect the appearance of the statements, but not the economic reality. And even if we had more information about Vermilion's assets, it would not be possible to definitively conclude that a particular amortization method was superior to the others. The fact is, there is no way of knowing which amortization method is "right" and which measure of net income is "best."

Does this mean that accounting choice doesn't matter? No. It can matter very much. Whether it matters depends on who is using the financial statements, how the statements are being used, and for what reason they are being used. It is unlikely that any but the most unsophisticated users of financial statements would be misled by a company's amortization policy. Research shows that reporting a higher income by changing amortization methods does not result in a higher stock price. However, if a contract depends on the numbers in the financial statements, then the amortization method could make a difference.

While income in individual years differs under the three amortization methods, notice that total net income for the four years is the same for all the methods (see Panel E of Table 9–1). The cumulative income statements highlight the fact that the different accounting choices affect the timing of revenues and expenses, but not the totals.

So how does a manager decide which method to use? Practically, no amortization method can be justified over all others because in almost all cases it is impossible to know how a capital asset contributes to earning revenue. Indeed, some people have argued that the choice of amortization method is arbitrary—one method of amortization cannot be proven to be superior to any other. It can also be difficult to estimate the useful life of an asset or its residual value with any precision. As long as an estimate is reasonable under the circumstances, it is acceptable. As a result, managers

TABLE 9-1 ⠇ **Vermilion Corp.: Summarized Financial Statement Information Using Three Different Amortization Methods**

Panel A

Vermilion Corp.
2009

	Straight-Line	40% Declining Balance	Unit-of-production
Revenue	$ 800,000	$ 800,000	$ 800,000
Expenses	425,000	425,000	425,000
Amort. Exp.	250,000	400,000	176,471
Operating Inc.	125,000	(25,000)	198,529
Taxes	38,500	38,500	38,500
Net Income	$ 86,500	$ (63,500)	$ 160,029
Capital assets (at cost)	$1,000,000	$1,000,000	$1,000,000
Accum. amort.	(250,000)	(400,000)	(176,471)
Capital Assets (net)	$ 750,000	$ 600,000	$ 823,529
Total Assets	$1,586,500	$1,436,500	$1,660,029

Panel D

Vermilion Corp.
2012

	Straight-Line	40% Declining Balance	Unit-of-production
Revenue	$ 700,000	$ 700,000	$ 700,000
Expenses	371,875	371,875	371,875
Amort. Exp.	250,000	216,000	205,882
Operating Inc.	78,125	112,125	122,243
Taxes	8,828	8,828	8,828
Net Income	$ 69,297	$ 103,297	$ 113,415
Capital Assets (at cost)	$1,000,000	$1,000,000	$1,000,000
Accum. amort.	(1,000,000)	(1,000,000)	(1,000,000)
Capital Assets (net)	$ 0	$ 0	$ 0
Total Assets	$1,838,107	$1,838,107	$1,838,107

Panel B

Vermilion Corp.
2010

	Straight-Line	40% Declining Balance	Unit-of-production
Revenue	$ 900,000	$ 900,000	$ 900,000
Expenses	478,125	478,125	478,125
Amort. Exp.	250,000	240,000	264,706
Operating Inc.	171,875	181,875	157,169
Taxes	105,222	105,222	105,222
Net Income	$ 66,653	$ 76,653	$ 51,947
Capital assets (at cost)	$1,000,000	$1,000,000	$1,000,000
Accum. amort.	(500,000)	(640,000)	(441,177)
Capital Assets (net)	$ 500,000	$ 360,000	$ 558,823
Total Assets	$1,653,153	$1,513,153	$1,711,976

Panel E

Vermilion Corp.
2007–2012

	Straight-Line	40% Declining Balance	Unit-of-production
Revenue	$3,400,000	$3,400,000	$3,400,000
Expenses	1,806,250	1,806,250	1,806,250
Amort. Exp.	1,000,000	1,000,000	1,000,000
Operating Inc.	593,750	593,750	593,750
Taxes	255,643	255,643	255,643
Net Income	$ 338,107	$ 338,107	$ 338,107
Capital Assets (at cost)	$1,000,000	$1,000,000	$1,000,000
Accum. amort.	(1,000,000)	(1,000,000)	(1,000,000)
Capital Assets (net)	$ 0	$ 0	$ 0
Total Assets	$1,838,107	$1,838,107	$1,838,107

Panel C

Vermilion Corp.
2011

	Straight-Line	40% Declining Balance	Unit-of-production
Revenue	$1,000,000	$1,000,000	$1,000,000
Expenses	531,250	531,250	531,250
Amort. Exp.	250,000	144,000	352,941
Operating Inc.	218,750	324,750	115,809
Taxes	103,093	103,093	103,093
Net Income	$ 115,657	$ 221,657	$ 12,716
Capital assets (at cost)	$1,000,000	$1,000,000	$1,000,000
Accum. amort.	(750,000)	(784,000)	(794,118)
Capital Assets (net)	$ 250,000	$ 216,000	$ 205,882
Total Assets	$1,768,810	$1,734,810	$1,724,692

have considerable leeway in choosing the amortization methods, useful lives, and residual values for their entity's capital assets. The managers' decision can be influenced by their knowledge of how the assets in question are actually used, by what is used by other firms in the industry, by the information needs of users, and by the interests of the managers themselves.

In the case of Vermilion Corp., if the managers had a bonus plan based on net income, they might prefer unit-of-production because their bonus would be higher in the first year. For appearances, perhaps if loans were required, managers might be reluctant to use the declining balance method because of the loss it produces in the first year. The managers may believe that lenders may be less willing to invest in an unprofitable entity. For tax purposes, none of these methods is appropriate because the ITA specifies how amortization must be calculated for tax purposes (as will be discussed in the appendix to this chapter).

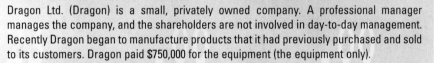

Knowledge Check

Dragon Ltd. (Dragon) is a small, privately owned company. A professional manager manages the company, and the shareholders are not involved in day-to-day management. Recently Dragon began to manufacture products that it had previously purchased and sold to its customers. Dragon paid $750,000 for the equipment (the equipment only).

■ What decisions must Dragon's manager make regarding the accounting for the new equipment before she can calculate the amortization expense for the current year?

■ Using the following assumptions, calculate the amortization expense for each year and the ending balance in the accumulated amortization expense using the straight-line, declining balance, and unit-of-production amortization methods. For declining balance, use a rate of 50 percent.

   i.   The cost of buying and getting the equipment operating was $800,000 ($750,000 cost + $50,000 in delivery, set-up, and ancillary costs).

   ii. The residual value of the equipment is estimated to be $80,000.

   iii. The useful life of the equipment is three years.

   iv. The equipment will produce 20,000 units in the first year, 32,000 in the second year, and 28,000 units in the third year.

■ Prepare the journal entries that would be required for each of the three years for the straight-line method.

www.mcgrawhill.ca/olc/friedlan

Summary

In summary, there are a number of amortization issues to be aware of:

1. There are a number of different, acceptable methods of amortizing capital assets, with little restriction on which can be used. None of the methods stand out clearly as the best.

2. Because it is difficult to estimate the useful life or the residual value of an asset, one can expect variation in the choices that managers make. The appropriate estimates depend on how the asset is used and how it is cared for, and these can be difficult to figure out from financial statements.

3. As a result of points 1 and 2, managers can make choices that serve their reporting objectives.

4. Amortization has no effect on cash flow.

5. The choices that managers make can have economic consequences, for example by affecting contracts such as management bonuses and debt covenants that are dependent on accounting measurements.

EXHIBIT 9-2 :

Comparison of Depreciation Methods— WestJet versus Air Canada

Panel A: WestJet Airlines Ltd.

1. Significant accounting policies

(h) Property and equipment:

Asset	Basis	Rate
Aircraft net of estimated residual value – Next-Generation	Cycles	Cycles flown
Live satellite television included in Aircraft – Next-Generation	Straight-line	10 years/lease term
Aircraft net of estimated residual value – 200-series	Flight hours	Hours flown
Ground property and equipment	Straight-line	5 to 25 years
Spare engines and parts net of estimated residual value – Next-Generation	Straight-line	20 years
Spare engines and parts net of estimated residual value – 200-series	Flight hours	Fleet hours flown
Aircraft under capital lease	Straight-line	Term of lease
Other assets under capital lease	Straight-line	Term of lease
Buildings	Straight-line	40 years
Leasehold improvements	Straight-line	Term of lease

Panel B: Air Canada (ACE Aviation Holding Inc.)

2. BASIS OF PRESENTATION AND SUMMARY OF SIGNIFICANT ACCOUNTING POLICIES

U) PROPERTY AND EQUIPMENT

Property and equipment are depreciated to estimated residual values based on the straight-line method over their estimated service lives. Property and equipment under capital leases and variable interest entities are depreciated to estimated residual values over the life of the lease. Air Canada aircraft and flight equipment are depreciated over 20 to 25 years, with 10 to 15% estimated residual values. Jazz aircraft and flight equipment are depreciated over 20 to 30 years, with 20% estimated residual values. Aircraft reconfiguration costs are amortized over 3 years. Betterments to owned aircraft are capitalized and amortized over the remaining service life of the aircraft. Betterments to aircraft on operating leases are amortized over the term of the lease.

Because of these issues, it is common for similar entities to use different amortization methods and make different assumptions regarding useful life and residual value. As a result, comparability of financial statements can be impaired. Users must pay careful attention to the accounting choices made by entities so that they can understand whether differences between entities reflect actual differences in economic activity or simply differences in how the accounting is done. The same holds true for interpreting the performance of or evaluating an entity. The amortization choices can have a significant effect on the reported numbers such as net income and the NBV of assets.

For example, Exhibit 9–2 shows the notes to the financial statements of Air Canada and WestJet Airlines Inc. (WestJet). Air Canada amortizes the aircraft and flight equipment that it owns on a straight-line basis over 20–25 years (Jazz aircraft and flight equipment are amortized on a straight-line basis over 20–30 years), whereas WestJet amortizes the aircraft it owns on cycles flown (a usage measure) or hours flown. These methods are significantly different and as a result the comparability of the financial statements is impaired. Both airlines amortized leased aircraft over the term of the lease.[3]

Even though amortization can be considered "arbitrary," as discussed above, the impact of amortization on the financial statements can be significant, especially for capital-intensive businesses. Figure 9–7 shows the percentage that capital assets are of total assets for a number of entities in different capital-intensive industries. Large amounts of capital assets mean that the amortization expense might also be large, meaning that the accounting choices made by the managers can have a significant impact on income.

Financial Statement Disclosure

Companies that adhere to GAAP and the *CICA Handbook* are required to disclose the following information about their capital assets:

- cost of capital assets
- amortization method and amortization period or rate
- accumulated amortization
- amortization expense

Company	Industry	Ratio of capital assets to total assets	Ratio of amortization expense to net income	Ratio of amortization expense to revenue
Brookfield Properties Corporation	Real Estate	85%	99%	10.5%
Canfor Corporation	Forest Products	58%	157%	4.0%
Clublink Corporation	Hospitality (golf courses)	94%	Not Determinable*	11.5%
Dofasco Inc.	Steel	48%	161%	5.1%
Newfoundland Power Inc.	Utility	77%	103%	7.7%
Rogers Communications Inc.	Communications	85%	Not Determinable*	19.8%

*The percentage is not determinable because Clublink Corporation reported a net loss for the year.

FIGURE 9–7

Ratios of Capital Assets to Total Assets in Capital-Intensive Industries

Exhibit 9–3 provides an example of capital asset disclosure for Shaw Communications Inc. (Shaw).[4] Shaw provides cable television, satellite television, Internet, digital telephone, and other communications services. Shaw's balance sheets only provide a small part of the capital asset story, showing only the net amount (cost less accumulated amortization) of the company's property, plant, and equipment (PPE) and intangible assets. The notes must be examined to get the full story about these assets.

The two notes under significant accounting policies describe how PPE and intangibles are accounted for, including how PPE is amortized (Shaw's intangibles are not amortized). Note 6 breaks down property, plant, and equipment into a number of subcategories, including assets under construction. The note provides the cost, accumulated amortization, and the NBV for each category. Note 8 provides similar information for the intangible assets.

Shaw's statements of income (loss) report the amortization expense for PPE of as $408,866,000 for 2005, $403,395,000 for 2004, and 413,381,000 for 2003. The significant accounting policy note PPE states that Shaw uses straight-line amortization for all capital assets (except for land, which isn't amortized), and states the amortization period for each category of capital asset.

The information in Shaw's financial statements provides some context for understanding the accounting it uses for capital assets. The information does not give an idea about whether the accounting methods used are reasonable or appropriate. That insight comes from familiarity with the business. Shaw provides fairly detailed information about its capital assets. Managers have considerable discretion for deciding how to present details about their entities' capital assets.

www.shaw.ca

EXHIBIT 9–3

Shaw Communications Inc. Financial Statements

Shaw Communications Inc.

CONSOLIDATED BALANCE SHEETS

As at August 31

[thousands of Canadian dollars]	2005 $	2004 $
ASSETS [note 9]		
Current		
Cash	1,713	–
Accounts receivable [note 3]	114,664	119,519
Inventories [note 4]	45,224	42,973
Prepaids and other	19,116	16,975
	180,717	179,467
Investments and other assets [notes 5 and 11]	36,229	43,965
Property, plant and equipment [note 6]	2,189,235	2,292,340
Deferred charges [note 7]	237,999	267,439
Intangibles [note 8]		
Broadcast licenses	4,684,647	4,685,582
Goodwill	88,111	88,111
	7,416,938	7,556,904

EXHIBIT 9-3 :

(continued)
Shaw
Communications
Inc. Financial
Statements

472

CHAPTER 9

CONSOLIDATED STATEMENTS OF INCOME (LOSS) AND DEFICIT

Years ended August 31

[thousands of Canadian dollars except per share amounts]	2005 $	2004 $	2003 $
Service revenue *[note 15]*	**2,209,810**	2,079,749	1,998,421
Operating, general and administrative expenses	**1,227,817**	1,153,814	1,180,780
Service operating income before amortization *[note 15]*	**981,993**	925,935	817,641
Amortization –			
Deferred IRU revenue *[note 10]*	**12,999**	12,098	11,984
Deferred equipment revenue *[note 10]*	**71,677**	82,711	91,863
Deferred equipment costs *[note 7]*	**(210,477)**	(229,013)	(251,103)
Deferred charges *[note 7]*	**(6,337)**	(7,796)	(21,125)
Property, plant and equipment *[note 6]*	**(408,866)**	(403,395)	(413,381)
Operating income	**440,989**	380,540	235,879
Interest *[notes 7, 9, 10 and 13]*	**(214,408)**	(219,472)	(259,702)
	226,581	161,068	(23,823)
Gain on sale of investments *[note 5]*	**32,163**	356	1,957
Write-down of investments *[note 5]*	**(1,937)**	(651)	(15,000)
Gain on redemption of SHELS *[note 5]*	**–**	–	119,521
Loss on sale of satellite assets *[note 2]*	**–**	–	(3,800)
Debt retirement costs *[note 9]*	**–**	(2,598)	(10,634)
Foreign exchange gain on unhedged long-term debt	**6,260**	3,963	32,617
Fair value loss on forward currency forward contracts	**(19,342)**	–	–
Loss on sale and write-down of assets *[note 8]*	**–**	–	(124,674)
Other gains *[note 1]*	**11,016**	3,753	9,338
Income (loss) before income taxes	**254,741**	165,891	(14,498)
Income tax expense *[note 14]*	**93,870**	74,732	30,445
Income (loss) before the following	**160,871**	91,159	(44,943)
Equity loss on investees *[note 5]*	**(286)**	(250)	(1,921)
Net income (loss)	**160,585**	90,909	(46,864)

NOTES TO CONSOLIDATED FINANCIAL STATEMENTS

Property, plant and equipment

Property, plant and equipment are recorded at purchase cost. Direct labour and direct overhead incurred to construct new assets, upgrade existing assets and connect new subscribers are capitalized. Repairs and maintenance expenditures are charged to operating expense as incurred. Amortization is recorded on a straight-line basis over the estimated useful lives of assets as follows:

Asset	Estimated useful life
Cable and telecommunications distribution system	10-15 years
Digital cable terminals and modems	5-7 years
Satellite audio, video and data network equipment and DTH receiving equipment	2-10 years
Buildings	20-40 years
Data processing	4 years
Other	3-10 years

The Company reviews property, plant and equipment for impairment whenever events or changes in circumstances indicate that the carrying value may not be recoverable. An impairment is recognized when the carrying amount of an asset is greater than the future undiscounted net cash flows expected to be generated by the asset. The impairment is measured as the difference between the carrying value of the asset and its fair value calculated using quoted market prices or discounted cash flows.

Intangibles

The excess of the cost of acquiring cable and satellite businesses over the fair value of related net identifiable tangible and intangible assets acquired is allocated to goodwill. Net identifiable intangible assets acquired consist of amounts allocated to broadcast licenses which represent identifiable assets with indefinite useful lives.

Goodwill and intangible assets with an indefinite life are not amortized but are subject to an annual review for impairment which consists of a comparison of the fair value of the assets to their carrying value.

6. PROPERTY, PLANT AND EQUIPMENT

	2005			2004		
	Cost $	Accumulated amortization $	Net book value	Cost $	Accumulated amortization $	Net book value
Cable and telecommunications distribution system	2,932,741	1,314,268	1,618,473	2,740,234	1,119,735	1,620,499
Digital cable terminals and modems	443,051	350,677	92,374	426,308	291,910	134,398
Satellite audio, video and data network equipment and DTH receiving equipment	338,204	214,925	123,279	296,020	166,006	130,014
Buildings	244,172	58,478	185,694	221,774	47,309	174,465
Data processing	89,902	42,911	46,991	51,678	24,690	26,988
Other assets	183,856	100,743	83,113	196,476	107,575	88,901
	4,231,926	2,082,002	2,149,924	3,932,490	1,757,225	2,175,265
Land	32,103	–	32,103	29,060	–	29,060
Satellite transponders under construction	–	–	–	43,200	–	43,200
Shaw Tower under construction	7,208	–	7,208	44,815	–	44,815
	4,271,237	2,082,002	2,189,235	4,049,565	1,757,225	2,292,340

Included in the cable and telecommunications distribution system assets is the cost of the Company's purchase of fibers under IRU agreements with terms extending to 60 years totalling $61,811 (2004 – $61,811; 2003 – $61,811).

8. INTANGIBLES

	Carrying amount	
	2005 $	2004 $
Broadcast licenses		
Cable systems	3,701,515	3,702,450
DTH and satellite services	983,132	983,132
	4,684,647	4,685,582
Goodwill – non-regulated satellite services	88,111	88,111
Net book value	4,772,758	4,773,693

The changes in the carrying amount of intangibles are as follows:

	Broadcast licenses $	Goodwill $
August 31, 2003	4,627,728	88,111
Business acquisitions *[note 2]*	57,854	–
August 31, 2004	4,685,582	88,111
Business divestiture *[note 2 and 18]*	(935)	–
August 31, 2005	4,684,647	88,111

Loss on sale and write-down of assets

In 2003, the Company determined that a write-down of $50,000 was required in respect of goodwill attributed to the non-regulated business operations of the satellite division. In addition, as described in note 2, the Company recorded a write-down, net of a final gain on sale, of $74,674 on the sale of the US cable systems. This resulted in a total loss on sale and write-down of assets of $124,674 in 2003.

EXHIBIT 9–3 :

(continued)
Shaw
Communications
Inc. Financial
Statements

473

CAPITAL ASSETS

Some people argue that the amortization of the cost of capital assets is arbitrary. Explain.

Answer: The purpose of amortization is to match the cost of capital assets to the revenues they help generate. But what is the relationship between a delivery vehicle and revenue, a lawn mower and revenue, a computer and revenue, or a machine and revenue? Clearly, these capital assets make contributions to earning revenue, but it is impossible to know exactly what that contribution is. Nevertheless, accrual accounting requires that capital assets have to be amortized, so it is necessary to develop methods to amortize them. As a result, different amortization methods can be justified in terms of the facts, as long as they are reasonable. It is impossible to argue that the method selected allocates the cost of capital assets to expense better than any other method. In other words, the choice is arbitrary.

INTANGIBLE ASSETS

Intangible assets—including knowledge assets or intellectual capital—are capital assets that have no physical qualities. Intangible assets cannot be seen, touched, or felt like a machine, a building, or a table, but they are often crucial to the success of an entity. Examples of intangible assets include patents, copyrights, trademarks, franchise rights, brand names, customer lists, software, licences, human resources, and goodwill.

One of the great challenges currently facing accounting is intangible assets. In the "new economy" of the 21st century, more and more of the investments made by entities are for knowledge assets. Yet investments that build brand names, investments in research that result in new, competitive products, and investments in human resources that allow people to do their jobs more efficiently, more effectively, and more profitably are all but ignored in traditional accounting.

Money spent creating knowledge assets is normally expensed when incurred. These investments are rarely reported as assets on an entity's balance sheet. However, it is difficult to argue that these investments are not assets, at least conceptually. There is no doubt that investments in creating knowledge assets provide an expectation of future benefits. The future success of technology companies depends on the research that they do to develop their products of the future. Without ongoing research, technology companies would quickly become worthless as their products became obsolete. Successful brand names, customer lists, and skilful personnel clearly provide future benefits to an entity. Yet the current accounting model fails to effectively account for these important assets. The *CICA Handbook* explicitly requires that research costs be expensed when incurred—these costs cannot be capitalized. The *CICA Handbook* does allow for capitalization of development costs if certain strict criteria are met.

In the United States, both research and development costs must be expensed when incurred. This creates a difference between Canadian and U.S. financial statements. Companies that have their securities traded in the U.S. as well as Canada must provide a note that reconciles from net income according to Canadian GAAP to net income according to U.S. GAAP. Exhibit 9–4 shows financial statement information for MDS Inc. (MDS), a Canadian company in the pharmaceutical and life sciences industry.[5] The Exhibit shows the accounting policy that MDS uses for its development costs and that during fiscal 2005 the company deferred (capitalized) $17 million of development costs and amortized $2 million of previously deferred development costs. Note 28 shows the reconciliation from Canadian to U.S. GAAP. Notice that $15 million is subtracted from the Canadian net income ($17 million deferred in 2005 – $2 million amortized in 2005). This adjustment makes a significant contribution to the $48 million difference in net income between Canadian and U.S. GAAP.

EXHIBIT 9–4 :

MDS Inc.
Accounting for
Development
Costs: Canada vs
the U.S.

1. Accounting Policies

Research and development
The Company carries on various R&D programs, some of which are funded in part by customers and joint venture partners. Funding received is accounted for using the cost reduction approach. Net research costs are expensed in the periods in which they are incurred.

Development costs that meet certain criteria, including reasonable assurance regarding future benefits, are deferred and amortized on a straight-line basis over periods ranging from three to five years, commencing in the year that the new product development is completed and commercial production commences.

12. **Research and Development**

	2005	2004	2003
Gross expenditures	$ 87	$ 100	$ 100
Investment tax credits	(5)	(20)	(15)
Recoveries from partners	(32)	(23)	(25)
Development costs deferred	(17)	(6)	(7)
Amortization of costs previously deferred	2	3	4
	35	54	57
Depreciation and amortization set out as a separate component of net income	(4)	(16)	(10)
Research and development expense	$ 31	$ 38	$ 47

28. **Differences Between Canadian and United States Generally Accepted Accounting Principles**

The consolidated financial statements have been prepared in accordance with Canadian GAAP. The principles adopted in these financial statements conform in all material respects to those of US GAAP except as summarized below. Significant differences between Canadian and US GAAP would have the following effect on net income of the Company:

	2005	2004[1]	2003[1]
Net income from continuing operations in accordance with Canadian GAAP	$ 42	$ 63	$ 82
US GAAP adjustments:			
Unrealized gains (losses) on foreign exchange contracts and interest rate swaps (i)	(39)	(10)	46
Deferred development costs (ii)	(15)	-	(2)
Dilution gains (iii)	-	(8)	-
Impairment of long-term investment (iv)	-	-	21
Acquired in-process research and development (v)	-	(3)	-
Stock-based compensation (vi)	-	-	(2)
(Increase) reduction in income tax expense arising from GAAP adjustments	17	8	(15)
Net income from continuing operations in accordance with US GAAP	5	50	130
Net income from discontinued operations in accordance with Canadian and US GAAP - net of tax	(11)	(12)	(34)
Net income in accordance with US GAAP	(6)	38	96

ii) Deferred Development Costs - Under Canadian GAAP, qualifying product development costs are capitalized and amortized over the future periods benefited. Under US GAAP, such costs are expensed as incurred.

475

CAPITAL ASSETS

There are a number of reasons why contemporary accounting fails to recognize knowledge assets. One reason is conservatism. Because the future benefits associated with investments in knowledge assets can be very difficult to measure, conservatism prevails and the expenditures are expensed. Part of the problem is that many knowledge assets are developed internally by entities over time, and in many or most cases, it is not at all clear that a valuable resource will ultimately emerge. In contrast, most tangible capital assets are purchased in a completed form—ready or almost ready for use.

Expensing investments in knowledge assets when they are incurred has significant implications for the financial statements. The first is that the matching principle is violated. A major cost associated with earning revenues—the cost of knowledge assets—is not matched to the revenue it helps generate. For example, a pharmaceuticals company will expense all expenditures that it makes in developing a new drug. By the time the new drug has been developed, tested, and approved by Health Canada and other regulators around the world, many years will have passed. When the drug finally makes it to market, most of the costs incurred to develop it would have been expensed. What does profit mean if the costs incurred to earn the revenues are not reported in the period the revenues are recognized? Clearly, net income does not represent the change in wealth that we traditionally think of. This would be similar to expensing the cost of a retailer's inventory when it is purchased rather than when it is sold.

Also, many financial ratios are adversely affected by the accounting treatment used for knowledge assets. Gross margin, profit margin, return on assets (net income ÷ total assets), return on equity (net income ÷ shareholders' equity), and many others tend to be distorted as a result of the accounting used for intangibles. Research has shown that return on assets and return on equity both tend to be higher than they would be if knowledge assets were capitalized.

Let's look at Ballard Power Systems Inc.'s (Ballard) income statement to get an idea of the magnitude of the issue. Ballard is trying to develop a fuel cell that will be a practical alternative to internal combustion car engines. A viable fuel cell would be significant because it would help address problems associated with global warming and the increasing cost of oil and gas. Ballard's income statement is shown in Exhibit 9–5.[6] In the year ended December 31, 2005 Ballard spent $75,492,000 on research and development (R&D), representing over 140 percent of revenues for the year and almost 48 percent of total operating expenses. In fiscal 2004 and 2003, respectively, Ballard spent $91,737,000 and $103,863,000 on R&D. These are large sums of money and they will not be expensed if and when Ballard's products become successful. Instead,

www.ballard.com

EXHIBIT 9–5 :

Ballard Power Systems Inc. Income Statement— Research and Development Costs

BALLARD POWER SYSTEMS INC.

CONSOLIDATED STATEMENTS OF OPERATIONS AND ACCUMULATED DEFICIT

(Expressed in thousands of U.S. dollars, except per share amounts and number of shares)
Years ended December 31

	2005	2004	2003
Revenues:			
Product revenues	$ 37,366	$ 67,575	$ 79,828
Engineering service and other revenue	16,367	13,798	39,738
Total revenues	53,733	81,373	119,566
Cost of revenues and expenses:			
Cost of product revenues	31,292	59,594	76,063
Research and product development	75,492	91,737	103,863
General and administrative	17,543	15,671	17,711
Marketing	8,012	10,028	9,454
Depreciation and amortization	26,094	40,094	46,408
Total cost of revenues and expenses	158,433	217,124	253,499
Loss before undernoted	(104,700)	(135,751)	(133,933)
Investment and other income	11,153	3,670	29,191
Loss on disposal and write-down of long-lived assets (notes 7, 8 and 9)	(7,787)	(17,678)	(13,274)
Gain (loss) on assets held for sale (note 2)	18,294	(23,051)	—
Equity in loss of associated companies	(3,738)	(2,175)	(2,067)
Minority interest	—	—	4,578
Business integration and restructuring costs	—	—	(8,838)
Loss before income taxes	(86,778)	(174,985)	(124,343)
Income taxes (note 15)	205	422	749
Net loss for the year	(86,983)	(175,407)	(125,092)
Accumulated deficit, beginning of year	(663,264)	(487,857)	(362,765)
Accumulated deficit, end of year	$ (750,247)	$ (663,264)	$ (487,857)
Basic loss per share	$ (0.73)	$ (1.48)	$ (1.07)
Weighted average number of common shares outstanding	119,701,260	118,461,114	117,438,962

1. **SIGNIFICANT ACCOUNTING POLICIES**

   (m) Research and product development expenditures:

   Research costs are expensed as they are incurred. Product development costs are expensed as incurred except when they meet specific criteria for deferral as set forth under Canadian GAAP.

they are treated as period costs and expensed when incurred. As a result of this treatment, there is a clear and significant mismatching of revenues and expenses. In addition, if we assume that the money Ballard is investing in research has future benefit, then assets on the December 31, 2005 balance sheet are understated. If the $271,092,000 that was spent on research and expensed in 2003 through 2005 had instead been capitalized, Ballard's total assets would be almost 52 percent higher than they are. But the big question is, will all the money Ballard is investing pay off?

Another example: Coca-Cola is one of the best-known brand names in the world. If the Coca-Cola Company were to be purchased, the buyer would pay a lot of money for the rights to the Coca-Cola name. Yet if you examine Coca-Cola's balance sheet there is no mention of this valuable asset. On December 31, 2005 Coca-Cola's shareholders' equity, as reported on the company's balance sheet, was US$16.355 billion. In contrast, the value of Coca-Cola's shares on the New York Stock Exchange (which is a market measure of the value of the company's shareholders' equity) was about $95 billion. Why this vast difference in these measures of the owners' interest in the company? The missing value of the Coca-Cola brand name certainly plays a significant role.

An introductory financial accounting textbook is not the place to go into detail about this problem. However, students of accounting, even at the introductory level, must be aware of this shortcoming in the current reporting model, especially given the importance of knowledge assets in the contemporary economy. The problem is under investigation by academic researchers and regulators, but it is not clear what the resolution will be.

It's worth noting that most knowledge assets don't appear on an entity's balance sheet if the entity creates the asset. But if a knowledge asset is purchased—for example, a patent, a copyright, a research project—it would appear on the balance sheet and be accounted for in the traditional way. For example, if an entity purchases the rights to a patent, the cost is capitalized and amortized over its useful life, just as is done with tangible capital assets.

Let's look at an example. Zangwill Ltd. purchased a patent from Roach Research Corp. for $6,000,000. The patent has a remaining life of 12 years and Zangwill's management believes that it will be able to sell products that rely on the patent for that long. When it purchases the patent, Zangwill would record the following journal entry:

Dr. Patent (asset +)   6,000,000
    Cr. Cash (asset −) or Liability (liability +)   6,000,000
To record the purchase of a patent.

Each year Zangwill would amortize a portion of the cost of the patent:

Dr. Amortization expense (expense +, shareholders' equity −)   500,000
    Cr. Accumulated amortization—patent (contra-asset +)   500,000
To record amortization of the patent ($600,000,000 ÷ 12 years).

If Zangwill had developed the patent internally, there would be no recognition of it on the balance sheet. The costs of developing the patent would have been expensed as they were incurred.

Intangible assets are not all amortized under GAAP. The GAAP rules on intangibles and goodwill have been shifting in recent years. Intangibles don't have to be amortized if there aren't any factors (for example, legal, economic, regulatory, competitive, or contractual) that limit their useful life. Intangibles that have limited lives should be amortized.

Goodwill

Most intangible or knowledge assets, regardless of how they are accounted for, can be identified. An entity will own a patent, a copyright, a franchise, a licence, and so on. Goodwill, probably the most commonly seen intangible asset on balance sheets, is different. Goodwill does not really represent anything in particular. To understand why goodwill does not represent anything in particular, we need to understand how goodwill arises.

Goodwill arises only when one entity purchases all or a majority of another entity. When an entity is purchased, the purchaser must allocate the purchase price to the specific assets and liabilities that were purchased. In effect, the purchaser must determine the market value of each asset and liability on the date of the purchase. **Goodwill** is the amount that the purchaser pays for another entity over and above the fair value of the purchased entity's identifiable assets and liabilities on the date the entity is purchased. That is,

$$\text{Goodwill} = \text{Purchase price} - \text{Fair value of identifiable assets and liabilities purchased}$$

Identifiable assets and liabilities are tangible and intangible assets and liabilities that can be specifically identified. Identifiable assets include cash, inventory, land, buildings, patents, copyrights, and research and development.

For example, assume that Rushoon Inc. (Rushoon) purchased 100 percent of the outstanding shares of Molanosa Ltd. (Molanosa) for $12,000,000. The fair of Molanosa's net assets (assets − liabilities) on the date of the purchase was $10,500,000. The goodwill that arose as a result of the purchase of Molanosa's shares by Rushoon is calculated as:

$$\begin{aligned}\text{Goodwill} &= \text{Purchase price} - \text{Fair value of identifiable net assets} \\ &= \$12,000,000 - \$10,500,000 \\ &= \$1,500,000\end{aligned}$$

Why would Rushoon pay $1,500,000 more than the fair value of the identifiable assets and liabilities for Molanosa? What does the goodwill actually represent? Well, it is hard to be sure because goodwill is a residual—it is the amount that is left over after the identifiable assets and liabilities have been valued. It is assumed that if a purchaser paid more than the fair value of the identifiable assets and liabilities for a company, the extra amount paid is for something of value, even if it isn't clear exactly what. Goodwill is often attributed to things such as management ability, location, synergies created by the acquisition, customer loyalty, reputation, and benefits associated with the elimination of a competitor—all things that are of value but that are very difficult to specifically identify and measure.

Of course, another possible explanation for paying more than the fair value of the identifiable assets and liabilities is that the investor paid too much. However, it would probably be imprudent for a manager to admit that too soon after the purchase of a subsidiary!

It is interesting to observe that assets such as management skill, location, reputation, and so on that are considered goodwill all exist before a subsidiary is purchased. However, according to GAAP, internally generated goodwill cannot appear on the balance sheet. This is the nature of historical cost, transactions-based accounting: Goodwill can be recognized only when one entity purchases another—it is determined only on the date a subsidiary is purchased. Because of conservatism and reliability, costs incurred to generate goodwill internally are expensed when incurred because it's difficult to measure the future benefits associated with the money spent. This treatment is also consistent with the accounting used for other intangible assets such as research and development, and copyrights.

It is important to emphasize that, conceptually, goodwill is an asset. The existence of greater management ability, reputation, customer loyalty, and so on should lead to higher profits than would be earned in their absence. The challenge with the accounting is determining the existence and the value of the future benefit.

According to GAAP, goodwill is not amortized. Instead, management must estimate the fair value of the goodwill each year. If the fair value is less than the book value, the goodwill must be written down to its fair value. The amount of any write-down of goodwill is expensed in the income statement in the year.

The *CICA Handbook* provides guidelines for estimating the fair value of goodwill. However, because of its nature, estimating the fair value of goodwill is very subjective and requires judgment. Because so much judgment is required to determine if goodwill's value is impaired, management has considerable leeway in deciding the timing and amount of any write-down.

Goodwill can represent a significant proportion of a company's assets. For example, on December 31, 2005 goodwill represented almost 22 percent of Rogers' assets. Goodwill on the balance sheet doesn't tell the reader of consolidated financial statements very much. It provides information about the amount that was spent for an investment, but nothing about what the goodwill represents, or if it represents anything at all. Financial statement readers can only speculate whether it represents a wise expenditure of company resources.

Why is it difficult to say for sure what goodwill is? Do you think goodwill meets the definition of an asset under GAAP? (See Chapter 2 for the criteria for an asset.)

Answer: It is difficult to say for sure what goodwill is because goodwill is a residual—it's the amount left over after identifiable assets and liabilities have had fair values assigned to them. Therefore, it's not possible to determine what the goodwill that an entity reports on its balance sheet represents. Also, other than faith in GAAP's requirement to estimate the fair value of goodwill, it's not possible to know whether an entity's goodwill really has any future benefit because it is hard to assess future benefit if you don't know what it is you are assessing.

The three GAAP criteria for an asset that were identified in Chapter 2 are:

1. An asset must be the result of a transaction with another entity;

2. The cost of an asset can be determined; and

3. An asset must provide a future benefit to the entity and the benefit must be reasonably measurable. (If you are not sure what the benefit is or that there will be a benefit, you cannot call an item an asset.)

The first criterion is met because goodwill is recorded only when another company is purchased. Whether the second criterion is met can be questioned. Since the cost of goodwill itself is not determined—rather, it is the portion of the purchase price that is not assigned to specific assets and liabilities—one can question whether the cost of goodwill can actually be determined. The cost of goodwill depends on how well the cost of the identifiable assets and liabilities can be determined. The third criterion is the most debatable. If we don't really know what goodwill is, how can we be reasonably sure that there is a future benefit and reasonably measure what that future benefit is?

The rationale for classifying goodwill as an asset is that since goodwill is purchased when an entity is acquired, it should be accounted for as an asset.

A Contrast with Oil and Gas Accounting

An interesting contrast with accounting for knowledge assets is the accounting that is used by companies that explore for oil and gas. Oil and gas exploration companies must spend large amounts of money to find new sources of fossil fuels in the same way that technology companies must invest heavily in research and development to develop new products. In both of these industries, a significant amount of money is spent before anything is sold. Unlike investments on research and development and other knowledge assets, expenditures on oil and gas exploration and development can be capitalized and amortized over the period that the oil or gas is extracted.

The *CICA Handbook* requires that expenditures on research must be expensed when incurred. Under no circumstances can research costs be capitalized. Why do you think the Handbook requires the expensing of research costs when they are incurred? Do you agree with this requirement?

Answer: Research costs represent important and valuable assets to an entity. Without them, many entities would quickly fail because they would be unable to compete. The problem is that it is not clear what the payoff is for investing in research. Investments in research might pay off handsomely or they might not pay off at all. Given the uncertainty,

(continued)

Question for Consideration (Continued)

accountants are reluctant to call expenditures made on research assets because they may prove to have no future benefit. This is an application of conservatism.

If one accepts the importance of conservatism as an accounting concept, then the existing treatment for research makes sense. However, it is clear that investments in research pay off, on average (although not necessarily for any particular investment or for any particular entity). In that case, expensing a research when it is incurred results in a mismatching of expenses and revenues and an understatement of assets on the balance sheet.

There are two methods that oil and gas companies can use to account for their exploration costs: **successful efforts** and **full costing.** Under full costing, a company capitalizes all costs incurred to find new sources of oil and gas, even if some of those costs do not result in successful projects. In contrast, under successful efforts accounting, only the costs associated with successful projects are capitalized. The costs associated with failed projects are expensed when they are incurred.

For example, Divide Corp. (Divide) invests $14,000,000 exploring for oil over 50,000 square kilometres in northern Alberta. The exploration efforts result in the drilling of seven test wells, of which two have oil. The cost of each well is $2,000,000. Under full costing, the $14,000,000 would be capitalized, even though $10,000,000 was spent on five wells that do not have any oil. The $14,000,000 would be amortized over the production of the two productive wells. If Divide used the successful efforts method, it would capitalize only the $4,000,000 cost associated with the two wells that have oil. The $10,000,000 associated with the dry wells would be expensed once it was clear they had no oil. With successful efforts the $4,000,000 would be amortized over the production of the two successful wells.

Exhibit 9–6 shows the notes to the financial statements of two companies, Petro-Canada, which uses successful efforts, and Bow Valley Energy Ltd., which uses full cost accounting.[7]

EXHIBIT 9–6	

Petro-Canada and Bow Valley Energy Ltd.

Petro-Canada—Extracts from the 2005 Annual Report

Note 1 **SUMMARY OF SIGNIFICANT ACCOUNTING POLICIES**

(j) Property, Plant and Equipment

Investments in exploration and development activities are accounted for using the successful efforts method. Under this method, the acquisition cost of unproved acreage is capitalized. Costs of exploratory wells are initially capitalized pending determination of proved reserves. Costs of wells which are assigned proved reserves remain capitalized, while costs of unsuccessful wells are charged to earnings. All other exploration costs, including geological and geophysical costs, are charged to earnings as incurred. Development costs, including the cost of all wells, are capitalized.

The interest cost of debt attributable to the construction of major new facilities is capitalized during the construction period.

Producing properties and significant unproved properties are assessed annually, or as economic events dictate, for potential impairment. Impairment is assessed by comparing the estimated net undiscounted future cash flows to the carrying value of the asset. If required, the impairment recorded is the amount by which the carrying value of the asset exceeds its fair value.

Bow Valley Energy Ltd.—Extracts from the 2005 Annual Report

NOTES TO CONSOLIDATED FINANCIAL STATEMENTS
FOR THE YEARS ENDED DECEMBER 31, 2005 AND 2004

1. **Significant Accounting Policies**

    (b) **Property, Plant and Equipment**

    The Company follows the full cost method of accounting, whereby all costs associated with the exploration for and development of oil and gas reserves are capitalized and accumulated in country-by-country cost centres. Such costs include land acquisition, geological and geophysical, carrying of non-producing properties, drilling productive and non-productive wells, and plant and equipment.

Insight

The difference between the accounting rules that oil and gas exploration companies can use versus what companies that invest in research and development must do is striking. The differences in the accounting for these conceptually similar expenditures can result in significantly different financial statements. Oil and gas companies will have lower expenses and more assets than companies investing in research and development. Lenders who rely on financial ratios to assess loan applications may have difficulty with the financial statements of research and development companies because of their low incomes and low asset balances. However, there is a difference between the two. An oil and gas company has the oil in the ground that it will be able to extract and sell. The revenue prospects for a lot of research projects is much more uncertain. This doesn't mean that the difference between the accounting treatments is for the best, but there is a reason for it.

DISPOSAL OF CAPITAL ASSETS

In Chapter 4, we discussed the gains and losses that arise on the sale of capital assets. When an entity sells an asset that is not usually sold in the ordinary course of its business for an amount that is different from the asset's NBV, a gain or a loss arises. In Chapter 4, the examples were limited to situations where land—an asset that is not amortized—was sold. In this section, the discussion is expanded to include amortizable assets.

When an amortizable asset is sold, the cost of the asset and the accumulated amortization associated with the asset must both be removed from the books. A gain or loss on the sale of a capital asset arises when the asset is sold for an amount that is different from its NBV. If the amount received is greater than the NBV, a gain is recorded. If the amount received is less than the NBV, there is a loss.

Before recording the disposal of the asset, it is necessary to record the amortization expense related to the part of the year the asset was sold. The entries to record the amortization expense and accumulated amortization usually take place at the end of a period, whereas sales of capital assets can take place any time, so in most cases, part of a year's amortization will not have been recorded. If the amortization expense is not recorded, amortization expense will be understated and the gain or loss on sale will be misstated. Net income will not be affected.

Let's look at an example. At the beginning of 2003, Ycliff Inc. (Ycliff) purchased equipment for $1,200,000. Management estimated that the equipment would have a residual value of $200,000 and useful life of 10 years. Ycliff amortized the equipment on a straight-line basis. In 2010, one-quarter of the way through the year, Ycliff sold the equipment for $400,000 in cash. At the end of 2009, the NBV of the assets was $500,000:

Cost	$1,200,000
Accumulated amortization	700,000
NBV	$ 500,000

Since the equipment was sold one-quarter of the way into 2010, an amortization expense of $25,000 is necessary for 2010. The journal entry is:

Dr. Amortization expense (expense +, shareholders' equity −)	25,000	
Cr. Accumulated amortization (contra-assets +)		25,000

To record the part-year amortization expense for equipment sold during 2010. $(((\$1,200,000 - 200,000) \div 10) \times 0.25)$

On the date of the sale, accumulated amortization on the equipment was $725,000 ($700,000 + $25,000) and the NBV was $475,000 ($1,200,000 − $725,000). The journal entry to record the sale is:

Dr. Cash (asset +)	400,000	
Dr. Accumulated amortization (contra-asset −)	725,000	
Dr. Loss on sale of equipment	75,000	
(income statement −, shareholders' equity −)		
Cr. Equipment (asset −)		1,200,000
To record the sale of equipment at a loss.		

The journal entry removes the cost of $1,200,000 and the accumulated amortization of $725,000 from the books. The gain or loss is equal to the proceeds from the sale of the asset less its NBV. In the example,

Proceeds from sale	$400,000
NBV	475,000
Loss	($ 75,000)

In this scenario, there is a loss because the proceeds from sale are less than the NBV. It is interesting to observe that the amount of the gain or loss on the sale of a capital asset is simply a function of how the asset is accounted for. We should assume that the selling price of a capital asset is fixed—that is, the amount a buyer would pay for the asset is not affected by its NBV. The amount of the gain or loss is then determined only by the asset's NBV, which in turn is determined by the amount that was capitalized in the first place for the asset and the amount of amortization that has accumulated over its life.

If, for example, Ycliff amortized the equipment over 12 years instead of ten, the NBV when the equipment was sold would have been $595,833 ((($1,200,000 − $200,000) ÷ 12) × 7.25) and the loss would have been $195,833 ($400,000 − $595,833). Any changes that affect the NBV of an asset will change the amount of the gain or loss reported (assuming that the selling price is a constant). In some cases, a manager's decision to sell an asset may be affected by the amount of any gain or loss. For example, if an entity requires higher net income to meet the requirements of a loan covenant, the managers may be unwilling to sell a capital asset at a loss, preferring instead to hold on to the asset.

Look at the income statement of Shaw Communications Inc. (Shaw) in Exhibit 9–3 on pages 471–472. In the section of the statement below operating income, you will see a number of gains and losses reported. By reporting these items below what Shaw calls operating income, the company tries to show that these items are not part of ordinary, day-to-day operations.

www.mcgrawhill.ca/
olc/friedlan

Knowledge Check

Suppose that in the Ycliff example (pages 481–482) the company had sold the equipment for $750,000 instead of $400,000.

■ How much amortization would be recorded on the asset for 2010?

■ What would be the gain or loss that Ycliff would report for the sale of the equipment in 2010?

■ Prepare the journal entry required to record the sale.

WRITE-DOWNS

Sometimes situations arise that impair the value of capital assets. A capital asset is impaired when two conditions are met: First, the asset's **net recoverable amount**—the net cash flow the asset is expected to generate from use over its remaining life, plus its residual value—is less than its NBV. When this condition occurs, it means that the entity will not be able to recover in cash the amount that the asset is valued at on the books. Second, the asset's fair value—its net realizable value (NRV)—is less than its NBV. Examples of impaired capital assets include a building destroyed by fire, a plant that is no longer productive, and reductions in the earnings expected from a mine.

According to GAAP, when capital assets become impaired they should be written down to their fair value. A write-down reduces the NBV of the capital asset and reduces income. It is important to recognize that capital assets are not assessed in the same way as inventory in the application of the lower of cost and market rule. With the lower of cost and market rule, the cost of inventory must be compared to its market value at the end of each period, and if the market value is less than cost, the inventory must be written down. The assessment of capital assets takes a longer-term perspective—cash flows over the entire life of an asset are considered, not a short-term measure of market value. A short-term decline in net realizable value or replacement cost, or a short-term reduction in net cash flows, is not enough to trigger the write-down of a capital asset. Once a write-down is made, it is not reversed.

For example, Overflow Ltd. (Overflow) owns a small office building. The building is recorded in the accounting records at its cost of $12,000,000, less accumulated amortization of $5,000,000. In recent years the building has become less attractive to potential tenants because the building has become rundown and its neighbourhood has deteriorated. As a result, the rents that Overflow can obtain have declined. Management now estimates that the building will generate $4,000,000 in net cash flows over its remaining life and will be sold at the end of its life for $1,000,000, so the net recoverable amount is $5,000,000 ($4,000,000 + $1,000,000). In addition, an independent real estate appraisal estimated that the fair value of the building to be $5,250,000. Therefore, according to GAAP Overflow must write down the building because the net recoverable amount is less than the NBV and the fair value is less than the NBV. The building should be written down to its fair value of $5,250,000, which means a write down of $1,750,000. The journal entry to record the write-down would be:

Dr. Loss due to impairment of building	1,750,000	
(income statement −, shareholders' equity −)		
Cr. Accumulated amortization (contra-asset +)		1,750,000
To write down the building to its net recoverable amount.		

The write-down is credited to Accumulated Amortization, which serves to decrease the NBV of the asset. Notice from the journal entry that a write-down doesn't affect cash. A write-down decreases the book value of assets, but cash isn't involved.

While the rules for determining whether a capital asset is impaired are clear, management has considerable discretion in deciding the timing and amount of a write-down because the actual determination of the impairment is very subjective. There is ample evidence that managers will time write-downs of capital assets to accomplish reporting objectives. For example, managers might write down capital assets as part of a big bath. (Big baths were introduced in Chapter 4.) A big bath will usually go along with difficult times for the company, but by taking a bath the entity gets rid of a lot of the bad news right away, paving the way for higher earnings in the future because there will be fewer expenses. Remember that writing down assets in a current period means that expenses that would have been recognized in a future period will no longer be recognized and income in the future will be higher than it would have been. A company must be able to justify a big bath—assets cannot be written off on the whim of management. That said, management can usually provide a "reasonable" justification because of the emphasis in GAAP accounting on conservatism.

Exhibit 9–7 (page 485) gives an example of an asset write-down. Onex Corporation (Onex) is a company that buys other companies and helps manage them. Among the companies that Onex owns are Cineplex theatres and Celestica.[8] In 2004, Onex wrote down $393,000,000 in goodwill and other intangibles, mostly pertaining to Celestica Inc. and $94,000,000 in long-lived assets, also mostly pertaining to Celestica Inc. The notes to the financial statements don't provide much information about the nature or reason for the write down other than to say they occurred. Exhibit 9–7 shows the presentation of the write-down on the income statement and the note explaining what happened.

www.onexcorp.com

EXHIBIT 9–7 :

**Onex
Corporation—
Write-Downs**

484

CHAPTER 9

CONSOLIDATED STATEMENTS OF EARNINGS

Year ended December 31 *(in millions of dollars except per share data)*	2004	2003
Revenues	$ 16,244	$ 12,119
Cost of sales	(14,510)	(10,859)
Selling, general and administrative expenses	(953)	(766)
Earnings Before the Undernoted Items	$ 781	$ 494
Amortization of property, plant and equipment	(416)	(407)
Amortization of intangible assets and deferred charges	(94)	(91)
Interest expense of operating companies (note 13)	(253)	(191)
Interest and other income	111	81
Equity-accounted investments	(8)	–
Foreign exchange loss	(116)	(122)
Stock-based compensation	(104)	14
Derivative instruments	29	–
Gains on shares of operating companies, net (note 15)	182	129
Acquisition, restructuring and other expenses (note 16)	(211)	(151)
Debt prepayment costs (note 17)	(8)	(11)
Writedown of goodwill and intangible assets (note 18)	(393)	(402)
Writedown of long-lived assets (note 19)	(94)	(88)
Loss before income taxes, non-controlling interests and discontinued operations	(594)	(745)
Provision for income taxes (note 20)	(347)	(67)
Non-controlling interests of operating companies	781	256
Loss from continuing operations	(160)	(556)
Earnings from discontinued operations (note 2)	195	224
Net Earnings (Loss) for the Year	$ 35	$ (332)
Net Earnings (Loss) per Subordinate Voting Share (note 21)		
Basic and Diluted:		
Continuing operations	$ (1.12)	$ (3.62)
Discontinued operations	$ 1.37	$ 1.46
Net earnings (loss)	$ 0.25	$ (2.16)

18. WRITEDOWN OF GOODWILL AND INTANGIBLE ASSETS

Year ended December 31	2004	2003
Celestica[a]	$ 388	$ 33
J.L. French Automotive[b]	–	214
Performance Logistics Group[c]	–	142
Radian[d]	–	8
ClientLogic[e]	5	5
	$ 393	$ 402

a) During the fourth quarter of 2004, Celestica performed its annual impairment tests of goodwill and intangible assets and determined that writedowns of $351 in goodwill and $37 in other intangibles was required. The majority of the writedowns were due to restructuring plans and the continued transfer of major customer programs from higher cost to lower cost geographies whereby these actions reduced the forecasted revenue and net cash flows for many sites. In 2003, the impairment tests resulted in writedowns of $24 in intellectual property and $9 in other intangibles due to prolonged declines in the computing and communications end-markets that affected the fair value of the reporting units.

b) During the third quarter of 2004, J.L. French Automotive performed its annual impairment tests of goodwill and intangible assets and determined that no writedowns were required. In 2003, the impairment tests resulted in a writedown of $214 in goodwill due to lower than anticipated production volumes and a relocation of certain assets within the reporting units.

c) In 2003, the impairment tests at PLG resulted in a writedown of $142 in goodwill as a result of the competitive nature of the industry.

d) In 2003, Radian performed impairment tests that resulted in a writedown of $8 in goodwill due to the slowdown in the telecommunications sector arising from tighter capital markets and capital-spending restrictions by wireless service providers. During 2004, Radian did not have any recorded goodwill or intangible assets.

e) During 2004, ClientLogic performed its annual impairment tests of goodwill and intangible assets and determined that a writedown of $5 in intangible assets was required due to the loss of certain client contracts. In 2003, the impairment tests resulted in a writedown of $5 in intangible assets due to a component of the existing client contracts being impaired.

19. WRITEDOWN OF LONG-LIVED ASSETS

Year ended December 31	2004	2003
Celestica[a]	$ 84	$ 75
J.L. French Automotive[b]	8	10
Other	2	3
	$ 94	$ 88

a) In 2004, Celestica recorded an impairment of $84 (2003 – $75) against property, plant and equipment. In 2003, $18 of the impairment related to the buyout of a leased facility.

b) In 2004, J.L. French Automotive implemented restructuring plans for its U.K. operations which resulted in an impairment of $8 against property, plant and equipment. In 2003, J.L. French Automotive recorded an impairment of $10 against property, plant and equipment, of which $7 related to a Mexican facility that was not producing an acceptable profit margin, and it was decided that the business would be resourced to another supplier.

CAPITAL ASSETS AND THE CASH FLOW STATEMENT

When capital assets are bought or sold for cash, the amount is reported as an investing activity in the cash flow statement. Purchases appear as negative amounts because they use cash, and disposals are positive because they generate cash. One complexity with the sale of capital assets is the treatment of gains and losses on the cash flow statement. Gains and losses are included in the calculation of net income but they do not affect cash flow, so gains must be subtracted from net income and losses added back when reconciling from net income to cash from operations (CFO) using the indirect method. The only cash flow effect of the sale of a capital asset is the cash received, and the cash received is treated as an investing activity. Write-downs of capital assets do not affect cash flows, so they are added back when calculating CFO, using the indirect method.

Does the Way Capital Assets Are Accounted for Affect the Cash Flow Statement?

It may come as a surprise, but how certain expenditures are accounted for can affect the cash flows reported in the cash flow statement. Accounting choices do not affect the actual amount of cash that enters and leaves an entity, but the choices can affect the classification of cash flows. If an expenditure is capitalized, the outlay appears in the cash flow statement as an investing activity. If that same expenditure is expensed when incurred, the expenditure is included in CFO.

Suppose that in 2008 Balaclava Ltd. (Balaclava) spends $1,000,000 in cash on the development of a new product. If the expenditure meets the requirements for capitalization under GAAP, Balaclava could make the following journal entry:

Dr. New product development (asset +) 1,000,000
    Cr. Cash (asset −) 1,000,000
To capitalize development costs associated with a new product.

If Balaclava decides to amortize the development costs over four years, there will be an annual amortization expense of $250,000 in each year from 2008 through 2011:

Dr. Amortization expense (expense +, shareholders' equity −) 250,000
    Cr. Accumulated amortization (contra-asset +) 250,000
To record amortization of new product development costs.

If instead Balaclava decides to expense the new product costs when they are incurred, the journal entry would be:

Dr. New product development expense 1,000,000
    (expense +, shareholders' equity −)
    Cr. Cash (asset −) 1,000,000
To expense expenditures associated with a new product.

Table 9–2 provides summarized income statements for Balaclava Ltd. for 2008 and 2009, for both capitalizing and expensing the new product development costs. It is assumed in the income statements that revenues and expenses other than the amortization expense are in cash, and that the revenues and expenses are the same in both 2008 and 2009. In 2008, if the expenditure is capitalized, net income is reduced by $250,000, the amount of the amortization expense. Net income is also reduced in 2009 (as well as 2010 and 2011) by $250,000 because the $1,000,000 is being amortized over four years. If the product development costs are expensed in full in 2008, income is reduced by $1,000,000 in 2008. In 2009 (as well as 2010 and 2011) the new product costs have no effect on income.

But what is the effect on the cash flow statement? Table 9–3 provides summarized cash flow statements for Balaclava Ltd. for 2008 and 2009 for both capitalizing and expensing the new product development costs. If the $1,000,000 is capitalized, the outlay is classified as an investing activity and the $250,000 amortization expense is added back to net income in the calculation of CFO using the indirect method. If the cost is expensed in full in 2008, it is classified as CFO. (The product development costs do not appear explicitly in the cash flow statement under the expensing alternative because the costs have already been deducted in the calculation of net income.)

TABLE 9-2 ::: Balaclava Ltd.: Summarized Income Statementes

Balaclava Ltd.
Income Statement
For the Years Ended December 31, 2008 and 2009

	December 31, 2008		December 31, 2009	
	Capitalize	Expense	Capitalize	Expense
Revenues	$25,000,000	$25,000,000	$25,000,000	$25,000,000
Expenses	15,000,000	15,000,000	15,000,000	15,000,000
Amortization of product development costs	250,000		250,000	
Product development expense		1,000,000		0
Net Income	$ 9,750,000	$ 9,000,000	$ 9,750,000	$10,000,000

TABLE 9-3 ::: Balaclava Ltd.: Summarized Cash flow Statements

Balaclava Ltd.
Cash flow Statements
For the Years Ended December 31, 2008 and 2009

	December 31, 2008		December 31, 2009	
	Capitalize	Expense	Capitalize	Expense
Cash Flow Operations				
Net Income	$9,750,000	$9,000,000	$9,750,000	$10,000,000
Add back:				
Amortization of product development costs	250,000	0	250,000	0
Cash from Operations	10,000,000	9,000,000	10,000,000	10,000,000
Investing Activities:				0
Cost of product development	1,000,000	0	0	0
Increase in Cash	$ 9,000,000	$ 9,000,000	$ 10,000,000	$10,000,000

Notice the effect of the accounting choice on the cash flow statement. In 2008, the overall increase in cash is $9,000,000 under both methods, but CFO is $10,000,000 when the product development costs are capitalized and $9,000,000 when the costs are expensed when incurred. If the costs are capitalized, investing activities reflect a $1,000,000 cash outlay, whereas if the costs are expensed, cash expended for investing activities is zero. In 2009, CFO and investing activities are the same under both alternatives because the only financial statement impact of the new product development costs is amortization, which has no effect on cash.

Even the cash flow statement, a statement designed to neutralize the effects of accounting choices by managers, is affected by accounting choices. In evaluating CFO, a user of the information has to consider the accounting policies used, because if some companies capitalize certain outlays as capital assets while similar entities expense them, the ability to compare the companies' CFO is impaired.

WHY ACCOUNTING CHOICE?

Let's take a moment to re-emphasize a central theme of this book. One of the most difficult issues for students of accounting to understand is the reason why there is so much choice available to managers. Accounting choice is a double-edged sword. Choice provides managers with the opportunity to present information in ways that are useful to stakeholders. Choice also provides an effective means for managers to achieve their own reporting objectives. There is nothing inherently sinister in allowing managers the ability to tailor information to suit their own needs and the needs of users. However, the other edge of the sword is that managers can use the flexibility inherent in accounting to mislead and manipulate the users of the information. It is not always possible for users to tell how the managers are using accounting choice. This is one of the dangers users face.

Some might ask why a single set of accounting rules couldn't be applied to every situation. This issue has been argued throughout the book, but it bears repeating through an example. Consider a small business wholly owned and operated by a husband-and-wife team. The financial statements have been used exclusively for management decision making and tax purposes. As such, the owners have always prepared its financial statements with the purpose of minimizing taxes. All accounting choices have been made with the purpose of paying as little tax as possible. This approach makes perfect sense. Why pay more taxes than necessary? Why make the book-keeping more complicated than necessary?

Then the husband and wife decide to sell the business. A prospective purchaser would want to see financial statements to assess the attractiveness of the business. Are the statements that the couple has been preparing for tax purposes appropriate for the prospective purchaser? Probably not! The financial statements prepared for tax purposes are inappropriate for the purpose of valuing a business because they will tend to understate the performance of the entity. Financial statements for a prospective buyer should reflect the economic activity of the business for the purpose of predicting future performance. In other words, a purchaser wants information to help evaluate how much money he or she will make. Tax-based financial statements don't do that.

Insight

The issue of how to deal with accounting policy choice has no easy answer. A system that allows choice opens itself up for abuse by managers. A system with no choice reduces the likelihood for abuse but may render financial statements useless. For now, Canada allows a lot of choice and emphasizes the exercise of judgment. Users should recognize the opportunity for abuse and use accounting information cautiously. Thus far, we have seen the effect that the choice of revenue recognition method, inventory cost flow assumption, and amortization method, along with a number of other estimates that the managers make, have on the financial statements. With these accounting issues alone, a wide range of numbers could appear in the financial statements of an entity, depending on the choices by the managers, each of which represents the identical underlying economic activity.

Accounting plays a very important role in communicating information about an entity. For the efficient and effective operation of the economy, it is essential that managers and any external accountants (including auditors) behave ethically. Users must be able to use accounting information with confidence. If they are unable to do so, the costs of doing business will increase and economic performance will decline.

Users must recognize that it is not always possible to "see through" the financial statements numbers to the "truth." Financial statements should rarely be the finishing point of an investigation. If they have the opportunity, users should ask detailed questions. (For example, if someone is planning to buy a business, he or she should ask the seller detailed questions about the business and the financial statements.) Other sources of information should also be consulted.

FINANCIAL STATEMENT ANALYSIS ISSUES

Despite the importance of capital assets to many entities, there are limits to the insights about an entity that can be gained from analyzing the historical cost information about them in the financial statements. First, as we discussed earlier in the chapter, the usefulness of historical cost information about capital assets for many decisions is questionable. Second, even under GAAP there is extensive choice for how to account for capital assets. How capital assets are accounted for can have significant effects on the numbers in the financial statements. The list below summarizes the areas of choice that were discussed in the chapter:

- what costs get capitalized

- how capital assets are amortized

- estimates of useful life and residual value

- the existence of unrecorded assets (especially intangible assets)

- write-downs and write-offs of capital assets

These policy and estimate choices will affect expenses, net income, assets and retained earnings, and any ratios that depend on these measures. However, a ratio often used to measure the performance and operating efficiency of an entity is **return on assets (ROA)**. ROA is defined as:

$$\text{Return on assets} = \frac{\text{Net income} + \text{After-tax interest expense}}{\text{Total assets}}$$

The numerator of the ratio is a measure of how the entity has performed—in this case, net income with the after-tax interest expense added back. The after-tax interest expense is the cost of interest after taking into consideration the fact that the government picks up part of the cost of interest because interest is deductible for tax purposes. That is, if an entity incurs $10,000 in interest and the entity's tax rate is 25 percent, the actual cost of interest to the entity is $7,500 ($10,000 × [1 − tax rate] = $10,000 × [1 − 0.25]). The reason after-tax interest expense is added back is so that the ratio is a measure of return on assets independent of how the assets are financed. If the interest expense were included in the numerator, the return on assets would be affected by the amount of debt the entity had.

The denominator is the investment—in this case the entity's investment in assets. The denominator can be expressed as average assets for the year or year-end assets. Both the numerator and denominator introduce some problems. In addition to the effect of the accounting choices made by management, the ratio will also be affected by when the assets were purchased. Assets purchased at different times will have different costs. As a result, comparing the ROA of different entities must be done with a great deal of caution.

This ratio can be thought of in the context of a bank account. The denominator—the investment or the assets invested—is the amount of money that you put in your bank account. The numerator—the return—is the interest that the bank pays you over the year. The return on assets is the rate the bank account earned. If you invested $1,000 in a bank account and over the following year the bank paid you $50 in interest, your return would be 5 percent ($50 ÷ $1,000).

ROA is a measure of how efficiently an entity uses its assets to generate a profit. A company can improve its ROA in two ways: it can lower its asset base or increase its profits. For example, if a company is able to reduce the amount of inventory it needs to operate or decrease the time it takes to collect its receivables (increase accounts receivable turnover) without affecting profits, ROA will increase. Similarly, if an entity has capital assets that it isn't using, it will be able to increase its ROA by selling its assets. Another way to think of ROA is if a company has a poorly performing division—the division has suffered losses for several years and shows no signs of improvement. If the division is sold or closed (and the assets sold off), the company will become more profitable (because the poorly performing division's losses will be eliminated) and will have less in assets. As a result, ROA will increase. There are other factors to consider before a company would close or sell a division, but it would be a good strategy to consider only ROA.

		2009	2010	2011	2012
Profit Margin	Straight-line	10.8%	7.4%	11.6%	9.9%
	Declining balance	−7.9%	8.5%	22.2%	14.8%
Return on Assets	Straight-line	5.5%	4.0%	6.5%	3.8%
	Declining balance	−4.4%	5.1%	12.8%	5.6%

FIGURE 9–8 ::

Vermilion Inc.: Effect of Using Straight-Line and Declining Balance Amortization Methods on Profit Margin and ROA

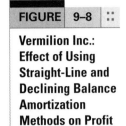

Rogers' return on assets for the year ended December 31, 2005 is:

$$\text{Return on assets} = \frac{\text{Net income} + \text{After-tax interest expense}}{\text{Total assets}}$$

$$= \frac{-\$44,658,000 + (\$710,079,00 \times (1 - 0.361)}{\dfrac{\$13,834,289,000 + \$13,272,738,000}{2}}$$

$$= \frac{\$409,082.5}{13,535,513.5}$$

$$= 3.0\%$$

The tax rate of 36.1 percent for fiscal 2005 can be found in Note 14 to Rogers' financial statements (see page A-34). Rogers' ROA for the year ended December 31, 2004 was 2.8 percent, so this measure of performance improved slightly in 2005 from 2004.

To illustrate the effect of policy choices on financial statement analysis, we will examine the effect of using different amortization methods on two financial ratios for Vermilion Corp. Vermilion Corp.'s financial statements are provided in Table 9–1 of this chapter (see page 468). The two ratios we will examine are profit margin and ROA. For simplicity, we assume that Vermilion incurred no interest expense and we use year-end total assets (instead of the year average) as the denominator in the calculation of ROA. The two ratios are calculated using straight-line and declining-balance amortization.

The results are shown in Figure 9–8. Observe how different the ratios are in each year. In 2009 the profit margin is over 10 percent when straight-line amortization is used and it is –7.9 percent when declining balance is used. Comparing 2009 to 2010, the profit margin ratio fell when straight-line is used but increased when declining balance is selected. ROA shows a similar pattern.

Similar results can be expected with other ratios and other accounting choices regarding capital assets. While the economic condition of an entity is unaffected by these accounting choices, the pictures that those ratios paint can be very different. Without being aware of the impact of accounting choices, the conclusions one might draw about the entity may be very different simply because of its accounting choices. Any type of financial analysis must be based on an understanding of the accounting choices that went into the financial statements. If comparisons are being made between entities or for a particular entity over time, it is important to ensure that like things are being compared.

:: Solved Problem

This chapter's solved problem is a case analysis in an unusual setting. The case will give readers an opportunity to apply the material that has been covered thus far in the book. The case is challenging and readers should not be discouraged if they struggle in places. Readers are encouraged to take the time to do a complete and thorough analysis before reading the solution.

High-Tech Industries Inc.

High-Tech Industries Inc. (Hi-Tech) develops and manufactures highly sophisticated technical equipment for mining companies. Over the years, High-Tech has developed a worldwide reputation for the quality and reliability of its products. For many years, High-Tech was the only company in this market, but in recent years a number of competitors have entered the industry. All these competitors have been supported by their national governments. In the last three years, High-Tech has seen its profits and its margins decline drastically in the face of the new competition. In its most recent fiscal year, High-Tech reported a loss of $42,000,000.

The management of High-Tech has approached government officials for support so that the company can compete on a "level playing field" with its competitors. High-Tech has suggested that it may be forced to move some or all of its operations to another country if it does not obtain adequate support and has asked for immediate subsidies of between $50 and $75 million.

The government has formed a committee to examine whether High-Tech should receive government funding. While the government itself and many members of the committee seem to support High-Tech, there is at least one member of the committee who strongly believes that governments should not be subsidizing private businesses. The dissenting member of the committee has asked you to prepare a report evaluating whether High-Tech's financial information provides a true picture of its financial position. Your report will be used to present the dissenting member's side of the story to the committee, so it is important that your report clearly detail any problems that you identify with the accounting information. Your report should also discuss alternative treatments for the problems you identify and consider the quantitative impact.

The committee member has supplied you with the information in Figure 9–9.

FIGURE 9–9 ::

Additional Information about High-Tech Industries Inc.

1. High-Tech is a private company. Normally its financial statements are not publicly available, but in an effort to support its position, High-Tech has provided a summarized income statement for its 2010 fiscal year to the government committee.

High-Tech Industries Inc.
Summarized Income Statement for the Year Ended October 31, 2010

Revenue		$225,000,000
Cost of sales		106,000,000
Gross margin		119,000,000
Expenses:		
Salaries and benefits	$59,000,000	
Selling, general, marketing and administration	25,000,000	
Loss on sale of technology	22,000,000	
Research and development	40,000,000	
Amortization	15,000,000	161,000,000
Net loss		($ 42,000,000)

2. High-Tech normally uses the percentage-of-completion method for recognizing revenue on its long-term contracts.

3. In 2010 the company entered into a large contract with an Asian company to develop a unique type of mining equipment. Work has begun on the project and it is expected to be completed in 2012. Because of the economic problems in the Asian country, High-Tech has decided to recognize revenue on a completed-contract basis for this contract. Management believes that there is a higher than normal probability that the customer will be unable to pay in full for the technology.

   High-Tech expensed the costs of obtaining the contract in its 2010 income statement. Some other costs pertaining to the contract have also been expensed in the current year. The contract will generate $33,000,000 in revenue and incur estimated costs of $17,000,000. The Asian company has already made $7,000,000 in payments to High-Tech.

4. The majority shareholder of High-Tech owns a company that provides testing and other consulting advice to High-Tech. During 2010 High-Tech paid $18,000,000 to the company owned by the majority shareholder.

5. In 2007 High-Tech purchased the rights to a technology developed by a British company. The technology has proven not to be useful to High-Tech and in 2010 it sold the rights to the technology to another company at a loss of $22,000,000.

6. High-Tech invests heavily in research and development. Research and development expenditures have been increasing significantly in each recent year and this trend is expected to continue. Research and development costs are expensed when they are incurred.

Required:

Prepare the report requested by the dissenting committee member.

This is a user-oriented case. This means that you are to approach the analysis from the perspective of a specific user of the financial statements—in this situation as an advisor to a member of a government committee who strongly opposes government subsidies to businesses.

High-Tech Industries Inc. (High-Tech) has approached the government for a large subsidy and the committee member wants to make an argument against granting a subsidy. Your task is to assist the committee member by providing an analysis of the income statement that serves the interests of the committee member. Remember that interpreting financial statements requires judgment. Simply because an entity reports a loss does not mean it is in financial distress. The role requires that you look at the financial statements to identify areas where the accounting used by High-Tech does not give a reasonable indication of its need for government support. In other words, you must assess whether High-Tech's income statement is appropriate for the stated purpose.

The report should make clear that High-Tech has incentives to understate its performance, and it should identify situations where High-Tech has taken advantage of accounting to make its situation look bad. The report must establish some criteria for assessing the performance of High-Tech. It could be cash flow (low income does not necessarily mean poor liquidity or financial problems), it could be accrual income adjusted for unusual items or some other measure of performance. Some criteria are necessary so that there is a context for interpreting financial statements.

An important aspect of this case is that GAAP have no role to play in this case. It might be necessary for High-Tech to prepare GAAP financial statements, but GAAP statements may not provide the information needed for the intended purpose. Because of GAAP's rules, it is possible that High-Tech's income statement does not reasonably reflect its need for a subsidy. Remember that managers who prepare the financial statements are often constrained by GAAP, but users are not. Users may adjust and modify financial statements to whatever form they please. If GAAP's rules do not provide information that provides that support, then those rules should not be followed. This does not imply a free-for-all. Any basis of accounting must be supported and supportable. So, whatever accounting choices are selected, each choice must be well explained and justified so that it will be convincing to other committee members and to High-Tech's representatives.

Solution:

REPORT TO COMMITTEE MEMBER ON HIGH-TECH INDUSTRIES INC.

I have examined the income statement and explanatory information provided by High-Tech Industries. In my opinion, that statement is not appropriate for evaluating the economic condition of High-Tech for purposes of determining whether High-Tech should be provided with a government subsidy. The statement tends to understate the actual economic performance of the company because of the measurement conventions used. The statement takes a conservative approach to reporting and includes at least one item that is not representative of ongoing performance. In addition, the statement is not a good indication of whether High-Tech actually needs cash. The statement is prepared on what is known as an accrual basis, which measures economic flows rather than cash flows.

The usual basis for preparing financial statements in Canada is generally accepted accounting principles or GAAP and it appears that High-Tech followed GAAP. While GAAP are a useful set of rules and guidelines for preparing financial statements, they are not useful for all decisions in all situations. In the case of High-Tech, application of GAAP served to understate its income in the current period. The reason is that GAAP are inherently conservative. In my analysis below, I suggest treatments that may deviate from GAAP. In my opinion, this is acceptable because GAAP treatments do not give a reasonable view of the economic situation of the company. Overall, I will use accrual accounting as the basis for evaluating High-Tech's performance, although not necessarily GAAP-based accrual accounting. I think it is also important to assess High-Tech's liquidity.

My review of the statements assesses the information provided. However, there is considerable additional information that would be very useful in assessing High-Tech. Thus, my conclusions can only be considered preliminary. Additional information that should be requested includes: comparative financial statements, cash flow statements, balance sheets, details on specific transactions such as related-party transactions, and notes to the financial statements. I have provided my analysis in the absence of a more complete set of information so that you can participate in the upcoming committee meeting in an informed way.

Use of completed-contract method

The impact of the completed-contract method is to reduce revenue and income by deferring revenue recognition to 2012 when the contract is completed. There is no theoretical problem with using different revenue recognition methods for different contracts, provided that the facts justify the different treatments. That is, the circumstances surrounding the contract with the Asian country must be such that the revenue or costs are difficult to reasonably estimate or collection of cash is questionable.

In this situation, it does not appear that the completed-contract method is justified. High-Tech contends that the completed-contract method is justified because cash collection is quite uncertain. The facts do not appear to support this claim. High-Tech has already collected $7,000,000 from the country, which suggests a willingness and an ability to pay. Therefore, there does not seem to be good reason to deviate from the percentage-of-completion method. Since the contract spans three years, I suggest recognizing one-third of the revenue and the expenses related to the contract in 2010. This treatment will add over $5,000,000 to income during the year. (The exact amount may change pending additional information on the work done through the end of 2010.)

Non-arm's length transactions

The non-arm's length transactions raise serious concerns but not answers. If the services provided by the related company have an actual market value of $18,000,000 and were required by High-Tech, then recording them at their transaction value is acceptable. However, it is impossible to determine whether the services provided had a market value of $18,000,000, $8,000,000, $1,800,000, or something else.

Non-arm's length transactions introduce the opportunity for the major shareholder to overstate the value of the services provided to High-Tech, with the purpose of understating High-Tech's income to make its financial situation look poorer. There are no negative economic consequences to High-Tech's major shareholder because she has an economic interest in both transacting entities. Additional information is required to evaluate these transactions. It is necessary to know extensive details on the services provided to High-Tech and an indication of their market value. Indeed, it is necessary to confirm the actual existence of these transactions. For the time being, I recommend that these costs be completely removed from the income statement until additional information is provided. This treatment will reduce the reported loss by $18,000,000.

Loss on sale of purchased technology

During 2010, High-Tech sold technology at a significant loss. That loss represents more than half of the reported net loss. A number of issues arise from this loss. First, the loss is likely not recurring. That means that future periods will not reflect this loss. Therefore, if everything else stayed exactly the same as this year, the loss in 2011 would be $20,000,000 instead of $42,000,000. Also, the loss is an accounting loss, not a cash loss. High-Tech paid for this technology a few years ago. Sale of the technology does not leave the company out of pocket in the current period. In fact, by selling the technology it is actually $22,000,000 better off in a cash sense. I recommend that this loss be disregarded when evaluating the company's income statement. Instead, the analysis should focus on earnings before non-recurring items. This treatment would reduce High-Tech's loss by $22,000,000.

The question can also be raised as to when the loss in value actually occurred. While the loss was realized in 2010, the actual economic loss may have been suffered in a previous period. This means that the loss should have been recognized earlier. There are a number of possible reasons why the loss might have occurred in previous periods but not recorded. If this is the case, income for 2010 is understated. Finally, there is the question of whether taxpayers should be subsidizing a company for its poor decisions.

Research and development costs

Research and development (R&D) is an investment by an entity in future revenue-generating resources. Standard accounting practice (GAAP) expenses R&D when it is incurred because of conservatism. The future benefits of R&D expenditures are considered too difficult to measure, which is why they are expensed. Conceptually, no one would dispute that R&D is an asset. By expensing R&D currently, High-Tech understates its income because expenses are not being matched to the revenues they generate. Those revenues will presumably be earned sometime in the future.

It makes better sense to capitalize the R&D costs and amortize them over some (probably short) period of time (say four years). That means that only $10,000,000 of the year's expenditures should be expensed this year. This adjustment will increase income by $30,000,000. However, for consistency, R&D expensed in previous years should be capitalized and amortized. Given that R&D spending is increasing, the net effect of these adjustments will be to increase income in the current period. However, it is not possible to state an amount that should be amortized in the current period.

Summary

Net income as reported		($42,000,000)
Add:	Adjustment to percentage-of-completion method	5,000,000
	Loss on sale of technology	22,000,000
	Non-arms length transactions	18,000,000
	Research and development costs	30,000,000
	Change in revenue recognition method	5,000,000
Deduct:	Amortization of previous years' R&D	?
Revised net income		$38,000,000

Revised net income shows that High-Tech was profitable in 2010. Even with additional adjustments for R&D amortization and for the non-arm's length transactions, income will likely continue to be positive. This approach is also more representative of its ongoing economic performance.

Please contact me if you have any questions about my report and if you require assistance at the upcoming hearing.

Insight

A good analysis should have included:

■ effective role playing

■ an indication of a basis for evaluating whether High-Tech should receive a subsidy

■ a solid discussion of the accounting issues and recommendations on appropriate treatments

■ an attempt to quantify the impact of the proposed accounting changes

Remember that this analysis represents only one approach. Different ones are possible. The preceding problem is intended to give an idea how this case could be approached, not to serve as the definitive answer.

SUMMARY OF KEY POINTS

▶ **LO 1** GAAP require that entities report their capital assets at historical cost. While historical cost accounting serves the purpose of matching, for the purpose of making projections or other future-oriented decisions it is difficult to understand how the historical cost of capital assets can be useful for most uses and to most users of financial statements. There are three alternatives to historical cost accounting for capital assets: net realizable value, replacement cost, and value-in-use. A main objection to these alternatives is that the measures are not as reliable as historical cost. None of these measurement bases is ideal for all purposes.

▶ **LO 2** The cost of an asset that is reported on an entity's balance sheet should include all the costs associated with purchasing the asset and getting it ready for use. Costs incurred by employees of the entity purchasing the asset, including their wages, should also be capitalized. Costs incurred to improve an existing asset should be capitalized and amortized, whereas costs incurred to maintain an asset should be expensed when incurred.

▶ **LO 3** The process of allocating the cost of a capital asset to expense over time to reflect the consumption of the asset is known as amortization. According to the *CICA Handbook*, the cost of an asset less its residual value should be amortized over its useful life in a "systematic and rational" manner. There are three major methods of amortization: straight-line, accelerated, and usage-based. All of the amortization methods result in the same amount of amortization over the life of the asset. Only the timing of the expense is affected. Different amortization methods do not affect an entity's cash flow, but the method used can affect the outcomes that are based on financial statement numbers.

▶ **LO 4** Intangible assets—also known as knowledge assets or intellectual capital—are capital assets that have no physical qualities. Investments in knowledge assets are all but ignored in traditional accounting, mainly because of conservatism. Money spent on knowledge assets is normally expensed when incurred. However, it is difficult to argue that these investments are not assets, at least conceptually. Expensing investments in knowledge assets when they are incurred has significant implications for the financial statements, including violation of the matching principle, which impairs the meaningfulness of net income.

▶ **LO 5** When an amortizable asset is sold, the cost of the asset and the accumulated amortization associated with it must be removed from the accounting records. If the proceeds received on disposal of a capital asset are different from the NBV of the asset, a gain or loss is reported on the income statement. The amount of the gain or loss on the sale of a capital asset is simply a function of how the capital asset is accounted for.

Sometimes situations arise that impair the value of capital assets. A capital asset is impaired when its net recoverable amount and its fair value are less than its NBV. According to GAAP, when capital assets become impaired they should be written down to their fair value. Management has considerable discretion in deciding the timing and amount of a write-down because determining the impairment of a capital asset is very subjective.

▶ **LO 6** How expenditures for capital assets are accounted for affects the cash flows reported in the cash flow statement. Accounting choices do not affect the actual amount of cash that enters and leaves an entity, but the choices can affect the amount reported as CFO. If an expenditure is capitalized, the outlay will appear in the cash flow statement as an investing activity. If that same expenditure is expensed when incurred, the expenditure is included in CFO.

▶ **LO 7** Despite the importance of capital assets to many entities, there are limits to the insights about an entity that can be gained from analyzing the historical cost information about capital assets in the financial statements. Despite the limitations, a ratio often used to measure the performance and operating efficiency of an entity is return on assets.

▶ **LO 8** (appendix). The *Income Tax Act* (*ITA*) uses the term capital cost allowance (CCA) to describe amortization for tax purposes. The mechanics of CCA are the same as they are for financial accounting—the cost of capital assets is somehow expensed over time—but the *ITA* is very detailed about the method and rate that must be used for each type of asset. For most assets, the *ITA* requires the declining balance method, though straight line is used for some assets. There is no choice or discretion available to the managers—the rules in the *ITA* must be followed exactly.

APPENDIX: AMORTIZATION AND TAXES

The *Income Tax Act* (*ITA*) is very specific about how capital assets can be amortized for tax purposes. The *ITA* uses the term **capital cost allowance** (CCA) to describe amortization for tax purposes. The mechanics of CCA are the same for tax as they are for financial accounting—the cost of capital assets is somehow expensed over time—but the *ITA* is very detailed about the method and rate that must be used for each type of asset. For most assets, the *ITA* requires the declining balance method, though straight-line is required for some assets. Examples of CCA Classes are provided in Figure 9–10. There is no choice or discretion available to the managers—the rules in the *ITA* must be followed exactly. Managers can do whatever they please for financial reporting purposes, but when the entity's income tax return is prepared, the amortization expense in the general purpose financial statements is replaced with CCA.

While for many assets the CCA rules would be acceptable for accounting purposes, in some cases they might not satisfy the *CICA Handbook*'s requirement that amortization of capital assets must be done in a systematic and rational manner because the government can use the *ITA* to achieve policy objectives. For example, the government might try to encourage investment by allowing entities to expense certain assets quickly. This treatment is fine for tax purposes, but may not achieve the matching objective under GAAP

Another example is the half-year rule. The **half-year rule** allows an entity to deduct for tax purposes, in the year an asset is purchased, only one-half the amount of CCA that would otherwise be allowable. If an entity purchases a vehicle for $20,000, it should be allowed to deduct 30 percent of the cost of the vehicle for tax purposes or $6,000 ($20,000 × 0.3) in the first year (because vehicles are a CCA class that allows a 30 percent declining balance rate). The half-year rule allows the entity to deduct only one-half of that amount in the year the vehicle is purchased, or in this case only $3,000 ($20,000 × 0.3 × 0.5). The half-year rule prevents entities from getting the full tax benefit from a new capital asset if the asset is purchased late in the year. On the other hand, an entity that purchases and uses an asset starting in the early part of the year would only be able to deduct 50 percent of the allowable amount of CCA in the year the asset is purchased. While this treatment may satisfy the policy objectives of the government, it does not really satisfy some of the basic concepts of GAAP, such as matching.

Insight

It is easy to make the mistake of thinking that by choosing an amortization policy that minimizes income for financial reporting purposes, taxes are minimized. However, amortization for financial reporting purposes is irrelevant for tax. If an entity uses different methods and rates for financial reporting than what is specified in the *ITA*, an adjustment is required when preparing the entity's tax return. Some companies will use the CCA methods for financial reporting, especially private companies that use their financial statements mainly for tax purposes, to reduce their bookkeeping costs. The irrelevance of amortization for tax purposes contrasts with the *ITA* treatment of inventory. Because the *ITA* does not specify how to account for inventory for tax purposes, the accounting method selected for the general purpose financial statements is usually used for tax purposes.

This discussion highlights the relationship between the *ITA* and financial reporting. Sometimes the *ITA* is very specific about how accounting must be done for tax purposes. In these situations, accounting and tax are completely separate. A company can pursue an objective other than tax minimization and still pay as little tax as possible. In other situations, such as inventory valuation, the *ITA* requires companies to use the same policies for tax purposes as they use in their general purpose financial statements. In that case, a company must choose whether it wants to follow tax minimization or some other objective of accounting.

FIGURE 9–10 ::

Examples of CCA Classes and Rates

CCA Class	Example	CCA Rate allowed
Class 1	Buildings acquired after 1987	4%
Class 7	Canoes, boats and other vessels, including their furniture, fittings or equipment.	15%
Class 10	Automobiles, vans, trucks, buses, computers and system software.	30%
Class 16	Automobiles for lease or rent, taxicabs and coin-operated video games or pinball machines.	40%

KEY TERMS

accelerated amortization, p. 463

amortization, p. 460

betterment, p. 458

capital asset, p. 454

capital cost allowance, p. 495

capitalize, p. 454

declining balance, p. 464

depletion, p. 460

depreciation, p. 460

full costing, p. 480

goodwill, p. 477

half-year rule, p. 495

identifiable assets and liabilities, p. 478

intangible asset, p. 460

maintenance, p. 458

net recoverable amount, p. 482

repair, p. 458

residual value, p. 460

return on assets (ROA), p. 488

straight-line amortization, p. 463

successful efforts, p. 480

tangible asset, p. 460

value-in-use, p. 455

SIMILAR TERMS

The left column gives alternative terms that are sometimes used for the accounting terms introduced in this chapter, which are listed in the right column.

fixed asset, long-lived asset — **capital asset, p. 454**

depreciation — **amortization, p. 460**

knowledge asset, intellectual capital — **intangible asset, p. 460**

diminishing balance — **declining balance, p. 464**

ASSIGNMENT MATERIALS

Questions

Q9-1. For each of the following entities, describe the types of capital assets you would expect the entity to have:
a. gas station
b. university
c. convenience store
d. hotel
e. dairy farm
f. electric utility
g. golf course

Q9-2. What is an intangible asset? How do intangible assets differ from tangible ones? Give examples of each.

Q9-3. Why do intangible assets often not appear on a balance sheet? Under what circumstances will intangible assets be reported on the balance sheet?

Q9-4. What is goodwill? How does it arise?

Q9-5. Why are capital assets amortized?

Q9-6. What costs should be included in the amount capitalized for the purchase of a new delivery vehicle?

Q9-7. What characteristics distinguish capital assets from inventory?

Q9-8. What effect does amortization have on an entity's cash flow? Why is amortization added back to net income when the indirect method of calculating cash from operations is used?

Q9-9. Academic research has shown that the stock price of a public company is not affected by the amortization method an entity uses. Does the amortization method an entity uses matter? Explain.

Q9-10. Why is the amortization of the cost of an asset considered arbitrary?

Q9-11. Identify and explain the two main reasons why capital assets have to be amortized.

Q9-12. Why is the selection of an amortization method never an issue if tax minimization is the main objective of financial reporting?

Q9-13. Why is accounting for knowledge assets such a difficult problem under existing GAAP?

Q9-14. To make room for new equipment that it was installing, Sandwich Inc. had to knock down a wall. The cost of knocking down the wall was $32,000. While the installation was in progress another wall was accidentally knocked down. The cost of replacing that wall was $44,000. Which, if any, of these costs should be capitalized? Explain.

Q9-15. An accounting firm purchases used office furniture for its support staff. For each of the following, would the expenditure be capitalized or expensed? Explain.
  a. The office furniture cost $18,000.
  b. Some of the furniture required repairs before it could be used. The repairs cost $4,000.
  c. Soon after the furniture was delivered, some was damaged because of mishandling by the accounting firm's staff. Additional repairs costing $1,300 were required.
  d. The accounting firm had to hire people to help rearrange the furniture to make room for the new furniture. The work cost $1,500.

Q9-16. Explain why repairs are expensed whereas betterments are capitalized.

Q9-17. An uncle of yours explains that amortization is important because it ensures that money is set aside for replacing the capital assets that are being used up. What would be your response to your uncle?

Q9-18. What effect does a write-down of capital assets have on cash flow? Explain.

Q9-19. What criteria are applied when deciding whether a capital asset should be written down? How does the approach to writing down capital assets differ from the approach used for writing down inventory?

Q9-20. Explain the difference between full cost and successful efforts accounting used by oil and gas exploration companies.

Q9-21. Why do you think GAAP allow the capitalization of oil and gas exploration costs but not research costs?

Q9-22. For each business identified below, explain how the capital asset contributes to generating revenue by the business:

Business	Asset
a. Lawn care	Lawn mower
b. Bank	Banking machine
c. Arena	Zamboni machine
d. Jewellery store	Display cases
e. Doctor's office	Waiting room furniture
f. Auto parts manufacturer	Warehouse

Q9-23. Why does judgment by the managers who prepare financial statements play such an important role in determining the amortization expense that an entity incurs? Be specific.

Q9-24. You are the accountant for a restaurant. The restaurant has recently started a home delivery service and purchased a car to make deliveries. You have to prepare the year-end financial statements for the restaurant and have to decide how to amortize the car. What useful life and residual value would you assign to the car? Explain your decision fully and discuss the factors you considered. Assume the restaurant prepares its financial statements in accordance with GAAP. The car costs $24,000.

Q9-25. Explain how accounting policies can affect the cash from operations an entity reports when we know that different accounting policies have no effect on cash flow.

Q9-26. Explain the following bases for valuing capital assets. Provide examples of how each might provide useful information to a user:
a. historical cost
b. replacement cost
c. net realizable value
d. value-in-use

Q9-27. Company A owns a world-renowned trademark, but it does not appear on its balance sheet. Company B owns a world-renowned trademark, which is valued on the company's balance sheet at $125,000,000. Explain why this difference might arise.

Q9-28. Wisdom Inc. tries to use very conservative accounting methods. For example, it tends to make conservative estimates of the useful lives of capital assets (shorter lives rather than longer ones) and residual value (lower estimates of residual value).
a. What is the impact of these conservative accounting policies on income? Explain.
b. How could these conservative policies have unconservative effects when Wisdom Inc. disposes of capital assets? Explain.

Q9-29. What is capital cost allowance? How does capital cost allowance differ from amortization?

Q9-30. Define and explain the use of the following terms. Provide examples of when each would be used:
a. amortization
b. depreciation
c. depletion

Q9-31. Is it possible for an entity to use a capital asset that is completely amortized? Explain. What would be the net book value of such an asset?

Q9-32. Esk Ltd. (Esk) recently purchased a fully equipped restaurant at an auction for $500,000. The restaurant included all the equipment, furniture, and fixtures. The building itself is rented. Now Esk must allocate the purchase price to the items purchased. Explain how Esk should allocate the purchase price to the specific items. Why is it necessary for the purchase price to be allocated to the specific items? What motivations might influence the allocations that Esk makes?

Exercises

E9-1. **(Straight-line amortization, LO 2, 3, 5)** Roxana Inc. (Roxana) recently purchased new display cases for its retail stores. The display cases cost $150,000, taxes were $22,000, delivery cost $5,000, and set-up cost $8,000. Roxanna's management expects to use the display cases for five years, at which time they will be replaced. Management uses straight-line amortization on assets of this type and estimates that the new display cases will have a residual value after five years of $5,000.

Required:

    a. Prepare the journal entry to record the purchase of the new display cases.

    b. Prepare an amortization schedule showing the amortization expense for each of the five years Roxana expects to keep the display cases and the NBV of the display cases at the end of each year. Assume that the display cases were purchased midway through the fiscal year and only a half-year's amortization is to be expensed in the first year.

    c. Suppose the display cases were sold at the end of the third year for $25,000. Prepare the journal entry to record the sale and any other journal entries required with respect to the display cases in the third year.

E9-2. **(Accelerated amortization, LO 2, 3, 5)** Examine the information provide in E9-1 and respond to parts a, b, and c assuming that Roxanna will use declining balance amortization at a rate of 40 percent for the display cases.

E9-3. **(Accelerated amortization, LO 2, 3, 5)** In early 2008 Jupitagon Ltd. (Jupitagon) purchased new computer equipment. Jupitagon does cutting-edge graphic design work and requires highly sophisticated computer hardware and software. The new equipment cost $400,000 plus $15,000 in taxes, $25,000 for installation, $50,000 for training, and $75,000 for a three-year insurance policy on the equipment.

    Jupitagon's management expects to be able to use the computer equipment for about four years, although with the passage of time the equipment will likely be less useful for more sophisticated work because better equipment becomes available very quickly. Accordingly, management has decided to amortize the equipment using the declining-balance method at a rate of 50 percent per year. Management has indicated that it hopes to be able to sell the equipment at the end of four years for $35,000.

Required:

    a. Prepare the journal entry to record the purchase of the new equipment.

    b. Prepare an amortization schedule showing the amortization expense for each of the four years Jupitagon expects to use the computer equipment, and the NBV of the equipment at the end of each year.

    c. Suppose the computer equipment was sold at the end of 2010 for $55,000. Prepare the journal entry to record the sale and any other journal entries required with respect to the computer equipment in 2010.

E9-4. **(Straight-line amortization, LO 2, 3, 6)** Examine the information provide in E9-2 and respond to parts a, b, and c assuming that Jupitagon Ltd. will use straight-line amortization for the computer equipment.

E9-5. **(Unit-of-production amortization, LO 2, 3, 6)** Grindstone Corp. (Grindstone) produces fad toys for children. In 2010 Grindstone purchased a new stamping machine to produce the latest fad toy. The machine cost $60,000 plus taxes of $4,200, and delivery and installation of $2,000. Grindstone's management estimates that the market for the toy is about 500,000 units and demand for the toy will last no more than four years. Management expects that it will be able to produce and sell 60,000 units in 2010, 300,000 units in 2011, 130,000 units in 2012, and 10,000 units in 2013. Once the fad dies, the machine will not be useful for any purpose and will have to be sold for scrap, about $4,000. Grindstone will use unit-of-production amortization for the machine.

a. Prepare the journal entry to record the purchase of the new machine.

b. Prepare an amortization schedule showing the amortization expense for each year and the NBV of the machine at the end of each year.

c. Suppose that at the end of 2011, Grindstone's management realized that the fad had died more quickly than expected and that there was no more demand for the toy. Prepare the journal entry to record the sale and any other journal entries required with respect to the machine in 2011. Assume that Grindstone produced and sold 300,000 units in 2011 and received $10,000 from a scrap dealer for the machine.

E9-6. **(Straight-line amortization, LO 2, 3, 5)** Examine the information provide in E9-3 and respond assuming that Grindstone will use straight-line amortization for the machine.

E9-7. **(Accelerated amortization, LO 2, 3, 5)** Examine the information provide in E9-3 and respond assuming that Grindstone will use declining balance amortization at a rate of 50 percent for the display cases.

E9-8. **(Accounting for a basket purchase, LO 2)** In January 2009 Bath Inc. (Bath) purchased an office building on a one hectare piece of land in Saskatoon for $13,500,000. An appraiser valued the land at $5,250,000. The building is eight years old and Bath's management expects the building to last for another 16 years, after which time it will have to be demolished. Management has decided to use straight-line amortization.

Required:

Prepare the journal entries that Bath would make to record the purchase of the land and building. What entry would be made to record the amortization expense for the year ended December 31, 2009?

E9-9. **(Determining the gain or loss on the sale of land, LO 5)** In 2005 Chin Corp. purchased a piece of land for $2,500,000. In 2010 the land was sold for $3,500,000.

Required:

Prepare the journal entry to record the sale of Chin Corp's land.

E9-10. **(Determining the gains or loss on the sale of capital assets, LO 5)** For each of the following situations, calculate any gain or loss that would arise on the sale of the asset and prepare the journal entries that would be required at the time of the sale. Assume that in each case the assets were amortized on a straight-line basis and that a full year's amortization was expensed in the year the asset was acquired. All sale transactions occur in the fiscal year ended December 31, 2009.

a. Equipment purchased in 2004 for $100,000 is sold on June 30 2009 for $37,000. When the equipment was acquired it was estimated to have a 10-year life and residual value of $8,000.

b. A building purchased in 1995 for $5,000,000 is sold on March 31, 2009 for $7,500,000. When the building was purchased it was estimated to have a 25 year life and a residual value of $1,000,000.

c. A delivery van purchased in 2007 for $60,000 is sold on December 31, 2009 for $30,000. When the van was purchased it was estimated to have a five year life and a residual value of $10,000.

E9-11. **(Classifying capital assets, LO 3)** Indicate whether the following assets would be considered tangible or intangible. Explain your reason for the classification:

a. unique design for office furniture

b. office furniture

c. right to access another entity's property to enter and leave a lake

d. land

e. exclusive right to open and operate Tim Hortons shops in a city

g. building that houses a Tim Hortons shop

E9-12. **(Calculation of goodwill, LO 4)** On December 31, 2009 Resolute Inc. (Resolute) purchased 100 percent of the common shares of Uno Ltd. (Uno) for $22,000,000. At the time of the purchase, Resolute's management made the following estimates of the fair values of Uno's assets and liabilities:

Assets	$25,000,000
Liabilities	6,000,000

Required:

Calculate the amount of goodwill that Resolute would report on its December 31, 2009 consolidated balance sheet as a result of its purchase of Uno. How much goodwill would Resolute report on its unconsolidated balance sheet on December 31, 2005 as a result of the purchase? Explain.

E9-13. **(Calculate the amount of goodwill, LO 4)** On April 15, 2003 Cashtown Inc. (Cashtown) purchased 100 percent of the common shares of Shakespeare Ltd. (Shakespeare) for $16,000,000. At the time of the purchase, Cashtown's management made the following estimates of the fair values of Shakespeare's assets and liabilities:

Current assets	$7,000,000
Tangible capital assets	17,000,000
Patents	3,500,000
Current liabilities	4,750,000
Long-term debt	10,250,000

Required:

a. Calculate the amount of goodwill that Cashtown recorded when it purchased Shakespeare on April 15, 2003.

b. In fiscal 2007, management determined that the goodwill associated with the purchase of Shakespeare was impaired and that it should be written down to $2,500,000. Prepare the journal entry that Cashtown would make to record the impairment of the goodwill. What amount would be reported on the fiscal 2007 balance sheet for goodwill and what expense would be reported in the income statement?

E9-14. **(Determining cost, LO 2)** Mr. Bogan operates a dairy farm in Québec. Recently, one of his cows gave birth to a female calf. The calf will eventually join the dairy herd that produces the milk that Mr. Bogan sells to dairies. When the calf was born, Mr. Bogan had the veterinarian check the calf. For the first while after its birth, the calf drinks its mother's milk. As the calf gets older, it will graze in the pasture, eating the grass that grows there. During the winter, the calf will eat hay that Mr. Bogan grows on another part of his farm. Eventually the calf will mature and join the herd as a milk-producing cow.

Required:

a. How would you report the dairy herd on Mr. Bogan's farm's balance sheet? Explain.

b. What cost will appear on the farm's balance sheet for the new calf when she is old enough to produce milk? Explain.

c. Explain any limitations you see using GAAP to account for the new calf.

E9-15. **(Calculation of gains and losses on sale of capital assets, LO 3, 5)** On July 4, 2009 Vroomanton Inc. (Vroomanton) purchased new equipment for its print shop. Vroomanton's accountant determined that the capital cost of the equipment was $102,000. The accountant also estimated that the useful life of equipment would be five years and the residual value $12,000. Assume that Vroomanton took a full year of amortization for the equipment in the year ended June 30, 2010.

Required:

    a. Prepare an amortization schedule for the new equipment, assuming the use of straight-line amortization. Set up your amortization schedule like Figure 9–4 in the chapter (page 464).

    b. Prepare an amortization schedule for the new equipment assuming the use of declining-balance amortization using an amortization rate of 40 percent. Set up your amortization schedule like Figure 9–5 in the chapter (page 465).

    c. Assume that on June 30, 2013, after the amortization expense had been recorded for the year, Vroomanton sold the equipment for $33,000. Prepare the journal entry that is required to record the sale assuming that:

       i. the amortization schedule in (a) was used, and

       ii. the amortization schedule in (b) was used.

    d. Explain the reason for the different income statement effects for the journal entries you recorded in (c).

E9-16. **(Preparing amortization schedules, LO 3)** In July 2010 Savory Inc. (Savory) purchased new equipment for $200,000. Savory's management estimates that the equipment's useful life will be eight years and that its residual value will be $10,000. Savory's year end is June 30.

Required:

    a. Prepare an amortization schedule for each year of the new piece of equipment's life using:

       i. straight-line amortization

       ii. declining balance amortization (30 percent)

       iii. unit-of-production method

       Your amortization schedule should show the amortization expense for each year and the net book value of the equipment and accumulated amortization at the end of each year. For the unit-of-production method, assume that 10 percent of the production is produced in each of fiscal 2011, 2012, 2017, and 2018, and 15 percent in each of the remaining years.

    b. Which method do you think Savory's managers would prefer if they have a bonus based on the company's net income? Explain.

E9-17. **(Repairs and maintenance, or betterments, LO 2)** For each of the following independent items, indicate whether the expenditure should be capitalized or expensed. Provide your reasoning.

    a. A courier company changes the oil, oil filters, spark plugs, and air filters of the trucks in its delivery fleet.

    b. An airline paints its aircraft with its new colours.

    c. An office building replaces broken windows with new, energy-efficient windows.

    d. An office suite is rewired to allow for more phone lines to be installed so customer service can be improved.

    e. The CPUs of 12 computers are replaced because of a defect.

    f. The carpets in a law office are cleaned.

    g. An extension is added to a building.

    h. Staff is sent on a training program to develop their customer service skills.

E9-18. **(Choosing an amortization period, LO 3)** Wandby Inc. (Wandby) recently replaced the roof on its 32-year-old building. The roofing company guarantees the roof for 15 years and advised Wandby's management that the roof should last 25 years with no problems. Wandby is amortizing the building on a straight-line basis over 40 years and it is expected that the building will have to be demolished and replaced before it is 45 years old.

Required:

How should Wandby amortize the new roof (method, useful life, and residual value)? Explain your answer fully.

E9-19. **(Determine the cost of a capital asset, LO 2)** The Nameless Cove Hotel (Nameless Cove) is a luxury resort in Atlantic Canada. Recently Nameless Cove built a new, Olympic-size swimming pool on its grounds. The pool was constructed by Deep and Sure Pool Company (Deep and Sure). The following costs were incurred to build the pool:

i.	Building permits	$ 1,000
ii.	Design costs	8,000
iii.	Redesign costs required to make changes that Nameless Cove wanted after construction began	5,000
iv.	Cost of clearing the land of trees and bushes	12,000
v.	Amount paid to Deep and Sure for construction of the pool	150,000
vi.	Damage and repairs to an adjacent property caused when heavy equipment was brought onto the site to do the excavation	22,000
vii.	Cost of meals served to workers	2,000
viii.	Penalties paid to Deep and Sure because Nameless Cove did not want construction to be done on certain regular working days	9,000
ix.	Damage and repair of underground telephone lines that Nameless Cove neglected to advise Deep and Sure about	5,500
x.	Construction of a patio	45,000
xi.	Electrical wiring installed for pool equipment and lighting around the patio	15,000
xii.	Cost of new plants for the patio	9,200

Required:

Determine the amount that should be capitalized as part of the cost of the pool. Explain your reasoning for including or excluding each item in the capitalized cost.

E9-20. **(Effect of transactions and economic events on ratios, LO 4, 5, 7)** Complete the table below by indicating whether the transactions or economic events would increase, decrease, or have no effect on the financial ratios listed in the period they occur. Assume the current ratio is greater than 1.0 before considering each of the situations.

		Return on assets	Profit margin percentage	Current ratio	Debt-to-equity ratio	Gross margin percentage
a.	Write-off of a capital asset.					
b.	Sell a building for cash. The NBV of the building is greater than the selling price.					
c.	Change in the estimate of the residual value of an asset from $10,000 to $15,000.					
d.	Expense R&D costs. Costs were incurred in cash.					
e.	Capitalize R&D costs. Costs were incurred in cash and amortization of the costs will begin in a future period.					
f.	Determine that the net recoverable amount associated with a factory is less than the factory's NBV, but the fair value of the factory is greater than its NBV.					
g.	A new intangible asset was acquired for cash and it was determined that no factors limit its useful life.					

E9-21. **(Effect of transactions and economic events on accounting measures, LO 4, 5, 6, 7)** Complete the following table by indicating whether the transactions or economic events would increase, decrease, or have no effect on the financial ratios listed in the period they occur.

	Net income	Gross margin	Total assets	Owners' equity	Cash from operations	cash from used in investing activities	Total cash flow
a. Write-off of a capital asset.							
b. Sell a building for cash. The NBV of the building is greater than the selling price.							
c. Change in the estimate of the residual value of an asset from $10,000 to $15,000.							
d. Expense R&D costs. Costs were incurred in cash.							
e. Capitalize R&D costs. Costs were incurred in cash and amortization of the assets will begin in a future period.							
f. Determine that the net recoverable amount associated with a factory is less than the factory's NBV, but the fair value of the factory is greater than its NBV.							
g. Determine that there are no factors that limit the useful life of a newly acquired intangible asset.							

E9-22. **(Evaluating the effect of the sale of a capital asset, LO 5, 6)** In 2006 Triangle Corporation purchased a piece of heavy equipment for $450,000. The equipment was estimated to have a ten-year life and it was amortized on a straight-line basis. In 2010 (after four years of amortization was recorded) the equipment was sold for $210,000 in cash. What journal entry would be made to record the sale of the equipment? How would the sale be reflected in the cash flow statement? Would there be any effect of this transaction on the calculation of cash generated from operations?

E9-23. **(Impact of capital asset transactions on the cash flow statement, LO 6)** For each of the following items, indicate whether it would appear on the cash flow statement as cash from operations, an investing cash flow, or a financing cash flow, or that it would not have an effect on cash flows:
a. loss on the sale of furniture and fixtures
b. purchase equipment in exchange for a long-term note payable
c. purchase of a patent for cash
d. amortization expense
e. proceeds from the sale of land
f. research costs
g. gain on the sale of equipment

E9-24. **(CCA versus amortization—Appendix)** On January 3, 2009 Goglin Inc. (Goglin) purchased new equipment to process fresh fruit into jams and jellies for retail sale. The equipment cost $25,000, fully installed, and the amount was capitalized for accounting and tax purposes. Goglin's equipment is classified as class 43, which has a CCA rate of 30 percent declining balance. Goglin's year end is December 31.

Required:

a. What is the maximum amount of CCA that could be claimed for tax purposes in 2009? Explain.
b. What is the maximum amount of CCA that could be claimed for tax purposes in 2010? Explain.
c. What is the maximum amount of amortization for financial reporting purposes that could be expensed in 2009?

d. If Goglin decides to amortize the equipment on a straight-line basis over 15 years, what would be the maximum amount of amortization that could be expensed in 2009?

e. How does the useful life estimated by Goglin's management affect the amount of CCA that can be claimed? Explain.

f. Why are the amounts calculated in (a) and (c) likely different? Explain.

Problems

P9-1. **(Interpreting a write-down, LO 4, 5, 7)** Fiscal 2009 was an outstanding year for Esterhazy Inc. (Esterhazy). For a variety of reasons, the company's sales surged and net income was going to exceed financial analysts' expectations by more than 20 percent or $13,000,000. Esterhazy's management recognized that the high earnings during the year were due to some unusual business circumstances and were not likely to be repeated in the foreseeable future.

Before finalizing its financial statements, Esterhazy's management evaluated the company's assets and determined that several were overvalued. As a result, Esterhazy's assets were written down by a total of $12,000,000 so that the assets would not be reported on its books at more than their market value. All of the assets written down were being amortized, and their remaining useful lives ranged between five and eight years. Esterhazy is a public company that is traded on a Canadian stock exchange.

Required:

a. Explain the effect on the current year's financial statements, as well as the implications for future years' financial statements, of the write-down.

b. Explain how users of the financial statements would be affected by the write-down and how the financial statements should be interpreted as a result of recording the write-down.

c. Why do you think Esterhazy chose to write down the assets?

d. Does it matter that Esterhazy wrote down these assets? Explain.

P9-2. **(Interpreting a write-down, LO 4, 5, 7)** In fiscal 2010, Plumas Technologies Inc. (Plumas) purchased a company that owned a technology that Plumas believed was extremely valuable for its future success. Plumas paid $900,000,000 for the company. Among the assets that Plumas obtained by purchasing the company were "technologies under development" that Plumas estimated to have a fair value of $350,000,000. This means that Plumas estimated that the technologies under development would generate net revenues of at least $350,000,000.

Plumas decided to expense the technologies under development in full in fiscal 2010. As an alternative, Plumas could have treated the technologies under development as an asset and amortized them over about 10 years. Plumas is a public company that is traded on a Canadian stock exchange.

Required:

Explain the effect on the current year's financial statements, as well as the implications for future years' financial statements, of fully expensing the technologies under development. Also, explain how users of the financial statements would be affected by how Plumas accounted for the acquired technologies and how the financial statements should be interpreted as a result of how the acquired technologies were accounted for. Why do you think Plumas chose to account for the technologies in the way it did?

P9-3 **(Repairs, maintenance, and betterments, LO 2)** In March 2005, Hazlet Inc. (Hazlet) purchased a new piece of equipment that was expected to increase the efficiency of the company's production process and the quality of its output. The equipment cost $150,000. The equipment was estimated to have a six-year useful life and a residual value of $15,000. In April 2009, Hazlet paid $98,000 to overhaul the equipment. The overhaul upgraded the technology of the equipment and extended its useful life by an additional two years. In July 2009 the equipment broke down and required servicing to get it to operate properly. The servicing cost $10,000. Hazlet's year end is February 28.

Required:

a. Provide the journal entry to record the purchase of the equipment in March 2005.
b. How would you account for the overhaul done in April 2009? Explain your reasoning.
c. How would you account for the servicing done in July 2009? Explain.
d. What effect would the events in b. and c. have on Hazlet's amortization expense?
e. What would be the amortization expense in each year of the equipments life, assuming that Hazlet uses straight-line amortization.

P9-4. (**Calculate missing information, LO 2, 3, 5**) Use the following information and determine the NBV of the capital assets of June Inc. (June) on September 30, 2010, the end of its 2010 fiscal year. An accounting equation spreadsheet may help you do this question.

i. On October 1, 2009 the cost of June's capital assets was $1,125,000 and the accumulated amortization was $337,500.
ii. During fiscal 2010 June sold capital assets with a cost of $165,000 at a loss of $30,000. June received $45,000 for the assets.
iii. During fiscal 2010 June sold land, which is included in the capital asset account, for $217,500 cash, which generated a gain for accounting purposes of $60,000.
iv. During fiscal 2010 capital assets were purchased for $285,000 cash, plus long-term debt of $337,500.
v. During fiscal 2010 June wrote down capital assets by $48,000.
vi. June recorded an amortization expense of $127,500 for fiscal 2010.

P9-5. (**Calculate missing information, LO 2, 3, 5**) Use the following information and determine the NBV of the capital assets of Ziska Ltd. (Ziska) on July 1, 2008, the first day of its 2009 fiscal year. An accounting equation spreadsheet may help you do this question.

i. On June 30, 2009 the cost of Ziska's capital assets was $1,125,000 and the accumulated amortization was $512,500.
ii. During fiscal 2009 Ziska purchased capital assets for $237,500 in cash plus $100,000 in notes payable.
iii. During fiscal 2009 Ziska sold capital assets with a cost of $135,000 at a gain of $30,000. Ziska received $50,000 cash for the assets.
iv. During fiscal 2009 Ziska sold land, which is included in the capital asset account, for $107,500 cash, which produced a loss for accounting purposes of $40,000.
v. During fiscal 2009 Ziska wrote down capital assets by $41,500.
vi. Ziska recorded an amortization expense of $115,000.

P9-6. (**Effect of capitalizing versus expensing R&D costs, LO 3, 4, 6, 7**) Utopia Inc. (Utopia) is a biotechnology company located in Montréal. Utopia has successfully marketed a number of products since it went public three years ago. Biotechnology is a highly competitive industry and a company's decline in the marketplace is no further away than a competitor's dramatic scientific breakthrough. To remain competitive, companies must invest heavily in research and development to ensure that they have a pipeline of new medicines to bring to market.

Utopia prepares its financial statements in accordance with GAAP, so it expenses all research costs and any development costs that do not meet the criteria for capitalization. To date, none of Utopia's development costs have met the criteria for capitalization. The following information has been summarized from Utopia's financial statements:

| | **Utopia Inc.** | | | | |
| | **Extracts from Financial Statements** | | | | |
	2011	**2010**	**2009**	**2008**	**2007**
Summarized from the income statement					
Revenue	$15,939,000	$ 9,955,000	$ 6,710,000	$ 1,870,000	$ 55,000
Expenses*	7,172,000	4,778,400	3,421,000	2,211,000	1,650,000
Research and develop expenditures	9,900,000	7,700,000	4,400,000	1,650,000	1,100,000
Net loss	$ (1,133,000)	$ (2,523,400)	$ (1,111,000)	$ (1,991,000)	$ (2,695,000)
Summarized from the balance sheet					
Total assets	$27,775,000	$24,717,000	$23,210,000	$ 7,150,000	$ 3,080,000
Total liabilities	10,832,250	8,898,120	8,123,500	3,003,000	1,386,000
Total shareholders' equity	16,942,750	15,818,880	15,086,500	4,147,000	1,694,000
Summarized from the cash flow statement					
Cash from operations	$ 1,375,000	$ (1,980,00)	$ (902,000)	$ (1,540,000)	$ (3,300,000)
Cash expended on investing activities	(2,201,100)	(2,717,000)	(11,770,000)	(3,850,000)	(2,090,000)

*Includes all expenses incurred by Utopia except for research and development.

Required:

a. Recalculate net income for 2009 through 2011, assuming that research and development costs were capitalized and expensed over three years using straight-line amortization.

b. What would total assets be at the end of 2009 through 2011 if research and development costs were capitalized and expensed over three years?

c. What would shareholders' equity be at the end of 2009 through 2011 if research and development costs were capitalized and expensed over three years?

d. What would cash from operations and cash expended on investing activities be if research and development costs were capitalized and expensed over three years?

e. What would the following ratios be, assuming that (1) research and development costs were expensed as incurred and (2) research and development costs were capitalized and expensed over three years? Assume that Utopia did not have an interest expense over the period 2007–2011.
   i.   return on assets
   ii. debt-to-equity ratio
   iii. profit margin percentage

f. How would your interpretation of Utopia differ depending on how research and development costs are accounted for? Which accounting approach do you think is more appropriate? Explain. Your answer should consider the objectives of the users and the managers who prepare the accounting information, as well as the accounting concepts discussed in Chapter 5.

P9-7.   **(Effect of capitalizing versus expensing R&D costs, LO 3, 4, 6, 7)** Florze Software Inc. (Florze) is a software development company located in Kanata, Ontario. Software is a highly competitive industry and the life of a software product is usually quite short. To remain competitive, companies must invest heavily in research and development to keep their existing products up to date and to develop new ones. Florze expenses all research costs and any development costs that do not meet the criteria for capitalization. Florze has never capitalized any development costs. The following information has been summarized from Florze's financial statements:

Florze Software Inc.					
Extracts from Financial Statements					
	2012	2011	2010	2009	2008
Summarized from the income statement					
Revenue	$ 8,983,800	$ 5,611,000	$ 3,782,000	$ 1,054,000	$ 899,000
Expenses*	4,105,950	3,262,750	2,805,500	2,123,500	2,084,750
Research and develop. expenditures	3,487,500	2,712,500	1,550,000	581,250	387,500
Net income (loss)	$ 1,390,350	$ (364,250)	$ (573,500)	$(1,650,750)	$(1,573,250)
Summarized from the balance sheet					
Total assets	$ 9,784,375	$ 8,707,125	$ 8,176,250	$ 2,518,750	$ 1,085,000
Total liabilities	4,011,595	3,047,495	2,452,875	730,438	271,250
Total shareholders' equity	5,772,780	5,659,630	5,723,375	1,788,313	813,750
Summarized from the cash flow statement					
Cash from operations	$ 465,000	$ (775,000)	$ (232,500)	$(1,085,000)	$(2,325,000)
Cash expended on investing activities	(1,395,000)	(1,085,000)	(5,425,000)	(1,550,000)	(883,500)

*Includes all expenses incurred by Florze except for research and development.

Required:

a. Recalculate net income for 2010 through 2012, assuming that research and development costs were capitalized and expensed over three years using straight-line amortization.

b. What would total assets be at the end of 2010 through 2012 if research and development costs were capitalized and expensed over three years?

c. What would shareholders' equity be at the end of 2010 through 2012 if research and development costs were capitalized and expensed over three years?

d. What would cash from operations and cash expended on investing activities be for 2010 through 2012 if research and development costs were capitalized and expensed over three years?

e. What would the following ratios be, assuming that (1) research and development costs were expensed as incurred and (2) research and development costs were capitalized and expensed over three years? Assume that Florze did not have an interest expense over the period 2008–2012.
   i. return on assets
   ii. debt-to-equity ratio
   iii. profit margin percentage

f. How would your interpretation of Florze differ depending on how research and development costs are accounted for? Which accounting approach do you think is more appropriate? Explain. Your answer should consider the objectives of the users and the managers who prepare the accounting information, as well as the accounting concepts discussed in Chapter 5.

P9-8. **(Impaired asset, LO 3, 5)** In January 2007, Coaticook Inc. (Coaticook) purchased a patent for a pharmaceutical designed to allow bald people to grow hair. The drug behind the patent was considered revolutionary at the time and Coaticook's management thought that purchasing the patent would provide it with a product that would re-invigorate sales and the company's stock price. Coaticook purchased the patent for

$125 million. At the time of the purchase, the patent had 10 years left before it expired and it was being amortized on a straight-line basis over that period. Management estimated when it purchased the patent that it would generate an average $22 million in net revenue (revenue less the cost of producing and selling the drug) per year over the remaining life of the patent. In 2007 and 2008, net revenues significantly exceeded expectations, but in mid-2009 a competing product came to market that in independent tests was more effective at growing hair than Coaticook's product, with fewer side effects. As a result of the new product, management slashed its estimate of the net revenues the product would generate by 50 percent. A present value analysis of the estimated future cash flows produced an estimated fair value of the product in mid-2009 of $42 million.

Required:

Coaticook's management has approached you for advice on how it should account for, if at all, the change in market conditions for its hair growth product. Management would like you to fully explain your reasoning and to provide any journal entries that are required to deal with the problem. They would also like your opinion on what effect this information will have on the company's stock price and on its performance for the year.

P9-9. (**Effect of a recording error on the financial statements, LO 2, 3, 6, 7**) In 2006 Zumbro Ltd. (Zumbro) purchased a small delivery truck for $36,000. In error, Zumbro's bookkeeper recorded the purchase as an expense rather than capitalizing the cost and recording it on the balance sheet as an asset. The error went unnoticed until late in 2009, when the truck was sold for $6,000 and no record could be found of it in the accounts.

Required:

a. Show the entry that Zumbro's bookkeeper made to record the purchase of the truck. Show the entry that the bookkeeper should have made.
b. Zumbro uses the straight-line method for amortizing its vehicles and the useful life assigned to similar vehicles in the past has been five years with a $5,000 residual value. What would have been the effect of the error on net income and total assets (amount and direction of the error) in 2006, 2007, and 2008?
c. What would have been the effect of the error on net income and total assets (amount and direction of the error) in 2009, the year the truck was sold?
d. What would have been the effect of the error on the cash flow statement in each of years 2006 through 2009?
e. Assuming the error is material, what would the implications of this error be for users of the financial statements? Explain.

P9-10. (**Effect of a recording error on the financial statements, LO 2, 3, 6, 7**) In 2010 We-Non-Cha Woodworking Ltd. (We-Non-Cha) purchased and installed a new state-of-the-art lathe line in its woodworking shop in British Columbia. The new lathe line cost $1,750,000 to purchase and install, all of which was capitalized. The line is being amortized on a declining balance basis at 20 percent per year. We-Non-Cha used its own employees to install the line. Because of errors made by We-Non-Cha's employees, it was necessary to remove parts of the lathe line after they were already installed to reinforce the building to meet safety standards. The extra work added $200,000 to the cost of the lathe line and is included in the $1,750,000 cost.

Required:

a. How should the cost of the extra work have been accounted for? Explain.
b. What would be the effect of capitalizing the cost of the extra work instead of expensing it on net income and total assets (amount and direction of the error) in 2010, 2011, and 2012? Explain your reasoning.

c. What would be the effect of capitalizing the cost of the extra work instead of expensing it on the cash flow statement in each of years 2010 through 2012?

d. Assuming the effect is material, what would be the implications of capitalizing the cost of the extra work instead of expensing it for users of the financial statements? Explain.

P9-11. **(Effect of accounting on business decisions, LO 5, 7)** Judge Ltd. (Judge) operates a small chain of auto supply shops. The company has been in business for many years and for most of that time it was owned and operated by the Judge family. In recent years Judge has been in financial difficulty and management has been turned over to a team of professional managers. The managers own 10 percent of the shares of Judge. The Judge family owns the remainder of the shares. As a result of the financial difficulties, Judge agreed to a number of strict accounting-based covenants with its creditors, including a requirement that Judge's debt-to-equity ratio not go above 1.5:1 at the end of any quarter over the term of either its bank loan or its long-term debt. If the covenant is violated, all loans become payable in full in 30 days.

Judge owns a piece of land and a building that it has not used for four years. The building housed the first of Judge's shops, but it is no longer appropriate for use. The building is in very poor condition and is not in a very good part of town. Judge has not been able to find a tenant or a buyer, even though it has been looking for both for over two years. The land and building have a NBV of $3,370,000. Judge Ltd. has received an offer of $2,000,000 for the land and building. The offer is attractive, especially because it would provide some urgently needed cash. The offer expires on June 30, 2010, the last day of Judge's fiscal year, and it appears unlikely that it will be renewed.

It is now June 27, 2010. Judge's management estimates that net income for the year will be about $450,000. Management also projects that on June 30, 2010 current liabilities will be $1,150,000 and long-term debt will be $3,350,000. Capital stock on June 30, 2010 will be $1,600,000 and retained earnings on June 30, 2009 were $1,450,000.

You have been asked by Judge's president to prepare a report discussing all the business and accounting issues relevant to the land and building.

Required:

Prepare the report requested by Judge's president.

P9-12. **(Effect of accounting on business decisions, LO 2, 3, 5)** Togo Ltd. (Togo) and Fairfax Inc. (Fairfax) are small property development companies. Ms. Bessnerdium owns 60 percent of the shares of each of the companies and the rest of the shares are owned by separate consortiums of investors in the cities where the companies own properties. Togo owns several small apartment buildings in Ottawa and Fairfax owns a number of apartments in Windsor. Recently, Togo and Fairfax traded buildings. Fairfax received from Togo a building that had a cost of $3,765,000 and accumulated amortization of $1,950,000, and Togo received from Fairfax a building that had a cost of $4,720,000 and accumulated amortization $1,425,000. Both buildings were appraised by independent appraisers, who estimated that the market value of each building was between $9,300,000 and $10,500,000.

Required:

a. Prepare the journal entries that Fairfax and Togo would have to make to record the exchange of the buildings.

b. What would be the effect of the exchange on each company's financial statements in the year of the exchange? Explain.

c. What would be the effect of the exchange on each company's financial statements in the year following the transactions? Explain.

d. Why do you think Fairfax and Togo entered into the exchange?

e. Do you think the accounting treatments you prescribed in (a) make sense? Use the accounting concepts from Chapter 5 to support and oppose the accounting treatment you prescribed.

f. If you were responsible for setting accounting standards, how would you require companies in the situation of Fairfax and Togo to account for these transactions? Explain your reasoning.

P9-13. **(Basket purchase, LO 2, 3, Appendix)** Quabbin Corp. (Quabbin) is a small manufacturing company in Regina. It is owned by five shareholders, two of whom manage the company. The other three are silent investors who invested when the company was struggling financially. The three silent investors live in British Columbia. Quabbin also has significant borrowings from the bank and it anticipates that it will have to request a significant increase in its line of credit in the next few months.

Recently, Quabbin purchased some land, a building, and a number of pieces of used equipment from a bankrupt company. The total cost of the bundle of goods was $5,200,000. For accounting purposes Quabbin estimates that the building will last about 12 years and the equipment should last about five years. It is expected that neither the building nor the equipment will have any residual value. For tax purposes CCA on the building can be charged at 4 percent per year on a declining balance basis. CCA on the equipment is 30 percent per year declining balance. CCA cannot be claimed on the land.

The land, building, and equipment were appraised by Quabbin to ensure it was getting a good deal before they were purchased. The land was appraised at between $950,000 and $1,300,000, the building at between $2,100,000 and $2,800,000, and the equipment at between $1,500,000 and $2,000,000.

You have been asked for advice by Quabbin's controller about how to account for the purchase of the land, building, and equipment. The controller has requested that you explain your recommendation fully so that he can in turn explain the situation to the managers. Your report should also provide the journal entry that Quabbin would make to record its purchase of the land, building, and equipment.

Required:

Prepare the report.

P9-14. **(Preparing amortization schedules, LO 2, 3, 4, 5)** In July 2007 Yreka Palladium Mines Inc. (Yreka), a public company, began operation of its new palladium mine. Geologists estimate that the mine contains about 310,000 ounces of palladium. Yreka incurred the following capital costs in starting up the mine:

Exploration and development	$25,000,000
Mine extraction equipment	18,000,000
Buildings	5,000,000

The exploration and development costs were incurred to find the mine and prepare it for operations. The mine extraction equipment should be useful for the entire life of the mine and Yreka should be able to sell the equipment for $3,500,000 when the mine is exhausted in ten years. The buildings are expected to last much longer than the ten-year life of the mine, but they will not be useful once the mine is shut down.

The production engineers estimate that all the palladium can be removed from the mine over ten years. They estimate the following year-by-year production for the mine:

2008	5,000 ounces
2009	25,000 ounces
2010–2015	40,000 ounces
2016	30,000 ounces
2017	10,000 ounces

Yrkeka's year end is June 30.

Required:

a. Show the journal entries necessary to record the purchase of the extraction equipment and the construction of the buildings.
b. Prepare amortization schedules using the straight-line, declining balance (20 percent per year), and unit-of-production methods for the three types of capital costs.
c. Which method would you recommend that Yreka use to amortize its capital assets? Explain. Do you think the same method should be used for each type of capital asset? Explain
d. The mine is viable as long as the cash cost of extracting the palladium remains below the price Yreka can obtain for its palladium. If the price falls below the cash cost of extraction, it may be necessary to close the mine temporarily until prices rise. What would be the effect on amortization if the mine were temporarily shut down?
e. Under some circumstances it may become necessary to shut the mine permanently. How would you account for the capital assets if the mine had to be shut down permanently? Show the journal entries that you would make in regard to the capital assets in the event the mine had to close permanently. State any assumptions you make.

P9-15. **(Full costing versus successful efforts, LO 3, 4, 7)** Forillon Exploration Ltd. (Forillon) and Gullbridge Gas Inc. (Gullbridge) are natural gas exploration and development companies. In 2009 both companies did extensive exploration in northern Alberta. Each company drilled seven wells and each found gas in three of the wells. The cost of exploring for the gas and drilling the wells was $2,500,000 per well. During 2009 each successful well produced $1,250,000 in gas revenue.

Both companies paid royalties to the Alberta government equal to 25 percent of the revenues from gas sales. In addition, for both companies the cost of producing the natural gas was $120,000 per well, general and administrative costs totalled $320,000, and interest costs were $215,000. Geologists estimate that in 2009, 10 percent of the gas reserves in the wells was extracted and sold. The only difference between the two companies is that Forillon uses the successful efforts method for accounting for gas exploration costs and Gullbridge uses full costing.

Required:

a. Prepare income statements for 2009 for Forillon and Gullbridge. Assume that both companies use the unit-of-production method to amortize exploration costs.
b. Prepare the journal entry required by each company to record the cost of exploring for natural gas. Assume that all expenditures were paid in cash.
c. Suppose that total assets before accounting for gas exploration costs was $29,000,000 for both companies. How would the balance sheets of the two companies differ?
d. Calculate the return on assets and profit margin for the two companies for 2009. Explain the difference between the two companies.
e. Which company is more successful? Explain. Which company would you invest in if you could only invest in one of them? Explain.

P9-16. **(Full costing versus successful efforts, LO 3, 4, 7)** Droxford Exploration Ltd. (Droxford) and Bartibog Inc. (Bartibog) are oil exploration and development companies. In 2010 both companies did extensive exploration in Alberta. Each company drilled 12 wells and each found oil in four of the wells. The cost of exploring for the oil and drilling the wells was $1,500,000 per well. During 2010 each successful well produced $2,000,000 in revenue.

Both companies paid royalties to the Alberta government equal to 25 percent of the revenues from oil sales. In addition, for both companies the cost of producing the oil was $326,000 per well, general and administrative costs totalled $550,000, and interest costs were $425,000. Geologists estimate that in 2010, 15 percent of the oil reserves in the wells was extracted and sold. The only difference between the two companies is that Droxford uses the successful efforts method for accounting for oil exploration costs and Bartibog uses full costing.

Required:

    a. Prepare income statements for 2010 for Droxford and Bartibog. Assume that both companies use the unit-of-production method to amortize exploration costs.

    b. Prepare the journal entry required by each company to record the cost of exploring for oil. Assume that all expenditures were paid in cash.

    c. Suppose that total assets before accounting for oil exploration costs was $42,000,000 for both companies. How would the balance sheets of the two companies differ at the end of 2010?

    d. Calculate the return on assets and profit margin for the two companies for 2010. Explain the differences between the two companies.

    e. What difference does it make which method of accounting for exploration a company uses? Why do you think Droxford and Bartibog would choose one over the other? Explain fully. Remember that both methods are allowed by GAAP.

P9-17. **(Observing the effects of accounting choices on the cash flow statement, LO 4, 6)**
Barkway Inc. (Barkway) is in the process of finalizing its cash flow statement for 2010. The statement has been completely prepared except for the new product development costs that the controller has not decided how to account for. Preliminary net income, *before* accounting for the development costs, is $242,500. The product development costs for the year are $205,000. Based on the controller's interpretation of the *CICA Handbook*, an argument could be made for either capitalizing the costs or expensing them. Barkway's preliminary cash flow statement is shown below (the product development costs are not reflected in the cash flow statement):

Barkway Inc. Cash Flow Statement For the Year Ended August 31, 2006	
Cash from operations	
Net income	$
Add: Amortization	92,500
Less: Gain on sale of capital assets	52,500
Less: Net increase in non-cash working capital	87,500
Cash from operations	
Investing activities	
Proceeds from the sale of capital assets	122,500
Purchase of capital assets	(245,000)
Cash from (used for) investing activities	
Financing activities	
Increase in long-term debt	187,500
Repayment of mortgage loan	(62,500)
Dividends	(25,000)
Cash from (used for) financing activities	
Change in cash during 2010	
Cash and equivalents, beginning of the year	55,000
Cash and equivalents, end of the year	$

Required:

    a. Complete the cash flow statement (shaded boxes) assuming that:
       i. the new product development costs are capitalized and amortized, and
       ii. the new product development costs are expensed when incurred.
      Assume that if the product development costs are capitalized, it is not necessary to amortize any of the costs in 2010.

    b. Compare the two cash flow statements. How is your evaluation of Barkway influenced by the two statements?

c. How are the balance sheet and the income statement affected by the different accounting treatments for the new product development costs?

d. If Barkway's management received their bonuses based on net income, which treatments for the product development costs do you think they would prefer? Explain.

P9-18. **(Observing the effects of accounting choices on the cash flow statement, LO 4, 6)** Juskatla Ltd. (Juskatla) is in the process of finalizing its cash flow statement for 2008. The statement has been completely prepared except for some costs that the controller is not sure whether to classify as repairs or betterments. Normally these types of costs are relatively minor, but this year they were significant and so the classification will have an impact on the financial statements. The preliminary net loss, *before* accounting for the repairs/betterments, is $212,500. The repair/betterment costs for the year are $105,000. The nature of the costs is ambiguous so the controller will likely be able to classify them as either repairs or betterments. The costs are not reflected in the preliminary cash flow statement shown below:

Juskatla Ltd.	
Cash Flow Statement	
For the Year Ended April 30, 2008	
Cash from operations	
Net loss	$
Add: Amortization	137,500
Add: Loss on sale of capital assets	47,5000
Add: Net decrease in non-cash working capital	56,000
Cash from operations	
Investing activities	
Proceeds from the sale of capital assets	155,000
Purchase of capital assets	(662,500)
Cash from (used for) investing activities	
Financing activities	
Increase in long-term debt	500,000
Repayment of long-term loan	(375,000)
Sale of common stock	525,000
Cash from (used for) financing activities	
Change in cash during 2004	
Cash and equivalents, beginning of the year	49,000
Cash and equivalents, end of the year	$

Required:

a. Complete the cash flow statement (shaded boxes) assuming that:
  i. the costs are treated as betterments, and
  ii. the costs are treated as repairs.
  Assume that if the costs are treated as betterments, it will be necessary to amortize $20,000 in 2008.

b. Compare the two cash flow statements. How is your evaluation of Juskatla influenced by the two statements?

c. How are the balance sheet and the income statement affected by the different accounting treatments for the repairs/betterments?

d. Assuming that the controller is correct in her belief that the costs can be reasonably classified as either repairs or betterments, what factors would you advise the controller to consider in making her decision? Explain.

P9-19. **(Evaluating and interpreting the effects of a write-down, LO 4, 5)** Mildmay Ltd. (ML) is a public company that manufactures machine parts. In its most recent financial statements ML wrote down $175,000,000 of its assets. The assets will continue to be used by ML. The new president and CEO of ML announced that the write-downs were the result of competitive pressures and poor performance of the company in the last year. The write-downs were reported separately in ML's income statement as a "non-recurring" item. A non-recurring item is "an item that results from transactions or events that are not expected to occur frequently over several years, or do not typify normal business activities of the entity." Mildmay does not include the write-off in its calculation of operating income.

ML's summarized income statement for the year ended December 31, 2009 is (amounts in millions of dollars):

Revenue		$625
Operating expenses		
Cost of goods sold	$470	
Amortization	87	
Selling, general, and administrative costs	82	639
Operating income		(14)
Other expenses		
Non-recurring item	175	
Interest expense	33	
Income tax expense	(53)	155
Net income		($169)

The write-downs will reduce the amortization expense by $22,000,000 per year for each of the next eight years. After the announcement and release of the income statement, analysts revised their forecasts of earnings for the next three years to:

Year ended December 31, 2010	$15,000,000
Year ended December 31, 2011	$47,000,000
Year ended December 31, 2012	$95,000,000

Required:

a. What would net income be in each of 2009 through 2012 had ML not written off the assets and continued to amortize them? Assume that the operations of ML do not change regardless of the accounting method used.

b. Why do you think the new management might have made the decision to write off the assets?

c. As an investor trying to evaluate the performance and predict future profitability, what problems do asset write-downs of this type create for you? Consider how the write-off is reflected in the income statement and use the ML case as a basis for your discussion.

Using Financial Statements

PRINTERA CORPORATION

Printera Corporation (Printera) provides high-quality labels for the consumer packaged goods market. Serving a global marketplace, Printera is recognized for its quality products, innovation, and exceptional customer service standards. Based in Toronto, Printera is strategically located to serve both the North American and global marketplaces. Its plant is fully equipped with rotogravure and lithographic printing and finishing equipment. Printera's production capacities are able to serve its existing customer base and support additional growth.

www.printera.com

Printera's consolidated statements of operations and consolidated statements of cash flow, and extracts from its consolidated balance sheets, along with extracts from the notes to the financial statements, are provided in Exhibit 9–8.[9] Use this information to respond to questions FS9-1 to FS9-9.

EXHIBIT 9-8 :

Printera
Corporation
Extracts from
Financial
Statements

CONSOLIDATED STATEMENTS OF OPERATIONS

YEAR ENDED SEPTEMBER 30 (in thousands of dollars)	NOTE	2005	2004
Sales		$ 31,269	$ 33,506
Cost of sales		25,614	28,662
Gross profit		5,655	4,844
Selling, general and administrative expenses		2,913	2,680
		2,742	2,164
Amortization expense		2,422	2,003
Interest expense	4, 5	2,059	1,775
Foreign exchange loss (gain)	11	(1,018)	(999)
Write-down on impairment of plant and equipment	12	5,053	3,472
Termination costs		201	313
Write-down of goodwill	13	4,666	-
Loss before income taxes		(10,641)	(4,400)
Write-down of future tax assets	9	2,749	-
Net loss		$ (13,390)	$ (4,400)
Net loss per share (basic and fully-diluted)	14	(0.12)	(0.06)

CONSOLIDATED BALANCE SHEETS

AS AT SEPTEMBER 30 (in thousands of dollars)	NOTE	2005	2004
ASSETS			
Current assets			
Accounts receivable		$ 4,372	$ 4,150
Inventory	2	3,901	4,207
Prepaid expenses		111	105
		8,384	8,462
Plant and equipment	3	9,048	16,430
Future income tax assets	9	-	2,749
Goodwill	13	-	4,666
		$ 17,432	$ 32,307

CONSOLIDATED STATEMENTS OF CASH FLOWS

YEAR ENDED SEPTEMBER 30 (in thousands of dollars)	2005	2004
Cash flows from operating activities		
Net loss	$ (13,390)	$ (4,400)
Items not involving cash:		
Amortization expense	2,422	2,003
Write-down of Goodwill	4,666	-
Foreign exchange gain	(1,018)	(999)
Write-down of future tax assets	2,749	-
Write-down on impairment of plant and equipment	5,053	3,472
	482	76
Changes in non-cash working capital	(148)	464
	334	540
Cash flows from investing activities		
Acquisition of plant and equipment	(135)	(276)
Proceeds from sale of equipment	40	-
	(95)	(276)
Cash flows from financing activities		
Repayment of long-term debt	(921)	(1,355)
Bank indebtedness	682	1,191
Share issuance costs	-	(100)
	(239)	(264)
Net cash flows	-	-
Cash, beginning of year	-	-
Cash, end of year	$ -	$ -

EXHIBIT 9-8 :

(continued)
Printera
Corporation
Extracts from
Financial
Statements

Plant and Equipment

Plant and equipment are recorded at cost. The Company provides for amortization of cost from the time the assets are placed into production on a straight-line basis over the expected useful lives of the assets. Amortization on manufacturing equipment varies from twelve to fourteen years. Amortization on computer and office equipment ranges from two to five years. Leasehold improvements are amortized over the term of the lease and one additional renewal period.

Goodwill

Goodwill is not amortized and is tested for impairment based on the fair value of the Company's reporting unit at least annually using the capitalization of cash flow method and an impairment loss is recognized when the carrying amount exceeds its fair value.

Impairment of long-lived assets

On September 1, 2003, the Company adopted CICA Handbook Section 3063, "Impairment of Long-Lived Assets", which requires the Company to test for impairment loss of long-lived assets whenever events or changes in circumstances occur which may cause their carrying value to exceed the total undiscounted cash flows expected from their use and eventual disposition. An impairment loss, if any, is determined as the excess of the carrying value of the asset over its fair value.

3. PLANT & EQUIPMENT

(in thousands of dollars)	2005			2004		
Asset Type	**Cost**	**Accumulated Amortization**	**Net Book Value**	**Cost**	**Accumulated Amortization**	**Net Book Value**
Manufacturing	$24,269	$16,260	$8,009	$30,851	$16,014	$14,837
Equipment Under Capital Lease	241	96	145	241	48	193
Office equipment	1,200	1,147	53	1,167	1,095	72
Leasehold improvements	1,604	763	841	1,938	610	1,328
	$27,314	$18,266	$9,048	$34,197	$17,767	$16,430

The above includes manufacturing assets with net book values of $651,000 that are not currently in production ($450,000 in 2004). For further reference see Note 12.

12. WRITE-DOWN ON IMPAIRMENT OF PLANT AND EQUIPMENT

The Company engaged in a valuation of certain production equipment and portions of the facility that were not in use during the year and are not anticipated to be utilized in the foreseeable future based on current capacity requirements. In light of the future uncertainty as to the use of this equipment or the timing of the potential use, in accordance with Section 3063 of the CICA Handbook "Impairment of Long-lived Assets", the Company recorded an impairment of $5.1 million against these assets. The impairment was determined in accordance with the above handbook section, which requires establishing the estimated realizable fair value of the held assets. Due to the future uncertainty of the use of the assets, the estimated realizable fair value was determined by an external equipment valuator as opposed to discounted future cash flows.

13. WRITE-DOWN OF GOODWILL

In line with the Company policy for the valuation of goodwill, and following testing for impairment, the carrying amount of goodwill has been written down by $4.7 million to zero. The write down is a result of the allocation of the enterprise value of the Company on a pre-debt basis to the existing book values of the various assets of the business.

FS9-1. Find or determine the following from the information provided about Printera:
   a. What amount of plant and equipment does Printera report on its September 30, 2005 balance sheet?
   b. What amount of goodwill does Printera report on its September 30, 2005 balance sheet?
   c. What amount of plant and equipment was written down during fiscal 2005?
   d. What amount did Printera expense for amortization during 2005?
   e. What is the cost of Printera's manufacturing equipment on September 30, 2005?
   f. Over what period is Printera's manufacturing equipment being amortized?
   g. How much cash did Printera spend on the purchase of new manufacturing equipment?
   h. How much cash did Printera receive from the sale of manufacturing equipment?

FS9-2. What was Printera's net loss for fiscal 2005? What was its cash from operations (CFO)? How do you explain the large difference between the net loss and CFO? Based on your assessment of net income and CFO, did Printera have a good year or a bad year in 2005? Based on the information provided, are you concerned about Printera's liquidity position? Explain.

FS9-3. What is the net book value of Printera's leasehold improvements? What is the cost of the leasehold improvements? How does Printera amortize its leasehold improvements? Do you think that this is a reasonable basis for amortizing the leasehold improvements? Explain. Do you think that it would be more appropriate to amortize the leasehold improvement over the life of the asset being leased? Explain.

FS9-4. How much cash did Printera spend on plant and equipment during 2005? Does this also tell you the cost of the plant and equipment that Printera acquired in 2005? How does Printera account for purchases of new plant and equipment on its balance sheet? How does Printera amortize its plant and equipment?

FS9-5. What amount of plant and equipment does Printera report on its September 30, 2005 balance sheet? What does the amount on the balance sheet represent (how would you explain what the amount means to a novice user of financial statements)? What proportion of Printera's assets are capital assets? Why do you think the proportion is so large? (When you answer, consider the nature of the business.)

FS9-6. How much goodwill did Printera report on September 30, 2005? How much did it report on September 30, 2004? What happened to all of Printera's goodwill? Explain. Normally, how does Printera amortize its goodwill?

FS9-7. By how much did Printera write-down its plant and equipment in fiscal 2005? Why was this write-down necessary? What effect did the write-down have on cash? Explain. How does Printera determine that a write-down of plant and equipment is necessary?

FS9-8. What was Printera's return on assets for the year ended September 30, 2005? What would the return on assets be for the year ended September 30, 2004 if total assets on September 30, 2003 were $36,951,000?

FS9-9. What method(s) does Printera use to amortize its capital assets? What is the basis that Printera (or any entity) uses to determine the period over which capital assets are amortized? What was Printera's amortization expense for 2005? How much amortization has been accumulated against the manufacturing plant and equipment? Why does Printera amortize its capital assets (aside from the fact it is required by GAAP)?

○ ROGERS Analyzing Rogers Communications Inc.

R9-1. Find or determine the following amounts in Rogers' financial statements:
a. The cost of property, plant, and equipment on December 31, 2005.
b. Depreciation and amortization expense for 2005.
c. Accumulated amortization on December 31, 2005.
d. The cost and net book value of wireless network equipment on December 31, 2005
e. Depreciation expense for 2005 on property, plant, and equipment.
f. The amount reported for Toronto Blue Jays player contracts on December 31, 2005 and the period over which the contracts are being amortized.
g. The period over which leasehold improvements are being amortized.
h. The period over which wireless network radio base station equipment is being amortized.
i. The amount of goodwill that was written off in 2005.

R9-2. How much does Rogers report on its December 31, 2005 balance sheet for intangible assets? What is the cost of the intangible assets on hand on December 31, 2005? Why is the cost of spectrum licences the same as their net book value on December 31, 2005? What amount was amortized for intangible assets in 2005? What amount of new intangible assets was added in 2005? What was the source of these intangibles?

R9-3. How much goodwill does Rogers report on its December 31, 2005 balance sheet? How much new goodwill was added in 2005? What were the major sources of this new goodwill? How much goodwill was written off during 2005? Why was this write-off necessary? What is goodwill and why does it arise?

R9-4. How often does Rogers review its long-lived assets for impairment? What condition does Rogers state must occur for a long-lived asset to be considered impaired? If an asset is considered to be impaired, how is the impairment loss determined? How much did Rogers expense in 2005 for impairments? Why is it necessary to test long-lived assets for impairment?

R9-5. What methods does Rogers use to amortize its capital assets? What is the basis that Rogers (or any entity) uses to determine the period over which capital assets are amortized (this is explained in the notes to Rogers' financial statements?) What was Rogers' depreciation and amortization expense for 2005? How much was amortized for property, plant, and equipment? Why does Rogers amortize its capital assets (aside from the fact it is required by GAAP)?

R9-6. Under what circumstances do you think how Rogers amortizes its capital assets would matter to some of its stakeholders? Explain.

R9-7. How much cash did Rogers spend on additions to property, plant, and equipment during fiscal 2005? Where did you find the answer?

R9-8. In 2004 Rogers purchased the outstanding shares of Rogers Wireless Communications. What was the total price of Rogers Wireless Communications? What individual asset acquired in the acquisition was assigned the highest value? What do you think that asset represents and why do you think it is so valuable? What amount of the purchase price was goodwill? How was the amount of goodwill determined?

R9-9. How much property, plant, and equipment was not yet in service on December 31, 2005? Why do you think these amounts aren't amortized?

ENDNOTES

1. Clarence Byrd, Ida Chen, and Joshua Smith, *Financial Reporting in Canada*, 30th Edition. The Virtual Professional Library. 2005.

2. Extracted from Aur Resources Inc.'s 2005 annual report.

3. Extracted from ACE Aviation Holdings Inc.'s and WestJet Airlines Ltd.'s 2005 annual reports.

4. Extracted from Shaw Communications Inc.'s 2005 annual report.

5. Extracted from MDS Inc.'s 2005 annual report.

6. Extracted from Ballard Power Systems Inc.'s 2005 annual report.

7. Panel A extracted from Petro-Canada's 2005 annual report. Panel B extracted from Bow Valley Energy Ltd.'s 2005 annual report.

8. Extracted from Onex Corporation's 2004 annual report.

9. Extracted from Printera Corporation's 2005 annual report.

LIABILITIES

November 2004 was a month the top managers at Rogers Communications would probably like to forget. A handful of prestigious bond rating agencies, including Moody's, Standard and Poor's, and Dominion, slapped downgrades on the company's credit rating. That's because Rogers added $3.4 billion to their already large debt load to make

some big strategic moves: buy back all of Rogers Wireless that it didn't own from AT&T, and gobble up Microcell Telecommunications (FIDO) and Call-Net (Sprint).

At one point, Rogers had five times more debt than earnings, before counting interest, taxes, depreciation, and amortization. By the end of 2004, Rogers reported debt of close to $9 billion dollars.

Investors and credit agencies were howling. After all, in 1998 investors sent the stock price down below $5 a share because Rogers was paying so much to service its debt that it wasn't making any money. CEO Ted Rogers promised in 1998 to improve his company's financial position by 2002, according to published reports in the *Toronto Star*.

Report on Business Magazine said of Ted Rogers' strategy that "he's always preferred to borrow and buy then obsess over present day profit" (March 2005).

But that worries money managers and research analysts alike.

Dvai Ghose, a telecom and cable equity analyst and partner at Genuity Capital Markets in Toronto, fears that being so much in debt could "negatively impact Rogers' ability to compete in new segments such as telefony, particularly as its telco competitors (Bell Canada, for instance) have much stronger balance sheets."

Rogers Communications has lost about $600 million since the company began and has been profitable only half the time since 1995.

Other critics wonder why, with such a massive debt, and rare profits, investors are still bullish on Rogers, willing to lend even more money each year, and sending the stock price up to $43.00 by spring 2006. Wade Burton, a former commercial banker, now with Cundill Investment Research in Vancouver, says he thinks companies founded by one family and controlled by the founder, should be run more like Magna International, the conglomerate controlled by auto parts magnate Frank Stronach.

"That business is run for profits," said Burton. "Rogers? I don't know why it's run."

But Ted Rogers himself is unapologetic. He has pledged to whittle down the debt "the old fashioned way," in his words, through improved earnings. And by

LEARNING OBJECTIVES

After studying the material in this chapter you will be able to:

▶ **LO 1** Explain what liabilities are and how they are valued.

▶ **LO 2** Describe the nature and type of current liabilities and how current liabilities are accounted for.

▶ **LO 3** Recognize the characteristics of bonds and other forms of long-term debt. Determine the value of bonds and understand how they are accounted for.

▶ **LO 4** Explain the fundamentals of leasing and how leases are accounted for and reported in the financial statements.

▶ **LO 5** Characterize the basics of pensions and pension accounting.

▶ **LO 6** Recognize the nature of contingencies, commitments, and subsequent events, and understand the reporting issues surrounding each.

▶ **LO 7** Analyze and interpret information about liabilities in financial statements.

▶ **LO 8** Describe future income taxes and explain how they arise. (Appendix)

mid-2006, there had been some improvement in the debt picture. Rogers Communications paid off some of its outstanding debts to the bond market and refinanced some debt, getting better terms as a result. Overall debt fell to about $7 billion. And the credit rating agencies responded with favourable reviews. Which is important, because better ratings make it cheaper and easier for Rogers to get new loans in the future.

INTRODUCTION

We now turn our attention to liabilities. Liabilities are obligations—to provide cash, goods, or services to customers, suppliers, employees, governments, lenders, and anyone else an entity "owes something to." A liability can be very short-term; for example, a loan that a lender can demand repayment of at any time or payments that must be made to suppliers within 10 days. Or a liability can exist for 10, 20, 30, or more years, such as a mortgage from a bank or bonds sold to investors to finance a capital asset.

Information about liabilities is very important for assessing the liquidity and solvency of an entity. Liabilities often represent obligations to pay significant amounts of cash at specified times, and the amounts and timing of the payments are usually not negotiable. As a result, knowing the timing and terms of these commitments can be crucial for evaluating the ability of an entity to meet its obligations and achieve its objectives. Of course, like most of the other accounting issues that we have discussed in this book, accounting for liabilities is not always straightforward. For example, some of an entity's "obligations" may not be reported on its balance sheet.

Accounting for some liabilities according to GAAP involves the application of complex rules. Accounting for leases, pensions, and future income taxes are among the most difficult topics of GAAP accounting. This chapter will introduce these topics to provide you with an understanding of what the amounts that appear on the balance sheet—amounts that can sometimes be very large—mean and where they come from. These are areas that a private company might choose not to follow if it isn't adhering to GAAP because the benefit to the users of these companies' financial statements may be limited.

WHAT ARE LIABILITIES?

A liability is an obligation. It can be an obligation to pay money to suppliers, lenders, employees, shareholders, or governments, or to provide goods or services to customers. A liability can be current, i.e., the obligation has to be fulfilled within a year, or one operating cycle or a liability can be non-current, i.e., it may not have to be settled for many years. One might think that identifying liabilities is pretty straightforward, but like so many of the topics we have addressed in the book, the matter isn't always clear. To establish a framework for thinking about liabilities, let's look at the criteria GAAP use to determine whether a liability exists.

According to GAAP, liabilities have three characteristics:

1. They require the sacrifice of resources.

2. They are unavoidable.

3. They are the result of past transactions or economic events.

By these criteria, an amount owed to a supplier for inventory purchased—an account payable—is a liability because:

a. The supplier will have to be paid cash to satisfy the obligation. The entity is sacrificing a resource—cash—to meet its obligation.

b. There is a legal obligation to pay. The goods have been delivered and an invoice has been received. The supplier has a right to the money. The entity has to pay or face possible legal action.

c. The amount is owed because the supplier has already delivered the requested goods. This criterion reflects transactions-based historical cost accounting.

Accrued liabilities also meet the GAAP criteria for liabilities. At the end of a reporting period, entities must often make adjusting journal entries to accrue expenses and payables for costs such as interest, warranties, and amounts owing to suppliers. The purpose is to reflect these costs in the period they are incurred so the costs can be matched to revenue. For example, an interest expense is accrued so the cost of borrowing money is reflected in the period the borrower used the money.

Some "obligations" aren't recorded as liabilities. Agreements that commit an entity to purchase goods or services in the future are not reported as liabilities, according to GAAP. These types of arrangements are called executory contracts. When neither party to a contract has performed its part of the bargain, then neither the liability to pay for nor the asset representing the goods or services to be received is recorded. For example, it is common in professional sports for athletes to sign long-term, high-value, guaranteed contracts. Under traditional GAAP, the liability to pay the athlete and its right to the athlete's services are not reported on the sport team's balance sheet. This transaction is not reported as a liability because criterion (3) has not, according to GAAP, been met. The signing of the contract does not trigger recognition of the liability. Performance by the athlete triggers recognition. Once the athlete has played (assuming that he or she was not paid in advance), a liability for wages can be set up.

Then there are items that are reported in the liability section of the balance sheet that probably do not meet the GAAP criteria. One example of these "non-liability" liabilities is future income taxes, which are reported as liabilities on many entities' balance sheets. We will discuss this topic in the appendix of the chapter.

Valuation of Liabilities

In principle, liabilities should be valued at their present value. For many liabilities, the timing and amount of the cash flows are known, and in most other cases it is possible to make a reasonable estimate of the cash flows. In contrast, it is usually very difficult to estimate the timing and amount of cash flows that assets, especially capital assets, will produce. It is also possible to identify an appropriate rate for discounting the cash flows associated with liabilities. Long-term liabilities such as bonds and other long-term debt are valued at the present value of the cash flows that will be paid to the creditors. However, not all liabilities are discounted to their present value. Unearned revenue, future income taxes, and, generally, all current liabilities are not discounted.

Let's look at an example that examines how liabilities are valued. On December 31, 2009 Rowena Inc. (Rowena) purchased heavy equipment from a dealer. The dealer, through the manufacturer, financed the purchase by giving Rowena a three-year, $300,000 interest-free loan. Under the terms of the loan Rowena is required to pay $100,000 on December 31 of each of the next three years. How much should Rowena report as a liability for the loan on its balance sheet on December 31, 2009 through 2012?

One possibility is for Rowena to report a liability equal to the actual number of dollars that it owes the dealer on each December 31. The amount that would be reported on each balance sheet can be seen in Column 1 of Table 10–1. With this approach, Rowena would not report an interest expense on its income statement (since the loan is interest free) and the liability would decrease each year by $100,000.

TABLE 10–1 ::: Valuation of Rowena Inc.'s Loan from the Equipment Dealer

	Column 1	Column 2
	Amount of liability using the nominal value of the liability	Amount of liability using the discounted value of the liability
December 31, 2009	$300,000	$244,371
December 31, 2010	200,000	171,252
December 31, 2011	100,000	90,090
December 31, 2012	0	0

This approach is useful because it informs users of the exact number of dollars that are owed. It is also simple to use and understand. The problem is that it ignores the time value of money. (See Chapter 7 to refresh your understanding of the time value of money.) Even though the loan agreement states that the loan is interest-free, the economic reality is that there is a cost to borrowing: people don't lend money interest-free. When the time value of money is ignored, assets and liabilities are overstated.

Rowena's assets are overstated because the present value of three annual $100,000 instalments is less than $300,000. The dealer would have accepted less than $300,000 if the cash was going to be paid right away. By recording the full amount owed to the dealer, Rowena is, in effect, capitalizing interest as part of the cost of the heavy equipment. Similarly, liabilities are overstated because the present value of the three $100,000 payments is less than $300,000. In addition, net income is overstated because the cost of borrowing is not expensed.

When the time value of money is considered, the amount that is reported on the December 31, 2009 balance sheet is equal to the present value of the payments that must be made to the dealer of the equipment. Assuming a discount rate of 11 percent, the amount that should be reported on December 31, 2009 is equal to the present value of three $100,000 payments made at the end of each of the next three years. Using the formula for the present value of an annuity, we find that the liability that should be recorded on December 31, 2009 is $244,371. The calculation is shown below:

$$\text{PV of an annuity}_{n,\,r} = \frac{1}{r} \times \left[1 - \frac{1}{(1+r)^n} \right] \times \text{Amount to be paid in each period}$$

$$\text{PV of an annuity}_{3,\,0.11} = \frac{1}{0.11} \times \left[1 - \frac{1}{(1+0.11)^3} \right] \times \$100,000$$

$$= \$244,371$$

The amounts that would be reported on the balance sheets over the life of the loan are shown in Column 2 of Table 10–1. The calculations for the other years are left to the reader to figure out in the Knowledge Check below.

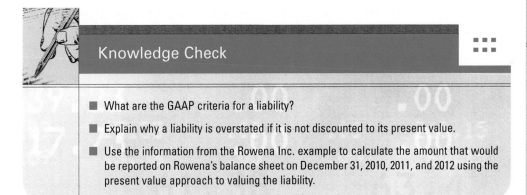

Knowledge Check

- What are the GAAP criteria for a liability?

- Explain why a liability is overstated if it is not discounted to its present value.

- Use the information from the Rowena Inc. example to calculate the amount that would be reported on Rowena's balance sheet on December 31, 2010, 2011, and 2012 using the present value approach to valuing the liability.

www.mcgrawhill.ca/olc/friedlan

CURRENT LIABILITIES

Current liabilities are obligations that will be satisfied in one year or one operating cycle. Information about current obligations is important for assessing the short-term liquidity of an entity. Current liabilities are usually not discounted to their present value because the amount of time until they are settled is relatively short. As a result, the difference between the present value and the stated value will be small. In this section, we will look at a number of different types of current liabilities and discuss the issues that affect accounting for them.

Bank and Other Current Loans

Loans are reported as current liabilities if the amount borrowed must be repaid within the next year or operating cycle. For example, Rogers classifies $286,139,000 of its long-term debt as a

current liability because it is to be repaid within one year. You can see this amount on Rogers' balance sheet (see page A-4) and in Note 11 to the financial statements (see page A-23).

Entities can also have short-term borrowing arrangements that they can use to meet its day-to-day operating needs. A **line of credit** is an arrangement with a lender that allows an entity to borrow up to a specified maximum amount when and if the entity requires the money. A **demand loan** is a loan that must be repaid whenever the lender requests or demands repayment. Lenders often never demand repayment and the loans remain on the books for a long time, but because demand loans are payable at any time, they are classified as current. Loans from banks are often demand loans.

Accounts Payable

Accounts Payable represents amounts that an entity owes to suppliers for goods and services. These goods and services include anything that the entity uses in the course of its business operations, including inventory, supplies, utilities, cleaning services, and so on. We have seen numerous examples of the recording and settlement of accounts payable throughout this book. Measuring the amount of accounts payable is usually not difficult because the recording is triggered by receipt of an invoice from the supplier. The amount of the invoice is recorded as an account payable, and when the amount owing is paid, the balance in Accounts Payable is reduced.

Collections on Behalf of Third Parties

Most entities act as tax collectors for various government taxation authorities. For example, when we purchase merchandise in a store, in addition to the selling price of the merchandise, we also pay the GST (goods and services tax) or the HST (harmonized sales tax) and, in some provinces, provincial sales tax. Employers withhold amounts from their employees' pay for items such as income taxes, employment insurance, and Canada or Québec Pension Plans. Employers also withhold amounts on behalf of employees for items such as employee shares of benefits, union dues, and so on.

GST/HST and provincial sales taxes collected from buyers and money withheld from an employee's pay do not belong to the entity. The entity has an obligation to send these amounts to the appropriate government agency, union, pension plan, and so on, and a liability is set up to reflect the obligation. For example, suppose a Rogers' customer in Alberta buys new wireless equipment online for $400. In addition to charging $400 for the merchandise, Rogers will also collect $24 of GST. The entry that would be made to record the sale (assuming the purchase was charged to his Rogers account) is:

Dr. Accounts receivable (assets +)	424	
Cr. Revenue (revenue +, shareholders' equity +)		400
Cr. GST payable (liabilities +)		24
To record the sale of merchandise and collection of GST.		

The $24 is a liability because the money does not belong to Rogers. It belongs to the government. Rogers is acting as a collector for the government. When Rogers remits the money to the government, it would make the following entry:

Dr. GST payable (liabilities −)	24	
Cr. Cash (assets −)		24
To record remittance of GST to the government.		

An entity must also record liabilities when it withholds money from an employee's pay, again because the money withheld does not belong to the employer, it has been collected from the employee on behalf of third parties. For example, Mr. Barrows is a crane operator for Eyremore Inc. (Eyremore). Mr. Barrows earned $7,000 in May. From his May paycheque, Eyremore withheld $2,000 for income taxes, $313 for Canada Pension Plan (CPP), $169 for Employment Insurance (EI), $90 in union dues, $450 for his employee contribution to the company pension plan, $100 for long-term disability insurance, and a $10 contribution to the United Way.

The journal entry that Eyremore would make to record Mr. Barrows' wages and the withholdings is:

Dr. Wages expense (expenses +, shareholders' equity −)	7,000	
Cr. Income taxes payable—employee (liabilities +)		2,000
Cr. CPP payable (liabilities +)		313
Cr. EI payable (liabilities +)		169
Cr. Union dues payable (liabilities +)		90
Cr. Pension plan contribution payable (liabilities +)		450
Cr. Disability insurance payable (liabilities +)		100
Cr. Charitable donation payable (liabilities +)		10
Cr. Cash (assets −)		3,868

To record wages and employee withholdings.

Of his $7,000 in wages, Mr. Barrows receives $3,868. The rest is collected and distributed on his behalf. The amount for income taxes payable is not for income taxes owed by Eyremore. These taxes are Mr. Barrows' income taxes that Eyremore must collect, by law, on behalf of governments. An entity would not make this entry for each employee. The entry would reflect wages and withholdings for the entire payroll of the company. When Eyremore sends the money owed to the appropriate parties, it would make the following entry:

Dr. Income taxes payable—employee (liabilities −)	2,000	
Dr. CPP payable (liabilities −)	313	
Dr. EI payable (liabilities −)	169	
Dr. Union dues payable (liabilities −)	90	
Dr. Pension plan contribution payable (liabilities −)	450	
Dr. Disability insurance payable (liabilities −)	100	
Dr. Charitable donation payable (liabilities −)	10	
Cr. Cash (assets −)		3,132

To record remittance of payroll withholdings.

Income Taxes Payable

Canadian businesses are required to pay tax on their income to both the federal and provincial governments. Most businesses are required to pay instalments throughout the year, based on their estimate of the amount of tax that will have to be paid for the year. A corporation does not have to file its tax return until six months after its fiscal year end, and an unincorporated business' taxes are included in the tax return of the proprietor or partner. In an entity's financial statements, the amount of income taxes that are owed should be accrued. The amount accrued should be the difference between the estimated amount of income tax the entity must pay and the amount already paid for the year. The accrued amount is classified as a current liability.

Dividends Payable

Dividends payable is an obligation to pay the corporation's shareholders a dividend that has been declared. Once the board of directors has declared a dividend, the amount of the dividend is classified as a liability until it is paid.

Accrued Liabilities

An accrued liability is a liability that is recognized and recorded in the financial statements, but for which the recording is not triggered by an external event such as receipt of a bill or invoice. Accrued liabilities must be recorded with adjusting journal entries. It is necessary to accrue liabilities so that expenses associated with revenues earned in the period are recorded. Examples of accrued liabilities include:

■ wages and salaries for employees that are unpaid at the end of a period

■ interest costs incurred but not payable until a later period

- goods and services that have been acquired but not invoiced (and have not been recorded)
- warranty liabilities
- liabilities for affinity programs (for example, airline frequent flyer programs)
- liabilities to redeem coupons (for example, discount coupons for grocery products, Canadian Tire money)

All of these accrued liabilities require the managers of the entity to determine the amount of the expense and associated liability, and record them with an adjusting journal entry. Some accrued liabilities can be estimated quite accurately. Accrued wages and salaries can be determined by referring to the number of hours worked or the proportion of salary earned from the end of the last pay period to the end of the reporting period.

Accrued interest payable can be calculated using the following formula:

$$\text{Accrued interest payable} = \frac{\text{Amount of}}{\text{loan}} \times \frac{\text{Interest}}{\text{rate}} \times \frac{\text{Proportion of the year since the}}{\text{last payment date}}$$

For example, Fordyce Ltd. (Fordyce) has a $250,000 bank loan that carries an interest rate of 8 percent per year. Interest payments must be made quarterly on the first business day of January, April, July, and October. Fordyce has a December 31 year end. On December 31, 2009 Fordyce must accrue a $5,041($250,000 × 0.08 × 92 ÷ 365) accrued interest payable liability so that the cost of borrowing money is matched to the proper period. The adjusting journal entry that Fordyce would make on December 31, 2009 to accrue the interest expense and interest payable is:

Dr. Interest expense (expenses +, shareholders' equity −)	5,041	
Cr. Accrued interest payable (liabilities +)		5,041
To accrue interest expense and accrued interest payable on the bank loan.		

On January 3, 2010 (the first working day in January 2010) Fordyce would record the following entry to record the payment of interest (the entry assumes that the interest expense incurred on January 1 and 2 will be paid in April):

Dr. Accrued interest payable (liabilities −)	5,041	
Cr. Cash (assets −)		5,041
To record the payment of interest on the bank loan.		

Some accrued liabilities are more difficult to estimate. To accrue a warranty liability, managers must estimate the average cost of providing warranty service to customers. If the entity has experience with a good or service, it can use historical information as a basis for making the estimate. It is more difficult to estimate the cost of providing warranty service for new products. It can also be difficult to make accurate estimates about frequent flyer programs, other affinity programs, and coupon programs. With these types of liabilities, the redemption rate and cost must be estimated and there is the potential for significant errors. For example, a pizza chain might distribute $200,000 in discount coupons, but how many of those coupons will be redeemed by customers? It is the value of the redeemed coupons that should be accrued as a liability.

Accrued liabilities for warranties and affinity programs can have non-current as well as current components. Carmakers, for instance, offer warranties of three or more years on their vehicles. The warranty cost must be estimated for each year that the warranty is offered.

Let's look at an example. Irricana Inc. (Irricana) offers a three-year warranty on its high-definition plasma televisions. The television is a new product and a new technology for Irricana, so it does not have much experience estimating the cost of the warranty service. Based on an analysis by the company's engineers and data from the first sets sold, management has estimated that the average cost per television of warranty service will be $175. During 2008, Irricana sold 22,000 of its high-definition televisions. The estimated warranty expense and liability for televisions sold during 2008 is \$3,850,000 (22,000 × \$175). The engineers further estimate that 40 percent of warranty costs will be incurred in the next 12 months. The entry that Irricana would make to accrue the warranty expense and liability for 2008 would be:

Dr. Warranty expense
 (expenses +, shareholders' equity −)   3,850,000
     Cr. Warranty liability—current (liabilities +)   1,540,000
     Cr. Warranty liability—non-current (liabilities +)   2,310,000
To accrue warranty expense and liability for television sets sold during 2008.

During 2009 Irricana incurred actual warranty costs of \$1,625,000, so the journal entry to record all warranty costs would be:

Dr. Warranty liability-current (liabilities −)   1,625,000
     Cr. Cash (assets −)   1,625,000
To record the payment for repairs of high-definition televisions under warranty.

That the actual cost of warranty repairs was not exactly the same as the amount accrued is not surprising nor is it a problem. Estimates by their nature are imprecise, and over time annual deviations will either average out or will be corrected with adjusting entries in later periods. At the end of 2010, in addition to accruing an expense and liability for warranty costs for televisions sold in 2010, Irricana will also need to reclassify part of the warranty liability accrued in 2009 from non-current to current.

Insight

Estimation is integral to accounting. Simply because certain amounts are difficult to estimate does not mean that the estimates should not be made, or that they do not provide useful information to users of the financial statements. It is, however, important to be aware that these measurements are imprecise and that financial statement numbers vary with the estimates that the managers make. In addition, because it is difficult to know exactly what the actual costs will be, these difficult-to-estimate accruals are attractive for earnings management. Remember in Chapter 7 we discussed how managers can use hidden reserves to manage earnings. Managers can use their estimates of warranty liabilities or coupon usage to set up reserves that managers can use to manage their earnings. For example, if managers wanted to smooth their income over time they could make slightly higher warranty or coupon expenses in years where net income was higher (the effect of doing this would be to lower income) and make slightly lower warranty or coupon expenses in years where net income was lower (the effect of doing this would be to increase income). It is possible for management to do this because it is very difficult to be precise with many of the estimates that must be made.

Unearned Revenue

When an entity receives cash in advance of providing goods or services, it has an obligation to provide those goods or services. Since cash is in hand but revenue has not been recognized, a liability equal to the amount of cash received is required. Examples of unearned revenue include:

- rent payments received in advance

- deposits for goods and services to be provided in the future

- tickets purchased in advance to sporting events, concerts, and the theatre

- gift certificates

For example, on December 4, 2010, Mr. Wayne purchased a $100 gift certificate at Dromore Books Ltd. (Dromore) as a gift for his daughter. The gift certificate entitles the holder to purchase books in the store worth up to $100. The gift certificate can't be exchanged for cash. Dromore would make the following entry to record the purchase of the gift certificate:

Dr. Cash (assets +)	100	
Cr. Unearned revenue—gift certificate (liabilities +)		100
To record the sale of a gift certificate on December 4, 2010.		

When Mr. Wayne's daughter purchases books using the gift certificate, Dromore would make the following entry:

Dr. Unearned revenue—gift certificate (liabilities −)	100	
Cr. Revenue (revenue +, shareholders' equity +)		100
To record the use of a $100 gift certificate.		

Since the gift certificate can be used at any time, the liability is classified as current even though it might not be used over the course of the next year. In general, the timing of converting unearned revenue into revenue is determined by when the entity recognizes its revenue.

Disclosure

Disclosure requirements for liabilities by entities that follow GAAP are quite general, and the financial statements of public companies show a wide variation in the classification and the amount of detail that is provided. The *CICA Handbook* requires that current liabilities be segregated by main class (i.e., bank loans, accounts payable and accrued liabilities, taxes payable, unearned revenue, current portion of long-term debt, and so on). Most entities segregate current and non-current liabilities, but not all. A survey of 200 Canadian firms in 2004 found that 13 of the firms surveyed did not segregate current and non-current liabilities (or assets).[1]

www.cn.ca
www.bombardier.com

Rogers does not provide very much detail about its current liabilities. Current liabilities are shown separately, with main classes shown as required by GAAP. Accounts Payable and Accrued Liabilities, shown as a single account representing about 71 percent of current liabilities, probably represent a wide variety of different obligations, but it is not possible to tell. The amount of detail that Rogers provides about its current liabilities is not unusual—many firms provide similar information.

An example of somewhat more detailed disclosure of current liabilities can be seen in the Canadian National Railway Company's (CN Rail) annual report. CN Rail provides a detailed breakdown of its accounts payable and accrued liabilities in the notes to the financial statements. CN Rail's disclosure on current liabilities can be seen in Panel A of Exhibit 10–1. An example of an entity that does not segregate current and non-current liabilities is Bombardier Inc. (Bombardier), the transportation equipment manufacturer. The liability section of Bombardier's balance sheet is shown in Panel B of Exhibit 10–1. Bombardier explains in the notes to the financial statements that because the company operates in two distinct businesses, each with a specific operating cycle, it is not meaningful to segregate current and non-current liabilities. The problem with not segregating current liabilities is that it is more difficult to assess the liquidity of an entity because it is not clear what is current and what isn't.[2]

BONDS AND OTHER FORMS OF LONG-TERM DEBT

Debt is amounts borrowed and owed by an entity. Debt can be long-term (non-current) or current. In this chapter, we will examine a number of aspects of long-term debt, including how to account for it.

Note 11 to Rogers' financial statements (pages A-23 to A-29) provides information on its debt. On December 31, 2005 Rogers reported long-term debt of $7,739,551,000, of which $286,139,000 was classified as current because it was due to be repaid within the next year. Many entities use

Panel A—Canadian National Railway Company

Consolidated Balance Sheet

In millions December 31,	2005	2004
Liabilities and shareholders' equity		
Current liabilities:		
Accounts payable and accrued charges *(Note 8)*	$ 1,478	$ 1,605
Current portion of long-term debt *(Note 10)*	408	578
Other	72	76
	1,958	2,259

8 Accounts payable and accrued charges

In millions December 31,	2005	2004
Trade payables	$ 475	$ 491
Income and other taxes	261	310
Accrued charges	226	179
Payroll-related accruals	207	259
Personal injury and other claims provision	115	118
Accrued interest	101	106
Workforce reduction provisions	49	90
Other	44	52
	$1,478	$1,605

Panel B—Bombardier Inc.

(IN MILLIONS OF U.S. DOLLARS) **CONSOLIDATED BALANCE SHEETS**

AS AT JANUARY 31	NOTES	2006	2005
			(RESTATED - NOTE 1)
Liabilities			
Accounts payable and accrued liabilities	9	$ 6,866	$ 7,085
Advances and progress billings in excess of related costs	4	2,191	2,359
Fractional ownership deferred revenues		325	163
Deferred income taxes	16	9	41
Long-term debt	10	4,747	5,716
Accrued benefit liabilities	21	877	897
Liabilities related to assets held for sale	1	42	1,571
		15,057	17,832
Shareholders' equity		2,425	2,298
		$17,482	$20,130

SUMMARY OF SIGNIFICANT ACCOUNTING POLICIES

FOR THE FISCAL YEARS ENDED JANUARY 31, 2006 AND JANUARY 31, 2005

BASIS OF PRESENTATION

Bombardier Inc. and its subsidiaries now carry out their operations in two distinct segments, Aerospace and the Corporation's transportation segment ("Transportation"), each one characterized by a specific operating cycle; therefore, the consolidated balance sheets are unclassified.

long-term debt as a way of financing their businesses. Rogers uses debt to finance the investment to develop and maintain it wireless and cable businesses. Rogers uses much more debt than equity to finance its businesses (see Rogers' balance sheet and Notes 11 and 13). Different entities and firms in different industries will use different combinations of debt and equity to finance their activities.

Debt comes in all different shapes and sizes. Money can be borrowed from banks. Debt can be issued to the public at large or to private organizations such as insurance companies or pension funds. Borrowers can provide receivables, inventory, equipment, buildings, or land to lenders as collateral for loans. The collateral provides the lenders with some protection should the borrower be unable to pay back the loan. If the borrowers can't pay, the lenders get the collateral or the proceeds from its sale. The interest rate can be fixed or it can vary with changes in interest rates in the economy. A loan whose interest rate varies with market conditions is called a **variable-rate loan**. If the interest rate does not change, the loan is called a **fixed-rate loan**. The period the debt is outstanding can be long or short. In sum, a debt arrangement can include whatever terms the borrowers and lenders can agree on. Look at the list of outstanding debt in Note 11 to Rogers financial statements (page A-23) and you will see a variety of different interest rates and maturity dates.

Examples of debt instruments include:

■ **bond:** A formal borrowing arrangement in which a borrower agrees to make periodic interest payments to lenders as well as repay the principal at a specified time in the future.

■ **debenture:** A bond with no collateral provided to the lenders.

■ **mortgage:** A loan that provides the borrower's property as collateral.

■ **note payable:** A formal obligation signed by the borrower, promising to repay a debt.

In this section we will focus our attention on bonds, although there are many similarities between bonds and other forms of debt.

There are two ways to finance an entity—debt and equity. Equity represents ownership in the entity. Debt is borrowings that have to be repaid.

Each form of financing has a number of advantages and disadvantages. Interest on debt is tax deductible, which means that the actual cost of borrowing is lower than the interest rate stated in the loan. (The tax deductibility of interest will be explained later in the chapter.) Also, debt is less costly to the entity than equity. However, debtholders do not have a say in the management of the entity; only equity investors, the owners of the entity, do. Debt is riskier for the issuing entity because the interest and principal payments have to be made when required by the loan agreement. That means that interest and principal payments on debt must be made regardless of how well the entity is doing. Defaulting on interest or principal payments (failing to make interest or principal payments when they are due) can have significant and costly economic and legal consequences for an entity. But debt is less risky for investors because debt investors must be satisfied before equity investors. If an entity goes out of business, the creditors must be fully repaid before the equity investors receive anything.

An attractive (and risky) feature of debt to an entity is leverage. **Leverage** is the use of debt to increase the return earned on equity. Debt can increase the return on equity because the cost of debt (interest) is fixed, so if an investment earns a return that is greater than the cost of debt, the return above the interest rate belongs to the equity investors. Of course, if the investment earns less than the cost of debt, the lenders still have to be paid the agreed amount. (We will look at an example of the effect of leverage in Chapter 11.)

Characteristics of Bonds

A bond is a formal borrowing arrangement in which a borrower agrees to make periodic interest payments to the lenders and to repay the principal at a specified time in the future. When a bond is issued, there is an agreement that lays out the terms and conditions of the bond. Each bond certificate will have a face value. The **face value of a bond** is the amount that the holder of the bond, the investor, will receive when the bond matures. The **maturity date of a bond** is the date on which the borrower has agreed to pay back the principal (the face value of the bond) to the bondholders. A bond will specify an interest rate or **coupon rate**, which is the percentage of the face value that the issuer pays to investors each year. These are the essentials of a bond. A bond with a face value of $1,000, coupon rate of 10 percent, and maturity of September 15, 2020 pays the holder of the bond $100 per year in interest and will repay the principal of $1,000 on September 15, 2020.

The face value of a bond is not necessarily the amount of money that the issuer receives from the sale of the bond to an investor. The amount of money that an issuer receives, or the **proceeds**, is determined by the market interest rate or effective interest rate that is appropriate for the bond being issued. The **effective interest rate** is the real or market rate of interest that is required by investors. If the coupon rate is different from the effective interest rate, the bond must be sold at a price that allows investors to earn the effective interest rate. If the coupon rate on a bond is lower than the effective interest rate, then the proceeds will be less than the face value. If the coupon rate is greater than the effective interest rate, then the proceeds from the issue will be greater than the face value. Only if the effective interest rate is the same as the coupon rate will the proceeds be the same as the face value. How the price of a bond is determined is discussed in the next section.

There are many other features that a bond can have in addition to the basic ones described above. Any other characteristics are bells and whistles that are added on to meet the needs of the lenders and the borrowers. The additional features come at a price—the price being a change in the interest rate. If a feature is beneficial to the investors who buy the bonds, the entity issuing the bonds should be able to offer a lower interest rate. If a feature is beneficial to the issuing entity, then investors will require a higher interest rate.

For example, some bonds are callable. A **callable bond** gives the bond issuer the option to repurchase the bond from investors at a time other than the maturity date under conditions that are specified in the bond agreement. This feature is attractive to an issuer because if interest rates fall, the issuer can call the bond and then make another issue at a lower interest rate. This feature is not attractive to investors because they lose an investment that was paying a higher-than-market rate of interest. A callable bond will have a higher market rate of interest associated with it than an equivalent bond without the call feature. A **convertible bond** may be exchanged by the investor for other securities of the issuing entity, such as common stock. The investor may be given the option to cash in the bond before the maturity date under certain conditions. This type of bond is called a **retractable bond**.

A bond agreement can also impose restrictions on the activities of the issuer. These restrictions are intended to reduce the risk of the investors and thereby reduce the cost of borrowing. Many restrictions are stated in accounting terms. For example, a borrowing agreement may set a maximum debt-to-equity ratio or a minimum current ratio. Restrictions may prohibit the payment of dividends if retained earnings falls below a certain amount. Violation of restrictive covenants can have significant economic consequences for the entity. These consequences can include an increase in the interest rate on the debt, an increase in the collateral required, additional covenants, or immediate repayment of the loan. Because violating restrictive covenants is costly, managers will take steps to avoid violating them. These steps can involve operating decisions—for example, reducing spending—or accounting choices.

Pricing of Bonds

Determining the price of a bond or other long-term debt involves the use of the present value tools discussed in Chapter 7. The price of a bond is equal to the present value of the cash flows that will be paid to the investor, discounted at the effective interest rate. The effective interest rate is not the same for all bonds. The effective interest rate is determined by market forces, and depends on the risk of the bond. The riskier the bond, the higher the effective interest rate. The risk for bond investors is whether they will receive their interest and principal. The higher the risk that the investors will not get paid, the higher the effective interest rate the market will apply to the bonds.

Let's consider an example to examine the pricing of long-term debt. Bardal Ltd. (Bardal) plans to issue a bond to raise about $5,000,000 to finance a major expansion. The bonds have a face value of $5,000,000 and will be issued on October 1, 2010. The bonds will carry a coupon rate of 9 percent, with interest paid semi-annually on March 31 and September 30 of each year, and will mature in five years, on September 30, 2015. Each semi-annual interest payment will be $225,000 ($5,000,000 × 0.09 × 1/2). For a bond of this type (risk, features, maturity), the effective interest rate is 10 percent. Therefore, the discount rate that should be used to value the cash flows from this bond is 10 percent. Bardal's year end is September 30. The cash flows that will be generated by the bond are shown in Figure 10–1.

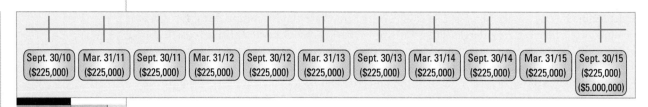

FIGURE 10–1 ::

Interest and Principal Payments for Bardal Ltd.'s $5,000,000 Bond Issue

The proceeds from this bond issue is the present value (discounted at the effective interest rate of 10 percent) of (a) a series of 10 payments of $225,000 paid semi-annually and (b) a payment of $5,000,000 on September 30, 2015, the maturity date of the bond. Because the interest payments are made semi-annually, there is a little twist from our discussion in Chapter 7. Instead of discounting the interest payments at 10 percent over five years, we use a 5 percent discount rate over 10 six-month periods. From the formula for the present value of an annuity, the present value of the interest payments is:

$$\text{PV of an annuity}_{n,\,r} = \frac{1}{r} \times \left[1 - \frac{1}{(1+r)^n}\right] \times \text{Amount to be paid in each period}$$

$$\text{PV of an annuity}_{10,\,0.05} = \frac{1}{0.05} \times \left[1 - \frac{1}{(1+0.05)^{10}}\right] \times \$225,000$$

$$= \$1,737,390$$

We also have to consider the present value of the principal that will be repaid on September 30, 2015. Using the formula for the present value of a single payment to be received in the future:

$$\text{PV}_{n,\,r} = [1+r]^n \times \text{Amount to be received or paid in each period}$$

$$\text{PV}_{10,\,0.05} = \frac{1}{(1+0.05)^{10}} \times \$5,000,000$$

$$= \$3,069,566$$

The proceeds from the bond is the sum of these two present value calculations:

Proceeds from bond issue	=	Present value of interest payments	+	Present value of principal repayment
	=	$1,737,390	+	$3,069,556
	=	$4,806,946		

Once the terms of the bond have been set (interest rate, maturity, other features), the proceeds that Bardal receives are a function of the discount rate that is used. The discount rate is the effective interest rate, which is set by the market. If we assume that the effective interest rate appropriate for Bardal's bond is 8 percent instead of 10 percent, the proceeds from the bond would be:

$$\text{PV of an annuity}_{n,\,r} = \frac{1}{r} \times \left[1 - \frac{1}{(1+r)^n}\right] \times \text{Amount to be paid in each period}$$

$$\text{PV of an annuity}_{10,\,0.04} = \frac{1}{0.05} \times \left[1 - \frac{1}{(1+0.04)^{10}}\right] \times \$225,000$$

$$= \$1,824,952$$

$$\text{PV}_{n,\,r} = [1+r]^n \times \text{Amount to be received or paid}$$

$$\text{PV}_{10,\,0.04} = \frac{1}{(1+0.04)^{10}} \times \$5,000,000$$

$$= \$3,377,821$$

$$\text{Proceeds from the bond issue} = \text{PV of interest payments} + \text{PV of the principal repayment}$$
$$= \$1,824,952 + \$3,377,821$$
$$= \$5,202,773$$

If we repeat the calculation using an effective interest rate of 9 percent, the same rate as the coupon rate on the bond, the proceeds would be $5,000,000. Try that calculation on your own to prove it! This result isn't a coincidence. When the effective interest rate and the coupon rate of a bond are the same, the proceeds and the face value of the bond will be the same.

Accounting for Bonds

Now that we've seen how bonds are priced in the marketplace, let's look at how we account for them. We will continue with the example of Bardal Ltd.'s $5,000,000 bond offer that we began in the previous section. We will examine the three scenarios we used for pricing the bonds. The first scenario will be when the effective interest rate is the same as the coupon rate on the bond, the second will be when the effective interest rate is greater than the coupon rate, and the third will be when the effective interest rate is less than the coupon rate.

Scenario 1: Selling Bonds at Face Value When the market rate of interest is the same as the coupon rate, the bonds sell at their face value, so Bardal will receive $5,000,000 from the offering. The journal entry that Bardal would make on October 1, 2010 to record the issue of the bonds is:

Dr. Cash (asset +)	5,000,000	
Cr. Long-term debt—bonds (liability +)		5,000,000
To record the issue of bonds on October 1, 2010.		

On March 31 and September 30 of each year, Bardal would make the following journal entry to record the payment of interest and the interest expense:

Dr. Interest expense (expense +, shareholders equity −)	225,000	
Cr. Cash (asset −)		225,000
To record the interest expense on the $5,000,000 bond offering.		

(This entry is made on March 31 and September 30 of each year from 2010 through 2015.)

On September 30, 2015, when the bond matures, Bardal would make the following journal entry to record the retirement of the bond. Retirement of a bond occurs when the liability is settled by paying the principal to the investors:

Dr. Long-term debt—bonds (liability −)	5,000,000	
Cr. Cash (asset −)		5,000,000
To record the retirement of the bonds on September 30, 2015.		

The accounting in this scenario is straightforward. The bonds would be reported as a $5,000,000 non-current liability on Bardal's balance sheet. The bonds would be reclassified as a current liability on the September 30, 2014 balance sheet because the bond would be payable in the next fiscal year. The income statement would show an interest expense of $450,000 (2 × $225,000) each year over the life of the bond.

Scenario 2: Selling Bonds at a Discount In this scenario the effective interest rate for Bardal's bonds is greater than the coupon rate. Similar bonds provide investors with a return of 10 percent per year, while the coupon rate on Bardal's bond is only 9 percent. As a result, Bardal has to sell its bonds for less than their face value so that investors can earn the 10 percent effective interest rate they require. Recall from the previous section that the price for Bardal's bond when the effective interest rate is 10 percent is $4,806,946. What this amount means is that investors earn a 10 percent return by investing $4,806,946 now in exchange for a series of ten $225,000 semi-annual payments, plus a $5,000,000 payment at the end of five years.

When a bond is sold to investors for less than its face value, the bond is said to have been sold at a **discount**. The discount is equal to the difference between the face value of the bonds and the proceeds from their sale. Now the question is, how do we account for the discount? When the bond is issued, the discount is recorded in a contra-liability account. The entry that Bardal would make to record the issue of its bonds is:

Dr. Cash (asset +)	4,806,946	
Dr. Bond discount (contra-liability +)	193,054	
Cr. Long-term debt—bonds (liability +)		5,000,000
To record the issue of bonds on October 1, 2010 at a discount.		

The net book value of the bonds—the face value of the bonds less the bond discount—is the net present value of bonds discounted using the effective interest rate when the bonds were sold. The discount can be thought of as extra interest that investors must receive to earn the effective rate of interest. By paying less than the face value for the bonds, investors are compensated for the low coupon rate. The discount of $193,061 is amortized over the life of the bonds and the portion of the discount amortized each period is reported on the income statement as part of the interest expense.

The bonds might be reported on Bardal's balance sheet, if it prepared one on October 1, 2010, as shown in Panel A of Table 10–2 (page 535). Panel A and the journal entry above treat the discount as a contra-liability account, which would be netted against the face value of the bonds to give the net book value of the bonds on the liability side of the balance sheet.

An alternative approach is to include the discount on the asset side of the balance sheet, reported as a deferred charge or other assets. The deferred charge represents interest paid in advance. In this approach, the bonds would be shown at their face value on the liability side of the balance sheet and the discount would appear separately on the asset side. This approach is shown in Panel B of Table 10–2. Both methods are seen in practice.

There are two methods for amortizing the discount: the straight-line method and the effective-interest method. The effective-interest method is required under GAAP. However, the key point to understand is that the discount is amortized over the life of the bond and becomes part of the interest expense. To demonstrate, the straight-line method will be used because the effective-interest method is much more complicated. With the straight-line method, the discount is spread evenly over the life of the bond. For the Bardal bond discount, $38,612 would be amortized each year or $19,306 when each semi-annual interest payment is made. The entry made each semi-annual period would be:

Dr. Interest expense (expense +, shareholders equity −)   244,306
    Cr. Bond discount (contra-liability −)   19,306
    Cr. Cash (asset −)   225,000

Note that even though the interest expense recorded at the time of each semi-annual payment is $244,306, the cash payment each time is only $225,000. With the effective interest method, the amount amortized each period would be different, but the concept is the same.

At maturity, Bardal would make the same as in Scenario 1 to record the retirement of the bond. At maturity, the discount would be completely amortized.

www.mcgrawhill.ca/
olc/friedlan

Knowledge Check

On January 1, 2009 Krydor Inc. (Krydor) issued a two-year, $1,000,000 bond with a 10 percent coupon, interest paid annually on December 31. The bond matures on December 31, 2010. The effective interest rate for this bond is 11 percent.

■ What price will Krydor sell the bond for?

■ What journal entry will Krydor make to record the issue of the bond?

■ Record journal entries that would be made on December 31, 2009 and 2010 to record the interest expense for the year.

■ What journal entry will Krydor make when the bond is retired and the investors are repaid the principal? Do not include the interest portion of the entry.

Scenario 3: Selling Bonds at a Premium In this scenario, the bonds are sold to investors for more than their face value; that is, the bonds are sold at a **premium**. A bond is sold at a premium when the coupon rate is greater than the effective rate of interest for a bond of that type. Recall from the section on pricing bonds that Bardal's bond had a coupon rate of 9 percent,

TABLE 10-2 ::: Methods of Reporting Bond Discount

Panel A: Discount Reported as a Contra-Liability Account

Bardal Ltd.
Extracts from the October 1, 2010 Balance Sheet

Long-term debt—Bonds payable	$5,000,000
Unamortized discount on October 1, 2010	193,054
Net book value of Long-term debt—Bonds payable	$4,806,946

Panel B: Discount Reported as "Other Assets"

Bardal Ltd.
Extracts from the October 1, 2010 Balance Sheet

Non-current assets:		Non-current liabilities:	
Other assets	$193,054	Long-term debt—Bonds payable	$5,000,000

while the effective interest rate was 8 percent (4 percent semi-annually). The amount of the premium is the difference between the cash received from investors and the face value of the bonds. The price for the bonds in this scenario was $5,202,773 and the premium $202,773 ($5,202,773 – $5,000,000). The entry that Bardal would make to record the issue of the bonds at a premium is:

Dr. Cash (asset +)	5,202,773	
Cr. Bond premium (contra-liability +)		202,773
Cr. Long-term debt—bonds (liability +)		5,000,000

To record the issue of bonds on October 1, 2010 at a premium.

Accounting for a premium is essentially the same as for a discount, except that the bond premium account carries a credit balance (instead of a debit balance as with a discount) and the amortization of the premium decreases the interest expense (instead of increasing the expense, as with a discount). A premium lowers the interest rate that the investors earn from the coupon rate to the effective rate. By paying a premium, investors are, in effect, repaying in advance the interest they will collect over the life of the bonds that is over and above the effective interest rate.

As with a discount, a premium is amortized over the life of the bonds using the straight-line method or effective-interest method. Again, the accounting for the amortization of the premium will be demonstrated using the straight-line method. Each year $40,554 of the premium would be amortized or $20,277 when each semi-annual interest payment is made. The entry made each semi-annual period would be:

Dr. Interest expense (expense +, shareholders' equity −)	204,723	
Dr. Bond premium (contra-liability −)	20,277	
Cr. Cash (asset −)		225,000

At maturity, Bardal would make the same entry as in Scenario 1 to record the retirement of the bond. At maturity, the premium would be completely amortized.

The straight-line and effective-interest methods give different measurements for the interest expense, NBV of bonds, and unamortized amounts of discounts and premiums. The coupon rate on a bond is typically the same as or very close to the effective interest rate so premiums and discounts tend to be small (although this isn't always true). Because the premiums and discounts tend to be small, there will be no material difference between the straight-line and effective-interest methods and so, in practice, the straight-line method is commonly used.

According to GAAP, bonds and other forms of long-term debt should be valued at the present value of the cash payments to investors, discounted using the effective interest rate on the date the bond is issued. However, interest rates can and do change over the life of a bond, but the financial statements do not reflect the effect of a change. By ignoring changes in interest rates, financial statements do not reflect real economic gains and losses on long-term debt.

For example, if interest rates increase after a bond is issued, the issuer benefits because its interest cost is now lower than the new market interest rate. The benefit of having to pay less than the going market interest rate would be reflected in a decrease in the market value of the liability. (Remember, when the discount rate increases, the present value of a given series of cash flows decreases. As a result, an increase in the effective-interest rate decreases the value of the bond.) The decrease in the market value of the debt can be thought of as an economic gain because the entity now has less debt and is therefore better off (less debt is better than more debt). The journal entry to record a decrease in the market value of debt would be:

Dr. Long-term debt (liability −)	xxx	
Cr. Gain on decrease in market value of long-term		
debt (income statement +, shareholders' equity +)		xxx
To record a decrease in the market value of long-term debt.		

The opposite logic applies if interest rates decrease. In that case, an entity would be paying a higher-than-market interest rate. As a result, the present value of the debt would increase and the entity would suffer an economic loss.

These gains and losses are **not** recognized under GAAP because of GAAP's transactional nature and because it is difficult to objectively determine the appropriate effective interest rate in the absence of a transaction. However, GAAP now require disclosure of the market value of debt in the notes to the financial statements.

Accruing Interest on Long-Term Debt

What happens if an entity's year end is not the same as the date that interest is paid? If we are using accrual accounting, it is necessary to accrue the interest expense at the end of the period so that the cost of borrowing is recognized in the appropriate period, even though the interest is not paid until later. This is the accrued expense/accrued liability adjusting entry that was discussed in Chapter 3.

If we assume that Bardal's year end is December 31 instead of September 30, an adjusting entry is necessary on December 31 of each year of the bond's life to accrue the interest expense and interest payable for October 1 to December 31. We will use the facts from Scenario 1 (page 533) to show the adjusting entry that has to be made. We will use the December 31, 2012 year end as the basis for the example.

Between October 1 and December 31, 2012, Bardal incurs three months of interest costs that should be matched to the 2012 fiscal year, so on December 31, 2012 the following adjusting entry is required:

Dr. Interest expense (expense +, shareholders' equity −)	112,500	
Cr. Interest payable (liability +)		112,500
The amount is one-quarter of the interest cost for a year ($450,000 × 0.25).		

On March 31, 2013, when Bardal actually pays interest to the investors, it would record the following entry:

Dr. Interest expense (expense +, shareholders' equity −)	112,500	
Dr. Interest payable (liability −)	112,500	
Cr. Cash (asset −)		225,000

This entry records the following information:

1. The interest expense for the first three months of fiscal 2013.

2. The reduction in the interest payable liability that was accrued on December 31, 2012.

3. The payment of interest earned by investors from October 1, 2012 through March 31, 2013 (part of the payment is for interest that was expensed in fiscal 2012 and part is being expensed in fiscal 2013).

Early Retirement of Debt

Entities sometimes retire their long-term debt before it matures. For example, lower market interest rates can make it worthwhile to retire existing high-interest-rate debt and then reissue at a lower rate. An entity can do this relatively easily if the debt has a provision that gives the issuer the option to redeem the debt. Alternatively, an entity could repurchase its debt on the open market if it is publicly traded.

Accounting for the early retirement of debt requires that any unamortized discount or premium be removed from the books when the debt is retired. The impact is that the unamortized premium or discount is included on the income statement in full when the debt is retired, instead of being amortized. A gain or loss will arise on the early retirement of long-term debt if the NBV of the debt is different from the amount that has to be paid to retire it. A gain arises if the cost of retiring the debt is less than its NBV. A loss occurs if the cost of retiring the debt is greater than its NBV.

For example, on December 31, 2009 Aklavik Ltd. (Aklavik) retired its bonds by paying $1,250,000 to investors. The bonds had a face value of $1,000,000 and there was an unamortized discount of $58,000 at the time the bonds were retired. Aklavik would record the following journal entry to record the retirement of the bonds (note that this entry assumes that the interest expense for the period ended December 31, 2009 was recorded before the bonds were retired):

December 31, 2009

Dr. Long-term debt—bonds (liability −)	1,000,000	
Dr. Loss on redemption of bond		
(income statement +, shareholders' equity −)	308,000	
Cr. Bond discount (contra-liability −)		58,000
Cr. Cash (asset −)		1,250,000

To record the early retirement of bonds on December 31, 2009.

A similar approach would be used if there was an unamortized premium recorded on the date the bonds were retired. If there was no unamortized discount or premium, the gain or loss would be the difference between the face value of the bonds and the amount paid to retire them.

Disclosure

The balance sheet itself usually only reveals the total amount of long-term debt outstanding and the amount of that long-term debt that is maturing within the next year. Many stakeholders need more information than that. The totals might provide a small bit of information about the riskiness of the entity, but much more information is required so that stakeholders can estimate future cash flows, funding requirements, and earnings, and evaluate the management and stewardship of the entity. The notes to Rogers' financial statements provide additional detail on its long-term debt that may be useful in assessing these areas.

The table at the beginning of Note 11 to Rogers' financial statements (page A-23) identifies the different long-term debt obligations that were outstanding on the balance sheet date, along with the amounts outstanding, the interest rates, and the year each matures. For example, Rogers Wireless had senior secured notes due in 2014 of $874,425,000 outstanding on December 31, 2005. The interest rate on these notes is 6.375 percent. The table shows that Rogers Cable and Wireless have borrowed huge amounts to finance the networks needed for those businesses. In contrast, Rogers Media has relatively little debt.

The text that follows the table provides additional information about the long-term debt. For example, the bank credit facility available to Wireless allows borrowing up to $700 million. This facility has restrictions that require that certain financial ratios be maintained (the actual ratios aren't stated but perhaps they are the current ratio or debt-to-equity ratio). The facility had restrictions on capital expenditures and dividends, but these have been removed. At the end of 2005, Rogers Wireless had $71 million in borrowings from this facility. This detail can be very useful in assessing the liquidity of Rogers Wireless.

The table at the very end of Note 11 discloses the principal repayments that Rogers will have to make in each of the next five years and thereafter on its long-term debt. This information is

◇ ROGERS

important for assessing future cash flows, cash requirements, and financing needs. According to this disclosure, Rogers has relatively little debt to repay through 2009, but in 2010 almost $1.25 billion is due to be repaid.

Most public companies provide similar disclosure about their long-term liabilities, though the extensiveness of the disclosure will vary from entity to entity. Private companies may provide less information than what appears in Rogers' statements because the users of the statements don't require, or the managers don't wish to provide, the information. However, powerful stakeholders of the financial statements may require and therefore request additional detail on liabilities.

LEASES

When an entity purchases an asset, it will often finance the purchase by borrowing money. When an asset purchase is financed this way, an asset and a liability are reported on the balance sheet. The asset, of course, is recorded at its cost and is amortized over its useful life. The liability is the amount owed to the lender and the liability decreases as repayments of principal are made.

However, financial arrangements can be sophisticated. What happens if, instead of borrowing money to buy the asset, the entity leases it? (A **lease** is a contractual arrangement in which one entity, the lessee, agrees to pay another entity, the lessor, a fee in exchange for the use of an asset. A **lessee** is an entity that leases an asset from the asset's owner and a **lessor** is an entity that leases assets that it owns to other entities.) A lease can be short- or long-term. An asset can be leased for an hour, a day, a week, a year, five years, or any term the parties agree to. Many different assets are available through leasing—individuals lease or rent homes, cars, and garden equipment.

The lessor owns the leased asset, but the lessee has certain rights and obligations that are defined in the lease agreement. Leasing has become a very common way for entities to obtain the use of assets without actually buying them. Air Canada, Canada's largest airline in 2005, had a fleet of 201 aircraft, of which it only owned 32; the rest were leased.

There are a number of reasons why entities prefer to lease assets instead of buying them. With a lease an entity does not have to obtain separate financing for the purchase. This can be important when the entity already has a lot of debt and lenders such as banks are reluctant to lend more. Leasing also allows for financing of 100 percent of the cost of the asset. A lender will often lend only a portion of the amount required to purchase the asset. Leases can also provide flexibility to lessees. For example, a lease agreement could allow a lessee to exchange leased computer equipment during the term of the lease for more up-to-date equipment. This arrangement provides the lessee some protection from technological obsolescence. Leasing is attractive for entities that do not need certain assets continuously. For example, a company may require heavy equipment only at certain stages of a project. A lease allows the entity to use the equipment when it is needed but not incur the cost of owning assets that are idle for a significant amount of time. The terms of a lease are the outcome of negotiation between the lessee and the lessor—any terms are possible if both parties agree.

Leasing has accounting implications. When leasing began to be popular, some entities used it to achieve a "trick" called off-balance-sheet financing. **Off-balance-sheet financing** occurs when an entity incurs an obligation without reporting a liability on its balance sheet. Leasing allowed for off-balance-sheet financing because the lessee would only have to record a lease or rent expense when payment to the lessor was paid or payable. The lessee could have use of the leased asset in much the same way a purchaser would, but neither the leased asset nor the lease liability had to be reported on the balance sheet.

Off-balance-sheet financing allows an entity to have the benefit of incurring a liability without suffering balance sheet consequences, such as a higher debt-to-equity ratio. This can be attractive to entities that are in danger of violating debt-to-equity covenants or for simply limiting the amount of debt the entity appears to have. Also, since the debt-to-equity ratio is a measure of an entity's risk, off-balance-sheet financing makes an entity appear less risky. Of course, an entity's risk is not affected by how liabilities are accounted for, but the ways of measuring the risk are affected.

Eventually, accounting standard-setters recognized that many of these leasing contracts were actually purchases in disguise that allowed entities to avoid recording liabilities on their balance sheets. To attempt to remedy the perceived abuse of the financial statements, rules were established in the *CICA Handbook*. The *CICA Handbook* requires that if a lease results in the transfer of the "benefits and risks of ownership to the lessee," the leased asset and associated liability must be reported on the lessee's balance sheet. Effectively, a lease transaction would be accounted for in the same way as a purchase of assets if the criteria in the *CICA Handbook* are met.

The *CICA Handbook* defines two categories of leases: capital leases and operating leases.

A **capital lease** is a lease that transfers the benefits and risks of ownership to the lessee. Assets associated with a capital lease are capitalized on the balance sheet of the lessee and a liability that is equal to the present value of the lease payments to be made over the life of the lease is recorded. At the beginning of a capital lease the amount recorded for the asset and the related liability are both equal to the present value of the lease payments. In most cases, the lessor treats the lease as a sale, removes the leased asset from its books, and reports a receivable equal to the present value of lease payments to be received. Under a capital lease the lessee amortizes the leased asset.

If the rights and risks of ownership are not transferred to the lessee but are retained by the lessor, then the lease is an **operating lease**. With an operating lease, the lessee does not record the assets or the associated liability on its balance sheet. Instead, the lessee recognizes an expense when the payment to the lessor is paid or payable and the lessor recognizes revenue from the lease when payments are received or receivable. When a lease is classified as an operating lease, the lessee has off-balance-sheet financing.

The key to lease accounting is whether the "benefits and risks of ownership" are transferred to the lessee. The *CICA Handbook* does not precisely define the term, but the idea is that if the lease is, for all intents and purposes, a sale and purchase, it should be accounted for as a sale and purchase. This notion is conceptually reasonable, but under what circumstances are the "benefits and risks of ownership" transferred? The *CICA Handbook* provides some criteria for determining the type of lease.

For a lessee, a lease should be classified as a capital lease if any of the following three criteria are met:

1. It is likely that the lessee will ultimately get ownership of the asset;

2. The lease term is long enough that the lessee receives most of the economic benefits available from the asset (usually defined as 75 percent or more of the leased asset's life); or

3. The lessor is assured of recovering its investment in the leased asset and earning a return on the investment (usually defined as the present value of the lease payments being greater than or equal to 90 percent of the asset's fair value).

These criteria are intended to provide guidance for classifying leases, but the classification of a lease is supposed to be a matter of judgment. In practice, the existence of concrete criteria are often interpreted as hard and fast rules. In the United States, the same criteria exist, but they are rules—judgment is not required. The criteria provide managers with the ability to design lease contracts that allow them to achieve their reporting objectives. If managers want to avoid accounting for a lease as a capital lease, the terms can be negotiated so that the criteria are not met.

Let's look at an example to see how lease accounting works. On March 31, 2009 Outram Inc. (Outram) signed an agreement to lease 200 computers from Cheekye Computer Leasing Corp. (Cheekye) for its new head office and distribution centre in Edmonton. The computers were leased for four years and Outram agreed to pay Cheekye $80,000 on March 31 of each year, beginning in 2010. Outram took delivery of the computers immediately upon the signing of the lease. At the end of the lease, Outram can purchase the computers for $1 each. Outram is responsible for maintaining, repairing, and insuring the computers. If Outram had purchased the computers, they would have cost $250,000. Outram's year end is March 31.

Outram should account for this lease as a capital lease because not one, but all three, *CICA Handbook* criteria appear to be met.

- First, Outram is likely to gain title of the computers at the end of the lease because it can purchase them for $1 each. At such a low price, Outram would certainly purchase the computers if they could still be used or if they could be sold for more than $1.

- We do not know the useful life of these computers, but it's hard to imagine that the life of a computer would be much longer than four years. Certainly five years would be a reasonable maximum for the life of a computer, in which case the lease term is 80 percent of the five-year life.

- The third criterion is also met. The present value of a series of four payments of $80,000 beginning in 2010 is $253,589 ($1/0.10 \times [1 - 1/(1 + 0.10)^4] \times$ $80,000), assuming a discount rate of 10 percent, so the present value of the lease payments is over 101 percent ($253,589 ÷ $250,000) of the purchase price of the computers. Note, though, that the third criterion is sensitive to the discount rate used. If a discount rate of 16 percent were used instead, the present value of the lease payments would be only about 89 percent of the purchase price of the computers, which would mean that the third criterion wouldn't be met.

TABLE 10–3 ::: Income Statement Effect of Capital Versus Operating Leases

| | Capital Lease | | | | | | Operating Lease |
| | Column A | Column B | Column C | Column D | Column E | Column F | Column G |
	Liability on March 31	NBV of the computers on March 31	Principal repayment	Interest expense	Amortization expense	Total expense	Lease expense
2009	$253,589	$253,589					
2010	198,948	202,871	$54,641	$25,359	$50,718	$76,077	$80,000
2011	138,843	152,154	60,105	19,895	50,718	70,613	80,000
2012	72,727	101,436	66,116	13,884	50,718	64,602	80,000
2013	0	50,718	72,727	7,273	50,718	57,991	80,000
2014	0	0	0	0	50,718	50,718	0

The amount that Outram should capitalize for the computers is the present value of the lease payments that will be made over the life of the lease, which is $253,589. The journal entry to record the acquisition of the computers by a capital lease is:

Dr. Assets under capital lease (asset +)   253,589
     Cr. Lease liability (liability +)   253,589
To record the acquisition of 200 computers under a capital lease.

After the initial recording of the leased asset and the related liability, the asset and liability are accounted for separately. (The accounting effects are summarized in the complicated-looking Table 10–3.) Leased capital assets are accounted for in much the same way as any capital asset—they are amortized over their useful lives. Amortization does present some interesting issues, though. If the term of the capital lease is shorter than the useful life of the asset and the lessee is not likely to take title of the leased asset at the end of the lease, the asset should be amortized over the term of the lease.

Since Outram will likely own the computers at the end of the lease, amortizing them over an estimated five-year life is reasonable. If Outram uses straight-line amortization, the annual amortization expense will be $50,718 ($253,589/5). The amortization expense is shown in Column E of Table 10–3 and the NBV of the computers at the end of each fiscal year is shown in Column B. If Outram chose a different amortization method or made different estimates of the useful life or residual value of the computers, the annual amortization expense would be different. The journal entry to record the amortization expense each year is:

Dr. Amortization expense (expense +, shareholders' equity −)   50,718
     Cr. Accumulated amortization (contra-asset +)   50,718
To record the amortization of leased computers.

The interest expense is calculated by multiplying the liability outstanding at the beginning of the year by the interest rate. Lease agreements typically don't state the interest rate so the rate has to be assumed. The same rate that was used to calculate the present value of the lease payments should be used. In this example, a rate of 10 percent has been assumed. Again, remember that the numbers in the financial statements will be affected by the rate chosen and that managers have some flexibility in choosing the rate.

Throughout fiscal 2010, Outram's liability to Cheekye was $253,589, so the interest expense for 2010 is $25,359 ($253,589 × 0.10). The remainder of the $80,000 paid to Cheekye (the portion that is not for interest) is repayment of principal and it reduces the amount of the liability. In 2010 the liability is reduced by $54,641 ($80,000 − $25,359), so the liability on March 31, 2005 is $198,948 ($253,589 − $54,641). For 2011 the interest expense is calculated on the $198,948 liability that is outstanding for the entire fiscal year.

Notice that as time passes, the interest portion of the annual payment decreases and the principal portion increases. This happens because, as the liability decreases, less interest must be paid and more of the payment is applied to paying down the liability. This effect can be seen in Columns A, C, and D of Table 10–3.

The journal entry that would be recorded to record the lease payment in 2010 is:

Dr. Interest expense (expenses +, shareholders' equity −)	25,359	
Dr. Lease liability (liability −)	54,641	
Cr. Cash (asset −)		80,000

To record the lease payment to Cheekye for 2010.

Notice in Table 10–3 that the NBV of the computers (Column B) and the associated liability (Column A) are different in each of the years shown, except when the lease is initially recorded and in the last year. This is expected because the asset and liability are accounted for separately after the initial recording of the lease.

If Outram were able to treat the lease as an operating lease (which in this example it could not if it had to follow GAAP), the only entries required would occur when a payment to Cheekye was made or became payable. The entry that Outram would make on March 31, 2010 (and in 2011 through 2013) if the lease were classified as an operating lease would be:

Dr. Lease expense (expense +, shareholders' equity −)	80,000	
Cr. Cash (asset −)		80,000

To record the annual payment to Cheekye for the computers leased under an operating lease.

The annual lease expense for Outram under an operating lease is shown in Column G of Table 10–3.

The *CICA Handbook* requires extensive disclosure about an entity's lease transactions. The *CICA Handbook* is our source for what should be disclosed because lease accounting is strictly a *Handbook* requirement. For operating leases, an entity should disclose in the notes to the financial statements the minimum lease payments that must be made under operating leases in each of the next five years. For capital leases, an entity should disclose the amount of assets it has under capital leases, along with accumulated amortization associated with those assets, as well as information about capital lease liabilities.

Rogers provides disclosure information about its operating leases in Note 20(g). The note shows that Rogers has lease obligations that are not on the balance sheet of in excess of $840 million, including over $214 million that has to be paid in 2006. More will be said about the importance and impact of off-balance sheet financing issues later in this chapter.

Lease accounting is an area where a private company might choose not to follow GAAP. For example, if the main or only reason for preparing financial statements is for tax purposes, then not following GAAP for leases makes sense if capital leases for accounting purposes are considered operating leases for tax purposes. It may also be sensible for small businesses to avoid the complexities of lease accounting if the users of the financial statements do not require them.

It is important to remember that whether a lease is classified as operating or capital affects many numbers in the financial statements. With a capital lease, total assets and liabilities will be higher than under an operating lease and expenses can be different (as can be seen by comparing Columns F and G in Table 10–3). These differences can affect many different financial ratios that are used in financial analysis. For example, with a capital lease total assets will be greater (compared with an operating lease), so ROA will be lower (though the exact impact will

⬡ ROGERS™

depend on how net income is affected). Similarly, as mentioned earlier, with an operating lease an entity's debt-to-equity ratio will be lower because there will be fewer liabilities.

Let's look at an example to see the effect of leasing on financial ratios. Consider the information about Outram's lease of computer shown in Table 10–3. Assume that

a. Outram's 2010 income before considering costs related to the lease $425,000;

b. Outram's interest expense for 2010 before considering interest pertaining to the lease was $50,000;

c. Total assets on March 31, 2009 before considering the effect of the lease was $2,250,000;

d. Total assets on March 31, 2010 before considering the effect of the lease was $2,500,000; and

e. Outram's tax rate is 20 percent.

Outram's ROA for 2010 using the two leasing arrangements are:

	Capital Lease	Operating Lease
Total assets, March 31, 2009	$2,503,589[1]	$2,250,000[2]
Total assets, March 31, 2010	2,702,871[3]	2,500,000[2]
Net income for fiscal 2010	348,923[4]	345,000[5]

[1] $2,250,000 + $253,589 (NBV of the computers on March 31, 2009—from Column B in Table 10–3).

[2] Total assets are not affected when the lease is classified as an operating lease.

[3] $2,500,000 + $202,871 (NBV of the computers on March 31, 2010—from Column B in Table 10–3).

[4] $425,000 − $76,077 (lease related expenses)

[5] $425,000 − $80,000 (lease expense)

$$ROA = \frac{\text{Net income} + \text{After-tax interest expense}}{\text{Total assets}}$$

$$ROA_{\text{Capital Lease}} = \frac{\$348,923 + (\$75,359 \times (1 - 0.2))}{\dfrac{(\$2,702,871 + \$2,503,589)}{2}}$$

$$= 15.7\%$$

$$ROA_{\text{Operating Lease}} = \frac{\$345,000 + (\$50,000 \times (1 - 0.2))}{\dfrac{(\$2,500,000 + \$2,250,000)}{2}}$$

$$= 16.2\%$$

The ROA using the capital lease is slightly lower than it is using the operating lease because average total assets are greater with the capital lease, but the numerator is also larger because of the interest expense related to the capital lease.

Question for Consideration

Explain why companies might prefer to have their leases classified as operating leases instead of capital leases. Explain why and how companies are able to arrange their leases to satisfy this preference under GAAP.

Answer: The disadvantage of a capital lease is that a liability equal to the present value of the lease payments must be reported on the balance sheet. This accounting treatment increases the amount of debt an entity reports on its balance sheet, which may affect the perceived risk of the entity and the perceived ability of the entity to carry additional debt. Measurements such as the debt-to-equity ratio increase when leases are capitalized, which may have economic consequences if a covenant exists that sets a limit

(continued)

on the debt-to-equity ratio and similar measures. Operating leases, on the other hand, have no effect on the liabilities of the entity. An operating lease allows the entity to keep its lease liabilities "off the balance sheet."

A lease is classified as a capital lease if the benefits and risks of ownership are transferred to the lessee. The *CICA Handbook* does not clearly define benefits and risks of ownership, but provides criteria for guiding managers. These criteria are often interpreted as firm rules and managers can structure leases so that none of the criteria are met, which allows the leases to be classified as operating.

PENSIONS AND OTHER POST-RETIREMENT BENEFITS

As part of their compensation packages, many employees receive pensions and other benefits after they retire. A **pension** is income provided to a person after he or she retires. Pensions are also provided to Canadians by government, through the Canada and Québec Pension Plans. Retired employees can also receive benefits such as extended medical coverage (medical costs not covered by a provincial health plan), as well as dental, vision, and prescription coverage. Employee pensions and other post-retirement employee benefits are negotiated between the employer and its employees.

Post-retirement benefits are an extremely important issue in Canada, for both economic and accounting reasons. The magnitude of the amounts that are involved in pension plans gives an idea of their economic significance. For example, the fair value of the assets in Canadian National Railway Company's employee pension plan was in excess of $14.8 billion on December 31, 2005. The economic significance of pensions and other post-retirement benefits will continue to grow as Canada's population ages.

Accounting for pensions and post-retirement benefits can be complex and the reporting of the information in the financial statements can be confusing. Most of the issues in pension accounting are beyond the scope of this book. However, because of the economic significance of pensions and post-retirement benefits and their prominence in many entities' financial statements, a brief introduction to the subject is appropriate. Rogers provides an explanation of its pensions in Note 16 to its financial statements (pages A-36 to A-38).

Employees earn their pensions and other post-retirement benefits while they are working, even though they receive the money and benefits after they retire. In effect, instead of receiving their full compensation in cash while they are working, the employer funds a pension plan that provides income to employees after they retire. Since a pension is part of employees' compensation while they are working, for accounting purposes the cost of providing a pension should be expensed over the employee's working career. In other words, it is a question of matching. But how much should be expensed in any given period? How much should an employer expense in 2009 for a pension that will be paid beginning in 2040?

There are two types of pension plans: defined-contribution plans and defined-benefit plans. In a **defined-contribution plan** the employer makes cash contributions to the plan as specified in the pension agreement with the employees. For example, the employer's contribution to the plan might be a percentage of each employee's wage or salary. Employees are often able to make their own contributions to the plan to increase the amount invested. The pension benefits that an employee receives upon retirement depend on the amount contributed to the plan on behalf of that employee (by the employer and the employee) and on the performance of the investments made with the funds in the pension plan. The employer's obligation is limited to making the required contribution each year. The employee is entitled only to his or her share of what is in the plan on retirement.

Accounting for defined-contribution plans is fairly straightforward. The pension expense for a year is the contribution that the employer is required to make to the plan according to the agreement with the employees. A pension liability is reported on the employer's balance sheet if the full contribution to the plan has not been made by the end of the period.

Consider the following example. Under its employee defined-contribution pension plan, Nojack Ltd. (Nojack) is required to contribute $250,000 to the plan in 2009. On December 15, 2009 Nojack's treasurer wrote a cheque for $200,000 to the plan. The remaining $50,000 is to be paid in 2010. The entry that Nojack would make to record its contribution in 2009 is:

Dr. Pension expense (expense +, shareholders' equity −)	250,000	
Cr. Cash (asset −)		200,000
Cr. Pension liability (liability +)		50,000

To record the contribution to the employee defined-contribution pension plan for 2009.

The $50,000 pension liability would be reported on Nojack's December 31, 2009 balance sheet. The liability would be reduced when Nojack made payments to the plan.

The second type of pension plan is a defined-benefit plan. In a **defined-benefit plan** the employer promises to provide employees with certain specified benefits in each year they are retired. A defined-benefit plan might specify that employees receive 2.5 percent of the salary earned in the final year of employment for each year worked for the entity. For example, if an employee worked for 30 years and his/her salary in the last year was $125,000, the employee would receive an annual pension of $93,750 ($125,000 × 0.025 × 30 years). There are many ways that the pensions due employees can be determined. These are based on the outcome of negotiations between the employees and the entity.

With a defined-benefit plan, the employer is obligated to provide the specified benefits to employees, regardless of how the investments in the pension plan perform. If there is not enough money in the pension plan to pay employees their pensions, the employer is responsible for making up the difference.

There are two decisions that an entity must make about its defined-benefit pension plan. The first is the accounting question—what should the annual pension expense be? The second is the funding question—how much money should the employer contribute to the plan each year? The pension expense in a year does not have to be the same, and will usually not be the same, as the amount of cash that the employer contributes to the plan.

Determining the amount to expense and the amount to fund are complex present-value problems. The objective of a defined-benefit plan is to provide an employee with regular payments of a specified amount (an annuity) for the rest of the employee's life after he or she retires. The calculation itself is relatively straightforward, but the assumptions that must be made to do the calculation are difficult.

For example, consider the employee described previously who is to receive an annual pension of $93,750. Conceptually, the pension plan must have enough money on hand when the employee retires to purchase an annuity that will pay the employee $93,750 for the rest of his or her life. If the employee is expected to live for 15 years after retirement and the appropriate discount rate is 8 percent, the plan would have to have $802,451.13 ($1/0.08 × [1 − 1/(1 + 0.08)^{15}] × $93,750) to purchase an annuity that guaranteed an annual payment of $93,750 for 15 years.

Two crucial assumptions have been made to come up with this amount: the number of years that the employee would live after retirement and the appropriate discount rate. If either of these assumptions changes, the amount that must be available in the retirement year to purchase the annuity would change, possibly dramatically.

But hold on. We have addressed only part of the problem. We also have to determine the amount that must be invested in the pension plan each year over the employee's working life so that the $802,406.25 will be in the plan when the employee retires. Then consider that we have to figure this out for an entire workforce.

It can get very complicated. The whole exercise is dependent on a set of assumptions. These assumptions include:

■ the number of years employees will work for the employer

■ the number of employees who will qualify for benefits

- the number of employees who will die before they retire

- the age at which employees will retire

- the salary employees will earn in the year or years on which the pension is based

- the number of years employees will live after retirement

- the return the money in the pension fund will earn (the higher the expected return, the less money that needs to be invested in the pension fund by the employer)

Now remember that funding pension plans and calculating pension expenses is based on events that will take place over the many years until an employee retires—20, 25, 30, or even more years into the future! It is these assumptions and the length of time involved that makes pension accounting so complex.

Neither the assets in the pension plan nor the actual obligation that the entity has to employees appears on the entity's balance sheet. The only amount that appears on the balance sheet regarding a pension plan is the deferred pension asset or liability. This amount represents the difference between the value of the assets in the pension plan and the obligation the pension plan has to the employees. (This statement isn't exactly correct because there are some additional accounting adjustments that are made. However, this difference does give the idea.) The pension plan assets and obligation can be found in the notes to the financial statements. In Note 9 to Rogers' financial statements you can see that Rogers reports a deferred pension asset of $32,111,000. You can see the pension plan assets and obligation, and how the deferred pension asset amount was calculated in Note 16.

Accounting for other post-retirement benefits (other than pensions) is similar to the accounting for pensions. However, unlike pensions, companies are not required to fund non-pension post-retirement benefits. Most companies pay for these benefits as they as they go. These can also be significant obligations for entities and they will likely grow as the number of retired employees grows.

Information about pensions and other post-retirement benefits is important to many stakeholders. These benefits can represent very significant obligations to an entity and may even affect an entity's solvency. Increasingly, entities are questioning their ability to meet the commitments they have made to their employees, so they have attempted to reduce the size of their commitments. These stakeholders would want to assess the impact that these benefits would have on the entity's ability to survive, compete, and be profitable. Employees and retired employees would clearly have an interest in information about the benefit plans since the quality of their lives after retirement depends on these plans. The condition of a pension plan provides information about the cash flow requirements of an entity.

One final point about pension accounting. Because of the complexity of the assumptions that must be made to calculate the pension expense, managers must exercise considerable judgment in making those assumptions. Some critics have contended that the assumptions that some managers have made are unrealistic and that, by making unrealistic assumptions, they have significantly understated the pension expense and the deferred pension liability.

CONTINGENCIES

Suppose an entity realizes that it may incur a gain or a loss as a result of events that have already happened, but the amount of the gain or loss, or even the existence of the gain or loss, is uncertain and will not be known until some future event occurs? What, if anything, should the financial statement impact be?

For example, in 2008 Rosyth Ltd. (Rosyth) was sued for $10,000,000. As of the end of fiscal 2009, no settlement had been reached or judgment made by the courts, so the amount that Rosyth will ultimately have to pay is unknown. What, if anything, should Rosyth report in its 2009 financial statements about the lawsuit? These types of situations are known as contingencies. A **contingency** is a possible liability or asset whose existence and amount depend on some future event. The lawsuit against Rosyth is a contingency because whether Rosyth has to pay out as a result of the lawsuit and the amount it will have to pay out depend on a future event—a settlement or a judgment by the courts.

There are three possible ways to account for a contingency: it could be accrued, disclosed in the notes to the financial statements, or ignored for financial reporting purposes. Accruing allows the financial statements to reflect the economic impact of contingencies. But does it make sense to accrue contingencies if they have a low probability of being realized—for example, a frivolous lawsuit launched by a disgruntled employee? Such recognition in the accounts would have an impact on the financial statements but would eventually have to be reversed when the lawsuit failed. It can also be difficult to determine the cost ultimately to be incurred. After all, just because someone sues you for $10,000,000 doesn't mean they're going to get $10,000,000.

On the other hand, ignoring contingencies would deprive users of important information about risks that the entity faces. Failing to disclose significant contingencies could open entities and their auditors to lawsuits for failing to provide important information. Disclosure could provide information about the existence and significance of contingencies, but disclosure does not have any measurement implications—it doesn't affect the financial statement numbers—so outcomes such as bonus payments or covenants that depend on financial statement numbers are not affected. Clearly, accounting for contingencies is a tricky business, and there is no easy solution fabout what to do.

For entities that follow GAAP, the *CICA Handbook* provides guidance for accounting for contingencies. The recommendations for contingent losses are summarized in Table 10–4. The table shows that contingencies should be evaluated on their measurability and likelihood of occurrence. For example, contingencies that are considered likely to occur and are reasonably measurable should be accrued.

TABLE 10–4 ::: *CICA Handbook* Recommendations on Contingent Losses			
Likelihood of occurance Measurability	Likely	Unlikely	Likelihood not determinable
Reasonably measurable	Accrue	Ignore*	Disclose
Unmeasurable	Disclose	Ignore*	Disclose

*The *Handbook* suggests that significant unlikely contingencies be disclosed, but this treatment is not required.

Contingent gains should never be accrued, according to the *CICA Handbook*. This treatment is consistent with conservatism. The *Handbook* requires disclosure of a contingent gain if it is likely to occur. Managers often have to exercise considerable judgment in applying this *CICA Handbook* section. The terms "likely," "unlikely," and "reasonably measurable" are subjective, and the judgments made by management can have an impact on the numbers reported in and the information provided by financial statements.

EXHIBIT 10–2 : Contingent Gain	Dofasco Inc.—Contingent Gain **17. Contingent gain** Effective August 30, 2004, the Corporation gave notice to a customer of the termination of a contractual steel supply arrangement, in accordance with the terms of the supply agreement. The 2004 results reflect a $10 million liquidation payment related to the termination of this contract. To ensure that the supply chain is not disrupted, Dofasco is continuing to ship steel to the customer at a price that is reflective of current market conditions. The right of Dofasco to terminate the arrangement is being disputed by the customer through arbitration proceedings, which were initiated in the fourth quarter of 2004. As a result of the dispute, a provision against sales and accounts receivable has been recorded as the amount equal to the difference between the invoice price and the original contract price. The cumulative provision increased from approximately $37 million at December 31, 2004 to approximately $100 million as at December 31, 2005. The amount and timing of realization of the potential gain to date, if any, is not determinable at this time as it is dependent on the resolution of the dispute with the customer. Future revenues will be impacted by such resolution, by future market conditions and by the volume of future purchases by the customer.

According to *Financial Reporting in Canada,* 30th edition, lawsuits, environmental matters, guarantees of the debts of others, and possible tax reassessments were the most common contingent losses reported by entities in 2004. The *Financial Reporting in Canada* survey finds that the reporting of contingent gains is quite rare. In 2004, 11 of the 200 firms surveyed reported contingent gains, whereas six firms in 2003 and seven in 2002 disclosed contingent gains.[3]

Notes 21 and 22 to Rogers' financial statements (pages A-44 to A-45) provide excellent examples of contingent liabilities. In Note 21, Rogers explains that it may be responsible to make payments to other entities as a result of transactions it entered into to sell businesses, provide services, and purchase and develop assets. For example, if Rogers sells a business or assets to a third party and that third party is subsequently sued because of an environmental issue, Rogers may be responsible for compensating the third party for any costs it incurred as a result of the environmental issue.

Note 22 describes three specific contingent liabilities and a general one. Note 22(d) says that the company is being sued and will be sued in the future for unstated reasons, but that none of these lawsuits are expected to have a material impact on the company. Note 22(b) describes a $160 million lawsuit against Fido and its subsidiary, Fido Solutions Inc. and others. This proceeding is at an early stage. Rogers says in the note that it thinks it has good defences to the claim, which implies that it thinks it can win the case. This note is important to some stakeholders because if Rogers loses, it could incur significant costs as a result. Exhibit 10–2 provides an example of a contingent gain reported by steelmaker Dofasco Inc.[4]

Recognizing contingencies in the financial statements, either in the statements themselves or in the notes, is not a violation of historical cost accounting. The trigger for recognizing a contingency is an event that occurs in the past, before the financial statement date. The difficulty with accounting for contingencies is the uncertainty about the outcome—whether there will actually be a loss (and therefore a liability) or a gain (and therefore an asset).

COMMITMENTS

A **commitment** is a contractual agreement to enter into a transaction in the future. It was explained earlier in the chapter that when neither party to the commitment has performed its side of the bargain, under GAAP the contract is not recorded in the entity's accounting records. These types of arrangements are called executory contracts.

The GAAP approach is not the only way of accounting for executory contracts. An alternative would be to record the asset and liability associated with the contract (perhaps only when it is not possible for either party to cancel the contract). For example, in December 2010, Chopaka Inc. (Chopaka) signed a contract to purchase $400,000 of lumber that it requires for the construction of homes in a new subdivision. The lumber is to be delivered over the construction period between March and October 2011. The contract is not cancellable by either Chopaka or the supplier. Under GAAP, this contract would not appear in the financial statements. However, if executory contracts were recognized, Chopaka would report an asset representing the lumber to be delivered and a liability to pay for the lumber when it is delivered. The asset and liability would each be reported at $400,000. There are no income statement effects of this treatment, but it increases assets and liabilities. There is no effect on working capital (current assets − current liabilities), but the current ratio (current assets + current liabilities) is affected if the ratio is not equal to 1.0.

While Canadian GAAP generally do not allow for recognition of executory contracts, GAAP recognizes that information about significant commitments by an entity can be important to users of the financial statements. The *CICA Handbook* requires disclosure of information about contracts that are significant to the entity. The *Handbook* mentions that contracts should be disclosed when they (a) involve an unusual degree of risk, (b) commit the entity to significant expenditures, or (c) commit the entity to issue shares.

If Chopaka followed GAAP, it might disclose information about its contract to purchase lumber if the contract were considered significant. No entries would be made to the financial records until lumber was actually delivered. The decision to disclose a contract is a judgment call made by the managers. Managers could avoid disclosing contracts that might be of interest to stakeholders by exercising that judgment. The managers could contend that there was nothing significant about a contract that would merit separate disclosure.

Rogers describes its commitments in Note 20 (page A-43). Each specific commitment is described and an amount associated with it. Note 20(g) reports the minimum lease payments Rogers will have to make in each of the next five years and beyond. These were discussed earlier in the chapter. Rogers also discloses in Note 20(d) the committed cost of $US30.6 million for the rights to broadcast the Olympic Games. Exhibit 10–3 provides an example of a commitment for Air Canada. In the note, Air Canada describes commitments to spend over $6.0 billion to purchase new aircraft.[5]

CHAPTER 10

EXHIBIT 10–3 :

Air Canada Commitments

16. COMMITMENTS

In 2004, Air Canada signed definitive purchase agreements with Empresa Brasileira de Aeronautica S.A. ("Embraer"), and Bombardier Inc. ("Bombardier") for the acquisition of regional jet aircraft. In November 2005, Air Canada also concluded agreements with The Boeing Company ("Boeing") for the acquisition of Boeing 777 and Boeing 787 aircraft.

BOEING

On November 9, 2005, Air Canada announced agreements with Boeing for the acquisition of up to 36 Boeing 777s and up to 60 Boeing 787 Dreamliners. The 36 Boeing 777s include firm orders for 18 aircraft plus purchase rights for 18 more, in a yet-to-be determined mix of the 777 family's newest models. Delivery of the first seven 777 aircraft is scheduled for 2007, commencing in March. The 60 Boeing 787 Dreamliners includes firm orders for 14 aircraft plus options and purchase rights for an additional 46 aircraft. Air Canada's first 787 is scheduled for delivery in 2010. The Corporation has received financing commitments from Boeing and the engine manufacturer covering all firm aircraft orders for approximately 90 percent of the capital expenditure.

EMBRAER

The agreement with Embraer covers firm orders for 15 Embraer 175 series aircraft as well as 45 Embraer 190 series aircraft. The purchase agreement also contains rights to exercise options for up to 60 additional Embraer 190 series aircraft as well as providing for conversion rights to other Embraer models.

Deliveries of the 15 Embraer 175 series aircraft commenced in July 2005 and the last aircraft was delivered in January 2006. All Embraer 175 deliveries were 80 percent financed by a third party.

The Embraer 190 series deliveries commenced in December 2005. At December 31, 2005, three of the Embraer 190 series firm aircraft orders have been completed and the remaining 42 deliveries are planned to be completed by January 2008. For the first 18 firm Embraer 190 deliveries, the Corporation has received loan commitments from a syndicate of banks and the manufacturer covering 80 percent of the capital expenditure. For the remaining 27 firm Embraer 190 deliveries, the Corporation has received loan commitments from the manufacturer covering 85 percent of the capital expenditures.

BOMBARDIER

The agreement with Bombardier covered firm orders for 15 Bombardier CRJ700 Series 705 aircraft and 15 Bombardier CRJ200 aircraft, all of which were delivered by the end of 2005. The agreement with Bombardier contains orders for 15 additional Bombardier CRJ200 aircraft which can be cancelled without penalty. The agreement also contains options for an additional 45 aircraft. As of February 9, 2006, no commitments have been made on the cancellable orders or on the additional options for 45 aircraft. The Corporation will also receive financing commitments of 85 percent of capital expenditures from the manufacturer on the cancellable aircraft orders should the Corporation decide to commit to acquire these aircraft.

AIRCRAFT RECONFIGURATION

On November 10, 2005, Air Canada announced its intention to provide all-new seating across its entire fleet, featuring state-of-the-art lie-flat seats for its international Executive First customers. In addition, Air Canada is outfitting its Executive Class cabins on North American routes with new premium seats, and all of its Hospitality cabins fleet-wide will be reconfigured with new seats offering personal seat back entertainment systems with an increased choice of audio and video programming.

CAPITAL COMMITMENTS

The estimated aggregate cost of the future firm deliveries as well as other capital purchase commitments approximates $6,055 excluding the 15 Bombardier CRJ200 aircraft which may be cancelled without penalty. US dollar amounts are converted using the December 31, 2005 noon day rate of CDN$1.1659. The estimated aggregate cost of aircraft is based on delivery prices that include estimated escalation and, where applicable, deferred price delivery payment interest calculated based on the 90-day LIBOR rate at December 31, 2005. Committed payments are as follows:

2006	$	826
2007		1,950
2008		1,213
2009		428
2010		837
Thereafter		801
	$	6,055

SUBSEQUENT EVENTS

What happens if a significant economic event occurs after the end of an entity's fiscal year? Strictly speaking, transactions-based, historical cost accounting should ignore the event until the financial statements are prepared for the fiscal year in which the event took place. On the other hand, any information that is potentially useful to stakeholders should be provided on a timely basis. GAAP and the *CICA Handbook* recognize that it can be important to disclose certain economic events even if they occur after the end of the fiscal year being reported on. A **subsequent event** is an economic event that occurs after an entity's year end, but before the financial statements are released to users.

The *CICA Handbook* identifies two types of subsequent events:

1. Events that provide additional information about circumstances that existed at the year end; and

2. Events that happened after the balance sheet date.

When the first type of subsequent event occurs, the financial statements themselves should be adjusted to reflect the new information. The availability of the new information allows managers to make better estimates than they could at the financial statement date. For example, if a debtor filed for bankruptcy after the year end, the information could be used to improve the estimate of uncollectables. If new information about a contingent liability such as a lawsuit becomes available after the year end, the entity may be able to accrue the cost of the lawsuit rather than just disclosing it.

The second type of subsequent event is unrelated to circumstances that existed at year end and should be disclosed only in the notes to the financial statements. The financial statements are not adjusted in response to this type of subsequent event. Of course, many events occur after the year end and virtually none of them are disclosed as subsequent events. What should be disclosed is not well defined. The *CICA Handbook* states that events that will have a significant effect on the entity in a subsequent period should be disclosed. Ultimately, what constitutes a subsequent event of either type is a matter of judgment and in many cases managers have flexibility as to whether and how an event that occurs after the year end will be reported in the financial statements.

For public companies, most events of any consequence would be disclosed to the public by such means as newspaper reports or press releases long before the financial statements were released. Thus, disclosing the second type of subsequent event in the financial statements would be redundant. The usefulness of a subsequent event disclosure of the second type for private companies, especially those that get little media scrutiny or public attention, would be much more likely to be "news" to users of the financial statements. However, private companies might not disclose relevant subsequent events.

Information about subsequent events, regardless of the source a stakeholder learns about them, would be useful for forecasting future earnings or cash flows.

Rogers discloses four subsequent events in Note 24 (page A-51). The note explains that in early 2006, Rogers redeemed senior secured notes, completed the purchase of some real estate, paid a dividend, and redeemed senior secured notes when they matured.

DEBT AND TAXES

Earlier, we briefly discussed the tax implications of debt. Entities are allowed to deduct interest when calculating taxable income. This means the actual cost of borrowing money is less than the amount that is paid to the lender. In effect, taxpayers pay for part of the cost of borrowing. The **after-tax cost of borrowing** is the interest rate an entity pays after taking into consideration the savings that come from being able to deduct interest in the calculation of taxable income. The after-tax cost of borrowing is calculated using the following formula:

$$\text{After-tax cost of borrowing} = \text{Stated interest rate} \times (1 - \text{tax rate})$$

Estmere Inc. (Estmere) has a $10,000,000 long-term bond outstanding that has an interest rate of 11.5 percent. Estmere pays the bondholder $1,150,000 in interest on December 31 of each year. Its tax rate is 40 percent. Estmere's after-tax cost of borrowing is:

$$\text{After-tax cost of borrowing} = \text{Stated interest rate} \times (1 - \text{tax rate})$$
$$= 11.5\% \times (1 - 0.4)$$
$$= 11.5\% \times 0.6$$
$$= 6.9\%$$

Since Estmere is able to reduce its income by $1,150,000 each year because it can deduct the interest cost, it has to pay $460,000 ($1,150,000 × 0.4) less tax than it would if the cost of borrowing were not deductible.

Suppose Estmere's income for tax purposes before deducting interest and taxes were $5,000,000. Estmere would have to pay $2,000,000 ($5,000,000 × 0.4) in taxes if interest were not deductible, whereas it would have to pay $1,540,000 ([$5,000,000 − $1,150,000] × 0.4) if interest were deductible. The deductibility of interest makes debt a desirable way to obtain financing because the entity does not have to pay the full cost of borrowing. Dividends, on the other hand, are not tax deductible.

FINANCIAL STATEMENT ANALYSIS ISSUES

Analyzing an entity's liabilities can provide important information about its financial situation and its prospects. This analysis can also provide insight into the financial management of the entity. For example, creditors can obtain information that allows them to assess the amount that they would be willing to lend the entity and the terms of the loan, including interest rate, amount and type of collateral, and restrictive covenants. In addition, the evaluation of liabilities provides important information about an entity's liquidity. We have looked at tools for evaluating the liquidity of an entity in previous chapters. Below, tools for analyzing risk, capital structure, and the ability to carry debt are discussed.

Debt-to-Equity Ratio

The debt-to-equity ratio provides a measure of the amount of debt relative to equity that an entity uses for financing. The ratio gives an indication of the riskiness of the entity and its ability to carry more debt. More debt makes an entity riskier. As explained earlier in the chapter (see pages 528–530), debt is riskier for an entity because interest and principal payments on debt must be made, regardless of how well the entity is doing. An entity that has relatively little debt (compared with industry norms) suggests that it is able to assume more debt.

It is important to recognize that debt is not a bad way for an entity to be financed. As discussed earlier in the chapter, debt is less costly than equity and interest on debt is tax deductible, whereas dividends aren't. This isn't to say that an entity should carry the maximum possible amount of debt. Debt becomes more costly as the relative amount of debt increases because the debt is riskier to the lenders, and a higher interest rate is how lenders are compensated for risk. An entity should have a balance between debt and equity. The appropriate mix depends on the nature of the entity. The debt-to-equity ratio is an important tool for evaluating an entity's debt load or its capital structure. (**Capital structure** is the term used to describe how an entity is financed—it is the amount of debt and equity the entity has.)

The debt-to-equity ratio is defined as:

$$\text{Debt-to-equity ratio} = \frac{\text{Total liabilities}}{\text{Total shareholders' equity}}$$

Rogers' debt-to-equity ratio on December 31, 2005, using the numbers directly from the financial statements, was:

$$= \frac{\$10,306,674,000}{\$3,527,615,000}$$
$$= 2.92$$

The interpretation of the debt-to-equity ratio must be done carefully. Rogers' debt-to-equity ratio of 2.92 means that it has $2.92 of liabilities for every $1 of equity. Is that too much? It is not possible to answer without a context. Determining whether a ratio is too high depends on many factors, including industry and circumstances. Entities that have highly reliable cash flows can carry more debt because they can be confident that the cash flows will be available to make interest and principal payments as required. Examples of seven year average debt-to-equity ratios for different industries are shown in Table 10–5.[6] Notice the variation in the ratio across the industries. However, Rogers' ratio does look high compared with these industry averages, even against the average of other firms in Rogers' industry (media).

The use of the debt-to-equity ratio by simply using the numbers on the balance sheet can provide misleading results and interpretations. Leases and pensions (and future income taxes, which is discussed in the appendix) all present problems that can impair the interpretation of the debt-to-equity and other ratios that incorporate liabilities. If an entity makes extensive use of operating leases, liabilities and the debt-to-equity ratio will be understated because operating leases are a form of off-balance-sheet financing. This situation makes it difficult to compare debt-to-equity ratios of entities that have borrowed money to purchase assets or use capital leases. The same is true if an entity has a lot of commitments.

For example, WestJet Airlines Ltd. (WestJet) makes extensive use of operating leases to acquire aircraft for its fleet. On December 31, 2005, 18 of WestJet's fleet of 56 next-generation aircraft were under operating leases. Exhibit 10–4 shows information from WestJet's statements.[7] WestJet's debt-to-equity ratio on December 31, 2005 is 2.30. If the future lease payments shown in Note 6 are discounted at 6 percent and the total amount added to total liabilities, the debt-to-equity ratio increases to 3.28, a significant increase.

Pensions pose similar problems. As we discussed, the pension liability on the balance sheet doesn't necessarily reflect the amount the entity must invest in the pension plan to meet the obligations of the plan. Footnote disclosure may help assess this shortfall. In any case, an adjustment to liabilities may be required so that the condition of the pension plan is reflected in the ratio.

Interest Coverage Ratio

The **interest coverage ratio** is one of a number of coverage ratios designed to measure the ability of an entity to meet its fixed financing charges. In particular, the interest coverage ratio indicates the ease with which an entity can meet its interest payments. The interest coverage ratio is defined as:

$$\text{Interest coverage ratio} = \frac{\text{Net income + Interest expense + Tax expense}}{\text{Interest expense}}$$

The larger the ratio, the better able the entity is to meet its interest payments. The interest-coverage ratio is limiting in that it ignores the fact that entities have financial charges other than interest. Other fixed financial charges include debt repayment and payments on operating leases. This ratio can be modified to include these other charges, but for introductory purposes the interest coverage ratio is appropriate. The interest coverage ratio can also be calculated on a cash basis.

The interest coverage ratio for Rogers for the year ended December 31, 2005 is calculated as:

$$\begin{aligned}
\text{Interest coverage ratio} &= \frac{\text{Net income + Interest expense + Tax expense}}{\text{Interest expense}} \\
&= \frac{-\,\$44,658,000 + \$710,079,000 + \$2,155,000}{\$710,079,000} \\
&= 0.940
\end{aligned}$$

The interest coverage ratio of 0.940 means that Rogers' income before taxes and interest expense is not quite enough to cover its interest cost. Of course, earnings and cash flows can be volatile and coverage ratios can change dramatically from period to period. Rogers' interest coverage ratio for

CONSOLIDATED BALANCE SHEETS

WestJet Airlines Ltd.

December 31, 2005 and 2004
(Stated in Thousands of Dollars)

	2005	2004
Liabilities and Shareholders' Equity		
Current liabilities:		
Accounts payable and accrued liabilities	$ 100,052	$ 91,885
Advance ticket sales	127,450	81,991
Non-refundable guest credits	32,814	26,704
Current portion of long-term debt (note 4)	114,115	97,305
Current portion of obligations under capital lease (note 6)	2,466	6,564
	376,897	304,449
Long-term debt (note 4)	1,044,719	905,631
Obligations under capital lease (note 6)	1,690	–
Other liabilities (note 5)	16,982	10,000
Future income tax (note 8)	102,651	67,382
	1,542,939	1,287,462
Shareholders' equity:		
Share capital (note 7(b))	429,613	390,469
Contributed surplus (note 7(g))	39,093	21,977
Retained earnings	201,447	177,446
	670,153	589,892
Subsequent events (note 6)		
Commitments and contingencies (notes 6 and 9)		
	$ 2,213,092	$ 1,877,354

6. **Leases:**

The Corporation has entered into operating leases and agreements for aircraft, buildings, computer hardware and software licenses and satellite programming, as well as capital leases relating to aircraft and ground handling equipment. The obligations are as follows (see note 9 for additional commitments):

	Capital Leases	Operating Leases
2006	$ 2,622	$ 91,340
2007	411	96,821
2008	411	97,833
2009	411	94,350
2010	665	85,203
2011 and thereafter	–	373,670
Total lease payments	4,520	$ 839,217
Less imputed interest at 6.09%	(364)	
Net minimum lease payments	4,156	
Less current portion of obligations under capital lease	(2,466)	
Obligations under capital lease	$ 1,690	

TABLE 10–5 ::: **Seven Year Average Debt-to-Equity Ratios and Interest-Coverage Ratios for Several Industries**

Industry	Seven Year Average Debt-to-equity ratio	Seven Year Average Interest-coverage ratio
Media	1.25	32.71
Utilities	1.35	2.58
Retailing	0.68	24.59
Metals and mining	0.42	10.32
Computers and electronic equipment	0.21	30.93
Transportation	1.17	32.61

the year ended December 31, 2004 is 0.889. Interest coverage ratios for several industries are shown in Table 10–5. In comparison with these industries, Rogers interest-coverage ratio is quite low, so this is an indication of higher risk. However, over the two years shown, the ratio is stable.

Other Issues

Another characteristic of debt worth noting is the currency of the borrowed money. Canadian firms sometimes borrow money in currencies other than Canadian dollars and the interest and repayment of those debts are made in that foreign currency. Debt in foreign currency can add significant risk to an entity because of the fluctuations in currency exchange rates. For example, in 1997 it cost an average of $1.38 Canadian to buy one United States dollar. In early 2006, one United States dollar cost Cdn$1.16. If a Canadian firm borrowed US$1,000,000 when the exchange rate was $1.38, the firm would receive Cdn$1,380,000. If the firm then had to repay the loan in U.S. dollars when the exchange rate was $1.16, the firm would have to pay Cdn$1,160,000 so that the lender would receive US$1,000,000. In this example, the borrowing cost fell by $220,000 because of the fall in interest rates. If exchange rates increased, the borrowing cost would have increased. The effect of changing exchange rates adds risk because it makes the cost of borrowing less certain.

Loans that have interest rates that vary also add risk. Rogers' syndicated bank loans have interest rates that vary with the prime lending rate. This means that as interest rates in the economy increase, the interest rate on the loans increase. An increase in the interest rate on a loan, of course, increases the entity's cost of borrowing.

On December 31, 2005 a significant portion of Rogers' outstanding debt was denominated in U.S. dollars and $979,245,000 of its debt had a floating interest rate.

Solved Problem

The solved problem for this chapter provides another example of a user-oriented case. This case will give you more experience with and exposure to situations where you have to work with financial statements provided to you. The purpose is to learn how to look critically at what is done and apply your knowledge to satisfy your client.

BENITO CORP.

In October 2009 the Benito family sold its 100 percent interest in Benito Corp. (BC) to a corporation wholly owned by the Nampa family. Because the two families could not agree on an exact selling price, the contract of purchase and sale required that the corporation that purchased BC pay an amount equal to 20 percent of BC's audited net income for the fiscal year ended September 30, 2010. When BC was purchased, the Nampa family replaced the senior management of the company. The new CEO of BC is the son of the head of the Nampa family, Shayne Nampa. Shayne Nampa has explained that the acquisition of BC is an important step in the growth the Nampa family's corporate holdings. He said that an important objective of the family is to minimize the amount of tax that must be paid.

On October 25, 2010 Ellin Benito, a member of the Benito family, approached you for advice. She explained that the Benito family had received BC's financial statements and they were very concerned about some aspects of the statements. The Benito family believes that Mr. Shayne Nampa is not acting in good faith and is trying to cheat the Benito family of money that is rightfully owed to them. Ellin Benito has asked you for a detailed report that analyzes aspects of the financial statements that the Benito family find questionable. She would like thorough explanations of the issues and recommendations of alternative treatments that you think are more appropriate. Ellin wants you to provide clear explanations and support for your positions so that she will be able to explain her concerns when she meets Mr. Shayne Nampa. The outstanding items are described below:

a. During fiscal 2009 (before BC was sold), management began planning to offer its products online. Shayne Nampa continued the development of the new e-business and expects that it will be launched mid-way through fiscal 2011. Through the end of fiscal 2010, BC spent

$476,000 developing the new e-business. Costs were incurred for Web site design, market surveys, and so on. The costs incurred in 2009 had been capitalized but BC expensed the full amount in fiscal 2010.

b. In May 2010, BC signed a contract with Fong Inc. for a large order of specially-designed products. Fong Inc. did not want to take delivery of the products until the order was complete so BC agreed to deliver the products in September 2010. Representatives of Fong Inc. monitored production to ensure that all finished goods met Fong Inc.'s specifications. Fong Inc. agreed to pay BC as production of the product progressed. As a result, when production of the products was completed on schedule in August 2010, Fong Inc. had paid 80 percent of the agreed price. The remaining 20 percent was to be paid on final delivery of the products. The products were ready for shipping in the first week of September 2010. However, Ellin learned from an employee of BC that Benito Corp. requested and obtained permission from Fong Inc. to delay shipping until mid-October. The products were finally delivered to Fong Inc. on October 13, 2010 and revenue was recognized at that time. Fong Inc. normally recognizes revenue on delivery.

c. During fiscal 2010, BC wrote down by a significant amount the book value of some of the company's manufacturing equipment. BC explained in the notes to the financial statements that upon review, the equipment was becoming obsolete and, as a result, the net book value exceeded the net recoverable amount associated with equipment. Accordingly, the equipment was written down to its fair value. The equipment is still being used on the main production line of BC's manufacturing facility.

Required:

Prepare the report requested by Ellin Benito.

REPORT TO ELLIN BENITO ON THE SEPTEMBER 30, 2010 FINANCIAL STATEMENTS OF BENITO CORP.

Dear Ms. Benito:

Thank you for engaging me to examine the September 30, 2010 financial statements of Benito Corp. Based on the information you provided to me, it appears that Shayne Nampa is using generally accepted accounting principles (GAAP) to his advantage and to your detriment. You may find it surprising, but GAAP is quite flexible and often requires judgement, and managers can sometimes use those qualities to their own economic benefit. Since the final selling price for Benito Corp. depends on the company's income for fiscal 2010, it is in Mr. Nampa's interest to report as low a net income as he can justify. I will look at each of the issues in turn:

New e-business: BC expensed all the costs incurred for its proposed e-business in fiscal 2010. The effect of expensing this $476,000 is to reduce the proceeds from sale that the Benito family will receive by $95,200 ($476,000 × 0.20). By expensing the amount, management is saying that there is no future benefit associated with the money spent so far on the e-business, or at least that the future benefit is so uncertain that it warrants not treating the amount as an asset. Certainly, BC can use conservatism as a justification for expensing these costs since, according to GAAP, it isn't acceptable to overstate assets. However, GAAP doesn't mean that you can write off any costs incurred. If a case can be made that the amounts spent do have a future benefit, then it is appropriate to capitalize the costs and amortize them when revenue is being earned, that is, match the costs to the revenue. The key question is, what are the revenue prospects for the new e-business? Clearly, Mr. Nampa believes that it is beneficial to continue with development, which suggests that he thinks it will be successful. If reasonable evidence can be provided that supports the contention that the amount of money invested in the e-business will be recovered from its operation, it is appropriate to capitalize the costs. It is not possible to provide a definitive conclusion at this point, but it's also not necessary to accept the treatment used in BC's financial statements.

> GAAP can often be reasonably interpreted in different ways. Just because the managers who prepared the financial statements have made certain choices doesn't mean you shouldn't or can't question those choices. To serve the needs of your client, you need to consider alternative ways of accounting. However, it is essential that you provide valid support for your alternative. An alternative shouldn't be proposed just because it's better for your client. It should be proposed because it is better for your client *and* it can be supported with the constraints and facts.

Sale to Fong Inc.: It is my opinion that BC rearranged the terms of the contract with Fong Inc. so that it could avoid recognizing the revenue in fiscal 2010. According to the GAAP revenue recognition criteria, delivery is required in most sales of goods for revenue to be recognized. Strictly speaking, BC has followed GAAP. But by artificially delaying delivery, it has violated the spirit of the agreement that was made with the Benito family. As of September 30, 2010 all the conditions necessary for recognizing revenue had been achieved. Production was complete and representatives of Fong Inc. were satisfied that the goods met specifications. The goods were ready for shipment and 80 percent of the agreed price had already been paid. The only condition missing was delivery, and based on the evidence you have provided, the delay in shipment was at the request of BC. While it may not be possible or appropriate to recognize this revenue in fiscal 2010 for general purpose reporting, for purposes of the contract of sale, the revenue should be included in fiscal 2010.

Insight

∷∷

> This situation is an excellent example of how acceptable accounting according to GAAP leads to an undesirable outcome for a user. The revenue recognition criteria are designed to discourage entities from recognizing their revenue too early. For the sale of BC, the purposes of the new owners of BC are served by the conservative nature of the criteria. But simply because GAAP is followed doesn't automatically make the treatment appropriate in the circumstances. From the information provided, it is clear that BC modified the terms of the contract to reduce the amount it would pay the Benito family. As an advisor to Ms. Benito, it is appropriate to call into question the structure of and accounting for the transaction.

Write-down of manufacturing equipment: By writing down the equipment, BC lowers its income and reduces the payment to the Benito family. According to GAAP, assets should be written down when the book value of the assets is greater than both their net recoverable amount and fair value. Write-downs are very subjective and managers have some leeway determining when they are recorded. The reason is that determining that an asset is impaired is subjective, in part because determining the net recoverable amount and fair value are subjective. However, BC is still using the equipment on its main production line. This suggests that perhaps the equipment is not obsolete. I suggest that you contest the write-down on two grounds. First, the equipment is still in use on the main production line. This calls into question whether the asset is impaired. Second, write-downs are highly subjective and somewhat arbitrary. I think that a case can be made that out-of-the-ordinary events like write-downs should not be part of the determination of the selling price of BC since they are not an actual operating cost. The terms of your contract may work against you on this point but I think it is worthwhile pursuing.

Again, thank you for using my services. If you have any questions, please do not hesitate to contact me.

Sincerely,

John Friedlan, CA

SUMMARY OF KEY POINTS

▶ **LO 1** Liabilities are obligations to provide cash, goods, and services to customers, suppliers, employees, governments, lenders, and any other creditors. According to GAAP, liabilities have three characteristics: (i) they require the sacrifice of resources; (ii) they are unavoidable; and (iii) they are the result of past transactions or economic events. In principle, liabilities should be valued at their present value, and in many cases they are. However, there are some exceptions.

▶ **LO 2** Current liabilities are obligations that will be satisfied in one year or one operating cycle. Information about current obligations is important because it is relevant for assessing the short-term liquidity of an entity. Current liabilities are usually not discounted to their present value because the amount of time until they are settled is relatively short, and as a result the difference between the present value and the stated value will be small. There are many different types of current liabilities, including loans, accounts payable, collections on behalf of third parties, accrued liabilities, and unearned revenue.

▶ **LO 3** A bond is a formal borrowing arrangement in which a borrower agrees to make periodic interest payments to the lenders, as well as to repay the principal at a specified time in the future. The essential characteristics of a bond are its face value, maturity date, and coupon rate. In addition, a bond can have a large array of features and restrictions that are agreed to by the lender and borrowers. These features and restrictions will affect the price of the bond. The price of bonds and other long-term debt is determined by discounting the interest and principal payments to investors using the effective interest rate. The effective interest rate is the market rate of interest appropriate for the long-term debt and is influenced by the risk and other characteristics of the debt.

Long-term debt is usually recorded at its present value, discounted using the effective interest rate on the date the debt is issued. If the coupon rate is not the same as the effective interest rate, a premium or discount arises. The premium or discount is amortized over the life of the debt using the straight-line or the effective-interest method. The amount amortized each period is included in the interest expense for the period. Once long-term debt is recorded, its value is not adjusted for changes in market interest rates. If the end of the reporting period does not correspond with the date when interest payments are made, it is necessary to accrue the interest expense and accrued interest payable. When debt is retired early, any premium or discount must be removed from the books immediately and a gain or a loss may arise on retirement.

▶ **LO 4** A lease is a contractual arrangement whereby a lessee agrees to pay a lessor a fee in exchange for the use of an asset. Leases have a number of advantages to lessees, including 100 percent financing and flexibility. There are two types of leases—capital leases and operating leases. A capital lease is a lease that transfers the benefits and risks of ownership to the lessee. Assets associated with a capital lease are capitalized on the balance sheet of the lessee, along with a liability that is equal to the present value of the lease payments to be made over the life of the lease. An important accounting and reporting benefit of treating a lease as a capital lease is that it overcomes the problem of off-balance-sheet financing. If the rights and risks of ownership are not transferred to the lessee but are retained by the lessor, then the lease is an operating lease. Under an operating lease, the lessee recognizes an expense when the payment to the lessor is paid or payable. The assets and related liabilities do not appear on the lessee's balance sheet.

► **LO 5** A pension is income provided to a person after he or she retires. Employees earn their pensions and other post-retirement benefits while they are working, even though they receive the money after they retire. There are two types of pension plans: defined-contribution plans and defined-benefit plans. Accounting for defined-contribution plans is relatively straightforward, but accounting for defined-benefit plans is complex because it is necessary to estimate and accrue currently the cost of benefits that will be received many years in the future. The pension asset or liability does not provide information about the condition of the pension plan—the ability of a plan to meet the obligations to retirees. It is simply the difference between the accounting measure of the pension expense and the amount funded.

► **LO 6** A contingency is a possible liability or asset whose existence and amount depend on some future event. How contingencies are accounted for according to GAAP depends on the likelihood of them occurring, whether they can be reasonably measured, and whether the contingency will result in a gain or a loss.

A commitment is a contractual agreement to enter into a transaction in the future. Commitments are executory contracts and under GAAP these contracts are not recorded in the accounting records. Significant commitments should be disclosed in the notes to the financial statements.

A subsequent event is an economic event that occurs after an entity's year end, but before the financial statements are released to users. According to GAAP, when a subsequent event occurs that provides additional information about circumstances that existed at the year end, the financial statements should be adjusted to reflect the new information. When a subsequent event occurs that is unrelated to circumstances that existed at year end, the event should be disclosed only in the notes to the financial statements.

► **LO 7** Analyzing an entity's liabilities can provide important information about its financial situation and prospects. This analysis can also provide insight into the financial management of the entity. Two tools for analyzing liabilities are the debt-to-equity ratio and the interest coverage ratio. Caution must be taken in using ratios that incorporate liabilities because of measurement problems associated with leases, pensions, and future income taxes. Failure to adjust for these problems may result in misinterpretation of the ratios.

► **LO 8** (appendix) The future income tax method is a method of accounting for an entity's income taxes where the income tax expense is calculated using accounting measurements, not the actual amount of taxes payable. Future income taxes arise because the accounting policies used to prepare general purpose financial statements are sometimes different from the rules entities must follow when calculating the amount of income tax they must pay. The differences that give rise to future income taxes are temporary and they eventually reverse. Future income taxes do not represent money owed to or owed by the government.

APPENDIX—FUTURE INCOME TAXES

Perhaps one of the most confusing, misunderstood, and abused topics in accounting is *future income taxes*. The topic is worthy of attention in an introductory financial accounting course because it is very common to see future income taxes (or deferred income taxes, as they used to be called) reported on companies' balance sheets. Table 10–6 shows the future income tax asset or liability of some Canadian companies. With numbers this big it's important to understand where they come from, what they represent and, perhaps even more important, what they do not represent.

TABLE 10–6 ::: Future Income Tax Assets and Liabilities of Some Canadian Companies

Company	Future Income Tax Asset	Future Income Tax Liability
PetroCanada		$2,708,000,000
Research-in-Motion Limited	$150,200,000	
Magna International Inc.	195,000,000	288,000,000
WestJet Airlines Ltd.		67,382,000

The first point to make about future income taxes is that they have nothing to do with the amount of tax an entity has to pay. **Future income tax assets and liabilities** arise because the accounting methods used to prepare the general purpose financial statements are sometimes different from the methods used to calculate taxable income and the amount of income tax an entity must pay. **Taxable income** is the measure of income, as defined by the *Income Tax Act* (*ITA*), that is used to calculate the amount of tax an entity must pay. When the *ITA* specifies how an entity must account for a certain type of transaction and economic event for tax purposes, the method must be used for tax purposes regardless of what is done for financial reporting. In other words, an entity can do what it wants for financial reporting purposes, but for calculating its taxes it must use the rules in the *ITA*.

If you examine Rogers' statement of income (page A-5), you will notice that the *income tax expense* is split into two parts: current expense and future expense. The current expense is the income taxes that Rogers must pay to the federal and provincial governments now—it is the amount that is reported on Rogers' tax return. The current expense represents cash that either has already been paid or is currently payable to government. For the year ended December 31, 2005, Rogers had to pay income taxes of $10,730,000. The future expense (benefit) portion is the result of differences in how certain transactions and economic events are accounted for according to the *ITA* and GAAP. For the year ended December 31, 2005, Rogers' future income tax expense was −$8,575,000. Rogers' income tax expense for 2005 was $2,155,000 ($10,730,000 + (−8,575,000)).

There are two categories of differences between tax accounting and financial reporting: temporary differences and permanent differences. **Temporary differences** are a matter of timing. Many revenues and expenses are recognized at different times for tax and financial reporting. These revenues and expenses will be fully recognized for both tax and financial reporting purposes, but recognition will happen at different times. For example, a warranty expense is accrued for financial reporting purposes when the revenue from the sale of the good or service under warranty is recognized. For tax purposes, warranty costs are deducted when the cost is actually incurred—i.e., when the warranty work is actually done. When temporary differences exist between tax and financial reporting, future income taxes arise.

Permanent differences are revenues and expenses that are recognized for tax purposes but never recognized for financial reporting purposes, or are recognized for financial reporting purposes but never recognized for tax purposes. These differences between tax and financial reporting are permanent—they never reverse. For example, for tax purposes businesses can deduct only 50 percent of amounts spent on meals and entertainment when calculating taxable income. For financial reporting purposes, 100 percent of these costs are expensed when calculating net income. The 50 percent that is not deductible for tax purposes is a permanent difference between tax and financial reporting. Permanent differences do not have an effect on future income taxes. Examples of temporary and permanent differences between tax and financial reporting are listed in Table 10–7.

Let's now look at some specifics. We will start by looking at the journal entry an entity makes to record income taxes. The form of the journal entry is:

Dr. Income tax expense (expenses +, shareholders' equity −) xxx
    Cr. Future income tax asset or liability yyy
    Cr. Taxes payable (liabilities +) zzz
or
Dr. Income tax expense (expenses +, shareholders' equity −) xxx
Dr. Future income tax asset or liability yyy
    Cr. Taxes payable (liabilities +) zzz

Taxes payable is the amount that the entity has to pay in taxes and is obtained from the entity's tax return. Determining the amount of tax an entity must pay can be very complex. We will not deal with those complexities in this book. Our challenge will be determining the debit or credit to future income taxes. The entry to future income taxes increases or decreases the amount in the future income taxes account on the balance sheet. Finally, the income tax expense is the amount that is reported on the entity's income statement. As we will see, the income tax expense is a "plug." It is the amount that balances the journal entry and doesn't have to be calculated.

Issue	Type of difference	Tax	GAAP
Amortization of assets	Temporary	CCA (capital cost allowance) at prescribed rates	Amortization in a "rational" way over an asset's useful life
Revenue recognition	Temporary	Percentage of completion for contracts lasting more than two years	Completed contract allowable if consistent with the facts
Warranty costs	Temporary	Deduct when the warranty cost is incorrect	Accrue the expense when the revenue is recognized
Discounts and premiums on long-term debt repaid	Temporary	Recognized when the principal is repaid	Amortized over the term of the debt
Pension costs	Temporary	Deduct when money contributed to the pension fund	Expense based on accounting estimate of the pension obligation
Capital gains	Permanent	50 percent of capital gains and losses are taken into income for tax purposes	100 percent of capital gains and losses are taken into income for financial reporting purposes
Meals and entertainment expenses	Permanent	Only 50 percent of the amount spent is deductible for tax purposes	100 percent is expensed for financial reporting purposes
Interest and penalties on late payment of taxes	Permanent	Not deductible for tax purposes	Expensed for financial reporting purposes

The future income tax balance on the balance sheet reflects temporary differences between the accounting value of assets and liabilities and the tax value of assets and liabilities on the balance sheet date, multiplied by the entity's tax rate. We will now go through a (long) example to show how it's done. As the basis for the example, we will use the largest contributor to most entities' temporary differences—the difference between capital cost allowance (CCA) and amortization.

Askilton Inc. (Askilton) began business in 2010. The company owns a single asset that it purchased for $100,000 in early 2010. For tax purposes, the asset is in a CCA class that allows Askilton to deduct 100 percent of the capital cost of the asset. However, because of the half-year rule, Askilton can claim only one-half of the allowable amount in 2010 and the remainder in 2011. For accounting purposes, management has decided to amortize the asset on a straight-line basis over four years. Askilton has an income tax rate of 30 percent and its income before amortization and taxes is $300,000 in each year from 2010 through 2013. Askilton has no temporary differences between tax and financial reporting, except for the difference between amortization and CCA, and there are no permanent differences. Askilton's year end is December 31.

The first step will be to determine how much tax Askilton has to pay. Extracts from Askilton's tax returns are shown in Table 10–8. To calculate taxable income, CCA is deducted each year from income before CCA and taxes. CCA in 2010 is $50,000 ($100,000 × 100 percent × 0.5) and in 2011 $50,000 ([$100,000 − $50,000] × 100 percent). After 2011, the full capital cost of the asset has been deducted for tax purposes, so no CCA can be deducted in 2012 and 2013. Askilton's tax liability is calculated by multiplying taxable income by the tax rate of 30 percent. Askilton must pay $75,000 in taxes in 2010 and 2011, and $90,000 in 2012 and 2013.

The way to determine the balance in the future income taxes account at a point in time is to compare the tax basis of an asset or liability with the accounting basis. The accounting basis of an asset (or liability) is its NBV for financial reporting purposes. For a capital asset, NBV equals the cost of the asset less accumulated amortization. The tax basis of an asset (or liability) is a similar concept, except that it is determined using tax rules instead of accounting rules. For a capital asset, the tax basis or **undepreciated capital cost (UCC)** is the part of the cost of the asset that has not been deducted for tax purposes. UCC is the tax equivalent of NBV and equals the cost of the asset less the total amount of CCA that has been deducted.

Table 10–9 provides a comparison of the tax basis and the accounting basis for Askilton's asset in each of the four years.

Table 10–9 shows that at the end of 2010, the tax basis (UCC) of Askilton's asset is $50,000 and its accounting basis (NBV) is $75,000. To the Canada Revenue Agency (CRA) the value of the asset at the end of 2010 is $50,000. To Askilton's auditor, the value at the end of 2010 is $75,000. All this means is that the income tax people measure Askilton's assets differently than accountants do.

Different ways of measuring the same thing is nothing new to us. The reason for the difference at the end of 2010 is that Askilton could deduct $50,000 of CCA in 2010, while for accounting purposes Askilton amortized $25,000 of the cost of the asset ($100,000 ÷ 4). At the end of 2011, the tax basis is $0 and the accounting basis is $50,000. At the end of 2013, the tax basis and the accounting basis of the asset are the same because the asset is fully amortized for both accounting and tax purposes. At the end of 2013, UCC = NBV = 0.

TABLE 10–8 ::: **Extracts from Askilton Inc.'s Tax Return**

Askilton Inc.
Extracts from Tax Returns for the Years Ended December 31, 2010–2013

	2010	2011	2012	2013
Income before CCA and taxes	$300,000	$300,000	$300,000	$300,000
Less: CCA	50,000	50,000	0	0
Taxable income	250,000	250,000	300,000	300,000
Income taxes (30% of taxable income)	$75,000	$75,000	$90,000	$90,000

TABLE 10–9 ::: **Comparison of Tax Basis and Accounting Basis for Askilton Inc.'s Asset**

	Tax Basis			Accounting Basis		
	UCC at the beginning of the year	CCA claimed for the year	UCC at the end of the year	NBV at the beginning of the year	Amortization expense	NBV at the end of the year
2010	$100,000	$50,000	$50,000	$100,000	$25,000	$75,000
2011	50,000	50,000	0	75,000	25,000	50,000
2012	0	0	0	50,000	25,000	25,000
2013	0	0	0	25,000	25,000	0

With the information from Table 10–9, we can calculate the amount of future income taxes that should be reported on Askilton's balance sheet each year. Askilton's future income tax asset or liability is calculated by multiplying the difference between the asset's tax basis (UCC) and its accounting basis (NBV) by the tax rate. Table 10–10 shows the calculation.

The rightmost column of Table 10–10 shows the balance that will appear on Askilton's balance sheet each year for future income taxes. A future income tax liability arises when the tax basis of an asset is less than the accounting basis of the asset or when the tax basis of a liability is greater than the accounting basis of the liability. A future income tax asset arises when the tax basis of an asset is greater than the accounting basis of the asset or when the tax basis of a liability is less than the accounting basis of the liability. These relationships are summarized in Table 10–11 (page 561).

Whereas the right-hand column in Table 10–10 tells us the balance that is required on the balance sheet at the end of each year, it does not tell us what the debit or credit to future income taxes should be to give us that balance. At the beginning of 2010, the balance in the future income tax account is zero (Askilton began business in 2010). At the end of 2010, we need the future income tax account to be a liability of $7,500 (see Table 10–10). To obtain this balance, a credit to future income taxes of $7,500 is needed. At the end of 2011, a liability of $15,000 is required, so another credit to future income taxes of $7,500 must be made. In 2012, the credit balance in the account decreases from $15,000 to $7,500. To account for this change, a debit to the future income tax account of $7,500 is needed. A summary of the debits and credits needed is shown in Table 10–12.

TABLE 10–10 ::: **Calculating Askilton's Future Income Tax Asset or Liability**

| | Tax Basis | Accounting Basis | | | |
	UCC at the end of the year	NBV at the end of the year	Difference	Tax rate	Future income tax asset (liability)
2010	$50,000	$75,000	($25,000)	30%	($7,500)
2011	0	50,000	(50,000)	30%	(15,000)
2012	0	25,000	(25,000)	30%	(7,500)
2013	0	0	0	30%	0

TABLE 10–11 ::: **Tax Bases and Accounting Bases and the Balance in the Future Income Taxes Account**

			Future income tax balance
Tax basis of an asset	>	Accounting basis of an asset	Asset
Tax basis of an asset	<	Accounting basis of an asset	Liability
Tax basis of an liability	>	Accounting basis of an liability	Liability
Tax basis of an liability	<	Accounting basis of an liability	Asset

We now have all the pieces to the puzzle. We know the amount of tax that has to be paid (see Table 10–8) and the entries required to the future income tax account (Table 10–12). All we need now is the income tax expense that is reported on the income statement. That, as was pointed out earlier, is a plug, meaning that the income tax expense is the amount that is needed to balance the accounting equation. With the method described here, it is not actually possible to calculate the income tax expense directly.

The journal entries for each year are shown in Table 10–13. For 2010, we know that Askilton must pay taxes of $75,000 (credit Taxes Payable or Cash) and that to obtain the required balance in the Future Income Tax account on December 31, 2010, a credit of $7,500 to Future Income Taxes is required. Therefore, the Income Tax Expense for 2010 must be $82,500. Examine the entries in Table 10–14 and notice how the tax expense is determined from the other amounts that are known.

The income tax expense in Askilton's income statement would be reported as shown in Table 10–14. The *CICA Handbook* requires that the financial statements disclose the portion of the income tax expense that is attributable to future income taxes. The amount can be shown in the income statement as in Table 10–15 or in the notes to the financial statements.

Notice that taxable income (Table 10–8) and income before taxes (Table 10–15) are different in each year and that the tax expense reported on the income statement and the amount of tax that Askilton must pay (Table 10–8) are different in each year. These differences occur because the *ITA* required Askilton to calculate its CCA deduction one way and GAAP allowed it to calculate amortization on the asset another way.

TABLE 10-12 ::: Entries Required to Obtain the Desired Balance in Future Income Tax Account on December 31, 2010–2013

Year	Opening balance in future income tax asset (liability) account	Entry required to the future income tax account	Ending balance in future income tax asset (liability) account
2010	0	$7,500 Cr.	($7,500)
2011	($7,500)	7,500 Cr.	(15,000)
2012	(15,000)	7,500 Dr.	(7,500)
2013	(7,500)	7,500 Dr.	0

TABLE 10-13 ::: Tax Journal Entries for Askilton Inc.

Dr. Tax expense (expenses +, shareholders' equity −)	82,500	
Cr. Future income tax liability (liabilities +)		7,500
Cr. Taxes payable (liabilities +)		75,000
To record the tax expense and future income tax liability for 2010.		
Dr. Tax expense (expenses +, shareholders' equity −)	82,500	
Cr. Future income tax liability (liabilities +)		7,500
Cr. Taxes payable (liabilities +)		75,000
To record the tax expense and future income tax liability for 2011.		
Dr. Tax expense (expenses +, shareholders' equity−)	82,500	
Dr. Future income tax liability (liabilities −)	7,500	
Cr. Taxes payable (liabilities +)		90,000
To record the tax expense and future income tax liability for 2012.		
Dr. Tax expense (expenses +, shareholders' equity −)	82,500	
Dr. Future income tax liability (liabilities −)	7,500	
Cr. Taxes payable (liabilities +)		90,000
To record the tax expense and future income tax liability for 2013.		

Things would be simpler if the income tax expense were simply the amount of tax an entity actually had to pay—an approach we can call the taxes payable method. If the taxes payable method were used, there would be no future income taxes to account for because the income tax expense would be equal to income taxes payable. The problem with the taxes payable method for some accountants is that the income tax expense would be measured using a different method than the other numbers on the income statement. The income tax expense would be based on the requirements of the *ITA* and the rest of the numbers would be based on GAAP, accrual accounting, or whatever basis of accounting the entity chose to use. Of course, as we have seen throughout the book, a variety of different ways of measuring things is reflected in contemporary financial statements. The taxes payable method can have some interesting effects on net income.

Net income calculated using the taxes payable method for Askilton is shown in Table 10–15 (page 563).

Notice that in Table 10–15 net income varies over the four years, whereas in Table 10–14 net income is the same each year. In general, the taxes payable approach makes earnings more variable, which can make an entity look riskier. Which approach is better? That depends on the users and the uses of the information. The taxes payable method is the cash approach. The future income tax method is based on accounting measurement criteria. Remember, however, that, regardless of which method is used, the actual cash flow, the amount of tax the entity pays, remains the same.

The Askilton example only gives rise to future income tax liabilities. Future income tax assets are also commonly reported. As shown in Table 10–11 (page 561), whether a future

Askilton Inc.
Extracts from the Income Statement
December 31, 2010–2013

	2010	2011	2012	2013
Income before amortization				
and income taxes	$300,000	$300,000	$300,000	$300,000
Amortization expense	25,000	25,000	25,000	25,000
Income before taxes	275,000	275,000	275,000	275,000
Income tax expense				
Current expense	75,000	75,000	90,000	90,000
Future expense (benefit	7,500	7,500	(7,500)	(7,500)
	82,500	82,500	82,500	82,500
Net Income	$192,500	$192,500	$192,500	$192,500

TABLE 10–15 ::: Net Income Calculated Using the Taxes Payable Method

Askilton Inc.
Extracts from the Income Statement
December 31, 2010–2013

	2010	2011	2012	2013
Income before amortization				
and income taxes	$300,000	$300,000	$300,000	$300,000
Amortization expense	25,000	25,000	25,000	25,000
Income before taxes	275,000	275,000	275,000	275,000
Income tax expense	75,000	75,000	90,000	90,000
Net income	$200,000	$200,000	$185,000	$185,000

income tax asset or liability arises is simply a matter of the tax basis of assets and liabilities versus their accounting basis. If at the end of 2010, the NBV of Askilton's asset was $45,000 instead of $75,000, Askilton would have reported a future income tax asset of $1,500 ($[(UCC − NBV) \times \text{tax rate}] = [(\$50,000 − \$45,000) \times 30 \text{ percent}]$). Also, the example did not deal with current and non-current future income tax assets and liabilities. Current future income tax assets and liabilities are the result of differences between the tax and accounting bases of current assets and liabilities. Non-current future income tax assets and liabilities are the result of differences between the tax and accounting bases of non-current assets and liabilities.

The purpose of this discussion was to show with a "simple" example where a balance in the future income tax account comes from. In reality, a future income tax balance is a complex mix of differences between financial reporting and tax for many different assets and liabilities. But the more important question for introductory students of accounting is, how should a future income tax balance be interpreted when examining an entity's financial statements? Here are some points to consider:

■ Future income taxes (and its predecessor, deferred taxes) have long been misinterpreted and abused. Every now and then in the media or among politicians, the future income tax liability is pointed to as evidence that corporations are not paying "their fair share" of taxes. This interpretation is false and misleading. Future income taxes also do not represent actual claims of governments against a company's assets or refunds that are forthcoming. As we discussed, future income taxes are the result of differences between financial reporting and tax. By using the taxes payable method, future income tax liabilities would disappear, but entities would be paying exactly the same amount of income tax. Perhaps the new name, future income taxes, instead of deferred income taxes, will discourage people from misinterpreting the meaning of this account.

- Only the current portion of the income tax expense on the income statement represents a current cash flow. The future portion represents a non-cash accrual. As a result, future income tax accounting reduces the association between earnings and cash flows.

- In principle, future income tax balances give some insight into the remaining tax value of assets and liabilities because they bridge the difference between accounting and tax. This information can be important because an asset with CCA still available to be claimed is more valuable than an asset with no CCA available, because the remaining CCA will reduce the amount of tax the entity has to pay. For example, at the end of 2011 Askilton's asset had a tax value of zero and an accounting value of $50,000. From the accounting records alone, it isn't possible to tell that the asset had no tax value. Information about the tax value of an asset is useful because it helps users assess future cash flows. The future tax liability of $15,000 tells users that the tax value of the asset is $50,000 (future tax liability ÷ tax rate = $15,000 ÷ 0.3) less than the accounting value. On December 31, 2011 the accounting value of the asset is $50,000, so the tax value is zero.

Rogers provides a table in Note 14 (page A-34) that identifies the source of the temporary differences that give rise to future income tax assets and liabilities. This disclosure helps users figure out the tax value of different groups of assets and liabilities. An alternative to this approach would be to disclose the tax value of assets and liabilities in the notes to the financial statements.

- The temporary differences that give rise to future income taxes are often not very temporary. If an entity is growing, the temporary differences between the amount of CCA deducted and the amount of amortization expensed will usually grow as well, with the result that the future income tax liability will increase year after year. In those circumstances, it is questionable whether the credit balance should be considered a liability.

- Future income tax liabilities are not discounted. As a result, amounts reported on the balance sheet are overstated because the time value of money is not taken into consideration. If future income tax balances will not decrease for a long time, some of the very large future income tax liability balances can actually represent some relatively small liabilities in present value terms. For example, if Petro-Canada's $2.708 billion future income tax liability will not decrease for 50 years, the present value of the liability discounted at 8 percent is only about $58,700,000.

www.petro-canada.ca

- Future income taxes are affected by the accounting policies used. Assuming that the amount of income tax an entity pays is not affected by the accounting choices it makes for financial reporting purposes, accounting choices that increase income will increase the future income tax liability (or decrease the future income tax asset).

- Entities that do not have to follow GAAP might choose not to use future income tax accounting. A small private company whose financial statements are used for tax purposes and by a banker might choose to forego following this GAAP rule. Also, companies that are eligible to follow differential reporting can elect to use the taxes payable method of accounting for income taxes as allowed by the Differential Reporting section of the *CICA Handbook*. **Differential Reporting** allows private companies that follow GAAP and have unanimous consent of their shareholders to use a number of simplified accounting rules that are not available to public companies. Differential reporting applies to some of the more complex *Handbook* sections and so can lower the cost of financial reporting in certain situations. Future income tax accounting is complex and confusing, can be costly to use, and in many situations may provide little useful information to financial statement users.

- The financial statements of public companies provide additional disclosures that can be useful to understanding the tax status of an entity. Note 14 to Rogers' financial statements (page A-34) provides a reconciliation from the amount of tax Rogers would be expected to pay using the statutory tax rate to the actual tax.

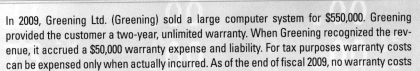
In 2009, Greening Ltd. (Greening) sold a large computer system for $550,000. Greening provided the customer a two-year, unlimited warranty. When Greening recognized the revenue, it accrued a $50,000 warranty expense and liability. For tax purposes warranty costs can be expensed only when actually incurred. As of the end of fiscal 2009, no warranty costs had been incurred on the computer system. Greening has an income tax rate of 35 percent.

What is the tax basis and accounting basis of the warranty liability at the end of fiscal 2009? What balance would there be in the future income tax account at the end of fiscal 2009?

Answer: The accounting basis of the warranty liability at the end of fiscal 2009 is $50,000. The NBV of the warranty liability is equal to the original accrual, less warranty costs incurred. Since no warranty costs had been incurred as of the end of 2009, the accounting basis of the warranty liability remains at the original amount of $50,000. The tax basis of the warranty liability is zero. The *ITA* does not recognize warranty accruals so for tax purposes there is no warranty expense and no warranty liability. The future income tax amount that would be reported on Greening's 2009 balance sheet is calculated as follows:

$$\text{Future income tax balance} = (\text{Tax basis of liability} - \text{Accounting basis of liability}) \times \text{Tax rate}$$
$$= (0 - \$50,000) \times 35 \text{ percent}$$
$$= \$17,500 \text{ Dr.}$$

Since the tax basis of the liability is less than the accounting basis, Greening's balance sheet will report a future income tax asset of $17,500 (from Table 10–11, page 561).

KEY TERMS

after-tax cost of borrowing, p. 549

bond, p. 530

callable bond, p. 531

capital lease, p. 539

capital structure p. 550

commitment, p. 547

contingency, p. 545

convertible bond, p. 531

coupon rate, p. 530

debenture, p. 530

debt, p. 528

defined-benefit plan, p. 544

defined-contribution plan, p. 543

demand loan, p. 524

differential reporting p. 564

discount (on debt), p. 533

effective interest rate, p. 531

face value of a bond, p. 530

fixed-rate loan, p. 530

future income tax assets and liabilities, p. 558

interest coverage ratio, p. 551

lease, p. 538

lessee, p. 538

lessor, p. 538

leverage, p. 530

line of credit, p. 524

maturity date of a bond, p. 530

mortgage, p. 530

note payable, p. 530

off-balance-sheet financing, p. 538

operating lease, p. 539

pension, p. 543

permanent differences, p. 558

premium (on debt), p. 534

proceeds, pp. 530–531

retractable bond, p. 531

subsequent event, p. 549

taxable income, p. 558

temporary differences, p. 558

undepreciated capital cost (UCC), p. 559

variable-rate loan, p. 530

SIMILAR TERMS

The left column gives alternative terms that are sometimes used for the accounting terms introduced in this chapter, which are listed in the right column.

long-term debt	**non-current debt**
deferred income taxes	**future income taxes**
provision for income taxes, income tax provision	**income tax expense**
security	**collateral**

ASSIGNMENT MATERIALS

Questions

Q10-1. What happens to the market value of a bond if the effective interest rate decreases after the bond is issued? Explain. How is the change in the effective interest rate reflected in the financial statements?

Q10-2. Explain the following terms as they relate to bonds:
a. effective rate of interest
b. coupon rate
c. maturity date
d. proceeds
e. face value

Q10-3. What is off-balance-sheet financing? Why is off-balance-sheet financing attractive for some entities? How does off-balance-sheet financing affect financial statement users' ability to interpret financial statements?

Q10-4. Hyannas Inc. has recently arranged financing for its planned expansion. The company arranged a $5,000,000 bank loan that is secured against inventory, receivables, and certain capital assets. The second loan is for $2,000,000 and is an unsecured loan. Which loan would you expect to have a higher interest rate? Explain.

Q10-5. Why does recording an "interest-free" loan at its face value result in the understatement of net income?

Q10-6. What is an executory contract? How are executory contracts accounted for according to GAAP? What is the reason for this treatment? What are some of the problems with it? Can you think of any executory contracts that are reported on GAAP-based financial statements?

Q10-7. What are bond discounts and premiums? Why are bonds sometimes sold at a discount or premium?

Q10-8. What are restrictive covenants? Why are restrictive covenants sometimes included as part of debt agreements? How does a borrower benefit from a restrictive covenant? Why would a borrower prefer to avoid having restrictive covenants in loan agreements, assuming nothing changes as a result?

Q10-9. Because of an increase in competition in the industry, a respected bond-rating agency recently downgraded its rating on Quaw Inc.'s (Quaw) corporate bonds. A downgrade means that the bonds are considered more risky. What do you think would be the effect of the downgrade on the market price of Quaw's bonds? Explain. What do you think the impact would be the next time Quaw issued bonds?

Q10-10. How do bond discounts and premiums affect an entity's interest expense? Explain.

Q10-11. Why do gains and losses arise when an entity redeems its bonds before they mature? How are the gains and losses calculated?

Q10-12. Explain the difference between a capital lease and an operating lease. Explain how each type of lease is accounted for and the effect that each has on the balance sheet and income statement.

Q10-13. What amount is reported on a lessee's balance sheet at the start of a lease for a leased asset and the associated liability? Why do the amounts reported for the asset and liability differ for balance sheets prepared after the start of the lease?

Q10-14. What is a subsequent event? How are subsequent events accounted for?

Q10-15. What is a commitment? How are commitments accounted for?

Q10-16. Distinguish between a defined-benefit pension plan and defined-contribution pension plan. Which plan is more attractive for employees? Explain. Which plan is less risky for employers? Explain.

Q10-17. What is a contingency in accounting? Under what circumstances should a contingency be accrued in the financial statements? Under what circumstances should a contingency be disclosed in the notes to the financial statements? Under what circumstances should a contingency not be reflected in the financial statements or notes? What do you think is the best way to account for a contingency? Explain.

Q10-18. What is an accrued liability? How does an accrued liability differ from an account payable? Under what circumstances are accrued liabilities required?

Q10-19. Because it is so difficult to estimate the cost of providing defined-benefit pensions to employees who will retire many years in the future, it would make more sense, and result in more accurate financial statements, to simply expense the pension when it is paid. Discuss this statement. In your discussion address relevant accounting concepts and the impact of the proposed approach on the financial statements.

Q10-20. What is a current liability? Why is it important to know the amount of current liabilities an entity has?

Q10-21. Why is the current portion of long-term debt classified separately as a current liability? What would be the impact on users of the financial statements if the current portion of long-term debt were not reported separately?

Q10-22. What is the interest coverage ratio? What information does the interest coverage ratio provide?

Q10-23. What is a liability? What are the three characteristics that, according to GAAP, a liability must have? Do you think these characteristics capture every obligation an entity has? Explain.

Q10-24. Rykerts Ltd. reports a pension liability of $3,250,000 on its December 31, 2010 balance sheet. Provide an interpretation of this account and the balance in the account.

Q10-25. Why do managers sometimes have incentives to understate liabilities? What are the implications for the financial statements of understating liabilities? Provide examples of how a manager could understate his or her entity's liabilities.

Q10-26. What are the characteristics of debt that make it risky? Why do these characteristics make debt risky?

Q10-27. Why are long-term liabilities such as bonds valued for financial reporting purposes at their present value, but capital assets are not?

Q10-28. What is the relationship between the coupon rate and effective interest rate when a bond is sold at a discount? What is the relationship when a bond is sold at a premium?

Q10-29. Why is the actual cost of borrowing usually lower than the stated rate of interest that the borrower pays to a lender such as a bank? Can you think of a situation where the actual cost of borrowing will not be lower than the stated rate of interest?

Q10-30. Why are the assets in a pension plan not reported on the balance sheet of the entity sponsoring the pension plan? Does this treatment result in an understatement of the sponsoring entity's assets?

Q10-31. What is unearned revenue? Why is it considered a liability?

Q10-32. Identify and explain the criteria that the *CICA Handbook* provides to assist in the classification of leases. What are the problems and benefits of providing preparers of the financial statements with these criteria?

Q10-33. In its most recent balance sheet, Vosburg Inc. reported a debt-to-equity ratio of 1.85 to 1. This ratio has increased slightly from the previous year when the ratio was 1.55 to 1. Assess Vosburg Inc.'s debt-to-equity ratio and the change in the ratio over the last year.

Q10-34 (appendix). A labour union leader said at a recent rally that there would be plenty of money for health care, education, and other social programs if governments simply collected the future income taxes that corporations owe and are reported on their balance sheets. A friend of yours asked you, in response to the union leader's comments, how it is that businesses can avoid paying their taxes whereas working people cannot.

Required:

Respond to your friend.

Q10-35 (appendix). What are future income taxes and what circumstances cause them to appear on an entity's balance sheet?

Q10-36 (appendix). According to the GAAP characteristics for liabilities, is a future income tax liability really a liability? Explain.

Q10-37 (appendix). One of the criticisms often made about accounting for future income taxes is that the amounts reported on the financial statements are not discounted. What is the problem with not discounting future income taxes? What problems do not discounting impose on users of the financial statements?

Q10-38 (appendix). Distinguish the future income tax method of accounting for income taxes from the taxes payable method.

Q10-39 (appendix). Entities that use future income tax accounting show two components of the income tax expense: the current expense and the future expense. Define and explain these two components of the income tax expense.

Exercises

E10-1. **(Determining the proceeds from a bond, LO 3)** On July 15, 2009, Dyce Inc. (Dyce) will be making a $4,000,000 bond issue to public investors. The bond matures in five years on July 14, 2014, has a coupon rate of 8 percent, and pays interest annually on July 14. Indicate how much Dyce will receive in proceeds from its bond if the effective interest rate when the bond is issued is:

a. 7%

b. 8%

c. 9%

E10-2. **(Determining the proceeds from a bond, LO 3)** On December 1, 2010 Koidern Inc. (Koidern) will be making a $3,000,000 bond issue to public investors. The bond matures in eight years on November 30, 2018 and pays interest annually on November 30. The effective interest rate on December 1, 2010 is expected to be 9 percent. Indicate how much Koidern will receive in proceeds from its bond if the coupon rate on the bond is:

a. 10%

b. 9%

c. 8%

E10-3. **(Accruing interest expense, LO 3)** For each of the following situations record the adjusting journal entry that would be required at year end to accrue the appropriate interest expense. In each case assume that the year end is December 31:

a. On October 1 a company issued a $100,000 bond that pays interest of 6 percent per year, payable on March 31 and September 30.

b. On December 1 a company issued a $10,000,000 bond that pays interest of 8 percent per year, payable annually on November 30.

c. On July 2 a company issued a $500,000 note that pays interest of 10 percent per year, payable quarterly on January 2, April 2, July 2, and October 2.

E10-4. **(Accounting for gift certificates, LO 2, 7)** Juno Boutique Inc. (Juno) operates a small chain of fashion boutiques. Juno usually opens its stores in upscale shopping malls in major cities. In 2009 Juno began offering gift certificates for sale to customers. The certificates can be exchanged for any merchandise in Juno's stores. The certificates cannot be redeemed for cash. During 2009 gift certificates worth $62,000 were sold. By the end of the year, $24,000 of the gift certificates had been redeemed by customers to purchase merchandise that cost Juno $15,000.

Required:

a. Prepare the journal entry required to record the sale of the gift certificates.

b. Prepare the journal entry required to record the redemption of the gift certificates.

c. How would the unused gift certificates be reported in Juno's financial statements?

d. What effect does the sale of gift certificates have on Juno's current ratio?

E10-5. **(Classifying liabilities, LO 2, 3)** How would each of the following items be classified on Atluck Grocery Store Corp.'s (Atluck) September 30, 2010 balance sheet? Explain your reasoning.

a. A $250,000 20-year mortgage on Atluck's land and building. The mortgage requires annual equal payments of $29,365.

b. $1,200 withheld from employee paycheques for income taxes.

c. A $2,500 deposit received from a customer for food platters to be served at a local company's annual meeting to be held on October 17, 2010.

d. $30,000 owed to a supplier for renovations on the store; $15,000 of the amount owed is due on December 15, 2010 and the remainder on November 1, 2011.

e. A $25,000 demand loan from the bank.

E10-6. **(Valuing liabilities, LO 1)** On March 31, 2009 Etzikom Inc. (Etzikom) purchased a corporate jet from the manufacturer for $3,750,000. Etzikom paid $250,000 in cash to the manufacturer and received a four-year, $3,500,000, interest-free loan for the remainder of the purchase price. The terms of the loan require Etzikom to pay the manufacturer $875,000 on March 31 of each of the next four years, beginning on March 31, 2010. Assume a discount rate of 5 percent when responding to the following questions.

a. What alternatives exist for reporting the liability to the manufacturer of the jet? What are the problems and benefits of the alternative approaches?

b. Prepare the journal entry that Etzikom should make to record the purchase of the jet. Explain the amount that you have recorded for the jet on the balance sheet.

c. Prepare the journal entries that Etzikom should make on March 31 of 2009 through 2013 to record payments on the loan.

d. How much should Etzikom report as a liability for the loan on its balance sheet on December 31, 2009 through 2013?

E10-7. **(Collections on behalf of third parties, LO 2)** For the following two independent situations, prepare the journal entry that Durrell Ltd. (Durrell) should record. Record the entry for both the amounts collected or withheld and for the remittances.

a. During November 2010, Durrell sold and delivered $220,000 of services to customers. In addition, customers were charged and paid 6 percent GST on the services provided. Durrell remits the GST it collects from customers on the tenth day of each month.

b. During November, Durrell's employees earned $42,000. From this amount Durrell withheld $13,000 for income taxes, $4,105 for Canada Pension Plan (CPP), $1,860 for Employment Insurance (EI), $750 in union dues, $1,450 for employee contributions to the company pension plan, $1,000 for long-term disability insurance, and $200 in contributions to local charities. Durrell remits the withholdings on the tenth day of each month.

E10-8. **(Classifying liabilities as current and non-current, LO 2)** The accountant of Hantsport Ltd. (Hantsport) is currently preparing the December 31, 2009 financial statements. She has asked you to help her classify the following items:

a. Hantsport withheld $20,000 in income taxes from employees during December 2009. Companies are required to remit these withholdings quarterly to the governments. The next remittance is due on February 28, 2010.

b. As of the end of December Hantsport owed suppliers $68,000 for inventory purchases during November and December 2009.

c. The company has a $50,000 note payable that is coming due in March. Hantsport has arranged a three-year, $50,000 loan from the bank that will be used to repay the loan.

d. Hantsport has received $10,000 in advances for goods that will be delivered during 2010.

e. Hantsport has a $100,000 outstanding with a private lender. $25,000 is scheduled to be repaid in 2010.

f. The company declared a $120,000 cash dividend on December 21, 2009. The dividend is to be paid on January 15, 2010.

Required:

Classify each of the items as a current or non-current liability (note that some may classified partially as current and partially as non-current). Provide your reasoning for each item.

E10-9. **(Calculating the interest expense, LO 3)** During 2009 Goffs Ltd. (Goffs) had the following amount of debt outstanding in each quarter of the year:

1st Quarter	$ 760,000
2nd Quarter	925,000
3rd Quarter	1,100,000
4th Quarter	535,000

The average interest rate that Goffs paid on its debt was 8.8 percent in the first and second quarters and 9.1 percent in the third and fourth quarters.

Required:

Calculate the interest expense that Goffs would report for 2009.

E10-10. (**Understanding bond accounting relationships, LO 3**) Assume the straight-line amortization method is used.

E10-11. (**Accounting entries for a defined-contribution pension plan, LO 5**) Iskut Inc. (Iskut) provides its employees with a defined-contribution pension plan. Each year the company is required to contribute $1,000 to an investment fund for each employee. In the year ended December 31, 2009 Iskut contributed $120,000 on behalf of its 200 employees.

Required:

a. What journal entry would Iskut make to record the contribution to the pension plan?
b. What other entries would be necessary? Explain. What would appear on the balance sheet with respect to the pension plan on December 31, 2009?

E10-12. (**Accounting entries for a defined-benefit pension plan, LO 5**) Brigus Corp. (Brigus) provides its employees with a defined-benefit pension plan. The plan was instituted three years ago. During the year ended March 31, 2010 Brigus contributed $150,000 to the plan. An evaluation of the plan as of the end of fiscal 2010 found that contributions of $250,000 were required in 2010 to have enough money in the plan to provide the benefits promised to employees when they retire.

a. What journal entry would Brigus have made in fiscal 2010 to record the cash it contributed to the pension plan.
b. How much pension liability should be reported on Brigus' balance sheet on March 31, 2010? Explain what this amount represents.

E10-13. (**Classifying transactions and economic events, LO 6**) Classify the following transactions and economic events that Floral Ltd. (Floral) was involved with as commitments, subsequent events, or contingencies. Some may fit more than one classification. Assume that the year end is December 31, 2009. Indicate how each should be reflected in the financial statements and explain your reasoning. In responding, consider the usefulness of the information to different users of the financial statements.

a. On January 15, 2010 Floral signed a three-year contract with a supplier to provide raw materials. The contract is the largest ever agreed to by Floral.
b. In November 2009, a company that Floral was suing for damages for breaching a contract made an offer of $200,000 to settle the case. As of the year end Floral had not decided whether to accept the offer or go to court. The offer is far below what Floral is suing for.
c. On January 21, 2010 Floral signed a five-year lease for storage space in a building near its main facility. The annual lease payments will be $5,000 per year.
d. On January 18, 2010 the company lost a lawsuit launched by a disgruntled former senior executive. Floral is required to pay the former employee $500,000 in damages.
e. In May 2009 Floral guaranteed a $1,000,000 bank loan made to a company Floral owns. Floral is responsible for paying the principal and any outstanding interest in the event that the company is unable to make its payments.

E10-14. (**Accounting for bonds, LO 3**) On November 1, 2010 Nordin Inc. (Nordin) issued a $5,000,000 bond with a 6 percent coupon rate and a maturity date of October 31, 2015. Interest is paid annually on October 31. The effective interest rate for a bond of this type on November 1, 2010 was 8 percent. Nordin's year end is October 31.

Required:

a. What will be the proceeds from the bond issue?
b. Prepare the journal entry to record issue of the bond on November 1, 2010.

c. Prepare an amortization schedule using the straight-line method for any premium or discount that arose on issue of the bond.

d. Prepare the journal entry required to record the interest expense and the interest payment to investors on October 31 of each year over the life of the bond.

e. Prepare the journal entry required to record the retirement of the bond on maturity.

E10-15. **(Accounting for bonds, LO 3)** On September 1, 2009 Yone Ltd. (Yone) issued a $2,000,000 bond with a 9 percent coupon rate and a maturity date of August 31, 2015. Interest is paid annually on August 31. The effective interest rate for a bond of this type on September 1, 2009 was 7 percent. Yone's year end is August 31.

Required:

a. What will be the proceeds from the bond issue?

b. Prepare the journal entry to record issue of the bond on September 1, 2009.

c. Prepare an amortization schedule using the straight-line method for any premium or discount that arose on issue of the bond.

d. Prepare the journal entry required to record the interest expense and the interest payment to investors on August 31 of each year over the life of the bond.

e. Prepare the journal entry required to record the retirement of the bond on maturity.

E10-16. **(Accounting for bonds, LO 3)** On February 1, 2011 Jura Corp. (Jura) issued a $8,000,000 bond with an 7 percent coupon rate and a maturity date of January 31, 2017. Interest is paid annually on January 31. The effective interest rate for a bond of this type on February 1, 2011 was 7 percent. Jura's year end is January 31.

Required:

a. What will be the proceeds from the bond issue?

b. Prepare the journal entry to record issue of the bond on February 1, 2011.

c. Prepare an amortization schedule using the straight-line method for any premium or discount that arose on issue of the bond.

d. Prepare the journal entry required to record the interest expense and the interest payment to investors on June 30 of each year over the life of the bond.

e. Prepare the journal entry required to record the retirement of the bond on maturity.

E10-17. **(Pensions, LO 8)** Orthez Inc. (Orthez) funds a defined-benefit pension plan for its employees. The plan began in 2008. Contributions to the pension plan are made in accordance with actuarial assumptions, while the pension expense that Orthez records each year is determined in accordance with GAAP. In the first three years of the plan Orthez contributed to the plan and expensed for financial reporting purposes the following amounts:

	Contributed to the plan	Pension expense
2008	$2,250,000	$2,000,000
2009	3,000,000	3,125,000
2010	3,250,000	3,000,000

Required:

a. Prepare the journal entry that Orthez would make each year to record the pension expense and the contribution to the pension plan.

b. What is the balance in the pension asset or liability account at the end of 2008 through 2010?

E10-18. **(Early retirement of bonds, LO 3)** In fiscal 2008 Ruthilda Inc. (Ruthilda) decided to exercise its option to redeem its outstanding bond issue before the bonds matured in 2015. The bonds had a face value of $6,000,000 and Ruthilda paid $6,400,000 to redeem them. The bonds were originally issued at a premium of $260,000, and at the time the bonds were redeemed $120,000 of the premium had been amortized.

Required:

a. Prepare the journal entry to record the early retirement of the bonds.
b. What would be the entry if Ruthilda were able to redeem the bonds on the open market at a cost of $5,600,000?
c. What is the economic significance of a gain or loss on the redemption of bonds? How do you think the gain or loss should be reported in the financial statements? Explain. In responding, consider the information needs of users of the financial statements.

E10-19. **(Early retirement of bonds, LO 3)** In fiscal 2009 Hurette Inc. (Hurette) decided to exercise its option to redeem its outstanding bond issue before the bonds matured in 2014. The bonds had a face value of $10,000,000 and Hurette paid $10,500,000 to redeem them. The bonds were originally issued at a discount of $500,000, and at the time the bonds were redeemed $200,000 of the discount had been amortized.

Required:

a. Prepare the journal entry to record the early retirement of the bonds.
b. What would be the entry if Hurette were able to redeem the bonds on the open market at a cost of $9,500,000?
c. What is the economic significance of a gain or loss on the redemption of bonds? How do you think the gain or loss should be reported in the financial statements? Explain. In responding, consider the information needs of users of the financial statements.

E10-20. **(Cost of borrowing, LO 3)** For each of the following situations, determine the entity's after-tax cost of borrowing:
a. A corporation has a $5,000,000 bond with a coupon rate of 8 percent. The corporation has a tax rate of 44 percent.
b. A small business has a three-year, $500,000, 5 percent note payable with a supplier. The small business has a tax rate of 18 percent.
c. A not-for-profit organization, which does not have to pay tax, has a $125,000 bank loan at the prime lending rate plus 2.5 percent. For the year just ended the prime lending rate was 4.5 percent.
d. What is the relationship between an entity's tax rate and its after-tax cost of borrowing? Is it more desirable for an entity to have a higher tax rate so that it can lower its after-tax cost of borrowing? Explain.

E10-21. **(Accounting for leases, LO 4)** On February 1, 2009 Flatwater Ltd. (Flatwater) signed a five-year lease for four delivery trucks. According to the terms of the lease, Flatwater must make annual lease payments of $87,500 on January 31, commencing in 2010. The interest rate that applies to the lease is 8 percent.

Required:

a. If Flatwater's lease were accounted for as an operating lease, what amount would be recorded as an asset for the leased delivery trucks on February 1, 2009?
b. If the lease were accounted for as an operating lease, prepare the journal entries that would have to be made in fiscal 2010 and fiscal 2012 to account for the lease.
c. If Flatwater's lease were accounted for as a capital lease, what amount would be recorded as an asset for the leased delivery trucks on February 1, 2009?
d. If the lease were accounted for as a capital lease, what journal entry would be required on February 1, 2009?

e. If the lease were accounted for as a capital lease, what journal entries would be required on January 31, 2010 to record the lease payment?

f. If the lease were accounted for as a capital lease, what journal entry would be required on January 31, 2010 to record the amortization of the delivery vehicles?

g. What would be the NBV of the leased delivery trucks and the lease liability on Flatwater's January 31, 2010 balance sheet if the lease were accounted for as a capital lease?

E10-22. (**The effect of interest rates on capital leases, LO 4**) On June 1, 2009 Grumbler Corp. (Grumbler) signed a six-year lease for heavy equipment. The lease requires Grumbler to make annual lease payments of $200,000 on May 31 of each year beginning in 2010. The lease is to be treated as a capital lease.

Required:

a. Indicate the amount that would be recorded for heavy equipment and for the lease liability on June 1, 2009 assuming:
   i. The appropriate interest rate for the lease was 8 percent.
   ii. The appropriate interest rate for the lease was 10 percent.
   iii. The appropriate interest rate for the lease was 12 percent.

b. Indicate the annual amortization expense for the heavy equipment, assuming straight-line amortization over six years and assuming:
   i. The appropriate interest rate for the lease was 8 percent.
   ii. The appropriate interest rate for the lease was 10 percent.
   iii. The appropriate interest rate for the lease was 12 percent.

c. Indicate the interest expense pertaining to the lease in the fiscal year ended May 31, 2010, assuming:
   i. The appropriate interest rate for the lease was 8 percent.
   ii. The appropriate interest rate for the lease was 10 percent.
   iii. The appropriate interest rate for the lease was 12 percent.

E10-23. (**The effect of bond transactions on the cash flow statement, LO 3**) Wivenhoe Ltd. (Wivenhoe) includes a cash flow statement in the financial statement package it prepares for the bank. Wivenhoe uses the indirect method for calculating cash from operations. For each of the following items, indicate whether it would be reported in Wivenhoe's cash flow statement as an operating, financing, or investing activity. Indicate how each item would be shown in reconciling from net income to cash from operations using the indirect method.
a. Amortization of a bond premium.
b. Proceeds from the issue of a bond.
c. Interest payment to investors.
d. Repayment of a bond on maturity.
e. Gain on early retirement of a bond.
f. Amortization of a bond discount.

E10-24. (**Lease accounting and financial ratios, LO 4, 7**) Zeballos Inc. (Zeballos) is planning to lease new equipment for its distribution centre. The terms that Zeballos has agreed to require that it pay $125,000 per year for the next five years. The interest rate for the lease is 9 percent. The lease comes into effect on the last day of the current fiscal year and the first payment is to be made in one year. Zeballos has provided you with the following balance sheet information before the new lease has been accounted for at the beginning of the lease.

Current assets	$ 392,500
Non-current assets	1,728,000
Current liabilities	272,500
Non-current liabilities	1,050,000
Shareholders' equity	798,000

Required:

    a. Calculate the current ratio and debt-to-equity ratio for Zeballos, assuming the lease is accounted for as an operating lease.

    b. Calculate the current ratio and debt-to-equity ratio for Zeballos, assuming the lease is accounted for as a capital lease.

    c. Which calculations provide a better representation of Zeballos' liquidity and underlying risk? Explain.

    d. Does it matter how Zeballos accounts for its lease (GAAP notwithstanding)? Explain.

E10-25. **(Accounting for bonds, LO 3)** On June 1, 2009 Joffre Inc. (Joffre) issued a $6,000,000, 10-year bond with an 8 percent coupon rate. Proceeds from the bond issue were $6,600,000. Interest is to be paid annually on May 31. Joffre's year end is December 31. Assume that Joffre uses the straight-line method to amortize any bond premiums or discounts.

Required:

    a. Prepare the journal entry to record the issue of the bond on June 1, 2009.

    b. Prepare the journal entry to accrue the interest expense on December 31, 2009.

    c. Prepare the journal entry to record the payment of interest to bondholders on May 31, 2010.

E10-26. **(Future income taxes, LO 8)** Use the following information to calculate the balance in the future income tax account for a machine owned by the entity:

Cost of the machine when it was purchased:	$1,400,000
Total amount of CCA deducted since the machine was purchased:	820,000
Total amount of amortization expensed since the machine was purchased:	1,150,000
Tax rate:	20 percent

E10-27. **(Future income taxes, LO 8)** Use the following information to calculate the balance in the future income tax account for a building owned by the entity:

Cost of the machine when it was purchased:	$5,000,000
Total amount of CCA deducted since the machine was purchased:	2,305,000
Total amount of amortization expensed since the machine was purchased:	1,787,500
Tax rate:	45 percent

E10-28. **(Future income taxes, LO 8)** For the fiscal year ended November 30, 2008 Vibank Ltd. (Vibank) has income before taxes of $2,250,000. Vibank's tax return shows taxable income of $2,475,000 for that year. The tax basis of Vibank's assets exceeded the accounting basis by $400,000 on November 30, 2008, and the balance in the future income tax account on November 30, 2007 was a credit of $150,000. Vibank has a tax rate of 25 percent.

Required:

    a. Prepare the journal entry that Vibank should make to record its income tax expense for fiscal 2008.

    b. What is Vibank's net income for fiscal 2008?

    c. What would Vibank's net income be if it used the taxes payable method?

    d. Explain the difference between (b) and (c).

E10-29. **(The effect of different amortization methods on future income taxes, LO 8)** Caycuse Inc. (Caycuse) has just completed its first year of operations on December 31, 2009. The company owns a single asset that cost $200,000. For tax purposes Caycuse can deduct $30,000 in CCA in calculating its taxable income in 2009. Assume that Caycuse's tax rate is 18 percent.

a. Determine the future income tax asset or liability on December 31, 2009 if Caycuse amortizes its asset on a straight-line basis over 10 years.

b. Determine the future income tax asset or liability on December 31, 2009 if Caycuse amortizes its asset on a straight-line basis over five years.

c. Determine the future income tax asset or liability on December 31, 2009 if Caycuse amortizes its asset on a declining balance basis at 30 percent per year.

d. Determine the future income tax asset or liability on December 31, 2009 if Caycuse amortizes its asset using the same basis used for tax purposes.

e. According to the three GAAP characteristics for determining whether a liability exists, is a future income tax liability really a liability? Should a future income tax asset be considered an asset? How would you interpret the future income tax assets or liabilities that you calculated in parts (a) through (d) above?

Problems

P10-1. **(Determining whether certain economic events are liabilities, LO 1)** Explain whether each of the following would be considered a liability according to GAAP (using the three criteria from the chapter) on December 31, 2009. Intuitively, would you consider each of these items a liability, regardless of how it is accounted for according to GAAP? Explain.

a. The cost of providing warranty services to a customer who purchased a product in 2009. The warranty covers parts and labour for three years from the date of purchase.

b. A company borrows $950,000 on January 8, 2010. The loan bears an annual interest rate of 7.5 percent and must be renewed each year.

c. A small business signs a two-year, non-cancellable lease on office space in a downtown building in December 2008. The lease requires the business to pay $10,000 in rent over the two years of the lease.

P10-2. **(Determining whether certain economic events are liabilities, LO 1)** Explain whether each of the following would be considered a liability according to GAAP (using the three criteria from the chapter) on December 31, 2010. Intuitively, would you consider each of these items a liability, regardless of how it is accounted for according to GAAP? Explain.

a. Interest on a bank loan outstanding on December 31, 2010. Interest is not payable until the loan must be repaid on September 30, 2011.

b. A $1,000,000 loan from a shareholder that bears no interest and has no scheduled repayment date.

c. The cost of closing a landfill when it is full. Significant costs will have to be incurred to ensure that it meets government standards. The landfill is expected to close in 15 years.

P10-3. **(Effect of transactions and economic events on ratios, LO 2, 3, 4, 6, 7)** The president of Oskelaneo Ltd. (Oskelaneo) wants to know the effect that a number of transactions and economic events will have on several financial measures for the company's fiscal year ended September 30, 2009. Complete the following table by indicating whether the listed transactions or economic events would increase, decrease, or have no effect on the financial measures listed. Explain your reasoning and state any assumptions that you make. Consider each item independently.

	Debt-to-equity ratio	Current ratio	Interest coverage ratio	Cash from operations	Return on assets
Ratio/amount before taking the transaction/economic event into effect.	1.3:1	1.67	3.98	$650,000	5.6%
a. Oskelaneo paid interest on a bank loan.					
b. Oskelaneo arranged a new capital lease.					
c. Oskelaneo repaid a bond that was classified as the current portion of long-term debt.					
d. Oskelaneo received cash from a customer for services that will be provided in February 2010.					
e. Oskelaneo retired a bond early and recognized a gain of $55,000 (the bond retired was classified as a non-current liability).					
f. A customer sued Oskelaneo in January 2009 for negligence. A decision by the court is not expected for at least two years. The company's lawyers state that it is unlikely the company will lose the lawsuit.					

P10-4. (**Effect of transactions and economic events on ratios, LO 3, 4, 5, 6, 7, 8**) The president of Ruskin Inc. (Ruskin) wants to know the effect that a number of transactions and economic events will have on several financial measures for the company's fiscal year ended April 30, 2010. Complete the following table by indicating whether the listed transactions or economic events would increase, decrease or have no effect on the financial measures listed. Explain your reasoning and state any assumptions that you make.

	Debt-to-equity ratio	Current ratio	Interest coverage ratio	Cash from operations	Return on assets
Ratio/amount before taking the transaction/economic event into effect.	0.7:1	0.85	4.21	$1,750,000	7.6%
a. Ruskin signed a contract to purchase raw materials beginning in 2011 at an agreed-to price.					
b. Ruskin provided services to a customer that were paid for in the previous fiscal year.					
c. Ruskin made a contribution to its defined-contribution pension plan.					
d. A fire destroyed a small building owned by Ruskin on May 4, 2010.					
e. Ruskin arranged a new operating lease.					
f. Ruskin paid $1,000,000 to settle a lawsuit that was launched three years ago.					

P10-5. (**Impact of covenants, LO 3, 7**) In late 2009 Bedeque Ltd. (Bedeque) arranged to borrow $1,000,000 from a local bank to provide $250,000 in needed working capital and $750,000 to finance the purchase of some new equipment. However, the terms of a previous loan require that the company maintain a current ratio greater than 1.5

and a debt-to-equity ratio of less than 1. If either of these restrictions is not met the loan would have to be repaid within 30 days. The previous loan agreement also states that for Bedeque to pay dividends, retained earnings must be greater than $1,700,000 after the dividend.

Bedeque's controller has asked you to figure out how the new loan will affect the restrictions on the December 31, 2009. Bedeque's shareholders are expecting a dividend in early 2010 so the controller also wants to know how much can be paid. The controller has provided you with a projected balance sheet for December 31, 2009. The balance sheet takes into consideration all expected economic activity through the end of the year (including the closing entry), except for the impact of the new loan.

Bedeque Inc.
Projected Balance Sheet
As of December 31, 2009

Current assets	$ 720,000	Current liabilities	$ 600,000
Non-current assets	5,250,000	Non-current liabilities	1,500,000
		Capital stock	2,000,000
		Retained earnings	1,870,000
Total assets	$5,970,000	Total liabilities and shareholders' equity	$5,970,000

Required:

Prepare a report that provides the information the controller wants. Explain you findings and reasoning.

P10-6. (**Accounting for possible unexpected warranty costs, LO 6**) Nouvelle Ltd. (Nouvelle) is a privately owned industrial-products manufacturer located in Sherbrooke, Québec. The president of Nouvelle owns 25 percent of the shares of the company and three investors who are not active in managing the company own the remaining 75 percent of the shares. The company has a large demand loan outstanding at the bank. The terms of the loan require that Nouvelle maintain a current ratio of greater than 1.5 and a debt-to-equity ratio of 1.25 to 1 or less. Nouvelle's senior executives have an employment contract that entitles them to share a bonus pool equal to 10 percent of the company's net income. The financial statements are also used for tax purposes.

On December 21, 2009 Nouvelle's quality control engineer presented a report to the president where she expressed concern about problems with a new line of the company's products. The engineer believes that these new products were rushed into production and as a result there are some technical flaws that have not been corrected in products that have been sold to customers. The engineer has reported that there has been an increase of about 20 percent in service calls required on the new products, as compared with other company products, but she believes that repairs will increase dramatically once the products have been used by customers for more than 2,500 hours. The engineer estimates that she expects to see a sharp increase in repairs on these products from 12 to 18 months from the date of purchase and that the cost of repairing these products will be $1,500,000 higher than the amount originally budgeted. To date, repair costs on the new product line are about $125,000 higher than budgeted. The engineer bases her concerns on extensive tests she has carried out in the quality control laboratory.

Nouvelle's product design engineer, who was responsible for development of the products, has stated flatly that there are no technical flaws and that the increase in service calls is reasonable for a new product line.

On December 15, 2009 Nouvelle's vice-president of finance provided the president with the following estimates of the December 31, 2009 financial statements:

Net income	$ 1,270,000	
Current assets	11,150,000	
Current liabilities	9,100,000	
Non-current liabilities	28,750,000	
Shareholders' equity	31,400,000	

Required:

Prepare a report to Nouvelle's president discussing the accounting and financial reporting issues regarding treatment of the concerns raised by the quality control engineer. Your report should identify alternative ways that the possible future costs could be treated and explain the implications of the alternatives. The president would also like your supported recommendations on what should be done.

P10-7. (Assessing debt load, LO 3, 6, 7) Lintlaw Ltd. (Lintlaw) recently released its December 31, 2009 financial statement. In a press release announcing the results Lintlaw's management proudly stated that the company had maintained its debt load well below the industry average of 2.5 to 1. Lintlaw's summarized balance sheet for the years ended December 31, 2008 and 2009, along with extracts from the notes to the financial statements are provided below.

Required:

Assess Lintlaw's debt position. Do you think management should be as proud of its financial situation as it is? Explain your thinking.

Lintlaw Ltd.
Balance sheets for the years ended December 31,
(in thousands of dollars)

	2009	2008		2009	2008
Cash	$350	$275	Accounts payable and accrued liabilities	$1,820	$1,700
Accounts receivable	750	720	Current portion of long-term debt	200	200
Inventory	1,300	1,210		2,020	1,900
Other	350	310	Long-term debt	1,200	1,400
	2,750	2,515	Other non-current liabilities	250	275
Property, plant and equipment (net)	1,970	2,010		3,470	3,575
Intangilbe assets (including goodwill)	1,750	1,850			
			Capital stock	1,800	1,800
			Retained earnings	1,200	1,000
Total assets	$6,470	$6,375	Total liabilities and shareholders' equity	$6,470	$6,375

Extracts from Lintlaw's financial statements:
- The company has leased most of the equipment that it uses in its production process. The leases generally are generally for four to five years and all are classified as operating leases. Minimum annual lease payments for the next five years are:

2010	$750,000
2011	775,000
2012	810,000
2013	850,000
2014	800,000

- The company has long-term binding commitments to purchase supplies from a Korean company. The commitments require a minimum purchase of $1,000,000 for the next three years.
- On January 15, 2010 the company signed an agreement to borrow $1.5 million from a local bank. The annual interest rate on the loan will be 7 percent for a term of three years. The loan comes into effect on February 19, 2010.

P10-8. **(Accounting for a rebate promotion, LO 1, 2, 6)** Urling Inc. (Urling) is a small public company that produces packaged consumer foods. Urling began operations about 22 years ago and has been a public company for eight years. The company is managed by professional managers, who own about 10 percent of Urling's stock. About 30 percent of the shares are owned by members of the family who originally founded the company and the rest are widely held by private and institutional investors. Urling stock has struggled in recent years. The company has failed to meet earnings targets for the last two fiscal years. For the current fiscal year management has projected earnings of $2,500,000, which is about a 2 percent increase from the previous year.

Recently, Urling introduced a new line of upscale frozen entrées to satisfy the tastes and lifestyles of busy baby boomers. For the first time, Urling's management decided to promote the sale of the new entrées by offering rebates to customers. In the past, the company had promoted its products through advertising and in-store price reductions. The new promotion entitles customers to a $5.00 rebate if they purchase four entrées and mail in the UPC labels from the packages. Urling used special packaging highlighting the promotion, provided in-store signs, and advertised it in newspaper and magazines. Since the promotion began several months ago, approximately 250,000 entrées have been sold and sales of an additional 70,000 are expected by year end. Approximately 1,500 customers have already mailed in their requests for rebates.

Because Urling has never used this type of promotion before, its marketing manager is not sure how to account for the promotion. The marketing manager has indicated that the number of rebate claims can be very difficult to estimate, especially because it is a new promotion and a new product. The manager has indicated that the number of claims can range between 2 percent and 25 percent of the product sold. Urling's controller has projected that net income before accounting for the new promotion will be about $2,555,000. Because projected earnings are so close to the forecast, the president is quite uneasy about the effect the new promotion will have.

Required:

a. Prepare a report to Urling's president outlining the accounting issues and problems with the new rebate promotion. Provide recommendations on how the promotion should be accounted for and provide support for your recommendations that can be used in any discussions with the company's auditors. Indicate how the rebate promotion will be reported in the financial statements.

b. Prepare a journal entry that will account for the rebate promotion in the current fiscal year.

P10-9. **(Accounting for a possible loss, LO 6)** Hoselaw Ltd. (Hoselaw) is a privately owned manufacturing company in eastern Ontario. The company is owned by five shareholders, three of whom are not active in management of the business. The company has a large demand loan outstanding at the bank.

The government recently informed Hoselaw's management that seepage from a dumpsite on its property might have polluted the ground water that is used by a local community. The company has denied responsibility, but the local community has launched a $2,000,000 lawsuit against Hoselaw to compensate the community for additional costs of obtaining fresh water and for cleaning up the contaminated water. The lawyers for the community and the company have met to discuss possible settlement terms, but little progress has been reported. Hoselaw's net income over the last five years has averaged $725,000 and its assets, as reported on the most recent balance sheet, have a NBV of $3,750,000.

Required:

Prepare a report to Hoselaw's president discussing the issues surrounding how to account for the environmental incident and the lawsuit. Your report should include a discussion of the alternative accounting treatments available and the implications of each.

P10-10. **(Accounting for a possible loss, LO 6)** In May 2008, a child was injured at a play area at the Kakisa Design Furniture Shoppe. The play area was provided so parents could leave their children while they shopped in the store. The parents of the child thought the injury was due to poor supervision and poor maintenance and so they are suing Kakisa for $1 million. As of December 31, 2009 (Kakisa's year end) the lawsuit has not been settled. Kakisa's lawyers believe that the company will probably lose the lawsuit if it goes to trial. The lawyers think that Kakisa stands to lose somewhere between $75,000 and $350,000.

Kakisa is a family-owned business but no family members are involved in management of the store. The financial statements are used by the members of the Kakisa family, for tax purposes, and by the store's banker. In January 2011, the lawsuit was finally settled with Kakisa paying the family of the injured child $150,000.

Required:

a. Prepare a report to Kakisa's president explain the accounting issues that must be considered in deciding how to account for the lawsuit in the December 31, 2009 financial statements. Provide a recommendation on how the lawsuit should be accounted for and explain your reasoning fully.

b. What are the accounting issues that would have to be considered when the December 31, 2010 financial statements are prepared?

P10-11. **(Accounting for leases, LO 4)** Vista Inc. (Vista) is a new manufacturing company that was formed in January 2009 to supply certain specialized machine parts to a large public company. Vista's managers decided to arrange long-term leases for the company's equipment, rather than to arrange financing and buy the equipment. Had Vista purchased the equipment, it would have cost about $2,000,000. Instead, Vista signed a 10-year lease for the equipment in January 2009 that required it to make annual payments of $300,000 on December 31, the company's year end. At the end of the lease, Vista has the option to purchase the equipment at its fair market value at the time. However, Vista's management thinks that it is unlikely that it will exercise the option, since after 10 years the equipment is likely to be technologically out of date. The interest rate appropriate for this lease is 9 percent.

On December 31, 2009 Vista had total liabilities (before accounting for the lease obligation) of $1,600,000, capital stock of $1,000,000, and income before lease-related expenses and taxes of $700,000. Vista's tax expense for 2009 is estimated to be $80,000.

Required:

a. What are some of the reasons that Vista might have leased rather than purchased the equipment?

b. Should the lease be accounted for as a capital lease or an operating lease? Explain.

c. What journal entry would be required when the lease agreement was signed if the lease were considered a capital lease? What entry would be required if it were classified as an operating lease?

d. Prepare a schedule showing the principal and interest components of each annual payment over the life of the lease, assuming the lease is treated as a capital lease. Prepare the journal entries that Vista would make on December 31, 2009 and December 31, 2012 to record the lease payment. What would the entries be if the lease were classified as an operating lease?

e. What amount would be reported on Vista's balance sheet for the machinery when the lease was signed in January 2009? What does this amount represent?

f. Over what period of time should the equipment be amortized? Explain. Prepare the journal entry to record the amortization expense for the year ended December 31, 2009. Assume Vista uses straight-line amortization.

g. How would Vista's debt-to-equity ratio be affected by accounting for the lease as a capital lease? Compare the debt-to-equity ratio on December 31, 2009 when the lease is classified as a capital lease versus an operating lease.

h. Compare the effect on the income statement of classifying the lease as a capital lease versus an operating lease. Make the comparison for the years ended December 31, 2009 and 2012.

i. What steps could Vista take to have the lease classified as an operating lease? Why might Vista prefer that classification?

j. For purposes of determining a bonus for Vista's managers, do you think it is more appropriate to treat the lease as a capital lease or an operating lease? In answering, focus on determining management's bonus, not how GAAP would require the lease to be classified.

P10-12. **(Accounting for leases, LO 4)** In May 2009 Isachsen Inc. (Isachsen) signed a four-year lease with an office supply company to supply Isachsen with all required office equipment over the lease period. Had Isachsen purchased the office equipment, it would have cost about $250,000. The lease requires Isachsen to make annual lease payments of $75,000 on April 30, the company's year end. At the end of the lease Isachsen will own the equipment. Isachsen's management believes that the office equipment will be useful for between six and eight years. The interest rate appropriate for this lease is 11 percent.

On April 30, 2010 Isachsen had total liabilities (before accounting for the lease obligation) of $1,375,000 and capital stock of $750,000. Isachsen's income before lease related-expenses and taxes for the year ended April 30, 2010 is $275,000. Isachsen's tax expense for fiscal 2010 is estimated to be $80,000 and retained earnings on April 30, 2009 was $450,000.

Required:

a. What are some of the reasons that Isachsen might have leased rather than purchased the office equipment?

b. Should the lease be accounted for as a capital lease or an operating lease? Explain.

c. What journal entry would be required when the lease agreement was signed if the lease were considered a capital lease? What entry would be required if it were classified as an operating lease?

d. Prepare a schedule showing the principal and interest components of each annual payment over the life of the lease, assuming the lease is treated as a capital lease. Prepare the journal entries that Isachsen would make on April 30, 2010 and April 30, 2012 to record the lease payment. What would the entries be if the lease were classified as an operating lease?

e. What amount would be reported on Isachsen's balance sheet for the equipment when the lease was signed in May 2009? What does this amount represent?

f. Over what period of time should the equipment be amortized? Explain. Prepare the journal entry to record the amortization expense for the year ended April 30, 2010. Assume Isachsen uses straight-line amortization.

g. How would Isachsen's debt-to-equity ratio be affected by accounting for the lease as a capital lease? Compare the debt-to-equity ratio on April 30, 2010 when the lease is classified as a capital lease versus an operating lease.

h. Compare the effect on the income statement of classifying the lease as a capital lease versus an operating lease. Make the comparison for the years ended April 30, 2010 and 2012.

i. What steps could Isachsen take to have the lease classified as an operating lease? Why might Isachsen prefer that classification?

j. Suppose you were considering buying all the shares of Isachsen. Which balance sheet and income statement would be more useful to you in assessing the company—statements where the lease was classified as a capital lease or as an operating lease?

P10-13. (**Effect of inaccurate accruals, LO 7**) In 2009 Ogoki Ltd. announced a major restructuring of its operations. The restructuring was in response to several years of poor performance and declining net income, the result of increased competition from Asia. The company announced that it would be downsizing its production facilities and reducing its workforce by 20 percent. Management estimated that the cost of reducing the workforce would be about $75 million. The reduction in the workforce and the related costs are to take place in 2010.

In 2010, Ogoki carried out its restructuring. When it was completed, the actual cost of reducing the workforce was $50 million. All of these costs were related to severance packages paid to and retraining of employees. Ogoki's year end is December 31.

Required:

a. Provide the journal entry that Ogoki would make in 2009 to record the estimated cost of reducing the workforce. Why do you think the entry would be made in 2009 when the reduction in the workforce was to actually take place in 2010? How would the amount be shown on the income statement? Explain.

b. What entry would be made to record the $50 million in cash costs incurred in 2010 to reduce the workforce. What effect would this entry have on the income statement in 2010? Explain.

c. What additional entry or entries would be needed in 2010 to adjust for the fact that management estimated the cost of reducing the workforce to be $75 million while the actual cost proved to be only $50 million? What is the effect of this difference on the financial statements in 2009 and 2010? Provide some possible explanations for the error in the estimate in 2009. When answering, consider the managers' financial reporting objectives.

P10-14. (**The effects of buying versus leasing on the financial statements, LO 4**) Winterton Rail Ltd. (Winterton) is considering obtaining some new locomotives. The purchase price of the locomotives is $59,724,975. Winterton is considering whether it should purchase the locomotives or lease them directly from the manufacturer. If Winterton buys the locomotives, it would borrow the full purchase price from a large institutional lender and repay the loan by making an annual payment of $7,500,000 on the last day of each of the next 20 years. If Winterton leases the locomotives, it would make annual lease payments of $7,500,000 to the manufacturer on the last day of each of the next 20 years.

Required:

a. Prepare the journal entries that Winterton would make if it borrowed the money and purchased the locomotives.

b. Prepare the journal entries that Winterton would make when the lease agreement is signed if it leased the locomotives and the lease were considered a capital lease.

c. Prepare the journal entries that Winterton would make when the lease agreement is signed if it leased the locomotives and the lease were considered an operating lease.

d. Compare the three alternatives in (a), (b), and (c). Explain the similarities and differences among them. Under what circumstances might one of the alternatives be preferred over the others? Explain.

P10-15. **(Lease accounting and financial ratios, LO 4, 7)** Uphill Corp. (Uphill) operates four amusement arcades in Calgary. Uphill's summarized balance sheet on March 31, 2009 is shown below.

The non-current liabilities of $115,000 include an $80,000 eight-year term note that matures in 2014. The terms of the note stipulate that Uphill must maintain a current ratio greater than 1.6 and a debt-to-equity ratio of less than 1.0. If either of these covenants is violated, the term note becomes payable immediately.

On April 1, 2009 management decided to upgrade the quality of the games in the arcades, many of which were no longer popular with the young people who are Uphill's primary customers. Uphill arranged a five-year lease for new games. The terms of the lease require annual payments of $22,000. The lease allows Uphill to replace up to 25 percent of the leased arcade games each year with newer games that are carried by the lessor.

Uphill Corp.
Balance Sheet
As of March 31, 2009

Assets		Liabilities and shareholders' equity	
Current assets	$ 45,000	Current liabilities	$30,000
Capital assets and		Non-current liabilities	115,000
other non-current assets	295,000		145,000
		Shareholders' equity	195,000
		Total liabilities and	
Total assets	$ 340,000	shareholders' equity	$340,000

Required:

a. Calculate the current ratio and debt-to-equity ratio on March 31, 2009.

b. Calculate the current ratio and debt-to-equity ratio on April 1, 2009 if the new lease is accounted for as an operating lease.

c. Calculate the current ratio and debt-to-equity ratio on April 1, 2009 if the new lease is accounted for as a capital lease. Assume that the appropriate interest rate that should be applied to the lease is 10 percent.

d. You are Uphill's controller. The president of the company has just informed you of his plan to lease the new arcade equipment. Write a memo to the president raising any concerns you have with the plan and providing advice and recommendations on how he should proceed.

P10-16. **(Accounting for bonds, LO 3)** On May 1, 2009 Kuldo Inc. (Kuldo) issued a $10,000,000 bond with a 6 percent coupon rate and a maturity date of April 30, 2013. Interest will be paid semi-annually on April 30 and October 31. Kuldo's year end is December 31. The effective interest rate for a bond of this type on May 1, 2009 was 8 percent.

Required:

a. What will be the proceeds from the bond issue?

b. Prepare the journal entry to record the issue of the bond on May 1, 2009.

c. Prepare an amortization schedule using the straight-line method for any premium or discount that arose from the issue of the bond.

d. Prepare the journal entry required to accrue the interest expense and interest payable on December 31, 2011. Make the entry assuming the straight-line amortization method.

e. Prepare the journal entry required to record the interest expense and the payment to investors on April 30, 2012. Make the entry for both the straight-line and effective interest amortization methods.

f. Prepare the journal entry required to record the retirement of the bond on maturity. Include the interest expense and amortization of any bond premium or discount in the entry.

g. Assume that Kuldo's bond agreement allowed the company to redeem the bond on April 30, 2012 for $11,250,000. Prepare the journal entry required to record early retirement of the bond.

h. Assume the role of a shareholder in Kuldo. How would you interpret the gain or loss that would be reported on Kuldo's income statement as a result of the early retirement of the bond? Explain.

P10-17. (**Accounting for bonds, LO 3**) On August 1, 2010 Quilty Inc. (Quilty) issued an $2,000,000 bond with an 8 percent coupon rate and a maturity date of July 31, 2016. Interest will be paid semi-annually on July 31 and January 31. Quilty's year end is December 31. The appropriate interest rate for a bond of this type on August 1, 2010 was 7 percent.

Required:

a. What will be the proceeds from the bond issue?

b. Prepare the journal entry to record the issue of the bond on August 1, 2010.

c. Prepare an amortization schedule using the straight-line method for any premium or discount that arose from the issue of the bond.

d. Prepare the journal entry required to accrue the interest expense and accrued interest payable on December 31, 2011.

e. Prepare the journal entry required to record the interest expense and the payment to investors on January 31, 2012.

f. Prepare the journal entry required to record the retirement of the bond on maturity. Include the interest expense and amortization of any bond premium or discount in the entry.

g. On July 31, 2013, Quilty was able to buy back all the outstanding bonds on the open market for $1,812,500. Prepare the journal entry required to record early retirement of the bond.

h. Do you think that the decision to buy back the bonds early was a good decision? Explain.

P10-18. (**Future income taxes, LO 8**) Noggle Inc. (Noggle) processes fresh apples that it purchases from local farmers into apple juice and applesauce. All of Noggle's processing equipment was purchased in 2007 for $900,000. For accounting purposes, Noggle is amortizing the equipment on a straight-line basis over 10 years. For tax purposes, the asset is in a CCA class that allows Noggle to deduct 30 percent of the capital cost of the asset on a declining-balance basis. Because of the half-year rule Noggle can deduct only one-half of the allowable amount (15 percent) of the cost in 2007. Noggle has an income tax rate of 18 percent and its income before amortization and taxes is $300,000 in each year from 2007 through 2009. Noggle has no temporary differences between tax and financial reporting except for the difference between amortization and CCA on the processing equipment, and there are no permanent differences.

Required:

a. Calculate Noggle's taxable income in 2007 through 2009.

b. Calculate the amount of income tax that Noggle must pay in 2007 through 2009.
c. Calculate the accounting and tax bases of the processing equipment in 2007 through 2009.
d. Calculate the future tax asset or liability that would be reported on Noggle's balance sheet at the end of 2007 through 2009.
e. Prepare the journal entry that Noggle would make each year to record its income tax expense in 2007 through 2009.
f. Calculate Noggle's net income in 2007 through 2009.
g. What would Noggle's net income be in 2007 through 2009 if it used the taxes payable method?
h. As a banker, which measure of net income is more useful to you? Explain.

Using Financial Statements

MDS INC.

www.mdsinc.com

MDS Inc. (MDS) is a global life sciences company that provides market-leading products and services that its customers need for the development of drugs and diagnosis and treatment of disease. It is a leading global provider of pharmaceutical contract research, medical isotopes for molecular imaging, radiotherapeutics, and analytical instruments. MDS' consolidated statements of financial position, statements of income and statements of cash flows, along with extracts from the notes to the financial statements from its 2005 annual report, are provided in Exhibit 10-5.[8] Use this information to respond to questions FS10-1 to FS10-7.

FS10-1. Use the information in Exhibit 10–5 to respond to the following questions:
a. What amount of current liabilities did MDS have on October 31, 2004 and 2005? What amount of non-current liabilities did it have?
b. What was MDS' debt-to-equity ratio on October 31, 2004 and 2005? Interpret the ratios you calculated.
c. Which liabilities on MDS' balance sheet are valued at their present value?
d. What was MDS' interest coverage ratio in 2005?
e. Calculate MDS' current and quick ratios on October 31, 2004 and 2005. What is your assessment of the company's liquidity? What other factors might you consider in assessing the company's liquidity?
f. What is MDS' cash from operations for 2004 and 2005? Why is cash from operations so different from net earnings?

FS10-2. How much does MDS report as deferred revenue on October 31, 2005? How much of the deferred revenue is current and how much is non-current? What does the deferred revenue represent and how does it arise? Why is the deferred revenue classified as a liability?

FS10-3. The following questions pertain to MDS' long-term debt:
a. How much long-term debt was outstanding on October 31, 2005? How much of that long-term debt was classified as current? What does it mean when long-term debt is classified as a current liability? What is the purpose of classifying long-term debt as current?
b. How much long-term debt did MDS issue in 2003, 2004, and 2005? How much long-term debt did it repay in each year?
c. How much of MDS' long-term debt is payable in US dollars? What are the risks that MDS faces because it borrows in U.S. dollars? What are the interest rates and maturities on its US debt?
d. What was MDS' interest expense in 2003, 2004, and 2005? How much interest did MDS pay in those years? Why are the interest expense and the amount of interest paid different?

CONSOLIDATED STATEMENTS OF FINANCIAL POSITION

As at October 31 (millions of Canadian dollars)		2005		2004 (Restated Notes 16 and 27)
ASSETS				
Current				
Cash and cash equivalents	$	265	$	296
Accounts receivable		278		278
Unbilled revenue		115		83
Inventories *(note 5)*		163		160
Income taxes recoverable		3		1
Current portion of future tax assets *(notes 2 and 15)*		19		14
Prepaid expenses and other		21		23
Assets held for sale *(note 16)*		114		51
		978		906
Capital assets *(note 6)*		841		785
Future tax assets *(notes 2 and 15)*		118		123
Long-term investments and other *(note 7)*		159		159
Goodwill *(note 8)*		541		548
Other intangible assets *(note 8)*		43		55
Assets held for sale *(note 16)*		-		61
	$	2,680	$	2,637
LIABILITIES AND SHAREHOLDERS' EQUITY				
Current				
Accounts payable and accrued liabilities	$	353	$	294
Deferred revenue		119		101
Income taxes payable		28		33
Current portion of unrealized benefit of future tax asset *(note 2)*		16		14
Current portion of long-term debt *(note 9)*		13		6
Liabilities related to assets held for sale *(note 16)*		50		27
		579		475
Long-term debt *(note 9)*		455		479
Deferred revenue *(note 10)*		26		41
Unrealized benefit of future tax asset *(note 2)*		64		82
Other long-term obligations		42		48
Future tax liabilities *(note 15)*		69		58
Minority interest *(notes 2 and 3)*		20		21
Liabilities related to assets held for sale *(note 16)*		-		12
		1,255		1,216
(Commitments and contingencies – notes 23 and 24)				
Shareholders' equity				
Share capital *(notes 11 and 19)*		847		833
Retained earnings		604		600
Cumulative translation adjustment *(note 26 and 27)*		(26)		(12)
		1,425		1,421
	$	2,680	$	2,637

CONSOLIDATED STATEMENTS OF INCOME

Years ended October 31 (millions of Canadian dollars except per share amounts)		2005		2004 (Restated Notes 16 and 27)		2003 (Restated Notes 16 and 27)
Net Revenues	$	1,489	$	1,479	$	1,388
Cost of revenues		(912)		(886)		(776)
Selling, general and administration		(307)		(267)		(260)
Research and development *(note 12)*		(31)		(38)		(47)
Depreciation and amortization		(69)		(65)		(68)
Restructuring charges *(note 13)*		(72)		(13)		(28)
Other income (expense) *(note 14)*		(17)		(74)		(26)
Equity earnings (loss) *(note 7)*		(5)		1		3
Operating income		76		137		186
Interest expense		(21)		(23)		(28)
Dividend and interest income		12		8		9
Income from continuing operations before income taxes and minority interest		67		122		167
Income taxes *(note 15)*						
- current		(21)		(57)		(48)
- future		4		-		(32)
Minority interest - net of tax		(8)		(2)		(5)
Income from continuing operations		42		63		82
Loss from discontinued operations - net of tax *(note 16)*		(11)		(12)		(34)
Net income	$	31	$	51	$	48

EXHIBIT 10–8 :

MDS Inc. Extracts from Financial Statements

EXHIBIT 10–8 :

(continued)
MDS Inc. Extracts
from Financial
Statements

CONSOLIDATED STATEMENTS OF CASH FLOWS

Years ended October 31 (millions of Canadian dollars)	2005		2004 (Restated Notes 16 and 27)		2003 (Restated Notes 16 and 27)
Operating activities					
Net income	$	31	$	51	$	48
Add back net loss from discontinued operations		(11)		(12)		(34)
Net income from continuing operations		42		63		82
Adjustments to reconcile net income to cash provided by operating activities relating to continuing operations (note 21)					
Items not affecting current cash flow		91		123		183
Changes in non-cash working capital balances		12		(4)		4
Cash provided by continuing operations		145		182		269
Cash provided by (used in) discontinued operations		16		(4)		(23)
		161		178		246
Investing activities					
Acquisitions (note 4)		(7)		(12)		(8)
Acquisition of tax assets (note 2)		-		(19)		-
Effect of deconsolidating MDS Proteomics (note 3)		-		(18)		-
Purchase of capital assets		(133)		(108)		(117)
Purchase of technology license (note 3)		(1)		(5)		-
Proceeds on sale of discontinued operations		11		35		-
Proceeds on sale of businesses and investments		-		2		31
Purchase of long-term investments and other		-		-		(48)
Increase in deferred development charges		(18)		-		(7)
Other		(5)		(1)		-
Cash used in investing activities of continuing operations		(153)		(126)		(149)
Cash used in investing activities of discontinued operations		(5)		(1)		(3)
		(158)		(127)		(152)
Financing activities					
Issuance of long-term debt		-		-		563
Repayment of long-term debt		(1)		(2)		(541)
Increase (decrease) in deferred income and other long-term obligations		(5)		14		(7)
Payment of cash dividends		(14)		(9)		(10)
Issuance of shares		11		18		8
Repurchase of Common shares		(13)		(17)		(7)
Distributions to minority interest		(11)		(11)		(11)
Cash used in financing activities of continuing operations		(33)		(7)		(5)
Cash used in financing activities of discontinued operations		-		(2)		-
		(33)		(9)		(5)
Effect of foreign exchange rate changes on cash and cash equivalents		(1)		(6)		(13)
Increase (decrease) in cash position during the year		(31)		36		76
Cash and cash equivalents, beginning of year		296		260		184
Cash and cash equivalents, end of year	$	265	$	296	$	260
See accompanying notes					
Cash interest paid	$	23	$	24	$	15
Cash income taxes paid	$	22	$	12	$	24

e. Described the terms of the loan MDS has received from the government. Why does the note explain that the loan is discounted at an effective interest rate of 7 percent?

f. Some of MDS' debt is secured and some is unsecured. Explain the difference between secured and unsecured debt. Do you think that the interest rate that an entity would have to pay on its debt is affected by whether it is secured or unsecured? Explain.

g. Describe MDS' revolving credit facility. How would this credit facility be reported on the balance sheet? Explain. Why is it useful to have the existence of the credit facility disclosed in the notes even though it was undrawn on October 31, 2005?

NOTES TO CONSOLIDATED FINANCIAL STATEMENTS
(All tabular amounts are in millions of Canadian dollars except where noted)

EXHIBIT 10–8 :

(continued)
MDS Inc. Extracts
from Financial
Statements

1. Accounting Policies

Pension, post-retirement and post-employment benefit plans
The Company offers a number of benefit plans that provide pension and other post-employment benefits. The current service cost of benefit plans is charged to income annually. Cost is computed on an actuarial basis using the projected benefits method and based on management's best estimates of investment yields, salary escalation and other factors.

The expected costs of post-employment benefits, other than pensions, for active employees are accrued in the consolidated financial statements during the years in which employees provide service to MDS. Adjustments resulting from plan amendments, experience gains and losses, or changes in assumptions are amortized over the remaining average service term of active employees. Other post-employment benefits are recognized when the event triggering the obligation occurs.

Revenues

A significant portion of the Company's pharmaceutical research services revenues are provided under the terms of long-term contracts that can extend from several months to several years. Revenues on these contracts are recognized using the percentage-of-completion method based on a proportional performance basis using output as a measure of performance. Losses, if any, on these contracts are provided for in full at the time such losses are identified. Services performed in advance of billings are recorded as unbilled revenue pursuant to the contractual terms. In general, amounts become billable upon the achievement of certain milestones or in accordance with predetermined payment schedules. Changes in the scope of work generally result in a renegotiation of contract terms. Renegotiated amounts are not included in net revenues until earned and realization is assured. Billings in excess of services performed to date or in excess of costs plus estimated profits on contracts in progress are recorded as deferred revenue. Customer advances on contracts in progress are shown as liabilities, and reimbursable costs in excess of billings are recorded as unbilled revenue.

Income taxes
The Company follows the liability method of income tax allocation. Under this method, future tax assets and liabilities are determined based on differences between the financial reporting and tax bases of assets and liabilities and are measured using substantively enacted tax rates and laws that will be in effect when the differences are expected to reverse.

Investment tax credits related to the acquisition of assets are deferred and amortized to income on the same basis as the related assets, while those related to current expenses are included in the determination of income.

9. Long-term Debt

	Maturity		2005		2004
Senior unsecured notes	2007 to 2015	$	368	$	379
Other debt	2005 to 2015		100		106
Total long-term debt			468		485
Current portion			(13)		(6)
		$	455	$	479

The Company has outstanding US$311 million of senior unsecured notes that bear interest at fixed rates between 5.15% and 6.19% and have various terms between five and twelve years.

h. The note provides a list of principal repayments that MDS must make over the next five years. How might users of the financial statements use this information? How would you assess the implications of the payments for MDS over 2006–2010?

FS10-4. The following questions pertain to MDS' income taxes:

a. What amount did MDS report as its income tax expense in the years ending October 31, 2004 and 2005? What portion was classified as a current expense and what portion was a future income tax expense? How much did MDS owe in income taxes on October 31, 2005? How much did the company actually pay in income taxes to government during 2005? How much was MDS expecting to recover in income taxes on October 31, 2005?

EXHIBIT 10-8 :

(continued)
MDS Inc. Extracts
from Financial
Statements

Note 9 (continued)

In 2004, MDS purchased assets from Applied Biosystems relating to the MALDI-TOF mass spectrometry operations for US$40 million, of which US$8 million was paid on closing and remaining consideration was in the form of a note payable, bearing an interest rate of 4%. Subsequent to closing, the purchase price was reduced by US$2 million, resulting in a reduction to the principal amount of this note payable. The amended note of US$30 million is payable evenly over four years beginning on October 2, 2006.

Other debt includes a non-interest-bearing government loan with a carrying value of $45 million (2004 - $50 million) discounted at an effective interest rate of 7%. A long-term investment has been pledged as security for the repayment of this debt (see note 7).

During 2005, the Company negotiated a $500 million, five-year, committed, revolving credit facility, replacing the $225 million credit facility existing in 2004. As at October 31, 2005, this facility was undrawn.

The remaining debt, amounting to $20 million (2004 - $26 million), bears interest at various fixed rates.

Principal repayments of long-term debt are as follows:

2006	$ 13
2007	23
2008	109
2009	22
2010	33
Thereafter	268
	$ 468

10. Deferred Revenue

Deferred revenue includes a $22 million deferred credit (2004 - $27 million), which is being amortized over 15 years using the sum of the years' digits method.

During 2004, the Company received $32 million from a customer as consideration for amending a supply agreement to eliminate certain minimum purchase commitments. The proceeds were recorded as deferred revenue and are being amortized over the remaining term of the contract. At October 31, 2005, the balance outstanding was $13 million, with $10 million classified as current deferred revenue.

13. Restructuring Charges

	Restructuring Charge	Cumulative drawdowns		Provision Balance at Oct. 31, 2005
		Cash	Non-cash	
2003:				
Workforce reductions	$ 17	$ (15)	$ (2)	$ -
Equipment and other asset writedowns - adjustment	11	-	(11)	-
	28	(15)	(13)	-
2004:				
Workforce reductions	$ 14	$ (11)	$ (1)	$ 2
Equipment and other asset writedowns - adjustment	(1)	-	1	-
	13	(11)	-	2
2005:				
Workforce reductions	$ 52	$ (24)	$ (1)	$ 27
Equipment and other asset writedowns - adjustment	8	-	(8)	-
Contract cancellation charges	12	-	-	12
	$ 72	$ (24)	$ (9)	$ 39
				$ 41

In 2005, the Company recorded restructuring charges related to a reduction in its management, administrative, and operations workforce, a realignment of its information technology infrastructure, and the reorganization of certain pharmaceutical research services operations. In 2004 and 2003, the Company recorded restructuring charges relating to the implementation of change initiatives affecting the provision of support services, systems implementation, senior management reductions, and certain other initiatives.

15. Income Taxes

a) Provision

The Company's effective income tax rate has the following components:

	2005 %	2004 %	2003 %
Combined Canadian federal and provincial tax rate	35.0	35.7	36.8
Increase (decrease) in tax rate as a result of:			
Research and development and pollution control incentives	(4.9)	(2.0)	(0.9)
Manufacturing and processing rate	(0.6)	(1.8)	(1.6)
Benefit of losses not previously recognized	(24.3)	(6.4)	-
Restructuring ineligible for tax recognition	10.3	-	1.7
Investment dispositions and writedowns	2.7	5.2	9.8
Tax rate on foreign operations	1.0	2.2	1.4
Federal capital taxes	2.7	1.4	1.2
Tax impact of minority interest and equity earnings	2.3	(2.7)	(0.2)
Stock option compensation	1.6	-	-
Other	(0.4)	(1.8)	(6.7)
	25.4	29.8	41.5
Impact of MDS Proteomics	-	16.9	6.4
	25.4	46.7	47.9

Tax recoveries were not recognized on elements of the restructuring provision that relate to foreign operations where full valuation allowances have been recorded with respect to existing tax assets.

b) Future tax assets and liabilities

Future tax assets and liabilities consist of the following temporary differences:

	2005	2004
Future tax assets		
Tax benefit of loss carryforwards	$ 160	$ 171
Book value in excess of tax basis	(4)	(1)
Investment tax credits	29	24
Provisions and reserves	15	4
Future tax assets before valuation allowance	200	198
Valuation allowance	(63)	(61)
	137	137
Future tax liabilities		
Book value in excess of tax basis	(73)	(72)
Tax on investment tax credits recognized for accounting purposes	(8)	(4)
Provisions and reserves	12	18
	(69)	(58)
Net future tax assets	$ 68	$ 79

20. Employee Future Benefits

The Company sponsors various post-employment benefit plans including defined benefit and defined contribution pension plans, retirement compensation arrangements, and plans that provide extended health care coverage to its employees. All defined benefit pension plans sponsored by the Company are funded plans. Other post-employment benefit plans are unfunded. Effective January 1, 2008, certain benefit plans were eliminated, resulting in a curtailment gain of $10 million, which was offset by a $6 million unamortized loss.

Defined Benefit Pension Plans - The formula for Canadian plans is based on the highest three or six average consecutive years' wages and requires employee contributions. A non-contributory Taiwanese plan is based on an employee's years of service and their compensation during the last month prior to retirement. A plan available to certain US employees is based on the participants' 60 highest consecutive months of compensation and their years of service.

The Company uses an October 31 measurement date for the majority of its plans. The most recent actuarial valuations of the majority of the pension plans for funding purposes were as of January 1, 2004, and the next required valuations will be as of January 1, 2007.

Defined Contribution Pension Plans - The Company sponsors a registered pension plan for certain senior executives. Contributions are based on 10%-15% of the employee's annual earnings. In addition, the Company sponsors a contributory pension plan for a subsidiary where the employees' contributions are based on a percentage of their pensionable earnings and the Company's contribution is based on the length of pensionable services. During 2005, the Company contributed $2 million (2004 - $2 million) to the defined contribution pension plans.

Other Benefit Plans – These include a supplemental retirement arrangement, a retirement/termination allowance and post-retirement benefit plans, which include contributory health and dental care benefits and contributory life insurance coverage. Individuals must retire to be eligible.

The net periodic benefit costs for the Company's post-employment benefit plans comprise the following components:

EXHIBIT 10–8 :

(continued)
MDS Inc. Extracts
from Financial
Statements

EXHIBIT 10–8 :

(continued)
MDS Inc. Extracts
from Financial
Statements

23. Commitments and Contingencies

As at October 31, 2005, the Company is obligated under premises and equipment leases and other long-term contractual commitments to make minimum annual payments of approximately:

	Operating Leases		Other Contractual Commitments
2006	$	35	$	90
2007		30		68
2008		24		62
2009		20		60
2010		18		55
Thereafter		25		147
	$	152	$	482

Rental expense under premises and equipment leases for the year ended October 31, 2005 was $47 million (2004 - $51 million; 2003 - $52 million).

Included in other contractual commitments above is $254 million associated with long-term supply arrangements and other long-term commitments with major electricity producers comprising the majority of the Company's expected cobalt purchase. In addition, the Company is party to a construction contract for the building of two special purpose reactors and a related processing facility.

Other contractual commitments included a remaining five-year commitment totalling $211 million (2004 - $256 million) relating to the outsourcing of the information technology infrastructure, and a $10 million commitment (2004 - $15 million) in the next year for the implementation of a common business system across the Company.

24. Guarantees

In 2003, the Company undertook to guarantee a bank loan of $20 million on behalf of an investee, Hemosol Corp. (the Borrower), in exchange for warrants in the Borrower. This loan is secured by a fixed and floating charge over all the assets of the Borrower. Under the guarantee, MDS was subrogated to and took an assignment of the rights and remedies of the bank under the loan. This guarantee initially expired on June 20, 2005. In consideration for providing the initial guarantee, MDS received 1.5 million warrants to purchase common shares of the Borrower, of which 1.25 million warrants were immediately exercisable at a price of $4.00 per share. As part of the reorganization of Labs LP, MDS surrendered 0.6 million warrants related to this guarantee.

In the second quarter of 2005, the term of the Borrower's credit facility was extended to May 25, 2007, and the guarantee was extended from June 20, 2005 to June 30, 2007. As consideration for the extension, the Company received warrants to purchase up to 0.7 million common shares of the Borrower at an exercise price of $3.36 per share with a term of five years from the date of issuance. The Company believed that the fair value of the units was nominal, and accordingly, ascribed no value to these units.

Subsequent to year-end, the Borrower entered receivership. As a result of the receivership, the Borrower's bank has requested payment by the Company of the amounts due on the bank loan. On December 8, 2005 the Company remitted $20 million to the bank and, in turn, assumed the loan and senior security position held by the bank. MDS has agreed to provide up to $1 million of debtor-in-possession financing in conjunction with another secured vendor who ranks second to MDS in preference. This funding will rank in preference to MDS's existing secured position. Due to measurement uncertainty, the Company is not able to determine if sufficient proceeds from the sale of the assets of the Borrower will be available to recover the Company's investment.

Other guarantees for which the Company is contractually obligated to make payments in the event of a default by a third party or due to its inability to meet certain performance-based obligations total approximately $11 million (2004 - $10 million).

b. What amount does MDS report on its October 31, 2004 and 2005 balance sheet for future income taxes? What do these amounts represent?

c. What was MDS' combined federal and provincial tax rates in 2003, 2004, and 2005? What is the tax rate using the income tax expense in 2003, 2004, and 2005? What is MDS' tax rate based on the actual amount of tax that it must pay for income earned in 2003, 2004, and 2005?

d. What journal entry did MDS make in 2003, 2004, and 2005 to record its income tax expense?

FS10-5. The following questions pertain to MDS' commitments:

    a. What is a commitment and how are they accounted for? Do you agree with how GAAP deals with commitments? Explain.

    b. Suppose the operating lease payments reported in Note 23 were to be reported as capital leases:

       i. What would be the journal entry that you would record on November 1, 2005 to record these leases as capital leases, assuming the leases went into effect on that date? Assume a discount rate of 7 percent and assume the payments to be made "thereafter" are evenly distributed over 2011 through 2015.

       ii. What effect would classifying these leases as capital leases have on MDS' debt-to-equity ratio? Explain and show your calculations.

       iii. Do you think that treating all leases as capital leases gives a better indication of an entity's debt load?

    c. Suppose the other contractual commitments reported in Note 23 were recorded in the financial statements:

       i. What would be the journal entry that you would make on November 1, 2005 to record these other contractual commitments? Assume a discount rate of 7 percent and assume the payments to be made "thereafter" are evenly distributed over 2011 through 2015.

       ii. What effect would recording these other contractual commitments have on MDS' debt-to-equity ratio? Explain and show your calculations.

       iii. Do you think that recording the other contractual commitments (rather than just noting them) gives a better indication of an entity's debt load?

       iv. Why would MDS enter into these long-term arrangements? What are some potential benefits and drawbacks of doing so? How does knowing about these commitments help you as a user of the financial statements?

FS10-6. The following questions pertain to MDS' guarantees:

    a. Describe the guarantee that MDS provided to Hemosol Corp.

    b. What are the implications for an entity making a guarantee on behalf of another company?

    c. What did MDS receive as compensation for the guarantee?

    d. What happened after October 31, 2005, MDS' year end? How do you think this event was reflected in the October 31, 2005 financial statements. Explain your thinking.

    e. What are the risks of providing a guarantee? How are guarantees accounted for? Under what circumstances would the company making a guarantee accrue the guarantee in the financial statements? Do you agree with this treatment? Explain.

FS10-7 What types of post-retirement benefit plans does MDS have? What is the basis of making contributions to these plans? What is the difference between defined contribution and defined benefit pension plans? Which type of plan would be preferred by employees? Explain. Which type of plan is less risky for employers? Explain. What types of non-pension post-retirement benefits does the company offer? Are these other post-retirement benefits funded? What does it mean if these plans aren't funded?

Analyzing Rogers Communications Inc.

ROGERS

R10-1. Examine Rogers' balance sheet, statement of earnings, and statement of cash flow (including the supplementary schedules):

a. How much does Rogers report in current liabilities on December 31, 2005?

b. What was the percentage increase in current liabilities from December 31, 2004 to December 31, 2005? What is the reason for the increase? Do you think the increase is reasonable? Explain.

c. What additional information might you want about Rogers' current liabilities? Explain what you would want that information for.

d. How much long-term debt did Rogers retire during fiscal 2005? How much new long-term debt did Rogers obtain during fiscal 2005?

e. How much interest did Rogers expense during fiscal 2005? How much interest was paid to lenders in cash? How do you explain the fact that these amounts are not the same?

R10-2. Examine Note 20 to Rogers' financial statements on commitments (page A-43).

a. What is a commitment? Why are commitments only reported in the notes to the financial statements and not in the financial statements themselves? If commitments were recorded in the financial statements, how might the commitment described in Note 20(a) be recorded? Prepare the journal entry that would be needed?

b. Explain the commitment described in Note 20(c). Why do you think this commitment is disclosed? Do you think the amount involved is material? Explain.

c. How much is Rogers committed to pay in operating lease payments in 2008 and 2009? Could this amount change in future years? How?

d. Suppose the operating lease payments reported in the note were to be reported as capital leases.

i. What would be the journal entry that you would record on January 1, 2006 to record these leases as capital leases, assuming the leases went into effect on that date? Assume a discount rate of 11 percent and assume the payments to be made in "2010 and thereafter" are evenly distributed over 2010 through 2014.

ii. What effect would classifying these leases as capital leases have on Rogers' debt-to-equity ratio? Explain and show your calculations.

iii. Does it matter how Rogers accounts for its leases? Explain.

R10-3. Examine Note 21 to Rogers' financial statements on guarantees (page A-44).

a. What is a guarantee and why are they disclosed in the notes to the financial statements? What would be the implications for stakeholders if guarantees were not disclosed?

b. Explain the guarantee described in Note 21(b). What do you think of the second paragraph of the note (which is repeated for the other two guarantees)? Does the second paragraph cause you any concerns? Explain.

R10-4. Examine Note 22 to Rogers' financial statements on contingent liabilities (page A-44).

a. Which users of financial statements would be interested in the information in Note 22? Explain. Answer by making reference to specific information disclosed in the notes. How helpful is the information provided to you in the note? What additional information would you want about the contingent liabilities? Explain how this additional information would help you.

b. Consider the contingent liability described in Note 22(b). Explain the circumstances giving rise to this item. Suppose Rogers lost this lawsuit in early 2006 and had to pay the plaintiff the full amount it is being sued for. What would be the implications of this outcome for Rogers? How would the decision be accounted for?

What would be the consequences for Rogers' financial position? Would Rogers be able to survive losing this suit? Explain.

c. Why are commitments only included in the notes to the financial statements and not in the financial statements themselves. Refer to Rogers' situation when responding.

R10-5. Examine Note 11 to Rogers' financial statements (pages A-23 to A-29).

a. How much long-term debt did Rogers have on December 31, 2005? How much of that debt was current?

b. How much long-term debt did Rogers Wireless have outstanding on December 31, 2005? How much of that debt was current? Why do you think Wireless has such a large amount of outstanding long-term debt?

c. What amount of principal repayments is Rogers required to make in 2007 and 2010? Why and to whom might this information be useful?

d. Describe the terms associated with the Wireless Senior Secured Debentures due in 2016. What is the amount owing on these debentures? When do they mature? What is the interest rate on them? Can Rogers redeem these debentures? What would Rogers have to do to redeem them? Are these debentures secured? Describe the security.

R10-6. Note 10 (page A-22) to Rogers' financial statements describes a $700 million bank credit facility available to Rogers Wireless from a consortium of Canadian chartered banks.

a. What is the interest rate that applies to this credit facility? Can the rate change? Explain.

b. Until the arrangement was amended on October 8, 2004 what were the conditions and restrictions on the facility? How did these conditions and restrictions change as a result of the October 8, 2004 amendment? Why do you think these types of terms and conditions exist and why do you think Rogers would negotiate to have them relaxed?

c. What amount of the credit facility is outstanding on December 31, 2005? What is the benefit of having this facility available even though Rogers is not currently using very much of it? How does the availability of the facility affect your assessment of Rogers' liquidity?

R10-7. Examine the financial statements and Note 14 (pages A-34 to A-35) to the financial statements.

a. What is the statutory income tax rate that applies to Rogers' income before income taxes and non-controlling interest in 2005?

b. How much was Rogers liable to pay in income taxes for the fiscal year ended December 31, 2005? How much was Rogers liable for the fiscal year ended December 31, 2004?

c. What would Rogers' income tax expense have been had the statutory income tax rate been applied to income before income taxes and non-controlling interest in 2005 (without any adjustments)? What is the actual tax rate that applies to income before income taxes and non-controlling interest?

d. Prepare the journal entry that Rogers would make to record its income tax expense for the year ended December 31, 2005. Prepare the entry for December 31, 2004.

e. What was the balance in the future income tax account on December 31, 2005 and on December 31, 2004?

f. Explain the difference between the income tax expense and taxes payable.

g. On Rogers' statement of cash flows, future income taxes (benefits) are deducted in the calculation of cash from operations. Explain why.

h. How much in income taxes did Rogers actually pay in cash to government in 2005? Why do you think this amount is different from the current portion of the income tax expense for 2005?

ENDNOTES

1. Clarence Byrd, Ida Chen, and Joshua Smith, *Financial Reporting in Canada*, 30th Edition. The Virtual Professional Library. 2005.

2. Panel A extracted from Canadian National Railway Company's 2005 annual report. Panel B extracted from Bombardier Inc.'s 2006 annual report.

3. Clarence Byrd, Ida Chen, and Joshua Smith, *Financial Reporting in Canada*, 30th Edition. The Virtual Professional Library. 2005.

4. Extracted from Dofasco Inc.'s 2005 annual report.

5. Extracted from ACE Aviation Holdings Inc.'s 2005 annual report.

6. Data obtained from *Financial Post Industry Report* at the *Financial Post Web site*, http://www.fpdata.finpost.com/suite/autologreports.asp (accessed February 14, 2006).

7. Extracted from WestJet Airlines Ltd. 2005 annual report.

8. Extracted from MDS Inc.'s 2005 annual report.

OWNERS' EQUITY

On a sunny but cool spring afternoon in April 2006, CEO Ted Rogers pored over some papers in a small boardroom next to his tenth-floor corner office, at the top of the Rogers Communications headquarters in Toronto. It was a regular Wednesday during the business week. But instead of a formal suit, Rogers was wearing shorts. And a sports shirt. Because he can. He's the boss.

Ted Rogers

At age 72, Rogers had been captain of the company he founded, and President and CEO since January of 1979. His office has floor-to-ceiling windows, a fireplace that takes up one wall, and a pale-colour couch. One small needlepoint pillow on the couch reads, "You can agree with me, or you can be wrong."

In December 2004, *Canadian Business* magazine, which he owns, ranked Ted Rogers the eleventh-richest man in Canada, worth $2.21 billion.

Rogers was originally supposed to retire in 2003. Then he pushed the date back to 2006. That year, he promised he would retire, for good, by December 31, 2008.

Ted and his family, and long-time associates, fill many of the company's director positions. The Rogers family also owns, or controls as a group, about 51.7 million Class A voting shares of Rogers Communications, which are listed on the Toronto Stock Exchange. That works out to about 91 percent of the Class A shares. Ted Rogers himself is the largest shareholder in the company, personally owning 23 percent of those shares, according to UBS Investment Research. (There are also about 250 million outstanding Class B shares available to the general public, but they are non-voting shares. That means non-voting shareholders are notified of upcoming Annual General Meetings, or special shareholders' meetings, but they can't vote.)

Rogers' wife Loretta and his children are also closely involved in the business: his wife is a director. Her paintings grace a small gallery down the hall from her husband's suite of offices. Two of their four children work for the company: Edward as head of Rogers Cable, and Melinda in strategic planning. Many observers believe Ted Rogers is grooming the pair to eventually take over the family firm after he's gone.

Some experts, like telecom consultant Eamon Hoey, have a lot of concern about family-owned companies that exercise block voting.

Hoey says big institutional investors such as mutual funds and pension plans now prefer to put their money in companies that are more widely held.

"The concern is," Hoey told the *National Post* Magazine in April 2003, "that if the family is well taken care of, what incentive do they have to take care of the other shareholders?"

INTRODUCTION

Entities finance their assets from two sources: debt and equity. These two sources of financing are seen in the structure of the accounting equation:

Assets = Liabilities + Owners' (Shareholders') Equity

Liabilities represent assets financed by debt and equity represents assets financed by the owners. Owners can invest in an entity in two ways. An investor can invest directly by purchasing an ownership interest from an entity in exchange for cash or other assets. Indirect investments are made when an entity reinvests the profits it earns into its own activities, instead of distributing those profits to owners as dividends or distributions.

The accounting equation provides another view of equity: equity as the residual interest of owners. When the accounting equation is rearranged as follows—

Assets − Liabilities = Owners' (Shareholders') Equity

—equity can be viewed as what is left over after the entity's assets have been used to satisfy the creditors. As we will see, the equity section of the balance sheet represents the owners' interest as measured by accountants; it does not represent the market value of the entity.

Many of the accounting issues we will look at in this chapter are straightforward and have been touched on earlier in the book (for example, accounting for the sale of shares to investors and payment of cash dividends). Other issues can be a bit trickier, such as accounting for when an entity buys back its own shares from investors. The chapter also uses an ongoing accounting controversy to highlight the important concept of economic consequences: the notion that how an entity reports its transactions and economic events has an economic impact on the entity and its stakeholders.

CORPORATIONS, PARTNERSHIPS, AND PROPRIETORSHIPS

The different types of accounting entities were introduced and discussed in Chapter 1. These accounting entities include proprietorships, partnerships, corporations, and not-for-profit organizations such as charities, social clubs, governments, professional organizations, universities, and so on. Readers might find it useful to return to Chapter 1 to review the section on the different types of accounting entities (pages 6–9).

Our focus throughout most of the book has been on corporations, so let's begin there. A corporation is a separate legal and taxable entity. The owners of a corporation are its shareholders. One of the main attractions of a corporation is the limited liability that is provided by its corporate status. Shareholders of a corporation are not liable for the obligations of and losses suffered by the corporation, beyond what they have invested in the corporation.

This limited liability is especially important for public companies, where most shareholders have little involvement in the management and operation of the entity. If the owner of 1,000 shares of a large public corporation were liable for fulfilling obligations that the corporation was not able to meet—for example, paying off a bank loan that the corporation was unable to pay—that shareholder would probably be much more reluctant to invest. If shareholders are responsible for a corporation's liabilities, they bear higher risks and investment in equity is less attractive. After all, how many people would want to hold stock in public companies if there were a chance they could lose their savings, cars, or houses?

In some circumstances, shareholders might agree to waive the limited liability protection of a corporation. For example, lenders often demand that the shareholders of smaller, private corporations personally guarantee to repay amounts borrowed by the corporation in the event it is not able to repay.

Corporations divide the shareholders' equity section of their balance sheets into two broad classifications: capital stock and retained earnings. Capital stock represents direct investments by shareholders—the purchase of shares by shareholders directly from the corporation. Retained earnings represents indirect investment by shareholders—earnings that are not distributed to the shareholders. The separation of direct and indirect investment on the balance sheet is important because the shareholders need to know whether the money being distributed to them is due to the profits earned by the corporation, or if it is just a return of the money that they invested. When a dividend is paid because the corporation has been profitable, it represents a sharing of the success of the corporation with the shareholders. When a dividend is paid from amounts directly invested, it is simply a return of the money that the shareholders have invested.

Partnerships and proprietorships aren't incorporated. Partnerships and proprietorships don't pay income taxes and don't file income tax returns. Instead, earnings are taxed in the hands of the proprietor or partners. At the end of each year a proprietor determines the income of the proprietorship and includes the amount in his or her personal tax return. The income of a partnership is divided among the partners at the end of each year in a way agreed to by the partners, and each partner includes that amount in his or her tax return. Because proprietorships and partnerships do not pay income taxes, their income statements do not report an income tax expense.

Partnerships and proprietorships do not have limited legal liability, which means that partners and proprietors are personally liable for any obligations that the partnership or proprietorship is unable to meet. However, there are exceptions to this unlimited liability rule. In partnerships known as **limited partnerships**, some of the partners have limited liability protection.

There are two types of partners in a limited partnership: limited partners and general partners.

- **Limited partners** have the same limited liability protection as they would if the entity were a corporation—they are not personally liable for the debts and obligations of the partnership.

- **General partners** do not have limited liability and are liable for all debts and obligations of the partnership. A limited partnership must have at least one general partner.

Limited partnerships are useful when a partnership is the preferred form of organizing a business, but some of the investors are not actively involved and would not be prepared to accept the risk associated with unlimited liability. Limited partners can't be involved in the management of the partnership or they risk losing their limited liability. There are also some tax benefits associated with using limited partnerships.

Another form of partnership that is commonly used by professionals such as accountants and lawyers is the limited liability partnership (LLP). A LLP is an ordinary partnership in which innocent partners are shielded from personal liability for the firm's malpractice liabilities. In other words, an individual partner of the LLP would not be liable for claims against the firm arising from negligence or other forms of malpractice unless the partner was personally involved. If you look at the websites of Canadian accounting and law firms, you will see that most have "LLP" after their names.

Most accounting done by partnerships and proprietorships is not very different from that done by corporations. There are no legal requirements that partnerships or proprietorships use GAAP, although GAAP would be used if, for example, a lender demanded it. However, the equity section of financial statements for partnerships and proprietorships is structured differently from that of corporations. See, for example, Table 11–1 (page 600), which shows the balance sheet of Luscar Energy Partnership, a large Canadian coal mining company that is organized as a partnership.[1]

In the equity section of the balance sheet in Table 11–1 there is a single line called Partners' Equity. The Statement of Partners' Equity provides additional detail about the partners' capital. Notice that the direct investment by the partners is not separated from the retained earnings of the partnership, as it is in a corporation. In a partnership, an account is kept for each partner. The partners' accounts keep track of the capital contributed by each, the portion of the partnership's earnings that is attributable to each partner, and the drawings made by each partner. (Drawings are amounts taken by the partners from the partnership.) This breakdown is not shown in Luscar's Statement of Partners' Equity.

An example of a statement of partners' equity with a column for each partner is shown in Table 11–2.

TABLE 11–1 ::: Luscar Energy Partnership

Luscar Energy Partnership
Consolidated Balance Sheets

(in thousands of Canadian dollars)	As at December 31, 2004	As at December 31, 2003 (Restated - Note 3)
ASSETS		
Current		
Cash and cash equivalents	$ 17,218	$ 21,750
Accounts receivable	52,221	62,087
Income taxes recoverable	1,269	1,096
Future income taxes *[note 16]*	4,850	3,896
Inventories *[note 6]*	40,005	43,816
Overburden removal costs	2,687	4,199
Prepaid expenses	2,310	2,073
	120,560	138,917
Capital assets *[note 7]*	1,346,249	1,405,306
Other assets *[note 10]*	27,905	27,704
	$1,494,714	$1,571,927
LIABILITIES AND PARTNERS' EQUITY		
Current		
Credit facility *[note 11]*	$ 12,000	$ 12,000
Trade accounts payable and accrued charges	41,229	38,648
Accrued interest payable	6,686	7,219
Accrued payroll and employee benefits	9,994	10,332
Due to related parties *[note 17]*	402	1,236
Income taxes payable	495	2,472
Current portions of		
Long-term debt *[note 11]*	7,796	46,342
Asset retirement obligations *[note 12]*	23,576	17,829
	102,178	136,078
Accrued pension obligations *[note 8]*	6,058	4,956
Long-term debt *[note 11]*	355,099	365,934
Asset retirement obligations *[note 12]*	76,707	90,509
Future income taxes *[note 16]*	332,710	354,428
	872,752	951,905
Guarantees, commitments and contingencies *[notes 24 and 25]*		
Partners' equity		
Partners' equity	621,962	620,022
	$1,494,714	$1,571,927

Luscar Energy Partnership
Consolidated Statements of Partners' Equity

Year ended December 31 (in thousands of Canadian dollars)	2004	2003 (Restated - Note 3)	2002 (Restated - Note 3)
Partners' equity, beginning of year, as previously stated	659,087	529,163	496,963
Change in accounting policy for asset retirement obligations *[notes 3 & 12]*	(39,065)	(39,160)	(35,975)
Partners' equity, beginning of year, as restated	620,022	490,003	460,988
Net earnings for the year	68,008	114,020	29,015
Distribution to partners	(66,068)	(33,962)	—
Net equity contribution from acquisition of SCAI *[note 4]*		49,961	—
Partners' equity, end of year	$ 621,962	$ 620,022	$ 490,003

Statement of Partners' Equity For the Year Ended December 31, 2009				
	Partner 1	**Partner 2**	**Partner 3**	**Total**
Capital on January 1, 2009	$85,000	$117,000	$49,000	$251,000
Share of net income	22,000	31,000	15,000	68,000
Withdrawals	(15,000)	(8,000)	(6,000)	(29,000)
Capital on December 31, 2009	$92,000	$140,000	$58,000	$290,000

Not-for-profit organizations (NFPO) are economic entities whose objective is to provide services, not to make a profit. NFPOs do not have owners or ownership shares that can be traded or sold. Any "net income" earned by the NFPO is reinvested in the organization. Because NFPOs are not organized to earn a profit, it is not appropriate to use the term net income when discussing an NFPO. Usually the "bottom line" on an NFPO's statement of operations (the term sometimes used for an NFPO's "income statement") is called the excess of revenues over expenses. The idea of this terminology is to convey whether the NFPO produced revenues that were greater than expenses or vice versa.

Revenues for an NFPO should not be thought of in the same way as revenues earned by a business. While some of the revenue of some NFPO's may be paid directly by those consuming the services, many NFPOs' revenues come from donations, contributions, and grants. For example, the Canadian Cancer Society provides support to cancer patients across Canada. The cancer patients do not pay for these support services. The services are paid for by contributors to the Cancer Society. Thus, the relationship that exists between expenses and revenues in a for-profit organization may not exist in an NFPO.

Because an NFPO does not have owners, it will not have an owners' or shareholders' equity section in its balance sheet. However, if a balance sheet is to be prepared, the difference between assets and liabilities must somehow be referred to. Different NFPOs use different terms; for example, the Heart and Stroke Foundation of Ontario refers to its "equity" as *net assets*, while the Canadian Cancer Society uses the term *resources*.

Most Canadian universities are not-for-profit organizations. The University of Ontario Institute of Technology's (UOIT) Statement of Financial Position and Statement of Operations are presented in Exhibit 11–1 (page 602).[2] Accounting for NFPOs is somewhat specialized and we will not be able to go into detail here. However, notice in the Net Assets section of Exhibit 11–1 that UOIT allocates its net assets—its assets less its liabilities—to a number of categories. These resource categories are *invested in capital assets, internally restricted, unrestricted*, and *endowments*.

■ Resources invested in capital assets represent the amount UOIT has invested in capital assets less the amount financed by long-term debt and capital contributions.

■ The use of internally restricted resources is limited by the university. The money in this category was restricted to academic and research purposes.

■ Unrestricted resources can be used in whatever way UOIT chooses.

Notice that the bottom line on the statement of operations is called "excess of revenue over expenses." Also notice that about two-thirds of the university's revenue comes from grants (from government). Unlike for-profit entities, it's common for the people who benefit from the services provided by the NFPO not to be the same ones who provide the revenue. In the case of UOIT, most of the revenue comes from government, but it is the students who benefit from the education provided by the university.

www.cancer.ca
www.heartandstroke.ca

UNIVERSITY OF ONTARIO INSTITUTE OF TECHNOLOGY
Statement of Financial Position
March 31, 2005

	2005	2004
ASSETS		
CURRENT		
Cash and short term investments	$ 44,794,217	$ 2,638,533
Restricted cash and short-term investments (Note 7)	7,500,000	-
Grant receivable	4,745,044	-
Other accounts receivable (Note 3)	1,386,334	2,416,653
Prepaid expenses	26,620	31,817
	58,452,215	5,087,003
CAPITAL ASSETS (Note 4)	243,077,177	164,708,782
OTHER ASSETS (Note 5)	4,071,389	-
	$ 305,600,781	$ 169,795,785
LIABILITIES		
CURRENT		
Demand loan (Note 6)	$ -	$ 76,259,980
Accounts payable and accrued liabilities	14,963,760	25,423,729
Deferred revenue (Note 8)	2,136,238	472,827
Current portion of long term debt (Note 7)	2,568,957	-
	19,668,955	102,156,536
LONG TERM DEBT (Note 7)	217,431,043	-
DEFERRED CONTRIBUTIONS (Note 9)	-	6,265,069
DEFERRED CAPITAL CONTRIBUTIONS (Note 10)	63,383,267	58,609,646
	300,483,265	167,031,251
NET ASSETS		
Unrestricted	3,287,215	(27,445,534)
Invested in capital assets (Note 11)	(2,388,528)	29,839,156
Internally restricted (Note 13)	2,224,582	-
Endowments (Note 14)	1,994,247	370,912
	5,117,516	2,764,534
	$ 305,600,781	$ 169,795,785

UNIVERSITY OF ONTARIO INSTITUTE OF TECHNOLOGY
Statement of Operations
Year ended March 31, 2005

	2005	2004
REVENUE		
Grants	$ 30,228,778	$ 15,122,601
Donations	185,626	60,371
Student tuition fees	7,150,028	3,719,047
Interest revenue	624,702	28,393
Student ancillary fees	4,248,052	1,599,555
Other income	727,713	491,676
Amortization of deferred capital contributions	3,026,379	1,988,805
	46,191,278	23,010,448
EXPENSES		
Salaries and benefits	18,960,874	11,679,946
Supplies and expenses	11,581,635	5,535,958
Professional fees	944,085	676,290
Interest expense	8,498,264	735,827
Amortization of capital assets	5,414,907	1,988,805
Amortization of deferred financing costs	61,866	-
	45,461,631	20,616,826
EXCESS OF REVENUE OVER EXPENSES	$ 729,647	$ 2,393,622

CHARACTERISTICS OF EQUITY

Unlike debt, equity offers no promises. When a corporation borrows money, the rate of interest, the timing of payments, and other terms of the loan are usually laid out in a contract. If the corporation is unable to meet the terms of the contract, it faces potentially significant economic and legal consequences. In contrast, a shareholder is not entitled to dividends or any other type of payments from the corporation, and no return of principal is guaranteed. The rights of shareholders come after those of debtholders. That means that if the corporation goes bankrupt, the debtholders must be paid what they are owed before shareholders receive anything.

From the corporation's standpoint, issuing equity is more attractive than debt because equity does not commit the corporation to make any payments at any time. The corporation has more flexibility to manage, particularly through difficult times.

However, there are drawbacks to issuing equity for the corporation and its existing shareholders. New shareholders have a voice in the corporation—not necessarily a say in its day-to-day affairs, but certainly the right to be heard on certain issues. In many situations, the shareholders of a corporation vote on important issues. The voice provided to new shareholders dilutes the voices of the existing ones. Consider a small business operated by a single entrepreneur. The entrepreneur needs money for expansion and finds an investor who is willing to invest in exchange for a 50 percent interest in the corporation. The new shareholder will own 50 percent of the corporation and will be able to participate in the key decision making of the company. The entrepreneur will no longer be able to act alone.

Unlike debt, the cost of equity is not deductible for tax purposes. This treatment raises the cost of equity relative to debt. Also, dividends are not expensed for accounting purposes. Dividends are not considered a cost of doing business but a distribution to the shareholders. Interest payments, in contrast, are expensed in the calculation of net income.

When a corporation is formed, it must file articles of incorporation with the appropriate government agency. The articles of incorporation define the terms of reference of the new corporation. Any changes to these terms of reference must be approved by the shareholders. The articles of incorporation define the types and characteristics of the shares the corporation can issue. The maximum number of each type of share that can be issued is the **authorized capital stock** of the corporation.

Rogers' authorized capital stock is 400 million preferred shares, 56,240,494 Class A voting common shares, and 1.4 billion Class B non-voting common shares. This means that Rogers can issue up to the indicated number of each type of share without having to consult the shareholders. The information about Rogers' shareholders' equity can be found in Note 13 to the financial statements.

The number of shares that have been distributed to shareholders is the **issued shares** of the corporation. The **outstanding shares** of a corporation are the number of shares currently in the hands of shareholders. The number of shares outstanding may differ from the number of shares issued because shares are sometimes repurchased by a corporation and retired. On December 31, 2005, Rogers had 56,233,894 Class A voting common shares, 257,702,341 Class B non-voting common shares, and no preferred shares outstanding.

Corporations or companies acts are laws of the federal and provincial governments that govern companies incorporated in a particular jurisdiction. For example, the *Canada Business Corporations Act* is the federal legislation that governs federally incorporated companies. These laws give shareholders certain rights and privileges, regardless of whether their investments are large or small. For example, shareholders of a corporation are entitled to attend its annual general meeting, where they can ask questions of management. Shareholders can usually vote on the composition of the board of directors, the appointment of auditors, amendments to the corporation's articles of incorporation, and other matters. For smaller shareholders, the annual general meeting of a public company may be the only place that their voices can be heard.

Even though every shareholder has the right to attend the annual meeting, the ability of smaller shareholders to exert any influence is limited. For example, a shareholder who owns 1,000 shares of BCE Inc. owns about 0.0001 percent of the votes. BCE had 927,318,916 shares outstanding on December 31, 2005.

Knowledge Check

■ What is a not-for-profit organization (NFPO)? Why don't NFPOs have "owners' equity"?

■ What are the characteristics that distinguish equity from debt?

■ Explain the terms *authorized capital stock* and *outstanding shares*.

Common and Preferred Shares

Broadly speaking, there are two types of shares that a corporation can issue: common shares and preferred shares. Because these shares can have various features added to them, many different varieties of shares are possible.

Common Shares **Common shares** represent the residual ownership in an entity. Common shareholders are entitled to whatever earnings and assets are left after obligations to debtholders and preferred shareholders have been satisfied.

For example, consider a one-year venture into which common shareholders invest $50,000 and creditors lend $50,000 at 10 percent interest for the year. If the venture earned $150,000, the creditors would receive $55,000—their $50,000 of principal plus $5,000 in interest. The common shareholders would get the rest—$95,000 ($150,000 − $55,000). The creditors are entitled only to the loan principal plus interest. They do not share in the profits of the venture. On the other hand, common shareholders are the last ones to be satisfied. If the venture earned $60,000, the common shareholders would receive only $5,000 because $55,000 would have to be used to satisfy the lenders.

Common shares do not have a specified dividend associated with them. Dividend declarations are made at the discretion of the board of directors. A corporation is under no obligation to pay a dividend at any time, and the board can eliminate or reduce dividends if it so chooses. Public companies don't like to cut their dividends because it suggests the company is in serious trouble. Usually, when a public company cuts its dividend its share price falls dramatically.

There can be more than one class of common shares. Some corporations issue common shares that have different voting rights and different dividends. As mentioned earlier, Rogers has two classes of common shares, Class A voting common shares and Class B non-voting common shares. The Class A common shares are multiple voting shares that have 50 votes per share while the Class B shares have no votes. This difference in voting power allows the Rogers family to control the company without owning more than 50 percent of the company's common shares. In addition, the Class A and B shares also have slightly different dividend rights (see Note 13(a)(ii)). Also, the Class A shares can be converted to Class B shares.

Some shares have a par value. **Par value** is a value assigned to each share of common stock in the articles of incorporation. At one time the par value of a share had legal significance, but that is no longer the case. The *Canada Business Corporations Act* and the corporations acts of a number of provinces do not permit par value shares. Par value shares are quite rare in Canada now (shares that do not have a par value are called **no par value** shares). The par value of a share has no economic significance and bears no relationship to its market value. Par value share are discussed in this chapter because Rogers' Class B common shares have a par value. Rogers is incorporated under the Company Act of British Columbia, which does allow par value shares. Rogers' Class A shares have no par value but its Class B shares have a par value of $1.62478 per share.

The accounting implication of par value versus no par value shares is quite minor, but there is an impact. When no par value shares are issued, the full amount of the proceeds is credited to the Common (or Capital) Stock account. When par value shares are issued, the par value of the shares is credited to the Common Stock account, and the difference between the proceeds from the sale of the shares and the par value is credited to an account called contributed surplus. **Contributed surplus** is a shareholders' equity account that shows the amounts an entity received from the sale of its shares in excess of the par value. You can see Rogers' contributed surplus account in the table at the beginning of Note 13.

If Rogers issued 1,000 shares of is Class A no par value common stock for $50 per share, it would make the following entry to record the sale of the shares:

Dr. Cash (assets +)	50,000	
Cr. Common stock (shareholders' equity +)		50,000
To record the issue and sale of 1,000 no par value		
common shares for $50 per share.		

If Rogers sold 100,000 shares of its Class B common shares (par value $1.62478) for $50 per share it would make the following entry:

Dr. Cash (assets +)	5,000,000	
Cr. Common stock (shareholders' equity +)		162,478
Cr. Contributed surplus (shareholders' equity +)		4,837,522
To record the issue and sale of 100,000 Class B common		
shares with par value of $1.62478 per share for $50 per share.		

The Common Stock account is credited for the par value of the shares (100,000 × $1.62478) and the amount in excess of par is credited to Contributed Surplus (100,000 × [$50.00 − $1.62478]). The Common Stock and Contributed Surplus accounts together equal the amount received from the sale of par value common shares.

While equity is usually sold for cash, it doesn't have to be. An investor can exchange property or expertise for an equity interest. In this situation, the challenge is to determine the amount that should be recorded for the property received and the shares issued. If a market value is available for the shares issued, then that amount should be used. For publicly traded companies, a share price is readily available. This is problematic for private companies since their shares are not actively traded. In those cases, it is appropriate to use the market value of the property received to value the transaction. In many situations, the market value of the shares and the property are not available, in which case estimates and/or appraisals have to be made. In these situations there could be a wide range of possible amounts.

Preferred Shares **Preferred shares** are shares of a corporation that have rights that must be satisfied before common shareholders' rights. Dividends on preferred shares must be paid before dividends can be paid to common shareholders. If the corporation is liquidated, preferred shareholders' claims to assets must be satisfied before the common shareholders' claims.

Preferred shares often have characteristics of debt. Some preferred shares specify a dividend payment that must be paid before the common shareholders can receive their dividends. However, a crucial difference between debt and preferred shares is that preferred shareholders can't take any action against the corporation if the dividend isn't paid. Dividends on shares are not guaranteed, and if the management of a corporation decides that it will not pay a dividend, then the shareholders are out of luck.

Preferred shares are often **cumulative**, which means that any dividends on the preferred shares that have not been paid in the current year or in previous years must be paid before the common shareholders can receive any dividends.

Preferred shares can have various other features. Some of the more common features of preferred shares include:

- **convertible:** Shareholders can choose to exchange their preferred shares for a specified number of common shares for each preferred share that they convert.

- **redeemable:** The issuer can repurchase the preferred shares from the shareholders if it chooses, according to specified terms.

- **retractable:** Shareholders can require the issuer to purchase the preferred shares from them, if they choose, according to specified terms.

- **participating:** The amount of the preferred share dividend increases above the stated amount if certain conditions are met. The amount of the preferred dividend is often tied to the dividend paid on the common shares.

One of the attractions of preferred shares for investors is that they can expect to receive periodic payments (as they would with debt), but the preferred dividends are taxed at a lower rate than interest. On the other hand, corporations that pay investors preferred dividends cannot

deduct them for income tax purposes. Private companies sometimes use preferred shares for tax and estate-planning purposes.

Exhibit 11–2 provides a description of the preferred shares that Bank of Montreal (BMO) has sold to investors.[3] BMO's articles of incorporation authorize it to issue an unlimited number of Class A or Class B preferred shares. The Class B shares can be issued in a foreign currency. The preferred shares are issued in series. Each series of preferred shares can have different features. The Class B—Series 10 preferred shares have the following features:

- redeemable by BMO beginning on February 25, 2012 for US$25 cash.

- convertible into BMO common shares at the bank's option starting on February 25, 2012.

- non-cumulative with a quarterly dividend of US$0.371875 per share.

The other series of Class B shares have similar features with some variations. The Series 5 preferred shares pays its dividend in Canadian dollars and the Series 4 preferred shares are convertible at the option of the shareholder, but the BMO can pay $25 cash instead.

Preferred shares are among a category of securities known as hybrid securities. **Hybrid securities** have characteristics of both debt and equity. (Convertible debt is another example of a hybrid security.) According to the *CICA Handbook*, entities must classify hybrid securities according to their economic nature, not simply by what they are called. The application of this accounting standard is complicated and beyond the scope of this book. Generally, the classification depends on whether a security has a mandatory payment associated with it (i.e., the issuer must make interest or dividend payments) and has to be repaid or converted by contract or at the option of the security holder. Some securities may have characteristics of both debt and equity and are split between the two categories.

Notice that in Exhibit 11–2 BMO classifies some of its Class B preferred shares as liabilities (Series 3, 4, and 6) and others as equity (Series 5 and 10). The reason the Series 3, 4, and 6 preferred shares are classified as liabilities is that they are convertible into BMO common shares at the option of the shareholder. In contrast, the Series 5 and 10 are classified as equity because they are convertible into commons shares at the option of the bank.

EXHIBIT 11–2

The Bank of Montreal's Preferred Shares

Note 20 ▸ Share Capital

Outstanding
(Canadian $ in millions, except as noted)

	2005			2004			2003		
	Number of shares	Amount	Dividends declared per share	Number of shares	Amount	Dividends declared per share	Number of shares	Amount	Dividends declared per share
Preferred Shares – Classified as Liabilities									
Class B – Series 3	–	$ –	$ –	–	$ –	$ 1.18	16,000,000	$ 400	$ 1.39
Class B – Series 4	8,000,000	200	1.20	8,000,000	200	1.20	8,000,000	200	1.20
Class B – Series 6	10,000,000	250	1.19	10,000,000	250	1.19	10,000,000	250	1.19
Preferred Shares – Classified as Liabilities		450			450			850	
Preferred Shares – Classified as Equity									
Class B – Series 5	8,000,000	$ 200	$ 1.33	8,000,000	$ 200	$ 1.33	8,000,000	$ 200	$ 1.33
Class B – Series 10	12,000,000	396	US$ 1.49	12,000,000	396	US$ 1.49	12,000,000	396	US$ 1.49
Preferred Shares – Classified as Equity		596			596			596	
Common Shares	500,219,068	4,022	$ 1.85	500,896,857	3,857	$ 1.59	499,632,368	3,662	$ 1.34
Share Capital		$ 4,618			$ 4,453			$ 4,258	

Preferred Shares
We are authorized by our shareholders to issue an unlimited number of Class A Preferred shares and Class B Preferred shares without par value, in series, for unlimited consideration. Class B Preferred shares may be issued in a foreign currency.
During the year ended October 31, 2004, we redeemed all of our Class B Preferred shares, Series 3, at a price of $25.50 per share plus any declared and unpaid dividends. The excess of the redemption price over carrying value of $8 million was charged to retained earnings in preferred share dividends.

Preferred Share Rights and Privileges
Class B – Series 4 shares are redeemable at our option starting August 25, 2005 for $25.00 cash per share, plus a premium if we redeem the shares before August 25, 2007, or an equivalent value of our common shares. They are convertible at the shareholder's option starting May 25, 2008 into our common shares; however, we have the right to pay $25.00 cash per share instead. The shares carry a non-cumulative quarterly dividend of $0.30 per share.

Class B – Series 5 shares are redeemable at our option starting February 25, 2013 for $25.00 cash per share, and are not convertible. The shares carry a non-cumulative quarterly dividend of $0.33125 per share.

Class B – Series 6 shares are redeemable at our option starting November 25, 2005 for $25.00 cash per share, plus a premium if we redeem the shares before November 25, 2007, or an equivalent value of our common shares. They are convertible at the shareholder's option starting November 25, 2008 into our common shares; however, we have the right to pay $25.00 cash per share instead. The shares carry a non-cumulative quarterly dividend of $0.296875 per share.

Class B – Series 10 shares are redeemable at our option starting February 25, 2012 for US$25.00 cash per share, and are convertible at our option starting February 25, 2012 into our common shares. The shares carry a non-cumulative quarterly dividend of US$0.371875 per share.

EXHIBIT 11–3 :

Torstar
Corporation's
Repurchase of
Shares

CONSOLIDATED STATEMENTS OF RETAINED EARNINGS
YEARS ENDED DECEMBER 31, 2005 AND 2004
(thousands of dollars)

	2005	2004
Retained earnings, beginning of year	$425,787	$395,758
Net income	118,843	112,703
Dividends	(57,869)	(55,387)
Premium paid on repurchase of shares for cancellation [note 8(c)]	(15,978)	(27,287)
Retained earnings, end of year	$470,783	$425,787

(See accompanying notes)

8. SHARE CAPITAL

(c) Under normal course issuer bids, the company has repurchased during 2005 904,100 Class B shares (2004 – 1,440,800) for cancellation at an average price of $23.07 per share (2004 – $24.28) for total consideration of $20,858,000 (2004 – $34,976,000). Retained earnings were reduced by $15,978,000 (2004 – $27,287,000) representing the excess of the cost of the shares repurchased over their stated value. The current issuer bid will terminate upon the company repurchasing a further 1,655,100 shares or May 5, 2006 whichever is earlier.

The journal entry to record the issuance of preferred shares is similar to the one made to record the issuance of common shares. The difference is that the credit is made to a Preferred Stock account, instead of the Common Stock account.

For example, on June 7, 2006 Nunalla Inc. issued 50,000 no par, cumulative preferred shares for $25 per share. The entry Nunalla Inc. would make to record the issuance is:

Dr. Cash (assets +)	1,250,000	
Cr. Preferred stock (shareholders' equity +)		1,250,000
To record the issue and sale of 50,000 no par,		
cumulative preferred shares for $25 per share.		

Share Repurchases

Sometimes a corporation will buy its own common stock from the shareholders. For example, during 2004, Torstar Corporation, the publisher of the *Toronto Star* repurchased some of its Class B non-voting shares. Exhibit 11–3 shows Torstar's statement of retained earnings and the note to the financial statements that explains the repurchase.[4] Why an entity repurchases its shares is not entirely clear, but some explanations have been suggested and investigated:

■ If an entity has excess cash, repurchasing shares is a way of distributing the cash to investors without establishing a precedent for paying regular or higher dividends.

■ Repurchasing shares increases the earnings per share (net income ÷ common shares outstanding) and should increase share price because there are fewer shares to participate in the company's earnings, assuming that the operating activity of the entity is not affected by the repurchase.

■ Repurchasing shares is a way for management to communicate to the market that it thinks the market is understating the value of its shares.

www.tsx.ca

When an entity repurchases its shares, there is no effect on the income statement. The accounting for share repurchases reduces the amount of cash and the amount in shareholders' equity.

In most jurisdictions in Canada, shares that are repurchased must be retired immediately. That means the shares no longer exist. In some jurisdictions in Canada, and in the United States, entities are allowed to own their own shares. Shares that were previously sold to investors and that the issuing corporation has repurchased but not retired are called **treasury stock**. Holders of treasury stock may not vote and cannot receive dividends, but treasury stock is available for resale by the entity.

Remember that an entry is made in the accounting records only when an entity issues shares to or repurchases shares from shareholders. For public companies in particular, the vast majority of purchase and sale transactions of shares takes place between individual investors in the secondary market. For example, most trades that take place on the Toronto Stock Exchange (TSX) occur between individual investors. The entity whose shares are being exchanged is not a party to these transactions and the transactions have no financial statement effect.

That is not to say that the managers of an entity are not keenly interested in its share price. The entity's share price can have an effect on the managers' wealth (because managers' compensation is sometimes related to share price and because managers are often shareholders), on their job prospects (managers of entities whose share price is not doing well will sometimes lose their jobs or may have fewer opportunities in the job market), and because market price provides information about the market's perceptions of the entity.

RETAINED EARNINGS, DIVIDENDS, AND STOCK SPLITS

Retained Earnings

Retained earnings represents the accumulated earnings of an entity, less all dividends paid to shareholders over its entire life. Retained earnings can be thought of as profits that have been reinvested in the entity by the shareholders. It represents an indirect investment by shareholders—indirect because investors do not decide for themselves to make the investment. While net income or loss and dividends are the most common economic events that affect retained earnings, there are others. A list of the transactions and economic events that affect retained earnings is provided in Figure 11–1. (There are actually a couple of other events that affect retained earnings, but they are beyond the scope of this book.)

Correction of errors affects retained earnings when an error made in a previous period is discovered. The prior years' financial statements are restated so that they appear in their corrected form. For example, in 2007 Auld Ltd. (Auld) purchased land for $700,000. The cost of the land was incorrectly expensed instead of capitalized. The error was not discovered until 2009. To correct the error, Auld would make the following journal entry in 2009:

FIGURE 11–1 ::

Transactions and Economic Events that Affect Retained Earnings

Economic event	Description
Net income or net loss	A measure of how the owners' wealth has changed over a period.
Dividends	Distributions of earnings to shareholders.
Correction of errors	When an accounting error is discovered that was made in a previous period, the error should be corrected retroactively.
Retroactive application of an accounting policy	When an entity is changing an accounting policy, the change in financial statements are restated as if the new accounting policy had always been used.
Share retirement	When an entity repurchases its shares from shareholders and pays more than the average price shareholders paid when they purchased them.

	Dr. Land (assets +)	700,000	
	Cr. Retained earnings (shareholders' equity +)		700,000

To correct an error in accounting for the purchase of land in 2007.

The credit to retained earnings is required because when the land was incorrectly expensed in 2007, net income was reduced by $700,000 (tax effects are ignored). At the end of 2007 retained earnings was then $700,000 lower than it should have been because the land should have been capitalized, not expensed. The entry shown above restates retained earnings so that the balance is what it would have been had the error not occurred.

Changes in accounting policy are discussed later in this chapter. As we will see, when an entity changes an accounting policy, the financial statements must be restated so that it appears as if the entity had always been using the new accounting policy. This means that current amounts in balance sheet accounts, including retained earnings, must be restated to reflect the new accounting policy.

Throughout the book, it has been emphasized that managers have considerable latitude, even under GAAP, in deciding how to account for many transactions and economic events. The effects of these differences accumulate in retained earnings. Over the life of an entity, retained earnings will not be affected by different accounting choices. However, at any point in time during the life of an entity, retained earnings can vary significantly, depending on the accounting choices made in the preparation of the financial statements.

The statement of retained earnings is probably the most overlooked of the financial statements. The purpose of the statement of retained earnings is to show the changes in the Retained Earnings account over the period. Rogers' statement of deficit is on page A-5). Rogers' statement shows two items: net loss and dividends. In addition, in 2004 there were two adjustments for the changes in accounting policies. A fourth effect can be seen in Exhibit 11–3 where Torstar Corporation reports the effect of a repurchase of shares.

Dividends

Dividends are distributions of a corporation's earnings to its shareholders. There are three types of dividends:

- cash

- property

- stock

Dividends are discretionary and must be declared by the board of directors. Dividends are declared on a per share basis and every share of a specific class must receive the same dividend. If, for example, an entity has a single class of common shares, it is not possible to pay some of the shareholders a dividend and not others. Once a dividend is declared, it is classified as a liability on the balance sheet until it is paid.

Corporations do not have an unlimited ability to pay dividends. There are legal limitations against paying dividends. The *Canada Business Corporations Act* prohibits the payment of dividends if it is reasonable to believe that the corporation would be unable to pay its liabilities if the dividends were paid. There can also be contractual restrictions against paying dividends. For example, a lending agreement might not allow the payment of dividends at all or only allow them if certain conditions are met. These conditions are often based on accounting numbers, so the accounting methods used by an entity can have an impact on whether dividends can be paid. For example, BCE Inc. (BCE) states that some of its debt agreements require it to meet certain requirements, including restrictions on dividends. Exhibit 11–4 (page 610) shows an extract from BCE's financial statements that describes the restrictions.[5]

For accounting purposes, there are three important dates pertaining to dividends:

- **Date of declaration**—the date when the board of directors of a corporation declares a dividend;

- **Date of record**—the registered owner of shares on the date of record receives the dividend. If a shareholder sells shares after the date of declaration but up to and including the date of

◇ ROGERS™

609

OWNERS' EQUITY

www.bce.ca

NOTE 18: LONG-TERM DEBT

Restrictions

Some of the debt agreements:

- require us to meet specific financial ratios
- impose covenants, maintenance tests and new issue tests
- restrict the payment of dividends
- restrict how we can dispose of Bell Canada voting shares.

We are in compliance with all conditions and restrictions.

record, the new shareholder is entitled to receive the dividend. If a shareholder sells shares after the date of record, the previous shareholder receives the dividend.

■ **Date of payment**—the date when the dividends are actually paid to shareholders.

For example, Rogers declared a dividend in December 2005 that was paid on January 6, 2006 to shareholders of record on December 28, 2005.

Cash Dividends Cash dividends are the most common form of dividend. A **cash dividend** is a cash payment from the corporation to its shareholders. It is sometimes said that dividends are "paid out of retained earnings." This expression means that retained earnings decrease when dividends are paid. However, to pay a cash dividend, the cash must be available. If an entity doesn't have cash or access to cash, it can't pay a cash dividend.

Let's look at an example of accounting for cash dividends. On December 15, 2009 Bankeir Inc. (Bankeir) declared a $0.10 quarterly dividend on its common shares and a $0.25 quarterly dividend on its preferred shares. On the date of declaration, Bankeir had 500,000 common shares and 250,000 preferred shares outstanding. Bankeir paid the dividend on January 12, 2010. The company's year end is December 31. The journal entries required to record the declaration and payment of the dividends are:

December 15, 2009

Dr. Retained earnings (shareholders' equity −)	112,500	
Cr. Dividend payable on common shares (liability +)		50,000
Cr. Dividend payable on preferred shares (liability +)		62,500

To record the declaration of a $0.25 per preferred share
and $0.10 per common share dividend on December 15, 2009.

January 12, 2010

Dr. Dividend payable on common shares (liability −)	50,000	
Dr. Dividend payable on preferred shares (liability −)	62,500	
Cr. Cash (asset −)		112,500

To record payment of the preferred and common share
dividends on January 12, 2010.

The first entry records the reduction of retained earnings and the liability to pay the preferred and common share dividends. The second entry records the cash payment to the shareholders and removes the liabilities to pay the dividends from the balance sheet. Bankeir's December 31, 2009 balance sheet would report the dividends payable on the preferred and common stock as current liabilities.

Property Dividends **Property dividends** are dividends paid with property instead of cash. In theory, a property dividend could be paid using any property the entity has: inventory, capital assets, investments, etc. In practice, for public companies or for private companies with many shareholders, there are practical limitations to declaring property dividends. Since every share of the same class must receive the same dividend, the entity must have property that can be divided to allow equal distribution. One type of property that can be readily used for a property dividend is shares of a corporation owned by the issuing entity (not its own shares).

If an entity pays a property dividend, the dividend is recorded at the market value of the property distributed on the date the dividend is declared. If the market value of the property is not equal to its book value on the date the dividend is declared, a gain or loss is reported on the income statement.

For example, Drook Corp. (Drook) decided to distribute the shares it owned of Rylstone Inc. (Rylstone) as a dividend. The book value of the shares was $5,000,000 and their market value on the date the dividend was declared was $7,200,000. The journal entries that Drook would make to record the property dividend are:

Dr. Investment in Rylstone (assets +)	2,200,000	
Cr. Gain on disposal of investments		
(income statement + shareholders' equity +)		2,200,000
To record the gain on the shares of Rylstone being		
distributed to shareholders as a property dividend.		
Dr. Retained earnings (shareholders' equity −)	7,200,000	
Cr. Property dividend payable (liability +)		7,200,000
To record the declaration of a property dividend.		
Dr. Property dividend payable (liability −)	7,200,000	
Cr. Investment in Rylstone (assets −)		7,200,000
To record payment of the property dividend.		

The first entry adjusts the value of the property to its market value on the date the dividend was declared. Because the market value of the dividend was greater than its book value, a gain is recognized on the income statement. The second entry records the declaration of the dividend. The amount of the property dividend is the market value of the property on the date the dividend is declared. The third entry records the actual payment of the dividend—the distribution of the Rylstone shares to Drook's shareholders.

Stock Dividends A **stock dividend** is the distribution of a corporation's own shares to its existing shareholders. Instead of cash, a shareholder receives company shares as the dividend. The number of shares a shareholder receives depends on the number of shares owned on the date of declaration.

For example, if Hylo Ltd. (Hylo) declared a 5 percent stock dividend, a shareholder that owned 1,000 shares would receive 50 shares of Hylo stock as the dividend. After the stock dividend, the investor would have 1,050 shares of Hylo stock. If Hylo had 100,000 shares outstanding before the distribution of the stock dividend, there would be 105,000 after the distribution. Each shareholder would own exactly the same proportion of Hylo before and after the dividend. The shareholder that owned 1,000 shares before the dividend and 1,050 shares after always owned 1 percent ($1,000 \div 100,000 = 1,050 \div 105,000$) of the outstanding shares. The market price of Hylo's shares should fall by 5 percent as a result of the stock dividend because nothing about the entity has changed except for the number of shares outstanding. Thus, the value of Hylo is spread over a larger number of shares (and therefore the value of each share is less after the stock dividend), but the total value of Hylo's shares should be the same before and after the stock dividend.

A stock dividend results in a decrease in Retained Earnings and an increase in Capital Stock, but there is more than one acceptable method of assigning an amount to the shares distributed. The shares can be valued at their market value just before they are issued or the board of directors can assign a value to the shares—for example, the average amount paid by shareholders for the shares already outstanding.

Returning to the Hylo Ltd. example, suppose that Hylo declared and distributed its stock dividend on June 23, 2009, when the market price of its common shares was $10 it would make the following entry, if it valued the shares at their market value:

Dr. Retained earnings (shareholders' equity −)	50,000	
Cr. Common stock (shareholders' equity +)		50,000
To record the declaration and distribution of a		
5 percent stock dividend.		

The form of the journal entry would be the same if a different value were assigned to the share. Only the amount would change. Note that no matter how the shares are valued, only the shareholders' equity section of the balance sheet is affected. There is no effect on assets, liabilities, or the income statement.

www.mcgrawhill.ca/
olc/friedlan

612

CHAPTER 11

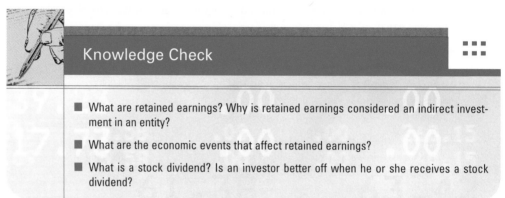

Knowledge Check

- What are retained earnings? Why is retained earnings considered an indirect investment in an entity?

- What are the economic events that affect retained earnings?

- What is a stock dividend? Is an investor better off when he or she receives a stock dividend?

Stock Splits

A **stock split** is the division of an entity's shares into a larger number of units, each with a smaller value. A stock split is really nothing more than a big stock dividend.

A stock split might split an entity's existing shares two-for-one, which means that a shareholder that previously had 1,000 shares would have 2,000 after the split. A three-for-two split means that a shareholder that initially had 1,000 shares would have 1,500 after the split.

The accounting for stock splits is different from accounting for stock dividends. There is no accounting effect of a stock split—the amounts in the retained earnings and common stock accounts are unchanged. No journal entries are required to record a stock split. What changes is the number of shares outstanding, so any measurements that are based on the number of shares will change. For example, if an entity's shares split three-for-one, retained earnings will be unchanged, but earnings per share will be one-third of what it was before the split.

Exhibit 11–5 (page 613) shows an example of the financial statement effects of a stock split. In 2004, the common shares of Talisman Energy Inc. (Talisman) split three for one. Exhibit 11–5 compares selected information about Talisman's 2003 fiscal year as reported in its 2003 annual report (before the stock split) and in its 2004 annual report (after the stock split). After a stock split, an entity restates the previous years' financial statements so that the comparable financial statements are prepared on the same basis. Notice that the number of shares tripled from the 2003 annual report to the 2004 annual report, but the dollar amounts in the Common Stock and Contributed Surplus accounts are the same. Earnings per share has been cut by one third because Talisman's earnings have been divided among three times as many shares. Retained Earnings is not quite the same because in 2004 Talisman made an accounting change that resulted in a restatement of 2003 retained earnings.[6]

Various explanations have been offered for stock dividends and stock splits. One explanation is that it allows shareholders to receive "something" when the entity is unable or unwilling to pay a cash dividend. Another explanation given for a stock split is that it lowers the price of a stock into a range that makes it accessible to more investors.

www.talisman-energy.com

Insight

The reality is that both stock splits and stock dividends are a bit of sleight of hand. Neither has any real economic significance—they merely divide the entity into a different number of pieces. In other words, there are more pieces of pie, not more pie. Stock dividends and stock splits have no effect on the assets, liabilities, or net income of an entity, and do not change the underlying value of a shareholder's interest in an entity. There is no evidence from research that suggests that shareholders are better off after a stock dividend or split than they were before.

9. SHARE CAPITAL

In 2004, the Company implemented a three-for-one share split of its issued and outstanding common shares. All references to net income per share, diluted net income per share, weighted average number of common shares outstanding, common shares issued and outstanding and options granted, exercised and forfeited/expired have been retroactively restated to reflect the impact of the Company's three-for-one split.

	2003 common share information As reported in the 2004 Annual Report		2003 common share information As reported in the 2003 Annual Report	
	Number of shares	Amount (in millions)	Number of shares	Amount (in millions)
Continuity of common shares				
Balance, beginning of year	393,118,305	2,725	131,039,435	2,785
Issued on exercise of options	884,679	5	294,893	11
purchased during year	(10,006,800)	(64)	(3,335,600)	(71)
Balance, end of year	383,996,184	2,666	127,998,728	2,725
Common Shares		2,725		2,725
Contributed surplus		73		73
Retained earnings		1,903		1,844
Earnings per share		2.56		7.65

EXHIBIT 11–5

Talisman Energy Inc.—The Effect of a Stock Split

Question for Consideration

Several years ago a friend of yours received 1,000 shares of a public company as a gift from her uncle. Recently the company shares split four-for-one and now she has 4,000 shares. Your friend is not sure what this means, but she is concerned that the shares that were trading for $104 per share before the split are now trading for around $26 per share.

Explain to your friend the meaning of a stock split and its economic significance. Should she be concerned about the decrease in the share price?

Answer: A stock split is the division of an entity's shares into a larger number of units, each with a smaller value. A stock split does not really have any economic significance. A stock split is like cutting a pie into six pieces and then, cutting the pie into 12 pieces when you realize that you will be having more than six guests. You have the same amount

(continued)

of pie, just more pieces. There is no difference between one slice of a pie cut into six pieces or two pieces of a pie cut into 12 pieces if the pies are the same size.

The same is true for a stock split. You have 4,000 shares instead of 1,000, but there are also four times as many shares outstanding. You own exactly the same percentage of the outstanding shares. The decrease in the share price makes perfect sense because after the split each share represents 25 percent of what it did before the split. Therefore, it is reasonable to expect that each share would be worth 25 percent of what it was before the split. The market value of your shares is the same before and after the split. Before the split the shares were worth $104,000 (1,000 × $104) and after the split they were worth $104,000 (4,000 × $26).

ACCOUNTING CHANGES—POLICIES AND ESTIMATES

Consistency in the application of accounting choices is an important principle. If an entity could change its accounting on a whim, the integrity and usefulness of the financial statements would be undermined and it would be much more difficult for users to understand and interpret the statements. However, consistency does not mean that an entity can never change how it does its accounting. Sometimes a change makes sense. An accounting change is necessary if GAAP change and the entity is required to use a different accounting policy. Or an entity may decide that a different way of accounting is appropriate because the facts underlying certain transactions have changed or the reporting objectives of the entity have changed.

There are two types of accounting changes—changes in policies and changes in estimates. **Accounting policies** are the methods that an entity selects for financial reporting. Accounting policies include the revenue recognition method, inventory cost flow assumption, and amortization method. **Accounting estimates** are the judgments about uncertain future events that managers must make to complete accrual accounting financial statements. Accounting estimates include the useful lives and residual values of capital assets, bad debt expenses, warranty expenses, and many more.

What happens if an entity decides to change an accounting policy or estimate? The two types of changes are dealt with differently. If a company decides to change an accounting policy—for example, switching from an accelerated method of amortization to the straight-line method—the change is applied retroactively. That is, previous years' financial statements are restated as if the new accounting method had always been used. This treatment also means that retained earnings would have to be restated to adjust for the difference in retained earnings between the old and new methods.

Consider the following example. In 2005, Justice Inc. (Justice) purchased a specialized piece of equipment for its manufacturing facility. The equipment cost $750,000. Management decided to use declining-balance amortization at 40 percent per year. In 2008, management decided to change from declining-balance to straight-line amortization because most firms in Justice's industry used straight-line. Management estimated that the equipment would continue to be useful until 2010 and would have no residual value at the end of its useful life.

Because this is a change in accounting policy, it must be applied retroactively. (The amortization schedules for the two methods are shown in Figure 11–1) When Justice prepares its annual report for 2008, the amortization expense reported for 2008 and for all comparative years would be the straight-line amount. That is, if Justice presented in its 2008 financial statements with comparative information for 2007, the amortization expense in each year would be $125,000, even though for 2007, $108,000 had been originally reported in financial statements.

It would also be necessary to adjust retained earnings at the end of 2006 to reflect the use of the straight-line method from the time the equipment was purchased (beginning retained earnings on January 1, 2007 would have to be adjusted for the change in accounting policy).

	2005	2006	2007	2008	2009	2010
40% Declining balance	$300,000	$180,000	$108,000	$ 64,800	$ 38,880	$ 58,320
Straight line, useful life six years	$125,000	$125,000	$125,000	$125,000	$125,000	$125,000

Current year

FIGURE 11–1 ::

Justice Inc.: Change in Accounting Policy from Declining Balance to Straight-Line

In 2005 and 2006, Justice would have expensed $480,000 ($300,000 + $180,000) for amortization of the equipment using the declining balance method. Had straight-line amortization been used from the date the equipment was purchased, $250,000 in amortization would have been expensed ($125,000 + $125,000). Since the declining balance method resulted in $230,000 ($480,000 − $250,000) "too much" amortization expense in 2005 and 2006, the balance in retained earnings on December 31, 2006 would have to be increased by $230,000 and accumulated amortization on the equipment reduced by $230,000 (thereby increasing the NBV of the equipment).

A change in accounting estimate is treated differently. If management decides that an accounting estimate made previously has to be revised—for example, if the initial estimate of an asset's useful life was too long—the change is reflected from the time of management's decision. Prior years are not revised.

Let's look at an example. In 2005, Aubigny Ltd. (Aubigny) purchased an asset for $48,000. Management decided to use straight-line amortization and assumed a zero residual value and a useful life of eight years. In each of years 2005, 2006, and 2007, Aubigny expensed $6,000 for amortization of the asset ($48,000 ÷ 8 years). In 2008, it became clear to Aubigny's management that the asset would only last for six years. Because the estimated life of the asset had decreased to six years, it was necessary to expense the unamortized portion of the cost of the asset over three years rather than five. At the end of 2007, Aubigny had amortized $18,000 of the cost of the asset (see Figure 11–2). The unamortized $30,000 ($48,000 − $18,000) would be amortized over the remaining three years on a straight-line basis, so the amortization expense in 2008, 2009, and 2010 would be $10,000 ($30,000 ÷ 3). No adjustment of retained earnings is necessary because the amortization expense in previous years is not restated—unlike changes in accounting policy, previous years' expenses are not changed. The year-by-year amortization expense and accumulated amortization for each year is shown in Figure 11–2.

	2005	2006	2007	2008	2009	2010
Amortization expense	$6,000	$ 6,000	$ 6,000	$10,000	$10,000	$10,000
Accumulated amortization	$6,000	$12,000	$18,000	$28,000	$38,000	$48,000

Current year

FIGURE 11–2 ::

Aubigny Ltd.: Change in Accounting Estimate

According to GAAP, accounting policy changes must be disclosed. In contrast, GAAP and the CICA Handbook do not require disclosure of changes in estimates. As a result, managers can manage their earnings by adjusting accounting estimates and it would be very difficult for a user to detect the existence and the extent of the change. The ability to manage earnings by adjusting estimates was also explored in Chapter 7 when we looked at hidden reserves. A proposed revision to the CICA Handbook would improve disclosure about changes in estimates so that financial statement users would be able to understand the effects on the financial statements of changes in accounting estimates. The change would require disclosure of the nature and amount of a change in an accounting estimate that has an effect in the current period or is expected to have an effect in later periods.

Note 2(s) to Rogers' financial statements explains the effect of the adoption of new accounting pronouncements on the financial statements.

O ROGERS

1 | SIGNIFICANT ACCOUNTING POLICIES

c) Recent accounting pronouncements and changes in accounting policies

i) Amortization of long-term assets

Effective September 1, 2003, the Corporation reviewed the useful life of its decoders and modems, commonly referred to as home terminal devices, and of certain other long-term assets. The useful life of decoders was changed from seven to five years while the useful life of modems was changed from seven to three years. These changes in accounting estimates, applied prospectively, increased amortization expense by $20.1 million for the year ended August 31, 2004.

Exhibit 11–6 gives an example of disclosure of a change in an accounting estimate. The note explains the Cogeco Cable Inc. shortened the estimated useful life of certain equipment.[7] The note also gives the effect on the amortization effect in fiscal 2004 and explains that the change is applied prospectively—there is no restatement of previous periods. This note is useful for users of financial statements because the change would likely have a significant effect on net income, but the *CICA Handbook* doesn't require it at this time.

COMPREHENSIVE INCOME

In 2005, the Accounting Standards Board issued a new *CICA Handbook* section entitled Comprehensive Income. Beginning with fiscal years beginning on or after October 1, 2006 companies will be required to report their comprehensive income. **Comprehensive income** includes all transactions and economic events that affect equity in a period that don't involve owners (transactions affecting equity that involve owners include sales of shares, dividends, and share repurchases). The purpose is to have a measure of performance that captures all transactions and economic events that don't involve owners, even ones that are not included in the calculation of net income.

Net income includes almost all changes in equity from non-owner sources, but there are some exceptions (Remember that net income is really a part of the equity section of the balance sheet.). Comprehensive income ensures that all transactions and economic events that affect equity are included in a measure of performance. Comprehensive income has two components: net income (which is calculated as it usually is) and other comprehensive income, which is revenues, expenses, gains, and losses that aren't included in the calculation of net income. We have not explored the types of items that are included in other comprehensive income, though in Chapter 12 we will look at one of the items, unrealized gains and losses on available-for-sale assets.

Research in Motion Limited (RIM), the Canadian creator of the Blackberry wireless device, included comprehensive income in its 2005 financial statements. RIM's comprehensive income information can be seen in Exhibit 11–7.[8] The equity section of RIM's balance shows accumulated other comprehensive income (it's like retained earnings except the amount only includes other comprehensive income). Note 17 shows the calculation of comprehensive income and the components of accumulated other comprehensive income on the balance sheet.

LEVERAGE

Leverage is the use of debt to attempt to increase the return earned on the equity investment of the owners. (The concept of leverage was introduced in Chapter 10.) Leverage is attractive because any profits earned from investing borrowed money, above the cost of borrowing, go to the owners. But leverage is risky because the cost of borrowing must be paid, regardless of how well or poorly the entity is performing.

Let's look at an example to demonstrate. Four Friends Partnership (FFP) was recently formed by four friends to operate a one-year business venture. The friends have decided that $100,000 of invested capital is required to safely launch the venture, but they are not sure how much debt and how much equity should be used. They have three possible financing arrangements in mind:

1. 100 percent equity financing: the friends invest $100,000 of their own money and do not borrow any from the bank.

2. 50 percent debt and 50 percent equity: the friends invest $50,000 of their own money and borrow $50,000 from the bank.

3. 90 percent debt and 10 percent equity: the friends invest $10,000 of their own money and borrow $90,000 from the bank.

The friends have predicted two possible outcomes for their venture: a good news outcome where revenues will be $80,000 and expenses $60,000 (excluding interest), and a bad news outcome where revenues will be $50,000 and expenses will be $48,000 (excluding interest). If the friends decide to borrow, the bank will charge them an interest rate of 10 percent. At the completion of the venture the friends will have to repay any money borrowed from the bank.

CONSOLIDATED BALANCE SHEETS

As at	March 4, 2006	February 26, 2005
Shareholders' Equity		
Capital stock (note 11)		
Authorized – unlimited number of non-voting, cumulative, redeemable, retractable preferred shares; unlimited number of non-voting, redeemable, retractable Class A common shares and an unlimited number of voting common shares		
Issued – 186,001,765 voting common shares (February 26, 2005 – 189,484,915)	1,852,713	1,892,266
Retained earnings	148,028	94,181
Accumulated other comprehensive income (loss) (note 17)	(1,974)	(2,771)
	1,998,767	1,983,676
	$2,312,156	$2,620,994

1. Summary of Significant Accounting Policies

(s) Statements of comprehensive income (loss)

U.S. GAAP, SFAS 130, *Reporting Comprehensive Income*, establishes standards for the reporting and display of comprehensive income and its components in general-purpose financial statements. Comprehensive income is defined as the change in net assets of a business enterprise during a period from transactions and other events and circumstances from non-owner sources, and includes all changes in equity during a period except those resulting from investments by owners and distributions to owners. The reportable items of comprehensive income are cash flow hedges as described in note 19, and changes in the fair value of investments available for sale as described in note 4. Realized gains or losses on available-for-sale investments are reclassified into earnings using the specific identification basis.

17. Comprehensive Income

The components of comprehensive net income are shown in the following table:

For the year ended	March 4, 2006	February 26, 2005	February 28, 2004
Net income	$ 382,078	$ 213,387	$ 51,829
Net change in unrealized gains (losses) on available-for-sale investments	(5,888)	(18,357)	1,854
Net change in derivative fair value during the year, net of income taxes of $9,539 (February 26, 2005 – $10,429; February 28, 2004 – $nil)	18,029	8,446	11,941
Amounts reclassified to earnings during the year, net of income taxes of $6,000 (February 26, 2005 – $5,359; February 28, 2004 – $nil)	(11,344)	(4,340)	(9,912)
Comprehensive income	$ 382,875	$ 199,136	$ 55,712

The components of accumulated other comprehensive income (loss) are as follows:

For the year ended	March 4, 2006	February 26, 2005	February 28, 2004
Accumulated net unrealized gains (losses) on available-for-sale investments	$ (18,233)	$ (12,345)	$ 6,012
Accumulated net unrealized gains on derivative instruments	16,259	9,574	5,468
Total accumulated other comprehensive income (loss)	$ (1,974)	$ (2,771)	$ 11,480

We will examine the effect of leverage by using return on equity (ROE). ROE was introduced in Chapter 3 and is defined as:

$$\text{Return on equity} = \frac{\text{Net income} - \text{Preferred dividends}}{\text{Average common shareholders' equity}}$$

ROE is a measure of the profitability of an entity and its effectiveness in using the assets provided by the owners of the entity to generate net income. The effects of leverage for FFP's venture are shown in Table 11–3. When 100 percent equity is used, the friends simply earn what the venture earns. If the good news outcome occurs, the friends earn $20,000, which is a 20 percent return on their $100,000 equity investment ($20,000 ÷ $100,000). If the bad news outcome occurs, the friends earn $2,000, a 2 percent ROE ($2,000 ÷ $100,000). With both outcomes, the friends get their original investment back.

If the friends borrow some money to finance their venture, they must pay interest. The effect of leverage is that they have to pay a fixed amount of interest to use the borrowed money, but anything the venture makes in excess of the interest cost belongs to them. When 50 percent debt and 50 percent equity is used, FFP must pay $5,000 ($50,000 × 10 percent) in interest, so net income is $15,000 in the good news outcome (see Table 11–3). While net income is lower than in the 100 percent equity alternative, the ROE earned by FFP increases from 20 percent to 30 percent. The reason is that the friends invested half as much money as before ($50,000) and earned 20 percent or $10,000 on their own investment. They also earned an additional $5,000 on the borrowed money. The bank supplied $50,000, that $50,000 earned 20 percent or $10,000, and FFP had to pay the bank $5,000 for the use of its money, so there is $5,000 left that goes to the four friends after the bank is paid. The friends' return is 30 percent because they earned $15,000 ($10,000 from their own investment and $5,000 from the bank's investment) on an investment of $50,000.

This is the effect of leverage: using "someone else's" money can increase equity investors' returns. Notice that the borrowed money does not increase the size of the venture. In all the alternatives the amount of capital invested is $100,000. What is different are the sources of the capital.

TABLE 11–3 ::: Scenarios Showing the Effect of Leverage on Performance

Four Friends Partnership Information Regarding New Venture			
	Financing Alternatives		
	100% equity	**50% debt and 50% equity**	**90% debt and 10% equity**
Debt	$ 0	$50,000	$90,000
Equity	100,000	50,000	10,000
	Projected performance outcomes		
	Good news outcome		
Revenue	$ 80,000	$80,000	$80,000
Expenses	60,000	60,000	60,000
Operating income	20,000	20,000	20,000
Interest expense	0	5,000	9,000
Net income	$ 20,000	$15,000	$11,000
Return on equity	20%	30%	110%
	Bad news outcome		
Revenue	$ 50,000	$50,000	$50,000
Expenses	48,000	48,000	48,000
Operating income	2,000	2,000	2,000
Interest expense	0	5,000	9,000
Net income	$ 2,000	$(3,000)	$(7,000)
Return on equity	2%	−6%	−70%

But there is a dark side to leverage. While leverage makes the good news better, it also makes the bad news worse. If the bad news outcome occurs, the four friends earn a small return of 2 percent on their $100,000 investment with the 100 percent equity investment. The friends get to take home $2,000 in profits and their initial investment is intact. With the 50 percent debt and 50 percent equity alternative, the cost of borrowing is more than what the borrowed money earned. The equity investors, the four friends, must pay this shortfall. The friends earn $1,000 ($50,000 × 2 percent) on their investment. The money from the bank also earns $1,000, but the bank has to be paid $5,000 in interest for the use of its money. To satisfy the bank, the $1,000 earned by the friends' investment and the $1,000 earned by the bank's investment goes to pay the bank. In addition, $3,000 of the friends' initial investment must be used to pay the bank. The $3,000 loss on the venture means that the friends lose some of their initial investment. In this scenario, the ROE is −6 percent (−$3000 ÷ $50,000).

The effect of leverage in the 90 percent debt and 10 percent equity alternative is even more dramatic. In the good news outcome, the four friends earn 110 percent on their $10,000 investment. They earn $2,000 on their equity investment (10,000 × 20 percent) and $9,000 on the bank loan (after interest) (($90,000 × 20 percent) − ($90,000 × 10 percent)). On the other hand, the friends have a return of −70 percent in the bad news outcome, because while the venture itself earned $2,000, the bank has to be paid $9,000. The loss on the venture is $7,000 and 70 percent of the friends' original $10,000 investment is lost.

How, you might ask, can the friends' return be increasing when the net income of the venture is decreasing? The answer is that the amount of income being earned as a proportion of the equity investment is increasing, even though the actual dollar amount of net income is decreasing. The friends will have more profit from the venture if only equity is used, but if the bank finances part of the venture, the friends will have a higher return and be able to keep some of their money for other purposes.

This example raises another interesting point. In all three financing alternatives, the amount invested was the same and the performance of the business activity itself—the operating income—was the same. (The operating income was $20,000 in the good news outcome and $2,000 in the bad news outcome.) What differed in the income statements under the three alternatives was the cost of financing. By separating operating income and the cost of financing, we can evaluate the performance of the entity separately from the cost of financing it.

It is also important to remember that there are limits to the amount of money that an entity can borrow. It is possible that if FFP wanted to borrow $90,000 when the owners were investing only $10,000, the bank might charge a higher interest rate or not lend at all.

Note that the FFP example ignores income taxes. This approach is sensible because FFP is a partnership and partnerships do not pay taxes. The individual partners take care of the taxes. Taxes are important, though. The tax implications of any decisions must be taken into consideration. (The tax implications of debt were discussed in Chapter 10.)

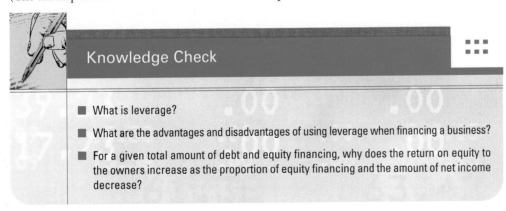

Knowledge Check

- What is leverage?
- What are the advantages and disadvantages of using leverage when financing a business?
- For a given total amount of debt and equity financing, why does the return on equity to the owners increase as the proportion of equity financing and the amount of net income decrease?

www.mcgrawhill.ca/
olc/friedlan

EMPLOYEE STOCK OPTIONS

Employees can be compensated in many ways. Common ones include salary and bonus, shares in the company, and stock options. In this section we will describe employee stock options and discuss the accounting issues surrounding this form of compensation.

Let's begin by covering some stock option basics:

- An **employee stock option** gives an employee the right to purchase a specified number of shares of the employer's stock at a specified price over a specified period of time. Employee stock options represent the right to purchase shares, not shares themselves.

- The price at which a stock option allows the employee to purchase shares is called the **exercise price**. For tax reasons, the exercise price of a stock option is usually the same as or greater than the market price of the shares on the date it is granted.

- The terms of a stock option also state an expiry date. The **expiry date** is the final date that the option can be exercised. If the employee has not exercised or used the option by its expiry date, the option is worthless—it cannot be used to purchase shares. An employee will exercise an option only if the exercise price is less than the market price because otherwise the employee would be buying shares for more than what they are worth in the open market.

- When the exercise price is less than the market price, the stock option is said to be "**in-the-money**."

- When the exercise price is greater than the market price, the stock option is said to be "**out-of-the-money**."

Stock options can be a very attractive way of compensating employees. From the entity's standpoint, an attractive feature of a stock option is that it doesn't cost it any cash. This can be very important for entities that are short of cash or are trying to conserve cash, as is common in growing or new businesses. Stock options give the employees the opportunity to make lots of money if the company is successful, without costing the company a lot of cash.

However, don't interpret the fact that stock options don't cost the entity any cash to mean that they aren't costly. In fact, stock options can have a significant economic cost. Stock options are exercised by employees when the exercise price is below the market value of the shares. By selling shares for below their market value, the value of the shares of other shareholders is diluted.

The significance of stock options as a form of compensation for senior executives can be seen in Figure 11–3. Figure 11–3 shows the compensation earned by the CEOs of eight Canadian companies. Figure 11–3 breaks down the CEOs' compensation into salary and bonus, stock option gains (the amount the CEO earned by exercising stock options), and other compensation. In addition, information about the number and value of new options granted to the CEO in 2005 is provided. Aside from the fact that these CEOs earn a lot of money, notice how significant a role stock options play in compensation.

Note 13(c) to Rogers' financial statements (page A-32) describes its incentive stock option plan. Under the terms of the plan the board of directors can grant stock options to purchase Class B non-voting common shares to employees, directors, and officers of the company. As of December 31, 2005, there were 13,239,424 options outstanding, which represented 5.1 percent of the number of Class B shares outstanding on December 31, 2005. If all of the options were exercised, an additional 13,239,424 shares in Rogers would be sold at prices below the market value of the shares.

Note 13(c) also describes the employee stock options that were outstanding on December 31, 2005. For example, on December 31, 2005 there were 2,393,115 options with an exercise price of between $5.78 and $8.92. The average exercise price of these options was $6.53. If 1,000,000 of these options were exercised, Rogers would receive $6,530,000 ($6.53 × 1,000,000) in cash and the employees would receive 1,000,000 shares of Roger's stock. If the market price of the shares on the date they were exercised was $45, the employees would be receiving, and Rogers would be giving up, shares worth $45,000,000 ($45 × 1,000,000) in exchange for $6,680,000 in cash. The difference between the $45 million market value and the $6.68 million exercise price is the cost borne by the shareholders. Overall, the 13,239,424 options outstanding on December 31, 2005 had an average exercise price of $19.24. Compare that price with the current market price of Rogers' Class B common shares to understand the potential cost to shareholders.

The question accountants ask is, how should employee stock options be accounted for? For many years the GAAP treatment for stock options was to ignore them. No compensation expense was recorded for stock options granted to or exercised by employees.

Accounting standard setters in the United States studied this issue for a long time and eventually tried to implement a standard that required entities to expense the economic value of stock options granted. There were very strong objections from the business community, especially in the high technology sector, to the proposed standard. In the end, the U.S. standard setters backed off and didn't require accrual of an expense for the value of stock options. Instead, companies in the U.S. were (and still are) only required to disclose the economic value of employee stock options in the notes to the financial statements. Eventually, Canada followed the U.S. lead.

In 2002, Canada revised its *Handbook* section to take a firm position on stock options. Now, Canadian GAAP requires that the value of stock options granted to employees be expensed as part of the compensation expense. Note 13(c) to Rogers' financial statements reports that for the year ended December 31, 2005 the company recorded a compensation expense of about $34.7 million for stock options granted to employees.

The Canadian treatment of stock options makes good economic sense. Some people argue that since stock options are usually out-of-the-money when they are granted, they have no value. This is clearly false. As long as there is time before the stock option expires, it has an economic value, even if it is out-of-the-money. For example, would you pay for the right to be able to purchase Rogers shares at $55 each sometime over the next three years if the current market price of the shares was $45? Many people would pay something for that right (they might not pay very much, but they would pay something).

Moreover, if stock options have no value, why would employees negotiate for and accept them as compensation? Clearly the options are worth something. The entity granting the option is giving something that is valuable: the opportunity to purchase stock at below-market prices.

	Salary + Bonus	Other Compensation[a]	Option Gains[b]	Total	New Options Granted in 2005	Value of New Options Granted in 2005[c]
Robert Milton ACE Aviation Holdings (Air Canada)	$1,897,289	$ 44,186	$ 5,550,370	$ 7,491,845	0	$ 0
Tony Comper Bank of Montreal	2,700,000	3,260,454	4,021,164	9,981,618	158,200	2,700,000
Michael Sabia BCE Inc.	1,250,000	5,457,826	0	6,707,826	0	0
Hunter Harrison Canadian National Railway	6,330,610	22,641,537	27,247,347	56,219,494	250,000	2,136,051
John Lederer Loblaw Companies	1,350,000	2,408,563	2,391,333	6,149,896	175,993	-
Mike Zafirovski Nortel Networks	305,785	37,123,512	0	37,429,297	5,000,000	10,695,000
Hank Swartout Precision Drilling Trust	4,200,000	15,589,000	55,035,331	74,824,331	403,038	3,345,215
Ted Rogers Rogers Communications	3,484,198	1,287	2,635,775	6,121,260	53,300	857,597

[a] Other compensation includes all other cash payments (e.g. insurance, car, housing) and the value of any equity awarded (e.g. shares).
[b] Option gains is the profit earned by the CEO by exercising stock options.
[c] Estimated market value of stock options granted in 2005.

FIGURE 11–3 ::

Compensation of CEOs of Major Canadian Companies, 2009[9]

A main objection to expensing the value of stock options is that doing so would significantly lower net income. As has been mentioned several times in the book, accounting has economic consequences and people will respond when they see themselves being disadvantaged by an accounting standard (or anything else). Some readers may find it surprising, but accounting standard setting can be very political. Accounting standard setting occurs in an environment of conflicting interests.

However, there are legitimate concerns about the requirement that the value of stock options be expensed. Conceptually, expensing stock options is correct; not doing so, as is possible in the U.S., results in the understatement of expenses and the overstatement of net income. Practically, there are a variety of problems with estimating the value of the options.

Let's look at an example to see how the accounting for stock options works. Ottertail Inc. (Ottertail) recently introduced an employee stock option plan whereby certain employees receive options to purchase shares of company stock. For the year ended December 31, 2010, Ottertail's board of directors granted employees 200,000 stock options to purchase Ottertail stock at $18.00 per share. The market price of the shares on the date the options were granted was $18.25. The market value of the options on the date of issue, calculated using an appropriate method for determining the economic value of stock options, was $2,925,000. (Note that determining the value of stock options is complicated and beyond the scope of this book. Methods exist for valuing options, including a model known as the Black-Scholes options pricing model.)

When the stock options are granted Ottertail would make the following entry:

Dr. Compensation expense (expense +, shareholders' equity −)   2,925,000
    Cr. Contributed surplus (shareholders' equity +)   2,925,000
To record the compensation expense for 2008.

With this entry, the full economic cost of the compensation being provided to the employees is being recognized when it is granted to the employees. The value of the stock options is credited to Contributed Surplus because the granting of the options does not mean that new shares were issued. Only when the shares are issued would the amount be credited to the Common Stock account. When the stock options are exercised in 2013, when Ottertail's shares are trading at $31, the following entry would be made:

Dr. Cash (assets +)   3,600,000
Dr. Contributed surplus (shareholders' equity −)   2,925,000
    Cr. Common stock (shareholders' equity +)   6,525,000
To record the exercise of 200,000 stock options at $18.

When the stock options are exercised, the amount that was credited to contributed surplus when the stock options were granted is moved to the common stock account.

Question for Consideration

Some people argue that employee stock options do not represent an economic cost to an entity and that is why it is reasonable not to record them as an expense.

Do you agree that employee stock options do not represent an economic cost to the entity that issues them? Explain.

Answer: Employee stock options do not require that an entity pay cash or any other assets to the employees. That does not mean there is no economic cost. The common shares of an entity represent valuable economic assets (although they are not accounted for as assets by the entity itself) and if they are "given away" or are sold for less than market value, the economic value of the shares held by existing shareholders decreases. The value of existing shares decreases because the ownership interest of the existing shares is being diluted. Since net income is intended to reflect the change in wealth of the shareholders, a real cost to the shareholders is ignored when the cost of employee stock options is not accounted for.

ECONOMIC CONSEQUENCES

Accounting matters. The discussion in the previous section about employee stock options and the controversy surrounding the attempt by United States standard setters to require that employee stock options be accrued provides an opportunity to emphasize that accounting does matter. If accounting didn't matter, why would people get so excited about a new accounting standard? Clearly, stopping the new accounting standard mattered to the people who objected to it.

But why does accounting matter? Accounting matters because it has economic consequences for an entity and its stakeholders. Economic consequences mean that the wealth of the stakeholders of an entity is affected by how the entity accounts for various transactions and economic events. Many decisions and outcomes can be affected simply by how an entity decides to represent its economic circumstances in its financial statements. Some of the decisions and outcomes affected by accounting include:

- management compensation
- compliance with debt covenants that are based on accounting measurements
- the selling price of an entity when the price is based on net income or other accounting measurements
- the amount of tax an entity pays
- rate changes for regulated companies when the rate is based on accounting measurements
- the ability of an entity to receive subsidies from government
- the ability of an entity to raise capital (some entities have argued that their ability to raise capital has been adversely affected by certain accounting standards)

This list does not include the effect that accounting choices might have on the decisions of individual stakeholders—decisions such as whether to buy shares of a particular entity, to sell shares already owned, or to lend money. While economic consequences mean that how an entity accounts affects the wealth of an entity and its stakeholders, the underlying economic activity is not affected by how the entity accounts. Whether employee stock options are accrued, disclosed, or ignored does not change the economic cost of those options. What is affected are the financial statements and the economic consequences of using those statements.

FINANCIAL STATEMENT ANALYSIS ISSUES

The equity section of an entity's balance sheet represents the book value of its equity. **Book value** is the amount recorded in the accounting records for the assets, liabilities, and equities—it is the accounting value of these items. The **book value of equity** is the balance sheet or accounting value of an entity's equity and is equal to assets minus liabilities as reported on the balance sheet. Book value of equity is also referred to as the net assets or net worth of the entity.

It is important to note that the book value of equity is not a measure of the market value of equity. As we have discussed throughout the text, there are many reasons why book values and market values do not correspond. The main reason is that historical cost, GAAP-based accounting is not designed or intended to measure the market value of all assets and liabilities. For example, assets are recorded at their cost and are not adjusted for changes in market value, and not all assets are even recorded on the balance sheet. (Remember that research and development, advertising, and human resources usually do not appear on a GAAP balance sheet.) However, book value is sometimes viewed as what would be left over for shareholders if a company shut down its operations, paid off all of its creditors, collected from all of its debtors, and liquidated itself. From this view, book value can be seen as the minimum amount an entity is worth. This interpretation makes more sense for entities that have most of their assets reflected on the balance sheet (like manufacturers and retailers) but less sense for knowledge-based entities that have not recorded many of their assets.

The **market value of equity** is the market price of an entity's shares multiplied by the number of common shares outstanding. For public companies, determining the market value of equity is straightforward because the shares trade publicly, so a market price is readily available.

The **price-to-book ratio** (PB ratio) is often examined by investors and analysts considering the desirability of a particular stock. The PB ratio is a measure of the stock market's valuation of a company's equity relative to its book value and is used as an indication of whether the shares are reasonably valued.

The PB ratio can be stated as:

$$\text{Price-to-book ratio} = \frac{\text{Market value of equity}}{\text{Book value of equity}}$$

A lower PB is an indication that a stock is undervalued and, therefore, an attractive investment. A low PB could also indicate significant problems with the company. Like most of the ratios we have considered in the book, how meaningful a particular amount is varies with the industry. For example, one would expect a software company to have a higher PB ratio than a steelmaker or bank because the software company has many assets that are not captured on the balance sheet.

For example, the market value of Rogers' equity on December 30, 2005 was $15,680,720,438.92 ($53.38 per Class A share × 56,233,894 shares + $49.20 per Class B share × 257,702,341 shares) and its book value on December 31, 2005 was $3,527,615,000, for a PB ratio of 4.4. Figure 7–2 shows the PB ratio for a number of Canadian industries. These ratios are the averages for the firms in the industry over seven years, 1999 through 2005. Notice the wide variation in both ratios across the industries.

Seven-Year Average Price-to-Book Ratios (1999–2005) for Selected Industries*			
Industry	**Ratio**	**Industry**	**Ratio**
Banks	1.77	Oil, Gas, and Consumable Fuels	2.68
Biotechnology	5.21	Paper and Forest Products	1.03
Computers and Electronic Equipment	3.61	Retailing	1.48
Food and Staples Retailing	2.77	Software	4.36
IT Services	4.17	Steel	0.80
Media	2.18	Telecommunications Services	3.13

*Data obtained from the 2006 Industry Reports published by the Financial Post.

Earnings Per Share

One of the most often quoted financial ratios is **earnings per share** or **EPS**. EPS is the amount of net income that is attributable to each individual share of common stock. The investing public pays close attention to EPS and anxiously awaits the announcement of companies' quarterly and annual earnings and EPS. Analysts project EPS, and whether an entity has had a successful quarter or year is often measured by whether it met the analysts' forecasts.

EPS comes in a number of variations. We will look at two of them. The first and most straightforward is **basic earnings per share**. Basic EPS is calculated using the following formula:

$$\text{Basic EPS} = \frac{\text{Net income} - \text{Preferred dividends}}{\text{Weighted-average number of common shares outstanding during the period}}$$

Preferred dividends are deducted from net income in the numerator of the formula because preferred dividends have preference over the rights of common shareholders. Therefore, the amount of preferred dividends is not available to common shareholders, but is not deducted in the calculation of net income. The denominator is the weighted-average number of shares that were outstanding during the year. The weighted-average number of common shares outstanding is the average number of shares outstanding during the period, taking into consideration when changes in the number of shares outstanding occurred during the period. For an example of how to calculate the weighted-average number of shares outstanding please visit the text's Companion Web site at www.mcgrawhill.ca/olc/friedlan.

For Rogers, basic EPS is:

$$\text{Basic earnings per share} = \frac{(\$44,658,000)}{288,668,000}$$
$$= \$(0.15)$$

EPS is reported at the bottom of Rogers' income statement and the calculation is detailed in Note 15 (page A-36). Since Rogers reported a loss for 2005, the EPS can be referred to as a loss per share. EPS is disclosed in virtually all financial statements that you are likely to examine.

The second EPS measure we will look at is called fully-diluted EPS. In this chapter and in Chapter 10, we discussed securities such as convertible bonds, convertible preferred shares, and stock options that can be converted into or exchanged for common shares. Some of these securities, if they are converted or exercised, will dilute an entity's earnings. They will increase the number of common shares that will share the entity's earnings and thereby lower EPS because the earnings would be spread over a larger number of shares. **Fully diluted earnings per share** is designed to show the effect that these dilutive securities would have on EPS if the securities were converted or exchanged for common stock.

The actual calculations can get complicated and will not be shown here, but fully diluted EPS can be thought of as a worst-case scenario of EPS. Fully diluted EPS is provided because one of the uses of financial statements is to help investors predict future earnings. Fully diluted EPS is intended to help users understand how EPS in future periods would be affected if the securities that can increase the number of common shares outstanding were converted or exercised.

Despite all the attention it receives in the media, EPS has significant limitations:

- First, like any ratio, EPS has no inherent meaning. It must be considered in relation to some benchmark. For example, current EPS could be compared with previous years' EPS to observe trends, or with forecasts of EPS that analysts who follow public companies often make.

- Second, EPS depends on the accounting policies and estimates reflected in the financial statements.

- Third, EPS may be affected by changes in the number of shares outstanding during a period. For example, if an entity repurchases some of its shares, EPS will increase. Another point worth noting is that EPS does not give an indication of the ability or willingness of an entity to pay dividends. It is simply the amount of earnings attributable to each common share.

- Fourth, it can also be very difficult to compare the EPS figures of different entities. Aside from the effect of different accounting choices, EPS is also affected by the way the entity is financed. Entities with identical assets and operating performance will have different EPS if they are financed differently—that is, if they have different proportions of debt and equity.

Insight

In Canada, the activities and performance of public companies get a lot of attention. For a lot of reasons, this is understandable. Many members of the public have an interest in these companies, either directly or indirectly through pension plans and mutual funds.

However, most corporations and businesses in Canada are private. That means that there is no market price to obtain a reasonable estimate of the market value of these entities. This is one of the reasons that accounting information is so important for evaluating an entity. For example, how much would you pay to buy a small business in your community? How much would you pay to join a partnership of accountants? Without a market-determined measure of value, it is difficult to know. It is why accounting information is relied on for determining the value of a private company for purposes of a purchase and sale, or in a divorce.

Return on Shareholders' Equity

In Chapter 9, return on assets (ROA) was introduced as a measure of the performance and operating efficiency of an entity. ROA provides a measure of the return the entity earns regardless of how the entity is financed. **Return on equity (ROE)** provides a measure of return earned by resources invested only by the common shareholders. ROE is defined as:

$$\text{Return on equity} = \frac{\text{Net income} - \text{preferred dividends}}{\text{Average common shareholders' equity}}$$

Because ROE is a measure of return to the common shareholders, preferred dividends are deducted from net income. Preferred dividends are not available to the common shareholders, but the amount is not deducted in the calculation of net income. The denominator, average common shareholders' equity, excludes equity contributed by the preferred shareholders. The denominator includes retained earnings since that amount belongs to the common shareholders. As was discussed in the section in this chapter on leverage, ROE will be affected by how the entity is financed. The more leverage or debt that an entity uses, the more volatile ROE will be.

For Rogers, ROE for 2005 was:

$$
\begin{aligned}
\text{Return on equity} &= \frac{\text{Net income} - \text{preferred dividends}}{\text{Average common shareholders' equity}} \\
&= \frac{\$(44,658,000)}{(\$3,527,615,000 + \$2,385,334,000) \div 2} \\
&= \frac{\$(44,658,000)}{\$2,956,474,500} \\
&= -1.51 \text{ percent}
\end{aligned}
$$

Rogers' common shareholders lost 1.51 percent on their investment in the company. ROE gives common shareholders an indication of the return they are earning on their investment in the company. Investors can compare the ROEs of different entities as part of their evaluation of investment alternatives.

Higher ROEs mean an investment is more attractive, but risk must be considered as well when evaluating investments. Generally, the higher the risk of an investment, the higher the return expected by investors. Thus, when comparing investments, a higher return may indicate more risk. At that point, the investor must decide whether he or she is willing to accept the additional risk in exchange for the higher return. This risk-return relationship—the trade-off that exists between risk and return—explains why interest rates that banks pay tend to be low, whereas expected returns on speculative investments tend to be high.

Solved Problem

You have been provided with the following information about Wrixon Ltd. (Wrixon):

■ Wrixon's year end is December 31.

■ Net income for the year ended December 31, 2009 was $3,250,000.

■ Wrixon had an unlimited number of common shares authorized and 100,000 outstanding on December 31, 2008.

■ There were 500,000 preferred shares with a dividend rate of $5 per share authorized and 400,000 outstanding on December 31, 2008.

■ Retained earnings on December 31, 2008 was $4,750,000.

■ Balance in the Common Stock account on December 31, 2008 was $1,000,000.

■ Balance in the Preferred Stock account on December 31, 2008 was $2,400,000.

During the year ended December 31, 2009 the following events occurred:

i. On March 15 Wrixon issued 50,000 preferred shares at $62 per share.

ii. On August 31 Wrixon declared a dividend of 0.25 shares of Battersea Corp. (Battersea), a public company, for each share of Wrixon stock an investor owned. On the date the dividend was declared, Battersea's shares were trading at $3.90. The dividend was distributed to investors on September 15, 2009. Wrixon originally paid $4.80 per share for the Battersea stock that it distributed to its investors.

iii. On October 1, 2009 Wrixon purchased 10,000 common shares from investors for $11 per share.

iv. On November 1, 2009 Wrixon declared and distributed a 10 percent stock dividend, with each shareholder receiving an additional share of Wrixon common stock for every 10 shares owned. The market value of Wrixon's shares on November 1, 2009 was $10.75.

v. On December 8, 2009 Wrixon announced a two-for-one stock split.

vi. On December 14, 2009 Wrixon exchanged 30,000 of its common shares for marketing rights for certain products produced by a European company. The price of Wrixon's shares on December 14 was $5.65.

vii. On December 31, 2009 Wrixon's board of directors declared a dividend of $5 per share on each outstanding preferred share. The dividend is to be paid on January 10, 2010.

Required:

a. Prepare the journal entries for each of the items described in the information about Wrixon Ltd.

b. How many common shares were outstanding on December 31, 2009?

c. Calculate the balances in the Preferred Stock and Common Stock accounts on December 31, 2009.

d. Calculate Retained Earnings on December 31, 2009.

e. Calculate basic earnings per share for the year ended December 31, 2009. Assume that the weighted-average number of common shares outstanding during 2009 was 198,000 shares, after taking into consideration the stock split on December 8.

f. Calculate return on equity for the year ended December 31, 2009.

Solution

a. Journal entries for Wrixon Ltd.:

    i. The following journal entry is made:

Dr. Cash (assets +)	3,100,000	
Cr. Preferred stock (shareholders' equity +)		3,100,000
To record the issuance and sale of 50,000 shares of preferred stock.		

    ii. The following journal entries are made:

Dr. Loss on disposal of investments (income statement −, shareholders' equity −)	22,500	
Cr. Investment in Battersea stock (assets −)		22,500
To record the loss on the shares of Battersea being distributed to shareholders as a property dividend.		
Dr. Retained earnings (shareholders' equity −)	97,500	
Cr. Property dividend payable (liability +)		97,500
To record the declaration of a property dividend on August 31, 2009.		
Dr. Property dividend payable (liability −)	97,500	
Cr. Investment in Battersea (assets −)		97,500
To record payment of the property dividend on September 15, 2009.		

iii. The average price paid by investors for Wrixon's shares was $10 per share ($1,000,000 ÷ 100,000). Since the price paid to purchase the shares is greater than the average price investors paid for the shares, Wrixon would make the following journal entry to record the transaction:

Dr. Common stock (shareholders' equity −)	100,000	
Dr. Retained earnings (shareholders' equity −)	10,000	
Cr. Cash (assets −)		110,000

To record the repurchase of 10,000 shares for $11 per share.

iv. Assume that Wrixon uses the market value method for accounting for stock dividends.

Dr. Retained earnings (shareholders' equity −)	96,750	
Cr. Common stock (shareholders' equity +)		96,750

To record the 10 percent stock dividend declared and paid on the 90,000 outstanding common shares.

v. According to GAAP, no entry is made when there is a stock split.

vi. The following journal entry is made:

Dr. Marketing rights (assets +)	169,500	
Cr. Common stock (shareholders' equity +)		169,500

To record the exchange of 30,000 Wrixon common shares for marketing rights for certain products.

vii. The following journal entry is made:

Dr. Retained earnings (shareholders' equity −)	2,250,000	
Cr. Preferred dividend payable (liabilities +)		2,250,000

To record payment of a $5 dividend per share on the 450,000 outstanding preferred shares.

b.
Common shares outstanding on December 31, 2008	100,000
Repurchase of shares	(10,000)
Stock dividend	9,000
Common shares outstanding on December 1, 2009 (before the stock split):	99,000
Common shares outstanding on December 8, 2009 (after the stock split)	198,000
Shares issued in exchange for marketing rights	30,000
Common shares outstanding on December 31, 2009:	228,000

c.
Balance in Preferred Stock account on December 31, 2008	$2,400,000
Preferred shares (50,000 @ $62 per share)	3,100,000
Balance in Preferred Stock account on December 31, 2009	$5,500,000
Balance in Common Stock account on December 31, 2008	$1,000,000
Repurchase of common shares	(100,000)
Stock dividend	96,750
Exchange of common shares for marketing rights	169,500
Balance in Common Stock account on December 31, 2009:	$1,166,250

d.
Retained earnings on December 31, 2008	$4,750,000
+ Net income	3,250,000
− Property dividend on common shares	(97,500)
− Premium paid on repurchase of shares	(10,000)
− Stock dividend	(96,750)
− Preferred share dividend	(2,250,000)
Retained earnings on December 31, 2009:	$5,545,750

e. Calculation of basic earnings per share:

$$\text{Basic EPS} = \frac{\text{Net income} - \text{Preferred dividends}}{\text{Weighted-average number of common shares outstanding during the period}}$$

$$= \frac{\$3,250,000 - \$2,250,000}{198,000}$$

$$= \$5.05$$

f. Calculation of return on equity:

$$\text{Return on equity} = \frac{\text{Net income} - \text{Preferred dividends}}{\text{Average common shareholders' equity}}$$

$$= \frac{\$3,250,000 - \$2,250,000}{\$6,231,000}$$

$$= 16.0\%$$

SUMMARY OF KEY POINTS

▶ **LO 1** A corporation is a separate legal and taxable entity. The shareholders of a corporation are not liable for the obligations of and losses suffered by the corporation beyond what they have invested in the corporation. Corporations divide the shareholders' equity section of their balance sheets into two broad classifications: capital stock and retained earnings.

Partnerships and proprietorships are not incorporated. Partnerships and proprietorships do not pay tax and do not file tax returns—earnings are taxed in the hands of the proprietor or partners. Partners and proprietors are personally liable for any obligations that the partnership or proprietorship is unable to fulfil, except in the case of limited liability partnerships. The equity section of a partnership has a separate account for each partner to keep track of the capital contributed by, the share of the partnership's earnings of, and the drawings made by each partner.

Not-for-profit organizations (NFPOs) are economic entities whose objective is to provide services and not to make a profit. NFPOs do not have owners or ownership shares that can be traded or sold.

▶ **LO 2** Common shares represent the residual ownership in an entity. Common shareholders are entitled to whatever earnings and assets are left after obligations to debtholders and preferred shareholders have been satisfied. Preferred shareholders have rights that must be satisfied before common shareholders' rights. These preferred rights pertain to the payment of dividends and/or to the distribution of assets in the event of liquidation. Unlike debt, the cost of equity is not deductible for tax purposes. Dividends are also not expensed for accounting purposes. Shareholders are not entitled to dividends or any other type of payments from the corporation, and no return of principal is guaranteed.

▶ **LO 3** Retained earnings represents the accumulated earnings of an entity over its entire life, less all dividends paid to shareholders over the entity's life. Retained earnings represents an indirect investment by shareholders. Dividends are distributions of a corporation's earnings to its shareholders. There are three types of dividends: cash, property, and stock. Dividends are discretionary and must be declared by the board of directors. Dividends are declared on a per share basis and every share of a specific class must receive the same dividend. Once a dividend is declared, it is classified as a liability on the balance sheet. A stock split is the division of an entity's shares into a larger number of units, each with a smaller value.

▶ **LO 4** There are two categories of accounting changes—changes in policies and changes in estimates. If a company decides to change an accounting policy, the change is applied retroactively.

A change in accounting estimate is adjusted in future periods, from the period of the change in estimate onward. Under GAAP, policy changes must be disclosed. GAAP and the *CICA Handbook* do not require disclosure of changes in estimates.

▶ **LO 5** Leverage is the use of debt to attempt to increase the return earned on the equity investment of the owners. Leverage is attractive because any profits earned from investing borrowed money, above the cost of borrowing, go to the owners. Leverage is risky because the cost of borrowing must be paid, regardless of how well or how poorly the entity is performing.

▶ **LO 6** Employee stock options give employees the right to purchase a specified number of shares of the employer's stock at a specified price over a specified period of time. Stock options have become an increasingly important way of compensating employees. In Canada, the economic value of stock options on the date they are granted to employees must be estimated and the amount expensed as a compensation expense.

▶ **LO 7** The equity section of an entity's balance sheet represents the book value of its equity. The book value of equity is the balance sheet or accounting value of an entity and is equal to assets minus liabilities as reported on the balance sheet. The book value of equity is not a measure of the market value of the equity.

Earnings per share (EPS) is the amount of net income that is attributable to each individual share of common stock. Basic earnings per share equals net income less preferred dividends divided by the weighted-average number of common shares outstanding during the period. Fully diluted EPS is designed to show the effect that dilutive securities would have on EPS if the securities were converted or exchanged for common stock. Return on equity provides a measure of return earned by resources invested only by the common shareholders.

KEY TERMS

accounting estimates, p. 614

accounting policies, p. 614

authorized capital stock, p. 603

basic earnings per share (basic EPS), p. 624

book value, p. 623

book value of equity, p. 623

Canada Business Corporations Act, p. 603

cash dividend, p. 610

common share, p. 604

comprehensive income, p. 616

contributed surplus, p. 604

convertible preferred share, p. 605

cumulative preferred share, p. 605

date of declaration of a dividend, p. 609

date of payment of a dividend, p. 610

date of record of a dividend, p. 609

earnings per share (EPS), p. 624

employee stock option, p. 620

exercise price, p. 620

expiry date, p. 620

fully diluted earnings per share, p. 625

general partner, p. 599

hybrid security, p. 606

in-the-money, p. 620

issued shares, p. 603

leverage, p. 616

limited liability partnership (LLP), p. 599

limited partner, p. 599

market value of equity, p. 633

no par value share, p. 604

out-of-the-money, p. 620

outstanding share, p. 603

par value, p. 604

participating preferred share, p. 605

preferred share, p. 605

price-to-book ratio, p. 623

property dividend, p. 611

redeemable preferred share, p. 605

retractable preferred share, p. 605

return on equity (ROE), p. 626

stock dividend, p. 611

stock split, p. 612

treasury stock, p. 608

SIMILAR TERMS

The left column gives alternative terms that are sometimes used for the accounting terms introduced in this chapter, which are listed in the right column.

additional paid-in capital	**contributed surplus, p. 604**
authorized share capital, authorized share	**authorized capital stock, p. 603**
dividend in kind	**property dividend, p. 611**
net assets, net worth	**book value of equity, p. 623**

ASSIGNMENT MATERIALS

Questions

Q11-1. Explain the difference between common and preferred shares.

Q11-2. Explain the following features that are sometimes associated with preferred shares:
   a. cumulative
   b. retractable
   c. redeemable
   d. participating
   e. convertible

Q11-3. What does it mean when an entity uses leverage to finance itself? What are the advantages and disadvantages of using leverage?

Q11-4. Describe and explain the characteristics that distinguish corporations from partnerships and proprietorships.

Q11-5. Why are common shares said to represent the residual interest in an entity?

Q11-6. Why is it important in a corporation's financial statements that contributed capital be separated from retained earnings?

Q11-7. Explain the differences between debt and equity. What are the advantages and disadvantages of each? Which do you think is preferable for an entity to use? Explain.

Q11-8. What is a not-for-profit organization? If the objective of not-for-profit organizations is not to make a profit, then what is their objective? Why is a traditional income statement not appropriate for a not-for-profit organization?

Q11-9. Explain why not-for-profit organizations do not have an owners' equity section on their balance sheets. What do they have instead? What does that section of the balance sheet represent? How should it be interpreted?

Q11-10. What is a limited partnership? What is the difference between limited partners and general partners? Why must a limited partnership have at least one general partner?

Q11-11. What are dividends? Why are dividends not expensed when calculating net income, whereas interest is expensed?

Q11-12. What does par value mean? How does the entry to record the issuance of common stock differ depending on whether the shares have a par value? Provide an example.

Q11-13. Grosvenor Ltd. has the following securities outstanding:
   i. $1,000,000 bond with 10 percent coupon rate.
   ii. $1,000,000 of cumulative preferred shares with a 6.5 percent dividend rate.

   What effect would payments to investors for each security have on the income statement? What would be the net cash cost of each security? Assume that Grosvenor Ltd. has a tax rate of 30 percent.

Q11-14. Over the last six months the price on the stock exchange of Ixworth Inc.'s (Ixworth) shares has fallen from a high of $32 per share to the current price of $18 per share. Ixworth does not plan to issue common shares in the foreseeable future, yet management has expressed concern about the falling share price. Explain why Ixworth's management might be concerned about its share price.

Q11-15. Distinguish between stock splits and stock dividends. How is each accounted for? What is the economic significance of stock splits and stock dividends?

Q11-16. What is retained earnings? What transactions and economic events have an effect on retained earnings? Why is retained earnings considered an indirect investment in an entity?

Q11-17. What are property dividends? How are they accounted for?

Q11-18. What are employee stock options? How are they accounted for? What are the advantages to an entity of issuing stock options to its employees?

Q11-19. You are a shareholder in a public company. The company is proposing to introduce an employee stock option program for its senior executives. Do you think that this proposal is a good idea? In your response, focus on the incentives that the stock option plan would create for the senior executives.

Q11-20. Why do employee stock options impose a cost on shareholders?

Q11-21. Car prices tend to increase over time. One car manufacturer has offered students the opportunity to lock in the price of a new car for when they graduate. By paying $500 today, a student can purchase any car made by the manufacturer at today's price at any time over the next three years. The $500 fee is not refundable once it is paid.

Required:

Do you think it is worthwhile to spend $500 to lock in the price of a car for three years? Explain. What are the risks associated with purchasing this price guarantee? Suppose you could sell the price guarantee to somebody else. What do you think would happen to the amount for which you could sell the price guarantee if the price of cars increased? What would happen to the amount you could receive if the price of cars decreased? Explain.

Q11-22. What is meant by the term "economic consequences"? Why does accounting have economic consequences?

Q11-23. Since the underlying economic activity of an entity is not affected by accounting choices such as when revenue is recognized or how capital assets are amortized, why does anyone care what accounting choices an entity makes?

Q11-24. Distinguish between the book value and market value of equity. Why are the two amounts usually different? How is book value per share calculated?

Q11-25. Corporations disclose the number of shares authorized and the number of shares outstanding. Explain what these terms mean.

Q11-26. How are preferred shares "preferred"? Are dividends on preferred shares guaranteed? If the preferred shares have a cumulative feature, are the dividends guaranteed? Explain.

Q11-27. Would you rather receive a cash dividend or a stock dividend from a corporation? Explain.

Q11-28. Why do most companies not pay out 100 percent of their earnings each year in dividends?

Q11-29. Why are preferred dividends deducted from net income when calculating earnings per share? Explain. Does earnings per share give an indication of the amount of dividends shareholders can expect to receive? Explain.

Q11-30. Explain why changes in accounting policies and corrections of errors have an effect on retained earnings.

Q11-31. Why might a loan agreement limit or prevent the payment of dividends by the borrower?

Q11-32. Why do you think that property dividends are accounted for at their market value instead of their book value? Why are property dividends relatively uncommon?

Q11-33. What are hybrid securities? Why do they sometimes pose a difficult accounting problem?

Q11-34. Explain the difference between a change in accounting policy and a change in accounting estimate. How is each accounted for in the financial statements?

Exercises

E11-1. (**Preparing journal entries, LO 2, 3, 5, 6**) For each of the following transactions or economic events, prepare the journal entry that would be required. Assume the year end in each case is December 31:

a. On April 2, 2010 Barthel Inc. issued 200,000 common shares for $4,500,000.

b. On May 17, 2010 Cayley Corp. announced a three-for-one stock split.

c. On December 11, 2010 Duro Ltd. declared a $0.25 per share cash dividend. The dividend was paid on February 11, 2011. Duro Ltd. had 1,000,000 shares outstanding on December 11, 2010.

d. On August 17, 2010 Gullies Inc. issued 300,000 common shares with a par value of $0.01 for $6,000,000.

e. On April 21, 2010 Quimper Corp. declared and distributed a 5 percent common stock dividend. On April 21, 2010 Quimper had 25,000,000 common shares outstanding and the market price per share was $2.75. The balance in the Common Stock account on April 21, 2010 was $20,000,000.

f. On February 19, 2010 Vidora Inc. granted 100,000 stock options with an exercise price of $12.00. The market price of the Vidora Inc.'s shares on February 19, 2010 was $11.75 and the value of the options was $120,000. The options were exercised on February 19, 2012, when the market price of Vidora Inc.'s shares was $14.20.

g. On December 4, 2010 Yarrow Ltd. declared a property dividend of some of the company's products. Each shareholder received an identical case of products that was taken directly from inventory. The book value of the inventory on December 4, 2010 was $1,200,000 and its market value, based on the most recent selling price to customers, was $2,100,000. The dividend was distributed to the shareholders on December 21, 2010.

E11-2. (**Accounting for equity transactions and preparing the shareholders' equity section of the balance sheet, LO 2, 3**) You are provided with the following information from the equity section of Aurora Ltd.'s balance sheet on December 31, 2009:

Preferred stock—Authorized, 200,000 shares; outstanding 60,000 shares	$1,500,000
Common stock—Authorized, unlimited; outstanding 400,000 shares	1,200,000
Retained earnings	9,110,000

During the year ended December 31, 2010, the following occurred (events are recorded in the order they occurred during the year):

i. Semi-annual dividend on common stock of $200,000 was declared and paid.

ii. 100,000 shares of common stock were issued for $3,000,000.

iii. 20,000 shares of preferred stock were issued for $1,000,000.

iv. 20,000 shares of common stock were issued in exchange for capital assets. The capital assets received had a list price on the vendor's price list of $380,000.

v. Preferred dividends were declared and paid, $200,000.

vi.   10 percent stock dividend was declared on the outstanding common shares.

vii.   Net income was $1,250,000.

viii.   Semi-annual dividend on common stock of $200,000 was declared. The dividend will be paid in January 2011.

Required:

a. Prepare the journal entries required to record the above events.

b. Prepare the shareholders' equity section of Aurora Ltd.'s balance sheet on December 31, 2010.

E11-3.   **(Correction of an accounting error, LO 3)** In fiscal 2009 Upshall Ltd. (Upshall) purchased land for $250,000. For some reason, the land was amortized over 10 years on a straight-line basis. A new employee in the accounting department who was asked to review the company's capital assets discovered the error in 2011. Retained earnings on December 31, 2010, Upshall's last year end, was $2,050,000.

Required:

Prepare the journal entry that must be made in Upshall's books to correct the error. What would retained earnings be on December 31, 2011 after the error had been corrected? Explain why the error is corrected in this way.

E11-4.   **(Correction of an accounting error, LO 3)** In fiscal 2004, Ioco Inc. (Ioco) purchased capital assets for $2,000,000. The capital assets were supposed to be amortized over five years on a straight-line basis. However, for some reason, these assets were not amortized. Ioco's new controller discovered the error while she was reviewing the accounting records in late 2010. Retained earnings on December 31, 2009, Ioco's last year end, was $24,680,000.

Required:

Prepare the journal entry that must be made in Ioco's books to correct the error. What would retained earnings be on December 31, 2009 after the error had been corrected? Explain why the error is corrected in this way.

E11-5.   **(Equity transactions, LO 2, 3, 7)** The shareholders' equity section of Fogo Ltd.'s balance sheet is shown below:

Fogo Ltd.

Extracts from the November 30, 2009 Balance Sheet

Shareholders' equity	
Preferred stock (Authorized 100,000; Outstanding 25,000)	$1,250,000
Common stock (Authorized 1,000,000; Outstanding 500,000)	1,800,000
Retained earnings	6,880,000
Total shareholders' equity	$9,930,000

During fiscal 2010, the following occurred:

i.   On January 31, 50,000 common shares were issued for $200,000.

ii.   On July 31, 75,000 common shares were issued for $350,000.

iii. Dividends on preferred stock of $100,000 were declared and paid.

iv. Dividends on common stock of $400,000 were declared and paid.

v.   Net income for fiscal 2010 was $1,950,000.

Required:

a. Calculate the weighted-average number of common shares outstanding during the year. (Learn how to calculate the weighted-average number of shares outstanding in the Online Learning Centre for this textbook at www.mcgrawhill.ca/olc/friedlan.)

b. Calculate basic earnings per share for the year ended November 30, 2010.

c. Calculate return on shareholders' equity for the year ended November 30, 2010.

d. Prepare the shareholders' equity section for Fogo Ltd.'s November 30, 2010 balance sheet.

E11-6. (**Calculating earnings per share, LO 6**) For each of the following situations calculate basic earnings per share for the year ended December 31, 2009:

	Situation A	Situation B	Situation C	Situation D	Situation E
Shares outstanding on December 31, 2008	100,000	250,000	1,000,000	800,000	10,000,000
Shares issued on July 1, 2009	0	50,000	0	0	2,000,000
Net income for 2009	$100,000	$525,000	($200,000)	$250,000	$25,000,000
Preferred shares outstanding during 2009	0	50,000	0	100,000	1000,000
Preferred dividends per share paid	0	$2	0	$5	$8

E11-7. (**Accounting for equity transactions, LO 2, 3**) During the year ended December 31, 2010 Oyama Corp. (Oyama) had the following equity-related transactions and economic events. On December 31, 2009 the balance in Oyama's Common Stock account was $4,000,000 with 1,000,000 shares outstanding, the balance in its Preferred Stock account was $0 with no shares outstanding, and Retained Earnings was $2,375,000.

i. On January 2 Oyama issued 200,000 common shares for $1,000,000.

ii. On February 28 Oyama issued 50,000 preferred shares for $1,250,000.

iii. On June 30 Oyama paid a dividend of $0.10 per common share.

iv. On September 30 Oyama declared a reverse stock split whereby the number of shares outstanding was reduced by half. A shareholder that had 1,000 shares before the reverse stock split would have 500 after the split.

v. On December 31 Oyama paid dividends to preferred shareholders of $2 per share.

vi. On December 31 Oyama paid a dividend of $0.10 per common share.

vii. Net income for 2010 was $1,150,000.

Required:

a. Prepare the journal entries required to record items (i) through (vi).

b. Prepare the equity section of Oyama's balance sheet on December 31, 2010 and provide comparative information for December 31, 2009.

c. Show the equity section of Oyama's balance sheet as it would have been reported in the December 31, 2009 financial statements. Explain the difference between the equity section for 2009 as reported in the 2010 annual report versus the 2009 annual report.

d. Calculate earnings per share and return on shareholders' equity for the year ended December 31, 2010. If earnings per share for 2009 had been reported as $1.75 per share, what amount would be reported for the year ended December 31, 2009 in the 2010 annual report?

e. How did the reverse stock split affect the performance of Oyama?

E11-8. (**Reporting shareholders equity and assessing the ability to pay dividends LO 2, 3, 7**) Kamsack Inc. (Kamsack) was formed in July 2009 to distribute imports from

China. During its first year Kamsack had the following transactions (these do not represent all the transaction during the year):

i. Issued 100,000 common shares to its two shareholders for $10 per share
ii. Issued 50,000 common shares to the owner of a Chinese company for the exclusive distribution rights in Canada for certain products made by companies she owned. The value of the shares and the exclusive rights is estimated to be about $400,000.
iii. Issued 1,500 preferred shares for $100 each. The preferred shares pay no dividends but must be repurchased by Kamsack within five years for $150 per share.
iv. For the year ended June 30, 2010 Kamsack reported a net loss of $50,000.

Required:

a. Prepare the journal entries need to recorded events i, ii, and iii.
b. Prepare Kamsack's equity section as it should be reported on its June 30, 2010 balance sheet.
c. Can Kamsack pay a dividend on June 30, 2010? Explain your answer. (Think carefully about your answer. This question is tricky.)

E11-9. **(Accounting for equity transactions, LO 2, 3)** During the year ended June 30, 2011, Utusivik Inc. (Utusivik) had the following equity-related transactions and economic events. On June 30, 2010 the balance in Utusivik's Common Stock account was $5,000,000 with 1,000,000 shares outstanding, the balance in its Preferred Stock account was $1,000,000 with 25,000 shares outstanding, and Retained Earnings was $8,200,000.

i. On August 1, 2010 Utusivik issued 200,000 common shares for $3,200,000.
ii. On November 30, 2010 Utusivik issued 50,000 preferred shares for $2,000,000.
iii. On December 31, 2010 Utusivik paid a dividend of $0.25 per common share.
iv. On April 30, 2011 Utusivik declared a two-for-one stock split.
v. On June 30, 2011 Utusivik paid dividends to preferred shareholders of $1.50 per share.
vi. On June 30, 2011 Utusivik paid a dividend of $0.25 per common share.
vii. On June 30, 2011 Utusivik obtained the rights to a patent in exchange for 50,000 shares of Utusivik common stock. The market value of Utusivik stock on June 30, 2011 was $12 per share.
viii. Net income for 2011 was $2,300,000.

Required:

a. Prepare the journal entries required to record items (i) through (vii).
b. Prepare the equity section of Utusivik's balance sheet on June 30, 2011 and provide comparative information for June 30, 2010.
c. Show the equity section of Utusivik's balance sheet as it would have been reported in the June 30, 2010 annual report. Explain the difference between the equity section for 2010 as reported in the 2011 annual report versus the 2010 annual report.
d. Calculate earnings per share and return on shareholders' equity for the year ended June 30, 2011. If earnings per share for 2010 had been reported as $1.75 per share, what amount would be reported for 2010 in the 2011 annual report?
e. How did the stock split affect the performance of Utusivik?

E11-10. **(Calculating earnings per share, LO 2, 3, 7)** For the year ended September 30, 2009 Queylus Inc. (Queylus) reported net income of $750,000. On September 30, 2008, Queylus had the following capital stock outstanding:

Preferred stock, no par, $5 annual dividend, cumulative, authorized 50,000 shares and 50,000 shares outstanding	$750,000
Common stock, no par, authorized 800,000 shares; issued and 400,000 shares outstanding	3,000,000

On January 31, 2009 Queylus issued 40,000 common shares for $480,000 and on April 30, 2009 it issued 50,000 common shares for $750,000.

Required:

a. Calculate Queylus's basic earnings per share for the year ended September 30, 2009.
b. How much of a dividend should Queylus's shareholders expect to receive in 2009?

E11-11. **(Impact of equity transactions on the statement of cash flows, LO 2, 3, 7)** For each of the following transactions and economic events, indicate whether it would appear in the cash flow statement. If the transaction or economic event does appear in the cash flow statement would it be reported as cash from operations, an investing cash flow, or a financing cash flow? Explain your reasoning.

a. Issuance of common shares for cash.
b. Declaration of a stock split.
c. Payment of cash dividends on preferred shares.
d. Issuance of preferred shares for cash.
e. Declaration of cash dividends on common shares.
f. Issuance of common shares for capital assets.
g. Distribution of a stock dividend.
h. Repurchase of common shares for cash.
i. Payment of cash dividends on common shares.
j. Granting of stock options to employees.
k. Exercise of stock options by employees.

E11-12. **(The difference between par and no par value shares, LO 2)** For each of the following transactions, record the required journal entry:

a. 25,000 shares of no par value shares are issued for $30 per share.
b. 25,000 shares of $0.10 par value shares are issued for $30 per share.
c. 25,000 shares of $1.00 par value shares are issued for $30 per share.
d. What effect does par value have on the financial statements? Does par value affect any ratios or the interpretation of the financial statements? Explain.

E11-13. **(Accounting for dividends, LO 3, 7)** Gogama Ltd. (Gogama) is planning on declaring a dividend for its common shareholders and is considering three alternatives:

i. Declare a cash dividend of $5.00 per share.
ii. Declare a property dividend. Shareholders would receive two shares of Judson Inc. (Judson) common stock for each share of Gogama stock owned. Judson's common stock has a market value of $2.50 per share and was originally purchased by Gogama for $1.00 per share.
iii. Declare a 5 percent stock dividend. Shareholders would receive one share of Gogama common stock for each 20 shares of Gogama stock owned. The current market value of Gogama's stock is $100.

Gogama's year end is December 31. The balances in the Common Stock and Retained Earnings accounts on December 31, 2009 are $7,500,000 and $12,500,000 respectively, after accounting for net income for the year but before accounting for the dividend. Gogama currently has 500,000 shares of common stock outstanding and net income for 2009 is $1,750,000.

Required:

a. Prepare the journal entries required to record each of the dividends. State any assumptions you make.
b. How would the equity section of Gogama's December 31, 2009 balance sheet be affected by the three dividends? Show the effect of each dividend separately.
c. What would basic earnings per share be under each dividend alternative?
d. What difference does it make which dividend alternative Gogama chooses? Is there an economic difference among the three? Explain. Under what circumstances might one dividend alternative be preferred over the others?

e. Suppose that instead of paying a property dividend, Gogama sold its shares in Judson and used the proceeds of the sale to pay a cash dividend. Prepare the journal entries required to record the sale of the Judson shares and the declaration and payment of the dividend. What is the difference between paying a property dividend and selling the shares and using the proceeds to pay a dividend?

E11-14. **(Accounting for a partnership, LO 1)** In July 2009 Mr. Irving and Ms. Ruth formed a partnership to offer consulting services. Mr. Irving contributed $40,000 in cash to the partnership and Ms. Ruth contributed non-cash assets to the partnership with a market value of $100,000. During its first year of operations the partnership earned revenues of $184,000 and incurred expenses of $100,000. Mr. Irving and Ms. Ruth agreed to divide the profits of the partnership in proportion to the value of their initial contributions. During the year Mr. Irving withdrew $10,000 in cash from the partnership and Ms. Ruth withdrew $14,000 in cash. The partnership's first year end is December 31, 2009.

Required:

a. Record the journal entries required to record formation of the partnership.
b. Prepare the statement of partners' capital on December 31, 2009.

E11-15. **(Change in accounting estimate, LO 4)** On November 12, 2004 Griffon Inc. (Griffon) purchased a new front-end loader for $275,000. Management estimated that the loader would have a useful life of eight years and a residual value of $25,000. Near the end of fiscal 2009, management reassessed the useful life of the loader and decided that because the workload of the loader was much lower than was originally expected, its useful life would probably be about 12 years and the residual value of the loader would be about $10,000. Griffon's year end is October 31 and the company uses straight-line amortization for this type of asset.

Required:

a. Prepare the journal entry to record the purchase of the loader in 2004.
b. What would be the amortization expense for the loader in fiscal 2005? Prepare the journal entry to record the amortization expense in 2005.
c. What would be the amortization expense for the loader in fiscal 2011? Prepare the journal entry to record the amortization expense in 2011.
d. Suppose the loader was sold in on January 31, 2013 for $22,000. Prepare the journal entry to record the sale.

E11-16. **(Unit-of-production amortization and change in accounting estimate, LO 4)** Grindstone Corp. (Grindstone) produces fad toys for children. In 2009, Grindstone purchased a new stamping machine to produce the latest fad toy. The machine cost $30,000 plus taxes of $2,100, and delivery and installation of $1,000. Grindstone's management estimates that the market for the toy is about 250,000 units and demand for the toy will last no more than four years. Management expects that it will be able to produce and sell 30,000 units in 2009, 150,000 units in 2010, 65,000 units in 2011, and 5,000 units in 2012. Once the fad dies, the machine will not be useful for any purpose and will have to be sold for scrap, about $2,000. Grindstone will use unit-of-production amortization for the machine.

Required:

a. Prepare the journal entry to record the purchase of the new machine.
b. Prepare an amortization schedule showing the amortization expense for each year and the NBV of the machine at the end of each year.

c. Suppose that early in 2011 Grindstone's management realized that the fad would last longer than expected and that it would be able to sell 100,000 units in 2011, 50,000 in 2012, and 10,000 in 2013, at which time the machine would be scrapped and Grindstone would receive $1,000. Prepare an amortization schedule showing the amortization expense for 2011, 2012, and 2013, and the NBV of the machine at the end of each year.

E11-17. **(Change in accounting policy, LO 4)** On April 21, 2003 Rustico Inc. (Rustico) purchased a new fishing trawler for $1,890,000. Rustico initially amortized the trawler on a straight-line basis over 20 years, assuming a residual value of $250,000. Near the end of fiscal 2010 management decided to switch to declining balance amortization using a 10 percent rate. Rustico's year end is March 31.

Required:

a. Prepare the journal entry to record the purchase of the trawler in 2003.
b. What would be the original amortization expense for the trawler in fiscal 2004, 2005, and 2006? Prepare the journal entry to record the amortization expense in each of these years.
c. What would be the amortization expense for the trawler in 2004, 2005, and 2006 after Rustico changed to the declining-balance method?
d. Suppose the trawler was sold in 2018 for $390,000. Prepare the journal entry to record the sale. Assume declining-balance amortization was being used by Rustico.

E11-18. **(Calculate financial ratios, LO 7)** Utterson Inc. (Utterson) is a small manufacturing company located in northern Ontario. Utterson's owner has approached you to take an equity position in the company. The owner has provided for your review balance sheets for the last two years. In addition you have learned that net income in 2009 was $35,000, interest expense was $11,000, $5,000 in dividends was paid on the preferred stock, and no dividends were paid on the common shares. Utterson's tax rate is 18 percent. The estimated market value of Utterson's shares on December 31, 2009 was $15 per share, the weighted average number of shares outstanding during 2009 was 20,000, and there were 25,000 shares outstanding on December 31, 2009.

Utterson Inc.
Balance Sheets
As of December 31,

	2009	2008		2009	2008
Assets			**Liabilities and Shareholders' Equity**		
Current assets	$100,000	$ 90,000	Current liabilities	$ 75,000	$ 73,000
Non-current assets	260,000	240,000	Long-term debt	110,000	127,000
			Preferred stock	25,000	25,000
			Common stock	70,000	50,000
			Retained earnings	80,000	55,000
			Total liabilities and		
Total assets	$360,000	$330,000	shareholders equity	$360,000	$330,000

Required:

Calculate the following ratios for 2009: Current ratio, debt-to-equity ratio, return on assets, return on equity, basic earning per share, and price-to-book ratio.

Problems

P11-1. (**Explaining the differences between preferred shares, LO 2**) Exhibit 11–2 (page 606) provides a description of Bank of Montreal's preferred shares. Class B—Series 4 and 5 were both issued in 1998 and have very similar features, yet the Series 5 shares pay a dividend that is about $0.13 more per year than the Series 4 shares. Examine the features of the Class B—Series 4 and Series 5 preferred shares and provide some possible explanations for why the dividends on the shares are different but they were sold for the same price.

P11-2. (**Effect of transactions and economic events on ratios, LO 2, 3, 5, 6, 7**) Complete the following table by indicating whether the listed transactions or economic events would increase, decrease, or have no effect on the financial ratios listed. Explain your reasoning and state any assumptions that you make.

	Debt-to-equity ratio	Current ratio	Return on equity	Basic earnings per share	Price-to-book ratio	Return on assets
Ratio/amount before taking into the transaction/economic event into effect	0.9:1	1.3	11.5%	$3.42	1.8	7.1%
1. Issuance of common shares for cash						
2. Granting of stock options to employees						
3. Stock dividend						
4. Issuance of common shares in exchange for capital assets						
5. Declaration of a cash dividend on common shares						

P11-3. (**Effect of transactions and economic events on ratios, LO 2, 3, 5, 6, 7**) Complete the following table by indicating whether the listed transactions or economic events would increase, decrease, or have no effect on the financial ratios listed. Explain your reasoning and state any assumptions that you make.

	Debt-to-equity ratio	Current ratio	Return on equity	Basic earnings per share	Price-to-book ratio	Return on assets
Ratio/amount before taking into the transaction/economic event into effect	1.8:1	1.6	9.8%	$1.82	2.5	6.5%
1. Three-for-one stock split						
2. Payment of a cash dividend that was declared in the previous fiscal year						
3. Repurchase of common shares for cash						
4. Issuance of preferred shares for cash						
5. Declaration of a property dividend. The property being distributed has a book value that is greater than its market value.						

P11-4. **(The effects of leverage, LO 5)** Chitek Inc. (Chitek) is an oil and gas exploration company operating in northern Canada. Chitek has not yet begun extracting oil or gas from the ground, but it is close to the stage when extraction will occur. When Chitek was formed about 18 months ago, shareholders contributed $3,000,000 in exchange for 1,500,000 common shares in the company. Chitek now requires $2,000,000 of additional capital to exploit the resources that it believes it has discovered.

Chitek's CEO is considering two options: selling additional shares in the company or borrowing the required funds. If the company borrows, it will have to pay 10 percent interest per year. If it uses equity, it will have to sell 500,000 shares to raise the required amount of money.

Oil and gas exploration is a risky business. The performance of an oil and gas exploration company is subject to many factors, including the quantity of oil and gas that can be economically extracted from a particular location, the market price of the resource, and the ability of the entity to control its costs. Chitek's CEO has projected two possible outcomes: a good outcome and a poor outcome. Under the good outcome, the CEO estimates that income from operations (income before considering financing costs) will be $500,000 in the first year. Under the poor outcome, the CEO estimates that income from operations will be $125,000 in the first year.

Assume that Chitek has a tax rate of 25 percent and that all tax effects are reflected in operating income except for the tax effect of the additional debt or equity.

Required:

    a. Prepare partial income statements for Chitek assuming:
        i.   Equity financing of the additional $2,000,000 and the good outcome.
        ii. Equity financing of the additional $2,000,000 and the poor outcome.
        iii. Debt financing of the additional $2,000,000 and the good outcome.
        iv. Debt financing of the additional $2,000,000 and the poor outcome.
    b. Calculate basic earnings per share and return on shareholders' equity for the four scenarios described in (a).
    c. Explain the advantages and disadvantages of Chitek using debt, and the advantages and disadvantages of it using equity.
    d. If you were a prospective lender, would you lend $2,000,000 to Chitek? Explain.
    e. Would you advise Chitek to use debt or equity to obtain the additional $2,000,000? Explain.

P11-5. **(The effects of leverage, LO 5)** Greenway Television (Greenway) owns licences to operate eight new digital specialty television channels. Greenway was recently granted the licences by the CRTC and plans to begin broadcasting within six to eight months. Greenway already has agreements in principle with cable and satellite operators to include Greenway's channels on their systems (although these agreements are not binding).

When Greenway was organized two years ago with the purpose of developing specialty channels, the company raised $10,000,000 by selling 4,000,000 common shares to investors. Now that Greenway has received its licenses from the CRTC, it is in need of an additional $10,000,000 to prepare the channels for going on air. Greenway's CEO is considering two options: selling additional shares in the company or borrowing the required funds. If the company borrows, it will have to pay 12 percent interest per year. If it uses equity, it will have to sell 2,000,000 shares to raise the required amount of money.

The success of Greenway has two main elements—subscribers and advertising revenues. The more subscribers it has and the more money advertisers are prepared to spend to buy advertising time on a channel, the more financially successful Greenway will be. Once the channels are operating, Greenway will receive a fixed fee for each person who subscribes to a channel. Cable and satellite operators sometimes bundle channels, so if a channel is bundled with other channels that are very attractive to viewers, the channel in question will generate revenues regardless of whether many people watch it.

Greenway's CEO has projected two possible outcomes: a good outcome and a poor outcome. Under the good outcome, the CEO estimates that income from operations (income before considering financing costs) will be $3,000,000 in the first year. Under the poor outcome, the CEO estimates that income from operations will be $600,000 in the first year.

Assume that Greenway has a tax rate of 35 percent and that all tax effects are reflected in operating income except for the tax effect of the additional debt or equity.

Required:

a. Prepare partial income statements for Greenway assuming:
   i. Equity financing of the additional $10,000,000 and the good outcome.
   ii. Equity financing of the additional $10,000,000 and the poor outcome.
   iii. Debt financing of the additional $10,000,000 and the good outcome.
   iv. Debt financing of the additional $10,000,000 and the poor outcome.
b. Calculate basic earnings per share and return on shareholders' equity for the four scenarios described in (a).
c. Explain the advantages and disadvantages of Greenway using debt, and the advantages and disadvantages of it using equity.
d. If you were a prospective lender, would you lend $5,000,000 to Greenway? Explain.
e. Would you advise Greenway to use debt or equity to obtain the additional $5,000,000? Explain.

P11-6. **(Effect of employee stock options, LO 6, 7)** At its annual meeting in March 2009 the shareholders of Jasper Inc. (Jasper) approved an employee stock option plan that allows the company's board of directors to grant stock options to certain employees as part of their compensation packages. During the year ended December 31, 2009 the board granted 200,000 options to its senior executives. The stock options were issued when Jasper's shares had a market price of $22 per share. The exercise price of the options is $24 per share.

During fiscal 2009, Jasper earned revenues of $37,345,000, and had cost of sales of $18,525,000; selling, general, and administrative expenses of $4,560,000; interest expense of $3,535,000; other expenses of $5,700,000; and an income tax expense of $1,340,000. The economic value of the stock options when they were issued was $1,200,000.

On December 31, 2008, the equity section showed the following:

Capital stock (unlimited number of common shares authorized; 7,000,000 outstanding)	$21,500,000
Retained earnings	18,950,000

During fiscal 2009 Jasper did not issue or repurchase any common shares. Dividends of $0.10 were declared and paid during the year.

Required:

a. Prepare Jasper's income statement for the year ended December 31, 2009.
b. Calculate basic earnings per share and return on shareholders' equity assuming that the value of the stock options is expensed when granted and assuming they are not expensed.
c. What effect on cash flow do the two accounting treatments for employee stock options have?
d. Which accounting approach do you think Jasper's managers would prefer? Explain.

e. Which accounting approach do you think gives a better representation of Jasper's economic performance?

f. If Jasper did not accrue the cost of the options in its financial statements, what information would you want disclosed about them? Explain.

P11-7. (**Stock splits and dividends, LO 3, 7**) During the year ended June 30, 2010 Ingonish Inc. (Ingonish) reported the following equity events:

September 15, 2009	10 percent stock dividend
December 15, 2009	Three-for-one stock split
May 15, 2010	$1 dividend per share

The equity section of Ingonish's balance sheet on June 30, 2009 was as follows:

Common stock (unlimited number of shares authorized; 1,000,000 issued and outstanding)	$5,750,000
Retained earnings	12,450,000

Net income for fiscal 2010 was $3,500,000. In previous years Ingonish has paid its shareholders annual dividends of $2.50 per share.

Required:

a. Prepare Ingonish's shareholders' equity section on June 30, 2010.

b. Calculate basic earnings per share for fiscal 2010. What would EPS have been had the stock split and stock dividend not occurred?

c. As an Ingonish shareholder, what is your reaction to the reduction in the per share dividend from $2.50 per share to $1 per share?

d. The market value of Ingonish's shares on June 30, 2010 was $18.20 per share. What do you estimate the market price of the shares would have been had the stock dividend and stock split not occurred? Explain your answer.

e. Calculate Ingonish's market-to-book ratio on June 30, 2010. What would the market-to-book ratio have been had the stock split and stock dividend not occurred?

P11-8. (**Stock splits and dividends, LO 3, 7**) During the year ended November 30, 2009 Aguanish Inc. (Aguanish) reported the following equity events:

February 15, 2009	10 percent stock dividend
March 15, 2009	Annual preferred dividend of $3 per share
May 15, 2009	Four-for-one stock split
August 15, 2009	$1 dividend per share

The equity section of Aguanish's balance sheet on November 30, 2008 was as follows:

Preferred shares (authorized, issued, and outstanding: 200,000	$4,000,000
Common stock (unlimited number of shares authorized; 2,000,000 issued and outstanding)	18,500,000
Retained earnings	23,450,000

Net income for fiscal 2009 was $6,500,000. In previous years Aguanish has paid its common shareholders annual dividends of $5 per share.

Required:

a. Prepare Aguanish's shareholders' equity section on November 30, 2009.

b. Calculate basic earnings per share for fiscal 2010. What would EPS have been had the stock split and stock dividend not occurred?

c. As an Aguanish shareholder, what is your reaction to the reduction in the per share dividend from $5 per share to $1 per share?

d. The market value of Aguanish's shares on November 30, 2009 was $20 per share. What do you estimate the market price of the shares would have been had the stock dividend and stock split not occurred? Explain your answer.

e. Calculate Aguanish's market-to-book ratio on November 30, 2009. What would the market-to-book ratio have been had the stock split and stock dividend not occurred? Explain your answer.

P11-9. **(Effect of employee stock options, LO 6, 7)** At its annual meeting in June 2010 the shareholders of Rusylvia Ltd. (Rusylvia) approved an employee stock option plan that allows the company's board of directors to grant stock options to certain employees as part of their compensation packages. During the year ended March 31, 2011 the board granted 200,000 options to its senior executives. The stock options were issued when Rusylvia's shares had a market price of $10 per share. The exercise price of the options is $10.25 per share.

During fiscal 2011, Rusylvia earned revenues of $34,500,000, and had cost of sales of $15,200,000; selling, general, and administrative expenses of $4,800,000; interest expense of $3,500,000; other expenses of $5,900,000; and an income tax expense of $1,220,000. The economic value of the stock options when they were issued was $1,800,000.

On March 31, 2010, the equity section showed the following:

Capital stock:

Preferred shares (unlimited number authorized; 400,000 outstanding, $3 annual dividend, cumulative)	$16,000,000
Common shares (unlimited number authorized; 8,000,000 outstanding)	9,000,000
Retained earnings	14,850,000

On February 1, 2011 Rusylvia issued 600,000 shares of common stock for $10 per share. In March 2011 Rusylvia declared and paid the dividend on the preferred shares and declared and paid a cash dividend of $0.25 per share on the common shares.

Required:

a. Prepare Rusylvia's income statement for the year ended March 31, 2011.

b. Calculate basic earnings per share and return on shareholders' equity assuming that the value of the stock options is expensed when granted and assuming they are not expensed.

c. What effect on cash flow do the two accounting treatments for employee stock options have?

d. Which accounting approach do you think Rusylvia's managers would prefer? Explain.

e. Which accounting approach do you think gives a better representation of Rusylvia's economic performance?

f. If Rusylvia did not accrue the cost of the options in its financial statements, what information would you want disclosed about them? Explain.

P11-10. **(Hybrid securities, LO 2)** In May 2009 Kugluktuk Ltd. (Kugluktuk) sold $200,000 in convertible bonds to investors. The bonds have a coupon rate of 9 percent and mature in May 2019. The bonds are convertible into common shares at the option of the company. The terms of the bond agreement make it highly likely that the bonds will be converted before they mature. Kugluktuk's summarized balance sheet just before the convertible bonds were sold was:

Kugluktuk Ltd.
Summarized Balance Sheet
(Just before the sale of convertible bonds)

Assets	$2,400,000	Liabilities	$1,000,000
		Shareholders' equity	1,400,000
		Total liabilities and shareholders'	
Total assets	$2,400,000	equity	$2,400,000

Required:

    a. Do you think that the convertible bonds are really debt or equity? Explain. (Consider the characteristics of debt and equity in your response.)

    b. Prepare the journal entry to record the issuance of the convertible bond and calculate the resulting debt-to-equity ratio, assuming that the bonds are classified as debt.

    c. Prepare the journal entry to record the issuance of the convertible bond and calculate the resulting debt-to-equity ratio, assuming that the bonds are classified as equity.

    d. How do you think Kugluktuk's management would want to classify the convertible bonds for accounting purposes? Explain.

    e. How do you think Kugluktuk's management would want to classify the convertible bonds for tax purposes? Explain.

    f. How do you think Kugluktuk's management would account for the convertible bonds if the classification for tax purposes had to be the same as the classification for accounting purposes?

    g. Does it matter how the convertible bonds are classified? Explain.

P11-11. **(Hybrid securities, LO 2)** In August 2010 Ethelbert Ltd. (Ethelbert) issued 10,000 shares of cumulative, redeemable preferred stock to investors for $500,000. The preferred shares pay an annual dividend of $4 per share and are redeemable beginning in 2015. Ethelbert must redeem the preferred shares before September 1, 2024. Ethelbert's summarized balance sheet just before the preferred shares were sold was:

Ethelbert Ltd.
Summarized Balance Sheet
(Just before the sale of preferred shares)

Assets	$4,400,000	Liabilities	$2,000,000
		Shareholders' equity	2,400,000
		Total liabilities and shareholders'	
Total assets	$4,400,000	equity	$4,400,000

Required:

    a. Do you think that the preferred shares are really debt or equity? Explain. (Consider the characteristics of debt and equity in your response.)

    b. Prepare the journal entry to record the issuance of the preferred shares and calculate the resulting debt-to-equity ratio, assuming that the shares are classified as debt.

    c. Prepare the journal entry to record the issuance of the preferred shares and calculate the resulting debt-to-equity ratio, assuming that the shares are classified as equity.

    d. How do you think Ethelbert's management would want to classify the preferred shares for accounting purposes? Explain.

    e. How do you think Ethelbert's management would want to classify the preferred shares for tax purposes? Explain.

    f. How do you think Ethelbert's management would account for the preferred shares if the classification for tax purposes had to be the same as the classification for accounting purposes?

    g. Does it matter how the preferred shares are classified? Explain.

P11-12. **(Analyzing the effects of different financing alternatives, LO 2, 7)** Owakonze Inc. (Owakonze) is in need of $2,000,000 to finance an expansion of its operations. Management is considering three financing alternatives:

    i. Issue 200,000 common shares to a group of private investors for $10 per share. In recent years dividends of $0.40 per share have been paid on the common shares.

ii. Issue 80,000 cumulative preferred shares with an annual dividend of $2 per share for $25 per share. The preferred shares are redeemable after 10 years for $27 per share.

iii. Issue a $2,000,000 bond with a coupon rate of 11 percent per year and maturity in 15 years.

It is now late July 2009. Owakonze's year end is July 31. Owakonze plans to raise the needed money at the beginning of its 2010 fiscal year, but management wants to know the financial statement effects and implications of each of the alternatives. Owakonze's accounting department has provided the right-hand side of the balance sheet as of July 31, 2009 and a summarized projected income statement for the year ended July 31, 2010. The projected statements do not reflect any of the proposed financing alternatives. If the current expansion plan is successful, Owakonze anticipates the need to raise additional money in the near future. One of Owakonze's loans has a covenant that requires the debt-to-equity ratio be below 1:1. Owakonze has a tax rate of 30 percent.

Owakonze Ltd.
Summarized Projected Income Statement as of July 31, 2010

Revenue	$3,800,000
Expenses	2,800,000
Income tax expense	300,000
Net income	$ 700,000

Owakonze Ltd.
Summarized Projected Liabilities and Shareholders' Equity as of July 31, 2009

Liabilities	$1,500,000
Shareholders' equity:	
Preferred stock (400,000 shares authorized, 0 issued)	0
Common stock (unlimited number of shares authorized, 400,000 outstanding)	1,900,000
Retained earnings	1,600,000
Total liabilities and shareholders' equity	$5,000,000

Required:

a. Calculate net income for Owakonze under the three financing alternatives.

b. Calculate basic earnings per share and return on shareholders' equity under the three financing alternatives.

c. Prepare a report to Owakonze's management explaining the effect of each of the financing alternatives on the financial statements. Include in your report a discussion of the pros and cons of each financing alternative. Also, make a recommendation as to which alternative it should choose. Support your recommendation.

P11-13. (**Different ways of looking at income, LO 2, 7**) In the traditional income statement prepared in accordance with GAAP, net income is thought of as the increase of wealth that belongs to the owners of the entity. In this view, interest is an expense, whereas dividends are a reduction of retained earnings. However, this is only one way to view an entity and its financial statements. Net income could also be calculated by expensing both interest and dividends. Another alternative would not treat interest, dividends, or income taxes as expenses.

During the year ended December 31, 2009 Atnarko Ltd. (Atnarko) had revenues of $1,225,000, expenses of $750,000, and income taxes of $118,500. In addition, Atnarko incurred interest costs of $75,000, and declared preferred share dividends of $35,000 and common share dividends of $55,000.

Required:

a. Prepare an income statement for Atnarko using the traditional GAAP approach. Explain why the measure of income is useful from the perspective of shareholders.

b. Devise three alternative measures of net income and prepare income statements on these bases. Explain which users of the income statement would find your alternative measures useful.

P11-14. **(Assessing the payment of dividends, LO 7)** Dunsinane Ltd. (Dunsinane) is a publicly traded manufacturing company that makes computer components for resale to end-product manufacturers. Extracts from the last five years' financial statements are shown below.

Dunsinane completed an expansion in 2009 that was financed by a share issuance made in late 2008. Management believes that cash from operations should now be fairly stable and the net cash outflows on investing activities should range between $450,000 and $750,000 per year. To date, Dunsinane has not faced the effects of any economic slowdowns. There is concern of the effects of a prolonged slowdown on Dunsinane's revenues, income, and cash flow. Dunsinane has access to a $500,000 line of credit secured against accounts receivable that it has not used to date. After two years of satisfactory and steady performance since the expansion was completed, the board of directors is considering a proposal to implement an annual common share dividend. Dunsinane has never paid dividends before.

	2011	2010	2009	2008	2007
Assets					
Cash	$ 256,000	$ 187,500	$ 215,000	$ 950,000	$ 87,500
All other assets	$4,454,000	$3,855,000	$3,387,500	$2,250,000	$1,525,000
Total assets	$4,710,000	$4,042,500	$3,602,500	$3,200,000	$1,612,500
Liabilities	1,450,000	1,300,000	1,200,000	1,100,000	700,000
Shareholders' equity					
Capital stock (unlimited number of common shares authorized, 1,000,000 outstanding)	1,882,500	1,812,500	1,780,000	1,712,500	600,000
Retained earnings	1,377,500	930,000	622,500	387,500	312,500
Total shareholders' equity	3,260,000	2,742,500	2,402,500	2,100,000	912,500
Total liabilities and shareholders' equity	$4,710,000	$4,042,500	$ 3,602,500	$3,200,000	$ 1,612,500
Extracts from the cash flow statement					
Cash from operations	$ 565,000	$ 487,500	$ (125,000)	$ (37,500)	$ 112,500
Cash spent on investing activities	(382,500)	(300,000)	(775,000)	(600,000)	(450,000)

Required:

Prepare a report to Dunsinane's board of directors, assessing the pros and cons of implementing an annual common share dividend. Identify additional information that you would want so you could make a definitive decision. If you recommend that a dividend should be paid, what amount per share should be paid? Provide support for your positions.

P11-15. **(Accounting for a change in accounting estimate, LO 4, 7)** On October 1, 2006 Independent Manufacturing Inc. (Independent) purchased a state-of-the-art mould-casting machine for its manufacturing facility for $4,100,000. Independent's management estimated that the machine would be useful for eight years, at which time it could be sold for $250,000. Independent uses straight-line amortization on all its capital assets. In September 2010, management realized that because of rapid technological changes, the machine would not likely be useful beyond fiscal 2012. Therefore, Independent decided to shorten its estimate of the machine's useful life to six years and reduce the estimated residual value to zero. Independent's year end is September 30.

Required:

a. Is the change being made by Independent considered a change in accounting policy or a change in accounting estimate? Explain. How would the change be accounted for?

b. What amortization expense would Independent have originally reported in fiscal 2007, 2008, and 2009 for the mould-casting machine?

c. What amortization expense would Independent have reported in fiscal 2007, 2008, and 2009 for the mould-casting machine after the accounting change had been made?

d. What amortization expense will Independent report for the year ended September 30, 2010?

e. What are the implications of this change to users of the financial statements? Explain.

f. Do you think that this type of change can be objectively made? Explain. What possible motivations could Independent's managers have for making the change? Explain.

P11-16. **(Accounting for a change in accounting policy, LO 4, 7)** On October 1, 2006, Eureka Corp. (Eureka) purchased state-of-the-art equipment for $5,100,000. Eureka's management estimated that the machine would be useful for six years, at which time the equipment could be sold for $250,000. Eureka's management decided that it would use declining-balance amortization at 25 percent per year for the equipment. In fiscal 2010 management decided that it would switch from declining-balance amortization to straight-line amortization. Management estimated that the equipment had a remaining useful life of four years from September 2010 (eight years from its initial purchase in 2006). Eureka's year end is September 30.

Required:

a. Is the change being made by Eureka considered a change in accounting policy or a change in accounting estimate? Explain. How should the change be accounted for?

b. What amortization expense would Eureka have originally reported in 2007, 2008, and 2009 for the equipment?

c. What amortization expense would Eureka have reported in fiscal 2007, 2008, and 2009 for the equipment after the accounting change had been made?

d. What amortization expense will Eureka report for the year ended September 30, 2010?

e. What are the implications of this change to users of the financial statements? Explain.

f. How do you think Eureka's management could justify the change in accounting? Is it possible that the change could satisfy the self-interests of Eureka's management? Explain.

P11-17. **(Examining financial statements, LO 1, 7)** The Convenience Store (or The Store) is a family-run, unincorporated business owned and operated by the Shar family. The Store offers food staples, basic household goods, newspapers and magazines, and candy, drinks, and snacks. The Store is operated 80 percent of the time by family members. Family members are not paid regular salaries. Instead, cash is distributed to family members as they require it. Income is allocated to family members with the purpose of minimizing taxes. Local people are hired to work in the store at other times, and they are paid the minimum wage.

The store is operated out of a building owned by the Shar family. The family lives in a large apartment above the store. The building has a 6 percent, $235,000 mortgage. The Shar family obtains most of its food and household needs from the shelves of The Convenience Store. The Shar family also often purchase goods and services through The Store for their own use. The Store has a fairly simple accounting system. Inventory is kept track of manually. Sales are recorded when a transaction is "rung up" on the cash register. Not all transactions are rung up.

The Shar family has earned a satisfactory living from The Convenience Store, but running a store of this type is difficult because it is necessary to be open for business 18 hours a day, seven days a week. A representative of a small chain of convenience stores has recently approached the Shar family with a proposal to buy The Convenience Store. The chain's executives feel the area where The Convenience Store operates has reached the necessary density to justify one of the chain's stores. The chain could open its store elsewhere in the area, but the executives feel that if it could buy The Convenience Store at a reasonable price it would obtain the best location in the area for the store and remove a source of competition.

As part of the negotiations, The Convenience Store has provided its income statements for the last two years to the chain. This is the first time that the chain has attempted to purchase an unincorporated, family-run store, and the controller is not sure what to make of the income statements. The controller has asked you to examine The Convenience Store's income statements and to prepare a report identifying and explaining any concerns you have with them. The controller would also like you to indicate any other information that should be obtained and explain the purpose of the information.

The Convenience Store
Income Statements
For the Years Ended December 31, 2006 and 2007

	2006	2007
Revenue	$285,000	$275,025
Cost of merchandise sold	151,050	152,364
Wages	11,900	11,662
Utilities	13,200	13,464
Supplies	11,300	11,074
Amortization of capital assets*	15,900	15,900
Advertising and promotion	7,500	7,000
Interest on bank loans and mortgage	18,100	17,738
Other expenses	20,200	21,000
Net income	$35,850	$24,823

*Amortization is based on rates specified in the *Income Tax Act*.

Required:

Prepare the report requested by the controller.

Using Financial Statements

FIRSTSERVICE CORPORATION

FirstService Corporation (FirstService) is a leader in the rapidly growing service sector, serving customers in the following areas: residential property management; commercial real estate; integrated security services; property improvement services; and business services. FirstService's business model is based on decentralized operations and management ownership, and grows through internal initiatives and selective acquisitions.

Market-leading brands include Continental, Wentworth and Prime Management in residential property management; Colliers International in commercial real estate; Intercon Security and SST in integrated security services; California Closets, Paul Davis Restoration, Pillar to Post Home Inspection, CertaPro and College Pro Painters in property improvement; and Resolve Corporation in business services. FirstService's annual revenues exceed US $1 billion.

FirstService's consolidated balance sheets, statements of earnings, retained earnings, and cash flow, and extracts from the notes to the financial statements are provided in Exhibit 11–5. Use this information to respond to questions FS11-1 to FS11-8.[10]

www.firstservice.ca

FS11-1. Examine the information provided in Exhibit 11–8 and find the following information:
   a. Retained earnings on March 31, 2004 and 2005.
   b. Dividends paid on common and preferred shares in 2004 and 2005.
   c. Total shareholders' equity on March 31, 2004 and 2005.
   d. Balance in the capital stock account on March 31, 2004 and 2005.
   e. Net income for the years ended March 31, 2004 and 2005.
   f. Net assets on March 31, 2004 and 2005.
   g. Contributed surplus on March 31, 2004 and 2005.
   h. Comprehensive earnings for fiscal 2004 and 2005.

FS11-2. Use the information provided in Exhibit 11–8 and calculate the following ratios for the years ended March 31, 2004 and 2005. Interpret and explain your findings. Assume that shareholders' equity on March 31, 2003 was $123,406,000:
   a. Earnings per share.
   b. Return on shareholders' equity.
   c. Debt-to-equity ratio.

FS11-3. Examine FirstService's Statement of Shareholders' Equity and Note 13 to the financial statements and respond to the following questions:
   a. Describe the different types of shares that FirstService is authorized to issue. How do the classes differ and how are they the same?
   b. How many shares of each class were outstanding on March 31, 2005?
   c. How many shares of each class were issued during fiscal 2005?
   d. How much capital (cash and property) was contributed by each class of share?
   e. Why do you think FirstService has these different classes of common shares?

FS11-4. FirstService's multiple voting shares are not traded publicly. They are closely held by of the company's CEO. What proportion of total shares are the multiple voting shares? What proportion of the total votes do the multiple voting shares have? Why do you think the multiple voting shares exist?

FS11-5. Use the information in Exhibit 11–8 to respond to the following questions:
   a. How many of its shares were repurchased by FirstService during fiscal 2005? What type of shares were repurchased?
   b. What was the total amount paid by FirstService to repurchase its shares? What was the average price paid for each share repurchased?
   c. What is the journal entry that FirstService would have made to record the repurchase of shares in fiscal 2005?
   d. How would you expect the repurchase of shares to appear in the cash flow statement? Explain.

FS11-6. Examine the information in Note 13 to FirstService's financial statements pertaining to the company's stock option plan and respond to the following questions:
   a. Describe the terms of the share compensation plan.
   b. How many employee stock options were outstanding on March 31, 2005? How many of the stock options could be exercised on March 31, 2005?

650

FirstService Corporation
Consolidated Statements of Earnings in thousands of US Dollars, except per share amounts
in accordance with generally accepted accounting principles in the United States

For the years ended March 31	2005	2004	2003
Revenues	$ 812,290	$ 593,782	$ 508,675
Cost of revenues (exclusive of depreciation shown below)	526,623	408,327	345,524
Selling, general and administrative expenses (note 5)	206,904	130,934	112,563
Depreciation	15,320	12,824	11,319
Amortization of intangibles other than brokerage backlog	3,140	2,212	1,837
Amortization of brokerage backlog	8,735	-	
	51,568	39,485	37,432
Other income, net (note 6)	(375)	(1,116)	(1,106)
Interest expense	11,019	7,900	8,934
Earnings before income taxes and minority interest	40,924	32,701	29,604
Income taxes (note 14)	11,338	9,815	8,036
Earnings before minority interest	29,586	22,886	21,568
Minority interest share of earnings	6,941	3,224	3,115
Net earnings from continuing operations	22,645	19,662	18,453
Net earnings (loss) from discontinued operations, net of income taxes (note 4)	562	(638)	(13)
Net earnings	$ 23,207	$ 19,024	$ 18,440

Net earnings (loss) per share (note 15)			
Basic			
Continuing operations	$ 0.76	$ 0.69	$ 0.66
Discontinued operations	0.02	(0.02)	-
	$ 0.78	$ 0.67	$ 0.66
Diluted			
Continuing operations	$ 0.72	$ 0.67	$ 0.64
Discontinued operations	0.02	(0.02)	-
	$ 0.74	$ 0.65	$ 0.64

FirstService Corporation
Consolidated Balance Sheets in thousands of US Dollars
in accordance with generally accepted accounting principles in the United States

As at March 31	2005	2004
Assets		
Current assets		
Cash and cash equivalents	$ 37,458	$ 15,620
Accounts receivable, net of an allowance of $8,471 (2004 - $3,976)	168,927	97,367
Income taxes recoverable	2,498	-
Inventories (note 7)	20,878	15,229
Prepaids and other (note 7)	12,591	15,659
Deferred income taxes (note 14)	6,418	3,358
	248,770	147,233
Other receivables (note 8)	7,077	5,397
Interest rate swaps (note 17)	283	6,805
Fixed assets (note 9)	57,241	49,826
Other assets (note 9)	6,402	2,829
Deferred income taxes (note 14)	8,992	2,167
Intangible assets (note 10)	61,423	37,717
Goodwill (note 11)	236,540	185,579
	377,958	290,320
	$ 626,728	$ 437,553
Liabilities		
Current liabilities		
Accounts payable	$ 41,905	$ 20,526
Accrued liabilities (note 7)	113,524	49,353
Income taxes payable	3,673	1,985
Unearned revenue	5,154	9,736
Long-term debt - current (note 12)	18,206	3,502
Deferred income taxes (note 14)	320	1,266
	182,782	86,368
Long-term debt - non-current (note 12)	201,809	160,386
Deferred income taxes (note 14)	29,802	19,594
Minority interest	26,464	16,104
	258,075	196,084
Shareholders' equity		
Capital stock (note 13)	73,542	68,557
Issued and outstanding: 28,867,094 (2004 - 28,174,036) Subordinate Voting Shares and 1,325,694 (2004 - 1,325,694) convertible Multiple Voting Shares		
Contributed surplus (note 13)	805	183
Receivables pursuant to share purchase plan (note 13)	(2,148)	(2,148)
Retained earnings	103,011	81,972
Cumulative other comprehensive earnings	10,661	6,537
	185,871	155,101
	$ 626,728	$ 437,553

EXHIBIT 11–8 :

(continued)
FirstService
Corporation
Extracts from
Financial
Statements

FirstService Corporation
Consolidated Statements of Shareholders' Equity in thousands of US Dollars
in accordance with generally accepted accounting principles in the United States

	Issued and outstanding shares (note 13)	Capital stock	Contributed surplus	Receivables pursuant to share purchase plan	Retained earnings	Cumulative other comprehensive earnings (loss)	Total shareholders' equity
Balance, March 31, 2002	27,550,530	$ 57,712	$ -	$ (2,630)	$ 44,765	$ (626)	$ 99,221
Comprehensive earnings:							
Net earnings	-	-	-	-	18,440	-	18,440
Foreign currency translation adjustments	-	-	-	-	-	2,947	2,947
Comprehensive earnings							21,387
Subordinate Voting Shares:							
Stock options exercised	843,250	3,002	-	-	-	-	3,002
Purchased for cancellation	(65,400)	(143)	-	-	(257)	-	(400)
Cash payments on share purchase plan	-	-	-	196	-	-	196
Balance, March 31, 2003	28,328,380	60,571	-	(2,434)	62,948	2,321	123,406
Comprehensive earnings:							
Net earnings	-	-	-	-	19,024	-	19,024
Foreign currency translation adjustments	-	-	-	-	-	4,216	4,216
Comprehensive earnings							23,240
Subordinate Voting Shares:							
Stock option expense	-	-	322	-	-	-	322
Stock options exercised	1,171,350	7,986	(139)	-	-	-	7,847
Cash payments on share purchase plan	-	-	-	286	-	-	286
Balance, March 31, 2004	29,499,730	68,557	183	(2,148)	81,972	6,537	155,101
Comprehensive earnings:							
Net earnings	-	-	-	-	23,207	-	23,207
Foreign currency translation adjustments (note 4)	-	-	-	-	-	4,124	4,124
Comprehensive earnings							27,331
Subordinate Voting Shares:							
Stock option expense	-	-	622	-	-	-	622
Stock options exercised	911,130	5,515	-	-	-	-	5,515
Purchased for cancellation	(218,072)	(530)	-	-	(2,168)	-	(2,698)
Balance, March 31, 2005	**30,192,788**	**$ 73,542**	**$ 805**	**$ (2,148)**	**$ 103,011**	**$ 10,661**	**$ 185,871**

FirstService Corporation
Consolidated Statements of Cash Flows in thousands of US Dollars
in accordance with generally accepted accounting principles in the United States

For the years ended March 31	2005	2004	2003
Cash provided by (used in)			
Operating activities			
Net earnings from continuing operations	$ 22,645	$ 19,662	$ 18,453
Items not affecting cash:			
Depreciation and amortization	27,195	15,036	13,156
Deferred income taxes	(5,287)	(683)	2,786
Minority interest share of earnings	6,941	3,224	3,115
Stock option expense	622	322	-
Other	341	(503)	(287)
Changes in operating assets and liabilities:			
Accounts receivable	(13,342)	(2,256)	9,661
Inventories	(6,425)	839	(4,292)
Prepaids and other	3,171	(1,069)	(1,042)
Accounts payable	(1,958)	(10,464)	(355)
Accrued liabilities	3,189	12,778	(6,629)
Income taxes payable	(1,028)	(1,670)	(1,503)
Unearned revenue	967	575	(3,033)
Net cash provided by operating activities	37,031	35,791	30,030
Investing activities			
Acquisitions of businesses, net of cash acquired	(56,869)	(16,019)	(9,561)
Purchases of minority shareholders' interests	(2,148)	(1,098)	(6,352)
Purchases of fixed assets	(17,028)	(13,121)	(9,335)
Purchases of intangible assets	(235)	(551)	(579)
Decrease (increase) in other assets	342	(163)	2,069
Decrease (increase) in other receivables	2,092	1,869	(578)
Net cash used in investing activities	(73,846)	(29,083)	(24,336)
Financing activities			
Increase in long-term debt	59,586	60,522	14,474
Repayment of long-term debt	(10,956)	(62,559)	(28,683)
Financing fees paid	(124)	(525)	-
Proceeds received on exercise of stock options	5,515	7,847	3,002
Repurchase of Subordinate Voting Shares	(2,698)	-	(400)
Collection of receivables pursuant to share purchase plan	-	286	196
Dividends paid to minority shareholders of subsidiaries	(606)	(510)	(191)
Net cash provided by (used in) financing activities	50,717	5,061	(11,602)
Net cash provided by (used in) discontinued operations	4,801	(1,052)	1,110
Effect of exchange rate changes on cash	3,135	(475)	2,844
Increase (decrease) in cash and cash equivalents during the year	21,838	10,242	(1,954)
Cash and cash equivalents, beginning of year	15,620	5,378	7,332
Cash and cash equivalents, end of year	$ 37,458	$ 15,620	$ 5,378

13. Capital stock

The authorized capital stock of the Company is as follows:

> An unlimited number of preference shares, issuable in series;
> An unlimited number of Subordinate Voting Shares having one vote per share; and
> An unlimited number of Multiple Voting Shares having 20 votes per share, convertible at any time into Subordinate Voting Shares at a rate of one Subordinate Voting Share for each Multiple Voting Share outstanding.

The following table provides a summary of total capital stock:

	Subordinate Voting Shares Number	Amount	Multiple Voting Shares Number	Amount	Total number	Total amount
Balance, March 31, 2003	27,002,686	$ 60,198	1,325,694	$ 373	28,328,380	$ 60,571
Balance, March 31, 2004	28,174,036	68,184	1,325,694	373	29,499,730	68,557
Balance, March 31, 2005	**28,867,094**	**73,169**	**1,325,694**	**373**	**30,192,788**	**73,542**

On December 15, 2004, the Company completed a 2 for 1 stock split effected in the form of a stock dividend. All stock balances for all periods presented have been retroactively adjusted to reflect the stock split.

In February 2004, the Company approved a long-term incentive plan ("LTIP") for the Chief Executive Officer ("CEO"). Under the LTIP, the CEO is entitled to receive a payment upon the arm's length sale of control of the Company or upon a distribution of the Company's assets to shareholders. The payment amount is determined with reference to the price per Subordinate Voting Share received by shareholders upon an arm's length sale or upon a distribution of assets. The right to receive the payment may be transferred among members of the CEO's family, their holding companies and trusts.

The Company's contributed surplus account relates to stock option compensation expense accounting under SFAS 123. Contributed surplus is credited at the time stock option compensation expense is recorded. As stock options are exercised, contributed surplus is reduced and capital stock is credited.

During the year ended March 31, 2005, the Company repurchased 218,072 (2004 - nil and 2003 - 65,400) Subordinate Voting Shares under a Normal Course Issuer Bid filed with the Toronto Stock Exchange, which allowed the Company to repurchase up to 5% of its outstanding shares on the open market during a twelve-month period.

The Company has $2,148 (C$3,034) (2004 - $2,148 (C$3,034)) of interest bearing loans receivable related to the purchase of 730,000 Subordinate Voting Shares (2004 – 730,000 shares). The loans, which are collateralized by the shares issued, have a ten-year term from the grant date; however, they are open for repayment at any time. The maturities of these loans are as follows, for the years ending March 31.

2006	$ -
2007	916
2008	467
2009	765
	$ 2,148

The Company has a stock option plan for certain officers and key full-time employees of the Company and its subsidiaries. Options are granted at the market price for the underlying shares on the date of grant. Each option vests over a four-year term and expires five years from the date granted and allows for the purchase of one Subordinate Voting Share. Options are exercisable in either US or Canadian dollars. At March 31, 2005, there were 1,844,000 options outstanding to 41 individuals at prices ranging from $6.00 to $17.29 (C$9.10 to C$21.40) per share, expiring on various dates through 2010. As at March 31, 2005, there were 333,500 options available for future grants.

The number of Subordinate Voting Shares issuable under options and the average option prices per share are as follows:

	Shares issuable under options			Weighted average price per share (US$)		
	2005	2004	2003	**2005**	2004	2003
Shares issuable under options - Beginning of year	**2,288,630**	3,565,980	4,238,230	**$ 8.01**	$ 7.98	$ 6.60
Granted	**496,500**	266,000	203,000	**13.63**	8.00	7.79
Exercised for cash	**(911,130)**	(1,171,350)	(843,250)	**6.42**	6.27	3.71
Expired or forfeited	**(30,000)**	(372,000)	(32,000)	**10.43**	11.83	9.50
Shares issuable under options - End of year	**1,844,000**	2,288,630	3,565,980	**$ 10.83**	$ 8.01	$ 7.98
Options exercisable - End of year	**915,500**	1,335,866	1,753,012			

	Weighted average price per share (C$)		
	2005	2004	2003
Shares issuable under options - Beginning of year	**$ 11.96**	$ 11.71	$ 10.53
Granted	**19.28**	11.95	12.07
Exercised for cash	**9.08**	9.37	5.74
Expired or forfeited	**14.75**	17.67	14.72
Shares issuable under options - End of year	**$ 15.31**	$ 11.96	$ 11.71

EXHIBIT 11–8 :

**(continued)
FirstService
Corporation
Extracts from
Financial
Statements**

The options outstanding as at March 31, 2005 to purchase Subordinate Voting Shares are as follows:

Range of exercise prices (US$)	Options outstanding			Options exercisable	
	Number outstanding	Weighted average remaining contractual life (years)	Weighted average exercise price (US$)	Number exercisable	Weighted average exercise price (US$)
$6.00 - $7.85	639,500	1.82	$ 6.93	449,750	$ 7.05
$9.82 - $11.02	475,000	3.83	11.36	124,000	11.28
$11.57 - $17.29	729,500	3.41	13.98	341,750	13.34
	1,844,000	2.91	$ 10.83	915,500	$ 10.12

Range of exercise prices (C$)	Options outstanding			Options exercisable	
	Number outstanding	Weighted average remaining contractual life (years)	Weighted average exercise price (C$)	Number exercisable	Weighted average exercise price (C$)
$9.10 - $12.50	639,500	1.82	$ 10.65	449,750	$ 10.82
$12.91 - $17.70	475,000	3.83	15.02	124,000	14.91
$18.44 - $21.40	729,500	3.41	19.58	341,750	18.69
	1,844,000	2.91	$ 15.31	915,500	$ 14.31

Prior to April 1, 2003, the Company had accounted for stock options under the intrinsic value method under APB 25. Had compensation expense for stock options been determined under the fair value method under SFAS 123 for all periods, pro forma reported net earnings and earnings per share would reflect the following:

	2005	2004	2003
Net earnings as reported	$ 23,207	$ 19,024	$ 18,440
Deduct: Stock-based compensation expense determined under fair value method, net of income taxes	(1,826)	(2,158)	(2,179)
Pro forma net earnings	$ 21,381	$ 16,866	$ 16,261
Pro forma net earnings per share:			
Basic	$ 0.72	$ 0.59	$ 0.59
Diluted	0.68	0.58	0.56
Reported net earnings per share:			
Basic	$ 0.78	$ 0.67	$ 0.66
Diluted	0.74	0.65	0.64
Assumptions:			
Risk-free interest rate	3.2%	3.0%	4.5%
Expected life in years	4.4	4.4	4.4
Volatility	30%	30%	30%
Dividend yield	0.0%	0.0%	0.0%

The weighted average fair values of options granted in 2005, 2004 and 2003 were $4.85 (C$6.20), $2.66 (C$3.59) and $2.55 (C$3.95) per share, respectively.

The Company has stock option plans at several of its subsidiaries. The impact of potential dilution from these plans is reflected in the Company's diluted earnings per share (note 15).

15. Earnings per share

Earnings per share information for all periods presented has been retroactively adjusted to reflect the 2 for 1 stock split that occurred on December 15, 2004.

The following table reconciles the numerators used to calculate diluted earnings per share:

	2005	2004	2003
Net earnings from continuing operations	$ 22,645	$ 19,662	$ 18,453
Dilution of net earnings resulting from assumed exercise of stock options in subsidiaries	(569)	-	-
Net earnings from continuing operations for diluted earnings per share calculation purposes	$ 22,076	$ 19,662	$ 18,453
Net earnings	$ 23,207	$ 19,024	$ 18,440
Dilution of net earnings resulting from assumed exercise of stock options in subsidiaries	(569)	-	-
Net earnings for diluted earnings per share calculation purposes	$ 22,638	$ 19,024	$ 18,440

The following table reconciles the denominators used to calculate earnings per share:

	2005	2004	2003
Shares issued and outstanding at beginning of year	29,499,730	28,328,380	27,550,530
Weighted average number of shares:			
Issued during the year	381,309	241,324	296,282
Repurchased during the year	(103,665)	-	(4,692
Weighted average number of shares used in computing basic earnings per share	29,777,374	28,569,704	27,842,120
Assumed exercise of stock options, net of shares assumed acquired under the Treasury Stock Method	689,597	621,952	1,152,970
Number of shares used in computing diluted earnings per share	30,466,971	29,191,656	28,995,090

c. How many options were granted during fiscal 2005? What was the average exercise price of the options granted during fiscal 2005? Prepare the journal entry that FirstService would have made to record the granting of the options.

d. How many options were exercised during fiscal 2005? What was the price paid for the shares purchased by the employees? Prepare the journal entry that FirstService would have made to record the exercise of the options in fiscal 2005.

e. How many options expired during fiscal 2005? Why would an employee allow an option to expire without exercising it?

f. What amount did FirstService expense in fiscal 2005 as a result of granting stock options to employees?

g. Why is the stock option expense added back to net income in the calculation of cash from operations?

h. What do you think is the purpose of FirstService's share compensation plan?

F11-7. What transactions or economic events gave rise to FirstService's contributed surplus balance on March 31, 2005. Provide the journal entries that resulted in the balance.

F11-8. During fiscal 2005, FirstService completed a stock split. Respond to the following questions about the stock split.
a. Describe the stock split.
b. What effect did the stock split have on the financial statements?
c. What journal entry would FirstService have recorded as a result of the stock split?
d. If you looked at the March 31, 2004 annual report, how many shares of each class of FirstService's common stock would you expect to see outstanding on March 31, 2004. Explain your answer.
e. What impact, if any, do you think the stock split would have on FirstService's earnings per share? Explain.
f. What impact, if any, do you think the stock split would have had on FirstService's stock price? Explain.

Analyzing Rogers Communications Inc.

◆ ROGERS™

R11-1. How much did shareholders contribute to Rogers in money and property for the purchase of common stock in the company as of December 31, 2005? What is the average amount paid per share by investors?

R11-2. What was Rogers' authorized capital stock on December 31, 2005? What is the par value of the authorized capital stock? How many shares were outstanding on December 31, 2005?

R11-3. On January 1, 2004 Rogers established an employee share accumulation plan. Describe the terms of the plan. How does Rogers account for its contribution to the purchase of shares by employees? Do you think that this treatment makes sense? Explain. Why do you think Rogers would offer such a plan?

R11-4. Calculate basic earnings per share and return on equity for 2004 and 2005. Assume shareholders' equity on December 31, 2003 was $1,109,594,000.

R11-5. How many new Class B non-voting common shares did Rogers issue during 2005? How much cash was raised from selling those shares? How would the transactions involving the sale of the shares be reported in the cash flow statement? How many shares were issued in non-cash transactions? Describe the non-cash transactions that gave rise to the issue of new Class B shares. How would these transactions be reported in the cash flow statement?

R11-6. How many Rogers' shares were purchased during fiscal 2005 by employees exercising their stock options? What was the average price paid for each share purchased? How much did Rogers receive in total from the employees exercising their stock options? Where in the statement of cash flows is this amount reported? Explain why it is reported there. Assuming that the average price during 2005 for Rogers' shares was $40, what was the economic gain employees enjoyed by exercising their options?

R11-7. How many stock options did Rogers grant its employees in fiscal 2005? What was the weighted-average exercise price of the options awarded in fiscal 2005? What journal entry did Rogers make during 2005 to record the effects that stock options had on the company during the year?

ENDNOTES

1. Extracted from Luscar Energy Partnership's 2004 annual report.

2. Extracted from the University of Ontario Institute of Technology's 2005 annual report.

3. Extracted from Torstar Corporation's 2005 annual report.

4. Extracted from the Bank of Montreal's 2005 annual report.

5. Extracted from BCE Inc.'s 2004 annual report.

6. Extracted from Talisman Energy Inc.'s 2004 and 2003 annual reports.

7. Extracted from Cogeco Cable Inc's 2004 annual report.

8. Extracted from Research In Motion Limited's 2006 annual report.

9. *The Globe and Mail*, May 9, 2006.

10. Extracted from FirstService Corporation's 2005 annual report.

INVESTMENTS IN OTHER COMPANIES

LEARNING OBJECTIVES

After studying the material in this chapter you will be able to:

▶ **LO 1** Understand why companies invest in other companies.

▶ **LO 2** Describe how corporations account for their subsidiaries.

▶ **LO 3** Discuss the accounting for investments where there is significant influence.

▶ **LO 4** Explain the accounting for passive investments.

In January 2004, Rogers Media bought a 50 percent interest in Dome Productions from Bell Globemedia's (BGM) CTV. The price? $21.3 million. Dome Productions was Canada's biggest mobile production and distribution company, based in Toronto and Montreal with a fleet of eight television trucks, including several that can transmit in High Definition.

Dome trucks and technicians broadcast Major League Baseball games, NHL hockey, and NBA basketball, as well as music concerts, including, in the summer of 2005, the Canadian portion of the Live-8 concert. For a whole day, Canadians could tune in to live performances by Sam Roberts, Neil Young, the Barenaked Ladies, and Blue Rodeo, among other performers who tried to raise awareness, and money, to fight hunger in Africa.

Sam Roberts at Live–8

Investing in Dome set Rogers up well for what is likely to be the company's most high-profile event yet: being co-host broadcaster with Bell Globemedia of both the 2010 Winter Olympics from Vancouver, and the 2012 Summer Olympics. Bell Globemedia and Rogers Communications paid $U.S. 153 million for the rights to broadcast both games, beating out the CBC. So what convinced the International Olympic Committee to give the Rogers–BGM consortium the winning bid?

"The overall coverage will be unprecedented in terms of quality and volume and will highlight the achievements of our athletes," said Tony Viner, then-President and CEO of Rogers Media Inc. at the time the winning bid was announced in February 2005.

Aside from fanning the Dome Production trucks out across Olympic venues to beam television to millions of viewers world-wide, BGM–Rogers planned to provide Olympics television coverage in Canada 24 hours a day, in English and French, totalling over 4,000 hours, using CTV, TQS (Tele-Quatre Saisons in Quebec) Omni.1, and Omni.2. They also planned to show Olympic sports on TSN, RDS, RIS Info Sports, and Rogers Sportsnet, as well as on the Outdoor Life Network. Rogers' local radio stations also had a role: to beef up Olympic coverage especially on Vancouver's News 1130, which plans to have games updates every 30 minutes.

Then there is the Rogers Wireless cell phone network and Bell Mobility's own wireless division, which are both likely to send Olympic content down the pipe to subscribers, not to mention coverage in magazines owned by Rogers and on other television stations like Discovery Channel, CTV Newsnet, Report on Business Television, and the Biography Channel.

But how did this Olympic marriage come about? Was it a meeting of strangers, or more a case of the girl-next-door? In fact, Rogers has long been partnered with Bell Globemedia in well-known initiatives before the investment in Dome Productions.

An earlier venture saw the pair set up Sportsnet, the all-sports channels seen from coast to coast. In 1998, Rogers, CTV, and Fox Cable Networks created the Sportsnet channels. Three years later, Rogers bought out the CTV stake, and in 2004, swallowed the remaining stake owned by Fox Cable. The Rogers Sportsnet studio in Ontario is located across the parking lot from the CTV National News with Lloyd Robertson's studios, in Scarborough, Ontario.

INTRODUCTION

◯ ROGERS™

One of the first things we pointed out when we looked at Rogers Communications Inc.'s (Rogers) financial statements for the first time in Chapter 2 was that the statements were consolidated. Rogers' financial statements combine the activities of Rogers Wireless, Rogers Cable, and Rogers Media, into a single set of financial statements.

Rogers isn't unusual. The financial statements of most public companies are consolidated. Consolidated financial statements are required under GAAP when one company (the parent) controls other companies (the subsidiaries).

Consolidated financial statements combine the financial statements of a parent and all its subsidiaries into a single set of financial statements. The idea behind consolidated financial statements is to provide financial information about an entire economic entity, rather than just the individual pieces. While the concept of consolidated financial statements is straightforward, it's among the most complicated topics in accounting. People who study to become accountants can spend an entire course on the subject.

Gaining control of another company is only one outcome of investment by one corporation in another. Some investments allow the investing corporation to influence the decisions of those companies, but not control them. Other investments, usually small ones, give the investing corporation no more influence than any small investor would have. These investments, with their different degrees of influence, are each accounted for differently.

In many ways, this topic, particularly the idea of consolidation, is beyond the scope of an introductory accounting course. However, because consolidated financial statements are encountered so frequently, and because accounts like Goodwill and Non-controlling Interest are so commonly seen in financial statements, it is important, even for the accounting novice, to be familiar with the subject.

To that end, this chapter will provide a discussion of how corporations account for investments in other corporations and how those investments affect the financial statements. The intent is to provide enough insight into how to account for investments so that you can understand and interpret financial statements, without being overwhelming. The appendix to this chapter will address some of the more complex aspects of this topic.

WHY DO COMPANIES INVEST IN OTHER COMPANIES?

There are many reasons why one company invests in another. The reason can be as simple as the need to find a place to invest a temporary surplus of cash. For example, companies in seasonal businesses may have excess cash on hand at certain points during a year. Or companies may accumulate cash over a period of time in anticipation of expansion or acquisitions. Prudent management requires that the cash not be idle—that it be invested to earn a reasonable return. This can be achieved by purchasing the debt or equity of other companies. Securities of other companies might be purchased because they represent good investment opportunities that will generate dividend, interest, and capital gains income for the investing company.

Companies might purchase competitors to reduce competition and expand its presence in a market. For example, in 2004 Rogers paid almost $1.4 billion in cash for the shares of Microcell Telecommunications Inc. This purchase made Rogers Canada's largest wireless service provider and increased its capacity to offer its wireless services across the country.

Some companies invest in other companies for strategic reasons—so that they can influence or control the decisions made by those companies. For example, in 2000 CanWest Global

Communications Corp. (CanWest) purchased the Canadian newspaper and Internet assets of Hollinger Inc. and a 50 percent partnership interest in the *National Post* newspaper for over $3 billion in cash, CanWest shares, and debt. (Soon afterwards, CanWest purchased the remaining 50 percent of the *National Post*.) CanWest made the investment to take advantage of media convergence by adding print and Internet businesses to its existing broadcasting and entertainment businesses.

Companies may also invest in their customers to provide markets for their products and in their suppliers to ensure the availability of needed inputs. For example, Imperial Oil Limited is a large producer, refiner, and marketer of petroleum products in Canada. By operating at all these levels, Imperial Oil ensures its refineries serve as guaranteed customers for the oil and gas it extracts from the ground, and its gas stations are customers for its gasoline and lubricants.

Companies may also purchase all or part of other companies to diversify. Some businesses are cyclical—their performance depends on where the economy is in the business cycle. Cyclical businesses will be profitable in some years and unprofitable in others. By diversifying their investments in different business and geographic areas, companies try to mitigate the effect of the business cycle. For example, Brascan Corporation has major investments in natural resources, energy, property, and financial management companies that are active in many parts of the world.

www.imperialoil.ca
www.brascancorp.com
www.canwest.com

ACCOUNTING FOR INVESTMENTS IN OTHER CORPORATIONS: INTRODUCTION

How an entity accounts for its investments in other corporations depends on the influence it has over those corporations. For accounting purposes, there are three levels of influence that an **investor corporation** (a corporation that has an investment in another corporation) can have over an **investee corporation** (a corporation in which an investor corporation has invested). (Throughout this chapter, the terms *investor* and *investee* will be used.) These levels of influence are:

1. Control. If an investor controls an investee, it can make all the investee's important decisions. An investee that is controlled is called a subsidiary of the investor, and the financial statements of the investor and investee are aggregated into a single set of consolidated financial statements.

2. Significant influence. If the investor does not control an investee, but can affect its important decisions, the investor corporation is said to have significant influence and, according to GAAP, should use the equity method of accounting.

3. Passive investment. If the investor has no influence over the decision making of the investee (or at least no more influence than any other small investor), the investment is called a passive investment and it is accounted for at cost or fair value, depending on the type of investment (we will discuss this further later in the chapter).

The different types of investments in other corporations are summarized in Figure 12–1. We will discuss each of the methods of accounting for investments in other corporations in detail in the following sections.

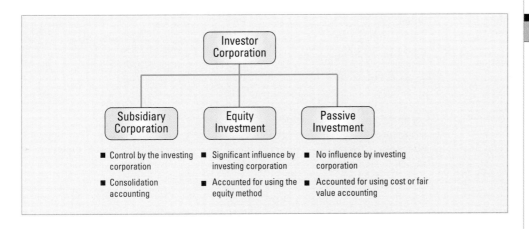

FIGURE 12–1

Types of Investments in Other Corporations

CONTROL: ACCOUNTING FOR SUBSIDIARIES

The first level of influence we will examine is control. When an investor has **control** of an investee, the investor is able to make the important decisions of the investee and determine its strategic operating, financing, and investing policies on an ongoing basis, without the support of other shareholders. In other words, the managers of the investor can set the key policies of the investee.

Control usually means that the investor owns more than 50 percent of the votes of the investee, although there are rare situations where an investor can have control with fewer than 50 percent of the votes. Note that 50 percent of the votes is not necessarily the same as 50 percent of the common shares. For example, Onex Corporation (Onex) controls a number of companies, despite owning less than 50 percent of the common shares. Onex owns 13 percent of the outstanding common shares of Celestica Inc., but has 79 percent of the votes. This is because each of the common shares that Onex owns has 25 votes, whereas the common shares held by other shareholders have only one vote each. Exhibit 12–1 lists the companies that Onex controls, the percentage of the common shares that it owns, and the percentage of the votes that it has.[1]

When an investor has control, it is often referred to as the **parent corporation** (parent) and the investee is called a **subsidiary corporation** (subsidiary). When an investor controls an investee, the investor prepares consolidated financial statements.

Consolidated financial statements aggregate the accounting information of a parent corporation and all of its subsidiaries into a single set of financial statements. This means that each line in a set of consolidated financial statements reflects the assets, liabilities, revenues, expenses, and cash flows of the parent and all its subsidiaries. A parent corporation may have many subsidiaries, each of which is reflected in the single set of consolidated financial statements. Figure 12–2 shows the corporate structure of Rogers. You can see that there are 15 separate corporations that are owned 100 percent and controlled by Rogers Communications Inc. and all of these are consolidated into the single set of financial statements that can be found in Appendix A.

Consolidated financial statements are an application of the entity assumption. The consolidated entity is a group of corporations that are under the control of a parent. The purpose of consolidated statements is to provide users who are interested in the parent—for example, shareholders of the parent—a single set of financial statements that reflect the assets, liabilities, equity, revenues, and expenses of all the corporations controlled by the parent.

EXHIBIT 12–1

Onex Corporation: Ownership and Voting Interests in Companies as Reported in its Consolidated Financial Statements

The principal operating companies and the Company's ownership and voting interests in these entities are as follows:

	December 31, 2005		December 31, 2004	
	Ownership	Voting	Ownership	Voting
Celestica	13%	79%	18%	84%
Cineplex Entertainment[a]	27%	100%	31%	100%
ClientLogic	68%	89%	68%	88%
J.L. French Automotive	77%	100%	77%	100%
Radian	90%	100%	89%	100%
Cosmetic Essence	22%	100%	21%	100%
Center for Diagnostic Imaging	20%	100%	–	–
Emergency Medical Services	29%	97%	–	–
Spirit AeroSystems	29%	100%	–	–
Skilled Healthcare	22%	100%	–	–
ONCAP	30%	100%	30%	100%
Magellan	–	–	6%	50%

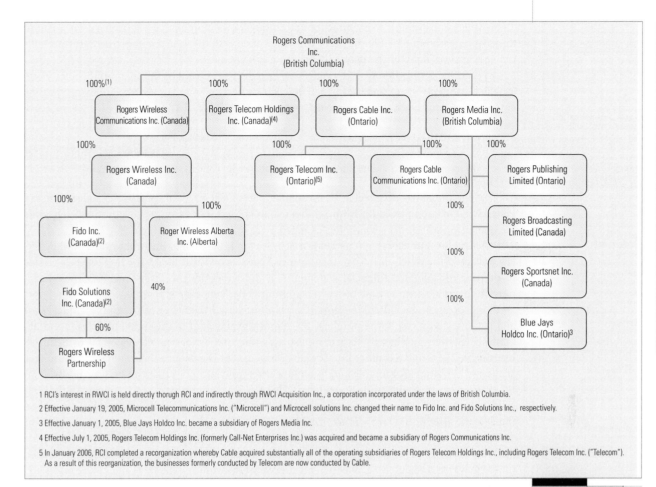

1 RCI's interest in RWCI is held directly thorugh RCI and indirectly through RWCI Acquisition Inc., a corporation incorporated under the laws of British Columbia.

2 Effective January 19, 2005, Microcell Telecommunications Inc. ("Microcell") and Microcell solutions Inc. changed their name to Fido Inc. and Fido Solutions Inc., respectively.

3 Effective January 1, 2005, Blue Jays Holdco Inc. became a subsidiary of Rogers Media Inc.

4 Effective July 1, 2005, Rogers Telecom Holdings Inc. (formerly Call-Net Enterprises Inc.) was acquired and became a subsidiary of Rogers Communications Inc.

5 In January 2006, RCI completed a reorganization whereby Cable acquired substantially all of the operating subsidiaries of Rogers Telecom Holdings Inc., including Rogers Telecom Inc. ("Telecom"). As a result of this reorganization, the businesses formerly conducted by Telecom are now conducted by Cable.

Rogers Corporate Organization

It is important to recognize that a consolidated group of companies is an accounting creation. The individual subsidiaries and the parent are each separate legal entities and each one must file its own tax return. Each corporation has its own limited legal liability. The consolidated group is not a legal entity and it does not file a tax return.

Conceptually, consolidated financial statements may sound simple—just a matter of adding together the individual financial statements of the parent and subsidiaries. In fact, preparing them is very complicated. Many adjustments must be made to arrive at the consolidated statements.

From an accounting perspective, the first event of consequence occurs when the investor purchases control of the investee. When the purchase is made, the investor records the investment at cost in its financial records. The investment is recorded in a single account that appears on the parent's balance sheet. (As we will see, the parent's financial statements are *not* the same as the consolidated financial statements.) In the consolidated balance sheet, the assets and liabilities of a subsidiary are recorded at the amount the parent paid for them. That is, the consolidated balance sheet reports the subsidiary's assets and liabilities at their cost to the parent on the date the subsidiary was purchased. However, on the subsidiary's own balance sheet, the assets and liabilities are reported at their cost to the subsidiary when the subsidiary purchased them.

There are, thus, two valuations for the subsidiary's assets and liabilities: the valuation used on the subsidiary's balance sheet, which is the cost to the subsidiary itself, and the valuation on the consolidated balance sheet, which is the cost to the parent. Both valuations are valid applications of GAAP. The two valuations represent the cost of the assets and liabilities at different times. Because the amounts that appear on the subsidiary's balance sheet are different from what is reported on the consolidated balance sheet, the balance sheets of the parent and the subsidiary can't simply be added together to get the consolidated amount.

We will use an example to examine the accounting for the purchase of a subsidiary. Throughout this chapter the examples assume that the investor used cash to make the investment. Investments can also involve shares of the parent, debt, and non-cash assets.)

On June 30, 2010 Pefferlaw Ltd. (Pefferlaw) bought 100 percent of the shares of Schuler Corp. (Schuler) from its shareholders for $20,000,000. Pefferlaw would make the following journal entry in its accounting records to record the investment in Schuler:

Dr. Investment in Schuler (asset +)	$20,000,000	
Cr. Cash (asset –)		$20,000,000

To record the purchase of 100 percent of the shares of Schuler Corp on June 30, 2010.

The investment has no effect at all on Schuler's accounting records or its financial statements. Pefferlaw purchased the shares from Schuler's shareholders, not from the corporation itself. Only the ownership of Schuler's shares has changed.

Pefferlaw has purchased 100 percent of Schuler for $20,000,000. But what exactly did Pefferlaw buy and how much did it pay for the specific assets and liabilities? For Pefferlaw to be able to prepare consolidated financial statements, it must identify the assets and liabilities that it purchased and determine their cost—the amount Pefferlaw paid for them.

This process can be difficult because Pefferlaw purchased an entire entity, not individual assets and liabilities. As a result, the purchase price must be allocated to the individual assets and liabilities that were purchased. To accomplish this, the market or fair values of all of Schuler's identifiable assets and liabilities must be determined as of the date of the purchase. (Identifiable assets and liabilities are tangible and intangible assets and liabilities that can be specifically identified and measured with some objectivity.) These are the amounts that are reported in the consolidated financial statements. (Remember, the cost of an asset or liability is its market value on the date the asset or liability was acquired.)

This is a straightforward application of GAAP's historical cost measurement convention. Since Pefferlaw has purchased Schuler, the assets and liabilities that were purchased should be treated the same way as any purchase, at cost. This process of determining the fair value of the assets and liabilities of a subsidiary occurs only once, when the subsidiary is purchased. After that, the consolidated financial statements are based on the amounts determined as of the date of the purchase.

(Throughout this chapter, the term **fair value** is used when referring to the estimated market value of the subsidiary's assets and liabilities on the date the subsidiary was purchased. This is the term commonly used in accounting for subsidiaries.)

Table 12–1 summarizes the book and fair values of Schuler's assets and liabilities on June 30, 2010.

There are a couple of things to notice in Table 12–1:

■ First, there are two measurements of Schuler's assets and liabilities. One measurement is the amount that actually appears in Schuler's own financial statements. The second measurement is the fair values on the date Schuler was purchased by Pefferlaw, which are the amounts Pefferlaw paid for Schuler's assets and liabilities. The fair values are the amounts that appear on Pefferlaw's consolidated balance sheet. The book values are the amounts that are reported on Schuler's balance sheet.

TABLE 12–1 ::: Fair Values and Book Values of Schuler Corp.'s Net Assets on June 30, 2010

	Fair Value on June 30, 2010	Book Value on June 30, 2010	Difference
Current assets	$ 5,500,000	$ 5,000,000	$ 500,000
Capital assets	21,500,000	14,000,000	7,500,000
Liabilities	(9,000,000)	(8,000,000)	(1,000,000)
	$18,000,000	$11,000,000	$7,000,000

■ Second, only $18,000,000 of the purchase price has been attributed to specific assets and liabilities. The remaining $2,000,000 is goodwill (remember from Chapter 9 that Goodwill = Purchase price − Fair value of identifiable assets and liabilities purchased).

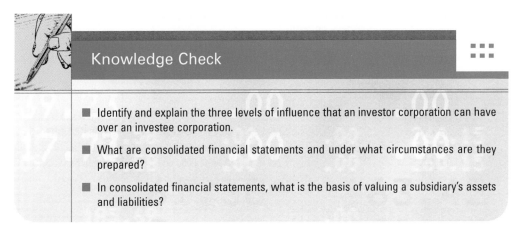

Knowledge Check

■ Identify and explain the three levels of influence that an investor corporation can have over an investee corporation.

■ What are consolidated financial statements and under what circumstances are they prepared?

■ In consolidated financial statements, what is the basis of valuing a subsidiary's assets and liabilities?

www.mcgrawhill.ca/
olc/friedlan

The Consolidated Balance Sheet on the Date the Subsidiary is Purchased

We now have the information to prepare Pefferlaw's consolidated balance sheet on June 30, 2010, the date that Pefferlaw purchased all of the shares of Schuler. Pefferlaw's consolidated balance sheet includes:

a. The amounts reported on Pefferlaw's own balance sheet (not the consolidated balance sheet) on June 30, 2010;

b. The fair value of Schuler's assets and liabilities (not the amounts on Schuler's own balance sheet) on June 30, 2010;

c. The goodwill from the acquisition of Schuler.

The Investment in Subsidiary account that is on the parent's financial statements doesn't appear on the consolidated financial statements. It's replaced by the actual assets and liabilities of the subsidiary. Also, the shareholders' equity of the subsidiary isn't included in the consolidated financial statements on the date the subsidiary is acquired. This is the case because the shareholders' equity of the parent already reflects the equity of the subsidiary.

It is important to understand that a parent's financial statements are not the same as its consolidated financial statements. The parent also prepares unconsolidated financial statements that report on the parent alone. All that is reported about a parent's subsidiaries in the unconsolidated financial statements is a single line reporting the investment in the subsidiaries. These unconsolidated statements are required for tax purposes and may be provided to other users, such as bankers. A parent's unconsolidated financial statements are not usually widely distributed.

The construction of Pefferlaw's consolidated balance sheet on June 30, 2010, the date Pefferlaw purchased the shares of Schuler, is shown in Table 12–2. Specifically,

■ Column 1 shows Pefferlaw's balance sheet (this information has not been shown before). Pefferlaw's balance sheet includes the account that records the investment in Schuler.

■ Column 2 shows the fair value of the Schuler's assets and liabilities on June 30, 2010. These are the amounts that will be included in Pefferlaw's consolidated balance sheet. These are **not** the amounts that appear on Schuler's own balance sheet. Schuler's own balance sheet will show the historical cost of the assets and liabilities to Schuler itself (these amounts can be seen in Table 12–1). Schuler's capital stock and retained earnings are not shown because

TABLE 12–2 ::: Consolidated Balance Sheet on June 30, 2010

	Column 1	Column 2	Column 3
	Balance Sheet of Pefferlaw Ltd. on June 30, 2010	**Fair value of Schuler Corp.'s Assets and Liabilities on June 30, 2010**	**Consolidated Balance Sheet on June 30, 2010**
Current assets	$ 29,000,000	$ 5,500,000	$ 34,500,000
Capital assets	52,000,000	21,500,000	73,500,000
Investment in Schuler	20,000,000		
Goodwill		2,000,000	2,000,000
	$101,000,000	$ 29,000,000	$110,000,000
Liabilities	$ 38,000,000	$ 9,000,000	$ 47,000,000
Capital stock	22,000,000		22,000,000
Retained earnings	41,000,000		41,000,000
	$101,000,000		$110,000,000

> The investment in Schuler account on Pentz's own balance sheet is eliminated when preparing the consolidated financial statements.

> The shareholders' equity section of the subsidiary's balance sheet isn't included in the consolidated financial statements.

they are not included in the calculation of consolidated shareholders' equity. Goodwill is calculated using the formula shown at the top of p. 663:

$$
\begin{aligned}
\text{Goodwill} &= \text{Purchase price} - \text{Fair value of identifiable assets and liabilities purchased} \\
\$2,000,000 &= \$20,000,000 - \$18,000,000
\end{aligned}
$$

■ Column 3 is the consolidated balance sheet.

The purchase of Schuler does not affect the consolidated income statement for the year ended June 30, 2010. The purchase took place on the last day of Schuler's fiscal year, and the revenues and expenses of a subsidiary are incorporated into the consolidated income statement only after the date of the purchase. The income statement effects of consolidation are discussed in the appendix.

Question for Consideration :::

When an entity purchases a subsidiary, the fair value of the subsidiary's assets and liabilities on the date the subsidiary is purchased are included in the consolidated balance sheet, not the amounts reported in the subsidiary's own balance sheet. Explain why this treatment is not a violation of the historical cost measurement convention.

Answer: Recording a subsidiary's assets and liabilities at their fair values in the consolidated balance sheet on the date the subsidiary was purchased is not a violation of the historical cost measurement convention because the subsidiary's assets and liabilities are purchased when the parent purchases the subsidiary.

Assigning fair values to the assets and liabilities of a subsidiary occurs only once—when the subsidiary is actually purchased. The fair values assigned on the date the subsidiary is purchased form the basis of valuing those assets and liabilities in the consolidated financial statements from then on. If the fair values were determined each time consolidated financial statements were prepared, the historical cost measurement convention would be violated.

Non-Controlling Interest

When a parent owns less than 100 percent of the shares of a subsidiary, but still controls it, accounts called "Non-controlling Interest" (or Minority Interest) appear in the consolidated financial statements. Non-controlling Interest accounts appear because of how the *CICA Handbook* requires parent corporations to account for subsidiaries that are less than 100 percent owned. The *CICA Handbook* requires that the consolidated balance sheet include 100 percent of the book values of the subsidiary's assets and liabilities, even if the parent owns less than 100 percent of those assets and liabilities. The *CICA Handbook* also requires that the consolidated income statement report 100 percent of the revenues and expenses of a subsidiary even if the subsidiary isn't 100 percent owned

The rationale for this approach is that since the parent controls 100 percent of the subsidiary's net assets, even if it doesn't own 100 percent of them, the consolidated statements should report what is under the parent's control. The problem with this approach is that the consolidated statements contain assets, liabilities, revenues, and expenses that don't belong to the parent's shareholders. If these amounts are going to be included in the consolidated financial statements, then what is to be done with the portions that are not owned by the parent's shareholders?

The answer is non-controlling interest. **Non-controlling interest** on the balance sheet represents the net assets of a subsidiary that are owned by the shareholders of the subsidiary other than the parent. Non-controlling interest on the income statement represents the portion of net income of the consolidated entity that belongs to the shareholders of subsidiaries other than the parent.

The number that is included in the consolidated balance sheet is a strange combination of measurements. What appears can best be shown with a simple example. On December 31, 2009 Pikwitonei Inc. (Pikwitonei) purchased 80 percent of the common shares of Sibbald Ltd. (Sibbald) for $1,000,000. The only asset Sibbald owned was a piece of land that had a book value of $800,000 (this is the amount that Sibbald actually paid for the land). The land had a fair value on December 31, 2009 of $1,000,000. Sibbald had no liabilities. The amount that would be recorded in the consolidated balance sheet on December 31, 2009 would be $960,000.

The reason for this amount is that GAAP allows the parent's share of the fair value of assets and liabilities to be included in the consolidated balance sheet, but only the non-controlling interest's share of the book values as shown on the subsidiary's balance sheet. Returning to the example, the $960,000 represents 80 percent of the fair value of the land ($1,000,000 × 80 percent = $800,000)—this is the parent's share of the land and 20 percent of the book value on Sibbald's balance sheet on December 31, 2009; ($800,000 × 20 percent = $160,000)—this is the non-controlling interest's share. What would appear on the consolidated balance sheet as non-controlling interest is $160,000, the amount of net assets included on the consolidated balance sheet that belong to the non-controlling interest. The non-controlling interest on the balance sheet is simply the book value of the non-controlling shareholders' interest in the net assets of the subsidiary.

Now let's look at the income statement. The consolidated income statement contains 100 percent of the revenues and expenses of a subsidiary even if the parent owns less than 100 percent of the subsidiary. As a result, the non-controlling interest entry to the income statement reduces net income by the amount that belongs to the non-controlling interest. If this entry was not made, net income would be overstated because it would include an economic gain that belongs to investors other than the shareholders of the parent. Returning to the Pikwitonei and Sibbald example, suppose that in fiscal 2010 Sibbald earned $100,000 in rent revenue from the land and incurred $20,000 of expenses related to the land. The consolidated income statement would include the $100,000 in revenue and the $20,000 in expenses, but it would also have an amount attributable to non-controlling interest of $16,000 (($100,000 − $20,000) × 20 percent). The $16,000 represents the non-controlling interest's share of the revenue less the expenses that were included in the consolidated income statement.

The non-controlling interest appears on the consolidated balance sheet between liabilities and shareholders' equity. Non-controlling interest is equity, but it is the equity of the non-controlling shareholders of the subsidiaries, not the equity of the parent's shareholders. It is not a liability because there is no obligation to anyone.

On the consolidated income statement, non-controlling interest appears as a deduction in the calculation of consolidated net income.

On the consolidated cash flow statement, the non-controlling interest reported on the consolidated income statement is added back to net income when calculating cash from operations using the indirect method. The non-controlling interest is added back because it does not represent cash distributed to the non-controlling shareholders—it is the allocation of income to the non-controlling shareholders. An example of consolidation when less than 100 percent of the subsidiary is acquired is provided in the appendix to this chapter.

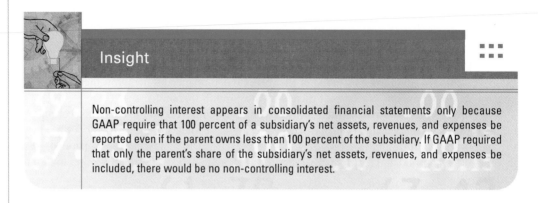

Insight

Non-controlling interest appears in consolidated financial statements only because GAAP require that 100 percent of a subsidiary's net assets, revenues, and expenses be reported even if the parent owns less than 100 percent of the subsidiary. If GAAP required that only the parent's share of the subsidiary's net assets, revenues, and expenses be included, there would be no non-controlling interest.

Knowledge Check

- What is goodwill and how is it calculated?
- What is non-controlling interest and why does it appear in some entities' consolidated financial statements?

www.mcgrawhill.ca/
olc/friedlan

Are Consolidated Financial Statements Useful?

Now that we have looked at the basics of accounting for subsidiaries (which aren't all that basic!), we can consider the usefulness of consolidated financial statements. Consolidated statements provide, in a single set of financial statements, financial information about a group of corporations that are under the control of a parent. This information might be useful to users who want stewardship information about the entire economic entity, or to evaluate the performance of the corporate group as a whole. Consolidated financial statements may be an effective way for a corporate group to communicate the "big picture" to various stakeholders. Since the parent company controls its subsidiaries, the parent is able to move assets from corporation to corporation and control the operations of the subsidiaries. For example, a parent company that is short of cash could have a subsidiary declare a dividend, make a loan, or pay management fees to the parent to help it meet its cash needs. Consolidated statements allow users to see the resources that are under the management of the entire corporate group.

Consolidated financial statements eliminate intercompany transactions and profits. This means that revenue and profit from exchanges between a parent and a subsidiary, or among the subsidiaries in a consolidated group, are not included reflected in the consolidated financial statements (this topic is explored in the appendix to this chapter). Intercompany transactions and profits can be misleading because they misstate the real economic activity and performance of the consolidated group. Transactions within a consolidated group do not have any economic significance from the perspective of the parent—such transactions are equivalent to moving money from one pocket to another. A parent could improve its reported economic performance or financial position, or that of a subsidiary, by ordering transactions between companies in the consolidated group (perhaps transactions that aren't required), or by dictating the terms of these transactions. The financial statements of the individual corporations in a consolidated group don't eliminate intercompany transactions, whereas consolidated statements don't report them.

For many users, however, consolidated financial statements are an obstacle to effective decision making because they aggregate information about the individual corporations in the consolidated group. The details about the different businesses that a parent and its subsidiaries are engaged in are lost in consolidated financial statements. It is virtually impossible to determine, by examining consolidated financial statements, which companies, lines of business, and geographical areas in a consolidated group are doing well and which are doing poorly.

Consolidated statements alone don't serve the interests of financial analysts and other sophisticated users who want to use historical accounting information as a starting point for predicting future earnings or cash flows. For example, consolidated financial statements can significantly limit the usefulness of ratio analysis. By combining the accounting information of several companies, often companies in different industries, ratios will not be representative of any industry. What sense can we make of Rogers' financial ratios when those ratios relate to companies in very different industries?

GAAP try to help users by requiring public companies to provide information about the different business activities and the different economic environments in which they operate. This disaggregation of information by types of products and services, geographic location, and major customers is called **segment disclosure**.

Rogers provides segment disclosure in Note 17 to its financial statements (see page A-xx). Rogers partitions its business into four segments: wireless, cable, media, and telecom. For each segment, an income statement is provided. Notice that there is also a column for eliminations. This is for transactions that took place among the different segments and are included in the amounts for each segment. Remember that intercompany transactions have to be eliminated when consolidated financial statements are prepared. Notice also that complete financial statements are not provided for each segment. Very limited balance sheet information is provided by segment. Note 17(b) breaks down the revenue earned by each segment into component parts.

Users can gain some very useful insights from the segment information. For Rogers, the segment information tells users that Wireless is the largest revenue producer and the most profitable segment. We also see that advertising is the largest source of revenue for the media segment.

For some users, consolidated financial statements, even with segment information, are not adequate for their needs. For lenders, consolidated financial statements and segment disclosure are not useful because loans are made to legal entities, not to consolidated ones. A lender will be concerned about the ability of the legal entity that borrowed the money to repay a loan. Consolidated financial statements don't provide information about individual subsidiaries, and segment disclosure provides information about business segments, not necessarily about separate corporations. Only if a loan is being made to the parent, or if the parent is guaranteeing a loan to a subsidiary, would the lender be interested in the consolidated statements. Otherwise, a lender needs the financial statements of the corporation actually borrowing the money.

Consolidated financial statements are of little interest to the non-controlling shareholders and other stakeholders of a subsidiary. The consolidated statements are intended for stakeholders of the consolidated entity. The non-controlling interest on the consolidated statements provides little useful information to users who are interested in subsidiaries. The non-controlling shareholders and other stakeholders in the subsidiary would want to see the financial statements of the subsidiary itself. The shareholders in the subsidiaries are entitled to receive financial statements of the subsidiaries in which they own shares.

Consolidated financial statements are not relevant for tax purposes. Each individual corporation is required to file tax returns with the Canada Revenue Agency and provincial taxation authorities. This means that each corporation must prepare financial statements for tax purposes regardless of who owns it.

◇ ROGERS™

Insight

Accounting for subsidiaries provides managers with significant opportunities to make choices that will influence the consolidated financial statements for many years. When a new subsidiary is acquired, the fair values of the assets and liabilities must be determined. A subsidiary is a bundle of assets and liabilities purchased for a single price, so the exact price paid for individual assets and liabilities is not known. Management must allocate the purchase price of the subsidiary to individual assets and liabilities and to goodwill. Because the process of assigning market values is imprecise, management can make choices that help it satisfy its reporting objectives. Different managers could come up with very different reasonable amounts of goodwill for the same acquisition and different reasonable valuations for the identifiable assets and liabilities. Because goodwill does not have to be amortized, managers who are concerned about net income might allocate less of the purchase price to amortizable assets and inventory so that more would be included in goodwill.

Purchasing Assets Instead of Shares

In this chapter, the focus is on situations where one corporation buys the shares of another corporation. An investor corporation can also buy another business's assets. These could be the assets of a corporation, partnership, or proprietorship.

The purchase of the assets of an entire business is accounted for in the same way as any purchase of assets—the assets are recorded at their cost. The accounting is a bit more complicated because, instead of a single asset being purchased, all the assets that comprise the business are acquired. As was discussed in Chapter 9, when a basket of assets is purchased, the purchase price must be allocated to the individual assets in the basket. If the amount paid for the assets was greater than the fair value of the identifiable assets on the date of the purchase, goodwill would be recorded. However, goodwill arises only if the assets of an entire business are purchased.

The purchase of the assets of a business does not require the preparation of consolidated financial statements. If the assets being purchased are included among the assets of the investor corporation, consolidated financial statements are not required because there is no subsidiary corporation to consolidate.

Whether to buy the assets or shares of another corporation is a complex decision. One of the main factors that must be considered is tax. Tax issues affect the buyer and the seller, and the ultimate terms of the purchase are the result of negotiations. One advantage of purchasing the assets is that the investor corporation does not acquire any unknown liabilities, such as lawsuits that have not yet been launched.

SIGNIFICANT INFLUENCE

When a corporation has significant influence on the decision making of another corporation as a result of its investment in that corporation, the *CICA Handbook* requires that the equity method of accounting be used. **Significant influence** means that the investor corporation can affect the strategic operating, investing, and financing decisions of the investee corporation, even though it does not have control.

The *CICA Handbook* suggests that owning between 20 percent and 50 percent of the votes of an investee company is an indication of significant influence. However, judgment must be used to determine whether significant influence exists in a particular situation. One investor corporation could own 30 percent of the voting shares of another company, but another investor could own more than 50 percent of the voting shares of that company and have control. In that case, significant influence may not exist. On the other hand, even with an investment of less than 20 percent, an investor corporation may be able to exert significant influence if, for example, the investor corporation has representation on the investee corporation's board of directors.

The **equity method of accounting** is essentially the same as accounting for subsidiaries using the consolidation method. However, the information appears in the financial statements in a very different way. Unlike accounting for subsidiaries, where the financial statements of the parent and subsidiary are combined line by line, information about investments accounted for using the equity method is presented on a single line on the balance sheet and a single line on the income statement.

An investment accounted for using the equity method is initially recorded on the investor's balance sheet at cost. The balance sheet amount is then adjusted each period by the investor's share of the investee's net income, less dividends declared by the investee. The income statement reports the investor's share of the investee's net income. The investor's share is determined by multiplying the investee's net income by the percentage of the investee that the investor owns. It is usually necessary to adjust the investee's net income for a number of effects resulting from the acquisition of the shares in the investee corporation.

The rationale for the equity method is that if an investor corporation has significant influence, it can affect the important policies of the investee, such as the timing and amount of dividends. By being able to influence the timing and amount of the investee's dividends, an investor can manage its own earnings by having the investee declare dividends when the investor wants them. Since dividends from an investment in an investee corporation accounted for using the equity method are not considered income, this type of income manipulation is not possible. A few points about the equity method of accounting are worth noting:

1. While an equity investment account changes to reflect the earnings of an investee and the dividends it declares, the amount reported on the balance sheet does not reflect the market value of the investment. The changes to the balance sheet amount are based on historical cost transactions-based accounting, not on changes in the investee's market value. Just as the shareholders' equity section of an entity's balance sheet does not provide the market value of its shares, the amount reported on the balance sheet for an investment accounted for using the equity method does not represent the market value of that investment.

2. The income reported from an investment accounted for using the equity method is not an indication of the amount of dividends or cash that will be forthcoming from the investee. The amount of income recorded is simply an allocation of the investor's share of the investee's income. An equity investment may not be very liquid and the investor may be limited in its ability to obtain cash from the investee.

3. The equity investment account on the investor's balance sheet provides virtually no information about the investee corporation. Information about investments over which the investor has significant influence is usually not included in the segment disclosures described earlier in the chapter. If the investee corporation is public, the financial statements of the investee can be examined. If the investee is private, then little will be known about it. An example of equity accounting can be seen in Exhibit 12–2.[2]

Exhibit 12–2 shows how Ivanhoe Mines Ltd. (Ivanhoe) reports its investments accounted for using the equity method. Ivanhoe reports a loss from equity-accounted investments in the year ended December 31, 2004 of $2,315,000 (the loss can be found on the line on the income statement called "Share of loss of significantly influenced investees"). Ivanhoe's balance sheet reports long-term investments of $16,281,000. Note 9 to Ivanhoe's financial statements shows that $5,024,000 of this amount is investments accounted for using the equity method while the remainder is classified as passive investments (Ivanhoe refers to these as portfolio investments).

The table in Note 9 shows Ivanhoe's equity and passive investments, its equity interest in each and the carrying (book) and market values on December 31, 2004 and 2003.

www.ivanhoe-mines.com

PASSIVE INVESTMENTS

Passive investments are investments for which the investor corporation can't influence the strategic decision making of the investee corporation. The term *passive investments* is not defined in the *CICA Handbook* but is intended to reflect investments that don't give the investing corporation control or significant influence. These investments are passive because the investing corporation has little say or influence on the decision making of the investee corporation.

All investments in non-voting securities—securities such as debt, preferred shares, or non-voting common shares—are accounted for as passive investments because without voting power, it is not possible to have influence. Voting shares are accounted for as passive investments when the investing company holds a relatively small proportion of the investee's voting shares.

EXHIBIT 12-2 :

Ivanhoe Mines
Ltd.—Equity
Accounting

IVANHOE MINES LTD.
Consolidated Balance Sheets
(Stated in thousands of U.S. dollars)

		December 31,		
		2004		2003
ASSETS				
CURRENT				
Cash (Note 5)	$	**122,577**	$	106,994
Investments (Note 6)		**-**		50,000
Accounts receivable (Note 7)		**10,286**		4,440
Broken ore on leach pads		**9,394**		6,181
Inventories (Note 8)		**5,516**		2,571
Prepaid expenses		**2,996**		1,639
Other current assets		**3,117**		2,107
Current assets held for sale (Note 3)		**34,918**		23,127
		188,804		197,059
LONG-TERM INVESTMENTS (Note 9)		**16,281**		14,716
MINING PROPERTY, PLANT AND EQUIPMENT (Note 10)		**132,599**		129,188
OTHER MINERAL PROPERTY INTERESTS (Note 11)		**50,316**		49,796
OTHER CAPITAL ASSETS (Note 12)		**8,909**		7,990
FUTURE INCOME TAXES (Note 16)		**782**		1,781
OTHER ASSETS (Note 13)		**7,472**		7,135
NON-CURRENT ASSETS HELD FOR SALE (Note 3)		**55,711**		48,057
	$	**460,874**	$	455,722

IVANHOE MINES LTD.
Consolidated Income Statements
(Stated in thousands of U.S. dollars, except per share amounts)

		Years ended December 31,		
		2004		2003
REVENUE	$	**44,091**	$	22,866
COST OF OPERATIONS		**(11,412)**		(12,428)
DEPRECIATION AND DEPLETION		**(5,177)**		(5,484)
OPERATING PROFIT		**27,502**		4,954
EXPENSES				
General and administrative		**(22,825)**		(17,393)
Interest on long-term debt		**(1,105)**		(1,444)
Exploration (Note 9 (a))		**(98,174)**		(67,989)
Depreciation		**(2,027)**		(1,501)
LOSS BEFORE THE FOLLOWING		**(96,629)**		(83,373)
OTHER INCOME (EXPENSES)				
Interest income		**3,177**		1,613
Foreign exchange gains		**4,442**		12,376
Mining property care and maintenance costs (Note 10)		**(3,755)**		(3,356)
Share of loss of significantly influenced investees (Note 9 (a) and (b))		**(2,315)**		(2,423)
Gain on sale of long-term investments (Note 9 (c) and (e))		**4,523**		4,625
Write-down of carrying values of other assets (Note 20)		**(5,277)**		(1,213)
Dilution gain on investment in subsidiary		**-**		4,210
Dilution loss on long-term investment in significantly influenced investee		**-**		(237)
Other		**(183)**		685
		612		16,280
LOSS BEFORE INCOME AND CAPITAL TAXES, NON-CONTROLLING INTEREST AND DISCONTINUED OPERATIONS		**(96,017)**		(67,093)
Provision for income and capital taxes (Note 16)		**(4,350)**		(1,756)
LOSS BEFORE NON-CONTROLLING INTEREST AND DISCONTINUED OPERATIONS		**(100,367)**		(68,849)
Non-controlling interest (Note 18)		**2,103**		546
NET LOSS FROM CONTINUING OPERATIONS		**(98,264)**		(68,303)
NET INCOME (LOSS) FROM DISCONTINUED OPERATIONS (Note 3)		**8,639**		(4,685)
NET LOSS	$	**(89,625)**	$	(72,988)

EXHIBIT 12–2 :

(continued)
Ivanhoe Mines
Ltd.—Equity
Accounting

9.   **LONG-TERM INVESTMENTS**

| | December 31, 2004 | | | December 31, 2003 | | |
	Equity Interest	Carrying Value	Quoted Market Value	Equity Interest	Carrying Value	Quoted Market Value
Investment in companies subject to significant influence:						
Jinshan Gold Mines Inc.						
(formerly Pacific Minerals Inc.) ("Jinshan") (a)	38.5%	$ 5,024	$ 10,267	35.5%	$ 9,027	$ 39,712
Portfolio investments:						
Intec Ltd. ("Intec") (b)	12.8%	1,446	2,915	23.2%	1,787	4,479
Olympus Pacific Minerals Inc. ("Olympus") (c)	19.6%	5,862	5,569	10.8%	2,587	3,342
Entrée Gold Inc. ("Entrée") (d)	9.0%	3,846	5,550	-	-	-
Resource Investment Trust ("RIT") (e)	-	-	-	6.2%	1,212	2,237
Other	-	103	-	-	103	-
		$ 16,281	$ 24,301		$ 14,716	$ 49,770

(a)   In 2003, the Company acquired 2.5 million units of Jinshan at a price of Canadian ("Cdn") $1.75 per unit, for a cost of Cdn$4.4 million ($3.3 million). Each unit consisted of one common share and one common share purchase warrant. Each warrant is exercisable for one common share at a price of Cdn$2.20 per share until December 2005.

In 2004, Ivanhoe Mines and Jinshan restructured their participating arrangements in respect of certain joint ventures. In consideration for the transaction, Jinshan issued to Ivanhoe Mines 2.5 million common shares with a fair value of $3,248,000. This amount has been included in operations as a recovery of prior exploration expenses.

During 2004, Ivanhoe Mines recorded a $1,974,000 (2003 - $2,333,000) equity loss on this investment, and an impairment provision of $5,277,000 (2003 – Nil) based on an assessment of the underlying book value of Jinshan's net assets. At December 31, 2004, the carrying value of the Company's investment in Jinshan exceeded its share of the underlying book value of Jinshan's net assets by approximately $2,709,000, which is being accounted for against the Company's share of Jinshan's post-acquisition net income or losses in accordance with the accounting policy described in Note 2(i).

At December 31, 2004, Ivanhoe Mines' equity interest in Jinshan on a fully diluted basis, which assumes that all of the outstanding share purchase warrants and stock options of Jinshan were exercised, amounts to 45.0%. At March 10, 2005, the quoted market value of the Company's investment in Jinshan was $11,327,000.

(b)   In 2003, Ivanhoe Mines acquired additional shares of Intec for cash of $493,000. This acquisition increased Ivanhoe Mines' holding in Intec from 19.9% to 23.2% and, accordingly, Ivanhoe Mines commenced equity accounting for its investment in Intec. In the fourth quarter of 2004, Ivanhoe Mines' interest in Intec was decreased to 12.8% as a result of the issuance of additional shares by Intec. As a result, Ivanhoe Mines ceased equity accounting for its investment in Intec.

During 2004, Ivanhoe Mines recorded a $341,000 (2003 - $90,000) equity loss on this investment.

The *CICA Handbook* suggests that if an investor corporation owns less than 20 percent of the voting shares of an investee, it should be treated as a passive investment. However, 20 percent is only a guideline. A 10 percent investment could give the investor corporation significant influence if, for example, the investee allows it to have representation on the board of directors.

There are three categories of passive investments, each with a different accounting treatment. The three categories are: held-to-maturity investments, trading investments, and available-for-sale investments.

Held-to-maturity investments—An investment with a maturity date, fixed or determinable payments (like interest payments), and the intent and ability of management to hold the investment to maturity. Because of the requirement of a maturity date, common shares and any other investments that do not have a specified life are excluded from this category. If management can't say whether the investment will be held to maturity, then the investment would be classified as available for sale.

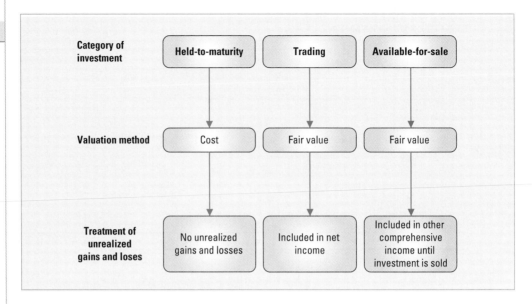

FIGURE 12–3

Accounting for Investments

Trading investments—Any investments that management designates as a trading investment. Investments in this category are actively bought and sold for profit making.

Available-for-sale investments—This is the default category. Any investment that does not give control or significant influence to the investing corporation, or that doesn't meet the criteria for classification as a held-to-maturity or trading investment, is considered an available-for-sale investment.

Notice that management intent plays an important role in the classification of investment. This requirement provides management with the opportunity to use this flexibility to achieve their reporting objectives. This is especially relevant because each of the types of investments is accounted for differently. The accounting treatments for the different categories of investment are summarized in Figure 12–3.

Held-to-maturity investments are accounted for at cost. Changes in the market value of an investment are ignored. The investment is reported on the balance sheet at its cost and gains and losses on the income statement would only be recognized if the investment were sold (which normally shouldn't occur since investments in this category are supposed to be held to maturity). Held-to-maturity investments can be written down if they are permanently impaired. Impairment would reduce the amount that the investor could expect to receive at maturity and so a write-down would be an appropriate conservative action to take.

Trading and available-for-sale investments are reported on the balance sheet at their market value. Changes in the market value of these investments while they are owned by the investor are known as unrealized holding gains or losses (this term was originally introduced in Chapter 4). Unrealized gains and losses are changes in the market value of an asset that aren't supported by a transaction. That is, the investment in question is not sold. Realization of a gain or loss occurs when there is a sale. The accounting for unrealized gains and losses is different for trading and available-for-sale investments.

For trading investments, unrealized gains and losses (and realized gains and losses) are recognized in the period they occur. If the market value of a trading investment increases by $100,000 during the year, a $100,000 gain is reported on the income statement regardless of whether the investment is sold. This treatment makes sense for trading investments because the investing entity is buying and selling investments so it can profit from changes in the value of the investments. By recognizing the changing market value as income, economic gains and losses are being reflected as they occur, so income is a better measure of the performance of the entity. However, this approach can add significant variability to reported income.

For available-for-sale investments, unrealized gains and losses are not reported in the income statement. Instead, they are included in the calculation of comprehensive income. Remember from Chapter 11 that comprehensive income is the change in equity from transactions and economic events from all sources that don't involve owners. Because available-for-sale investments can be sold if management decides to do so, the market value valuation on the balance sheet gives financial statement users an idea of how much would be realized from the sale. When a gain or loss is ultimately realized by selling the investment, the full amount of the unrealized gains and losses that were included in other comprehensive income are recorded in the income statement.

For all these investment categories, interest revenue is accrued as it is earned and dividend revenue is recognized when it is declared. There are no differences among the methods.

We can compare the accounting for the different methods with an example. On November 1, 2009 Elko Inc. (Elko) purchased $1,000,000 in corporate bonds as an investment. The bonds had a face value of $1,000,000 and a coupon rate of 7 percent with interest paid semi-annually on April 30 and October 31. Because of changes in the economy and a change in the issuing company's credit rating, the market value of the bonds on April 30, 2010 was $1,025,000. Recording the initial purchase of the bonds is the same with the three methods. The entry to record the purchase is:

Dr. Investment in Bonds	1,000,000	
Cr. Cash		1,000,000

The balance sheet and income statement for Elko using the three categories of passive investments is shown in Exhibit 12–3. Key differences to pay attention to in the statements are shaded in the Exhibit.

Notice that the balance sheet valuation of Elko's bonds is the market value if the bonds are classified as trading or available-for-sale investments. Also, retained earnings is greater when the bond is classified as a trading investment because the unrealized gain is reflected in earnings. Total equity is

EXHIBIT 12–3 :

Elko Inc.'s Financial Statements

Elko Inc. Balance Sheet As of April 30, 2010			
	Hold-to-Maturity	Trading	Available-for-Sale
Assets			
All Other Assets	$11,500,000	$11,500,000	$11,500,000
Investment in Bonds	1,000,000	1,025,000	1,025,000
	$12,500,000	$12,525,000	$12,525,000
Liabilities and Shareholders' Equity			
All Liabilities	$ 7,000,000	$ 7,000,000	$ 7,000,000
Shareholders' Equity			
Capital Stock	2,000,000	2,000,000	2,000,000
Retained Earnings	3,500,000	3,525,000	3,500,000
Other Comprehensive Income: Unrealized Holding gains			25,000
Total Shareholders' Equity	5,500,000	5,525,000	5,525,000
	$12,500,000	$12,525,000	$12,525,000

Elko Inc. Income Statement For the year ended April 30, 2010			
Revenue	$ 8,000,000	$ 8,000,000	$ 8,000,000
Expenses	6,870,000	6,870,000	6,870,000
Interest income from bonds	70,000	70,000	70,000
Unrealized Holding Gain on Bond Investment		25,000	
Net Income	$ 1,200,000	$ 1,225,000	$ 1,200,000
Other Comprehensive Income: Unrealized Holding Gains on Available-for-Trade Investments			25,000
Comprehensive Income	$ 1,200,000	$ 1,225,000	$ 1,225,000

the same for both trading and available-for-sale investments, but the available-for-sale balance sheet shows the increase in market value as other comprehensive income. On the income statement, notice that the unrealized gain is included in the calculation of net income when the bond is classified as a trading investment, whereas when the bond is classified as available-for-sale, the unrealized gains are shown as other comprehensive income (and not included in the calculation of net income).

If Elko sold the bonds on May 1, 2010 for $1,025,000 the financial statements would be as shown in Exhibit 12–4. (Exhibit 12–4 assumes a one-day period (May 1, 2010) and there is no economic activity on May 1 except the sale of the bonds.) The key points to notice in Exhibit 12–4 are:

■ The investment in bonds account is now zero because the bonds have been sold.

■ Retained earnings is the same for all three classifications of the investment. This occurs because, once gains are realized, there are no differences among the methods.

■ The balance in Other Comprehensive Income: Unrealized Holding Gains is now zero. Once gains or losses are realized, the unrealized amount is removed from this account.

■ There are no unrealized gains or losses reported on the income statement. Because the bonds were sold, the gain was realized.

■ There is no gain reported when the bonds are classified as trading investments. The gain was recognized in the year ended April 30, 2010.

EXHIBIT 12–4 :

Elko Inc.'s Financial Statements

Elko Inc. Balance Sheet As of May 1, 2010—After the Sale of the Bonds			
	Hold-to-Maturity	Trading	Available-for-Sale
Assets			
All Other Assets	$12,525,000	$12,525,000	$12,525,000
Investment in Bonds	0	0	0
	$12,525,000	$12,525,000	$12,525,000
Liabilities and Shareholders' Equity			
All Liabilities	$ 7,000,000	$ 7,000,000	$ 7,000,000
Shareholders' Equity			
Capital Stock	2,000,000	2,000,000	2,000,000
Retained Earnings	3,525,000	3,525,000	3,525,000
Other Comprehensive Income			0
Unrealized Holding gains			
Total Shareholders' Equity	5,525,000	5,525,000	5,525,000
	$12,500,000	$12,525,000	$12,525,000

Elko Inc. Income Statement For the one day period ended May 1, 2010			
Revenue			
Expenses			
Interest income from bonds			
Gain on the sale of bonds	25,000		25,000
Unrealized Holding Gain on Bond Investment			
Net Income	$ 25,000	$ 0	$ 25,000
Other Comprehensive Income: Unrealized Holding Gains on Available-for-Trade Investments			(25,000)
Comprehensive Income	$ 25,000	$ 0	$ 0

The valuation of investments is a significant departure from historical cost accounting, but a welcome one. While valuation at cost is useful for some purposes, by and large users will find market values more useful for decision making. For public companies' securities, there will be little controversy about the reliability of the valuation since publicly traded securities have readily available market prices. Reliability can be a question for private companies because there are no market prices readily available. However, there are methods for estimating the value of securities.

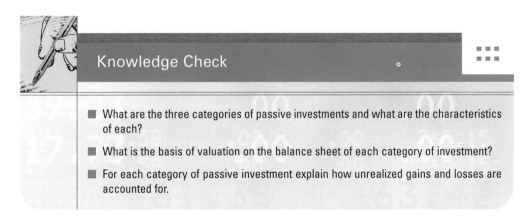

Knowledge Check

- What are the three categories of passive investments and what are the characteristics of each?

- What is the basis of valuation on the balance sheet of each category of investment?

- For each category of passive investment explain how unrealized gains and losses are accounted for.

www.mcgrawhill.ca/
olc/friedlan

⸪ Solved Problem

Tecumseh Inc. (Tecumseh) is a small diversified company in eastern Canada. The company is owned and operated by the Osler family. Tecumseh operates a restaurant in Moncton, New Brunswick, a potato farm in Prince Edward Island, a fish processing plant in Newfoundland, and a trucking company that operates throughout the Maritime provinces. The president of Tecumseh, Perry Osler, has approached your aunt for a $250,000 loan to update the potato farm operations. Your aunt recently won a lottery and she has set up an investment fund to invest in small Canadian businesses. She thinks it would be fun to be involved in these businesses and hopes that it will be a good way for her to make some money from her winnings.

As part of the preliminary investigation, Tecumseh has provided a consolidated balance sheet for the two years ended December 31, 2009. The balance sheet consolidates all of Tecumseh's activities. This is the first time your aunt has ever seen a consolidated balance sheet (the other companies she has considered were not consolidated) and she's not sure what to make of it. She has asked you to write a report identifying the key aspects of the consolidated balance sheet that she should be aware of when deciding whether to grant the loan to the potato farm. She would also like any other general observations you can make about the balance sheet. Tecumseh's consolidated balance sheets and some additional information are provided in Table 12–3.

Additional Information

- Tecumseh Inc. has four operations: a restaurant, a potato farm, a fish processing plant, and a trucking company. Each operation is organized as a separate corporation.

- The non-controlling interest relates to the potato farm. The farmer who operates the farm owns 25 percent of the shares of the farm.

- The goodwill arose when Tecumseh purchased the trucking company.

Tecumseh Inc.
Consolidated Balance Sheets
For the years ended December 31

	2009	2008		2009	2008
Cash	$ 55,000	$ 85,000	Bank loan	$ 125,000	$ 25,000
Accounts Receivable	1,250,000	850,000	Accounts Payable	1,110,000	985,000
Inventory	850,000	800,000	Unearned Revenue	125,000	99,000
Other Current Assets	35,000	45,000			
	2,190,000	1,780,000		1,360,000	1,109,000
Plant, property, and equipment	4,285,000	4,021,000	Long-term Debt	2,300,000	1,900,000
Goodwill	900,000	900,000	Future Income Taxes	310,000	275,000
			Non-controlling Interest	250,000	275,000
				4,220,000	3,559,000
			Capital Stock	2,000,000	2,000,000
			Retained earnings	1,155,000	1,142,000
			Total Liabilities and		
Total Assets	$ 7,375,000	$ 6,701,000	Shareholders' Equity	$ 7,375,000	$ 6,701,000

Solution:

Dear Aunt Meaghan:

Thank you for the opportunity to prepare this report for you. On my review of Tecumseh's balance sheets for the years ended December 31, 2009 and 2008, I note the following points for your consideration:

1. The first and most important point to remember is that you are being asked to lend money to the potato farm and that these financial statements apply to the entire corporate group. That is, the assets and liabilities reported in the balance sheet belong to all of Tecumseh's operations, not just the potato farm. This is important because you are being asked to lend money only to the farm, which may mean that many or most of the assets and liabilities reported in the balance sheet may not have any relationship to the entity to which you would be lending money. You must also obtain the financial statements of the potato farm.

2. The goodwill on the balance sheet is a large asset but it's not clear what it represents. The goodwill arose when Tecumseh bought the trucking company, which means it paid $900,000 more for the company than could be attributed to the net assets that could be specifically identified. This means that you can't tell what the goodwill represents or whether it represents anything at all. In addition, this goodwill is not related to the potato farm, the company to which you are being asked to lend.

3. The non-controlling interest on the liability side of the balance sheet represents the fact that Tecumseh does not own 100 percent of the potato farm. According to GAAP, the consolidated balance sheet should report 100 percent of the net assets controlled by Tecumseh, even though it doesn't own 100 percent of the farm's net assets. The additional information states that 25 percent of the farm is owned by another party. The non-controlling interest account is necessary to reflect the fact that 25 per cent of the potato farm's net assets do not belong to Tecumseh but are reported in Tecumseh's consolidated balance sheet. This account does not mean that money, goods, or services are owed to a third party but simply reflects the "equity" that the potato farm's non-Tecumseh's owners have in the assets and liabilities reported in the consolidated balance sheet.

4. The non-controlling interest does provide a small clue about how the potato farm is doing. The non-controlling interest decreased from 2008 to 2009, which means that the farm suffered a loss in 2009. You will have to get financial statements for the farm itself before making a decision about whether to make a loan to it, but this piece of information gives some insight about what to expect.

5. In general, the ability to analyze consolidated financial statements is quite limited. Tecumseh's balance sheet combines the assets and liabilities of four very different types of businesses, so it's very difficult to make much sense of any type of ratio analysis.

6. I notice from the balance sheet that Tecumseh's overall debt has increased significantly in 2009 over 2008. Long-term debt has increased by $400,000 and the bank loan by $100,000. As a result, the debt-to-equity ratio has increased from 1.13 to 1.34. The increase in the debt-to-equity ratio is not alarming, though consideration of the individual business lines is necessary, but you should investigate why there has been a need for such a large increase in debt, especially in light of a much smaller increase in property, plant, and equipment. In addition, you should find out whether the new debt is for the farm or for another part of the operation. Also, you should find out what security has been provided for the existing debt and whether the owners have personally guaranteed it. This is important information because it will give you some insight into how much protection (through collateral and personal guarantees) you can obtain if you decided to lend money to the farm.

7. Consolidated liquidity on the balance sheet seems strong (the current ratio is 1.61, which is about the same as in 2008) but I am very concerned about the large increase in accounts receivable. Not much analysis of receivables is possible without the income statement and other information, but this could be a concern if the increase is not matched by increases in revenues. The downside of the increase is that Tecumseh may be having trouble collecting its receivables or, perhaps, there is a receivable to a manager or shareholder in the reported balance. Once again, you need to find out whether this increase in receivable pertains to the farm.

8. As I have indicated throughout this report, you do not have nearly enough information to make a lending decision. You need the farm's financial statements and you must obtain additional information. However, it is always important to remember that these are historical financial statements; they report past transactions. Ultimately, a lending decision should be based on the ability of an entity to generate cash flows to pay the interest on the loan and to repay the principal.

Best wishes and thanks for letting me do this report for you.

Your nephew,

John

APPENDIX

The Consolidated Financial Statements in Periods after a Subsidiary Is Purchased

In periods after the acquisition of a subsidiary, the amounts that were included in the consolidated financial statements are the basis of accounting for the subsidiary in the consolidated statements. In other words, the amounts that are on the subsidiary's balance sheet are irrelevant for preparing the consolidated balance sheet in later periods. Recall the Pefferlaw-Schuler example from the main part of the chapter. In that example, the $21.5 million fair value of Schuler's capital assets that are included in Pefferlaw's consolidated balance sheet is what is amortized. It doesn't matter that these same assets are recorded on Schuler's own balance sheet at $14 million. For purposes of preparing the consolidated financial statements, it's the $21.5 million that matters. It's not even necessary for the same method of amortization to be used on the consolidated statements as is used in the subsidiary's statements. Similarly, if the fair value of Schuler's inventory on June 30, 2010 was $2,200,000, that's the amount that would be used in the consolidated financial statements.

Remember, a subsidiary's assets and liabilities are not fair valued each time consolidated financial statements are prepared. Fair valuing is done once, when the subsidiary is acquired, and those values become the historical costs for use in the preparation of future consolidated financial statements.

There are other considerations that go into the preparation of the consolidated financial statements.

Goodwill As mentioned earlier, according to the *CICA Handbook,* **goodwill** does not have to be amortized. Management must regularly evaluate the company's goodwill and write it down if its value is somehow impaired. The write-down would reduce the amount of goodwill on the consolidated balance sheet and the amount of the reduction would be expensed on the consolidated income statement.

The Income Statement For the most part, a consolidated income statement can be prepared by adding together the income statements of the parent and the subsidiaries. Some adjustments are needed, two of which we just discussed. First, the fair value of the subsidiaries' assets and liabilities on the date the subsidiaries are purchased are used to calculate the amortization expense. Second, it may be necessary to write down goodwill. (Remember, the goodwill only appears on the consolidated financial statements, not on the financial statements of the parent or the subsidiary.) Third, it may be necessary to adjust the consolidated financial statements for intercompany transactions.

An important and useful feature of how subsidiaries are accounted for is that **intercompany transactions**—transactions among the corporations in a consolidated group—are eliminated when consolidated financial statements are prepared. This means that sales and expenses, and changes in the value of assets and liabilities that occur as a result of transactions among subsidiaries and with the parent, are not reflected in the consolidated statements. Transactions that take place among the entities in a consolidated group are recorded in the accounting records of the individual corporations and will be part of the financial statements each entity prepares, but from the perspective of the consolidated entity, these transactions have no economic significance. Only transactions with entities external to the consolidated group have economic significance. After all, have there been any economic gains to the consolidated entity if a subsidiary sells merchandise to its parent at a profit? If sales among entities in a corporate group are not eliminated, sales and expenses in the consolidated income statement will be overstated, and receivables, inventory, and payables on the balance sheet may also be overstated.

Let's use an example to examine the effect on the consolidated financial statements of sales by a subsidiary to its parent. Seech Inc. (Seech) is a 100 percent-owned subsidiary of Pitaga Ltd. (Pitaga). During the year ended December 31, 2009, Seech sold merchandise costing $2,000,000 to Pitaga for $4,500,000. These were the only transactions that Pitaga and Seech entered into during 2009. Seech recorded the sale with the following journal entries:

Dr. Accounts receivable (asset +)	4,500,000	
Cr. Revenue (revenue +, shareholders' equity +)		4,500,000
To record the sale of merchandise to Pitaga.		

Dr. Cost of sales (expense +, shareholders' equity −)	2,000,000	
Cr. Inventory (asset −)		2,000,000
To record the cost of the merchandise sold to Pitaga.		

Pitaga recorded its purchase of the merchandise from Seech with the following journal entry:

Dr. Inventory (asset −)	4,500,000	
Cr. Accounts payable (liability −)		4,500,000
To record the purchase of merchandise from Seech.		

Notice the effect of this transaction. Seech has earned a profit of $2,500,000 ($4,500,000 − $2,000,000) and the inventory it sold to Pitaga is now valued at $4,500,000 on Pitaga's balance sheet. There are receivables and payables of $4,500,000. In the context of historical cost, transactions-based accounting, nothing has happened to justify reporting the revenue and profit and the increase in the value of inventory, accounts receivable, and accounts payable in the context of the consolidated entity. From the perspective of the consolidated entity, this is no different from recognizing a profit, increasing the value of inventory, and reporting payables and receivables when moving goods from one warehouse to another.

Table 12–4 sets out the effect of intercompany transactions between Pitago and Seech:

- Column 1 shows the summarized income statements and extracts from the balance sheets of the two companies. (These statements would be used for tax purposes and perhaps by a banker who loaned money to these entities.)

- Column 2 shows Pitaga's consolidated financial statements if the intercompany transactions are not eliminated. From the information in Column 2, consolidated Pitaga appears to be an active, perhaps successful enterprise with sales of $4,500,000 and net income of $2,500,000. It is not possible to tell from these statements that no real economic activity has occurred.

- Column 3 shows the consolidated statements if the intercompany transactions are eliminated. These statements show no activity: no revenues, no expenses, inventory reported at its cost to Seech, and no receivables or payables.

Because the transactions between Pitaga and Seech do not have economic significance to the consolidated entity, intercompany transactions are eliminated when the consolidated financial statements are prepared. Imagine the effect if Pitaga and Seech sold the same items back and forth many times. Sales would be huge, but would the transactions have any economic significance?

Now let's suppose that Pitaga sold the inventory it purchased from Seech to third parties for $6,200,000 during 2009, instead of having the inventory on hand at the end of the year. Pitaga would make the following journal entries to record the sale:

Dr. Accounts receivable (asset −)	6,200,000	
Cr. Revenue (revenue +, shareholders' equity +)		6,200,000
To record the sale of merchandise to customers.		

Dr. Cost of sales (expense +, shareholders' equity −)	4,500,000	
Cr. Inventory (asset −)		4,500,000
To record the cost of the merchandise sold to customers.		

Once the inventory has been sold to a third party, problems with intercompany transactions still exist. The consolidated financial statements should reflect only the effect of transactions with entities external to the consolidated entity. This means that only sales of merchandise to third parties by Pitaga and the cost of the merchandise to the consolidated entity should be recorded. This means that the effects of the sale by Seech to Pitaga still have to be eliminated.

The summarized income statements and extracts from the balance sheets of Pitaga and Seech and the consolidated information under this scenario are provided in Table 12–5. The inventory is no longer an issue because it has been sold. The accounts receivable and payable that were recorded when Seech sold the merchandise to Pitaga still have to be eliminated, unless they are actually settled by the two companies; otherwise, receivables and payables will be overstated. The only receivable that should appear on the consolidated statements is the amount owed by the third party customers ($6,200,000). The revenue recorded by Seech from the sale to Pitaga must still be eliminated. Otherwise, the sale of the inventory appears twice—once when it was sold to Pitaga and once when Pitaga sold it to the third parties.

TABLE 12–4 ::: The Effect of Intercompany Transactions: Scenario 1 (Seech Sells Merchandise to Pitaga—Merchandise Held by Pitaga at the End of the Year)

	Column 1 Accounting Information for the Year Ended and As of December 31, 2009		Column 2 Consolidated Statements (intercompany transactions not eliminated)	Column 3 Consolidated Statements (intercompany transactions eliminated)
	Pitaga Ltd.	Seech Inc.		
Revenue	$ 0	$4,500,000	$ 4,500,000	$ 0
Cost of Sales	0	2,000,000	2,000,000	0
Net Income	0	$2,500,000	$ 2,500,000	0
Accounts Receivable	0	$4,500,000	$ 4,500,000	$ 0
Inventory	$4,500,000	0	$ 4,500,000	$ 2,000,000
Accounts Payable	$4,500,000	0	$ 4,500,000	$ 0

Columns 2 and 3 of Table 12–5 compare the financial statement impact of not eliminating (Column 2) and eliminating (Column 3) the effects of the intercompany transactions. Column 3 shows only the effect of transactions with outside entities. Revenue is only revenue earned from third parties. Cost of sales reflects only the cost of the merchandise to the consolidated entity ($2,000,000). If intercompany transactions are not eliminated, then revenues, cost of sales, accounts receivable, and accounts payable are all overstated. The entity looks much more active than it really is when intercompany transactions are not eliminated. Clearly, from the perspective of the consolidated entity, Column 3 is a better representation of its economic activity than is Column 2.

These examples highlight the effect that intercompany transactions can have on the numbers in financial statements, and the difficulties that can be created for users who want to interpret and analyze the financial statements if intercompany transactions are not eliminated. Fortunately, GAAP requires elimination of these transactions. When the financial statements of a subsidiary are being examined (not the consolidated financial statements), it is important to be aware that intercompany transactions can have a significant effect on those financial statements.

TABLE 12–5 ::: The Effect of Intercompany Transactions: Scenario 2 (Pitaga Sells Inventory Purchased from Seech to Third Parties)

	Column 1 Accounting Information for the Year Ended and As of December 31, 2009		Column 2 Consolidated Statements (intercompany transactions not eliminated)	Column 3 Consolidated Statements (intercompany transactions eliminated)
	Pitaga Ltd.	Seech Inc.		
Revenue	$6,200,000	$4,500,000	$10,700,000	$ 6,200,000
Cost of Sales	4,500,000	2,000,000	6,500,000	2,000,000
Net Income	$1,700,000	$2,500,000	$ 4,200,000	$ 4,200,000
Accounts Receivable	$6,200,000	$4,500,000	$10,700,000	$ 6,200,000
Inventory	0	0	0	0
Accounts Payable	$4,500,000	0	$ 4,500,000	$ 0

Question for Consideration

Explain why including intercompany transactions in consolidated financial statements can make those statements misleading to users.

Answer: If intercompany transactions are not eliminated from consolidated financial statements, a number of problems exist that can mislead users.

1. Revenue from sales by one member of the consolidated entity to another will be included in the consolidated revenue reported on the income statement. This will overstate the economic activity of the entity, making it appear that the entity is generating more revenue than it really is.

2. If an entity purchases inventory from another entity in the consolidated group at a profit, the value of the inventory on the balance sheet is increased, which violates the historical cost measurement convention of GAAP. While there may be merit to changing the value of inventory, this is not in accordance with GAAP. As a result, a user who is assuming that GAAP's concepts are being followed could be misled.

3. If the transactions between the corporations in the consolidated entity are not settled in cash, receivables and payables will be increased by the amounts owing between the entities, thereby overstating current assets and liabilities.

4. As a result of the effects in (1) to (3), financial ratios will be distorted from the amounts that would be reported if intercompany transactions were eliminated.

EXAMPLE OF WHEN LESS THAN 100 PERCENT OF A SUBSIDIARY IS ACQUIRED—NON-CONTROLLING INTEREST

For example, on January 31, 2009, Padlei Ltd. (Padlei) purchased 80 percent of the common shares of Schyan Inc. (Schyan) for $800,000 cash. On January 31, 2009, Schyan's balance sheet reported net assets of $1,000,000 and on that date the book value of the net assets equalled their fair value. Table 12–6 shows how this transaction affects the consolidated balance sheet.

TABLE 12–6 ::: The Effect of Non-Controlling Interest: Scenario 1 (Book Value of Subsidiary's Net Assets Equals Their Cost on the Date the Subsidiary Is Purchased)				
	Summarized Balance Sheets As of January 31, 2009		**Adjustments**	**Summarized Consolidated Balance Sheet As of January 31, 2009**
	Padlei Ltd	**Schyan Inc.**		
Net assets	$5,500,000	$1,000,000		$6,500,000
Investment in Schyan (at cost)	800,000		−800,000	0
Non-controlling shareholders' interest in consolidated Padlei's net assets			+200,000	200,000
Shareholders' equity	$6,300,000	$1,000,000	$−1,000,000	$6,300,000

Notice that net assets on the consolidated balance sheet are $6,500,000, which includes the $1,000,000 of Schyan's net assets, even though Padlei's interest in those net assets is only $800,000 ($1,000,000 × 80 percent). The other $200,000 is the net assets that belong to the non-controlling shareholders of Schyan ($1,000,000 × 20 percent). The consolidated balance sheet is reporting 100 percent of the net assets that the parent controls, not just the 80 percent that the parent owns. The non-controlling interest represents the equity that Schyan's non-controlling shareholders have in Padlei's consolidated net assets. The non-controlling interest account appears on the liabilities and shareholders' equity side of the balance sheet.

Perhaps surprisingly, the amount reported for non-controlling interest on the balance sheet is not affected if the market value of the subsidiary's net assets is not the same as their book value on the date a subsidiary is purchased. The reason is that GAAP allows only the parent's share of the fair value adjustments and goodwill to appear on the consolidated balance sheet. The non-controlling interest on the balance sheet is simply the book value of the non-controlling shareholders' interest in the net assets of the subsidiary.

The result is that a consolidated balance sheet includes a potentially confusing mix of measurements—100 percent of the book value of a subsidiary's net assets (the parent's and the non-controlling interest's share), plus the parent's share of the difference between fair value and book value. The rationale for this treatment is an application of the historical cost measurement convention. Since only the parent's share of the subsidiary has been purchased, only the parent's share of the fair value is recorded.

Returning to the Padlei–Schyan example, suppose that the market value of Schyan's net assets was $1,125,000 and Padlei paid $900,000 for its 80 percent interest ($1,125,000 × 80 percent) in Schyan (assume no goodwill). The consolidated balance sheet would include 100 percent of the book value of Schyan's net assets ($1,000,000—the amount on Schyan's balance sheet) plus 80 percent of the difference between the fair value and book value of Schyan's net assets on the date the subsidiary was purchased—$100,000 ([$1,125,000 − $1,000,000]× 80 percent). The non-controlling interest would still be $200,000 ($1,000,0000 × 20 percent) because only the parent's share of the difference between the fair value and book value of the net assets is included in the consolidated balance sheet. Therefore, the non-controlling shareholders' equity in Padlei's net assets is $200,000.

The effects of this situation are shown in Table 12–7. As we will discuss next, non-controlling interest does change over time, reflecting the non-controlling shareholders' share of consolidated net income.

Now let's look at the income statement. The summarized income statements of Padlei and Schyan and the summarized consolidated income statement for fiscal 2010 are shown in

TABLE 12–7 ::: **The Effect of Non-Controlling Interest: Scenario 2 (Fair Value of Subsidiary's Net Assets Greater than Their Cost on the Date the Subsidiary is Purchased)**

	Summarized Balance Sheets As of January 31, 2009		Adjustments	Summarized Consolidated Balance Sheet As of January 31, 2009
	Padlei Ltd	Schyan Inc.		
Net assets	$5,400,000	$1,000,000	+$1,000,000	$6,500,000
Investment in Schyan (at cost)	900,000		−900,000	0
Non-controlling shareholders' interest in consolidated Padlei's net assets			+200,000	200,000
Shareholders' equity	$6,300,000	$1,000,000	$−1,000,000	$6,300,000

Table 12–8. Notice that 100 percent of Schyan's revenues and expenses are included in the consolidated income statement, even though 20 percent of those revenues and expenses belong to the non-controlling interest. Remember that net income is a measure of the change in wealth of the owners of an entity—in this case, the owners of Padlei. The $50,000 ($250,000 × 20 percent) of Schyan's net income that belongs to Schyan's non-controlling shareholder should not be included in Padlei's consolidated net income because it doesn't belong to the owners of Padlei. If it were included, Padlei's consolidated net income would be overstated. There would be $50,000 in net income that belonged to others. Therefore, $50,000 is deducted in the calculation of consolidated net income.

The amount deducted not only reduces consolidated net income, it also increases the balance in the non-controlling interest account on the balance sheet. The reason is that the non-controlling interest's equity in the consolidated entity's net assets has increased by $50,000. The non-controlling interest account on the consolidated balance sheet can be thought of as the non-controlling interest's equity in the consolidated entity's net assets.

The non-controlling interest appears on the consolidated balance sheet between liabilities and shareholders' equity. Non-controlling interest is equity, but it is the equity of the non-controlling shareholders of the subsidiaries, not the equity of the parent's shareholders. It is not a liability because there is no obligation to anyone.

On the consolidated income statement, non-controlling interest appears as a deduction in the calculation of consolidated net income.

On the consolidated cash flow statement, the non-controlling interest reported on the consolidated income statement is added back to net income when calculating cash from operations using the indirect method. The non-controlling interest is added back because it does not represent cash distributed to the non-controlling shareholders—it is the allocation of income to the non-controlling shareholders.

The amount of cash within the consolidated entity is not affected by the deduction of non-controlling interest on the income statement. Cash is affected only when a dividend is paid to the shareholders.

One final remark: Non-controlling interest appears in consolidated financial statements only because GAAP require that 100 percent of a subsidiary's net assets, revenues, and expenses be reported, even if the parent owns less than 100 percent of the subsidiary. If GAAP required that only the parent's share of the subsidiary's net assets, revenues, and expenses be included, there would be no non-controlling interest.

TABLE 12–8 ::: Non-Controlling Interest and the Income Statement

	Summarized Income Statement For the Year Ended January 31, 2010		Consolidated Income Statement For the Year Ended January 31, 2010
	Padlei Ltd	Schyan Inc.	
Revenues	$1,000,000	$750,000	$1,750,000
Expenses	700,000	500,000	1,200,000
Income before non-controlling interest			550,000
Non-controlling interest			(50,000)*
Net Income	$300,000	$250,000	$500,000

* The non-controlling interest's share of Padlei's net income is equal to 20 percent of Schyan Inc.'s net income ($250,000 × 20 percent).

SUMMARY OF KEY POINTS

▶ **LO 1** When an investor has control of an investee, the investor prepares consolidated financial statements. Consolidated financial statements aggregate the accounting information of a parent corporation and all of its subsidiaries into a single set of financial statements. On the consolidated balance sheet, the assets and liabilities of a subsidiary are reported at their fair value on the date the subsidiary was purchased. The consolidated income statement combines the revenues and expenses of the parent and its subsidiaries, but with three types of adjustments: amortization of fair value adjustments, possible write-down of goodwill, and elimination of the effects of intercompany transactions.

If a parent pays more than the fair value of the subsidiary's identifiable assets and liabilities on the date the subsidiary is purchased, goodwill arises. Goodwill can be recognized only when one entity purchases another and, according to GAAP, goodwill is not amortized. Instead, management must estimate the fair value of the goodwill each year, and if the fair value is less than the book value, the goodwill must be written down to its fair value.

When a parent company owns less than 100 percent of the shares of a subsidiary, but still controls it, accounts called non-controlling interest are reported on the consolidated balance sheet and income statement. Non-controlling interest arises because GAAP require that the consolidated balance sheet include 100 percent of the book values of a subsidiary's assets and liabilities, and 100 percent of the revenues and expenses, even though the parent owns less than 100 percent of those assets and liabilities.

▶ **LO 2** When one corporation has significant influence on the decision making of another corporation, the equity method of accounting is used. The equity method of accounting is essentially the same as accounting for subsidiaries using the consolidation method, except that the information about equity-accounted-for investments is presented on a single line on the balance sheet and a single line on the income statement. An investment accounted for using the equity method is initially recorded on the investor's balance sheet at cost. The balance sheet amount is then adjusted each period by the investor's share of the investee's net income, less dividends declared by the investee. The investor's share is determined by multiplying the investee's net income (after necessary adjustments) by the percentage of the investee that the investor owns.

The rationale for the equity method is that if an investor corporation has significant influence, it can affect the important policies of an investee corporation, such as the timing and amount of the dividends the latter pays.

▶ **LO 3** Passive investments are investments for which the investor corporation can't influence the strategic decision making of the investee corporation. All investments in non-voting securities are accounted for as passive investments. Voting shares are accounted for as passive investments when the investing company holds a relatively small proportion of the investee corporation's voting shares.

Passive investments can be classified as hold-to-maturity, trading, and available-for-sale. Held-to-maturity investments must have a maturity date, fixed or determinable payments, and the intent and ability of management to hold the investment to maturity. Hold-to-maturity investments are accounted for using the cost method. Trading investments are investments that management designates as a trading investment. Investments in this category are actively bought and sold for profit making. Available-for-sale investments is the default category. Any investment that does not give control or significant influence to the investing corporation, or that doesn't meet the criteria for classification as a held-to-maturity or trading investment, is considered an available-for-sale investment. Trading and available-for-sale investments are valued at their market value. All gains and losses on trading investments are recognized in the income statement in the period they occur, regardless of whether they are realized. Unrealized gains and losses on available-for-sale investments are treated as other comprehensive income.

The classification of passive investments depends in part on management intentions and, therefore, management's choices can affect the financial statements.

KEY TERMS

available-for-sale investments, p. 672

consolidated financial statement, p. 660

control, p. 660

equity method of accounting, p. 668

fair value, p. 662

held-to-maturity investments, p. 671

goodwill, p. 678

Identifiable assets, p. 662

Identifiable liabilities, p. 662

intercompany transaction, p. 678

investee corporation, p. 659

investor corporation, p. 659

non-controlling interest, p. 665

parent corporation, p. 660

passive investment, p. 669

segment disclosure, p. 667

significant influence, p. 668

subsidiary corporation, p. 660

trading investments, p. 672

SIMILAR TERMS

The left column gives alternative terms that are sometimes used for the accounting terms introduced in this chapter, which are listed in the right column.

minority interest   **non-controlling interest, p. 665**

market value   **fair value, p. 662**

ASSIGNMENT MATERIALS

Questions

Q12-1. What is goodwill? Under what circumstances is it recorded on financial statements?

Q12-2. Why is understanding the extent to which one corporation influences another important for accounting purposes? What impact does the degree of influence one entity has over another entity have on accounting?

Q12-3. Explain the following degrees of influence that one corporation can have over another and the implications of each for financial reporting:
a. control
b. significant influence
c. no influence

Q12-4. What are consolidated financial statements? What are some of the benefits and limitations of them?

Q12-5. Why do companies invest in other companies?

Q12-6. What are intercompany transactions? Why are the effects of intercompany transactions eliminated when consolidated financial statements are prepared?

Q12-7. What is a subsidiary? How are subsidiaries accounted for? Explain.

Q12-8. What is meant by the term "non-controlling interest"? What does the non-controlling interest on a company's balance sheet represent? What does non-controlling interest on the income statement represent?

Q12-9. Why is non-controlling interest added back to net income when calculating cash from operations using the indirect method?

Q12-10. Explain how a non-controlling shareholder in a subsidiary would use the non-controlling interest accounts on the parent's consolidated balance sheet and income statement.

Q12-11. When a subsidiary is acquired, the managers of the parent must allocate the purchase price to the subsidiary's identifiable assets and liabilities. Because the subsidiary's assets and liabilities are bought as a bundle, management has some flexibility in how it allocates the purchase price. Given this flexibility, how do you think the objectives of financial reporting would affect how management allocates the purchase price? Explain.

Q12-12. What is segment disclosure? Why is segment information required in the financial statements of public companies?

Q12-13. Explain the usefulness of the consolidated financial statements of a parent corporation for the following stakeholders:
a. shareholder of the parent corporation
b. major supplier of one of the subsidiaries
c. Canada Revenue Agency (for income tax determination)

Q12-14. What are the three categories of passive investments? Explain the differences in how each category is accounted for.

Q12-15. Explain why consolidated financial statements are not just the sum of the amounts reported on the parent's and subsidiaries' financial statements.

Q12-16. Explain the following terms:
a. investor corporation
b. investee corporation
c. parent corporation
d. subsidiary corporation

Q12-17. When the equity method of accounting for investments is used, dividends received from the investee corporation reduce the balance in the investment account on the investor's balance sheet. The dividends are not treated as investment income on the income statement. Explain.

Q12-18. Explain the difference between the parent's consolidated financial statements and the financial statements of the parent alone.

Exercises

E12-1. **(Accounting for different types of investments in securities, LO 2, 3, 4)** How should an investor corporation account for the following investments?
a. Ownership of 51 percent of the shares of a company.
b. Ownership of 20 percent of the outstanding common shares of a company. These common shares represent 60 percent of the votes.
c. Ownership of 25 percent of the shares of a company.
d. Ownership of 0.05 percent of the shares of a company.

E12-2. **(Accounting for different types of investments in securities, LO 2, 3, 4)** State how the investor corporation would account for the following investments. Explain your choice.
a. Purchase of $1,000,000 of bonds that management intends to hold until they mature in three years.
b. Investment in non-voting shares of a private corporation. Management hopes to sell the shares within six months.
c. Investment in voting shares of a private corporation. The investment represents 15 percent of the voting shares of the corporation. One person owns the remaining shares.
d. Investment in 52 percent of the voting shares of a private corporation. One person owns the remaining shares.
e. Investment in 30 percent of the voting shares of a public corporation. The investor corporation is the largest single investor in the public corporation and it has five representatives on its board of directors.
f. Investment in 60 percent of the voting shares of a public corporation. The investor corporation intends to sell its investment within six months.

E12-3. **(Impact of investments on the cash flow statement, LO 4)** For each of the following transactions and economic events explain how the cash flow statement would be affected:

a. A company purchases 1,000 shares of a public company for $50 per share. The company pays for the shares in cash.

b. A company receives a dividend cheque declared on shares that it owns.

c. The market value of an investment classified as a trading investment increases from $10 to $12 over the year. As of year end the shares are still owned by the company.

d. The market value of an investment classified as an available-for-sale investment increases from $10 to $12 over the year. As of year end the shares are still owned by the company.

e. The market value of an investment classified as a held-to-maturity investment increases from $10 to $12 over the year. As of year end the shares are still owned by the company.

f. A company sells 20,000 shares that it has been holding as a passive investment for $10 per share. The shares originally cost $7 per share.

g. A company exchanges 20,000 shares that it has been holding as a passive investment for equipment. The market value of the shares on the date of the exchange is $11 per share and the original cost of the shares was $9 per share.

E12-4. **(Non-controlling interest, LO 2)** On December 31, 2009, Kootuk Inc. (Kootuk) purchased 80 percent of the common shares of Grimmer Ltd. (Grimmer) for $1,750,000. At the time of the purchase, Kootuk's management made the following estimates of the fair values of Grimmer's assets and liabilities:

	Book Value of Grimmer's Assets and Liabilities on December 31, 2009	**Fair Value of Grimmer's Assets and Liabilities on December 31, 2009**
Assets	$2,500,000	$3,000,000
Liabilities	1,000,000	1,200,000

Required:

a. Calculate the amount of non-controlling interest that Kootuk would report on its December 31, 2009 consolidated balance sheet as a result of its purchase of Grimmer.

b. What amount would be included in the assets and liabilities on the Kootuk's December 31, 2009 consolidated balance sheet as a result of the purchase of Grimmer?

E12-5. **(Non-controlling interest, LO 2)** On August 31, 2010 Hoselaw Inc. (Hoselaw) purchased **75 percent** of the common shares of Upsalquitch Ltd. (Upsalquitch) for $16,000,000. At the time of the purchase, Upsalquitch's management made the following estimates of the fair values of Upsalquitch's assets and liabilities:

	Book Value of Upsalquitch's Assets and Liabilities on August 31, 2010	**Fair Value of Upsalquitch's Assets and Liabilities on August 31, 2010**
Current assets	$2,000,000	$2,500,000
Tangible capital assets	6,000,000	7,200,000
Patents	200,000	2,000,000
Current liabilities	1,750,000	1,800,000
Long-term debt	4,250,000	4,000,000

Required:

a. Calculate the amount of non-controlling interest that Hoselaw would report on its August 31, 2010 consolidated balance sheet as a result of its purchase of Upsalquitch.

b. What amount would be included in each asset and liability account on the August 31, 2010 consolidated balance sheet as a result of the purchase of Upsalquitch?

c. What does non-controlling interest on the balance sheet represent? Explain why it appears. How should users of financial statements interpret non-controlling interest?

E12-6. **(Accounting for passive investments, LO 4)** Chockpish Inc. (Chockpish) has provided you with the following list of transactions and economic events that involved its investment portfolio in 2010. For each of the items on the list, prepare any necessary journal entries required. Explain your entries fully. Chockpish's year end is December 31.

a. On January 15, 2,000 shares of Inwood Corp. were purchased at $37 per share.

b. On February 12, a cheque for $10,000 was received from Guthrie Inc. for dividends.

c. At the close of trading on December 31, bonds of Hydraulic Corp. were priced $980 per thousand dollar bond. Chockpish's 100 bonds have a book value of $1,000 per bond and the company plans to hold the bonds until they mature in 2013.

d. At the close of trading on December 31, shares of Kynoch Ltd. were priced at $12 per share. Chockpish's 5,000 shares of Kynoch Ltd. have a book value of $15 per share. Chockpish plans to continue holding these shares for the foreseeable future.

e. At the close of trading on December 31, shares of Jobrin Inc. were priced at $19 per share. Chockpish's 3,000 shares of Jobrin Ltd. have a book value of $22 per share. Chockpish plans to sell the shares by March 31, 2011.

E12-7. **(Accounting for portfolio investments, LO 4)** Yellek Inc. (Yellek) is a private corporation owned by the Yellek family. Yellek maintains a significant investment portfolio of publicly traded shares as a method of maximizing the return on surplus cash that the family keeps in the company. In March 2009, Yellek purchased 25,000 shares of Viking Corp. (Viking), a public company that trades on the Toronto Stock Exchange, for $20 per share. Then in May 2009, Yellek purchased an additional 10,000 shares of Viking for $23 per share. During 2009, Viking declared and paid a dividend of $0.12 a share on April 30 and a dividend of $0.12 a share on September 30. On November 12, 2009 Yellek sold 15,000 of its Viking shares for $25 per share because it needed cash to pay dividends to members of the family.

On December 12, 2009 Viking made an announcement that stunned the investment community. Viking was being forced to close one of its operating facilities permanently because of environmental concerns. The facility was responsible for about 20 percent of its annual production and the company said that it did not think it would be able to make up the lost production in the short term. Immediately after the announcement, Viking's share price fell to $13 per share. On December 31, 2009 Viking's shares closed at $13.25.

Required:

a. Prepare the journal entries to record the purchase of Viking shares during 2009.

b. Prepare the journal entries to account for the dividends declared and paid by Viking during 2009.

c. Prepare the journal entry to record the sale of Viking shares on November 12, 2009. Assume that Viking uses the specific identification method of accounting for its securities. Explain your entry.

d. How would you account for the effects of the announcement made by Viking on December 12, 2009? Explain. Prepare any journal entry required. Indicate the amount that would be reported on Yellek's balance sheet for its investment in Viking.

E12-8. **(Consolidation accounting, LO 2)** In order to expand its market penetration in the retail clothing market Balmoral Designs Ltd. (Balmoral) purchased 100 percent of the outstanding shares of Chipman Fine Clothiers Inc. (Chipman). Balmoral paid $2,100,000 for the shares and its management determined that at the time of acquisition the fair value of Chipman's identifiable assets and liabilities was $1,200,000. The following information was obtained as of the date Chipman was acquired:

	Balmoral	Chipman (Book Values)	Chipman (Fair Values)		Balmoral	Chipman (Book Values)	Chipman (Fair Values)
Current assets	$3,500,000	$ 950,000	$1,200,000	Current liabilities	$2,500,000	$ 375,000	$375,000
Non-current assets	2,500,000	25,000	585,000	Non-current liabilities	1,000,000	200,000	210,000
				Shareholders' equity	2,500,000	900,000	
Total assets	$6,000,000	$1,475,000		Total liabilities and shareholders' equity	$6,000,000	$1,475,000	

Required:

Calculate the amounts that would appear on Balmoral's consolidated balance sheet on the date it acquired Chipman.

E12-9. **(Consolidation accounting, LO 2)** In order to expand its product line Dorchester Manufacturing Ltd. (Dorchester) purchased 100 percent of the outstanding shares of Hardisty Inc. (Hardisty). Dorchester paid $7,000,000 for the shares. The following information was obtained as of the date Hardisty was acquired:

	Dorchester	Hardisty (Book Values)	Hardisty (Fair Values)		Dorchester	Hardisty (Book Values)	Hardisty (Fair Values)
Current assets	$ 8,500,000	$ 3,000,000	$ 3,800,000	Current liabilities	$ 6,500,000	$ 2,500,000	$2,700,000
Non-current assets	32,500,000	10,000,000	12,000,000	Non-current liabilities	18,000,000	6,300,000	7,100,000
				Shareholders' equity	16,500,000	7,000,000	
Total assets	$41,000,000	$13,000,000	$15,800,000	Total liabilities and shareholders' equity	$41,000,000	$15,800,000	

Required:

Calculate the amounts that would appear on Dorchester's consolidated balance sheet on the date it acquired Hardisty.

E12-10. **The equity method of accounting, LO 3, 4)** On January 1, 2009 Fletwode Corp. (Fletwode) purchased 1,125,000 common shares of Irvine Ltd. (Irvine) for $5,000,000. The investment represents a 30 percent interest in Irvine and gives Fletwode significant influence over Irvine. For 2009 Fletwode's share of Irvine's net income was $195,000 and during the year Irvine paid dividends of $0.20 per share. Both companies have December 31 year ends.

Required:

    a. Prepare the journal entry that Fletwode would make to record its investment in Irvine.

    b. What amount would be reported on Fletwode's December 31, 2009 balance sheet for its investment in Irvine? How much would Fletwode report on its December 31, 2009 income statement from its investment in Irvine?

E12-11. **(The equity method of accounting, LO 3)** On June 1, 2009 Wostok Corp. (Wostok) purchased 1,000,000 common shares of Griffin Ltd. (Griffin) for $2,000,000. The investment represents a 40 percent interest in Griffin and gives Wostok significant influence over Griffin. During fiscal 2010 Wostok's share of Griffin's net income was $440,000. Also, Griffin paid dividends during the year of $0.50 per share. Both companies have May 31 year ends.

Required:

    a. Prepare the journal entry that Wostok would make to record its investment in Griffin.

    b. How much would Wostok report on its May 31, 2010 income statement from its investment in Griffin?

    c. What amount would be reported on Wostok's May 31, 2010 balance sheet for its investment in Griffin?

E12-12. **(Consolidated income statement, LO 2—Appendix)** Explain how the following items would affect consolidated net income in the year the subsidiary is purchased and the year after it is purchased:

    a. Impairment of the value of goodwill.

    b. Land with a book value of $2,000,000 on the subsidiary's balance sheet on the date the subsidiary was purchased has a fair value of $5,000,000 on that date.

    c. Equipment with a book value of $1,000,000 on the subsidiary's balance sheet on the date the subsidiary was purchased has a fair value of $1,500,000 on that date. The equipment has a remaining useful life of five years.

    d. Inventory with a book value of $200,000 on the subsidiary's balance sheet on the date the subsidiary was purchased has a fair value of $230,000 on that date.

    e. Dividends paid by the subsidiary to the parent.

    f. Services sold at a profit by the subsidiary to the parent.

    g. The subsidiary is 80 percent owned by the parent.

Problems

P12-1. **(Accounting for passive investments, LO 4)** In June 2008, Jolicure Inc. (Jolicure) and Horsefly Inc. (Horsefly) each began operations. Each company was formed with an initial capital contribution of $200,000. During the year ended May 31, 2009, each company had revenue of $450,000 and total expenses of $350,000. In addition, during the first year of operations each company purchased 1,000 shares of Nictaux Ltd. (Nictaux), a public company, for $24 per share. In May 2009 Horsefly sold its shares in Nictaux for $40 per share and immediately repurchased them at the same price. Jolicure did not sell its shares during fiscal 2009. On May 31, 2009 each company had total assets (excluding the shares in Nictaux) of $336,000 and total liabilities of $60,000. For both companies, the investment was considered as available-for-sale. Assume that the market value of the investment was $40 per share.

Required:

    a. Prepare summarized balance sheets for Jolicure and Horsefly as of May 31, 2009.

    b. Prepare summarized income statements for Jolicure and Horsefly for the year ended May 31, 2009.

    c. Which company performed better in fiscal 2009?

    d. Why do you think Horsefly sold and repurchased the shares in Nictaux? Do you think that this was a wise transaction to enter into? Explain.

P12-2. **(Accounting for passive investments, LO 4)** On August 1, 2009 Lourdes Inc. (Lourdes) purchased 10,000 preferred shares of Matagami Ltd. for $100 per share. The shares have a dividend of $10 per share and must be repurchased by the Matagami on or before November 30, 2015 for $100 per share. On December 31, 2009, Lourdes' year end, the market value of the shares was $90 per share. On December 31, 2009 Lourdes had total assets (excluding the investment in the preferred shares) of $20 million, total liabilities of $15 million and capital stock of $2 million. In addition, Lourdes revenues and expenses for 2009 (excluding all income statement effects related to the preferred shares) were $4,200,000 and $3,100,000 respectively.

Required:

    a. Prepare a summarized balance sheet on December 31, 2009 assuming that Lourdes accounts for the shares as a (i) trading investment, (ii) held-to-maturity investment, and (iii) available-for-sale investment, assuming that Lourdes owned the shares on December 31, 2009.

    b. Prepare a summarized income statement and statement of comprehensive income for the year ended December 31, 2009 assuming that Lourdes accounts for the shares as a (i) trading investment, (ii) held-to-maturity investment, and (iii) available-for-sale investment, assuming that Lourdes owned the shares on December 31, 2009.

    c. Prepare a summarized balance sheet on December 31, 2009 assuming that Lourdes accounts for the shares as a (i) trading investment, (ii) held-to-maturity investment, and (iii) available-for-sale investment, assuming that Lourdes sold the shares on December 31, 2009 for $90 per share.

    d. Prepare a summarized income statement and statement of comprehensive income for the year ended December 31, 2009 assuming that Lourdes accounts for the shares as a (i) trading investment, (ii) held-to-maturity investment, and (iii) available-for-sale investment, assuming that Lourdes sold the shares on December 31, 2009 for $90 per share.

P12-3. **(Preparation of a consolidated balance sheet on the date a subsidiary is purchased, LO 2)** On August 31, 2009 Pacquet Inc. (Pacquet) purchased 100 percent of the common shares of Schwitzer Ltd. (Schwitzer) for $4,000,000 cash. Pacquet's and Schwitzer's balance sheets on August 31, 2009 just before the purchase were:

Balance Sheets As of August 31, 2009		
	Pacquet Inc.	**Schwitzer Ltd.**
Current assets	$ 7,000,000	$1,250,000
Capital assets	6,500,000	2,500,000
Total assets	$13,500,000	$3,750,000
Current liabilities	$ 2,700,000	$ 750,000
Non-current liabilities	2,500,000	1,000,000
Capital stock	4,000,000	500,000
Retained earnings	4,300,000	1,500,000
Total liabilities and shareholders' equity	$13,500,000	$3,750,000

Management determined that the fair values of Schwitzer's assets and liabilities were as follows:

	Fair Value of Schwitzer's Assets and Liabilities on August 31, 2009
Current assets	$1,750,000
Capital assets	3,900,000
Current liabilities	750,000
Non-current liabilities	1,100,000

Required:

a. Prepare Pacquet's balance sheet immediately following the purchase.
b. Calculate the amount of goodwill that would be reported on Pacquet's consolidated balance sheet on August 31, 2009.
c. Prepare Pacquet's consolidated balance sheet on August 31, 2009.
d. Calculate the current ratios and debt-to-equity ratios for Pacquet, Schwitzer, and for the consolidated balance sheet. Interpret the differences between the ratios. When calculating the ratios, use Pacquet and Schwitzer's balance sheets after the purchase had been made and recorded.
e. You are a lender who has been asked to make a sizeable loan to Schwitzer. Which balance sheets would you be interested in viewing? Explain. How would you use Pacquet's consolidated financial statements in making your lending decision?

P12-4. **(Preparation of a consolidated balance sheet on the date a subsidiary is purchased, LO 2)** On January 31, 2010, Paju Inc. (Paju) purchased 100 percent of the common shares of Shellmouth Ltd. (Shellmouth) for $5,000,000 in cash. Paju's and Shellmouth's balance sheets on January 31, 2010 just before the purchase were:

Balance Sheets As of January 31, 2010		
	Paju Inc.	Shellmouth Ltd.
Current assets	$ 6,000,000	$4,500,000
Capital assets	11,750,000	1,500,000
Total assets	$17,750,000	$6,000,000
Current liabilities	$ 1,200,000	$1,500,000
Non-current liabilities	6,000,000	500,000
Capital stock	7,500,000	3,000,000
Retained earnings	3,050,000	1,000,000
Total liabilities and shareholders' equity	$17,750,000	$6,000,000

Management determined that the fair values of Shellmouth's assets and liabilities were as follows:

	Fair Value of Shellmouth's Assets and Liabilities on January 31, 2010
Current assets	$3,900,000
Capital assets	1,900,000
Current liabilities	1,600,000
Non-current liabilities	750,000

Required:

a. Prepare Paju's balance sheet immediately following the purchase.
b. Calculate the amount of goodwill that would be reported on Paju's consolidated balance sheet on January 31, 2010.

c. Prepare Paju's consolidated balance sheet on January 31, 2010.

d. Calculate the current ratios and debt-to-equity ratios for Paju, Shellmouth, and for the consolidated balance sheet. Interpret the differences between the ratios. When calculating the ratios, use Paju's and Shellmouth's balance sheets after the purchase has been made and recorded.

e. You are a potential investor who has been asked to purchase a 25 percent equity interest in Shellmouth (you would purchase the shares from Shellmouth, not from Paju). Which balance sheets would you be interested in viewing? Explain. How would you use Paju's consolidated financial statements in making your investment decision? What concerns would you have about making an equity investment in Shellmouth?

P12-5. **(Preparation of a consolidated balance sheet on the date a subsidiary is purchased when less than 100 percent of the subsidiary is purchased, Appendix)** On March 31, 2010 Popkum Inc. (Popkum) purchased 60 percent of the common shares of Saguay Ltd. (Saguay) for $1,500,000. Popkum's and Saguay's balance sheets on March 31, 2010 just before the purchase were:

Balance Sheets As of March 31, 2010		
	Popkum Inc.	**Saguay Ltd.**
Current assets	$3,500,000	$ 625,000
Capital assets	3,250,000	1,250,000
Total assets	$6,750,000	$1,875,000
Current liabilities	$1,350,000	$375,000
Non-current liabilities	1,250,000	500,000
Capital stock	2,000,000	250,000
Retained earnings	2,150,000	750,000
Total liabilities and shareholders' equity	$6,750,000	$1,875,000

Management determined that the fair values of Saguay's assets and liabilities were as follows:

	Fair Value of Saguay's Assets and Liabilities on March 31, 2010
Current assets	$ 875,000
Capital assets	1,950,000
Current liabilities	375,000
Non-current liabilities	550,000

Required:

a. Calculate the amount of goodwill that would be reported on Popkum's consolidated balance sheet on March 31, 2010.

b. Calculate the amount of non-controlling interest that would be reported on the consolidated balance sheet on March 31, 2010.

c. Prepare Popkum's consolidated balance sheet on March 31, 2010.

d. Calculate the current ratios and debt-to-equity ratios for Popkum, Saguay, and for the consolidated balance sheet. Interpret the differences between the ratios.

e. Explain what the non-controlling interest on the balance sheet represents. How would you interpret it from the perspective of a shareholder of Popkum? How would you interpret it from the perspective of a shareholder in Saguay? How would you interpret it from the perspective of a lender?

P12-6. **(Preparation of a consolidated balance sheet on the date a subsidiary is purchased when less than 100 percent of the subsidiary is purchased, Appendix)** On October 31, 2009, Pahonan Inc. (Pahonan) purchased 75 percent of the common shares of

Seebe Ltd. (Seebe) for $1,500,000. Pahonan's and Seebe's balance sheets on October 31, 2009 just before the purchase were:

Balance Sheets As of October 31, 2009		
	Pahonan Inc.	Seebe Ltd.
Current assets	$2,000,000	$2,250,000
Capital assets	6,875,000	750,000
Total assets	$8,875,000	$3,000,000
Current liabilities	$ 600,000	$ 750,000
Non-current liabilities	3,000,000	250,000
Capital stock	3,750,000	1,500,000
Retained earnings	1,525,000	500,000
Total liabilities and shareholders' equity	$8,875,000	$3,000,000

Management determined that the fair values of Seebe's assets and liabilities were as follows:

	Fair Value of Seebe's Assets and Liabilities on October 31, 2009
Current assets	$1,950,000
Capital assets	950,000
Current liabilities	800,000
Non-current liabilities	375,000

Required:

a. Prepare the journal entry that Pahonan would prepare to record its purchase of Seebe's shares.
b. Prepare the journal entry that Seebe would prepare to record its purchase by Pahonan.
c. Calculate the amount of goodwill that would be reported on Pahonan's consolidated balance sheet on October 31, 2009.
d. Calculate the amount of non-controlling interest that would be reported on the consolidated balance sheet on October 31, 2009.
e. Prepare Pahonan's consolidated balance sheet on October 31, 2009.
f. Calculate the current ratios and debt-to-equity ratios for Pahonan and Seebe, and for the consolidated balance sheet. Interpret the differences between the ratios.
g. Explain what the non-controlling interest on the balance sheet represents. How would you interpret it from the perspective of a shareholder of Pahonan? How would you interpret it from the perspective of a shareholder in Seebe? How would you interpret it from the perspective of a lender?

P12-7. (Intercompany transactions, Appendix) Vonda Inc. (Vonda) is a 100 percent-owned subsidiary of Atik Ltd. (Atik). During the year ended March 31, 2009, Vonda sold, on credit, merchandise costing $1,000,000 to Atik for $2,000,000. These were the only transactions that Atik and Vonda entered into during fiscal 2009 (with each other or with third parties) and there were no other costs incurred.

Required:

a. Prepare an income statement for Vonda for the year ended March 31, 2009.
b. What amount of accounts receivable would Vonda report on its March 31, 2009 balance sheet?

c. What amount of inventory and accounts payable would Atik report on its March 31, 2009 balance sheet?

d. Prepare Atik's March 31, 2009 consolidated income statement assuming that intercompany transactions are not eliminated. How much would be reported for accounts receivable, inventory, and accounts payable on the March 31, 2009 consolidated balance sheet?

e. Prepare Atik's March 31, 2009 consolidated income statement, assuming that intercompany transactions are eliminated. How much would be reported for accounts receivable, inventory, and accounts payable on the March 31, 2009 consolidated balance sheet?

f. Discuss the differences in the information you prepared in parts (d) and (e). Which information is more useful to stakeholders? Explain.

P12-8. **(Intercompany transactions, Appendix)** Batteau Inc. (Batteau) is a 100 percent-owned subsidiary of Castaway Ltd. (Castaway). During the year ended May 31, 2010, Batteau sold, on credit, merchandise costing $700,000 to Castaway for $1,200,000. During fiscal 2010 Castaway sold, on credit, the merchandise it had purchased from Batteau to third parties for $2,000,000. These were the only transactions that Castaway and Batteau entered into during 2010 (with each other or with third parties) and there were no other costs incurred.

Required:

a. Prepare an income statement for Batteau for the year ended May 31, 2010.

b. What amount of accounts receivable would Batteau report on its May 31, 2010 balance sheet?

c. What amount of inventory and accounts payable would Castaway report on its May 31, 2010 balance sheet?

d. Prepare Castaway's May 31, 2010 consolidated income statement assuming that intercompany transactions are not eliminated. How much would be reported for accounts receivable, inventory, and accounts payable on the May 31, 2010 consolidated balance sheet?

e. Prepare Castaway's May 31, 2010 consolidated income statement, assuming that intercompany transactions are eliminated. How much would be reported for accounts receivable, inventory, and accounts payable on the May 31, 2010 consolidated balance sheet?

f. Discuss the differences in the information you prepared in parts (d) and (e). Which information is more useful to stakeholders? Explain.

P12-9. **(Intercompany transactions, Appendix)** Guilds Inc. (Guilds) is a 100 percent-owned subsidiary of Nutak Ltd. (Nutak). During the year ended August 31, 2009, Guilds sold merchandise costing $200,000 to Nutak for $500,000. These were the only transactions that Nutak and Guilds entered into during 2008 (with each other or with third parties) and there were no other costs incurred. The sale was on credit.

Required:

a. Prepare an income statement for Guilds for the year ended August 31, 2009.

b. What amount of accounts receivable would Guilds report on its August 31, 2009 balance sheet?

c. What amount of inventory and accounts payable would Nutak report on its August 31, 2009 balance sheet?

d. Prepare Nutak's August 31, 2009 consolidated income statement assuming that intercompany transactions are not eliminated. How much would be reported for accounts receivable, inventory, and accounts payable on the August 31, 2009 consolidated balance sheet?

e. Prepare Nutak's August 31, 2009 consolidated income statement assuming that intercompany transactions are eliminated. How much would be reported for accounts receivable, inventory, and accounts payable on the August 31, 2009 consolidated balance sheet?

f. Discuss the differences in the information you prepared in parts (d) and (e). Which information is more useful to stakeholders? Explain.

P12-10. **(Intercompany transactions, Appendix)** Dozois Inc. (Dozois) is a 100 percent-owned subsidiary of Yarbo Ltd. (Yarbo). During the year ended July 31, 2010, Dozois sold merchandise costing $2,200,000 to Yarbo for $3,000,000. During fiscal 2010, Yarbo sold, on credit, the merchandise it had purchased from Dozois to third parties for $3,200,000. These were the only transactions that Yarbo and Dozois entered into during 2010 (with each other or with third parties) and there were no other costs incurred.

Required:

a. Prepare an income statement for Dozois for the year ended July 31, 2010.

b. What amount of accounts receivable would Dozois report on its July 31, 2010 balance sheet?

c. What amount of inventory and accounts payable would Yarbo report on its July 31, 2010 balance sheet?

d. Prepare Yarbo's July 31, 2010 consolidated income statement assuming that intercompany transactions are not eliminated. How much would be reported for accounts receivable, inventory, and accounts payable on the July 31, 2010 consolidated balance sheet?

e. Prepare Yarbo's July 31, 2010 consolidated income statement assuming that intercompany transactions are eliminated. How much would be reported for accounts receivable, inventory, and accounts payable on the July 31, 2010 consolidated balance sheet?

f. Discuss the differences in the information you prepared in parts (d) and (e). Which information is more useful to stakeholders? Explain.

P12-11. **(Passive Investments, LO 4)** In July 2009 Roddickton Ltd. (Roddickton) purchased 100,000 shares of Kola Inc. (Kola), a publicly traded company, for $37 per share. Roddickton received dividends of $0.70 per share from its investment in Kola. On December 31, 2009 the closing price for Kola's shares was $34. There were 100,000,000 shares of Kola's common stock outstanding during 2009.

Required:

a. Prepare the journal entry that would be made to record the purchase of the shares.

b. Prepare the journal entry to record the dividends received by Kola during 2009.

c. How would you classify this investment for financial accounting purposes? How would you decide? Does it matter how the investment is accounted for?

d. If the investment in Kola were classified as available-for-sale, what amount would be reported on Roddickton's December 31, 2009 balance sheet? Explain. Would there be any impact on the income statement? Explain

e. If the investment in Kola were classified as a trading investment, what amount would be reported on Roddickton's December 31, 2009 balance sheet? Explain. Would there be any impact on the income statement? Explain

f. Do you think a management cares whether its investments are classified as available-for-sale or trading? Explain.

Using Financial Statements

BROOKFIELD ASSET MANAGEMENT CORPORATION INC.

Brookfield Asset Management Inc. (Brookfield) is an asset management company focused on property, power and other infrastructure assets. The company has approximately $50 billion under management. This includes 59 million square feet of property and 130 power generating plants. The company is listed on the New York and Toronto stock exchanges.[3]

Brookfield's consolidated balance sheet, statements of income, statement of cash flows, and extracts from the notes to the financial statements are provided in Exhibit 12–5 (pages 698–702). Use this information to respond to questions FS12–1 to FS12–6.

FS12-1. What are the companies that Brookfield accounts for using the equity method of accounting? What is Brookfield's ownership interest in each of these companies? Why are these companies accounted for using the equity method? What is the book value of each of the equity-accounted-for investments?

FS12-2. How much does Brookfield report on its December 31, 2005 balance sheet for securities? How the securities valued? What was the fair value of the securities at December 31, 2005? As a prospective lender to Brookfield, what is the most useful valuation of the securities the company owns? Explain.

FS12-3. How much did Brookfield receive in dividends from companies that it accounts for using the equity method? (This question is tricky and requires that you use information from the consolidated statement of income and consolidated statement of cash flows.)

FS12-4. The following questions pertain to Brookfield's non-controlling interest:
   a. What amount of non-controlling interest is reported on Brookfield's December 31, 2005 balance sheet? What does this amount represent? What parts of Brookfield's business is the non-controlling interest on the balance sheet attributable to?
   b. Where on the balance sheet is the non-controlling interest reported? Explain why it is reported there.
   c. What amount of non-controlling interest is reported on Brookfield's statement of income for the year ended December 31, 2005? What does this amount represent?
   d. Why is the non-controlling interest added back to income from continuing operations when calculating cash from operations?
   e. If you were an investor in Brookfield Properties Corporation, a company 51% owned by Brookfield, how would you use the non-controlling interest information included in Brookfield's financial statements?

FS12-5. Examine Note 25 to Brookfield's financial statements and answer the following questions on segment disclosure:
   a. Identify the business segments in which Brookfield operates. Which segment has the most revenues? Which has the most assets? Which has the most income?
   b. Identify the geographic segments that Brookfield reports in Note 25. Which segment has the most revenues? Which has the most assets? Why do you think segment income information isn't provided for the geographic segments?
   c. Is the segmented information provided only for the entities that are consolidated into Brookfield's consolidated financial statements? Explain.

EXHIBIT 12–5 :

Brookfield Asset
Management
Corporation
Financial
Statement Extracts

Consolidated Balance Sheet

AS AT DECEMBER 31
MILLIONS

	Note	2005	2004
			(Note 1)
Assets			
Cash and cash equivalents		$ 951	$ 404
Financial assets	2	2,171	1,220
Investments	3	595	1,944
Accounts receivable and other	4	4,148	1,551
Operating assets			
Property, plant and equipment	5	15,776	12,231
Securities	6	2,069	1,757
Loans and notes receivable	7	348	900
		$ 26,058	$ 20,007
Liabilities and shareholders' equity			
Non-recourse borrowings			
Property specific mortgages	8	$ 8,756	$ 6,045
Subsidiary borrowings	8	2,510	2,373
Corporate borrowings	9	1,620	1,675
Accounts payable and other liabilities	10	4,561	2,719
Capital securities	11	1,598	1,548
Non-controlling interests in net assets	12	1,984	1,780
Shareholders' equity			
Preferred equity	13	515	590
Common equity	14	4,514	3,277
		$ 26,058	$ 20,007

Consolidated Statement of Income

YEARS ENDED DECEMBER 31
MILLIONS, EXCEPT PER SHARE AMOUNTS

	Note	2005	2004
			(Note 1)
Total revenues		$ 5,256	$ 3,899
Fees earned		282	199
Revenues less direct operating costs	16		
Property		1,210	973
Power generation		469	268
Timberlands and infrastructure		64	26
Specialty funds		54	48
		1,797	1,315
Investment and other income		227	188
Disposition gains		49	123
		2,355	1,825
Expenses			
Interest		881	608
Current income taxes	18	162	86
Asset management		184	126
Other operating costs		103	83
Non-controlling interests in net income before the following	17	386	360
		639	562
Other items			
Equity accounted income from investments	19	219	332
Gains on disposition of Falconbridge	3	1,350	—
Depreciation and amortization		(374)	(251)
Future income taxes and other provisions	18	(324)	(260)
Non-controlling interests in the foregoing items	17	152	172
Net income		$ 1,662	$ 555
Net income per common share	14		
Diluted		$ 6.12	$ 2.02
Basic		$ 6.27	$ 2.06

d. Why is segment disclosure required under GAAP? As a user of Brookfield's annual report, how would your ability to use the financial statements be impaired by not having the segmented information?

e. What are the limitations of the segment disclosure provided by Brookfield?

Consolidated Statement of Cash Flows

YEARS ENDED DECEMBER 31 MILLIONS	Note	2005	2004
			(Note 1)
Operating activities			
Net income		$ 1,662	$ 555
Adjusted for the following non-cash items			
Depreciation and amortization		374	251
Future income taxes and other provisions		324	260
Gains on disposition of Falconbridge		(1,350)	—
Non-controlling interest in non-cash items	17	(152)	(172)
Excess of equity income over dividends received		(175)	(268)
		683	626
Special dividend from Norbord Inc.		42	48
Net change in non-cash working capital balances and other		105	198
		830	872

Notes to Consolidated Financial Statements

1.   SUMMARY OF ACCOUNTING POLICIES

These consolidated financial statements are prepared in accordance with generally accepted accounting principles ("GAAP") as prescribed by the Canadian Institute of Chartered Accountants ("CICA").

(a)   Basis of Presentation

All currency amounts are in United States dollars ("U.S. dollars") unless otherwise stated. The consolidated financial statements include the accounts of Brookfield Asset Management Inc. (formerly Brascan Corporation) and the entities over which it has voting control, as well as Variable Interest Entities ("VIEs") in which the company is considered to be the primary beneficiary (see Note 1(u)(i)).

The company accounts for its investments in Norbord Inc. ("Norbord"), Fraser Papers Inc. ("Fraser Papers"), Falconbridge Limited ("Falconbridge") (formerly Noranda Inc.) and other investments over which it has significant influence, on the equity basis. Interests in jointly controlled partnerships and corporate joint ventures are proportionately consolidated. The company sold its investment in Falconbridge in 2005.

(b)   Acquisitions

The company accounts for business combinations using the purchase method of accounting which establishes specific criteria for the recognition of intangible assets separately from goodwill. The cost of acquiring a company is allocated to its identifiable net assets on the basis of the estimated fair values at the date of purchase. The excess of acquisition costs over the underlying net book values of assets acquired is allocated to the underlying tangible and intangible assets with the balance being allocated to goodwill. The allocated amounts are amortized over the estimated useful lives of the assets. The company periodically evaluates the carrying values of these amounts based on reviews of estimated future operating income and cash flows on an undiscounted basis, and any impairment is charged against income at that time. Goodwill arising on acquisitions is allocated to reporting units and tested at least annually for impairment.

EXHIBIT 12–5 :

**(continued)
Brookfield Asset
Management
Corporation
Financial
Statement Extracts**

FS12-6.   What are the problems and limitations of analyzing financial ratios based on Brookfield's consolidated financial statements? Explain your reasons.

EXHIBIT | 12–5 | :

(continued)
**Brookfield Asset
Management
Corporation
Financial
Statement Extracts**

3. INVESTMENTS

Equity accounted investments include the following:

MILLIONS	Number of Shares		% of Investment		Book Values	
	2005	2004	**2005**	2004	**2005**	2004
Norbord Inc.	53.8	53.8	37%	36%	$ 199	$ 177
Fraser Papers Inc.	13.4	12.8	46%	42%	197	204
Falconbridge Inc.	—	122.6	—	42%	—	1,344
Other					199	219
Total					$ 595	$ 1,944

During the second quarter of 2005 there was a substantial reorganization of Falconbridge which involved the repurchase by Falconbridge (formerly Noranda) of approximately 64 million common shares in exchange for $1.25 billion of preferred shares and the subsequent issuance of 132.8 million shares to minority shareholders of Falconbridge to effect the privatization. As a result, Brookfield received $950 million retractable preferred shares in exchange for 48 million common shares and the company's common share interest in Falconbridge decreased to 20% from 42%. The company subsequently sold 73 million common shares, or substantially all of its remaining 20% ownership for proceeds of $1.7 billion, consisting of $1.3 billion cash and a $375 million convertible debenture. These transactions resulted in an aggregate pre-tax gain of $1,350 million. Falconbridge redeemed $380 million of the $950 million retractable preferred shares previously received by the company as part of the exchange. The company's remaining investment in these preferred shares is included in Financial Assets as at December 31, 2005.

6. SECURITIES

MILLIONS	**2005**	2004
Government bonds	$ 930	$ 684
Corporate bonds	480	170
Asset backed securities	195	142
Common shares	197	311
Canary Wharf Group common shares	267	450
Total	$ 2,069	$ 1,757

Securities represent holdings that are actively deployed in the company's financial operations and include $1,570 million (2004 – $917 million) owned through the company's Insurance operations, as described in Note 15(g).

The securities are carried at the lower of cost and their net realizable value. The fair value of securities at December 31, 2005 was $2,220 million (2004 – $1,895 million). During 2005, the company received dividends of $183 million from Canary Wharf Group (2004 – $nil) which were accounted for as a return of investment.

Corporate bonds include fixed rate securities totalling $284 million (2004 – $172 million) with an average yield of 5.5% (2004 – 6.5%) and an average maturity of approximately five years. Government bonds and asset backed securities include predominantly fixed rate securities.

12. NON-CONTROLLING INTERESTS IN NET ASSETS

Non-controlling interests represent the common and preferred equity in consolidated entities that is owned by other shareholders.

MILLIONS	**2005**	2004
Common equity		
Property operations	$ 1,196	$ 1,226
Power generation	213	194
Timberlands and infrastructure	257	—
Other	143	110
	1,809	1,530
Preferred equity	175	250
Total	$ 1,984	$ 1,780

17. NON-CONTROLLING INTERESTS

Non-controlling interests of others is segregated into the share of income before certain items and their share of those items, which include depreciation and amortization and taxes and other provisions attributable to the non-controlling interest.

MILLIONS	2005	2004
Distributed as recurring dividends		
Preferred	$ 12	$ 15
Common	109	73
Undistributed	113	100
Non-controlling interests expense	$ 234	$ 188
Non-controlling interests share of income prior to the following	$ 386	$ 360
Non-controlling interests share of depreciation and amortization, and future income taxes and other provisions	(152)	(172)
Non-controlling interests expense	$ 234	$ 188

During 2004, the company's residential home building subsidiary paid a special dividend of $140 million to the holders of non-controlling interests in addition to recurring dividends as noted above.

19. EQUITY ACCOUNTED INCOME

Equity accounted income (loss) includes the following:

MILLIONS	2005	2004
Falconbridge	$ 145	$ 205
Norbord	87	135
Fraser Papers	(13)	(8)
Total	$ 219	$ 332

25. SEGMENTED INFORMATION

The company's presentation of reportable segments is based on how management has organized the business in making operating and capital allocation decisions and assessing performance. The company has four reportable segments:

(a) property operations, which are principally commercial office properties, residential development and home building operations, located primarily in major North American cities;

(b) power generation operations, which are predominantly hydroelectric power generating facilities on North American river systems;

(c) timberlands and infrastructure operations, which are predominantly high quality private timberlands on the west coast of Canada and in Brazil and electrical transmission and distribution systems located in northern Ontario; and

(d) specialty funds, which include the company's bridge lending, real estate finance and restructuring funds along with the company's public securities operations and are managed for the company and for institutional partners.

Non-operating assets and related revenue, cash flow and income are presented as financial assets and other.

Revenue, net income and assets by reportable segments are as follows:

	2005			2004		
MILLIONS	Revenue	Net Income	Assets	Revenue	Net Income	Assets
Property						
Core office properties	$ 1,146	$ 690	$ 8,688	$ 1,070	$ 662	$ 7,089
Residential properties	1,936	496	1,205	1,603	305	818
Development properties	11	6	942	5	1	950
Real estate services	68	18	39	9	5	51
Power generation	800	469	3,568	469	268	2,951
Timberlands and infrastructure	170	64	1,018	99	26	184
Specialty funds	58	54	480	58	48	873
Other	282	147	6,523	199	196	3,597
	4,471	1,944	22,463	3,512	1,511	16,513
Financial assets and other	774	216	3,122	383	188	1,624
Investments	11	1,580	473	4	332	1,870
	$ 5,256	3,740	$ 26,058	$ 3,899	2,031	$ 20,007
Cash interest and other cash expenses		1,532			1,137	
Depreciation, taxes and other non-cash items		546			339	
Net income from continuing operations		$ 1,662			$ 555	

Revenue and assets by geographic segments are as follows:

	2005		2004	
MILLIONS	Revenue	Assets	Revenue	Assets
United States	$ 3,484	$ 12,633	$ 2,374	$ 9,943
Canada	1,323	9,463	1,172	6,729
International	449	3,962	353	3,335
Revenue / Assets	$ 5,256	$ 26,058	$ 3,899	$ 20,007

EXHIBIT 12–5 :

(continued)
Brookfield Asset
Management
Corporation
Financial
Statement Extracts

INVESTMENTS

We own direct interests in a number of investments which will be sold once value has been maximized, integrated into our core operations or used to seed new funds. Within our areas of expertise, we continue to seek new investments of this nature and dispose of more mature assets.

The following table sets out these investments, together with associated cash flows and gains:

| AS AT AND FOR THE YEARS ENDED DECEMBER 31 | | | | Assets Under Management | Invested Capital | | | | Operating Cash Flow | | | |
| | | | | | Total | | Net | | Total | | Net | |
MILLIONS	Location	Shares	Interest	2005	2005	2004	2005	2004	2005	2004	2005	2004
Forest products												
Norbord Inc.	North America / UK	33.8	23%	$ 199	$ 199	$ 177	$ (12)	$ (18)	$ 62	$ 19	$ 37	$ 19
Fraser Papers Inc.	North America	13.4	46%	197	197	204	197	204	—	—	—	—
Privately held	North America		100%	428	428	174	285	122	(35)	(1)	(41)	(1)
Business services												
Insurance	Various		80-100%	2,028	2,028	1,172	495	345	27	32	20	28
Banco Brascan, S.A.	Rio de Janeiro		51%	69	69	59	69	59	6	4	6	4
Privately held	Various		100%	304	304	299	133	172	32	17	20	11
Publicly listed	Canada		—	84	84	107	49	77	—	4	(2)	3
Mining and metals												
Coal lands	Alberta		100%	77	77	70	77	70	4	4	4	4
Falconbridge	Various		—	—	—	1,344	—	1,344	24	45	24	45
Net investment / operating cash flows				$ 3,386	$ 3,386	$ 3,606	$ 1,293	$ 2,375	$ 120	$ 124	$ 68	$ 113

We account for our non-controlled public investments such as Norbord and Fraser Papers using the equity method, and include dividends received from these investments in cash flow and our proportional share of their earnings in net income. We consolidate the results of our majority owned private companies and accordingly include our proportional share of their results in the operating cash flow shown above.

Analyzing Rogers Communications Inc.

R12-1. The following questions pertain to Rogers' goodwill.
  a. How much goodwill did Rogers report on its December 31, 2005 and 2004 balance sheets?
  b. How much new goodwill did Rogers acquire in 2005 and 2004? What were the main sources of that goodwill?
  c. How much goodwill did Rogers write off in 2005 and 2004? Why is it sometimes necessary to write down goodwill?
  d. Do you think Rogers' consolidated balance sheet fully reflects Rogers' goodwill? (In other words, if Rogers were purchased, would there be additional goodwill not currently reported on the balance sheet?) Why is this goodwill not currently reported on the consolidated balance sheet? What might be the sources of this unrecorded goodwill?

R12-2. In November 2004 Rogers purchased 100 percent of the outstanding shares of Microcell Telecommunications Inc. (Microcell). How much did Rogers pay for its purchase of Microcell? How much was paid in cash in 2004 to the sellers? What amount of the purchase price was allocated to identifiable assets and liabilities? How much of the purchase price was allocated to goodwill? How were acquisition costs accounted for? Does this treatment make sense to you?

R12-3. On July 1, 2005 Rogers purchased 100 percent of the shares of Call-Net Enterprises Inc. (Call-Net). How much did Rogers pay for its purchase of Call-Net? How much was paid in cash to the sellers? What amount of the purchase price was allocated to identifiable assets and liabilities? How much of the purchase price was allocated to goodwill? How were acquisition costs accounted for? Does this treatment make sense to you? If you examined the actual financial statements of Call-Net, how much would you find recorded for property, plant, and equipment? Explain your answer.

R12-4. Examine Note 17 to Rogers' financial statements (see page A-39). These questions pertain to Rogers' segment disclosures.

    a. Identify the different segments that Rogers reports. What was the operating revenue and net income for each segment in 2005?

    b. Which segment has the most sales in 2005? Which is the most profitable? If you could invest in one of Rogers' segments, which segment would it be? Explain fully.

    c. Which segment had the greatest growth in operating revenue in 2005? Which had the greatest growth in net income?

    d. Which product generates the most revenue for the cable division? Which product of the cable division showed the most growth?

    e. Are segment disclosures useful? Explain. Tie your answer to specific users of the financial statements.

    f. In the table showing the segmented disclosures there is a column called corporate items and eliminations. What do you think the eliminations are (provide some examples) and why do you think the eliminations are necessary?

R12-5 You are considering making an investment in Rogers Communications Inc. You sit down with the financial statements to do an in-depth analysis. Discuss how Rogers' consolidated financial statements help and hinder your work. Explain fully, using examples from the Rogers' financial statement package.

ENDNOTES

1. Extracted from Onex Corporation's 2005 annual report.

2. Extracted from Ivanhoe Mines Ltd.'s 2004 annual report.

3. Extracted from Brookfield Asset Management Corporation Inc.'s 2005 annual report.

ANALYZING AND INTERPRETING FINANCIAL STATEMENTS

LEARNING OBJECTIVES

After studying the material in this chapter you will be able to:

▶ **LO 1** Distinguish between permanent and transitory earnings, and discuss the concept of earnings quality.

▶ **LO 2** Analyze and evaluate entities through the use of financial ratios.

▶ **LO 3** Recognize the limitations of using financial statements and ratio analysis for evaluating an entity.

▶ **LO 4** Understand that because of the flexibility of accounting rules (even under GAAP) managers are able to manage the earnings of their entities and thereby affect the numbers that are reported in the financial statements and the information that is disclosed.

"April 25 (Bloomberg)—Rogers Communications Inc., Canada's biggest cable-television and mobile-telephone company, posted a first-quarter profit of C$14.8 million that missed analysts' estimates after wireless subscriber growth slowed. Net income was 5 cents a share, compared with a loss of $46 million, or 17 cents, a year earlier, Toronto-based Rogers said today in a statement. Sales jumped 28 percent to C$2.03 billion."

This is how Bloomberg News, a respected business news service, began its story the day Rogers Communications released first-quarter results on April 25, 2006. Bloomberg's reporter, like a lot of other business journalists, focused mostly on how the communications giant missed forecasts in areas like earnings per share and in wireless subscriber growth.

Shortly after the results were released, Rogers Communication's Class B shares fell 59 cents to $45.15 in mid-morning trading on the Toronto Stock Exchange.

But stock analysts at both UBS Investment Research and at Desjardins Securities, who spent 24 hours combing through the Rogers financial statements, told a much different story about Rogers' results when these two firms issued research reports the next day. They both recommended investors should buy the stock. Why?

Because the analysts were looking at the financial statements for more then just the headline numbers of earnings per share and subscriber growth. They wanted to see how healthy Rogers' balance sheets were, using more sophisticated data.

At UBS Investment Research for instance, Jeffrey Fan and Aryeh Bourkoff focused on things like free cash flow, and on whether Rogers was making progress reducing its debt. They also looked at operating margins in wireless, and at capital expenditures, and at something called ARPU, or average monthly revenue per user. That's a key measure of how a company is performing in the mobile phone company business.

UBS found that Rogers was earning $51.60 per subscriber per month, up 7.2 percent from the year before.

Rogers is "getting more money from each customer, as people took photos, e-mailed one another, text messaged, downloaded ring tones, etc.," said Linda Sims, business editor at CTV Newsnet and Report on Business Television.

Meanwhile, over at Desjardins Securities, their analysts also looked at ARPU, but they were also interested in something called churn, another key measure of how well the company is doing in the cell phone business. Churn is how many customers leave or cancel service: turnover, in other words. Desjardins's Joseph MacKay and Eric Bernofsky, who wrote the report April 26, 2006, said they were pleased with a .43 per cent decline in monthly churn for those customers who pay after they talk.

INTRODUCTION

Chapter 1 of this book began with the following statement:

Accounting is full of mystery and intrigue. The reader of an accounting report, like the reader of a good mystery, must sort through clues, interpret and analyze information, exercise judgment, decide which information is relevant and which should be ignored, and use the information to come to a conclusion. Solving an accounting mystery requires detective work. The numbers tell a story, but it is usually necessary to read between the lines.

The first 12 chapters of this book explained the mystery and intrigue of accounting. It should now be clear to readers that there is nothing straightforward about the information that is reported in financial statements. However, despite the complexity, ambiguity, and limitations of the information, financial statements are crucial for decision making. It would be extremely difficult for people to make their decisions without the information that is in the financial statements.

Without financial statements, it would be difficult to determine whether to purchase a business and how much to pay for it; to decide whether to lend money to an entity and how much to lend; and for regulators to set rates for regulated companies.

But using the information in financial statements for making decisions usually isn't easy. The answers to most questions are not laid out in the statements. Users must analyze and interpret the financial statements to help them get the answers they need. Even then, the financial statements do not usually provide the answers. They provide clues and insights, but rarely definitive answers.

This chapter begins by providing some perspective on how different stakeholders approach the task of analyzing financial statements. It discusses the importance of having a good understanding of an entity before beginning the analysis. The chapter also explains the concepts of permanent and transitory earnings, which are valuable for understanding how current earnings are useful for predicting future earnings.

Throughout the book, tools for analyzing and interpreting financial statements have been discussed. The chapter reviews those analytical tools and provides additional methods for interpreting financial statements. Two techniques that eliminate the impact of size from the financial statement numbers and restate them as proportions are introduced: common size financial statements and trend statements. The ratios and analytical tools are grouped into four analytical themes:

1. evaluating performance

2. liquidity

3. solvency and leverage

4. other common ratios

WHY ANALYZE AND INTERPRET FINANCIAL STATEMENTS?

Analysis and interpretation of financial information is not an end in itself. People analyze financial statements to help them make better decisions. The type of analysis that one does depends on the decisions one has to make. Different stakeholders need to resolve different questions. As a result, each stakeholder group will approach their analysis differently.

Let's look at some stakeholders and discuss reasons why they would want to analyze financial statements.

Creditors Creditors come in many shapes and sizes. They may be suppliers of goods and services that accept payment sometime (usually in a short time) after supplying the goods or services. Creditors may be banks that provide short-term or permanent working capital loans, or long-term financing through term loans. They may be suppliers of long-term financing through notes payable, bonds, debentures, or mortgages. Creditors may be public or private investors.

Creditors have two broad concerns:

■ First, they are concerned about the ability of the borrower to make payments. To assess this concern, creditors consider the resources the entity has and the reliability, timing, and stability of its future cash flows. Creditors will be particularly concerned about an entity's ability to make payments as economic conditions change—for example, if the economy enters a recession. A creditor will want to be confident that the borrower can weather poorer economic conditions and meet its obligations.

■ Second, creditors are concerned about security. Security can include assets that a creditor can sell if the borrower does not meet its obligations. For this reason, a creditor will want to know the fair market value of the assets that have been given as security. Security can also be provided through specified restrictions on the behaviour of the borrower. These restrictions can be in the form of actual limitations on the borrower's activities—for example, restrictions on the payment of dividends, additional borrowing, or the sale of certain assets. Restrictions can also require that borrowers comply with specified accounting measures, such as the current ratio or the debt-to-equity ratio, where the borrower agrees not to exceed specified levels of these measures.

Restrictions that impose limits on the actions of borrowers are known as **covenants**. Violating covenants can have significant economic consequences on the borrower, such as requiring immediate repayment of the loan or an increase in the interest rate charged on the loan.

The type of analysis required by a creditor depends on the nature of the credit being provided. Short-term creditors will be concerned about an entity's financial situation at the time the credit is offered, the liquidity of current assets, and how quickly the current assets turn over. Long-term creditors will want to forecast future cash flows and evaluate the borrower's ability to generate earnings. The ability of an entity to generate earnings is important because it serves as an indicator of the borrower's ability to generate cash flows to meet its obligations.

Equity Investors In many ways, equity investors need to know everything. That's because most events that affect an entity also affect the equity investors. Remember that equity investors have a residual interest in the entity. A residual interest means that equity investors are entitled to what is left over after all other interests, in particular creditors, have been satisfied. Because of their residual interest in the entity, equity investors' analyses are much more complex than those of creditors. Whereas a creditor has to assess the ability of an entity to make specified payments at specified times, payments to equity investors are not specified or required.

There are many questions that equity investors (or prospective equity investors) can ask. A fundamental question is the value of the entity or its shares. This is an extremely important question for people considering investing in or purchasing a privately owned entity. Privately owned companies don't have prices set by trading on a stock market to serve as a benchmark for evaluation, so financial statement analysis is crucial for determining a reasonable price for a prospective investment. Public companies are also thoroughly analyzed by individual investors, analysts for investment bankers, and mutual and pension fund managers to determine the attractiveness of investing in a particular company. Equity investors could analyze an entity to determine strengths and weaknesses in its performance, perhaps relative to competitors. Equity investors could also analyze an entity to assess its risk.

As well as creditors and equity investors, we should keep in mind the many stakeholders that were identified in Chapter 1 and that have been referred to throughout the book, including:

■ Employees and their representatives, who could analyze the financial statements of the employer to determine the employer's ability to pay increased wages.

■ The Canada Revenue Agency (CRA), which might analyze financial statements to assess the reasonableness of amounts reported in tax returns.

■ Regulators, which could use financial information to evaluate requests by regulated companies for permission to increase their prices.

There are others, but the point is that while stakeholders use financial accounting information in their decision making, in most cases the financial statements do not present the answers to stakeholders' questions "on a silver platter." Usually, the information in the financial statements must be analyzed, massaged, evaluated, and interpreted before it can provide insights about the entity.

KNOW THE ENTITY

Financial statements are only one source of information about an entity, albeit an important one. The successful analysis of an entity cannot be achieved only by examining its financial statements. In fact, the analysis of an entity shouldn't even begin with the financial statements.

Financial statements are nothing more than numbers on pages. To understand what those numbers are saying requires an understanding of the entity's business, its industry, and its environment. Much of that information will come from sources other than the financial statements. Chapter 2 of this book is titled *Financial Statements: A Window on an Entity*. Why is this title significant? Because it emphasizes that financial statements provide important information about an entity and are essential for investigating various aspects of the entity, but that while financial statements are *a* window on an entity, they are not the *only* window. Just as looking in only one window of a house cannot give the observer a complete view of all its rooms, examining only the financial statements cannot provide a complete view of the entity.

Information about entities can be obtained from many sources. The media often provide news items about entities. Brokerage firms provide research that analyzes the investment prospects of publicly traded companies. There are also many online services that provide information, such as Globeinvestor.com, Bloomberg.com, and Morningstar.ca.

Information about the entity itself might not be the only consideration. Recall the accounting environment, depicted in Figure 1–1. The different elements of the accounting environment could be relevant when evaluating an entity, depending on the decision the stakeholder is making. For example, information about competitors could provide a useful benchmark against which to evaluate the entity of interest.

Information about the entity's industry can also be relevant. Industry information can be obtained from industry and trade associations that represent the interests of all members of a particular industry. Statistics Canada, a department of the Government of Canada, provides extensive industry information. Statistics Canada also provides detailed economic and demographic data.

www.statcan.ca

There are many more possible sources and types of information available about an entity. Keep in mind, though, that not all of these sources provide information for free.

What does one need to know about an entity, its industry, and environment? The list could be endless and much depends on the entity being investigated and its environment. Some questions to consider include:

■ What does the entity do—what business or businesses is it in?

■ What strategies does the entity use to make money?

■ What is the entity's competitive environment? (Are there many competitors? Is it easy for new competitors to enter the market?)

■ What are the entity's competitive advantages?

■ Who are the managers of the entity? What experience do the managers have? What has their performance been?

■ What are the risks faced by the entity?

■ Is the entity regulated? How does regulation affect the way it can conduct business?

■ How do economic conditions and changes in economic conditions affect the entity?

- What are the conditions in the entity's businesses?

- How does the entity produce, market, and distribute its products?

- What are the key inputs for the entity and how does it obtain them? What are the conditions in the supplier market?

- What are the entity's key success factors?

While one should examine sources other than the annual report to learn about an entity, its industry, and its environment, the annual reports of public companies can provide considerable useful information beyond what is reported in the financial statements and notes. One very valuable section of an annual report is the **management discussion and analysis (MD&A)**. The MD&A must be prepared by publicly traded companies (but not by private companies). The MD&A is prepared by an entity's managers and provides them the opportunity to discuss its financial results, position, and future prospects. The MD&A is intended to provide readers with a view of the entity through the eyes of management.

In its 2005 annual report, the Rogers MD&A spanned 83 pages (look at a Rogers MD&A by downloading a recent annual report from sedar.com). Rogers' MD&A provides extensive interpretation, discussion, and analysis that complements and supplements the information in the financial statements.

Rogers' MD&A is broken down into six sections. Coverage includes:

- Corporate overview—discussion of the business, strategy, acquisitions, and presentation of financial and operating results.

- Segment review—discussion of each of the operating divisions (Wireless, Cable, Media, and Telecom)

- Financing and risk management—discussion of liquidity, commitments and obligations, and off-balance sheet financing issues.

- Operating environment—discussion of regulation, competition, and risks and uncertainties.

- Accounting policies and non-GAAP measures—description of key performance indicators and non-GAAP measures, critical accounting policies and estimates, and new accounting standards.

- Additional financial information—presentation of the five-year financial summary, quarterly results, and non-GAAP calculations.

A user of Rogers' financial statements would be in a much better position to understand the statements after having carefully read the MD&A. However, it should be noted that the quality of MD&As varies widely from entity to entity and depends on what management puts into it. Some entities provide very informative MD&As, whereas others do little more than state the obvious.

While the MD&A can be a very valuable source of information about an entity, it is important to remember that management prepares it. This raises an interesting paradox. Management is, for the most part, the best source of information and insight about the entity. But management will not likely be unbiased about how it presents information about the entity. That's not to say that the information provided by management is false. Rather, management is likely to focus on positive aspects of the entity, its performance, and its prospects, and provide favourable and optimistic interpretations of events.

Private companies are not required to provide a MD&A. In general, one can expect to find far less information about private companies than public ones, both from the private companies themselves and from non-company sources. To begin with, private companies are not required to disclose their financial statements to the public. Private companies can limit access to their statements to whichever entities they choose—for instance, the CRA, the company's bankers, and possibly suppliers who want to do a credit analysis. Also, there will usually be little interest in private companies by the investment community. People in the investment community gather information about public companies to gain insight into the desirability of investing in their equity and debt. The same incentives for gathering information about private companies do not exist.

ROGERS

There are other parts of annual reports that can provide useful information. Annual reports usually have a message from the CEO and/or the chair of the board of directors. They also typically include information about the entity's senior executives and the members of the board of directors. All this information can be useful, depending on the user and how the information is to be used.

Companies often issue press releases about their activities. While press releases and other disclosures by an entity are prepared by management and can therefore be biased, they can still be a useful source of information.

Of course, as a user of financial information you should evaluate all information you receive for its usefulness and credibility. You should recognize that just because information is provided by a source other than the entity itself, it does not mean that the information is unbiased. For example, information from industry associations would take views favourable to the interests of that industry. Also, research by brokerages and investment bankers has been assailed in recent years because these organizations have incentives not to offend entities that might use their services in the future. As a result, these organizations will not be inclined to make negative statements about potential future clients. There are many Internet discussion boards where investors exchange information about various investment opportunities. Information from these sources will be highly unreliable since the source of the information will usually be very difficult to verify.

PERMANENT EARNINGS AND THE QUALITY OF EARNINGS

Permanent Earnings

One of the themes emphasized throughout this book is that net income is not an absolute or true number. Net income reflects the economic gain or loss of the owners of the entity; it is a representation of the underlying economic performance of an entity, albeit not a complete or comprehensive representation. We have seen that measuring economic gains and losses is extremely complex. As a result, it is not possible to determine an entity's "true" net income. The amount of income an entity reports is a function of the accounting policies it chooses and the estimates it makes. Despite all the difficulties that exist in measuring income, the measurement of income is important because it provides information to stakeholders for decision making.

For many stakeholders, an use for current earnings is for forecasting future earnings. Many decisions that stakeholders want to make would be helped by knowing an entity's future net income. The *CICA Handbook* recognizes the importance of future-oriented information by stating that one objective of financial statements is for investors and creditors to predict earnings and cash flow.

However, Canadian GAAP, as well as financial reporting regulations in most jurisdictions around the world, do not require or support providing forecasted financial statements. As a result, stakeholders are left to their own devices in trying to make these forecasts. Stakeholders are not completely abandoned in Canada—disclosure requirements and information from other sources can improve stakeholders' ability to make forecasts.

For the purpose of forecasting future earnings, historical earnings can be used as a starting point. Historical earnings can be adjusted to reflect changes that are expected to affect the entity. An important aspect of interpreting historical earnings is being able to determine the components of earnings that can be expected to recur in future periods. These **permanent earnings**— earnings that are expected to be repeated in the future—are a good indicator of future earnings. In contrast, **transitory earnings** are earnings that are not expected to be repeated in future periods. The net income of an entity can have both permanent and transitory components.

The distinction between permanent and transitory earnings and their impact on forecasting future earnings can be shown with the following example.

In mid-2010, Rusagonis Ltd. (Rusagonis) signed a $100,000 contract with a customer. After considering all costs, Rusagonis' management expects to earn $31,000 as a result of the contract. If the revenue and earnings associated with this contract are repeated year after year, the contract will increase permanent earnings. This is an appropriate interpretation if Rusagonis' management expects that the customer is going to become permanent or if the contract is indicative of Rusagonis' growth. If we measure the value of a company as the present value of its future earnings, we would expect the value of Rusagonis to increase by the present value of a series of $31,000 payments to be received for the foreseeable future. (It is assumed here that the annual earnings increase translates into annual cash flows of $31,000.) To a lender, the new contract would mean that Rusagonis could support more debt. Because of the new contract, shareholders might anticipate increased dividends. The new contract might enable unions and employees to argue for increased wages and salaries.

But now let's suppose that the $100,000 contract was a just a one-time event. In this situation Rusagonis is clearly better off, but only by $31,000 (the amount of profit earned on the contract). This contract and contracts like it are not expected to occur in the future, so the contract has no implications for future earnings. If a stakeholder were estimating future earnings, the contract would be ignored because it has no effect on permanent or future earnings—it was simply a one-time event. In other words, the effect of this contract on earnings is transitory. There would be a one-year increase in earnings of $31,000, but everything else being equal, earnings would be expected to decrease in the next year by $31,000 and return to the pre-2010 level.

This discussion should highlight the importance to users of understanding the sources of an entity's earnings and the reason for changes in its earnings. Permanent and transitory earnings should be interpreted differently. As a result, it is desirable for financial statements to provide information that helps users distinguish permanent and transitory earnings.

GAAP and the *CICA Handbook* provide some help in this regard. The *CICA Handbook* requires or allows disclosure of information that is helpful for understanding the components of earnings. We will look at three areas:

1. extraordinary items

2. unusual items

3. discontinued operations

Extraordinary Items   An **extraordinary item** (EOI) is defined in the *CICA Handbook* as an event or transaction that is:

- not expected to occur frequently,

- not typical of the entity's business, and

- not primarily the result of decisions or determinations by the managers or owners of the entity.

The *CICA Handbook* requires that EOIs be disclosed separately in the income statement. The "extraordinary" designation clearly indicates that an event is transitory. Because of the stringent criteria for determining whether a transaction or event should be treated as extraordinary (particularly the third one), EOIs are rarely reported in Canada. *Financial Reporting in Canada,* 30th Edition reports that in its sample of 200 public companies, there were two EOIs reported in 2004 and none in 2001, 2002, and 2003.[1] The two reported in 2004 pertain to the purchase of one corporation by another. The *CICA Handbook* requires that these situations be treated as EOIs even though they don't meet the criteria. Examples of events and transactions that could be considered extraordinary include losses caused by natural disasters (earthquakes, tornadoes) and expropriations.

Exhibit 13–1 provides an example of an EOI. For its year ended December 31, 2004, BCE Inc. (BCE) reported a gain $69 million related to its purchase of 360Newtworks Corporation.[2] This is not an extraordinary item according to the criteria (but is appropriately classified as extraordinary according to the *CICA Handbook*) but it does show how extraordinary items are reported on the income statement.

Unusual Items   At one time, the criteria for classifying a transaction or event as extraordinary were much looser than they are today. Many events that were actually quite ordinary—for example, losses on the sale of capital assets—were classified as extraordinary. When the criteria for extraordinary items were tightened, standard setters recognized that it was necessary to allow preparers to distinguish between permanent and transitory events. As a result, Section 1520 of the *CICA Handbook,* the section on the income statement, was modified to require separate disclosure of "unusual" revenue, expenses, gains, and losses.

www.bce.com

EXHIBIT 13–1 :

BCE Inc.
Extraordinary Item

Consolidated Statements of Operations

FOR THE YEAR ENDED DECEMBER 31 (in $ millions, except share amounts)	NOTES	2004	2003	2002
Operating revenues		19,193	18,737	18,900
Operating expenses		(11,629)	(11,327)	(11,516)
Amortization expense		(3,108)	(3,100)	(3,024)
Net benefit plans (cost) credit	23	(256)	(175)	33
Restructuring and other items	4	(1,224)	(14)	(768)
Total operating expenses		(16,217)	(14,616)	(15,275)
Operating income		2,976	4,121	3,625
Other income	5	411	175	2,408
Impairment charge	6	–	–	(765)
Interest expense	7	(1,005)	(1,105)	(1,120)
Pre-tax earnings from continuing operations		2,382	3,191	4,148
Income taxes	8	(710)	(1,119)	(1,614)
Non-controlling interest		(174)	(201)	(663)
Earnings from continuing operations		1,498	1,871	1,871
Discontinued operations	9	26	(56)	536
Net earnings before extraordinary gain		1,524	1,815	2,407
Extraordinary gain	3	69	–	–
Net earnings		1,593	1,815	2,407

Unusual items are revenue, expenses, gains, and losses that do not meet the definition of an extraordinary item, but that are not expected to occur frequently, or that are not considered part of the normal business activities of the entity. While unusual items are included among the ordinary operating activities of the entity, identifying them separately is helpful because it allows users to distinguish events that are permanent, transitory, or a little of each. This classification allows users to forecast earnings and cash flows better.

How particular transactions and events are classified in the income statement is often a matter of judgment. Managers may have incentives to classify bad news as unusual and to not classify good news as unusual. The reason is that unusual items are more likely to be interpreted as transitory. For public companies, a transitory event should have less of an effect on an entity's stock price, so classifying bad news as unusual may lessen the stock price impact of the event. The logic is opposite for good news. If a good news event is not treated as unusual, the stock market may include the impact of the event in permanent earnings. Similarly, if managers' bonuses are based on earnings before unusual items, there would be incentives for them to classify bad news as unusual and good news as part of "ordinary" operations.

Financial Reporting in Canada, 30th edition, reports that the classification of transactions and events as unusual is not uncommon. In 2004, 159 of the 200 companies surveyed (almost 80 percent of the firms in the survey) reported unusual items. The percentage of firms reporting unusual items in other years was also high—62 percent in 2001, 76 percent in 2002, and 78 percent in 2003.[3]

The *CICA Handbook* does not require that a transaction or event be designated as unusual, just that it be separately disclosed. As a result, users of the financial statements must carefully evaluate and consider the items reported in the income statement and disclosed in the notes to assess the implications an event may have for future periods. Users should also consider the implications of information from other sources and from financial statement analysis in evaluating earnings.

On Rogers' statement of income, the loss on repayment of long-term debt might be considered unusual (take a look at Rogers' statements of income on page A-5). However, Rogers reported a loss on repayment of long-term debt in 2004 (and 2003 as well) so these may not really be unusual. Remember, the purpose of identifying unusual items is to be able to separate transitory income from permanent income. Events that happen year-after-year are not unusual, even if they are classified as such or are disclosed separately.

Exhibit 13–2 provides another example of unusual items. Exhibit 13–2 provides the statements of operations, the cash from operations section of the statements of cash flow, and extracts from

○ ROGERS™

Consolidated statements of operations

YEARS ENDED SEPTEMBER 24, 2005 AND SEPTEMBER 25, 2004
(in millions of dollars, unless otherwise noted)

	2005	2004 (Restated)
Sales	$ 3,585.0	$ 3,664.8
Freight and sales deductions	413.3	422.2
Countervailing and antidumping duties (note 14)	89.4	111.4
Cost of sales	2,885.6	2,784.1
Selling, general and administrative	171.6	178.6
Earnings before unusual items, interest, income taxes, depreciation and amortization, and other non-operating expenses (EBITDA) (note 15)	25.1	168.5
Depreciation and amortization (note 16)	243.7	234.7
Unusual items (note 17)	254.5	46.6
Operating loss	(473.1)	(112.8)
Interest, foreign exchange and other (note 18)	11.1	(99.0)
Exchange gain on long-term debt	(124.8)	(93.5)
Earnings (loss) before income taxes and minority interests	(359.4)	79.7
Income taxes (recovery) (note 19)	(55.1)	42.3
Minority interests	–	0.4
Net earnings (loss)	$ (304.3)	$ 37.0
Basic earnings (loss) per share (note 13)	$ (3.55)	$ 0.43
Diluted earnings (loss) per share (note 13)	$ (3.55)	$ 0.43

Consolidated statements of cash flows

YEARS ENDED SEPTEMBER 24, 2005 AND SEPTEMBER 25, 2004
(in millions of dollars)

	2005	2004 (Restated)
Cash flows from operating activities:		
Net earnings (loss)	$ (304.3)	$ 37.0
Adjustments for:		
Depreciation and amortization (note 16)	243.7	234.7
Amortization of deferred financing costs	5.4	5.3
Exchange gain on long-term debt	(124.8)	(93.5)
Amortization of deferred gain on foreign exchange contracts (note 22)	(117.9)	(149.3)
Derivative financial instruments gain (note 22)	(30.3)	(84.6)
Proceeds on sale of derivative financial instruments (note 22)	138.7	193.7
Loss on consolidation of foreign integrated subsidiaries	6.0	2.0
Future income taxes (note 19)	(61.8)	35.4
Unusual items (note 17)	223.1	46.6
Other	9.6	8.1
	(12.6)	235.4
Changes in non-cash working capital:		
Temporary investments	6.2	4.8
Accounts receivable	2.6	(25.9)
Inventories	(28.4)	(59.0)
Prepaid expenses	(3.6)	(6.5)
Accounts payable and accrued charges	(1.4)	58.0
	(24.6)	(28.6)
	(37.2)	206.8

Note 17 to the financial statements from the September 24, 2005 annual report of Tembec Inc. (Tembec), an integrated forest products company.[4] For its year ended September 24, 2005, Tembec reports $254.5 million in unusual losses, pertaining to the closure and restructuring of some of the company's facilities. The losses involve the write-down of assets, accruals for employee severance, and other closure costs. From the statements of cash flows, you can see that $223.1 million of the amount expensed didn't involve cash.

EXHIBIT 13–2 ⋮

(continued)
Tembec Inc.
Unusual Items

713

17. Unusual items:

2005

During the December 2004 quarter, as a result of a major restructuring of its sawmills in North Eastern Ontario, the Company recorded a non-cash charge of $15.5 million including $2.5 million for goodwill relating to the reduction of the carrying value of the fixed and other assets of two sawmills that were permanently closed. Employee severance and other closure costs amounting to $4.8 million were also recorded. The after-tax effect of theses charges was $14.2 million.

During the June 2005 quarter, the Company recorded a non-cash charge of $114.7 million relating to the reduction of the carrying value of the fixed and other assets of three sawmills, a papermill and a remanufacturing facility that were permanently or indefinitely closed. Employee severance and other closure costs amounting to $21.4 million were also recorded. The after-tax effect of these charges was $91.7 million.

During the September 2005 quarter, as a result of the permanent closure of the pressurized groundwood pulping line and one of the four paper machines at the St. Francisville, Louisiana papermill, the Company recorded a non-cash charge of $39.8 million relating to the reduction of the carrying value of the fixed and other related assets. Employee severance and other closure costs amounting to $5.2 million were also recorded. Also during the September 2005 quarter, the Company recorded a non-cash charge of $30.0 million relating to the reduction of the carrying value of a dismantled pulp machine and a dismantled paper machine. During the September 2005 quarter, the Company performed the required annual impairment test of goodwill and found that impairment did exist in relation to its hardwood flooring and its newsprint business. As a result, goodwill impairment charges of $1.5 million and $21.6 million, respectively were recorded. The after-tax effect of these charges was $87.5 million.

The following table provides the components of the unusual items by reportable segment:

		2005	
	Forest products	Paper	Consolidated
Fixed assets write-down	$ 34.0	$ 109.9	$ 143.9
Fixed assets depreciation	–	37.5	37.5
Goodwill impairment	4.0	21.6	25.6
Other assets (a)	–	6.6	6.6
Write-down of investments	0.2	–	0.2
Obsolescence of inventory and other current assets	2.8	6.5	9.3
Severance and other labour related costs	12.8	10.6	23.4
Idling and other costs	3.3	4.7	8.0
	$ 57.1	$ 197.4	$ 254.5

(a) Includes $3.8 million of other assets related to pulp segment.

The following table provides the reconciliation components of the mill closure provisions by reportable segment. No charges were incurred in 2004.

			2005	
		Forest products	Paper	Consolidated
Opening balance		$ –	$ –	$ –
Additions:	Severance and other labour-related costs	12.8	10.6	23.4
	Idling and other costs	3.3	4.7	8.0
Payments:	Severance and other labour-related costs	(6.6)	(3.4)	(10.0)
	Idling and other costs	(1.4)	(1.2)	(2.6)
Ending balance		$ 8.1	$ 10.7	$ 18.8

There are many ways that information about unusual items can be shown in the income statement. In Rogers' income statement, the items that were identified as possibly being unusual were reported below the line called "operating income." In contrast, the items Tembec identified as being unusual are included in the calculation of "operating income (actually, it's an operating loss)." There is no authoritative definition of operating income, so whether or not an item is included in the calculation of operating income doesn't really tell you whether it is unusual or not. Similarly, an entity calling an item unusual doesn't make it unusual and not referring to an item as unusual doesn't mean that it's not unusual. The *CICA Handbook* only requires that unusual items be included in the income statement before discontinued operations and extraordinary items. Stakeholders must assess the nature of a reported item to determine whether it is permanent or transitory.

www.tembec.com

Discontinued Operations Another helpful income statement classification that is required by the *CICA Handbook* is discontinued operations. A **discontinued operation** is a business segment that an entity has stopped operating or plans to stop operating. When management decides to discontinue operating a particular business segment, the *CICA Handbook* requires that the results be disclosed separately in the income statement. This means that the revenue and expenses associated with the discontinued operation are not included in normal operating revenue and expenses. Instead, these amounts are shown separately, usually toward the bottom of the income statement. Comparative years' information is also shown separately. Information about the assets and liabilities associated with the discontinued operation is also disclosed.

Once the decision is made to stop operating a business segment, information about the segment gets disclosed separately. It doesn't matter if the segment being discontinued continues operating after the decision is made. Also, the costs associated with ceasing to operate a business segment are included in the income statement. These costs can include termination pay for employees, costs of shutting or selling facilities, gains and losses on the disposition of assets, and so on. Discontinuing a business segment has implications for future revenues, expenses, and income of the entity, and prediction of earnings and cash flows must take into account the changes caused by the discontinued operation.

Exhibit 13–3 provides an example of discontinued operations.[5] In 2005, Stelco Inc. (Stelco), the troubled steelmaker, decided to close the mini-mill and manufactured product segments as part of its reorganization. As of the end of 2005, Stelco planned to sell (but had not yet sold) the businesses in these segments. As a result of the decision, Stelco reported the revenues and expenses pertaining to the discontinued businesses as discontinued operations. This information is reported in a single line near the bottom of Stelco's statement of earnings (loss). What is included in revenues and expenses in Stelco's statement of earnings (loss) are the revenues and expenses of the businesses that Stelco is continuing to operate. The revenues and expenses pertaining to the discontinued businesses are not included. As a result, net earnings from continuing operations includes only income from the continuing business segments. This separation of operating activities and discontinued operations is helpful for predicting future earnings and cash flows. Once an entity decides to discontinue part of its operations, the revenue and expenses for all years reported in the statement of earnings are reclassified as discontinued. It doesn't matter when management decides to discontinue part of its operations; once the decision is made, revenues and expenses affected must be reclassified on the income statement as discontinued for all years reported. This treatment is important because it makes the revenues and expenses related to ongoing operating activities comparable for the three reported years.

Also notice that on the balance sheet there are asset and liability categories for assets and liabilities held for sale. These accounts segregate the assets and liabilities that Stelco is trying to sell. The held-for-sale assets and liabilities are valued at the lower of their fair value and book value. Additional information about the amounts shown on the balance sheet and statement of earnings (loss) can be found in Exhibit 13–3 in the extracts from Note 10.

www.stelco.com

Question for Consideration

Explain the difference between transitory and permanent earnings. Why is it important for users of financial statements to distinguish between transitory and permanent earnings?

Answer: Permanent earnings are earnings that are expected to be repeated in the future, whereas transitory earnings are earnings that are not expected to be repeated. When forecasting future earnings and cash flows, it is important to distinguish between permanent and transitory earnings. For example, a lender that is trying to determine whether a prospective borrower will be able to meet interest and principal payments will want to focus on information about the entity's earnings and cash flows that are likely to be realized in the future. Permanent earnings provide information in this regard, whereas transitory earnings do not. This is not to say that transitory earnings are not important. Transitory earnings can provide useful insights about the performance of management and the performance of the entity, but the information is not useful for predictive purposes.

Consolidated Statement of Financial Position

(under Creditor Protection as of January 29, 2004 – Note 1)

At December 31, (in millions)	2005	2004
	(Note 26)	(Restated – Note 3)
Current assets		
Cash and cash equivalents	$ 25	$ 32
Restricted cash (Note 6)	17	11
Accounts receivable	294	470
Inventories (Note 12)	783	844
Prepaid expenses	29	38
Future income taxes (Note 11)	22	15
Assets held for sale (Note 10)	351	–
	1,521	1,410
Current liabilities		
Current liabilities not subject to compromise		
Bank and other short term indebtedness (Note 13)	191	216
Accounts payable and accrued	232	283
Employee future benefits (Note 22)	60	62
Income and other taxes	8	10
Long-term debt due within one year (Note 17)	23	44
Liabilities held for sale (Note 10)	206	–
	720	615
Working capital	801	795
Other assets		
Property, plant, and equipment (Note 14)	932	999
Intangible assets (Note 15)	72	66
Deferred pension cost (Note 22)	112	213
Future income taxes (note 11)	12	6
Other	21	24
	1,149	1,308
Total investment	1,950	2,103
Other liabilities		
Other liabilities not subject to compromise		
Employee future benefits (Note 22)	834	907
Long-term debt (note 17)	20	49
Future income taxes (Note 11)	92	120
Asset retirement obligations (Note 9)	15	12
	961	1,088
Liabilities subject to compromise (Note 7)	630	583
Shareholders' equity	$ 359	$ 432
Derived from:		
Convertible debentures conversion option (Note 17(b))	$ 23	$ 23
Capital stock (Note 19)	781	781
Contributed surplus	16	16
Retained deficit	(461)	(388)
	$ 359	$ 432

EXHIBIT 13–3 :

**Stelco Inc.
Discontinued
Operations**

715

ANALYZING AND INTERPRETING FINANCIAL STATEMENTS

Insight

Our discussion in this section has focused on the reporting requirements of the *CICA Handbook*. It's important to recognize that the interpretation of transactions and other economic events as permanent or transitory isn't just a GAAP and *CICA Handbook* issue. Regardless of the accounting basis being used, stakeholders should distinguish between events that have permanent and transitory implications for the financial statements. Stakeholders should also be aware of any information that will affect their predictions. nformation about commitments, contingencies, subsequent events, off-balance sheet financing, and environment changes such as the economy, labour issues, regulation, competition, and so on should also be taken into consideration.

EXHIBIT 13–3 :

(continued)
Stelco Inc.
Discontinued
Operations

Consolidated Statement of Earnings (Loss)
(under Creditor Protection as of January 29, 2004 – Note 1)

Years ended December 31, (in millions, except per share amounts)	2005	2004
		(Restated – Notes 3 and 10)
Net Sales	$ 2,553	$ 2,558
Costs	2,370	2,292
	183	266
Gain on sale of plate mill assets (Note 5)	(20)	–
Amortization of property, plant, and equipment	108	105
Amortization of intangible assets (Note 15)	3	3
Operating earnings	92	158
Reorganization items (Note 4)	(76)	(53)
	16	105
Financial expense		
Interest on long-term debt and debt subject to compromise	(42)	(44)
Other interest – net	(13)	(20)
Earnings (loss) before income taxes from continuing operations	(39)	41
Income tax expense (recovery) (Note 11)		
Current	19	–
Future	(33)	15
Future income tax asset valuation allowance (release)	(16)	(8)
Net earnings (loss) from continuing operations	(9)	34
Net earnings (loss) from discontinued operations (Note 10)	(64)	30
Net earnings (loss)	$ (73)	$ 64

Note 10. Discontinued Operations and Assets Held for Sale

All the businesses that comprised the Manufactured Product segment and Mini-mill segment were determined to be non-core upon the conclusion of the Corporation's strategic review in 2004. The decision was made to sell these businesses as part of a broader capital raising process aimed at generating the cash flow and financing required to implement the Corporation's strategic capital expenditure plan at its core-integrated steel making facilities.

All of these businesses have been presented as discontinued operations resulting in the retroactive restatement of the consolidated financial statements to isolate the earnings (loss) and cash flows associated with these businesses as discontinued operations.

Quality of Earnings

The discussion of permanent and transitory earnings leads us to another concept for evaluating the usefulness of the income statement and net income—earnings quality. **Earnings quality** refers to the usefulness of current earnings for predicting future earnings.

Earnings quality is high if there is a close relationship between current and future earnings. Earnings quality is low if the relationship between current and future earnings is not close. Another way of thinking about earnings quality is as the extent to which reported earnings are permanent. If an entity's earnings contains a lot of transitory elements, those earnings would be considered to be of low quality.

Low earnings quality isn't simply a matter of identifying and removing the transitory components of earnings that were discussed earlier. The lowering of earnings quality can be much more insidious than these obvious items. Managers can also lower earnings quality when they manage earnings through their accounting policies, estimates, and accruals. A crucial effect of earnings management is that it allows managers to move earnings among periods to achieve their reporting objectives, but in doing so lower earnings quality, distort the relationship between current and future earnings, and impair the usefulness of the financial statements for predicting future earnings and cash flow.

Managers are able to move earnings among periods and thereby manage earnings for two main reasons. The first is accrual accounting. Accrual accounting creates the need for judgment in determining when economic events occur and how they should be accounted for. The second is periodic reporting. Periodic reporting makes it necessary to provide financial information for

EXHIBIT 13–3 :

(continued)
Stelco Inc.
Discontinued
Operations

717

ANALYZING AND INTERPRETING FINANCIAL STATEMENTS

Summary

The following tables summarize the net sales, earnings (loss) before income taxes, and net earnings (loss) relating to all of the Corporation's discontinued operations:

Years ended December 31 (in millions)		2005					2004
		Manufactured				Manufactured	
	Mini-mills	Products	Total		Mini-mills	Products	Total
Net Sales	$ 446	427	873	$	462	505	967
Costs, amortization, and							
financial expense	419	445	864		412	493	905
	27	(18)	9		50	12	62
Write-down of property, plant							
and equipment	–	–	–		–	18	18
(Gain) loss on sale of assets / shares	–	17	17		–	(7)	(7)
Curtailment expense	22	15	37		–	–	–
Settlement expense	–	24	24		–	–	–
Earnings (loss) before income taxes	5	(74)	(69)		50	1	51
Current income taxes (recovery)	(3)	2	(1)		6	(1)	5
Future income taxes (recovery)	4	(10)	(6)		11	1	12
Future income tax							
valuation allowance	–	2	2		–	4	4
Net earnings (loss)	$ 4	(68)	(64)	$	33	(3)	30

The total assets and liabilities held for sale relating to all of the Corporation's discontinued operations are as follows:

At December 31 (in millions)			2005
		Manufactured	
	Mini-mills	Products	Total
Current assets	$ 145	69	214
Property, plant, and equipment (Note 14)	98	9	107
Deferred pension cost (Note 22)	(7)	26	19
Future income taxes	11	–	11
Total assets held for sale	247	104	351
Current liabilities	62	26	88
Employee future benefits (Note 22)	53	52	105
Long-term debt (Note 17)	12	–	12
Future income taxes	–	–	–
Other	1	–	1
Total liabilities held for sale	128	78	206
Net investment held for sale	$ 119	26	145

The total assets and liabilities that are not reflected as assets or liabilities held for sale on the Statement of Financial Position relating to all of the Corporation's discontinued operations are as follows:

Years ended December 31 (in millions)		2005					2004
		Manufactured				Manufactured	
	Mini-mills	Products	Total		Mini-mills	Products	Total
Current assets	$ –	18	18	$	147	179	326
Property, plant, and equipment	–	–	–		93	15	108
Deferred pension cost	–	25	25		9	61	70
Future income taxes	–	–	–		5	2	7
Total assets	–	43	43		254	257	511
Current liabilities	–	11	11		69	59	128
Employee future benefits	–	45	45		48	88	136
Long-term debt	–	–	–		16	–	16
Future income taxes	–	–	–		1	–	1
Total liabilities	–	56	56		134	147	281
Net investment (liability)	$ –	(13)	(13)	$	120	110	230

periods of time that are shorter than the life of the entity. These two factors provide managers with the flexibility for deciding when and how revenues and expenses will be reported.

As we know, accounting does not affect an entity's cash flows (at least not directly, although there can be secondary cash flow effects caused by taxes, bonus plans, and so on). Earnings during a period can be thought of as being comprised of two elements: cash flow and accruals. These components can be expressed in equation form as:

$$\text{Earnings} = \text{Cash from operations} + \text{Accruals}$$

Cash from operations is real. An entity collects and spends a specific number of dollars during the period. Accounting can do nothing to change that. Accruals represent the non-cash part of earnings. Accruals include things like amortization, bad debt expense, accrued liabilities, provisions for losses, write-downs of assets, and allowances for returns, to name a few. Accruals require judgment. The managers must estimate the amounts of the accruals because the actual amounts are not usually known.

Let's consider the case of the bad debt expense. Accrual of a little too much bad debt expense this year means that at some time in the future, a little bit less of an expense will be required. In other words, if managers make accruals that lower earnings in one period, earnings will have to be higher in another period to offset this. At the end of the life of an entity, the amount of receivables that will be collected will be known. The problem is that at the time a bad debt estimate is made, the amount that will be collected is not known. Over the life of an entity the "right" amount of bad debts will have to be expensed. The right amount is the amount of credit sales that were not collected. Earnings can't be managed over the life of an entity, but in the short term managers can use the uncertainty surrounding estimates and accruals to shift earnings among periods. Other examples of estimates that managers can shift earnings include: warranty provision, allowance for returns, unearned revenue, obsolete inventory, contingent liabilities, and useful lives of assets.

When managers use accruals to influence earnings in a given period, earnings quality can be reduced because by shifting earnings to satisfy short-term reporting objectives, the relationship between current and future earnings may be impaired. And remember, adherence to GAAP doesn't solve the problem. In most cases, earnings management is done in accordance with GAAP.

We have only covered part of the story. Earnings quality can also be affected by an entity's operating decisions—the timing of its actual transactions. For example, if an entity wants to increase its income in a period, it can defer discretionary expenditures to a later period. Expenditures on discretionary items such as research and development, advertising, and repairs and maintenance are possible candidates for this type of treatment. An important responsibility of management is to determine how to spend the entity's money. It makes sense to cut back spending that management does not believe is productive. However, cutting these expenditures just to boost the bottom line can be counter-productive, because while the cuts may provide a short-term boost to net income, they may reduce future earnings. As a result, the relationship between current and future earnings is weakened and earnings quality is reduced.

Remember that operational choices affect accounting but they do not represent accounting choice. Delayed or forgone discretionary spending is not recorded under GAAP. Thus following GAAP does not ensure that earnings are not being managed in these ways.

There are a number of ways that discretionary spending can be evaluated. One way is to look at an expenditure in relation to the sales of the entity. For example, for research and development costs the following ratio could be calculated:

$$\text{Ratio of research and development expense to sales} = \frac{\text{Research and development expense}}{\text{Sales}}$$

Similar ratios can be calculated for other discretionary expenses. A significant decrease in the ratio in a period could indicate an attempt by management to bolster earnings by cutting discretionary spending. Or there could be legitimate business reasons for the decrease. This conclusion reconfirms that financial statement analysis provides clues to potential problems but doesn't usually provide definitive answers.

Management can also affect the quality of earnings by recognizing sales in one period rather than another. For example, if management wanted to increase income, it could ship goods to customers early, or create incentives for customers to make purchases sooner than they otherwise would have. This "channel stuffing" has the effect of increasing sales and income legitimately in a strict accounting sense, but this action makes current sales and earnings a poorer indicator of future earnings. The impact of channel stuffing is that customers will not have to buy as much in future periods, or they will return merchandise in larger-than-expected amounts. This type of behaviour is difficult to identify from financial statements.

Earnings management will be discussed further later in the chapter once the different analytical tools have been discussed. However, below are some additional points to consider:

- Disclosure is one of the most effective ways of overcoming difficulties in understanding the effects of an entity's accounting choices on its financial statements. If users were informed about the impact of accounting choices and estimates, they would be better able to assess the quality of an entity's earnings and then be able to make better forecasts and to better assess the quality of information that management is providing. The *CICA Handbook* has disclosure requirements, as do securities regulations, and as we discussed in Chapter 5, the measurement convention of full disclosure requires that an entity provide all relevant information about the economic activities of the entity. The reality, however, is that all relevant information is not provided, so there will always be limitations to conducting comprehensive analyses.

- Accounting choices in one period often have implications that go beyond that period. For example, when an entity takes a big bath by writing off or writing down some of its assets, earnings in periods after the big bath will be higher than they would have been had the big bath not occurred, because there are fewer costs to expense. If, as part of a big bath, an entity wrote down equipment initially with a book value of $10,000,000 to $4,000,000, income in the year of the bath would be reduced by $6,000,000, but in subsequent years there would be $6,000,000 less equipment to amortize. If the equipment had a remaining useful life of ten years, amortization each year would be $600,000 lower than it would have been had the big bath not occurred. The big bath would likely have been interpreted as a transitory item, but the effect in subsequent years could easily be included in permanent earnings.

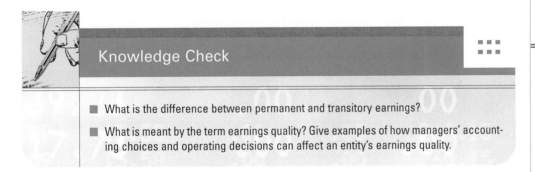

Knowledge Check

- What is the difference between permanent and transitory earnings?

- What is meant by the term earnings quality? Give examples of how managers' accounting choices and operating decisions can affect an entity's earnings quality.

www.mcgrawhill.ca/
olc/friedlan

USING RATIOS TO ANALYZE ACCOUNTING INFORMATION

Throughout this book we have discussed using financial statement information to analyze entities. In most chapters, ratios and other analytical tools were introduced. In this chapter, some of the same ratios and analytical tools are discussed, but here they are grouped into four analytical themes:

1. evaluating performance

2. liquidity

3. solvency and leverage

4. other common ratios

However, before that discussion begins, two new analytical tools, common size financial statements and trend analysis, are introduced.

If you have been working carefully with the financial statement analysis material in each chapter, you have probably already developed some good skills for analyzing and interpreting financial statements. Because the material from earlier chapters is not repeated in its entirety here, you may find it helpful to review the earlier parts of the book in which the ratio or tool was initially introduced. Figure 13–1 summarizes the financial statement analysis material covered in each chapter.

Before we begin our discussion, here are a few points to keep in mind:

- There are no GAAP for ratio analysis or financial statement analysis. A person can modify or create any ratios that he or she feels is appropriate for the analysis. What is important is making sure that the right tool is used.

- While many of the topics, ratios, and tools are presented separately in this section, they can't be considered independently. The information obtained from different analyses often has to be integrated to obtain the most informed insights.

- As was discussed earlier in this chapter, financial information has to be integrated with information from other sources to get a more complete picture of the entity and its circumstances.

- Materiality is important. Small changes in some accounts (such as gross margin) can be very significant and important, whereas large changes in other accounts may be unimportant.

FIGURE 13–1

Summary of Financial Statement Analysis Coverage in Chapters 2 Through 12

Chapter	Coverage
Chapter 2	■ Current ratio, pp. 41 ■ Debt-to-equity ratio, p. 43
Chapter 3	■ Profit margin ratio, p. 107 ■ Return on equity, p. 107
Chapter 4	■ The effect of accounting choices on financial statement numbers, pp. 168–172
Chapter 6	■ Interpreting the cash flow statement, pp. 306–308 ■ The effect of accrual accounting choices on the cash flow statement, pp. 308–311
Chapter 7	■ Hidden reserves, pp. 362–364 ■ Quick ratios and limitations of the current ratio for measuring liquidity, pp. 364–366 ■ Accounts receivable turnover ratio and average collection period of accounts receivable—limitations of these measures, pp. 366–368
Chapter 8	■ Inventory turnover ratio and average number of days inventory on hand—evaluation of inventory management, pp. 420–422 ■ A banker's view of inventory, p. 423
Chapter 9	■ Return on assets—measurement of performance and operating efficiency of an entity, pp. 488–489 ■ Limitations to using historical information about capital assets for decision making, pp. 454–456 ■ The effect of accounting policy choices on the cash flow statement, pp. 482–488 ■ The effect of accounting policy choice on ratios, pp. 488–489
Chapter 10	■ Debt-to-equity ratio—measure of risk and debt carrying ability, pp. 550–551 ■ Interest coverage ratio—ability to cover fixed financing charges, pp. 551–553
Chapter 11	■ Leverage, pp. 616–619 ■ Book value versus market value of equity—why the accounting value of equity can differ from the market value, p. 623–624 ■ Earnings per share (basic and fully diluted)—summary measure of performance, pp. 624–625 ■ Return on shareholders' equity—measure of return earned by common shareholders, pp. 625–626
Chapter 12	■ Limitations of consolidated financial statements for ratio analysis, pp. 666–668

- Financial statement information can't be interpreted in a vacuum. The information must be compared to previous years' information for the same entity, the performance of other entities, industry standards, forecasts, and other benchmarks.

Common Size Financial Statements and Trend Analysis

Interpreting the raw numbers—the numbers actually presented in a set of financial statements—can be a challenge. It is certainly necessary to examine the actual numbers that an entity reports, but it can be difficult to make sense of trends in and relationships among the numbers in the statements by examining only the raw numbers. It can also be difficult to compare the raw numbers of different entities.

In this section we will discuss two tools that make this type of analysis easier:

- common size financial statements or vertical analysis

- trend or horizontal analysis

These tools eliminate the impact of size from the financial statement numbers by restating them as proportions.

Common Size Financial Statements or Vertical Analysis **Common size financial statements** or **vertical analysis** is an analytical tool in which the amounts in the balance sheet and income statement are expressed as percentages of other elements in the same year's statements. On the balance sheet, amounts can be expressed as a percentage of total assets. On the income statement, amounts can be stated as a percentage of revenue. If amounts on the balance sheet are presented as percentages of total assets, the common size balance sheet will show the percentages that cash, inventory, capital assets, long-term debt, and so on are of total assets.

This presentation gives a good view of the asset and liability composition of the entity. Similarly, if income statement elements are stated as a percentage of revenues, the user can see the proportion of sales that each expense represents. This type of analysis can provide some useful insights into the relative importance of different expenses and allow comparisons over time and with other entities. For example, comparing common size income statements would allow users to see the percentage of each sales dollar that is expended for advertising, research and development, or wages. By examining the common size financial statements of an entity over a number of years, it may be possible to explain developments such as changes in profitability. Common size statements may also help identify problem areas by highlighting expenses that have changed significantly relative to sales.

Figure 13–2 shows common size financial statements for Rogers. On Rogers' statements of income, each line is presented as a percentage of sales for the year. As a result, the sales line in each is 100 percent (for fiscal 2005, sales $_{\text{fiscal 2005}}$ ÷ sales $_{\text{fiscal 2005}}$ × 100 percent = \$7,482,154,000 ÷ \$7,482,154,000 = 100 percent). Similarly, operating income for fiscal 2005 is 8.9 percent of sales (operating income $_{\text{fiscal 2005}}$ ÷ sales $_{\text{fiscal 2005}}$ × 100 percent = \$665,558,000 ÷ \$7,482,154,000 × 100 percent). For the common size balance sheets in Figure 13–2, each amount is stated as a percentage of total assets. For example, goodwill on December 31, 2005 is 21.9 percent of total assets (goodwill $_{\text{December 31, 2005}}$ ÷ total assets $_{\text{December 31, 2005}}$ × 100 percent = \$3,035,787,000 ÷ \$13,834,289,000 × 100 percent). Amounts on the liabilities side of the balance sheet are also shown as a percentage of total assets. Comparing the percentages year to year allows the user to see any changes in the relative proportion of assets and liabilities.

The common size statements make year-to-year comparisons very convenient. By comparing each row, we see proportionally how each amount has changed over time. For example, on the statements of income, Rogers' operating income as a percentage of sales decreased from 11.4 percent in 2004 to 8.9 percent in 2005. By looking at Rogers' actual statement of earnings, it is not possible to tell at a glance that the operating income as a percentage of sales has decreased. It is easy to see that operating income has increased because the dollar amount in fiscal 2005 is greater than in 2004, but you can't tell that operating costs have increased by a greater percentage than sales.

If we had more years of data our analysis could have been more informative. However, there were some changes in presentation from the 2004 to the 2005 annual report that made a

◆ ROGERS™

FIGURE 13–2 ::

Common Size Financial Statements for Rogers Communications Inc.

Rogers Communications Inc. Common Size Consolidated Balance Sheets		
	December 31, 2005	December 31, 2004
Assets		
Current assets:		
Cash and cash equivalents	0.0%	1.8%
Accounts receivable	6.4%	5.1%
Other current assets	2.2%	2.0%
Future tax asset	0.8%	0.0%
	9.4%	8.9%
Property, plant and equipment (note 5)	44.5%	41.3%
Goodwill	21.9%	25.5%
Intangible assets	19.0%	21.5%
Investments	1.0%	1.0%
Deferred charges	0.9%	1.0%
Future tax asset	2.5%	0.0%
Other long-term assets	0.7%	0.7%
	100.0%	100.0%
Liabilities and Shareholders' Equity		
Current liabilities:		
Bank advances, arising from outstanding cheques	0.8%	0.0%
Accounts payable and accrued liabilities	10.2%	10.8%
Current portion of long-term debt	2.1%	4.7%
Current portion of derivative instruments	0.1%	0.4%
Unearned revenue	1.3%	1.2%
	14.4%	17.0%
Long-term debt	53.9%	59.7%
Derivative instruments	5.7%	4.8%
Other long-term liabilities	0.5%	0.5%
	74.5%	82.0%
Shareholders' equity	25.5%	18.0%
	100.0%	100.0%

line-by-line comparison inappropriate without adjusting the amounts from previous years. (These changes would be possible to make but we will not do them in this book.) Some items that stand out from the two-year analysis are:

■ The percentage decrease in operating income is due mainly to the percentage increase in cost of sales and to a small extent the percentage increase in depreciation and amortization. These increases were offset by percentage decreases in operating, general, and administrative expenses, and selling and marketing expenses.

■ Interest as a percentage of sales decreased significantly in 2005. From the common size balance sheet, we can see that that debt as a percentage of total assets has also decreased. So the proportion of Rogers that is financed by debt is decreasing, along with the actual amount of debt that the company has.

■ The proportion of property, plant, and equipment increased significantly in 2005 while the proportion of goodwill and intangible assets decreased significantly.

FIGURE 13–2 ::

(continued)
Common Size
Financial
Statements for
Rogers
Communications
Inc.

Rogers Communications Inc. Common Size Consolidated Statements of Income		
	December 31, 2005	December 31, 2004
Operating revenue	100.0%	100.0%
Cost of sales	17.3%	14.2%
Sales and marketing expenses	15.0%	15.8%
Operating, general and administrative expenses	38.1%	39.0%
Integration expenses	0.9%	0.1%
Depreciation and amortization	19.8%	19.5%
Operating income	8.9%	11.4%
Interest on long-term debt	9.5%	10.3%
	(0.6%)	1.2%
Loss on repayment of long-term debt	(0.2%)	(0.5%)
Foreign exchange gain (loss) (note 2(g))	0.5%	(1.2%)
Change in the fair value of derivative instruments	(0.3%)	0.5%
Gain on dilution on issue of shares by a subsidiary	0.0%	0.3%
Other income, net	0.0%	0.1%
Income before income taxes and non-controlling interest	(0.6%)	0.3%
Income tax expense (reduction)	0.0%	0.0%
Current	0.1%	0.1%
Future	(0.1%)	0.0%
	0.0%	0.1%
Income before non-controlling interest	(0.6%)	0.2%
Non-controlling interest	0.0%	(1.4%)
Net income (loss) for the year	(0.6%)	(1.2%)

■ The largest expense line on the statements of income, operating, general, and administrative (OGA) expenses decreased by 0.9 percent, a significant amount as a proportion of sales, even though the actual number of dollars spent on this item increased significantly (by 30 percent from 2004 to 2005). This analysis of OGA expenses shows the usefulness of common size financial statements. If the analysis focuses only on the raw numbers in the income statement, the conclusion would simply be that Rogers spent a lot more money in 2005 on OGA expenses. With the common size analysis, some context for the increase is provided.

Though this point has been made many times in the book, it bears repeating again: *Financial statement analysis may help identify problems, but it will not usually explain them.* The last bullet point above is an example of this. Operating, general, and administrative expenses as a percentage of sales decreased from 2004 to 2005, but it isn't clear why. The decrease could be due to improved efficiencies or that some of the costs included in the expense category are fixed, so they don't increase proportionately with sales. Some answers may be found in the MD&A, but that may not always be the case. In many cases, explanations may not be found in the annual report at all. Users would have to look elsewhere for help to answer the question at hand.

Rogers' annual report provides selected data for the five-year period 2001–2005. Figure 13–3 provides a common-size analysis for Rogers' divisional revenue and operating profit. (The raw data used in Figure 13–3 can be found in Panel A of Figure 13–4.) In Figure 13–3, the revenue of each division is shown as a percentage of total revenue and the operating profit is shown as a percentage of total operating profit. The Exhibit shows the increasing dominance of the wireless division for producing revenues and operating profit. Both have grown steadily and significantly over the five-year period. Operating profit could have also been assessed as a percentage of divisional sales to show the operating margin for each division. Data can be analyzed in many different ways, depending on the question that is being asked.

FIGURE 13–3

Common-size Analysis for Rogers' Revenue and Operating Profit by Division

	2005	2004	2003	2002	2001
Revenue					
Wireless	53.5%	49.6%	46.1%	44.3%	43.0%
Cable	27.6%	34.7%	37.3%	37.8%	37.9%
Media	14.7%	17.1%	17.8%	19.0%	18.9%
Telecom	5.7%	0.0%	0.0%	0.0%	0.0%
Corporate and eliminations	(1.5%)	(1.4%)	(1.2%)	(1.2%)	0.1%
	100.0%	100.0%	100.0%	100.0%	100.0%
Operating Profit					
Wireless	62.4%	54.8%	50.2%	46.2%	43.2%
Cable	33.5%	40.9%	45.8%	49.4%	54.3%
Media	6.0%	6.7%	7.4%	7.7%	7.2%
Telecom	2.1%	0.0%	0.0%	0.0%	0.0%
Corporate and eliminations	(4.0%)	(2.3%)	(3.4%)	(3.3%)	(4.7%)
	100.0%	100.0%	100.0%	100.0%	100.0%

Common size financial statements are very useful for comparing the financial statements of different entities. It can be very difficult to compare raw financial statement numbers of different entities because the entities may differ in size. Common size financial statements eliminate the effects of size and allow users to see the financial statement components of different entities on a common basis. Of course, differences between entities have to be interpreted carefully because they can be due to different accounting choices, as well as to differences in the economic performance and nature of the entities.

Horizontal Analysis or Trend Statements Another type of analysis that eliminates the effects of size from financial statements is called horizontal analysis or trend statements. **Horizontal analysis** or **trend statements** is an analytical tool in which the amounts in the balance sheet and income statement are expressed as percentages of a base year set of financial statements.

Trend statements provide information that shows the change in each account in the financial statements relative to that account's base year. To construct trend statements, it is first necessary to specify a base year. The base year serves as the basis for determining the trend in each account in the financial statements. For each year reported in the financial statements, each account is stated as a proportion of that particular account's base year.

For our discussion of trend statements we will use Rogers' five-year financial summary that is included in its 2005 MD&A. The five-year financial summary provides extracts from the statements of income and balance sheets for the period 2001 to 2005. The summary doesn't provide the full income statements and balance sheets. The original data from the summary is shown in Panel A of Figure 13–4. Rogers' trend statements are presented in Panel B of Figure 13–4. For the trend data, 2001 was selected as the base year. Notice that each row in the 2001 column is 100 percent. The amounts for 2002 through 2005 are stated as percentages of the 2001 amounts. Calculations for 2001 and 2005 for Rogers' Wireless division revenue (Wireless) is shown below:

$$\text{Trend statement amount} = \frac{\text{Current year amount}}{\text{Base year amount}} \times 100\%$$

$$\text{Trend data amount for Wireless revenue for 2001} = \frac{\$1,640,889,000}{\$1,640,889,000} \times 100\% = 100.0\%$$

$$\text{Trend data amount for Wireless revenue for 2005} = \frac{\$4,006,658,000}{\$1,640,889,000} \times 100\% = 244.2\%$$

For each year the denominator is Wireless revenue for 2001 and the numerator is Wireless revenue for the year for which the trend statement is being calculated. Thus for 2005, Wireless revenue in 2005 is the numerator and revenue in 2001 is the denominator. When the trend statement amount is calculated for another line on the financial statements, the amounts from that line are used.

The trend data give a different view of the entity. These statements allow the user to view the change in each account over time relative to the base year. Thus, from 2001 to 2002 Wireless revenue increased by 15.3 percent. From fiscal 2001 to fiscal 2005, Wireless revenue increased by 144.2 percent (see Figure 13–4). If you want to know the growth in sales from fiscal 2003 to fiscal 2005, additional calculations are required.

Some issues that arise from an examination of Rogers' trend data are:

- For the five-year period total sales increased by 96.2 percent. The wireless division had the greatest percentage increase in revenue (144.2 percent) while the cable division had the smallest increase (42.9 percent).

- Growth in operating profit was 125 percent over the five years, with the wireless division again showing greatest growth by far over the period.

- Cash from operations (CFO) was 220.6 percent higher in 2005 than in 2001. Rogers is definitely a reliable producer of cash from operations, particularly over the five-year period 2001 through 2005.

- Total assets increased by 50.4 percent over the five-year period while liabilities increased by 40.7 percent. This indicates that over the five years, the increase in assets was financed more by equity than by debt.

Some interpretational issues with using trend statements should be noted. When the balance in an account changes from positive to negative, or from negative to positive—for example, Rogers' net income—the change can't be interpreted simply by looking at the percentage change relative to the base year. Also, if the balance in an account in the base year is zero, it is not possible to calculate a trend number for subsequent years because division by zero is infinity. In addition, very small balances in the base year can result in huge percentage changes that may not be meaningful.

FIGURE 13–4 ::

Trend Financial Statement Data for Rogers Communications Inc.

Panel A: Original Data[6]					
	2005	**2004**	**2003**	**2002**	**2001**
Income and Cash Flow					
Revenue					
Wireless	$4,006,658	$2,783,525	$2,207,794	$1,891,514	$1,640,889
Cable	2,067,733	1,945,655	1,788,122	1,614,554	1,446,599
Media	1,097,176	957,112	854,992	810,805	721,710
Telecom	423,890	—	—	—	—
Corporate and eliminations	(113,303)	(78,043)	(59,052)	(50,088)	4,772
Total	$7,482,154	$5,608,249	$4,791,856	$4,266,785	$3,813,970
Operating Profit					
Wireless	$1,337,049	$ 950,391	$ 727,572	$ 527,687	$ 411,945
Cable	718,603	708,659	663,474	563,480	516,805
Media	127,846	115,372	106,724	87,635	68,306
Telecom	45,940	—	—	—	—
Corporate and eliminations	(85,869)	(40,281)	(48,874)	(37,188)	(44,535)
Total	$2,143,569	$1,734,141	$1,448,896	$1,141,614	$ 952,521

FIGURE 13–3 ::

(continued)
Trend Financial Statement Data for Rogers Communications Inc.

Panel A: Original Data[6]					
	2005	**2004**	**2003**	**2002**	**2001**
Net Income (loss)	($ 44,658)	($ 67,142)	$ 79,358	$ 259,854	($ 515,721)
Cash flow from operations	$ 1,551,415	$ 1,305,019	$1,031,043	$ 682,839	$ 483,862
Additions to PP&E	$ 1,353,796	$ 1,054,938	$ 963,742	$1,261,983	$1,420,747
Basic earnings (loss) per share	($ 0.15)	($ 0.28)	$ 0.35	$ 1.05	($ 2.56)
Balance Sheet					
Assets					
Property, plant and equipment, net	$ 6,151,526	$ 5,486,837	$5,039,304	$5,051,998	$6,151,526
Goodwill	3,035,786	3,388,687	1,891,636	1,892,060	3,035,786
Intangible assets	2,627,467	2,855,689	400,219	423,674	2,627,467
Investments	138,212	139,170	229,221	223,937	138,212
Other assets	1,881,298	1,402,355	905,115	1,115,064	1,881,298
Total assets	$13,834,289	$13,272,738	$8,465,495	$8,706,733	$9,198,944
Liabilities and Shareholders' Equity					
Long-term debt	$ 7,739,551	$ 8,541,097	$5,440,018	$6,319,454	$5,809,497
Accounts payable and other liabilities	2,567,123	2,346,307	1,534,541	1,272,745	1,192,165
Future income taxes	—	—	—	27,716	137,189
Non-controlling interest	—	—	193,342	132,536	186,377
Total liabilities	10,306,674	10,887,404	7,167,901	7,752,451	7,325,228
Shareholders' equity	3,527,615	2,385,334	1,297,594	954,282	1,873,716
Total Liabilities and Shareholders' Equity	$13,834,289	$13,272,738	$8,465,495	$8,706,733	$9,198,944

Panel B: Trend Financial Statement Data					
	2005	**2004**	**2003**	**2002**	**2001**
Income and Cash Flow					
Revenue					
Wireless	244.2%	169.6%	134.5%	115.3%	100.0%
Cable	142.9%	134.5%	123.6%	111.6%	100.0%
Media	152.0%	132.6%	118.5%	112.3%	100.0%
Telecom					
Corporate and eliminations	−2,374.3%	−1,635.4%	−1,237.5%	−1,049.6%	100.0%
Total	196.2%	147.0%	125.6%	111.9%	100.0%
Operating Profit					
Wireless	324.6%	230.7%	176.6%	128.1%	100.0%
Cable	139.0%	137.1%	128.4%	109.0%	100.0%
Media	187.2%	168.9%	156.2%	128.3%	100.0%
Telecom					
Corporate and eliminations	192.8%	90.4%	109.7%	83.5%	100.0%
Total	225.0%	182.1%	152.1%	119.9%	100.0%
Net Income (loss)	8.7%	13.0%	−15.4%	−50.4%	100.0%
Cash flow from operations	320.6%	269.7%	213.1%	141.1%	100.0%
Additions to PP&E	95.3%	74.3%	67.8%	88.8%	100.0%
Basic earnings (loss) per share	5.9%	10.9%	−13.7%	−41.0%	100.0%

Panel B: Trend Financial Statement Data					
	2005	**2004**	**2003**	**2002**	**2001**
Balance Sheet					
Assets					
Property, plant and equipment, net	130.4%	116.3%	106.8%	107.1%	100.0%
Goodwill	177.4%	198.0%	110.5%	110.5%	100.0%
Intangible assets	620.6%	674.5%	94.5%	100.1%	100.0%
Investments	13.2%	13.3%	21.9%	21.4%	100.0%
Other assets	144.9%	108.0%	69.7%	85.9%	100.0%
Total assets	150.4%	144.3%	92.0%	94.6%	100.0%
Liabilities and Shareholders' Equity					
Long-term debt	133.2%	147.0%	93.6%	108.8%	100.0%
Accounts payable and other liabilities	215.3%	196.8%	128.7%	106.8%	100.0%
Future income taxes				20.2%	100.0%
Non-controlling interest			103.7%	71.1%	100.0%
Total liabilities	140.7%	148.6%	97.9%	105.8%	100.0%
Shareholders' equity	188.3%	127.3%	69.3%	50.9%	100.0%
Total Liabilities and Shareholders' Equity	150.4%	144.3%	92.0%	94.6%	100.0%

FIGURE 13–3 ::

**(continued)
Trend Financial
Statement Data for
Rogers
Communications
Inc.**

Trend statements give a better indication of growth and decline than common size financial statements because the proportion in the trend data is relative to another year. Trend statements remove the effects of size from the numbers, which facilitates comparisons among periods and entities. However, the actual numbers in a set of financial statements can't be ignored. Only by examining the actual numbers can one get a sense of the importance of a particular account.

Evaluating Performance

Many users of financial statements want to evaluate the performance of entities. They want to know how a particular entity "did." This is often easier said than done, because measuring performance can be very difficult. Performance is a multi-faceted concept that can be measured in different ways. Different performance indicators can often tell conflicting stories about how an entity is doing.

In this section, we discuss different ways of evaluating the performance of an entity. Before we do, it is important to keep in mind some of the measurement difficulties that exist with determining income. These points have been raised before, but they bear repeating:

■ There are many different choices available to managers in accounting for an entity's transactions and economic events. In many cases, it is not possible to point to one of the alternatives as being the best way of measuring income. As a result, many reasonable measures of income can be obtained, depending on the accounting policies used.

■ Another measurement problem relates to the use of estimates. While traditional GAAP reporting is historical and transactions-based, there is usually uncertainty reflected in the amounts reported in the financial statements. The amount of accounts receivable that will not be collected cannot be known with certainty on the financial statement date. The cost of fulfilling an entity's warranty obligations must be estimated when financial statements are prepared. The useful lives of capital assets must be estimated so that amortization can be calculated. The list goes on and on. The actual amount of cash that will be collected, costs incurred, and so on, depends on future, uncertain events. Management can make their best efforts to estimate these unknown amounts, but in the end they are still estimates.

■ As a result, we cannot contend that the current GAAP accounting system can provide an entity's true income. Thus, while there might be a "true" income or economic reality out there, it is not possible to know what it is. And while accountants, managers, and users do their best to find that "right" number, it is not possible to know whether it has been found. Only when an entity winds up, and all its liabilities are settled and its assets converted into cash, is it possible to know and understand the performance of the entity over its life.

But we evade the issue. While there are many problems associated with measuring performance, those problems don't take away the need to measure it. Despite all its limitations, measuring performance is essential to users so they can make decisions about how to invest their resources, evaluate how well managers have done their jobs, and address many other performance-related questions. How then, does one approach this task?

A logical place to start is with the income statement. The income statement was described in Chapter 2 as a statement of performance. In accrual accounting, the income statements provide an indication of an entity's economic gains (revenues) and the economic sacrifices (expenses) that were incurred to generate those gains. Net income is a representation of the net economic gain or loss to the owners of the entity over a period.

We can also look at subtotals within the income statement to get different indicators of performance. Gross margin (sales – cost of sales), operating income, income before taxes, and others are examples of different, potentially informative measures that are reported on an income statement.

One of the most commonly used tools for analyzing financial statements is ratios. Ratios allow people to examine relationships between numbers in the financial statements to gain insight about the entity. Also, like common size financial statements and trend statements, ratios eliminate the effect of size from the data.

Let's examine some of the common income statement performance measures.

Gross Margin Gross margin is the difference between sales and cost of sales. (Cost of sales is the cost of the goods or services actually provided to customers.) Gross margin is an important measure of performance. An entity must be able to cover all its other costs of operations and provide profit from gross margin. Gross margin is often stated as a percentage of sales and called the gross margin percentage. The gross margin percentage indicates the percentage of each dollar of sales that is available to cover other costs and return a profit to the entity's owners.

The gross margin percentage is defined as:

$$\text{Gross margin percentage} = \frac{\text{Sales} - \text{Cost of sales}}{\text{Sales}} \times 100\% = \frac{\text{Gross margin}}{\text{Sales}} \times 100\%$$

Rogers' gross margin in fiscal 2005 is $6,186,006,000 (sales – cost of sales = $7,482,154,000 – $1,296,148,000). The gross margin percentage for 2005 was 82.7 percent ($6,186,006,000 ÷ $7,482,154,000). Gross margin is not very meaningful for Rogers because it is mainly a provider of services—goods sold represents a very small proportion of Rogers' business activities. Gross margin and gross margin percentage are meaningful for retail, wholesale, and manufacturing businesses, where goods are actually sold as part of the entity's activities. A gross margin percentage of 82.7 percent means that for every dollar of sales, Rogers had $0.83 to apply to costs other than costs of goods and for profit.

An entity's gross margin percentage can be influenced in two ways:

1. An entity can increase its gross margin percentage by increasing the price it charges for its goods or services. It is not always possible for a business to raise its price without consequences. Customers must believe they are getting something in return to accept a higher price. For example, an entity might offer higher quality products or better service than its competitors. If an entity cannot somehow distinguish its products, customers may take their business elsewhere.

2. An entity can influence its gross margin percentage through cost control and efficiency. If an entity can obtain the inputs it requires to provide its goods or services at a lower cost, or use those inputs more efficiently, the entity will have a higher gross margin percentage.

Gross margin percentages can vary dramatically from entity to entity and industry to industry. For example, computer software companies often have very high gross margin percentages because a major cost of developing software—research and development—is expensed when incurred. Research and development is accounted for as a period cost and is therefore not included in cost of sales.

Gross margin percentages for a number of entities in different industries are shown in Figure 13–5.

A financial statement user can't always determine an entity's gross margin because some entities don't provide the information in their income statements. Retail businesses frequently don't disclose their gross margins for fear of giving valuable information to competitors. Some entities don't specifically show the gross margin on their income statements, but do provide cost of sales, making it possible to calculate the amount. Rogers is an example of this. Rogers doesn't show its gross margin, probably because it is a minor consideration for a business of this type.

Entity	Industry	Gross Margin in Most Recent Fiscal Period
Angoss Software Corporation	Software	99.7% (year ended November 30, 2005)
Domtar Inc.	Forest and paper products	12.7% (year ended December 31, 2005)
Falconbridge Limited	Mining	22.3% (year ended December 31, 2005)
Leon's Furniture Limited	Furniture retailing	40.9% (year ended December 31, 2005)
Mitec Telecom Inc.	Computer hardware	9.4% (year ended April 30, 2005)
Sleeman Breweries Ltd.	Beer brewer	51.3% (year ended December 31, 2005)
TransCanada Corporation	Pipeline	80.9% (year ended December 31, 2005)

FIGURE 13–5

Gross Margin Percentages for Selected Companies in Different Industries

729

Consolidated statements of earnings

EXHIBIT 13–4

Income Statement Presentation of Gross Margin— Sobeys Inc.

(in millions except per share amounts)	53 weeks ended May 7, 2005	52 weeks ended May 1, 2004 Restated (Note 1t)
Sales	$ 12,189.4	$ 11,046.8
Gain on sale of assets (Note 22)	–	14.6
Operating expenses		
Cost of sales, selling and administrative expenses	11,690.4	10,614.4
Depreciation	174.5	152.2
Amortization of intangibles	1.9	0.5
Earnings before interest and income taxes	322.6	294.3
Interest expense		
Long-term debt	35.0	40.0
Short-term debt	2.9	3.2
	37.9	43.2
Earnings before income taxes	284.7	251.1
Income taxes (Note 8)	98.0	84.6
Net earnings	$ 186.7	$ 166.5
Earnings per share basic and diluted (Note 10)	$ 2.85	$ 2.53
Basic and diluted weighted average number of common shares outstanding, in millions	65.5	65.9

Exhibit 13–4 provides the statement of earnings for Sobeys Inc., an operator and franchiser of grocery stores.[7] Sobeys Inc. reports virtually all its expenses on a single line on its statement of earnings, making calculation of gross margin impossible.

Profit Margin Ratio The profit margin ratio is a bottom line measure of performance. The ratio indicates the percentage of each sales dollar that the entity earns in profit. The ratio is defined as:

$$\text{Profit margin ratio} = \frac{\text{Net income}}{\text{Sales}} \times 100\%$$

ANALYZING AND INTERPRETING FINANCIAL STATEMENTS

www.sobeys.com

A higher profit margin ratio indicates greater profitability because the entity earns a larger proportion of each dollar of sales in profit. Rogers' profit margin for the fiscal year ended December 31, 2005 is calculated as:

$$\text{Profit margin ratio} = \frac{\text{Net income}}{\text{Sales}} \times 100\%$$

$$= \frac{\$(44,658,000)}{\$7,482,154,000} \times 100\%$$

$$= (0.6\%)$$

The profit margin ratio of –0.6 percent means that Rogers lost $0.006 for every dollar of sales that it made. Rogers' profit margin in 2004 was –1.2 percent.

There are some different variations of the profit margin ratio. The numerator can be defined as operating income or income before discontinued operations and non-controlling interest. These provide measures of profitability that reflect ongoing operations rather than overall profitability.

Figure 13–6 shows the profit margin ratios for a number of industries. The profit margins shown are seven-year averages (1999–2005) for firms in each industry. Figure 13–6 shows that there is a wide variation of profit margin among industries. Considerable variation can also be seen by the firms in each industry across the reported years.

Return on Investment Our discussion of performance to this point has focused on the income statement. We have looked at two measures of performance, each calculated as a percentage of sales. These measures provide some insight into the operating profitability of an entity. However, these income statement measures ignore what it cost to generate those sales and earn those profits. An entity could have a high gross margin and profit margin, but the amount of investment required to earn those margins—the amount of assets required—might indicate that the performance of the entity was unsatisfactory. In other words, a profit of $1,000,000 will be evaluated differently if the investment required to earn that profit was $5,000,000 or $50,000,000.

This is where our measures of return on investment come in. Earlier in the book, two measures of return on investment were discussed: return on assets (ROA) and return on equity (ROE). These two return measures allow us to assess the performance of an entity in relation to the investment made in the entity. They differ in the investment base that each uses. ROA uses all investment, debt and equity, to determine the return. ROA is a measure of the performance of the entity that is independent of how the entity's assets were financed. In contrast, ROE determines the return on the investment made by the common equity investors. Both are legitimate, valid, and widely used measures.

FIGURE 13–6

Profit Margins in Selected Canadian Industries

Industry	Seven-Year Average Profit Margin (1999–2005)* Profit margin equals net income before discontinued operations and non-controlling interest
Auto parts and components	(49.58)%
Banks	17.71%
Food and staples retailing	2.88%
Media	3.12%
Oil, gas, and consumable Fuels	10.15%
Paper and forest products	2.78%
Retailing	3.69%
Software	(41.83)%
Telecommunications services	8.50%

*Data from the *Financial Post Industry Reports*, http://www.fpdata.finpost.com/suite/autologreports.asp (accessed May 8, 2006).

Here are the definitions of ROA and ROE in equation form:

$$\text{Return on assets} = \frac{\text{Net Income} + \text{After tax interest expense}}{\text{Average total assets}} = \frac{\text{Net income} + \text{interest expense} \, (1 - \text{tax rate})}{\text{Average total assets}}$$

$$\text{Return on equity} = \frac{\text{Net income} - \text{preferred dividends}}{\text{Average common shareholders' equity}}$$

The numerator in ROA has after-tax interest expense added back because the ratio is a measure of return that is supposed to be independent of how the assets are financed. If the interest expense were included in the numerator, ROA would be affected by the amount of debt because the interest expense would increase with the amount of debt.

Preferred dividends are deducted from net income when calculating ROE because ROE is a measure of return to the common shareholders. Preferred dividends are paid to the preferred shareholders, so the amount paid is not available to the common shareholders. Remember that preferred share dividends are not expensed in the calculation of net income.

ROA and ROE for Rogers and the telecommunications services industry (the industry that Rogers is classified in) are shown in Figure 13–7.

○ ROGERS™

	2005	2004	2003
Return on assets—Rogers	3.01%	2.81%	4.53%
Return on equity—Rogers	−1.39%	−4.69%	4.82%
Return on assets—Telecommunications Services*	7.32%	7.62%	6.72%
Return on equity— Telecommunications Services*	10.55%	10.92%	10.21%

*Data from the *Financial Post Industry Reports*,
http://www.fpdata.finpost.com/suite/autologreports.asp (accessed May 8, 2006).

FIGURE 13–7 :: 731

Return on Assets and Return on Equity for Rogers and the Telecommunications Services Industry

Rogers' average ROE is negative over the three year period shown. Over the three years, the return earned by equity investors is less that what investors would have earned from investing in a GIC. Investors expect a higher return because investing in a telecommunications business like Rogers is much riskier than keeping money in the bank.

Both ROE and ROA are lower for 2005 than they were in 2003. We can also compare Rogers' returns with firms in the same industry. Figure 13–7 shows that Rogers' ROA and ROE were both significantly lower than the industry average for each of 2003–2005. (Despite the poor performance based on ROE and ROA, it is worth pointing out that Rogers' stock price was doing well in early 2006.)

It is important to keep in mind, of course, that these measures of return on investment are affected by the accounting choices the managers make. Different accounting choices mean different measures of return on investment. This means that comparisons among firms may not be valid, though it might be possible to interpret trends among different firms. Also, remember that the returns earned by an entity are related to risk. The higher the risk, the higher the return should be. Therefore, differences in returns may be reflecting differences in risk as well as different performance levels. It is important to remember that Rogers is in a number of different industries, which may impair the validity of the comparison with the industry average.

It is common to break down ROA into components to provide insight into how an entity is generating its returns and to help identify how its performance can be improved. ROA can be broken down into two components: profit margin and asset turnover. Generally then, ROA can be stated as follows:

$$\text{Return on assets} = \text{Asset turnover ratio} \times \text{Profit margin ratio} \times 100\%$$

$$= \frac{\text{Sales}}{\text{Average total assets}} \times \frac{\text{Net income} + \text{interest expense} \times (1 - \text{tax rate})}{\text{Sales}} \times 100\%$$

$$= \frac{\text{Net income} + \text{interest expense} \, (1 - \text{tax rate})}{\text{Average total assets}} \times 100\%$$

FIGURE 13–8 ::

How Different Combinations of Profit Margin and Asset Turnover Can Generate a Specific ROA

	Company A	Company B	Company C
Sales	$8,000,000	$1,000,000	$4,000,000
Net income	640,000	20,000	40,000
Average assets	8,000,000	250,000	500,000
Profit margin ratio	8%	2%	1%
Asset turnover ratio	1	4	8
Return on assets	8%	8%	8%

We discussed profit margin earlier in this section. Profit margin indicates the amount of each sales dollar the entity earns as profit. **Asset turnover** is a measure of how effectively an entity can generate sales from its asset base. The more sales an entity can generate from its asset base, the higher its asset turnover ratio and the higher its ROA. If an entity can produce the same amount of sales by carrying less inventory than its competitors, everything else being equal, that entity will have a higher asset turnover ratio and a higher ROA.

An entity can generate a given ROA through different combinations of profit margin and asset turnover. The objective for any entity will be to maximize the ROA. It is up to an entity's managers to design strategies to achieve this objective. Some businesses or industries might pursue a strategy of accepting a low profit margin but compensate by having a high asset turnover ratio. In other words, make a small amount of money on each sale, but make a lot of sales. Business and industries that have a relatively low asset turnover ratio would try to compensate with a higher profit margin.

In Figure 13–8, three combinations for earning an 8 percent ROA are shown. Company A generates its 8 percent ROA with a relatively high profit margin (8 percent) but a relatively low asset turnover ratio (1 percent). Company C does the opposite. Company C has a very small profit margin ratio but its assets turn over quickly. Company B is in between.

By breaking down ROA into its components, it is possible to identify sources of problems with an entity's performance. An entity with a low profit margin would require different corrective steps than an entity with a low asset turnover ratio. An entity with a low profit margin might focus on product pricing (for example, it might try to increase its prices) or find ways of controlling or reducing costs, identifying inefficiencies in the production and delivery of the entity's product, and so on. A company with a low asset turnover ratio might examine whether there are unproductive or idle assets, assets perhaps that could be sold, or whether some assets could be managed more efficiently and effectively (for example, inventory or receivables levels that are unreasonably high).

Of course, there are limits to the improvements management can make. If an entity is already performing well in either profit margin or asset turnover, there is only so much the managers can do to make improvements. Also, the nature of different industries imposes limits on the magnitude of these ratios. For example, industries that require very large capital investments tend to have lower asset turnover ratios.

Seven-year average asset turnover ratios for a number of industries are shown in Figure 13–9.

Now let's examine the components of Rogers' ROA. The information needed from Rogers' annual report to do the analysis is shown in Figure 13–10.

For 2005, the breakdown of ROA is calculated as follows:

$$\text{Return on assets for 2005} = \text{Asset turnover ratio} \times \text{Profit margin percentage} \times 100\%$$

$$= \frac{\text{Sales}}{\text{Average total assets}} \times \frac{\text{Net income} - (\text{interest expense} \times (1 - \text{tax rate}))}{\text{Sales}} \times 100\%$$

$$= \frac{\$7,482,154,000}{(\$13,834,289 + \$13,272,738,000)/2} \times \frac{\$(44,658,000) + (\$710,079,000 \times (1 - 0.361))}{\$7,482,154,000} \times 100\%$$

$$= 0.552 \times .0547 \times 100\%$$

$$= 3.01\%$$

Seven-Year Average Asset Turnover Ratios	
Industry	**(1999–2005)***
Auto parts and transportation equipment	1.08
Computers and electronic equipment	1.24
Food and staples retailing	2.70
Gold	0.26
Media	0.58
Paper and forest products	0.81
Retailing	2.44
Software	0.68
Telecommunications services	0.53
Utilities	0.40

*Data from the *Financial Post Industry Reports*,
http://www.fpdata.finpost.com/suite/autologreports.asp (accessed May 8, 2006).

FIGURE 13–9

Seven-Year Average Asset Turnover Ratios for Selected Industries

	2005	**2004**	**2003**
Revenue	$7,482,154,000	$5,608,249,000	$4,791,856,000
Net Income (loss)	(44,658,000)	(13,218,000)	129,193,000
Total assets	13,834,289	13,272,738,000	8,465,495,000
Interest expense	710,079	522,074,000	488,865,000
Tax rate	36.1%	35.3%	36.6%

FIGURE 13–10

Information From Rogers' Annual Report to Calculate Return on Investment

	Return on Assets	**=**	**Asset Turnover Ratio**	**×**	**Profit Margin Percentage***
2005	3.01%	=	0.552	×	5.47%
2004	2.81%	=	0.516	×	5.45%
2003	4.53%	=	0.558	×	8.12%

*Profit margin = (Net income + (Interest expense × (1 − tax rate)) ÷ Sales

FIGURE 13–11

Return on Assets for Rogers, 2003–2005

We can use the information in Figure 13–10 to calculate return on assets and its components for the fiscal years 2003 through 2005. The results are shown in Figure 13–11.

Over the period 2003 to 2005, Rogers' ROA declined each year. Over the three years, Rogers' profit margin percentage declined while its asset turnover remained fairly steady. We could further break down the asset turnover ratio into additional component parts such as receivables turnover (see Chapter 7) and inventory turnover (see Chapter 8) to gain further insight into changes in the asset turnover ratio. We can obtain further information about the profit margin percentage by examining the common size financial statements (see Figure 13–2, pages 722–723) to see changes in the income statement components.

Earnings per Share Earnings per share or EPS is the amount of net income that is attributable to each individual share of common stock. EPS was discussed in depth in Chapter 11. This section will serve as a brief summary of that discussion.

EPS comes in a number of variations. The first and most straightforward is basic EPS. Basic EPS is calculated using the following formula:

$$\text{Basic EPS} = \frac{\text{Net income} - \text{Preferred dividends}}{\text{Weighted-average number of common shares outstanding during the period}}$$

Preferred dividends are deducted from net income in the numerator because the amount of preferred dividends is not available to common shareholders, but is not deducted in the calculation of net income. The denominator is the weighted-average number of shares that were outstanding during the year (see the text web site at www.mcgrawhill.ca/olc/friedlan for an explanation of the weighted-average number of shares).

Another EPS measure is fully diluted EPS. Fully diluted EPS is designed to show the effect that dilutive securities (securities such as convertible bonds, convertible preferred shares, and stock options that can be converted into common stock) would have on EPS if they were converted or exchanged for common stock. Fully diluted EPS can be thought of as a worst-case scenario of EPS. It is provided because one of the uses of financial statements is to help investors predict future earnings.

www.mcgrawhill.ca/
olc/friedlan

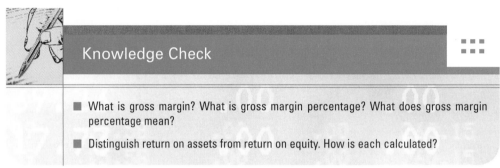

Knowledge Check

- What is gross margin? What is gross margin percentage? What does gross margin percentage mean?
- Distinguish return on assets from return on equity. How is each calculated?

Liquidity

Liquidity is an entity's ability to make payments as they come due. This means an entity must have adequate cash resources and/or the ability to generate cash to make payments to suppliers, creditors, lenders, employees, and so on. Lenders and creditors want to assess the liquidity of an entity to ensure that it will be able to pay amounts owed. If there is concern that the entity will not be able to meet its obligations, lenders and creditors may not want to provide credit. At the very least, they will attach terms to any credit offered that will reflect the level of risk associated with the entity.

In Chapter 7, two commonly used measures of liquidity were introduced:

- the current ratio
- the quick or acid test ratio

The current ratio provides a measure of the resources an entity has to meet its short-term obligations. The higher the current ratio, the more likely it is that an entity will be able to meet its existing current obligations. A larger current ratio also indicates greater protection in the event the entity's cash flow somehow becomes impaired. The ratio assumes that inventory, receivables, and other current assets can be converted to cash on a timely basis.

The current ratio is defined as:

$$\text{Current ratio} = \frac{\text{Current assets}}{\text{Current liabilities}}$$

The quick or acid test ratio is a stricter test of an entity's ability to meet its obligations because it excludes less liquid assets such as inventory and prepaids. The concept behind the quick ratio is that it can take a fairly long time to convert inventory into cash. Remember, in the normal course of events, inventory must be sold and the purchase price collected from the customer before cash is realized. For businesses in which inventory turns over relatively slowly, considerable time can pass before the inventory is realized in cash. In these cases, inventory cannot be considered very liquid. Other current assets (for example, prepaids and store opening costs) are not liquid at all. They will never be realized in cash, so it makes sense to exclude them from an assessment of liquidity.

The quick or acid test ratio is defined as:

$$\text{Quick ratio or acid test ratio} = \frac{\text{Quick assets*}}{\text{Current liabilities}}$$

*Quick assets include cash, temporary investments, accounts receivable, and any other current assets that can be quickly converted to cash.

A major problem with both the current and quick ratios is that they are static measures. These ratios reflect the existing current resources an entity has available to meet its existing obligations. But the ratios say nothing about an entity's ability to generate cash flow to meet existing and future obligations. Ultimately, an entity's liquidity depends on its ability to generate cash flows, so paying attention to cash from operations is important. As long as an entity has a steady and reliable flow of cash coming in, a low current ratio isn't going to be a concern. However, if cash flow is unpredictable—for example, if an entity is sensitive to changes in the economy or competitive changes in the industry—then the current ratio gives an indication of the entity's ability to weather any cash flow disturbances in the short term. A higher current (or quick) ratio means that an entity has some insurance in the event that cash flow becomes impaired.

It is important to understand that many of the liquidity problems that entities face arise because of changes in the environment. If an entity's environment remains stable and predictable, it is unlikely to face liquidity problems (assuming that it does not already have liquidity problems). Why? If an entity is operating successfully in a given environment, as long as that environment remains constant there is no reason for the entity's cash flows to change.

However, change is another matter. A changing environment can create significant liquidity pressures. Change can take many forms. It can be economy-wide (an economic slowdown) or specific to the entity (growth). Change in the environment can affect the timing and amount of cash flows. An economic slowdown might reduce an entity's sales, force a reduction in the prices it charges its customers, increase the amount of uncollectable accounts receivable, increase the time it takes to collect receivables, and make inventory less saleable. For example, suppose a retailer purchased inventory in anticipation of a certain level of sales. If the sales targets are not met, the retailer would be left with surplus inventory that it might not be able to sell, or that it would have to sell at discounted prices. Regardless of these problems, the retailer's suppliers would still have to be paid the full agreed-upon amount.

Additional insights into the liquidity of an entity can be obtained by examining the turnover of receivables and inventory. Depending on the industry, receivables and inventory can represent the major part of current assets, so understanding how long it takes to realize them in cash can help a user predict cash flows and identify liquidity problems. In Chapter 7, the accounts receivable turnover ratio and the average collection period of accounts receivable were introduced. In Chapter 8, the inventory turnover ratio and the average number of days inventory on hand were explained. For in-depth discussions of these ratios, you should review those chapters.

The accounts receivable turnover ratio indicates how quickly an entity is collecting its receivables. The larger the ratio, the more quickly receivables are being collected. The average collection period of receivables conveys the same idea as the receivables turnover ratio, except it is stated as the number of days, on average, it takes to collect receivables. A decrease in the receivables turnover ratio (or an increase in the average collection period) relative to previous years, or a deterioration in these measures relative to similar firms or industry benchmarks, may suggest a liquidity problem. A decrease may suggest that receivables have become less collectable (the amount of receivables that will not be collected has increased) and/or the period of time it takes to collect receivables has increased. A decrease in the receivables turnover ratio means that it takes more time for the entity to receive cash. As a result, it has less cash to meet its obligations.

The formulas for the accounts receivable turnover ratio and the average collection period for accounts receivable are:

$$\text{Accounts receivable turnover ratio} = \frac{\text{Credit sales}}{\text{Average accounts receivable}}$$

$$\text{Average collection period of accounts receivable} = \frac{365}{\text{Accounts receivable turnover ratio}}$$

The inventory turnover ratio indicates the number of times during a period the entity is able to purchase and sell (or use) its stock of inventory. The average number of days inventory on hand conveys the same idea as the inventory turnover ratio, except it is stated as the number of days, on average, it takes to sell or use inventory. A high turnover rate (or low average number of days inventory on hand) indicates that the inventory is more liquid because it is sold quickly and, therefore, cash is realized sooner than with slower-moving inventory. An inventory turnover ratio that is decreasing (or average number of days inventory on hand that is increasing) relative to previous years, or that is deteriorating relative to similar firms or industry benchmarks, may suggest a liquidity problem. Inventory may not be selling well or some could be obsolete. A decreasing inventory turnover ratio indicates that it is taking more time to sell inventory, which means that it will take more time to realize the inventory in cash. In the meantime, suppliers of inventory and other goods and services still have to be paid.

The formulas for the inventory turnover ratio and the average number of days inventory on hand are:

$$\text{Inventory turnover ratio} = \frac{\text{Cost of sales}}{\text{Average inventory}}$$

$$\text{Average number of days inventory on hand} = \frac{365}{\text{Inventory turnover ratio}}$$

A third turnover ratio can be added to the previous two, one we haven't examined before. The **accounts payable turnover ratio** provides information about how quickly an entity pays its accounts payable. The accounts payable turnover ratio is calculated using the following formula:

$$\text{Accounts payable turnover ratio} = \frac{\text{Credit purchases}}{\text{Average accounts payable}}$$

There are some practical difficulties with applying this ratio. First, credit purchases or purchases, for that matter, are not usually disclosed in the financial statements. It is possible to estimate inventory purchases during a period using the equation:

$$\text{Purchases} = \text{Cost of sales} - \text{Beginning inventory} + \text{Ending inventory}$$

This equation will provide a reasonable estimate of purchases for a retail business because cost of sales includes mainly the cost of inventory, which, we can reasonably assume, is purchased mainly on credit. For manufacturing companies, this estimate is less reliable because cost of sales will include much more than the cost of goods purchased on credit. It includes costs such as wages and, possibly, amortization. Second, accounts payable usually includes amounts owed to all suppliers, not just suppliers of inventory.

In its December 31, 2009 financial statements Bawlf Ltd. reported beginning inventory of $190,000, ending inventory of $225,000, and cost of sales of $1,100,000. Accounts payable on December 31, 2008 and 2009 were $127,000 and $135,000 respectively. All of Bawlf's accounts payable pertain to the purchase of inventory. The first step is to calculate the amount of inventory purchased during 2009:

$$
\begin{aligned}
\text{Purchases} &= \text{Cost of sales} - \text{Beginning inventory} + \text{Ending inventory} \\
&= \$1,100,000 \quad - \quad \$190,0006 \quad + \quad \$225,000 \\
&= \$1,135,000
\end{aligned}
$$

$$
\begin{aligned}
\text{Accounts payable turnover ratio} &= \frac{\text{Purchases}}{\text{Average accounts payable}} \\
&= \frac{\$1,135,000}{((\$127,000 + \$135,000) \div 2)} \\
&= 8.66
\end{aligned}
$$

The accounts payable turnover ratio can also be stated as the number of days that the entity takes to pay its accounts payable. This ratio, the **average payment period for accounts payable**, is calculated as follows:

$$\text{Average payment period for accounts payable} = \frac{365}{\text{Accounts payable turnover ratio}}$$

Bawlf's average payment period for accounts payable is:

$$
\begin{aligned}
\text{Average payment period for accounts payable} &= \frac{365}{\text{Accounts payable turnover ratio}} \\
&= \frac{365}{8.66} \\
&= 42.1 \text{ days}
\end{aligned}
$$

This amount means that, on average, Bawlf takes just over 42 days to pay its suppliers.

Examining these amounts for an entity over time may provide some reasonable insights. A decreasing accounts payable turnover ratio or increasing average payment period may indicate that the entity is having cash flow problems and is extending the time it takes to pay its accounts payable.

Taken together, these three turnover ratios, when expressed in number of days, give an idea of how well operating cash inflows and outflows are matched. Recall that in Chapter 6 we discussed the lag that exists between the expenditure of cash and the receipt of cash. The three turnover ratios allow us to estimate that lag. The lag can be estimated using the following equation:

$$\text{Cash lag} = \frac{\text{Average collection period}}{\text{of accounts receivable}} + \frac{\text{Average number of days}}{\text{inventory on hand}} - \frac{\text{Average payment period}}{\text{for accounts payable}}$$

The larger the cash lag, the longer the period of time the entity must finance its inventory and accounts receivable. In times of financial distress, the length of the lag will likely increase. This information can be important to users such as lenders, who want to predict cash flows and assess the risk associated with a loan.

The above ratios provide only part of the information required to analyze an entity's liquidity. Other tools, which we will not investigate here, are available. However, analyzing liquidity is not only a matter of using ratios. The notes to the financial statements often provide information that is useful for evaluating an entity's liquidity, even though the information is not reflected in the financial statements themselves. For example, many entities have access to lines of credit from which they can borrow money as it is needed. That is, a lender will make a specified amount of money available to an entity and it can borrow up to the amount specified if and when it is needed. If an entity has lines of credit available that have not yet been fully used, the amount not yet borrowed is not reported on the balance sheet. However, that available credit can be an important source of liquidity for the entity that should be taken into consideration when its liquidity position is analyzed.

Exhibit 13–5 provides Note 3 to the financial statements of Le Chateau Inc. (Le Chateau), the clothing retailer, which describes the credit that is available to it.[8] The lines of credit described in

www.lechateau.com

EXHIBIT 13–5 :

Disclosures About Le Chateau Inc. Available Credit

3. CREDIT FACILITIES

The Company has operating lines of credit totaling $11 million, which is increased to $16 million during the Company's peak period, April 15 to September 15. These operating lines of credit are collateralized by the Company's accounts receivable, inventories, the issued shares of a subsidiary company and a moveable hypothec providing a charge on the Company's assets. This credit agreement is renewable annually. Amounts drawn under these lines of credit are payable on demand and bear interest at rates based on the prime bank rate for loans in Canadian dollars, U.S. base rate for loans in U.S. dollars and banker's acceptance plus 1.25% for banker's acceptances in Canadian dollars. Furthermore, the terms of the banking agreement require the Company to meet certain non-financial covenants.

In addition, the Company has two credit facilities totalling $13 million available until September 30, 2005 to finance the renovation and re-fixturing of various stores throughout Canada. Draw downs under these facilities are repayable over 48 months and will bear interest at a fixed rate based on the three year Government of Canada bond interest rate. The facilities are collateralized by the store fixtures and equipment financed. As at March 25, 2005, no amounts had been drawn under these two credit facilities.

the note represent available liquidity that Le Chateau can draw on that isn't represented in the financial statements.

Entities sometimes make commitments that require them to make cash payments in the future. These were described earlier in the book as executory contracts—arrangements in which neither party to a contract has performed its side of the arrangement, so there are no financial statement effects. These commitments, such as payments required under operating leases, have implications for an entity's liquidity because they commit an entity to expend cash. Rogers discloses its commitments in Note 20 to its financial statements (see page A-43).

www.mcgrawhill.ca/
olc/friedlan

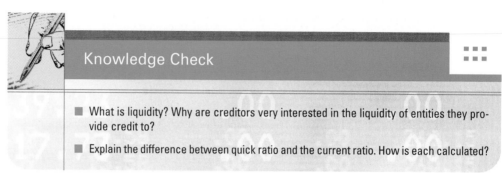

Knowledge Check

- What is liquidity? Why are creditors very interested in the liquidity of entities they provide credit to?

- Explain the difference between quick ratio and the current ratio. How is each calculated?

Example: Analyzing Leon's Furniture Ltd.'s Inventory

As an example of the insights that can be gained from analyzing financial statement information, let's take a look at inventory. Leon's Furniture Ltd. (Leon's) is Canada's largest retailer of home furnishings. On its Web site, Leon's points out that "with multi-million dollar inventory levels, Leon's provides customers with almost instant delivery." Clearly, good management of its inventory is an important function for the company. Leon's management must be sure that it has enough inventory on hand to meet the needs of customers without carrying too much of it. Remember, it costs money to carry inventory.

Exhibit 13–6 provides income statements for the five-year period 2001 to 2005 for Leon's, along with ending inventory, the inventory turnover ratio, the number of days inventory on hand, and gross margin percentage for each year.[9] Over the five-year period, the amount of inventory Leon's had on hand at the end of the year increased steadily. One would expect inventory and sales to grow at about the same rate absent any other significant changes and that's the pattern the data show. (The idea is that a certain amount of inventory is required to support a particular amount of sales, so as revenues increase, inventory should increase as well.) Rows 2 and 3 provide a trend analysis for inventory and sales over the five-year period, using 2001 as the base. The analysis shows that inventory and sales increased similarly, but inventory grew slightly more. The inventory turnover ratio and number of days inventory on hand highlight the impact of this difference. Over the five years, the inventory turnover ratio has steadily declined and the number of days inventory on hand has increased. This means that it's taking Leon's longer to sell its inventory, which increases the cost of operating the business. The financial statements do not explain this trend. Some possible explanations include: (i) The composition of the inventory has changed. Leon's carries a wide range of home furnishing items that may have different inventory management patterns. If, for example, the proportion of home electronics has increased while the proportion of kitchen furnishings has decreased (assuming these lines have different turnover rates), a change in the overall turnover rate would occur. (ii) The selection available in the stores has increased. More brands, styles, and colours means more inventory is needed to meet the demands of customers. (Remember, Leon's thinks it's important to be able to deliver to customers quickly.) (iii) Inventory is being managed less effectively. More investigation would be needed to come to a conclusion.

Another concern from the data in Exhibit 13–6 is the decreasing gross margin percentage. In 2005, the gross margin percentage is the lowest it's been over the five years. Over this period, gross

Income Statistics

($ in thousands, except earnings per share)	2005	2004	2003	2002	2001
Sales	$ 547,744	$ 504,591	$ 455,702	$ 449,693	$ 425,687
Cost of sales	323,629	295,241	267,323	261,265	248,445
Gross profit	224,115	209,350	188,379	188,428	177,242
Operating expenses (net of interest and sundry income)	127,980	118,622	108,933	108,086	99,293
Rent and property taxes	9,518	9,579	9,213	8,059	7,362
Amortization	11,892	10,412	9,881	8,552	7,742
	149,390	138,613	128,027	124,697	114,397
Income before income taxes	74,725	70,737	60,352	63,731	62,845
Provision for income taxes	25,761	24,633	21,914	25,211	26,522
Net income	$ 48,964	$ 46,104	$ 38,438	$ 38,520	$ 36,323
1 Inventory on December 31,	$ 72,644	$ 71,279	$ 58,841	$ 55,047	$ 51,079
2 Inventory growth (trend analysis)	1.29	1.19	1.07	1.06	1.00
3 Sales growth (trend analysis)	1.26	1.18	1.06	1.06	1.00
4 Inventory Turnover Ratio	4.497	4.538	4.694	4.924	4.957
5 Number of days inventory on hand	81.2	80.4	77.8	74.1	73.6
6 Gross Margin Percentage	40.9%	41.5%	41.3%	41.9%	41.6%

EXHIBIT 13–6 :

Financial Statement Information about Leon's Furniture

margin has tended to fluctuate a bit but the overall downward tendency is a cause for concern. Small changes in gross margin can have significant effects on the overall performance of the company. For Leon's, a 0.5 percent decrease in gross margin percentage means over $2.7 million less gross margin in 2005 (Sales × 0.005). If other costs remain the same in 2005 that would mean over $1.8 million less in net income (assuming a tax rate of 34 percent) (Sales × 0.005 × (1 – 0.34).

Much more analysis could be done here. However, the above discussion should give an idea of how information in the financial statements could be used to analyze a company. Also notice that the analysis does not provide firm conclusions. More investigation is needed to get better answers.

Solvency and Leverage

We discussed solvency and leverage in several places in the book. In Chapter 2, the debt-to-equity ratio was introduced. In Chapter 10, the debt-to-equity ratio and another tool for analyzing liabilities and credit worthiness, the interest coverage ratio, were discussed in detail. In Chapter 11, the nature and implications of leverage were explained. This section reviews the earlier coverage and adds some additional insights to the topic.

In the last section, liquidity was defined as an entity's short-term ability to make payments as they come due. In contrast, **solvency** refers to the financial viability of an entity—its ability to meet its long-term obligations.

One of the important sources of insight into an entity's solvency is its capital structure. **Capital structure** refers to an entity's sources of financing—its relative proportions of debt and equity. Capital structure is important in the assessment of solvency because the more debt an entity has in its capital structure, the more risk there is to its long-term solvency. A common tool for evaluating capital structure is the debt-to-equity ratio.

The debt-to-equity ratio provides a measure of the relative amount of debt to equity an entity is using. The ratio gives an indication of the riskiness of the entity and its ability to carry more debt. More debt makes an entity riskier. Why? More debt means there are more fixed interest charges that must be paid—regardless of whether the entity is performing well or poorly. If interest and principal payments are not paid when required, the entity faces significant economic and legal consequences. Also, as the proportion of debt increases, the cost of debt—interest—will also increase, because lenders will charge higher interest rates. Higher interest rates are how lenders are compensated for higher risk.

There are many variations of the debt-to-equity ratio. The debt-to-equity ratio we have discussed so far in the book is defined as:

$$\text{Debt-to-equity ratio} = \frac{\text{Total liabilities}}{\text{Total shareholders' equity}}$$

This ratio includes all liabilities and all equity. Other variations on the debt-to-equity ratio include:

$$\text{Long-term debt-to-equity ratio} = \frac{\text{Long-term debt}}{\text{Total shareholders' equity}}$$

$$\text{Debt-to-total-assets ratio} = \frac{\text{Total liabilities}}{\text{Total liabilities} + \text{Total shareholders' equity}} = \frac{\text{Total liabilities}}{\text{Total assets}}$$

We will not discuss these alternatives further, but recognize that there are different ways of measuring the same concept. The alternatives are not necessarily identical, however. For example, the long-term debt-to-equity ratio does not include current liabilities in the numerator.

The use of the debt-to-equity ratio by simply using the numbers on the balance sheet can provide misleading results and interpretations. Leases, pensions, and future income taxes all present problems that can impair the interpretation of the debt-to-equity and other ratios that incorporate liabilities. If an entity makes extensive use of operating leases, liabilities and the debt-to-equity ratio will be understated because operating leases are a form of off-balance-sheet financing. If this is the case, users might want to incorporate the operating lease "liability" into their assessment of the entity's capital structure. (The impact of leases, pensions, and future income taxes on the debt-to-equity ratio is discussed in Chapter 10.)

Because interest has to be paid regardless of whether an entity is performing well or poorly, debt makes an entity riskier. That does not mean, however, that entities should carry no debt. While debt does add risk, it offers some benefits as well:

■ Debt is usually less costly than equity because the payments to debt-holders are specified and debt-holders are entitled to be paid before equity investors.

■ Interest on debt is tax deductible, whereas dividends to shareholders are not.

An entity needs a balance between debt and equity financing. Too much debt may result in the entity being unable to pay its obligations. Also, at some point debt will become too expensive because of the increasing interest rates that are charged as the proportion of debt in the capital structure increases. The optimal amount of debt an entity should have depends on the entity. An entity with reliable cash flows can afford to carry more debt than an entity with less predictable cash flows. Factors that affect the reliability of cash flows include competition, threat of technological change, sensitivity to economic cycles, and predictability of capital expenditures.

Another important aspect for assessing the solvency of an entity is its ability to generate cash from operations. An entity that can reliably generate cash is best equipped to meet its obligations. Earnings are often used in place of cash flow to assess cash flow generating ability. While earnings are not cash flow, and while, in the short term, earnings and cash flow can differ significantly, earnings do tend to be a good indicator of long-term cash flow. A reliable flow of earnings or cash provides creditors with assurance that the entity will be able to meet its obligations.

The **interest coverage ratio (accrual basis)** is one of a number of coverage ratios designed to measure the ability of an entity to meet its fixed financing charges. In particular, the interest coverage ratio indicates the ease with which an entity can meet its interest payments. The interest coverage ratio is defined as:

$$\text{Interest coverage ratio} = \frac{\text{Net income} + \text{Interest expense} + \text{Tax expense}}{\text{Interest expense}}$$

The larger the ratio, the better able the entity is to meet its interest payments. However, the interest coverage ratio is limiting in that it ignores the fact that entities have fixed charges other than interest. Other fixed charges can include debt repayment and lease payments on operating leases. This ratio can be modified to include these other charges.

The interest coverage ratio can also be calculated on a cash basis. The **interest coverage ratio (cash basis)** is calculated as follows:

$$\text{Interest coverage ratio (cash-based)} = \frac{\text{Cash from operations excluding interest paid}}{\text{Interest paid}}$$

Some users prefer the cash-based interest coverage ratio because debt-holders have to be paid in cash, not in earnings. The cash-based measure shows the number of dollars of cash generated by operations for each dollar of interest that had to be paid.

The cash-based interest coverage ratio for Rogers for the year ended December 31, 2005 is:

$$
\begin{aligned}
\text{Interest coverage ratio (cash-based)} &= \frac{\text{Cash from operations excluding interest paid}}{\text{Interest paid}} \\
&= \frac{\$1,227,407,000 + \$705,816,000}{\$705,816,000} \\
&= 2.74
\end{aligned}
$$

This can be compared with the earnings-based interest coverage ratio of 0.94 that was calculated in Chapter 10 (see page 552). The cash-based interest coverage ratio shows that Rogers generated $2.74 of cash from operations for each dollar of interest that had to be paid. The amount of interest that Rogers paid can be found in Note 10(b) of the financial statements (see page A-22). Rogers' cash-based interest coverage ratio for the year ended December 31, 2004 was 3.38 and the earnings-based interest coverage ratio was 0.89.

The interest coverage ratio and other measures of an entity's ability to meet its fixed charges are very important indicators for creditors. A higher coverage ratio gives more assurance that the creditors will be paid. The acceptable level of a coverage ratio depends on the entity. A creditor can accept a lower coverage ratio for an entity with highly reliable earnings and cash flows. A creditor would want a higher coverage ratio for an entity in a cyclical industry or with highly variable earnings and cash flows.

It is important to remember that the interest coverage and similar ratios are historical measures. They show what has happened, not necessarily what will happen. Examining historical trends can help give users of financial information insight into the ability of an entity to generate adequate earnings to cover current and future obligations, but it is also important to consider any changes that may affect that ability. For example, increased competition or changing economic conditions could impair an entity's ability to generate earnings and cash flow in future, despite its historical success in doing so.

Other Common Ratios

Price-to-Earnings Ratio The **price-to-earnings** or **P/E ratio** is commonly mentioned and discussed. The stock market listings that are published daily in most major newspapers usually provide each entity's P/E ratio. The P/E ratio is defined as:

$$\text{P/E ratio} = \frac{\text{Market price per share}}{\text{Earnings per share}}$$

Conceptually, the P/E ratio gives an indication of how the market values an entity's earnings. The P/E ratio is seen as an indicator of the growth prospects of an entity. The higher the P/E ratio, the more the market expects earnings to grow in the future. Another way of thinking about this is that the higher an entity's P/E ratio, the more sensitive the entity's share price to changes in earnings. For example, a P/E ratio of 10 means that a $1 increase in EPS will result in a $10 increase in share price. A P/E ratio of 25 means that a $1 decrease in EPS will result in a $25 decrease in share price.

The P/E ratio is also an indicator of the risk associated with future earnings. The higher the risk of an entity, the lower will be its P/E ratio for a given level of earnings. (The reason for this is that when risk is higher, future cash flows are discounted at a higher rate to reflect the risk. See Chapter 7 for further discussion of the present value technique.)

For a number of reasons, the P/E ratio must be interpreted carefully. Remember from our discussion of earnings quality that earnings in any given period will contain permanent and transitory components. Permanent and transitory earnings will have different effects on the market price of shares, which in turn will have implications for the P/E ratio.

Also, conceptually, the market price of a share represents the present value of the cash flows that will be received by the shareholder. This is a future-oriented perspective. Earnings, on the other hand, is largely a historically focused measure. As a result, the link between GAAP earnings and share price is not perfect. Current information will be reflected in the price of an entity's shares immediately, whereas the information might not affect earnings until a later time. If an entity has very low but positive earnings in a period, the P/E ratio will be very large. In that case, the P/E ratio may not say anything about the prospective growth of an entity. It will simply be the mathematical result of division by a small number.

In addition, a P/E ratio is not meaningful if an entity has a loss. Finally, earnings are affected by the accounting choices an entity makes, so the P/E ratio will vary with different ways of accounting for the same underlying economic activity.

(Note that it is not possible to determine the P/E ratios of private companies because they do not have readily available market prices for their shares.)

Since share prices of companies change from day to day, while annual earnings for a given year are constant for that year, the P/E ratio will vary with share price. The P/E ratio for Rogers on December 31, 2005 can't be meaningfully calculated because the company reported a loss for the year.

Dividend Payout Ratio The **dividend payout ratio** indicates the proportion of earnings that is being paid to common shareholders as dividends. The dividend payout ratio is defined as:

$$\text{Dividend payout ratio} = \frac{\text{Common dividends paid}}{\text{Net income}}$$

A dividend payout ratio of 0.25 means that 25 percent of earnings is paid in dividends. The portion of earnings that is not paid out as a dividend is retained in the entity. In any given year, an entity does not have to report a profit to pay a dividend. In other words, an entity with a net loss can pay a dividend. If the losses continue, it is likely that the entity's cash flow will be affected, and eventually it will not have the resources to sustain the dividend. A dividend payout ratio greater than 1.0 is also possible. What is necessary for dividends is the cash to pay them. If net income is negative, the dividend payout ratio is not meaningful. In 2005, Rogers reported a net loss but declared dividends of $0.125 per share during the year. In fact, Rogers increased its semi-annual dividend in 2005 from $0.05 per share to $0.075 per share.

An entity's dividend payout ratio can vary quite a bit from period to period if it pays the same dividend every year, regardless of the amount of earnings. That is, an entity may decide to pay a certain dividend per share and it will attempt to maintain that dividend, regardless of any variation in year-to-year earnings. This approach is common with public companies. For public companies, dividends tend to be constant over time, increasing when the managers feel there will be adequate future cash flow to permanently support that level of dividends. Managers of public companies are very reluctant to decrease dividends because a decrease suggests to investors that current and future cash flows are declining and that the decline is expected to be permanent. The stock prices of public companies usually fall significantly when a decrease in dividends is announced.

Question for Consideration

Zehner Ltd. (Zehner) is a publicly traded Canadian company. On December 31, 2010, the last day of the company's fiscal year, Zehner's management announced the signing of a new, long-term contract with a customer. The contract will increase Zehner's revenue significantly, and management and financial analysts agree that the contract will be very profitable. The contract begins in the middle of 2011.

Required: How do you think Zehner's share price will be affected by the announcement of the new contract? How will Zehner's December 31, 2010 earnings be affected by the new contract? Explain.

Answer: Zehner's share price should increase because of the new contract. The new contract is expected to be very profitable, which means that the company is now more valuable. Larger earnings mean investors can ultimately expect more cash in the future. In contrast, the announcement of the contract will have no effect on Zehner's December 31, 2010 earnings. Earnings reflects mainly transactions that have occurred. As of December 31, 2011 Zehner has earned no revenue and would report no profits as a result of the new contract (under GAAP at least). Earnings will only be affected when the contract comes into effect, in the middle of 2011. Since the contract commences part way through 2011, the full effect will not be reflected in earnings until 2012.

Private companies will be much less concerned about maintaining a given level of dividends because they will not be concerned about the impact of dividend changes on the market value of the shares. The shareholders of private companies will likely consider tax issues, their personal cash needs, and the cash requirements of the entity in any dividend decisions.

SOME LIMITATIONS AND CAVEATS ABOUT FINANCIAL STATEMENTS AND FINANCIAL STATEMENT ANALYSIS

Financial ratios are powerful and informative tools for analyzing and evaluating entities. Financial ratios provide valuable insights into the performance and prospects of an entity. However, ratio analysis has limitations, some of them quite severe. The limitations of doing analysis on GAAP-based information are largely due to the limitations of the GAAP information itself.

It is important to remember that the existence of these limitations and caveats does not mean that financial statement and ratio analysis is not useful or should not be done. But to get the most out of financial statement and ratio analysis, it is important to understand the strengths and limitations of the tools being used. Let's examine some of the limitations and the caveats associated with financial statement and ratio analysis.

■ *GAAP financial statements are historical.* For many users and uses of financial statements, it's the future that matters. However, GAAP-based financial statements are not forecasts or predictions. They report on transactions and economic events that have already happened. Therefore, the results of analyzing GAAP financial statements may not be relevant for assessing what will happen in the future. In most cases, GAAP financial statements can be used as a starting point of an analysis, but the user has to incorporate his or her own future-oriented information to project the future.

GAAP financial statements have limitations because things change. Economic conditions change. Technology changes. An entity's marketplace changes. Entities themselves change. As a result, the future may be different from the past, which may limit the usefulness of analyzing historical financial statements. Historical financial statements will be most useful for entities that are stable and where the effects of change are predictable. They will be least informative about entities that are subject to rapid and unpredictable change. For example, entities in the high technology industries are subject to a rapidly changing environment and are often growing. These circumstances make the past a poor predictor of the future.

- *Managers prepare financial statements.* This is good news and bad news. Managers are the people best equipped to prepare financial statements because they are the ones who know and understand the entity best. They can incorporate their insights and understanding of the entity into the financial statements. However, managers' self-interests can influence the accounting choices they make. Also, because an entity can only prepare one set of general purpose financial statements, managers often have to choose among the information needs of the different stakeholders when deciding how to orient the financial statements.

- *Financial statements are not comprehensive.* Financial statements do not reflect all of an entity's assets and liabilities, or all of its economic activity. Many valuable resources and important obligations are not reported. As a result, financial statements do not give a complete picture of an entity.

  There are many examples. Human resources—for many entities the most valuable asset—are not reported as assets. Research, the lifeblood of many entities in the knowledge-based economy, is expensed as incurred, not classified as assets. Also, commitments are not recorded as liabilities, even though the entity may have significant and binding obligations to third parties. In addition, traditional financial statements ignore significant amounts of economic activity. For example, financial statements provide little in the way of information about market values or changes in market values. For the most part, assets are recorded at their cost and are left at cost, even though the market values of those assets may change, often significantly. As a result, potentially useful information is omitted from the financial statements.

- *Accounting policy choices and estimates affect ratios.* Under GAAP, there are often alternative acceptable accounting policies available. The implication of using these different policies is that similar underlying economic activity can appear very differently in financial statements, depending on the accounting policies chosen. GAAP require that an entity disclose its accounting policies in the notes to the financial statements. It is, therefore, important for users to carefully read the note that describes the entity's significant accounting policies. Even if the accounting policy choices of an entity are known, it can be very difficult to restate financial statements so that they conform to the accounting policies preferred by a user.

  Also, the nature of accrual accounting requires that managers make estimates of future, uncertain events that are reflected in the financial statements. Estimates require judgment by the managers. Because estimates are predictions, the actual amounts can't be known at the time they are made. As a result, the assumptions, information, biases, and self-interests of the managers will affect the estimates reflected in the financial statements and, therefore, the numbers reported in the financial statements. Even if self-interest does not play a role in the making of estimates, it is reasonable to expect that there will be a range of acceptable estimates that could be made for most circumstances. In addition, many of the accounting estimates an entity makes are not explicitly stated in the financial statements.

- *Comparing financial statements can be difficult to do.* One of the desirable uses of accounting is to compare entities. Tools such as common size financial statements and financial ratios are often used to make comparisons. However, comparing entities should always be done cautiously and steps should be taken to ensure that the comparison is valid (for example, by adjusting for differences in accounting policies and estimates).

- *Financial statements are not the only source of information.* It is not possible to analyze an entity by only relying on financial statements. A comprehensive analysis of an entity will integrate information from financial statements as well as from other sources. As explained above in this section, financial statements are not comprehensive. They generally do not include future-oriented information, market values, and information about some important assets and liabilities.

- *Financial analysis is a diagnostic tool. It does not necessarily provide explanations for problems that are identified.* The accounting information on which financial analysis is performed reflects the economic activity of an entity—the entity's strategies, management, operations, and environment. Problem areas identified using financial analysis reflect these factors, but to get to the root of the problem an analyst must understand the entity's strategies, operations, and environment.

EARNINGS MANAGEMENT

One of the main themes of this book is that the managers who are responsible for the preparation of accounting information, whether prepared in accordance with GAAP or on some other basis, often have choices to make when deciding how to account for, disclose, and present information about their entity's transactions and economic events. It has also been emphasized that the choices the managers make can have a significant impact on the numbers that appear in the financial statements and the information that is disclosed in the statements and the notes. These in turn can have significant economic consequences on the stakeholders who use the information for decision making. Earnings management has been defined many different ways, but a good definition comes from Professor William R. Scott who defines it as "the choice by a manager of accounting policies so as to achieve some specific objective."[10] This definition should be interpreted broadly to include accounting policies (e.g., revenue recognition, inventory valuation method, amortization method), accounting estimates (e.g., bad debts, returns, warranties, useful lives of assets), and disclosure. The term *earnings management* is also not limited to making choices to affect the bottom line on the income statement. The concept of earnings management also applies to choices that affect other lines on the income statement and the balance sheet, such as making choices to increase assets or reduce liabilities. Earnings management also applies to how management discloses information in the notes to the financial statements.

The flexible nature of accounting rules provides managers with the ability to manage earnings. The economic consequences of accounting information provide them with the motivation. The earnings of public companies are carefully studied by investors and analysts, and the managers of these companies are under pressure to meet investors' expectations and to maintain the stock price. Managers can help achieve these objectives by using accounting choices to increase or smooth earnings. Also, managers' compensation, opportunities in the job market, and job security can be affected by the results reported in the financial statements. Managers may also have incentives to pursue objective such as being able to sell company shares for as high a price as possible, obtain the best terms for a loan, avoid violation of debt covenants, obtain financial support from government, minimize taxes, and generally influence the outcome of decisions that rely on accounting information.

Many of the accounting scandals that have occurred in recent years are the result of the use of accounting rules to achieve the objectives of management. Enron and Worldcom were clear cases of fraud. Other cases such as Nortel occurred under highly questionable circumstances. However, it is a mistake to think that most or even many of the situations of earnings management are the result of fraud. In fact, most cases of earnings management occur within the rules. For example, when a manager decides that the useful life of a new piece of equipment is 10 years rather than eight years, she is making a choice that will affect assets, net income, and any ratios that rely on these measures (e.g., profit margin or return on assets), but there is nothing fraudulent about her choice, unless 10 years is not a reasonable estimate of the equipment's useful life.

Also remember that the numbers in the financial statements can be managed by operating decisions as well as by accounting choices.

It is essential for users of financial statements to be aware of how the choices that managers make can affect the reported information. The tools introduced in this chapter can be very helpful for identifying earnings management. By looking for changes in the trends of different financial ratios, it is possible to spot suspicious situations that require further investigation. Also, comparing an entity's information with industry norms and similar companies can also provide indications of problems. Of course, it is also essential to carefully read the notes to the financial statements.

Table 13–1 identifies some of the techniques that managers have to manage earnings. The table shows the different financial accounting reporting areas and identifies techniques as policies, estimates, and other. All of the techniques in the table have been addressed in this book.

TABLE 13–1 ::: Earnings Management Opportunies

	Policies	Estimates	Other
Revenue recognition	■ When to recognize revenue	■ Bad debts ■ Returns ■ Discounts	
Inventory	■ Inventory valuation method (FIFO, LIFO, average cost) ■ Costs included in inventory	■ Write-downs of obsolete and damaged inventory	
Capital assets	■ Amortization method	■ Useful lives ■ Timing and amount of write-downs and write offs	
Liabilities	■ Leases	■ Warranty provisions ■ Pensions ■ Accrued liabilities	
Assets versus expenses	■ Capitalization policies		
Other			■ Big baths ■ Income statement classifications as ordinary versus unusual ■ Off-balance sheet financing ■ Non-recurring items ■ Disclosure of commitments and contingencies

You've now completed your long and challenging journey through this book. Think back to what you knew about accounting when you first started. Now pick up the annual report of an entity and notice how you are able to make sense of the information in the financial statements. You should be able to interpret the numbers and recognize and understand the impact of the accounting choices. You should now be able to unravel some of the mysteries and intrigues of accounting.

:: Solved Problem

Esperanza Stores Corp. (Esperanza) operates two small retail stores in malls in Charlottetown. The two stores were opened in late 2003 and, according to Minh Tran, the president and majority shareholder, they have grown spectacularly over the last few years. To provide customers with the merchandise they want, Esperanza has moved into larger stores and further increased the size of its stores by taking over adjacent retail space as it became available. These expansions have significantly increased the amount of floor space in the stores and allowed Esperanza to expand the range and variety of products sold. Ms. Tran is currently thinking about opening additional stores.

Ms. Tran has approached the bank for an expanded line of credit. Esperanza's current line of credit is $30,000 and as of December 31, 2009 the line of credit has almost been fully used. Ms. Tran has provided the bank with Esperanza's financial statements for 2006 through 2009. The statements are available in Table 13–2. Additional information provided by Ms. Tran accompanies the financial statements.

TABLE 13–2 ::: Esperanza Stores Corp.: Financial Statements

Esperanza Stores Corp.
Balance Sheets
As of December 31, 2006–2009

	2009	2008	2007	2006
ASSETS				
Cash	$ 10,000	$ 25,000	$ 50,000	$ 75,000
Inventory	200,000	160,000	125,000	78,000
Other current assets	16,298	17,322	8,440	6,000
Total current assets	226,298	202,322	183,440	159,000
Capital assets	182,000	151,000	110,000	75,000
Accumulated amortization	(75,530)	(60,400)	(41,800)	(22,500)
	$332,768	$292,922	$251,640	$211,500
LIABILITIES AND SHAREHOLDERS' EQUITY				
Bank loan	$ 29,371	$ 23,821	$ 11,966	$ 0
Accounts payable	101,000	81,500	65,000	45,000
Other payables	3,000	13,000	19,000	24,000
Current portion of long-term debt	20,000	5,000	5,000	5,000
Total current liabilities	153,371	123,321	100,966	74,000
Long-term debt	20,000	40,000	45,000	50,000
Capital stock	50,000	50,000	50,000	50,000
Retained earnings	109,397	79,601	55,674	37,500
	$332,768	$292,922	$251,640	$211,500

Esperanza Stores Corp.
Income Statements
For the Years Ended December 31, 2006–2009

	2009	2008	2007	2006
Revenue	$535,000	$485,000	$450,000	$350,000
Cost of sales	299,600	264,325	238,500	182,000
Gross margin	235,400	220,675	211,500	168,000
Selling, general, and administrative costs	180,000	170,000	165,000	140,000
Interest expense	6,200	6,000	5,200	5,000
Other expenses	11,000	14,000	18,000	20,000
Income before taxes	38,200	30,675	23,300	3,000
Income tax\se	8,404	6,749	5,126	660
Net income	$ 29,796	$ 23,927	$ 18,174	$ 2,340

Additional information:

■ All sales of merchandise to customers are for cash or major credit card. No credit terms are offered to customers. Esperanza recognizes revenue at the time of sale.

■ All purchases of inventory from suppliers are purchased on credit.

■ The long-term loan is from a private lender. The loan must be repaid in full by 2012. Esperanza has been making payments on the loan since cash has been available to do so.

■ Esperanza has never paid dividends.

Required:

You are Ms. Tran's banker. Review the information provided and prepare a report for your manager assessing whether Esperanza should receive a larger credit line.

Solution:

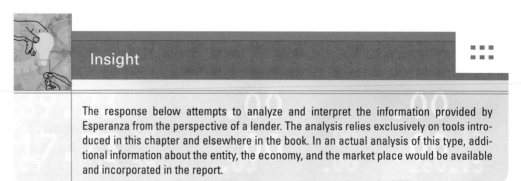

Insight

The response below attempts to analyze and interpret the information provided by Esperanza from the perspective of a lender. The analysis relies exclusively on tools introduced in this chapter and elsewhere in the book. In an actual analysis of this type, additional information about the entity, the economy, and the market place would be available and incorporated in the report.

REPORT ON ESPERANZA STORES CORP.

I have completed my examination of Esperanza Stores Corp. (Esperanza) and while, on the surface, the stores appear to be performing well, there are some serious concerns. In essence, it appears that Esperanza is facing a serious liquidity problem and may have difficulty generating the cash flows necessary to support a significant loan. It is possible that improvements could be made that make Esperanza a more viable candidate for a loan. This is not to say that Esperanza is a lost cause. It isn't. As my report details, there are many positive accomplishments. The data I refer to in my report are presented in Tables 13–3, 13–4, 13–5, 13–6, and 13–7 [pages 750–752].

Performance

Esperanza has performed well over the last four years. Net income has increased each year, from $2,340 in 2006 to $29,796 in 2009, a very significant improvement. In addition, Esperanza's profit margin (Table 13–3 or 13–5), return on assets (Table 13–5), and return on equity (Table 13–5) have all increased in each reported year. Sales have been growing over the four years as well, with sales in 2009 almost 53 percent greater than they were in 2006. In absolute numbers, sales have grown from $350,000 in 2006 to $535,000 in 2009. Clearly, the company has done a good job building its business.

On the other hand, gross margin percentage (Table 13–5) has decreased steadily over the last four years from 48 percent in 2006 to 44 percent in 2009. This is a significant and alarming drop. Had Esperanza been able to maintain its 48 percent gross margin in 2009, net income would have been more than $21,000 higher and there would have been significantly more cash coming in.

Further information is needed to explain the reason for the decline. Is it due to increased competition or a pricing strategy that tried to increase sales by lowering prices? Additional information is also required about what the gross margin percentage is likely to be in future, as this will have significant implications for cash flows.

Despite the decline in the gross margin percentage, the gross margin has increased each year because of the increase in sales. Also, despite the decline in the gross margin percentage, the profit margin percentage has increased each year. Esperanza has achieved a rising profit margin percentage, through cost control, even though its gross margin percentage has been decreasing. Selling, general, and administrative costs have increased at a much slower rate than sales, and the proportion of these costs as a percentage of revenue has fallen over the four-year period.

An important question is whether spending has been permanently reduced, or whether expenditures have been deferred. Also, there is a question about whether the reduction in spending will have implications for Esperanza's ability to maintain and increase sales in the future.

Overall, Esperanza has performed well. The company has grown its business with sales, profits, and profitability improving. The company's liquidity is another matter.

Liquidity

While the performance of Esperanza has been fine, I have serious concerns about its liquidity. All liquidity indicators have been deteriorating over the past four years and the company is in danger of running out of cash. The current ratio has decreased from 2.149 in 2006 to 1.475 in 2009. While a current ratio of 1.475 in and of itself is not a problem, the significant decline is.

The current ratio also masks the fact that an increasing proportion of Esperanza's assets is inventory. Since 2006, the proportion of total assets represented by inventory has increased from 36.9 percent to 60.1 percent. In addition, the amount of inventory on hand has increased much more rapidly than revenues. In most situations, one would expect inventory to grow at a rate similar to that of sales. Over the period 2006 to 2009, the amount of inventory on hand has increased 256 percent, while revenues have grown by only about 53 percent.

This difference in growth suggests that Esperanza may be carrying significant amounts of unsaleable inventory. If the inventory cannot be sold or can only be sold at a discount, the implication is that the current ratio overstates the liquidity of the company. There are other possible explanations for the large increase in inventory, such as failure to meet expected sales forecasts or because a wider range of merchandise is being carried in the stores. The increase could also be the result of poor inventory management.

The quick ratio, which focuses on the availability of very liquid current assets to cover current liabilities, supports a liquidity problem. Esperanza's only quick asset is cash, and over the last four years the amount of cash that the company is holding has declined significantly. As of December 31, 2009 the company had only $10,000 in cash with which to meet its obligations. If, for example, the current portion of long-term debt had to be paid immediately, Esperanza would not have the resources to do so.

The inventory turnover and accounts payable turnover ratios raise similar concerns. Since 2006 Esperanza has been taking much longer to sell its inventory and to pay suppliers. The average number of days inventory is held before being sold has increased from 155 days in 2007 to 219 days in 2009, an increase of over 40 percent. The average number of days the company takes to pay its suppliers has increased from 70 days in 2007 to 98 days in 2009. The increased number of days to pay suppliers suggests that Esperanza is responding to its liquidity problems by delaying payments to suppliers for as long as possible. Taking the average number of days inventory and the average payment period for accounts payable together, the period over which Esperanza is self-financing its inventory has increased from 85 days in 2007 (155 – 70) to 121 days in 2009 (219 – 98).

From the information provided, I constructed cash flow statements for 2007 through 2009. These statements are rough because of missing information, particularly about the amortization expense. It seems likely that, given the small change in accumulated amortization year to year, some capital assets were sold during some of the years. As a result, using the change in the accumulated amortization account as an estimate of the amortization expense may be in error. If my assumption regarding the sale of assets is correct, cash from operations in my cash flow statements is likely lower than it actually is.

Cash from operations in each of the three years has been positive, i.e., growing, but is still quite small. Depending on sales in 2010, the company might not have enough cash to make its planned payment on the long-term debt. The company's operating cash flow is crucial for assessing a loan. While the current and quick ratios suggest liquidity problems, the problems could be mitigated if the business were generating enough cash flow. At this point, the cash flow statement and my interpretation of the turnover ratios do not relieve my uneasiness. Even so, despite the liquidity problems, Esperanza has been able to reduce its long-term debt over the last three years. However, it has done so by increasing its bank loan each year.

There is also potential for trouble if suppliers become more aggressive trying to collect amounts owing to them or if they stop providing credit. If this were the case, any loan that our bank makes could be in jeopardy. In the event a loan is made, Esperanza has little to offer in the way of security. There are no receivables, and it is possible that capital assets and inventory will not produce much cash if they had to be sold.

Over the last three years, Esperanza has made significant investments in capital assets. An important question is whether additional expenditures for capital assets will continue to be required.

Esperanza has been expanding and, as a result, additional capital assets are required. However, the depletion of the company's cash can be largely attributed to the purchases of capital assets each year.

Overall, Esperanza seems to be an attractive and successful business. Its challenge is to survive its liquidity problems. At this point I do not recommend extending additional credit to the company. I think that Esperanza should take immediate steps to reduce its inventory levels to free up cash and reduce its investment in working capital. Also, the company should limit its spending on capital assets until its liquidity position becomes more solid.

TABLE 13–3 ::: **Common Size Financial Statements**

Esperanza Stores Corp.
Common Size Balance Sheets
As of December 31, 2006–2009

	2009	2008	2007	2006
Cash	0.030	0.085	0.199	0.355
Inventory	0.601	0.546	0.497	0.369
Other current assets	0.049	0.059	0.034	0.028
Total current assets	0.680	0.691	0.729	0.752
Capital assets	0.547	0.515	0.437	0.355
Accumulated amortization	−0.227	−0.206	−0.166	−0.106
	1.000	1.000	1.000	1.000
Bank loan	0.088	0.081	0.048	0.000
Accounts payable	0.304	0.278	0.258	0.213
Other payables	0.009	0.044	0.076	0.113
Current portion of long-term debt	0.060	0.017	0.020	0.024
Total current liabilities	0.461	0.421	0.401	0.350
Long-term debt	0.060	0.137	0.179	0.236
Capital stock	0.150	0.171	0.199	0.236
Retained earnings	0.329	0.272	0.221	0.177
	1.000	1.000	1.000	1.000

Esperanza Stores Corp.
Common Size Income Statements
For the Years Ended December 31, 2006-2009

	2009	2008	2007	2006
Revenue	1.000	1.000	1.000	1.000
Cost of sales	0.560	0.545	0.530	0.520
Gross margin	0.440	0.455	0.470	0.480
Selling, general, and administrative costs	0.336	0.351	0.367	0.400
Interest expense	0.012	0.012	0.012	0.014
Other expenses	0.021	0.029	0.040	0.057
	0.071	0.063	0.052	0.009
Income tax expense	0.016	0.014	0.011	0.002
Net income	0.056	0.049	0.040	0.007

TABLE 13-4 ::: Trend Financial Statements

Esperanza Stores Corp.
Trend Balance Sheets
As of December 31, 2006–2009

	2009	2008	2007	2006
Cash	0.133	0.333	0.667	1.000
Inventory	2.564	2.051	1.603	1.000
Other current assets	2.716	2.887	1.407	1.000
Total current assets	1.423	1.272	1.154	1.000
Capital assets	2.427	2.013	1.467	1.000
Accumulated amortization	3.357	2.684	1.858	1.000
	1.573	1.385	1.190	1.000
Bank loan	—	—	—	—
Accounts payable	2.244	1.811	1.444	1.000
Other payables	0.125	0.542	0.792	1.000
Current portion of long-term debt	4.000	1.000	1.000	1.000
Total current liabilities	2.073	1.667	1.364	1.000
Long-term debt	0.400	0.800	0.900	1.000
Capital stock	1.000	1.000	1.000	1.000
Retained earnings	2.917	2.123	1.485	1.000
	1.573	1.385	1.190	1.000

Esperanza Stores Corp.
Trend Income Statements
For the Years Ended December 31, 2006–2009

	2009	2008	2007	2006
Revenue	1.529	1.386	1.286	1.000
Cost of sales	1.646	1.452	1.310	1.000
Gross margin	1.401	1.314	1.259	1.000
Selling, general, and administrative costs	1.286	1.214	1.179	1.000
Interest expense	1.240	1.200	1.040	1.000
Other expenses	0.550	0.700	0.900	1.000
	12.733	10.225	7.767	1.000
Income tax expense	12.733	10.225	7.767	1.000
Net income	12.733	10.225	7.767	1.000

| TABLE | 13–5 | ::: | Table of Financial Ratios |

Esperanza Stores Corp.
Selected Financial Ratios, 2006–2009

	2009	2008	2007	2006
Current ratio	1.475	1.641	1.817	2.149
Quick ratio	0.065	0.203	0.495	1.014
Inventory turnover ratio	1.664	1.855	2.350	
Average number of days inventory on hand	219.292	196.775	155.335	
Accounts payable turnover ratio	3.722	4.086	5.191	
Average payment period for accounts payable	98.075	89.322	70.315	
Purchases (= cost of sales – beginning inventory + ending inventory)	$339,600	$299,325	$285,500	$260,000
Gross margin percentage	0.440	0.455	0.470	0.480
Profit margin percentage	0.056	0.049	0.040	0.007
Asset turnover	1.710	1.781	1.943	
Return on assets	0.111	0.106	0.096	
Return on equity	0.206	0.203	0.188	
Debt-to-equity ratio (liabilities ÷ shareholders' equity)	1.088	1.260	1.381	1.417

| TABLE | 13–6 | ::: | Cash Flow Statements |

Esperanza Stores Corp.
Cash Flow Statements
For the Years Ended December 31, 2007–2009

	2009	2008	2007
Net income	$29,796	$23,927	$18,174
Add: Amortization expense	15,130	18,600	19,300
	44,926	42,527	37,474
Adjustments for changes in current operating accounts			
Increase in inventory	(40,000)	(35,000)	(47,000)
Decrease/(increase) in other current assets	1,024	(8,882)	(2,440)
Increase in accounts payable	19,500	16,500	20,000
(Decrease) in other payables	(10,000)	(6,000)	(5,000)
Increase in current portion of long-term debt	15,000	0	0
Cash from operations	30,450	9,145	3,034
Investing activities—purchase of capital assets	(31,000)	(41,000)	(35,000)
Financing activities			
Repayment of long-term debt	(20,000)	(5,000)	(5,000)
Bank loan	5,550	11,855	11,966
	(14,450)	6,855	6,966
Decrease in cash during year	(15,000)	(25,000)	(25,000)
Cash balance at beginning of year	25,000	50,000	75,000
Cash balance at end of year	$10,000	$25,000	$50,000

SUMMARY OF KEY POINTS

▶ **LO 1** An important use for current income is for forecasting future income. For the purpose of forecasting future earnings, historical earnings can be used as a starting point. Permanent earnings are earnings that are expected to be repeated in the future. As a result, permanent earnings are a useful indicator of future earnings. Earnings that are not considered permanent are called transitory. An entity's net income can have both permanent and transitory components. GAAP and the *CICA Handbook* require disclosure of information that is helpful for understanding the components of earnings. These disclosures include extraordinary items, unusual items, and discontinued operations.

Earnings quality refers to the usefulness of current earnings for predicting future earnings. Earnings quality is high if there is a close relationship between current earnings and future earnings. Earnings quality is low if the relationship between current and future earnings is not close. Another way of thinking about earnings quality is the extent to which reported earnings are permanent. Managers lower earnings quality when they manage earnings through their accounting policies, estimates, and accruals, and through the timing of actual transactions, such as discretionary expenditures and sales.

▶ **LO 2** To gain insight into the numbers and other information provided in a set of financial statements, it is usually necessary to analyze them. Financial ratios are a common tool used for examining, evaluating, and assessing an entity. There is a vast number of different ratios that have been developed for various purposes. In this chapter, ratios and analytical tools are grouped into four analytical themes: (1) evaluating performance, (2) liquidity, (3) solvency and leverage, and (4) other common ratios. Two tools that make this type of analysis easier are common size financial statements and trend analysis. These tools eliminate the impact of size from the financial statement numbers and restate them as proportions.

▶ **LO 3** Financial ratios are a powerful and informative tool for analyzing and evaluating entities. Financial ratios provide valuable insights into the performance and prospects of an entity. However, ratio analysis has limitations, some of them quite severe. To get the most out of financial statement analysis it is important to understand the strength and limitations of the tools being used. The limitations include:

■ GAAP financial statements are historical.

■ Managers prepare financial statements.

■ Financial statements are not comprehensive.

■ Accounting policy choices and estimates affect ratios.

■ Comparing financial statements can be difficult to do.

■ Financial statements are not the only source of information.

■ Financial analysis is a diagnostic tool. It does not necessarily provide explanations for problems that are identified.

▶ **LO 4** Managers often have choices to make when deciding how to account for, disclose, and present information about their entity's transactions and economic events. These choices can have a significant impact on the numbers that appear in the financial statements and the information that is disclosed in the statements and the notes, which in turn can have significant economic consequences on the stakeholders who use the information for decision making. The economic consequences of accounting information provide them with the motivation. Managers will make choices that will allow them to meet their objectives of financial reporting. The selection of accounting methods that serve the reporting objectives of the managers is known as earnings management.

KEY TERMS

accounts payable turnover ratio, p. 736

asset turnover, p. 732

average payment period for accounts
   payable, p. 737

capital structure, p. 739

common size financial statement
   (vertical analysis), p. 721

covenant, p. 706

discontinued operation, p. 714

dividend payout ratio, p. 742

earnings quality, p. 716

extraordinary item, p. 710

horizontal analysis (trend statement), p. 724

interest coverage ratio (accrual basis),
   p. 740

interest coverage ratio (cash basis), p. 741

management discussion and analysis
   (MD&A), p. 708

permanent earnings, p. 709

price-to-earnings (P/E) ratio, p. 741

solvency, p. 739

transitory earnings, p. 709

trend statements (horizontal analysis), p. 724

unusual item, p. 711

vertical analysis (common size financial
   statement), p. 721

SIMILAR TERMS

The left column gives alternative terms that are sometimes used for the accounting terms introduced in this chapter, which are listed in the right column.

horizontal analysis   **trend analysis, p. 724**

sustainable earnings, recurring earnings,
   core earnings, persistent earnings   **permanent earnings, p. 709**

vertical analysis   **common size financial statements, p. 721**

ASSIGNMENT MATERIALS

Questions

Q13-1. What is gross margin? Why can it be important to determine an entity's gross margin? Why is it often difficult to determine an entity's gross margin from its financial statements?

Q13-2. What is the difference between permanent and transitory earnings? Why might it be important to distinguish between these different types of earnings?

Q13-3. Suppose you were considering making an investment in one of Canada's major grocery chains, Loblaw Companies Ltd. or Sobeys Inc. As part of your research, you obtained each company's annual report. What concerns would you have in comparing the information presented in each company's financial statements when making your decision? What steps could you take to overcome these concerns?

Q13-4. Why is it important to learn as much as you possibly can about an entity when doing an analysis of it? Explain.

Q13-5. Would it be possible to gain useful insights into making a loan to an entity by looking *only* at the entity's financial statements? Explain. Assume that, except for what you could obtain from the financial statements, you had no access to other information about the entity and did not otherwise know anything about the entity.

Q13-6. For each of the following situations, explain why GAAP-transactions-based financial statements would be of limited use for predicting the entity's future performance:

a. The entity purchases a major new operating division near its year end in a new line of business for the entity.

b. A large and successful U.S. firm in the same line of business as the entity enters the Canadian market late in the fiscal year.

c. The entity just began operations and is growing rapidly.

d. The entity is in a declining industry and has just closed down a number of its plants.

e. The entity is a producer of software.

Q13-7. Identify and explain the limitations and caveats associated with using financial ratio analysis on GAAP-based financial statements.

Q13-8. What are the implications for financial statement analysis of the fact that preparers of financial statements can often choose among different, acceptable accounting methods? Provide examples of some of the accounting choices that preparers have to make.

Q13-9. How do different objectives of financial reporting affect financial statement analysis?

Q13-10. Explain how the follow events would affect the usefulness of current earnings as a basis for predicting future earnings:

a. An entity has a two-month strike during the year.

b. An entity writes off a significant amount of capital assets.

c. An entity receives a large payment from a competitor as part of the settlement of a lawsuit. The entity sued the competitor for infringement of a patent.

d. An entity records a gain on the disposal of one of its vehicles.

Q13-11. Is it possible for an entity to be too liquid? Explain.

Q13-12. Explain why the quick ratio might be a better indicator of an entity's liquidity than the current ratio.

Q13-13. Explain the following and explain why it might be useful for a user of financial statements to have information about these items separately disclosed in the financial statements:

a. extraordinary items

b. unusual items

c. discontinued operations

Q13-14. Describe a situation where the user of a private corporation's financial statements would be interested in segregating permanent and transitory earnings. Explain why the separation of the two types of earnings would be important in the situation.

Q13-15. Explain the concept of quality of earnings. What distinguishes high quality earnings from low quality earnings?

Q13-16. Explain how each of the following would affect the quality of an entity's earnings:

a. Management decides to increase advertising in the current period as part of a special event. Management expects that the increase will occur only in the current year and spending levels will return to historical levels in the future.

b. Management increases the estimated useful life of some of the entity's capital assets.

c. Management decides to write down certain capital assets to reflect changes in market conditions.

Q13-17. Explain the significance of the fact that over the life of an entity, the accruals that are made must add up to zero.

Q13-18. What are common size financial statements? Explain why they can be useful for analyzing an entity over and above the actual financial statements of the entity.

Q13-19. What are trend financial statements? Explain why they can be useful for analyzing an entity over and above the actual financial statements of the entity.

Q13-20. What is liquidity? Why are suppliers concerned about the liquidity of an entity?

Q13-21. Why is it not adequate for stakeholders to focus their analyses of entities only on the financial statements? What type of information about an entity that is not included in financial statements might be desirable for a stakeholder? What other sources of information might a stakeholder turn to?

Q13-22. What are covenants? Why are covenants often included in lending agreements? What purpose do they serve? Why are covenants often stated in accounting terms?

Q13-23. Explain the two broad concerns that creditors have about the credit they provide to entities. Describe the different types and sources of information that creditors would require to evaluate these concerns.

Q13-24. What is the difference between short-term and long-term creditors? Why would each approach financial statement analysis differently? What type of information would each require for making a decision to supply credit to a prospective customer? Explain.

Q13-25. The text states, "In many ways equity investors need to know everything." Explain why this is the case.

Q13-26. Would information about each of the following be useful to a prospective long-term creditor of an entity? Explain. Would information about each item be available from the financial statements? Explain.
a. competitive advantages and disadvantages
b. risks faced by the entity
c. source of supplies and conditions in the supplier market
d. regulatory environment

Q13-27. Would information about each of the following be useful to a prospective equity investor in an entity? Explain. Would information about each item be available from the financial statements? Explain.
a. quality, experience, and performance of the managers
b. strategies for making money
c. competitive environment
d. lines of business

Q13-28. What is the management discussion and analysis (MD&A)? Why do you think public companies are required to provide an MD&A, whereas private companies are not?

Q13-29. Contrast the benefits and limitations of information provided to stakeholders by management versus information from a financial analyst who is independent of the entity.

Q13-30. Explain the implications of using only the financial statements when analyzing an entity.

Q13-31. What are factors that allow managers to manage earnings? What is it about these factors that allows for the management of earnings?

Q13-32. Explain the difference between return on assets and return on equity. Which measure is a more useful measure of the performance of an entity? Explain.

Q13-33. Why is it necessary to evaluate financial ratios on a comparative basis rather than in absolute terms? What bases of comparison can be used?

Q13-34. Why is it not possible to carry out an effective financial analysis without knowing the decision that the decision-maker is making?

Exercises

E13-1. **(Classifying transactions and economic events as permanent or transitory, LO 1)**
Would you classify each of the following as transitory or permanent in the entity's financial statements? Explain your reasoning.
a. severance pay to a number of executives who were fired during a reorganization
b. increase in wages paid to employees as a result of a union contract settlement
c. costs associated with closing a manufacturing facility
d. gains on the sale of equipment

E13-2. **(Classifying transactions and economic events as permanent or transitory, LO 1)**
Would you classify each of the following as transitory or permanent in the entity's financial statements? Explain your reasoning.
  a. increase in raw materials costs
  b. payment associated with the settlement of a lawsuit
  c. revenues associated with a discontinued operation
  d. bonuses paid to senior executives

E13-3. **(Preparing common size financial statements, LO 2)** Examine the balance sheets and income statements for Fairplay Inc. (Fairplay).

Fairplay Inc.
Balance Sheets
As of December 31

	2010	2009	2008
Asssets			
Cash	$ 18,000	$ 24,000	$ 20,000
Accounts receivable	105,200	92,800	70,000
Inventory	118,500	92,000	90,000
Other current assets	24,000	22,000	16,000
Total current assets	265,700	230,800	196,000
Capital assets (net of amortization)	510,000	420,000	370,000
Total assets	$ 775,700	$ 650,800	$ 566,000
Liabilities and shareholders' equity			
Bank loans	$ 96,620	$ 54,800	$ 46,000
Accounts payable and accrued liabilities	91,800	82,000	76,000
Total current liabilities	188,420	136,800	122,000
Long-term liabilities	140,000	124,000	100,000
Capital stock	250,000	250,000	250,000
Retained earnings	197,280	140,000	94,000
Total liabilities and shareholders' equity	$ 775,700	$ 650,800	$ 566,000

Fairplay Inc.
Income Statements
For the Years Ended December 31

	2010	2009	2008
Revenue	$1,040,256	$ 963,200	$ 860,000
Cost of sales	492,134	457,800	420,000
Gross margin	548,122	505,400	440,000
Selling, general, and administrative expenses	251,790	231,000	220,000
Amortization	60,000	56,000	46,000
Other expenses	126,490	117,120	96,000
Interest expense	30,000	24,000	16,000
Income before taxes	79,842	77,280	62,000
Income tax expenses	17,566	20,000	16,000
Net income	$ 62,276	$ 57,280	$ 46,000

Additional information:
■ All sales are on credit.
■ All purchases of inventory are on credit.
■ Fairplay must begin repaying its long-term debt in 2012.

Required:

a. Prepare common size balance sheets and income statements for 2008, 2009, and 2010.

b. Analyze and interpret the common size financial statements you prepared.

c. How are these common size statements more useful than the statements originally prepared by Fairplay?

d. Why would it be unwise to examine the common size financial statements without considering the financial statements originally prepared by Fairplay?

E13-4. **(Preparing trend financial statements, LO 2)** Use the financial statements for Fairplay Inc. provided in Exercise E13-3 to respond to the following:

a. Prepare trend balance sheets and income statements for 2008, 2009, and 2010. Use 2010 as the base year to prepare the trend statements.

b. Analyze and interpret the trend financial statements you prepared.

c. How are these trend statements more useful than the statements originally prepared by Fairplay?

d. Why would it be unwise to examine the trend financial statements without considering the financial statements originally prepared by Fairplay?

E13-5. **(Calculating liquidity ratios, LO 2)** Use the information provided about Fairplay Inc. in Exercise E13-3 to respond to the following:

a. Calculate the following for 2009 and 2010:
   i.   current ratio
   ii.   quick ratio
   iii. accounts receivable turnover ratio
   iv.   average collection period of accounts receivable
   v.   inventory turnover ratio
   vi.   average number of days inventory on hand
   vii. accounts payable turnover ratio
   viii. average payment period for accounts payable
   ix.   cash lag

b. Assume the role of an important new supplier to Fairplay. Use the amounts calculated in part a. and prepare a report assessing whether Fairplay should be granted credit terms for purchases from your company. Explain the conclusions you make.

E13-6. **(Using common size and trend statements to evaluate performance, LO 2)** The income statements of Kronau Corp. (Kronau) for the years ended March 31, 209 through 2011 are shown below:

Kronau Corp.
Income Statements
For the Years Ended March 31

	2011	2010	2009
Sales	$2,875,000	$2,612,500	$2,425,000
Cost of sales	1,575,000	1,375,000	1,280,500
Gross margin	1,300,000	1,237,500	1,144,500
Selling, general, and administrative expenses	675,000	575,000	555,500
Amortization expense	129,000	105,000	95,000
Interest expense	150,000	137,500	130,000
Unusual income	250,000	—	—
Income before income taxes	596,000	420,000	364,000
Income tax expense	100,000	80,000	75,000
Net income	$ 496,000	$ 340,000	$ 289,000

Required:

a. Prepare common size and trend financial statements for Kronau. (For the trend statements, use 2009 as the base year.)
b. Use the information from part a. to evaluate the performance of Kronau. Explain fully. Your evaluation should include a comparison of Kronau's performance from year to year.
c. How does the unusual income affect your ability to evaluate the performance of Kronau and to interpret your common size and trend financial statements?

E13-7. **(Calculating accounts payable turnover, LO 2)** You have been provided with the following information from the balance sheets and income statements of Batchawana Inc. (Batchawana). Accounts Payable and Inventory are from the balance sheet as of December 31 of the stated year, and Cost of Sales is for the stated year ended December 31. Assume that all purchases of inventory are made on credit, and cost of sales includes only the cost of inventory sold:

Batchawana Inc. Financial Statement Information				
	2010	**2009**	**2008**	**2007**
Accounts payable	$ 2,509,200	$ 2,132,820	$1,919,538	$1,535,630
Inventory	3,261,960	3,156,574	2,898,502	2,272,732
Cost of sales	10,112,076	10,416,692	9,623,028	7,227,290

Required:

a. Calculate the accounts payable turnover ratio for 2008, 2009, and 2010.
b. Calculate the average payment period for accounts payable for 2008, 2009, and 2010.
c. What circumstances could explain a declining accounts payable turnover ratio (or increasing average payment period for accounts payable)?

E13-8. **(Determining the effects of transactions on ratios, LO 2)** Complete the following table by indicating whether the transactions or economic events would increase, decrease, or have no effect on the financial ratios listed. Consider each item independently. State any assumptions you make. Explain your reasoning.

	Current ratio	Inventory turnover ratio	Return on assets	Gross margin percentage	Debt-to-equity ratio
Ratio before the transactions/ economic events	1.47	3.5	12%	48%	1.8:1
a. Payment of a $500,000 dividend.					
b. Accrual of an extraordinary loss on expropriation of land.					
c. Early retirement of a long-term liability.					
d. Payment of an obligation by supplying inventory instead of paying cash.					
e. Write-down of a capital asset to net realizable value.					
f. Purchase of inventory on credit.					

E13-9. (**Determining the effects of transactions on ratios, LO 2**) Complete the following table by indicating whether the transactions or economic events would increase, decrease, or have no effect on the financial ratios listed. Consider each item independently. State any assumptions you make. Explain your reasoning.

	Interest coverage ratio	Accounts receivable turnover	Price-to-earnings ratio	Return on assets	Gross margin percentage
Ratio before the transactions/economic events	5.35	5.5	18.5	10%	52.5%
a. Declaration and payment of preferred shares.					
b. Write-off of an accounts receivable.					
c. Sale of goods costing $11,000 for $24,000. Payment is to be made within 45 days.					
d. Disposal of an asset that was not being used. The asset had a book value of $390,000 when it was disposed of.					
e. Announcement of a new long-term contract with a new customer. The announcement was unexpected by the capital markets.					
f. Write-off of obsolete inventory. The company does this each year.					

E13-10. (**Determining the effects of transactions on ratios, LO 2**) Complete the following table by indicating whether the transactions or economic events would increase, decrease, or have no effect on the financial ratios listed. Consider each item independently. State any assumptions you make. Explain your reasoning.

	Quick ratio	Average payment period for accounts payable	Return on equity	Profit margin percentage	Earnings per share
Ratio before the transactions/economic events	0.82	45	16.5%	4%	$1.10
a. Repayment of a bond on the first day of the fiscal year.					
b. Conversion of a bond with a 10% coupon rate into common stock.					
c. Purchase of equipment for cash.					
d. Sale of 2,000 common shares for cash.					
e. Sale of inventory on credit.					
f. Payment of accounts payable.					

E13-11. (**Evaluating accounts receivable, LO 2**) Oungre Inc. (Oungre) is a small printing business that provides a wide range of printing services to retail and commercial clients. Retail customers pay cash, while Oungre offers its commercial customers 30 days from the delivery date to pay amounts owing. You have been provided with the following information from Oungre's accounting records (Oungre's year end is December 31):

	2006	2007	2008	2009
Accounts receivable (on December 31)	$67,500	$75,000	$85,000	$93,750
Sales (for the year ended)		950,000	1,006,250	1,093,750
Proportion of sales to commercial customers		60.0%	66.0%	75.0%

Required:

    a. Calculate Oungre's accounts receivable turnover ratio for 2007, 2008, and 2009.

    b. Calculate Oungre's average collection period of accounts receivable for 2007, 2008, and 2009.

    c. Assess how well Oungre is managing its accounts receivable over the three-year period.

    d. What are some possible explanations for why Oungre's collection is not less than 30 days? What steps might Oungre's management take to reduce the collection period?

    e. Suppose you did not know what the proportion of Oungre's sales to commercial customers was. How would your calculation of the accounts receivable turnover ratio and the average collection period of accounts receivable be affected? How would your interpretation of the performance of Oungre's management be affected?

E13-12. **(Evaluating inventory management, LO 2)** Zawale Ltd. (Zawale) is a wholesaler of fresh fruits and vegetables. Zawale purchases fruits and vegetables from growers and supplies them to small grocery stores. You have been provided with the following information from Zawale's accounting records (Zawale's year end is December 31):

	2007	2008	2009	2010
Inventory (on December 31)	$ 48,750	$ 54,750	$ 60,750	$97,500
Cost of sales (for the year ended)		3,150,000	3,622,500	3,441,375

Required:

    a. Calculate Zawale's inventory turnover ratio for 2008, 2009, and 2010.

    b. Calculate Zawale's average number of days inventory on hand for 2008, 2009, and 2010.

    c. Evaluate how well Zawale's management is managing the inventory. Explain.

    d. What are some possible explanations for the amounts you calculated in parts (a) and (b)?

    e. What are the implications for Zawale's performance of the results you found in parts (a) and (b)? Explain.

E13-13. **(Evaluating accounts payable management, LO 2)** Guisachan Books Inc. (Guisachan) is a small book retailer. Guisachan has approached your company, a large publishing house, requesting credit terms on purchases. Guisachan has never purchased from your company. If credit is approved, Guisachan would be given 60 days to pay outstanding amounts. You have been provided with the following information from Guisachan's accounting records (Guisachan's year end is March 31):

	2007	2008	2009	2010
Accounts payable (on March 31)	$67,200	$ 72,800	$ 85,400	$100,800
Credit purchases (for the year ended)		448,000	462,000	455,000

Required:

    a. Calculate Guisachan's accounts payable turnover ratio for 2008, 2009, and 2010.

    b. Calculate Guisachan's average payment period for accounts payable for 2008, 2009, and 2010.

    c. Assume you are the credit manager for the large publishing house. How would you interpret the information you received about Guisachan's accounts payable? How would this information influence your decision about whether to offer credit to Guisachan? Explain. What additional information would you request before making a final decision? Explain.

    d. What effect will the results you calculated in parts a. and b. have on Guisachan's cash from operations? Explain. Is this a good situation? Explain. How might Guisachan's suppliers respond? Explain.

E13-14. **(Calculating EPS, price-to-earnings ratio, and dividend ratios, LO 2)** Junor Inc. (Junor) is a publicly traded company. During its year ended July 31, 2010 Junor reported net income of $1,879,500. During fiscal 2010, Junor declared and paid quarterly dividends of $0.05 per share on its 10,000,000 outstanding common shares. During the year, no shares were issued and none were repurchased from investors. In addition, Junor paid $500,000 in preferred dividends. On July 31, 2010 Junor's share price was $5.75.

Required:

Calculate the following ratios for 2010. Explain and interpret the meaning of each ratio:
i.   basic earnings per share for fiscal 2010
ii. price-to-earnings ratio on July 31, 2010
iii. dividend payout ratio for fiscal 2010

E13-15. (Calculating EPS, price-to-earnings ratio, and dividend ratios, LO 2) Kovach Ltd. (Kovach) is a publicly traded company. During its year ended March 31, 2009 Kovach reported a net loss of $37,500,000. During fiscal 2009 Kovach declared and paid quarterly dividends of $0.05 per share on its 24,000,000 outstanding common shares. During the year no shares were issued and none were repurchased from investors. In addition, Kovach paid $5,000,000 in preferred dividends. On March 31, 2009 Kovach's share price was $6.75.

Required:

a. Calculate the following ratios for 2009. Explain and interpret the meaning of each ratio:
   i.   basic earnings per share for fiscal 2009
   ii. price-to-earnings ratio on March 31, 2009
   iii. dividend payout ratio for fiscal 2009
b. Explain how it is possible for Kovach to pay a dividend when it reported a loss during fiscal 2009.
c. Explain why Kovach would have a share price that is greater than zero when the company is losing money.

E13-16. (Examining the effect of debt covenants on debt and dividends) During fiscal 2010, Husavick Inc. (Husavick) borrowed $250,000 from a private lender. The loan agreement requires that Husavick's debt-to-equity ratio not exceed 2:1 at any time. The loan is repayable in 2016. You have been provided with the following information from Husavick's accounting records:

Husavick Inc.
Summarized Balance Sheet
For the Year Ended July 31, 2010

Assets:	
Current assets	$150,000
Non-current assets	615,000
Total assets	$765,000
Liabilities and shareholders' equity:	
Current liabilities	$115,000
Non-current liabilities	375,000
Shareholders' equity	275,000
Total liabilities and shareholders' equity	$765,000

Required:

a. Calculate Husavick's debt-to-equity ratio on July 31, 2010.
b. How much additional debt could Husavick have borrowed without violating the debt covenant on July 31, 2010?
c. How much could Husavick have paid in dividends during fiscal 2010 without violating the debt covenant?
d. What would be the effect on Husavick's debt-to-equity ratio if it declared a $50,000 dividend on July 31, 2010 that was to be paid on August 15, 2010?

E13-17. (Computing ratios, LO 2) Hurstwood Wineries Ltd. (Hurstwood) produces and markets wines from its vineyards in Ontario and B.C. You have been provided with the following income statements and balance sheets for Hurstwood:

Hurstwood Wineries Ltd.
Income Statements
For the Years Ended March 31
(in thousands of dollars except per share amounts)

	2009	2008
Sales	$87,333	$86,865
Cost of goods sold	55,463	54,816
Gross profit	31,870	32,049
Selling and administration	22,561	21,294
Earnings before interest and amortization	9,309	10,755
Interest	1,435	1,563
Amortization	2,700	2,481
Earnings before unusual items	5,174	6,711
Unusual items	(667)	4,739
Earnings before income taxes	4,507	11,450
Provision for (recovery of) income taxes:		
Current	2,168	3,634
Future	(295)	463
	1,873	4,097
Net earnings for the year	2,634	7,353
Retained earnings—beginning of year	39,395	33,970
Dividends on common shares	1,928	1,928
Retained earnings—end of year	$40,101	$39,395

Hurstwood Wineries Ltd.
Balance Sheets
As of March 31
(in thousands of dollars)

	2009	2008
Assets		
Current assets:		
Accounts receivable	$7,542	$7,844
Inventories	30,736	31,241
Prepaid expenses	702	557
	38,980	39,642
Capital assets and goodwill	43,884	38,844
Investment	3,565	3,565
	$86,429	$82,051
Liabilities		
Current liabilities:		
Bank indebtedness	$17,883	$13,665
Accounts payable and accrued liabilities	8,548	6,862
Dividends payable	482	482
Income and other taxes payable	928	2,009
Current portion of long-term debt	1,552	1,370
	29,393	24,388
Long-term debt	11,346	12,384
Future income taxes	2,716	3,011
	43,455	39,783
Shareholders' equity		
Capital stock (weighted average number of shares outstanding during 2009 was 3,953,050 and during 2008 was 3,875,200)	2,873	2,873
Retained earnings	40,101	39,395
	42,974	42,268
	$86,429	$82,051

Required:

  a. Compute the following ratios and amounts for Hurstwood for 2009 and 2008:
    i.   gross margin
    ii. gross margin percentage
    iii. profit margin
    iv. profit margin percentage
    v.   earnings per share
    vi. working capital
    vii. current ratio
    viii. quick ratio
    ix. debt-to-equity ratio
    x.   interest coverage ratio
    xi. dividend payout ratio

  b. Compute the following ratios and amounts for Hurstwood for 2009:
    i.   asset turnover
    ii. return on equity
    iii. return on assets
    iv. inventory turnover ratio
    v.   average number of days inventory on hand
    vi. accounts receivable turnover ratio
    vii. average collection period of accounts receivable
    viii. accounts payable turnover ratio
    ix. average payment period for accounts payable
    x.   cash lag

  c. How do the unusual items reported on the 2009 and 2008 income statements affect your ability to predict Hurstwood's future performance?

  d. Comment on Hurstwood's liquidity, based on amounts you calculated in parts a. and b. Be sure to consider the nature of Hurstwood's business in your response.

E13-18. **(Understanding return on assets, LO 2)** You are provided with the following information about Unwin Corp. (Unwin), a small manufacturing company.

	2010	2009	2008	2007	2006
Sales	$1,309,440	$1,223,776	$1,165,500	$1,050,000	
Net income	56,306	51,398	44,290	36,750	
Total liabilities (at year end)	346,274	326,674	294,300	272,500	250,000
Shareholders' equity (at year end)	381,680	325,376	273,976	229,688	192,938

Required:

  a. Calculate Unwin's return on assets by determining its profit margin and asset turnover ratio. Assume that profit margin equals net income divided by sales.

  b. Calculate Unwin's return on equity.

  c. Assess the profitability of Unwin. In your response, explain the reasons for any changes in Unwin's profitability.

E13-19. **(Understanding return on assets, LO 2)** You are provided with the following information about Wha Ti Inc. (Wha Ti), a vehicle repair company.

	2009	2008	2007	2006	2005
Sales	$957,264	$854,700	$763,125	$687,500	
Net income	33,504	32,479	30,525	28,875	
Total liabilities (at year end)	159,535	151,938	144,703	137,813	131,250
Shareholders' equity (at year end)	318,623	285,119	252,641	222,116	193,241

Required:

a. Calculate Wha Ti's return on assets by determining its profit margin and asset turnover ratio. Assume that profit margin equals net income divided by sales.

b. Calculate Wha Ti's return on equity.

c. Assess the profitability of Wha Ti. In your response, explain the reasons for any changes in Wha Ti's profitability.

E13-20. (**Classifying transactions and economic events, LO 1**) Explain whether you would classify each of the following transactions and economic events as extraordinary, unusual, or ordinary.

a. An entity's property is destroyed in a terrorist attack.

b. A manufacturer sells its old equipment so that it can purchase new equipment.

c. A business settles a large lawsuit by paying $1,000,000.

d. A chain of restaurants closes five of its poorly performing locations.

e. An earthquake destroys a factory of a large company.

f. An entity sells one of its operating divisions.

Problems

P13-1. (**Find the missing information, LO 2**) Use the information provided about Kynocks Inc. (Kynocks) to determine the missing information from its December 31, 2009 balance sheet and for the income statement for the year ended December 31, 2009. For all final amounts determined for the balance sheet and income statement, round to the thousands of dollars.

Kynocks Inc.
Balance Sheets
As of the Years Ended December 31, 2008 and 2009

	2009	2008
Cash	$	$110,000
Accounts receivable		105,000
Inventory		248,000
Capital assets (net)		146,000
Total assets:	$	$609,000
Accounts payable	$	$184,000
Long-term debt		100,000
Capital stock		75,000
Retained earnings		250,000
Total liabilities and shareholders' equity:	$	$609,000

Kynocks Inc.
Income Statement
For the Year Ended December 31, 2009

Revenue	$
Cost of sales	1,500,000
Gross margin	
Selling, general, and administrative expenses	
Interest expense	
Income before taxes	
Income tax expense	
Net income	
Number of common shares outstanding during 2009	$

Additional information:
- No dividends were paid during the year.
- There are no preferred shares outstanding.
- All sales and purchases of inventory are on credit.
- No new common shares were issued during the year and no common shares were repurchased during the year.
- Tax rate = 20.63%.

- Gross margin percentage = 40%.
- Profit margin percentage = 2%.
- Interest coverage ratio = 6.2085.
- EPS = $0.40.
- ROA = 9.85.
- Inventory turnover ratio = 5.474.
- Accounts receivable turnover ratio = 21.739.
- Accounts payable turnover ratio = 7.589.
- Debt-to-equity ratio = 0.733.
- Current ratio = 2.222.

P13-2. **(Find the missing information, LO 2)** Use the information provided about Voligny Inc. (Voligny) to determine the missing information from its December 31, 2010 balance sheet and for the income statement for the year ended December 31, 2010. For all final amounts determined for the balance sheet and income statement, round to thousands of dollars.

Voligny Inc.
Balance Sheets
As of the Years Ended December 31, 2010 and 2009

	2010	2009
Cash	$	$ 25,000
Accounts receivable		125,000
Inventory		185,000
Capital assets (net)		925,000
Total Assets	$	$1,260,000
Accounts payable	$	$70,000
Long-term debt		450,000
Capital stock		200,000
Retained earnings		540,000
Total Liabilities and Shareholders' Equity	$	$1,260,000

Voligny Inc.
Income Statement
For the Year Ended December 31, 2010

Revenue	$
Cost of sales	
Gross margin	
Selling general and administrative expenses	
Interest expense	
Income before taxes	
Income tax expense	
Net income	$ 100,000

Additional information:
- No dividends were paid during the year.
- There are no preferred shares outstanding.
- All sales and purchases of inventory are on credit.
- No new common shares were issued during the year and no common shares were repurchased during the year.
- Tax rate = 20%.
- Gross margin percentage = 45%.

- Profit margin percentage = 10%.
- Interest coverage ratio = 4.906
- EPS = $0.75.
- Inventory turnover ratio = 2.716
- Accounts receivable turnover ratio = 7.547
- Accounts payable turnover ratio = 7.222.
- Debt-to-equity ratio = 0.586
- Current ratio = 4.293

P13-3. **(Considering the debt-to-equity ratios of different industries, LO 2)** Consider the following industries and indicate whether you think each would have a low or high current ratio (for example above or below 1.25). Explain your thinking.
  a. Telecommunications (like Rogers Communications)
  b. Airline
  c. Retail furniture store
  d. Software developer
  e. Real estate developer (builds and operates apartment buildings)
  f. Car manufacturer

P13-4. **(Considering the debt-to-equity ratios of different industries, LO 2)** Consider the following industries and indicate whether you think that the debt-to-equity ratios of entities in the industry would tend to be high or low (e.g. above one or below one). In answering consider whether you would want to lend money to an entity in the industry. Explain your answer.
  a. Oil and gas exploration company
  b. Software development company
  c. Auto parts manufacturer
  d. Cattle farmer
  e. Biotechnology company
  f. Electricity utility
  g. Furniture retailer

P13-5. **(Determining the effect of a big bath on future earnings and financial ratios, LO 1, 2, 4)** Vogar Ltd. (Vogar) is a public company that manufactures machine parts. In its most recent financial statements Vogar wrote down $10,000,000 of its capital assets. The assets will continue to be used by Vogar. The new president and CEO of Vogar announced that the write-downs were the result of competitive pressures and poor performance of the company in the last year. The write-downs were reported separately in Vogar's income statement as a "non-recurring" item. The write-off is not included in the calculation of operating income. In addition, Vogar wrote down its inventory in fiscal 2009 by $1,000,000. The amount is included in cost of sales.

Vogar's summarized income statement for the year ended December 31, 2009 is (amounts in thousands of dollars):

Vogar Ltd.
Summarized Income Statement
for the Year Ended December 31, 2009
(in thousands of dollars)

Revenue		$47,500
Operating expenses:		
Cost of sales	$26,000	
Amortization	7,000	
Selling general and administrative costs	9,000	
Operating income		5,500
Other expenses:		
Non-recurring item	10,000	
Interest expense	2,500	
Income tax expense	1,000	13,500
Net income		($8,000)

The write-downs will reduce the amortization expense by $1,250,000 per year for each of the next eight years. After the announcement and release of the income statement, analysts revised their forecasts of earnings for the next three years to:

Year ended December 31, 2010 $2,000,000
Year ended December 31, 2011 $4,500,000
Year ended December 31, 2012 $6,000,000

You also obtained the following information from Vogar's December 31, 2008 and 2009 balance sheets:

Vogar Ltd.
Summarized Balance Sheet Information
As of December 31, 2008 and 2009
(in thousands of dollars)

	2009	2008
Current assets	$16,487.5	$18,750.0
Total assets	71,383.5	75,798.5
Current liabilities	12,110.0	11,075.0
Non-current liabilities	19,125.0	16,575.0
Shareholders' equity	40,148.5	48,148.5

Required:

a. What would net income be in each of 2009 through 2012 had Vogar not written off the assets and continued to amortize them? Assume that the operations of Vogar do not change regardless of the accounting method used. Interpret the differences in net income under the two scenarios. Use the analysts' forecasts to determine net income.

b. What would Vogar's gross margin, profit margin, debt-to-equity ratio, return on assets, and return on equity be in 2009 assuming (i) that the assets had been written off and (ii) assuming that the assets had not been written off and they were continuing to be amortized? Interpret the results under each assumption.

c. How would the write-downs in 2009 affect Vogar's gross margin, profit margin, debt-to-equity ratio, return on assets, and return on equity in 2010 through 2012? How is your ability to analyze and interpret the financial statements affected?

P13-6. **(Evaluating the effect of R&D accounting on financial statement analysis, LO 1, 2, 3)** One controversial accounting issue is accounting for research costs. In Canada, research costs must be expensed as incurred. This treatment is an application of the conservatism measurement convention. Some people argue that research is a legitimate asset and requiring that it be expensed results in an understatement of assets and income, violates matching, and makes companies that invest heavily in research appear less successful than they actually are.

Chortitz Ltd. (Chortitz) is a large and successful software development company. You have been provided with Chortitz's balance sheets and income statements for 2008 through 2010. In addition, Chortitz expensed (and expended) $15,812,000 for research in 2007 and $13,224,000 in 2006.

Chortitz Ltd.
Summarized Balance Sheet Information
As of June 30, 2007–2010
(000s)

	2010	2009	2008	2007
Current assets	$ 95,906	$103,126	$ 82,204	$ 69,630
Total assets	$210,432	$190,872	$170,094	$141,178
Current liabilities	$ 64,308	$ 66,440	$ 44,466	$ 37,138
Non-current liabilities	$ 23,100	$ 18,480	$ 12,376	$ 8,662
Shareholders' equity	$123,024	$105,952	$113,252	$ 95,378

Chortitz Ltd.
Income Statements
For the Years Ended June 30,
(000s)

	2010	2009	2008
Revenues	$ 243,704	$ 186,360	$ 152,686
Cost of revenues:			
License & networking	9,698	4,430	3,002
Customer support	12,592	9,456	5,200
Service	41,192	37,950	24,510
Total cost of revenues	63,482	51,836	32,712
	180,222	134,524	119,974
Operating expenses:			
Research and development	40,114	29,276	18,766
Sales and marketing	84,674	70,832	60,128
General and administrative	21,766	32,722	9,770
Depreciation	10,356	9,172	8,450
Total operating expenses	156,910	142,002	97,114
Income (loss) from operations	23,312	(7,478)	22,860
Interest expense	2,010	1,530	996
Income before income taxes	21,302	(9,008)	21,864
Provision for (recovery of) income taxes	4,230	(1,708)	3,990
Net income for the year	$ 17,072	($7,300)	$ 17,874
Weighted average number of common shares outstanding during the year	40,064,184	44,698,536	41,828,730

Required:

a. Recalculate Chortitz's net income in 2008, 2009, and 2010, assuming that research is capitalized and amortized over three years. Also calculate total assets and shareholders' equity, assuming research is capitalized and amortized. What amount would be reported on the balance sheet for research if research were capitalized instead of expensed? (Assume that one-third of the amount expended on research is expensed each year, including the year of the expenditure.)

b. Calculate Chortitz's profit margin, interest coverage ratio, earnings per share, debt-to-equity ratio, ROA, and ROE for 2008, 2009, and 2010 using the information as presented in the company's financial statements. Calculate the same ratios, assuming that Chortitz capitalizes and amortizes its research costs over three years.

c. Evaluate the performance and solvency of Chortitz under the "expense" and "capitalize" scenarios. What are the implications of the differences between the two scenarios? Do you think there is merit in the criticisms some people have expressed about the current GAAP treatment of research costs? Explain fully.

P13-7. **(Evaluating performance, LO2)** Nywening Ltd. (Nywening) operates in a highly competitive industry. Price is very important to most customers and it is very difficult for small operators such as Nywening to differentiate themselves on product quality. It is possible to differentiate based on service, but most competitors offer reasonably comparable service packages.

The president of Nywening is reviewing the company's performance in 2009. During 2009 sales increased by 15 percent to $875,000. Average total assets for the year were $487,500, net income was $50,000, and interest expense was $15,000. Nywening's tax rate is 20 percent.

The president believes that Nywening can improve its performance in 2010. She would like to see a 12 percent growth in sales in 2010 and a return on assets of 20 percent. The president estimates that it will be necessary to increase assets by 10 percent in 2010. The president does not think that any additional borrowing will be required and, as a result, the interest expense for 2010 will be the same as for 2009.

Required:

a. Calculate Nywening's profit margin, asset turnover, and return on assets for 2009.
b. What asset turnover ratio is required in 2010 to achieve the president's objectives? What net income is needed to achieve her objectives? What would the profit margin be if the objectives are achieved? For purposes of this question use net income plus the after tax cost of interest to calculate profit margin.
c. Do you think the president's objectives are reasonable?

P13-8. **(Determining the effects of transactions on ratios, LO 2)** You have been provided with the following information about Everell Inc. (Everell).

	2007	2008	2009	2010
Accounts receivable	$ 300,000	$ 315,000	$ 330,750	$ 347,288
Inventory	200,000	210,000	220,500	231,526
Accounts payable	150,000	157,500	165,376	173,644
Revenue	2,000,000	2,100,000	2,310,000	2,541,000
Cost of sales	1,100,000	1,155,000	1,282,050	1,423,076

Required:

a. Calculate the accounts receivable, inventory, and accounts payable turnover ratios for 2008 through 2010.
b. Calculate the average collection period of accounts receivable, average number of days inventory on hand, and average payment period for accounts payable for 2008 through 2010.
c. Determine Everell's cash lag for 2008 through 2010.
d. Interpret the results you obtained in parts a. through c. What do these results tell you about Everell's liquidity over the last three years?
e. What are some possible explanations for the results?
f. Suppose you are a banker Everell's management has approached about an expanded line of credit. How would the results you obtained in parts a. through c. affect your decision? Explain.

P13-9. **(Determining the effects of transactions on ratios, LO 2)** You have been provided with the following information about Yarker Ltd. (Yarker).

	2006	2007	2008	2009
Accounts receivable	$ 3,375,000	$ 3,645,000	$ 3,827,250	$ 4,018,614
Inventory	7,500,000	7,800,000	8,190,000	7,780,500
Accounts payable	300,000	305,760	314,628	292,917
Revenue	30,000,000	31,500,000	30,870,000	29,326,500
Cost of sales	12,000,000	12,537,000	12,224,829	11,555,520

Required:

a. Calculate the accounts receivable, inventory, and accounts payable turnover ratios for 2007 through 2009.
b. Calculate the average collection period of accounts receivable, average number of days inventory on hand, and average payment period for accounts payable for 2007 through 2009.
c. Determine Yarker's cash lag for 2007 through 2009.

d. Interpret the results you obtained in parts a. through c. What do these results tell you about Yarker's liquidity over the last three years?

e. What are some possible explanations for the results?

f. Suppose you are a banker whom Yarker's management approached about an expanded line of credit. How would the results you obtained in parts a. through c. affect your decision? Explain.

P13-10. (The effect of leverage on ROA and ROE, LO 2) Three companies, Company A, Company B, and Company C, are identical in every respect except for how they are financed. You are provided with the following information about each company.

	Company A			Company B			Company C		
	Jan. 1, 2009	Dec. 31, 2009	Dec. 31, 2010	Jan. 1, 2009	Dec. 31, 2009	Dec. 31, 2010	Jan. 1, 2009	Dec. 31, 2009	Dec. 31, 2010
Income before interest and taxes		$22,400	$2,400		$22,400	$2,400		$22,400	$ 2,400
Interest expense		0	0		2,400	2,400		5,600	5,600
Income tax expense		4,928	528		4,400	0		3,696	(704)
Net income		17,472	1,872		15,600	0		13,104	(2,496)
Dividends paid		8,000	4,368		6,128	2,496		3,632	0
Total assets	80,000	89,472	86,976	80,000	89,472	86,976	80,000	89,472	86,976
Shareholders' equity	80,000	89,472	86,976	56,000	65,472	62,976	24,000	33,472	30,976
Tax rate		22%	22%		22%	22%		22%	22%

Required:

a. Calculate ROA and ROE for each company for the years ended December 31, 2005 and 2006.

b. Explain the differences in performance among the three companies.

c. Explain the effect of leverage on the performance measures.

P13-11 (The effect of leasing on ratios, LO 2, 4) Fodhia Inc. (Fodhia) is a small manufacturing company operating in eastern Canada. Fodhia is a public company. In 2010 Fodhia's management decided to acquire additional manufacturing equipment so that it would be able to meet the increasing demand for its products. However, instead of purchasing the equipment, Fodhia arranged to lease the equipment. The lease came into effect on December 1, 2009. In its 2010 financial statements Fodhia accounted for the leases as operating leases. You have obtained Fodhia's summarized balance sheets and income statements for 2009 and 2010.

Fodhia Inc.
Summarized Balance Sheets
As of November 30, 2009 and 2010

	2010	2009
Cash	$ 159,000	$ 206,250
Accounts receivable	521,250	456,000
Inventory	1,368,750	1,160,250
Capital assets (net)	2,171,250	1,989,000
Other non-current assets	281,250	331,500
Total assets	$ 4,501,500	$ 4,143,750
Current liabilities	$ 1,296,000	$ 1,367,250
Long term debt	742,500	712,500
Capital stock (750,000 shares outstanding)	900,000	900,000
Retained earnings	1,563,000	1,163,250
Total liabilities and shareholders' equity	$ 4,501,500	$ 4,143,750

Fodhia Inc.
Income Statements
For the Years Ended November 30, 2009 and 2010

	2010	2009
Revenue	$12,937,500	$10,875,000
Cost of sales	7,163,250	5,997,000
Selling, general, and administrative expenses	4,884,000	4,162,500
Amortization expense	232,500	206,250
Lease expense for equipment	56,250	
Interest expense	69,000	64,500
Income tax expense	132,750	111,000
Net income	$ 399,750	$ 333,750

Had Fodhia accounted for the equipment leases as capital leases, the following differences would have occurred in the 2010 financial statements:

■ No lease expense would have been recorded.
■ The leased equipment would have been recorded on the balance sheet as capital assets for $345,000. The equipment would have been amortized straight line over 12 years.
■ A liability of $345,000 would have been recorded at the inception of the lease. On November 30, 2010 the current portion of the liability would have been $23,925. The interest expense arising from the lease in fiscal 2010 would have been $34,500. On November 30, 2010 the remaining liability, including the current portion, would have been $323,250.
■ There would be no effect on the tax expense for the year.

Required:

a. Prepare revised financial statements, assuming that Fodhia treated the leases as capital leases instead of as operating leases.
b. Calculate the following ratios, first using the financial statements as initially prepared by Fodhia and then using the revised statements you prepared in part (a):
   i.   debt-to-equity ratio
   ii.   return on assets
   iii. return on equity
   iv.   profit margin ratio
   v.   current ratio
   vi.   asset turnover
   vii. earnings per share
   viii. interest coverage ratio
c. Discuss the differences between the two sets of ratios you calculated in part (b). Why are the ratios different? How might users of the financial statements be affected by these differences? Which set of ratios gives a better perspective on the performance, liquidity, and leverage of Fodhia? Explain.

P13-12. (**Determining the effect of a big bath on future earnings, LO 1, 2, 4**) Quirpon Inc. (Quirpon) is a large mining company. In 2006, Quirpon wrote down $20,000,000 in costs that it incurred finding and developing certain mining properties. If Quirpon had not written down the $20,000,000 in costs, $4,000,000 in amortization would have been expensed in each year from 2006 through 2010. The summarized financial statement information for the years 2006 through 2009 is:

Quirpon Inc.
Summarized Financial Statement Information
(in thousands of dollars)

	2005	2006	2007	2008	2009
Revenue		$61,000	$56,000	$62,000	$ 66,000
Operating expenses		24,000	22,000	26,000	29,000
Amortization expense		14,000	14,400	14,800	15,600
Interest expense		2,400	2,400	2,400	2,400
Income tax expense		5,150	4,300	4,700	4,750
Net income		$15,450	$12,900	$14,100	$ 14,250
Total assets	$74,000	$69,450	$82,350	$96,450	$110,700
Total shareholders' equity	$50,000	$45,450	$58,350	$72,450	$ 86,700

Additional information:

- Quirpon has no preferred shares outstanding.
- The amortization expense does not include the amortization of the written-down assets and the write-down is not reflected in the presented information.
- Quirpon's tax rate is 20 percent.
- Assume that the write-down and any additional amortization expense do not affect Quirpon's tax expense.

Required:

a. Determine Quirpon's net income for 2006 through 2009, assuming that the $20,000,000 write-down (i) occurred and (ii) did not occur. For (ii) amortization of the assets must be expensed each year.
b. Calculate Quirpon's profit margin, return on assets, and return on equity, assuming that the write-down (i) occurred and (ii) did not occur.
c. Should the write-down be considered permanent or transitory earnings? Explain.
d. As an equity investor in Quirpon, how would your evaluation of the company be affected by whether the write-down occurred versus if the assets were amortized over their remaining life? In responding you should consider permanent versus transitory earnings.

P13-13. (Forecasting future earnings, LO 1, 4) You have been presented with Peverel Ltd.'s (Peverel) income statement for the year ended September 30, 2009.

Peverel Ltd.
Income Statement
For the Year Ended September 30, 2009

Sales	$ 5,100,000
Cost of sales	2,295,000
Gross margin	2,805,000
Expenses:	
Salaries and wages	1,101,600
Amortization	394,800
Selling and administrative	580,000
Interest	200,000
Other	130,000
Unusual items—lawsuit revenue	400,000
Income before income taxes	798,600
Income tax expense	239,580
Net income	$ 559,020

In addition, you have learned the following:

- Cost of sales in 2009 includes a write-down of inventory of $118,000. The amount of the write-down is about three times larger than the amount usually written down each year to account for non-saleable inventory or inventory that will have to be sold at a deep discount.
- Sales includes $500,000 for a one-time-only sale to the government of a foreign country. The gross margin percentage on this sale was 60 percent, which is significantly higher than what Peverel normally experiences.
- Selling and administrative costs includes a $80,000 retirement bonus paid to the former CEO.
- Peverel signed a contract with its employees that goes into effect on October 1, 2009. The contract increases union employees' wages and benefits by 4 percent. Wages to employees covered by the contract represent 70 percent of salaries and wages expense in 2009. Wages to other employees are not expected to change during 2010.
- During 2009, Peverel won a lawsuit against a former employee for divulging confidential information to her new employer. The employee and her new employer are required to pay damages to Peverel of $400,000.
- Sales (excluding the one-time sale note above) are expected to grow by 7 percent during 2010. Inventory costs are expected to increase by 8 percent, selling and administrative expenses are expected to decrease by 2 percent, interest expense is not expected to change, amortization expense is expected to increase by 3 percent, and other expenses are expected to increase by 5 percent.

Required:

a. Use Peverel's 2009 income statement and the additional information to forecast an income statement for 2010.
b. Explain and interpret Peverel's actual performance in 2009 and the performance that you forecast for 2010.
c. Discuss the difficulties that can occur with forecasting the future performance of an entity and the problems with using GAAP financial statements for forecasting.

P13-14. (Evaluating liquidity and solvency, LO 2) Yekooche Inc. (Yekooche) is a small manufacturer of home environmental products such as humidifiers, air cleaners, and ionizers. Yekooche's products are sold across Canada and about 20 percent of its sales are outside of Canada, mainly in the United States. The president of Yekooche feels that the company has a good product and established markets, and has performed well over the last few years. However, the president is concerned that Yekooche is chronically tight on cash. She has approached your organization for a significant loan to provide the company with additional working capital, as well as to purchase capital assets that need to be replaced. The president of Yekooche has provided income statements and balance sheets for recent years.

Yekooche Inc.
Income Statements
For the Years Ended July 31, 2007–2009

	2009	2008	2007
Sales	$3,704,000	$3,963,280	$3,923,646
Cost of sales	2,077,944	2,199,620	2,150,158
Selling, general, and administrative expenses	1,304,108	1,341,516	1,312,422
Amortization	220,000	204,000	196,000
Research and development	90,000	176,000	250,000
Gain on sale of investment	126,000	0	0
Income tax expense	26,000	6,000	2,000
Net Income	$ 111,948	$ 36,144	$ 13,066

Yekooche Inc.
Balance Sheets
For the Years Ended July 21, 2006–2009

	2009	2008	2007	2006
Cash				
Receivables	11,158	53,210	11,066	80,000
Inventory	630,000	420,000	364,000	330,000
Prepaid expenses	102,000	56,000	162,000	30,000
Current assets	1,293,160	959,212	897,066	730,000
Capital assets (net of amortization)	1,298,000	1,220,000	1,080,000	820,000
Investment, at cost	0	150,000	150,000	0
	$2,591,158	$2,329,210	$2,127,066	$1,550,000
Bank loans	$ 250,000	$ 184,000	$ 94,000	$ 0
Accounts payable and accrued liabilities	700,000	616,000	540,000	420,000
Current liabilities	950,000	800,000	634,000	420,000
Long-term debt	350,000	350,000	350,000	0
Capital stock	1,000,000	1,000,000	1,000,000	1,000,000
Retained earnings	291,158	179,210	143,066	130,000
	$2,591,158	$2,329,210	$2,127,066	$1,550,000

Additional information:
- The long-term debt is due to be repaid in early 2011. The amount is owed to a large bank and is secured against certain capital assets.
- Yekooche has a $260,000 line of credit available from its bank. Bank loans represent the amount borrowed against the line of credit.
- All sales to customers and purchases of inventory are made on credit.
- Interest expense is included in selling, general, and administrative expenses. Interest expense was $62,000 in 2009, $102,000 in 2008, and $48,000 in 2007.

Required:

Prepare a report to the corporate lending department evaluating the liquidity and solvency of Yekooche. Provide a preliminary recommendation on whether the loan should be made. Provide support for your recommendation. What additional information would you want before reaching a final decision on the loan application? In your analysis consider Yekooche's cash flow.

P13-15. (**Evaluating an equity investment, LO 2**) Refer to the information about Yekooche Inc. provided in Problem P13-14.

You are an investment analyst for Qualicum Investment Group, Inc. (Qualicum). Qualicum raises capital from individual investors and invests in promising small businesses, with the expectation that the businesses will grow and that it will ultimately be able to sell the investments at a profit. The president of Yekooche has approached your organization to make a significant equity investment in the company.

Required:

Prepare a report to Qualicum's executive board analyzing Yekooche's performance over the last few years and assessing its attractiveness as an investment. What additional information would you want before reaching a final decision on whether to invest? In your analysis consider Yekooche's cash flow.

P13-16. (**Assessing inventory, LO 1, 2**) My Secrets Inc. is a Canadian women's wear retail chain with stores located in major cities across Canada. The company is looking for new equity investment to help finance a major expansion. A private investment fund is looking to place some money in the Canadian retail industry and so is considering My Secrets Inc. You are an analyst for a private investment fund and your manager has asked you to analyze the company's inventory information for any trends and insights you can obtain. You have been given information relevant to inventory for the last 10 years as well as other financial statement information that might be useful.

	2009	2008	2007	2006	2005	2004	2003	2002	2001	2000
Inventories	$ 35,371	$ 28,702	$ 36,123	$ 24,378	$ 34,936	$ 29,904	$ 34,278	$ 31,450	$ 38,618	$ 36,689
Accounts Receivable	7,846	5,099	6,691	4,146	5,247	3,414	3,035	3,659	3,017	1,650
Total Revenue	296,635	256,245	242,970	208,730	280,671	266,326	255,789	242,139	233,224	341,380
Cost of goods sold	157,217	133,760	127,559	113,758	151,843	143,284	138,126	130,513	126,174	184,345
Other Operating Expenses	101,390	93,726	92,594	68,391	98,608	98,214	96,522	91,563	86,052	134,979
Net Income	12,806	58	(9,293)	(2,726)	16,140	11,327	4,383	9,737	(8,803)	32,037

Required:

Prepare the report requested by your manager. Provide any ratios that you think appropriate. Be sure to interpret your results and explain the tools that you use to do the analysis.

Using Financial Statements

THE FORZANI GROUP LTD.

The Forzani Group Ltd. (Forzani) is Canada's largest sporting goods retailer. FGL currently operates 260 corporate stores under the banners: Sport Chek, Sport Mart, Coast Mountain Sports and National Sports. The Company is also the franchisor/licensor of 204 stores under the banners: Sports Experts, Intersport, RnR, Econosports, Atmosphere, Tech Shop/Pegasus, Nevada Bob's Golf, and Hockey Experts. FGL operates four websites, dedicated to the Canadian online sporting goods market, www.sportchek.ca, www.sportmart.ca, www.sportsexperts.ca, and www.nationalsports.com.

FGL's unique, multi-banner concept is designed to provide the largest group of Canadian consumers a collection of technically superior sporting goods at all price points. Quality products and customer service are two of the hallmarks of the FGL shopping experience, tailored specifically to the needs and preferences of our broad base of consumers.

The Company is dedicated to continuously growing its retail store base and customer service in order to provide expert advice, quality products and value pricing to our customers.

Forzani's consolidated balance sheets, statements of operations and retained earnings, statements of cash flows, and extracts from the notes to the financial statements are provided in Exhibit 13–7.[11] Use this information to respond to questions FS13-1 to FS13-7.

FS13-1. Prepare common size and trend statements from Forzani's balance sheets and statements of operations. Analyze the statements you prepared to identify any issues that you think might require additional explanation. Explain why you identified the issues you did.

FS13-2. Compute and interpret the following ratios for Forzani for fiscal years 2005 and 2006. Use these ratios to assess Forzani's liquidity. Be sure to use the information provided from Forzani's February 1, 2004 balance sheet.
a. current ratio
b. quick ratio
c. accounts receivable turnover ratio
d. average collection period of accounts receivable

THE FORZANI GROUP LTD.

THE FORZANI GROUP LTD.
Consolidated Balance Sheets
(in thousands)

As at	January 29, 2006	January 30, 2005
ASSETS (note 6)		
Current		
Cash	$ 19,266	$ 26,018
Accounts receivable	68,927	58,576
Inventory	278,002	278,631
Prepaid expenses	2,647	3,022
	368,842	366,247
Capital assets (note 3)	193,594	179,702
Goodwill and other intangibles (note 4)	75,805	52,790
Other assets (note 5)	10,080	9,415
Future income tax asset (note 9)	4,885	-
	$ 653,206	$ 608,154
LIABILITIES		
Current		
Accounts payable and accrued liabilities	$ 244,293	$ 238,239
Current portion of long-term debt (note 6)	5,135	1,580
	249,428	239,819
Long-term debt (note 6)	58,805	40,278
Deferred lease inducements	62,883	62,613
Deferred rent liability	3,810	2,213
Future income tax liability (note 9)	-	384
	374,926	345,307
SHAREHOLDERS' EQUITY		
Share capital (note 8)	138,131	137,811
Contributed surplus	4,271	2,915
Retained earnings	135,878	122,121
	278,280	262,847
	$ 653,206	$ 608,154

Additional Information from Forzani's February 1, 2004 Balance Sheet (in thousands of dollars):

Accounts receivable	$36,319
Inventory	258,816
Total assets	549,038
Accounts payable	217,777
Total shareholders equity	233,396
Preferred shares	0
Preferred dividends	0
Dividends on common shares	0

e. inventory turnover ratio

f. average number of days inventory on hand

g. accounts payable turnover ratio

h. average payment period for accounts payable

FS13-3. Compute and interpret the following ratios for Forzani for fiscal 2006 and 2005. Use these ratios to assess Forzani's performance:

a. gross margin

b. profit margin

c. return on assets

d. return on equity

FS13-4. Compute and interpret the following ratios for Forzani for fiscal year 2006 and 2005. Use these ratios to assess Forzani's solvency and liquidity. Do not restrict your evaluation to the ratios that you are required to calculate.

a. debt-to-equity ratio

b. interest coverage ratio (earnings based)

c. interest coverage ratio (cash based)

FS13-5. Forzani does not pay dividends. Why do you think that is the case? Do you think that Forzani could pay a regular dividend to its shareholders? What would be the implications to Forzani of paying a regular dividend?

EXHIBIT 13-7 :

(continued)
The Forzani Group
Ltd. Extracts from
Financial
Statements

F2006 ANNUAL REPORT

THE FORZANI GROUP LTD.
Consolidated Statements of Operations and Retained Earnings
(in thousands, except share data)

	For the 52 weeks ended January 29, 2006	For the 52 weeks ended January 30, 2005
Revenue		
Retail	$ 856,149	$718,820
Wholesale	273,255	266,234
	1,129,404	985,054
Cost of sales	746,313	651,158
Gross margin	383,091	333,896
Operating and administrative expenses		
Store operating	225,218	190,891
General and administrative	88,720	66,536
	313,938	257,427
Operating earnings before undernoted items	69,153	76,469
Amortization	41,343	35,885
Interest	6,145	4,447
Loss on write-down of investment (note 14)	-	2,208
	47,488	42,540
Earnings before income taxes	21,665	33,929
Provision for income taxes (note 9)		
Current	8,784	10,207
Future	(876)	2,177
	7,908	12,384
Net earnings	13,757	21,545
Retained earnings, opening	122,121	101,528
Adjustment arising from normal course issuer bid (note 8(b))	-	(952)
Retained earnings, closing	$ 135,878	$ 122,121
Earnings per share (note 8(c))	$ 0.42	$ 0.66
Diluted earnings per share (note 8(c))	$ 0.42	$ 0.66

(b) Inventory

Inventory is valued at the lower of laid-down cost and net realizable value. Laid-down cost is determined using the weighted average cost method and includes invoice cost, duties, freight, and distribution costs. Net realizable value is defined as the expected selling price.

Volume rebates and other supplier discounts are included in income when earned. Volume rebates are accounted for as a reduction of the cost of the related inventory and are "earned" when the inventory is sold. All other rebates and discounts are "earned" when the related expense is incurred.

(h) Revenue recognition

Revenue includes sales to customers through corporate stores operated by the Company and sales to, and service fees from, franchise stores and others. Sales to customers through corporate stores operated by the Company are recognized at the point of sale, net of an estimated allowance for sales returns. Sales of merchandise to franchise stores and others are recognized at the time of shipment. Royalties and administration fees are recognized when earned, in accordance with the terms of the franchise/license agreements.

(i) Store opening expenses

Operating costs incurred prior to the opening of new stores, other than rent incurred during the fixturing period, are expensed as incurred.

FS13-6. You are the credit analyst for a company that Forzani has approached to become a major supplier of hockey equipment. Prepare a report to the manager of the credit department assessing the credit-worthiness of Forzani and recommending whether the company should extend credit. Be sure to consider the information provided in the notes to the financial statements provided in Exhibit 13–7.

FS13-7. You are considering purchasing an equity interest in Forzani. Use the information provided in Exhibit 13–7 to assess the attractiveness of such an investment. What additional information would you want to make a decision?

THE FORZANI GROUP LTD.
Consolidated Statements of Cash Flows
(in thousands)

	For the 52 weeks ended January 29, 2006	For the 52 weeks ended January 30, 2005
Cash provided by (used in) operating activities		
Net earnings	$ 13,757	$ 21,545
Items not involving cash		
Amortization	41,343	35,885
Amortization of deferred finance charges	637	828
Amortization of deferred lease inducements	(10,661)	(10,459)
Rent expense (note 7)	2,281	4,565
Stock-based compensation (note 8(d))	1,356	27
Write-down of investment and other assets	-	2,213
Future income tax expense	(876)	2,177
	47,837	56,781
Changes in non-cash elements of working capital (note 7)	(1,979)	(6,545)
	45,858	50,236
Cash provided by (used in) financing activities		
Net proceeds from issuance of share capital	320	967
Increase in long-term debt	23,573	3,563
Decrease in revolving credit facility	-	-
Debt assumed on acquisition (note 15(c))	(17,922)	-
Proceeds from deferred lease inducements	9,368	13,402
	15,339	17,932
Changes in non-cash elements of financing activities (note 7)	(2,450)	(4,375)
	12,889	13,557
Cash provided by (used in) investing activities		
Net addition of capital assets	(50,837)	(45,726)
Net addition of other assets	(3,751)	(7,112)
Acquisition of wholly-owned subsidiary (note 15)	(12,428)	(9,589)
	(67,016)	(62,427)
Changes in non-cash elements of investing activities (note 7)	1,517	1,337
	(65,499)	(61,090)
Increase (decrease) in cash	(6,752)	2,703
Net cash position, opening	26,018	23,315
Net cash position, closing	$ 19,266	$ 26,018

7. Supplementary Cash Flow Information

	2006	
Changes in non-cash elements of working capital		
Accounts receivable	$ (10,038)	$(22,257)
Inventory	24,544	(13,607)
Prepaid and other expenses	1,140	8,270
Accounts payable and accrued liabilities	(17,761)	20,363
Non-cash free rent	136	686
	$ (1,979)	$ (6,545)

3. Capital Assets

		2006			2005	
	Cost	Accumulated Amortization	Net Book Value	Cost	Accumulated Amortization	Net Book Value
Land	$ 3,173	$ -	$ 3,173	$ 3,173	$ -	$ 3,173
Buildings	20,007	3,197	16,810	17,637	2,498	15,139
Building on leased land	4,564	2,330	2,234	3,159	1,898	1,261
Furniture, fixtures, equipment and automotive	176,670	104,254	72,416	145,838	84,042	61,796
Leasehold improvements	205,519	106,595	98,924	187,141	89,177	97,964
Construction in progress	37	-	37	369	-	369
	$ 409,970	$ 216,376	$193,594	$ 357,317	$ 177,615	$179,702

4. Goodwill and Other Intangibles

		2006			2005	
	Cost	Accumulated Amortization	Net Book Value	Cost	Accumulated Amortization	Net Book Value
Goodwill	$ 47,818	$ 1,187	$ 46,631	$ 25,243	$ 1,187	$ 24,056
Trademarks/Tradenames	28,693	626	28,067	25,715	561	25,154
Non-competition agreements	4,000	2,893	1,107	5,680	2,100	3,580
	$ 80,511	$ 4,706	$ 75,805	$ 56,638	$ 3,848	$ 52,790

EXHIBIT 13–7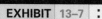

**(continued)
The Forzani Group
Ltd. Extracts from
Financial
Statements**

6. Long-term Debt

	2006	2005
G.E. term loan	$ 50,000	$ 25,000
Vendor take-back, unsecured with interest rate of prime plus 1% due August 1, 2006	4,606	4,428
Mortgages, with monthly blended payments of $79,625, including interest at rates from approximately 4.9% to 6.2%, compounded semi-annually, secured by land and buildings, expiring between September 2006 and October 2009 (each with a fifteen year amortization).	9,078	9,658
Amounts due under non-competition agreements, (payment negotiated and retired in 2006)	-	2,680
Asset retirement obligation	97	92
Other	159	-
	63,940	41,858
Less current portion	5,135	1,580
	$ 58,805	$40,278

Principal payments on the above, due in the next five years, are as follows:

2007	$ 3,810
2008	$ 523
2009	$50,519
2010	$ 529
2011	$ 557

10. Commitments

(a) The Company is committed, at January 29, 2006 to minimum payments under long-term real property and data processing hardware and software equipment leases, for the next five years, as follows:

	Gross
2007	$ 75,904
2008	$ 73,146
2009	$ 70,366
2010	$ 63,921
2011	$ 54,517

In addition, the Company may be obligated to pay percentage rent under certain of the leases.

(b) As at January 29, 2006, the Company has open letters of credit for purchases of inventory of approximately $4,579,000 (2005 - $3,108,000).

12. Contingencies and Guarantees

In the normal course of business, the Company enters into numerous agreements that may contain features that meet the Accounting Guideline ("AG")14 definition of a guarantee. AG-14 defines a guarantee to be a contract (including an indemnity) that contingently requires the Company to make payments to the guaranteed party based on (i) changes in an underlying interest rate, foreign exchange rate, equity or commodity instrument, index or other variable, that is related to an asset, a liability or an equity security of the counterparty, (ii) failure of another party to perform under an obligating agreement or (iii) failure of a third party to pay its indebtedness when due.

The Company has provided the following guarantees to third parties:

(a) The Company has provided guarantees to certain franchisees' banks pursuant to which it has agreed to buy back inventory from the franchisee in the event that the bank realizes on the related security. The Company has provided securitization guarantees for certain franchisees to repay equity loans in the event of franchisee default. The terms of the guarantees range from less than a year to the lifetime of the particular underlying franchise agreement, with an average guarantee term of 5 years. Should a franchisee default on its bank loan, the Company would be required to purchase between 50% – 100%, with a weighted average of 65%, of the franchisee's inventory up to the value of the franchisee's bank indebtedness. As at January 29, 2006, the Company's maximum exposure is $32,034,000 (2005 - $31,506,000). Should the Company be required to purchase the inventory, it is expected that the full value of the inventory would be recovered. Historically, the Company has not had to repurchase significant inventory from franchisees pursuant to these guarantees. The Company has not recognized the guarantee in its financial statements.

(b) In the ordinary course of business, the Company has agreed to indemnify its lenders under its credit facilities against certain costs or losses resulting from changes in laws and regulations and from any legal action brought against the lenders related to the use, by the Company, of the loan proceeds, or to the lenders having extended credit thereunder. These indemnifications extend for the term of the credit facilities and do not provide any limit on the maximum potential liability. Historically, the Company has not made any indemnification payments under such agreements and no amount has been accrued in the financial statements with respect to these indemnification agreements.

(c) In the ordinary course of business, the Company has provided indemnification commitments to certain counterparties in matters such as real estate leasing transactions, securitization agreements, director and officer indemnification agreements and certain purchases of assets (not inventory in the normal course). These indemnification agreements generally require the Company to compensate the counterparties for costs or losses resulting from any legal action brought against the counterparties related to the actions of the Company or any of the obligors under any of the aforementioned matters or failure of the obligors under any of the aforementioned matters to fulfill contractual obligations thereunder. The terms of these indemnification agreements will vary based on the contract and generally do not provide any limit on the maximum potential liability. Historically, the Company has not made any payments under such indemnifications and no amount has been accrued in the financial statements with respect to these indemnification commitments.

(d) Claims and suits have been brought against the Company in the ordinary course of business. In the opinion of management, all such claims and suits are adequately covered by insurance, or if not so covered, the results are not expected to materially affect the Company's financial position.

16. Segmented Financial Information

The Company operates principally in two business segments: corporately-owned and operated retail stores and as a wholesale business selling to franchisees and others. Identifiable assets, depreciation and amortization and interest expense are not disclosed by segment as they are substantially retail in nature, with the exception of accounts receivable of $58.9 million (2005 - $48.1 million), capital assets of $16.8 million (2005 – $13.4 million) and goodwill/other assets of $8.1 million (2005 - $6.9 million) which are wholesale in nature.

In determining the reportable segments, the Company considered the distinct business models of the Retail and Wholesale operations, the division of responsibilities, and the reporting to the Board of Directors.

	2006	2005
Revenues:		
Retail	$ 856,149	$718,820
Wholesale	273,255	266,234
	1,129,404	985,054
Operating Profit:		
Retail	78,236	68,433
Wholesale	23,547	27,583
	101,783	96,016
Non-segment specific administrative expenses	32,630	19,547
Operating activities before under-noted items	69,153	76,469
Amortization	41,343	35,885
Interest expense	6,145	4,447
Loss on write-down of investments	-	2,208
	47,488	42,540
Earnings before income taxes	21,665	33,929
Income tax expense	7,908	12,384
Net earnings	$ 13,757	$ 21,545

Analyzing Rogers Communications Inc.

R13-1. It is January 4, 2006. You have been approached by Rogers to replace a line of credit that had been previously supplied by another lender.

    a. What information would you want that is not provided in Rogers' annual report in Appendix A?

    b. What sources might you approach to find the additional information?

    c. Would Rogers itself be a good source of additional information? Would it be prepared to supply the additional information to you? Explain. If you were a small investor interested in buying 100 shares in Rogers, would the company be prepared to supply information to you over and above what was included in the annual report? Explain.

R13-2. Calculate the following ratios for Rogers for fiscal 2004 and 2005. Explain what these ratios tell you individually and collectively. Assume the following values on December 31, 2003: total assets = $8,465,495,000; shareholders' equity = $1,297,594,000; preferred securities = $188,000,000:

    a. gross margin

    b. profit margin

    c. return on assets

    d. return on equity

R13-3. Calculate the following ratios for Rogers for fiscal 2005 and 2004. Explain what these ratios tell you individually and collectively. Assume that accounts receivable on December 31, 2003 was $550,830,000:

    a. current ratio

    b. quick ratio

    c. accounts receivable turnover ratio

    d. average collection period of accounts receivable

R13-4. You are the credit analyst for a company that Rogers has approached to become a major supplier. Prepare a report to the manager of the credit department assessing the credit-worthiness of Rogers and recommending whether the company should extend credit.

R13-5. How much did Rogers pay in dividends to common shareholders in 2005 and 2004? Do you think that Rogers should be paying dividends to its shareholders? Explain.

R13-6. You are considering purchasing an equity interest in Rogers. Use the information provided from Rogers' financial statements to assess the attractiveness of such an investment. You should analyze and investigate all aspects of Rogers' business when responding to this question.

R13-7. Use the information provided in Note 17 to Rogers' 2005 annual report to assess the performance of the company's business segments. Which segment has performed best in the last two years and which has performed worst? What additional information would you want to conduct a more comprehensive assessment of the performance of the business segments? You can also use the information Figure 13–3 in this chapter.

ENDNOTES

1. Clarence Byrd, Ida Chen, and Joshua Smith, *Financial Reporting in Canada*, 30th Edition. The Virtual Professional Library. 2005.

2. Extracted from BCE Inc.'s 2004 annual report.

3. Clarence Byrd, Ida Chen, and Joshua Smith, *Financial Reporting in Canada*, 30th Edition. The Virtual Professional Library. 2005.

4. Extracted from Tembec Inc.'s 2004 annual report.

5. Extracted from Stelco Inc.'s 2005 annual report.

6. Extracted from Rogers Communications Inc.'s 2005 annual report

7. Extracted from Sobeys Inc.'s 2005 annual report.

8. Extracted from Le Chateau Inc.'s fiscal 2005 annual report.

9. Extracted from Leon's Furniture Ltd.'s 2005 annual report.

10. William R. Scott, *Financial Accounting Theory, Second Edition*. Prentice Hall, 2002.

11. Extracted from The Forzani Group Ltd.'s fiscal 2006 annual report and from www.forzani-group.com.

APPENDIX A

you...

Rogers Communications Inc.
2005 Annual Report

ROGERS COMMUNICATIONS INC. AT A GLANCE ▶

Management's Responsibility for Financial Reporting

DECEMBER 31, 2005

The accompanying consolidated financial statements of Rogers Communications Inc. and its subsidiaries and all the information in Management's Discussion and Analysis are the responsibility of management and have been approved by the Board of Directors.

The financial statements have been prepared by management in accordance with Canadian generally accepted accounting principles. The financial statements include certain amounts that are based on the best estimates and judgments of management and in their opinion present fairly, in all material respects, Rogers Communications Inc.'s financial position, results of operations and cash flows. Management has prepared the financial information presented elsewhere in Management's Discussion and Analysis and has ensured that it is consistent with the financial statements.

Management of Rogers Communications Inc., in furtherance of the integrity of the financial statements, has developed and maintains a system of internal controls, which is supported by the internal audit function. Management believes the internal controls provide reasonable assurance that transactions are properly authorized and recorded, financial records are reliable and form a proper basis for the preparation of financial statements and that Rogers Communications Inc.'s assets are properly accounted for and safeguarded. The internal control processes include management's communication to employees of policies that govern ethical business conduct.

The Board of Directors is responsible for overseeing management's responsibility for financial reporting and is ultimately responsible for reviewing and approving the financial statements. The Board carries out this responsibility through its Audit Committee.

The Audit Committee meets periodically with management, as well as the internal and external auditors, to discuss internal controls over the financial reporting process, auditing matters and financial reporting issues; to satisfy itself that each party is properly discharging its responsibilities; and, to review Management's Discussion and Analysis, the financial statements and the external auditors' report. The Audit Committee reports its findings to the Board for consideration when approving the financial statements for issuance to the shareholders. The Committee also considers, for review by the Board and approval by the shareholders, the engagement or re-appointment of the external auditors.

The financial statements have been audited by KPMG LLP, the external auditors, in accordance with Canadian generally accepted auditing standards on behalf of the shareholders. KPMG LLP has full and free access to the Audit Committee.

February 7, 2006

Edward "Ted" S. Rogers, OC
President and Chief Executive Officer

Alan D. Horn. CA
Vice President, Finance and Chief Financial Officer

Auditors' Report to the Shareholders

We have audited the consolidated balance sheets of Rogers Communications Inc. as at December 31, 2005 and 2004 and the consolidated statements of income, deficit and cash flows for the years then ended. These financial statements are the responsibility of the Company's management. Our responsibility is to express an opinion on these financial statements based on our audits.

We conducted our audits in accordance with Canadian generally accepted auditing standards. Those standards require that we plan and perform an audit to obtain reasonable assurance whether the financial statements are free of material misstatement. An audit includes examining, on a test basis, evidence supporting the amounts and disclosures in the financial statements. An audit also includes assessing the accounting principles used and significant estimates made by management, as well as evaluating the overall financial statement presentation.

In our opinion, these consolidated financial statements present fairly, in all material respects, the financial position of the Company as at December 31, 2005 and 2004 and the results of its operations and its cash flows for the years then ended in accordance with Canadian generally accepted accounting principles.

KPMG LLP

Chartered Accountants
Toronto, Canada
February 7, 2006, except as to notes 23 and 24 which are as of March 1, 2006

Consolidated Balance Sheets

(IN THOUSANDS OF DOLLARS)

December 31, 2005 and 2004	2005	2004
Assets		
Current assets:		
Cash and cash equivalents	$ —	$ 243,993
Accounts receivable, net of allowance for doubtful		
accounts of $98,464 (2004 — $94,035)	890,701	673,936
Other current assets (note 4)	297,846	260,517
Future tax asset (note 14)	113,150	—
	1,301,697	1,178,446
Property, plant and equipment (note 5)	6,151,526	5,486,837
Goodwill (note 6(a))	3,035,787	3,388,687
Intangible assets (note 6(b))	2,627,466	2,855,689
Investments (note 7)	138,212	139,170
Deferred charges (note 8)	129,119	134,466
Future tax asset (note 14)	347,252	—
Other long-term assets (note 9)	103,230	89,443
	$ 13,834,289	$ 13,272,738
Liabilities and Shareholders' Equity		
Current liabilities:		
Bank advances, arising from outstanding cheques	$ 103,881	$ —
Accounts payable and accrued liabilities	1,411,045	1,428,296
Current portion of long-term debt (note 11)	286,139	618,236
Current portion of derivative instruments (note 12)	14,180	58,856
Unearned revenue	176,266	152,723
	1,991,511	2,258,111
Long-term debt (notes 2(s)(i) and 11)	7,453,412	7,922,861
Derivative instruments (note 12)	787,369	641,545
Other long-term liabilities	74,382	64,887
	10,306,674	10,887,404
Shareholders' equity (notes 2(s)(i) and 13)	3,527,615	2,385,334
	$ 13,834,289	$ 13,272,738

Commitments (note 20)
Guarantees (note 21)
Contingent liabilities (note 22)
Canadian and United States accounting policy differences (note 23)
Subsequent events (note 24)

See accompanying notes to consolidated financial statements.

On behalf of the Board:

Edward "Ted" S. Rogers
Director

Ronald D. Besse
Director

Consolidated Statements of Income

(IN THOUSANDS OF DOLLARS, EXCEPT PER SHARE AMOUNTS)

Years ended December 31, 2005 and 2004	2005	2004
Operating revenue	$ 7,482,154	$ 5,608,249
Cost of sales	1,296,148	797,857
Sales and marketing expenses	1,122,348	883,622
Operating, general and administrative expenses	2,853,613	2,188,214
Integration expenses (note 3(e))	66,476	4,415
Depreciation and amortization	1,478,011	1,092,551
Operating income	665,558	641,590
Interest on long-term debt (note 2(s)(i))	710,079	575,998
	(44,521)	65,592
Loss on repayment of long-term debt (note 11(f))	(11,242)	(28,210)
Foreign exchange gain (loss) (note 2(g))	35,477	(67,555)
Change in fair value of derivative instruments	(25,168)	26,774
Gain on dilution on issue of shares by a subsidiary	—	15,502
Other income, net	2,951	3,783
Income (loss) before income taxes and non-controlling interest	(42,503)	15,886
Income tax expense (reduction) (note 14):		
Current	10,730	3,447
Future	(8,575)	—
	2,155	3,447
Income (loss) before non-controlling interest	(44,658)	12,439
Non-controlling interest	—	(79,581)
Loss for the year (note 2(s)(i))	$ (44,658)	$ (67,142)
Loss per share (note 15):		
Basic	$ (0.15)	$ (0.28)
Diluted	(0.15)	(0.28)

See accompanying notes to consolidated financial statements.

Consolidated Statements of Deficit

(IN THOUSANDS OF DOLLARS)

Years ended December 31, 2005 and 2004	2005	2004
Deficit, beginning of year:		
As previously reported	$ (519,441)	$ (339,436)
Change in accounting policy related to stock-based compensation (note 2(p))	—	(7,025)
Change in accounting policy related to Convertible Preferred Securities (note 2(s)(i))	—	(81,786)
As restated	(519,441)	(428,247)
Loss for the year	(44,658)	(67,142)
Dividends on Class A Voting and Class B Non-Voting shares	(37,449)	(24,052)
Deficit, end of year	$ (601,548)	$ (519,441)

See accompanying notes to consolidated financial statements.

A-5

ROGERS COMMUNICATIONS INC. 2005 ANNUAL REPORT

Consolidated Statements of Cash Flows

(IN THOUSANDS OF DOLLARS)

Years ended December 31, 2005 and 2004	2005	2004
Cash provided by (used in):		
Operating activities:		
Loss for the year	$ (44,658)	$ (67,142)
Adjustments to reconcile loss to net cash flows from operating activities:		
Depreciation and amortization	1,478,011	1,092,551
Program rights and video rental inventory depreciation	90,184	88,328
Future income taxes	(8,575)	—
Non-controlling interest	—	79,581
Unrealized foreign exchange loss (gain)	(34,964)	66,943
Change in fair value of derivative instruments	25,168	(26,774)
Loss on repayment of long-term debt	11,242	28,210
Stock-based compensation expense	38,949	15,389
Accreted interest on Convertible Preferred Securities (note 2(s)(i))	17,783	20,924
Amortization on fair value increment of long-term debt and derivatives	(14,907)	—
Other	(6,818)	7,009
	1,551,415	1,305,019
Change in non-cash working capital (note 10(a))	(324,008)	(62,090)
	1,227,407	1,242,929
Investing activities:		
Additions to property, plant and equipment ("PP&E")	(1,353,796)	(1,054,938)
Change in non-cash working capital related to PP&E	(37,883)	59,994
Cash and cash equivalents acquired on acquisition of Rogers Telecom Holdings Inc. (note 3(a))	43,801	—
Acquisition of Rogers Wireless Communications Inc. (note 3(b))	—	(1,772,840)
Acquisition of Microcell Telecommunications Inc., net of cash acquired (note 3(b))	(51,684)	(1,148,637)
Investment in Toronto Blue Jays Baseball Club (note 7(a))	—	(99,235)
Other acquisitions	(38,092)	(66,700)
Other	2,177	(2,566)
	(1,435,477)	(4,084,922)
Financing activities:		
Issue of long-term debt	1,369,208	8,982,443
Repayment of long-term debt	(1,509,577)	(6,092,721)
Proceeds on termination of cross-currency interest rate exchange agreements	402,191	58,416
Payment on termination of cross-currency interest rate exchange agreements	(470,825)	(64,602)
Financing costs incurred	(4,940)	(66,071)
Issue of capital stock	100,348	302,231
Dividends paid on Class A Voting and Class B Non-Voting shares	(26,209)	(23,422)
	(139,804)	3,096,274
Increase (decrease) in cash and cash equivalents	(347,874)	254,281
Cash and cash equivalents (deficiency), beginning of year	243,993	(10,288)
Cash and cash equivalents (deficiency), end of year	$ (103,881)	$ 243,993

Cash and cash equivalents (deficiency) are defined as cash and short-term deposits, which have an original maturity of less than 90 days, less bank advances.

For supplemental cash flow information and disclosure of non-cash transactions see note 10(b) and (c).

See accompanying notes to consolidated financial statements.

Notes to Consolidated Financial Statements

(TABULAR AMOUNTS IN THOUSANDS OF DOLLARS, EXCEPT PER SHARE AMOUNTS)
FOR THE YEARS ENDED DECEMBER 31, 2005 and 2004

Note 1. **Nature of the business:**

Rogers Communications Inc. ("RCI") is a Canadian communications company, carrying on business on a national basis, engaged in cable television, high-speed Internet access, cable telephony and video retailing through its wholly owned subsidiary, Rogers Cable Inc. ("Cable"); wireless voice, messaging and data services through its wholly owned subsidiary, Rogers Wireless Communications Inc. ("Wireless"); radio and television broadcasting, televised home shopping, publishing, and sports entertainment through its wholly owned subsidiary, Rogers Media Inc. ("Media"); and circuit-switch telephony, data networking, and high-speed Internet access through its wholly owned subsidiary, Rogers Telecom Holdings Inc. ("Telecom"). RCI and its subsidiary companies are collectively referred to herein as the "Company".

Note 2. **Significant accounting policies:**

(a) **BASIS OF PRESENTATION:**
The consolidated financial statements are prepared in accordance with Canadian generally accepted accounting principles ("GAAP") and differ in certain significant respects from United States GAAP as described in note 23.

The consolidated financial statements include the accounts of RCI and its subsidiary companies. For the period from January 1, 2004 to October 13, 2004, the non-controlling interest of Wireless represented approximately 44.7% of Wireless' net income, after dilutions of the Company's ownership over that period. For the period from October 14, 2004 to December 31, 2004, the non-controlling interest represented approximately 11.2% of Wireless' net income, after dilutions of the Company's ownership over that period. Subsequent to December 31, 2004, there was no non-controlling interest in Wireless. Intercompany transactions and balances are eliminated on consolidation. When RCI's subsidiaries issue additional common shares to unrelated parties, RCI accounts for these issuances as if RCI had sold a portion of its interest in that subsidiary and, accordingly, records a gain or loss on dilution of RCI's interest.

Investments over which the Company is able to exercise significant influence are accounted for by the equity method. Other investments are recorded at cost. Investments are written down when there is evidence that a decline in value that is other than temporary has occurred.

Certain comparative figures have been reclassified to conform with the current year's presentation.

(b) **PROPERTY, PLANT AND EQUIPMENT:**
Property, plant and equipment ("PP&E") are recorded at purchase cost. During construction of new assets, direct costs plus a portion of applicable overhead costs are capitalized. Repairs and maintenance expenditures are charged to operating expenses as incurred.

The cost of the initial cable subscriber installation is capitalized. Costs of all other cable connections and disconnections are expensed, except for direct incremental installation costs related to reconnect Cable customers, to the extent of reconnect installation revenues. Deferred reconnect revenues and expenses are amortized over the related service period of approximately four years.

(c)   **DEPRECIATION:**

PP&E are depreciated annually over their estimated useful lives as follows:

Asset	Basis	Rate
Buildings	Mainly diminishing balance	5% to 6²/₃%
Towers, head-ends and transmitters	Straight line	6²/₃% to 25%
Distribution cable, subscriber drops and network equipment	Straight line	5% to 33¹/₃%
Wireless network radio base station equipment	Straight line	12¹/₂% to 14¹/₃%
Computer equipment and software	Straight line	14¹/₃% to 33¹/₃%
Customer equipment	Straight line	20% to 33¹/₃%
Leasehold improvements	Straight line	Over shorter of estimated useful life and term of lease
Other equipment	Mainly diminishing balance	20% to 33¹/₃%

(d)   **ASSET RETIREMENT OBLIGATIONS:**

Asset retirement obligations are legal obligations associated with the retirement of long-lived tangible assets that result from their acquisition, lease, construction, development or normal operations. The Company records the estimated fair value of a liability for an asset retirement obligation in the year in which it is incurred and when a reasonable estimate of fair value can be made. The fair value of a liability for an asset retirement obligation is the amount at which that liability could be settled in a current transaction between willing parties, that is, other than in a forced or liquidation transaction and, in the absence of observable market transactions, is determined as the present value of expected cash flows. The Company subsequently allocates the asset retirement cost to expense using a systematic and rational method over the asset's useful life, and records the accretion of the liability as a charge to operating expenses.

(e)   **LONG-LIVED ASSETS:**

Long-lived assets, including PP&E and intangible assets with finite useful lives, are amortized over their useful lives. The Company reviews long-lived assets for impairment annually or more frequently if events or changes in circumstances indicate that the carrying amount may not be recoverable. If the sum of the undiscounted future cash flows expected to result from the use and eventual disposition of a group of assets is less than its carrying amount, it is considered to be impaired. An impairment loss is measured as the amount by which the carrying amount of the group of assets exceeds its fair value. At December 31, 2005 and 2004, no impairments in the carrying value of these assets existed.

(f)   **GOODWILL AND INTANGIBLE ASSETS:**

(i)   **Goodwill:**

Goodwill is the residual amount that results when the purchase price of an acquired business exceeds the sum of the amounts allocated to the tangible and intangible assets acquired, less liabilities assumed, based on their fair values. When the Company enters into a business combination, the purchase method of accounting is used. Goodwill is assigned as of the date of the business combination to reporting units that are expected to benefit from the business combination.

Goodwill is not amortized but instead is tested for impairment annually or more frequently if events or changes in circumstances indicate that the asset might be impaired. The impairment test is carried out in two steps. In the first step, the carrying amount of the reporting unit, including goodwill, is compared with its fair value. When the fair value of the reporting unit exceeds its carrying amount, goodwill of the reporting unit is not considered to be impaired and the second step of the impairment test is unnecessary. The second step is carried out when the carrying amount of a reporting unit exceeds its fair value, in which case, the implied fair value of the reporting unit's goodwill, determined in the same manner as the value of goodwill is determined in a business combination, is compared with its carrying amount to measure the amount of the impairment loss, if any.

(ii)   **Intangible assets:**

Intangible assets acquired in a business combination are recorded at their fair values. Intangible assets with finite lives are amortized over their estimated useful lives and are tested for impairment, as described in note 2(e). Intangible assets having an indefinite life, such as spectrum licences, are not amortized but instead are tested for impairment on an annual or more frequent basis by comparing their fair value with book value. An impairment loss on indefinite life intangible assets is recognized when the carrying amount of the asset exceeds its fair value.

Intangible assets with determinable lives are amortized on a straight-line basis annually over their estimated useful lives as follows:

Subscriber bases	$2\frac{1}{4}$ to $4\frac{2}{3}$ years
Brand names – Rogers	20 years
Brand names – Fido	5 years
Dealer networks	4 years
Wholesale agreements	38 months
Roaming agreements	12 years
Player contracts	5 years

The Company has tested goodwill and intangible assets with indefinite lives for impairment during 2005 and 2004 and determined that no impairment in the carrying value of these assets existed.

(g)   FOREIGN CURRENCY TRANSLATION:

Monetary assets and liabilities denominated in a foreign currency are translated into Canadian dollars at the exchange rate in effect at the balance sheet date and non-monetary assets and liabilities and related depreciation and amortization expenses are translated at the historical exchange rate. Revenue and expenses, other than depreciation and amortization, are translated at the average rate for the month in which the transaction was recorded. The accounting for the effect of cross-currency interest rate exchange agreements used to hedge long-term debt is described in note 2(m). Exchange gains or losses on translating long-term debt are recognized in the consolidated statements of income. In 2005, foreign exchange gains related to the translation of long-term debt totalled $33.3 million (2004 – losses of $66.9 million).

(h)   DEFERRED CHARGES:

The costs of obtaining bank and other debt financings are deferred and amortized on a straight-line basis over the life of the debt to which they relate.

During the development and pre-operating phases of new products and businesses, related incremental costs are deferred and amortized on a straight-line basis over periods of up to five years.

(i)   INVENTORIES:

Inventories are primarily valued at the lower of cost, on a first-in, first-out basis, and net realizable value. Video rental inventory, which includes videocassettes, DVDs and video games, is depreciated to its estimated residual value. The residual value of the video rental inventory is recorded as a charge to operating expense upon the sale of the video rental inventory. Depreciation of video rental inventory is charged to cost of sales on a diminishing-balance basis over a six month period.

(j)   PENSION BENEFITS:

The Company accrues its pension plan obligations as employees render the services necessary to earn the pension. The Company uses the current settlement discount rate to measure the accrued pension benefit obligation and uses the corridor method to amortize actuarial gains or losses (such as changes in actuarial assumptions and experience gains or losses) over the average remaining service life of the employees. Under the corridor method, amortization is recorded only if the accumulated net actuarial gains or losses exceed 10% of the greater of accrued pension benefit obligation and the value of the plan assets at the beginning of the year.

The Company uses the following methods and assumptions for pension accounting:

(i)   The cost of pensions is actuarially determined using the projected benefit method prorated on service and management's best estimate of expected plan investment performance, salary escalation, compensation levels at the time of retirement and retirement ages of employees. Changes in these assumptions would impact future pension expense.

(ii)   For the purpose of calculating the expected return on plan assets, those assets are valued at fair value.

(iii)   Past service costs from plan amendments are amortized on a straight-line basis over the average remaining service period of employees.

A-9

ROGERS COMMUNICATIONS INC. 2005 ANNUAL REPORT

(k) **ACQUIRED PROGRAM RIGHTS:**

Acquired program rights are carried at the lower of cost less accumulated amortization, and net realizable value. Acquired program rights and the related liabilities are recorded when the licence period begins and the program is available for use. The cost of acquired program rights is amortized over the expected performance period of the related programs. Net realizable value of acquired program rights is assessed using the industry standard daypart methodology.

(l) **INCOME TAXES:**

Future income tax assets and liabilities are recognized for the future income tax consequences attributable to differences between the financial statement carrying amounts of existing assets and liabilities and their respective tax bases. Future income tax assets and liabilities are measured using enacted or substantively enacted tax rates expected to apply to taxable income in the years in which those temporary differences are expected to be recovered or settled. A valuation allowance is recorded against any future income tax asset if it is not more likely than not that the asset will be realized. Income tax expense is the sum of the Company's provision for current income taxes and the difference between opening and ending balances of future income tax assets and liabilities.

(m) **DERIVATIVE INSTRUMENTS:**

The Company uses derivative financial instruments to manage risks from fluctuations in exchange rates and interest rates. These instruments include cross-currency interest rate exchange agreements, interest rate exchange agreements, foreign exchange forward contracts and, from time-to-time, foreign exchange option agreements. All such instruments are only used for risk management purposes.

Effective January 1, 2004, the Company adopted Accounting Guideline 13, "Hedging Relationships" ("AcG-13"), which established new criteria for hedge accounting for all hedging relationships in effect. Effective January 1, 2004, the Company re-assessed all relationships to determine whether the criteria for hedge accounting were met, and applied the new guidance on a prospective basis. The Company formally documents the relationship between derivative instruments and the hedged items, as well as its risk management objective and strategy for undertaking various hedge transactions. At the instrument's inception, the Company also formally assesses whether the derivatives are highly effective at reducing or modifying currency risk related to the future anticipated interest and principal cash outflows associated with the hedged item. Effectiveness requires a high correlation of changes in fair values or cash flows between the hedged item and the hedging item. On a quarterly basis, the Company confirms that the derivative instruments continue to be highly effective at reducing or modifying interest rate or foreign exchange risk associated with the hedged items. Derivative instruments that meet these criteria are carried at their intrinsic value.

For those instruments that do not meet the above criteria, variations in their fair value are marked-to-market on a current basis, with the resulting gains or losses recorded in or charged against income.

See note 12 for a discussion of the impact of the adoption of this standard in 2004.

(n) **REVENUE RECOGNITION:**

The Company offers certain products and services as part of multiple deliverable arrangements. The Company divides multiple deliverable arrangements into separate units of accounting. Components of multiple deliverable arrangements are separately accounted for provided the delivered elements have stand-alone value to the customers and the fair value of any undelivered elements can be objectively and reliably determined. Consideration for these units is then measured and allocated amongst the accounting units based upon their fair values and then the Company's relevant revenue recognition policies are applied to them. The Company recognizes revenue once persuasive evidence of an arrangement exists, delivery has occurred or services have been rendered, fees are fixed and determinable and collectibility is reasonably assured.

The Company's principal sources of revenue and recognition of these revenues for financial statement purposes are as follows:

(i)   Monthly subscriber fees in connection with wireless and wireline services, cable, telephony, Internet services, rental of equipment, network services, and media subscriptions are recorded as revenue on a pro rata basis over the month as the service is provided;

(ii)   Revenue from wireless airtime, roaming, long distance and optional services, pay-per-view and video-on-demand services, video rentals, and other sales of products are recorded as revenue as the services or products are delivered;

(iii)   Revenue from the sale of wireless and cable equipment is recorded when the equipment is delivered and accepted by the independent dealer or customer. Equipment subsidies provided to new and existing subscribers are recorded as a reduction of equipment revenues upon activation of the service;

(iv)   Installation fees and activation fees charged to subscribers do not meet the criteria as a separate unit of accounting. As a result, these fees are recorded as part of equipment revenue or, in the case of Cable and Telecom, are deferred and amortized over the related service period, as appropriate. The related service period for Cable is determined to be approximately four years while that of Telecom ranges from 26 to 33 months, based on subscriber disconnects, transfers of service and moves. Incremental direct installation costs related to re-connects are deferred to the extent of deferred installation fees and amortized over the same period as these related installation fees. New connect installation costs are capitalized to PP&E and amortized over the useful life of the related assets;

(v)   Advertising revenue is recorded in the period the advertising airs on the Company's radio or television stations and the period in which advertising is featured in the Company's media publications;

(vi)   Monthly subscription revenues received by television stations for subscriptions from cable and satellite providers are recorded in the month in which they are earned;

(vii)   The Blue Jays' revenue, which is composed primarily of home game admission and concession revenue, is recognized as the related games are played during the baseball season. Revenue from radio and television agreements is recorded at the time the related games are aired. The Blue Jays also receive revenue from the Major League Baseball ("MLB") Revenue Sharing Agreement which distributes funds to and from member clubs, based on each club's revenues. This revenue is recognized in the season in which it is earned, when the amount is estimable and collectibility is reasonably assured; and

(viii)   Multi-product discounts are incurred as Cable, Wireless, Media and Telecom products and services are provided, and are charged directly to the revenue for the products and services to which they relate.

Unearned revenue includes subscriber deposits, installation fees and amounts received from subscribers related to services and subscriptions to be provided in future periods.

(o)   **SUBSCRIBER ACQUISITION COSTS:**
Except as described in note 2(n)(iv), the Company expenses the costs related to the acquisition of new subscribers upon activation and costs related to the retention of existing subscribers are expensed as incurred.

(p)   **STOCK-BASED COMPENSATION AND OTHER STOCK-BASED PAYMENTS:**
Effective January 1, 2004, Canadian GAAP requires the Company to calculate the fair value of stock-based compensation awarded to employees and to expense the fair value over the vesting period of the stock options. In accordance with the transition rules, the Company adopted the standard retroactively to January 1, 2002 without restating prior periods. The Company determined the fair value of stock options granted to employees since January 1, 2002 using the Black-Scholes option pricing model and recorded an adjustment to opening retained earnings in the amount of $7.0 million, representing the expense for the 2003 and 2002 fiscal years, with a corresponding increase in contributed surplus.

The Company accounts for all stock-based payments to non-employees and employee awards that are direct awards of stock, call for settlement in cash or other assets, or are stock appreciation rights that call for settlement by the issuance of equity instruments using the fair value-based method. The estimated fair value is amortized to expense over the vesting period.

Stock-based awards that are settled in cash or may be settled in cash at the option of employees or directors, including restricted stock units, are recorded as liabilities. The measurement of the liability and compensation cost for these awards is based on the intrinsic value of the awards. Compensation cost for the awards is recorded in operating income over the vesting period of the award. Changes in the Company's payment obligation prior to the settlement date are recorded in operating income over the vesting period. The payment amount is established for these awards on the date of exercise of the award by the employee.

The Company also has an employee share accumulation plan. Under the terms of the plan, participating employees with the Company can contribute a specified percentage of their regular earnings through regular payroll deductions. The designated administrator of the plan then purchases, on a monthly basis, Class B Non-Voting shares of the Company on the open market on behalf of the employee. At the end of each quarter, the Company makes a contribution of 25% of the employee's contribution in the quarter. Certain employees are eligible for a higher percentage match by the Company. The administrator then uses this amount to purchase additional shares of the Company on behalf of the employee. The Company records its contribution as compensation expense. The share accumulation plan is more fully described in note 13.

The Company has a directors' deferred share unit plan, under which directors of the Company are entitled to elect to receive their remuneration in deferred share units. Upon resignation as a director, these deferred share units will be redeemed by the Company not later than December 15 of the year following resignation as a director at the then-current market price of the Class B Non-Voting shares. Compensation expense is recognized in the amount of the directors' remuneration as their services are rendered. The related accrued liability is adjusted to the market price of the Class B Non-Voting shares at each balance sheet date and the related adjustment is recorded in operating income. At December 31, 2005, a total of 132,698 (2004 – 160,372) deferred share units were outstanding. At December 31, 2004, as a result of the acquisition of Wireless, the Company converted 16,517 Wireless deferred share units into 28,905 RCI deferred share units (note 3(b)).

(q) **EARNINGS PER SHARE:**

The Company uses the treasury stock method for calculating diluted earnings per share. The diluted earnings per share calculation considers the impact of employee stock options and other potentially dilutive instruments, as described in note 15.

(r) **USE OF ESTIMATES:**

The preparation of financial statements requires management to make estimates and assumptions that affect the reported amounts of assets and liabilities and disclosure of contingent assets and liabilities at the date of the financial statements and the reported amounts of revenue and expenses during the year. Actual results could differ from those estimates.

Key areas of estimation, where management has made difficult, complex or subjective judgments, often as a result of matters that are inherently uncertain, include the allowance for doubtful accounts, the ability to use income tax loss carryforwards and other future tax assets, capitalization of internal labour and overhead, useful lives of depreciable assets, discount rates and expected returns on plan assets affecting pension expense and the pension asset and the recoverability of long-lived assets, goodwill and intangible assets, which require estimates of future cash flows. For business combinations, key areas of estimation and judgment include the allocation of the purchase price, related integration and severance costs, as well as the determination of useful lives for amortizable intangible assets acquired, including subscriber bases, brand names, roaming agreements, dealer network and wholesale agreements.

Significant changes in the assumptions, including those with respect to future business plans and cash flows, could materially change the recorded amounts.

(s) **ADOPTION OF NEW ACCOUNTING PRONOUNCEMENTS:**

(i) **Financial instruments – disclosure and presentation:**

On January 1, 2005, the Company adopted the amended provisions of The Canadian Institute of Chartered Accountants' ("CICA") Handbook Section 3860, Financial Instruments – Disclosure and Presentation ("CICA 3860") with retroactive application and, as a result, has reflected the impact of this new accounting policy in the consolidated balance sheet as at December 31, 2005 and 2004 and in the consolidated statements of income and cash flows for each of the years in the two-year period ended December 31, 2005. CICA 3860 was amended to provide guidance for classifying as liabilities certain financial obligations of a fixed amount that may be settled, at the issuer's option, by a variable number of the issuer's own equity instruments. Any financial instruments issued by an enterprise that give the issuer unrestricted rights to settle the principal amount for cash or the equivalent value of its own equity instruments are no longer presented as equity.

As a result of retroactively adopting CICA 3860, the Company reclassified the liability portion of its Convertible Preferred Securities to long-term debt and the related interest expense has been included as interest expense in the consolidated statements of income (notes 11 and 13).

These changes resulted in the following adjustments to the 2004 comparative amounts:

	2004
Increase (decrease):	
Consolidated balance sheet:	
Liabilities:	
Long-term debt	$ 490,710
Shareholders' equity:	
Convertible Preferred Securities	(388,000)
Deficit, beginning of year	81,786
Deficit, end of year	102,710
Consolidated statement of income:	
Interest on long-term debt	53,924
Loss for the year	(53,924)
Consolidated statement of cash flows:	
Cash provided by operating activities	(33,000)
Cash provided by financing activities	33,000

These changes do not affect loss per share since the related interest expense has, in prior years, been deducted from the loss for the year in determining loss per share.

(ii)   Consolidation of variable interest entities:

Effective January 1, 2005, the Company adopted Accounting Guideline 15, "Consolidation of Variable Interest Entities" ("AcG-15"). AcG-15 addresses the application of consolidation principles to certain entities that are subject to control on a basis other than ownership of voting interests. AcG-15 addresses when an enterprise should include the assets, liabilities and results of activities of such an entity in its consolidated financial statements. There was no impact to the consolidated financial statements of the Company as a result of adopting this standard since the Company does not have an interest in any entities subject to control on a basis other than ownership of voting interests.

(iii)   Arrangements containing a lease:

CICA Emerging Issues Committee ("EIC") Abstract 150, Determining whether an Arrangement Contains a Lease ("EIC 150"), addresses a situation where an entity enters into an arrangement, comprising a transaction that does not take the legal form of a lease but conveys a right to use a tangible asset in return for a payment or series of payments. EIC 150 was effective for arrangements entered into or modified after January 1, 2005. There was no impact to the consolidated financial statements of the Company as a result of the adoption of this new standard since the Company has not entered into such arrangements.

(t)   RECENT CANADIAN ACCOUNTING PRONOUNCEMENTS:

(i)   Non-monetary transactions:

In 2005, the CICA issued Handbook Section 3831 Non-monetary transactions ("CICA 3831"), replacing Section 3830, Non-monetary transactions. CICA 3831 requires that an asset exchanged or transferred in a non-monetary transaction must be measured at its fair value except when: the transaction lacks commercial substance; the transaction is an exchange of a product or property held for sale in the ordinary course of business for a product or property to be sold in the same line of business to facilitate sales to customers other than the parties to the exchange; neither the fair value of the asset received nor the fair value of the asset given up is reliably measurable; or the transaction is a non-monetary non-reciprocal transfer to owners that represents a spin-off or other form of restructuring or liquidation. In these cases the transaction must be measured at the carrying value. The new requirements are effective for transactions occurring on or after January 1, 2006. The Company does not expect that this new standard will have a material impact on its consolidated financial statements.

(ii)   Financial Instruments:

In 2005, the CICA issued Handbook Section 3855, Financial Instruments – Recognition and Measurement, Handbook Section 1530, Comprehensive Income, and Handbook Section 3865, Hedges. The new standards will be effective for interim and annual financial statements commencing in 2007. Earlier adoption is permitted. The new standards will require presentation of a separate statement of comprehensive income. Derivative financial instruments will be recorded in the balance sheet at fair value and the changes in fair value of derivatives designated as cash flow hedges will be reported in comprehensive income. The existing hedging principles of AcG-13 will be substantially unchanged. The Company is assessing the impact of these new standards.

Note 3. **Business combinations:**

(a) 2005 ACQUISITIONS:

The Company has completed the following acquisitions during the year which were accounted for by the purchase method:

(i) Call-Net Enterprises Inc.:

On July 1, 2005, the Company acquired 100% of Call-Net Enterprises Inc. ("Call-Net") in a share-for-share transaction (the "Call-Net Acquisition"). Call-Net, primarily through its wholly owned subsidiary Sprint Canada Inc., is a Canadian integrated communications solutions provider of home phone, wireless, long distance and Internet access services to households, and local, long distance, toll free, enhanced voice, data and Internet access services to businesses across Canada. The operations of Call-Net were consolidated with those of the Company as of July 1, 2005.

Under the terms of the arrangement, holders of common shares and Class B Non-Voting shares of Call-Net received a fixed exchange ratio of one Class B Non-Voting share of the Company for each 4.25 common shares and/ or Class B Non-Voting shares of Call-Net held by them. All outstanding options to purchase Call-Net shares vested immediately prior to the Call-Net acquisition. In addition, each holder of outstanding Call-Net options received fully-vested options of the Company using the same 4.25 exchange ratio. As a result, 8.5 million Class B Non-Voting shares and 0.4 million options were issued as consideration. The Class B Non-Voting shares issued were valued at the average market price over the period two days before and two days after the May 11, 2005 announcement date of the transaction. This resulted in share consideration valued at $316.0 million. The options issued as consideration were valued at $8.5 million using the Black-Scholes model.

Also under the terms of the arrangement, the only outstanding preferred share of Call-Net was deemed to be redeemed by Call-Net for $1.00, being the redemption price thereof. Subsequently, Call-Net was renamed Rogers Telecom Holdings Inc. and Sprint Canada Inc. was renamed Rogers Telecom Inc.

Prior to completion of the acquisition, the Company began to develop a plan to restructure and integrate the operations of Call-Net. As a result of the restructuring and integration, a liability of $3.7 million was recorded in the acquisition balance sheet of Call-Net for severance and other employee related costs. Including direct incremental acquisition costs of approximately $4.0 million, the aggregate purchase price for the acquisition of Call-Net shares and options totalled $328.5 million.

The allocation of the purchase price is preliminary and subject to finalization of the restructuring and integration plan. The allocation of the purchase price reflects management's best estimate at the date of preparing these financial statements. The purchase price allocation is expected to be finalized by early 2006.

The Call-Net subscriber bases acquired is being amortized over its weighted average estimated useful life of 29 months. A change in the fair value of the Call-Net subscriber bases of $10.0 million acquired would have impacted depreciation and amortization expense and net income by $2.1 million for the year ended December 31, 2005. An increase in the weighted average useful life of six months would have reduced depreciation and amortization expense and decreased the loss for the year by approximately $4.3 million for the year ended December 31, 2005. A decrease in the weighted average useful life of six months would have increased depreciation and amortization expense and increased the loss for the year by approximately $6.6 million for the year ended December 31, 2005.

As at December 31, 2005, the purchase price allocation was adjusted upon revisions of the valuation of the intangible assets acquired and for a severance accrual. Amortization will be adjusted on a prospective basis over the estimated remaining useful life of the intangible assets. This will result in an increase in amortization expense of $7.6 million, on an annualized basis, over the remaining useful life relative to that originally determined under the preliminary valuation.

Goodwill related to the Call-Net Acquisition has been assigned to the Telecom reporting segment.

(ii)   Other:

On January 31, 2005, the Company completed the acquisition of Rogers Centre, a multi-purpose stadium located in Toronto, Canada for a purchase price of approximately $26.6 million, including acquisition costs, plus $4.8 million of assumed liabilities. The purchase price has been allocated on a preliminary basis to working capital and property, plant and equipment pending finalizing the valuation of its tangible and intangible assets. The operations of Rogers Centre were consolidated with those of the Company as of January 31, 2005.

Two other acquisitions occurred during 2005 for cash consideration of approximately $11.7 million.

(b)   2004 ACQUISITIONS:

The Company completed the following acquisitions during 2004 which were accounted for by the purchase method:

(i)   Wireless minority interests:

On October 13, 2004, the Company acquired the 34% interest of Wireless owned by JVII General Partnership, a partnership wholly owned by AT&T Wireless Services, Inc. ("AWE"), for cash consideration totalling $1,767.4 million. With this transaction, the Company increased its ownership in Wireless from 55.3% to 89.3%. Wireless is a subsidiary of the Company whose results were already consolidated with those of the Company prior to this transaction.

On November 11, 2004, the Company announced that it would launch an exchange offer for any and all of the remaining outstanding shares of Wireless owned by the public, with consideration being 1.75 Class B Non-Voting shares of the Company for each share of Wireless. For accounting purposes, the value of the consideration was calculated as the average price of the Class B Non-Voting shares of the Company over a period of two days before and after the November 11, 2004 announcement date of the exchange offer. At December 31, 2004, the Company completed the acquisition of all of the publicly-held shares of Wireless in exchange for 28,072,856 Class B Non-Voting shares of the Company valued at $811.9 million. This represented an acquisition of an approximate 11.2% interest in Wireless. As a result, at December 31, 2004, the Company owned 100% of Wireless.

On December 31, 2004, the Company issued stock options to purchase Class B Non-Voting shares of the Company in exchange for both vested and non-vested stock options to purchase shares of Wireless, using the same conversion ratio of 1.75. The fair value of the vested options issued totalled approximately $29.3 million, and was included as part of the purchase price. The fair value of the unvested options issued of approximately $43.9 million will be amortized to expense over the vesting period. The fair values of the Company's options were calculated using the Black-Scholes model.

Including direct incremental acquisition costs of approximately $10.2 million, the aggregate purchase price for the acquisition of the Wireless shares and options totalled $2,618.8 million.

Goodwill related to the step acquisitions of Wireless has been assigned to the Wireless reporting segment.

(ii)   Microcell Telecommunications Inc.:

On November 9, 2004, the Company acquired the outstanding equity securities of Microcell Telecommunications Inc. ("Fido") for cash consideration. The results of Fido were consolidated effective November 9, 2004. Fido is a provider of wireless telecommunications services in Canada. With this acquisition, the Company now operates the only Global System for Mobile communications ("GSM") network in Canada.

Including direct incremental acquisition costs of approximately $14.9 million, the purchase price totalled $1,318.4 million, including $51.7 million paid for warrants in 2005.

Prior to completion of the acquisition, the Company developed a plan to restructure and integrate the operations of Fido. As a result of the restructuring and integration, $129.0 million was originally accrued as a liability assumed on acquisition in the allocation of the purchase price as at December 31, 2004. As at December 31, 2004, no payments had been made related to this liability. This liability included severance and other employee-related costs, as well as costs to consolidate facilities, systems and operations, close cell sites and terminate leases and other contracts. During 2005, management finalized its plan and revised the estimated restructuring and integration costs. As restructuring activities progressed and the Company was able to assess such matters as the extent of its network coverage, management was able to finalize those cell site and facility leases to be terminated and negotiate lease termination costs with the landlord where applicable. The negotiations related to the termination of other contracts were completed during 2005 as well. Additionally, as the dismantling of cell sites progressed, the Company was able to estimate the costs involved in dismantling sites with greater accuracy. With the continued integration of Fido's operational and administrative functions, the Company was able to finalize the list of those employees who would be retained and those whose employment would be severed in order to avoid the duplication of functions within the integrated enterprise.

The resulting adjustments to the liabilities assumed on acquisition and payments made against such liabilities during 2005 are as follows:

	As at December 31, 2004	Adjustments	Revised liabilities	Payments	As at December 31, 2005
Network decommissioning and restoration costs	$ 52,806	$ (18,505)	$ 34,301	$ (18,496)	$ 15,805
Lease and other contract termination costs	48,329	(21,648)	26,681	(22,997)	3,684
Involuntary severance	27,891	(15,557)	12,334	(10,156)	2,178
	$ 129,026	$ (55,710)	$ 73,316	$ (51,649)	$ 21,667

The remaining liability as at December 31, 2005 will be paid over the course of 2006.

(iii)   Other:

On December 23, 2004, the Company purchased the remaining 20% interest of Rogers Sportsnet for $45 million. The purchase price was allocated to goodwill on a preliminary basis pending completion of the valuations of the net identifiable assets acquired. In October 2005, an adjustment was made to allocate $23.6 million of the purchase price to broadcast licence with an offsetting reduction to goodwill. The broadcast licence has an indefinite life.

On January 2, 2004, the Company acquired 50% of CTV Specialty Television Inc.'s mobile production and distribution business ("Dome Productions") for cash of $21.3 million, net of cash acquired of $3.5 million. Dome Productions has been proportionately consolidated with the Company since acquisition of the 50% interest on January 2, 2004.

Goodwill related to the acquisitions of Sportsnet and Dome Productions has been assigned to the Media reporting segment.

During 2004, the Company had other acquisitions with purchase consideration of $0.4 million.

(c)   ADJUSTMENTS TO PRELIMINARY PURCHASE ALLOCATIONS RELATED TO 2004 ACQUISITIONS:

During 2005, the purchase price allocations related to the 2004 acquisitions were adjusted to reflect final valuations of tangible and intangible assets acquired as well as updated information and estimates related to Fido restructuring and integration plans. The following table summarizes the adjustments made to the purchase price allocations from those disclosed at December 31, 2004:

	Wireless	Fido	Other	Total
Increase (decrease) in estimated fair value of net assets acquired:				
Subscriber bases	$ 15,263	$ 31,500	$ —	$ 46,763
Brand names	903	2,500	941	4,344
Roaming agreements	(10,160)	1,500	—	(8,660)
Dealer networks	27,140	13,500	—	40,640
Wholesale agreements	—	13,000	—	13,000
Spectrum licences	(1,768)	(91,600)	—	(93,368)
Broadcast licence	—	—	23,600	23,600
PP&E	1,020	5,590	—	6,610
Deferred revenue	—	(5,654)	—	(5,654)
	32,398	(29,664)	24,541	27,275
Decrease in liabilities assumed on acquisition	—	55,710	—	55,710
Decrease (increase) in acquisition costs	1,078	—	(63)	1,015
Adjustment to fair value of unvested options	20,456	—	—	20,456
Decrease in goodwill	$ 53,932	$ 26,046	$ 24,478	$ 104,456

(d) **PURCHASE PRICE ALLOCATIONS:**

The table below summarizes the estimated fair values of the assets acquired and liabilities assumed for the acquisitions in 2005 and 2004. The final purchase price allocations for Wireless and Fido are presented below. The final purchase price allocations for Call-Net and Rogers Centre are expected to be completed in early 2006.

	2005			2004			
	Call-Net	Other	Total	Wireless	Fido	Other	Total
Consideration:							
Cash	$ —	$ 36,308	$ 36,308	$ 1,767,370	$ 1,251,819	$ 70,200	$ 3,089,389
Class B Non-Voting shares	315,986	—	315,986	811,867	—	—	811,867
Amounts due in 2005	—	—	—	—	51,705	—	51,705
Options issued as consideration	8,495	—	8,495	73,228	—	—	73,228
Less fair value of unvested options	—	—	—	(43,896)	—	—	(43,896)
Acquisition costs	4,000	1,996	5,996	10,200	14,888	—	25,088
Purchase price	$ 328,481	$ 38,304	$ 366,785	$ 2,618,769	$ 1,318,412	$ 70,200	$ 4,007,381
Cash and cash equivalents	$ 43,801	$ 212	$ 44,013	$ —	$ 118,070	$ 3,500	$ 121,570
Short-term investments	21,666	—	21,666	—	—	—	—
Accounts receivable	29,040	4,968	34,008	—	86,179	4,118	90,297
Other current assets	27,561	4,537	32,098	—	31,796	674	32,470
Inventory	—	1,023	1,023	—	47,292	—	47,292
Long-term investments	584	—	584	—	3,823	—	3,823
Deferred charges	—	—	—	(17,197)	—	—	(17,197)
Other long-term assets	4,604	—	4,604	—	—	—	—
Subscriber bases	123,000	—	123,000	807,779	171,500	5,000	984,279
Brand names	—	—	—	303,459	102,500	—	405,959
Roaming agreements	—	—	—	486,574	36,500	—	523,074
Broadcast licence	—	—	—	—	—	23,600	23,600
Spectrum licences	—	—	—	201,909	319,000	—	520,909
Dealer networks	—	—	—	27,140	13,500	—	40,640
Wholesale agreement	—	—	—	—	13,000	—	13,000
PP&E	339,984	32,239	372,223	33,143	337,029	7,768	377,940
Accounts payable and accrued liabilities	(147,153)	(11,207)	(158,360)	—	(144,692)	(3,881)	(148,573)
Deferred revenue	—	(2,426)	(2,426)	—	(50,956)	—	(50,956)
Liabilities assumed on acquisition	(3,655)	(5,997)	(9,652)	—	(73,316)	—	(73,316)
Long-term debt	(292,532)	—	(292,532)	(56,509)	(352,651)	—	(409,160)
Derivative instruments	—	—	—	(20,090)	(64,602)	—	(84,692)
Other long-term liabilities	(9,396)	—	(9,396)	—	—	—	—
Non-controlling interest	—	—	—	290,878	—	—	290,878
Fair value of net assets acquired	$ 137,504	$ 23,349	$ 160,853	$ 2,057,086	$ 593,972	$ 40,779	$ 2,691,837
Goodwill	$ 190,977	$ 14,955	$ 205,932	$ 561,683	$ 724,440	$ 29,421	$ 1,315,544

APPENDIX A

(e) **INTEGRATION EXPENSES:**

As part of the acquisition of Call-Net and Fido, the Company incurred certain integration costs that did not qualify to be included as part of the purchase price allocation as a liability assumed on acquisition. Rather, these costs are recorded within operating expenses. These expenses include various severance, consulting and other incremental restructuring costs directly related to the acquisitions.

During 2005, the Company incurred $12.9 million in integration expenses related to the Call-Net acquisition and $53.6 million in integration expenses related to the Fido acquisition (2004 – $4.4 million).

(f) **PRO FORMA RESULTS OF OPERATIONS:**

The pro forma results of operations had the Company acquired Call-Net on January 1, 2004 and Wireless and Fido on January 1, 2003, would have been as follows:

(Unaudited)	2005	2004
Operating revenue	$ 7,909,771	$ 6,958,303
Loss for the year	$ (175,684)	$ (661,726)
Loss per share:		
Basic and diluted	$ (0.60)	$ (2.66)

Note 4. **Other current assets:**

	2005	2004
Inventories	$ 117,182	$ 123,457
Video rental inventory	35,309	31,132
Prepaid expenses	111,908	88,288
Acquired program rights	20,984	13,651
Other	12,463	3,989
	$ 297,846	$ 260,517

Depreciation expense for video rental inventory is charged to operating, general and administrative expenses and amounted to $64.3 million in 2005 (2004 – $62.5 million). The costs of acquired program rights are amortized to operating, general and administrative expenses over the expected performances of the related programs and amounted to $25.9 million in 2005 (2004 – $25.8 million).

Note 5. **Property, plant and equipment:**

Details of PP&E are as follows:

	2005			2004		
	Cost	Accumulated depreciation	Net book value	Cost	Accumulated depreciation	Net book value
Land and buildings	$ 405,489	$ 76,816	$ 328,673	$ 349,029	$ 62,364	$ 286,665
Towers, headends and transmitters	743,349	361,958	381,391	670,229	340,197	330,032
Distribution cable and subscriber drops	4,081,473	2,070,422	2,011,051	3,707,609	1,816,561	1,891,048
Network equipment	3,870,411	1,889,486	1,980,925	3,091,614	1,455,907	1,635,707
Wireless network radio base station equipment	1,501,961	1,105,396	396,565	1,459,153	994,341	464,812
Computer equipment and software	1,567,927	1,129,387	438,540	1,310,068	906,645	403,423
Customer equipment	714,028	404,592	309,436	625,130	389,301	235,829
Leasehold improvements	260,055	152,402	107,653	210,810	123,827	86,983
Other equipment	532,315	335,023	197,292	495,036	342,698	152,338
	$13,677,008	$ 7,525,482	$ 6,151,526	$11,918,678	$ 6,431,841	$ 5,486,837

Depreciation expense for 2005 amounted to $1,074.8 million (2004 – $984.0 million).

PP&E not yet in service and therefore not depreciated at December 31, 2005 amounted to $364.5 million (2004 – $305.8 million).

Note 6. **Goodwill and intangible assets:**

(a) **GOODWILL:**

	2005	2004
Goodwill	$ 3,035,787	$ 3,388,687

A summary of the changes to goodwill is as follows:

	2005	2004
Opening balance	$ 3,388,687	$ 1,891,636
Additions/adjustments to goodwill related to:		
Acquisition of Call-Net (note 3(d))	190,977	—
Acquisition of Wireless (note 3)	(53,932)	615,615
Acquisition of Fido (note 3)	(26,046)	750,487
Other acquisitions (notes 3(a) and (b))	(9,525)	53,021
Blue Jays (note 7)	—	95,509
Reductions to goodwill related to:		
Reduction in valuation allowance for acquired future tax assets (note 14)	(451,827)	—
Write-off of divisions	(2,547)	(12,225)
Dilution of interest in Wireless	—	(5,356)
	$ 3,035,787	$ 3,388,687

The Company wrote-off goodwill of $2.5 million during 2005 (2004 – $12.2 million) related to the closure of two of its divisions.

(b) **INTANGIBLE ASSETS:**

	2005			2004		
	Cost	Accumulated amortization	Net book value	Cost	Accumulated amortization	Net book value
(i) Spectrum licences	$ 928,553	$ —	$ 928,553	$ 1,017,157	$ —	$ 1,017,157
(ii) Brand names	410,740	43,292	367,448	406,396	6,927	399,469
(iii) Subscriber bases	1,112,479	321,799	790,680	942,716	42,648	900,068
(iv) Player contracts	119,926	112,392	7,534	119,926	105,587	14,339
(v) Roaming agreements	523,074	50,623	472,451	531,734	7,078	524,656
(vi) Dealer networks	40,640	11,751	28,889	—	—	—
(vii) Wholesale agreements	13,000	4,689	8,311	—	—	—
(viii) Broadcast licence and other	23,600	—	23,600	—	—	—
	$ 3,172,012	$ 544,546	$ 2,627,466	$ 3,017,929	$ 162,240	$ 2,855,689

Amortization of subscriber bases, brand names, player contracts, roaming agreements, dealer networks and wholesale agreements in 2005 amounted to $382.3 million (2004 – $64.3 million).

(i)   As a result of the acquisitions of Fido and Wireless, the Company determined the value of the spectrum licences acquired to be $520.9 million (note 3(d)). In a spectrum auction conducted by Industry Canada in February 2001, the Company purchased 23 personal communications services licences of 10 megahertz ("MHz") or 20 MHz each, in the 1.9 gigahertz ("GHz") band in various regions across Canada at a cost of $396.8 million, including costs of acquisition. During 2005, the Company acquired spectrum in various licence areas for an aggregate cost of $4.8 million (2004 – $6.1 million). These amounts have been recorded as spectrum licences. The Company has determined that these licences have indefinite lives for accounting purposes and are therefore not being amortized.

(ii)   The Fido brand names were acquired in 2004 as a result of the acquisition of Fido (note 3(b)). The fair value of the brand names was determined to be $102.5 million and is being amortized straight-line over five years. The Rogers brand names were acquired in 2004 as a result of the acquisition of 100% of Wireless (note 3(b)). The fair value of the portion of the brand names acquired was determined to be $303.5 million and is being amortized straight-line over 20 years.

(iii)   The subscriber bases were acquired as a result of the acquisitions of Fido and Wireless in 2004 (note 3(b)) and the acquisition of Call-Net in 2005 (note 3(a)). The fair value of the customer base for Fido is being amortized straight-line over 2.25 years, the fair value of the customer base for Wireless is being amortized straight-line over a weighted average of 4.6 years and the fair value of the customer base for Call-Net is being amortized straight-line over a weighted average period of 2.4 years.

(iv)   Player contracts are related to the value of contracts associated with the Toronto Blue Jays Baseball Club ("Blue Jays") and are being amortized straight-line over five years.

(v)   Roaming agreements are related to the value of roaming contracts associated with Fido and Wireless (note 3(b)). These agreements are being amortized straight-line over 12 years.

(vi)   The dealer networks were acquired in 2004 as a result of the acquisitions of Fido and Wireless (note 3(b)). The dealer networks are being amortized straight-line over four years.

(vii)   Wholesale agreements are related to the value of contracts acquired as part of the Fido acquisition (note 3(b)). These agreements are being amortized straight-line over a period of 38 months.

(viii)   The broadcast licence was acquired as part of the acquisition of the remaining 20% of Sportsnet (note 3(b)). The broadcast licence has an indefinite life and is therefore not being amortized.

Note 7. **Investments:**

			2005		2004	
	Number	Description	Quoted market value	Book value	Quoted market value	Book value
Investments accounted for by the equity method			$ 9,047		$ 9,348	
Investments accounted for by the cost method, net of write-downs:						
Publicly traded companies:						
Cogeco Cable Inc.	6,595,675 (2004 – 6,595,675)	Subordinate Voting Common	$ 161,594	68,884	$ 169,179	68,884
Cogeco Inc.	3,399,800 (2004 – 3,399,800)	Subordinate Voting Common	81,595	44,438	76,190	44,438
Other publicly traded companies			11,998	2,845	23,772	3,551
			255,187	116,167	269,141	116,873
Private companies				12,998		12,949
				$ 138,212		$ 139,170

(a)   **BLUE JAYS:**

On January 5, 2004, the Company paid the remaining amount related to the purchase of the 20% minority interest in the Blue Jays of approximately $39.1 million. This payment had no impact on the carrying value or the control of the investment since this liability was recorded at the original date of acquisition.

Effective April 1, 2001, Rogers Telecommunications Ltd. ("RTL"), a company controlled by the controlling share-holder of the Company, acquired the Class A Preferred shares of a subsidiary of RCI that owns the Blue Jays ("Blue Jays Holdco Inc.") for $30.0 million. On July 31, 2004, Blue Jays Holdco Inc. redeemed and cancelled the 30,000 Class A Preferred shares for $30.0 million, resulting in the control of Blue Jays Holdco Inc. being transferred to the Company. Accordingly, commencing July 31, 2004, the Company began to consolidate its investment in Blue Jays Holdco Inc. This had no impact on net income since the Company had previously equity accounted for 100% of the losses of Blue Jays Holdco Inc.

While they were outstanding, the Class A Preferred shares of Blue Jays Holdco Inc. had a cumulative divi-dend rate of 9.167% per annum. These dividends were satisfied in kind by transferring income tax losses to RTL. During 2004, Blue Jays Holdco Inc. transferred income tax losses to RTL in the amount of $27.4 million with an agreed value of $2.7 million.

From January 1, 2004 to July 30, 2004, cash contributions of $30.1 million were made to Blue Jays Holdco Inc.

(b)   **COGECO INC. AND COGECO CABLE INC. (COLLECTIVELY "COGECO"):**

In November 2004, the Company entered into an agreement with a group unaffiliated with Cogeco, to exchange 658,125 Subordinated Voting shares of Cogeco Cable Inc. ("CCI") for 675,000 Subordinated Voting shares of Cogeco Inc. ("CI"). This transaction was based on the December 13, 2004 closing price and resulted in an increase in the Company's investment in CI of $15.8 million, a decrease in the Company's investment in CCI of $6.9 million and a gain on the exchange of $8.9 million. The Company's total investment in CI represents an approximate 21% equity ownership, representing a 7% voting interest, and in CCI an approximate 16.5% equity ownership, representing a 4% voting interest. Therefore, the Company does not exercise significant influence over either CI or CCI.

Note 8.   **Deferred charges:**

	2005	2004
Financing costs	$ 66,858	$ 81,229
Pre-operating costs	12,126	3,506
CRTC commitments	34,403	44,746
Other	15,732	4,985
	$ 129,119	$ 134,466

Amortization of deferred charges for 2005 amounted to $34.8 million (2004 – $35.3 million). Accumulated amortization as at December 31, 2005 amounted to $116.0 million (2004 – $123.9 million).

Financing costs of $4.9 million were deferred in connection with the amendments to certain credit facilities in 2005. Financing costs of $66.1 million were deferred in connection with the issuance of long-term debt in 2004.

In connection with the repayment of certain long-term debt during 2005 and amendments made to certain credit facilities, the Company wrote off deferred financing costs of $3.0 million (2004 – $19.2 million) (note 11(f)).

The Company has committed to the Canadian Radio-television and Telecommunications Commission ("CRTC") to spend an aggregate of $77.4 million in operating funds to provide certain benefits to the Canadian broadcasting system. In prior years, the Company agreed to pay $50.0 million in public benefits over seven years relating to the CRTC grant of a new television licence in Toronto, $6.0 million relating to the purchase of 13 radio stations and the remain-der relating to a CRTC decision permitting the purchase of Sportsnet, Rogers (Toronto) Ltd. and Rogers (Alberta) Ltd. The amount of these liabilities, included in accounts payable and accrued liabilities and other long-term liabilities, is $68.6 million at December 31, 2005 (2004 – $48.3 million). Commitments are being amortized over periods ranging from six to seven years.

Note 9. **Other long-term assets:**

	2005	2004
Deferred pension	$ 32,111	$ 24,184
Program rights	23,420	45,188
Long-term deposits	46,392	14,072
Long-term receivables	1,307	3,632
Other	—	2,367
	$ 103,230	$ 89,443

Note 10. **Consolidated statements of cash flows:**

(a) **CHANGE IN NON-CASH WORKING CAPITAL:**

	2005	2004
Decrease (increase) in accounts receivable	$ (182,756)	$ 15,496
Increase (decrease) in accounts payable and accrued liabilities	(61,532)	13,525
Increase (decrease) in unearned revenue	15,463	(1,811)
Increase in deferred charges and other assets	(95,183)	(89,300)
	$ (324,008)	$ (62,090)

(b) **SUPPLEMENTAL CASH FLOW INFORMATION:**

	2005	2004
Income taxes paid	$ 15,662	$ 13,446
Interest paid	705,816	523,061

(c) **SUPPLEMENTAL DISCLOSURE OF NON-CASH TRANSACTIONS:**

	2005	2004
Class B Non-Voting shares issued on conversion of Series E Convertible Preferred shares	$ —	$ 1,752
CCI shares exchanged for CI shares (note 7(b))	—	(6,874)
CCI shares acquired in exchange for CI shares (note 7(b))	—	15,801
Class B Non-Voting shares issued in exchange for Wireless shares (note 3(b))	—	811,867
Options to acquire Class B Non-Voting shares issued in exchange for Wireless options (note 3(b))	—	73,228
Options to acquire Class B Non-Voting shares Issued in exchange for Call-Net options (note 3(a))	8,495	—
Class B Non-Voting shares issued in consideration for acquisition of shares of Call-Net (note 3(a))	315,986	—
Class B Non-Voting shares issued in consideration upon the conversion of convertible debt (note 11(a))	271,197	—
Class B Non-Voting shares issued in consideration upon the conversion of Preferred Securities (note 11(a))	696,494	—

Refer to note 13(a) for details of other non-cash transactions.

A-22

APPENDIX A

Note 11. **Long-term debt:**

	Interest rate	2005	2004
(a) Corporate:			
(i) Convertible Debentures, due 2005	5.75%	$ —	$ 261,810
(ii) Senior Notes, due 2006	10.50%	75,000	75,000
(iii) Convertible Preferred Securities, due 2009 (note 2(s)(i))	5.50%	—	490,710
		75,000	827,520
(b) Wireless:			
(i) Bank credit facility	Floating	71,000	—
(ii) Senior Secured Notes, due 2006	10.50%	160,000	160,000
(iii) Floating Rate Senior Secured Notes, due 2010	Floating	641,245	661,980
(iv) Senior Secured Notes, due 2011	9.625%	571,291	589,764
(v) Senior Secured Notes, due 2011	7.625%	460,000	460,000
(vi) Senior Secured Notes, due 2012	7.25%	547,973	565,692
(vii) Senior Secured Notes, due 2014	6.375%	874,425	902,700
(viii) Senior Secured Notes, due 2015	7.50%	641,245	661,980
(ix) Senior Secured Debentures, due 2016	9.75%	180,598	186,438
(x) Senior Subordinated Notes, due 2012	8.00%	466,360	481,440
(xi) Fair value increment arising from purchase accounting		44,326	55,232
		4,658,463	4,725,226
(c) Cable:			
(i) Bank credit facility	Floating	267,000	—
(ii) Senior Secured Second Priority Notes, due 2005	10.00%	—	350,889
(iii) Senior Secured Second Priority Notes, due 2007	7.60%	450,000	450,000
(iv) Senior Secured Second Priority Notes, due 2011	7.25%	175,000	175,000
(v) Senior Secured Second Priority Notes, due 2012	7.875%	408,065	421,260
(vi) Senior Secured Second Priority Notes, due 2013	6.25%	408,065	421,260
(vii) Senior Secured Second Priority Notes, due 2014	5.50%	408,065	421,260
(viii) Senior Secured Second Priority Notes, due 2015	6.75%	326,452	337,008
(ix) Senior Secured Second Priority Debentures, due 2032	8.75%	233,180	240,720
(x) Senior Subordinated Guaranteed Debentures, due 2015	11.00%	—	136,819
		2,675,827	2,954,216
(d) Media:			
Bank credit facility	Floating	274,000	—
(e) Telecom:			
(i) Senior Secured Notes, due 2008	10.625%	25,703	—
(ii) Fair value increment arising from purchase accounting		1,619	—
		27,322	—
Mortgages and other	Various	28,939	34,135
		7,739,551	8,541,097
Less current portion		286,139	618,236
		$ 7,453,412	$ 7,922,861

Further details of long-term debt are as follows:

(a) **CORPORATE:**

(i) **Convertible Debentures, due 2005:**
On May 13, 2005, 1,031 Class B Non-Voting shares were issued upon conversion of US$0.03 million face amount of the Company's 5.75% Convertible Debentures.

On June 30, 2005, the Company issued a notice of redemption for all of its US$224.8 million face value amount (accreted amount – US$221.5 million) of 5.75% convertible debentures due November 26, 2005 for an aggregate redemption amount of approximately US$223.0 million. Debenture holders converted an aggregate US$224.5 million face amount of debentures into 7,715,417 Class B Non-Voting shares of the Company with a value of $271.2 million. The remaining US$0.3 million face amount was redeemed in cash.

(ii)   Senior Notes, due 2006:

The Company's $75.0 million Senior Notes mature on February 14, 2006. Interest on the Senior Notes is paid semi-annually.

The Company's Senior Notes and debentures described above are senior unsecured general obligations of the Company ranking equally with each other.

(iii)   Convertible Preferred Securities, due 2009:

Convertible Preferred Securities were issued in 1999 with a face value of $600.0 million to Microsoft R-Holdings, Inc. ("Microsoft"), a subsidiary of Microsoft Corporation. These Convertible Preferred Securities bore interest at 5½% per annum, payable quarterly in cash, Class B Non-Voting shares or additional Convertible Preferred Securities, at the Company's option. The Convertible Preferred Securities were convertible, in whole or in part, at any time, at Microsoft's option, into 28.5714 Class B Non-Voting shares per $1,000 aggregate principal amount of Convertible Preferred Securities, representing a conversion price of $35 per Class B Non-Voting share. In August 2004, the Company and Microsoft agreed to amend the terms of such securities, whereby certain transfer restrictions would have terminated on March 28, 2006 unless a qualifying offer to purchase these securities was made by the Company. In the event such transfer restrictions terminated, during a three-month period subsequent to March 28, 2006, the Company had the option to extend the maturity of these securities for up to three years from the original August 11, 2009 maturity date. The Company had the option of repaying the Convertible Preferred Securities in cash or Class B Non-Voting shares.

As part of the transaction to issue the Convertible Preferred Securities, the Company issued 5,333,333 warrants to Microsoft, each exercisable into one Class B Non-Voting share. Since the proceeds of $600.0 million included the 5,333,333 warrants, these were recorded as a separate component of shareholders' equity at their fair value of $24.0 million. These warrants expired on August 11, 2002 and the $24.0 million book value of these warrants was transferred to contributed surplus.

In addition, Canadian GAAP requires that the fair value of the conversion feature of $188.0 million be recorded as a separate component of shareholders' equity. The remaining $388.0 million represented the fair value of the principal amount of the Convertible Preferred Securities at the date of issuance. The $388.0 million principal element was being accreted up to the $600.0 million face value over the term to maturity. The accretion and the 5½% interest were charged to interest expense (note 2(s)(i)).

On October 11, 2005, the Company gave a notice of redemption to Microsoft, stating its intention to redeem $600 million 5½% Convertible Preferred Securities due August 2009 in accordance with the terms of such securities. Under the terms of the Convertible Preferred Securities, following the October 11, 2005 notice of redemption, Microsoft had 27 days in which to give notice of its intention to convert the Preferred Securities into an aggregate 17,142,857 RCI Class B Non-Voting shares, at the conversion price of $35 per share. On October 17, 2005, the Company received a notice of conversion from Microsoft stating that it had elected to convert its Preferred Securities into Class B Non-Voting shares, and pursuant to such notice, on October 24, 2005, the Company issued to Microsoft 17,142,857 Class B Non-Voting shares with a value of $696.5 million and recorded contributed surplus for the difference between the carrying values of the debt plus conversion feature and the total par value (note 13(a)(iii)(iv)).

(b)   WIRELESS:

(i)   Bank credit facility:

On October 8, 2004 Wireless and its bank lenders entered into an amending agreement to Wireless' $700.0 million bank credit facility that provided among other things, for a two year extension to the maturity date and the reduction schedule so that the bank credit facility now reduces by $140.0 million on each of April 30, 2008 and April 30, 2009 with the maturity date on the April 30, 2010. In addition, certain financial ratios to be maintained on a quarterly basis were made less restrictive, the restriction on the annual amount of capital expenditures was eliminated and the restriction on the payment of dividends and other shareholder distributions was eliminated other than in the case of a default or event of default under the terms of the bank credit facility.

At December 31, 2005, $71.0 million (2004 – nil) was outstanding under the bank credit facility, which provides Wireless with, among other things, up to $700.0 million from a consortium of Canadian financial institutions.

Under the credit facility, Wireless may borrow at various rates, including the bank prime rate or base rate to the bank prime rate or base rate plus 1³⁄₄% per annum, the bankers' acceptance rate plus 1% to 2³⁄₄% per annum and the London Inter-Bank Offered Rate ("LIBOR") plus 1% to 2³⁄₄% per annum. Wireless' bank credit facility requires, among other things, that Wireless satisfy certain financial covenants, including the maintenance of certain financial ratios.

This credit facility is available on a fully revolving basis until the first date specified below, at which time, the facility becomes a revolving/reducing facility and the aggregate amount of credit available under the facility will be reduced as follows:

On April 30:
2008	$ 140,000
2009	140,000
2010	420,000

Borrowings under the credit facility are secured by the pledge of a senior bond issued under a deed of trust, which is secured by substantially all the assets of the Company and certain of its subsidiaries, subject to certain exceptions and prior liens.

(ii) Senior Secured Notes, due 2006:
Wireless' $160.0 million Senior Secured Notes mature on June 1, 2006. These notes are redeemable, in whole or in part, at Wireless' option, at any time, subject to a certain prepayment premium.

(iii) Floating Rate Senior Secured Notes, due 2010:
On November 30, 2004, Wireless issued US$550.0 million of Floating Rate Senior Secured Notes, which mature on December 15, 2010. These notes are redeemable in whole or in part, at Wireless' option, at any time on or after December 15, 2006 at 102.0% of the principal amount, declining ratably to 100.0% of the principal amount on or after December 15, 2008, plus, in each case, interest accrued to the redemption date. The Company pays interest on the Floating Rate Notes at LIBOR plus 3.125%, reset quarterly.

(iv) Senior Secured Notes, due 2011:
Wireless' US$490.0 million Senior Secured Notes mature on May 1, 2011. These notes are redeemable, in whole or in part, at Wireless' option, at any time, subject to a certain prepayment premium.

(v) Senior Secured Notes, due 2011:
On November 30, 2004, Wireless issued $460.0 million Senior Secured Notes which mature on December 15, 2011. These notes are redeemable, in whole or in part, at Wireless' option, at any time, subject to a certain prepayment premium.

(vi) Senior Secured Notes, due 2012:
On November 30, 2004, Wireless issued US$470.0 million Senior Secured Notes which mature on December 15, 2012. These notes are redeemable, in whole or in part, at Wireless' option at any time, subject to a certain prepayment premium.

(vii) Senior Secured Notes, due 2014:
On February 20, 2004, Wireless issued US$750.0 million of Senior Secured Notes due on March 1, 2014. These notes are redeemable, in whole or in part, at Wireless' option at any time, subject to a certain prepayment premium.

(viii) Senior Secured Notes, due 2015:
On November 30, 2004, Wireless issued US$550.0 million of Senior Secured Notes which mature on March 15, 2015. These notes are redeemable, in whole or in part, at Wireless' option at any time, subject to a certain prepayment premium.

(ix)   Senior Secured Debentures, due 2016:

Wireless' US$154.9 million Senior Secured Debentures mature on June 1, 2016. These debentures are redeemable, in whole or in part, at Wireless' option, at any time, subject to a certain prepayment premium.

Each of Wireless' Senior Secured Notes and Debentures described above is secured by the pledge of a senior bond that is secured by the same security as the security for the bank credit facility described in note 11(b)(i) and ranks equally with the bank credit facility.

(x)   Senior Subordinated Notes, due 2012:

On November 30, 2004, Wireless issued US$400.0 million Senior Subordinated Notes due on December 15, 2012. These notes are redeemable in whole or in part, at Wireless' option, at any time up to December 15, 2008, subject to a certain prepayment premium and at any time on or after December 15, 2008 at 104.0% of the principal amount, declining ratably to 100.0% of the principal amount on or after December 15, 2010.

Interest is paid semi-annually on all of Wireless' notes and debentures with the exception of Wireless' Floating Rate Senior Secured Notes due 2010 for which Wireless pays interest on a quarterly basis.

(xi)   Fair value increment arising from purchase accounting:

The fair value increment on long-term debt is a purchase accounting adjustment required by GAAP as a result of the acquisition of the minority interest of Wireless during 2004. Under GAAP, the purchase method of accounting requires that the assets and liabilities of an acquired enterprise be revalued to fair value when allocating the purchase price of the acquisition. This fair value increment is recorded only on consolidation at the RCI level and is not recorded in the accounts of Wireless. The fair value increment is amortized over the remaining term of the related debt and recorded as part of interest expense. The fair value increment, applied against the specific debt instruments of Wireless to which it relates, results in the following carrying values at December 31, 2005 and 2004 of the Wireless debt in the Company's consolidated accounts:

		2005	2004
Senior Secured Notes, due 2006	10.50%	$ 161,632	$ 165,572
Senior Secured Notes, due 2010	Floating	643,857	665,119
Senior Secured Notes, due 2011	9.625%	605,875	630,090
Senior Secured Notes, due 2011	7.625%	461,648	461,925
Senior Secured Notes, due 2012	7.25%	550,871	569,006
Senior Secured Notes, due 2014	6.375%	857,172	883,551
Senior Secured Notes, due 2015	7.50%	644,409	665,488
Senior Secured Debentures, due 2016	9.75%	193,290	200,349
Senior Subordinated Notes, due 2012	8.00%	468,709	484,126
Total		$ 4,587,463	$ 4,725,226

(c)   CABLE:

(i)   Bank credit facility:

In June 2005, Cable amended its bank credit facility (the "Bank Credit Facility"). The maximum amount of the facility has been reduced by $75.0 million to $1.0 billion comprised of $600.0 million Tranche A and $400.0 million Tranche B. The amendment served to extend the maturity dates of both Tranche A and Tranche B from January 2, 2009 to "bullet" repayments on July 2, 2010 and eliminate the amortization schedule for Tranche B; reduce interest rates and standby fees and relax certain financial covenants.

At December 31, 2005, $267.0 million (2004 — nil) was outstanding under the Bank Credit Facility.

The Bank Credit Facility is secured by the pledge of a senior bond issued under a deed of trust which is secured by substantially all of the assets of Cable and its wholly owned subsidiary, Rogers Cable Communications Inc. ("RCCI"), subject to certain exceptions and prior liens. In addition, under the terms of an inter-creditor agreement, the proceeds of any enforcement of the security under the deed of trust would be applied first to repay any obligations outstanding under the Tranche A Credit Facility. Additional proceeds would be applied pro rata to repay all other obligations of Cable secured by senior bonds, including the Tranche B Credit Facility and Cable's senior secured notes and debentures.

The Bank Credit Facility requires, among other things, that Cable satisfy certain financial covenants, including the maintenance of certain financial ratios. The interest rate charged on the Bank Credit Facility ranges from nil to 2.0% per annum over the bank prime rate or base rate or 0.625% to 3.25% per annum over the bankers' acceptance rate or LIBOR.

(ii)   Senior Secured Second Priority Notes, due 2005:
On March 15, 2005, Cable repaid US$291.5 million aggregate principal amount of its 10.0% Senior Secured Second Priority Notes due March 15, 2005.

(iii)   Senior Secured Second Priority Notes, due 2007:
Cable's $450.0 million Senior Secured Second Priority Notes mature on February 6, 2007. The Notes are redeemable at Cable's option, in whole or in part, at any time, subject to a certain prepayment premium.

(iv)   Senior Secured Second Priority Notes, due 2011:
On November 30, 2004, Cable issued $175.0 million Senior Secured Second Priority Notes due on December 15, 2011. These Notes are redeemable at Cable's option, in whole or in part, at any time, subject to a certain prepayment premium.

(v)   Senior Secured Second Priority Notes, due 2012:
Cable's US$350.0 million Senior Secured Second Priority Notes mature on May 1, 2012. The Notes are redeemable at Cable's option, in whole or in part, at any time, subject to a certain prepayment premium.

(vi)   Senior Secured Second Priority Notes, due 2013:
On June 19, 2003, Cable issued US$350.0 million Senior Secured Second Priority Notes due June 15, 2013. The Notes are redeemable at Cable's option, in whole or in part, at any time, subject to a certain prepayment premium.

(vii)   Senior Secured Second Priority Notes, due 2014:
On March 11, 2004, Cable issued US$350.0 million Senior Secured Second Priority Notes due March 15, 2014. The Notes are redeemable at Cable's option, in whole or in part, at any time, subject to a certain prepayment premium.

(viii)   Senior Secured Second Priority Notes, due 2015:
On November 30, 2004, Cable issued US$280.0 million Senior Secured Second Priority Notes, due on March 15, 2015. The Notes are redeemable at Cable's option, in whole or in part, at any time, subject to a certain prepayment premium.

(ix)   Senior Secured Second Priority Debentures, due 2032:
Cable's US$200.0 million 8.75% Senior Secured Second Priority Debentures mature on May 1, 2032. The debentures are redeemable at Cable's option, in whole or in part, at any time, subject to a certain prepayment premium.

Each of Cable's Senior Secured Notes and Debentures described above is secured by the pledge of a senior bond which is secured by the same security as the security for the Bank Credit Facility described in note 11(c)(i) and rank equally in regard to the proceeds of any enforcement of security with the Tranche B Credit Facility.

(x)   Senior Subordinated Guaranteed Debentures, due 2015:
During 2005, Cable redeemed the US$113.7 million aggregate principal amount outstanding of the 11% Senior Subordinated Guaranteed Debentures due 2015 at a redemption price of 105.5% of the aggregate principal amount together with accrued and unpaid interest. This resulted in a loss on redemption of debt of $9.8 million including the premium on redemption as well as the write-off of the related deferred financing costs.

Interest is paid semi-annually on all of Cable's notes and debentures.

(d)   **MEDIA:**
Bank credit facility:
In September 2005, Media amended its bank credit facility which is provided by a consortium of Canadian financial institutions. The maximum amount of the facility has been increased by $100.0 million to $600.0 million. The amendment also served to extend the maturity date by four years to September 30, 2010; reduce interest rates and standby fees and relax certain financial covenants.

At December 31, 2005, Media had $274.0 million (2004 – nil) outstanding under its bank credit facility. Borrowings under this facility are available to Media for general corporate purposes. Media's bank credit facility is available on a fully revolving basis until maturity on September 30, 2010 and there are no scheduled reductions prior to maturity.

The interest rates charged on this credit facility range from the bank prime rate or U.S. base rate plus nil to 2.0% per annum and the bankers' acceptance rate or LIBOR plus 1.0% to 3.0% per annum. The bank credit facility requires, among other things, that Media satisfy certain financial covenants, including the maintenance of certain financial ratios.

The bank credit facility is secured by floating charge debentures over most of the assets of Media and three of its subsidiaries, Rogers Broadcasting Limited ("RBL"), Rogers Publishing Limited ("RPL") and Rogers Sportsnet Inc. ("Sportsnet"), subject to certain exceptions. Each of RBL, RPL and Sportsnet has guaranteed Media's present and future liabilities and obligations under the credit facility.

(e)   **TELECOM:**
During 2005, Telecom redeemed $237.9 million (US$200.9 million) aggregate principal amount of its 10.625% Senior Secured Notes due 2008. Premiums and related expenses aggregated $17.5 million and a loss of $1.5 million, net of the adjustment to the fair value of debt on acquisition of $16.0 million, was recorded. As a result, $25.7 million (approximately US$22.0 million) aggregate principal amount of these Notes remain outstanding as at December 31, 2005 (note 24).

(f)   **DEBT REPAYMENTS:**
        (i)   During 2005, the Company redeemed an aggregate US$606.1 million principal amount of Senior Secured Second Priority Notes, Senior Secured Notes and Senior Subordinated Guaranteed Debentures by cash and converted US$224.8 million face value amount of Convertible Debentures by issuing 7,716,448 Class B Non-Voting shares and paying US$0.3 million in cash. The Company also converted the $600.0 million face value of its Convertible Preferred Securities and issued 17,142,857 of Class B Non-Voting shares in return. The Company paid aggregate prepayment premiums and other expenses of US$20.8 million, wrote off deferred financing costs of $3.0 million and wrote off $16.0 million of the fair value increment related to Telecom's Senior Secured Notes that arose on the acquisition of Telecom. As a result, the Company recorded a loss on the repayment of debt of $11.2 million.
        (ii)   During 2004, the Company redeemed an aggregate US$708.4 million and C$300.0 million principal amount of Senior Notes and Debentures and repaid $1,750.0 million related to the bridge credit facility established in connection with the Company's acquisition of Wireless. The Company paid aggregate prepayment premiums of $49.2 million, and wrote off deferred financing costs of $19.2 million, offset by a $40.2 million gain on the release of the deferred transition gain related to the cross-currency interest rate exchange agreements that were unwound during the year, resulting in a loss on the repayment of debt of $28.2 million.

(g)   **WEIGHTED AVERAGE INTEREST RATE:**
The Company's effective weighted average interest rate on all long-term debt, as at December 31, 2005, including the effect of all of the derivative instruments, was 7.76% (2004 – 7.98%).

(h)   **PRINCIPAL REPAYMENTS:**
As at December 31, 2005, principal repayments due within each of the next five years and in total thereafter on all long-term debt are as follows:

2006	$ 286,139
2007	451,218
2008	865
2009	760
2010	1,253,904
Thereafter	5,700,720

The provisions of the long-term debt agreements described above impose, in most instances, restrictions on the operations and activities of the companies governed by these agreements. Generally, the most significant of these restrictions are debt incurrence and maintenance tests, restrictions upon additional investments, sales of assets and payment of dividends. In addition, the repayment dates of certain debt agreements may be accelerated if there is a change in control of the respective companies. At December 31, 2005, the Company is in compliance with all terms of the long-term debt agreements.

Note 12. **Derivative instruments:**

Details of the liability for derivative instruments is as follows:

2005	U.S. $ notional	Exchange rate	Cdn. $ notional	Carrying amount	Estimated fair value
Cross-currency interest rate exchange agreements accounted for as hedges	$ 4,190,000	1.3313	$ 5,577,998	$ 710,275	$ 1,307,451
Cross-currency interest rate exchange agreements not accounted for as hedges	611,830	1.2021	735,479	27,095	27,095
Interest exchange agreements not accounted for as hedges	–	–	30,000	791	791
	4,801,830		6,343,477	738,161	1,335,337
Transitional gain	–		–	63,388	–
	4,801,830		6,343,477	801,549	1,335,337
Less current portion	326,830	1.2045	393,672	14,180	14,180
	$ 4,475,000		$ 5,949,805	$ 787,369	$ 1,321,157

2004	U.S. $ notional	Exchange rate	Cdn. $ notional	Carrying amount	Estimated fair value
Cross-currency interest rate exchange agreements accounted for as hedges	$ 4,473,437	1.3363	$ 5,977,998	$ 613,667	$ 932,538
Cross-currency interest rate exchange agreements not accounted for as hedges	661,830	1.2183	806,304	10,882	10,882
Interest exchange agreements not accounted for as hedges	–	–	30,000	2,347	2,347
	5,135,267		6,814,302	626,896	945,767
Transitional gain	–		–	73,505	–
	5,135,267		6,814,302	700,401	945,767
Less current portion	283,437	1.4112	400,000	58,856	61,530
	$ 4,851,830		$ 6,414,302	$ 641,545	$ 884,237

Effective January 1, 2004, the Company determined that it would not account for its cross-currency interest rate exchange agreements as hedges for accounting purposes and consequently began to account for such derivatives on a mark-to-market basis, with resulting gains or losses recorded in or charged against income.

The Company adjusted the carrying value of these instruments from $338.1 million at December 31, 2003 to their fair value of $385.3 million on January 1, 2004. The corresponding transitional loss of $47.2 million was deferred and was being amortized to income over the remaining life of the underlying debt instruments.

Effective July 1, 2004, the Company met the requirements for hedge accounting under AcG-13 for certain of its derivative instruments and, consequently, on a prospective basis, began to treat approximately US$2,773.4 million notional amount of the aggregate US$2,885.3 million, or 96.1% of these exchange agreements, as hedges for accounting purposes on US$2,773.4 million of U.S. dollar-denominated debt.

A transition adjustment arising on the change from mark-to-market accounting to hedge accounting was calculated as at July 1, 2004, resulting in a deferred transitional gain of $80.0 million. This transitional gain is being amortized to income over the shorter of the remaining life of the debt and the term of the exchange agreements.

Amortization of the net transitional gain for the year ended December 31, 2005 was $10.8 million (2004 — $3.2 million).

On March 15, 2005, a cross-currency swap of US$50.0 million notional amount matured. Cable incurred a net cash outlay of $10.5 million upon settlement of this swap.

Cable repaid its US$291.5 million 10.0% Senior Secured Second Priority Notes at maturity on March 15, 2005. Including the $58.1 million net cash outlay on the settlement of the cross-currency interest rate swap of US$283.4 million notional amount, Cable paid a total of $409.8 million.

On November 30, 2004, the Company entered into an additional aggregate US$1,700.0 million notional principal amount of cross-currency interest rate exchange agreements that meet the requirements of hedge accounting as hedges against foreign exchange fluctuations under AcG-13.

Note 13. Shareholders' equity:

	2005	2004
Capital stock:		
Common shares:		
56,233,894 Class A Voting shares (2004 — 56,235,394)	$ 72,311	$ 72,313
257,702,341 Class B Non-Voting shares (2004 — 218,979,074)	418,695	355,793
Total capital stock	491,006	428,106
Convertible Preferred Securities (notes 2(s)(i) and 13(b))	—	188,000
Contributed surplus	3,638,157	2,288,669
Deficit	(601,548)	(519,441)
	3,036,609	1,957,228
	$ 3,527,615	$ 2,385,334

(a)   CAPITAL STOCK:

(i)   Preferred shares:

Rights and conditions:

There are 400 million authorized Preferred shares without par value, issuable in series, with rights and terms of each series to be fixed by the Board of Directors prior to the issue of such series. The Preferred shares have no rights to vote at any general meeting of the Company.

(ii)   Common shares:

Rights and conditions:

There are 56,240,494 authorized Class A Voting shares without par value. Each Class A Voting share is entitled to 50 votes per share. The Class A Voting shares are convertible on a one-for-one basis into Class B Non-Voting shares.

There are 1.4 billion authorized Class B Non-Voting shares with a par value of $1.62478 per share.

In December 2005, the Company declared a 50% increase to the dividend paid for each outstanding Class A Voting share and Class B Non-Voting share. Accordingly, the annual dividend per share increased from $0.10 per share to $0.15 per share. During 2005, the Company declared dividends in aggregate of $0.125 per share on each of its Class A Voting shares and Class B Non-Voting shares.

The Class A Voting shares may receive a dividend at a semi-annual rate of up to $0.05 per share only after the Class B Non-Voting shares have been paid a dividend at a semi-annual rate of $0.05 per share. The Class A Voting and Class B Non-Voting shares share equally in dividends after payment of a dividend of $0.05 per share for each class.

(iii)   During 2005, the Company completed the following capital stock transactions:

I.   In 2005, the Company issued 8,464,426 Class B Non-Voting shares with a value of $316.0 million in exchange for the issued and outstanding common and Class B Non-Voting shares of Call-Net (note 3(a));

II. During 2005, the Company issued 7,716,448 Class B Non-Voting shares with a value of $271.2 million upon the conversion of convertible debt (note 11(a));

III. On July 25, 2005, 1,500 Class A Voting shares were converted to 1,500 Class B Non-Voting shares;

IV. On conversion of the Convertible Preferred Securities on October 24, 2005, the Company issued 17,142,857 Class B Non-Voting shares with a value of $696.5 million and recorded contributed surplus of $668.6 million for the difference between the carrying values of the debt of $508.5 million plus conversion feature of $188.0 million and the total par value of the Class B Non-Voting shares of $27.9 million (note 11(a)(iii) and note 13(b)); and

V. During 2005, 5,398,036 Class B Non-Voting shares were issued to employees upon exercise of options for consideration of $106.1 million.

As a result of the above transactions, $1,326.8 million of the issued amounts related to Class B Non-Voting shares were recorded in contributed surplus. In addition, $22.7 million was recorded in contributed surplus related to stock-based compensation, including the adjustment of $20.5 million to the fair value of the RWCI unvested options and the $8.5 million related to the options issued in exchange for Call-Net options (notes 3 and 13(c)).

(iv) During 2004, the Company completed the following capital stock transactions:

I. On December 31, 2004, 28,072,856 Class B Non-Voting shares with a value of $811.9 million were issued in exchange for Class B Restricted Voting shares of Wireless (note 3(b));

II. On April 15, 2004, the Company filed a final shelf prospectus in all of the provinces in Canada and in the U.S. under which it will be able to offer up to aggregate of US$750 million of Class B Non-Voting shares, preferred shares, debt securities, warrants, share purchase contracts or units, or any combination thereof, for a period of 25 months;

III. On June 16, 2004, 9,541,985 Class B Non-Voting shares were issued under the shelf prospectus for net cash proceeds of $238.9 million;

IV. 4,019,485 Class B Non-Voting shares were issued to employees upon the exercise of stock options for cash of $62.3 million;

V. 103,102 Series E Convertible Preferred shares with a value of $1.8 million were converted to 103,102 Class B Non-Voting shares, and 1,386 Series E Convertible Preferred shares were cancelled upon their expiry in April 2004;

VI. On December 31, 2004, the Company redeemed for cancellation its Series XXVII Preferred shares held by a subsidiary company;

VII. On December 1, 2004, the Series XXX Preferred shares held by a subsidiary company were cancelled as a result of the windup of the subsidiary company; and

VIII. On December 31, 2004, the Company redeemed for cancellation its Series XXXI Preferred shares held by a subsidiary company.

As a result of the above transactions, $1,046.8 million of the issued amounts related to Class B Non-Voting shares was recorded in contributed surplus. In addition, $72.0 million was recorded in contributed surplus related to stock-based compensation (note 13(c)).

IX. The Articles of Continuance of the Company under the Company Act (British Columbia) impose restrictions on the transfer, voting and issue of the Class A Voting and Class B Non-Voting shares in order to ensure that the Company remains qualified to hold or obtain licences required to carry on certain of its business undertakings in Canada.

The Company is authorized to refuse to register transfers of any shares of the Company to any person who is not a Canadian in order to ensure that the Company remains qualified to hold the licences referred to above.

(b) CONVERTIBLE PREFERRED SECURITIES AND WARRANTS:

As part of the issuance of the Convertible Preferred Securities (note 11(a)(iii)), the Company issued 5,333,333 warrants to Microsoft, each exercisable into one Class B Non-Voting share. These warrants were recorded as a separate component of shareholders' equity at their fair value of $24.0 million. Upon expiration of these warrants on August 11, 2002, $24.0 million was transferred to contributed surplus.

The balance of $188.0 million represented the value of the conversion feature of the Convertible Preferred Securities and was recorded as a separate component of shareholders' equity. As described in note 11(a)(iii), on October 24, 2005, the Company issued 17,142,857 Class B Non-Voting shares and recorded contributed surplus for the difference between the carrying values of the debt plus conversion feature and the total par value of the Class B Non-Voting shares.

(c)   **STOCK OPTION AND SHARE PURCHASE PLANS:**

I.   **Stock option plans:**

Details of the RCI stock option plan are as follows:

The Company's stock option plan provides senior employee participants an incentive to acquire an equity ownership interest in the Company over a period of time and, as a result, reinforces executives' attention on the long-term interest of the Company and its shareholders. Under the plan, options to purchase Class B Non-Voting shares of the Company on a one-for-one basis may be granted to employees, directors and officers of the Company and its affiliates by the Board of Directors or by the Company's Management Compensation Committee. There are 15 million options authorized under the 2000 plan, 12.5 million options authorized under the 1996 plan, and 4.75 million options authorized under the 1994 plan. The term of each option is 7–10 years; the vesting period is generally four years but may be adjusted by the Management Compensation Committee on the date of grant. The exercise price for options is equal to the fair market value of the Class B Non-Voting shares determined as the five-day average before the grant date as quoted on The Toronto Stock Exchange.

On December 31, 2004, all stock options of Wireless were exchanged for options of RCI (note 3(b)).

On July 1, 2005, all stock options of Call-Net were exchanged for fully-vested options of RCI (note 3(a)).

At December 31, 2005, a summary of the RCI option plan is as follows:

	2005		2004	
	Number of options	Weighted average exercise price per share	Number of options	Weighted average exercise price per share
Outstanding, beginning of year	18,075,849	$ 18.37	18,981,033	$ 19.06
Granted	602,534	37.27	303,666	25.88
Exercised	(5,398,036)	18.55	(4,019,485)	16.97
Forfeited	(470,197)	21.36	(1,154,959)	26.62
Exchanged from Wireless options	—	—	3,965,594	15.48
Exchanged from Call-Net options	429,274	24.37	—	—
Outstanding, end of year	13,239,424	19.24	18,075,849	18.37
Exercisable, end of year	9,570,203	$ 18.75	12,184,543	$ 18.69

At December 31, 2005, the range of exercise prices, the weighted average exercise price per share and the weighted average remaining contractual life are as follows:

		Options outstanding		Options exercisable	
Range of exercise prices	Number outstanding	Weighted average remaining contractual life (years)	Weighted average exercise price per share	Number exercisable	Weighted average exercise price per share
$ 2.76 – $ 5.00	1,869	3.6	$ 2.76	1,869	$ 2.76
$ 5.78 – $ 8.92	2,393,115	2.0	6.53	2,360,302	6.52
$ 9.38 – $13.17	2,275,434	4.7	11.28	1,658,475	11.80
$ 14.83 – $20.59	1,722,454	7.2	16.88	663,156	17.38
$ 20.60 – $26.00	4,663,852	6.4	22.98	3,290,935	23.62
$ 26.01 – $38.18	2,004,728	4.6	34.50	1,595,466	34.63
$ 39.00 – $46.89	177,972	6.9	45.08	—	—
	13,239,424	5.2	$ 19.24	9,570,203	$ 18.75

For the year ended December 31, 2005, the Company recorded compensation expense of approximately $34.7 million (2004 — $15.1 million), including the Wireless options, related to stock options granted to employees.

The weighted average estimated fair value at the date of the grant for RCI options granted during 2005 was $16.09 (2004 — $12.64) per share. No Wireless options were granted in 2004. The fair value of each option granted was estimated on the date of the grant using the Black-Scholes option pricing model with the following assumptions:

	2005	2004
RCI's risk-free interest rate	4.00%	4.36%
RCI's dividend yield	0.27%	0.38%
Volatility factor of the future expected market price of RCI's Class B Non-Voting shares	42.30%	44.81%
Weighted average expected life of the RCI options	5.4 years	6.0 years

The weighted average estimated fair value at the date of exchange of Wireless options to RCI options was $22.15 per share. The weighted average estimated fair value at the date of exchange of Call-Net options to RCI options was $19.79 per share. The fair value of each RCI option granted upon exchange and included in the purchase price equations was estimated at the date of the announcements to acquire the remaining shares of Wireless and Call-Net (note 3). The fair value of the unvested options which will be amortized to expense was calculated as at the closing date (note 3(b)). The following assumptions were used in the Black-Scholes fair value option pricing model:

	Wireless		Call-Net
	Vested options	Unvested options	Vested options
Risk-free interest rate	4.12%	4.07%	3.91%
Volatility factor of the future market price of RCI's Class B Non-Voting shares	43.06%	43.26%	31.50%
Dividend yield	0.35%	0.32%	0.27%
Weighted average expected life of the options	5.33 years	5.71 years	5.23 years

At December 31, 2004, as a result of the exchange offer, the following Wireless' stock options were exchanged for RCI options:

	Number of options	Weighted average exercise price
Options outstanding, beginning of year	4,227,097	$ 24.22
Granted	—	—
Exercised	(1,875,547)	20.70
Forfeited	(85,496)	25.31
Exchanged for RCI options	(2,266,054)	27.09
Options outstanding, end of year	—	—

II.   Employee share accumulation plan:

Effective January 1, 2004, the Company established an employee share accumulation program that allows employees to voluntarily participate in a share purchase program. Under the terms of the program, employees of the Company can contribute a specified percentage of their regular earnings through regular payroll deductions. The designated administrator of the plan then purchases, on a monthly basis, Class B Non-Voting shares of the Company on the open market on behalf of the employee. At the end of each quarter, the Company makes a contribution of 25% of the employee's contribution in the quarter. The administrator then uses this amount to purchase additional shares of the Company on behalf of the employee, as outlined above.

The Company records its contribution as compensation expense, which amounted to $3.0 million for the year ended December 31, 2005 (2004 — $1.2 million).

In addition, employees of Wireless were able to participate in Wireless' employee share accumulation plan until December 31, 2004. The terms were the same as the RCI plan, except the designated administrator of the plan purchased Class B Restricted Voting shares of Wireless on the open market on behalf of the employee. On December 31, 2004, as a result of the Company's acquisition of 100% of the outstanding Class B Restricted Voting shares of Wireless, Wireless employees had the option of using their contributions and Wireless' contributions to purchase RCI Class B Non-Voting shares, or to have their contributions refunded.

III.   Restricted share unit plan:

During 2004, the Company established a restricted share unit plan which enables employees, officers and directors of the Company to participate in the growth and development of the Company by providing such persons with the opportunity, through restricted share units, to acquire a proprietary interest in the Company. Under the terms of the plan, restricted share units are issued to the participant and the units issued vest over a period not to exceed three years from the grant date.

On the vesting date, the Company, at its option, shall redeem all of the participants' restricted share units in cash or by issuing one Class B Non-Voting share for each restricted share unit. The Company has reserved 2,000,000 Class B Non-Voting shares for issuance under this plan.

At December 31, 2005, 297,767 (2004 – 50,916) restricted share units were outstanding. These restricted share units vest at the end of three years from the grant date. The Company records compensation expense equally over the vesting period, taking into account fluctuations in the market price of the Class B Non-Voting shares of the Company. Compensation expense for the year ended December 31, 2005 related to these restricted units was $4.3 million (2004 – $0.3 million).

Note 14.   Income taxes:

The income tax effects of temporary differences that give rise to significant portions of future income tax assets and liabilities are as follows:

	2005	2004
Future income tax assets:		
Non-capital income tax loss carryforwards	$ 1,393,897	$ 1,219,699
Deductions relating to long-term debt and other transactions denominated in foreign currencies	86,491	98,523
Investments	58,890	64,081
Other deductible differences	149,825	172,759
Property, plant and equipment and inventory	86,755	—
Total future income tax assets	1,775,858	1,555,062
Less valuation allowance	617,838	696,833
	1,158,020	858,229
Future income tax liabilities:		
Property, plant and equipment and inventory	—	(35,309)
Goodwill and intangible assets	(679,556)	(795,603)
Other taxable differences	(18,062)	(27,317)
Total future income tax liabilities	(697,618)	(858,229)
Net future income tax asset	460,402	—
Less current portion	(113,150)	—
	$ 347,252	$ —

In assessing the realizability of future income tax assets, management considers whether it is more likely than not that some portion or all of the future income tax assets will be realized. The ultimate realization of future income tax assets is dependent upon the generation of future taxable income during the years in which the temporary differences are deductible. Management considers the scheduled reversals of future income tax liabilities, the character of the income tax assets and the tax planning strategies in place in making this assessment. To the extent that management believes that the realization of future income tax assets does not meet the more likely than not realization criterion, a valuation allowance is recorded against the future tax assets.

In making an assessment of whether future income tax assets are more likely than not to be realized, management regularly prepares information regarding the expected use of such assets by reference to its internal income forecasts. Based on management's estimates of the expected realization of future income tax assets, during 2005 the Company reduced the valuation allowance to reflect that it is more likely than not that certain future income tax assets will be realized. Approximately $451.8 million of the future income tax assets recognized in 2005 relate to future income tax assets arising on the acquisitions of Fido and Sportsnet (note 6(a)). Accordingly, the benefit related to these assets has been reflected as a reduction of goodwill. Any reduction in the valuation allowance related to the remaining unbenefited Fido future income tax assets, aggregating $61.4 million at December 31, 2005, will be recorded as a reduction to purchased goodwill.

As a result of the acquisition of Call-Net, the Company acquired tax assets of approximately $389.9 million against which a valuation allowance has been recorded. Any reduction in the valuation allowance related to the Call-Net future income tax assets will first reduce acquired goodwill, then acquired intangible assets and income tax expense.

The valuation allowance at December 31, 2005 includes $516.7 million of income tax assets primarily relating to non-capital loss carryforwards and $101.1 million of income tax assets relating to losses on capital account.

Total income tax expense (reduction) varies from the amounts that would be computed by applying the statutory income tax rate to income before income taxes for the following reasons:

	2005	2004
Statutory income tax rate	36.1%	35.3%
Income tax expense (reduction) on income before income taxes and non-controlling interest	$ (15,344)	$ 5,607
Increase (decrease) in income taxes resulting from:		
Change in the valuation allowance for future income tax assets	10,880	(13,440)
Adjustments to future income tax assets and liabilities for changes in substantively enacted rates	(23,293)	(920)
Non-taxable portion of capital gains	(1,750)	(2,391)
Non-deductible foreign exchange on debt and other items	2,167	2,491
Non-deductible portion of accreted interest on Convertible Preferred Securities	—	7,387
Recovery of prior years' income taxes	—	(6,660)
Non-deductible (non-taxable) amounts from investments accounted for by the equity method	(1,140)	3,715
Stock-based compensation	13,862	5,432
Other items	6,907	(7,995)
Large corporations tax	9,866	10,221
Income tax expense	$ 2,155	$ 3,447

As at December 31, 2005, the Company has the following non-capital income tax losses available to reduce future years' income for income tax purposes:

Income tax losses expiring in the year ending December 31:

2006	$ 479,833
2007	659,371
2008	1,116,873
2009	305,033
2010	197,163
2011	—
2012	—
2013	2,794
2014	706,473
2015	364,616
2016	28,791
	$ 3,860,947

Note 15. **Loss per share:**

The following table sets forth the calculation of basic and diluted loss per share:

	2005	2004
Numerator:		
Loss for the year, basic and diluted	$ (44,658)	$ (67,142)
Denominator (in thousands):		
Weighted average number of shares outstanding – basic and diluted	288,668	240,435
Loss per share:		
Basic and diluted	$ (0.15)	$ (0.28)

For 2005 and 2004, the effect of potentially dilutive securities, including the Convertible Debentures and the Convertible Preferred Securities, were excluded from the computation of diluted loss per share as their effect was anti-dilutive. In addition, options totalling approximately 13.2 million (2004 – 18.1 million) that are anti-dilutive are excluded from the calculation for the year ended December 31, 2005.

Note 16. **Pensions:**

The Company maintains both contributory and non-contributory defined benefit pension plans that cover most of its employees. The plans provide pensions based on years of service, years of contributions and earnings. The Company does not provide any non-pension post-retirement benefits.

Actuarial estimates are based on projections of employees' compensation levels at the time of retirement. Maximum retirement benefits are primarily based upon career average earnings, subject to certain adjustments. The most recent actuarial valuations were completed as at January 1, 2004 for certain of the plans and January 1, 2005 for one of the plans. The next actuarial valuation for funding purposes must be of a date no later than January 1, 2006 for one of the plans. For certain other plans, the next actuarial valuation for funding purposes must be of a date no later than January 1, 2007.

The Company also provides supplemental unfunded pension benefits to certain executives. The accrued benefit obligation relating to these supplemental plans amounted to approximately $18.0 million at December 31, 2005 (2004 – $14.1 million) and related expense for 2005 was $3.4 million (2004 – $2.9 million).

The estimated present value of accrued plan benefits and the estimated market value of the net assets available to provide for these benefits measured at September 30 for the year ended December 31 are as follows:

	2005	2004
Plan assets, at fair value	$ 483,822	$ 402,433
Accrued benefit obligations	574,388	453,318
Deficiency of plan assets over accrued benefit obligations	(90,566)	(50,885)
Employer contributions after measurement date	6,165	4,851
Unrecognized transitional obligation	(38,234)	(48,108)
Unamortized past service	4,145	4,974
Unamortized net actuarial loss	150,601	113,352
Deferred pension asset	$ 32,111	$ 24,184

Pension fund assets consist primarily of fixed income and equity securities, valued at market value. The following information is provided on pension fund assets measured at September 30 for the year ended December 31:

	2005	2004
Plan assets, beginning of year	$ 402,433	$ 339,071
Actual return on plan assets	66,730	43,053
Contributions by employees	13,871	13,237
Contributions by employer	20,152	25,572
Benefits paid	(19,364)	(18,500)
Plan assets, end of year	$ 483,822	$ 402,433

Accrued benefit obligations are outlined below measured at September 30 for the year ended December 31:

	2005	2004
Accrued benefit obligations, beginning of year	$ 453,318	$ 368,306
Service cost	15,094	11,746
Interest cost	29,538	24,003
Benefits paid	(19,364)	(18,500)
Contributions by employees	13,871	13,237
Actuarial loss	81,931	54,526
Accrued benefit obligations, end of year	$ 574,388	$ 453,318

Net plan expense is outlined below:

	2005	2004
Plan cost:		
Service cost	$ 15,094	$ 11,746
Interest cost	29,538	24,003
Actual return on plan assets	(66,730)	(43,053)
Actuarial loss on benefit obligation	81,931	54,526
Costs	59,833	47,222
Differences between costs arising in the period and costs recognized in the period in respect of:		
Return on plan assets	37,177	17,900
Actuarial gain	(74,377)	(49,537)
Plan amendments/prior service cost	830	829
Transitional asset	(9,875)	(9,875)
Net pension expense	$ 13,588	$ 6,539

(a) **ACTUARIAL ASSUMPTIONS:**

	2005	2004
Weighted average discount rate for accrued benefit obligations	5.25%	6.25%
Weighted average discount rate for pension expense	6.25%	6.25%
Weighted average rate of compensation increase	4.00%	4.00%
Weighted average expected long-term rate of return on plan assets	7.25%	7.25%

Expected return on assets represents management's best estimate of the long-term rate of return on plan assets applied to the fair value of the plan assets. The Company establishes its estimate of the expected rate of return on plan assets based on the fund's target asset allocation and estimated rate of return for each asset class. Estimated rates of return are based on expected returns from fixed income securities which take into account bond yields. An equity risk premium is then applied to estimate equity returns. Differences between expected and actual return are included in actuarial gains and losses.

The estimated average remaining service periods for the plans range from 9 to 13 years. The Company does not have any curtailment gains or losses.

(b) **ALLOCATION OF PLAN ASSETS:**

Asset category	Percentage of plan assets, December 31, 2005	Percentage of plan assets, December 31, 2004	Target asset allocation percentage
Equity securities	59.5%	58.9%	50% to 65%
Debt securities	39.9%	40.2%	35% to 50%
Other (cash)	0.6%	0.9%	0% to 1%
	100.0%	100.0%	

Plan assets are comprised primarily of pooled funds that invest in common stocks and bonds. The pooled Canadian equity fund has investments in the Company's equity securities comprising approximately 1% of the pooled fund. This results in approximately $0.8 million (2004 – $0.7 million) of the plans' assets being indirectly invested in the Company's equity securities.

The Company makes contributions to the plans to secure the benefits of plan members and invests in permitted investments using the target ranges established by the Pension Committee of the Company. The Pension Committee reviews actuarial assumptions on an annual basis.

(c) **ACTUAL CONTRIBUTIONS TO THE PLANS ARE AS FOLLOWS:**

	Employer	Employee	Total
2004	$ 19,423	$ 13,238	$ 32,661
2005	21,466	14,088	35,554

Expected contributions by the Company in 2006 are estimated to be $31.7 million.

Employee contributions for 2006 are assumed to be at levels similar to 2004 and 2005 on the assumption staffing levels in the Company will remain the same on a year-over-year basis.

(d) **EXPECTED CASH FLOWS:**
Expected benefit payments for fiscal year ending:

2006	$ 24,600
2007	24,300
2008	24,200
2009	24,000
2010	23,900
	121,000
Next 5 years	124,800
	$ 245,800

Blue Jays and Fido each have defined contribution plans with total pension expense of $5.3 million in 2005 (2004 – $0.9 million).

Note 17. **Segmented information:**

(a) **OPERATING SEGMENTS:**

The Company provides wireless services, cable services and, through Media, radio and television broadcasting and the publication of magazines and periodicals. All of these operating segments are substantially in Canada. With the acquisition of Call-Net in 2005, the Company also provides wireline long distance, data and local telecommunication services reported in the Telecom segment. Effective January 1, 2005, Blue Jays Holdco Inc. became a reporting unit of Media and as a result, is reported as part of the Media operating segment commencing in 2005 (restated for 2004). Information by operating segment for the years ended December 31, 2005 and 2004 are as follows:

2005	Wireless	Cable	Media	Telecom	Corporate items and eliminations	Consolidated Total
Operating revenue	$ 4,006,658	$ 2,067,733	$ 1,097,176	$ 423,890	$ (113,303)	$ 7,482,154
Cost of sales	773,215	157,466	157,710	207,757	—	1,296,148
Sales and marketing expenses	603,823	262,764	199,442	56,319	—	1,122,348
Operating, general and administrative expenses	1,238,964	928,900	612,178	109,272	(35,701)	2,853,613
Integration expenses	53,607	—	—	4,602	8,267	66,476
Management fees	12,025	41,355	15,322	—	(68,702)	—
Depreciation and amortization	615,710	483,946	52,019	70,653	255,683	1,478,011
Operating income (loss)	709,314	193,302	60,505	(24,713)	(272,850)	665,558
Interest on long-term debt	(405,344)	(244,859)	(8,813)	(6,702)	(44,361)	(710,079)
Intercompany: Interest expense	37,050	(18,796)	(4,337)	(5,760)	(8,157)	—
Loss on repayment of long-term debt	—	(9,799)	—	(17,460)	16,017	(11,242)
Change in fair value of derivative instruments	(27,324)	2,151	—	—	5	(25,168)
Foreign exchange gain (loss)	25,697	2,373	1,326	10,418	(4,337)	35,477
Investment and other income (expense)	(5,669)	4,043	2,120	(1,691)	4,148	2,951
Income tax reduction (expense)	84,358	(4,837)	14,298	64	(96,038)	(2,155)
Net income (loss) for the year	$ 418,082	$ (76,422)	$ 65,099	$ (45,844)	$ (405,573)	$ (44,658)
Additions to PP&E	$ 584,922	$ 676,243	$ 39,635	$ 37,352	$ 15,644	$ 1,353,796
Goodwill acquired/ adjustments (note 6(a))	$ (527,044)	$ —	$ (14,286)	$ 190,977	$ (2,547)	$ (352,900)
Goodwill	$ 1,212,422	$ 926,445	$ 705,943	$ 190,977	$ —	$ 3,035,787
Identifiable assets	$ 8,792,781	$ 4,065,782	$ 1,320,774	$ 561,716	$ (906,764)	$ 13,834,289

2004	Wireless	Cable	Media	Corporate items and eliminations	Consolidated Total
Operating revenue	$ 2,783,525	$ 1,945,655	$ 956,962	$ (77,893)	$ 5,608,249
Cost of sales	509,540	145,936	142,381	—	797,857
Sales and marketing expenses	444,379	248,754	190,489	—	883,622
Operating, general and administrative expenses	874,800	842,306	508,720	(37,612)	2,188,214
Integration expenses	4,415	—	—	—	4,415
Management fees	11,675	38,913	13,661	(64,249)	—
Depreciation and amortization	497,674	486,038	67,342	41,497	1,092,551
Operating income (loss)	441,042	183,708	34,369	(17,529)	641,590
Interest on long-term debt	(219,366)	(247,365)	(14,043)	(95,224)	(575,998)
Intercompany:					
Interest expense	(7,196)	(552)	(42,225)	49,973	—
Dividends	—	—	42,915	(42,915)	—
Loss on repayment of long-term debt	(2,313)	(18,013)	—	(7,884)	(28,210)
Change in fair value of derivative instruments	(7,796)	34,570	—	—	26,774
Foreign exchange gain (loss)	(46,714)	(41,089)	(154)	20,402	(67,555)
Investment and other income (expense)	7,939	(872)	(19,522)	31,740	19,285
Income tax reduction (expense)	(6,487)	(1,196)	(2,606)	6,842	(3,447)
Non-controlling interest	—	—	—	(79,581)	(79,581)
Net income (loss) for the year	$ 159,109	$ (90,809)	$ (1,266)	$ (134,176)	$ (67,142)
Additions to PP&E	$ 439,157	$ 587,906	$ 20,322	$ 7,553	$ 1,054,938
Goodwill acquired/adjustments (note 6(a))	$ 1,360,746	$ —	$ 148,530	$ (12,225)	$ 1,497,051
Goodwill	$ 1,739,465	$ 926,445	$ 720,229	$ 2,548	$ 3,388,687
Identifiable assets	$ 5,054,803	$ 3,861,925	$ 1,224,559	$ 3,131,451	$ 13,272,738

(b)   **PRODUCT REVENUE:**

Revenue from external customers is comprised of the following:

	2005	2004
Wireless:		
Post-paid (voice and data)	$ 3,383,444	$ 2,361,128
Prepaid	209,588	116,658
One-way messaging	19,628	24,480
Equipment sales	393,998	281,259
	4,006,658	2,783,525
Cable:		
Cable	1,298,956	1,253,053
Internet	440,664	378,912
Rogers Home Phone	4,938	—
Video store operations	326,926	316,954
Intercompany eliminations	(3,751)	(3,264)
	2,067,733	1,945,655
Media:		
Advertising	503,948	470,768
Circulation and subscription	137,247	126,852
Retail	251,792	230,865
Other	55,496	71,278
Blue Jays	148,693	57,199
	1,097,176	956,962
Telecom:		
Consumer	149,010	—
Business	274,880	—
	423,890	—
Corporate items and intercompany eliminations	(113,303)	(77,893)
	$ 7,482,154	$ 5,608,249

As a result of changes to the Company's internal management reporting in January 2006, the Company's reporting segments will change.

Note 18. **Related party transactions:**

The Company entered into the following related party transactions:

(a) The Company has entered into certain transactions in the normal course of business with AWE, a shareholder of Wireless until October 13, 2004, and with certain broadcasters in which the Company has an equity interest.

   The programming rights acquired from the Blue Jays in 2004 represent the rights acquired from January 1, 2004 to July 30, 2004, after which time, the Blue Jays were consolidated.

   The amounts billed (paid) to AWE represent amounts to October 13, 2004, after which AWE was no longer a related party.

	2005	2004
Roaming revenue billed to AWE	$ —	$ 12,146
Roaming expenses paid to AWE	—	(8,977)
Fees paid to AWE for over air activation	—	(31)
Programming rights acquired from the Blue Jays	—	(7,972)
Access fees paid to broadcasters accounted for by the equity method	(18,424)	(19,011)
	$ (18,424)	$ (23,845)

These transactions are recorded at the exchange amount, being the amount agreed to by the related parties.

(b) The Company has entered into certain transactions with companies, the partners or senior officers of which are directors of the Company and/or its subsidiary companies, which are measured at their exchange amounts, being the amounts agreed to by the related parties. Total amounts paid by the Company to these related parties are as follows:

	2005	2004
Legal services and commissions paid on premiums for insurance coverage	$ 5,358	$ 4,042
Telecommunication and programming services	1,555	6,340
Interest charges and other financing fees	21,960	37,809
	$ 28,873	$ 48,191

(c) The Company made payments to (received from) companies controlled by the controlling shareholder of the Company as follows:

	2005	2004
Dividends paid on Class A Preferred shares of Blue Jays Holdco Inc. (note 7(a))	$ —	$ 2,744
Charges to the Company for business use of aircraft	606	473
Charges by the Company for rent and reimbursement of office and personnel costs	(148)	(125)
	$ 458	$ 3,092

During 2005, with the approval of the Board of Directors, the Company entered into an arrangement to sell to the controlling shareholder of the Company, for $13 million in cash, the shares in two wholly owned subsidiaries whose only asset will consist of tax losses aggregating approximately $100 million. The terms of the transaction were reviewed and approved by a Special Committee of the Board of Directors comprised of independent directors. The Special Committee was advised by independent counsel and engaged an accounting firm as part of their review to ensure that the sale price was within a range that would be fair from a financial point of view. The sale of the tax losses will be completed by mid-2006. For accounting purposes, the Company has recorded in the consolidated balance sheet at December 31, 2005 a future tax asset of $13 million, representing the amount the Company will receive from the controlling shareholder for the tax losses when the sale is completed. In addition, a corresponding $13 million was recorded as a reduction of income tax expense in 2005 in the consolidated statement of income.

Note 19. **Financial instruments:**

(a) **FAIR VALUES:**

The Company has determined the fair values of its financial instruments as follows:

(i)   The carrying amounts in the consolidated balance sheets of cash and cash equivalents, accounts receivable, amounts receivable from employees under share purchase plans, mortgages and loans receivable, bank advances arising from outstanding cheques and accounts payable and accrued liabilities approximate fair values because of the short-term nature of these instruments.

(ii)   Investments:

The fair values of investments that are publicly-traded, are determined by the quoted market values for each of the investments (note 7). Management believes that the fair values of other investments are not significantly different from their carrying amounts.

(iii) Long-term receivables:

The fair values of long-term receivables approximate their carrying amounts since the interest rates approximate current market rates.

(iv)   Long-term debt:

The fair values of each of the Company's long-term debt instruments are based on the period-end trading values, except as noted below.

(v)   Derivative instruments:

The fair values of the Company's interest exchange agreements, cross-currency interest rate exchange agreements and other derivative instruments are based on values quoted by the counterparties to the agreements.

The estimated fair values of the Company's long-term debt and related derivative instruments as at December 31, 2005 and 2004 are as follows:

	2005		2004	
	Carrying amount	Estimated fair value	Carrying amount	Estimated fair value
Liability:				
Long-term debt	$ 7,739,551	$ 8,095,057	$ 8,541,097	$ 8,861,038[1]
Derivative instruments[2]	738,161	1,335,337	626,896	945,767
	$ 8,477,712	$ 9,430,394	$ 9,167,993	$ 9,806,805

(1) The fair value of the Convertible Preferred Securities was not readily determinable and are, therefore, included at their carrying value of $490.7 million at December 31, 2004.

(2) Excludes deferred transitional gain of $63.4 million (2004 — $73.5 million).

Fair value estimates are made at a specific point in time, based on relevant market information and information about the financial instruments. These estimates are subjective in nature and involve uncertainties and matters of significant judgment and, therefore, cannot be determined with precision. Changes in assumptions could significantly affect the estimates.

At December 31, 2005, 85.2% of U.S. dollar-denominated debt (2004 — 81.1%) was protected from fluctuations in the foreign exchange between the U.S. and Canadian dollars by the total derivative instruments.

The credit risk of the interest exchange agreements and cross-currency interest rate exchange agreements arises from the possibility that the counterparties to the agreements may default on their respective obligations under the agreements in instances where these agreements have positive fair value for the Company. The Company assesses the creditworthiness of the counterparties in order to minimize the risk of counterparty default under the agreements. All of the portfolio is held by financial institutions with a Standard & Poor's rating (or the equivalent) ranging from A+ to AA. The Company does not require collateral or other security to support the credit risk associated with the interest exchange agreements and cross-currency interest rate exchange agreements due to the Company's assessment of the creditworthiness of the counterparties. The obligations under US$4,801.8 million (2004 — US$5,135.3 million) aggregate notional amount of the cross-currency interest rate exchange agreements are secured by substantially all of the assets of the respective subsidiary companies to which they relate and generally rank equally with the other secured indebtedness of such subsidiary companies.

(vi)   Other long-term liabilities:
The carrying amounts of other long-term liabilities approximate fair values as the interest rates approximate current rates.

(b)   OTHER DISCLOSURES:

The Company does not have any significant concentrations of credit risk related to any financial asset.

Note 20. **Commitments:**

(a)   On September 16, 2005, the Company announced a joint venture with Bell Canada to build and manage a nationwide fixed wireless broadband network. The companies will jointly and equally fund the initial network deployment costs estimated at $200 million over a three-year period. The Company will also contribute its broadband wireless spectrum in the 2.3 GHz, 2.5 GHz and 3.5 GHz frequency ranges, subject to approvals from Industry Canada.

(b)   RCI enters into agreements with suppliers to provide services and products that include minimum spend commitments. The Company has agreements with certain telephone companies that guarantee the long-term supply of network facilities and agreements relating to the operations and maintenance of the network.

(c)   In the ordinary course of business and in addition to the amounts recorded on the consolidated balance sheets and disclosed elsewhere in the notes, the Company has entered into agreements to acquire broadcasting rights to programs and films over the next three years at a total cost of approximately $57.7 million. In addition, the Company has commitments to pay access fees over the next year totalling approximately $18.4 million.

(d)   On February 7, 2005, the Company was awarded a share of the broadcast rights to the 2010 Olympic Winter Games and the 2012 Olympic Summer Games at a cost of US$30.6 million.

(e)   The Company has a 33.33% interest in each of Tech TV Canada and Biography Channel Canada, which are equity-accounted investments. The Company has committed to fund its share of the losses and PP&E expenditures in these new channels to a maximum of $8.8 million, through equity financing and shareholder loans. As at December 31, 2005, the Company has funded a total of $5.9 million.

(f)   Pursuant to CRTC regulation, the Company is required to make contributions to the Canadian Television Fund ("CTF"), which is a cable industry fund designed to foster the production of Canadian television programming. Contributions to the CTF are based on a formula, including gross broadcast revenues and the number of subscribers. The Company may elect to spend a portion of the above amount for local television programming and may also elect to contribute a portion to another CRTC-approved independent production fund. The Company estimates that its total contribution for 2006 will amount to approximately $34.1 million.

(g)   In addition to the items listed above, the future minimum lease payments under operating leases for the rental of premises, distribution facilities, equipment and microwave towers and commitments for player contracts and other contracts at December 31, 2005 are as follows:

Year ending December 31:		
2006	$	214,123
2007		187,992
2008		143,284
2009		126,154
2010		90,012
2011 and thereafter		80,191
	$	841,756

Rent expense for 2005 amounted to $194.3 million (2004 – $134.2 million).

Note 21. **Guarantees:**

The Company has entered into agreements that contain features which meet the definition of a guarantee under GAAP. A description of the major types of such agreements is provided below:

(a) **BUSINESS SALE AND BUSINESS COMBINATION AGREEMENTS:**
As part of transactions involving business dispositions, sales of assets or other business combinations, the Company may be required to pay counterparties for costs and losses incurred as a result of breaches of representations and warranties, intellectual property right infringement, loss or damages to property, environmental liabilities, changes in laws and regulations (including tax legislation), litigation against the counterparties, contingent liabilities of a disposed business or reassessments of previous tax filings of the corporation that carries on the business.

The Company is unable to make a reasonable estimate of the maximum potential amount it could be required to pay counterparties. The amount also depends on the outcome of future events and conditions, which cannot be predicted. No amount has been accrued in the consolidated balance sheets relating to this type of indemnification or guarantee at December 31, 2005 or 2004. Historically, the Company has not made any significant payments under these indemnifications or guarantees.

(b) **SALES OF SERVICES:**
As part of transactions involving sales of services, the Company may be required to pay counterparties for costs and losses incurred as a result of breaches of representations and warranties, changes in laws and regulations (including tax legislation) or litigation against the counterparties.

The Company is unable to make a reasonable estimate of the maximum potential amount it could be required to pay counterparties. No amount has been accrued in the consolidated balance sheets relating to this type of indemnification or guarantee at December 31, 2005 or 2004. Historically, the Company has not made any significant payments under these indemnifications or guarantees.

(c) **PURCHASES AND DEVELOPMENT OF ASSETS:**
As part of transactions involving purchases and development of assets, the Company may be required to pay counterparties for costs and losses incurred as a result of breaches of representations and warranties, loss or damages to property, changes in laws and regulations (including tax legislation) or litigation against the counterparties.

The Company is unable to make a reasonable estimate of the maximum potential amount the Company could be required to pay counterparties. The amount also depends on the outcome of future events and conditions, which cannot be predicted. No amount has been accrued in the consolidated balance sheets relating to this type of indemnification or guarantee at December 31, 2005 or 2004. Historically, the Company has not made any significant payments under these indemnifications or guarantees.

(d) **INDEMNIFICATIONS:**
The Company indemnifies its directors, officers and employees against claims reasonably incurred and resulting from the performance of their services to the Company, and maintains liability insurance for its directors and officers as well as those of its subsidiaries.

Note 22. **Contingent liabilities:**

(a)   On August 9, 2004, a proceeding under the Class Actions Act (Saskatchewan) was brought against Wireless and other providers of wireless communications services in Canada. The proceeding involves allegations by Wireless customers of breach of contract, misrepresentation and false advertising with respect to the system access fee charged by Wireless to some of its customers. The plaintiffs seek unquantified damages from the defendant wireless communications service providers. Wireless believes it has good defences to the allegations. The proceeding has not been certified as a class action and it is too early to determine whether the proceeding will qualify for certification as a class action. In addition, on December 9, 2004, Wireless was served with a court order compelling it to produce certain records and other information relevant to an investigation initiated by the Commissioner of Competition under the misleading advertising provisions of the Competition Act with respect to its system access fee.

(b)   On April 21, 2004, a proceeding was brought against Fido and its subsidiary, Fido Solutions Inc. and others alleging breach of contract, breach of confidence, misuse of confidential information, breach of a duty of loyalty, good faith and to avoid a conflict of duty and self-interest, and conspiracy. The plaintiff is seeking damages in the amount of $160 million. The proceeding is at an early stage. Wireless believes it has good defences to the claim.

(c)   The Company believes that it has adequately provided for income taxes based on all of the information that is currently available. The calculation of income taxes in many cases, however, requires significant judgment in interpreting tax rules and regulations. The Company's tax filings are subject to audits which could materially change the amount of current and future income tax assets and liabilities, and could, in certain circumstances, result in the assessment of interest and penalties.

(d)   There exist certain other claims and potential claims against the Company, none of which is expected to have a material adverse effect on the consolidated financial position of the Company.

Note 23. **Canadian and United States accounting policy differences:**

The consolidated financial statements of the Company have been prepared in accordance with GAAP as applied in Canada. In the following respects, GAAP, as applied in the United States, differs from that applied in Canada.

If United States GAAP were employed, loss for the year in each year would be adjusted as follows:

	2005	2004
Loss for the year based on Canadian GAAP	$ (44,658)	$ (67,142)
Gain on sale of cable systems (b)	(4,028)	(4,028)
Pre-operating costs (c)	(8,621)	5,348
Equity instruments (d)	15,818	18,526
Capitalized interest, net (e)	2,879	3,061
Financial instruments (h)	(285,775)	(188,420)
Stock-based compensation (i)	14,113	15,091
Income taxes (k)	(2,090)	8,374
Installation revenues, net (l)	1,706	2,744
Loss on repayment of long-term debt (m)	—	(28,760)
Interest expense (n)	(2,499)	—
Non-controlling interest	—	(36,630)
Other	559	1,211
Loss for the year based on United States GAAP	$ (312,596)	$ (270,625)
Basic and diluted loss per share based on United States GAAP	$ (1.08)	$ (1.13)

The cumulative effect of these adjustments on the consolidated shareholders' equity of the Company is as follows:

	2005	2004
Shareholders' equity based on Canadian GAAP	$ 3,527,615	$ 2,385,334
Gain on sale and issuance of subsidiary shares to non-controlling interest (a)	46,245	46,245
Gain on sale of cable systems (b)	116,909	120,937
Pre-operating costs (c)	(12,127)	(3,506)
Equity instruments (d)	—	(98,098)
Capitalized interest (e)	43,927	41,047
Unrealized holding gains on investments (f)	139,384	152,267
Acquisition of Cable Atlantic (g)	34,673	34,673
Financial instruments (h)	(533,788)	(248,013)
Minimum pension liability (j)	(20,423)	(20,970)
Income taxes (k)	(253,567)	(253,567)
Installation revenues, net (l)	4,450	2,744
Loss on repayment of long-term debt (m)	(28,760)	(28,760)
Acquisition of Wireless (n)	3,095	2,927
Non-controlling interest effect of adjustments	(95,031)	(95,031)
Other	(15,270)	(15,829)
Shareholders' equity based on United States GAAP	$ 2,957,332	$ 2,022,400

The areas of material difference between Canadian and United States GAAP and their impact on the consolidated financial statements of the Company are described below:

(a) GAIN ON SALE AND ISSUANCE OF SUBSIDIARY SHARES TO NON-CONTROLLING INTEREST:
Under United States GAAP, the carrying value of the Company's investment in Wireless would be lower than the carrying value under Canadian GAAP as a result of certain differences between Canadian and United States GAAP, as described herein. This results in an increase to the gain on sale and dilution under United States GAAP.

(b) GAIN ON SALE OF CABLE SYSTEMS:
Under Canadian GAAP, the cash proceeds on the non-monetary exchange of the cable assets in 2000 were recorded as a reduction in the carrying value of PP&E. Under United States GAAP, a portion of the cash proceeds received must be recognized as a gain in the consolidated statements of income on an after-tax basis. The gain amounted to $40.3 million before income taxes.

Under Canadian GAAP, the after-tax gain arising on the sale of certain of the Company's cable television systems in prior years was recorded as a reduction of the carrying value of goodwill acquired in a contemporaneous acquisition of certain cable television systems. Under United States GAAP, the Company included the gain on sale of the cable television systems in income, net of related future income taxes.

As a result of these transactions, amortization expense under United States GAAP was increased in subsequent years.

(c) PRE-OPERATING COSTS:
Under Canadian GAAP, the Company defers the incremental costs relating to the development and pre-operating phases of new businesses and amortizes these costs on a straight-line basis over periods up to five years. Under United States GAAP, these costs are expensed as incurred.

(d) EQUITY INSTRUMENTS:
Under Canadian GAAP, the fair value of the liability component of the Convertible Preferred Securities of $388.0 million at the date of issuance was recorded as long-term debt. This liability component was being accreted up to the $600.0 million face value of the Convertible Preferred Securities over the term to maturity. This accretion was charged to interest expense. Under Canadian GAAP, the value of the conversion feature of $188.0 million was recorded in shareholders' equity.

Under United States GAAP, the fair value of the conversion feature was not permitted to be separately recorded. The fair value of the liability component of $576.0 million at issuance was recorded outside of shareholders' equity and was being accreted up to the $600.0 million face value of the Convertible Preferred Securities over the term to maturity. This accretion was charged to interest expense.

During 2005, the Convertible Preferred Securities were converted to Class B Non-Voting shares (note 11(a)(iii)).

(e)   **CAPITALIZED INTEREST:**

United States GAAP requires capitalization of interest costs as part of the historical cost of acquiring certain qualifying assets that require a period of time to prepare for their intended use. This is not required under Canadian GAAP.

(f)   **UNREALIZED HOLDING GAINS AND LOSSES ON INVESTMENTS:**

United States GAAP requires that certain investments in equity securities that have readily determinable fair values be stated in the consolidated balance sheets at their fair values. The unrealized holding gains and losses from these investments, which are considered to be "available-for-sale securities" under United States GAAP, are included as a separate component of shareholders' equity and comprehensive income, net of related future income taxes.

(g)   **ACQUISITION OF CABLE ATLANTIC:**

United States GAAP requires that shares issued in connection with a purchase business combination be valued based on the market price at the announcement date of the acquisition, whereas Canadian GAAP had required such shares be valued based on the market price at the consummation date of the acquisition. Accordingly, the Class B Non-Voting shares issued in respect of the acquisition of Cable Atlantic in 2001 were recorded at $35.4 million more under United States GAAP than under Canadian GAAP. This resulted in an increase to goodwill in this amount, with a corresponding increase to contributed surplus in the amount of $35.4 million.

(h)   **FINANCIAL INSTRUMENTS:**

Under Canadian GAAP, the Company accounts for certain of its cross-currency interest rate exchange agreements as hedges of specific debt instruments. Under United States GAAP, these instruments are not accounted for as hedges, but instead changes in the fair value of the derivative instruments, reflecting primarily market changes in foreign exchange rates, interest rates, as well as the level of short-term variable versus long-term fixed interest rates, are recognized in income immediately. Foreign exchange translation gains and losses arising from change in period-end foreign exchange rates on the respective long-term debt are also recognized in income.

Under United States GAAP, as a result of the adoption of United States Financial Accounting Standard Board's ("FASB") Statement ("SFAS") No. 133, Accounting for Derivative Instruments and Hedging Activities ("SFAS 133") effective January 1, 2001, the Company recorded a cumulative transition adjustment representing the adjustment necessary to reflect the derivatives at their fair values at that date, net of the offsetting gains/losses on the associated hedged long-term debt. In March 2004, $11.4 million of this cumulative transition adjustment was written off as a result of the repayment of the long-term debt to which it relates (note 23(m)).

(i)   **STOCK-BASED COMPENSATION:**

Under Canadian GAAP, effective January 1, 2004, the Company adopted the fair value method of recognizing stock-based compensation expense. For United States GAAP purposes, the intrinsic value method is used to account for stock-based compensation of employees. Compensation expense of $34.7 million (2004 – $15.1 million) recognized under Canadian GAAP would not be recognized under United States GAAP for the year ended December 31, 2004. The exercise price of stock options is equal to the market value of the underlying shares at the date of grant; therefore, there is no expense under the intrinsic value method for United States GAAP purposes for the years ended December 31, 2005 and 2004.

Effective January 1, 2004, the Blue Jays were determined to be a variable interest entity for United States GAAP purposes and, as a result, their results were consolidated from that date (note 23(o)). As such, the employees of the Blue Jays were considered employees of the Company effective January 1, 2004 for United States GAAP purposes. The intrinsic value of the options of Blue Jays' employees was calculated as at January 1, 2004 as nil. Prior to 2004, the Blue Jays' employees were not considered employees of the Company.

Under United States GAAP, unvested options that were issued as consideration for the acquisition of the remaining shares of RWCI on December 31, 2004 were revalued at this date with the resulting intrinsic value of $38.3 million recorded as unearned compensation cost. Unearned compensation cost is recognized as compensation expense over the remaining vesting period. During 2005, under United States GAAP, $20.7 million of compensation expense was recorded related to these options.

(j)   MINIMUM PENSION LIABILITY:

Under United States GAAP, the Company is required to record an additional minimum pension liability for one of its plans to reflect the excess of the accumulated benefit obligation over the fair value of the plan assets. Other comprehensive income has been increased by $0.4 million (2004 – charged with $8.5 million), which is net of income taxes of $0.2 million (2004 – $4.6 million). No such adjustments are required under Canadian GAAP.

(k)   INCOME TAXES:

Included in the caption "Income taxes" is the tax effect of various adjustments where appropriate. Under Canadian GAAP, future income tax assets and liabilities are remeasured for substantively enacted rate changes, whereas under United States GAAP, future income tax assets and liabilities are only remeasured for enacted tax rates.

(l)   INSTALLATION REVENUES AND COSTS:

For Canadian GAAP purposes, cable installation revenues for both new connects and re-connects are deferred and amortized over the customer relationship period. For United States GAAP purposes, installation revenues are immediately recognized in income to the extent of direct selling costs, with any excess deferred and amortized over the customer relationship period.

(m)   LOSS ON REPAYMENT OF LONG-TERM DEBT:

On March 26, 2004, the Company repaid long-term debt resulting in a loss on early repayment of long-term debt of $2.3 million. This loss included, among other items, a $40.2 million gain on the realization of the deferred transitional gain related to cross currency interest rate exchange agreements which were unwound in connection with the repayment of long-term debt. Under United States GAAP, the Company records cross currency interest rate exchange agreements at fair value. Therefore, under United States GAAP, the deferred transition gain realized under Canadian GAAP would be reduced by $28.8 million, representing the $40.2 million gain net of realization of a gain of $11.4 million, related to the deferred transition adjustment that arose on the adoption of SFAS 133 (note 23(h)).

(n)   ACQUISITION OF WIRELESS INTEREST:

At December 31, 2004, the Company acquired the outstanding shares of Wireless not owned by the Company and exchanged the outstanding stock options of Wireless for stock options in the Company (note 3(b)). United States GAAP requires that the intrinsic value of the unvested options issued be determined as of the consummation date of the transaction and be recorded as deferred compensation. Canadian GAAP requires that the fair value of unvested options be recorded as deferred compensation. Under United States GAAP, this results in an increase in goodwill in the consolidated accounts of the Company of $5.6 million, with a corresponding adjustment to contributed surplus.

Under Canadian GAAP, as part of the purchase price equation, the derivative instruments of Wireless were recorded at their fair value at the date of acquisition (note 3(b)). The fair value increment is amortized to interest expense over the remaining terms of the derivative instruments. Under United States GAAP, the derivative instruments are recorded at fair value. Therefore, under United States GAAP, the fair value increment related to derivative instruments is reduced by $20.1 million with an offsetting decrease to goodwill. As a consequence, the amortization of the fair value increment is not required under United States GAAP.

(o)   **BLUE JAYS:**

Under United States GAAP, FASB Interpretation No. 46, Consolidation of Variable Interest Entities, requires the Company to consolidate the results of the Blue Jays effective January 1, 2004. Under Canadian GAAP, the Company consolidated the Blue Jays effective July 31, 2004. Therefore, the United States GAAP consolidated balance sheet as at December 31, 2004 and net income of the Company for the year then ended would be unchanged from that of Canadian GAAP as the Company recorded 100% of the losses of the Blue Jays. Under United States GAAP, consolidation from January 1, 2004 to July 31, 2004 would result in an increase in revenues of $75.0 million, cost of sales would increase by $70.1 million, sales and marketing costs would increase by $3.8 million, operating general and administrative expenses would increase by $17.8 million, depreciation and amortization would increase by $5.8 million, operating income would be reduced by $22.6 million and losses from equity method investments would decrease by $22.6 million.

(p)   **STATEMENTS OF CASH FLOWS:**

(i)   Canadian GAAP permits the disclosure of a subtotal of the amount of funds provided by operations before change in non-cash operating items in the consolidated statements of cash flows. United States GAAP does not permit this subtotal to be included.

(ii)   Canadian GAAP permits bank advances to be included in the determination of cash and cash equivalents in the consolidated statements of cash flows. United States GAAP requires that bank advances be reported as financing cash flows. As a result, under United States GAAP, the total increase in cash and cash equivalents in 2004 in the amount of $254.3 million reflected in the consolidated statements of cash flows would be decreased by $10.3 million and financing activities cash flows would decrease by $10.3 million. The total decrease in cash and cash equivalents in 2005 in the amount of $347.9 million reflected in the consolidated statements of cash flows would be decreased by $104.0 million and financing activities cash flows would be increased by $104.0 million.

(q)   **STATEMENT OF COMPREHENSIVE INCOME:**

United States GAAP requires the disclosure of a statement of comprehensive income. Comprehensive income generally encompasses all changes in shareholders' equity, except those arising from transactions with shareholders.

	2005	2004
Net loss based on United States GAAP	$ (312,596)	$ (270,625)
Other comprehensive income, net of income taxes:		
Unrealized holding gains (losses) arising during the year, net of income taxes	(1,138)	69,586
Realized gains included in income, net of income tax	(9,463)	(10,567)
Realized losses included in income	–	1,650
Minimum pension liability, net of income taxes	354	(8,483)
Comprehensive loss based on United States GAAP	$ (322,843)	$ (218,439)

(r)   **OTHER DISCLOSURES:**

United States GAAP requires the Company to disclose accrued liabilities, which is not required under Canadian GAAP. Accrued liabilities included in accounts payable and accrued liabilities as at December 31, 2005 were $1,068.6 million (2004 – $1,100.9 million). At December 31, 2005, accrued liabilities in respect of PP&E totalled $104.0 million (2004 – $116.0 million), accrued interest payable totalled $113.1 million (2004 – $117.6 million), accrued liabilities related to payroll totalled $176.6 million (2004 – $173.3 million), and CRTC commitments totalled $40.4 million (2004 – $56.5 million).

(s) **PENSIONS:**

The Company implemented SFAS No. 132, Employers Disclosures about Pensions and Other Post-retirement Benefits — an amendment of FASB Statement No. 87, 88 and 106 in 2004. The following summarizes the additional disclosures required and different pension-related amounts recognized or disclosed in the Company's accounts under United States GAAP:

	2005	2004
Current service cost (employer portion)	$ 15,094	$ 11,746
Interest cost	29,538	24,003
Expected return on plan assets	(29,554)	(25,153)
Amortization:		
Transitional asset	(9,875)	(9,875)
Realized gains included in income	830	829
Net actuarial loss	7,555	4,989
Net periodic pension cost	$ 13,588	$ 6,539
Accrued benefit asset	$ 12,944	$ 3,214
Accumulated other comprehensive loss	19,167	20,970
Net amount recognized in balance sheet	$ 32,111	$ 24,184

Under United States GAAP, the accrued benefit liability related to the Company's supplemental unfunded pension benefits for certain executives was $15.6 million (2004 — $12.5 million), the intangible asset was $5.0 million (2004 — $6.5 million) and the accumulated other comprehensive loss was $1.3 million (2004 — nil).

(t) **RECENT UNITED STATES ACCOUNTING PRONOUNCEMENTS:**

SFAS 123(R), Share-Based Payment, as revised, is effective for fiscal 2006 of the Company. This revised standard requires companies to recognize in the income statement, the grant-date fair value of stock options and other equity-based compensation issued to employees. The fair value of liability-classified awards is remeasured subsequently at each reporting date through the settlement date while the fair value of equity-classified awards is not subsequently remeasured. The alternative to use the intrinsic value method of Accounting Principles Board ("APB") Opinion 25, which the Company has chosen for United States GAAP purposes, is eliminated with this revised standard. The Company is currently evaluating the impact of this revised standard.

In November 2004, the FASB issued SFAS No. 151, Inventory Costs, an amendment of ARB No. 43, Chapter 4. This statement amends the guidance in ARB No. 43, Chapter 4, "Inventory Pricing" to clarify the accounting for abnormal amounts of idle facility expense, freight, handling costs, and wasted material (spoilage). SFAS 151 requires that those items be recognized as current-period charges. In addition, this statement requires that allocation of fixed production overheads to costs of conversion be based upon the normal capacity of the production facilities. The provisions of SFAS 151 are effective for inventory cost incurred in fiscal years beginning after June 15, 2005. As such, the Company is required to adopt these provisions at the beginning of fiscal 2006. The Company is currently evaluating the impact of this revised standard.

SFAS 153, Exchanges Of Non-Monetary Assets — an Amendment of APB Opinion 29, was issued in December 2004. APB Opinion 29 is based on the principle that exchanges of non-monetary assets should be measured based on the fair value of assets exchanged. SFAS 153 amends APB Opinion 29 to eliminate the exception for non-monetary exchanges of similar productive assets and replaces it with a general exception for exchanges of non-monetary assets that do not have commercial substance. The standard is effective for the Company for non-monetary asset exchanges occurring in fiscal 2006 and will be applied prospectively. The Company is currently evaluating the impact of this revised standard.

In June 2005, the FASB issued SFAS No. 154, Accounting Changes and Error Corrections, a replacement of APB Opinion No. 20, Accounting Changes, and FASB Statement No. 3, Reporting Accounting Changes in Interim Financial Statements ("SFAS 154"). The Statement applies to all voluntary changes in accounting principle, and changes the requirements for accounting for and reporting of a change in accounting principle. SFAS 154 requires retrospective application to prior periods' financial statements of a voluntary change in accounting principle unless it is impracticable. SFAS 154 requires that a change in method of depreciation, amortization, or depletion for long-lived, non-financial assets be accounted for as a change in accounting estimate that is affected by a change in accounting principle. Opinion 20 previously required that such a change be reported as a change in accounting principle. SFAS 154 is effective for accounting changes and corrections of errors made in fiscal years beginning after December 15, 2005. The Company is currently evaluating the impact of the new standard.

Note 24. **Subsequent events:**

On January 3, 2006, the Company redeemed all of Telecom's remaining 10.625% Senior Secured Notes due 2008. The total redemption amount was US$23.2 million including a redemption premium of US$1.2 million.

On January 4, 2006, the Company completed the acquisition of certain real estate assets in Brampton, Ontario, Canada for $96.3 million in cash, net of adjustments, and including taxes and title insurance. The total purchase price for the acquisition was $99.3 million including a $3.0 million deposit made in 2005.

On January 6, 2006 the Company paid a semi-annual dividend of $23.5 million to the shareholders of record on December 28, 2005.

Upon maturity on February 14, 2006, the Company redeemed its $75.0 million Senior Notes.

A-51

APPENDIX B

COMPREHENSIVE CASES

1. Richibucto Rattlesnakes and Sports Complex, Ltd.
2. GAAP Air Ltd.
3. Angela Kellett, Barrister and Solicitor
4. International Productions Corporation
5. Vulcanzap Inc.
6. Shmevan Stores Ltd.
7. Good Quality Auto Parts Limited
8. Jeremy Langer
9. Kenaston Convenience Store
10. Dymo Manufacturing
11. Discount Stores Limited
12. Ontario Printing Limited

CASE 1: RICHIBUCTO RATTLESNAKES AND SPORTS COMPLEX, LTD.

Max Lee is a successful dentist in southern Ontario. He began his practice fifteen years ago. Recently, Max has been looking for an investment to indulge his lifelong interest in sports. He and a group of like-minded people have begun seeking out a minor league sports franchise to purchase. All the members of the group are mainly interested in the fun and excitement of owning a sports team, but they don't want to be spending much of their own money beyond the initial amount they pay for the franchise. None of the people in the group has experience in business, accounting or operating a sports franchise. All members of the group will continue in their present occupations after a team is purchased.

The group has begun preliminary discussions with the owner of a hockey franchise in Atlantic Canada, the Richibucto Rattlesnakes (Rattlesnakes). The owner of the franchise, Jane Bowen, says the franchise has been quite successful but she wants to sell the Rattlesnakes because of her failing health. Bowen has owned and operated the team since its formation in 1984, when she purchased the franchise rights for the city from the league. In 1989, Jane built a 6,000 seat arena in the city to house the team. The arena is also used for other events such as concerts that are promoted by Jane, or by third parties who rent the facility. Revenue is also generated from concessions (food, souvenirs, and parking).

The group has obtained the Rattlesnakes' most recent year's financial statements. Jane has indicated that the statements are prepared strictly for tax purposes as there are no other users for the statements. The statements are, by and large, prepared according to GAAP, but not exclusively.

Max Lee has come to you for advice on interpreting the financial statements. He has indicated that he does not understand them very well and wants to get some insights into what the statements tell and what they do not tell his. He would also like your advice on what additional accounting and financial information he should request from Bowen before deciding on how much he and his group are prepared to pay for the team and its facility.

Required:

Prepare a report to Max Lee providing the advice he requested. Be specific and provide full explanations.

Richibucto Rattlesnakes and Sports Complex, Ltd.
Balance Sheet
As at July 30, 2009

Cash	$ 125,000	Bank Loan	$225,000
Accounts Receivable	5,000	Accounts Payable	100,000
Prepaids and Other Assets	15,000		
Capital Assets	8,450,000		
Less: Accumulated Amortization	(6,337,500)		
	2,112,500	Common Stock	1,100,000
Hockey Team Franchise	400,000	Retained Earnings	1,232,500
Total Assets	$2,657,500	Total Liabilities and Shareholder's Equity	$2,657,500

Richibucto Rattlesnakes and Sports Complex, Ltd.
Income Statement
For the year ended July 30, 2009

Revenue			
	Hockey	$3,200,000	
	Concessions and parking	1,200,000	
	Other events	1,500,000	
	Other revenue	210,000	$6,110,000
Expenses			
	Hockey operations	1,760,000	
	Concessions and parking	540,000	
	Other events	1,125,000	
	Building costs	2,550,000	$5,975,000
Expansion Fee Revenue			250,000
Income tax expense			77,000
Net Income			$308,000

Richibucto Rattlesnakes and Sports Complex, Ltd.
Notes to the Financial Statements

1. Fixed assets include the arena and land, along with the equipment necessary to operate the arena and hockey team.

2. The Hockey Team Franchise account is the cost of the franchise. The amount is not amortized.

3. Hockey revenue includes $355,000 for the radio broadcast rights to the team's home games. The radio network is owned separately by Bowen and her family.

4. Revenue is recognized for hockey games and other events when the event occurs.

5. During fiscal 2009 the league expanded by two teams. The Rattlesnakes received $250,000 as its share of the expansion fees.

6. The Rattlesnakes has a working arrangement with a major league professional hockey team. The major league team supplies players and pays their salaries, but is entitled to use those players at its discretion. Approximately 60 percent of the players used by the Rattlesnakes are supplied by the major league team. The contract with the major league team expires in two years.

7. The bank loan is personally guaranteed by Jane Bowen and is secured against company assets as well as Jane's personal assets.

CASE 2: GAAP AIR LTD.

GAAP Air Ltd. (GAAP Air) is an airline that was started five years ago to take advantage of the popular brand name associated with The GAAP clothing chain. GAAP Air was incorporated as a separate entity in 2005 and went public two years ago in 2008. GAAP Air has struggled financially over the past few years due to depressed demand and intense competition in the airline industry. In fact, several of GAAP Air's competitors have been forced into bankruptcy over the past few years.

It is now February 2010 and industry experts are projecting a turnaround in the airline industry by 2011. Unfortunately, negative operating cash flows over the past few years have eaten up GAAP Air's cash and available credit. GAAP Air has approached a major bank for a loan to allow it to continue operating for another year, until the industry conditions improve. The bank is waiting for the 2009 audited financial statements to make a final decision on whether or not to lend the funds.

You are a Senior Accountant at GAAP Air. Your boss, the Chief Financial Officer (CFO), has given you the following summary of new transactions undertaken by the company during the year. He would like you to provide a report discussing how GAAP Air should account for each of the transactions. He would like you to discuss alternative policies, where applicable, and give your opinion on which policy the company should select. The CFO would like you consider all of the financial statement users and their objectives, as well as any constraints on accounting policy choices in your analysis. He will use your report in his discussion with the company's auditors. GAAP Air has a December 31st year end.

1. In an attempt to increase ticket sales, GAAP Air introduced a unique loyalty program. For every mile a customer flies, he or she gets one GAAP Mile. The customer can then redeem GAAP miles for free flights or merchandise at The GAAP, Old Army or Papaya Republic. The CFO would like to know when and how the cost of GAAP miles should be recognized.

2. In an effort to reduce employee turnover, the company has introduced a signing bonus for new employees. The company pays new employees a signing bonus of 5 percent of annual salary. Employees must repay the entire bonus if they do not stay with the company for at least two years. After the initial two year period, employees are not obligated to repay any of the bonus. The CFO would like to know how this bonus should be accounted for.

3. GAAP Air has a fleet of 14 planes. Two of the planes are more than 20 years old and were taken out of service in 2009. GAAP Air has contacted several shipping companies in an effort to sell the planes for use carrying cargo. To date, none of the companies have made an offer. The Chief Executive Officer (CEO) is confident that the planes will eventually be sold. The planes are currently carried on the balance sheet at a cost of $12,000,000 less accumulated depreciation of $10,500,000 (total for both planes). The CFO would like you to consider whether a write-down is required.

4. GAAP Air entered a contract on July 1, 2009 with the Toronto Towers hockey team. The contract states that GAAP Air will fly the Toronto Towers hockey players and support staff to all 40 "away games" for a lump sum payment of $800,000. The payment was received on July 31st 2009. The hockey season runs from September through April. The contract is non-cancellable and GAAP Air will keep the $800,000 if for any reason the Towers chooses not to use the flights. In addition, as part of the contract, GAAP Air agreed to display the Towers logo on their planes until the end of the hockey season. The CFO would like to know when the revenues related to this contract should be recognized.

CASE 3: ANGELA KELLETT, BARRISTER AND SOLICITOR*

Angela Kellett is a recent law school graduate. She opened her practice six months ago and her client base has been growing steadily over that time. Ms. Kellett was recently approached

---

*This case was written by Angela Kellett of the University of Ontario Institute of Technology and is used with permission.

by a new client, Ferdinand Jones, who wanted advice about selling his business. Mr. Jones and the buyer are in the final stages of negotiations. So far they have agreed on all terms except the final selling price. The buyer has proposed that an earnout arrangement be included in the contract whereby Mr. Jones would receive a fixed payment plus a share of net income for one or two years after the sale is complete. The buyer has stipulated that for purposes of the earnout arrangement the financial statements would be prepared in accordance with GAAP consistently applied and that the financial statement would have to receive an unqualified audit opinion from an independent auditor.

Ms. Kellett took some business courses while at law school, including a course in financial accounting, and she's very worried about the earnout arrangement. She remembers from her accounting course that managers have a lot of leeway when it comes to preparing the financial statements and she thinks that her client may be significantly disadvantaged by the earnout arrangement. Ms. Kellett has come to see you to obtain information and advice about the earnout. She would like you to review the information she has about her client's business and provide advice about the terms that should be included in sale agreement to minimize the risks to her client of being affected by accounting choices made by the new owner of the company.

Mr. Jones' company, Inuvik Technologies Inc. (Inuvik), is a manufacturer of sophisticated components for heavy equipment. The company is small but is well known in the industry for producing high-quality, reliable components. Mr. Jones believes that the reasons for Inuvik's success include the extensive testing the company does of its components before they are shipped to customers, the warranty and after-sales support provided, and the ongoing investment in research and development to improve existing technologies and discover new ones.

Ms. Kellett has provided you with the following additional information about Inuvik and its operations:

- One of the reasons the buyer is buying Inuvik is because it is complementary to other businesses that he owns. The buyer expects that Inuvik will be a major supplier to some of these other businesses.

- Inuvik values its inventory at the lower of FIFO cost and net realizable value. It uses specific identification for components that are specially designed for customers. The company has a large inventory of parts that are used to construct its products and for repairs and maintenance of products sold. Some of the inventory is quite old and is kept to ensure that Inuvik can support some of its older products that are still in use.

- A new generation of production equipment will be introduced within the next six to 12 months and to remain competitive Mr. Jones thinks that Inuvik will have to make a significant investment in new equipment (Inuvik would purchase the new equipment after it is sold to the new owner. The existing equipment would still be usable (in fact Mr. Jones says it has another three years of life left) but it will not be capable of producing output of the same quality as the new equipment. The old equipment would only be useable on a limited basis and its value in the used equipment market would be very low.

- Inuvik generally recognizes its revenue on delivery. However, customers have the right to return components that do not meet specifications. Returns have never been a large problem though from time to time a major order will be returned for modification. Inuvik offers customers 45 days to pay. Most customers pay on time and bad debts have been predictable in each of the past five years at about 1 percent to 1.5 percent of revenues.

- Inuvik reports a significant amount of development costs on its balance sheet that are being amortized over five years. The costs are related to new technologies that Inuvik has developed for integration into its products.

- Inuvik provides a five-year warranty on all its components. The warranty covers all repairs that are required as a result of manufacturer's defects. Warranty costs have averaged about 4 percent of sales over the last five years and have been relatively stable. Last year the company utilized a new technology in some of its components and Mr. Jones is unsure what warranty costs will be for that line.

■ In 1998, Inuvik purchased a competitor and merged its operations with its own. As a result of the purchase, $250,000 of goodwill is reported on Inuvik's balance sheet as of the most recent year end. The company no longer amortizes its goodwill in accordance with GAAP. Inuvik evaluates the goodwill annual to ensure that it is not overvalued.

■ Inuvik will be managed by the son of the new owner. To date, the amount of compensation taken by Mr. Jones in any year was determined by the amount of cash available in the company and his personal needs. The form of the compensation also varied, sometimes paid in salary and bonus and other times as a dividend. The way compensation was paid usually depended on tax cost and benefits.

Required:

Prepare the report requested by Angela Kellett. In your report you should discuss the problems that could arise for Ferdinand Jones if an earnout arrangement is used to determine the selling price of Inuvik. You should also propose accounting recommendations that would minimize the problems and risks that Mr. Jones could face if the earnout is used.

CASE 4: INTERNATIONAL PRODUCTIONS CORPORATION[1]

International Productions Corporation (IPC) is a diversified, privately owned entertainment company with operations throughout Canada. IPC's operations include movie theatres, live theatre productions, and television productions. IPC has been expanding rapidly, financed mainly by large bank loans and by debt and equity investments by private investors. The CEO of IPC owns 30 percent of the shares of the company and is the largest single investor. The CEO is also the founder and main creative force behind the company. IPC is in the process of finalizing its fiscal 2009 financial statements (year end October 31). The CEO has asked you for advice on a number of outstanding accounting issues that need to be resolved before the financial statements can be issued to the various stakeholders. The CEO informed you of the following issues:

a. IPC purchases real estate in prime locations where an existing theatre chain does not adequately serve the market. After purchasing the real estate, IPC engages a contractor to build a theatre complex. During fiscal 2009, IPC received a $2,000,000 payment from a contractor who had built a theatre complex in Montreal. The payment represents a penalty for not completing the theatre complex on time. Construction began in February 2008 and was to have been completed by December 2008. Instead, the complex was not completed until the end of May 2009.

b. The company is staging the Canadian version of "Accounting: What Could be Better!!" which is to open in January 2010. The smash-hit musical has been running in Paris for three years and is still playing to sold-out audiences. IPC started receiving advance bookings in November 2008, and the first 40 weeks of the show's run are completely sold out. Average ticket prices are $65 and the show will play seven nights a week. The theatre used for the production is relatively small, with about 1,200 seats. As of October 31, 2009, IPC had included in revenue $900,000 of interest collected on the funds received from advance ticket sales. IPC has already invested $4,000,000 advertising the production. It will have invested $15,000,000 in pre-production costs by January 2010 and will incur weekly production costs of $250,000 once the show opens. (Pre-production costs are the costs incurred before a show is actually presented to audiences.)

c. IPC started selling some of its movie theatres a couple of years ago. Each theatre's contribution to long-run operating cash flow is assessed and, if the value of the real estate is greater than the present value of future theatre operating cash flows, the theatre is sold. In the past, revenue from these sales has been relatively minor, but this year 25 percent of net income, about $6,000,000, came from the sale of theatres. Since these sales are considered an ongoing part of the company's operations, proceeds from the sale of theatres are recorded as revenue in the income statement.

d. During November 2008, IPC purchased a library of "classic" movies and television programs for $5,000,000. Management thought that the library would be a good source of revenue for IPC because of the many new television channels that would be looking to find suitable programming. Management is now concerned that its decision to purchase the library was a poor one because there has been little interest from broadcasters to purchase the rights to show movies and programs from IPC's library. In October 2009, a large broadcaster signed a contract to use certain movies in the library over the next four years. The contract guarantees IPC $1,000,000 over the four years, but payment is only required when the broadcaster actually shows one of the movies. At the end of the four years the broadcaster must make a payment to IPC so that the total payments over the life of the contract are $1,000,000. The contract with the broadcaster is the only interest that has been shown in the contents of the library.

Required:

Prepare a report for the CEO of IPC advising him on these accounting issues. Your report should clearly explain the reasoning for your recommendations and should address possible alternatives. The CEO may use your report as the basis for discussions with IPC's auditors.

CASE 5: VULCANZAP INC.[2]

Vulcanzap Inc. (VZAP) is a high-technology company that develops, designs, and manufactures telecommunications equipment. VZAP was founded in 2002 by the former assistant head of research and development at a major telephone company, Dr. Jordan Warman. He and the director of marketing left the company to found VZAP. VZAP has been very successful. Sales reached $5.3 million in its first year and have grown by 80 percent annually since then. The key to VZAP's success has been the sophisticated software contained in the equipment it sells.

VZAP's board of directors recently decided to issue shares to raise funds for strategic objectives through an initial public offering of common shares. The shares will be listed on a major Canadian stock exchange. VZAP's underwriter believes that an offering price of 18 to 20 times the most recent fiscal year's earnings per share can be achieved.

VZAP has announced its intention to go public, and work has begun on the preparation of a preliminary prospectus. The prospectus will be filed with the relevant securities commission in 40 days. The offering is expected to be completed in about 75 days. The company has an October 31 year end. It is now November 9, 2010.

Dr. Warman has provided you with the following information regarding a number of unresolved accounting issues. He has asked you for a report that analyzes the issues and makes recommendations on how they should be treated in the October 31, 2010 financial statements.

1. The job market for top software and hardware engineering talent is very tight. As a result, VZAP has turned to information technology "head hunters" to attract key personnel from other high-technology companies. During the year, VZAP paid $178,000 in placement fees. The search firm offers a one-year money-back guarantee if any of the people hired leaves the company or proves to be unsatisfactory.

2. On July 29, 2010, the company made a payment of $250,000 to a computer hacker. The hacker had given the company ten days to pay her the funds. Otherwise, she said she would post on the Internet a security flaw she had detected in VZAP's Firewall Plus software. Disclosure of the security flaw would limit the usefulness of the software. VZAP has been aware of the flaw for some time but has not been able to figure out a solution for it. The hacker did not provide any information that would be useful in correcting the security flaw. VZAP currently has $500,000 in unamortized development costs pertaining to Firewall Plus classified as assets on the balance sheet.

3. Jordan Warman had been working on a photon phaser when he left the telephone company. He has moved this technology ahead significantly at VZAP and the product is close to being brought to market. To date, VZAP has capitalized $1,750,000 in development costs. In September, a competitor introduced a product very similar to the photon phaser and the product has already captured significant attention from customers. Jordan Warman thinks the product will still be

successful but it is not likely that VZAP will be able to command the market share that it originally anticipated.

4. One of VZAP's products, the ATM 4000, has been a flop. High rates of failures and customer dissatisfaction led VZAP to issue an offer, dated July 30, 2010, to buy back all units currently in service for a total of $1,467,500. Southwestern Utah Telephone is suing VZAP for $4,000,000 for damages related to two ATM 4000 devices that it had purchased through a distributor. The devices broke down, affecting telephone traffic for two weeks before they were replaced.

5. During the first two years of operation, VZAP expensed all desktop computers (PCs) when purchased, on the grounds that they become obsolete so fast that their value after one year is almost negligible. In the current year, VZAP bought $429,000 worth of PCs and plans to write them off over two years.

Required:

Prepare the report requested by Jordan Warman.

CASE 6: SHMEVAN STORES LTD.[3]

Shmevan Stores Ltd. (Shmevan) is a national chain of franchised business supply stores. Currently, there are 75 stores in the chain, each owned and operated by people who live in the communities where the stores operate. The stores sell a complete line of business supplies, office furniture, computer hardware and software, and other business related products. Shmevan supplies all merchandise to the stores. Shmevan is able to obtain lower prices because of its significant buying power. Shmevan receives a royalty on all sales made by the franchise stores.

In May 2008, in response to the tough and increased competition in the business supplies market, Shmevan's management introduced a contest to motivate franchise store owners and to encourage innovation of new and profitable business practices. The winner of the contest is to receive a cash prize of $150,000. The prize is to be awarded to the store that reported the highest percentage increase in net income before taxes for the year ended October 31, 2009.

On a preliminary review of the financial statements by Shmevan's management, the franchise store in Saskatoon was the winner. The Saskatoon store reported a percentage increase in income before taxes of 278 percent using the formula used for the contest. However, the panel that was made up of Shmevan's management, along with five people representing the owners of the franchise stores, has concerns about the results reported by the Saskatoon store. Some members of the committee believe that Saskatoon has misrepresented its financial position. As a result of the concerns, a number of stores have protested the awarding of the prize to the Saskatoon store. The second place finisher in the contest, the store in Fredericton, reported a percentage increase in income before taxes of 201 percent.

You have been engaged by Shmevan to review the financial information prepared by the Saskatoon store. Shmevan would like a report assessing the appropriateness of the accounting methods Saskatoon used and whether the accounting methods used by the Saskatoon store were "fair in the context of the contest." In preparing to write your report, you have gathered the following information:

1. The formula used to calculate the percentage increase in net income before taxes is:

$$\frac{\text{Income before taxes in 2009} - \text{Income before taxes in 2008}}{\text{Income before taxes in 2008}}$$

In the event that income before taxes in 2008 is below $100,000, for purposes of the formula, net income before taxes in 2008 is assumed to be $100,000.

2. For the year ended October 31, 2008, the Saskatoon store reported income before taxes of $42,000.

3. The Saskatoon store normally recognizes revenue when goods are delivered to customers.

4. During 2009, the Saskatoon store changed its inventory valuation method from average cost to FIFO. Saskatoon's owner explained that the change was made to make the store's accounting records consistent with other stores in the chain. As of October 31, 2009, 58 of the Shmevan stores used FIFO. The effect of the change was to increase income by $18,000 in 2008 and by $21,000 in 2009 versus the amount that would have been reported using average cost.

5. During the fiscal year ended October 31, 2008, the Saskatoon store wrote off $50,000 of inventory because management deemed that the inventory could not be sold. In February 2009, the inventory was sold to three separate customers for $72,000.

6. In October 2009, the president of the Saskatoon store made three television commercials that are to be broadcast in the Saskatoon area beginning in December. As of October 31, the commercials have not been shown on television, although they have been completed. The commercials cost $15,000 to produce and the amount has been capitalized and is reported on the October 31, 2009 balance sheet.

7. In September and October 2009, the Saskatoon store ran a promotion that offered significant discounts to customers who made large purchases. These customers were assured that they could return any purchases after 90 days for a full refund for any reason if the customer decided that the merchandise was not required. Sales in September and October 2009 were significantly higher than the same months the year before and preliminary evidence suggests that sales in November 2009 have declined from 2008.

8. In October 2008, the Saskatoon store paid employees $22,000 in advances against commissions that would be earned in fiscal 2009. The advances were accounted for as wage expenses in 2008. The amount was paid because some employees were facing financial difficulties and the owner of the store wanted to help them out.

9. During fiscal 2009, the Saskatoon store sold a delivery vehicle, some furniture and fixtures, and a number of miscellaneous other assets. Most items were sold for more than their net book values (gains), but some were sold at a loss. Overall, the sales produced a gain of $17,000.

Required:

Prepare the report requested by Shmevan.

CASE 7: GOOD QUALITY AUTO PARTS LIMITED[4]

Good Quality Auto Parts Limited (GQAP) is a medium-sized, privately-owned producer of auto parts which are sold to car manufacturers, repair shops, and retail outlets. In March 2008, the union negotiated a new three-year contract with the company for the 200 shop-floor employees. At the time, GQAP was in financial difficulty and management felt unable to meet the contract demands of the union. Management also believed that a strike of any length would force the company into bankruptcy.

The company proposed that, in exchange for wage concessions, the company would implement a profit-sharing plan whereby the shop floor employees would receive 10 percent of the company's annual after-tax profit as a bonus in each year of the contract. Although the union generally finds this type of contract undesirable, it believed that insisting on the prevailing industry settlement would jeopardize GQAP's survival. As a result, the contract terms were accepted.

The contract specifies that no major changes in accounting policies may be made without the change being approved by GQAP's auditor. Another clause in the contract allows the union to engage an accountant to examine the accounting records of the company and meet with GQAP's management and auditor to discuss any issues. Under the terms of the contract, any controversial accounting issues are to be negotiated by the union and management to arrive at a mutual agreement. If the parties cannot agree, the positions of the parties are to be presented to an independent arbitrator for resolution.

On April 10, 2009, GQAP's management presented to the union its annual financial statements and the unqualified audit report for the year ended February 28, 2009, the first year that the profit sharing plan was in effect. The union engaged you to examine these financial statements and determine whether there are any controversial accounting issues. As a result of your examination, you identified a number of issues that are of concern to you. You met with the GQAP's controller and obtained the following information:

1. GQAP wrote off $250,000 of inventory manufactured between 2002 and 2005. There have been no sales from this inventory in over two years. The controller explained that up until this year she had some hope that the inventory could be sold as replacement parts. However, she now believes that the parts cannot be sold.

2. The contracts GQAP has with the large auto manufacturers allow the purchaser to return items for any reason. The company has increased the allowance for returned items by 10 percent in the year just ended. The controller contends that, because of stiff competition faced by the auto manufacturers with which GQAP does business, there will likely be a significant increase in the parts returned.

3. GQAP has a policy of writing off any small tool acquisitions, even though the tools will be used over several periods. For the year just ended, small tools costing $170,000 were acquired.

4. In April 2008, GQAP purchased $500,000 of new manufacturing equipment. To reduce the financial strain of the acquisition, the company negotiated a six-year payment schedule. GQAP decided to use accelerated depreciation at a rate of 40 percent for the new equipment. The controller argued that because of the rapid technological changes occurring in the industry, equipment purchased now is more likely to become technologically, rather than operationally, obsolete. The straight-line depreciation method applied to the existing equipment has not been changed. Existing equipment similar to that purchased is amortized over 10 years.

5. In 2003, GQAP purchased a small auto parts manufacturer and merged it into its own operation. At the time of acquisition, $435,000 of goodwill was recorded. The company has written off the goodwill in the year just ended. The controller explained that GQAP's poor performance in particular has made the goodwill worthless.

6. In February 2009, the president and the chairman of the board, who between them own 75 percent of the voting shares of the company, received bonuses of $250,000 each. GQAP did not pay any dividends during the current year. In the prior year, dividends amounting to $650,000 were paid. The controller said that the board of directors justified the bonuses as a reward for keeping the company afloat despite extremely difficult economic times.

7. Until this year, GQAP calculated its tax expense based on the actual amount of income tax it had to pay. In all previous years, the company received a qualified audit opinion from the auditors due to this deviation from generally accepted accounting principles (GAAP). This year, the company has used future income tax accounting as required by GAAP. The change has been made retroactively. The effect of the change has been to reduce net income for fiscal 2009 by a significant amount. The controller argued that, because the company is likely to need significant external financing from new sources in the upcoming year, a clean audit opinion would reduce any fears prospective lenders might have about the company. The controller also believed that in light of the contract with the union, the financial statements should be prepared in accordance with GAAP.

The union has asked you to prepare a report on the position it should take on the issues identified when discussing them with management. The union also wants to know what additional information you require in order to support this position.

Required:

Prepare the report.

CASE 8: JEREMY LANGER

Jeremy Langer is a young entrepreneur who lives in a large Canadian city. In early 2010, he saw a good opportunity to make some money selling souvenirs designed especially for the upcoming International World Festival, a six-week event that was going to be held in June and July, 2010. The International World Festival is held every three years in a different city. The Festival has never been held in Canada and it was last held in North America in 1982. The city was expecting a large influx of tourists for the event. You obtain the following information on Jeremy's venture:

- In January, Jeremy opened a bank account in the name of his business venture and deposited $15,000 of his own money into the account. Jeremy also developed a number of designs for the souvenirs that he plans to sell. The designs cost $1,200 and he paid cash from the venture's bank account.

- In early February, Jeremy presented his designs to the Festival organizing committee. Use of the Festival name or logos on souvenirs required approval by the committee if they were to be legally sold. Jeremy's designs were approved and he paid a licensing fee of $2,000 that allows him to legally sell the souvenirs.

- In late February, Jeremy borrowed $30,000 from the bank. Jeremy agrees to pay the bank its money back plus $1,500 in interest on August 1, 2010.

- In May, Jeremy signed a contract with a company to produce the souvenirs. Because of the nature of the souvenirs, it will be necessary to produce them all before the Festival begins. Jeremy has 5,000 souvenirs produced at a cost of $10 each. It will not be possible to produce additional souvenirs. Jeremy pays the producer $40,000 in cash and agrees to pay an additional $5,000 on June 30 and the remainder at the end of the festival.

- Jeremy purchased an old van to transport the souvenirs for $5,000 in cash.

- Jeremy hired a number of vendors who operate street carts who will sell merchandise. He agrees to pay the vendors $5 for each souvenir sold. The selling price of Jeremy's souvenirs is $19 each. The vendors pay Jeremy $14 for each souvenir they sell (they keep the $5 they earn from each sale).

- On June 30, Jeremy makes the $5,000 payment to the producer of the souvenirs.

- On July 3, Jeremy has 3,500 unsold souvenirs.

- Jeremy has incurred other costs of $1,000 to date, all in cash.

It is July 3, 2010. The festival has been underway for three and half weeks and Jeremy hasn't had a chance to sit down and take stock of how his venture is doing. He asks you to help him.

Required:

a. Prepare an income statement and balance sheet for Jeremy's venture as of July 3, 2010. Explain the accounting choices you made and why you made them. Be sure to discuss the users and uses of the income statement in your response.

b. Assume the role of Jeremy's banker. Jeremy has provided you with the statements that were prepared in part (a). Are these statements useful to you? Explain. What concerns do you have about the venture at this point? Explain. What suggestions would you give to Jeremy?

c. Use the statements you prepared in (a) to advise Jeremy about how his venture has performed to date. What suggestions would you give to Jeremy for operating the venture for the remainder of the Festival? Jeremy has asked whether he can withdraw money from the venture for some personal needs. What would you advise Jeremy?

CASE 9: KENASTON CONVENIENCE STORE

The Kenaston Convenience Store (KCS) is a local convenience store located near a subdivision in Regina. KCS opened about three years ago and is owned and operated by the Wu family. The store has been very successful and now that the neighbourhood has matured and the population is large enough, a major chain of convenience stores, Community Mart Ltd. (CML), is interested in buying KCS so that it can establish a presence in the area. It is CML's usual practice to only move into an area once the population density has reached a certain level. It prefers to buy out an existing convenience store in an area because it gets the benefit of an established location and eliminates a competitor.

You are CML's location evaluator. It's your job to make contact with the owners of established convenience stores that CMS might be interested in and evaluate their suitability for acquisition. Your preliminary evaluation of KCS is that it is a potential candidate for acquisition and your initial discussions with Mr. Wu were favourable. Mr. Wu has agreed to allow you to look at KCS's most recent income statements. The income statements are presented below:

Kenaston Convenience Store
Income Statements for the years ended March 31

	2009	2008
Revenue	$417,250	$368,425
Cost of sales	258,695	225,845
Gross Margin	158,555	142,580
Expenses		
Amortization of capital assets	32,000	34,200
Interest	15,200	17,400
Utilities	14,700	13,900
Other	7,500	6,200
Advertising and promotion	6,200	4,500
Salaries and wages	2,000	2,200
Repairs and maintenance	4,150	2,750
Income taxes	12,565	5,400
Total expenses	94,315	86,550
Net income	$64,240	$56,030

In addition, you obtained the following information from your discussion with Mr. Wu and from observing the business:

■ KCS is located in a two-storey, 30-old building located at the edge of the new subdivision. The building cost $300,000 and there is a $210,000 mortgage on it. The Wu family lives in a spacious apartment above the store. Mortgage payments and all utilities and property taxes for the entire building are included in KCS's income statements. The Wu's own the building.

■ The store is open seven days a week from 7 AM to 11 PM. The store is always staffed by Mr. or Mrs. Wu or one of their children. All work in the store is also done by family members. No one gets paid for the work they do but money is provided as it is needed, often just taken from the cash register.

■ The financial statements are prepared for the bank, which has provided a small loan in addition to the mortgage on the building, and for tax purposes.

■ KCS amortizes its capital asset on the same basis as is required for tax purposes, using the rates specified in the Income Tax Act.

■ All sales are for cash (no credit sales) and are recorded on the cash register. Not all sales are rung up on the register.

■ KCS had printed a large quantity of flyers that it has distributed in the neighbourhood from time to time to promote the store. Mr. Wu estimated that there would be enough flyers to last about a year when they were printed. About 30 percent of the flyers remained at the end of the year. However, Mr. Wu noted that some of the remaining flyers might not be usable because they were damaged when water leaked into the storage room during a recent storm. The full cost of the flyers was expensed in 2009.

■ Inventory is counted on the last day of the year. Cost of goods sold is calculated by adding the opening inventory to purchases made during the year and then subtracting ending inventory. Family members often take store items for their own use.

Required:

Prepare a report for your manager, the vice-president of acquisitions, outlining your evaluation of the KCS's income statements. In your report, identify and discuss whether the statements are representative of KCS's activity and whether they give a good indication of how the store would perform if CML purchased and operated it. Be sure to identify and discuss any adjustments you would recommend to make the financial statements more useful.

CASE 10: DYMO MANUFACTURING LIMITED

Dymo Manufacturing Limited (Dymo) is a small manufacturer of appliances. Its products are manufactured under the brand names of the stores that buy from Dymo. (Dymo does not sell any appliances under its own brand name.) The company is wholly owned and managed by Jon and Crystell Karpoff, a married couple. Recently, the Karpoffs have been considering retiring and they have been approached by a prospective buyer. The prospective buyer has requested a set of financial statements so that she can analyze the company. The buyer is a sophisticated business person. Until now, the only use of the financial statements has been for calculation of income taxes and internal management purposes.

In your discussion with the Karpoffs, you learn the following:

1. Dymo manufactures several different types of household appliances. It usually carries enough inventory so that it is able to respond to most orders quickly. For these products, when a store places an order with Dymo the goods are shipped within days.

2. Dymo also carries a significant inventory of parts and supplies used in the production of the appliances. Mr. Karpoff observed on a recent examination of the inventory that there was some stock (both input materials and finished goods) that has been on hand for some time, including some relating to products that are no longer made.

3. Dymo allows retailers to return for any reason up to 20 percent of the appliances purchased.

4. Dymo offers a two-year warranty on the appliances it makes. Appliances requiring repairs are returned to the retailer, which ships them to Dymo for repair. All costs are paid by Dymo.

5. Dymo uses CCA rates, the rates prescribed in the Income Tax Act, to calculate depreciation.

6. One of Dymo's major suppliers is a sheet metal manufacturer that is owned by the Karpoff's son.

7. Recently, Dymo agreed to produce a significantly modified version of an existing product for a local chain of appliance stores. The chain promised to purchase a minimum of 7,000 appliances per year for three years. Dymo incurred $75,000 in costs modifying the design of the existing appliance. Production of the new product is scheduled to begin in about a month.

8. The Karpoffs pay themselves enough to cover their living requirements.

Required:

The Karpoffs have come to you requesting advice on the selection of appropriate accounting policies for the financial statements that will be prepared for the prospective buyer. They would like full explanations for the recommendations (in case the buyer questions the choice) you make.

CASE 11: DISCOUNT STORES LIMITED

Discount Stores Limited (Discount) is a chain of retail stores with locations in several medium-sized Ontario communities. Discount sells a wide range of clothing and household items that it obtains at discounts from wholesalers and jobbers. The company is wholly owned by Ruth and

Irving Bogan, who use the cash generated by Discount to live on. Two years ago, the Bogans hired Harry Highpaid as the chief executive officer of the company to help turn the company around after a number of unprofitable years. At the time Harry was hired, the Bogans were worried that Discount would go bankrupt and they would lose their main source of income. Harry was well known as an excellent manager, and the Bogans were prepared to pay for someone who could reverse the fortunes of their business. The Bogans agreed to pay Harry a salary plus 25 percent of income after taxes in each year of a three-year contract. In his first year with Discount, Harry made significant improvements in the business, but it still suffered a small loss. This year, the company has continued to improve, and the Bogans once again feel confident about the viability of Discount.

Harry has just presented the financial statement for the current year to the Bogans for their approval. The Bogans are pleased about Discount's improvement, but they are concerned about some accounting treatments that appear to have contributed to a significant increase in net income.

1. Harry launched an extensive advertising campaign to improve the image of Discount and to attract new customers. According to Harry, the campaign has been a success and as a result Discount has been able to increase its profit margins and has increased the flow of customers through all stores. Harry has capitalized 50 percent of the advertising costs and is amortizing them over five years, arguing that they will benefit the firm over a number of years. In the past, Discount has expensed all advertising costs as they were incurred.

2. Discount has had a policy of writing off slow-moving inventory at the end of each fiscal period. Slow-moving inventory is defined as merchandise that has been on hand for six months or more. Harry has suspended the policy and now only writes off inventory that he believes cannot be sold.

3. To attract more customers, Harry has begun offering credit to customers. He has not, however, recorded an allowance for bad debt or a bad debt expense for the period.

Ruth Bogan has come to you for advice on the above accounting issues. Since Ruth and Irving are the only members of Discount's board of directors, they can make any changes they wish to the financial statements. However, they are not very sophisticated about financial issues and are not sure what to do.

Required:

Prepare a report for the Bogans providing them with the advice they seek.

CASE 12: ONTARIO PRINTING LIMITED

In September 2009, Alex Jesse and Evan Shayne decided to end their 10-year business relationship as owners of Ontario Printing Limited (OPL). OPL is a commercial printing business that Alex and Evan organized in 1999. They each own 50 percent of the common shares of OPL but Alex operates and manages it. Evan participates in major decisions but, for the most part, is not involved in day-to-day operations. Alex and Evan have agreed that Alex will purchase the shares of OPL from Evan at fair market value. They have agreed that fair market value will be equal to five times average net income for the past two years, including the fiscal year ending October 31, 2009. Alex and Evan also agree that the accounting policies should be in accordance with generally accepted accounting principles. Alex and Evan recognize that adjustments to the final selling price might be necessary to take specific circumstances into consideration. Since their decision to part ways, Evan has not been involved in any way in the activities and operation of OPL.

You obtain the following information about OPL:

1. OPL has used its financial statements primarily for tax purposes. The company writes off any expenditures that it makes that can be justified for tax purposes, regardless of whether they have any future benefit.

2. The company owns a small building in the north end of the city. Its offices occupy the ground floor of the building and the rest of the building is leased to tenants. Since the building was acquired, its market value has increased from $800,000 to $950,000, based on increases in neighbouring property values.

3. OPL has two copying machines that do not produce high-quality copies compared with more technologically current equipment. The equipment is used infrequently and only for jobs that do not require high-quality work. The equipment has a net book value of $12,920.

4. Alex and Evan have charged many personal expenses to the business over the years.

5. Alex took a salary of $125,000 during the year. A manager doing Alex's work at a competitor's company would be paid between $50,000 and $75,000, depending on the size of the company and responsibilities. Evan agreed to this salary several years ago.

6. In mid-October 2009, Alex launched a major advertising campaign to increase business. Alex hopes the advertising will allow OPL to increase utilization of its equipment and allow it to expand capacity in the near future. During the last two weeks of October, OPL spent several thousand dollars for media and direct contact with potential clients.

7. In early October 2009, OPL shut down for two days for annual maintenance of equipment. This work is done each year to ensure the equipment operates at maximum efficiency and to avoid costly breakdowns. The annual maintenance was last done in November 2009.

8. In late October 2009 Alex sold some equipment at a loss of $37,000.

9. During the summer of 2009, Evan negotiated a contract with a customer on behalf of OPL to produce instruction manuals for its products. The contract begins in January 2010. In exchange for lower printing rates the customer has guaranteed a *minimum* of $200,000 of work over two years. The customer will pay as work is done. Any shortfall from the $200,000 will be paid at the end of the contract term.

Required:

Alex and Evan have engaged you to prepare a report that they can use to determine the selling price of Evan's shares. The report should state the accounting policies that should be used for preparing the financial statements that should be used specifically to set the selling price of OPL, as well as any adjustments that should be made to the final price as a result of other information and concerns you have. You should explain your reasoning fully so that lawyers for the respective parties will have a basis for discussion.

ENDNOTES

1. Adapted from the 1997 Uniform Final Examination, Canadian Institute of Chartered Accountants

2. Adapted from the 1998 Uniform Final Examination, Canadian Institute of Chartered Accountants.

3. Adapted from the 2000 Uniform Final Examination, Canadian Institute of Chartered Accountants.

4. Adapted from the 1991 Uniform Final Examination, Canadian Institute of Chartered Accountants.

PHOTO CREDITS

Chapter 1
Page 1, Corbis Images / JupiterImages

Chapter 2
Page 32, Courtesy Rogers Communications Inc.

Chapter 3
Page 87, Courtesy Rogers Communications Inc.

Chapter 4
Page 167, Courtesy Rogers Video

Chapter 5
Page 232, Courtesy Rogers Communications Inc.

Chapter 6
Page 285, J.P. Moczulski

Chapter 7
Page 335, Used with permission from FLARE Magazine.

Chapter 8
Page 392, Reprinted with permission from Pierre Lalande.

Chapter 9
Page 453, Used with permission of Fido Solutions Inc.

Chapter 10
Page 520, Royalty-Free/CORBIS

Chapter 11
Page 597, CP/Jacques Boissinot

Chapter 12
Page 657, CP/Aaron Harris

Chapter 13
Page 704, Keith Brofsky/Getty Images

Appendix A
Pages A-1–A-51, courtesy of Rogers Communications Inc.

Throughout
Rogers logo courtesy of Rogers Communications Inc.

GLOSSARY

Accelerated amortization (page 463) Amortization methods that allocate more of the cost of an asset to expense in the early years of its life and less in the later years.

Account (page 95) A category of asset, liability, or owners' equity.

Accounting (page 3) A system for producing information about an entity and communicating that information to people who want or need the information for making decisions.

Accounting cycle (page 88) The process by which data about economic events are entered into an accounting system, processed, organized and used to produce information such as financial statements.

Accounting equation (page 35) The conceptual foundation of modern accounting that states assets = liabilities + owners' equity.

Accounting estimates (pages 196, 614) Estimated amounts that must be used when financial statements are prepared because the actual amounts pertaining to many economic events and transactions are not known with certainty at the time. Examples of accounting estimates include the amount of accounts receivable that will not be collected, the useful lives of capital assets, and the cost of warranty services that have not yet been provided.

Accounting policies (pages 54, 614) The methods, principles, and practices used by an entity to report its financial results.

Accounts payable (page 40) Amounts owed to suppliers for goods and services acquired.

Accounts payable turnover ratio (page 736) A ratio that provides information about how quickly an entity pays its accounts payable. Defined as credit purchases ÷ average accounts payable.

Accounts receivable (page 38) Usually, amounts owed to the entity by customers for goods and services provided on credit. Can also be amounts owed for other reasons such as loans to shareholders and employees, interest due on investments, etc.

Accounts receivable turnover ratio (page 366) A measure of how well an entity's credit program is being managed by giving an idea of how quickly the entity is collecting its receivables. The accounts receivable turnover ratio is defined as credit sales divided by average receivables.

Accrual basis of accounting (page 44) A system of accounting that measures the economic performance of an entity rather than just its cash flows. Under the accrual system revenue is recognized when it is earned and expenses matched to revenue, regardless of when the cash is received or spent.

Accrued asset (page 119) An asset that is recognized and recorded in the financial statements but the recording is not triggered by an external event.

Accrued expense (page 117) An expense that is recognized and recorded in the financial statements before the cash payment is made

Accrued liabilities (page 117) A liability that is recognized and recorded in the financial statements but the recording is not triggered by an external event such as receipt of a bill or invoice.

Accrued revenue (page 119) Revenue that is recorded before cash is received.

Accumulated amortization (page 115) A contra-asset account used to accumulates deductions from capital asset and other amortizable asset accounts.

Acid test ratio (page 365) A measure of entity's liquidity. Defined as an entity's most liquid assets (cash, cash equivalents, temporary investments, receivables) divided by current liabilities.

Adjusting entries (page 112) Journal entries recorded at the end of a reporting period that reflect economic changes that may have occurred during the period that have not been recorded in the accounting system. Adjusting entries are not triggered by exchanges with outside entities.

Adverse opinion (page 254) The audit opinion given when the financial statements are so materially misstated or misleading that they do not present fairly the financial position, results of operations, and/or cash flows of the entity.

After-tax cost of borrowing (page 549) The interest rate an entity pays after taking into consideration the tax deductibility of interest. The after-tax cost of borrowing is calculated as: Actual interest rate * (1−tax rate).

Aging schedule (page 355) A schedule that classifies accounts receivable by the length of time they have been outstanding.

Allowance for uncollectable accounts (page 353) A contra asset account to accounts receivable or other receivables account that represents the portion of the receivables that management estimates will not be collected.

Amortization (pages 104, 460) The allocation of the cost of a capital asset of a to expense over time to reflect the consumption of the asset while it helps to earn revenue. Also used specifically for the amortization of intangible assets.

Annuity (page 346) A series of equal cash flows (inflows or outflows), usually made at equally spaced time intervals.

Arm's length transaction (page 249) A transaction that takes place between unrelated parties, each of whom is acting in his or her own self interests and, therefore, the exchange amount is considered to be fair market value.

Asset turnover (page 732) A measure of how effectively an entity can generate sales from its asset base. Defined as sales ÷ average total assets.

Assets (page 34) Economic resources that provide future benefits to an entity for carrying out its business activities.

Authorized capital stock (page 603) The maximum number of each type of share that can be issued by a corporation.

Available-for-sale investments (page 672) Any investment that does not give control or significant influence to the investing corporation, or that doesn't meet the criteria for classification as a held-to-maturity or trading investment.

Average collection period of accounts receivable (page 366) A measure of how well an entity's credit program is being managed by giving the number of days receivables are outstanding before they are collected. The average collection period of accounts receivable is calculated by dividing the accounts receivable turnover ratio into 365.

Average cost method (page 400) An inventory cost flow assumption that determines the average cost of all goods on hand during the period and uses that average to calculate cost of sales and the balance in ending inventory.

Average number of days inventory on hand ratio (page 421) A ratio used to evaluate the efficiency of inventory management. The average number of days inventory on hand ratio indicates the number of days it takes an entity to sell its inventory. The ratio is defined as 365 divided by the inventory turnover ratio.

Average payment period for accounts payable (page 737) The average number of days that the entity takes to pay its accounts payable.

Balance sheet (page 34) The financial statement that provides information about the financial position—its assets, liability and owners' equity—of an entity at a moment in time.

Bank overdraft (page 295) Occurs when an entity removes more money from their bank account than there is in the bank account, effectively creating an amount owing to the bank. The amount of the overdraft is treated as a liability.

Basic earnings per share (page 624) Net income minus preferred share dividends divided by the weighted-average number of shares outstanding during the period.

Betterment (page 458) An expenditure made that improves an existing capital asset, thereby making it more valuable to the entity. A betterment might increase a capital asset's useful life or improve its efficiency.

Big bath (page 194) The expensing of a significant amount assets that would normally have been amortized or otherwise expensed in future periods.

Bond (page 530) A formal borrowing arrangement in which a borrower agrees to make periodic interest payments to

lenders as well as repay the principal at a specified time in the future.

Book value (page 623) The amount shown in the accounting records for an asset, liability, or equity item.

Book value of equity (page 623) The balance sheet value of the equity section of the balance sheet and is equal to assets – liabilities from the balance sheet. Book value of equity is also referred to as the net assets or net worth of the entity.

Callable bond (page 531) A bond that gives the bond issuer the option to repurchase the bond from investors at a time other than the maturity date under conditions that are specified in the bond agreement.

Canada Business Corporations Act (page 603) The federal legislation that governs federally incorporated companies.

Canada Revenue Agency (page 8) The Canadian government department responsible for administration and enforcement of the Canadian federal tax laws.

Capital assets (page 39) Economic resources that are used on an ongoing basis to earn revenue, but that are not sold in the ordinary course of business.

Capital assets (page 454) Resources that contribute to the earning of revenue over more than one period by helping an entity to produce, supply, support, or make available the goods or services it offers to its customers. Capital assets contribute indirectly to the earning of revenue—indirectly because selling capital assets is not part of the ordinary activities of the entity.

Capital cost allowance (page 495) Amortization for tax purposes.

Capital expenditure (page 306) Money spent to purchase capital assets.

Capital lease (page 539) A lease that transfers the benefits and risks of ownership to the lessee. Assets associated with a capital lease are capitalized on the balance sheet of the lessee along with liability representing the lease payments to be made over the life of the lease.

Capital stock (page 42) A balance sheet account that shows the amount of money that shareholders have paid to the corporation in exchange for shares in the corporation.

Capital structure (pages 550, 739) The term used to describe how an entity is financed—the amount of debt and equity the entity has.

Capitalize (page 454) An amount expended or accrued that is recorded on the balance sheet as an asset.

Cash basis of accounting (page 44) A system of accounting where revenue is

recognized when cash is received and expenses recognized when cash is spent.

Cash cycle (page 287) The cycle by which an entity begins with cash, invests in resources, provides goods or services to customers using those resources, and then collects cash from customers.

Cash dividend (page 610) A distribution in cash of a corporation's earnings to its shareholders.

Cash flow statement (pages 51, 293) The financial statement that shows how cash was obtained and used during a period and classifies cash flows as operating, investing or financing.

Cash from financing activities (pages 52, 293) The cash an entity raises and pays to equity investors and lenders.

Cash from investing activities (pages 52, 293) The cash an entity spent buying capital and other long-term assets and cash received from selling those assets.

Cash from operations (pages 51, 293) The cash an entity generates from or uses in its regular business activities.

Closing journal entries (page 121) The journal entry required for resetting temporary account balances to zero and transferring the balances in the temporary accounts to Retained Earnings or Owners' Equity.

Collateral (page 242) Assets that are pledged by a borrower and that are turned over to the lender in the event the borrower is unable to repay a loan.

Commission (page 419) A payment made to a seller as compensation for making a sale. A commission can be based on the selling price of the item, on the gross margin, or be a fixed fee.

Commitment (page 547) A contractual agreement to enter into a transaction in the future.

Common shares (page 604) Shares representing the residual ownership in an entity. Common shareholders are entitled to whatever earnings and assets are left after obligations to debtholders and preferred shareholders have been satisfied.

Common size financial statement (vertical analysis) (page 721) An analytical tool in which the amounts in the balance sheet and income statement are expressed as percentages of other elements in the same year's statements

Comparability (pages 19, 239) The qualitative characteristic of accounting information under Canadian GAAP that states that users should be able to compare the accounting information provided by different entities and the information of a particular entity from period to period.

Completed-contract method (page 183) A critical-event approach to revenue recognition that recognizes revenue in full when a contract is completed.

Compound interest (page 342) Interest that is calculated on the principal amount and on interest accumulated in previous periods.

Comprehensive income (page 616) The change in equity from transactions and economic events from all sources that don't involve owners.

Conservatism (page 104) A fundamental GAAP accounting concept that serves to ensure that assets, revenue, and net income are not overstated and that liabilities and expenses are not understated. The implication is that when preparers are faced with reasonable alternative accounting treatments, they should choose the one that is more conservative.

Consignment inventory (page 419) Inventory that is held for sale by an entity, but not owned by the selling entity. Consignment inventory is included in the inventory account of the entity that owns the inventory (not in the inventory account of the entity selling the inventory) and revenue on the sale of consignment inventory is not recognized until is sold to the final customer.

Consignment sale (page 174) A transaction in which the producer or distributor of goods transfers the goods to another entity for sale but for which the rights and risks of ownership do not transfer. The producer or distributor to recognize revenue when the other entity actually sells the merchandise to somebody else.

Consistency (page 240) Use by an entity of the same accounting policies from period to period.

Consolidated financial statements (page 34) Financial statements that combine the financial information of two or more entities into a single set of statements.

Consolidated financial statements (page 660) A single set of financial statements that aggregate the accounting information of a parent corporation and all of its subsidiaries.

Contingency (page 545) A possible liability or asset whose existence and amount depend on some future event.

Contingent liability (page 283) A liability that may arise in the future if future events occur.

Contra-asset account (page 115) An account that is used to accumulate subtractions from a related asset account.

Contributed surplus (page 604) A shareholders' equity account that shows amounts received by the entity from the sale of shares that are greater than the par value of the shares.

Control (page 660) When an investor is able to make the important decisions of the investee and determine its strategic operating, financing, and investing policies on an ongoing basis, without the support of other shareholders.

Convertible bond (page 531) May be exchanged by the investor for other securities of the issuing entity, such as common stock.

Convertible preferred shares (page 605) Preferred shares that shareholders can choose to exchange for a specified number of common shares for each preferred share that they convert.

Corporation (page 7) A separate legal entity created under the corporation laws of Canada or of a province. A corporation has many of the rights and responsibilities of an individual.

Cost of sales (page 48) The cost of an entity's inventory that was sold during a period.

Cost/benefit trade-off (page 4) The concept of comparing the benefits of an action with the costs of the action, and taking action only if the benefits exceed the costs.

Coupon rate (page 530) The percentage of the face value that the issuer pays to investors each year as interest.

Covenant (page 706) Restrictions that impose limits on the actions of borrowers.

Credit (page 109) An entry to an account that has the effect of decreasing assets and expenses, and increasing liabilities, owners' equity, and revenues.

Creditor (page 35) An entity to whom the reporting entity has an obligation to provide cash or other assets in the future.

Critical-event approach (page 169) A revenue recognition approach where an entity recognizes revenue when a specified instant in the earnings process, called the critical event, occurs. When the critical event occurs, 100% of the revenue is recognized.

Cumulative preferred shares (page 605) Preferred shares that require payment of any dividends on the shares that have not been paid in respect of the current year or previous years before the common shareholders can receive any dividends.

Current assets (page 39) Assets that will be used up, sold, or converted to cash within one year or one operating cycle.

Current liabilities (page 39) Liabilities that will be paid or satisfied within one year or one operating cycle.

Current ratio (page 41) A measure of entity's liquidity. Defined as current assets divided by current liabilities.

Date of declaration of a dividend (page 609) The date when the board of directors of a corporation declares a dividend.

Date of payment of a dividend (page 610) The date when the dividends are actually paid to shareholders.

Date of record of a dividend (page 609) The registered owner of shares on the date of record is entitled to receive a dividend declared by a corporation.

Debenture (page 530) A bond with no collateral provided to the lenders.

Debit (page 109) An entry to an account that has the effect of increasing assets and expenses, and decreasing liabilities, owners' equity, and revenues.

Debit card (page 99) A method of payment that allows a customer to pay for goods and services by transferring money directly from the customer's bank account to the vendor's bank account. Payment by debit card is equivalent to payment by cash.

Debt (page 528) Amounts borrowed and owed by an entity.

Debt-to-equity ratio (page 43) A ratio that provides a measure of the amount of debt relative to equity an entity uses for financing. The ratio gives an indication of the riskiness of the entity and its ability to carry more debt. Defined as Total liabilities ÷ Total shareholders' equity.

Declining balance (page 464) An accelerated method of amortization. The method applies an amortization rate to the NBV of the asset at the beginning of the year to calculate the amortization expense.

Deferred expenses (page 114) Assets that are acquired in one period but not expensed, at least in part, until a later period.

Deficit (page 42) When retained earnings is negative.

Defined-benefit plan (page 544) A pension plan in which the employer promises to provide employees certain specified benefits in each year they are retired.

Defined-contribution plan (page 543) A pension plan in which the employer makes a cash contribution to the pension fund as specified in the agreement with the employees. The pension benefits that an employee receives upon retirement are dependent on the amount contributed to the plan on behalf of the individual (by the employer and the employee) and on the how well the investments that are made with the funds in the pension fund perform.

Deflation (page 339) A period when, on average, prices in the economy are falling.

Demand loan (page 524) A loan that must be repaid whenever the lender requests or demands repayment.

Denial of opinion (page 255) The audit opinion given when the auditors do not have enough evidence to support an opinion on the financial statements. In that case, the auditors do not give an opinion.

Depletion (page 460) The term used to describe the amortization of the cost of natural resources.

Depreciation (page 460) Amortization of the cost of tangible capital assets.

Development stage companies (page 307) Companies that are in the process of developing their products and markets, and have not yet begun its planned business activity.

Differential reporting (page 564) Allows private companies that follow GAAP and have unanimous consent of their shareholders to use a number of simplified accounting rules that are not available to public companies.

Direct method of calculating cash from operations (page 297) A method of calculating/reporting cash from operations by showing cash collections and cash disbursements from operations during the period.

Direct write-off method (page 353) A method of accounting for uncollectable receivables where the receivable is removed from the list of accounts receivable and an expense is recorded when management decides that a receivable will not be collected.

Discontinued operations (page 714) The parts of an entity's operations that the entity has sold or plans to sell in the near future.

Discount (on debt) (pages 343, 533) When a bond is sold to investors for less than its face value. Occurs when the coupon rate is greater than the effective rate of interest for the bond.

Dividend payout ratio (page 742) The proportion of earnings that is being paid to common shareholders as dividends.

Dividends (page 42) Distributions of a corporation's earnings to shareholders.

Double-entry bookkeeping (page 94) An accounting system in which each transaction or economic event is recorded in two places in the accounts.

Earnings per share (EPS) (page 624) The amount of net income that is attributable to each individual share of common stock.

Earnings quality (page 716) The usefulness of current earnings for predicting future earnings.

Effective interest rate (page 531) The real or market rate of interest that is paid or earned on debt.

Efficient Market Hypothesis (page 246) A hypothesis that suggests that all publicly available information is reflected quickly in the price of publicly traded securities such as stocks and bonds.

Employee stock option (page 620) A right granted to an employee to purchase a specified number of shares of the employer's stock at a specified price over a specified period of time.

Entity (page 3) An economic unit such as an individual, proprietorship, partnership, corporation, government, not-for-profit organization etc. In an accounting environment an entity is an economic unit that a stakeholder wants accounting information about.

Equity method of accounting (page 668) An investment accounted for using the equity method is initially recorded on the balance sheet at cost. The balance sheet amount is adjusted each period for the investor's share of the investee company's income less dividends declared. The income statement reports the investor company's share of the investee's net income.

Exchange rate (page 340) The price to buy one currency stated in terms of another currency.

Executory contract (page 99) An exchange of promises where one party promises to supply goods or services and the other party promises to pay for them, but neither side has fulfilled its side of the bargain.

Exercise price (page 620) The price at an employee holding an employee stock option is allowed to purchase the shares.

Expenses (page 46) Economic sacrifices made to earn revenue. Sacrifices can be the result of using up an asset or incurring a liability. Expenses result in a decrease in owners' equity.

Expiry date (page 620) The final date that an option can be exercised. After an option expires, it cannot be used to purchase shares.

External audit (page 12) The process of examining, on behalf of stakeholders who are external to the entity, an entity's financial statements and the data supporting the information in the financial statements

for the purpose of determining whether the statements adhere to principles such as fairness and GAAP.

External auditors (page 12) The people who examine entities' financial information on behalf of stakeholders who are external to the entity.

Extraordinary item (page 710) An event or transaction that is not expected to occur frequently, not typical of the entity's business, and not primarily the result of decisions or determinations by the managers or owners of the entity.

Face value of a bond (page 530) The amount that the holder of the bond, the investor, will receive when the bond matures.

Fair value (page 662) In accounting for a subsidiary, the estimated market value of the subsidiary's assets and liabilities on the date the subsidiary was purchased.

Financial accounting (page 5) The field of accounting that provides information to people who are external to an entity— people who do not have direct access to an entity's information.

Financing activities (page 52) the cash an entity raises and pays to equity investors and lenders; reported on the cash flow statement.

Finished goods inventory (page 394) Inventory that has been completed and is ready for sale.

First-in, first-out (FIFO) (page 399) An inventory cost flow assumption in which the cost of inventory that is purchased or produced first is expensed first. For raw materials that are used in a manufacturing process, the cost of the raw materials that were purchased first is the cost that is used in the production process first. With a FIFO system the cost of inventory reported on the balance sheet represents the cost of inventory that was purchased or produced most recently.

Fiscal year (page 34) The 12-month period over which performance is measured and at the end of which a balance sheet is prepared.

Fixed-rate loan (page 530) A loan whose interest rate does not change.

Free cash flow (page 307) The cash that is remaining after reducing cash from operations by cash spent on capital expenditures and dividends.

Full costing (page 480) An accounting method used by oil and gas exploration companies in which all costs incurred to find new sources of oil and gas are capitalized, including costs associated with unsuccessful projects.

Full disclosure (page 245) The accounting principle that requires that financial statements include all relevant information about the economic activities of the entity.

Fully diluted earnings per share (page 625) An earnings per share measure that reflects the effect that dilutive securities would have on basic EPS if the dilutive securities were converted or exchanged for common shares.

Future income tax assets and liabilities (page 558) Assets and liabilities that arise because the accounting methods used to prepare the general purpose financial statements are sometimes different from the methods used to calculate taxable income and the amount of income tax an entity must pay.

Future value (page 341) The amount of money you will receive in the future by investing it today at a given interest rate.

General journal (page 128) The chronological record of the journal entries that have been entered into the accounting system.

General ledger (page 129) A record of all the accounts of an entity.

General partner (page 599) Member of a limited partnerships who does not have limited liability and is liable for all debts and obligations of the partnership. A limited partnerships must have at least one general partner.

General purpose financial statements (page 33) Financial statements that are prepared for a wide range of stakeholders, but not necessarily tailored to the needs of any or all of them.

Generally Accepted Accounting Principles (GAAP) (pages 18, 234) The broad principles and conventions that provide guidance to accountants and managers for making accounting choices as well as rules and procedures that are established as accepted accounting practices at a particular time.

Generally accepted auditing standards (GAAS) (page 253) A set of general guidelines that are stated in the *CICA Handbook* that provide guidance to auditors in the conduct of their audits.

Going-concern assumption (page 236) One of the basic assumptions underlying GAAP that states an entity that will be continuing its operations for the foreseeable future.

Goodwill (pages 477, 678) The amount that a parent pays for a subsidiary over and above the fair value of the subsidiary's identifiable assets and liabilities on the date the subsidiary is purchased.

Gradual approach (page 169) A revenue recognition approach that results in revenue being recognized gradually over a period of time.

Gross margin (page 48) Sales minus cost of goods sold.

Gross margin percentage (page 48) Gross margin divided by sales.

Half-year rule (page 495) A requirement in the *Income Tax Act* that allows an entity to deduct for tax purposes in the year an asset is purchased only one-half the amount of CCA that would otherwise be allowable.

Held-to-maturity investments (page 671) An investment with a maturity date, fixed or determinable payments (like interest payments), and management must have the ability and intention to hold the investment to maturity.

Hidden reserves (page 362) Undisclosed accounting choices used to manage earnings and other financial information with the intention of satisfying the self-interests of the preparers.

Historical cost principle (page 245) The accounting principle that requires that transactions and economic events be valued in the financial statements at the actual dollar amounts involved when the transaction or economic event took place.

Holding gain or loss (page 415) A change in the value of inventory or some other asset while the asset is owned by the entity. A holding gain or loss is called a realized holding gain or loss if the asset is sold before the financial statement date and the holding gain or loss is called an unrealized holding gain or loss if the asset is still owned by the entity on the financial statement date.

Horizontal analysis (trend statement) (page 724) An analytical tool in which the amounts in the balance sheet and income statement are expressed as percentages of a base year set of financial statements.

Hybrid securities (page 606) Securities that have characteristics of debt and equity.

Identifiable assets and liabilities (page 478) Tangible or intangible assets and liabilities that can be specifically identified and measured with some objectivity.

In-the-money (page 620) A stock option whose exercise price is greater than the market price.

Income statement (page 44) The financial statement that provides a measure of the economic performance of an entity over a period of time. The income statement summarizes an entity's revenues and expenses for a period.

Indirect method of calculating cash from operations (page 297) A method of calculating/reporting cash from operations by reconciling from net income to cash from operations by adjusting net income for non-cash amounts that are included in the calculation of net income and for operating cash flows that are not included in the calculation of net income.

Inflation (page 339) A period when, on average, prices in the economy are rising.

Installment method (page 174) A revenue recognition method that recognizes revenue when each payment in a series of payments is received. The expenses incurred to earn the revenue are matched to the revenue on a proportional basis to the revenue recognized.

Intangible asset (page 460) A capital asset that does not have physical substance, such as patents, copyrights, trademarks, brand names and goodwill.

Intercompany transactions (page 678) Transactions among the corporations in a consolidated group. Intercompany transactions are eliminated when preparing consolidated financial statements. This means that sales and expenses, and changes in the value of assets and liabilities that occur as a result of transactions among subsidiaries and with the parent are not reflected in the consolidated statements.

Interest (page 43) The cost of borrowing money.

Interest coverage ratio (accrual basis) (page 740) A ratio that measures the ability of an entity to meet its fixed financing charges. Defined as (Net income + Interest expense + Tax expense) ÷ Interest expense

Interest coverage ratio (cash basis) (page 741) A ratio that measures the ability of an entity to meet its fixed financing charges. Defined as Cash from operations excluding interest paid ÷ Interest paid

Internal control (page 338) The processes that management implements to provide reasonable assurance that that an entity will be able to achieve its objectives regarding the reliability of financial reporting, the effectiveness and efficiency of its operations, and compliance with relevant laws and regulations.

Inventory (page 393) Goods that are available for sale by an entity, or goods that will be used to produce goods that will be sold when they are completed. Inventory can also include materials used in supplying a service to customers.

Inventory turnover ratio (page 421) Provides information on how efficiently inventory is being managed by measuring how quickly the entity is able to sell its inventory. The inventory turnover ratio is defined as cost of sales divided by average inventory.

Investee corporation (page 659) A corporation that an investor corporation has invested in.

Investing activities (page 52) The cash an entity spent buying capital and other long-term assets and cash received from selling those assets; reported on the cash flow statement.

Investor corporation (page 659) A corporation that has an investment in another company.

Issued shares (page 603) The number of authorized shares that have been distributed to shareholders.

Journal entries (page 93) The method used to enter information about economic events into the accounting system.

Laid-down cost (page 394) All costs that are incurred to purchase or make products and get them ready for sale to customers.

Last-in, first-out (LIFO) (page 400) An inventory cost flow assumption in which the cost of inventory that was purchased or produced most recently is matched to revenue first. For raw materials that are used in a manufacturing process, the cost of the raw materials that were purchased last or most recently is the cost that is used in the production process first. With LIFO, the cost of inventory reported on the balance sheet represents the cost of old, sometimes very old inventory.

Lease (page 538) A contractual arrangement where one entity (the lessee) agrees to pay another entity (the lessor) a fee in exchange for the use of an asset.

Lessee (page 538) An entity that leases an asset from the asset's owner.

Lessor (page 538) An entity that leases assets that it owns to other entities.

Leverage (page 530) The use of debt to increase the return earned on equity.

Leverage (page 616) The use of debt to increase the return earned on the equity investment of the owners.

Liabilities (page 35) Obligations an entity has to pay debts or provide goods or services.

Limited liability (page 7) Shareholders of a corporation are not liable for the obligations of and losses suffered by the corporation.

Limited liability partnerships (LLP) (page 599) An ordinary partnership in which innocent partners are shielded from

personal liability for malpractice liabilities of the firm. An individual partner of the LLP would not be liable for claims against the firm arising from negligence or other forms of malpractice unless the partner was personally involved in the negligence or malpractice.

Limited partners (page 599) Members of a limited partnerships who have limited liability protection and as a result are not personally liable for the debts and obligations of the partnership.

Limited partnerships (LLP) (page 599) Partnerships in which some of the partners have limited liability protection.

Line of credit (page 295) A prearranged loan that can be drawn on as required by the entity.

Line of credit (page 524) An arrangement with a lender that allows an entity to borrow up to a specified maximum amount when and if the entity requires the money.

Liquidity (page 40) An entity's ability to make payments as they come due.

Long-term debt (page 40) Money borrowed that has to be repaid in more than one year.

Lower of cost or market (LCM) rule (page 409) Requires that when the market value of inventory at the end of a reporting period is lower than the cost of the inventory, the inventory must be reported on the balance sheet at its market value. The amount of the write-down, the difference between the cost of the inventory and its market value, is reported as a loss in the income statement. The loss is recorded in the period the inventory decreases in value, not when the inventory is sold.

Maintenance (page 458) Expenditures that allow an asset to operate as intended—to do what it is designed to do. Maintenance costs should be expensed when incurred.

Management discussion and analysis (MD&A) (page 708) The MD&A is prepared by an entity's managers and provides them the opportunity to discuss its financial results, position, and future prospects. It is intended to provide readers with a view of the entity through the eyes of management.

Managerial accounting (page 5) The field of accounting that provides information to the managers of the entity and others decision makers who work for the entity to assist them in making decisions related to operating the entity.

Market value of equity (page 623) The market price of an entity's shares multiplied by the number of shares outstanding.

Matching (matching concept) (page 91) The process of recording and reporting expenses in the period that the revenue those expenses help earn is recorded and reported.

Materiality (page 251) The significance of financial information to users. Information is material if its omission or misstatement would affect the judgement of a user of the information.

Maturity date of a bond (page 530) The date that the borrower or bond issuer has agreed to pay back the principal (the face value of the bond) to the bondholders.

Mortgage (page 530) A loan that provides the borrower's property as collateral.

Net assets (page 47) assets–liabilities

Net book value (NBV) (page 115) The cost of a capital asset less the accumulated amortization.

Net income (page 51) A measure of the economic performance of an entity over a period of time. Net income reported on the income statement and equals an entity's revenue less all the expenses incurred to earn that revenue.

Net realizable value (page 244) The amount of cash that is expected to be received from the sale or realization of an asset after taking into consideration any additional costs.

Net recoverable amount (page 482) The net cash flow a capital asset is expected to generated from use over its remaining life plus its residual value. A capital asset should be written down to its net recoverable amount when its net recoverable amount is less than its NBV.

No par value shares (page 604) Shares that do not have a par value assigned to them.

Non-controlling interest (page 665) An account on a consolidated balance sheet that represents the net assets of a subsidiary that are owned by entities other than the shareholders of the parent corporation. On a consolidated income statement non-controlling interest represents the portion of net income of the consolidated entity that belongs to entities other than the shareholders of the parent. Non-controlling interest arises in consolidated financial statements when a parent owns less than 100% of the commons shares of a subsidiary because GAAP requires that the consolidated statements include 100% of the subsidiary's assets, liabilities, revenues, and expenses.

Non-current assets (page 39) Assets that will not be used up, sold, or converted to cash within one year or one operating cycle.

Non-current liabilities (page 39) Liabilities that will be paid or satisfied in more than one year or one operating cycle.

Non-monetary transaction (page 99) An exchange of goods or services that does not involve cash.

Not-for-profit organization (page 8) An entity whose objective is to provide services and not to make a profit. Examples include hospitals, charities, churches, mosques and synagogues, unions, clubs, daycare centres, and universities.

Note payable (page 530) A formal obligation signed by the borrower promising to repay a debt.

Off-balance-sheet financing (page 538) A financing arrangement that occurs when an entity can borrow money without a liability appearing on its balance sheet.

Operating cycle (page 39) The time it takes from the initial investment an entity makes in goods and services until cash is received from customers.

Operating expenses (page 48) The usual expenses an entity incurs for its main business activities.

Operating income (page 48) The income the entity earned from its main business activities. Operating income can give stakeholders some insight into the performance of an entity's actual business activities.

Operating lease (page 539) A lease that does not transfer the rights and risks of ownership to the lessee. Assets associated with an operating lease remain on the books of the lessor, the lessor recognizes revenue from the lease when payments are received or receivable, and the lessee recognizes an expense when the payment to the lessor is paid or payable.

Out-of-the-money (page 620) A stock option whose exercise price is less than the market price.

Outstanding shares (page 603) The number of shares of a corporation currently in the hands of shareholders.

Overhead (page 395) The costs in a manufacturing process other than direct labour and direct materials. Overhead costs are more difficult or even impossible to associate directly with the product being made.

Owners' equity (page 35) The investment the owners of an entity have made in the entity.

Par value (page 604) A value assigned to each share of common stock in the articles of incorporation. The Canada Business Corporations Act and the corporations acts provincial of a number of provinces do not permit par value shares.

Parent corporation (page 660) An investor corporation that controls an investee corporation.

Participating preferred shares (page 605) The amount of the preferred share dividend increases above the stated amount if certain conditions are met. The amount of the preferred dividend is often tied to the dividend paid on the common shares.

Partner (page 8) An entity that is one of two or more owners of a partnership.

Partnership (page 8) An unincorporated business owned by two or more entities. (Partners can be corporations or individuals persons.) A partnership is not legally separate from the partners who own it.

Passive investments (page 669) Investments where the investor corporation cannot influence the strategic decision making of the investee corporation.

Pension (page 543) Income provided to a person after they retire.

Percentage-of-completion method (page 182) A method of revenue recognition used with the gradual approach to revenue recognition. The percentage-of-completion method allocates revenues and related expenses among more than one reporting period based on a measure of the effort completed in each period.

Percentage-of-credit-sales method (page 357) A method of estimating uncollectable receivables that is based on management's estimate of the percentage of credit sales that will not be collected in a period.

Percentage-of-receivables method (page 354) A method of estimating uncollectable receivables that is based on management's estimate of the percentage of the period ending receivables balance that will not be collected.

Period costs (page 188) Costs that are expensed in the period that in which they are incurred.

Periodic inventory control system (page 395) An inventory control system where the inventory account is not adjusted whenever a transaction affects inventory. The balance in the inventory account at the end of period and cost of goods sold for the period are determined by counting the inventory on hand on the period ending date.

Periodic reporting assumption (page 238) One of the basic assumptions underlying GAAP that states that meaningful financial information about an entity can be provided for periods of time that are shorter than the life of an entity.

Permanent differences (page 558) Revenues and expenses that are recognized for tax purposes but never recognized for financial reporting purposes, or are recognized for financial reporting purposes but never recognized for tax purposes.

Permanent earnings (page 709) Earnings that are expected to be repeated in the future.

Perpetual inventory control system (page 395) A system of inventory control that keeps an ongoing record of purchases and sales of inventory. When inventory is purchased or sold, the inventory account is immediately debited or credited to record the change. When inventory is sold, cost of sales is immediately debited.

Posting (page 129) The process of transferring each line of a journal entry to the corresponding account in the general ledger.

Preferred shares (page 605) Shares of a corporation that have rights that must be satisfied before common shareholders'. These preferred rights pertain to the payment of dividends and/or to the distribution of assets in the event of liquidation.

Premium (on debt) (page 534) When a bond is sold to investors for more than its face value. Occurs when the coupon rate is greater than the effective rate of interest for the bond.

Prepaid expenses (page 114) Assets that are acquired in one period but not expensed, at least in part, until a later period or periods.

Preparers (page 11) The people responsible for deciding what, how, and when information is going to be presented in an entity's financial statements and other accounting information are presented. The preparers are the people who make the decisions—senior managers such as controllers, chief financial offers and even chief executive officers—not to the people who do the physical preparation of the statements.

Present value (page 341) The worth today of money that will be received in the future.

Price-to-book ratio (page 623) A measure of the stock market's valuation of a company's equity relative to its book value. Used as an indication of whether the shares are reasonably valued.

Price-to-earnings (P/E) ratio (page 741) Conceptually, the P/E ratio gives an indication of how the market values an entity's earnings. The P/E ratio is seen as indicator of the growth prospects of an entity. Defined as Market price per share ÷ Earnings per share

Principal (page 43) The amount borrowed from a lender.

Private corporation (page 7) A corporation whose shares and other securities are not available for purchase without agreement with the private corporation or its shareholders.

Proceeds (page 530) The amount of money a bond issuer receives from selling bonds to investors.

Product costs (page 188) Costs that can be matched to specific revenues and that are expensed when the revenue they help generate is recognized.

Profit margin ratio (page 107) A measure of how effective the entity is at controlling expenses and reflects the amount of income earned for each dollar of sales. Equal to net income/revenue.

Property dividend (page 611) Dividends paid with property instead of cash.

Property, plant, and equipment (page 38) Tangible capital assets that are used on an ongoing basis to earn revenue, but that are not sold in the ordinary course of business.

Proprietor (page 8) A person who owns a proprietorship.

Proprietorship (page 8) An unincorporated business owned by one person. A proprietorship is not legally separate from the person who owns it.

Prospectus (page 179) A legal document that provides detailed information about a company that is offering its shares for public sale.

Public corporation (page 7) A corporation whose shares or other securities are available for purchase by any entity that has an interest in owning the securities and money to buy them. The securities of public corporations are usually traded on a stock exchange.

Qualified opinion (page 254) The audit opinion given when, overall, the financial statements present the entity's situation fairly, but the statements do deviate from GAAP (or from whatever set of accounting standards the auditor is auditing to). A qualified audit opinion always contains the term "except for", which prefaces the explanation why the qualified audit report was given.

Quick ratio (page 365) A measure of entity's liquidity. Defined as an entity's most liquid assets (cash, cash equivalents, temporary investments, receivables) divided by current liabilities.

Raw materials inventory (page 394) The inputs into the production process of a manufacturer or processor.

Realized holding gain or loss (page 415) A holding gain or loss that has been

realized because the asset has been sold before the financial statement date.

Receivables (page 348) Amounts owed to an entity. The amounts can be due from customers (accounts receivable), taxation authorities (taxes receivable), investments (interest and dividends receivable), shareholders or employees (shareholder/employee loans receivable), etc.

Recognition (page 246) The process whereby any financial statement element—asset, liability, equity, expense or revenue—is entered into the accounting system and reported in the financial statements.

Redeemable preferred shares (page 605) Preferred shares that that the issuer can purchase back from investors if it chooses, according to specified terms.

Related parties (page 249) The relationship between entities when one entity has the ability to influence the decision making of another other. Examples of related parties include close family members, corporations owned or controlled by a single shareholder, and senior management.

Related party transactions (page 250) Transactions between related parties.

Relevance (pages 19, 240) The qualitative characteristic of accounting information under Canadian GAAP that states that the information provided to users must be relevant or useful for the decisions they have to make.

Reliability (page 19) (5, 241) The qualitative characteristic of accounting information under Canadian GAAP that states that the information provided to users must be a reasonable measure of what it is intended to measure.

Repairs (page 458) Expenditures that allow an asset to operate as intended—to do what it is designed to do. Repair costs should be expensed when incurred.

Replacement cost (page 244) The current price that would have to be paid to purchase an identical or equivalent asset.

Residual value (page 460) The amount a capital asset can be sold for at the end of its useful life.

Retained earnings (page 42) A balance sheet account that shows the amount of earnings a corporation has earned over its life less the amount of dividends paid to shareholders over the corporation's life.

Retractable bond (page 531) A bond that gives the investor the option to cash in the bond before the maturity date under certain conditions.

Retractable preferred shares (page 605) Preferred shares that shareholders can

require the issuer to purchase the preferred shares from them, if they choose, according to specified terms.

Return on assets (page 438) A measure of the performance and operating efficiency of an entity. ROA is defined as net income + after tax interest expense/total assets.

Return on equity (ROE) (pages 107, 626) A measure of the profitability of an entity and its effectiveness in using the assets provided by the owners of the entity to generate net income. Equal to net income/owners' equity. Owners' equity can be the period end amount or the average for the period.

Revenue (page 45) Economic benefits earned by providing goods or services to customers. Revenue results in an increase in owners' equity.

Revenue recognition (page 91) The point in time when revenue is recorded in the accounting system and is reported in the income statement.

Review engagement (page 255) A form of assurance that provides less assurance to users than an audit does about whether an entity's financial statements are in accordance with GAAP. Review engagements are never performed on public companies because securities laws require audits. A review will be done for private companies when external stakeholders are satisfied with less assurance than is provided by an audit.

Segment disclosure (page 667) Disaggregations of information about an entity by types of products and services, geographic location, and major customers.

Segregation of duties (page 339) An internal control procedure that requires that people who handle an asset should not be responsible for the record keeping for the asset.

Share (page 7) A unit of ownership in a corporation.

Shareholder (page 7) An entity that owns shares of a corporation and that is therefore an owner of the corporation.

Significant influence (page 668) An ownership interest in an investee corporation that allows the investor corporation to affect the strategic operating, investing, and financing decisions of the investee corporation even though it does not have control.

Simple interest (page 342) Interest that is paid or earned on the principal amount only.

Solvency (page 739) The financial viability of an entity—its ability to meet its long-term obligations.

Special purpose report (page 56) Accounting reports that are prepared to meet the needs of specific stakeholders and/or a specific purpose.

Specific identification method (page 401) An inventory valuation method that assigns the actual cost of a unit of inventory to that unit of inventory.

Stakeholder (page 9) A group or individual that is interested in or has a "stake" in an entity.

Start-up companies (page 307) Companies are companies that are in the process of developing their products and markets, and have not yet begun its planned business activity.

Statement of retained earnings (page 50) The financial statement that summarizes the changes to retained earnings during a period.

Statistics Canada Canada's national statistical agency. Statistics Canada has a mandate to collect, compile, analyze, abstract and publish statistical information on virtually every aspect of the nation's society and economy.

Stock dividend (page 611) The distribution of a corporation's own shares to its existing shareholders.

Stock exchange (page 7) A place (physical or virtual) where entities can trade securities of publicly traded entities.

Stock split (page 612) The division of an entity's shares into a larger number of units, each with a smaller value.

Straight-line amortization (page 115) An amortization method where the amortization expense is the same in each period.

Straight-line amortization (page 463) A method of amortization that allocates an equal amount of the cost of a capital asset to expense in each year of the asset's life.

Subsequent event (page 549) An economic event that occurs after an entity's year end, but before the financial statement are released.

Subsidiary corporation (page 660) An investee corporation that is controlled by an investor corporation.

Successful efforts (page 480) An accounting method used by oil and gas exploration companies in which only the costs associated with successful projects are capitalized.

T-account (page 129) An accounting textbook device used to represent general ledger accounts. Each T-account corresponds with a general ledger account.

Tangible asset (page 460) A capital asset with physical substance, such as land,

buildings, equipment, vehicles, and furniture.

Taxable income (page 558) The measure of income that is used, as defined by the Income Tax Act, to calculate the amount of tax an entity must pay.

Temporary accounts (page 120) Accounts whose balances are reset to zero at the end of a period by closing them to retained earnings or owners' equity. All income statement accounts are temporary accounts. The balances in temporary accounts are not carried forward from one period to the next.

Temporary differences (page 558) Revenues and expense that are fully recognized for both tax and financial reporting purposes, but the recognition happens at different times.

Time value of money (page 341) The concept that people would prefer to receive a given amount of money sooner rather than later.

Trading investments (page 672) Any investments that management designates as a trading investment. Investments in this category are actively bought and sold for profit making. All gains and losses (realized and unrealized) are recognized in the income statement in period they occur.

Transactional entry (page 113) An entry that is triggered by an exchange with another entity.

Transitory earnings (page 709) Earnings that are not expected to be repeated in future periods.

Treasury stock (page 608) Shares that were previously sold to investors and that the issuing corporation has repurchased but not retired.

Trend statements (horizontal analysis) (page 724) An analytical tool in which the amounts in the balance sheet and income statement are expressed as percentages of a base year set of financial statements.

Trial balance (page 131) A listing of all the accounts in the general ledger by their balances. The main purpose of the trial balance is to ensure that the debits equal the credits.

Undepreciated capital cost (page 559) The portion of the cost of a capitalized asset that has not been deducted for tax purposes.

Understandability (page 19) The qualitative characteristic of accounting information under Canadian GAAP that states that users must be able to understand information if it is to be useful to them.

Unearned revenue (page 117) A liability that results from receiving cash before the recognition of revenue.

Unit-of-measure assumption (page 237) One of the basic assumptions underlying GAAP that states that economic activity of an entity can be effectively stated in terms of a single unit-of-measure. The unit-of-measure that is almost always used is money, and in Canada the monetary unit used is usually the Canadian dollar.

Unqualified opinion (page 253) The audit opinion that is given when the auditors are satisfied that the financial statements present the financial situation of the entity fairly and that statements follow GAAP.

Unrealized holding gain (loss) (page 175) (8, 415) Increases or decreases in the market value of assets that are not supported by a transaction with an outside party.

Unusual item (page 711) Revenue, expenses, gains, and losses that do not meet the definition of an extraordinary item, but that are not expected to occur frequently, or that are not considered part of the normal business activities of the entity.

Value-in-use (page 455) The net present value of the cash an asset would generate over its life or the net present value of the cash the asset would allow the entity to avoid.

Variable rate loan (page 530) A loan whose interest rate changes with market conditions.

Vertical analysis (common size financial statements) (page 721) An analytical tool in which the amounts in the balance sheet and income statement are expressed as percentages of other elements in the same year's statements.

Warranty (page 174) A promise by a seller or producer of a product to correct specified problems with the product.

Work-in-process inventory (WIP) (page 394) Inventory that is partially completed on the financial statement date.

Working capital (page 40) Current assets minus current liabilities.

Working capital ratio (page 41) A measure of entity's liquidity. Defined as current assets divided by current liabilities.

Write-down (page 248) A reduction in the net book value of an asset to some measure of the market value of the asset. A write-down is achieved by debit an expense and crediting the asset.

Write-off (page 248) The write-down of an asset to zero.

INDEX

A
accelerated amortization, 463–464, 465f
account
    contra-asset account, 115
    described, 94, 95
    temporary accounts, 120
accounting
    accrual basis of accounting, 44
    cash basis of accounting, 44
    defined, 3
    economic consequences, 622–623
    financial accounting, 5
    managerial accounting, 5
    for measurement, 14–18
    role of, 487
    rules. See generally accepted
        accounting principles (GAAP)
accounting changes, 614–616, 719
accounting choices
    analysis of accounting
        problems, 201–202
    awareness of, 409
    capital assets, 486–487
    cash flow implications, 310–311
    and cash flow statement, 308–311
    constraints, 199–200, 200f
    cost flow assumption, 423
    as double-edged sword, 487
    facts, 199–200, 200f
    financial reporting, objectives of,
        190–198
    financial statement analysis,
        effect on, 489
    hidden reserves, 362–364
    inventory valuation methods, 409
    issues, 487
    objectives, 199–200, 200f
    ratios, effects on, 744
    undisclosed, 362–364
accounting cycle
    accounting equation spreadsheet,
        93, 128
    adjusting entries, 112–120, 131,
        133–134
    comprehensive example, 131–137
    defined, 88
    described, 88–89

journal entry, 93–94, 109–112
    steps in, 128–131, 128f
accounting environment
    described, 5–6, 6f
    entities, 6–9, 10
    environment, 6
    preparers, 11–13
    stakeholders, 9–10
accounting equation
    defined, 35
    double-entry bookkeeping, 94
    financing sources, 598
    tool for recording information, 37
accounting equation spreadsheet
    described, 93, 128
    format, 95
    formula for, 35, 94
    illustration of use, 94–109
accounting estimates
    changes in, 614–616
    defined, 196
    errors in, 358
    examples of, 196–197
    measurement problem, 727
    necessity of, 527
    as prediction, 355–356
    uncollectibles, 363–364
accounting information
    and accounting environment, 5–14
    cash information, 308–311
    challenges of analysis, 126
    comparability, 19–20
    constraints, 10–11
    credibility of, 13–14
    financial statements. See financial
        statements
    need for, 3–5
    other accounting information, 56
    qualitative characteristics, 19–20,
        239–244
    relevance, 19
    reliability, 19
    reliance on, 197
    understandability, 19
    up-to-date information, 238
accounting policies
    see also accounting choices

arbitrary changes, protection
    from, 240
changes in, 614–616
defined, 54
disclosure of, 196
accounting principles. See generally
    accepted accounting principles
    (GAAP)
accounting scandals, 13–14
Accounting Standards Board (ASB),
    19, 232, 235
accounting system
    accrual accounting system. See
        accrual basis of accounting
    double-entry bookkeeping, 94
    overview, 89f
    timing, 93
    use of, 14
accounts payable, 40, 524
accounts payable turnover ratio, 736
accounts receivable
    aging schedule, 355
    described, 351–352
    examples of, 356f
    financial statement analysis
        issues, 362–368
    long-term receivables, 360–361
    reporting of, according to
        GAAP, 351–352
    uncollectible receivables, 353–360
accounts receivable turnover
    ratio, 366–368, 735
accrual accounting. See accrual basis
    of accounting
accrual basis of accounting
    adjusting entries, 112–120
    appropriateness of, 102
    versus cash basis of accounting,
        90–92, 286
    and cash flow statement, 308–311
    defined, 44
    described, 90–92
    matching. See matching concept
    recording sales, 100
    revenue recognition, 91–92
accrued asset, 113, 119–120
accrued expense, 113, 117–119

accrued liabilities, 40, 113, 117–119, 522, 525–527
accrued revenue, 113, 119–120
accumulated amortization, 115
acid test ratio, 365–366, 735
actual use, 465–466
Adelphia, 232
adjusting entries
    accrued asset, 119–120
    accrued expense, 117–119
    accrued liabilities, 117–119
    accrued revenue, 119–120
    deferred expense, 114–116
    deferred revenue, 116–117
    described, 112
    necessity of, 113
    prepaid expense, 114–116
    preparation and posting, 131, 133–134
    purpose of, 112
    types of, 113, 114–120
adverse opinion, 254–255
affinity programs, 526
after-tax cost of borrowing, 549
aging schedule, 355
Air Canada, 538, 548, 548f
allowance for uncollectible accounts, 353
amortization
    accumulated amortization, 115
    as allocation of cost, 104
    defined, 47, 104, 460
    half-year rule, 495
    issues, summary of, 469–473
    and market values, 461
    matching, 104
    obsolescence, 461
    physical use, 461
    reasons for, 461
    and taxes, 495–496
amortization expense, 463
amortization methods
    accelerated amortization, 463–464, 465f
    comparison of, 466–469
    declining balance, 464
    example, 462f
    relative use in Canada, 463f
    straight-line amortization, 115, 463, 464f
    types of, 462
    unit-of-production, 465–466, 466f
    usage-based amortization, 465–466, 466f
analysis of financial statements.
    See financial statement analysis
annual report, 708
annuity, 346–348
Arthur Andersen, 252
asset turnover, 732

assets
    accrued asset, 113, 119–120
    on balance sheet, 38–39
    capital assets. See capital assets
    current assets, 39
    defined, 34
    future income tax assets and liabilities, 557–564
    historical cost, 456–460
    identifiable assets, 478, 662
    intangible assets, 460
    net assets, 47
    net book value (NBV), 115–116, 248
    non-current assets, 39
    purchase of other business' assets, 668
    replacement cost.
        See replacement cost
    tangible assets, 460
    types of, 38
assumptions of GAAP, 236–239
ATI Technologies Inc., 448–451
AT&T, 33, 520
audit, 12
audit environment, 252–255
auditors
    Canada Revenue Agency (CRA), 12
    external auditors, 12
    internal auditors, 12
auditors' report, 253–255
Aur Resources Inc., 466, 467f
Aurizon Mines Ltd., 173, 173f
authorized capital stock, 603
available-for-sale investments, 672
average collection period of accounts receivable, 366–368, 735
average cost method, 400–401, 403, 408–409
average number of days inventory on hand, 421, 736
average payment period for accounts payable, 737

B
bad debt expense, 189, 353
balance sheet
    see also financial statements
    assets, 34, 38–39
    book value of equity, 623
    consolidated balance sheet, 663–664
    defined, 34
    liabilities, 35, 39–40
    liquidity analysis, 40–41
    long-term debt, 537
    owners' equity, 35, 41–43
    as photograph, 37
balance sheet approach, 354–356
Ballard Power Systems Inc., 330–333, 476–477, 476f

bank loans, 523–524
Bank of Montreal, 34, 251, 606, 606f
bank overdraft, 295
bank reconciliation, 339
barter transaction. See non-monetary transaction
basic assumptions of GAAP, 236–239
basic earnings per share, 624
basket purchases, 459–460
Bayton Ltd. (solved problem), 20–22
BC Ferries, 10
BCE Inc., 251, 609, 610f, 710, 711f
Beeston, Paul, 11
Bell Canada, 453, 520
Bell Globemedia, 657
Bell Mobility, 657
Benito Corp. (solved problem), 553–556
Bernofsky, Eric, 705
betterment, 458
bias, freedom from, 242
big bath, 194, 719
Bloomberg News, 704
Bloomberg.com, 707
Blue Jays Holdco Inc., 237
bond agreement, 531
bond rating agencies, 520
bonds
    accounting for bonds, 533–536
    callable bond, 531
    characteristics of, 530–531
    convertible bond, 531
    coupon rate, 530
    debenture, 530
    defined, 530
    effective interest rate, 531
    face value, 530
    maturity date, 530
    net book value, 535
    pricing, 531–533
    proceeds, 530–531
    retractable bond, 531
    sale at discount, 533–534
    sale at face value, 533
    sale at premium, 534–536
book value, 623
book value of equity, 623
Bourkoff, Aryeh, 704
Bow Valley Energy Ltd., 480, 480f
Bramalea Telecable Limited, 453
brokerage firms, 707
Brookfield Asset Management, 697–702
Burnett, A.J., 285
Burton, Wade, 520
business newspapers, 2

C
Call-Net (Sprint), 520
callable bond, 531
Camco Inc., 248–249

Canada Business Corporations Act, 11, 234, 603, 604, 609
Canada Revenue Agency (CRA)
  auditors, 12
  completed-contract accounting, 184
  cost flow assumptions, 419
  described, 8
  financial statement analysis, 706
  inventory accounting, 420
  as user of accounting information, 10, 54
Canadian Business, 597
Canadian Cancer Society, 601
Canadian Institute of Chartered Accountants (CICA), 19, 232, 235
Canadian National Railway Company (CN), 235, 236f, 528, 529f
Canadian Public Accountability Board (CPAB), 252
Canadian Radio-television and Telecommunications Commission (CRTC), 10
Canadian Securities Administrators, 252
Canadian Tire Corporation, Limited, 348–351, 350f
Canfor Corporation, 393–394, 394t, 416, 418f
CanWest Global Communications Corp., 307f
capital assets
  accounting choices, 486–487
  allocation of costs, 461f
  amortization. *See* amortization
  basket purchases, 459–460
  betterment, 458
  and cash flow statement, 485–486
  defined, 454
  described, 39
  disclosure of information, 470
  disposal of, 481–482
  financial statement analysis issues, 488–489
  forms of, 454
  historical costs and, 454–455
  impaired capital assets, 482–483
  intangible assets, 460, 474–480
  maintenance, 458
  measurement of, 454–455
  net book value, 461
  net realizable value, 455
  net recoverable amount, 482
  repairs, 458
  replacement cost, 455
  reporting of, 98
  residual value, 460
  return on assets (ROA), 488–489
  tangible assets, 460
  types of, 461f

undepreciated capital cost (UCC), 559–560
value-in-use, 455
write-down, 482–483
capital cost allowance (CCA), 495–496, 559
capital expenditure, 306
capital-intensive businesses, 454, 471
capital lease, 539, 541–542
capital markets, 246
capital stock, 42, 603
capital structure, 550, 739
capitalized costs, 454
carrying value. *See* net book value (NBV)
cases
  Angela Kellett, Barrister and Solicitor, B-3–B-5
  Discount Stores Limited, B-12–B-13
  Dymo Manufacturing Limited, B-12
  GAAP Air Ltd., B-3
  Good Quality Auto Parts Limited, B-8–B-9
  International Productions Corporation, B-5–B-6
  Jeremy Langer, B-10
  Kenaston Convenience Store, B-10–B-12
  Ontario Printing Limited, B-13–B-14
  Richibucto Rattlesnakes and Sports Complex Ltd., B-1–B-2
  Shmevan Stores Ltd., B-7–B-8
  Vulcanzap Inc., B-6–B-7
cash
  as asset, 38
  attractiveness of, to thieves, 338
  controls, 338–339
  definition of, and GAAP, 295
  foreign currencies, 340–341
  management of, 338–339
  purchasing power, 339–340
  restrictions on, 336–337
  segregation of duties, 339
  unit-of-measure, 339–341
cash accounting. *See* cash basis of accounting
cash basis of accounting, 44, 90–92, 286
cash collection, 173–174, 302–303
cash cycle, 286–293, 288f
cash dividends, 610
cash flow
  versus earnings, 286
  evaluation of, 306–307
  example scenarios, 289–293
  examples of, 294f
  free cash flow, 307
  future value, 341–343
  interest payment and collection, 294
  prediction, 193
  present value, 341, 343–346

and recognition of revenue and expense, 92f
cash flow statement
  see also financial statements
  accrual accounting choices, effect of, 308–311
  capital assets, 485–486
  cash from operations (CFO), 51–52, 293, 297–305
  consolidated cash flow statement, 666
  cost of goods sold, 304–305
  defined, 51, 293
  direct method, 297–298, 297f
  financing activities, 52, 293, 296
  gains and losses, treatment of, 301
  indirect method, 297, 297f, 298–300
  information provided by, 293
  interpretation, 306–308
  inventory, 304–305
  investing activities, 52, 293, 296
  manipulation of cash flow information, 308–311
  overview of, 293–296
  parts of, 51–52
  private companies and, 293
  specific activities, 296–305
  use of, 306–308
cash from financing activities, 52, 293, 296
cash from investing activities, 52, 293, 296
cash from operations (CFO), 51–52, 293, 297–305, 306
cash lag, 287, 287f
Celestica Inc., 660
Centennial College, 32
CEO compensation, 621
Certified General Accountants (CGAs), 14, 235
Certified Management Accountants (CMAs), 14, 235
changes in accounting policies and estimates, 614–616
changes to accounting policies, 240
Chartered Accountants (CAs), 14, 252–253
Chedder Inc. (solved problem), 423–426
Child First Safety Ltd. (CFS) (solved problem), 122–126
churn, 705
CICA Handbook
  see also generally accepted accounting principles (GAAP)
  accounting estimate changes, 615
  amortization, 495
  auditors and, 253
  capital asset disclosure, 470
  capitalization of development costs, 474
  changes to accounting policies, 240
  comprehensive income, 616

contingencies, 546
cost flow assumptions, 398, 406, 407
current liabilities, 528
described, 19
differential reporting, 564
direct method, 297
disclosure requirements, 719
discontinued operations, 714
equity method of
    accounting, 668
extraordinary items, 710
future income taxes, 561
generally accepted auditing
    standards (GAAS), 253
goodwill, 478
hybrid securities, 606
indirect method, 297
interest payment and
    collection, 294
inventory accounting,
    394–395
inventory disclosures, 415
inventory valuation
    methods, 398
leases, 539, 541
market definition, 413
non-controlling interest, 665
passive investments, 669–671
private companies and
    cash flow statements, 293
qualitative characteristics of
    financial statements,
    19–20
related party transactions,
    250–251
relevance, 240–241
reliability, 241–242
research costs, 474, 479
residual value, 460
role of, 181
significant commitments, 547
significant influence, 668
as source of GAAP, 234
stewardship, 193
stock options, 621
subsequent events, 549
understandability, 239
unusual items, 710–713
clean audit opinion. See unqualified
    opinion
Clearly Canadian Beverage
    Corporation, 278–283, 307f
closing journal entries,
    120–121, 135–137
Coca-Cola Company, 477
code of conduct, 14
Cogeco Cable Inc., 616, 616f
collateral, 242–243
collections for third
    parties, 524–525
commission, 419

commitments, 547–548
common shares, 604–605
common size financial
    statements, 721–724
common stock, 61
comparability, 19–20, 239–240
completed-contract method,
    183–185, 185t
completion of production,
    172–173
completion of warranty
    period, 174–175
compliance, 195–197
compound interest, 342
comprehensive income, 616
conservatism, 104, 247–249
consignment inventory,
    416–419
consignment sale, 174
consolidated balance sheet,
    663–664
consolidated cash flow
    statement, 666
consolidated financial
    statements, 34, 660,
    666–667, 677–681
consolidated income
    statement, 666, 676
constraints, 199–200, 200f
constraints, facts, and
    objectives model, 201–202
consumers, 10
contingencies, 545–547
contra-asset account, 115
contract compliance, 193–194
contributed surplus, 604
control (subsidiaries), 660–668
controls over cash, 338–339
convertible bond, 531
convertible shares, 605
core earnings. See permanent
    earnings
corporation, 7, 234, 598–599
cost-benefit trade-off, 4
cost flow assumptions,
    398, 423
    see also inventory valuation
cost-methods of inventory
    valuation. See inventory
    valuation
cost of goods sold, 61, 304–305
cost of sales, 48, 398, 410
costs
    of bad debt, 353
    capitalized costs, 454
    historical cost, 245, 456–460
    inventory. See inventory
        valuation
    laid-down cost, 394
    maintenance costs, 260–261
    of management, 262

overhead, 395
period costs, 188
product costs, 188
replacement cost, 244, 413,
    414–415, 455
reporting of, 456–457
research costs, 474, 479
for tax purposes, 419–420
transaction cost, 245
of vandalized equipment, 262
warranty costs, 189
Cott Corporation, 387–390
coupon rate, 530
coupons, 526
covenants, 706
credit, 110
credit card transactions, 352
credit cards, 351
creditors
    concerns of, 706
    financial statement
        analysis, 706
    as user of financial
        statements, 54
critical-event approach
    cash collection, 173–174
    completion of production,
        172–173
    completion of warranty
        period, 174–175
    delivery, 172
    described, 169, 171–172
    determination of critical
        event, 176
    unrealized gains, 175–176
CTV, 657, 658
cumulative shares, 605
Cundill Investment
    Research, 520
current assets, 39
current liabilities
    accounts payable, 524
    accrued liabilities, 525–527
    bank and other current loans,
        523–524
    collections for third
        parties, 524–525
    defined, 523
    described, 39
    disclosure, 528
    dividends payable, 525
    income tax payable, 525
    unearned revenue, 527–528
current loans, 523–524
current ratio, 364–366, 734

D
date of declaration, 609
date of payment, 610
date of record, 609
debenture, 530

debit, 110
debit card, 137
debt
  after-tax cost of borrowing, 549
  bonds. *See* bonds
  and currency of borrowed
    money, 553
  described, 528
  disclosure, 537–538
  early retirement of, 537
  financing, 530, 598
  hybrid securities, 606
  leverage, 530, 616–619
  long-term debt, 40, 536, 537–538
  and taxes, 549–550
  types of, 529–530
debt instruments, 530
debt-to-equity ratio, 43,
  550–551, 552t, 740
debt-to-total-assets ratio, 740
decision-making, 201–202
declining balance, 464
deferred charge. *See* prepaid expense
deferred cost. *See* prepaid expense
deferred debit. *See* prepaid expense
deferred expense, 113, 114–116
deferred income taxes, 557–564
deferred revenue, 113, 116–117
deficit, 42
defined-benefit plan, 544
defined-contribution plan, 543–544
deflation, 339
delayed discretionary spending, 718
delivery, 172
demand loan, 524
denial of opinion, 255
depletion, 460
  see also amortization
depreciation, 460
  see also amortization
Desjardins Securities, 705
development costs, 474
development-stage companies, 307–308
differential reporting, 564
Digital Theater Systems,
  410, 411f
diminishing balance. *See* declining
  balance
direct method, 297–298, 297f
direct write-off method, 353
disclosure
  accounting estimate changes, 615
  accounting policies, 196
  of accounting policies, 240
  accounting policy changes, 615
  capital asset information, 470
  full disclosure, 245–246, 251
  inventory, 415–416
  lease transactions, 541
  liabilities, 528
  long-term debt, 537–538

materiality, 251–252
  requirements, 719
  segment disclosure, 667
  significant commitments, 547
  undisclosed accounting
    choices, 362–364
discontinued operations, 714–716
discount (on debt), 533–534
discount rate, 343
Discount Stores Limited
  (case), B-12–B-13
discounting, 346, 348
discretionary expenses, 718
disposal of capital assets, 481–482
dividend payout ratio, 742–743
dividends
  cash dividends, 610
  date of declaration, 609
  date of payment, 610
  date of record, 609
  defined, 42, 609
  and net income, 106
  property dividends, 611
  retained earnings, effect on, 105
  stock dividend, 611–612, 613
  types of, 609
dividends payable, 525
Dofasco Inc., 546
Dome Productions, 657–658
Dominion, 520
double-entry bookkeeping, 94
Dymo Manufacturing Limited
  (case), B-12

E
early retirement of debt, 537
earnings
  versus cash flow, 286
  permanent earnings, 709–715
  sources of, 710
  transitory earnings, 709
earnings management,
  194–195, 197, 745–746, 746t
earnings per share (EPS),
  624–626, 733–734
earnings quality, 716–719
economic consequences, 622–623
effective interest rate, 531
Efficient Market Hypothesis
  (EMH), 246
Eldorado Gold Corporation, 357
employee stock options, 619–622
employee wages, 101, 303–304, 525
employees, 706
Enron Corporation, 13, 232,
  252, 338, 745
entities
  accounting policies, 54
  accounting policies,
    disclosure of, 240
  attributes of, 14

capital structure, 550
  characteristics, 10
  constraints on, 10–11
  and GAAP, 234–235
  know the entity, 707–709
  measurement of economic
    performance, 44
  types of, 6–9
entity assumption, 237–238
Eppel, Mike, 87
equity
  see also owners' equity
  authorized capital stock, 603
  basic earnings per share, 624
  book value of equity, 623
  characteristics of, 603–607
  common shares, 604–605
  cost of, and tax deductibility, 603
  dividends, 609–612
  earnings per share (EPS), 624–626
  employee stock options, 619–622
  financial statement analysis
    issues, 623–626
  financing, 530, 598
  fully-diluted earnings per share, 625
  hybrid securities, 606
  leverage, 616–619
  market value of equity, 623
  preferred shares, 605–607
  price-to-book ratio, 623–624
  return on equity (ROE), 625–626
  share repurchases, 607–608
  stock splits, 612–613
equity investors, 706
equity method of accounting, 668–669
error corrections, 608
errors in estimates, 358
Esperanza Stores Corp.
  (solved problem), 746–752
estimates. *See* accounting estimates
ethics
  accounting scandals, 13–14
  big bath, 194
  earnings management, 194
  and non-arm's length
    transactions, 251
  smoothing income, 186, 195
exchange rates, 340–341, 553
executory contract, 99
exercise price, 620
expense recognition
  described, 188–190
  maintenance costs, 260–261
  personal expenses, 237–238
expenses
  accrued expense, 113, 117–119
  bad debt expense, 189, 353
  deferred expense, 113, 114–116
  defined, 46
  discretionary expenses, 718
  matching to revenue, 92

operating, general, and administrative expenses, 723
operating expenses, 48
prepaid expense, 113, 114–116
rent expense, 262
expiry date, 620
external audit, 12
external auditors, 12
external auditors' opinion, 252

F
face value of a bond, 530
facts, 199–200, 200*f*
fair value, 662, 664
Fan, Jeffrey, 704
federal corporations acts, 234
feedback value, 241
FIFO (first in, first out), 398*f*, 399, 402–403, 407–408
financial accounting, 5
financial information, 2–3
financial ratios. *See* ratios
financial reporting
    audits, 252–255
    cash flow prediction, 193
    earnings management, 194–195, 197
    impact of objective chosen, 197
    management evaluation, 193
    minimum compliance, 195–197
    monitoring contract compliance, 193–194
    objectives of, 190–198
    performance evaluation, 193
    rules for. *See* generally accepted accounting principles (GAAP)
    statement of management's responsibility, 338
    stewardship, 193
    tax minimization, 192–193
Financial Reporting in Canada, 413, 463, 547, 711
financial statement analysis
    see also ratios
    accounting choices, effect of, 489
    accounts receivable turnover ratio, 366–368
    acid test ratio, 365–366
    annual report, 708
    average collection period of accounts receivable, 366–368
    average number of days inventory on hand, 421
    basic earnings per share, 624
    capital assets, 488–489
    common size financial statements, 721–724
    cost flow assumption, effect of, 423
    current ratio, 364–366
    debt-to-equity ratio, 550–551, 552*t*
    as diagnostic tool, 744–745
    earnings per share (EPS), 624–626

earnings quality, 716–719
fully-diluted earnings per share, 625
hidden reserves, 362–364
historical analysis, 724–727
identification of problem, 723
interest coverage ratio, 551–553, 552*t*
inventory issues, 420–423
inventory turnover ratio, 421
know the entity, 707–709
liabilities, 550–553
limitations and caveats, 743–745
management discussion and analysis (MD&A), 708
owners' equity, 623–626
performance evaluation, 727–734
permanent earnings, 709–715
purpose of, 705–707
quick ratio, 364–366
receivables issues, 362–368
return on assets (ROA), 488–489
return on equity (ROE), 625–626
stakeholders and, 705–707
summary of coverage, 720*f*
trend statements, 724–727
vertical analysis, 721–724
financial statements
    backward-looking nature of, 241
    balance sheet, 34–43
    see also balance sheet
    cash flow statement, 51–52
    see also cash flow statement
    comparability, 19–20, 239–240
    comparison difficulties, 744
    consolidated, 34
    consolidated financial statements, 660, 666–667, 677–681
    disclosures. *See* disclosure and financial reporting objective, 197
    fiscal year, 34
    format of, 55–56
    full disclosure, 245–246
    general purpose financial statements (GPFS), 33–34, 55–56
    gross margin, 48–50
    historical nature of, 743
    income statement, 44–48
    see also income statement
    limitations and caveats, 743–745
    non-comprehensive nature of, 744
    notes to financial statements, 52–54
    and owners' personal transactions, 237–238
    preparation, 131, 135, 744
    qualitative characteristics, 19–20, 239–244
    qualitative characteristics of, 19–20
    relationships among, 52
    relevance, 19, 240–241, 242–244

reliability, 19, 241–244
review engagement, 255
statement of retained earnings, 50–51
understandability, 19, 239
users of, 54–55
financing activities, 52, 293, 296
finished goods inventory, 394
first in, first out (FIFO), 398*f*, 399, 402–403, 407–408
FirstService Corporation, 649–655
fiscal year, 34
fixed assets. *See* capital assets
fixed-rate loan, 530
Flare, 335
foregone discretionary spending, 718
foreign currencies, 340–341, 553
Forzani Group Ltd., 777–781
Four Seasons Hotels Inc., 356*f*
Fox Cable Networks, 658
free cash flow, 307
freedom from bias, 242
full costing, 480
full disclosure, 245–246, 251
fully-diluted earnings per share, 625
future income tax assets and liabilities, 557–564
future value, 341–343

G
GAAP. *See* generally accepted accounting principles (GAAP)
GAAP Air Ltd. (case), B-3
gains and losses
    described, 187–188
    examples, 187
    holding gain or loss, 415
    separate reporting of, 188
    treatment of, 301
    unrealized gains and losses, 175–176
    unrealized holding gain or loss, 415
gas, 479–480
Geac Computer Corporation Limited, 336–337, 337*f*
general journal, 128, 128*f*
general ledger, 129–131, 132–133
general partners, 599
general purpose financial statements (GPFS), 33–34, 55–56
generally accepted accounting principles (GAAP)
    see also CICA Handbook
    accounting estimate changes, 615
    accounting for transactions and economic events, 609
    accounting policy changes, 615
    adjusting entries, 112
    appropriateness of, 102
    assets, 38–39, 40
    audit environment, 252–255
    auditors' report, 253–255
    backward-looking nature of, 241

basic assumptions, 236–239
bonds and other long-term
    debt, 535–536
Canadian *versus* U.S., 232–233, 235
capital asset disclosure, 470
capital assets, 98, 458
cash, 295
comparability, 19–20, 239–240
conservatism, 104, 247–249
as constraint, 11
cost flow assumptions, 406
critical events under, 175
defined, 18, 234
described, 18–20, 234–235
entity assumption, 237–238
executory contract, 99
full disclosure, 245–246
future of Canadian
    GAAP, 235
going-concern assumption, 236, 238
goodwill, 478
historical cost, 454, 662
impaired capital assets, 483
interpretation variations, 555
inventory, 394–395
inventory valuation methods, 398
latitude provided by, 11
liabilities, 521
management accounting choices,
    168, 194
measurement conventions, 244–252
non-arm's length
    transactions, 249–252
non-controlling interest, 666, 683
periodic-reporting
    assumption, 238–239
qualitative characteristics,
    19–20, 239–244
receivables, 351–352
recognition, 246
recording sales, 100
related parties, 249–252
relevance, 19, 240–241, 242–244
reliability, 19, 241–244
revenue recognition criteria, 170–171
review engagement, 255
as rules of accounting, 233
shortcomings of, 102
sources of, 234
stewardship, 193
understandability, 19, 239
and undesirable outcomes, 555
unit-of-measure assumption, 237,
    339–341
and unrealized gains and losses, 175
valuation, 244–245
generally accepted auditing standards
    (GAAS), 253
Genesis Land Development Corp, 175,
    175*f*, 416, 417*f*
Genuity Capital Markets, 520

GGL Diamond Corp., 307*f*
Ghose, Dvai, 520
Glaus, Troy, 285
*The Globe and Mail's Report
    on Business*, 2, 520
Globeinvestor.com, 707
going-concern assumption, 236, 238
Good Quality Auto Parts
    Limited (case), B-8–B-9
goodwill, 477–478, 678
Google Inc., 179–181
Gossling, John, 232
government
    collections for, 524–525
    role of, 8
    as stakeholder, 10
Government of Canada, 308, 310*f*
gradual approach
    completed-contract method,
        183–185, 185*t*
    described, 169, 182
    percentage-of-completion
        method, 182–185
gross margin, 48–50, 728–729
gross margin percentage, 48–50
gross profit, 61
Grosvenor Park Rogers Video, 167
GST (goods and services tax), 524

H
half-year rule, 495
Halladay, Roy, 285
Heart and Stroke Foundation
    of Ontario, 601
held-to-maturity investments, 671
Hemosol Corp., 308, 309*f*
hidden reserves, 362–364
high earnings quality, 716
High-Tech Industries Inc.
    (solved problem), 490–493
historical analysis, 724–727
historical cost, 245, 456–460, 662
historical cost accounting, 454–455
holding gain or loss, 415
Home Depot, 351
HST (harmonized sales tax), 524
Hudson's Bay Company, 238, 351
hybrid securities, 606

I
identifiable assets and liabilities, 478, 662
impaired capital assets, 482–483
in-the-money, 620
income
    comprehensive income, 616
    net income, 44
    operating income, 48
    taxable income, 558
income smoothing. *See* smoothing
    income
income statement

see also financial statements
consolidated income statement,
    666, 676
defined, 44
example, 47–48
expenses, 46
format, 45
and matching of costs and
    benefits, 188
revenue, 45
income statement approach, 357–360
Income Tax Act, 10, 419, 495, 558
income tax expense, 48
income tax payable, 525
income taxes. *See* taxes
income trusts, 8
Indigo Books & Music Inc.,
    393, 394*t*, 454
indirect method, 297, 297*f*, 298–300
individuals, 8–9
inflation, 339
initiation fees, 259
instalment method, 174
intangible assets
    accounting challenges, 474–476
    described, 460, 474
    financial ratios and, 476
    goodwill, 477–478
intellectual capital. *See* intangible assets
intercompany transactions, 676–680
interest
    accrued, on long-term debt, 536
    capitalization of, 457
    compound interest, 342
    costs, 525
    defined, 43
    effective interest rate, 531
    payment and collection of, 294
    simple interest, 342
    variable interest rates, 553
interest coverage ratio, 551–553, 552*t*
interest coverage ratio
    (accrual basis), 740–741
interest coverage ratio (cash basis), 741
interest expense, 102, 540–541
internal auditors, 12
internal controls
    cash, 338–339
    inventory, 397
internally generated goodwill, 478
International Accounting Standards
    Board (IASB), 19, 235
International Financial Reporting
    Standards (IFRS), 19, 235
International Productions
    Corporation (case), B-5–B-6
interpretation of financial statements.
    See financial statement analysis
inventory
    bankers' view of, 423
    on cash flow statement, 304–305

consignment inventory, 416–419
defined, 393
described, 393–394
in different companies, 394t
disclosures, 415–416
financial statement analysis
    issues, 420–423
finished goods inventory, 394
generally accepted accounting
    principles (GAAP), 394–395
and income taxes, 419–420
internal controls, 397
laid-down cost, 394
lower of cost and market
    (LCM) rule, 409–414
overhead, inclusion of, 395
periodic inventory control
    system, 395–396
perpetual inventory control
    system, 395, 397
raw materials inventory, 394
services industry, 416
types of, 393–394
work-in-process (WIP), 394
inventory turnover ratio, 421, 736
inventory valuation
    average cost method,
        400–401, 403, 408–409
    best method, 406–409
    comparison of, 402–406
    cost flow assumptions, 398
    described, 397–399
    first in, first out (FIFO), 398f, 399,
        402–403, 407–408
    last in, first out (LIFO), 400,
        401f, 403, 408, 419, 420
    lower of cost and market
        (LCM) rule, 409–414
    net realizable value, 415
    non-cost methods, 414–415
    replacement cost, 414–415
    specific identification method,
        401–402, 405
investee corporation, 659
investing activities, 52, 293, 296
investments in other companies
    asset purchases, 668
    available-for-sale investments, 672
    consolidated balance sheet, 663–664
    consolidated financial
        statements, 677–681
    control, 660–668
    held-to-maturity investments, 671
    introduction to, 659
    non-controlling interest,
        665–666, 681–683
    passive investments, 669–675
    reasons for, 658–659
    significant influence, 668–669
    subsidiaries, accounting for, 660–668
    trading investments, 672

types of, 659f
valuation of, 675
investor corporation, 659
investors, 706
issued shares, 603
itravel2000.com, 88
Ivanhoe Mines Ltd., 669, 670f

J
journal entries
    adjusting entries, 112–120,
        131
    closing journal entries,
        120–121, 135–137
    defined, 93–94
    illustration of, 110–112
    information provided by, 109–110
    posting to general ledger,
        129–131, 132–133
    preparation of, 128–129, 132
    purpose of, 109
    transactional entry, 113

K
Kellett, Angela (case), B-3–B-5
Kenaston Convenience Store (case),
    B-10–B-12
know the entity, 707–709
knowledge assets. See intangible assets
KPMG, 253
Kreuger, Ivar, 42

L
laid-down cost, 394
Lalande, Pierre, 392
land market value, 176
Langer, Jeremy (case), B-10
last in, first out (LIFO), 400, 401f,
    403, 408, 419, 420
Le Chateau Inc., 737, 739f
leases, 538–542
lenders
    collateral, 242–243
    inventory, view of, 423
    as stakeholders, 9
    as user of financial statements, 55
Leon's Furniture Limited, 49, 49f,
    421–422, 738–739, 738f
lessee, 538
lessor, 538
leverage, 530, 616–619
leverage ratios, 739–741
liabilities
    accounts payable, 524
    accrued liabilities, 40, 113,
        117–119, 522, 525–527
    on balance sheet, 39–40
    bank and other current loans, 523–524
    bonds and other long-term
        debt, 528–538
    characteristics, 521

collections for third parties,
    524–525
commitments, 547–548
contingencies, 545–547
current liabilities, 39, 523–528
debt. See debt
debt-to-equity ratio, 550–551, 552t
defined, 35, 521
described, 521–522
disclosure, 528
dividends payable, 525
financial statement analysis
    issues, 550–553
future income tax assets
    and liabilities, 557–564
identifiable liabilities, 478, 662
income tax payable, 525
interest coverage ratio,
    551–553, 552t
leases, 538–542
non-current liabilities, 39
pensions, 543–545
post-retirement benefits, 543–545
subsequent events, 549
types of, 40
unearned revenue, 40, 117, 527–528
valuation, 522–523
LIFO (last in, first out), 400, 401f,
    403, 408, 419, 420
limited liability, 7
limited liability partnership
    (LLP), 599
limited partners, 599
limited partnerships, 599
line of credit, 295, 524
liquidity, 40–41
liquidity problems, 288
liquidity ratios, 734–739
Livent, 13
loans, 523–524, 530, 553
Loblaw Companies Limited, 50, 50f
long-lived assets, 61
    see also capital assets
long-term assets, 61
long-term debt, 40, 536, 537–538
    see also bonds
long-term debt-to-equity ratio, 740
long-term liabilities. See long-term debt
long-term receivables, 360–361
loss. See gains and losses
low earnings quality, 716
lower of cost and market
    (LCM) rule, 409–414

M
MacKay, Joseph, 705
Magna International Inc., 394t,
    415–416, 417f, 520
maintenance, 458
maintenance costs, 260–261
Major League Baseball, 11, 285

management
  accounting choices, and
    GAAP, 168, 194
  constraints faced by, 198–199
  costs, 262
  earnings management, 194–195
  evaluation of, 193
  financial reporting, objectives
    of, 190–198
  judgment, 93
  limit on accounting
    choices, 190–192, 191f
  revenue recognition choices, 181
  stakeholders' reporting
    demands, 198
management discussion and
  analysis (MD&A), 708
managerial accounting, 5
manipulation of cash flow
  information, 308–311
market definitions, 413
market value of equity, 623
market values, 461
MasterCard, 351
matching concept
  amortization, as example of, 104
  challenges of, 92
  cost of capital assets, 460
  defined, 91
  described, 246
  and expense recognition,
    188–190
  practical problems, 246–247
materiality, 251–252, 258
maturity date of a bond, 530
MDS Inc., 474, 475f, 586–593
measurement
  with accounting, 14–18
  capital assets, 454–455
measurement conventions
  conservatism, 247–249
  full disclosure, 245–246
  matching, 246–247
  materiality, 251–252
  non-arm's length
    transactions, 249–251
  recognition, 246
  valuation, 244–245
Microcell Telecommunications
  (FIDO), 520
Microsoft Corporation, 185–187
minimum compliance, 195–197
minority interest. See non-controlling
  interest
Molina, Benjie, 285
Molson Coors Brewing
  Company, 238
Molson's Breweries, 238
monitoring contract compliance,
  193–194
monthly membership fees, 259–260

Moody's, 520
Morningstar.com, 707
mortgage, 530

N
National Energy Board (NEB), 10
The National Post's Financial Post, 2
negative cash from operations
  (CFO), 306
negative working capital, 41
net assets, 47
net book value (NBV)
  of assets, 115–116, 248
  bonds, 535
  capital assets, 461
net earnings. See net income
net income
  see also earnings
  defined, 44
  exceptions, 616
net profit. See revenue
net realizable value
  as alternative to historical cost, 455
  capital assets, 455
  defined, 244, 413
  impaired capital assets, 483
  inventory valuation, 415
  and percentage-of-credit-sales
    method, 357
  and percentage-of-receivables
    method, 354
  receivables, 351–352
net recoverable amount, 482
neutrality, 242
New York Stock Exchange, 232
Newfoundland Power Inc., 55–56, 55f
News 95.7, 87–88
newspaper editorial process, 89, 90f
no par value, 604
nominal account. See temporary
  accounts
nominal dollar, 237
non-arm's length transactions, 249–252
non-cash items, 300f,
  301–302
non-controlling interest,
  665–666, 681–683
non-cost methods of inventory
  valuation, 414–415
non-current assets, 39
non-current liabilities, 39
non-monetary transaction, 99
non-profit organization. See not-for-
  profit organizations
Nortel Networks Corporation,
  13–14, 237, 307f, 453, 745
not-for-profit organizations, 8,
  194, 601
note payable, 530
notes to financial statements, 52–54
Nuwata Inc. (solved problem), 368–369

O
objectives, 199–200, 200f
obsolescence, 461
off-balance-sheet financing, 538
Office of the Superintendent
  of Financial Institutions, 252
oil and gas accounting, 479–480
Onex Corporation, 483, 484f,
  660, 660f
Ontario Printing Limited
  (case), B-13–B-14
Ontario Securities
  Commission, 252
Open Text Corporation, 454
operating, general, and
  administrative expenses, 723
operating cycle, 39
operating expenses, 48
operating income, 48
operating lease, 539, 541–542
out-of-the-money, 620
outstanding shares, 603
Overbay, Lyle, 285
overhead, 395
owners, 9
owners' equity
  see also equity
  in balance sheet, 41–43
  contributed surplus, 604
  defined, 35
  financial statement analysis
    issues, 623–626
  retained earnings, 608–609
owner's salary, 262

P
par value, 604
parent corporation, 660
Parmalat, 13
participating shares, 605
partners' equity, 42, 599, 600f
  see also owners' equity
partnership, 8, 234, 599
passive investments, 669–675
Peace Arch Entertainment
  Group Inc., 188, 189f
pensions, 543–545
percentage-of-completion
  method, 182–185
percentage-of-credit-sales
  method, 357–360
percentage-of-receivables
  method, 354–356
performance evaluation, 193,
  727–734
period costs, 188
periodic inventory control
  system, 395–396
periodic-reporting assumption,
  238–239
permanent differences, 558, 559t

permanent earnings
  defined, 709
  discontinued operations, 714–716
  extraordinary items, 710
  sources of, 710
  versus transitory earnings, 709
  unusual items, 710–713
perpetual inventory control system, 395, 397
persistent earnings. *See* permanent earnings
personal expenses, 237–238
Pet Valu, Inc., 225–230
Petro-Canada, 480, 480*f*
physical use, 461
Pizzazz Pizza Parlours Ltd. (PPPL) (solved problem), 202–208
positive working capital, 41
post-retirement benefits, 543–545
posting
  adjusting entries, 131, 133–134
  to general ledger, 129–131, 130*f*, 132–133
prediction of cash flow, 193
predictive value, 240–241
preferred shares, 605–607
premium (on debt), 534–536
prepaid expense, 113, 114–116
prepaid rent, 98
preparers, 11–13
present value
  annuity, 346–348
  and bond pricing, 532
  defined, 341
  described, 343–346
  discount rate, 343
  examples of, 345–346
price-to-book ratio, 623–624
price-to-earnings (P/E ratio), 741–742
pricing of bonds, 531–533
principal, 43
Printera Corporation, 515–518
private corporation
  accounts receivable, 352
  and cash flow statements, 293
  defined, 7
  examples of, 7*t*
  lease accounting, 541
  market value, 625
proceeds, 530–531
product costs, 188
production, 172–173
professional accountants, 14
professional code of conduct, 14
professional partnerships, 599
profit. *See* revenue
profit margin ratio, 107, 729–730
property, plant, and equipment, 38
  see also capital assets
property dividends, 611

proprietor, 8
proprietor's equity, 42
proprietorship, 8, 234, 599
prospectus, 179
provincial corporations acts, 234
public corporations, 7*t*
purchase of assets, 668
purchasing power, 339–340
pyramid scheme, 42

Q

qualified opinion, 254
qualitative characteristics, 19–20, 239–244
quick ratio, 364–366, 735

R

ratios
  see also financial statement analysis
  accounting choices, effects of, 744
  accounts payable turnover ratio, 736
  accounts receivable turnover ratio, 366–368, 735
  acid test ratio, 365–366, 735
  analysis with, 41
  asset turnover, 732
  average collection period of accounts receivable, 366–368, 735
  average number of days inventory on hand, 736
  average payment period for accounts payable, 737
  basic earnings per share, 624
  cost flow assumption, effect of, 423
  current ratio, 41, 364–366, 734
  debt-to-equity ratio, 43, 550–551, 552*t*, 740
  debt-to-total-assets ratio, 740
  dividend payout ratio, 742–743
  earnings per share (EPS), 624–626, 733–734
  fully-diluted earnings per share, 625
  gross margin, 728–729
  gross margin percentage, 48–50
  and intangible assets, 476
  interest coverage ratio, 551–553, 552*t*
  interest coverage ratio (accrual basis), 740–741
  interest coverage ratio (cash basis), 741
  inventory turnover ratio, 421, 736
  leverage ratios, 739–741
  liquidity ratios, 734–739
  long-term debt-to-equity ratio, 740
  price-to-book ratio, 623–624
  price-to-earnings (P/E ratio), 741–742
  profit margin ratio, 107, 729–730
  quick ratio, 364–366, 735

return on assets (ROA), 488–489, 730–733
return on equity (ROE), 107, 625–626, 730–733
solvency ratios, 739–741
use of, 719
working capital ratio, 41
raw materials inventory, 394
reasonable assurance, 254
receivables
  accounts receivables, 351–352
  aging schedule, 355
  defined, 348
  financial statement analysis issues, 362–368
  long-term receivables, 360–361
  net realizable value, 351–352
  private companies, 352
  reporting of, according to GAAP, 351–352
  returns, 360
  uncollectible receivables, 353–360
  writing-off a receivable, 359
recognition, 168, 246
  see also expense recognition; revenue recognition
recurring earnings. *See* permanent earnings
redeemable shares, 605
regulators, 10, 54, 707
related parties, 249–252
related party transactions, 250–251
relevance, 19, 240–241, 242–244
relevance-reliability trade-off, 243*f*
reliability, 19, 241–244
renovations, 97–98
rent expense, 262
repairs, 189, 458
replacement cost
  capital assets, 455
  defined, 244, 413
  inventory valuation, 414–415
representational faithfulness, 242
research costs, 474, 479
Research in Motion Limited, 237, 616, 617*f*
residual value, 460
retained earnings, 42, 608–609
retractable bond, 531
retractable shares, 605
return on assets (ROA), 488–489, 730–733
return on equity (ROE), 107, 618, 619, 625–626, 730–733
returns, 360
revenue
  accrued revenue, 113, 119–120
  deferred revenue, 113, 116–117
  defined, 45
  matching to expenses, 92
  for not-for-profit organizations, 601

sales revenue. *See* capital stock
unearned revenue, 117, 527–528
revenue recognition
cash collection, 173–174
choices, 181
completed-contract method,
183–185, 185*t*
on completion of warranty
period, 174–175
conservative approach, 170
criteria for recognizing
revenue, 170–171
critical-event approach, 169,
171–176
on delivery, 172
described, 91–92, 168–169
gradual approach, 169, 182–185
initiation fees, 259
at Microsoft Corporation, 185–187
non-universal nature of criteria, 171
percentage-of-completion
method, 182–185
on production, 172–173
on right-of-return period, 174–175
timing of, 169, 176–181, 260
unrealized gains, 175–176
review engagement, 255
Ricciardi, J.P., 285
Richibucto Rattlesnakes and Sports
Complex Ltd. (case), B-1–B-2
right-of-return period, 174–175
RIM. *See* Research in Motion Limited
Rogers, Ted, 232, 453, 520, 597
Rogers AT&T Wireless, 33
Rogers Cable Inc., 34, 172, 237, 453
Rogers Communications Inc.
accounting, effect of, 12–13
accounting changes, 615–616
accounts receivable turnover
ratio, 367*t*
accrual accounting system, 90–92
adding value to services, 169
analysis, 594–595, 655–656,
702–703, 781–782
annual report (2005), A-1–A-51
auditors' report, 253
authorized capital stock, 603
average collection period of
accounts receivable, 367*t*
balance sheet, 34–43, 336
basic EPS, 624–625
capital assets, 453
cash and cash equivalents, 296
cash flow patterns, 307*f*
cash flow statement, 51–52,
293, 296, 297, 302, 306
commitments, 548
common-size analysis, 723–724, 724*f*
common size financial
statements, 722*f*
compliance with U.S. GAAP, 232–233

consolidated balance sheet, A-4
consolidated financial statements, 237
consolidated statements of
cash flows, A-6
consolidated statements of
deficit, A-5
consolidated statements of
income, A-5
contingent liabilities, 547
control of, 597
corporate organization, 661*f*
currency of borrowed
money, 553
current liabilities, 528
debt, 520–521, 528–529
employee stock options, 620
first-quarter results, 2006, 704
fiscal year end, 241
five-year financial summary,
724–725, 725*f*
goodwill, 478
gross margin, 728
historical cost, 245
income statement, 47–48
inventory, 394*t*
long-term debt obligations, 537
management discussion and
analysis (MD&A), 708
media empire, 1
News 95.7, 87
notes to consolidated
financial statements, A-7–A-51
notes to financial statements,
53–54, 246
operating leases, 541
other current assets, 365
overview, 34
related party transactions, 251
return on assets, 489
return on equity (ROE), 626
Roger Wireless, and
company growth, 32–33
segment disclosure, 667
The Shopping Channel, 393
statement of retained earnings, 51
Toronto Blue Jays, 285
unusual items, 711
users of, 54–55
Rogers Media, 87, 335, 392,
657–658
Rogers Sportsnet Inc., 237
Rogers UR Music, 32
Rogers Video, 167, 245, 287, 392
Rogers Wireless, 230–231, 237,
520, 537, 657
Rogers Wireless Inc., 34
Rozsell, Tim, 87
rules of accounting. *See* generally
accepted accounting principles
(GAAP)
Ryan, B.J., 285

S
salaries, 101, 303–304, 525
sales. *See* capital stock
sales revenue. *See* capital stock
Sarbanes-Oxley Act, 232, 252, 338
Savoy Health Club Ltd.
(solved problem), 256–262
scandals, 13–14, 745–746
scope paragraph, 254
Scott, Lisa, 335
Sears Canada Inc., 351
segment disclosure, 667
segregation of duties, 339
self-interest, 190–192
service companies, 393, 416
share capital. *See* owners' equity
share repurchases, 607–608
shareholders
investments, 42
rights of, 603
as stakeholder, 7
as user of financial statements, 54
shareholders' equity, 42
see also cash flow statement
shares, 7, 603, 604–607
see also equity
Shaw Communications Inc., 471, 471*f*,
472*f*, 482
Shmevan Stores Ltd. (case), B-7–B-8
Shoppers Drug Mart Corporation,
196, 196*f*
The Shopping Channel, 392
significant influence, 668–669
simple interest, 342
Sleeman Breweries Ltd., 307*f*
smoothing income, 186, 195
Snowflake's Snow Removal
Company (SSRC) (solved
problem), 56–59
Sobeys Inc., 729
sole proprietors. *See* proprietorship
solved problems
Bayton Ltd., 20–22
Benito Corp., 553–556
Chedder Inc., 423–426
Child First Safety Ltd.
(CFS), 122–126
Esperanza Stores Corp., 746–752
High-Tech Industries Inc., 490–493
Nuwata Inc., 368–369
Pizzazz Pizza Parlours Ltd.
(PPPL), 202–208
Savoy Health Club Ltd., 256–262
Snowflake's Snow Removal
Company (SSRC), 56–59
Tecumseh Inc., 675–677
Trendy Tee-Shirts Inc., 311–314
Wrixon Ltd., 626–629
solvency, 739
solvency ratios, 739–741
special purpose reports, 56

specific identification method, 401–402, 405
Sportsnet, 658
stakeholders
versus preparers, 11–13
reporting demands, 198
types of, 9–10
up-to-date information, 238
Standard and Poor's, 520
start-up, 307–308
statement of cash flow. See income statement
statement of changes in financial position. See cash flow statement
statement of financial position. See balance sheet
statement of management's responsibility, 338
statement of retained earnings, 50–51
see also financial statements
Statistics Canada, 9, 707
Stelco Inc., 55, 55f, 714, 715f
stewardship, 193
stock dividend, 611–612, 613
stock exchange, 7
stock market. See stock exchange
stock options, 619–622
stock splits, 612–613
stockholder. See shareholders
stockholders' equity. See owners' equity
straight-line amortization, 15, 463, 464f
Stronach, Frank, 520
subsequent events, 549
subsidiary corporation
accounting for, 660–668
consolidated balance sheet, 663–664
consolidated financial statements, 677–681
intercompany transactions, 676–680
successful efforts, 480
suppliers, 9–10
sustainable earnings. See permanent earnings
Swedish Match King, 42

T
T-account, 129, 133, 133f
Talisman Energy Inc., 612, 613f
tangible assets, 460
tax minimization, 192–193
taxable income, 558
taxation authorities, 10
taxes
and accounting choices, 192
after-tax cost of borrowing, 549
amortization, 495–496
capital cost allowance (CCA), 495–496, 559

completed-contract method, 184, 185t
costs, for tax purposes, 419–420
and debt, 549–550
equity, cost of, 603
future income tax assets and liabilities, 557–564
GST (goods and services tax), 524
half-year rule, 495
historical costs, 245
HST (harmonized sales tax), 524
income tax expense, 48
inventory, 419–420
minimization of, 192–193
undepreciated capital cost (UCC), 559–560
Tecumseh Inc. (solved problem), 675–677
Tembec Inc., 712, 712f
temporary accounts, 120
temporary differences, 558, 559t
TimberWest Forest Corp., 454
time value of money
described, 341
future value, 341–343
present value, 341, 343–346
present value of an annuity, 346–348
timeliness, 241
timing, 93
Toronto Blue Jays, 1, 11, 34, 285
Toronto Star, 520
Toronto Stock Exchange (TSX), 7, 246, 608
Torstar Corporation, 607, 607f
trading investments, 672
transaction cost, 245
transactional entry, 113
transitory earnings, 709
treasury stock, 608
trend statements, 724–727
Trendy Tee-Shirts Inc. (solved problem), 311–314
trial balance, 131, 134

U
uncollectible receivables
accounting for, 353–360
aging schedule, 355
allowance for uncollectible accounts, 353
balance sheet approach, 354–356
comparison of methods, 359–360
direct write-off method, 353
hidden reserves, 362–364
income statement approach, 357–360
percentage-of-credit-sales method, 357–360
percentage-of-receivables method, 354–356
writing-off a receivable, 359

undepreciated capital cost (UCC), 559–560
understandability, 19, 239
undisclosed accounting choices, 362–364
unearned revenue, 40, 117, 527–528
unit-of-measure assumption, 237, 339–341
unit-of-production amortization method, 465–466, 466f
United States
leases, 539
research and development costs, 474
stock options, 621, 622–623
US GAAP, 232–233, 235
universities, 601
University of Ontario Institute of Technology (UOIT), 601, 602f
unqualified opinion, 253
unrealized gains and losses, 175–176
unrealized holding gain or loss, 415
unusual items, 710–713
usage-based amortization, 465–466, 466f
USB Investment Research, 704

V
valuation
inventory. See inventory valuation
of investments, 675
of liabilities, 522–523
methods of, 244–245
value-in-use, 245, 455
vandalized equipment, 261
variable interest rates, 553
variable-rate loan, 530
verifiability, 241
vertical analysis, 721–724
Via Rail, 454
Visa, 351
Vulcanzap Inc. (case), B-6–B-7

W
wages, 101, 303–304, 525
Warner, Justin, 32
warranty, 174–175, 526
warranty costs, 189
websites for financial information, 2–3
WestJet Airlines Inc., 161–165, 174, 393, 394t, 551, 552f
work-in-process (WIP), 394
working capital, 40–41
working capital ratio, 41
WorldCom, 13, 232, 745
write-down, 248, 482–483
write-off, 248
writing-off a receivable, 359
Wrixon Ltd. (solved problem), 626–629